Praise for Peter Baker's

DAYS OF FIRE

"Poignant. . . . The story of those eight years would seem far too vast to contain inside a single volume. Yet here that volume is. Peter Baker neither accuses nor excuses. He writes with a measure and balance that seem transported backward in time from some more dispassionate future."

—David Frum, *The New York Times Book Review*

"A fine new book about [Bush's] time in office. . . . [Baker's] shrewd, meticulous reporting offers a useful corrective to tales of a puppet-master deputy manipulating an inexperienced boss."

—*The Economist*

"Baker draws out each development in this tangled relationship in much the same way that Robert Caro wrote about the relationship between John F. Kennedy and Lyndon Johnson."

—James Mann, *The Washington Post*

"An encyclopedic and even-handed account of the Bush years. . . . Baker offers clear-eyed perspective on the fateful decisions of a decade ago. . . . [A] kaleidoscopic, behind-the-scenes narrative."

—*The Christian Science Monitor*

"Baker's approach works well . . . [he] is an impressive stylist."

—*Minneapolis Star Tribune*

"Magisterial. . . . [A] remarkable achievement. . . . Baker has done a tremendous job of knitting together the disparate strains of a complex and multilayered narrative. For all its density, the book proceeds at a beach-read velocity that makes it a pleasure to peruse."

—*The National Interest*

"The first comprehensive narrative history of what will surely remain one of the most controversial presidential administrations in U.S. history. . . . All subsequent writers dealing with the subject will find this book indispensable." —Walter Russell Mead, *Foreign Affairs*

"Baker's book is red meat for political junkies. . . . Mr. Baker's fair book is an admirable attempt to put a polarizing administration into perspective. But it's not designed to forgive and forget. If anything, it resurrects the consequential days of an administration that dealt with unprecedented problems and tensions in a uniquely headstrong, American way." —*Pittsburgh Post-Gazette*

"The new book with all the buzz is *Days of Fire*. . . . A magisterial study of the way [Bush and Cheney] influenced each other, waxing and then waning, during the fateful eight-year presidency of George W. Bush." —*US News & World Report*

"This is an amazing book, a deeply reported, wonderfully written and—crucially—wholly fair and penetrating review and critique of the Bush-Cheney years, their turmoil and tragedy, their great successes and their great failures. I can't think of a book produced so close to a presidency that has done quite what Baker does in this book. . . . You will be inside the Bush White House in a way you could never have hoped to see inside until decades from now."

—Hugh Hewitt, host of *The Hugh Hewitt Show*

"On each page, there are stories that I remember well from my days in the Bush White House; stories that I'm surprised Peter discovered, and revelations that I read about for the first time."

—Nicolle Wallace,
former White House Communications Director

"Peter Baker's superb biography of George W. Bush and Dick Cheney will stand as the most complete and balanced discussion of the men and their administration for decades. . . . No one has drawn the complicated Bush-Cheney relationship more convincingly than Baker. Anyone eager to understand our current dilemmas would do well to read this book." —Robert Dallek,
author of *Nixon and Kissinger: Partners in Power*

"Peter Baker tells the story of Bush and Cheney with the precision of a crack reporter and the eye and ear of a novelist. . . . A splendid mix of sweeping history and telling anecdotes that will keep you turning the page." —Chris Wallace, anchor of *Fox News Sunday*

"It turns out George W. Bush was no puppet, and Dick Cheney no puppet master. *Days of Fire* takes us inside a relationship that came to define American conflict, peace, and politics. . . . This excellent book tells us what really happened, from the mouths of the players themselves." —Gwen Ifill, coanchor of *PBS NewsHour*

"Peter Baker's *Days of Fire* is a book for every presidential hopeful and every citizen." —Tom Brokaw, author of *The Greatest Generation*

"You may or may not agree with George W. Bush's actions as president, but by the time you put *Days of Fire* down, you will understand them, and him, as never before." —Richard Norton Smith, author of *Thomas E. Dewey and His Times*

"Steeped in facts, and the writing is clear and crisp. . . . [*Days of Fire*] offers breathtaking insights into power, passion and politics at the highest levels of our government." —*BookPage*

"A fast-paced read that deftly weaves the trials and tribulations of the Bush presidency into a monumental tale of hubris and missed opportunities for greatness." —*Publishers Weekly* (starred review)

"A thorough, objective and surprisingly positive examination of the Bush-Cheney years. . . . This briskly written but exhaustively detailed account defies expectations. . . . A major contribution to the rehabilitation of our forty-third president."

—*Kirkus Reviews* (starred review)

"Ambitious, engrossing, and often disturbing. . . . A superbly researched, masterful account of eight critical, history-changing years."

—*Booklist* (starred review)

ALSO BY PETER BAKER

The Breach: Inside the Impeachment and Trial
of William Jefferson Clinton

Kremlin Rising: Vladimir Putin's Russia and the End of Revolution
(with Susan Glasser)

Peter Baker

DAYS OF FIRE

Peter Baker is the Chief White House Correspondent for *The New York Times* and a regular panelist on *Washington Week* on PBS. He is the author of the *New York Times* bestseller *The Breach*, about Bill Clinton's impeachment, and, with his wife, Susan Glasser, of *Kremlin Rising*, about Vladimir Putin's Russia.

DAYS OF FIRE

BUSH AND CHENEY IN THE WHITE HOUSE

Peter Baker

ANCHOR BOOKS
A Division of Random House LLC
New York

To Susan and Theo

And to my parents
for a lifetime of love

FIRST ANCHOR BOOKS EDITION, JUNE 2014

The Library of Congress has cataloged the Doubleday edition as follows:
Baker, Peter.
Days of fire : Bush and Cheney in the White House / Peter Baker.—
First edition.
pages cm
1. United States—Politics and government—2001–2009.
2. Bush, George W. (George Walker), 1946–
3. Cheney, Richard B. I. Title.
E902.B353 2013
973.931092—dc23
2013018745

Anchor Trade Paperback ISBN: 978-0-385-52519-0
eBook ISBN: 978-0-385-53692-9

Author photograph © Doug Mills
Book design by Maria Carella

www.anchorbooks.com

Printed in the United States of America
10 9 8 7 6 5 4 3 2 1

For a half a century, America defended our own freedom by standing watch on distant borders. After the shipwreck of communism came years of relative quiet, years of repose, years of sabbatical. **AND THEN THERE CAME A DAY OF FIRE.**

PRESIDENT GEORGE W. BUSH,
SECOND INAUGURAL ADDRESS, JANUARY 20, 2005

CONTENTS

DAYS OF FIRE

PROLOGUE

"Breaking china"

George W. Bush was sitting behind his desk in the Oval Office, chewing gum, staring, and listening—in fact listening longer than usual. He did not like long discursive reports. But this one weighed on him.

"Do you think he did it?" Bush asked.

"Yeah," the lawyer said, "I think he did it."

The nation's forty-third president had just days left in office, and the Decider, as he had memorably dubbed himself, was struggling with one final decision. His vice president, the man who had been at his side through every crisis for eight tumultuous years, was pressing him as never before. For two months, Dick Cheney had been lobbying for a pardon for his former chief of staff, I. Lewis Libby, who was known to all as Scooter and had been convicted of perjury and obstruction of justice in a case that had its roots in the origins of the Iraq War. Cheney would not let it go. He brought it up again and again, to the point that the president did not want to talk with him about it anymore.

Bush's gut told him no pardon, and he usually followed his gut. He had long bristled at the notion of people trading on connections to win executive clemency. The whole pardon process seemed corrupted to him, and now here was the ultimate insider seeking a special favor. Yet how could he tell Cheney no? How could he reject his partner of two terms on the one thing Cheney cared about most? For a man who valued loyalty above almost all else, it cut against the grain.

To help make a decision, Bush personally asked White House lawyers to reexamine the case to see if a pardon was justified. Fred Fielding, the White House counsel who had also served in the same role for Ronald Reagan, and William Burck, his deputy who had been a federal prosecutor in New York, pored over trial transcripts and studied evidence that Libby's lawyers had raised. Now they were in the Oval Office to report back that the jury had ample reason to find Libby guilty.

"I don't know. I wasn't there," Burck was saying to Bush, tempering his "he did it" judgment just a bit. "But if I were on that jury, I would probably have agreed with them. You have to follow the law, and the law says if you say something that is untrue, knowingly, to a federal official in the context of a grand jury investigation and it is material to their investigation, that's a crime."

Libby had been convicted of lying to federal investigators about whether he had divulged to journalists the name of a CIA officer married to a critic of the vice president. Libby insisted he simply remembered events differently from other witnesses. However, his story clashed not just with that of one person but with those of eight other people, including fellow administration officials. To believe Libby, the lawyers concluded, would be to believe that all those other people were wrong in their recollections or that Libby's memory was so faulty that he did not remember repeated conversations about a topic that clearly consumed the office of the vice president.

"All right, all right," the president said finally, which his aides took to mean he would not grant the pardon. "So why do you think he did it? Do you think he was protecting the vice president?"

"I don't think he was protecting the vice president," Burck said.

"So why do you think he did it?" Bush asked.

Burck said he thought Libby assumed his account of events would never be contradicted because prosecutors would not force reporters to violate vows of confidentiality to their sources. "I think he thought that would never be broken, and I think also Libby was concerned because he took to heart what you said back then, which is that you would fire anybody that you knew was involved in this," Burck said. "I just think he didn't think it was worth falling on the sword."

Bush took that in but did not seem convinced. "I think he still thinks he was protecting Cheney," the president said. He did not say so, but it seemed that Bush believed that Cheney had a personal stake in this, that in effect it was a conflict of interest. Now the vice president was just one more supplicant trading on personal connections in the pardon process, in this case seeking forgiveness for the man who had sacrificed himself for Cheney.

Bush sighed. "Now I am going to have to have the talk with the vice president," he said gloomily. That was the sort of unpleasant business that for eight years he had left to Cheney. It was the vice president who had delivered the bad news to people like Paul O'Neill and Donald Rumsfeld when they were fired.

Joshua Bolten, the president's chief of staff, spoke up: "I can do it."

"Nah, nah, I can do it," Bush said.

But he was dreading it.

FOR EIGHT YEARS, George Walker Bush and Richard Bruce Cheney had been partners in an ambitious joint venture to remake the country and the world. No two Americans in public office had collaborated to such lasting effect since Richard M. Nixon and Henry Kissinger.

Together they had accomplished significant things. They lifted a nation wounded by sneak attack on September 11, 2001, and safeguarded it from further assault, putting in place a new national security architecture for a dangerous era that would endure after they left office. At home, they instituted sweeping changes in education, health care, and taxes while heading off another Great Depression and the collapse of the storied auto industry. Abroad, they liberated fifty million people from despotic governments in the Middle East and central Asia, gave voice to the aspirations of democracy around the world, and helped turn the tide against a killer disease in Africa. They confronted crisis after crisis, not just a single "day of fire" on that bright morning in September, but days of fire over eight years.

Yet for all that, their misjudgments and misadventures left them the most unpopular president and vice president in generations. They had unwittingly unleashed forces that led to the deaths of perhaps a hundred thousand Iraqis while squandering America's moral authority, failing to rescue a great American city from a biblical flood, presiding over the worst financial crisis in eight decades, and leaving behind a fiscal mess that would hobble the country for years. For good or ill, theirs was a deeply consequential administration that would test a country and play out long after the two men at its center exited the public stage.

That their final hours together would be consumed by their private argument over the pardon underscores the distance the two men had traveled. Theirs is a story that may seem familiar on the surface, but in fact the real tale of Bush and Cheney and their eight years together is far more complicated than the simplistic narrative that developed over time. Hundreds of interviews with key players, including Cheney, and thousands of pages of never-released notes, memos, and other internal documents paint a riveting portrait of a partnership that evolved dramatically over time. Even in the early days, when a young, untested president relied on the advice of his seasoned number two, Bush was hardly the pawn nor Cheney the puppeteer that critics imagined. But if the vice president won most of the fights in the first term, he had grown increasingly marginalized by the second. Restless and disaffected, Bush sought out new paths to right his presidency and no longer paid as much heed to his vice president on everything from North Korea to gun rights. Cheney became alienated sitting in his West Wing office watching their efforts in his view run off course, undermining much of what he had accomplished. His fight for Libby was in a sense, then, a fight for redemption from a president who had turned away from him. In pressing for clemency, Cheney was seeking one last validation of their extraordinary tandem—one that Bush was ultimately unwilling to give.

"Friendship" is a word that does not fully capture the relationship between Bush and Cheney. They did not see each other out of the workplace. Cheney did not spend social weekends at Camp David, and they did not dine together with their wives. They did not typically exchange birthday gifts. Bush did not go hunting with Cheney, and the vice president visited the president's ranch in Texas only for official meetings, although the two men would occasionally slip out to fish for bass in a pond on the property. On election night in 2000 and again in 2004, they watched the returns separately, coming together only late in the evening when they thought they were about to head to a public party to claim victory. "They weren't personally close," reflected Ari Fleischer, the president's first White House press secretary. "They didn't go bowling together or to Camp David. Cheney didn't go jogging with George Bush. He was everything that Bush designed when he chose Dick Cheney to be counselor."

Cheney thought of their relationship as a business one. "It was professional, more than personal," Cheney said after leaving office. "We weren't buddies in that sense." Bush had a hard time defining their relationship. "You know, I would, I would say friends," he finally concluded. "But on the other hand, we run in separate circles. Dick goes home to his family, and I go home to mine. I wouldn't call him a very social person. I'm certainly not a very social person either. So we don't spend a lot of time socially together. But, uh, friends."

Partners might be a more apt description, although even that is freighted. Some Bush advisers objected because in their view partnership implied an equal footing, and the vice president was, in the end, the *vice* president. Cheney never forgot that and made a point of showing nothing but deference to Bush. While Bush called him "Dick," Cheney always called Bush "Mr. President." Even out of his presence, Cheney referred to him as "the Man," as in "Let's take this to the Man." Bush, more irreverently, sometimes referred to Cheney as "Vice." Karl Rove came to call Cheney "Management," as in "Better check with Management."

Cheney was just five years Bush's senior but carried himself with the gravitas of a much older man, and Bush treated him with more respect than anyone else in the inner circle. Yet in any meeting, it was clear who was in charge: Bush led the discussion, asked the questions, and called on people to speak, while Cheney largely remained quiet. "If you spent any time around

President Bush, you quickly realize he's not a guy who can be led around in that way, not at all," observed Matthew Dowd, his campaign strategist. "And Cheney's not the type who operates that way, not at all." Still, that silence seemed to connote a power all its own; everyone else in the room understood that when they left, Cheney stayed behind, offering advice one-on-one when nobody could rebut him. What Cheney actually thought, at times, remained mysterious. "He was a black box to a lot of us," said Peter Wehner, the White House director of strategic initiatives.

They were, of course, starkly different men, Bush an outgoing former college cheerleader from a privileged family background who delighted in bestowing nicknames, conquered his own demons with a ferocious midlife discipline, and preferred the big picture; Cheney a onetime electrical lineman who worked his way up to some of the most important jobs in Washington by mastering the intricacies of governance, ultimately becoming the grim eminence of a wartime White House.

But they shared more in their backgrounds than many recognized. Both were raised in the West and identified with its frontier spirit. Both made their way east to the halls of Yale University, only to become disenchanted by what they found to be an elitist culture. Both partied robustly as young men and had run-ins with the law, only to get their acts together after the women in their lives finally put their feet down. Both admired Winston Churchill to the point of displaying busts of the legendary prime minister, seeking to emulate his relentless strength in the face of overwhelming odds.

They both had a sense of humor too, though of markedly different brands. Where Bush was jocular and sometimes goofy, making faces on his campaign plane or enjoying an aide's whoopee cushion prank, Cheney was dry and understated, slipping in an ironic comment and then lifting the corner of his mouth into his trademark crooked grin. As it happened, they shared the same target for their humor: Cheney. Bush enjoyed poking fun at his vice president's bad aim and penchant for secrecy. "Dick here sent over a gift I could tell he'd picked out personally," Bush said when his daughter Jenna got engaged to be married. "A paper shredder." Cheney embraced his own dark reputation. Once his friend David Hume Kennerly greeted him teasingly by saying, "Hi, Dick. Have you blown away any small countries this morning?" Without missing a beat, Cheney replied, "You know, that's the one thing about this job I really love." At one point, he puckishly tried on a Darth Vader mask his aides had bought and posed for a picture. When Cheney later tried to put the picture in his memoir, Lynne Cheney talked him out of it.

Popular mythology had Cheney using the dark side of the force to manipulate a weak-minded president into doing his bidding. The image took on such power that books were written about "the co-presidency" and "the hijacking of the American presidency." Late-night comedians regularly turned to the same theme. Conan O'Brien joked that Cheney had told an interviewer, "I'll really miss being president." Jimmy Kimmel joked that Cheney "doesn't regret any of the decisions he made, and if he had to do it all over again, he would order President Bush to do exactly the same thing."

Cheney did not seem to mind, but it got under Bush's skin. When he published his own memoir after leaving office, Bush disclosed that Cheney had volunteered to drop off the 2004 election ticket. "Accepting Dick's offer," Bush mused, "would be one way to demonstrate that I was in charge." Yet while Bush stewed, Cheney came to see the reputation as an advantage. "Am I the evil genius in the corner that nobody ever sees come out of his hole?" he once asked sardonically. "It's a nice way to operate, actually."

The cartoonish caricature, however, overstated the reality and missed the fundamental path of the relationship. Cheney was unquestionably the most influential vice president in American history. He assembled a power base through a mastery of how Washington worked and a relationship of trust with Bush, who viewed him as his consigliere guiding him through a hostile and bewildering capital. Cheney subordinated himself to Bush in a way no other vice president in modern times had done, forgoing any independent aspiration to run for president himself in order to focus entirely on making Bush's presidency successful. In return, Bush gave him access to every meeting and decision, a marked contrast to his predecessors. Harry Truman as vice president met alone with Franklin D. Roosevelt just twice after Inauguration Day. When asked in 2002 how many times he had met privately with Bush, Cheney reached into his suit pocket and pulled out his schedule. "Let me see," he said. "Three, four, five, six, seven—seven times." Then he paused for effect. "Today."

As a result, Cheney played an outsized role in driving decisions in the early years of the administration, expertly employing a network of loyalists placed strategically throughout the government. When he ran into opposition, Cheney instituted controversial environmental, energy, and counterterrorism policies by circumventing the internal process. He pressed, and even badgered, an inexperienced president to go after Saddam Hussein in Iraq over any reservations Bush might have harbored. "Are you going to take care of this guy or not?" Cheney demanded impatiently at one of their private lunches.

For all that, Cheney was largely pushing on an open door, taking Bush where the president himself was already inclined to go. The president's closest friends and advisers do not recall him ever complaining that Cheney had convinced him to do something he would not have done otherwise. "He never did anything in his time serving George W. that George W. didn't either sanction or approve of," said Alan Simpson, a former Republican senator from Wyoming and a close friend of Cheney's. "So when people say that Cheney was running the show, that is bullshit." General Richard Myers, who as chairman of the Joint Chiefs of Staff was on hand for some of the most critical moments, agreed. "This whole notion that the vice president was the puppet master I find laughable," he said. "He was an active vice president because I think he was empowered, but he wasn't a dominant factor. The alpha male in the White House was the president."

Even in the first term, Bush rebuffed Cheney on more than one occasion. While agreeing to confront Iraq, Bush refused to attack in the spring of 2002, when Cheney first pushed him to do so, nearly a year before the eventual invasion. He accepted Colin Powell's recommendation to first seek UN support and rejected a plan to create a post-Hussein government led by Iraqi exiles like Ahmad Chalabi. By the second term, Bush had moved even further away from Cheney. Frustrated by the failure to find weapons of mass destruction in Iraq and the crescendo of violence that greeted the "liberators," unhappy to find the United States isolated from its allies, and eager for breakthroughs that would shape his legacy, Bush increasingly turned not to his vice president but to Condoleezza Rice, who as secretary of state supplanted Cheney as the president's most influential lieutenant.

That's not to say he was neutered. Cheney managed to preserve much of what he had started. But he was on defense more than offense in the second term, trying to fend off changes that he thought would weaken the country or unravel the policies he had brought to pass. "Perhaps my clout was diminished," he conceded after leaving office. "That's possible. I wouldn't quarrel about that." Indeed, by the time Bush and Cheney stepped out of the White House for the final time, they had disagreed on North Korea, gun rights, same-sex marriage, tax cuts, Guantánamo Bay, interrogation practices, surveillance policy, Iran, the auto industry bailout, climate change, the Lebanon War, Harriet Miers, Donald Rumsfeld, Middle East peace, Syria, Russia, and federal spending.

All of that came before the Scooter Libby pardon.

THE VICE PRESIDENT'S lobbying campaign started in earnest after the 2008 election that picked their successors. With the final weeks of the administration now at hand, Cheney decided he would invest whatever fading capital he had left in winning a pardon for his onetime right-hand man.

To Cheney, it was simple justice. Libby had been pursued by an unprincipled prosecutor bent on damaging the White House. Neither Libby nor anyone else had been charged with the leak that precipitated the investigation in the first place, and it turned out the special prosecutor had known virtually from the start that someone else had been the original source. The fact that the prosecutor kept investigating anyway made Cheney feel that he was the real target and Libby collateral damage. In the end, he felt, the charges against Libby were built on nothing more than a faulty memory. Libby had loyally served Cheney and Bush, and for that matter his country, only to be made into a criminal.

Cheney brought up the case incessantly. In eight years, he had never pushed Bush as hard on any other matter. Cheney raised it with Bush during a meeting before a Thanksgiving round of pardons, then again before a Christmas round. Bush told Cheney he would hold off more controversial pardons until near the end of their term, a comment the vice president took as an indication that Libby would be among them. But Bush never believed he had made any commitment, and he was skeptical of a pardon from the start. He had already commuted Libby's prison sentence after it was handed down in 2007 so the former aide never had to spend a minute behind bars. But at the time, Fred Fielding had written a public statement for Bush saying he was not substituting his judgment for the jury's on the question of guilt or innocence. How could he change his mind eighteen months later?

That was the argument Cheney heard from Ed Gillespie, the presidential counselor and top political adviser who came to see the vice president one day to explain why he was advising Bush against a pardon. As with many in the White House, the Libby case had proved personally painful for Gillespie. He had been among the first to contribute to Libby's legal defense fund. But given what Bush had said in commuting the sentence, Gillespie told Cheney he did not think the president should now grant a full pardon.

"On top of that, Mr. Vice President, the lawyers are not making the case for it," Gillespie said. "We'll be asked, did the lawyers recommend it? And if the lawyers didn't, it's going to be hard to justify for the president."

Cheney said he thought Gillespie was wrong and shared his views about why the prosecution was illegitimate. The two agreed to disagree, and Gillespie got up and left after what he thought was the hardest thing he had had to do while in the White House.

THE CONTROVERSY THAT surrounded Cheney's role invited a question that would mark his time in office: Had he changed? What happened to the sensible, moderate Republican people thought they knew? Brent Scowcroft, who had served as national security adviser to two Republican presidents, famously said he no longer recognized his friend. Others wondered whether the vice president had somehow been affected by his multiple heart attacks or by the trauma of September 11, 2001.

Perhaps so many thought he had changed because they mistook his low-key demeanor, friendships across party lines, and service for moderate presidents as indications that he was more moderate than he really was. The record suggests he was always more conservative than his reputation. In Gerald R. Ford's White House, he was at odds with Secretary of State Henry Kissinger and Vice President Nelson Rockefeller. In Congress during the 1980s, he compiled one of the most conservative voting records; when the *Washington Post* referred to him as a moderate, Cheney instructed an aide to call for a correction. As defense secretary for George H. W. Bush, he was deeply suspicious of the reformist Soviet leader Mikhail Gorbachev. After all this, Cheney scoffed at the notion that he was any different than he had been as a young man. "I didn't change," he said. "The world changed."

Having participated in doomsday war-game scenarios in the 1980s mapping out the consequences of catastrophic attack, Cheney had long nursed dark views about the world's dangers, views that seemed ratified on September 11. He spent the rest of his time in office consumed not with another September 11 but with a much worse scenario where terrorists would be armed with nuclear or chemical weapons instead of box cutters. By the end of his tenure, the country had largely forgotten its fears from the days after the World Trade Center fell, but Cheney had not. What happened on September 11 was a wrenching tragedy, but ultimately survivable for a nation; an attack with weapons of mass destruction could pose a much more existential threat. In that view, almost anything it took to protect the country seemed justified. While some Americans began thinking they had overreacted to September 11, Cheney lived in the shadowy world of intelligence reports that projected threats around every corner, the "dark side," as he memorably put it. What was the moral cost of waterboarding three terrorists against the chance of a mushroom cloud in Manhattan?

If anything transformed, it was Cheney's public persona. "He went from the wise man, the Yoda character, to Colonel Jessup from *A Few Good Men*," said Adam Levine, who worked in the White House in the first term. Levine then channeled Cheney as the gravelly voiced Jack Nicholson playing the you-can't-handle-the-truth colonel lecturing the lawyer played by Tom Cruise on a rough-and-tumble world: "'You want me on that wall. Who is going to do it? You, Colin Powell? You, Condi Rice? I don't have the time or inclination to explain myself to somebody who rises and sleeps under the blanket of freedom I provide and then questions the manner in which I provide it.' Cheney embodied that feeling of it—'I don't have to fucking explain to you what I am doing. I am saving the country, you asshole. I am saving lives. As much as you might hate me, you need me here.' Bush was never like that."

From the days after September 11 at least, it was Cheney who did not change. He remained focused unwaveringly on the threat he perceived. It was Bush who changed, not in his core beliefs or his general personality, but in his approach toward the same goals. By the latter half of his presidency, he had grown more confident in his own judgments and less dependent on his vice president. He was willing to compromise on his most controversial terror policies in order to build a bipartisan foundation that would outlast his administration. He was more interested in rebuilding alliances and trying diplomacy than in preemptive wars. Condoleezza Rice, the architect of the shift, said Bush viewed it not as a sharp pivot but as more of a natural evolution along a continuum following the necessarily aggressive actions of the first term. "We had broken a lot of china," she reflected. "But at that point, you have to leave something in place. That is true with allies. It is true with the Middle East. It is true in putting together an international consensus on North Korea and international consensus on Iran. And I don't think that is how the vice president saw it. I think he would have liked to have kept breaking china."

Bush and Cheney headed into their final months in office resigned to their differences. Bush remained respectful of his number two and was rarely heard to utter a disparaging word, although there were occasions when he was known to roll his eyes at something Cheney did or said. Cheney seemed tired, physically spent after four heart attacks on his way to a fifth and politically spent after eight years in the trenches. When it came to one of the last major foreign policy decisions of the administration—what to do about a secret Syrian nuclear reactor—Cheney's isolation was made plain when he urged an American air strike. "Does anyone here agree with the vice president?" Bush asked at the critical meeting. Not a single hand went up.

A few weeks before the inauguration, even as Cheney was lobbying Bush for the Libby pardon, Joshua Bolten invited all of his living predecessors as chief of staff to his West Wing office to meet with his successor, Rahm Emanuel. Thirteen of the sixteen men to have served in that unique role attended, including Cheney, who had been Ford's top assistant. They went around one by one to offer advice.

When it came to Cheney, a devilish look crossed his face. "Whatever you do," he said, pausing for effect, "make sure you've got the vice president under control."

AS HE HEADED into his final days in the White House, it was clear to Bush that he did not exactly have his vice president under control. The president had decided he would not pardon Scooter Libby, and he now had to break the news to his estranged partner.

Bush welcomed Cheney into the small private dining room off the Oval Office for their final one-on-one lunch on January 15, culminating a tradition they had kept up for their entire time in office. Around this table, they had discussed some of the epic decisions of their tenure, war and peace, life and death. They had bonded over family talk, personal observations, and political gossip. But this lunch would go like none of the others before.

There would be no pardon for Libby, Bush announced to Cheney. It was a hard choice, but that was his decision.

"You are leaving a good man wounded on the field of battle," Cheney snapped at the president, abandoning eight years of deference.

Bush was taken aback. It might have been the harshest thing Cheney had ever said to him, and in language designed to attack Bush's self-identity, his sense of loyalty to his own troops in a time of war.

"The comment stung," Bush wrote in his memoir. "In eight years, I had never seen Dick like this, or even close to it. I worried that the friendship we had built was about to be severely strained, at best."

He had reason to worry. To Cheney, this was the final evidence that Bush had lost his will. The president who had been buffeted by critics for so long would not stand up for what was right and jeopardize the relatively positive media attention he was receiving for a smooth transition with Barack Obama, his successor. Perhaps it was even one last attempt to show who was actually in charge after all.

"Scooter was somebody, you know, he didn't have to be there," Cheney said years later. "He came to serve. He worked for me before at the Pentagon. He had done yeoman duty for us." The conviction, he added, was a deep scar. "He has to live with that stigma for the rest of his life. That was wrong, and the president had it within his power to fix it, and he chose not to. It is obviously a place where we fundamentally disagree. He knows how I felt about it." Cheney suggested the president did not want to take the heat. "I am sure it meant some criticism of him, but it was a huge disappointment for me."

Wounded, the president wondered if he had made the right decision. Famed for never second-guessing himself, Bush began reconsidering. Maybe he should grant the pardon after all.

PART ONE

1

"One of you could be president"

George W. Bush had already dropped by to see three congressmen when he strode down the high-ceilinged corridor of the Cannon House Office Building to find the fourth on his list. It was June 17, 1987, and the son of the vice president was making the rounds to gather support for his father's presidential campaign, or at least build goodwill with Republicans on Capitol Hill. His 3:30 p.m. appointment was with a low-key congressman from Wyoming named Dick Cheney.

This next-generation Bush was a tall, rangy man, handsome with an easy smile and a face that bore a striking resemblance to that of his famous father. Just a couple weeks shy of his forty-first birthday, he had moved his wife and twin daughters to Washington for the campaign, appointing himself "loyalty enforcer" to ensure a growing staff of political operatives was laboring on behalf of George H. W. Bush's interests rather than their own.

Along the way, he was becoming a surrogate for his father and was surprised how much he enjoyed his new role. This family business had gotten into his blood. He had none of his father's smoothness, though, and none of those polished New England sensibilities. Junior, as some called him, although he was not technically a junior, lived closer to the edge, the "Roman candle of the family," as the campaign chronicler Richard Ben Cramer would call him, "the biggest and most jagged chip off the old block."

By temperament, the man he was visiting was quite the opposite. Cheney, a former White House chief of staff now in his fifth term in Congress, was as quiet as Bush was voluble, as stoic as the younger man was expressive. He would say what he had to and then stop, perfectly comfortable with the silences that disquieted others. "He's not necessarily what you would call the life of the party," observed Dennis Hastert, who served with him in the House and went on to become Speaker. Cheney's wife, Lynne, thought the way to understand him was to remember how much he loved fly-fishing, standing without a sound for hours casting for a bite—"not a sport for the impatient," as she put it, and "definitely not a sport for chatterboxes." He refused to go fishing with his friend Kenneth Adelman because "he talks too much." At forty-six, Cheney had just been promoted to chairman of the House Republican Conference, the number-three position in the party leadership. He had his eye on someday becoming Speaker.

Neither man in the years to come would remember the first time they met, but it was likely this encounter in the summer before the Republican primaries. Never mind that Cheney had no intention of taking sides in the Republican contest featuring Bush's father. To a congressman eyeing further moves up the leadership ladder, becoming a partisan for a presidential candidate would be "asking for grief I didn't need," as Cheney later put it. Indeed, his neutrality would cause a years-long rift with his good friend and mentor, Donald Rumsfeld, who had been contemplating his own run for president. But Cheney got along well with his guest that day. "He and Bush hit it off," recalled Wayne Berman, the campaign's congressional relations director who organized the meeting.

Berman would go on to become one of Washington's premier lobbyists and Republican fund-raisers, as well as one of the few men close to both Bush and Cheney. He raised millions of dollars for them, promoted their campaigns, and hosted dinners for them at his house. His wife, Lea Berman, would work in the White House first for Cheney's wife and then for Bush's wife. But even Wayne Berman never imagined what would eventually come of the acquaintance that began in that courtesy call one summer afternoon. "Bush in those days was a really interesting guy," he observed years later. "A little insecure, had a bit of a chip on his shoulder. Very skeptical of everything in Washington, something I think he retained. Skeptical of a lot of people around his dad." As for Cheney, he was more comfortable with Washington yet also kept his distance. The only ones he truly relaxed around were his wife and two daughters. "Cheney has three confidantes, and all their last names are Cheney," Berman noted. "One is related by marriage and two by blood." He could be unguarded with friends, "but if he told you something and it leaked and he suspected you leaked it, you didn't get a second chance. Finished."

Bush at that point had yet to win public office and was still evolving into the politician he would later become. When he visited the West Wing in those days, he would stop by offices of aides he knew, plop down on a couch, and put his cowboy boots on the coffee table. Ronald Reagan, who had met the Bush children, thought that if any of them had a bright political future, it would be George's brother Jeb. Their brother Marvin once gave his assessment of each sibling. "George?" he said. "George is the family clown."

Indeed, after their father won the presidency, the younger George attended a state dinner for Queen Elizabeth II, lifted his pant legs to show her his cowboy boots, and proudly declared that he was the black sheep in the family. "Do you have any in yours?" he asked. What was certainly a defense mechanism for a son and grandson of accomplished men also became a conscious strategy of lowering expectations. "It is always better to lowball these things," he once told a general years later in a revealing moment during a conference call about Iraq. "If you perform, people are surprised." He added, "I really enjoy it when somebody says, that son of a bitch just got out a coherent sentence."

The day Bush met Cheney came less than a year after a radical midlife course correction. Although he never accepted the word "alcoholic," Bush's decision to quit drinking the day after his fortieth birthday reshaped his outlook on life, manifesting itself as both empathy and determination. The man who conquered his own weakness would stop whatever he was doing upon meeting an addict. "His cadence would change," said David Kuo, a former aide. "He would put both of his hands on the man's shoulders and look into his eyes. Any swagger disappeared. Something softer and perhaps more genuine took its place." At the same time, the iron discipline it took to stop cold turkey would become a never-look-back approach to the Oval Office; he could be at once maddeningly stubborn about revisiting decisions and indefatigably upbeat in the face of crises that would leave other presidents talking to the paintings.

It may have also fueled an urgent idealism that would characterize his presidency for better or worse; on some level, he believed he had been saved to accomplish great things. His zeal inspired supporters with its promise of transformation while dismaying critics as dangerously messianic. Bush's favorite book was *The Raven*, a Pulitzer Prize–winning biography that traced the life of Sam Houston from drunkard to president of the Republic of Texas. "His first thought, his constant thought, was to atone for the period of his delinquency," the author, Marquis James, wrote of Houston. "He would do something grand. He would capture an empire."

Grandiosity never defined Cheney. He was, as the writer Todd Purdum once observed, "a never-complain, never-explain politician who reminded many of the younger officials and journalists who came to know him of their fathers." A man who would survive five heart attacks, the first at age thirty-seven, Cheney demonstrated a grit he rarely got credit for, one that fostered a single-minded intensity to get things done regardless of others' sensibilities. "I suppose it gives him a sense of you can't count on being here forever and you have to accomplish what you can accomplish while you can," his daughter Liz observed. His own mortality never far from mind,

Cheney adopted a cold-eyed view of what was needed to protect the life of the country, never entertaining a moment of doubt over tactics that would cause others to recoil.

Trent Lott, who served with him in the House before becoming Senate majority leader, remembered skiing with Cheney once in Jackson Hole, Wyoming, where the future vice president had a vacation home. Lott was decked out in a fancy outfit and red coat, while Cheney showed up at the lift in jeans, red scarf, and ragged old jacket that "looked like something a sailor would have worn in 1945." Cheney took off "and all I saw for the next two miles was that red scarf flapping in the breeze as I skidded down the run on my butt," Lott recalled. "He came up, very unimpressive looking, nothing fancy, skied like a wild man going down that run. I said that's the real Dick Cheney. I *looked* good and he *skied* good."

Cheney's DNA was missing that politician's gene attuned to reputation, a trait that served him well for decades, only to betray him at the end as he allowed himself to be reduced to a cartoon figure in the public mind. "I think years ago, the rooms in his brain that normal people devote to keeping score of slights and Beyoncé and popular culture, he moved all the furniture out of those rooms and stuffed them full of file cabinets about GDP and throw weights and all that kind of stuff," said Pete Williams, who worked for Cheney on Capitol Hill and at the Pentagon. "He is fundamentally a very serious man." And because Cheney flunked out of Yale and never became part of the club, he never felt beholden. "He didn't have the blue blazer, he didn't have the crest, and he didn't have the whale belt and the purple pants and all that stuff," Williams said. "There is no Ivy League thing, there is no big city thing, there is no prep school thing. He went to a public high school. So I think what that means is he came here pretty much on his own two feet. I think that that has always given him a great deal of self-confidence. That plays out in a number of ways. I think it liberated him to follow his own conscience. He didn't have chits to repay, he didn't have errands to run, he didn't have to worry about being ostracized if he took a view that was unorthodox. He just took the measure of himself and that was enough."

GEORGE WALKER BUSH and Richard Bruce Cheney were born five and a half years and a world apart. Bush arrived on July 6, 1946, in New Haven, Connecticut, joining a blue-blazer-and-whale-belt family with a rarefied history dating back to the *Mayflower*. His mother, the former Barbara Pierce, was a distant cousin of President Franklin Pierce's, while his father, George Herbert Walker Bush, had roots tied by researchers to fifteen American presidents and the British royal family. His grandparents traveled in the same circles as the Rockefellers, Tafts, Luces, Grahams, Harrimans, Lodges, Fulbrights, and Kennedys. Cheney was born on January 30, 1941, in Lincoln, Nebraska, to a family of New Deal Democrats who struggled through the Great Depression and were proud their oldest son was born on Franklin Roosevelt's birthday. His grandparents had lost everything in the crisis except their house. His father, Richard Herbert Cheney, dropped out of college and worked for decades for the Soil Conservation Service teaching farmers how to rotate crops. His mother, Marjorie Dickey, waited tables at the family-owned Dickey's Café in Syracuse, Nebraska, until meeting the young public servant. At various points growing up, Dick lived on an uncle's farm and in a family friend's basement.

Yet from such disparate beginnings, the two future partners would travel familiar paths. Bush's parents eschewed the easy life in the East to move to hardscrabble Texas oil country, and the Cheneys headed to the frontier of Wyoming, with the boys raised in settings not all that different. "There is a similarity, to a certain extent, between West Texas and Casper, Wyoming, in look and feel," observed Dean McGrath, who spent years working for Cheney. "It is a long, long way between places. There was openness and expanse that when people in the West talk about, people on the East Coast don't get." From their western upbringings came strong views about the American ethos and an equally strong detachment from the coasts that dominated national life. As McGrath put it, "They are both pretty conservative, they are both pretty free market, they are both pretty free trade, and they both have pretty strong social values."

Nostalgia naturally shrouded the places that shaped Bush and Cheney in romantic hues, but friends describe them in similar terms, as towns where doors were left unlocked, boys played baseball day after day, and everyone knew each other's business. Midland was a "little Mayberry type of town," as Bush's lifelong friend Joe O'Neill remembered it, while Joe Meyer, Cheney's high school pal, described Casper as something out of *Happy Days*. They were towns on the rise, flush with oil and the entrepreneurs who chased it. Midland was the capital of the Permian Basin, which produced nearly 20 percent of America's oil in the 1950s. Casper was called the oil capital of the Rockies. Both towns were formed in the 1880s and topped twenty thousand residents in 1950; Casper had doubled in size since 1920, while Midland had quadrupled since 1930 and would triple again over the next decade. By the time the Bushes bought their first house in Midland, 215 oil companies had opened offices there. Both towns were arid, but Midland was flat and brown, prone to tumbleweed and sandstorms, while Casper was greener, perched at the base of a mountain and nearly as high as Denver.

The Bushes came from money, of course, but family tradition dictated that each generation make its own. Prescott Bush, young George's grandfather, who went by Pres, had refused his father's inheritance and helped round up investors in early American icons like CBS, Prudential, and Pan Am. He helped Dresser Industries reorganize and go public with a Yale University friend, Neil Mallon, at the helm. George H. W. Bush, the youngest commissioned navy combat pilot in World War II and a star baseball player at Yale, set off for Texas in 1948 to make his own mark. That's not to say family connections were unavailable. It was Mallon who gave him a job at a Dresser subsidiary in Odessa. But he had to start as an equipment clerk. It was a hard, peripatetic life in modest homes for years until oil began paying off. Settling in Odessa, the family rented a two-room duplex, sharing a bathroom with a mother-and-daughter prostitute team next door. After a yearlong transfer to California, where the family bounced around five different homes, they returned to Texas in 1950, this time to Midland. Pres Bush, meanwhile, embarked on a political career, losing a close Senate race in Connecticut that same year after an erroneous news report that he headed a birth control advocacy group, souring the family view of the media. He tried again in 1952 and this time won. In Washington, he became a friend and golfing partner of President Dwight D. Eisenhower's, stood up to Joseph McCarthy, helped write the interstate highway bill, and blazed a path for pro-business, pro-civil-rights moderate Republicanism. He was a stiff man, insisting that his grandchildren wear coat and tie to dinner and address him as "Senator" instead of "Grandpa."

The younger Bush family lived in a succession of houses in Midland, each time trading up as George H. W. Bush's fortunes rose. The house where they spent most of their time was a cozy, one-floor home with knotty pine walls on Ohio Street that Bush bought for $9,000 in 1951. With three bedrooms, one bathroom, no shower, wall heaters, but no air conditioners, it hardly looked like the home of a future president, much less two. It might have fit inside one wing of the family compound in Kennebunkport, Maine, that Bush would later purchase.

For Georgie, as the son was called at the time, life was carefree, a time of bicycles and baseball. "He lives in his cowboy clothes," his father wrote to a friend. With the elder Bush often away on business, Georgie bonded with his mother. He would grow up like her, straightforward, tough, acerbic. He would later joke that he had his father's eyes and his mother's mouth. He was not above troublemaking. Once he stole a pack of his mother's cigarettes, and the football coach caught him smoking in an alley; the principal at another point paddled him three times for drawing a mustache, beard, and sideburns on his own face with an ink pen. At fourteen, he wrecked the family car—twice. "Georgie aggravates the hell out of me at times (I am sure I do the same to him)," the elder Bush wrote to his father-in-law in 1955, "but then at times I am so proud of him I could die."

The "starkest memory of my childhood" came when he was seven. Georgie's younger sister, Robin, was diagnosed with leukemia, and their parents took her to New York in a losing battle to save her. Georgie was never told what was going on, so when he walked down a covered walkway at Sam Houston Elementary School carrying a phonograph to the principal's office one day, he was excited to see his parents' green Oldsmobile pull up on the gravel driveway with what he thought was Robin's head in the back. "My mom, dad, and sister are home," he told a teacher. "Can I go see them?" But when he got to the car, Robin was not there. "She died," his mother whispered.

As for any boy his age, processing such a loss was hard. "Why didn't you tell me?" he asked. But with his father back on the road for business and Jeb too young to understand, Georgie focused on helping his mourning mother. When a friend came by, the young Bush said, "I can't come over to play because I have to play with my mother. She's lonely." Barbara overheard. "That started my cure," she later said. "I realized I was too much of a burden for a little seven-year-old boy to carry." She went on to have three more children, Neil, Marvin, and Dorothy.

Nearly eight hundred miles to the north, Dick Cheney experienced a similar childhood, though without the tragedy. His first years had been spent in Nebraska, listening to *The Lone Ranger* on the radio, playing Little League, and joining the Cub Scouts. The family moved around until finding an eight-hundred-square-foot house with a bedroom that he would share with his brother, Bob. His parents did not own a car until Dick was eight, and even then it was a twelve-year-old Buick coupe with no backseat, forcing the boys to ride in boxes on floorboards. His father was transferred in 1954 to Casper, where the family bought a small $15,000 house on Texas Place on the eastern edge of town. Out the window was prairie as far as the eye could see. "His father had a wry sense of humor but was a man of few words," recalled Pete Williams. "His mom was the real ripsnorter of the family," said Joe Meyer. "She was the athlete, just a ball of fire."

Dick learned to fish and hunt, the beginning of lifelong avocations. He and friends would shoot jackrabbits with .22-caliber rifles and give them to his mother to fry for school lunch boxes. As they got older, they went to ten-cent movies and cruised the small city. "We had an A&W on one side of town and a drive-in on the other side, and for fifty cents' worth of gas you could drive back and forth all night just to see who was driving around," recalled Bernie Seebaum, who grew up a block away. Like the young Bush, Dick got in trouble on occasion. Once he and a friend were taken to the police station for throwing snowballs at passing cars and hitting a driver who had left her window open. While he had been on the honor roll in Nebraska, he was not impressing teachers in Casper. One complained of "too much time wasted foolishly" and wrote that "he needs to get over his very smarty attitude." He and his friends played poker, smoked cigars, and once in a while snuck a beer. "We thought we were pretty hot stuff," Seebaum said.

At Natrona County High School, Dick became a star halfback and linebacker on the football team and caught the eye of Lynne Vincent, a state champion baton twirler and ace student. When he gathered the nerve to ask her out, she exclaimed, "You're kidding!" But she meant it as surprise, not disinterest, and the two soon became the school's leading couple, the senior class president and football co-captain who crowned the homecoming queen at the dance. It was a simple and satisfying life, "like a classic fifties movie," as he remembered it. Dick delivered newspapers, cut lawns, and even worked at the rodeo grounds. "We didn't know we were poor and that we were missing things," said Mick McMurry, a longtime friend.

THEIR PATHS ALMOST crossed in New Haven, Connecticut, where Bush enrolled in Yale just two years after Cheney left. Neither one of them found Yale to his liking, and in some ways their campus stays would shape their views of the Eastern establishment for life.

Leaving behind Lynne, his parents, and his siblings, Bob and Susan, Cheney took the train across the country in 1959 with his friend Tom Fake. He and Fake were tight; during high school, they double-dated, played football together, took up boxing, and spent weeks learning how "to beat the crap out of each other." They received scholarships through Thomas Stroock, a classmate of George H. W. Bush's who operated an oil company in Casper and employed Lynne as a part-time secretary.

It was Cheney's first time east of Chicago, and getting off the train was like stepping into a foreign country where "they were speaking another language." He was used to open spaces and western sensibilities where people looked you in the eye. More significantly, he realized he was not prepared academically. "We went from being the big fish in a small puddle to being thrown into Yale with all the fifth-year boys and really sixth-year boys who had gone to prep school," Fake recalled. "We were just struggling to stay afloat." It was a shock. "You'd come home dragging your tail between your legs when everything else for eighteen years had gone so well."

Moreover, like many young men, Cheney believed that "beer was one of the essentials of life." A dean wrote to his parents, "Dick has fallen in with a group of very high-spirited young men." After freshman year, his grades were so bad the university cut off the scholarship. He paid for the first semester of sophomore year through loans, but after that the school would no longer provide even those and told him to take a year off. He returned to Wyoming and worked as a $3.10-an-hour electrical lineman before returning to Yale for spring semester in 1962. Once again, he flunked out and returned to the lineman job, spending off-hours consuming life's essential and getting arrested for drunk driving in October 1962 and again in June 1963. The second time he found himself nursing a hangover in jail around the time his Yale classmates were graduating. Lynne put her foot down. "She made it clear eventually that she had no interest in marrying a lineman for the county," Cheney said. He got his act together, enrolled in community college, and then transferred to the University of Wyoming. They were married in August 1964, but he got sick and spent the honeymoon money on treatment.

Bush arrived at Yale that fall, following the footsteps of his father and his father's father. His family had moved from Midland to Houston, where he attended the Kinkaid School, and then at fifteen he had gone off to Phillips Academy in Andover, Massachusetts. "Andover was cold and distant and difficult," he said later. Like Cheney, he was out of place academically and culturally. Writing a paper about Robin's death, he looked up a synonym for "tears." When he wrote that "lacerates" fell from his eyes, the teacher marked a big zero in red ink on the paper. So he threw himself into the study of people, becoming a cheerleader and forming a stickball league with himself as high commissioner. He called himself "Tweeds Bush," a play off Boss Tweed, the nineteenth-century political boss, and gave teams names like Crotch Rots and Nads (as in "Go, Nads!"). Classmates called him "Lip" for his active mouth.

Yale was much the same. With neither the academic nor the athletic gifts to match his father, Bush set about making friends, developing skills that would later prove critical to his rise. He knew the names of all fifty pledges to Delta Kappa Epsilon. But he was turned off by what he saw as the intellectual superiority around him. When his father launched his political career in Texas with a losing challenge to Senator Ralph Yarborough in 1964, George headed home for election night and cried at the result. Returning to Yale, he ran into William Sloane Coffin, the university chaplain. "I knew your father," Coffin told him, "and your father lost to a better man." Bush was crushed. As the Vietnam War heated up and the campus turned increasingly activist, Bush grew more alienated. "He was a guy out of water when he was at Yale," Joe O'Neill said. "He felt uncomfortable as hell."

As with Cheney, Bush's Yale days were better remembered for their extracurricular exploits. Lubricated by beer, he and his fraternity brothers were arrested for stealing a Christmas wreath from a local hotel, although disorderly conduct charges were dropped. When Yale beat Princeton at football, Bush led others onto the New Jersey field to tear down the goalpost. Police found him on the crossbar and put him into a cruiser, whereupon Yale friends started rocking the car, shouting, "Free Bush!" The officers ultimately let him go but ordered him never to return.

While he was tapped for the Skull and Bones secret society like his father and grandfather, Bush was ambivalent; asked what he wanted his Bones name to be, he could not think of one, so he was dubbed "Temporary," and it ended up sticking. A Bonesman was a "good man," and for a lifetime that became Bush's ultimate endorsement. Still, he was more at home at the Deke House, where he became president and forged a connection with other students. Once when a classmate believed to be gay walked by, someone made a mean remark. As Lanny Davis, later a prominent Democratic lawyer, recalled it, Bush told the wisecracker to knock it off. "Why don't you try walking in his shoes and seeing how it feels?"

Unlike Cheney, Bush graduated in 1968, albeit with a solid-C record. For decades, that would fuel questions about his intellect. "I went to school with him for six or seven years, and he's a very smart guy," said Jack Morrison, a fellow Andover and Yale graduate. "He's not a philosopher. He's not going to go to bed reading Plato at night. But he's very smart." Bush would long play off his reputation to lower expectations. When he returned to Yale in 2001 to deliver the commencement address, he joked about the experiences he and Cheney shared there. "If you graduate from Yale, you become president," Bush told the crowd. "If you drop out, you get to be vice president."

THE YEARS AFTER Yale became what Bush would call his "nomadic" period. During summers and after graduation, he held a series of jobs without any real sense of where he was going; he worked on an oil rig off Louisiana, spent time on the trading floor of a stock brokerage, sold sporting goods at Sears, Roebuck, herded cows on a cattle ranch in Arizona, helped out on a couple of political campaigns, and mentored troubled young boys at a poverty program in Houston.

The elder Bush had won a seat in the House of Representatives in 1966, and George W. felt pressure to live up to his standard. He joined the Texas Air National Guard to become a fighter pilot like his father, helped by the Speaker of the Texas House of Representatives, who called the National Guard commander on his behalf. But while the father fought in World War II, the son stayed stateside during Vietnam, and even then questions would arise about how often he reported to duty. "I would guess that probably he did have some desire to see if he could live up to his father's—I would not say expectations because I don't think his father ever put those types of expectations on him, but in his own mind live up to his own father's achievements and record," said Charlie Younger, his lifelong friend from Midland. Bush had broken off an engagement with a Houston woman during school and was now dating without much commitment. His father, while mounting a second losing Senate campaign in 1970 with George's help on the campaign trail, even set him up on a date with Tricia Nixon. The younger Bush showed up nervously at the White House in a purple Gremlin to take out the president's daughter. "We went to dinner," he said afterward. "It wasn't a very long date."

The subtle tension between father and son finally erupted around Christmas 1972 when George W. took his sixteen-year-old brother, Marvin, out drinking. Driving home, he smashed into a neighbor's trash can and noisily dragged it down the block. His father sent Jeb to bring George to the study.

"I hear you're looking for me," the inebriated young man snapped. "You want to go mano a mano right here?"

Jeb tried to defuse the moment by telling his father that George had gotten into Harvard Business School.

The elder Bush, caught off guard, asked if he would go.

"No," the son said. "I'm not going. I just did it to show you that I could."

Cheney at that point was in the middle of one of the most extraordinary rises to power in modern American history. After graduating from the University of Wyoming, he had an internship in the state legislature and then won an internship with Governor Warren Knowles of Wisconsin. He and Lynne drove their black 1965 Volkswagen Beetle to Madison, and Lynne enrolled in the University of Wisconsin to work on a doctorate, while Dick kept working on a master's degree that he finished in June 1966. A month later their first daughter arrived, Elizabeth, who came to be called Liz. Cheney began work on a PhD, and he and Lynne planned a life as college professors. With fighting in Vietnam escalating, his academic work, marriage, and fatherhood helped secure him five deferments. "I had other priorities in the '60s than military service," he explained blandly when the question came up later.

Offered a fellowship in Washington in 1968, Cheney put aside his studies and headed to the capital, where at an orientation he saw an impressive Republican congressman named Donald Rumsfeld. He sought an interview that did not go well. "It was clear that we hadn't hit it off," Cheney said. "He thought I was some kind of airhead academic and I thought he was rather an arrogant young member of Congress. Probably we were both right." Cheney went to work instead for another Republican congressman, William Steiger.

The next year, as Cheney's family grew with the birth of another daughter, Mary, Rumsfeld was tapped by President Richard Nixon to run the Office of Economic Opportunity overseeing the war on poverty. Cheney took it upon himself to write a twelve-page memo with suggestions. Rumsfeld summoned him back with equal brusqueness but a different outcome.

"You," Rumsfeld barked at Cheney, never looking up. "You're congressional relations. Now get the hell out of here."

An FBI background check later turned up Cheney's drunk-driving arrests, which he had disclosed. "But he stood by me," Cheney said of Rumsfeld, "and I have never forgotten that."

It was the start of a decades-long relationship that would prove enormously significant for both men, and the country. Cheney stayed with Rumsfeld when he took over the inflation-fighting Cost of Living Council. Both jobs soured Cheney on government intervention in the economy, and the son of New Deal Democrats became a conservative Republican. But when Rumsfeld was sent to Europe as ambassador to NATO, Cheney went to work at Bradley Woods, a consulting firm. That did not last long. In August 1974, as Nixon was preparing to resign, Cheney picked up the phone and heard Rumsfeld's secretary telling him to meet his old boss at the airport the next day. The new president, Gerald Ford, needed Rumsfeld, and Rumsfeld needed Cheney.

DESPITE HIS TESTY response to his father, Bush did go to Harvard Business School in the fall of 1973. "Here you are at the West Point of capitalism," said the taxi driver who dropped him off. Like Yale, it proved aggravating for a Texas conservative, especially one whose father had become chairman of the Republican National Committee in the midst of the Watergate scandal. Two thousand people celebrated Nixon's resignation with an impromptu flag-waving snake dance through Harvard Square. Bush had a "rotten time" at Harvard during Watergate, according to his aunt Nancy Ellis, who lived nearby and often hosted him when he escaped campus.

Bush rebelled against Harvard. At the buttoned-down, exclusive New England school, he defiantly wore cowboy boots and his National Guard flight jacket while spitting tobacco into a cup during classes. He later described Harvard as "claustrophobic, intellectually and physically." But it also provided what his mother called "structure." In her view, it "was a great turning point for him." And the first glimpses of his own ambition came through. When some students objected to an assignment to study paper flow in Senator Ted Kennedy's office, the instructor told them not to count out politics: "One of you could be president one day." Bush, in the back row, grinned, mischievously thrust his arms in the air, and flashed the Nixonian V-for-victory sign.

What seemed farcical to Bush came closer to reality for his father. Taking over for Nixon, Gerald Ford considered George H. W. Bush and Rumsfeld for vice president, before settling instead on the former governor Nelson A. Rockefeller of New York. Rumsfeld became chief of staff, and he tapped Cheney as his deputy. Just thirty-three years old, Cheney had never met the new president but now was helping him run the nation. "All I really had going for me was the good opinion of Don Rumsfeld," Cheney said later. Ford was impressed, viewing the young man as a "pragmatic problem solver" who "worked eighteen-hour days" and was "absolutely loyal to me." For all of his later reputation for militancy, Cheney was as sick of Vietnam as anyone else. As North Vietnamese forces closed in on Saigon for the final act of the conflict in April 1975, Ford flew to New Orleans to wash the country's hands of it, declaring it "a war that is finished as far as America is concerned." The mood on Air Force One back to Washington was one of relief, even celebration. Cheney raised a glass and offered a pungent toast. "Fuck the war," he declared.

But a low-key, laid-back demeanor masked a strong conservative streak, often pitting him against moderates like Rockefeller and Henry Kissinger. Cheney struck Robert Hartmann, the president's longtime adviser, as "somewhat to the right of Ford, Rumsfeld or, for that matter, Genghis Khan." A tough-minded anti-Communist and skeptic of détente, Cheney pushed Ford to meet with the Soviet dissident Aleksandr Solzhenitsyn, only to lose to Kissinger's don't-rock-the-boat argument. Cheney had more success burying Rockefeller's activist-government ideas. "He didn't care much for me, because I was the roadblock to his doing what he wanted to do and thought ought to be done, because everything got filtered through me and he never liked the outcome of those policy debates," Cheney said years later. He also thought a vice president should not participate in meetings of advisers because it would warp the discussion.

Heading into a difficult election year with Ford facing a challenge from Ronald Reagan on the right, Cheney and Rumsfeld decided the White House had grown dysfunctional and drafted a blistering twenty-six-page memo urging Ford to stop speaking bureaucratically, "be presidential," and "fire someone visably [*sic*]." To clear the way, they offered their own resignations. "The bulk of the problems," they wrote, "involve Hartmann, the Vice President or Kissinger." Hartmann "simply seems not to work well with other people," Cheney and Rumsfeld wrote. Hartmann did not think much of them either, referring to them as "the Praetorians" and writing that Cheney's "most distinguishing features were snake-cold eyes." After repeated turf battles, Hartmann concluded, "I could never trust Dick Cheney."

Ford did not accept their resignations but shook up the team. He stripped Kissinger of his second title of national security adviser and gave the job to Brent Scowcroft. He forced out Secretary of Defense James Schlesinger and the CIA director, William Colby, nominating George H. W. Bush to take over the spy agency, sending Rumsfeld to run the Pentagon, and promoting Cheney to chief of staff. To defend against Reagan, Cheney urged the president to dump Rockefeller from the ticket in 1976, and the vice president agreed to step aside.

It was a pivotal moment that would reverberate a quarter century later when Bush's son put together his own government. By sending the elder Bush to the CIA, Ford effectively took him out of the vice presidential sweepstakes in 1976 since Senate Democrats insisted the nominee forswear a candidacy in exchange for confirmation. The move drove a permanent wedge between Bush and Rumsfeld; Bush assumed Rumsfeld had orchestrated the appointment to sideline him, something Rumsfeld and Cheney would spend decades denying. Either way, the effect was to clear Rumsfeld's path of rivals for vice president; Rockefeller and Bush were out of the picture.

Now thirty-four, Cheney took over as the youngest White House chief of staff in history. "I knew that I could ask Cheney to step into Rumsfeld's shoes and that the White House would function just as efficiently," Ford wrote. Cheney took a modest profile, initially continuing to drive his old Volkswagen Beetle with a missing front fender to work instead of accepting the traditional car and driver. The Secret Service gave him the code name Backseat. But from the backseat, he wielded enormous influence and tackled the discipline problems he and Rumsfeld had identified. He was easygoing and "intelligent without displaying the arrogance and studied aloofness of Rumsfeld" and "doesn't press his opinions on others, and particularly the president, as Rumsfeld did," John J. Casserly, a White House speechwriter, recorded in his diary. Cheney had friendships with reporters, although he disdained the conservative columnists Rowland Evans and Robert Novak, whom he dubbed "Errors and No Facts." He oversaw the campaign, leaning on a crafty Texas operative named James A. Baker III to wage a delegate-by-delegate battle staving off Reagan. Cheney, more in tune politically with the challenger, made a secret trip to Camp David in August 1976 to convince Ford to put Reagan on the ticket. But the scars of their primary contest were too deep.

The battle went all the way to the convention, where Reagan forces extracted one last concession, a "morality in foreign policy" plank in the platform denouncing agreements with the Soviet Union—in effect, denouncing Ford's own policies. Kissinger insisted on fighting it, but Cheney advised standing down. "We're going to take a dive," he told his fellow Ford aide Ron Nessen in a van bumping across Kansas City, where the convention was held. "Principle is okay up to a certain point, but principle doesn't do any good if you lose the nomination." With Cheney and Baker's leadership, Ford eked out victory with 1,187 delegates, to 1,070 for Reagan. But Cheney's patron, Rumsfeld, had fallen off the list for running mate, and Ford picked a candidate he thought would help rally the divided party behind him, Senator Bob Dole of Kansas. Rockefeller, nursing his wounds, called Cheney a "son of a bitch" when Dole was slated to be brought onstage before him.

Weakened by the primary battle, Ford started the general election campaign far behind the Democrat Jimmy Carter. After Ford claimed during a debate that the Soviet Union did not dominate Eastern Europe, it fell to Cheney to force him to backtrack. He headed into the president's cabin on Air Force One the next day, only to be rebuffed. So he enlisted the campaign adviser Stuart Spencer to return with him to the cabin. It took several statements to finally douse the furor. Still, Ford closed the margin in the final days, and on election night the balloting remained close enough that he went to bed not knowing for sure that he had lost.

The next morning, Cheney went over the numbers.

"Gentlemen," he proclaimed, "we have to hoist our flag—the white flag of surrender."

Shortly after 9:00 a.m., he delivered the verdict to Ford. "Mr. President, we lost," he said.

The result was close, but Ford rejected a recount, reasoning that since he lost the popular vote, "it would be very hard for me to govern if I won the presidency in the Electoral College through a recount," as James Baker recalled it. Baker thought "he was right, of course," never imagining he would go on to help another candidate who lost the popular vote win the presidency through the Electoral College.

Ford called Carter. "Governor, my voice is gone, but I want to give you my congratulations," he said. "Here's Dick Cheney. He will read you my concession statement."

He handed the phone to Cheney.

ON THE DAY Carter was sworn in, Cheney went to Andrews Air Force Base to see off Ford, then took his family to lunch at McDonald's to talk about the future. They then went on a Bahamas vacation with Donald Rumsfeld and his family. After a dozen years away from Wyoming, Cheney decided to return home, hitching his old Volkswagen Beetle to a moving truck and heading west in June 1977.

Cheney's days in the Ford White House proved formative to his governing philosophy. In the post-Watergate, post-Vietnam era, he served at the nadir of the presidency, when Congress was chipping away at executive power through the War Powers Resolution and other legislation that altered the balance of power in American government. The Church Committee investigation into abuses by the CIA, he felt, undercut the nation's premier spy agency. Bryce Harlow, a veteran of the Eisenhower White House and a colleague in Ford's, warned Cheney about the need to protect the prerogatives of the executive. "One of the things he would say is, 'Look, we have to make sure we leave this institution of the presidency with the same authorities and powers that the Constitution intended,'" Rumsfeld later recalled. "Once an executive acquiesces in something that infringes on that because it is politically expedient or is weak or the Congress is a quid pro quo for something, it doesn't just affect your presidency; it affects the institution." That, Rumsfeld said, made a lasting impression on him and Cheney. "I felt that way, and I know he felt that way," Rumsfeld said. Cheney later told reporters as vice president, "A lot of the things around Watergate and Vietnam, both, in the '70s served to erode the authority, I think. The president needs to be effective, especially in a national security area."

George W. Bush, meanwhile, was far from such weighty questions. While Cheney helped run the country, Bush could barely run his own life. After earning his MBA from Harvard, he returned to Midland, where like his father he dove into the oil business seeking his fortune. He trolled courthouses searching land records for properties adjacent to wells and lived a carefree existence. He wore hand-me-down shirts and relied on his friend Don Evans's wife to do his laundry. His alley-side apartment resembled a "toxic waste dump," remembered his friend Charlie Younger, and he drank prodigiously. Bush and Younger once bolted onstage during a Willie Nelson concert with a pack of beer. At dinner with his parents, Bush blurted out to a woman who was their close friend, "So, what's sex like after fifty, anyway?" While visiting Kennebunkport in September 1976, he was arrested for drunk driving, later paying a $150 fine and temporarily losing driving privileges in Maine.

He was the "Bombastic Bushkin," as friends called him, though there were limits. "He always lived on the edge," Younger said. "He would get on the brink and then pull back in. But he would never really go over the edge. I mean, he would have a lot of fun and his IQ would go up the more he drank and get a little boisterous. But he never really did really crazy stuff that other people did."

2

"To be where the action is"

Gerald Ford's defeat proved a turning point for both Bush and Cheney. Each had been tied to the ousted government, and now with Republicans in the wilderness, controlling neither the White House nor Congress, they began to explore their own ambitions. As it happened, in separate parts of the country, they both set sights on the same goal: the House of Representatives.

The 1978 midterm election campaign came during a moment of transition in American politics as the conservative movement found its champion in Ronald Reagan and positioned itself for a new era of influence. Both Bush and Cheney were part of the old order, and even if their personal philosophies might have aligned more with the emerging Reaganism, they had to prove their ideological bona fides and fight off carpetbagging charges.

They both targeted seats vacated by longtime incumbents, but neither was embraced by the local establishment. In Texas, Bush found himself discouraged by the former governor Allan Shivers when it was clear a popular Democratic state legislator would seek the House seat representing Midland, Odessa, and Lubbock. "Son, you can't win," Shivers told Bush. "This district is just made for Kent Hance." As Bush later told his sister, Doro, "I listened to him, said okay, and decided to run anyway." In Wyoming, Cheney talked with the former governor Stanley K. Hathaway about running for the Senate but also found a state legislator standing in his way. "Dick, if you run for Senate, Al Simpson will kick your fanny," Hathaway told him. Unlike Bush, Cheney took the advice and backed off, only to get another opportunity when the state's lone House member unexpectedly retired.

For Bush, the looming campaign came at a time of significant change in his personal life. One day in July 1977, he went to a barbecue at the Midland home of his friend Joe O'Neill, whose wife, Jan, had invited a friend, Laura Welch, a local librarian. Laura and George had actually grown up ten blocks away from each other, attended San Jacinto Junior High together, and at one point lived in the same apartment complex in Houston without knowing each other well. As they grilled hamburgers in the backyard that night, though, Laura in her blue sundress caught Bush's eye. She was thirty years old with an easy smile and the shoulder-length feathered hair common to that era, the daughter of a loan company manager and a homemaker. The O'Neills realized he was serious when the early-to-bed Bush would not leave. "He stayed almost past midnight, which is unheard of for him," O'Neill said later. "They hit it off right away." That they were so different was part of the appeal. She liked to listen; he liked to talk. She curled up with a good book; he was in perpetual motion. "Laura stays in her own space," he noticed. "I've always invaded other people's spaces." Four months later they were married.

Far apart as they were, Bush and Cheney found their campaigns playing out in similar ways. They both had to show they were homegrown, they both had to translate what they had seen at the national level to the local level, and they both had something to learn about themselves. Bush tapped his parents' card file of supporters for campaign cash, including Rumsfeld, while striving to be his own man. Still mastering the art of the stump, he was driving home from a speech one day and asked Laura how it had gone; not well, she answered, shocking him so much that he crashed the car into a garage. Cheney, for his part, drove around the state listening to eight-track tapes of the Carpenters. Like Bush, Backseat was trying to make the transition to the front. He addressed crowds in a monotone, with none of the rhetorical flourishes or applause lines of most politicians. Pete Williams, then a young reporter covering the campaign, thought, "This guy doesn't give a speech; he briefs the audience."

Looming over both races was Ronald Reagan. Bush's primary opponent had worked for Reagan, who in turn sent a letter supporting him for the Texas seat, a move that might have been rooted in loyalty but also reflected the chess match then under way for the 1980 presidential nomination with Bush's father. Cheney, for his part, had to live down his work in the 1976 primaries against Reagan, who carried the Wyoming delegation at the convention. Reluctant to "run as Jerry Ford's guy in Wyoming," Cheney asked his former boss not to endorse him.

For Cheney, the seminal event of the campaign came late one night. He had been at his friend Bill Thomson's house in Cheyenne, talking late into the evening. Then he and Lynne retired back to Joe Meyer's house, where they were spending the night. About two or three in the morning on June 18, Cheney woke up complaining that two fingers on his left hand were tingling. Lynne rushed downstairs and woke Meyer, who drove them to a hospital.

At thirty-seven, Cheney had had a heart attack and was confronted with a medical reality that would haunt him the rest of his life. "That was devastating to them," Meyer recalled. "They didn't have any money set aside. They had two young girls. Neither one of them came from rich families. Lynne, I saw her at the kitchen table; she was kind of weepy."

Cheney stuck with the campaign. "Look, hard work never killed anybody," his doctor told him. "What takes a toll is spending your life doing something you don't want to do." Cheney quit his three-pack-a-day smoking habit and pared back on coffee, but viewed it "as a one-off event" and "was in denial to some extent." He sent a letter to voters assuring them of his fortitude and ultimately overcame two name brands for the Republican nomination: Ed Witzenburger, the state treasurer; and Jack Gage, son of a former governor. Cheney won the primary with a 42 percent plurality, then the general election with 59 percent. He was heading back to Washington.

Not so Bush. A "feisty fighter," in his father's judgment, Bush won the Republican nomination by overcoming Jim Reese, a former mayor of Odessa. But as warned, Kent Hance proved a formidable opponent in the fall. Both of his opponents painted Bush as an outsider. Reese brandished Bush's birth certificate to prove he was born in Connecticut. Hance ran a radio ad noting Bush's pedigree from Andover, Yale, and Harvard. "I don't think he's ever been in the back of a pool hall in Dimmitt, Texas," Hance told an audience.

At another appearance, Hance said Bush was trying "to ride the coattails, I think, of his father."

Bush was frustrated. "Would you like me to run as Sam Smith?" he replied. "The problem is I can't abandon my background."

Bush joked that he would have preferred being born in Texas but he thought he ought to be close to his mother that day and she happened to be in Connecticut. He distinguished himself from his famous father by establishing his Texas pedigree. "He went to Greenwich Country Day School," the candidate said repeatedly, "and I went to San Jacinto Junior High." Never mind that he went there for just a year.

When a conservative radio talk show host asked him if he was associated with the Trilateral Commission, Bush snapped, "I won't be persuaded by anyone, including my father." Leaving the interview, he refused to shake the host's hand, muttering, "You asshole."

His loss was sealed when a student supporter placed an ad in a campus newspaper promising free beer at a Bush rally and the Hance camp sent a letter criticizing it to religious voters. Advisers urged Bush to retaliate by pointing out that Hance leased property to a bar near campus, but he refused, deeming that dishonorable. Hance beat Bush with 53 percent, instilling a lesson for life. "He allowed Hance to define him as an easterner carpetbagger, which was not the case," Joe O'Neill said. Bush resolved "never to get out-countried again."

Years later, Bush and Cheney would trade notes on that 1978 election. "We talked on more than one occasion about his campaign for Congress" and his vow to never be painted as an outsider again, Cheney said. "I could identify with that because I always believed, and still do to this day, that I benefited politically when it was time for me to run for office by virtue of the fact that I had graduated not from Yale but from the University of Wyoming."

BUSH THREW HIMSELF back into the oil business through a company he started with the help of investors referred by his uncle Jonathan Bush. He called it Arbusto, the Spanish word for "bush," and began drilling holes with modest success. Intent on work, he devoted little time to his father's presidential campaign in 1980 and only learned of his selection as Reagan's running mate from television while dining with investors at New York's '21' Club. George H. W. Bush got the nod after Cheney and others talked Gerald Ford out of joining Reagan's ticket.

George W. and Laura were having trouble conceiving and had begun exploring adoption when she finally became pregnant with twins. Jenna and Barbara were born in November 1981, and suddenly the Bombastic Bushkin was forced to be a responsible father. But business was problematic. Wells came up empty, oil prices fell, and Bush felt the pressure of losing money invested by family friends. Arbusto was looking more like Ar-*bust*-o, so he changed the name to Bush Exploration Company. By the end of 1983, it ranked 993rd in oil production in Texas. Nearly half of the ninety-five holes it drilled were dry. In 1984, Bush merged it with Spectrum 7, a Dallas-based company looking for distressed oil firms. Bush was made chairman with a $75,000-a-year salary and 1.1 million shares.

While Bush struggled in Texas, Cheney was accumulating influence in Washington. Young and smart with a sober demeanor, Cheney was tapped in December 1980 by Robert H. Michel, the House Republican leader, to run for chairman of the House Republican Policy Committee, the party's number-four position. Cheney won and became the youngest member of the leadership in a century. Michel picked him to balance his own conservatism, and the Wednesday Club, a group of moderates, invited Cheney to join. But Michel and his colleagues misjudged personality for policies. When it came time to vote, Cheney supported tax cuts, prayer in school, and the contra rebels in Nicaragua and, in his own words, "never met a weapons system he didn't vote for." He opposed abortion, the Equal Rights Amendment, creation of the Education Department, a ban on armor-piercing bullets, and anti-apartheid sanctions on South Africa. He voted against funding for the Clean Water Act, the Safe Drinking Water Act, and the Endangered Species Act. He opposed Head Start and Superfund. He earned a 91 percent lifetime rating from the American Conservative Union, edging out his classmate Newt Gingrich, with 90 percent. "I had no idea he was that conservative," Michel said later. "Nobody ever checked the voting record," Cheney said. "I was consistently one of the most conservative members of the House in terms of how I voted."

Cheney had respect for government, though. The son of a career government worker, he would cross out the word "bureaucrat" in news releases produced by aides and insert "public servant" instead. Nor was he a deficit hawk. When red ink flowed in Reagan's first year in office, he advised riding it out. "The deficit isn't the worst thing that could happen," he said. Indeed, fiscal conservatism took a backseat to national security. He was an ardent supporter of Reagan's anti-Communist defense buildup and proxy wars in Central America. During a 1983 congressional trip to Moscow, Representative Tom Downey, a Democrat, needled him. "You can't expect them to accept all our terms," Downey said. "You can't expect them to surrender." Cheney answered, "Yeah, yes I can."

Cheney was absorbed with the struggle with the Soviet Union and the prospect of Armageddon-like war. Unknown to almost anyone at the time, he was a regular participant in a secret program conducted by the Reagan administration intended to reestablish a rudimentary government in the event of a nuclear holocaust. Every year, Cheney would disappear for three or four days, spirited out of Washington in the middle of the night along with a team of several dozen federal officials and a single Reagan cabinet secretary to a remote military base or underground bunker. The cabinet secretary would play the president, and Cheney would reprise his role as White House chief of staff. Leading one of the other continuity-of-government teams was his old friend Donald Rumsfeld as they prepared for the ultimate doomsday scenario.

The exercises reinforced Cheney's views about the need for a strong executive. When Reagan tripped up with the Iran-contra scandal, Cheney came to his defense, seeing the affair through the lens of his Ford experience. Congress had no right to bar a president from arranging funding for the contras, he argued, and he called Lieutenant Colonel Oliver North, the White House aide at the heart of the scheme, "the most effective and impressive witness" of the congressional hearings. Cheney, who spent a lot of time on his assignment to the House Intelligence Committee, served on an investigative commission and collaborated with a tall, aggressive staff lawyer named David Addington. Cheney signed a 155-page minority report in 1987 that provided a template for his views of a muscular presidential authority in the areas of national security and foreign policy.

Along the way, Cheney kept moving up the ranks despite continuing health problems. He suffered a second heart attack in 1984 and a third one in 1988. He watched George H. W. Bush deliver his "read my lips" acceptance speech at the Republican convention from a hospital bed as a male nurse shaved his body for bypass surgery. But after recovering he was poised to become Republican whip, the number-two position. His eye on the top spot, he and Lynne wrote a book, *Kings of the Hill*, profiling famous Speakers.

His friend Joe Meyer once asked why. "Dick, what in the hell would possess anybody to fly every other weekend back to here?"

"To be where the action is," Cheney replied. "I just truly get a buzz out of the policy side of all this stuff."

Lynne Cheney liked the action as well, becoming a leader of the culture wars as the outspoken chairwoman of the National Endowment for the Humanities.

While Dick Cheney's star rose, Bush was still aimless and irresponsible, ricocheting from one venture to another. He remained the family scamp, the contrarian who would keep his father's motorcade waiting because he had not dressed yet. "Go get George," an irritated Barbara Bush would shout to one of her husband's aides. The aide would roust the younger Bush. "George, goddamn it, get in that car! You are pissing everyone off!"

Now with his father again running for president, Bush tried to get his act together. He joined the rest of his family at Camp David in the spring of 1985 to hear from Lee Atwater, the rough-and-tumble political strategist from South Carolina.

"How do we know we can trust you?" George asked.

"If someone throws a grenade at our dad," Jeb added, "we expect you to jump on it."

Atwater responded with a challenge: if they were so worried about his loyalty, then one of them should move to Washington to keep an eye on him. George took the dare.

His life was changing in other ways too. That summer, as Bush later recalled the moment, he took a walk with the Reverend Billy Graham, who was visiting the family compound in Kennebunkport and talked about seeking salvation by embracing Jesus Christ. Graham, he later said, "planted a seed in my heart and I began to change." Bush started weekly Bible studies that fall. In recounting his religious awakening, Bush generally leaves out an earlier encounter with a flamboyant evangelist named Arthur Blessitt, who traveled the world by foot carrying a twelve-foot cross. While Blessitt was in Midland in 1984, Bush went to meet with him. "I want to talk to you about how to know Jesus Christ and how to follow him," Bush told him.

With the collapse in oil prices, Bush was still struggling. "I'm all name and no money," he ruefully observed to a reporter at the time. In 1986, he sold Spectrum 7 to Harken Energy, a Texas firm, which gave him $600,000 in shares and a title as director and consultant earning up to $120,000 a year. That would free him to move to Washington, where he and his family rented a town house near the vice president's residence. Bush's drinking worsened, though. When he saw the journalist Al Hunt in a Mexican restaurant in Dallas in April 1986, Bush marched over and berated him in front of his family for predicting that Jack Kemp would win the nomination. "You no good fucking sonofabitch," he shouted. "I will never fucking forget what you wrote!"

Laura pressed him about the alcohol. "Can you remember the last day you didn't have a drink?" she challenged him.

"Of course, I can," he replied. But he realized he could not. He regularly indulged in what he called the four *B*s—beer, bourbon, and B&B.

That summer proved a pivot point. Celebrating his and Laura's fortieth birthdays with friends at the Broadmoor in Colorado, the group emptied $60 bottles of Silver Oak and repeated the same toast, by Laura's count, twenty times. "We made a little noise in the dining room that night," conceded Joe O'Neill. After waking up the next day with a pounding hangover that did not begin to dissipate until halfway through his daily run, Bush made the resolution that changed him forever, vowing to give up drinking. Bush later joked that Laura insisted, "It's either Jim Beam or me," although she never actually put it that starkly. Either way, friends understood his father's campaign also played a part. "He said one day I might be an embarrassment to my father, and he never picked up another drop," said O'Neill.

In Washington, Bush claimed an office at campaign headquarters. "He was a big, booming personality," recalled Debra Dunn, his assistant. "He's an action guy. He liked to make decisions." He showed up in his jogging suit, chewing tobacco and making friends. "Everyone loved him because he treated everyone the same way," Dunn said. His humor still leaned to the juvenile. A driver named Payne was nicknamed "Payne-is." But the experience was a lesson in power. He learned that by showing up for a meeting with his father twenty minutes before anyone else, other advisers would arrive and take note of his access, even if they had just been talking sports. He also developed a taste for the crowd.

"Yeah, I killed them in Atlanta," he was saying into the phone the day the author Richard Ben Cramer was first brought into his office. "I *killed* them. They were saying, 'Junior! Junior!' "

And then "Junior" made the crowd noise into the phone. "He was fully alive to who he was and how he was," observed Cramer, who became a friend.

It fell to the younger Bush to publicly quash talk of adultery by his father. "You've heard the rumors," he recounted asking his father. "What about it?" His father answered, "They're just not true." Atwater then arranged a call between the younger Bush and Howard Fineman of *Newsweek*. "The answer to the Big A question is N-O," Bush told him. His parents were later chagrined at that, especially his mother. But he was tough on those who crossed or embarrassed his father. When an *Esquire* magazine profile of Atwater reported that he answered his hotel door wearing only underwear and socks, then kept talking to the writer while using the bathroom, à la Lyndon B. Johnson, George W. reamed him out. When *Newsweek* ran a cover on his father with the headline "Fighting the 'Wimp Factor,' " Bush was "red hot" and called the reporter Margaret Warner to accuse her of "a political ambush." Just as the false news report on Prescott Bush in 1950 colored his son's view of journalism, so did this episode shape the younger Bush's.

If Bush was a fiercely loyal son, he was also a nervous one. During the second presidential debate, he could not bear to watch, so he took Marvin to the movies. But he kept sending Marvin out to phone for updates, eventually giving up and leaving to watch for himself. He did not have to avert his eyes on election night. His father swept to a forty-state victory. More important, working together seemed to wipe away at least some of George's complex about his father. Bush declared that he had gotten over his "self-pity" about "being George Bush's son." As Laura put it, "If there was any sort of leftover competition with being named George Bush and being the eldest, it really at that point was resolved."

WITH THE WIN, Bush headed home to Texas. Cheney, however, became one of the new president's most important advisers. He was not the first choice to be secretary of defense, but even before John Tower's nomination crashed in March 1989, the phone rang in Cheney's office summoning him to the White House.

Cheney proved an easy confirmation, although not before lawmakers questioned him in closed session about his own raucous past. How did you clean up your act? asked Senator John Glenn, the Ohio Democrat. "I got married and gave up hanging out in bars," Cheney answered.

Having never served in uniform, Cheney was eager to make clear who was in charge. On his eighth day on the job, he saw a *Washington Post* story about General Larry Welch, the air force chief of staff, negotiating a compromise ballistic missile plan on Capitol Hill. "My instinct is to cut him off at the knees," Cheney growled to the Pentagon press secretary before heading into his first news conference to do just that. "General Welch was freelancing," Cheney told reporters. "He was not speaking for the department." He added, "I'm not happy with it, frankly. I think it's inappropriate for a uniformed officer to be in a position where he's in fact negotiating an agreement." In fact, Welch was not freelancing. He had cleared his discussions with the White House and the acting defense secretary before Cheney's confirmation. Even Cheney later concluded that Welch "got a bit of a bum rap." But "it was a target of opportunity if you wanted to sort of reassert civilian control."

His most important personnel move came later in 1989 when he reached deep into the ranks to select the most junior of fifteen eligible four-star officers, General Colin L. Powell, as chairman of the Joint Chiefs of Staff, the first African American to hold the post. Powell, a Vietnam veteran with a magnetic bearing and political savvy, had vaulted through a series of Washington jobs until he found himself in the White House at the very moment when Ronald Reagan needed a new national security adviser. Cheney thought picking someone with that combination of backgrounds to run the Joint Chiefs was "a stroke of genius." As for Powell, he viewed Cheney as "a cerebral Wyoming cowboy" who was "supremely self-confident," or at least gave that impression, at bottom "a loner who would take your counsel, but preferred to go off by himself to make up his mind." The two proved to be great partners, though not without tension. At one point when Powell argued for cutting tactical nuclear weapons, Cheney said none of his civilian advisers agreed. "That's because they're all right-wing nuts like you," Powell said half jokingly.

Cheney faced early tests, most notably the brief war in Panama to arrest the drug-running dictator Manuel Noriega. But it was the attempted military coup in the Philippines in December 1989 that brought to the fore questions of authority. When the White House got word of the attempt to seize power in Manila, the president was flying to a Middle East summit, so Vice President Dan Quayle called a National Security Council meeting at the White House. Cheney, at home, refused to attend, arguing that the vice president was not in the chain of command. Instead, he stayed in contact directly with the president on Air Force One. Once again, Cheney was fighting a vice president he thought was overstepping his bounds. From the plane, Scowcroft juggled telephone calls from Cheney and Quayle, but the power struggle was never fully resolved.

In Dallas, the younger Bush had largely checked out of his father's administration. He nursed his own political ambitions but confronted the harsh reality that he had no record. "George, everybody likes you, but you haven't done anything," a Texas Republican operative told him. "You need to go out in the world and do something, the way that your father did when he left Connecticut and the protection of his family. You just haven't done shit. You're a Bush and that's all." His opportunity came when Bush heard the owner of the Texas Rangers wanted to sell. He worked his contacts, played off his family name, and put together an investor group to buy the ailing baseball team in April 1989. Bush himself ultimately put in just $606,000 of the $86 million but would be the public face as co-managing partner. "How cool is this?" he asked his partner Rusty Rose on the pitcher's mound on opening night.

The baseball venture relaunched his political career. No hands-off owner, Bush regularly sat in Section 109, Row 1, Seat 8, behind the Rangers' dugout, signing autographs. He printed baseball cards with his face on them and traveled Texas giving speeches. "I can't tell you how many Rotary lunches and Kiwanis lunches he would do," recalled his driver, Israel Hernandez. "It was baseball, baseball, baseball. He loved talking about baseball." But it also helped build a foundation for his political career. Bush orchestrated a referendum approving a temporary tax increase to pay for a new stadium that would open in the spring of 1994, just months before a governor's election. While he traded away the future slugging star Sammy Sosa to his later regret, the Rangers went from a losing team to winning records in seven of the next ten seasons, nearly doubling attendance and increasing revenues. The success "solved my biggest political problem in Texas," he reflected. "My problem was, 'What's the boy ever done?' "

Cheney's defining test came in a far different arena when in August 1990 Iraq invaded Kuwait. While Powell questioned whether anyone cared enough about Kuwait to commit troops, Cheney clearly did. His question was whether President Bush would go for it. "Did the president have the balls to call out the Reserves?" Cheney wondered. He did. Cheney wanted to prove he had balls too. When he read another *Washington Post* article quoting another air force chief speaking out of turn, he again took action. This time it was General Michael Dugan discussing plans to target Saddam Hussein and other sensitive details. Cheney read the article twice, went for a walk along the C&O Canal to cool down, returned home, reread the story, and got mad all over again. He called the president at Camp David, pulling him off the tennis court to tell him he might relieve Dugan. The next morning he did. "It sent a hell of a message," Cheney said later. "Dugan was a gift from that perspective."

Cheney also found himself at odds with Powell. The general did not think it was worth going to war over Kuwait and made that point in a White House meeting, only to be dressed down by Cheney, who made clear that his job was to offer military, not policy, advice. Likewise, Cheney rejected the first war plan sent to him by Powell, an up-the-middle assault that he and James Baker, by then the secretary of state, derisively called the "Washington Monument plan." Bypassing Powell, Cheney ordered a rewrite that envisioned a left hook to cut off Iraqi forces. Worried about "bugs and gas," Cheney also ordered contingency plans to use tactical nuclear weapons if Iraqi forces employed biological and chemical weapons. The notion was so sensitive that Powell later had the study destroyed. As for the war itself, Cheney argued against asking Congress for permission, but the president disregarded him and won authorization. Cheney later admitted he had been wrong.

Two nights before the Gulf War began, Cheney made a secret visit to the Vietnam Veterans Memorial in Washington to contemplate mistakes of the past and pray he did not repeat them. But he was no tortured soul. The night the war started, he ordered Chinese food and calmly monitored reports. He spent so much time schooling himself on military techniques that his uniformed staff later jokingly awarded him an honorary war college degree. He did not like everything he learned. When military attorneys barred a strike on a Hussein memorial, he scoffed, "Lawyers running a war?"

In any case, American forces easily expelled the Iraqis from Kuwait. When retreating Iraqis were being slaughtered on what was now called the Highway of Death, the president asked whether it was time to end the war. "The unanimous view of those of us who were there, civilian and military, was yes," Cheney later said. "Our objective was to liberate Kuwait." The war was over with just 148 American battle deaths.

In years to come, critics dismissed by Powell as "simple solutionists" would deem it a profound mistake not to have taken out Hussein. But Cheney never publicly expressed second thoughts. A few months before the 1992 election, he defended the decision and predicted America would have gotten "bogged down" running Iraq if it had deposed Hussein. "Once we had rounded him up and gotten rid of his government, then the question is what do you put in its place?" Cheney asked. "You know, you then have accepted responsibility for governing Iraq." He added, "The question in my mind is how many additional American casualties is Saddam worth? And the answer is not very damned many." Eight years later, just before joining George W. Bush's ticket in 2000, he had not changed his mind. "I still think we made the right decision there," Cheney said in a secret oral history taped that year but not released until after his vice presidency. "I don't think we should have gone to Baghdad."

As successful as the Gulf War was, it was the zenith for the Bush team. From Texas, George W. was tapped by his father to help sort out a dysfunctional West Wing, starting at the top. John Sununu, the chief of staff, had burned bridges. "Smart guy, arrogant, didn't know what he didn't know," as Cheney later described him. The president wrote notes to seven or eight longtime allies seeking advice. His son then put them inside envelopes with his own return address in Dallas and followed up with telephone calls. The verdict was unmistakable, and so the day before Thanksgiving the younger Bush arrived at the West Wing to deliver the message.

"You know," he told Sununu, "I've talked to a lot of people. They're down on you. It's going to be tough for you to work with these people."

But Sununu did not take the hint. Only after Bush's father sent three aides, Andy Card, Dorrance Smith, and C. Boyden Gray, to deliver the same message one after another did the headstrong chief resign.

George W. Bush was even less successful in dislodging the vice president, whom he deemed a drag on reelection. Much as Cheney helped orchestrate the replacement of Nelson Rockefeller, Bush tried to persuade his father to dump Dan Quayle from the 1992 ticket. In his place? He recommended Cheney. The defense secretary knew nothing about this, but he had made clear through intermediaries like Baker that he also thought Quayle should go. While the president privately acknowledged that he "blew it" by picking Quayle in the first place, he was unwilling to cut loose a loyal lieutenant.

"But," George W. Bush wrote waggishly after his own presidency, "I never completely gave up on my idea of a Bush-Cheney ticket."

THE DEFEAT OF the president in 1992 disappointed both Bush and Cheney, but it also proved liberating. For the first time in years, each of them could again pursue an independent path.

Bush had been eyeing the Governor's Mansion in Texas but put off a run while his father was in office. With his father now retired, he was free to run—not that anyone thought he could beat the incumbent governor, Ann Richards, a folksy, well-liked Democrat. "George, you can't win," his mother told him with characteristic bluntness. His friends told him the same thing. "I thought she was unbeatable," said Charlie Younger.

Undaunted, Bush threw himself into the campaign, eager both to prove himself and, friends thought, perhaps even to avenge his father against Richards, who had memorably mocked the president for being "born with a silver foot in his mouth," and Bill Clinton, who had prematurely ended his father's presidency. When the sportswriter Randy Galloway sidled up to the candidate in the dugout and asked why he was running against Richards since she would beat him, Bush said, "I'm not running against her. I'm running against the guy in the White House." His motivation increased when Richards turned her taunts on him, calling him "some jerk" and "shrub." When Bush found himself in an elevator with Richards heading to a debate, he wished her luck. She responded, "This is going to be rough on you, boy."

It proved rougher on her and a surprise to the nation. With a youthful message of change much like the one Clinton had used successfully against his father, Bush barnstormed the state focusing on four campaign issues: education, juvenile crime, welfare reform, and litigation limits. With the help of Kenneth Lay of Enron and other deep-pocketed contributors, Bush competed financially. "He just flat outworked her," said Joe O'Neill. As it happened, his upset victory with 53 percent in November 1994 came the same night Jeb Bush lost his first race for governor of Florida. George was disappointed that his parents were focused on consoling Jeb. "Why do you feel bad about Jeb?" he asked his father over the phone. "Why don't you feel good about me?" His parents did feel good about him, of course, as did Republicans far from Texas who saw a new star.

Also working the campaign circuit that fall was Cheney, who had cleared out his desk at the Pentagon and left without even saying good-bye to his partner, Powell, who later admitted being "disappointed, even hurt, but not surprised." Cheney decided to test his own possible run for the presidency, driving eight thousand miles across the country to appear at nearly 160 fund-raisers and political events for Republican candidates. Cheney raised $1.3 million for a political action committee run by David Addington and spent so much time on the road that he mailed dirty shirts home to be laundered. At Christmas, he retreated to snowy Jackson Hole to talk it over with his family. Ultimately, he decided against it.

When Cheney announced his decision in January 1995, Sean O'Keefe, a former aide, asked why. Cheney said he would explain when they had more time, so the two arranged to go fishing in Pennsylvania one day. As they stood there in Spring Creek, Cheney was "beating the water as hard as you can imagine," as O'Keefe recalled it, but hours passed without an explanation. Finally, O'Keefe couldn't stand it.

"Mr. Secretary, you told me you were going to tell me why you didn't do this," he said. "We were in the foxhole ready to do this."

Cheney cast his line and looked at O'Keefe. "You know," he said, "the idea of spending the rest of my life begging for money was just unappealing."

And then he flipped the fly right back in. *That's it?* O'Keefe thought. "Caught a lot of fish that day," he later recalled, "and one nugget of insight."

Cheney was somewhat more expansive with other former aides. Grilling steaks one afternoon in the backyard of his Wyoming home, he told Pete Williams, "I just decided I didn't want to do this to my family and they didn't want to have this done to them. And there was the health issue. But at the end of the day, I just didn't have the fire in the belly for fixing the Social Security system." Over lunch with another former aide, Stephen Hadley, Cheney articulated a three-part test: "You have to first be able to visualize yourself in the office. Then you have to be able to decide that you are prepared and able to put together the organization and the money that you need to win it. Then you have to make sure that you have the fire in the gut to see it through. I couldn't check all three of those boxes."

For Cheney, this was to be the end of his political career. He received a call from Tom Cruikshank, with whom he had gone fishing a few months earlier. Cruikshank, chief executive officer of Halliburton, was retiring. Would Cheney be interested in taking over the oil services giant? Cheney accepted and told a Wyoming newspaper that his political career was "over with." Asked whether he might think about the vice presidency, he scoffed. It was, he said, a "cruddy job."

Arriving in Dallas in the fall of 1995, he took over a $5.7 billion company with nearly sixty thousand employees, while Lynne became co-host of CNN's *Crossfire* political show. For the first time in Cheney's life, he was making big money, and when he flew back to Wyoming in the company jet, his friend Bill Thomson reminded him of his complaints about schlepping around the campaign trail. "I see you have solved your transportation problems," Thomson told him. Cheney set out to expand business with the federal government and became an active voice opposing unilateral sanctions against countries like Iran, arguing that it made no sense to deprive American companies of business.

His biggest move at Halliburton grew out of a quail-hunting trip in January 1998 with Bill Bradford, chairman of Dresser Industries—the same company that Prescott Bush helped go public and that gave George H. W. Bush his start fifty years earlier. Out of their conversation, Halliburton bought Dresser for $7.7 billion, a merger that expanded the company. Only later would it seem questionable. The purchase came at the top of the market, with Halliburton paying a 16 percent premium; by the time the merger was complete, Cheney had to cut ten thousand jobs right away. Moreover,

Dresser brought vast liability for past asbestos use that forced Halliburton to put part of the company into bankruptcy and pay out billions of dollars to victims. Still, it was a period of great growth; over the course of Cheney's tenure, Halliburton would expand to an $11.9 billion giant.

Cheney now lived just up the highway from Bush, who had moved his collection of autographed baseball cards into the governor's office and was proving to be an effective executive, pushing through his legislative program with the help of a bipartisan alliance he forged with Bob Bullock, the powerful Democratic lieutenant governor. Bullock was "an irascible, crazy old Texas politician," as Sandy Kress, a Bush adviser, described him, but he took a fatherly liking to the governor. Bush courted Bullock and the Democratic House Speaker, Pete Laney, at weekly breakfasts and roamed the capitol popping his head into the offices of other lawmakers.

His irreverence worked. Once Bullock declared that he was on the opposite side of a bill. "Governor, on this I'm going to have to fuck you," he said.

Bush got up from his chair and leaned over to plant a kiss on Bullock's mouth. "If you are going to fuck me, you've at least got to kiss me first," Bush said playfully.

Bullock proved to be such a close ally that he endorsed the Republican governor for reelection in 1998, even though he was godfather to the son of the Democratic nominee, Garry Mauro.

With Newt Gingrich the harsh-edged, shut-the-government face of the Republican Party in Washington, Bush stood out as a different kind of Republican, one trying not only to forge bipartisan alliances but to break out of the old paradigm of a seemingly heartless conservatism. He drew attention for disagreeing with Governor Pete Wilson's attempts in California to limit public benefits for illegal immigrants, and he implemented policies intended to address social ills but through more conservative means. His willingness to buck party orthodoxy attracted the likes of Mark McKinnon, a Democratic media consultant who switched parties to work for Bush.

In February 1998, Bush visited a juvenile detention center in Marlin, Texas, and was surprised when a fifteen-year-old African American boy locked up for petty theft asked, "What do you think about us?" Bush, searching for an answer, said, "The state of Texas still loves you all. We haven't given up on you. But we love you enough to punish you when you break the law." He was still dwelling on the encounter the next day when a young political operative named David Kuo came down from Washington to talk about a job. "I didn't have an answer," Bush told Kuo. "I still don't. I said something, but I don't remember exactly what it was. But I have to have an answer to that. There has to be something done about the gap between the rich and the poor. There has to be something done about racial justice, economic justice, social justice."

Bush told Kuo that day that he was not sure he wanted to run for president. "I just don't know if I can spend the rest of my life in a security bubble," he said. "I'll never walk down a street alone. Never again." It was a theme of his conversations that year. He told Karen Hughes, his communications director, "I'll never again be able to just walk into Wal-Mart and buy fishing lures." As Bush cruised to an easy victory over Mauro, becoming the first Texas governor to win a second consecutive term, the real drama was what he would do about national office. The Rangers were sold, and he received a check for $14.9 million, a healthy return on his $606,000 investment and enough for him to pursue his political dreams without financial worry. But his teenage daughters had no ambivalence about the notion: they were against it.

"I'm not going to run," he told his friend Doug Wead one day.

"And why not?" Wead asked. "You are at the head of the pack."

"Because of the girls," he said. "They would be in college then and it would ruin their lives."

"Did it ruin your life?"

Bush paused. "No," he said. "It made my life."

3

"The fire horse and the bell"

For George W. Bush, the idea of running for president in 2000 was both eminently logical and utterly far-fetched. While Americans disapproved of Bill Clinton's character, they were content with the way he governed the country. In this interregnum following the Cold War, the United States was largely at peace, the emerging information age economy was generating jobs, wealth, and innovation, and the federal treasury was overflowing with surplus money for a change. The brief war in Kosovo had demonstrated America's capacity to assert its will without a single American casualty. The warning signs of a gathering terrorist threat, manifested in attacks on American embassies, a military barracks, and a navy ship overseas, had done little to shake the public out of its satisfaction. Vice President Al Gore could run on that record.

And yet here was Bush, with just one term as governor of Texas and the same first and last names as the last president rejected by American voters, seriously eyeing a run for America's highest office. He found himself leading polls for the nomination, albeit largely due to his familiar name. Every time he turned around, someone was telling him he could be president. "I feel like a cork in a raging river," he said over dinner with a couple of reporters in October 1998.

It was intoxicating, and unlike Dick Cheney, who found the idea of hustling for the 1996 nomination too unpleasant, Bush enjoyed the feel of the campaign trail. Besides, the more he looked at the other possible candidates, the more he came to the conclusion that he was as good as, or better than, any of them. There were not many times in life, he told his cousin John Ellis, when the main thing standing between you and a presidential nomination was Steve Forbes, the nebbishy magazine publisher. Ellis was not so sure. He thought the timing was bad, that Al Gore would run the campaign his father did in 1988, and that even if Bush won, a recession was overdue and he would inherit it.

But there were other signs, ones that a deeply religious man would see and vest with great meaning. In January 1999, he sat in church in Austin preparing to take the oath for a second term as governor. The Reverend Mark Craig delivered a sermon on leadership, recalling that Moses was reluctant when called upon to lead his people but assumed the duty. "We have the opportunity, each and every one of us, to do the right thing, and for the right reason," the pastor said. Barbara Bush leaned over and mouthed to her son, "He is talking to you." Her son thought so too. "I feel as if God were talking directly to me," he mentioned at a family gathering. It took Laura to temper his grandiosity. "I think that's a bit of a stretch," she told him. And other family members thought a presidential run seemed ludicrous. "Are you nuts?" his brother Marvin asked.

As he prepared his campaign, Bush had a core team from Texas centered on the so-called Iron Triangle of Karen Hughes, Joe Allbaugh, and Karl Rove. Hughes, tall and booming, was a former television reporter who became Bush's communications guru and styled herself the voice of soccer moms and other everyday people. Allbaugh, six feet four and gruff with a military-style flattop haircut and a gift for bringing order to chaos, had come from Oklahoma to serve as chief of staff for the governor, who called him "Big Country." First among equals, though, was Rove, with spectacles and round cheeks that gave him an owlish look. A longtime Republican consultant who had worked for Bush's father, Rove had built a reputation as a latter-day Lee Atwater, a political genius with a touch of deviousness, a searching intellect, and manic energy, someone "who makes the Energizer Bunny seem lethargic," as Hughes put it. Rove practically worshipped Bush, recalling his first impression: "Huge amounts of charisma, swagger, cowboy boots, flight jacket, wonderful smile, just charisma—you know, wow."

From his father's team, Bush enlisted people who could school him in foreign policy, starting with Condoleezza Rice, a former National Security Council aide who was now provost of Stanford University. A black minister's daughter, she grew up in Bull Connor's Birmingham and knew one of the girls killed in the 1963 bombing that galvanized the civil rights movement. But through bristling determination and a series of eager mentors, she trained as a Soviet scholar and concert pianist who endeared herself to President George H. W. Bush and later bonded with his son over workouts and sports talk. To educate him about the world, she assembled a group of experts she called the Vulcans, named for a statue in Birmingham. "I need your help," Bush told them at their first meeting in Austin. "Not to become president. I will take care of that. But I need your help to be a good president."

Bush also brought in people with no connection to his family past like Marvin Olasky, author of the influential book *The Tragedy of American Compassion*, and Sandy Kress, a former Dallas School Board president he had been working with on education reform. Olasky, a onetime Marxist who now argued that private organizations, particularly Christian churches, do a better job than government at tackling social ills, brought a group of policy wonks to see Bush in Austin in early 1999 for a three-hour briefing on poverty. "It was very much like a graduate school seminar," Olasky remembered.

His father's old crowd was a mixed blessing. Bush liked to joke that he "inherited half of his friends and all of his enemies." But he knew he could not be seen as simply his father's son. When Ron Kaufman, White House political director for the first president Bush, sent a fund-raising letter urging donors to "send an important signal about the strength of the Bush network," Rove slapped him down—and then leaked it to the columnist Robert Novak. "Rove let me know that the boarding party had been repelled," Novak said later, "and that Kaufman and the rest of the Bush Senior entourage would not be on the son's ship." The senior Bush entourage got the message. "We had to be the back-of-the-bus guys," Kaufman recalled, "and we had to be onboard help but know our place, and we did that very effectively."

Indeed, Bush seemed more interested in assuming the mantle of Ronald Reagan than that of George Bush. In April 1999, he went to the Palo Alto, California, home of George Shultz, Reagan's secretary of state, for cookies and coffee with many of the former president's circle. In Shultz's living room, Bush impressed the elder statesmen of American conservatism with his talk of Social Security reform, the rise of India, and the need to control federal spending. He told them he wanted to achieve big things. Shultz gave him the blessing he was seeking, taking him aside and telling Bush that he had brought Reagan to the same spot in the same home in 1979 and given him the same message: run.

Two months later, he did. Bush kicked off his campaign on June 12, 1999, with a flight to Iowa filled with national journalists and skyrocketing anticipation. Well aware that he now had to justify that, Bush cheekily dubbed his inaugural foray the Great Expectations tour. As he boarded a chartered MD-80 just after sunrise, he came on the public address system. "This is your candidate speaking," he started. "Please stow your expectations securely in the overhead bin as they may shift during the trip and they could fall and hurt someone—especially me." The maiden voyage went so well that Karl Rove said over dinner one night that "the only thing we haven't done well is to lower expectations."

While keeping distance from his father's crew, Bush wanted at least one person from the first Bush administration: Dick Cheney. He had served on a business advisory council for the Texas governor and had occasionally joined Rice's foreign policy group. But Bush wanted more. In November, while Cheney and his wife, Lynne, hosted a benefit for Barbara Bush's literacy campaign at their Dallas house, the governor took Cheney aside.

In Cheney's library, Bush asked the former defense secretary to chair his presidential campaign.

Cheney said no. "Look, I'm really committed here at Halliburton," he said. But if there was anything else he could do, he told Bush, just call. "I'm eager to do what I can to be helpful."

IF BUSH STARTED out with well-defined thoughts about domestic policy, he was a virtual blank slate on foreign policy. But there were plenty of competing factions eager to claim him, including neoconservatives like Paul Wolfowitz and Richard Perle and more traditional Republicans like Richard Armitage and Robert Zoellick, all in Rice's Vulcans.

When they sat down at one point in the spring of 1999 just as American-led NATO air strikes were driving Serbian forces out of Kosovo, Bush asked whether they would have advocated the original Balkans intervention in Bosnia. All but two supported it. The dissenters were Dov Zakheim, a former Pentagon official under Reagan, and Dick Cheney. Bush told them that "his heart was with the minority," as Zakheim recalled it, "but his head told him it was the right thing to do." And now that the United States was committed, he added, it had to complete the task.

Bush laid out his thinking about the nation's armed forces in a speech at the Citadel military academy in South Carolina in September. It was a blueprint for a humbler, more restrained use of American power, a rejection of Clinton's humanitarian interventionism and nation building, which Bush considered distractions from the mission of the military. "That mission is to deter wars—and that mission is to win wars when deterrence fails," Bush told the cadets. "Sending our military on vague, aimless and endless deployments is the swift solvent of morale." While disavowing an isolationist "retreat from the world," Bush said he would be more "selective in the use of our military" to relieve "the tension on an overstretched military," sentiments that would not survive long into his presidency. But Bush foresaw what would become the defining challenge of his time. "I will put a high priority on detecting and responding to terrorism on our soil. The federal government must take this threat seriously."

Just as Clinton had sought to shift the Democratic Party away from its liberal, soft-on-crime, weak-on-defense, pro-welfare identity, Bush was now trying to redefine the Republican Party, sanding off the harsher edges of the Gingrich revolution. Instead of what Karen Hughes called "grinchy old Republican" promises to abolish the Department of Education and deport illegal immigrants, Bush advocated more federal intervention in schools to fight the "soft bigotry of low expectations" and more acceptance of the millions of undocumented workers. Hughes was a driving force behind this approach. An army brat born in Paris, she moved with her family to Texas, where she studied journalism at Southern Methodist University and then went into television news. Eventually, she became a political operative and went to work for Bush, bonding over their shared devotion to religion. She called his brand of politics "compassionate conservatism," a term that unbeknownst to her had actually been used for years by others, including Bob Dole and Jack Kemp. Doug Wead, an Assemblies of God minister who befriended Bush while working as his father's liaison to evangelicals, had popularized the phrase, which was adopted by Ron Kaufman for the elder Bush's campaigns.

But no one had put the notion as front and center as George W. Bush. By branding his conservatism "compassionate," he was summoning the Samaritan legacy of Christianity while signaling to secular voters a more humane ideology. Behind the slogan was the idea of pursuing liberal goals through conservative means. Bush would fight poverty with "armies of compassion" by using government resources to help churches, synagogues, and mosques do charity work. He would steer more money to schools to bridge the gap between rich and poor in exchange for accountability measured by standardized tests. Even his centerpiece domestic promise, a sweeping package of tax cuts with plenty of benefits for the wealthiest Americans such as eliminating the inheritance tax and reducing top marginal tax rates, also included ideas targeted at those with less means, like doubling the child tax credit and reducing the lowest tax bracket for the working poor. For conservative economists, such ideas made no sense because they would not trigger economic growth. "Somewhat different from many conservatives, certainly at the time, he asked a lot of questions about fairness and safety nets," recalled Glenn Hubbard, who advised him on economics. "He's a little bit of a hybrid."

The notion turned off many Republicans, who considered compassionate conservatism an insult to traditional party values or believed it "sounded less like a philosophy than a marketing slogan," as David Frum, who would work for Bush, put it after leaving the White House. But it drew others to

Texas hoping that Bush's idealistic talk was more than a campaign tactic, people like Michael Gerson, who became his chief speechwriter, a low-key, bespectacled evangelical Christian uncomfortable with Texas swagger and locker-room humor. "It took a little getting used to for me because I am not much of a towel snapper," Gerson said.

For all the speeches he would give and policy papers he would issue, Bush crystallized his image as a different kind of Republican with a single sentence one day that fall when congressional Republicans proposed stretching out earned income tax credits to the working poor.

Hughes went to Bush's hotel room. "You're going to get asked about this," she said. "It doesn't sound like something you would do."

Bush agreed, and when a reporter did ask, he responded, "I don't think they ought to balance their budget on the backs of the poor."

He could get away with the overt appeal to independents and moderates in part because of his own ties to the Christian conservative wing of the party. While his father's faith was the traditionally quiet Episcopalianism of New England, the new Bush had publicly embraced the evangelical notion of Jesus Christ as his personal savior. "I'm always amazed when I read that George Bush is moving this way or that way for the religious right," his cousin John Ellis once said. "George W. Bush *is* the religious right."

When Bush said at a Republican debate in December that his favorite philosopher was Jesus, his father was chagrined. "I don't think your answer will hurt you too much," the elder Bush told him.

"Which answer?"

"You know, that one on Jesus."

Rather than hurt, it served as a powerful message to a section of the party that voted most often. Consciously or not, Bush was again emulating Ronald Reagan, who once said that Christ was the historical figure he most admired. And Bush was distancing himself from his father, who lost reelection after breaking his famous "read my lips, no new taxes" pledge. "This is not only no new taxes," the younger Bush said of his economic plan during a debate in January 2000. "This is tax cuts so help me God."

ON THE CAMPAIGN plane, Bush acted playful, even goofy with the reporters following him. He enjoyed a winking, mischievous relationship with Alexandra Pelosi, daughter of the Democratic congresswoman Nancy Pelosi and a documentary filmmaker following him with her camera. He showed her his boots and Texas-seal belt buckle, performed an Elvis Presley impression, and grabbed her camera to quiz her about her dating life. "I can see a little chemistry there," he teased her about another reporter. "You know what I mean by 'chemistry there'?" At times, he was too loose. Talking with the conservative writer Tucker Carlson, he mocked Karla Faye Tucker, the first woman put to death in Texas in more than a century. "Please, don't kill me," he whimpered in imitation.

That was, for the most part, an aberration. As a campaigner, Bush described himself as "a uniter, not a divider," and largely meant it. He rejected advice to demonize gays and lesbians. "I'm not going to kick gays, because I'm a sinner," he told Doug Wead. "How can I differentiate sin?" He complained about the Christian Coalition's divisive tactics. "This crowd uses gays as the enemy. It's hard to distinguish between fear of the homosexual political agenda and fear of homosexuality." He added, "I think it is bad for Republicans to be kicking gays."

Still, Bush was rough on the campaign trail, a walking gaffe machine at times, mocked for bringing his own pillow on the road. He mangled various nationalities, referring to "Grecians" and "Kosovarians." He confused Slovakia and Slovenia and failed a pop quiz by a radio reporter who asked him to name the leaders of Taiwan, Chechnya, Pakistan, and India. Words had a way of coming out in all the wrong places. "Rarely is the question asked, is our children learning?" he said one day in South Carolina. "I know how hard it is for you to put food on your family," he said a couple weeks later in New Hampshire. Bush was okay with it if it meant his rivals thought less of him. "They misunderestimated me," he declared.

And yet, backed by money, charm, and a famous name, Bush quickly outdistanced most of the Republican field, including not just Steve Forbes but also Dan Quayle, the former transportation secretary Elizabeth Dole, and the former education secretary Lamar Alexander. To win the nomination, Bush still had to vanquish Senator John McCain, a war hero from his years as a prisoner in North Vietnam and the embodiment of a maverick reformer. Bush did not take McCain seriously at first. "He's going to wear very thin when it is all said and done," he told Wead. The scale of that misjudgment became clear when McCain thrashed Bush by eighteen percentage points in the New Hampshire primary on February 1, 2000. Not used to conceding defeat, Bush left it to Karl Rove to call McCain, which did not go over well with the senator's consultant John Weaver. "Consultants don't concede to candidates," Weaver instructed an aide to tell Rove. A few minutes later, Bush himself called to talk with McCain. The conversation lasted about ninety seconds. "We said good-bye as friends," McCain recalled. "We would soon be friends no more."

Bush took the loss better than his advisers, who were summoned to his hotel room expecting to be fired. Instead, the candidate bucked them up. "This is my fault, not yours," he told them. Every president stumbles on the way to the White House. His father had lost Iowa in 1988 before winning the nomination. Such defeats strengthened a campaign. "He really was like a coach whose team had a bad first half," said Senator Judd Gregg, who led the New Hampshire effort. "He was telling everyone to suck it up and get back in the game. There was virtually no self-pity or woe is me. Just the opposite." But in private, Laura Bush put her finger on the problem; he had gotten away from his core message of changing Washington. "You got defined," she told him. "And you need to make up your mind whether or not you're going to go down there and tell people who *you* are, instead of letting people define you."

The campaign's crucible was South Carolina. Karen Hughes called Rove to vent about how a longtime senator and chairman of the Commerce Committee had somehow co-opted their outsider status. "McCain has managed to steal our reform mantra," she said. They came up with a new slogan, "Reformer with Results," and resolved to refer to McCain as "Chairman" to paint him as a creature of Washington. Then the campaign in the Low Country took a decidedly low turn. Bush, who had rejected divisive politics against gays, visited Bob Jones University, the conservative Christian school known to almost everyone but him apparently for its ban on interracial dating. He also stood by as a surrogate at another campaign event accused McCain of forgetting fellow veterans when he returned after five and a half years of captivity in Hanoi. At McCain headquarters, reports poured in about flyers and phone calls insinuating scurrilous things about the senator—that he had fathered a black child out of wedlock, beat his wife, was mentally unstable, had a secret Vietnamese family, was a Manchurian candidate. Bush denied involvement.

Bush all but ended McCain's threat with a strong victory in South Carolina on February 19. McCain did little to hide his anger, calling Bush "a combination of the Cowardly Lion, the Tin Man and the Scarecrow"—in other words, a man with no courage, no heart, and no brain. Eventually, McCain backed Bush for the general election without enthusiasm. He grew testy at reporters parsing his words, at one point blurting out, "I endorse Governor Bush, I endorse Governor Bush, I endorse Governor Bush," repeating it seven times as if he were scrawling his punishment on a chalkboard. For years afterward, a debate would rage over whether McCain actually voted for Bush. Several liberal celebrities claimed he told them at a dinner once that he did not. McCain denied it.

Either way, the bad blood ensured that Bush would not follow Reagan's precedent of picking his toughest competitor to join the ticket in the fall.

WHILE BUSH WAS securing the nomination, he began thinking ahead to the general election. Weeks after South Carolina, he sent Joe Allbaugh to visit Dick Cheney with a question: Would he agree to be considered for the vice presidential nomination?

Cheney said no. "I cited all the reasons why that was a bad idea," he said later. He had had three heart attacks, he would reinforce the notion of a Big Oil ticket, and he brought no geographic balance to the campaign. Indeed, there could even be a constitutional problem because under the Twelfth Amendment electors cannot cast ballots for both presidential and vice presidential candidates from their own state. Since Cheney at the time lived in Dallas, that would mean Texas's electors could vote for Bush but not for Cheney.

Undeterred, Bush came back a few weeks later with another request. If you won't be my vice president, he asked, will you find one for me? This time, Cheney said yes. He figured at most that assignment would last a few months and he could then return to Halliburton full-time.

He set out to cull names, relying on the help of his daughter Liz, David Addington, and a few others. He eliminated the most obvious candidates, including McCain. Cheney's old Pentagon partner, Colin Powell, now one of the most popular figures in the country, made clear he was not interested and insisted on a public statement that he was not under consideration. Senator Connie Mack of Florida told Cheney that if he was put on a list, he would never speak to him again. Cheney wanted his old mentor, Donald Rumsfeld, to be considered, but Bush personally shot that down. Cheney assured Bush that Rumsfeld really had not been out to get his father in the 1970s, but it was a nonstarter.

Cheney soon assembled a list of nine candidates: Governors Frank Keating of Oklahoma, Tom Ridge of Pennsylvania, and John Engler of Michigan; Senators Bill Frist of Tennessee, Chuck Hagel of Nebraska, and Jon Kyl of Arizona; Representative John Kasich of Ohio, former governor Lamar Alexander of Tennessee, and former senator John Danforth of Missouri. Each agreed to fill out a seventy-nine-part questionnaire and turn over tax returns, medical records, employment and residential history, and every speech and interview ever given.

Helping put together voluminous binders on the candidates, Addington joked that if Cheney did a good enough job, maybe Bush would ask him to be the running mate. Cheney just laughed.

He deflected friends who suspected something was up. When former senator Alan Simpson quizzed him about who was on the short list, Cheney refused to say.

"Are you on it?" Simpson asked.

"No. Lynne isn't going to go for that. I'm not going to go for that."

When his old aide and friend Pete Williams, now at NBC News, called to ask, Cheney said, "I am so glad to be out of public life. Forget it."

What happened from there usually falls into two competing narratives. The official version is that Bush never gave up on the idea of having Cheney as his running mate and wore him down. "If someone says no, do they mean it?" he asked his father at one point. The more conspiratorial version is that Cheney actually did want the nomination and manipulated the process to uncover the flaws of the others, leaving himself the only logical candidate without ever being vetted himself.

In the years that followed, Cheney offered a powerful rebuttal to the suspicions. "He didn't have any desire to be vice president," Liz said, "otherwise he would have agreed the first time Joe Allbaugh asked him if he wanted to be on the list." And Bush by his own account told Cheney every time they talked that he was the solution to his problem. Yet some losing candidates and even some Cheney friends were convinced it was all an elaborate orchestration. "Cheney engineered the whole vice president thing," said one friend. "The brilliance of Cheney is he let the other alternatives just light themselves on fire, one after the other. It was perfect." Cheney never said as much to this friend, but it says something that someone close to him would come to this conclusion.

By summer, Cheney was certainly entertaining the idea. In June, he flew to South America for a hunting trip with his daughter Mary. They spent a week sitting in duck blinds, talking about family and Mary's school plans and their home in Jackson Hole. Only on the flight home on July 1 did he reveal what really was on his mind.

"What do you think about me running for vice president?" he asked.

Mary thought he was kidding. She knew he headed the search committee but did not realize until then that Allbaugh had sounded him out or that Bush still wanted him.

Cheney asked what she thought. Mary had come out to her parents in high school and was now in a committed relationship with another woman, Heather Poe, a former park ranger. Her private life was sure to come under public scrutiny if he were to run.

"Personally, I'd rather not be known as the vice president's lesbian daughter," she told him frankly. "But if you're going to run, I think the country would be lucky to have you. I want to do whatever I can to help out on the campaign. And you'd better win."

When they got home, the family had several conversations about the idea. Lynne Cheney was unexcited. She liked their life. She had her own career writing fiction, appearing on television, and serving on boards, still leaving her time for grandchildren. For months, she had been asking her husband, "You're not going to do this, right?" And he would answer, "No, no"—right until he said yes. Liz Cheney, on the other hand, was bursting with enthusiasm, joking that she had already started painting "Cheney for Veep" signs.

Two days after the flight home from South America, Cheney went to visit Bush at his ranch outside Crawford, Texas.

LAURA BUSH AND her friend Nancy Weiss made sandwiches while Bush and Cheney went through binders in the other room. It was July 3, and the Republican National Convention was only a few weeks away. Time was running short, and Bush had conducted no formal interviews for the job. Bush and Cheney then joined Laura, Weiss, and Karen Hughes for lunch.

Laura asked how the search was going.

"The man I really want to be the vice president is here at the table," Bush said as he ate his sandwich.

Cheney said nothing. The others at the table were stunned.

The two men then retired to the back porch on what Cheney described as a "punishingly hot" day to keep talking amid the cactus and sagebrush. Cheney would later joke that the heat overcame his good sense because he finally agreed to consider joining the ticket. He would have to consult with Halliburton's board and see a doctor, plus talk with Lynne again. He mentioned that Mary was gay. He also said he wanted a chance to go through all the arguments against his selection. Bush said fine.

Bush told Hughes on the way out to her car that afternoon that he was serious about Cheney, and soon he began telling other top advisers. But there was resistance. Hughes warned that they did not know enough about Cheney, who after all had not been vetted. She favored Tom Ridge. Karl Rove also harbored "real doubts" about Cheney and leaned toward John Danforth, as did Joshua Bolten, the campaign policy director. Matthew Dowd, a campaign strategist, still wanted Connie Mack. During a run with Bush, Mark McKinnon, the media consultant, argued for John McCain. Bush invited Rove, Hughes, and Joe Allbaugh to the Governor's Mansion on July 15 to present the case against Cheney. Gathering in the Austin Library, decorated with portraits of famous Texans, they were joined by Cheney himself.

"Tell me why you think I shouldn't pick Dick Cheney," Bush said to Rove.

Stealing a nervous glimpse at Cheney, Rove gamely plowed ahead.

The strategist mentioned the gamut of objections, from Cheney's health and congressional voting record to oil industry ties and the constitutional residency conflict. Unlike Danforth, Cheney brought no battleground state to the table; Bush would obviously have conservative Wyoming's three electoral votes no matter what, while Missouri looked close. And picking Cheney would look as if he were "falling back on his father's administration for help."

After a half hour, Bush asked Cheney if he had anything to ask Rove. Cheney shook his head. "He'd looked at me impassively the entire time, with a poker face that betrayed not a hint of emotion," Rove recounted. "If he was amused, dismissive, angry, or impressed, I couldn't tell." Rove worried he had made an enemy for life out of someone who was about to become vice president.

But Cheney made the same arguments to Bush and mentioned as well his two drunk-driving convictions and flunking out of Yale. Finally, he emphasized to Bush how conservative he was.

"Dick," Bush said dismissively, "we know that."

"No," Cheney said. "I mean *really* conservative."

Bush was unbothered. Cheney was his man. He had gotten to know Cheney and grown to appreciate his quiet command. He found it amusing when Cheney told him that a personality test had determined his ideal job would be funeral director. Bush emphasized to advisers that here was someone eminently qualified to step into the presidency, and he liked the fact that Cheney did not seem to actually want it. He had talked with his father about Cheney, although the elder Bush later said it was "absolutely inaccurate" that he drove the choice.

For the younger Bush, Cheney was the lesson from his father's mistakes, the un-Quayle who would never be accused of being a lightweight. And Bush understood that a neophyte on the world stage like himself could use a seasoned veteran like Cheney at his side. Cheney was "the mature person sitting next to him," Dennis Hastert, then the House Speaker, said years later. "He was the most prominent adult in the room," agreed Sean O'Keefe, the former Cheney aide who would go on to work in the White House. Details like Cheney's voting record were less important. "You know, I really wasn't looking that closely at it," Bush later told an ally.

Although he had made up his mind, Bush went through with plans to interview another candidate. If nothing else, it could reinforce that he had made the right choice while also throwing a head fake to the media. Cheney flew to St. Louis to pick up John Danforth and his wife, Sally, and accompany them to Chicago, where he spirited them unseen into a hotel on July 18 to meet with the governor. Bush was intrigued with Danforth, an ordained Episcopal priest and former three-term senator known for his probity and sometimes called "St. Jack," both admiringly and derisively.

For three and a half hours, Bush chatted with both Danforths, mainly about personal issues rather than grand political philosophy. For Danforth and his wife, joining the ticket would mean a wholesale change in lifestyle, and that was on the top of their minds. "You'd think it would be about what should happen with taxes or foreign policy or the budget or something global," Danforth recalled a little ruefully. "And it was, well, how often could we get back to St. Louis? Dumb stuff like that." Bush did ask Danforth about the role of faith in his public life, and the former senator demurred. "I just wanted to make clear that I didn't see my religion translating into a political agenda," Danforth said.

Danforth had no idea the Sherpa who had escorted him to the interview had already been secretly tapped for the job ostensibly under discussion. Cheney even sat in on the interview until he was told that Liz was on the phone. Excusing himself, he picked up the line, and Liz told him Pete Williams had called to say that NBC was about to report that he was the pick for vice president. Cheney told Liz to call back and say no decision had been made. That might have been technically true, but reporters were picking up the scent, and the secret could not hold long. Bush left his meeting with Danforth impressed, but he had not changed his mind.

Cheney set about clearing away the underbrush. His longtime friend and aide David Gribbin called another Cheney friend, Joe Meyer, now Wyoming's secretary of state, to ask what had to be done to be a voter in the state; Meyer said a recent state supreme court case had made clear that someone who had a home in the state could declare it his primary residence and register. The deadline for the Republican primaries, though, was fast approaching. So Cheney and his wife made a secret trip on July 21 to Teton County, where their vacation home was located, and went to the courthouse to fill out paperwork. It did not take long for word to leak, setting off a flood of speculation. Caught off guard, Karen Hughes tried to find out what was going on by calling Liz Cheney, who was getting a haircut and had to slip into a utility closet to explain the Twelfth Amendment problem. Rove was eager to preserve surprise for Bush's decision. On July 22, he found a fellow campaign aide often suspected of leaking to the media and lied to him by saying Danforth was the choice. By that evening's network news, Danforth was being reported as a leading candidate.

Cheney, of course, knew better, even if he had not been formally offered the job or formally accepted. He confided in only a few trusted friends and presented himself as the reluctant candidate.

"Look," he said when he reached his friend David Hume Kennerly, who had been the Ford White House photographer. "You're going to hear something tomorrow that Bush has asked me to be his running mate."

Kennerly didn't miss a beat. "You told him no, right?"

"Well, not exactly."

"Not exactly? Let's get this clear—you helped him find his vice president and it's like a bad love story and it turns out to be you?"

"He kind of twisted my arm."

"Oh, bullshit, how's that one going to play?"

They would find out. At 6:22 a.m. on July 25, Bush called Cheney at home and formally offered him the nomination. Cheney, reportedly on the treadmill, accepted. He hung up the phone and turned to Lynne. "Honey, let's sell the house," he said. "I quit my job. We're going back into politics."

The Cheneys flew to Austin for the 2:00 p.m. announcement and then later to Wyoming for a raucous rally in the Natrona County High School gymnasium. During their speeches, both Bush and Cheney referenced Cheney's initial refusal to be considered and suggested their months working on the selection brought them together. "I was impressed by the thoughtful and thorough way he approached his mission, and gradually I realized that the person who was best qualified to be my vice presidential nominee was working by my side," Bush told supporters.

Cheney offered a similar account. "I was deeply involved in running a business, enjoying private life, and I certainly wasn't looking to return to public service," he said. "But I had an experience that changed my mind this spring. As I worked alongside Governor Bush, I heard him talk about his unique vision for our party and for our nation. I saw his sincerity. I watched him make decisions, always firm and always fair. And in the end, I learned how persuasive he can be."

PERSUASIVE OR NOT, it was still unclear why Cheney would want the job. Vice presidents have historically found themselves consigned to political exile, deprived of real power unless the most awful thing happened. John Adams, the first to hold the job, called it "the most insignificant office" ever invented, and John Nance Garner, one of Franklin Roosevelt's vice presidents, called it "not worth a bucket of warm spit," or something even more graphic. Lyndon B. Johnson was so despondent about the job that he stared at the television the morning after the 1960 election palpably depressed at having won the vice presidency and later declared, "I detested every minute of it." Walter F. Mondale called it a job "characterized by ambiguity, disappointment, and even antagonism."

Cheney knew that firsthand. "It is a crappy job," he said. "Jerry Ford often told me that it was the worst eight months of his life." Moreover, Cheney said, "I had been there in the Nixon administration and seen Agnew go down in flames, and I had been on the receiving end of Nelson Rockefeller's frustration, which was wide and deep; he hated the damn job." As the instrument of that frustration, Cheney understood intimately the office's limitations. The only constitutional duty beyond succession is to preside as president of the Senate, casting no votes except in case of ties. As Cheney had made clear with Dan Quayle during the attempted coup in the Philippines, the vice president is not in the chain of command.

But the vice presidency had been expanding since the days of Adams and Garner. Johnson was the first with an office in the White House complex, in the Old Executive Office Building next to the West Wing; John F. Kennedy gave it to him to separate Johnson from his old power base in the Senate, where vice presidents typically had an office. Jimmy Carter moved Mondale into the West Wing itself, finally installing him and every vice president who followed just steps from the Oval Office. Bill Clinton gave Al Gore broad responsibility over policy areas like the environment, Russian-American relations, and reorganizing government. Yet for all that, any vice president's influence is strictly derivative, dependent entirely on the beneficence of the president.

So why did Cheney accept? For all of his skepticism, the vice presidency ultimately appealed to him because it offered the prospect of shaping policy without having to endure the hassles required to be elected president. Cheney once said he had no appetite to run for president, but he would happily accept if someone wanted to simply offer it to him by fiat. The more Bush talked about making Cheney a real partner, the closer he came to such a scenario. Bush could be the front man, the baby kisser and rope-line worker, while Cheney focused on what he cared about most. Cheney surely understood that a president with as little knowledge or interest in details as Bush would leave him plenty of room to maneuver. "I was impressed and believed that he was serious," Cheney said years later, "that he was looking for somebody of consequence to do the job and he wasn't just worried about the Electoral College."

Cheney was also a competitive man, despite his quiet manner, and he had been turned off by what he saw of Clinton's White House. "The idea of not wearing a tie in the Oval Office and running around in jeans and just the whole style thing and Clinton's policies struck him as wrong," said Pete Williams. "I think he felt so viscerally that Clinton was pushing things in the wrong direction, that there was a part of him that said, this has got to be fixed. There was a part of him that's a little bit of the fire horse, and the bell rang."

Answering the bell, though, would require adjustment. It had been twelve years since Cheney last faced voters, twenty-two since his only competitive race, and that was a Republican primary in Wyoming, far from the harsh glare of the modern political-media culture. A decade earlier, while he was defense secretary, activists had threatened to out Mary if Cheney did not end the ban on gays and lesbians serving in uniform. He had ignored it. But there would be no ignoring such issues now.

On the day of the announcement, the new environment confronted him right away. Just after the speeches, Howard Fineman of *Newsweek* approached Mary with questions. She rebuffed him. Then he spoke with Cheney.

"Your daughter's sexual orientation and views on same-sex marriage have become a topic in the campaign," Fineman remembered saying. "What do you say to those who point out the conflict between her views and those of the party and the campaign?"

Cheney brushed it off. It was nobody's business, he said. "He did not snap at me or snarl," Fineman recalled. "He was grim as usual, but subdued. More sad and smoldering about politics and the world than visibly or volubly angry."

Overhearing the exchange, Bush leaned over and took it upon himself to answer the question Cheney did not want to. "The secretary loves all of his family very deeply," Bush volunteered.

The issue came up within the campaign operation when Cheney decided Mary would travel as his campaign aide. Two Bush advisers, Dan Bartlett and Ari Fleischer, were concerned it would invite media attention. The two agreed to talk with Cheney and rehearsed their approach. The next day they got into a car with the future vice president heading to the site of the Republican National Convention in Philadelphia, where the nominations would be ratified. Bartlett expected Fleischer to raise the issue, but when the moment came, he was reading a newspaper and not paying attention. So Bartlett, all of twenty-nine years old, jumped in.

"There is one issue we need to talk about," he told Cheney. "We heard that maybe your daughter was going to be on the campaign trail with you. Perfectly fine, but I just want you to know that the press is really going to focus on this. They're going to maybe intrude more into her life than you would be prepared for."

Bartlett paused and noticed what he thought were darts shooting from Lynne Cheney. Nobody said anything for a minute. Bartlett looked to Fleischer for help, but he kept quiet too.

"Well," Bartlett ventured again, "I just wanted to put this on the table for you."

Cheney looked at him with impassive eyes. "We won't be talking about my daughter," he said flatly, shutting down the discussion.

"Okay," Bartlett said, retreating quickly. "Thank you very much."

No sooner had his selection been announced than Cheney and Lynne sat down with two speechwriters, John McConnell and Matthew Scully, to talk about his convention speech. It was Lynne who came up with the most cutting line. Recalling Al Gore's "it's time for them to go" riff from the 1992 Democratic convention, she suggested turning it against him. The speechwriters incorporated that into their draft.

As the planning for the convention advanced, Bush advisers concluded the governor's speech was too harsh and put the toughest lines in Cheney's instead. It was the time-honored role of the vice presidential candidate to be the attack dog. Cheney had no problem with that. But Andy Card, a former lieutenant for the elder Bush who had been tapped to run the convention, decided Cheney's speech was too negative as well and sent edits toning it down. Cheney ignored them and never got back to Card. When he got up before the cheering delegates at Philadelphia's First Union Center on the night of August 2, Cheney simply delivered the original speech as written, word for word. "I came up and gave them a little bit of red meat," he said later.

To raucous applause, Cheney argued that the Clinton-Gore administration had "done nothing to help children" in mediocre schools, "never once" offered a serious plan to save Social Security, and starved the military while demanding more of it than ever. To the armed forces, Cheney said, "I can promise them now help is on the way." He dismissed the Democratic team as full of "lectures and legalisms and carefully worded denials" and did his best, without explicitly mentioning Monica Lewinsky or Whitewater, to tie Clinton's scandals to Gore. "As the man from Hope goes home to New York, Mr. Gore tries to separate himself from his leader's shadow," Cheney said. "But somehow we will never see one without thinking of the other. Does anyone, Republican or Democrat, seriously believe that under Mr. Gore the next four years would be any different from the last eight?" Three times he used the line "It is time for them to go." Lynne beamed from the audience.

It was Bush's turn the next night, August 3. He accepted the nomination with a host of Bushes on hand to witness his triumph, most notably, of course, the father who had stood there eight years before. Even with his speech toned down, the new nominee offered a harsh indictment, arguing that the outgoing administration had "coasted through prosperity" and wasted opportunities. "Our current president embodied the potential of a generation," Bush declared. "So many talents. So much charm. Such great skill. But in the end, to what end? So much promise, to no great purpose." Seeking to distance himself from Clinton and Newt Gingrich at the same time, Bush promised a new "responsibility era" and touted "compassionate conservatism." He noted, "I have no stake in the bitter arguments of the last few years," and he vowed to "change the tone of Washington to one of civility and respect."

It was an effective speech. But in a time of peace and prosperity, it was, as Scully put it, "just straining for big themes." If Bush and Cheney won, what would this presidency be about?

4

"We wrapped Bill Clinton around his neck"

Governor Bush," the CIA man said, "if you are elected president, there will be a major terrorist attack during your time in office."

With the nominations in hand, life around George W. Bush and Dick Cheney began to change. Their security details increased, their perimeters expanded, the advance operations became more elaborate, the events bigger. And the prospect of actually becoming president and vice president loomed ever larger.

Within days, Bush welcomed to Crawford a team of CIA briefers sent by Bill Clinton to give him a classified tour of the world. What the briefers expected to be a one-hour session stretched into four hours as Bush peppered them with questions. Bush jumped in so assertively and proved so interactive that after ten minutes the briefers put aside their binder and engaged in an expansive conversation with the candidate about trouble spots around the globe.

For Bush, this was a tutorial like no other. He proved familiar with Latin America and the Balkans and was especially interested in Russia and China, but he had little of his father's grasp of the world and had traveled little himself. "There were some issues on which he was quite well briefed and others on which he wasn't, and he used the occasion to get smart about things that he didn't know a lot about," recalled John McLaughlin, the deputy CIA director who led the briefing.

At one point, terrorism came up, and McLaughlin and his team had brought charts and graphs, as well as a briefcase that was set down in front of Bush and opened to expose a timing device with red digits counting down as if it were a chemical bomb. McLaughlin offered the prediction that terrorism would mark his presidency. After all, during Clinton's tenure, radicals had bombed the World Trade Center in New York, a housing complex full of American military personnel in Saudi Arabia, and two American embassies in East Africa, and intelligence agencies had broken up a plot to blow up Los Angeles International Airport. The nation's intelligence agencies were hunting down a shadowy Islamic terrorist group called al-Qaeda and its leader, Osama bin Laden. Bush was attentive, though no more than on other topics like Russia. "He absorbed it and was interested and took it on board," McLaughlin said.

None of that played out on the campaign trail, where the issues were domestic. Bush and his team recognized his challenge of taking on Al Gore in a prosperous moment. Stuart Stevens, a consultant to the campaign, jokingly suggested the slogan "Times Have Never Been Better, Vote for Change." But Bush had little respect for his opponent, privately dismissing Gore as "pathologically a liar," and he anticipated an abrasive fall campaign. "I may have to get a little rough for a while," he told Doug Wead, "but that is what the old man had to do with Dukakis, remember?" While the elder George Bush had assailed Michael Dukakis on prison furloughs and his supposed lack of zeal for the Pledge of Allegiance, the younger Bush's strategy was simple. "What we did with Gore was we wrapped Bill Clinton around his neck and never talked about one without talking about the other," Cheney said later. Gore played into that by viewing the scandal-tarred Clinton as an albatross and keeping him on the sidelines. Bush baited the president to come out of hiding. "If he decides he can't help himself and gets out there and starts campaigning against me, the Shadow returns," Bush said.

For Cheney, the return to the stump proved rocky. The basics eluded him. Bush aides watched him walking with Lynne to a rally and thought he needed to learn how to hold her hand. Cheney cared more about the issues than atmospherics and spent hours boning up. "The binders came back fully consumed," remembered Stuart Holliday, an aide dispatched by the Austin headquarters to staff the new candidate. But it would take a while to find his best role on the trail, and with Cheney never vetted the way he had vetted other candidates, the campaign was ill-equipped to respond when Democrats attacked his conservative votes in Congress. "The whole thing was a surprise to him," said his friend Alan Simpson. "He hadn't prepared for it at all."

Heading out on the trail, Cheney was sent to South Florida, where he visited a couple of schools on August 31, only to realize he was delivering a speech on school bond financing to an audience of grade schoolers. He thought it was a fiasco and resolved to take control of his own schedule. "He basically sort of laid down the law to a certain degree and became, I think, an active partner in the overall process of determining what states, what events, what messages, and so forth," said Holliday. As the campaign progressed, Austin eventually got the message—no reading to children, not a lot of rope lines, no cocktail parties, no tailgating at college football games. Aides in Austin joked that they would just make a cardboard cutout of Cheney and send it on the trail.

Cheney joined up with Bush a few days later for a Labor Day event in Naperville, Illinois, on September 4. Waving to a boisterous crowd, Bush in a casual blue shirt turned to Cheney in a blazer and nodded toward the press section.

"There's Adam Clymer, major league asshole from the *New York Times*," Bush said.

"Oh yeah," Cheney responded. "He is, big time."

Neither realized that the microphones picked up the remarks; the audience could not hear, but journalists plugged into the sound system could and quickly asked whether Bush was living up to his vow of civility. Back aboard the campaign plane, Cheney's staff debated whether to smooth it over by inviting Clymer to the front for a drink with the candidate. Cheney had no interest. But from then on, his staff delighted in playing the Peter Gabriel song "Big Time" at campaign rallies.

Bush had been preparing for weeks to debate Gore, tapping Senator Judd Gregg to play the Democratic candidate in rehearsals in Kennebunkport and Crawford. Gregg spent hundreds of hours studying Gore tapes and transcripts. He badgered and interrupted and "was careful to break almost every rule of the debate agreement," as Stuart Stevens, the consultant playing the moderator, put it, just as he presumed Gore would. "There was no quarter given in these debate preps," Gregg said. "I was not deferential at all." But they were relatively loose affairs, with Bush not going through a full ninety-minute evening rehearsal until just days before the first debate. When he did, he was "flat," Stevens recalled. Bush looked as tired as anyone had seen him. Mark McKinnon fretted. "Lambs to the slaughter," he told Stevens.

Afraid of protesters in a liberal state, Karl Rove decided Bush should not fly to Boston the night before the first debate and should instead stay over in West Virginia. But when the governor and his entourage arrived at the hotel and found a table in the restaurant, the kitchen was empty of everything but chicken, and the staff was overwhelmed, making the increasingly impatient candidate wait an hour for his food. Don Evans, his friend and campaign chairman, kept going back to the kitchen to prod the staff, passing out $20 bills to speed up the service. Already irritated, Bush headed to his room to lie down, only to hear train whistles and barge horns outside the window all night.

Not well rested, he flew to Boston the next day, October 3. To avoid protesters, Bush's staff arranged for him to arrive at the University of Massachusetts campus by boat. In the holding room beforehand, he called Kirbyjon Caldwell, a minister from Texas, and prayed with him over the phone, beginning what would become a tradition before big events. He headed onstage and shook hands with Gore, who squeezed hard as if trying to intimidate him. Bush took his watch off and placed it on the podium rather than repeat his father's mistake from eight years earlier, when he was caught glancing at his timepiece in the middle of a debate.

Bush used the opportunity to lay out his vision of a humbler America stepping more gingerly on the world stage. "He believes in nation building," Bush said of Gore. "I would be very careful about using our troops as nation builders. I believe the role of the military is to fight and win war and therefore prevent war from happening in the first place." Overall, he added, "I believe we're overextended in too many places."

In the end, though, as often happens in modern presidential debates, the words mattered less than the pictures. Gore, his makeup caked on too thick, was caught reacting scornfully to Bush's comments in split-screen images. Gore rolled his eyes and sighed in exasperation at Bush's answers, making him look haughty to many viewers. Bush won mainly by keeping his sighs to himself.

NEXT UP WAS Cheney, who had not faced an opponent in years and now confronted Senator Joseph Lieberman, a confident and skilled debater. Cheney watched Lieberman's debates from his 1988 Senate race and studied thick briefing books on plane rides. By late September, he had retreated to his home in Wyoming, where Liz ran a more rigorous preparation than Bush's.

They practiced at a local theater with overstuffed red velvet seats that "felt like a cross between a frontier opera house and a bordello," as Stuart Stevens remembered it. After drawing too much attention, they retreated to the house, where they conducted a mock debate each night at a round table covered by a bedsheet against Representative Rob Portman of Ohio playing Lieberman. Portman needled Cheney about Halliburton and other issues, getting under the candidate's skin. The advisers tutored him on making his answers more digestible. "His tendency is to give a very long, substantive, heavy answer," Liz said. "We'd be like, 'Let's think about how we can personalize that.'" Liz also learned to keep her mother out of Cheney's line of sight because "she would throw him off."

Cheney cleared his mind the day before the debate by taking Portman fly-fishing and telling stories about the Nixon-Ford days. Then he flew to Kentucky the morning of October 5 and called Matthew Dowd, Bush's campaign strategist. How should he handle Lieberman? he asked. "He was getting all kinds of advice to be an attack dog," Dowd recalled. Dowd thought that would backfire and urged Cheney to resist what seemed to be pressure from his family.

"Whatever you want to do, Mr. Cheney," Dowd said, "but if you do that, you are making a huge mistake."

Cheney paused for a moment before finally saying, "Okay."

Lieberman came to the same conclusion. His staff had drafted attack lines against Cheney, including a hit on his growing wealth at Halliburton. Lieberman should note that most people were better off than eight years earlier and "I think that probably includes you too," according to a campaign memo. In years to come, though, Lieberman said he was later urged to stand down. "It is a loser, don't attack him," Lieberman remembered his political adviser, Stan Greenberg, telling him. Greenberg and his colleague, Robert Shrum, recalled it differently, saying they urged the candidate to go after Cheney vigorously and were surprised when he did not.

The two candidates met onstage at Centre College in Danville, Kentucky, sitting at a table as if on a Sunday talk show, a format Cheney had insisted on. The seating arrangement had the effect of turning the showdown into a civil conversation. Indeed, the only time Lieberman turned to one of the scripted attack lines, it backfired.

Lieberman said most Americans were better off. "I'm pleased to see, Dick, from the newspapers that you're better off than you were eight years ago too," he added.

"I can tell you, Joe, that the government had absolutely nothing to do with it," Cheney responded, provoking laughter in the hall.

Lieberman, realizing Cheney had gotten the better of him, tried humor too. "I can see my wife and I think she's thinking, 'Gee, I wish he would go out into the private sector.'"

Cheney took the opening. "Well, I'm going to try to help you do that, Joe," he said.

Of course, when Cheney said the government had nothing to do with his financial success, that conveniently overlooked the $763 million in federal contracts Halliburton received in 2000 alone. But Cheney's dry wit turned Lieberman's attack back on him. Cheney was deemed to have won, frustrating Democrats who considered it a missed opportunity. Both Cheney and Lieberman for years would take pride in the discussion. "The debate was actually very high-toned, I thought," Lieberman said. "I was proud of it, civil debate."

Bush emerged unscathed from his second debate with Gore on October 11 at Wake Forest University in Winston-Salem, North Carolina, and then set about preparing for the final debate with a town-hall-style format, this time with Portman serving as his practice opponent. Stools were set up in the Governor's Mansion to simulate the setting. Portman, who had been studying Gore's primary debates with Bill Bradley, surprised Bush by standing up in the middle of a rehearsal and walking over into the governor's space. Bush reacted playfully, leaning over and kissing Portman on the head, but he scoffed at the idea that Gore would try it.

"He's not going to do that," Bush said. "It's ridiculous."

"You bet he will," Portman responded. "He's going to try to intimidate you. Gore did it to Bradley."

Sure enough, at Washington University in St. Louis on October 17, Gore got up from his stool in the middle of a Bush answer on health care, walked over, and stood right next to him. Bush, looking surprised, gave Gore a quick nod and then returned to his answer. It was just the right dismissive reaction, and once again a debate dominated by body language favored Bush. "He put the move on me," Bush exclaimed to aides afterward.

By the end of October, Bush was feeling confident. He was ahead in the polls and saw no obstacle to victory. "I'll be the most surprised man in America if I don't win," he told Governor Tommy Thompson of Wisconsin. His mother was not so sure. "'Miss Pessimistic' (me) really doesn't think he is going to win as we are at peace and because we have a strong economy," Barbara Bush wrote in her diary on October 31.

She had reason to worry. Two days later, on November 2, with just five days until the election, Karen Hughes rushed into Bush's room to tell him a reporter had found out about his drunk-driving arrest in Maine. "His face didn't change, but his body slumped a little," Hughes recalled. Bush had kept the arrest secret from all but a handful of trusted advisers and ignored their advice to disclose it earlier in his campaign autobiography, where it would have been received in the context of a redemption narrative. He rationalized by saying he did not want his teenage daughters to know. He likewise refused to say whether he had tried cocaine. At one point during the campaign, his press aide Scott McClellan overheard him telling someone on the phone, "You know, the truth is I honestly don't remember whether I tried it or not," which McClellan considered an act of elaborate self-deception.

The report on Bush's arrest broke as a huge scandal days before the vote. Without telling anyone, Matthew Dowd commissioned last-minute polls in three states and found that Bush's lead had disappeared in Florida and Ohio, while Michigan was now out of reach. Swing voters might not have cared, but social conservatives were disturbed. "This thing has gone from probably-win to I-have-no-idea," Dowd told Dan Bartlett as they went golfing on the morning of Election Day. Karl Rove would later calculate that four million evangelical voters stayed home. Stuart Stevens concluded the story might have shifted enough votes to cost Bush the states of New Mexico, Iowa, Oregon, and Maine—and almost Florida.

Still, when the campaign's lawyers got together for brunch in Austin just before the election, they chewed over all sorts of scenarios—all but one. "The one thing on which there was absolute unanimity," recalled Michael Toner, the campaign's general counsel, "was we didn't have to worry about a recount."

BUSH AND CHENEY organized separate dinners for separate entourages on election night, November 7, expecting to join together late in the evening to declare victory. The campaign was confident enough to distribute a schedule showing that Bush would deliver his victory speech at precisely 10:39 p.m. Texas time, but the candidate himself was not so sure.

Bush and his family went to dinner at the Shoreline Grill, a restaurant in Austin. "It could be a long night," he told his parents on the way.

At the restaurant, tables were set and appetizers ready, but Bush kept checking out the television in the corner. At 6:48 p.m. in Texas, or 7:48 p.m. back east, the networks began calling Florida for Gore. Bush and his brother Jeb, the Florida governor, were irritated; polls were still open for another twelve minutes in the conservative panhandle, where Bush had strong support. More important, Florida was critical to a Republican majority in the Electoral College.

Jeb Bush had tears in his eyes as he hugged his brother apologetically. "I felt like I had let him down," Jeb told his sister, Doro, afterward.

Already antsy, the candidate grew more agitated when the restaurant's television broke. "I'm not going to stay around," he whispered to his father. "I want to go back to the mansion."

Skipping dinner, Bush, his wife, and his parents headed out. As the car made its way through the dark, rainy night, the ride struck Bush as ominously quiet.

At the mansion, the family headed upstairs and flipped on the television. Rove, who had confidently predicted that Bush and Cheney would win with 320 electoral votes and a four- to seven-point margin in the popular vote, examined and reexamined the numbers and concluded the networks had gotten it wrong in Florida. He called to berate network executives, and eventually they began to back off.

Jeb Bush, in touch with officials back in Florida, realized his state was still in play and rushed over to the Governor's Mansion, bounding up the stairs.

"Back from the ashes!" he shouted.

At 8:54 p.m. in Texas (9:54 p.m. in the East), CNN and CBS News retracted the Florida call but were not yet ready to put the state in Bush's column.

In a suite across town at the Four Seasons Hotel, Cheney was following the same roller-coaster results with an electoral map of the country he clipped out of the newspaper and a yellow legal pad on which he was scratching out tallies. Joining him were friends and advisers like James Baker, Donald Rumsfeld, Alan Simpson, Nick Brady, Scooter Libby, and David Addington. Bush called Cheney at one point to declare, "We're still alive."

Bush's family crowded into the relatively cramped upstairs of the Governor's Mansion. Laura Bush made coffee in the kitchen and kept loading the dishwasher ("when she's stressed, she cleans," according to her daughter Jenna). Barbara Bush sat on a couch stitching a needlepoint canvas and listening through earphones to an audio version of a Sandra Brown novel. The elder George Bush was nervous and, in Barbara's eyes, "suddenly looked old, tired, and so worried." Another person who talked with the former president that night recalled him popping antacids, tormented by suspense.

By midnight Texas time, Bush had picked up West Virginia, Arkansas, and Tennessee—the first a state that had voted Democratic in fourteen of the previous seventeen presidential elections and the other two the home states of the incumbent Democratic president and vice president. If Florida held, victory seemed assured. *If.*

Just before 1:00 a.m. Texas time, Bush got a call from his cousin John Ellis, who had worked for network election units for years and this night was running the election desk for Fox News.

"What do you think?" John Ellis asked.

"What do *you* think?" Bush retorted.

"I think you've got it."

Not long after that, at 1:15 a.m. Texas time (2:15 a.m. East Coast time), Fox called Florida for Bush and Cheney, bringing them to 271 electoral votes, one more than needed. All other networks followed within five minutes.

About fifteen minutes later, Bush got the call he had long awaited.

"Congratulations," Gore told him, conceding the election.

"You're a formidable opponent and a good man," Bush said.

"We gave them a cliff-hanger," Gore said.

"I know it's hard, and hard on your family. Give my best to Tipper."

With that, Bush thought he had been elected president and called his running mate. At the Four Seasons, Cheney was as drained as Bush was restless and had ducked into the bedroom to lie down a few minutes earlier. He would later remember his daughter Liz waking him up. "Dad, you just got elected vice president. The president-elect wants to talk to you."

Mary Cheney remembered her mother being the one to wake Cheney, while Alan Simpson and Nick Brady each recalled being the one to rouse him.

"Get up, bastard!" Simpson remembered calling out. "You're the vice president of the United States."

Cheney, in this recollection, reacted cautiously. "It isn't over yet, Al," he said.

He emerged from the bedroom with his shirttail hanging out but enough presence of mind to tell his friend David Hume Kennerly, the photographer, not to take his picture when he was looking so disheveled. After Bush told him about the call from Gore, the Cheneys left for the Governor's Mansion. The Secret Service spirited them through the hotel kitchen for security purposes, and as they passed the cooking stations, Lynne Cheney noticed her husband was the only one not smiling.

"You've just been elected vice president of the United States," she said. "You could at least look happy about it."

"This just doesn't feel right," he said.

His instincts were on target. When they arrived at the mansion, everyone was calling Bush "Mr. President" or "Mr. President-elect." But they soon noticed Gore had not come out to publicly concede. At 2:30 a.m., Gore called Bush back.

"Circumstances have changed dramatically since I first called you," he started. "The state of Florida is too close to call."

Bush could not believe it. "Are you saying what I think you're saying? Let me make sure I understand. You're calling back to retract that concession?"

"Don't get snippy about it," Gore retorted. "Let me explain." He went on to say that if Florida did go for Bush, he would concede, but it was too early to be making statements with the final result still in doubt.

Bush noted that the governor of Florida was standing right there. "My little brother says it's over," he said.

"I don't think this is something your little brother gets to decide," Gore shot back.

"Do what you have to do," Bush said sharply.

Incredulous, Bush hung up. He went back downstairs, slipping through the kitchen to rejoin the others, and looked as if he were in a state of shock.

"He took it back," he said. "He took it back."

"Who took what back?" asked Kennerly.

"Gore just called and took back his concession."

Bush was not sure what to do now. Maybe, he suggested, he should go out to the crowd that had been waiting in the rain for hours and declare victory anyway. The numbers were on their side. Why should he have to defer to Gore?

Jeb talked him out of it. "George, don't do it," he said. "The count is too close." Don Evans went instead to address the crowd and put things on hold.

Finally, Laura Bush walked over to her husband and put her arm around him. She knew how exhausted he must be and wanted him to rest.

"Bushie," she said teasingly, "would you rather win or go to bed?"

He laughed. "Go to bed," he said.

NOT SINCE Rutherford B. Hayes squared off against Samuel Tilden in 1876 had the result of a presidential election been seriously contested. As lawyers for both sides flew to Florida in the early morning hours, Bush and Cheney woke to an uncertain future.

With Florida set to be a legal and political war, Bush turned to his party's greatest field marshal, James Baker, the close friend of his father and Cheney, to lead the fight. But Bush opted not to appear too involved personally and to proceed as if he really had won. He headed to the ranch, while Cheney spent ten days at the Four Seasons in an improvised war room before heading back to his house outside Washington. Bush affected a pose of quiet confidence and almost indifference to the daily machinations as lawyers in Florida argued over hanging chads and other ballot irregularities. He had no cable television and made sure his staff let it be known that he was reading a biography of Joe DiMaggio.

He also had time to get to know Andy Card, who would be his new chief of staff if he won, as they cleared brush, ate Blue Bell ice cream, and discussed what they would do in office. "We spent literally hours together talking about how would you like the White House organized? Who are the people you're comfortable with? Who are the people you're not that comfortable with but you want them in the administration just not that close?" Card recalled. Card considered it "almost a gift," because with attention focused on Florida, Bush had a chance to stop and think, and reenergize, in a way he would not have had after a clear election night victory.

When Bush returned to Austin to handle state business, he joined friends for a dinner of Chinese carryout one night but refused to open his fortune cookie. A friend opened it for him: "You are entering a time of great promise and overdue rewards." Laura Bush exclaimed, "You made that up!"

Bush of course was following developments in Florida. He and Cheney held a conference call each morning with Baker to review the latest, and he peppered his sister, Doro, and others with instant messages asking what was going on. He was constantly on the phone with his father. "We talk all the time," the former president wrote a friend. One day after an adverse decision by the Florida Supreme Court, Karen Hughes thought Bush "seemed worn down for the first time." When he saw Ari Fleischer at the ranch before sending the spokesman off to Washington, Bush sounded almost resigned to a fate beyond his control. "If they're going to steal the election, they're going to steal it," he said. "If they do, I'll get on with my life here." He was hardly a passive bystander, though. He authorized Baker to go to the U.S. Supreme Court to stop the recount despite doubts on his team.

Baker and Don Evans tracked down John Danforth on vacation in Cancún to ask him to represent the man who had passed him over for Cheney just months earlier. But Danforth thought it was a fool's errand and said so.

"I just can't conceive that a federal court's going to take jurisdiction over a matter relating to state election law," Danforth said. "I just can't believe that." Bush was still a young man and could have a future if he lost. If he brought an unworthy case to court, "it could affect his reputation."

Baker asked him to do it anyway, and Danforth reluctantly agreed. Minutes after he checked out of the hotel, however, Baker called back. "It sounds like your heart's not in it," he said, "so we'll get somebody else."

Instead, the campaign tapped Theodore Olson, a well-known Republican lawyer, and he proved Danforth wrong. The court took the case.

While all this was going on, Bush told Cheney to organize the transition. No incoming president had ever delegated the construction of his administration to his vice president before. Cheney started in Austin by reaching for the only paper around, a Bush-Cheney news release on Palm Beach County ballots, flipped it over, and mapped out what had to be done in the ten weeks until the inauguration. After returning to Washington, Cheney with the help of Liz and David Addington based his operation at the kitchen table in his town house in McLean, Virginia, since the government would not hand over space for a transition office. His communications network consisted of three cell phones, which sometimes had to be taken outside to get a signal. For calls too sensitive for wireless phones, Lynne brought down an old beige Princess dial phone from the attic. Cheney had experienced five presidential transitions but never one like this.

In the early morning of November 22, just hours after the Florida Supreme Court extended the deadline for recounts, Cheney woke with discomfort in his chest and was rushed to George Washington University Hospital, where he was checked in under the pseudonym Red Adair. At first, a heart attack was ruled out, which Bush conveyed to reporters. But as a stent was inserted to open up a clogged artery, further tests indicated he did have a heart attack. Briefing the media, doctors used technical terminology. Concerned that they had not said the words "heart attack," Karen Hughes ordered the doctors to hold a second news conference so no one could suspect a cover-up.

This was Cheney's fourth heart attack, and it revived questions about whether he was up to the job. In the midst of the recount, perceptions mattered, and the last thing the campaign wanted was the image of a medically unfit would-be vice president. So Cheney called in to Larry King's show on CNN from the hospital.

"I feel good and everything's looking good," Cheney reported. "I should be out of here in a day or two."

"How about the stress?" King asked.

"Frankly, it may sound hard to believe, but I have not found this last couple of weeks as stressful, for example, as, say, the Gulf War."

Any doubt about doing the job should they win?

"No doubt about my serving," he insisted.

After a Thanksgiving dinner in the hospital prepared by Colin Powell's wife, Alma, Cheney returned to transition duties. The campaign secured private offices in McLean, and Cheney began stocking the emerging government with people he trusted.

Uncertainty was growing. If the dispute could not be resolved soon, it was conceivable Inauguration Day would arrive without a president to swear in. The CIA began briefing House Speaker Dennis Hastert, next in the line of succession, in case he had to become acting president.

Finally, the U.S. Supreme Court ended the matter. At about 10:00 p.m. on December 12, it ruled 7 to 2 in *Bush v. Gore* that recounts under way in selected counties had to stop because of inconsistent standards that violated the Constitution's equal protection clause; by a 5-to-4 vote, the court ruled there was not enough time to establish standards for new recounts before the deadline for Florida's electors to cast their votes. The complicated rulings confused television reporters who grabbed the copies and went right on the air without digesting the details.

Cheney was at his town house in McLean when David Hume Kennerly called. Kennerly had just left after a visit and heard that the court was issuing its ruling.

"Dick, the Supreme Court is going to give their ruling tonight," he said.

"Come back, come back over," Cheney said.

Kennerly was only a few blocks away drinking with a friend, Michael Green, an Associated Press photographer, so they rushed over to the house.

Lynne and Mary were upstairs fighting the flu, and Cheney was sitting alone in the kitchen watching the news when they arrived. He flipped around until he found Pete Williams reporting on NBC. "If anybody knows, it'll be Pete," Cheney said. Sure enough, Williams figured out the rulings faster than most: Bush and Cheney had won.

Cheney called James Baker.

"Hello, Mr. Vice President–elect," Baker said.

"Thank you, Jim," Cheney said. "And congratulations to you. You did a hell of a job. Only under your leadership could we have gone from a lead of 1,800 votes to a lead of 150 votes."

After hanging up, Cheney turned to his guests. "I'm going to open the good bottle of wine," he said. Soon after, Liz and her husband, Phil Perry, arrived with champagne. "It was not a wild celebration," Kennerly recalled. "He's a fly fisherman. That's a Zen-like thing."

Bush was at the Governor's Mansion already in bed when the ruling came out. The phone rang, and it was Karl Rove, who told him to turn on the television. Bush flipped on CNN, but its correspondents were struggling with the import of the decision and reading the dissent at the moment.

"Congratulations, Mr. President," Rove said. "This is great news."

"What are you talking about?" Bush asked. "This is terrible."

"What channel are you watching?" Rove asked.

Bush told him. Rove told him to switch to NBC.

Bush switched and watched for a minute, then hung up to call Baker for a legal opinion. Baker confirmed Rove's take.

Bush called his father. "I'm not a lawyer," he told him, "but I think this means I won."

Gore took the night to consider his options, then called Bush the next morning to concede, this time for good. "I'm not calling back this time," he told Bush.

After thirty-six frenzied days, it was over. The final tally showed Bush and Cheney winning Florida by 537 votes out of nearly 6 million cast and winning the presidency with 271 electoral votes, one more than the minimum needed. The Florida recount had become a raw struggle for power as both sides abandoned long-held philosophical positions in a desperate bid to claw their way into the White House. Gore's campaign insisted on counting all ballots, but only in Democratic-friendly counties where they were likeliest to pick up votes; they were less interested in counting all ballots from military service members stationed overseas who were more likely to vote for the other side. Republicans insisted on following the letter of the law to exclude ballots that were even potentially questionable—except those from soldiers who should be given the benefit of the doubt. Liberals who had long championed an assertive federal judiciary argued for state sovereignty. Conservatives traditionally skeptical of equal protection claims and federal court intervention in state disputes were suddenly at the doors of the Supreme Court demanding it step in. Judges and justices who presented themselves as apolitical justified positions that just happened to suit their philosophical allies.

The process was so palpably cynical that it was bound to feel discredited no matter who won. The Supreme Court ruling was widely ridiculed by the Left, and Bush's critics deemed him an illegitimate president because the election was "stolen" by unelected conservatives in robes. But however reasoned or flawed its findings may have been, the Supreme Court did not elect Bush and Cheney; it stopped a recount process that would not have changed the outcome. Two extensive recounts conducted later by media organizations showed that Bush and Cheney would still have won even if the hand recount ordered by the Florida Supreme Court or the more limited recount in four Democratic counties sought by Gore had gone forward.

Still, Bush understood that his victory would always come with an asterisk, and regardless of Florida it was true he had lost the popular vote nationally. The disputed nature of his ascension was like "pouring alcohol in an open wound" for those who did not support Bush, as Karen Hughes saw it. So Bush made a point of giving his victory speech on December 13 from the chamber of the Texas House of Representatives, introduced by the Democratic Speaker. "Here in a place where Democrats have the majority, Republicans and Democrats have worked together to do what is right for the people we represent," Bush said. "We've had spirited disagreements. And in the end, we found constructive consensus." Bush praised Gore for a "spirited campaign" and expressed empathy with him for "how difficult this moment must be." He promised to work with Democrats to save Social Security and Medicare, improve schools, cut taxes, and produce a "bipartisan foreign policy."

"The spirit of cooperation I have seen in this hall," he added, "is what is needed in Washington, D.C. It is the challenge of our moment."

5

"I'm going to call Dick"

Whatever spirit of cooperation George W. Bush saw in that Texas hall eluded Dick Cheney back in Washington. On the same day Bush accepted Gore's concession and delivered a conciliatory speech, Cheney was roaming the halls of Capitol Hill delivering a far different message: a new team was coming to town, and there would be no compromise.

If the chattering class thought the freshly anointed president and vice president would be chastened, abandon fundamental ideas, and hew to a centrist path, Cheney planned to disabuse them. "Our attitude was hell no," he later recalled. "We got elected. You don't now go for half tax reform. We're not going to leave half the children behind. No, it's full speed ahead." Cheney thought acting weak would make them weak. They should proceed as if they had a mandate and force Washington to accept their legitimacy.

Cheney had received a lunch invitation with five moderate Republican senators for December 13 in the hideaway office of Senator Arlen Specter of Pennsylvania. The Senate had split 50 to 50, meaning Republicans retained control through the tie-breaking vote of the new vice president. With the balance so close, Specter and the other moderates—James Jeffords of Vermont, Lincoln Chafee of Rhode Island, and Susan Collins and Olympia Snowe of Maine—assumed they would play a vital role. But just as Cheney defied his recent heart attack by ordering fried chicken—polishing off the bird and even dropping a piece that stained the hideaway's white carpet—he defied any suggestion of retreat. Instead, he outlined a bold agenda to cut taxes, back out of the Kyoto climate change treaty, renounce the International Criminal Court, and abrogate the Anti-Ballistic Missile Treaty with Russia to develop a missile defense system.

"What really unnerved me was his attitude," Chafee recalled. "He welcomed conflict." Chafee wondered where Cheney got the nerve to come to the Hill and dictate results; he was issuing orders, not soliciting input.

"Our votes at this table are important," Chafee told Cheney.

Cheney dismissed the moderates. "*Every* vote is important," he said.

That was not just Cheney being pugnacious. Bush agreed. For all the talk of Texas-style bipartisanship, he made clear that his call for "constructive consensus" really meant forcing others to accept his ideas. Compromise was reserved for when it was really necessary. As Karl Rove argued, John F. Kennedy did not scale back his agenda after winning a razor-thin victory, nor did Bill Clinton after winning with less than a majority of the popular vote.

Nowhere was that more true for Bush than on taxes, the centerpiece of his campaign and the issue that helped sink his father's presidency. The federal government was projected to take in $5.6 trillion more than it would spend over the next ten years. Much of that would be reserved for Social Security and Medicare, but Bush thought it reasonable to return less than a third of it, $1.6 trillion, to taxpayers.

"How will this work?" Bush asked Nick Calio, his father's legislative affairs director, who would reprise the role in the new White House.

Calio described the state of play on Capitol Hill. Implicit was that at some point they would have to give ground.

Bush interrupted and leaned across the table. "Nicky," he said, "we're going to say $1.6 trillion. And when anybody says anything else, we're going to say $1.6 trillion. And we're going to keep saying $1.6 trillion. I'm not saying at some point we might not accept something else. But we're never going to say it. We're just going to keep saying $1.6 trillion. We're going to see how long it takes us to get it.

"You get that?" Bush asked.

"Yes, sir, loud and clear," Calio said.

With just thirty-eight days for a truncated transition, Cheney moved his operation to government office space and accelerated efforts to build a new team. He recruited Paul O'Neill, a Ford administration colleague, as Treasury secretary. Senator John Ashcroft, a former Rove client defeated for reelection by a challenger who died before Election Day, was picked for attorney general. The former New Jersey governor Christine Todd Whitman, who worked with Cheney in the Nixon White House, would head the Environmental Protection Agency. While Bush wanted Condoleezza Rice for national security adviser, Cheney promoted his former aide Stephen Hadley as her deputy and recruited another, Sean O'Keefe, as deputy budget director. He eventually found positions for others like Paul Wolfowitz, Douglas Feith, John Bolton, and Robert Joseph, all known as leaders of the most hawkish wing of the Republican Party. Cheney knew how to build an administration to his liking, and whispers were already spreading about who was really in charge. Bush was still figuring it all out. When Whitman asked whether she or the CEQ, shorthand for the White House Council on Environmental Quality, would call the shots, Bush asked, "What's CEQ?"

Bush had already decided on Colin Powell for secretary of state, tapping one of the nation's most admired figures, but the retired general's expansive performance at the announcement overshadowed his putative bosses and only reinforced their instinct to find someone else for the cabinet who could counterbalance him. As Powell saw it, Cheney became intent on "keeping me on a much shorter leash than we had during" the first Bush administration. For a moment, Cheney toyed with the idea of serving simultaneously as secretary of defense. No vice president had headed a cabinet department before, but nothing in the Constitution barred it. There was even a precedent of sorts when Henry Kissinger served as both national security adviser and secretary of state in the Nixon and Ford administrations.

But Cheney had been at Ford's side when he stripped Kissinger of his White House title to establish clearer lines of authority, and he concluded any such arrangement now would be unwise. A defense secretary was subject to Senate confirmation and oversight by Congress. He could be summoned to testify, his papers subpoenaed. Protecting executive privilege while serving in the cabinet seemed problematic. "To be in a position where you would have to step down in a sense and take off your constitutional hat and go up and be a cabinet member who has been through confirmation by the Senate, it really puts a strain on the system," Cheney said later.

Instead, Bush's first choice for the Pentagon was Frederick Smith, founder of FedEx, but he underwent emergency heart bypass surgery during the Thanksgiving holiday. Bush's second choice was the former senator Dan Coats of Indiana, who had the support of Senator Trent Lott, the majority leader. But when they met, Coats did not impress Bush or Cheney as forceful enough to handle Powell. So they went to the third choice, Donald Rumsfeld. In his memoir, Bush attributed the idea to Condoleezza Rice, but Cheney clearly played an important role. In late December, Cheney sent a car to bring Rumsfeld to the Madison Hotel in Washington, where he was slipped in through a basement to avoid witnesses. When the old friends sat down, Cheney told Rumsfeld he was thinking about him for Defense or CIA.

Rumsfeld flew to Austin to meet with the president-elect on December 22. The same "awkward issue" that Bush identified in ruling out Rumsfeld for vice president loomed over a cabinet appointment too. "All I'm going to say to you is, you know what he did to your daddy," James Baker told Bush. But even if Rumsfeld had maneuvered his father out of contention for vice president a quarter century earlier, the younger Bush was no longer going to hold it against him. "I had no way of knowing if this was true," he later wrote, evidently choosing not to ask his father or, if he had, not taking his version on faith. "Whatever disagreements he and Dad might have had twenty-five years earlier did not concern me so long as Don could do the job." Rove also argued against Rumsfeld, warning that the appointment would feed impressions that Cheney was in charge. Bush brushed him off.

Four days later, Cheney called Rumsfeld, who had gone to New Mexico for the holidays. Rumsfeld started suggesting other possibilities.

"Dick, here's an interesting idea," he said. "What if—"

Cheney interrupted. "Hold on, Don, I've got another call. Let me get back to you."

Cheney called back ten minutes later. "That was the president-elect calling. He told me to tell you he wants you to be secretary of defense."

"Actually," Rumsfeld interjected, "before we were interrupted, I was going to suggest *you* as SecDef."

Cheney did not seem surprised. "The president-elect had the same idea," he said, attributing the idea to Bush. But Rumsfeld was the choice.

To some around Washington, it seemed as if the old gang was getting back together. Alan Greenspan, the chairman of the Federal Reserve, thought it was like the second coming of the Ford administration, where he had worked along with Cheney, Rumsfeld, and O'Neill. Prince Bandar bin Sultan, the longtime ambassador from Saudi Arabia and man-about-town in Washington, thought it was more like the return of the first Bush administration, when he worked with Cheney and Powell to organize the Gulf War. "My God, talk about a replay," the prince said. It was "too good to be true."

Still, the new president was torn between the work-across-the-aisle instincts of Ford and his father, and the no-compromise resolve of his new vice president. Bush yearned for a Bob Bullock, a Democrat he could work with the way he did with the lieutenant governor in Texas. But a Texas Democrat was more like a Republican in Washington. Bush was looking less for someone to compromise with than a Democrat who would agree with him.

His search took him to the Capitol Hill office of Senator Tom Daschle, the Democratic leader. The two sat in front of a fireplace on a cold, dark January day, and Bush quickly cited Bullock as proof of his bipartisan spirit.

"We got to be very close," Bush said. "I'd like to see if we could do that too."

As Daschle weighed his response, Bush added, "I hope you'll never lie to me."

Surprised, Daschle replied, "Well, I hope you'll never lie to *me*."

Bush was edgier than Daschle anticipated. Then the president implicitly raised Cheney's role in his White House.

"I know there's been a lot of talk out there about who's in charge around here," Bush said. "There's not ever going to be any question about who's in charge. Decisions are going to come to my desk, and I'm going to be the one making them."

It struck Daschle as a little defensive, even insecure.

A LIGHT FREEZING RAIN fell on the Capitol on January 20, 2001, as Bill Clinton prepared to hand power to the son of the man he had taken it from eight years earlier. Bush and Cheney were both kept in their limousines as they waited for Clinton, ever behind schedule, to get ready to receive them for the traditional White House coffee that preceded the inaugural ceremony.

After an abbreviated visit, Cheney and Al Gore climbed into the limousine they would share to the Capitol for the ceremony. Gore noted that Clinton had been busy with last-minute pardons. "How many more do you think he can get signed before noon?" he asked sarcastically. After eight years together, Clinton and Gore were parting on sour terms, a president and a vice president ending their partnership in schism.

At the Capitol's West Front, the steps were narrower than Bush expected, and he forced himself to pay special attention to avoid falling. As he stared at the sea of overcoats, Bush focused on the cacophony of sounds and images and worried that the sleet might make it hard for him to read his inaugural address on the teleprompter. He took the thirty-five-word oath, then offered a vision for his presidency that suited the moment. "I will live and lead by these principles—to advance my convictions with civility, to pursue the public interest with courage, to speak for greater justice and compassion, and to call for responsibility and try to live it as well," he said. Cheney watched from a leather chair several feet away. A tear rolled down Bush's face as he hugged his father.

It was a unifying speech at a time when many liberals viewed Bush as a usurper. Hendrik Hertzberg, who was President Jimmy Carter's speechwriter, called it "shockingly good" as a piece of writing, "by far the best Inaugural Address in forty years," and "better than all but a tiny handful of all the Inaugurals of all the Presidents since the republic was founded."

Like others, Kirbyjon Caldwell, the African American pastor from Texas who performed the benediction, took it as a sign that Bush would steer to the political center. "Had you closed your eyes, you would not have known if it was a Republican or a Democrat that had given the speech," he said. He buttonholed Bush afterward to ask about some policy—he later forgot the specifics—and was struck by the answer.

"Did you hear my speech?" Bush asked.

"Yes, I did."

"Well, that is where I am going to be."

Caldwell took that to be the middle of the road.

After traveling down the Pennsylvania Avenue parade route, Bush arrived in the White House for the first time as president. He looked around with a familiarity many predecessors did not have, but somehow it felt different. He asked someone to find his father, who had already settled into the Queen's Bedroom in the residential quarters and slipped into a hot bath to chase away the cold. Told his son wanted him, the elder Bush jumped out of the tub, dressed again, and raced to the Oval Office.

"Welcome, Mr. President," his son greeted him when he arrived.

"It's good to see you, Mr. President," the father replied, his hair still damp.

It was a mind-spinning experience for a onetime screw-up from Midland. It all took some adjusting. The younger Bush did not even know how to react when two men introduced themselves as his valets.

"I don't think I need a valet," he confided to his father.

The elder Bush smiled. "Don't worry," he said. "You'll get used to it."

FROM THE START, Bush intended to put his own mark on the White House. He kept the *Resolute* desk, built from the timbers of the HMS *Resolute* and sent as a gift by Queen Victoria to President Rutherford B. Hayes. He kept the bust of Abraham Lincoln. But he replaced the carpet, designing a new one with a sunburst pattern to send a signal of optimism, and he replaced the Andrew Jackson bust Clinton favored with one of Dwight Eisenhower. He also hung a portrait of Eisenhower in the Cabinet Room. In his private study, as an inside joke with his father, he put up a painting of John Quincy Adams, the only other son of a president to reach the White House. The two would come to call each other 41 and 43, after their order in the presidency, and the dining room would come to be called the "Johnny Q Room."

For the central piece of art in the Oval Office, Bush borrowed a painting from his friend Joe O'Neill called *A Charge to Keep*. The painting, by W. H. D. Koerner, showed a rugged cowboy racing a horse up a wooded mountain trail, followed by a couple of other roughriders, and rushing so fast his hat has fallen off. Bush thought it had been inspired by the Charles Wesley hymn of the same title, which began, "A Charge to keep I have, A

God to glorify." He had hung the painting in the governor's office too, and described it to visitors as a portrait of a circuit rider spreading Methodism in the Alleghenies. He liked it so much he made it the title of his campaign autobiography, *A Charge to Keep*.

Later research, however, determined that the painting had no religious meaning and nothing to do with the hymn. In fact, it was commissioned in 1916 to accompany a *Saturday Evening Post* story about a horse thief escaping a lynch mob in Nebraska. It was later reprinted in another magazine to illustrate another story, titled "A Charge to Keep," about a son who inherits a forest from his father and must protect it from timber barons. Whatever its origins, much meaning would be attached to the imagery. While Bush identified with the heroic qualities he saw in the mysterious rider, David Gergen, who worked for four presidents and was once hired by Cheney, later wrote that critics saw "a lone, arrogant cowboy plunging recklessly ahead, paying little heed to danger, looking neither left nor right, listening to no voice other than his own."

For Cheney, the inauguration meant a return to the West Wing twenty-four years after he left. This time he took the suite down the hall and around the corner from the Oval Office, somewhat smaller than the corner office next door that he had occupied as chief of staff. His office had large bay windows, a mahogany desk, a deep blue carpet, and a series of flags, including one with the vice presidential seal. He hung portraits of John Adams and Thomas Jefferson, the first two vice presidents. During his second week on the job, as a sixtieth birthday gift, his daughters gave him a hand-painted map they had commissioned showing all the battles that his great-grandfather Samuel Fletcher Cheney had fought in on the side of the Union during the Civil War. That would hang on his wall for the next eight years.

Unlike the Bushes, who moved into their new quarters on Inauguration Day, the Cheneys remained at their suburban town house. The vice president's residence on the grounds of the Naval Observatory was in need of renovation, especially the flooring. While some Republicans groused that Gore had run down the place, Cheney considered it nothing more than the typical wear and tear of a family with children, and he made no protest about the delay. For a while, he even still headed over to the supermarket in McLean to do his own grocery shopping, albeit trailed by Secret Service agents.

Both Bush and Cheney had ideas about how to run things, based on experiences with past White Houses. Bush wanted to return the West Wing to traditions observed under his father—always a coat and tie in the Oval Office, none of the casual, late-night, college pizza-party atmosphere that sometimes prevailed in the Clinton days. Yet he had his own fraternity-boy style; he delighted in those early days at popping into meetings to see aides jump to their feet, then leaving and popping back in a moment later to see them do it again. He eschewed formalities like state dinners. He preferred lunch from the White House chef to be a bacon, lettuce, and tomato sandwich, or a grilled cheese sandwich with Kraft singles on white bread, or a peanut butter and honey sandwich, with Lay's potato chips on the side. For dinner, he favored anything Tex-Mex, no soup or salad and no "wet fish," meaning poached, steamed, or boiled.

Organizing his staff, he took lessons from his father's time. He wanted a flatter structure, granting more access to more aides, a recipe for a relatively weak chief of staff, unlike the domineering John Sununu. But he also wanted a disciplined team that resisted being buffeted by outside events. His staff had laid out his first twenty-one days in office by the time he took the oath. He believed fervently in punctuality and obsessively worried about keeping others waiting, to the point of abruptly ending a meeting at its designated time regardless of where the conversation was. "It was probably the good breeding from his family," observed John Bridgeland, an aide. Others who did not share that Bush punctuality were quickly taught a lesson. When Colin Powell showed up late for the first cabinet meeting, Bush had the door locked. When the doorknob jiggled a few minutes later, the room burst out laughing. But the point was made.

Perhaps the most important lesson was the insistence on complete loyalty, with none of the freelancing by appointees out to puff themselves up that he saw in his father's White House. He surrounded himself with confidants from Texas, including Karen Hughes as counselor, Karl Rove as senior adviser, Dan Bartlett as communications director, Alberto Gonzales as White House counsel, Harriet Miers as staff secretary, and Margaret Spellings as domestic policy adviser. In tapping Andy Card as chief of staff, Bush was easing Joe Allbaugh out of the inner circle, making him director of the Federal Emergency Management Agency. Other campaign veterans transitioning into new roles included Ari Fleischer as press secretary, Michael Gerson as speechwriting director, and Joshua Bolten and Joe Hagin as deputy chiefs of staff. The twin poles in the inner circle were Hughes, who considered herself the champion of everyday Americans, and Rove, who viewed politics through a more Machiavellian prism.

Cheney likewise valued loyalty and brought several longtime advisers with him to the West Wing. He asked Scooter Libby to be his national security adviser; Libby asked to also serve as chief of staff, and the incoming vice president agreed. David Addington would be his counsel. Mary Matalin, a media-savvy veteran of the first Bush White House, would be his counselor. John McConnell, who helped write the convention address, would be his speechwriter. Cheney's focus on national security issues was clear when

Libby sent him Cesar Conda to interview for domestic policy adviser. The session lasted no more than ten minutes, with a television on in the background, and the only question Cheney asked was if Conda had ever done anything that would embarrass the administration. "No, sir," Conda said, and got the job.

Most notable was how Cheney integrated his staff with the president's. Both Libby and Matalin also carried the rank of assistant to the president, making them equivalent to Card and Condoleezza Rice. McConnell would be part of Gerson's speechwriting shop also writing for the president. Addington would work closely with Gonzales, to the point of dominating the counsel's office. National Security Council aides were told to make their computer calendars accessible to the vice president's staff. "We said great, do we get to see their calendar?" recalled Michael Green, an Asia adviser. "The answer was no. At first people were a little bit intimidated by it." Green would sometimes put "Meeting with Vice President" on his calendar as a joke on Cheney aides.

But Cheney's efforts to establish himself as more than the typical vice president got away from him at times. Addington decided Cheney ought to chair cabinet-level national security meetings whenever the president did not attend. That was not unheard of; Richard Nixon had done so under Eisenhower. But in modern times, such meetings were typically chaired by the national security adviser.

Rice took the issue to Bush. "Mr. President, this is what the NSA does: convene the national security principals to make recommendations to you," she said. He agreed.

Her new deputy, Stephen Hadley, approached Cheney. "Mr. Vice President, your staff is pushing the notion that you should be chair of the Principals Committee," Hadley said, using the formal title for the group. "I don't believe that is what you want to do."

"That is exactly right," Cheney said, attributing the idea to overzealous aides. "I don't want to do that. That is Condi's job."

The episode was blamed on Libby, but in fact he was chagrined when he learned. The proposal had actually come from Addington, who had not cleared it with his bosses. Cheney and Libby said it was a stupid idea. Still, not everyone believed Cheney; at least one Rice aide saw a memo mentioning the idea signed by Cheney. Rice took it as an early warning sign that Cheney's staff "seemed very much of one ultra-hawkish mind" and "was determined to act as a power center of its own." For their part, Cheney's staff saw a red flag when Rice's intramural victory was leaked to the media, building her up at his expense.

While he would not chair the Principals Committee, Cheney made clear he would not sit quietly on the sidelines. He would attend meetings of the principals, even though he once believed Gerald Ford's vice president should not participate in meetings with advisers because his presence would warp the discussion. He got Bush to agree to have lunch once a week, and the new president told aides to invite Cheney to any meeting he wanted to attend. Bush's scheduling director would later estimate that Cheney attended 75 percent to 80 percent of Bush's meetings. Cheney even arranged to have the intelligence report known as the President's Daily Brief presented to him first in the library of his residence each morning at 6:30. Then, having already read the materials, he would join Bush for the official briefing at 8:00 a.m., led by the CIA director, George Tenet, a Clinton appointee kept on at the urging of Bush's father. Cheney expressed so much interest in intelligence that his CIA briefers began preparing a second part just for him dubbed "Behind the Tab" that the president never saw.

The extent of the vice president's influence proved sensitive from the start. When his press secretary, Juleanna Glover, suggested he conduct weekly background briefings for reporters, even without being identified, the White House staff rejected it. "I think those guys are always just a little more insecure about a strong force in the White House," observed Neil Patel, another Cheney aide. Cheney was fine keeping out of the spotlight, but he was not about to be locked into silos like Gore or Dan Quayle. When Joshua Bolten proposed that he take on three main subject areas—homeland security, energy, and the reinventing government project Gore had led—Cheney and Libby agreed to head a task force on the first but rejected the other two.

Indeed, when Quayle visited shortly after the inauguration, he was surprised to hear Cheney's description of the job. Quayle assumed he would be doing a lot of fund-raisers and funerals as he had.

"We've all done it," he said.

"I have a different understanding with the president," Cheney replied serenely.

"Well, did you get that directly from Bush?" Quayle asked.

"Yes."

THE DECISION NOT to move to the political center despite the close election was reinforced by a detailed study of the electorate. Matthew Dowd, the campaign strategist, compared the November results with those of five previous presidential elections and found that the long-sought-after "swing voters" were a vanishing breed in American politics.

Dowd reclassified voters who called themselves independents but actually voted reliably as Democrats or Republicans and determined that the fraction of the electorate genuinely open to persuasion had shrunk since 1980 from 22 percent to 7 percent. Dowd charted his findings in a memo to Rove, a memo that would profoundly shape the thinking behind the Bush presidency for the next four years. If compassionate conservatism had been aimed at independents, Dowd's numbers suggested they were not the decisive bloc. "You could lose the 6 or 7 percent and win the election, which was fairly revolutionary, because everybody up until that time had said, 'Swing voters, swing voters, swing voters, swing voters, swing voters,' " Dowd said later. Just as important was motivating the Republican base and driving up turnout of those already inclined to support the candidate.

Yet Bush's instinct for unyielding principle, as he saw it, clashed with his self-image as a bridge builder. Among his first actions in office was to sign two executive orders pleasing conservatives, one limiting taxpayer money for organizations that promoted abortions overseas and the other creating a White House office of faith-based initiatives to help religious groups do charitable work. At the same time, on his second full workday as president, Bush invited Senator Ted Kennedy, the nation's most prominent liberal, to the Oval Office to talk about education reform.

Searching for his new Bob Bullock, Bush was in full courtship mode, showing Kennedy that he had chosen the *Resolute* desk that his brother had used as president. Bush "was eager and fervent and knowledgeable and caring," observed Sandy Kress, the former Dallas School Board chief who had followed Bush from Texas to serve as an education adviser. Bush described a more aggressive federal involvement in the nation's schools than ever before. The trade-off for more funding would be rigorous testing to hold schools accountable for results. But it was Bush's animated discussion about closing the achievement gap between white and minority children that really sealed the partnership. When Bush used a term of art, "disaggregation of data," to describe the importance of breaking out minority test scores so school districts could not hide their problems, Kennedy concluded this was a president who was serious.

As Kennedy got up to leave, Bush noted the reporters outside. "You know, Senator, they are going to ask you when you walk out of here about vouchers and other things that might divide us," Bush said, "and I just want you to know I want to do a deal with you, I want to work with you on this, I don't want any issue to keep us from working together."

Kennedy agreed. "I hear you," he said. "I won't let that happen." Speaking with reporters outside the building, Kennedy said there were areas of agreement and he was "interested in getting some action."

Bush, watching, concluded this was someone he could trust. "I don't think the two expected to like each other," Kress concluded, "but they did."

AS BUSH SOUGHT new allies at home, he made a series of introductory phone calls to American allies abroad. He was so unschooled in foreign policy that he was thrown off by the time differences of those with whom he spoke. He tried to cover for his lack of preparation with brashness.

On January 25, he was on the line with President Kim Dae Jung of South Korea, who explained his "Sunshine Policy" of reaching out to the hostile and volatile North Korea.

Bush covered the mouthpiece with his hand. "Who is this guy?" he asked aides. "I can't believe how naive he is."

Charles Pritchard, a veteran diplomat listening to the call, couldn't believe how naive Bush was.

Kim, of course, understood the complexities of Korean politics a hundred times better than a rookie president five days on the job. Kim had spent four decades in Korean politics, mostly in opposition to authoritarian governments; he spent years in prison or under house arrest, survived several attempts on his life, and went into exile in the United States before helping to bring democratic reform to South Korea and winning the presidency in 1997 and the Nobel Peace Prize in 2000. Later that day, Pritchard was asked to write a paper for Bush about "who is this guy," which he did overnight. "It did not change the president's views," Pritchard concluded.

Others were trying to get Bush's attention in those early days. Richard Clarke, the counterterrorism coordinator held over from Clinton, gave Condoleezza Rice a memo on the same day as the Kim phone call saying "we *urgently* need" a cabinet-level review of the fight with al-Qaeda. Using a different spelling, he wrote that "al Qida is not some narrow, little terrorist issue that needs to be included in broader regional policy," adding, "We would make a major error if we underestimated the challenge al Qida poses." The CIA had put together what it called a "Blue Sky" plan for additional authorities to go after Osama bin Laden and his cohorts more aggressively, and Clarke wanted the new president to sign off on aid to the Northern Alliance, an anti-Taliban rebel group in Afghanistan, and to neighboring Uzbekistan. Rice authorized him to develop a strategy, but no such meeting would be held for months. And the new administration did no more than its predecessor to retaliate for al-Qaeda's bombing of the USS *Cole* the previous fall, deciding it would wait for its review rather than lob more cruise missiles ineffectually as Clinton had done during his presidency.

Bush convened the first meeting of his National Security Council at 3:35 p.m. on January 30 and made clear he was not letting Cheney chair such sessions in his absence. "Condi Rice will run these meetings," Bush announced. "I'll be seeing all of you regularly, but I want you to debate things out here and then Condi will report to me."

With that settled, the discussion turned to the intractable Israeli-Palestinian conflict that had consumed Clinton in his final days in office. On the way out of office, Clinton had called Powell to vent angrily about Yasser Arafat, the Palestinian leader he said could not be trusted. Bush had watched as a deal eluded Clinton and had no interest in heading into that snake pit.

"We're going to correct the imbalances of the previous administration on the Mideast conflict," Bush declared. "We're going to tilt it back toward Israel. And we're going to be consistent. Clinton overreached and it all fell apart. That's why we're in trouble. If the two sides don't want peace, there's no way we can force them."

Powell was alarmed. He agreed Clinton had overreached, but pulling back too far could be dangerous. It could give Ariel Sharon, the Israeli prime minister, a green light to send the Israeli army into Palestinian territories and escalate the situation. Cheney countered that Bush was right and should not waste his time.

The conversation turned to Iraq, where a decade after the end of the Gulf War, American forces still enforced two no-fly zones and the United Nations program of sanctions had been terribly corrupted. As Rice put it later, "Almost from the very beginning, Iraq was a preoccupation of the national security team." Official U.S. policy, set by Congress and signed by Clinton, called for regime change, but there was no obvious route to achieve that, and no one at this point was advocating war.

Powell suggested it was time to revamp sanctions to make them more effective.

"Why are we even bothering with sanctions?" retorted Rumsfeld. What mattered was finding and destroying Iraqi weapons of mass destruction.

George Tenet, the CIA director, unrolled oversized surveillance photographs on the table showing antiaircraft batteries around Baghdad and what he called chemical weapons factories.

Secretary of the Treasury Paul O'Neill studied the photographs but was unconvinced. "Factories all over the world look like this," he said. "Tell me how you can tell this is a factory that creates weapons of mass destruction?"

Tenet cited what he considered telltale signs, and few others in the room seemed to doubt they were what he said they were.

Bush ended the meeting by instructing Powell to work on a better sanctions regime and Rumsfeld to review existing military options.

BUSH DECIDED TO make Mexico his first foreign destination, a sign of commitment to America's southern neighbor and a trip he could take without worry since his experience in Texas had left him with a working understanding of the place. He arrived on February 16 and greeted President Vicente Fox like an old friend, certain that a fresh era in Mexican-American relations would be a cornerstone of his foreign policy. But the reality of what his presidency would become intruded. About an hour into the meeting with Fox, Bush noticed that Rice had been called away from the table, then Powell and finally Karen Hughes. "What's going on?" Bush asked, clearly irritated. Rice whispered in his ear that something was happening in Iraq.

American and British warplanes were bombing radar and command-and-control facilities around Baghdad in response to what the military considered an escalated threat to aircraft patrolling no-fly zones. Bush was stunned. How had this happened without his knowing in advance? Heading to a news conference with Fox, Bush knew the questions would now be about Iraq. Aides advised him not to let on that he did not know about it and to use the word "routine" to describe it. Bush followed the advice, informing the world that "a routine mission was conducted to enforce the no-fly zone."

From there, the president flew to his Texas ranch. On television were scenes of bombing in Baghdad.

"I'm going to call Dick," the restless president said.

Cheney came on the line and told the president that this was a good action that would reinforce American resolve against Saddam Hussein.

Rice was struck that in a moment of uncertainty the first person Bush thought to consult was Cheney. "That said something to me, that he was sort of looking for reassurance," she said later.

The main partners in the strike were the British, and Bush was determined to make common cause with Prime Minister Tony Blair. A center-left Labour politician and fast friend of Clinton's, Blair was hardly the most natural partner for a conservative Republican from Texas. But Bush invited him to Washington so the two could take each other's measure.

It was an awkward opening. Before meeting with Bush, Blair was first asked to sit down with Cheney in the White House on February 23. Cheney struck the British as "relaxed while at the same time emanating tension," as Blair's adviser Alastair Campbell put it. The meeting "had a certain Soviet woodenness to it," thought Christopher Meyer, the British ambassador, and Blair's team was chagrined that Cheney "did not seem to have been instantly felled by the prime minister's fabled charm." By the time Blair and his entourage flew to Camp David, they were wary enough that Blair's wife, Cherie, looked out the helicopter window to spot the Bushes waiting for them and muttered, "I don't expect that they are looking forward to this any more than we are."

But they were struck by the contrast with Cheney. Bush laughed easily and treated them as long-lost friends. "He was a curious mix of cocky and self-deprecating, relaxed and hyper," Campbell observed. "He liked to see everything in very simple terms, let others set out complicated arguments and then he would try to distill them in shorter phrases." Blair found him "self-effacing and self-deprecatory" with "a great sense of humor." Still, it was not a deep discussion; one American official noticed the president stuck closely to his note cards lest he wander outside his comfort zone.

After the meetings, the leaders met with reporters focused on the transatlantic odd couple. One journalist asked if they had anything in common.

"Well," Bush said, "we both use Colgate toothpaste."

As everyone laughed, Blair interjected with a smile: "They're going to wonder how you know that, George."

Then the two and their spouses and aides enjoyed a relaxed dinner. "Why don't we all watch a movie?" Bush suggested. He picked *Meet the Parents,* the decidedly lowbrow Ben Stiller–Robert De Niro comedy. Bush roared with laughter, particularly when it turned out Stiller's character was named Gay Focker, while Rice nodded off in her chair.

Not every early effort to make acquaintances went according to plan. After seeing the Blairs off, Bush returned to the White House, where he planned to host an overnight stay for Republican governors in town for the annual National Governors Association meeting. But as the evening wore on, no one showed up.

"Well, what did they say when you invited them?" Bush finally asked Laura.

"When *I* invited them?" she said. "I thought *you* did."

WHILE THE BUSHES got used to their new home, Cheney and his wife were finally moving into theirs. With the new floors finished at the vice president's official residence, the last of a hundred boxes of books and other belongings arrived on March 2, and the Cheneys spent their first night in the house after dinner with Liz, her husband, Phil Perry, and their three children. While the books included all the predictable volumes on history and national security, the ones Cheney would keep most accessible were on fly-fishing. A visitor later in his tenure would count thirty-seven fishing books on the shelves and forty-three more in the stacks.

Amid the unpacking, Cheney began to feel uncomfortable. The next day, March 3, he was getting off the treadmill when he felt a twinge in his chest. It did not last, and he did not respond to it. In fact, on the CNN show *Late Edition* the next day, he offered a good report on his health. "Well, I feel great," he said. "I am well-behaved. They've taken control of my food supply. So I'm trying to do all those things you need to do to be a responsible individual with a history of coronary artery disease and somebody who's sixty years old. So far, so good."

That afternoon, he felt another twinge, but went to a birthday party for Alan Greenspan and did not call his doctor until the next morning, when the pain returned more sharply while he was dressing. Even then, he headed to the White House for meetings without mentioning the pain to anyone. By afternoon, it had worsened, and he was rushed to George Washington University Hospital, where doctors operated and found his artery clogged again. They cleared it out and allowed Cheney to go home the next morning.

Cheney planned to join the president the next day, March 7, for a meeting with Kim Dae Jung, the South Korean president Bush had scorned while on the phone in January. With Cheney's backing, Bush took a more jaded view of North Korea than Clinton, who negotiated a deal called the Agreed Framework to compensate Pyongyang for halting its nuclear program. But when Bush woke up that morning, he found a headline in the *Washington Post* that declared, "Bush to Pick Up Clinton Talks on N. Korean Missiles." It was based on a news conference by Colin Powell. No way, Bush thought. That was the opposite of his approach.

Bush picked up the phone and dialed Rice's temporary apartment, not bothering to go through the White House operator. It was 5:15 a.m., and she was still asleep.

"Have you seen the *Washington Post*?" he demanded.

"No, Mr. President, I haven't," the groggy adviser said.

"Go outside and get it," Bush ordered tersely.

Rice put on a robe and retrieved the paper.

"Go to page A20," Bush instructed.

She did and quickly read the headline and beginning of the article.

"Do you want me to take care of this, or do you want to?" Bush asked.

It was hardly a question. "I'll take care of it, Mr. President," Rice answered.

She called Powell at home and told him to fix it before the meeting with Kim. Powell did not think it was such a problem. All he meant was they were reviewing the North Korea situation and would not automatically toss aside everything Clinton had done. He concluded the real problem was what he later called "the fatal word: 'Clinton.'" Later that morning, Powell fell on his sword. "There was some suggestion that imminent negotiations are about to begin," he told reporters. "That is not the case."

A few weeks later, Powell explained away the confusion by saying, "Sometimes you get a little too far forward on your skis." But the episode proved an early warning sign of Bush's relationship with his secretary of state. "That spooked the president and confirmed Cheney's view that a leash was in order," Powell concluded.

BY THE TIME Bush and Cheney took office, California was in the throes of a full-fledged energy crisis. Years of deregulation combined with a growing economy and market manipulation had caused prices to shoot up as demand increased. So in the first few months of the new administration, California utilities were forced to resort to rolling blackouts, turning out the lights in the nation's largest and most important state.

Against that backdrop, Cheney switched gears and agreed to head an energy policy task force. But he did not wait for its conclusions to undo what he saw as an ill-advised campaign pledge to fight climate change. Bush had promised to impose a cap on carbon emissions, but with the need for energy seemingly more pressing by the day, Cheney argued it was the wrong time to add to industry's burden.

With a letter in hand from Senator Chuck Hagel and three other Republicans requesting the president's position, Cheney went to Bush on the morning of March 13 and argued it was time to drop the carbon pledge and renounce the Kyoto climate change treaty signed by Clinton. Bush agreed and signed a letter Cheney had drafted responding to the senators. "I oppose the Kyoto Protocol," the letter said, since the agreement did not cover rising economies like China and India, was "unfair and ineffective," and would "cause serious harm to the U.S. economy." It added that Bush did not believe that "government should impose on power plants mandatory emissions reductions for carbon dioxide, which is not a 'pollutant' under the Clean Air Act."

Bush's rejection of the Kyoto treaty was hardly a surprise—he had made that point during the campaign—and in some ways was not a fundamental change in American policy, since even Clinton had not submitted it for Senate ratification after senators of both parties voted 95 to 0 for a nonbinding resolution opposing such an agreement. But Bush's letter made only passing mention of working with other countries to find alternatives to the flawed pact, and no one had prepared the allies for what was coming, feeding the impression of a go-it-alone attitude on the part of the new president. Just as significantly, the position on the carbon cap reversed a campaign promise that had the strong support of some members of his team.

Having sided with Cheney, Bush now had to explain his position to Christine Todd Whitman, his Environmental Protection Agency director. Whitman arrived at the Oval Office at 10:00 a.m. prepared to make the case for keeping the promise. As she sat down, she realized she was there not to make arguments but to be informed that the decision was already made.

As she left the Oval Office, Whitman ran into Cheney with his overcoat on. "Do you have it?" Cheney asked an aide, who handed him the Bush-signed letter. Cheney stuffed it in his pocket and headed out. Only later would she learn what was in the letter; Bush had not mentioned it. "That one was a done deal," she concluded later. Bush probably did not tell her about the letter because "he felt he was cutting my legs out from under me, which he did pretty effectively."

Cheney took the letter straight to Capitol Hill, hand delivering it to the weekly lunch of Republican senators. When he announced the president's decision, the assembled senators broke out into cheers and shouted, "Hoo-rah!" One senator yelled triumphantly, "Somebody better tell Christie!"

Somebody had, of course, but not in time for her to do anything about it. Nor were Powell or Rice consulted ahead of time. Each of them was sent a copy of the letter just as Whitman was heading to the Oval Office, and both had similar reactions: there was nothing wrong with the policy necessarily, but the language was unnecessarily provocative. They should rewrite the letter to make clear the rejection of Kyoto was not a rejection of the issue altogether and emphasize that the United States was committed to finding ways of tackling climate change. "Slow this thing down until I get there," Powell told Rice as he rushed to his car.

By the time she reached the Oval Office, it was too late. "But the letter is already gone," Bush told her. "The vice president is taking it up to the Hill because he has a meeting up there. I thought you cleared the letter."

Rice was taken aback. She had not cleared it.

Powell arrived a few minutes later.

"It's gone," Rice told him.

"What's gone?" Powell asked.

"The letter."

"Gone where?"

Rice explained that Cheney was delivering the letter.

Bush looked at Powell. "Well," he said, "we wanted to get it up to the Hill to Hagel right away."

"Well," Powell responded, "you're going to see the consequences of it."

The consequences were more profound than Bush anticipated. Fairly or not, the decision would haunt him for years as he sought international help in places like Afghanistan and Iraq. "The way they did it was just flipping the bird to the rest of the world," Whitman believed. What Bush did not understand was how invested many European and Asian allies felt in Kyoto. As Rice put it to her aides, "They had built this beautiful crystal sculpture, and we walked in and, 'Oh, I am sorry, did I break something?'" Bush came to understand later. "While he was right on Kyoto, we were just wrong on the way we did it," Stephen Hadley said. "We lived with that one; that is really where this 'Bush unilateralism' starts from."

There was also the question of Cheney unilateralism. In an institution that cherished process, the vice president had achieved a major decision with little input from those who disagreed. Rice told Bush she was "appalled" the vice president had been allowed to take a letter to Congress on a significant international policy without the input of the national security adviser or secretary of state. "It wasn't that the vice president was 'running the country' the way a lot of people say," Whitman later observed, "but he certainly did have a lot of influence, and this may have been one of those where the president just decided it wasn't worth the fight."

Paul O'Neill, the Cheney friend serving as Treasury secretary and a supporter of more assertive action on climate change, commiserated with Whitman. He told her Hagel's letter sounded as if it were written by Cheney himself and speculated that the vice president might even have asked Hagel to send it to provide an excuse to press Bush.

"We thought we knew Dick," O'Neill later reflected. "But did we? About this time, people first started to ask—has Dick changed? Or did we just not know him before?"

MANY WOULD LOOK to Cheney's repeated health scares as one possible cause of change. After his latest angioplasty, Cheney focused on his own mortality. More than most vice presidents, he had given a lot of thought to succession issues often called "continuity of government." He had seen up close the ascension of a vice president to the Oval Office during the Nixon-Ford administration and participated in what-if Cold War exercises during the Reagan administration.

At Cheney's request, David Addington did some studying and reported that the Constitution provided a mechanism to remove an incapacitated president but not an incapacitated vice president. So if Cheney were to fall into a coma, the nation would be stuck with a vice president it could not replace. Worse, should that happen and the president then died in office, the nation would be stuck with an incapacitated acting president. Or if the president were incapacitated, there would be no way to remove him because the Constitution required the assent of the vice president.

So on March 28, Cheney secretly signed a letter of resignation effective upon delivery to the secretary of state. At Addington's recommendation, it included no conditions for taking effect, out of concern that could become fodder for disputes over meaning. So Cheney pulled out a piece of stationery emblazoned "The Vice President" and scrawled out a separate letter:

> *Dave Addington,*
> *You are to present the attached document to President George W. Bush if the need ever arises.*
> *Richard B. Cheney*

The vice president then made clear to Addington that it would be up to Bush to submit the letter to the secretary of state. "This is not your decision to make," Cheney told him. "This is not Lynne's decision to make. The only thing you are to do, if I become incapacitated, is get this letter and give it to the president. It's his decision, and his alone, whether he delivers it to the secretary of state."

"Yes, Mr. Vice President," said Addington, who inserted the letter into two manila envelopes and kept it in a desk drawer at home in case something happened at the White House. (As it happened, his home later burned down in a fire; Addington saved two things, a folder of family financial information and birth certificates and Cheney's resignation letter.)

Cheney never discussed the contingent resignation with anyone other than Bush and Addington until he revealed it in his memoir after leaving office.

6

"Iron filings moving across a tabletop"

President Bush was at Camp David on Saturday, March 31, when Condoleezza Rice, who had joined him and the first lady for the weekend, notified him about 10:00 p.m. that an American spy plane had made an emergency landing on Chinese soil after a midair collision with one of Beijing's jet fighters.

The navy's EP-3E Aries II reconnaissance plane was gathering intelligence over the South China Sea seventy nautical miles off the coast when a Chinese pilot shadowing it got too close. The American four-engine turboprop plummeted thousands of feet before its pilot reasserted control and managed to land at a Chinese base on Hainan Island. Its crew of twenty-four destroyed as much sensitive equipment as they could before being detained. The Chinese F-8 fighter was sliced by a propeller on the American plane into two pieces; the pilot ejected and was missing and presumed dead. For a new president barely two months in office, it would be the first test on the international stage.

Bush resolved not to let the episode escalate. "He was not going to be jingoistic about it," recalled Senator Judd Gregg, who was at Camp David that weekend. "That was the tone of the discussion: we've got to be firm, but we can't let this blow up what should be a more positive relationship." While making firm statements at first demanding release of the crew and plane, Bush avoided inflammatory language and turned the conflict largely over to Colin Powell. But his efforts were complicated for days as Chinese officials did not answer phones or return messages, in what Americans interpreted as internal disarray in Beijing.

The key to unlocking the crisis was a Chinese demand for an apology. On April 2, Bush discussed it with Powell, Rice, and Donald Rumsfeld in the Oval Office. Rice and Powell were open to some sort of statement, and Powell added that the State Department favored a suspension of the reconnaissance flights that had provoked the Chinese. Rumsfeld argued against any apology or suspension. The American crew did nothing wrong; the Chinese pilot caused the accident. Besides, he said, capitulating would only embolden the Chinese and make the United States look weak. Vice President Cheney agreed.

Over succeeding days, Bush inched closer to language satisfying the Chinese. On April 5, he said, "I regret that a Chinese pilot is missing," but did not apologize for American actions. Three days later, Powell said "we're sorry" about the death of the pilot, but added that "that can't be seen as an apology accepting responsibility." Rumsfeld privately mocked the discussions, at one point joking that Powell should say "pretty please." Eventually, a middle ground was worked out, where the American ambassador would say in a letter that the United States was "very sorry" the Chinese pilot died and the American plane entered Chinese airspace and landed without verbal clearance but would not apologize or accept responsibility for the collision. The seven-paragraph letter was delivered on April 11 to the Chinese, who called it "a letter of apology" and released the crew.

The resolution disappointed Cheney and Rumsfeld, who felt the president's language "was unfortunate" and "was in effect an apology." It generated criticism from neoconservatives like Robert Kagan and William Kristol, who concluded that "they have won and we have lost." It would take three more months to secure the return of the plane. The Chinese refused to allow it to be flown home and instead required American technicians to dismantle it and send it back in boxes. But Bush took pride in navigating the crisis without a bigger rupture, believing he had passed the commander-in-chief test; some advisers even assumed this would be seen as a signal foreign policy triumph during his bid for reelection in 2004, not realizing there were bigger tests to come.

AS THE PRESIDING officer of the Senate, the vice president typically had a ceremonial office in the Capitol and played a role in pushing legislation. But Cheney took it further than any of his predecessors. He secured permission to attend the weekly luncheon of Senate Republicans, something Democrats had rejected when Lyndon Johnson tried it after becoming vice president. And Cheney became the first vice president given an office on the House side of the Capitol, where he could monitor the lower chamber too. Bush made clear Cheney had his proxy. "When you're talking to Dick Cheney, you're talking to me," the president told one Republican senator. "When Dick Cheney's talking, it's me talking."

It fell to Cheney to put out fires. When Senator Trent Lott lobbied for a

Mississippian to head the Tennessee Valley Authority, a White House aide made the mistake of telling him it was the president's decision. "Yes," Lott replied, "and I'm the majority leader of the Senate, and I can guarantee you that if I decide to hold it, he won't be confirmed." Word quickly reached Cheney, who called Lott to invite him to the Oval Office to see Bush. "We're going with your guy," the president told him.

Just as often, though, Cheney was the enforcer. "It was good news if the president called you," recalled Dennis Hastert, the House Speaker. "It was bad news if the vice president called you."

Cheney proved a useful intervener as well when the president's political aides needed to recruit a candidate, or even discourage one. On April 18, Cheney called Tim Pawlenty, a Minnesota state lawmaker, just ninety minutes before he was scheduled to kick off a campaign for Senate. Karl Rove had determined that Norm Coleman, the mayor of St. Paul, would be a stronger challenger to Senator Paul Wellstone in 2002. "We're asking you for the good of the overall effort to stand down," Cheney said. Pawlenty backed off.

Cheney's portfolio kept expanding. On May 8, Bush asked him to conduct a thorough review of homeland security, an area that had long interested the vice president. His experience with continuity-of-government exercises had convinced Cheney the country was ill-prepared for what he saw as the gathering threat of biological and chemical weapons. It was an issue that animated him like no other. Just days earlier, he had told an interviewer that the new national security paradigm in the post–Cold War era was "the threat of terrorist attack against the U.S., eventually, potentially, with weapons of mass destruction—bugs or gas, biological or chemical agents, potentially even, someday, nuclear weapons."

Cheney was also finalizing an energy report calling for expanded oil and gas production while reviving the nuclear power industry. But he was fighting on several fronts. Congress was demanding information about his energy task force, which had met extensively with executives and lobbyists for utilities and energy companies, including Enron, whose chief, Kenneth Lay, was a strong Bush supporter. But with Cheney's blessing, David Addington had structured the task force to be exempt from freedom-of-information laws, and he delighted in rejecting requests from Democratic lawmakers and the General Accounting Office.

When Andrew Lundquist, the task force executive director, went to Cheney suggesting they hand over the information anyway because they had nothing to hide, he was sharply rebuffed. Others like Karen Hughes and Dan Bartlett also argued for disclosure. For Cheney, this was the first test of reinvigorating the executive branch against what he saw as a quarter century of post-Watergate encroachment. If critics thought the energy report was too friendly to industry, they could judge its recommendations, he reasoned; they did not need to know everyone he spoke with.

When the issue was presented to Bush in the Oval Office, he listened, thought about it for a few seconds, and then sided with Cheney against the inquisitive lawmakers.

"Stiff 'em," Bush said.

Cheney was also arguing with Hughes about the substance of the report itself. He was already under fire for a speech he gave in Toronto that seemed to denigrate the need to conserve energy. "Now, conservation is an important part of the total effort," he had said. "But to speak exclusively of conservation is to duck the tough issues. Conservation may be a sign of personal virtue, but it is not a sufficient basis all by itself for sound, comprehensive energy policy. We also have to produce more." Hughes thought everyday Americans wanted solutions beyond production, and the two "battled over the energy policy page by page," according to the speechwriter David Frum. When the report was issued on May 16, what would be remembered would be the controversy; the recommendations would languish without action for years. The personal virtue phrase "literally defined the next three years," said Jim Connaughton, head of the White House Council on Environmental Quality.

For all that, these were relatively carefree days for a White House that did not realize what was to come. Bush was focused on issues like judicial selections, recognizing that an important legacy he would leave behind would be on the bench. Karl Rove personally participated in weekly review sessions in the Roosevelt Room to screen candidates, and Bush was so committed to picking like-minded nominees that he personally called everyone nominated even for district judgeships, usually not on a president's radar screen. "It was a way of establishing a connection with his nominees and letting them know that he had personally chosen them," said Brad Berenson, a White House lawyer involved in the process.

Bush still had the mirthful, mischievous streak of the campaign trail, though more cloaked in public. One day while reviewing nominations, aides from the counsel's office brought up the candidacy of Strom Thurmond Jr., the twenty-eight-year-old namesake of the South Carolina senator, for U.S. attorney. An aide explained the young man's background in the prosecutor's office.

Bush interrupted. "Strom Thurmond Jr., huh?" he said. "Is that Strom Thurmond Jr. as in Strom Thurmond?"

"Yes, Mr. President."

Bush thought for a second, then said with a smile, "I hate a fellow who trades on his daddy's name."

THE TAX CUT plan was proving to be a defining test for the new president. He had flown to twenty-six states in his first hundred days in office to rally the public behind him. Success would breed success; if he demonstrated he could push through his tax cut plan, he believed, it would help with education, Medicare, Social Security, and every other priority. And never far from his mind was his father's read-my-lips reversal. That was one mistake he would not repeat.

Secretary of the Treasury Paul O'Neill had urged him to consider triggers that would scale back the tax cuts if the government's fiscal situation worsened. But Bush resisted. "I won't negotiate with myself," he said. Alan Greenspan, the Federal Reserve chief who had collaborated with O'Neill on the triggers idea, had assumed Bush's unyielding stance was a bargaining position as with any White House. "I did not foresee how different the Bush White House would be," he said later.

So when Nick Calio, Bush's chief lobbyist on Capitol Hill, came to the president and reported they could get a deal that fell short of $1.6 trillion, Bush sent him back with a firm no.

"Nicky," he said, "don't wobble. One-point-six, keep saying one-point-six."

Not long after, Calio returned. If Bush wanted it, Calio had an agreement with two conservative Democratic senators, John Breaux and Ben Nelson, for $1.375 trillion. But Calio told Bush that Senate Republican leaders thought they could get more.

Bush turned to Cheney. "What do you think?" he asked.

"Well, I think at this point," Cheney said, "we have to stick with our horses."

Bush agreed and sent Calio back again to keep pushing for more.

The tax cut issue would soon cost Bush politically. As debate opened on the Senate floor on April 2, the body was sharply divided along party lines. Cheney watched on television from his Senate office as a vote came down to the wire on a budget amendment that would preserve the $1.6 trillion in tax cuts against Democratic efforts to trim it. Senator Lincoln Chafee, one of the moderate Republicans who met with Cheney after the recount, switched his aye to nay. Cheney stood up, strode into the chamber, and cast his first tie-breaking vote.

But the war was not over, and Cheney was still trying to lock down enough votes for the tax legislation itself. His main target was Senator James

Jeffords, another of the moderates, who was now demanding the tax cut be pared back and $200 billion be devoted to special education for children with disabilities. Cheney summoned Jeffords to his Senate office. Exactly what happened in the flurry of conversations that followed became a point of dispute. Trent Lott thought Jeffords had committed to voting for the tax cut; Jeffords thought he had a deal with Lott to divert some of the tax cut money to special education. By the end of the day, it was clear neither understood the other. Cheney later summoned Jeffords back to his Senate office, which Jeffords's staff had begun calling "the Torture Chamber," but the two got nowhere. Karl Rove would later suggest that Jeffords, chairman of the Education Committee, had been jealous that Bush bypassed him to work with Senator Judd Gregg on the No Child Left Behind education legislation. From Jeffords's point of view, the president and the vice president were unreasonably governing from the right even after losing the popular vote. Jeffords began contemplating his options.

On the evening of May 21, Andy Card got an urgent message from Senator Olympia Snowe, a Maine Republican, warning that Jeffords was preparing to leave the party and hand control of the 50–50 Senate to Democrats. Alarmed, Card invited Jeffords to the White House to meet with Bush at two the next afternoon. The meeting did not go well. Jeffords found Bush "relaxed and charming," but he had clearly made up his mind on the tax plan and was not open to persuasion.

"Here we are in the Oval Office," Bush told him, "and you are contemplating something that's going to have a profound impact on the country—something that will affect my ability to get things done on behalf of the American people, and I just want to know: Why? This is a historic move; can you tell me why?"

Jeffords talked about his support for special education and argued that Bush should govern from the center. He warned that Bush would follow in his father's footsteps and become "a one-term president if he didn't go beyond the conservative Republican base on such issues as providing greater resources for education."

Bush countered that the senator was already positioned to advocate for his issues. "You are the swing vote," he said. "You can have enormous influence."

Jeffords was not moved. Bush and Cheney thought it was less about the way they were governing and more about the committee chairmanship Democrats were offering. "It was clear that the deal had been cooked," Nick Calio recalled. Cheney argued against giving in to what he saw as blackmail. If they caved to Jeffords to keep him in the majority, then it was not really a workable majority. "He just said there will be no end to it and that's not what he wants us to do, it's not defensible, we're not going to do it," recalled Lott, "and I could have kissed him."

On May 24, Bush watched on a television on Air Force One en route to a speech in Cleveland as Jeffords announced his decision to leave the party and caucus with the Democrats. Just like that, Bush had lost control of the Senate, four months after taking office. "It was a big body blow," Ari Fleischer concluded.

Still, Jeffords agreed not to block the tax cut. Cheney brokered the final deal, scribbling down $1.425 trillion on a yellow napkin and passing it to Senator Ben Nelson in a meeting; ultimately, it was negotiated down to $1.35 trillion, and included a clause making the tax cuts expire after a decade unless renewed. But it was a major victory. The final version lowered the top rate from 39.6 percent to 35 percent and the three next-highest rates by three percentage points each. A new, lower 10 percent bracket was created for the working poor, child tax credits were increased, the estate tax was to be phased out, and the so-called marriage penalty reduced. The bulk of the cut would go to the highest-income Americans; however, as a percentage, their share roughly mirrored their share of the tax burden. The lowest-income Americans, who do not pay income taxes but do pay payroll taxes, were not affected. On May 26, the House approved the plan 240 to 154, and the Senate followed barely an hour later with a 58-to-33 vote.

After passage of the tax cuts, Lincoln Chafee, one of just two Republicans to vote no in the Senate, asked to see Bush, and it proved a testy meeting. Chafee warned Bush that his sharply conservative agenda was risking Republican seats in 2002, including those of Senators Susan Collins of Maine and Gordon Smith of Oregon.

"Don't worry about Susan and Gordon," Bush told him.

Chafee asked why he was so uncompromising on abortion. "Even Laura is pro-choice," Chafee said, guessing the first lady's position without really knowing it.

Bush grew irritated but did not deny it. "Don't you bring my wife into this," he said.

Although the Senate was back in the Democrats' hands, their 51-to-49 edge was as perilous as the Republicans' had been. Bush decided to reach out again to Senator Tom Daschle, the new majority leader, renewing his peripatetic search for another Bob Bullock. He invited Daschle and his wife, Linda, to dinner with Laura in the White House. At the last minute the first lady flew to Texas to be with one of their daughters. Over enchiladas, Bush talked at length about how lonely the White House could be, especially on weekends. He felt like a prisoner, unable to leave his own house without a spectacle. "That's the reason I like to go back to Texas," he said. As Bush walked the Daschles to the elevator on the third floor to say good night, it occurred to the senator how disarmingly charming Bush could be. "I'd finally gotten a firsthand taste of George Bush at his best," he later reflected.

But the pressures against bipartisan cooperation were powerful. Although he had secured the tax cuts, Bush was facing a revolt from within his own party over his education program. The House Republican leadership showed up in the Oval Office one day over the summer to tell him conservatives were balking at the No Child Left Behind initiative. For a party that had long urged the elimination of the Education Department, voting to expand the federal role in schools was a lot to swallow.

Dennis Hastert, the Speaker; Dick Armey, the majority leader; and Tom DeLay, the majority whip, pressed Bush to abandon his alliance with Ted Kennedy.

"Mr. President, conservatives are very unhappy with this; they don't agree with it," DeLay said. "We can get all the votes on the Republican side. We need to go partisan on this, not bipartisan."

Bush understood that going with only Republican votes would mean big compromises in the program. But he also felt he had to trust his party's leadership. Simply disregarding their advice would be problematic.

But Nick Calio urged him to stick with his plan. "Mr. President, I got to tell you, I think on this one, you started it out bipartisan. I think you have to see the course through."

AS SUMMER ARRIVED, Bush prepared for his first trip to Europe. He had agreed to meet with Vladimir Putin, the former KGB colonel turned president of Russia.

The relationship with Russia had changed drastically since his father's presidency, when the Soviet Union was collapsing. A decade later, the rocky 1990s had soured Russia on democracy, and the ascension of Putin heralded a new era of centralized power. Bush was wary of Putin—"one cold dude," he had called the Russian leader—but he was interested in forging a working relationship with Putin if only because he saw the real threat to the United States elsewhere. When he met with Russian scholars invited by Condoleezza Rice, Bush agreed with Michael McFaul, a Stanford University professor, who told him that keeping Russia "inside our tent" was the best course.

"You're absolutely right," McFaul remembered Bush answering, "because someday we're all going to be dealing with the Chinese."

On June 16, Bush arrived in Ljubljana, Slovenia, for his introduction to Putin. The two met in a gold-draped room in a sixteenth-century castle. Putin immediately showed that he had done his homework.

"I *did* play rugby," Bush replied. "*Very* good briefing."

Bush recalled his own briefing on Putin. "Let me say something about what caught my attention, Mr. President, was that your mother gave you a cross which you had blessed in Israel, the Holy Land," Bush said.

Putin was caught by surprise. "It's true," he said.

"That speaks volumes to me, Mr. President," Bush said. "May I call you Vladimir?"

Though baptized by his mother secretly during Communist times, Putin had made little public demonstration of religiosity, and as she watched the exchange, Rice found it hard to believe he was genuinely a man of faith. If so, it was hardly in the same wear-it-on-your-sleeve way that Bush was. But his time in the KGB stationed in East Germany had taught him how to gain trust and cooperation from a contact. So, sensing that Bush judged others in part through the lens of his own Christian faith, Putin launched into a story about how his country house once burned to the ground and the only thing he recovered was the cross.

Bush came away encouraged. While he had excoriated Bill Clinton for personalizing the Russian-American relationship through his friendship with Boris Yeltsin, Bush began to do the same with Putin. When reporters asked Bush if he trusted Putin, it occurred to Rice that they had not prepared the president for that question. Bush winged it, calling Putin "an honest, straightforward man." He added, "I looked the man in the eye," and "I was able to get a sense of his soul." Rice stiffened, worried the answer might be too effusive, but said nothing.

Back in Washington, Cheney and his staff were even more disturbed. The vice president saw Russia as simply a weaker version of the Soviet Union, a view that traced back to the fight over Aleksandr Solzhenitsyn in the Ford White House, and the skepticism about Mikhail Gorbachev in the first Bush administration. Every time Cheney saw Putin, he privately told people, "I think KGB, KGB, KGB." The president's soul-gazing comment provoked disbelief. "A lot of us were kind of rolling our eyes about that," Eric Edelman, Cheney's deputy national security adviser, said later.

Cheney had other things to worry about. On June 30, he checked into the hospital for an operation to insert a pacemaker and defibrillator. The sophisticated device, implanted near his left collarbone, would act as both a traditional pacemaker speeding up a heart that beat too slowly and a miniature defibrillator that could stabilize an irregular heartbeat. The decision to insert the device reinforced concerns about his health, making White House aides nervous. He left the hospital the same day and to prove his vigor gave three radio interviews when he returned to work on July 2.

Cheney then slipped away for a fishing trip out west. Out on a boat with his friend Jack Dennis, Cheney nodded off. Just days after the defibrillator surgery, Dennis was nervous enough to check to see if he was still breathing.

"Well, so what?" Cheney snapped. "What would happen if I wasn't? Will you just not worry about me? Leave me alone and whatever happens happens. I can't think of a better place to die."

AS THE VICE president recovered his strength, the nation's intelligence agencies were collecting increasingly alarming reports suggesting a major al-Qaeda plot in the works. There was no hard information about where and when, but it was chilling enough that George Tenet later said it "literally made my hair stand on end." On July 10, he called Rice and asked to see her immediately. Tenet and a couple of aides raced to the White House and told Rice, Stephen Hadley, and Richard Clarke that a "spectacular" attack seemed likely in weeks or months.

"What should we do?" Rice asked.

"This country needs to go on a war footing now," said Cofer Black, the CIA's counterterrorism chief.

Rice said she would take it to the president. In her own memoir years later, she remembered the warning more vaguely but said alerts were raised and efforts made to prod allies to help pick up extremists like Abu Zubaydah. Still, it would take another two months for new strategies against al-Qaeda and the Taliban to reach a point of decision. By then it would be too late.

IN JULY, BUSH made his first visit to see Tony Blair in Britain. As a gift, Blair had sent Bush a Jacob Epstein bust of Winston Churchill for the Oval Office that the British government lent him for the remainder of his presidency. Realizing from their Camp David meeting that the president did not care for stuffy diplomatic formalities, Blair invited the Americans to Chequers, the sixteenth-century mansion used as a country getaway by British prime ministers. Intent on keeping the visit relaxed, Blair and his wife, Cherie, decided that while aides could join official meetings, only family would stay at the estate. When Rice asked to stay as well, the Blairs said no.

Cherie Blair was later surprised when the person running Chequers told her, "I've managed to accommodate Mr. Bush's doctor. I've put him in my room."

"What doctor?" Cherie Blair asked.

"Dr. Rice."

The Bushes arrived by helicopter on July 19. The president had doffed his tie, and the two leaders went for a long walk alone, then joined aides upstairs for a discussion of the Middle East. Over dinner, they were joined by their wives and the Blairs' children. One of the kids brought up capital punishment. As governor of Texas, Bush had presided over 152 executions, more at that point than any other politician since the Supreme Court reinstated the death penalty in 1976.

Cherie Blair, a formidable lawyer, jumped in. The death penalty was inherently wrong, she argued. If a mistake was made, it could not be corrected.

"Well, that's not the way it is in America," she remembered Bush saying. "We take the eye-for-an-eye view."

A good-natured debate persisted through much of the meal; it was unusual for a president to be challenged so frontally at dinner.

"Give the man a break, Mother," said Euan, the Blairs' son.

BACK IN WASHINGTON, Rumsfeld was trying to force a broader reassessment of Iraq policy. In a four-page memo marked "Secret" that he sent to Cheney, Rice, and Powell on the afternoon of July 27, the defense chief proposed meeting to discuss three options: give up the no-fly zones and sanctions since they were no longer effective; approach "our moderate Arab friends" to explore "a more robust policy" aimed at toppling Saddam Hussein; or open a dialogue with Hussein to see if he was ready "to make some accommodation." Rumsfeld painted a picture of gathering danger.

"Within a few years the U.S. will undoubtedly have to confront a Saddam armed with nuclear weapons," he wrote. While he did not suggest direct military action, Rumsfeld concluded that "if Saddam's regime were ousted, we would have a much-improved position in the region and elsewhere." But the meeting he sought never happened.

BUSH AND CHENEY were finding a good working rhythm. Cheney exercised his greatest influence in the weekly lunches with Bush and on other occasions when the two met alone. Cheney usually showed up with three or four items he wanted to talk about, and sometimes Bush came with something on his mind as well. "I always felt there wasn't anything that I couldn't talk about," Cheney said. "It was an opportunity, sometimes, to argue issues." The conversations ranged widely. "Sometimes it was family; sometimes it would be personnel matters related to the cabinet and the Congress," Cheney said later. “Sometimes it would be policy where he would tell me about decisions he had made.” Whatever was said at those sessions, though, remained among the biggest secrets in the White House. Sometimes Bush or Cheney might share a bit with aides, but more often they did not.

How much Cheney was quietly steering decisions through those private meetings or by shaping choices before they were presented to Bush became a constant source of speculation in the West Wing. Cheney got three bites at any major decision: his staff sat on committees that developed policies, the vice president participated in cabinet-level meetings that debated proposals, and then he had a chance to talk with Bush about them alone. Sometimes his impact was clear; other times it was just assumed. “Cheney’s role was like watching iron filings moving across a tabletop,” said David Frum, the speechwriter. “You know there is a magnet down there. You know the magnet is moving. You never see the magnet.”

The vice president’s unparalleled influence, and more important the perception of it, bothered Bush aides like Karl Rove and Karen Hughes, who chafed at the implication that the president was led around by the nose. But Bush at that point was not bothered. “He could care less,” Ari Fleischer remembered. “It rolled off his back.” Indeed, Bush pulled Hughes aside one day to reassure her. “You don’t get it,” he told her. “The stronger Cheney is, the better it is for me. It means we get more stuff done.”

Cheney picked his battles. The ones he cared most about were no secret. He was intensely interested, for instance, in an environmental policy debate over what was called new source review. Power plants were required to install scrubbing equipment to clean up their emissions if they expanded but not during basic repairs. The industry naturally wanted the most expansive definition of what counted as basic repair. Under pressure from Cheney, Christine Todd Whitman’s EPA was rethinking the aggressive approach the Clinton administration had taken. Cheney kept calling, even tracking her down on vacation in Colorado. “He was on me all the time,” Whitman recalled. On other issues, like education and entitlements, Cheney did not engage. “The vice president didn’t have to get involved in every issue. The president did,” said Dean McGrath, Cheney’s deputy chief of staff. “This afforded the vice president a little more freedom.”

IN THE EARLY months of the administration, perhaps the toughest issue Bush faced was stem-cell research. For months, he struggled with whether federal money should be used to target the ravages of diseases like Alzheimer’s and Parkinson’s by experimenting on stem cells from embryos grown in a laboratory. No one was talking about banning such research altogether, only whether taxpayer money should pay for it. The tension between Bush's anti-abortion convictions and the prospect of saving or improving the lives of millions weighed on him. He received a poignant letter from Nancy Reagan, who had become an activist since her husband's diagnosis with Alzheimer's. Yet many of Bush's conservative friends and advisers were deeply uncomfortable with destroying embryos. Where was the line?

Advisers sent Bush memo after memo, and he grew so engaged that he began calling Jay Lefkowitz, the aide assigned to lead the review, almost every day with follow-up questions or requests for information. He asked all sorts of people he encountered for their opinion—a doctor who showed up for an unrelated Rose Garden ceremony, the White House medical staff at a birthday party, junior aides at an event in Virginia. Lefkowitz brought a copy of *Brave New World*, the Aldous Huxley science fiction novel in which humans are bred in hatcheries, and read passages to Bush. "We have got to be really cautious," Bush responded, "because it is like stepping off a cliff. If you step off a cliff and you have made a mistake, by the time you realize it, you are at the bottom."

Andy Card set aside thirty-minute blocks of time for Bush to meet with ethicists and scientists. Doug Melton, a leading stem-cell researcher from Harvard University, told Bush that embryos were not alive, and while he agreed they should not "be treated cavalierly," he believed the research could make a world of difference to real people. He mentioned that his son suffered from juvenile diabetes.

"I'm committed to doing everything I can to help my son," Melton told Bush.

The president said he understood, mentioning his sister's death from leukemia.

On July 9, he met in the Oval Office with two bioethicists, Leon Kass of the University of Chicago and Daniel Callahan of the Hastings Center, a research institution dedicated to bioethics.

"I must confess, I am wrestling with a difficult decision," Bush told them. "I worry about a culture that devalues life. I think my job is to encourage respect for life. On the other hand, I believe technologies and science will help solve many medical problems, and I have great hope for cures."

His guests sympathized. But unlike Melton, Kass viewed frozen embryos as living human beings, even if at a very early stage of development.

"We at least owe them the respect not to manipulate them for our own purposes," he told Bush.

But what about existing lines of stem cells from embryos that had already been destroyed?

Kass found no ethical compunction about that since "you are not necessarily complicit in their destruction," provided that Bush make clear he opposed such destruction and would not reward it in the future.

Maybe Bush had found the middle ground he was seeking.

As the meeting broke up, he stopped Karen Hughes. "Are you comfortable with this?" he asked.

She nodded, but uncertainly.

"No, you're not, I can tell," he said. "I want your opinion."

"I'm increasingly uncomfortable with additional destruction," she said.

"Me too," he agreed.

In late July, Bush summoned Hughes and Lefkowitz. He would allow funding for existing lines—he was told there were about sixty—but prevent federal money from being used to create additional lines. It was not universally supported inside the White House. "A number of people internally didn't like that idea, because they thought it would tick off everyone," recalled Kristen Silverberg, a White House aide. Conservatives would object to any federally funded research, while liberals would be unhappy that it was limited to existing lines.

It was a mark of the moment that Bush would give a prime-time address to the nation explaining his decision. Nighttime presidential speeches were usually reserved for war or national emergency, and this was, at its core, a policy decision—one fraught with difficult questions, but not on the same level as sending troops into combat. Yet after seven months in office, it was the hardest choice Bush had made. His staff viewed it as so momentous that Hughes wrote it herself, the only speech she would draft start to finish during her time in the White House.

At his ranch on August 9, Bush settled into a cushioned chair with a brown-and-white flower pattern in front of a window with an American flag to his right. Hughes hoped doing it from home would seem more natural, less stiff than in the Oval Office. Addressing the camera, Bush described his decision. "This allows us to explore the promise and potential of stem cell research without crossing a fundamental moral line, by providing taxpayer funding that would sanction or encourage further destruction of human embryos that have at least the potential for life." For a leader who prided himself on crisp decisions, he hinted at the doubt that still racked him. "I have made this decision with great care," he said, "and I pray it is the right one." As aides predicted, he made both sides mad. But in presenting his decision in moderate, reasoned terms, he had advanced what his speechwriter David Frum called "the most unflinchingly pro-life position ever expressed by a president before a mass audience." Frum considered it "a masterstroke—and Hughes's finest hour."

ON AUGUST 6, even as he was preparing the stem-cell speech, Bush received a memo in the President's Daily Brief titled "Bin Ladin Determined to Strike in US." For months, intelligence agencies had been picking up signs of danger, and "the system was blinking red," as George Tenet later described it. Bush had asked his CIA briefer whether there were indications that the American homeland was being targeted. This memo, just a little over one page, was the response.

The document would later become famous, or infamous, but on this morning it seemed maddeningly unspecific, offering information that was sketchy and mostly three or four years old. Nothing on the first page cited current intelligence. The memo said bin Laden had "implied in US television interviews in 1997 and 1998" that he wanted to attack the United States and in 1998 he had "told followers he wanted to retaliate in Washington" for cruise missile strikes on his base in Afghanistan. It said al-Qaeda members "have resided in or traveled to the US for years, and the group apparently maintains a support structure that could aid attacks."

Beyond that, the memo said intelligence agencies had "not been able to corroborate some of the more sensational threat reporting," including a 1998 report that bin Laden "wanted to hijack a US aircraft to gain the release" of those convicted in the 1993 bombing of the World Trade Center. Only on the second page did the memo hint at what was really going on: "Nevertheless, FBI information since that time indicates patterns of suspicious activity in this country consistent with preparations for hijackings or other types of attacks, including recent surveillance of federal buildings in New York." That sentence cried out for elaboration. What suspicious activity? What surveillance? It said nothing more about that and hardly constituted "actionable intelligence," the phrase used by security officials to describe information specific enough to guide a specific response. Bush was told the FBI was conducting seventy investigations throughout the United States related to bin Laden, although that was not completely accurate.

Looking back, Bush admitted that he did not react with the alarm he should have. He did not summon the directors of the FBI and the CIA. He did not order heightened alerts. Nor was any action requested of him in the memo. "I didn't feel that sense of urgency," Bush said. The thinness of the memo and his faith in the FBI lulled him into a false sense of security.

IN THE STEAMY Texas of August, Bush settled in for a relaxing few weeks at the ranch. He got a charge out of the heat and took a perverse pleasure inflicting it on others. He jokingly called himself a "windshield rancher," but the ranch was a refuge, the only place other than Camp David where he could wander around, go fishing, even drive a white pickup truck around the property. "I fell in love with it the minute I saw it," he said.

It was a sprawling, untamed piece of land, filled with trees and creeks and seven canyons, and populated by turkeys, doves, and the occasional cottonmouth water snake. Two experts from Texas A&M University came out that August and identified seventeen or eighteen different varieties of hardwood trees. The main house had been built with an environmentally friendly geothermal heating and cooling system: water was pumped three hundred feet into the ground to keep it at a constant temperature, allowing the house to use 75 percent less electricity than traditional systems. The ranch had been outfitted with a twenty-five-thousand-gallon rainwater cistern for irrigation. Bush had a second building that came to be called the Governor's House for guests like Condoleezza Rice and Karen Hughes. After his ascension to the presidency, a couple of double-wide trailers were brought in for staff to stay in during his long sojourns away from the capital.

Bush's days started early, and he was reading Nathaniel Philbrick's *In the Heart of the Sea* and planned to dig into David McCullough's *John Adams* next. He still found Washington intruding, but the location made that bearable. The Joint Chiefs of Staff came for a daylong meeting, and he had briefings each morning. On August 25, for instance, he got up at 5:45 a.m., read his briefing books, went for a run at 7:00 a.m., returned to the house by 7:45 a.m., and then had his hour-long CIA briefing on the porch overlooking a lake, followed by another hour-long briefing with national security aides. By late morning, he decided to give a tour to the reporters assigned to wait out his vacation. Dressed in a brown T-shirt, blue jeans, boots, and a cowboy hat, Bush seemed in no rush as he spent an hour and a half showing them the ravines and walking paths that animated him.

"What we're doing here, we're cleaning this out," he said. "We're making a trail from the top to come down over here. Do you all want to walk in here? It's kind of neat in here. These cliffs are pretty unusual, from this perspective."

He piled several of the journalists into his pickup truck and took off. His main occupation, sometimes three hours a day, was taking a chain saw to all the cedar, which took up too much of the property's water and was considered a plague on the rest of the wildlife, he explained.

He took them to the area he called the Cathedral and warned the photographers to look out for poison ivy. He showed them the waterfall he discovered one day after a run. ("It's a wonderful spot to come up in here and just kind of think about the budget," he joked.) He showed them the lake that he had stocked with black bass and the small boat he used to while away hot afternoons. He showed them the spots where his dog Barney would chase armadillo and the pool he built after much imploring by his young daughters and then dubbed the Whining Pool.

"What is it you like about coming out here?" one reporter asked.

"It is one of the few places where I can actually walk outside my front door and say, I think I'm going to go walk two hours," Bush said.

Still, a reporter noted, his friends were surprised such a social person would retreat to "the middle of nowhere and just kind of be by yourself."

"I guess they don't know what it's like to be the president," he said.

RECHARGED, BUSH RETURNED to Washington in September. His staff worried that his presidency was drifting. With the tax cuts behind him and education reform on track, they sensed a lack of purpose. "There wasn't any galvanizing issue," recalled Peter Wehner, a speechwriter. Michael Gerson was working on what he was calling a "character of communities" speech to frame government as a catalyzing force for civic institutions, although Wehner thought "it seemed awfully thin."

On national security, after months of study and delay, the administration was finally cranking toward consensus on issues of terrorism and Afghanistan. Rice gathered the cabinet-level principals on the day after Labor Day, September 4, to approve a plan to go after al-Qaeda, one that largely resembled the one waiting for Bush and Cheney when they arrived in office. Richard Clarke, the frustrated counterterrorism adviser, vented in a chilling memo he sent Rice that day before the meeting. "Decision makers should imagine themselves on a future day when the CSG," the Counterterrorism Security Group, "has not succeeded in stopping al Qida attacks and hundreds of Americans lay dead in several countries, including the US," he wrote. "What would those decision makers wish that they had done earlier? That future day could happen at any time."

Six days later, on September 10, Rice forwarded the al-Qaeda strategy to Bush, while her deputy, Stephen Hadley, convened the number-two officials of the national security departments to advance a separate but complementary plan to target the Taliban in Afghanistan by helping their opponents and devising covert action to topple the government from within and eliminate al-Qaeda bases. The meeting came the day after Ahmed Shah Massoud, the legendary Lion of Panjshir who led the anti-Taliban Northern Alliance, was assassinated. Some in the room wondered whether they might be too late.

But if the warning lights had been blinking red over the summer, they were dark again in the season's fading days. In none of the morning intelligence briefings in the days after Bush returned from Crawford did George Tenet recall discussing a possible domestic attack.

Bush left for Florida to promote his education plans.

PART TWO

7

"Somebody's going to pay"

It was still dark but already a temperate seventy-five degrees when President Bush emerged in jogging clothes from his villa at the oceanfront Colony Beach and Tennis Resort outside Sarasota, Florida. It was 6:30 a.m. He wanted to run along the beach, but the Secret Service had nixed that. Too exposed. Instead, they drove him in a fourteen-car motorcade to the resort golf course, where he jumped out and began circling paths marked off and cleared in advance by agents. His staff had arranged for him to run with Richard Keil, a tall, affable Bloomberg reporter Bush had come to like during the grueling hours on the campaign trail.

"C'mon, Stretch!" the president called out, using his nickname for the journalist. "C'mon!"

With the sun peeking above the horizon that Tuesday, September 11, Bush and Keil powered along the paths, trailed by an agent running behind them and another riding a bicycle with an assault rifle. Keil was a college cross-country runner who was all-American in track, and Bush wanted to know how fast he thought they were running.

"Feels like we're going about 7:15, 7:20 a mile," Keil said.

"Really?" Bush asked. "You think?"

With no elections or other big events coming up that fall, Bush said he had resolved to step up his running so he was covering a mile in under seven minutes for a three-mile run.

Keil said he thought he would reach his goal.

Why? Bush asked.

"Because we're running almost that fast now and you're talking normally while you run, no wheezing or gasping," he said. "If you can converse now, you could run seven minutes a mile if you'd just be quiet for a little bit."

Bush laughed and then listened attentively as an agent called out a time when they passed a chalk mark. The agents had already marked out the course so that Bush could calculate his pace as he ran.

"What's that work out to?" he asked, then did the math in his head. "That's 7:15 a mile!"

By 8:00 a.m., Bush was back in the villa, showered, and dressed in his suit. His morning intelligence briefing included items on China, Russia, and the Palestinian turmoil. His staff filled him in on the upcoming education event—who would be there, what would happen when, how he should deliver his message. Bush nodded. Then instead of getting up to head to the motorcade, the famously punctual president did something odd: he began chatting idly with his advisers, including Sandy Kress, the Texas lawyer who had come to Washington to help out on No Child Left Behind. None of the talk would survive the passage of time, just stories about people in Texas, catching up on who was doing what. Bewildered at Bush's unusually languid state, Kress kept glancing at his watch—*three minutes late, five minutes late, ten minutes late.* Still, it was clear Bush was enjoying the moment, the only time Kress could remember him being relaxed and unprogrammed since arriving in the White House. "Those were the last carefree moments he had in his presidency," Kress recalled.

The motorcade pulled up to Emma E. Booker Elementary School at 8:54 a.m. As the president headed into the building, Karl Rove told him a plane had hit one of the towers of the World Trade Center in New York. Bush assumed it was a small propeller plane. But then Condoleezza Rice called and said it was a commercial airliner. Thinking back to his days in the Texas Air National Guard, Bush assumed the pilot must have had a heart attack. "This must be a horrible accident," he said.

Bush entered a classroom accompanied by the principal, Gwendolyn Tosé-Rigell, and met the teacher Sandra Kay Daniels. He sat down, and Daniels led the students in a reading exercise. He was in a good mood, smiling, following along. But then he felt a presence behind him on his right. Andy Card was leaning down to whisper in his ear.

"A second plane hit the second tower," he said in his distinctive Massachusetts accent. "America is under attack." Then Card stepped back.

Bush's face tightened, his mouth narrowed, and his eyes hardened. A second plane meant this was no freak accident. This was an act of war.

For whatever reason, he did not jump up and leave the room. Acutely aware of the television cameras trained on him and the students in front of him, he remained seated as the mostly African American students read *The Pet Goat*, a children's story. Bush picked up a copy and opened it, but his eyes were staring at the back of the room. He forced a weak smile as the children read, but grew distracted, and his mouth curled up with an intense expression.

Bush could see reporters' cell phones going off in the back of the room. It felt strangely like a silent movie, he thought. Bush caught sight of Ari Fleischer, the press secretary, holding up a notebook on which he had written out in block letters: "DON'T SAY ANYTHING YET."

Minutes passed as the students read and Bush focused on what was happening to the country.

"Whoo, these are great readers," Bush said, trying to stay in the moment. "Very impressive. Thank you all so much for showing me your reading skills."

He kept up the banter a few more seconds, asking if the children spent more time reading than watching television. Several hands went up. "Oh, that's great. Very good."

Then he signaled the end. "Thanks for having me. Very impressive."

The five minutes between Card's whisper and Bush's unhurried exit would become the most criticized five minutes of his presidency and the subject of endless mockery. Told that America was under attack, why did he not get up and leave? Critics found a metaphor for a president who did not know what to do. Bush later explained he wanted to maintain an air of calm, both for the children in the room and for the national television audience. But it was a moment of transition. Bush was a man who cherished order and structure; he believed in showing up on time and leaving on time, and he did not like disruptions to the schedule. It clearly took a few minutes for it to dawn on him how much his life, and his presidency, had just been turned upside down.

AT THE WHITE HOUSE, it had been a slow morning with the boss away. "Nothing much is happening," Peter Wehner, the speechwriter, e-mailed his boss, Michael Gerson. Vice President Cheney arrived at 7:57 a.m. for a typically full schedule of meetings. Sean O'Keefe, the deputy budget director, stopped by the vice president's office to talk about a spending issue. John McConnell, the speechwriter, followed him in to ask about an upcoming speech.

Cheney's secretaries, Debbie Heiden and Ashley Snee, had the television on in the outer office. When they saw the news about a plane hitting the tower, they called in to the vice president. "Turn on the TV right away," Cheney heard.

He flipped it on and saw the north tower of the World Trade Center billowing smoke. Like Bush, he assumed it was a small plane. "Boy, it's going to be a bad day at the FAA today," Cheney said. "This is a tragedy."

Cheney watched as the second plane smashed into the south tower, and it became clear this was no accident. He jumped up and marched to Andy Card's office next door.

"I want to talk with him when he calls in," Cheney told the chief of staff's secretary.

He returned to his own office and picked up the direct hotline. "I need to talk to the president," Cheney said, then hung up to wait for the call to be put through.

Others were gathering in his office, including Scooter Libby, Condoleezza Rice, Joshua Bolten, Richard Clarke, and Mary Matalin. They agreed to coordinate federal agencies from the Situation Room. On the television was Peter Jennings in shirtsleeves for ABC News. The phone rang and it was Bush, now in a holding room at the Florida elementary school. He was going to make a statement and then head immediately to Air Force One.

In the holding room, Bush pulled out his Sharpie pen and scratched out some words on a yellow pad. He was sitting at a student desk, back to the television. While everyone else stared at the images, Bush focused on the notepad. When the television replayed the footage of the second plane hitting the south tower, Dan Bartlett pointed and exclaimed, "Look!"

Bush, on the phone with Robert Mueller, the FBI director, turned and looked for just a moment, very matter-of-fact, before swinging back to work on his statement. He began reading it aloud.

"Today, we've had a national tragedy," he said. "Two airplanes have crashed into the World Trade Center in a terrorist attack on our country."

Bartlett interjected. "We don't know for sure it was a terrorist attack."

"Sure it is," Bush said. "What else do you think it is?"

Fleischer and Scott McClellan, the deputy press secretary, agreed.

"I'm just saying we have not confirmed anything yet," Bartlett said. "We don't know who is responsible."

"Then just say 'apparent' terrorist attack," McClellan said.

On the notepad, Bush wrote that the FBI was working to catch those responsible. "We will punish them," he wrote, then crossed out that line. Instead, he wrote, "Terrorism against Amer will not succeed."

A few minutes later, Bush strode into the school gymnasium filled with students and teachers who did not realize what was happening. He told them about the "apparent" terrorist attack and vowed to "hunt down and find those folks who committed this act," choosing an oddly casual way of describing mass murderers. "Terrorism against our nation will not stand," he added, misreading the notes, which said "will not succeed," and in the process unconsciously echoing words his father had used when Saddam Hussein invaded Kuwait. It was a shaky performance that left advisers worried that he had not been reassuring or commanding enough.

Barely a minute after he was done, Bush headed out the door. Just after 9:30 a.m., his motorcade took off for the airport at what seemed like eighty miles per hour. "We were flying, faster than any motorcade I can remember," recalled the White House photographer, Eric Draper.

A minute later, back in the White House, Secret Service agents burst into Cheney's office. "Mr. Vice President, we've got to leave now," barked Special Agent Jimmy Scott, racing around the desk.

The Secret Service had gotten a report of an airplane heading toward the White House. The agent grabbed Cheney's belt from behind with one hand and his shoulder with another and physically rushed him out of the room. "Doors flew open, Secret Service guys came in, and he vanished," O'Keefe remembered. Oddly, Cheney grabbed a copy of the *Economist* on the way out, thinking for a moment that he might be taken somewhere for a long wait with nothing to do. Rice and Bolten were left staring at each other in shock.

The agents, bristling with guns and urgency, had maneuvered Cheney into the tunnel beneath the White House by 9:37 a.m., just as the plane smashed into the Pentagon instead. Some concluded later that the hijackers tried to find the White House but from the air could not see it amid taller nearby buildings and struck at the military headquarters instead. If so, it saved Cheney's life because the plane would have hit the White House before the agents got him into the tunnel.

The rest of the White House was evacuated. "Women, take off your heels and run!" agents shouted. Outside the gates, frightened aides were told to take off their White House badges in case there were snipers looking for targets. Not knowing what to do, some simply walked home in a daze. Others, alerted by colleagues, headed two blocks to the offices of Daimler Chrysler, where Tim McBride, a veteran of the first Bush White House, sent his own staff home and ordered sandwiches to create a makeshift White House headquarters for seventy-two dislocated presidential aides.

In the tunnel under the White House, Cheney paused when he came across a television, bench, and telephone. While he waited, word arrived of the crash at the Pentagon.

"Get me the president," he ordered an agent.

Bush was in the car heading to the airport when Rice called to tell him about the Pentagon attack. He arrived at Air Force One at 9:45 a.m., bounded up the stairs, and told his agents to make sure his wife and daughters were safe. Laura Bush, hosted by Ted Kennedy on Capitol Hill to testify on behalf of the education program, had been rushed by her security detail to Secret Service headquarters. Their daughters would not be secured for another hour. Lynne Cheney had been brought to the tunnel outside the bunker, joining her husband.

Bush called Cheney. "Sounds like we have a minor war going on here," Bush said. "I heard about the Pentagon. We're at war." He added, "Somebody's going to pay."

Cheney, standing in the tunnel, told Bush to stay away from Washington until they could determine it was safe. Bush argued, but Cheney, Andy Card, and Edward Marinzel, the lead Secret Service agent traveling with the president, prevailed upon him. Eric Draper, the photographer, could see frustration on Bush's face, but he still tried to pump everyone up. "This is what they pay us for, boys," he said.

Air Force One rocketed into the air at 9:54 a.m. without a destination, the pilots aiming to get as high as possible as quickly as possible. By the time they leveled out, they were at forty-five thousand feet, far above normal cruising altitude. Bush, his coat now off, emerged from his cabin. "I just heard Angel is the next target," he said, using the code name for Air Force One. Bush could feel the plane bank sharply to the west and away from Washington.

CHENEY HEADED INTO the bunker three stories under the East Wing, a pair of massive steel doors closing behind him with a loud hiss, forming an airtight seal. Officially known as the Presidential Emergency Operations Center, the bunker was first built in 1934 along with the East Wing; Franklin Roosevelt converted it into an air raid shelter in 1942 during World War II. It was equipped with secure telephones, kept in drawers under the conference table, that looked as if they were from the 1960s, two television screens embedded in the back wall and another couple on a side wall, several bunks for sleeping, and days' worth of food and supplies. But it had never been used in an actual crisis and was "shockingly low-tech," as Joshua Bolten put it.

At some point shortly after stepping into the bunker, Cheney said he talked with Bush again about fighter jets being scrambled to protect Washington. Both he and Bush recalled the vice president asking for authority to shoot down hijacked airliners if they did not follow instructions. "You bet," Bush recalled answering. Rice on the ground and Karl Rove in the air recalled overhearing a call like that, and a military aide remembered Cheney calling Bush shortly after entering the bunker. But none of about a dozen sets of logs and notes kept that day recorded the call, leading some to wonder later whether Cheney did get permission before deciding what to do about further attacks.

When a military aide reported that United Airlines Flight 93 was eighty miles away and heading toward Washington, he asked Cheney whether it should be shot down. In "the time it takes a batter to decide to swing," as Scooter Libby put it, Cheney said yes.

When the plane was believed to be sixty miles away, the aide asked again.

Cheney repeated the order.

Finally, the aide came back a third time.

"Just confirming, sir. Authority to engage?"

"I said yes," Cheney replied, his voice betraying irritation.

Silence came over the room as the gravity of the moment sank in. The vice president had just ordered military warplanes to shoot down a commercial airliner with scores of innocent passengers on board.

Cheney never flinched. "I don't want it to sound heartless, but there was no alternative," he explained later. "It wasn't the kind of thing you agonized over." Thousands of lives were at stake.

On the other side of the table, Bolten, who had not heard any earlier conversation with Bush about shoot-down authority, quietly suggested the vice president call the president to inform him about the order. That call was logged at 10:18 a.m., and Bush ratified the vice president's decision. Bolten later said he was not questioning whether Cheney had permission to give the order but merely thought the president would want to know it had been issued.

A few minutes later, a report came back that United Airlines Flight 93 had crashed. Cheney wondered whether he had just shot down a civilian plane.

In fact, the United jet had gone down in Shanksville, Pennsylvania, at 10:03 a.m., before any order was given. Passengers had staged a revolt. No one knew that yet, but it occurred to Cheney that maybe it was not his shoot-down order that brought down the plane. "I think an act of heroism just took place on that plane," he said to no one in particular.

But he was frustrated not to get a precise report. "You must know whether or not we engaged, whether or not a fighter engaged a civilian aircraft," Cheney said into the phone to the Pentagon. "You *have* to know the answer to that."

As it turned out, in the confusion of the day, Cheney's order never got passed along to the pilots in the air. F-16 fighters scrambled out of Andrews Air Force Base so quickly they had no missiles. The pilots resolved that if they did receive orders to stop a hijacked plane, they would ram their jets into the target. One of the pilots, Lieutenant Heather Penney, was prepared to do it even knowing that her father, a United Airlines pilot, might be on board.

Cheney looked up to see his deputy national security adviser, Eric Edelman. "Mr. Vice President," Edelman said, "Steve Hadley asked me to come down here." Hadley and Richard Clarke thought Cheney should be evacuated to a remote site in case the White House was still a target.

Cheney, who had been telling Bush to stay away, refused to go himself. "You know, I have got communications with the president here and I have been on the phone with him and this place was meant to be able to operate in a nuclear environment. And if I leave now and go off to one of these other sites, with my helicopters, it will be forty-five minutes before we get on the ground and reestablish contact. There is just too much going on right now. We don't understand the full dimensions of this. So I am staying here. Convey that back to Hadley and Clarke."

Edelman turned around and started to leave.

"Where are you going?" Cheney called after him.

"Well, sir, I am going to carry out your instruction," Edelman said.

"No, I need you here," he said. "Call Hadley."

So Edelman got Hadley on the phone and told him the vice president was staying. Cheney tried to join the secure videoconference Clarke was running out of the Situation Room, but the audio was impossible to make out.

Cheney was exasperated. "Get that off the screen," he finally ordered. "Put up CNN so I can actually find out what is going on around here."

He told Edelman to get on the phone and monitor the Situation Room conference call. But after trying to listen for a while, Edelman finally gave up.

"This is like listening to Alvin and the Chipmunks in the bottom of a swimming pool," he fumed.

Screw it, Cheney said. Get off the phone.

By this point the south tower had collapsed. At 10:28 a.m., Cheney looked up to see the north tower crumble in a smoky heap. Everyone in the room gasped, shock etched on their faces—all except for Cheney, who stared stoically at the television.

Just then came a report of another plane heading to Washington.

"Take it out," Cheney ordered. "If it looks threatening, take it out."

In the end, it turned out to be a medevac helicopter.

Cheney worked with Norman Mineta, the transportation secretary, to ground the four thousand planes in American airspace. Among them was one carrying the president's parents, forced to put down in Milwaukee. With three separate pads of paper in front of him, Cheney kept track of how many planes were still in the air as Mineta called out tail numbers. Other erroneous reports arrived of a bomb at the State Department, a fire on the Mall, airplanes heading toward Camp David and the Crawford ranch. Falling back on his continuity-of-government exercises, Cheney ordered officials to fly congressional leaders to a prearranged secure location.

At 10:39 a.m., Cheney got hold of Donald Rumsfeld, who had rushed outside to help with victims when the Pentagon was hit. Cheney updated him.

"There's been at least three instances here where we've had reports of aircraft approaching Washington—a couple were confirmed hijack," Cheney told him. "And pursuant to the president's instructions, I gave authorization for them to be taken out."

The vice president was not sure Rumsfeld was still there. "Hello?"

"Yes, I understand," Rumsfeld said. "Who did you give that direction to?"

"It was passed from here through the center at the White House."

"Okay," Rumsfeld said. "Let me ask the question here. Has that directive been transmitted to the aircraft?"

"Yes, it has," Cheney said.

"So we've got a couple of aircraft up there that have those instructions at this present time?" Rumsfeld asked.

"That is correct. And it's my understanding they've already taken a couple of aircraft out."

"We can't confirm that," Rumsfeld said. "We're told that one aircraft is down but we do not have a pilot report that did it."

Rumsfeld ordered the defense readiness condition elevated to DefCon 3, the highest since the Yom Kippur War of 1973, and several members of the Bush team talked with Russian officials, who were conducting military exercises. Vladimir Putin later made much of being the first foreign leader to call Bush to offer support, although he did not initially get through. Rice took the call. "We have canceled our exercises," he told her.

But as Cheney managed the crisis in the bunker, another danger loomed. His doctors that day received back a blood test showing the vice president with a "potentially lethal" level of potassium that suggested hyperkalemia, which could trigger cardiac arrest that even the defibrillator in his chest would not stop.

AIR FORCE ONE raced west at full throttle, hitting 630 miles per hour, surprising even some of its crew who did not know it could go that fast. Bush was sobered to look out the window on the left side and see F-16 fighters escorting him, so close he could spot the stubble on the chin of one of the pilots, who saluted him.

The plane headed to Barksdale Air Force Base in Louisiana. It was an aggravating flight. Without its own television stream, the plane picked up feeds from local stations as it flew over various cities and then lost them again. Phone calls got cut off. But Bush saw one of the towers fall and thought to himself that no American president had ever seen so many of his people die all at once before. Three thousand had been killed in the deadliest sneak attack in American history, all on his watch. At the time, he thought it was even more.

The plane landed at Barksdale about 11:45 a.m. East Coast time, and Bush was further taken aback to see the base filled with armed bombers and guarded by rifle-toting troops. "It was surreal," he remembered later. "It was like flying in the midst of a combat zone." With no motorcade waiting for him, Bush climbed into a military vehicle that drove off at great speed.

"Slow down, son," Bush called out. "There are no terrorists on this base."

Bush taped another statement to be played to the nation and called Rumsfeld. "The ball will be in your court," Bush told him.

But the statement was no more reassuring than the earlier one. David Frum, the speechwriter, thought Bush "looked and sounded like the hunted, not the hunter." The communications at Barksdale were inadequate, so at Cheney's suggestion Bush took off again for Offutt Air Force Base in Nebraska, headquarters of Strategic Command, or Stratcom, which was equipped to run a war if need be. On the plane, Bush kept up a running argument over returning. "We need to get back to Washington," he told his Secret Service agent. "We don't need some tinhorn terrorist to scare us off. The American people want to know where their dang president is."

He also grilled Michael Morell, his CIA briefer.

"Who do you think did this?" Bush asked.

"There are two terror states capable, Iran and Iraq, but both have everything to lose and nothing to gain," Morell said. "If I had to guess I'd put a lot of money on the table that it was al-Qaeda."

"So when will we know?"

"We could know it soon, or it could take a while."

Barksdale was not the only place with communications problems. The White House bunker was supposed to have an open phone line with the Situation Room upstairs, but it kept cutting out. Richard Clarke in the Situation Room kept calling back asking for Major Mike Fenzel. The person answering the phone just grunted and passed the phone.

"Who is the asshole answering the phone for you, Mike?" Clarke asked.

"That would be the vice president, Dick," Fenzel said.

While the working assumption was that Osama bin Laden's al-Qaeda was behind the attacks, it did not take long for Iraq to come up. During a meeting at the Pentagon at 2:40 p.m., just five hours after the building was hit, Rumsfeld broached the idea of attacking Saddam Hussein, even though there was no evidence of his involvement. Stephen Cambone, a Rumsfeld aide, scribbled notes, using abbreviations for Hussein and bin Laden: "Best info fast. Judge whether good enough hit S.H. @ same time—Not only UBL."

At the White House, the air in the bunker had grown stale and heavy with carbon dioxide. Secret Service agents tried to clear space around Cheney. David Addington asked nonessential people to leave. Cheney had grown concerned that the president's brief statements were not enough to let Americans know that their government was operating. He was loath to make a public appearance himself, knowing it would fuel the impression that he was really running the show. "We were at war," he said later. "Our commander in chief needed to be seen as in charge, strong, and resolute—as George W. Bush was. My speaking publicly would not serve that cause." So he assigned Karen Hughes to conduct a briefing.

He wanted to make sure she had the best information when she did. By now, he knew just one plane had gone down, but he was still unsure whether it was because of his order.

"Call the NMCC," Cheney told his aide Eric Edelman, referring to the National Military Command Center, "and make sure we didn't shoot that plane down. We only get one chance to have the first take on the story, and if we get it wrong, we'll pay an enormous price. So make sure we didn't shoot it down."

Edelman made the call. The military staff at the center said no, there was no contact between air force fighters and the plane that went down in Pennsylvania.

Edelman reported back.

"Go ask them again," Cheney instructed.

"But, sir, I just asked them."

"Go ask them to check again."

Edelman got back on the phone and asked the military center to double-check. No, came the response, we had nothing to do with it. Edelman reported back to Cheney again.

Still unsatisfied, Cheney said, "I want you to go make sure."

Edelman made a third call and for the third time came back with the same answer.

Only then was Cheney satisfied.

BUSH LANDED AT Offutt at 2:50 p.m. East Coast time and headed into a command center like the one in the movie *WarGames*. At 3:15 p.m., the president convened a secure videoconference with top advisers. Appearing on separate video feeds were Cheney, Rumsfeld, George Tenet, and Robert Mueller, who had been FBI director for just a week.

"We're at war," Bush began. "We will find these people and they will suffer the consequence of taking on this nation. We will do what it takes."

Tenet told him it did indeed look as if al-Qaeda were responsible. A check of the manifests of the four hijacked planes had found three passengers who were known members, and electronic surveillance had picked up congratulatory communications among al-Qaeda figures.

Even as they discussed the response, a voice interrupted the videoconference to announce that a plane from Madrid was not responding to radio calls; permission to shoot it down was requested. *When is this going to end?* Bush thought. He authorized lethal action if necessary. Soon the voice interrupted again to report that the Madrid flight had landed in Lisbon.

Bush understood it was not going to end and that his presidency as he knew it was over. "We are at war against terror," he declared. "From this day forward, this is the new priority of our administration."

After the conference, he ordered his plane back to Washington so he could address the nation from the Oval Office. "If I'm in the White House and there's a plane coming my way, all I can say is I hope I read my Bible that day," he said.

Before taking off, he called Theodore Olson, the lawyer who had handled *Bush v. Gore* and later became his solicitor general. Olson's wife, Barbara, a lawyer and well-known political figure in Washington, had been on the plane that hit the Pentagon. Bush promised Olson he would find the people responsible.

After landing at Andrews Air Force Base, Bush boarded his marine helicopter to fly the last few miles to the White House. As it banked over Washington, he saw the plumes of smoke still emerging from the Pentagon. "The mightiest building in the world is on fire," he muttered. "That's the twenty-first-century war you just witnessed."

Marine One touched down at 6:55 p.m. on the South Lawn, where picnic tables and chuckwagons had been set up only that morning for a congressional picnic that was to be held that evening. Bush met with aides for a few minutes and then headed to the bunker, which he had never visited before. He found Laura waiting for him and hugged her, then caught up with Cheney.

At 8:30 p.m., Bush sat at his desk in the Oval Office as cameras transmitted his first extensive remarks on the crisis. The speechwriters had hashed through multiple drafts, but in the end Hughes put her pen through most of it. Bush did not declare war that night, because he wanted to reassure Americans, and he uttered lines that made the speechwriters cringe, such as "These acts shattered steel but they cannot dent the steel of American resolve." The speechwriters called it the "Awful Office Address." Michael Gerson, who had been stuck in highway traffic near the Pentagon when the hijacked plane hurtled into the building, thought it was "unequal to the moment" and made Bush look "stiff and small."

But one line from the speechwriter Matthew Scully survived: "We will make no distinction between the terrorists who committed these acts and those who harbored them."

Just like that, Bush declared a sweeping new doctrine in American security, one that he had not discussed in advance with Cheney, Rice, Rumsfeld, or Colin Powell. This would not be "pounding sand," as he often characterized what he saw as Bill Clinton's feckless responses to terrorist attacks of the past. This would be going after anyone and any nation that had anything to do with it, including Afghanistan, where al-Qaeda had bases, and possibly even Iraq, which was a designated state sponsor of terrorism.

After another meeting, Cheney, his wife, and his top aides headed out to the South Lawn, where they boarded a white-topped marine helicopter and took off at 9:57 p.m. Like Bush hours earlier, Cheney saw the damaged Pentagon, a searing image that to him evoked the War of 1812, the last time foreign forces attacked the American capital. During the flight, a White House doctor handed a note to Cheney asking to repeat the blood test that had indicated danger of cardiac arrest. "Not tonight," Cheney said. "You can have it in the morning." (The next morning the retest came back normal.)

The Cheneys headed to what would be called an undisclosed secure location—in this case, Camp David, where they landed at 10:30 p.m. and settled into Aspen, the president's cabin. Liz Cheney and her family had already been brought to the camp. As a general rule, only the president lands or takes off from the South Lawn; even when Ronald Reagan was shot in 1981, George H. W. Bush, rushing back to town, refused to land on the South Lawn. But Cheney was implementing protocols he had learned during the 1980s, keeping the president and the vice president apart in case of a devastating attack. He returned to the White House during the day but slept much of the next week at Camp David, the beginning of a months-long period of quasi-seclusion.

As for Bush, Carl Truscott, head of his Secret Service detail, told him to sleep that night in the bunker. Bush saw an old couch with a fold-out bed that he imagined Harry Truman himself had put in. "There is no way I'm sleeping there," he declared, and headed upstairs to his own room.

As he lay in bed, images of the day flashed through his mind, planes crashing into the symbols of the nation's might, passengers realizing the end was near, some even fighting back, firefighters and police officers rushing in to help, buildings collapsing into so much dust. *Why had this happened? What was the right response? How could he balance reassurance with resolve? How could he find a shadowy enemy that waged a secret war from caves halfway around the world?* Lying next to him, Laura sensed him staring into the darkness.

Then the president noticed a silhouette in the door and heard heavy breathing.

It was a Secret Service agent. "Mr. President! Mr. President! You've got to come now. The White House is under attack."

Bush threw on a pair of running shorts and Laura a robe. He scooped up Barney, the Scottish terrier, while she grabbed Kitty the cat, and they called for Spot, the springer spaniel, to follow. The first lady was virtually blind without her contacts, so the president led her down the hallway.

Agents armed with assault rifles rushed them down to the bunker. Neil Bush was there, as were Andy Card, Condoleezza Rice, and the president's housekeeper. Bush heard the slam and hiss of the pressurized metal doors closing behind them.

After a minute or two, an air force enlisted man announced, "Don't worry, Mr. President, it's one of ours."

An F-16 had the wrong transponder code on. The president in his running shorts and the blurry-eyed first lady in her robe trudged back upstairs with their pets and tried to rest.

8

"Whatever it takes"

When the Bushes woke the next morning, the first lady noticed piles of strollers on the lawn. Tourists visiting the White House had abandoned them and grabbed their children when the building was evacuated. It seemed nothing would ever be the same again. Suddenly the White House was brimming with guns, and military units were in the streets of the capital. Many people who worked for them were afraid to come back. And her husband was to be tested in a way he never expected.

President Bush had not fared well the day before. His decision to remain in the Florida classroom listening to children read, his peripatetic journey from air base to air base, his long disappearance from the public stage, and his unsteady statements had not sent a reassuring message in a moment of crisis. His advisers understood that and were defensive. Karl Rove tracked down the presidential historian Robert Dallek and the columnist William Safire, after they were critical of the president's slow-motion return to Washington, to tell them that Air Force One had been targeted. Dallek interpreted the call as an act of intimidation against anyone questioning the president. At the very least, it reflected a recognition that impressions harden quickly, and if the memory that day was of Bush in a seeming flight from danger, it could hobble his presidency.

Bush began a series of meetings to fashion a response to the attacks. As he sat with top officials reviewing the damage, he grew increasingly angry and suddenly turned in the direction of Attorney General John Ashcroft.

"Don't ever let this happen again," Bush said.

It was not clear whether he meant that as a message specifically for the attorney general or for everyone in the room, but Ashcroft "took it personally."

George Tenet reported that he was certain now that Osama bin Laden's network was behind the hijackings. Going after it would require expanded powers and money, he said.

"Whatever it takes," Bush said.

He turned to Robert Mueller, the new FBI director.

"Give me a brief," Bush instructed. "Where are we on what's happening?"

Mueller agreed that al-Qaeda was to blame, noting that hijackers could be heard over air traffic control radio calling on Allah. He reported on the latest in the investigation. But as the conversation moved forward, Mueller grew concerned by talk of aggressive action at the expense of traditional procedures.

"Wait a second," he said at one point. "If we do some of these things, it may impair our ability to prosecute."

Ashcroft cut him off. "We simply can't let this happen again," he said, echoing Bush. "Prosecution cannot be our priority. If we lose the ability to prosecute, that's fine, but we have to prevent the next attack. Prevention has to be our top priority."

Ashcroft paused to see if Bush agreed and, deciding that he did, plunged ahead. "The chief mission of U.S. law enforcement is to stop another attack and apprehend any accomplices and terrorists before they hit us again," he said. "If we can't bring them to trial, so be it."

At 11:30 a.m., leaders of Congress joined Bush in the Cabinet Room. To some, he seemed drained both mentally and physically. But as he briefed the lawmakers, he took a decisive tone. "This is the beginning of war in the twenty-first century," he began. "It will require a new strategy." He talked about rescue efforts in New York, mentioned emerging details about the passengers on United Airlines Flight 93 who fought back, and broached the need for additional law enforcement powers, emergency spending, and authorization to use force.

"We will answer the bloodlust of the American people that is rightly at boil," Bush said. "We'll spend our capital wisely and make it stick. We'll be patient. We are at war. The dream of the enemy was for us not to meet in this building. They wanted the White House in rubble."

Bush laid out his evolving new doctrine that stated that harboring terrorists would be held just as accountable. "These guys are like rattlesnakes," he said, falling back on Texas aphorisms. "They'll go back into their hole. Not only will we strike the hole, we'll strike the rancher." At the same time, he emphasized that Arab Americans should not be scapegoated.

Tom Daschle grew concerned by the talk of war. Not that he did not regard what happened as a singular assault on the United States, but he noted that the term "war" had been used indiscriminately over the years—the war on poverty, the war on cancer, the war on drugs. Daschle felt they should avoid once again using a term that might not result in a tangible victory.

"*War* is a very powerful word," he told Bush. "This war is so vastly different. Take great care in your rhetorical calculations."

Some Bush advisers were quietly stunned. *Careful about calling it war? If this was not war, what was?* But Bush chose not to engage in a debate.

He got more support from the other Democratic leader, Representative Richard Gephardt. "Mr. President, the most important thing here now is that we trust one another," he said. "That doesn't mean we are going to agree on everything—we never do—but our commitment to the American people is to keep them safe, and to do that, we have to really work together and basically put politics aside in making these decisions as much as we can."

Late that afternoon, Bush traveled across the Potomac River to the Pentagon. The building was still burning, and crews were still pulling bodies from the wreckage. Bush put his arm around Rumsfeld's shoulder. He shook hands and reaffirmed that America would "not be cowed by terrorists." Making his way back to his car, he found soldiers from the morgue detail who had approached Joe Hagin, the deputy White House chief of staff, to meet the president. Bush talked at length with the men in their protective suits and rubber gloves and boots. "He went down that line, took a long, long time with them," Hagin recalled.

By the time Bush returned to the White House, he found himself with a few minutes and wandered down to the Situation Room alone. "He looked like he wanted something to do," thought Richard Clarke, the counterterrorism chief. As Clarke remembered it, Bush grabbed him and a few others and closed the door.

"Look, I know you have a lot to do and all," Bush said, "but I want you, as soon as you can, to go back over everything, everything. See if Saddam did this. See if he's linked in any way."

Clarke was incredulous. "But, Mr. President, al-Qaeda did this."

"I know, I know, but see if Saddam was involved. Just look. I want to know any shred."

Clarke found the request disturbing, an indication of what he considered to be Bush and Cheney's obsession with Saddam Hussein. Bush later disputed the details of Clarke's account but told an investigating commission that he might have spoken to Clarke and asked about Iraq. To Bush, it was a logical question; Iraq was an enemy of America's and had sponsored terrorists before, even if not al-Qaeda. It was worth checking.

Later that evening, White House officials finished draft legislation to authorize force and faxed it to Capitol Hill. The draft declared "that the

President is authorized to use all necessary and appropriate force" against those linked to the attacks and to "preempt any related future acts of terrorism or aggression against the United States." Democrats like Daschle saw it as a blank check. Hurried negotiations ensued to find language that would satisfy both sides.

But in terms of the public leadership Americans expect from their president in moments of crisis, Bush had yet to find his footing, and advisers were worried. Michael Gerson went to Karl Rove's office that evening to express his concern.

"If we think our response has been a success so far," Gerson told him, "we're wrong."

"MR. PRESIDENT, by the time we're through with these guys, they're going to have flies walking across their eyeballs."

Cofer Black, the CIA's counterterrorism chief, was briefing Bush and Cheney on the morning of September 13. Balding, chubby-cheeked, and bespectacled, Black looked more like an accountant than the Hollywood version of a spymaster, but he was seen inside the agency as "something of a cross between a mad scientist and General George Patton," and his tough words were a balm to a president and a vice president hungry for action.

Still, everything at this point was an act of improvisation. Cheney pulled Karen Hughes aside and suggested Bush visit New York as soon as possible. The country needed to see its leader at the site. Bush had been reluctant to get in the way of rescue efforts, but it was becoming apparent that work was shifting toward recovering bodies rather than finding survivors. The president had been talking about going to New York the following Sunday; Hagin had been urging him to wait until Monday. The White House was organizing a prayer service at the Washington National Cathedral for Friday. "Maybe we should go tomorrow after the prayer service," Bush suggested.

Shortly afterward, Bush called Governor George Pataki and Mayor Rudy Giuliani of New York, inviting reporters into the Oval Office to record the moment. As he expressed condolences and offered support, the president surprised his staff by declaring on the spot that he would visit the next day.

"You've extended me a kind invitation to come to New York City," he said. "I accept. I'll be there tomorrow afternoon."

As shocked aides whispered to each other—*what did he just say?*—the president finished the call and took questions from reporters. They asked whether it was safe to fly, whether he had determined who was responsible, and what kind of international coalition he might assemble. Then Francine Kiefer of the *Christian Science Monitor* cut through the professional veneer.

"Could you give us a sense as to what kind of prayers you are thinking and where your heart is for yourself?" she asked.

Bush, his hands still planted on the desk, tried to find words. "Well, I don't think about myself right now," he said. "I think about the families, the children." The image of the Pentagon morgue team and the sound of Theodore Olson's voice came into his head.

It took eight seconds for him to start again, an eternity with television cameras rolling. "I am a loving guy," Bush said, "and I am also someone, however, who has got a job to do—and I intend to do it. And this is a terrible moment. But this country will not relent until we have saved ourselves and others from the terrible tragedy that came upon America."

Then he swept out of the office, his face contorted in grief.

Later he saw Gerson. Bush was uncertain about almost losing it on live television.

Was that okay? he asked.

"I thought it was an important moment for the country," Gerson told him.

Bush apologized to Hughes. "Sorry about that," he said.

"You don't need to apologize for having a big heart," she told him.

His aides wanted to reassure Bush, knowing how much weight he carried on his shoulders. As his speechwriters filed out of the Oval Office at one point so he could take a call from President Hosni Mubarak of Egypt, John McConnell couldn't help noticing that the president was sitting there just tapping his wedding ring against his desk in a steady rhythm, mentally lost in thought.

The impact hit closer to home when Andy Card mentioned that Brad Blakeman, the president's scheduling director, was missing a nephew in the World Trade Center. Bush couldn't believe it. It had been two days, and he was only learning now that one of the aides he worked with most closely had family directly involved. Blakeman's nephew Thomas Jurgens, a combat-trained army medic working as a court officer, had commandeered a jury van with supplies when he heard about the attacks and raced to the scene. He had not been heard from since.

Bush picked up the phone and called Blakeman. "How come you didn't tell me your nephew is missing?" he demanded.

"Because you have a lot going on," Blakeman replied.

"We are going to pray for a safe return," Bush said. "And I want your family to know that we are going to find the people who did this and bring them to justice."

"Thank you," Blakeman said. "We are going to hope that he returns."

Bush hung up. But he was still upset. He stood up and marched out of the Oval Office to Blakeman's office. "I want you to tell your family that I am going to find the people who did this and bring them to justice," he told Blakeman, repeating in person what he said over the phone. Blakeman busied himself in the days to come assembling a study of how past presidents responded to crises. His nephew's badge and gun were later found but not his body.

The president and first lady made a quick trip that day to Washington Hospital Center to visit people wounded in the Pentagon. Bush met Lieutenant Colonel Brian Birdwell, who had been badly burned on his hands and back. Bush saluted him, and it took a painful fifteen or twenty seconds or so for Birdwell to bring his bandaged arm up to salute back. Bush held his arm up the entire time.

When the motorcade arrived back at the White House just after noon, Card jumped into Bush's car before he could get out.

"We've got another threat on the White House," Card said. "We're taking it seriously."

Bush was mad. "Why are you telling me in here?" he asked, knowing that news photographers would notice. "You could have waited until I got into the Oval Office."

He marched back into the building and continued the conversation in the Oval Office. He was tired and surly. Whatever intelligence they had, he was not going to respond. If they were worried, they could send home nonessential personnel and make sure Cheney was at a separate location.

"I'm not leaving," Bush said irritably. "If a plane hits us, I'll just die."

Then he turned to the navy steward Ferdinand Garcia. "And, Ferdie, I'm hungry. I'll have a hamburger."

Karen Hughes interjected with fatalistic humor, "You might as well add cheese."

THE THREAT WAS one of many in the hours and days after the attack. Over the course of just four hours that afternoon, according to a Secret Service log, the city's main mosque reported a bomb threat, the Eisenhower Executive Office Building next to the White House was evacuated because of fire alarms, the British embassy received a suspicious package, a Cessna airplane violated airspace over Washington and was intercepted by F-16s, and the Capitol was evacuated when a police dog reacted to a package. It was a city on edge.

Bush and Cheney were confronted with a dizzying array of other challenges, from dealing with national heartache to plotting out economic recovery. They had to figure out when to allow airplanes to fly again, when to reopen the stock market, how to rebuild New York, even how to keep the auto industry from collapsing since closing the borders had blocked supplies. They had to figure out how to force the Taliban to give up Osama bin Laden and shut down al-Qaeda camps and how to make its sponsors in Pakistan realize the equation had changed.

What Bush had going for him was a public eager to follow his lead and a world for once united behind America. "Nous sommes tous Américains," headlined *Le Monde*. "We are all Americans." NATO for the first time in its history invoked Article 5 of its charter declaring an attack against one as an attack against all. Condoleezza Rice cried when she saw a television clip of the Coldstream Guards playing "The Star-Spangled Banner" during a changing of the guard at Buckingham Palace in London.

Bush met with his cabinet on September 14. Entering the room, he was surprised by sustained applause. Bush choked up, and tears came down his face for the second time in two days. He asked Donald Rumsfeld to lead a prayer. "We seek your special blessing today for those who stand as sword and shield, protecting the many from the tyranny of the few," the defense secretary said. "Our enduring prayer is that you shall always guide our labors and that our battles shall always be just."

Colin Powell worried that the president seemed in a fragile state heading into the cathedral speech that afternoon and slipped Bush a note. "Dear Mr. President," he wrote. "When I have to give a speech like this, I avoid those words that I know will cause me to well up, such as Mom and Pop."

Bush was both touched and amused and held it up for the group. "Let me tell you what the secretary of state just told me," Bush said with a grin. " 'Dear Mr. President, don't break down!' "

Everyone laughed, defusing the tension.

"Don't worry," Bush added. "I'm not losing it."

Michael Gerson, John McConnell, and Matthew Scully put together a simple, elegant, and moving speech for Bush, one they hoped would steady his presidency after the halting efforts so far. McConnell inserted a line about the war starting on the timing of others but ending at an hour of our choosing, adopting the phrase from a Franklin Roosevelt speech after German U-boats sank an American destroyer in 1941. Laura Bush thought music would be comforting, but Hughes also wanted a note of defiance, so she selected the "Battle Hymn of the Republic," not the usual fare for a mourning service. Bush agreed. "Defiance is good," he said. When he was told that the Washington National Cathedral wanted him to follow a verger to the pulpit, as was customary, he refused. He would approach the pulpit on his own, the solitary leader he had become the moment the planes hit the towers.

Arriving at the cathedral on a rainy day that seemed to reflect the country's grief, Bush visited a holding room to thank the clergy leading the service. He found his friend from Texas, the Reverend Kirbyjon Caldwell.

"May I come with you to Ground Zero?" Caldwell asked.

"Yeah," Bush answered, "that would be good."

As he headed into the main cathedral, he found an extraordinary assemblage of the nation's leaders—former presidents, senior members of Congress, the cabinet, and the military, Democrats and Republicans, even his vanquished foe, Al Gore, all united in this moment. The one not there was Cheney, who had flown to Camp David to preserve the line of succession should the unthinkable happen again.

When Bush saw three soldiers crying, he knew Powell had a point and resolved that whatever he did, he would not look at his parents when he spoke. "We are here in the middle hour of our grief," he began. "So many have suffered so great a loss, and today we express our nation's sorrow." Bush summoned an eloquence and capacity for inspiration that had eluded him on the day of the attacks. "Just three days removed from these events, Americans do not yet have the distance of history," he said. "But our responsibility to history is already clear—to answer these attacks and rid the world of evil. War has been waged against us by stealth and deceit and murder. This nation is peaceful, but fierce when stirred to anger. This conflict was begun on the timing and terms of others. It will end in a way, and at an hour, of our choosing."

He spoke for a mere seven minutes, but it was one of the signal moments of his presidency. He did not cry, but when he sat back down, the first president Bush, without looking at him, simply reached over across Laura Bush to squeeze his son's arm in a fatherly gesture of love and pride. Both Bushes were stirred as the battle hymn concluded the service. *He hath loosed the fateful lightning of His terrible swift sword, His truth is marching on . . .*

After the service, the president strode out of the cathedral and got into his armored limousine with Laura and Kirbyjon Caldwell to head to New York.

Bush noticed a bulge in Caldwell's sock. "What is that?" he asked.

"That is my phone," Caldwell said.

"Oh," Bush said. "Kind of looks like a gun."

Caldwell harked back to Bush's work in a Houston poverty program as a young man. "That must have taken you back to your Fifth Ward days," he joked.

Bush laughed, glad for a light moment on a heavy day.

AS AIR FORCE One approached New York, Bush could see the giant scar in the middle of a great city. It was worse than the pictures, worse than he could have imagined.

The plane landed at McGuire Air Force Base in New Jersey, and Bush boarded Marine One for the short helicopter flight into Manhattan. After an overnight rain, the day had turned bright and sunny, much like the one three days earlier. The helicopter flew low and fast toward the city, and as the Statue of Liberty came into view, the air turned noxious, filled with a stench of ignited jet fuel and burning bodies. "You could literally smell the carnage," Caldwell recalled.

The helicopter touched down at the Wall Street landing pad, and Bush joined Rudy Giuliani and George Pataki for the motorcade to what was already being called Ground Zero. As they turned the corner onto West Street, piles of ruins came into view. The rubble was still burning despite the rain. Dust and debris covered everything and everyone. As Bush emerged from the vehicle, sloshing through wreckage still wet from rain and fire hoses, he thought it was "like walking into hell."

Rescue workers chanted, "U-S-A, U-S-A!"

"Make 'em pay, George!" someone yelled.

"Whatever it takes!"

One rescue worker pointed at Bush and said, "Don't let me down!"

Bush was taken aback. He could sense the palpable thirst for vengeance. *Don't let me down. Whatever it takes.* The words stayed with him for years.

Bush encountered a former New York firefighter named Rocco Chierichella, who had jumped into his car in Pennsylvania and raced to Manhattan to help.

Chierichella put his arm around Bush's shoulder, turned him around, and pointed to a pile of ash.

"Mr. President," he said, "look what they've done to us. You can't let them get away with it."

Bush whispered in his ear. "You must have patience. I'm going to get every one of them."

No remarks were scheduled, but an advance person, Nina Bishop, approached Karl Rove. "They want to hear from their president," she said. Rove agreed and sent her to find a bullhorn while he tracked down Andy Card, who suggested it to the president.

Bush climbed onto a crushed fire truck, helped up by Bob Beckwith, a sixty-nine-year-old retired firefighter who had put his old uniform on and rushed to the scene to help search for survivors. Once Bush was up, Beckwith started to climb down.

"Where are you going?" Bush asked.

"I was told to get down," Beckwith said.

"No, no, you stay right here," Bush said.

Bush draped his arm around Beckwith as he started to speak into the bullhorn: "I want you all to know that America today, America today is on bended knee in prayer for the people whose lives were lost here, for the workers who work here, for the families who mourn. This nation stands with the good people of New York City and New Jersey and Connecticut."

Someone kept shouting, "I can't hear you!" It was Chierichella.

Instinct kicked in. "I can hear *you*!" Bush responded. "The rest of the world hears you. And the people who knocked these buildings down will hear *all* of us soon."

Presidencies are built on random, unscripted moments, and this was the most iconic of Bush's. For all of Michael Gerson's poetry, for all of the solemnity of a cathedral service, those few seconds of unvarnished bravado in the face of tragedy would most move a nation.

Joe Hagin had agreed with New York officials that the president would stop by the Jacob Javits Convention Center for a half hour to meet people waiting for word of missing relatives. A half hour turned into two hours and twenty minutes as Bush worked his way through the tableau of grief, hugging people with bloodshot eyes holding up signs that said, "Have you seen my brother?" He embraced a little boy clutching a teddy bear and signed pictures of the missing so their family members could prove to them that they met the president when they were found—even though he knew most never would be.

The scene was so intense that even Secret Service agents had tears in their eyes. Karen Hughes had to leave after twenty minutes because she could not take the overpowering grief. When she returned, a man approached, saying the mother of a dead Port Authority officer wanted to give her son's badge to the president. Bush met Arlene Howard, who reached into her purse and pressed the metal object into his hand.

"This is my son's badge. His name is George Howard. Please remember him."

The president promised he would.

As Bush left to return to Washington, Ari Fleischer told him Congress had passed the resolution authorizing force in response to the attacks and asked if it was okay to put out a statement welcoming the vote.

Bush looked weary. "Put it out," he said simply.

Aides had never seen him so drained. "You could tell he was wiped out," Eric Draper, the White House photographer, said later. As the motorcade made its way back to the helipad, thousands of normally jaded New Yorkers lined the route eight- and nine-deep, holding candles, applauding, cheering. "I didn't vote for you," read one sign, "but thank you so much for coming."

When Bush got back to his helicopter, he collapsed into the seat, slumping down, thoroughly spent.

THE PRESIDENT AND first lady flew that night to Camp David, where he would spend the weekend conferring with Cheney and the rest of what was becoming known as the war cabinet. Camp David, a 148-acre compound in the Maryland mountains, was first used by Franklin Roosevelt as a getaway named Shangri-La, then rechristened by Dwight D. Eisenhower after his grandson, David.

By the time Bush inherited it, there were eleven stone-and-wood cabins, plus tennis courts, swimming pools, a dining facility, movie theater, bowling alley, skeet range, gymnasium, chapel, and putting green. Most important, there was solitude. The deeply secluded rustic retreat, not recorded on official maps, was one place where a president could get away. While Bill Clinton did not care for the place, Bush like his father relished the woodsy escape and retreated there any weekend he could; he liked surrounding himself with family and told his two siblings living in the Washington area, Marvin and Doro, that any weekend he went up, they were always welcome to join him. His brother came often enough that Bush jokingly renamed the place "Camp Marvin."

But this would be a different kind of getaway. Bush wanted to use the setting to spark a broader conversation about how to respond to September 11 over the long run. Cheney was already there when other cabinet officers began arriving for the meeting the next day, and the vice president invited Donald Rumsfeld, Colin Powell, and Condoleezza Rice to join him in Holly Lodge for a private dinner. Over buffalo steak, a Cheney favorite, the four informally discussed the decisions to come. It was a powerful tandem; three of the four of them had served in multiple high-ranking positions through a multitude of crises before. Rice for once felt out of place.

The next morning, Bush convened the war cabinet in Laurel, the main lodge used for office work and meetings. He wore a casual blue shirt and a rugged olive jacket with a presidential seal on it and sat at the middle of a long oak table in a wood-paneled conference room. To his right were Cheney, John Ashcroft, and Scooter Libby. To his left were Powell, Rumsfeld, and Paul Wolfowitz, Rumsfeld's deputy. Also present were Rice, Andy Card, George Tenet, John McLaughlin, Cofer Black, Robert Mueller, Paul O'Neill, Alberto Gonzales, General Hugh Shelton, chairman of the Joint

Chiefs of Staff, and General Richard Myers, the vice chairman. Laid across the table was a large map of Afghanistan, a place so remote and forbidding that Rice, the Russia expert, could not help but think of it as "the place where great powers go to die."

Bush started the discussion by turning to Powell, who reported on his efforts to build a coalition for the war to come. O'Neill talked about reopening the stock market and going after terrorist finances. Tenet handed out a package titled "Going to War" with information about al-Qaeda and a draft presidential order authorizing the agency to go after it in a way the agency never had before. Rumsfeld turned the table over to Wolfowitz, who began making the case for going after Saddam Hussein. He declared that there was a 10 percent to 50 percent chance that Hussein had been involved in the attacks, although he presented no evidence. Afghanistan would not be a particularly satisfying place to wage a war since it was so primitive that there were few targets; Iraq, on the other hand, had plenty of targets and military action there would be a powerful demonstration that the United States would not sit by idly while a danger like Hussein operated with impunity.

Powell, Rice, Card, and Shelton were aggravated. "No one will understand or support us doing anything but going after those who attacked us," Powell said. Going after Iraq would shatter the emerging coalition.

If it was a coalition unwilling to face Iraq, Rumsfeld countered, maybe "it is not a coalition worth having."

Moving back to Afghanistan, Shelton outlined three military options. The first was a cruise missile strike. The second was a cruise missile strike accompanied by manned bombers.

Before Shelton could even get to his third option, Wolfowitz interrupted. "But we really need to think broader than that right now," he said. "That's not big enough. We've got to make sure we go ahead and get Saddam out at the same time—it's a perfect opportunity."

By Shelton's later account, Bush became incensed. "How many times do I have to tell you we are *not* going after Iraq right this minute?" he snapped at Wolfowitz. "We're going to go after the people we know did this to us. Do you understand me?"

Shelton's third option combined the cruise missile strike with bombers and ground forces, although of course that would be the one that would require the most preparation and it was not entirely clear what troops would be used for. Bush and Cheney, determined not to repeat Clinton's approach to fighting al-Qaeda, found the first two options unacceptable and the third unimaginative.

Only toward the end did they return to the matter of preventing future attacks on American soil. Ashcroft said it was important to disrupt terrorists immediately. Someone asked what he suggested. "I'm so glad you asked," he said, pulling out a framework for legislation greatly expanding law enforcement powers.

After more than three hours of unusually freewheeling discussion, Bush finally called for lunch and told his team to take a few hours to walk around, exercise, and think. After lunch, Bush pulled Card aside and told him to tell Wolfowitz not to interject like that again; he expected to hear from his cabinet secretaries, not the deputies. Cheney went back to his cabin and called Lyzbeth Glick, the widow of Jeremy Glick, a passenger on United Airlines Flight 93 who had been among those who rushed the hijackers, to express appreciation for her husband's heroism. The conversation kept him centered on what he considered the primary mission. *Never again. This could never happen again.*

THEY RECONVENED AT 4:30 p.m., and Bush kept a tighter rein on the conversation as he went around the table soliciting recommendations. Powell again went first, suggesting they give Afghanistan an ultimatum to hand over bin Laden and al-Qaeda figures or face war. He argued again for sticking to Afghanistan for fear of pushing away the allies. "Whatever problem Iraq is, it is not the cause of what happened," Powell said.

Rumsfeld said the military options all seemed antiquated, but he made no concrete recommendation, flabbergasting Powell. Card and Tenet, on the other hand, agreed with Powell about going after Afghanistan, not Iraq. Rice, at Bush's request, withheld her opinion to share privately with him. Going last was Cheney, who agreed that now was not the time to focus on Iraq. "If we go after Saddam Hussein, we lose our rightful place as good guy," he said. Bush thanked everyone and said he would let them know what he decided.

That night, the team gathered for a social hour and dinner. Standing near the fireplace, Bush and Cheney listened as Wolfowitz again pressed his case. He was not arguing for an invasion of Iraq at that point, he said, but demanding that Hussein hand over terrorists known to be on his territory and readmit UN inspectors. If he refused, the United States could take action that would be more imaginative than a full-scale war, like establishing an enclave in the south that would deprive Hussein of most of his oil fields and give Shiites a base to wage their own rebellion against him.

"Well, that is imaginative," Bush said.

That wasn't the word Powell would use; privately, he would come to lampoon the notion as the "Bay of Goats."

Finally, talk of war receded momentarily. Ashcroft noticed a piano and sat down to play spirituals. Rice sang "His Eye Is on the Sparrow," a gospel hymn popular in African American church services. Sitting down to dinner later, Bush asked Rice to lead a prayer. "We have seen the face of evil," she began, "but we are not afraid."

The next morning, September 16, Cheney was taken to Camp Greentop, not far from Camp David, where he sat down with Tim Russert of *Meet the Press* for his first interview since September 11. The purpose was to use Cheney's credibility from a career in government to reassure the country that all was under control, but the interview emphasized the centrality of his role in the emerging new era. It also signaled where Cheney would help take the nation in his drive to guard against future attacks.

"If you provide sanctuary to terrorists, you face the full wrath of the United States of America," he told Russert, his aggressive words belied by his calm, low-key tone. He warned this would be a war unlike any other, unlike the Gulf War he had led, one that would go beyond simply marshaling armies and air forces.

"We also have to work sort of the dark side, if you will," he said. "We're going to spend time in the shadows in the intelligence world. A lot of what needs to be done here will have to be done quietly, without any discussions, using sources and methods that are available to our intelligence agencies if we're going to be successful. That's the world these folks operate in."

He hinted at the new security architecture he had in mind, casting aside old barriers that seemed quaint in the face of this new enemy. "It's going to be vital for us to use any means at our disposal, basically, to achieve our objective," Cheney said. "It is a mean, nasty, dangerous, dirty business out there, and we have to operate in that arena. I'm convinced we can do it. We can do it successfully. But we need to make certain that we have not tied the hands, if you will, of our intelligence communities in terms of accomplishing their mission."

Cheney did draw one limit, for the moment, the same one the president had drawn that weekend. When Russert raised Iraq, the vice president batted it down.

"At this stage, the focus is over here on al-Qaeda and the most recent events in New York," he said. "Saddam Hussein's bottled up at this point."

Asked if there was evidence linking Saddam Hussein to the attacks, Cheney answered simply, "No."

Bush flew back to the White House on Sunday afternoon. As Marine One touched down on the South Lawn just after 3:20, he found a clutch of reporters waiting, and he paused long enough to take a few questions. "This crusade, this war on terrorism is going to take a while," he said. "And the

American people must be patient. I'm going to be patient. But I can assure the American people I am determined. I'm not going to be distracted."

With that, Bush had, unthinkingly, branded the war on terror a "crusade." To the Muslim world, the word evoked the religious wars fought until the end of the thirteenth century, Christian armies marching to recapture the Holy Land from Islamic infidels. Bush meant no historical allusion, but a leader more seasoned in foreign policy might have anticipated the consequences of using such a freighted term. After advisers explained it to him, Bush never again used the word to describe the war on terror, but the onetime unscripted utterance proved a defining moment to many Muslims for years.

That night Bush kept a social engagement scheduled long before the attacks, a tenth-anniversary dinner for his longtime friend and aide Debra Dunn and her husband, Alan. Dunn had worked for Bush during his father's presidential campaign and was now working in the White House for Cheney. Everyone had expected the dinner to be canceled, but Laura Bush insisted they go ahead to provide her husband with a break from the tension and a small window of normalcy in those crazed, confused days. Dunn could not believe they were still having the dinner. "No, we want to do this," Bush told her. "You know me—I wouldn't do it if I didn't want to."

Seven couples sat at the table in the Family Dining Room, Dunn on one side of the president and her six-year-old daughter, Helen, on the other. Bush led them in a brief prayer for the country and the Americans who had died the week before but then turned the conversation to the sorts of things that come up at an anniversary dinner. The wear on his face was evident, but no one brought up the obvious.

Bush, always good with children, lavished attention on young Helen. He cut her roast beef for her and advised her not to drink from the finger bowl.

"So what are you reading?" he asked her. "Are you reading?"

"Yes, I'm just beginning to read."

"I read books too," he said with a twinkle, "though nobody thinks I do."

Afterward, Bush went downstairs with some of the guests as they filed out to the South Lawn. Bush had brought Spot. It was eerily quiet, no sound of traffic, or much else. Suddenly a plane roared overhead.

Bush looked up. "Is that supposed to be there?" he asked. It was the question on everyone's mind. The plane disappeared in the distance, and it would later turn out to be a fighter jet patrolling the skies.

Bush did not know that. He looked down and said quietly, "I'm fighting an enemy that I can't see."

THE NEXT DAY, September 17, Bush began the fight. He started the morning by visiting the Eisenhower Executive Office Building adjacent to the White House, where most people who worked for him actually spent their days. "Thanks for coming to work," he said, shaking hands in the cafeteria. He understood how frightened everyone was.

Heading back to the West Wing, Bush spotted Richard Keil, the Bloomberg correspondent. Bush reached out to grab his hand and remarked how hard it was to believe they were running together less than a week before.

"You were the last person I was with," Bush said softly. "Before—before we were attacked."

Keil, normally the most professional of reporters, broke with journalistic detachment. "Just know, Mr. President, that I'm praying for you," he said. "Everyone is praying for you, sir."

Bush squeezed his hand and turned to go.

Bush joined his war cabinet at 9:35 a.m. and announced the strategy he had settled on over the weekend. "The purpose of this meeting," he said, "is to assign tasks for the first wave of the war against terrorism. It starts today."

Bush laid out the tasks. John Ashcroft, Robert Mueller, and George Tenet would coordinate plans to bolster defense of the homeland. Colin Powell would deliver an ultimatum to the Taliban to stop harboring al-Qaeda, one so tough they will be "quaking in their boots." Assuming the Taliban refused, Donald Rumsfeld and Hugh Shelton would develop contingencies to "attack with missiles, bombers and boots on the ground." Paul O'Neill would go after al-Qaeda financing. And Bush signed a classified order giving the CIA vast new authority to conduct covert operations and use lethal force.

As to the points Rumsfeld and Paul Wolfowitz had been making at Camp David, Bush made clear he agreed with them in spirit, just not on timing. "I believe Iraq was involved," he said, evidently more from supposition than proof, "but I'm not going to strike them now. I don't have the evidence at this point."

With that, Bush headed over to the Pentagon to give a pep talk to Defense Department workers back on duty just yards from the rubble where their colleagues had died. Later, he visited the Islamic Center of Washington, the largest mosque in the American capital, to make the point just a day after using the word "crusade" that the coming war on terror in fact was not a war on Islam.

But once again, his off-the-cuff remarks came under scrutiny for their bravado. When a reporter at the Pentagon asked if he wanted Osama bin Laden dead, he looked down and said, "I want justice." Then, leaning back in his chair, he continued: "There's an old poster out west, as I recall, that said, 'Wanted: Dead or Alive.'"

Some aides thought the comment was fine; Ari Fleischer thought it captured the mood of the country. Laura Bush did not agree. When she next saw Bush, she ribbed him as only she could. "Bushie, you gonna git 'im?" she asked. He got the message. He asked Condoleezza Rice whether it had been a mistake. "The language was a little white hot for the president of the United States," she replied. He nodded. His top national security lawyer, John Bellinger, went so far as to send an e-mail to Alberto Gonzales warning that such a comment could be seen as instigating an illegal assassination. David Addington, Cheney's counsel, erupted and told Gonzales "to get control of Bellinger."

While Bush disavowed any attack on Iraq for now, that did not end the debate. Wolfowitz sent Rumsfeld a memo that day arguing that if there was even a 10 percent chance that Saddam Hussein was behind the 9/11 attack, they should focus on eliminating that threat. Richard Clarke, responding to Bush's request, sent a memo of his own to Rice the next day, reporting only anecdotal evidence linking Iraq to al-Qaeda and concluding that there was no "compelling case" that Iraq had planned or carried out the attacks. Unsatisfied, Bush told Tenet that he wanted to know about links between Hussein and al-Qaeda and told him to consult with Cheney, who had heard something about Mohamed Atta, the suspected leader of the hijackers, meeting with an Iraqi agent in Prague months before the attacks.

To defend against further attacks, Bush decided he needed a homeland security adviser. The name that came up was Governor Tom Ridge of Pennsylvania, one of the candidates on Cheney's list during the vice presidential selection process. In that role, Ridge was problematic because of his support for abortion rights. But in this job, that would not matter. Plus, as a military veteran, manager of a state government, and governor of one of the states affected on September 11, Ridge seemed the right fit.

Speaker Dennis Hastert had been urging Bush to address a joint session of Congress, much as Franklin Roosevelt had done after Pearl Harbor. Karl Rove and Karen Hughes agreed, but Michael Gerson opposed it, and Bush was reluctant without something to say. Gerson and his fellow speechwriters, Matthew Scully and John McConnell, were told to produce a draft by 7:00 p.m. They objected that it was impossible but were given no choice.

As the three men huddled over a computer screen, they tried to frame the emerging war and the enemy they now faced. Each contributed memorable lines. McConnell, for instance, came up with the idea of predicting terrorism would be relegated to "history's graveyard of discarded lies." When

Bush read the draft and saw another line quoting Roosevelt, he ordered it removed. "I don't want to quote anyone," he said. "I want to lead. I want to be the guy they quote." He was not happy either with a line about not yielding or resting, seeing that as too negative, but let it remain. He agreed with Hughes, who was pushing to keep a line urging Americans to "live your lives and hug your children," over the objections of the speechwriters, who thought it trite. Hughes also suggested Bush hold up the badge Arlene Howard had given him.

With his black Sharpie pen, Bush could be a tough editor of speeches. He was far more involved in crafting them than Cheney, who generally did not invest as much energy in the art of speech making. Bush had set ideas about writing he remembered from a Yale language class. He liked active verbs and emphatic statements; he hated passive construction. He refused to begin a sentence with the word "it" and scratched out throat-clearing phrases like "I am here to say" or "As I mentioned before." He did not like "I think" or "I believe." He took out adjectives. He wanted a beginning, middle, and end and was intolerant of repeating the same point. For lyricists like Gerson, Bush's Texas cadence and vernacular could be a challenge.

In this case, though, Gerson's concern was more prosaic. The speech had no real takeaway, no news. Then Rice showed up with several paragraphs laying down an ultimatum to the Taliban.

"Is this news enough for you?" she asked.

Yes, he said. That would do.

WHILE BUSH THOUGHT about how to reassure and yet prepare the country for a new era of warfare, Cheney found himself absorbed by the danger of a biological attack. It showed up in the intelligence briefings with unnerving regularity, and it was all the more frightening because the impact could be more powerful than hijacked aircraft. Indeed, it had been a preoccupation of Cheney's since long before September 11. As soon as a few moments allowed on his schedule, the vice president summoned experts to a conference room in the Eisenhower Executive Office Building on September 20.

Cheney listened impassively but intently as the specialists told him about a two-day exercise called Dark Winter conducted by several academic institutes at Andrews Air Force Base in June examining what would happen in the event of a smallpox outbreak in Oklahoma. The former senator Sam Nunn played the president, the former White House aide David Gergen played the national security adviser, the former deputy defense secretary John White played the defense secretary, the former CIA director James Woolsey and the former FBI director William Sessions reprised their old jobs, and Governor Frank Keating of Oklahoma played himself. A handful of reporters participated, including Judith Miller of the *New York Times*. The results were ominous. Within thirteen days, the disease had spread to twenty-five states and fifteen other countries; within months, three million people were infected and one million dead. The exercise concluded that government response plans were inadequate.

"What does a biological weapon look like?" Cheney asked the experts.

Randall Larsen, a retired air force colonel who had studied biological warfare, pulled a test tube from his briefcase. "Sir," he said dramatically, "it looks like this."

The test tube contained what he said was a weaponized powder of *Bacillus globigii*, a biological agent. It was harmless but nearly identical to *Bacillus anthracis*, which causes anthrax, and no more difficult to make. "And by the way," Larsen said, "I did just carry this into your office."

As Cheney delved deeper into the dark side, Bush prepared for a speech that he knew would define the remainder of his presidency. For his first rehearsal in the family theater of the White House, he was wearing a sweat suit and was in a casual mood. When he came to the point where he was to hold up the badge, he held up a water bottle instead. By his final practice, though, he seemed different, more sober, more serious, as if steadying himself. A cap had fallen off a back tooth, but he ignored the discomfort.

After he practiced the speech on the afternoon of September 20, Bush went upstairs to rest but ended up on a series of phone calls. By evening, Prime Minister Tony Blair of Britain arrived, straight from a transatlantic flight. Bush was glad to see Blair, who was rapidly becoming his closest friend on the world stage. Bush's steady demeanor surprised Blair. "He was unbelievably, almost preternaturally calm," Blair recalled. Worried about a precipitous reaction to the attacks that could alienate the rest of the world, Blair asked Bush about Iraq. Bush reassured him that Saddam Hussein was not the immediate problem. Blair's chief of staff, Jonathan Powell, found it ironic that Margaret Thatcher had warned Bush's father after the Iraqi invasion of Kuwait not to "go wobbly," and now, as he saw it, another British prime minister was telling another president Bush, "This *is* a time to wobble."

The two leaders joined advisers for a dinner of scallops, veal, and salad. Bush, relaxed, picked up the thin ring of pastry on top of the scallop.

"God dang, what on earth is that?" he asked.

The server, misunderstanding, said it was a scallop.

Bush said it looked like a halo over an angel.

Over dinner, Bush expressed concern that others were using September 11 for their own purposes, naming in particular Israel and Russia, both of which were fighting Muslim militants. Bush told Blair he had pressed Prime Minister Ariel Sharon of Israel not to go after Yasser Arafat. "I said Arafat is not bin Laden and you do nothing," Bush said. Likewise, Vladimir Putin seemed to be angling to escalate his military operation against Chechen rebels. At home, Bush said his advisers feared another attack and worried Hollywood might be the next target since Islamic radicals believed it was dominated by Jewish executives spreading decadent material around the world.

Blair said they needed to keep public opinion behind them and urged him to focus on al-Qaeda and the Taliban.

"I agree with you, Tony," Bush said. "We must deal with this first. But when we have dealt with Afghanistan, we must come back to Iraq."

The speech was not long away, and Blair tried to excuse himself to give Bush time to collect himself. But Bush would not let him go, insisting he stay and talk. He did not want to be alone. The presence of a friend was reassuring.

As they got into the White House elevator to head to the motorcade, Blair asked Bush if he was nervous. This would be the biggest speech of his presidency to date.

"No, not really," Bush answered. "I have a speech here and the message is clear."

Indeed, Bush looked to Blair as if he were comfortable not only with the speech but, more broadly, with his new mission.

Bush arrived at the Capitol and privately greeted congressional leaders, who were struck by his presence and confidence. Bush had made an important transition from the awkward uncertainty of September 11 to the leader of a wartime nation, some thought. "He *looked* more like a commander in chief than ever before," Tom Daschle reflected. "It was as if he had actually grown a suit size or two."

Mounting the rostrum in the House chamber, Bush began to turn the nation from grief to determination. He explained to Americans who had never heard of al-Qaeda or Osama bin Laden what he saw as the roots of the attacks. He vowed tolerance for peaceful Muslims. And he laid down his ultimatum to Afghanistan's leadership.

"Tonight, the United States makes the following demands on the Taliban," he intoned. Among them was to hand over al-Qaeda leaders and shut down their training camps. "These demands are not open to negotiation or discussion. The Taliban must act, and act immediately. They will hand over the terrorists, or they will share their fate."

Bush defined al-Qaeda as an enemy of American freedom, ignoring bin Laden's own statements about specific grievances against the United States, such as the troops still present in Saudi Arabia a decade after the Gulf War. "Americans are asking why do they hate us?" Bush said. "They hate what we see right here in this chamber—a democratically elected government. Their leaders are self-appointed. They hate our freedoms—our freedom of religion, our freedom of speech, our freedom to vote and assemble and disagree with each other."

Joining Blair in the House gallery were Tom Ridge, who had agreed to head the new White House Office of Homeland Security, and Lisa Beamer, widow of Todd Beamer, whose reported words "Let's roll" came to stand for the determination of the passengers who attempted to retake United Airlines Flight 93 and inspired the nation. Bush warned that the war would be long and arduous, sometimes visible, and sometimes in the shadows. He held up the police badge Arlene Howard had given him. "I will not forget this wound to our country or those who inflicted it," he said. Then, summoning a Churchillian tone, he uttered the line he had resisted but that would become a memorable statement of resolve: "I will not yield. I will not rest. I will not relent in waging this struggle for freedom and security for the American people."

He spoke for forty-one minutes and was interrupted thirty-one times by applause, and if the nation was not sure what to think of him when he started, many millions came to agree with Daschle by the end. The speech hit all the right notes and generated a standing ovation. Even some of his harshest Democratic critics believed he had hit a home run. As Bush made his way out of the chamber, he encountered Daschle, and the two embraced, the conservative president and the liberal senator swept up in the emotion of the moment. Unwittingly, they created a symbolic statement of national unity as newspapers transmitted pictures of "The Hug" across the world.

Afterward, Bush learned that the speech had drawn rapt audiences across the country; even a game between the Philadelphia Flyers and the New York Rangers at First Union Center in Philadelphia was suspended when fans insisted on watching the president speak on the Jumbotron rather than proceed with the third period.

After all the stumbling moments, the scripted statements that came across as stilted or forced, Bush now seemed to be in the zone. Nine days after the calamity, he had found his voice. He was almost exuberant afterward, in a way he rarely was following a speech.

"What do you think, Barty?" Bush asked Dan Bartlett.

"You did a great job," Bartlett responded.

"I've never been more comfortable in my life giving a speech," Bush said.

He called Gerson, who made a point of never actually attending the big addresses he helped write. The president was upbeat. "I have never felt more comfortable in my life," Bush repeated.

The next morning, Bush got on the phone with Daschle. "Did we get into trouble last night for hugging each other?" he asked lightly. After all, this was a town where that could cause either of them political grief.

"I don't think so," Daschle responded. "It just seemed like the natural thing to do. I think that was what the American people expected."

9

"The first battle of the war"

In the weeks after September 11, Vice President Cheney, the commanding presence at every table, suddenly became a disembodied voice emanating from a video screen. The fear of a "second wave" consumed the White House, and Cheney spent much of his time removed from the building to maintain presidential succession in case the worst happened. To avoid overlap, a special color-coded schedule showed the future locations of Trailblazer and Angler, as the Secret Service called the president and the vice president.

The notion of the vice president disappearing to an "undisclosed secure location" captured the public imagination, first as a chilling sign of the way life had changed and later as fodder for a thousand late-night jokes. In truth, the infamous undisclosed location was often no more mysterious than the vice president's residence. Since it was several miles up the road from the White House, as long as no one knew that was where he was, that was good enough. "The whole goal was to keep them separate," said Neil Patel, a top Cheney aide. Scooter Libby would join the vice president in the office on the third floor of his official residence on the Naval Observatory grounds, and a couple of other aides like Patel would squeeze into a tiny office to the side or borrow space in a larger office on the main floor where Lynne Cheney's staff was located.

More often, the secret hideout was Camp David, for once in its history serving as a de facto headquarters and refuge from danger rather than the scene of family holidays and the occasional Middle East summit. Accompanied by Libby, a personal aide, secretary, military aide, doctor, and either Patel or David Addington, Cheney would fly up by helicopter on Sunday nights, then fly back to Washington on Friday evenings. He and his staff got their own cabins, and they would join each other for breakfast and lunch in Laurel Lodge, then work out of the president's office space all day. Cheney would usually retire for dinner by himself in his cabin. Sometimes he used a secret military compound bristling with satellite dishes and antennas known as Site R and located not far from Camp David on the Pennsylvania border. And his vacation house in Wyoming served the same purpose at times.

The attention to security affected almost everything. The president's and the vice president's schedules were no longer distributed by e-mail, and the passwords to access them were restricted. Cheney, who at first had still escaped to the grocery store, now lived in a tighter security bubble than any vice president before; his motorcade no longer stopped at traffic lights, and his armored vehicle was equipped with a protective suit in the event of chemical or biological attack.

The physical constraints took Cheney away at the very moment when he was most engaged. He participated in most meetings via a secure video hookup that proved disconcerting. A curtain would be set up behind him so no one would know his location; once, it was jostled, and aides recognized the backdrop as Cheney's own home. In another surreal moment, the vice president nodded off on-screen.

The phrase "undisclosed secure location" quickly entered the cultural lexicon. One day when he emerged from what aides called "the Cave" to return to the White House, one of Cheney's domestic policy advisers, Ron Christie, gave him a recording of a *Saturday Night Live* sketch in which the vice president's secret location was revealed as Kandahar, Afghanistan, and he was presented as a "one-man Afghani wrecking crew" demolishing the Taliban and al-Qaeda single-handedly. The comic Cheney, played by Darrell Hammond, explained how he could do this with a weak heart by tearing open his shirt to reveal a metal device attached to his chest.

"I got me a bionic ticker!" the impersonator crowed. "This thing regulates my heartbeat, it gives me night vision and renders me completely invisible on radar!"

Then, pushing a button, he said, "Check this out." Coffee began pouring from the mechanical heart. "I brew my own Sanka! Oh yeah, now that's good coffee."

What a difference a few months had made. Before September 11, the running joke on *Saturday Night Live* had been Cheney's monotonous demeanor: giving a speech on energy policy, the ersatz Cheney said he had personally demonstrated conservation by putting his personality into an "energy-saving mode." Cheney, unsurprisingly, enjoyed the revamped version, describing the bionic-heart skit as one of his favorites.

Even beyond the vice president's absences, the West Wing in the weeks following the attacks was almost unrecognizable. Large, menacing men swathed in black and armed with assault rifles and shotguns suddenly showed up everywhere. Tours were cut off. Access to the West Wing was restricted. The staff table at the White House mess was largely empty many days, as if aides were "either unable or unwilling to be seen" taking a break from work. "We were all under an almost suffocating amount of tension and stress," as Christie put it. Staff members went to work thinking they might never get married or have children because there was a decent chance they might be killed—all very dramatic sounding years later and yet the way it felt at the time. "You had brothers, sisters, mothers, fathers, spouses, telling people you can't work there anymore," Joe Hagin said. Bush's schedule was thrown out, and it took three weeks for his schedulers to get it back in order. The White House chef began preparing comfort food for the president, a lot of Black Angus beef fillet with gratin of silver corn or garlic-scented chicken breast with asparagus.

Each morning greeted Bush and Cheney with a new Threat Matrix, a compendium of potential horrors, as many as a hundred threats a day culled from a broad array of intelligence sources. They included everything from wiretap surveillance to anonymous tips; almost nothing, it seemed, was left out, no matter how far-fetched. In the post–September 11 world, no one wanted to take a chance of missing anything. But the shotgun approach undercut the usefulness of the reports since separating the real from the phantom was virtually impossible. The president and the vice president understood it was in part a "cover-your-ass kind of bureaucratic procedure," as Cheney put it. But bombarding the commander in chief and his number two with endless reports of possible mayhem and tragedy naturally influenced the approach they took to defending the country. "It had a huge impact on our psyches," Condoleezza Rice recalled. George Tenet later said it was impossible to read what crossed his desk "and be anything other than scared to death." Laura Bush remembered the effect on her husband. "He didn't bring it all home," she said, "but he brought enough that I could see the lines cut deeper in his face and could hear him next to me lying awake at night, his mind still working."

For Bush, this was his new mission. Until September 11, "Bush lacked a big organizing idea," observed David Frum, his speechwriter. Now this war on terrorism would define his tenure. His domestic agenda, compassionate conservatism, all of it would take a backseat. "Nine-eleven blew him away, like it blew all of us away," said Joe O'Neill, his friend. "All of a sudden, that overrode everything, getting reelected, everything. We were attacked, and so he was going to go after them." And with his approval rating hitting 90 percent, the highest of any president ever recorded, he had considerable latitude.

For Cheney, this was not so much a new mission as the mission for which he had long prepared. All those years focusing on continuity of government and homeland security seemed validated. "I think he has a certain level of fatalism and a feeling that the world is not a safe place," said Anne Womack, who served as his press secretary, "and when 9/11 happened, my guess is that it confirmed a lot of things that he had felt for a long time." From then on, nothing else would matter as much. "How are the bad guys going to get us?" said Kevin Kellems, another press secretary. "He woke up every morning with that first thing on his mind." Pete Williams, his friend and former aide, said the vice president concluded that "the country was fundamentally unprepared" and "it was really kind of up to him."

Despite the surreal physical separation, Bush turned to Cheney in a way he had not before. Bush had let the vice president handle the transition during the recount, manage legislative strategy on Capitol Hill, and drive decisions on issues like energy. But as a former governor, Bush had command of most of the issues that dominated the national conversation until September 11. Now he was heading into unfamiliar territory and happy to have Cheney as his guide. "In the period after that," recalled Neil Patel, the Cheney aide, "they were almost closer than ever."

THE DAYS THAT followed the address to Congress were a blur of meetings and decisions, many of them improvisational as Bush and Cheney cobbled together a war plan that combined traditional military action, special forces, diplomacy, law enforcement, financial tools, and intelligence operations.

On September 21, the day after the speech, Bush invited Cheney and the military team to the study on the second floor of his living quarters to talk about attacking Afghanistan, assuming the Taliban did not comply with his ultimatum. He cleared two hours from his schedule, an unusually long stretch in any president's day, and seemed in no rush even when the discussion went long. "We're okay, Don," he assured Rumsfeld when the defense secretary hurried the generals briefing him. "This is important information."

General Tommy Franks, head of Central Command, which had responsibility for the region, presented a four-phase plan of attack on Afghanistan. Franks was from Midland, Texas, like Bush, and had gone to school with Laura. He bonded with the president in Lone Star fashion. Once, when Bush asked how he was doing, Franks answered, "I'm sharper than a frog hair split four ways." Shucking his jacket and lighting up a cigar, Bush listened intently as the general outlined the succession of actions and basing rights he would need. The president's dog Barney wandered around the room. Bush struck aides as focused but more relaxed than he had been since the attack.

Rumsfeld warned that the plan was crude and quickly assembled. "You are not going to find this plan completely fulfilling," he said. "We don't."

General Hugh Shelton, the Joint Chiefs chairman appointed by Bill Clinton, thought that Bush, like his predecessor, "had a solid grasp of the tactical, operational specifics as well as the overall strategic concerns." Bush wanted the operation to demonstrate an enduring commitment. He wanted a sense of progression, not just a single strike.

Bush asked Franks how soon he could begin.

"Mr. President, in about two weeks," he said.

"I understand," Bush said. "Two weeks."

Franks noted that they could begin an air campaign sooner but wanted to launch Special Forces operations simultaneously and that would require negotiations for basing and transit rights with neighbors like Uzbekistan.

"I understand," Bush said. "A large air operation would make a statement."

He paused for a moment and then added, "On the other hand, I'm willing to wait. When we do this, we'll do it right. My message to the American people is to be patient."

But patience was difficult with Americans itching for action. Bush worried that the longer it took to respond, the harder it would be to keep the public behind him. So when he heard that weekend that Secretary of the Treasury Paul O'Neill was planning to announce moves to freeze assets of people and groups linked to terrorism, the president tracked down Karen Hughes at Sunday school.

"This financial action is the first battle of the war," he said. "Why am I not announcing this?"

The next morning, September 24, Bush appeared in the Rose Garden with O'Neill and Colin Powell to announce the order. "Money is the lifeblood of terrorist operations," he declared. "Today, we're asking the world to stop payment."

FOR YEARS, BUSH had started each day reading the Bible, and in the days following September 11 he sought comfort from the holy book. One morning shortly after the attacks, he read Proverbs 21:15: *When justice is done, it brings joy to the righteous but terror to evildoers.*

The phrase may have stuck in Bush's head. On September 25, he took a short motorcade ride over to FBI headquarters, which served as a venue for a speech urging Congress to pass the new law enforcement powers he was seeking. "I see things this way," Bush said. "The people who did this act on America, and who may be planning further acts, are evil people. They don't represent an ideology. They don't represent a legitimate political group of people. They're flat evil. That's all they can think about, is evil." He later used the word "evildoers" twice to describe terrorists.

The speech bothered Ari Fleischer, who worried it might sound unsophisticated. In the car back to the White House, Fleischer advised Bush to go easy on the word "evil," suggesting it was too simple.

"If this isn't good versus evil, what is?" Bush countered. He reminded Fleischer that Ronald Reagan had not gone to Berlin to say "put a gate in this wall" or "take down a few bricks." He said "tear down this wall," all of it. Sometimes simple was best.

Bush was getting second-guessed at every turn. Not much later, Hughes broached his use of the word "folks" to describe the attackers.

"Mr. President, I'm not sure you ought to be calling the terrorists 'folks.' It sounds like the nice people next door."

"Folks aren't all good," he said. "There are a lot of bad folks in the world."

"But it just sounds too familiar, too folksy," she said. "These are trained killers and it just doesn't sound right to call them folks."

Bush, irritated, turned to Andy Card, Condoleezza Rice, and Karl Rove. "Anybody else not like anything else I say?"

On September 26, Bush and Cheney got word that the first CIA paramilitary operatives had arrived in Afghanistan. Fifteen days after September 11, the United States was ready to take the fight to the enemy, implementing a strategy to dislodge the Taliban by using local Afghan forces on the ground aided by the power of American munitions from the air. Arriving in a Russian-made helicopter with a suitcase filled with $3 million in $100 bills, the CIA operatives were to hook up with the Northern Alliance, the ragtag collection of mainly Tajik and Uzbek fighters who had been waging a largely ineffective rebellion against the Taliban government since its inception but now had the world's only superpower behind them.

But as war in Afghanistan loomed, Bush also had his mind on something else. Even though he had shut down Paul Wolfowitz at Camp David, he had been pondering what to do about Iraq. After the National Security Council meeting that morning, Bush asked Rumsfeld to stay behind. The two talked alone in the Oval Office.

"I want you to develop a plan to invade Iraq," Bush said. "Do it outside the normal channels. Do it creatively so we don't have to take so much over."

Rumsfeld was surprised. The Pentagon's on-the-shelf plan for Iraq was basically just Desert Storm redux. But since he was already reviewing all of the military's stock war plans anyway, he told Bush, he could have Tommy Franks update the Iraq plan without drawing too much attention.

The meeting, which would remain secret until Rumsfeld revealed it in his memoir in 2011, was the first time Bush set in motion the action that would ultimately shape his presidency. How intent he was at that point to go all the way was uncertain. Iraq had been a preoccupation of Bush and Cheney's from the start, but that did not mean they always intended to invade. There was little public appetite for war with Iraq, and Bush had done nothing in his first eight months in office to build a case for it. "No one in the discussions at that time was pushing for an invasion of Iraq," said Zalmay Khalilzad, a national security aide who would later go on to become ambassador to Baghdad. When Rumsfeld urged a high-level meeting to craft a new Iraq strategy in July, Bush did not follow up. It is possible he might have found cause for war eventually anyway, but it is also possible he would have simply waged a more aggressive version of the shadow campaign that had been going on since his father's time, with covert operations to undermine Hussein and aid to opposition groups seeking regime change, everything short of troops on the ground.

Either way, the experience of September 11 changed the dynamics. Even if Iraq did not have a relationship with al-Qaeda, as Cheney suspected, Hussein now looked more dangerous in a world where the United States could no longer afford to let threats fester. If Hussein once seemed manageable in the box Washington had constructed for him, it no longer seemed reasonable to Bush or Cheney to leave in power an openly hostile enemy of the United States who might have chemical, biological, or even possibly nuclear weapons that he could use himself or potentially pass along to terrorists.

In years to come, that calculation would look different, but at that moment it seemed logical. Bush gave Rumsfeld his marching orders.

But before letting him leave, Bush raised a personal matter.

"Dick told me about your son," Bush said. Rumsfeld's grown son, Nick, had been struggling with drug addiction and just checked into a treatment facility.

Rumsfeld, the tough man, unexpectedly broke down and cried. He could not even speak. Finally, recovering a bit of composure, he said, "I love him so much."

Bush was struck by the unusual display of emotion. "I can't imagine the burden you are carrying for the country and your son," he told Rumsfeld.

Then Bush stood up, came from around his desk, and hugged him.

Rumsfeld later jotted down notes in his day calendar about the meeting with the president. "Amazing day," he wrote. "He is a fine human being." And then at the bottom of the page, he scribbled, "Joyce says I have to let Nick go."

WHILE CIA OPERATIVES went to work, Bush and Cheney braced for more attacks at home. Every night when Bush went to bed, he felt a moment of relief that another day had passed without incident. Al-Qaeda had America on its heels, and now was surely the time it would press that advantage. It would take weeks, months, and even years to tighten security for a country as large and open as the United States, and it seemed implausible that terrorists would not mount follow-up attacks. "There was a pervasive feeling that 9/11 itself was not the end of the story," remembered John McLaughlin, the deputy CIA director.

On September 28, McLaughlin sat in for Tenet to deliver the daily intelligence briefing to Bush and Cheney. They went through the various threats and tidbits of information picked up in the previous twenty-four hours.

Finally, the president, anxious and edgy, asked, "Why do you think nothing else has happened?"

McLaughlin did not have a certain answer. "Tighter security matters," he offered. What they were doing made a difference. Their aggressive efforts to disrupt al-Qaeda, he theorized, might have militants scattered and in hiding.

Bush hoped so. But he soon had reason to doubt it. On the morning of October 4, Bush got word of an attack in Florida using anthrax, a deadly biological agent. A photo editor at the *Sun*, the supermarket tabloid, had been hospitalized after opening an envelope containing the spores that had been mailed to the newspaper. No one knew if it was the work of terrorists, but Bush was anxious that this was the beginning of something much worse. Tightening security at airports was one thing. How could they stop a weapon they could not even see?

Bush was heading to the State Department for a speech, but his mind was elsewhere. He looked haggard and worried, his shoulders slouched as he stared out the window of his car. "When Bush got the first information about Florida, nobody knew what the facts were yet," remembered Ari Fleischer, who accompanied him. "That was the lowest I ever saw Bush."

Bush picked up the phone and called Karen Hughes, who was at home working on a statement. "I'm here with Ari," Bush said. "Are you on a secure line?"

No, she said.

He went ahead anyway. "Well, we may have a case of anthrax in Fort Lauderdale, Florida. We don't know the source, it appears to be a high concentration in one person. This is a critical moment. We'll need to calm people. I may need to make a statement."

In the end, they decided not to have the White House issue a statement but to have it come from the Department of Health and Human Services to avoid a panic. The statement emphasized that "so far this appears to be an isolated case." At least they hoped it was. The Florida photo editor, Bob

Stevens, died the next day, the first anthrax death in the United States in twenty-five years. The question was who was next. "There was a real, almost fatalistic concern that we were going to get hit again," remembered Dean McGrath, Cheney's deputy chief of staff. "In that atmosphere, the anthrax attack threw people for a loop."

AMID THE FEARS of a second wave, Bush and Cheney cast about for any advantage they could find, pressing intelligence agencies to push further. The National Security Agency, which operated spy satellites and tapped telephones and e-mail servers overseas, lifted some of its self-imposed restrictions. For years, in the interest of protecting civil liberties, it had employed a practice called "minimization"; if American citizens not under suspicion turned up in overseas eavesdropping, names and identifying information were generally omitted from reports. But after September 11, Lieutenant General Michael Hayden, the agency director, removed those safeguards on communications out of Afghanistan.

All of this was deemed legal by government lawyers. But when George Tenet mentioned the move to Bush and Cheney during a morning briefing, he made light of longtime sensitivities about the agency's activities.

Oh, by the way, Tenet said, Hayden is going to jail.

Tell him we will bail him out, Cheney replied dryly.

Turning serious, Tenet explained the process. Bush and Cheney had no objection and wondered if Hayden was going far enough.

Is there anything else he could do? Cheney asked.

Tenet said he would find out.

After the meeting, Tenet called Hayden. "Is there anything else you could do?"

"Not with my current authorities," Hayden said.

"That is not what I asked you," Tenet said. "Is there anything else you could do?"

Hayden said he would call back. After huddling with his staff, he came up with a plan to vastly widen the net. Under the Foreign Intelligence Surveillance Act of 1978, the NSA could target communications involving someone inside the United States only with a warrant from a secret court. But with so many foreign telephone calls and e-mail now coming through American communications trunks, it was impractical, Hayden and his team concluded, to seek individual warrants. The average wait when the NSA asked the Justice Department to obtain covert permission was four to six weeks. Even using emergency authorization under the current law usually involved a delay of a day or so.

A plan was devised to bypass the FISA law by citing the president's inherent power under Article II of the Constitution to defend the nation. The NSA would be authorized to collect the data and content of telephone calls and e-mail when there was probable cause to believe one person in the communication was in Afghanistan or preparing for terrorist acts.

"Mr. Vice President," Hayden said, "we can do this, but you know, we really have to be careful. Ever since the Church Committee, my agency up there, NSA, we have been at bat with a one-ball, two-strike count on us, you know. We aren't taking close pitches."

"Okay," Cheney said. "I understand."

The reference to the Church Committee touched directly on Cheney's long-standing concern about limits placed on executive power. Named for Senator Frank Church, an Idaho Democrat, the committee exposed abuses by the CIA, FBI and NSA in the 1970s, leading to reforms, including the FISA law. The committee was a thorn in the side of the Ford White House run by Cheney, who considered its queries an intrusion into executive activities.

Bush summoned Hayden to the Oval Office to hear about his plan. Clearly Cheney had already briefed him.

"Mike, thank you for coming," the president began. "I understand your concerns, but you know, if there are things we could be doing, we ought to be doing them."

With the World Trade Center still smoldering and body parts still being recovered, the imperative was to do anything conceivable to avoid another attack. If the government had the ability to track communications of terror cells, Bush and Cheney reasoned, they had to do it. No legal niceties should stand in the way of that. If there were another attack, how could they explain not doing everything in their power to prevent it? *Whatever it takes*, the men at Ground Zero had told Bush.

Hayden went home that evening and took a walk with his wife. "I have some choices here," he told her. Without disclosing details, he said, "I can't not do what I am being asked, but this is not without risk."

Bush signed an order on October 4 authorizing the new program. He built safeguards into it, requiring it be recertified roughly every thirty or forty-five days. But in the rush to start, Attorney General John Ashcroft was asked to certify the program on the same day he was told about it, and the first formal Office of Legal Counsel opinion supporting its legality by a young lawyer named John Yoo was not drafted until a month later, on November 2.

There was discussion about whether Congress should be told. Bush agreed to inform only the leadership. Cheney invited the Gang of Eight—

leaders of both parties from both houses, plus chairmen and ranking minority members of the Intelligence Committees. Cheney and Hayden explained the program and what it could do.

"Do we need legislation?" Cheney asked.

Speaker Dennis Hastert said later that "everybody looked around the room and said no, I don't think we need to."

The lawmakers were forbidden to discuss the program with colleagues or aides, so they had no way to research more rigorously its legality. Indeed, virtually no one else would know about the program for years, not even some of Bush's closest advisers. David Addington personally drafted the reauthorization orders and delivered them to the NSA himself. When NSA lawyers asked to see the Justice Department memo outlining the program's legal basis, Addington refused. Even Donald Rumsfeld was not informed at first, although the NSA reported to him. This would remain for four years one of the most protected secrets of Bush and Cheney's war on terror.

10

"We're going to lose our prey"

President Bush was on the couch in his office in the Laurel Lodge at Camp David the following weekend as Michael Gerson sat at the desk typing a statement. The military was ready to begin operations in Afghanistan. Bush did not want a piece of rhetoric, just a straightforward message describing what was happening in firm tones.

While Gerson composed, Bush worked the phones notifying Senator Trent Lott and other congressional leaders. The secure lines kept cutting out, aggravating Bush.

At one point, Bush put his hand over the phone. "Are you cleared for any of this?" he asked Gerson.

"I don't think so," Gerson answered.

"You are now," Bush said.

Events were moving so quickly that much was happening on the fly. Bush had canceled a visit from friends the previous weekend because of reported threats, but this weekend Michael and Nancy Weiss from Texas were with him at Camp David along with Gerson, Karen Hughes, Andy Card, and Condoleezza Rice. He went through the motions without giving away to his friends what was about to happen. Laura Bush had comfort food made for dinner that night, October 6: chicken-fried steak with mashed potatoes and banana pudding for dessert. During the meal, friends noticed, an aide would bring notes to Bush and Rice, and they would scribble on them and send them back. The next morning Bush took his friends with him by helicopter to Emmitsburg, Maryland, where he marked the twentieth annual tribute to fallen firefighters. When they boarded the helicopters again, Bush began practicing his statement. "You can surmise that we started bombing Afghanistan," he told the Weisses.

Back at the White House, the red light on the camera in the Treaty Room went on at 1:00 p.m. "Good afternoon," Bush said. "On my orders, the United States military has begun strikes against al-Qaeda terrorist training camps and military installations of the Taliban regime in Afghanistan. These carefully targeted actions are designed to disrupt the use of Afghanistan as a terrorist base of operations and to attack the military capability of the Taliban regime." He had given the Taliban a chance. "And now the Taliban will pay a price."

He recognized others would pay a price too. "I recently received a touching letter that says a lot about the state of America in these difficult times—a letter from a 4th-grade girl, with a father in the military. 'As much as I don't want my Dad to fight,' she wrote, 'I'm willing to give him to you.' " He wrapped up in seven minutes, closing with the line from his address to Congress. "The battle is now joined on many fronts. We will not waver. We will not tire. We will not falter. And we will not fail."

The bombs that rained down on Kabul brought into vivid relief the anger and retribution of a superpower, but days would pass without substantial movement as twenty-first-century technology met fifteenth-century battleground. In relying on Northern Alliance fighters clad in plastic sandals and flowing robes rather than inserting a large American ground force, Bush and Cheney were hostage to some extent to a primitive army they could not control. And as Rumsfeld and Paul Wolfowitz predicted, the bombing quickly took out the few legitimate targets from the air.

At the same time, the home front felt increasingly vulnerable. On October 15, Bush was told that Tom Daschle's Senate office had received a letter with anthrax powder in it. Since the first attack in Florida, anthrax had also been found in a letter sent to the NBC News anchorman Tom Brokaw. Like the Florida letter, the Daschle and Brokaw letters were marked by hand "09–11–01" and mailed from Trenton, New Jersey. Mail rooms were shut down and bags of mail deposited in the vice president's office on Capitol Hill since it was not used as regularly as other space; antibiotics were snapped up all over town. Bush and Cheney wanted to know who was behind it, and suspicions turned to al-Qaeda and Iraq.

In Afghanistan, the new form of warfare was bound to foster territorial tension and command confusion. The CIA had taken the lead in organizing the Northern Alliance on the ground, while the military would stick to a "light footprint" and concentrate its energies on bombing targets identified by the agency's operatives and allies. Sure enough, the unprecedented arrangement boiled over at a National Security Council meeting the next day, October 16.

Rumsfeld complained this was the CIA's strategy and "we're just executing the strategy."

John McLaughlin, the deputy CIA director sitting in for George Tenet, said the agency was simply supporting the regional military commander, Tommy Franks, and had made clear that once Afghanistan became a war zone, he would have the final word.

"No," Rumsfeld shot back, "you guys are in charge."

Bush noticed Richard Armitage, the deputy secretary of state sitting in for Colin Powell, shaking his head and asked what he thought.

"Well, sir, I think it's all FUBAR," he said, an old-fashioned acronym for "fucked up beyond all recognition."

Bush, frustrated, turned to Condoleezza Rice. "Condi, fix it," he ordered.

VICE PRESIDENT CHENEY was about to die. Or so he was told.

More than five weeks after the September 11 attacks, he was finally going to New York to view the damage for the first time. He had accepted an invitation to address the Alfred E. Smith Memorial Foundation Dinner, an annual white-tie dinner benefiting Catholic charities.

But as Air Force Two raced north to New York on October 18, Cheney got word of another possible threat. Scooter Libby told him that biological sensors at the White House had detected the possibility of botulinum toxin, an agent so powerful and lethal that, Cheney was told, as little as a single gram could theoretically kill one million people. Anyone who had been in the White House could have been exposed—including the president and the vice president. Bush had just arrived for a summit in Shanghai, where it was the middle of the night, so Cheney decided not to wake him until there was more information.

When his jet landed, Cheney instructed Libby to stay on board and learn more while the vice president flew by helicopter to Ground Zero. The site was as horrific as it had been the day it happened. If mere box cutters were enough to cause this, Cheney could only imagine the swath of death and destruction that terrorists with biological weapons like botulinum toxin could wreak. By the time he got to the Waldorf Astoria hotel to get ready for the dinner, he found Libby waiting to update him. There had indeed been two positive hits on a White House detector. Further tests were being conducted that would provide more definitive results by noon the next day.

Cheney already had a secure videoconference scheduled with Bush for when he woke in Shanghai.

Bush strode into a specially designed blue tent set up inside the Ritz-Carlton to block Chinese eavesdropping.

"Good morning, Dick," Bush said.

Gazing at the video screen, he saw Cheney in white tie and tails for the speech, but the vice president seemed stricken. Bush asked if everything was all right.

"Mr. President," Cheney started soberly, "the White House biological detectors have registered the presence of botulinum toxin and there is no reliable antidote. Those of us who have been exposed to it could die."

Bush, taken aback, sought to understand what he had just heard. "What was that, Dick?" he asked.

Colin Powell jumped in. "What is the exposure time?" he asked.

Bush and Condoleezza Rice assumed he was calculating his last time in the White House, trying to figure out whether he had been exposed too. It turned out he had been there within the possible exposure window.

Since all they could do was wait for tests, the discussion soon moved on to Afghanistan, but the possible biological outbreak remained on everyone's mind. After the conference, Bush asked Rice to find out when they would know. It turned out mice were being injected, and if there was a presence of the agent, they would die. So, Rice told Bush, conveying Stephen Hadley's explanation, if the mice's feet were up, they were all exposed; if they were feet down, they were fine.

Cheney learned separately from John Ashcroft and Tom Ridge that fifty-eight hours had passed since the last sensor went off, meaning they would probably be showing symptoms by now if they had been exposed. He went ahead with his speech at the charity dinner, joking that "it's nice, for a change, to be at a disclosed location." He went on to vow a relentless war on terrorists that will "only end with their complete and permanent destruction." But in China, the hours stretched on agonizingly slowly as Bush, Rice, and Powell waited to learn their fate. Finally, Rice got word from Washington. "Feet down, not up," she told Bush. It was a false alarm; there was no botulinum toxin.

The fear inside the West Wing grew on October 23, when Bush and Cheney were told that Pakistan had arrested two nuclear scientists who had been in contact with Osama bin Laden, possibly to help al-Qaeda build a bomb. It was heart-stopping news, everything Cheney had feared since the moment the planes hit the Twin Towers. The Pakistanis had picked up the two scientists in response to a tip from American intelligence agencies. When Bush and Cheney sat down with the rest of the National Security Council in the Situation Room that morning, they presented the most alarming variant of what they had been told.

Bin Laden "may have a nuclear device" that could destroy half of Washington, Bush told the team, and there was enough unaccounted-for Russian-made weapons-grade fissile material to produce a bomb.

Cheney looked pale, thought General Richard Myers, who had succeeded Hugh Shelton as chairman of the Joint Chiefs.

"We have to intensify the hunt for Osama bin Laden," the vice president insisted.

Later that day, Bush learned that two U.S. Postal Service workers in Washington had died from anthrax poisoning. They had evidently handled poisoned letters coming through their facility. Since the tainted letter arrived in Daschle's office a week before, several other exposures had been reported as well. But Bush and Cheney still had no answer about who was behind it.

Bush was "deeply affected" by the anthrax attacks, his aide Scott McClellan observed. It was an unsettling time—the botulinum scare, the rogue Pakistani nuclear scientists, and the anthrax. When Bush's cousin John Ellis came to visit, the two went out to the South Lawn after dinner to walk the dog. The president noticed a plane approaching Ronald Reagan Washington National Airport. If it turned left and headed toward the White House, he observed, they would have less than a minute before being killed.

To Cheney, the latest events confirmed what he already felt. "The threat going forward wasn't just another 9/11-style attack," he observed later. "It was, and remains, the possibility that the next one could be far deadlier and more devastating than anything we have ever seen."

BUSH HAD JUST finished his workout on the evening of October 25 when Rice came to see him in the White House residence. He was still in his gym shorts and socks. She said she was worried about the mood among his war cabinet advisers, who were nervous about a quagmire in Afghanistan, a prospect that increasingly flavored media accounts.

"You know, Mr. President," she said, "the mood isn't very good among the principals and people are concerned about what's going on. And I want to know if you're concerned about the fact that things are not moving."

"Of course I'm concerned about the fact that things aren't moving."

"Well, do you want to start looking at alternative strategies?"

"Well, what alternative strategies would we be looking at?" he asked.

"Well, you know, there always is the thought that you could use more Americans in this. You could Americanize this up front."

"You know," Bush said, "it hasn't been that long."

"That's right."

"Do you think it's working?"

She ducked but suggested he address the matter with his team.

He agreed. But before he did, he asked Cheney's advice. "Is there any qualm in your mind about this strategy we've developed?" Bush asked.

Cheney answered flatly, "No, Mr. President."

At the National Security Council meeting the next morning, October 26, Bush let the participants make their routine presentations before raising the point.

"I just want to make sure that all of us did agree on this plan, right?"

He went around the table, asking the cabinet secretaries one by one, and then their deputies on the back wall. Everyone agreed; they had embraced the strategy.

"Anybody have any ideas they want to put on the table?" he asked.

No one did.

Fine, Bush said, then they should stick with the plan and not let the press panic them. It had only been nineteen days. "We're going to stay confident and patient, cool and steady," he said.

Bush and Rice thought they sensed relief. Perhaps that had defused the tension.

The same day, Bush signed legislation providing the kinds of expanded powers John Ashcroft had first broached at Camp David. The measure allowed the government to obtain "roving wiretaps" targeting individuals regardless of which telephone they used. It empowered federal agents to obtain orders allowing them to seize "any tangible things" related to a security investigation, including business customer records. It expanded the power to seize assets and deport suspects while lengthening the statute of limitations and sentences for terrorism-related crimes. Terrorism investigators would gain powers already available in drug and racketeering prosecutions. But the language was expansive enough that the government would have vast new abilities to peer into the lives of citizens it suspected of extremist ties. Congress set some provisions to expire unless renewed after several years but otherwise brushed off objections that the measure violated civil liberties. The Senate passed it with just one no vote and the House with just sixty-six.

Lawmakers were in a rush to bolster the nation's defenses and to show how tough they were at the same time. "Hardly able to restrain themselves, the Committee labeled the bill the 'PATRIOT Act,'" a White House memo noted after it cleared its first hurdle. Bush never retreated from the measure, but he did regret the name because it implied that its opponents "were unpatriotic." After leaving office, he concluded, "I should have pushed Congress to change the name of the bill before I signed it."

The drumbeat of security threats reached a crescendo a few days later when intercepted conversations of al-Qaeda operatives indicated something big on the way, possibly a radiological attack that would be more devastating than September 11. At the National Security Council meeting on October 29, Bush was in a defiant mood.

"Those bastards are going to find me exactly here," he said. "I'm not going anywhere. And if they get me, they're going to get me right here."

Cheney pushed back gently. "This isn't about you," the vice president told him. "This is about our Constitution."

The Constitution, though, sometimes seemed to depend on the eye of the beholder. It was around this time that the NSA warrantless surveillance program came up for reauthorization for the first time. Michael Hayden, the agency director, believed the program was producing results. But as he discussed the reauthorization with David Addington, he learned something he did not know.

"Now, you know the order allows you to do domestic to domestic?" Addington asked. The order had been written so broadly that it authorized the NSA to tap not just calls or e-mails with at least one person overseas without warrants but even communications entirely within the United States.

Hayden was surprised. "No, I didn't know that, David," he said. Then he asked that it be taken out. "My personal view, number one, we are a foreign intelligence agency. It is not what we do. Number two, my personal metric for doing that is if we are doing domestic to domestic, I am going to court. Okay?"

"Okay," Addington said, and then swung around in his chair back to his computer to rewrite the order. Bush signed it November 2.

OF ALL THE duties in those first weeks of the war, one that took an inordinate toll on Bush's stress level was the prospect of throwing out the first pitch at the third game of the World Series in New York. It was meant to be a powerful display of resolve during a time of crisis, and what better place than the city that had borne the brunt of the attacks. But Bush was nervous. The first time he threw out a pitch as president, way back in April at the opening of Miller Park in Milwaukee, the ball hit the dirt. Not many were paying attention then. Now the eyes of the world would be on him.

Dressed in a New York Fire Department windbreaker, the zipper pulled all the way up to his neck to cover the Kevlar vest the Secret Service made him wear, Bush greeted the players in the Yankees' dugout before the game on October 30. In case he did not feel anxious enough, he ran into the star shortstop Derek Jeter.

"Mr. President, are you going to throw from the base of the mound or are you going to take the rubber?" Jeter asked.

"From the base of the mound," Bush answered.

"I wouldn't do that if I were you," Jeter warned.

"Why not?"

"This is New York. If you throw from the base of the mound, they're going to boo you."

"Do you really think they'll do that?"

"This is New York. They'll boo you."

Resigned, Bush said, "I guess I'll take the mound."

Then, as Jeter headed off, Bush heard him call out, "If you take the rubber, Mr. President, don't bounce it. They'll boo you."

Bush took the pitcher's mound amid the cheering crowd and flashing cameras, his adrenaline racing as some 55,820 sets of eyes trained on him. He offered a stiff wave and a stiffer thumbs-up. "USA Fears Nobody, Play Ball," read a hand-painted banner in the stands. Bush's eyes looked a little moist as he took in the moment. Then he sent the ball sailing sixty and a half feet cleanly over the plate and right into the glove of the catcher Todd Greene. The crowd roared. Plainly relieved, Bush did not smile but had a look of satisfaction on his face, as if to say, *Take that, Jeter.* As he headed off the field, the crowd chanted, "U-S-A, U-S-A!"

THE NEXT MORNING, Bush was brought back to earth when he picked up the *New York Times* and saw a pessimistic front-page story on Afghanistan by R. W. "Johnny" Apple Jr., the renowned correspondent who had covered Vietnam before a long career in Washington. "The ominous word 'quagmire' has begun to haunt conversations" about Afghanistan, Apple wrote.

Bush was aggravated. "They don't get it," he vented at his morning meeting with advisers. "How many times do you have to tell them it's going to be a different kind of war?" He later told a sympathetic biographer, "I mean, we were at this thing for three weeks and all of a sudden there was kind of a breathless condemnation of the strategy." If it were just the media, that would be one thing. His own team remained beset by doubts despite his earlier pep talk.

With the outbreak of hostilities in Afghanistan, the administration needed to figure out what to do with Taliban and al-Qaeda fighters captured on the battlefield. An interagency task force had wrestled with the issue for weeks, much to the frustration of Cheney and Addington, who had little patience for foot-dragging. When Brad Berenson, a White House lawyer assigned to the task force, reported back to his bosses, Alberto Gonzales, and his deputy, Tim Flanigan, that good progress was being made but no order would be ready before Thanksgiving, their "jaws dropped."

Gonzales was a Bush favorite, one of eight children of a Mexican American construction worker who grew up in a two-room house in a Texas town actually named Humble; he joined the air force, earned his way into Harvard Law School, and became a successful Houston attorney. Bush had brought him into his inner circle in Texas, nicknaming him Fredo and calling him *mi abogado* in his rough Spanish. But Gonzales was a quiet, unassuming, even passive figure. So as Cheney grew alarmed by the glacial pace of the detention task force, it fell to Flanigan and Addington, who stepped in and "kind of took control of it personally." The two adapted the military tribunal order signed by Franklin Roosevelt to prosecute Nazi saboteurs in World War II, an order later upheld by the Supreme Court. If it was good enough then, it should be good enough now. But decades of international and domestic law on the subject had been enacted in the interim, most significantly the Geneva Conventions.

On November 10, Cheney convened a small meeting in the Roosevelt Room with Addington and others. Among those uninvited and unaware were Colin Powell, Condoleezza Rice, and the uniformed leaders of the military. When the order drafted by Flanigan and Addington was presented, John Ashcroft objected, arguing that as attorney general he oversaw prosecutions and it should not be up to a defense secretary to take away suspects. Cheney told him he already had legal concurrence from Ashcroft's own Justice Department, in the name of John Yoo. Ashcroft erupted. Every time Cheney tried to get in a word, the attorney general talked over him. The vice president saw Ashcroft's concerns as old-fashioned turf battling, but to assuage him, Cheney had the order tweaked to make clear that the president himself would "reserve the authority" to decide when to transfer suspects to a military commission. For Cheney, the need for swift action was reinforced the next day, November 11, when Ibn al-Shaykh al-Libi, an al-Qaeda commander, was captured in Pakistan.

Cheney showed up at the Oval Office two days later with a four-page order drafted by Addington and Flanigan authorizing military commissions. Bush readily agreed, and Cheney took the order back to Addington, who gave it to Flanigan, who gave it to Berenson and told him to have it formalized for the president's signature. Berenson, not knowing that Rice and Powell had been bypassed, took the order to the staff secretary, the office that handled presidential paperwork. Stuart Bowen, the deputy staff secretary on duty, insisted on distributing the order around the building for review according to usual procedure. Berenson left and returned with Flanigan. "Don't worry about it," Flanigan told Bowen. "The president's already been briefed by the vice president." Then he added, "The president's waiting for it right now."

Bowen figured if the president was waiting, then it was not for him to get in the way. He put the order in proper format, and the lawyers headed to the Oval Office, where Bush was preparing to leave for Texas to host Vladimir Putin at his ranch. The rotor blades of Marine One were already spinning on the South Lawn outside the building.

"This is it?" Bush asked.

"Yes," Andy Card said.

Bush gave the order a quick read, "more like a scan or a skim than a word-for-word read," Berenson remembered, since he had already looked at it earlier that day. Still standing, he pulled a Sharpie pen out of his pocket, signed it, and handed it back. Then he and Card headed to the helicopter.

Berenson chased after them to ask about a public announcement. "What do you want us to do by way of the rollout?" he asked.

"Nothing," Card answered. "Just let it go."

In the end, a copy of the order was released without ceremony. But once again, as on climate change, Cheney had outflanked rivals to push through a far-reaching decision. Cheney's relationship with Bush and understanding of how to work the system had established his office as "a real power center and a place to be feared," Berenson said. Yet that did not mean Cheney manipulated the president, as some assumed. Bush was sometimes influenced by moderating views when he heard them, but by and large when he went along with Cheney, it was because he agreed with him. "I never got the sense that Cheney was dragging Bush to the right on these issues," said Berenson. "To me, they always appeared very unified in a two-man scull rowing hard in the same direction."

CHENEY WAS SIMULTANEOUSLY engaged in another debate. Powell felt they should keep their Afghan allies, the Northern Alliance, composed mainly of Tajiks and Uzbeks, from taking Kabul for fear of alienating Pashtuns in the south and their patrons in Pakistan, and to avoid absorbing all available manpower. Cheney and Donald Rumsfeld thought that was foolish. They needed a victory, and they should let the Northern Alliance move.

The debate culminated the same day Bush signed the military commission order. Rumsfeld fired off a testy two-page memo. "Mr. President," he wrote, "I think it is a mistake for the United States to be saying we are not going to attack Kabul. To do so, tells the Taliban and the Al Qaida that Kabul can be a safe haven for them. The goal in this conflict is to make life complicated for the Taliban and the Al Qaida, not to make it simple."

But even as he wrote that, the Northern Alliance was already swarming into Kabul, making the point moot. Whatever commitments were made to stay out of the capital were disregarded when Northern Alliance commanders heard the Taliban had slipped out of the city in the middle of the night to retreat south. Moving into the city, the Northern Alliance commanders explained to their American patrons, was simply a matter of providing security for an abandoned population.

However it happened, the fall of Kabul capped an extraordinary five-week campaign to topple the Taliban, and Bush and Cheney were struck by the images of cheering Afghan men, raising fists, throwing off turbans, cutting off beards, and shouting, "Long live America!" This was not the end of the war. But the capture of the capital represented the first tangible victory in the emerging war on terror. The sensitivities of the Pashtun population and the Pakistani government would need to be managed, but despite the doubts the war strategy had worked. The challenge now was to pursue the remnants of Taliban forces to finish them off, destroy remaining al-Qaeda bases, and track down Osama bin Laden. It all seemed possible that day.

For the moment, it looked as though Bush and Cheney had accomplished what Britain and Russia had failed to do. Afghanistan, after all, was the place where empires went to die, as Condoleezza Rice, the Russia scholar, knew well. For the Russians, the disastrous, decade-long war in the twilight years of the Soviet Union was recent enough to remain deeply scarring. So there was some irony that even at this moment of triumph for the United States, Vladimir Putin was at the White House visiting.

Bush and Putin talked about Afghanistan and the future there. Putin certainly knew that military victories had a way of being ephemeral in the forbidding mountains and valleys of Afghanistan. And he had his own interests in what happened next. In the years since the Soviet withdrawal, Moscow had kept ties to the Afghans who now ran the Northern Alliance, financing their long fight against the Taliban. So while Pakistan resisted the Northern Alliance taking control in the capital, Russia was backing its allies against the Pashtuns. Afghanistan was once again at the center of a great game.

Bush and Putin had other issues to hash over during a working lunch as well. Bush had made clear since his campaign that he wanted to build a more limited version of Ronald Reagan's proposed Star Wars antimissile system to guard against rogue states like Iran, and to do so, he was ready to abrogate the Anti-Ballistic Missile Treaty of 1972. To Russia, no longer able to keep up with American military advances, throwing out the ABM Treaty seemed inherently destabilizing; no matter what Bush or anyone else said, any American missile defense system seemed certain to be aimed at neutralizing Russia's strategic nuclear strength.

But in the two months since the September 11 attacks, Bush and Putin had resolved to redefine the Russian-American relationship for a new era, and they were determined not to let the ABM dispute sour that. To put down a marker on a new partnership, they agreed to dramatically slash their nuclear arsenals, bringing them down to the lowest levels since the early years of the Cold War. In an exchange of unilateral but reciprocal announcements, each side committed to reducing its deployed strategic warheads to between seventeen hundred and twenty-two hundred, down from the six thousand allowed under the Strategic Arms Reduction Treaty, or START, signed by Bush's father in 1991.

The next day, November 14, Bush met again with Putin, this time at his Crawford ranch. Bush was annoyed that a gusty downpour was marring the visit as he drove the Russian leader around the ranch in his pickup truck for forty-five minutes while his staff scrambled to move tables and the cowboy cooks hired for the occasion grilled in the rain. Bush grew more irritated later when Putin arrived an hour early for dinner. Realizing the mistake, Putin retreated back to the guesthouse until the appointed hour, but Bush barked at Condoleezza Rice and Karen Hughes. "Somebody forgot to tell Vladimir about the time change," he snapped. Rice knew that was aimed at her but could not help laughing at a former KGB officer flummoxed over something as simple as a time zone.

When another hour passed, the two leaders, their wives, and their advisers made the most of the intemperate weather, casting aside suits and ties for blue jeans and sweaters and a relaxed dinner of fried catfish and corn bread, followed by mesquite-grilled beef tenderloin and then birthday cake for Rice. The birthday girl entertained by playing piano, and some of the guests danced. Putin's wife, Lyudmila, wore a sequined vest in red, white, and blue. Bush chatted in broken Spanish with Igor Ivanov, the Russian foreign minister, to the consternation of aides from both sides who could not understand them.

"We are seeing a historic change in relationship between Russia and the United States," Bush said in his toast. "Usually you only invite friends to your home, and I feel that is the case here."

"I've never been to the home of another world leader," Putin responded, "and it's hugely symbolic to me and my country that it's the home of the president of the United States."

The visit smoothed the way for Bush to formally pull out of the ABM Treaty a few weeks later. Putin told Bush he would publicly oppose the decision but would not let it disrupt their relationship. Still, he wanted something too—a new treaty codifying the nuclear arms cuts they had just announced. To the Russians, treaties ratified their importance on the world stage long after the years of Soviet dominance. Bush, on the other hand, had no taste for drawn-out Geneva negotiations, and Cheney argued strongly against it. But Bush was eager to accommodate Putin and agreed to draft a treaty.

"**MR. VICE PRESIDENT,** this is the thing we all feared the most. This changes everything."

George Tenet was briefing Bush, Cheney, and Rice on the investigation into the Pakistani scientists accused of helping Osama bin Laden figure out how to build a nuclear device. The situation, he told them, was every bit as chilling as feared when the scientists were arrested a month earlier.

One of the scientists was Sultan Bashiruddin Mahmood, a former chairman of the Pakistan Atomic Energy Commission and an open admirer of the Taliban. Mahmood had met twice with bin Laden, who grilled him on how to build a bomb. Mahmood was an expert in enriching uranium but had no experience creating a weapon, so bin Laden pressed him to connect him with other Pakistani scientists who did. Bin Laden hinted he had already obtained black-market fissile material from the former Soviet Union with the help of an allied radical group, the Islamic Movement of Uzbekistan. Mahmood told interrogators he had not helped bin Laden, but he failed half a dozen lie detector tests.

Cheney asked if they thought that meant al-Qaeda did have a nuclear weapon. A CIA analyst accompanying Tenet said no, probably not, but he could not say for certain.

"If there's a one percent chance that Pakistani scientists are helping al-Qaeda build or develop a nuclear weapon," Cheney replied, "we have to treat it as a certainty in terms of our response."

He meant not that they should overlook evidence to the contrary but that the consequences of terrorists with a nuclear weapon were so unimaginable that the normal risk calculations did not apply. Judgments like "high confidence" or "low confidence" used by intelligence agencies or legal concepts like "preponderance of the evidence" had no meaning in a world of weapons that could wipe out a city in an instant. With that, he outlined a new way to evaluate the dangers he saw confronting the nation.

In that context, Cheney believed, it was not enough to simply keep a dangerous figure like Saddam Hussein in a box. The policy of containment over the past dozen years no longer seemed adequate. Hussein had been found after the Gulf War not only to have chemical weapons but to be pursuing nuclear bombs. What if he eventually succeeded? Even if he did not use them himself, what if he gave them to the likes of bin Laden? With the fall of Kabul, Bush and Cheney began thinking more seriously about what to do about Iraq.

After the National Security Council meeting on November 21, Bush pulled aside Donald Rumsfeld.

"Where do we stand on the Iraq planning?" he asked.

Rumsfeld told him he had reviewed the plan and, as expected, it was just a version of Desert Storm. To revamp it, Rumsfeld said, he needed to bring more people into the loop.

Fine, Bush said, but keep it in the building.

Later that day, a fifth and final victim of the anthrax attacks died in Connecticut. Investigators were still years away from cracking the case, but the attacks had subsided. This was, somehow, an isolated case, not the existential threat Cheney feared, not the 1 percent peril. That, he worried, could still come.

But while attention moved to Iraq, the war in Afghanistan was hardly over. A prison uprising in Mazar-e Sharif left a CIA operative named Johnny Micheal Spann dead on November 25, the first American killed in action in the war on terror. Captured at Mazar was a young American Muslim, John Walker Lindh, who would be brought home to face charges for joining the Taliban. And American Special Forces and their Afghan allies had chased bin Laden and hundreds of his followers to the forbidding mountain stronghold of Tora Bora near the Pakistani border.

Before them lay the chance to capture or kill the mastermind of the attacks on America. But Rumsfeld and Tommy Franks were sticking to their strategy of using American airpower while relying on Afghan troops on the ground. Fewer than a hundred American special operations troops and CIA operatives were in the area, and while B-52s dropped 700,000 pounds of ordnance, the Afghan warlords recruited by the Americans simply pocketed bags of U.S. cash, then let bin Laden escape.

Some in Washington pressed Bush and Cheney to send more American troops. The marines had landed near Kandahar the same day as Spann's death, and Brigadier General James Mattis believed he could swing up to Tora Bora. Hank Crumpton, who was leading the CIA's operations in Afghanistan, brought his concerns to the White House, imploring Bush to send the marines to block escape routes.

"We're going to lose our prey if we're not careful," he said.

"How bad off are these Afghani forces, really?" Bush asked. "Are they up to the job?"

"Definitely not, Mr. President," Crumpton said. "Definitely not."

But Bush deferred to Franks, who argued it would take weeks to deploy significant numbers of American troops and even then they could never seal the area. Sending enough forces quickly enough to make a difference would have been a formidable challenge—commanders estimated that deploying one thousand to three thousand troops would have required hundreds of helicopter flights over a week—and still might not have stopped bin Laden from escaping. But relying on the Afghans had clearly backfired. On December 16, bin Laden and a phalanx of his fighters slipped out of Tora Bora and disappeared into Pakistan. In his desire to let the military call the shots, Bush had missed the best opportunity of his entire presidency to catch America's top enemy.

AS BUSH SETTLED into Camp David for the holidays, friends noticed that he seemed more distant than usual. "He was totally disengaged with anything around him other than what was happening" overseas, noticed Charlie Younger, the president's childhood friend. "He would walk in the woods and walk with his dog, very contemplative and distant, a lot on his mind. He wasn't his usual self even when it was time to eat." In the eight years of his presidency, this was the only time Younger saw him this way.

He had plenty on his mind. On December 22, an al-Qaeda follower, Richard Reid, tried to ignite explosives in his shoes on a flight bound for Miami, only to be tackled by alert fellow passengers. The country clearly was still at risk. That "had a big impact on me," Bush said later. The same day, a courageous Pashtun tribal leader named Hamid Karzai was installed as Afghanistan's interim president. But that only prompted Bush to turn attention again to Saddam Hussein, summoning Franks to Crawford on December 28 for an update on contingency plans to invade Iraq.

It was a cold Texas morning, and Bush was wearing jeans, a plaid shirt, and boots when he took the general and his operations director, Major General Victor "Gene" Renuart of the air force, into a double-wide trailer that had been turned into a secure communications center. The men sat at a small oak table facing a plasma screen at the other side of the room, and with the touch of a button the screen opened into separate rectangles showing other members of the war cabinet. Cheney joined the teleconference from the second-floor study of his Wyoming home. Rumsfeld was at his home in Taos, New Mexico, while Colin Powell, Condoleezza Rice, George Tenet, Andy Card, and Richard Myers were in the Situation Room at the White House.

They started with a quick briefing on Afghanistan, and Bush took the opportunity to rib Franks about reports of his recent visit. "Tommy, what's this I hear about your dodging missiles over Kabul?" he asked.

"Nothing serious, Mr. President," he replied. "Been shot at before."

"Tommy," he replied, "I don't want you to go getting yourself killed. That's the last thing we need. Got work for you, important work."

The "important work" Bush had in mind for him was Iraq. The military had not significantly updated its contingency plan for Iraq, Operations Plan 1003, since 1998, and it essentially advanced the same sort of strategy used in the Gulf War—an assault force of 400,000 assembled over a six-month buildup. No one thought that was suitable anymore, including Franks. The general noted that Iraq's army had shrunk from 1 million men to about 350,000 today.

"General Franks," interrupted Cheney, who had overseen the last assault on Iraq. "You've described an Iraqi force around half the size it was when the Gulf War began. Does that mean it is only half as effective?"

"Sir, smaller does not necessarily mean weaker," Franks replied. He noted that the Republican Guard, while fewer in number, was still well manned and armed.

"What do you think of the plan, Tommy?" Bush asked.

"Mr. President, it's outdated," he answered. Aside from the long buildup, he said, it did not account for the fact that American weaponry was tremendously more effective than a decade earlier.

Franks presented what he called a new commander's concept, a four-phase plan with three different options. He could begin a ground war with as few as 100,000 troops while other forces continued to flow into the region, building up to 145,000; if necessary, the force could grow to 275,000. Tenet noted that Iraq would be significantly different from Afghanistan. While Afghanistan was a primitive land governed by tribes and warlords commanding untrained fighters, Iraq was relatively modern with an organized, equipped army. Moreover, there was no Northern Alliance for the United States to team up with in Iraq. American intelligence had burned a lot of bridges since the end of the Gulf War because of a failure to help Shiites during their 1991 uprising and various failed plots to topple Hussein later in the 1990s.

Bush told Rumsfeld and Franks to keep working on the plan. He hoped diplomacy and pressure would force Hussein to disarm, but he said they needed to prepare in case that did not happen. "We cannot allow weapons of mass destruction to fall into the hands of terrorists," Bush declared. "*I* will not allow that to happen."

With that, the meeting ended. While bin Laden was escaping in the mountains, Bush and Cheney were focusing on Iraq.

THE SEPTEMBER 11 attacks managed to change the dynamics even on Bush's domestic program at least for a while. For months before the attacks, working with his new friend Ted Kennedy, Bush had been pushing Congress to pass an education reform program called No Child Left Behind, after a campaign slogan. In exchange for an infusion of money, schools would test students in math and reading from grades three to eight and once in high school, with the goal of every child meeting basic proficiency by 2014. States would set their own standards and tests. Schools that did not measure up would face sanctions, and their students would be allowed to transfer. Kennedy, deeming it "flawed but necessary," considered it the most important education law in a quarter century. Yet it had run into strong headwinds from left and right. Liberals did not like the emphasis on testing, while conservatives did not like Washington dictating how schools run. Republican lawmakers cobbled together a plan to derail the program with an amendment giving states more flexibility. Bush summoned the sponsor to the White House to pressure him to drop it.

But in the weeks after September 11, Bush and Kennedy suddenly found lawmakers more pliant. "There was almost a feeling of what can we do in our area to come together?" recalled Sandy Kress, the president's education adviser. "Oddly," he added, remembering that Bush's trip to Florida was to promote education reform, "the feeling of the need to come together and do something together kind of partly, as a response to this, was far more powerful than any talk we would have given that day." With many opponents swallowing misgivings, Congress passed the plan by large margins just before Christmas in perhaps the most significant bipartisan domestic victory of Bush's presidency. And now, on January 8, Bush embarked on a fly-around with Kennedy, John Boehner, and other legislative architects to celebrate the victory. He signed the bill in Boehner's state of Ohio, then flew to Boston in the late afternoon to showcase his partnership with Kennedy.

On this one issue at least, he had found his Bob Bullock. "You know," he told a crowd at Boston Latin School, "I told the folks at the coffee shop in Crawford, Texas, that Ted Kennedy was all right. They nearly fell out." He smiled as the crowd laughed. "But he is. I've come to admire him. He's a smart, capable senator. You want him on your side, I can tell you that." Bush went on to recall how Kennedy hosted and comforted Laura Bush during the September 11 attacks. "Not only are you a good senator, you're a good man," the president said, using the highest form of compliment in the Bush lexicon.

By the time he got back to Washington, though, Bush's mind was already drifting back to other weighty issues. Kress recognized that education, as important as it was to Bush, would recede for a time.

"The president is in another place," he told colleagues.

As it happened, the fly-around with Kennedy marked the end of the post–September 11 unity in Washington. Even before the two boarded Air Force One together, the bipartisan spirit had begun to fray. Democrats blamed Bush for not doing enough for an economic stimulus package that failed to pass, while the president took umbrage at an anonymous quotation in the *New York Times* attributed to a Democratic aide calling him "disengaged." Bush's advisers blamed that on Tom Daschle, once the president's hope for a partner but increasingly the White House poster boy for obstructionism. Daschle attacked Bush's economic policies in a speech on January 4, 2002, indicting him for the "most dramatic fiscal deterioration in our nation's history." Bush fired back the next day at a town hall meeting in California, declaring, "Not over my dead body will they raise your taxes." It was a long time since his spontaneous hug with Daschle.

Tension between the White House and the Senate Democratic leader rose even further when Cheney called one day in January. The vice president was concerned about Senate hearings into what happened before September 11 and pressed Daschle to rein them in.

"This would be a very dangerous and time-consuming diversion for those of us who are on the front lines of our response today," Cheney told him. "We just can't be tied down with the problems that this would present for us. We've got our hands full."

Cheney had a legitimate point; hearings would consume enormous time at a perilous moment. But they also represented a profound political risk. Washington loved finding a scapegoat, and there was plenty of potential for second-guessing how the government failed to stop the deadliest attack on American soil.

Democrats knew that too, and if the vice president's resistance to inquiry invariably involved a mix of substantive and political calculations, so did the opposition's interest in investigating. And to the extent there was any hesitation to inject politics into national security, that faded on January 18 when Karl Rove addressed the Republican National Committee's winter meeting in Austin.

"Americans trust the Republicans to do a better job of keeping our communities and our families safe," Rove told the party faithful. "We can also go to the country on this issue, because they trust the Republican Party to do a better job of protecting and strengthening America's military might and thereby protecting America." On the one hand, Rove's statement was unremarkable—the president's chief political strategist talking to a political audience about an upcoming election and an issue that historically had been a Republican strength. But coming just four months after the attacks, Rove's remarks gave the impression that the White House was using the war on terror for partisan advantage. Democrats reacted with equal parts outrage and eagerness to accuse the other side of politicizing the war. A "shameful statement," declared Richard Gephardt. "Nothing short of despicable," exclaimed Terry McAuliffe, the Democratic National Committee chairman.

INSIDE THE ADMINISTRATION, Bush was mediating another intense clash. Cheney and other advisers were debating what to do with prisoners captured in Afghanistan and elsewhere. With no appetite to bring them to American soil, where they might be given rights by American courts, the Bush team settled on the navy base on the tip of Cuba, a legal no-man's-land where prisoners could theoretically be held beyond the reach of judges. Some might be put on trial in the military commissions Cheney had gotten Bush to authorize in November, but others might not be, and the vice president did not want judges second-guessing the White House's decisions.

Hooded, chained, and clad in orange jumpsuits, the first twenty prisoners arrived on the sunny, warm island after a long flight from Afghanistan on January 11. Navy engineers had hastily assembled several dozen outdoor cells made from chain-link fences on a cement slab, an open-air prison that came to be called Camp X-Ray. Pictures of their arrival were beamed around the world, signaling a new era. Whatever the legal wisdom behind choosing Guantánamo, releasing photographs of those first arrivals backfired, searing an image of a crude and even barbaric place, an image that would linger long after modern, humane facilities were constructed.

Bush decided after their arrival that neither al-Qaeda nor Taliban captives would be covered under the Geneva Conventions, adopting the reasoning of a forty-two-page memo drafted by John Yoo at the Justice Department and dispensing with the thirty-seven-page rebuttal from William H. Taft IV, the top lawyer at the State Department and great-grandson of a president, who called Yoo's factual assumptions and legal analysis "seriously flawed." Both Richard Myers, at the Pentagon, and Colin Powell, traveling in Asia, were alarmed when they learned of Bush's decision. The general and the retired general were deeply invested in the notion of laws of war. That the United States, which had done more than any nation to institute international standards, would simply toss them aside when they were inconvenient struck them as unwise and potentially even dangerous to American troops if they were ever captured. Powell made his case in the Oval Office with Bush, who agreed to let the issue be debated before the full National Security Council.

Soon after, Bush and Cheney sat down with the National Security

Council to discuss detainee policy. Powell and Myers teamed up to argue for Geneva. Even if fighters were not deemed prisoners of war under Geneva's definition, they should have hearings to determine whether they qualified. Cheney and his allies were appalled that what they saw as a slavish devotion to process would prevent them from interrogating prisoners who might have information that would stop another September 11. Al-Qaeda was not a party to Geneva, and its fighters did not wear uniforms or constitute a legitimate army waging legal warfare. Cheney's team adopted Yoo's analysis that while Afghanistan had signed Geneva years ago, the country had since become a failed state and therefore no longer constituted a party to the conventions, a novel interpretation not explicitly envisioned by treaty provisions.

"We have an image to uphold around the world," Powell countered. "If we don't do this, it will make it much more difficult for us to try and encourage other countries to treat people humanely."

Myers seconded him on moral terms. "Mr. President," he said. "You'll notice that everybody here's with a lawyer. I don't have a lawyer with me. I don't think this is a legal issue."

But John Ashcroft now advanced the Yoo analysis, saying Afghanistan was no longer a real nation and al-Qaeda and the Taliban were essentially a "coalition of pirates."

"Would you apply the Geneva Conventions to Iraq?" Bush asked Ashcroft.

"Yes, Mr. President," Ashcroft said. Iraq was a legitimate nation.

"But you can say that Saddam Hussein is a pirate too," Bush said.

Cheney said the Taliban and al-Qaeda were not lawful combatants. "We all agree that they'll be treated humanely," he said. "But we don't want to tie our hands."

In the end, Bush backed off the original interpretation somewhat, but his compromise made little practical difference. He signed an executive order on February 7 finding that while Geneva did not apply to al-Qaeda terrorists, it did cover the war against the Taliban government. But Bush then determined that even under Geneva's own definitions, Taliban soldiers across the board were illegal combatants and therefore did not qualify as prisoners of war. The United States would treat detainees, "to the extent appropriate and consistent with military necessity, in a manner consistent with the principles of Geneva," he ruled, language that gave the government all the wiggle room it needed to write its own rules.

Bush was preparing to thrust the issue of war onto the national table in an even more dramatic way. With his State of the Union address coming up, he asked his speechwriters to outline a doctrine for a new age when the United States must confront terrorism and unconventional weapons like chemical, biological, or nuclear arms. Michael Gerson assigned David Frum to come up with a line or two about Iraq. Frum thought about the alliance between terror states and terror organizations, and for whatever reason it made him think about the Axis powers of World War II. He scribbled down the phrase "axis of hatred" to describe the modern-day nexus confronting the United States. Gerson liked it but, playing off a favorite Bush word, changed it to "axis of evil."

At first, Iraq was the only country named, but Condoleezza Rice and Stephen Hadley worried that would make it look as if the president were ready to go to war with Iraq. So the speechwriters added Iran, the sponsor of Hamas and Hezbollah, and North Korea, an aspiring nuclear state suspected of spreading dangerous weapons and technology to rogue nations. Hadley then had second thoughts about including Iran, since there were stirrings of democracy there. "No, I want it in," Bush said. "I want to turn up the pressure on Iran." Gerson made no objection. "It didn't seem particularly controversial to use these as examples of state sponsors of terror," he said. Powell and his deputy, Richard Armitage, read the speech and had no problem with the phrase either.

On the evening of January 29, Bush strode into the House chamber and delivered perhaps the most memorable line of his presidency. "States like these and their terrorist allies constitute an axis of evil, arming to threaten the peace of the world," he said. "By seeking weapons of mass destruction, these regimes pose a grave and growing danger. They could provide these arms to terrorists, giving them the means to match their hatred. They could attack our allies or attempt to blackmail the United States. In any of these cases, the price of indifference would be catastrophic."

When Bush finished to applause, his staff thought the major takeaway would be his commitment to "the non-negotiable demands of human dignity" in the Muslim world, including rule of law, free speech, religious tolerance, and women's rights. To the extent that anyone picked up on "axis of evil," they misjudged what would provoke controversy. "We were more focused on the 'evil' part of it as opposed to the 'axis' part of it," Dan Bartlett said later. The word "evil" consistently rubbed some on the left the wrong way. It never dawned on them that the word "axis" would become the issue. They meant an axis between rogue states and terrorists, not a link between three disparate countries nor a target list. "The reason it was an axis was not because they were in alliance. The reason it was an axis was because they were all three separately doing the same thing, both pursuing weapons of mass destruction and supporting terror," Hadley said later. "We thought it was a figure of speech, and nobody thought that somebody would think that we were alleging that they were actually in league with one another."

The phrase bothered even some hawks, like Paul Wolfowitz. But Bush did not care. He liked it and had no regrets. "It was not the president's habit to feel like, let's back off because of criticism," Gerson reflected. Indeed, Bush grew irritated when he picked up the *New York Times* on January 31, two days after the speech, and saw that some aides had tried to tone down the language. On the road for a post–State of the Union trip to promote a new volunteerism initiative that would eventually become the USA Freedom Corps, Bush called Rice in Washington to tell her there would be no retreat from the line. When Ari Fleischer arrived in his hotel suite, Bush told him to quash any suggestion that the White House was backing off. Bush thought it was "quite cowardly for people to read into my intentions when they don't know me."

11

"Afghanistan was too easy"

The presidential limousine pulled up to the Badaling section of China's Great Wall on a Friday afternoon in February. President Bush got out for a quick tour. He had last visited twenty-seven years earlier while his father was the American envoy. Now he was back as president, fresh from lunch with China's leader.

Bush was taken to a section of the wall that Richard Nixon had visited in 1972 during his historic opening to the Middle Kingdom.

"Where did Nixon stop?" Bush asked his guide.

Right where you are, the guide said.

"Let's go about a hundred yards more," Bush said.

Bush was nothing if not competitive. He spent his youth competing against his father's legacy, as a student at Andover and Yale, as a military pilot, as an oilman, as a candidate for Congress, almost always falling short. He finally found success as the owner of the Texas Rangers. As president, Bush prided himself on outlasting Secret Service agents on the running trail and challenged aides to earn their way into the Hundred Degree Club reserved for those who finished three miles on the ranch with the thermometer in triple digits. Later in his presidency, he would get into a reading contest with Karl Rove, measured not just by the number of books read but by the number of pages and even square inches of text.

Of course, it requires a certain competitive streak to run for president in the first place. How many people look in the mirror and conclude that in a country of 300 million, there is no one better to lead it? Once reaching the White House, a president invariably compares himself with the forty or so other men who held the office. How did Abraham Lincoln save the country? How did Theodore Roosevelt earn his way onto Mount Rushmore? How did Franklin Roosevelt take on depression and war? Bush was determined to be not just a good president but a great president. No "small ball" for him, as he put it, derisively referring to his predecessor's strategy of advancing incremental initiatives. He came to office with expansive visions: he would transform education, Medicare, Social Security, the military, the culture in Washington even. The attacks of September 11 gave him a chance to transform the world. It was not enough to quote Franklin Roosevelt. He wanted to be the one others quoted.

On that at least, he had succeeded. His "axis of evil" phrase had reverberated across the globe. The members of the theoretical axis unsurprisingly denounced him for "political immaturity and moral leprosy," as the North Korean Foreign Ministry put it. But American allies were also perturbed. While willing to help in Afghanistan, they were not eager for war elsewhere and saw Bush's rhetoric as saber rattling. The European Community's foreign policy commissioner warned America against "unilateralist overdrive." When Bush arrived in South Korea on his way to China, he was greeted by demonstrators holding up banners that read, "Who Is in Axis of Evil? You, Mr. Bush!"

His trip to South Korea, Japan, and China was his first chance to see up close the ripple effects of his speech. The truth was he did not mind all the consternation. If three simple words had managed to focus attention on the world's outliers and perhaps even scare them into thinking they faced possible American action, so much the better. He used the trip to calm allies without retreating from the sentiments he had expressed. Indeed, while visiting the South Korean side of the demilitarized zone, he was told that a museum on the other side exhibited axes used to kill two American service members in 1976. "No wonder I think they're evil," Bush said.

But it was not the North Koreans who were at the top of Bush's and Cheney's minds. From the start, they had seen Saddam Hussein as the nation's central threat. The "axis of evil" speech was not a declaration of war, and there were still plenty of ways to avoid an armed showdown, but it set Bush and Cheney on a course that would dominate the rest of their time in office.

The looming confrontation brought to a head a long, complicated conflict between the Bush family and Saddam Hussein. The relationship actually began as one of pragmatic friendship in the 1980s when Hussein was at war with Iran, the main American enemy in the region, and George H. W. Bush was vice president in an administration that offered to help. Through Arab intermediaries, Bush advised Hussein to intensify the bombing of Iran, according to a 1992 *New Yorker* article. Hussein's invasion of Kuwait in August 1990, though, proved a strategic miscalculation that put him on the opposite side of a Bush and Dick Cheney at the Pentagon.

In April 1993, after the Gulf War, the former president went to Kuwait for a hero's welcome, and a group of Iraqis crossed the border in what was called a thwarted attempt to kill him. Among those on the trip who could have been killed were Barbara Bush and Laura Bush. George W. Bush had stayed in Texas, where he was preparing to run for governor. Some later questioned the seriousness of the assassination attempt or its connections to Baghdad, but the incident was a jarring moment for the Bush family. Running for president, the younger Bush in November 1999 said he would not repeat his father's mistake of leaving Hussein in power. "No one envisioned him still standing," he said. "It's time to finish the task." At a debate a couple of weeks later, Bush was more explicit. "If I found in any way, shape, or form that he was developing weapons of mass destruction," he said, "I'd take them out."

As Bush and Cheney turned up the pressure on Iraq in the beginning of 2002, many could not help wondering how much it was due to the president's desire to finish what his father started—or to succeed where he had failed. "He cut and run early," Bush once said of his father. While he steadfastly denied any personal motivations, even some of his best friends wondered if Bush targeted Hussein out of a sense of unfinished family business. "Whether he did or not, only God can tell," said Joe O'Neill, his lifelong Texas friend. "I don't know if we'll ever know that."

Still, even if that was a part of it, however subconsciously, it was not the whole picture. For one thing, Cheney and others, like Rumsfeld, Paul Wolfowitz, Scooter Libby, and Douglas Feith, were vigorous proponents of action against Iraq without any paternal interest. Cheney had served in the previous Bush administration and had agreed to halt the Gulf War without marching to Baghdad on the assumption that Hussein would eventually be toppled anyway, a decision that now haunted him.

The sense that Hussein was a menace who could not be left in power was shared across party lines. Bill Clinton signed legislation declaring regime change American policy toward Iraq. Hussein was the only one in the world taking shots at American service members on a regular basis in the no-fly zones. He had flouted UN resolutions calling for disarmament and maintained a murderous grip over his people. As far as anyone knew, he still harbored ambitions for chemical, biological, and nuclear weapons far more devastating than box cutters, and he had demonstrated a ruthless willingness to use deadly gas on his Iranian neighbors and on his own people during a Kurdish uprising.

In the aftermath of September 11, Bush and Cheney fell back on the thinking of their generation, the nation-state paradigm. Going after a stateless, formless enemy like a terrorist network was unfamiliar. Going after Iraq fit more neatly into their experience. "Every one of us, our entire worldview of foreign affairs was put together in an era of great-power conflict—good versus evil, us versus them," said one administration official who worked on Iraq and supported action, only to regret it later. "Fundamentally, the problems we faced after 9/11 did not lend themselves to the great-power conflict model. Stateless enemy. And so people have said, why did George Bush use this language—us versus them, smoke them out, hunt them down? It's because that's all he knew and that's all everybody knew."

His success at toppling the Taliban fed the desire to hit another target. Bush did not want to be like Clinton flailing ineffectually at shadows. Taking on tyrants, rooting out terrorists, confronting rogue states with weapons of mass destruction, and perhaps even planting a seed for democracy were missions worthy of a great president. Afghanistan seemed to show that America could force change in a region swarming with people who wanted to do it harm—never mind that Special Forces were still chasing al-Qaeda fighters from Tora Bora into the treacherous mountains of Shahikot south of Kabul.

The anger over September 11 seemed to demand more. Afghanistan was not enough. While Bush and Cheney had Iraq in their sights for a long time, they were responding to public appetite for action. For the first time in more than a generation, the country was willing to be assertive overseas. A poll taken just before the "axis of evil" speech showed that 77 percent of Americans supported military action in Iraq and just 17 percent opposed it. In a separate poll, almost an identical number, 76 percent, thought Hussein provided help to al-Qaeda, and another poll released around then found that 72 percent said it was very or somewhat likely that Hussein was "personally involved in the September 11 attacks." Memories of the Twin Towers were still fresh. "The only reason we went into Iraq, I tell people now, is we were looking for somebody's ass to kick," said the administration official who worked on Iraq. "Afghanistan was too easy."

ON A CHILLY, dry day in February, Cheney sat down with his CIA briefer to go through the latest intelligence. While Bush preferred a more interactive briefing, Cheney tended to read the documents while the briefer sat quietly waiting in case he had any questions. He usually did. On this morning, Cheney found a report from the Defense Intelligence Agency, or DIA, titled "Niamey Signed an Agreement to Sell 500 Tons of Uranium a Year to Baghdad."

The report, dated February 12, 2002, caught Cheney's eye. Niamey was the capital of Niger, an African country with significant uranium deposits. Iraq had no civilian nuclear energy program, and the only reason it could want uranium from Africa was to fuel a bomb. The uranium would have to be enriched, no easy task and not one that Iraq had mastered. But if it were, five hundred tons by one calculation would be enough to make fifty weapons. The report was based on information from a foreign intelligence service, and Cheney asked his briefer to find out what the CIA thought of it.

By this point, Cheney was hunting for evidence that Iraq had chemical, biological, and even nuclear weapons in violation of its obligations under the UN Security Council resolutions that followed the Gulf War. For years, American intelligence agencies had assumed that Saddam Hussein was developing weapons, but they had been without a window into Iraq ever since UN inspectors left at the end of 1998 just before Clinton launched a four-day bombing attack for failing to cooperate adequately. Nothing in the interim had made intelligence analysts in the United States or Europe think Hussein had abandoned his weapons programs or his ambitions for them. The request from Cheney put the CIA on high alert to confirm the Niger report.

A couple days later, the CIA briefer gave Cheney the agency's assessment, which was more skeptical than the DIA report. The CIA analysis noted that the "information on the alleged uranium contract between Iraq and Niger comes exclusively from a foreign government service report that lacks crucial details." Moreover, it said, "some of the information in the report contradicts reporting from the U.S. Embassy in Niamey." Niger's uranium mines were operated by a consortium led by the French government, which was unlikely to permit an illegal sale to Iraq. The analysis named the Italians as the foreign intelligence agency that provided the tip, a red flag in the intelligence community since Italy's was not the most highly regarded spy agency in Europe. Back at CIA headquarters, analysts decided to send the husband of one of their own, Joseph Wilson, a former ambassador with contacts in Niger, to see if he could unearth more.

WHILE ALL THIS took place out of public view, Bush and Cheney had challenges on the domestic front. The steel industry was hurting from foreign competition, and the White House, despite its free-market philosophy, was debating whether to step in. During the 2000 campaign, Bush and Cheney had promised to help steelworkers in West Virginia, a normally Democratic state that then went Republican.

Karl Rove was focused as well on larger steel-producing states like Pennsylvania and Ohio, states that were key to any Electoral College victory in the future. But most of the economic team, including Paul O'Neill, Glenn Hubbard, and Mitch Daniels, the budget director, opposed a steel tariff as a sellout of principle. "If you can't do the right thing when you're at 85 percent approval," Daniels said at a meeting on February 11, "then when can you do the right thing?"

Cheney's own staff peppered him with op-ed articles arguing against steel tariffs. One from the *Wall Street Journal* sent to the vice president on January 25 argued that tariffs would be "dangerously protectionist." A memo sent to him on February 28 summarized six editorials opposing tariffs. Hubbard showed Bush a map of states that would be affected by resulting higher costs to consumers. "I'm no politician, but I would dispute that it was a good idea even politically, and was clearly a bad idea economically," he recalled arguing.

But Bush and Cheney were united. On March 5, Bush imposed quotas of up to 30 percent on most imported steel, what he called "temporary safeguards" to offset subsidies from foreign governments. While reaffirming his free-market ideals, Bush said in a written statement that "sometimes imports can cause such serious harm to domestic industries that temporary restraints are warranted." He and Cheney hoped to use the move to win congressional authorization to negotiate new free-trade agreements without line-item interference by lawmakers.

BUSH HAD TAKEN to keeping a chart of top al-Qaeda figures in his desk, and as they were captured or killed, he would draw a big *X* through them. On March 28, after a gunfight, American and Pakistani agents captured Abu Zubaydah, a man considered the highest-ranking al-Qaeda operative seized since the attacks the previous fall. Zubaydah was shot in the chest, groin, and thigh as he tried to escape but was being treated by American doctors. For Bush, the chart was looking better.

A moment of triumph, though, quickly became a moment of decision. Figuring out what to do with a captured terrorist would prove to be a defining moment for Bush and Cheney. In the six months since the World Trade Center was destroyed, the president and the vice president had thrown out the old rule books when it came to prisoners in this twenty-first-century war. Now the CIA had concluded that ordinary interrogation techniques were not enough and asked Bush for permission to use abusive methods.

Amid concern about more attacks like September 11, and worse, Bush and Cheney considered traditional law-enforcement-style questioning inadequate to the threat. It would take months for the CIA and the Justice Department to figure out how to introduce a new, more brutal form of interrogation and to justify it under the law. But in the end, at Cheney's urging, Bush by his own account approved all but two of the proposed techniques. *Whatever it takes,* the people at Ground Zero had told him. Now he was doing whatever he thought it would take to protect the country. At what cost would not become clear for some time.

In a secret overseas prison, Bush's order had tangible consequences. CIA officers strapped Zubaydah to a board, inclined his feet slightly above his head, covered his mouth and nose with a cloth, and then poured water over it for up to forty seconds to simulate drowning. Then they did it again. And again. All told, Zubaydah would be waterboarded eighty-three times over the next month.

Zubaydah talked. In the years to come, Bush and Cheney, backed by intelligence officials, would claim that Zubaydah provided critical information that led them to the capture of Ramzi bin al-Shibh, a top aide to Khalid Sheikh Mohammed, the mastermind of September 11, and José Padilla, an al-Qaeda plotter in the United States. But his case was a touchstone for a debate that would last for years. FBI agents said Zubaydah was already cooperating under normal questioning before they were shunted aside by CIA operatives with their board and hood and that he said nothing after waterboarding that could not have been gotten out of him anyway. Some claimed Zubaydah was mentally unstable, citing diaries that seemed to feature multiple personalities. George Tenet disputed that, saying such a conclusion was overblown and the diaries reflected a literary device Zubaydah was using.

Either way, Zubaydah's case had taken Bush and Cheney down a road to what the vice president had called the "dark side." While waterboarding eventually captured the public imagination, or horror, it was just one of several harsh methods. Detainees were stripped nude, forced to stand for prolonged periods, deprived of sleep for days on end, put on a liquid diet, slapped in the face or belly, and doused with water. A memo drafted largely by John Yoo at the Justice Department but signed by Assistant Attorney General Jay Bybee determined that such actions did not constitute torture under the law as long as they did not result in pain equivalent to organ failure, impairment of bodily function, or death. The CIA came up with the euphemistic phrase "enhanced interrogation techniques" to describe them.

Bush and Cheney also authorized some detainees to be seized and turned over to allied countries like Egypt, which could apply their own interrogation techniques, a process called extraordinary rendition. Some of the most sensational allegations that Iraq had trained al-Qaeda operatives to use explosives and chemical weapons came from such an interrogation of a prisoner named Ibn al-Shaykh al-Libi, who later recanted the statements, saying he lied to stop brutal interrogations.

The military had its own rules for interrogations at Guantánamo. By the end of the year, Donald Rumsfeld was presented with options for interrogation techniques broken down into three categories. Rumsfeld accepted the two less aggressive categories but unlike the CIA rejected the most forceful category except for "mild, non-injurious physical contact such as grabbing, poking in the chest with the finger, and light pushing." No one would be waterboarded at Guantánamo.

Rumsfeld wrote his name on the approval line. "However," he then added by hand, "I stand for 8–10 hours a day. Why is standing limited to four hours?"

IN MARCH, CHENEY made his first overseas trip as vice president to round up support for a possible war against Iraq. As he boarded Air Force Two at Andrews Air Force Base, it felt like a repeat of a mission he had made to the Middle East for the president's father. Now returning, Cheney stopped in twelve countries over the course of ten days—Britain, Jordan, Egypt, Yemen, Oman, the United Arab Emirates, Saudi Arabia, Bahrain, Qatar, Kuwait, Israel, and Turkey—all with the same message: Bush had not made up his mind about Iraq, but if he did go to war, the result would be decisive.

Accompanying Cheney was Lynne, who in addition to providing companionship and counsel proved a useful decoy. Worried about security, the Secret Service concocted a ruse to allow the vice president to land safely in Yemen, the ancestral home of Osama bin Laden and one of the most dangerous destinations in the world. After meetings in Sharm el-Sheikh in Egypt, Cheney and his wife both approached the modified Boeing 757 used as Air Force Two, but only Lynne got on board. The plane then took off for Sanaa, the Yemeni capital, and swooped over the city before climbing again and flying on to Oman. The vice president slipped aboard a less obvious C-17 and landed in Yemen after a corkscrew approach to avoid fire from the ground.

As the exhausting trip wound down, Cheney headed to Israel to meet with America's closest ally in the region. During the plane ride, he and his advisers debated whether to meet with Yasser Arafat. William Burns, the assistant secretary of state for the region, recommended he sit down with Arafat because meeting only with the Israelis would send a bad signal. Cheney's own advisers, Scooter Libby, John Hannah, and Eric Edelman, objected, arguing that a meeting would reward a known terrorist. Cheney held off deciding until landing, whereupon he got into a car with General Tony Zinni, the special envoy to the region trying to set up a cease-fire. Zinni described his travails, and Cheney asked if it would be helpful to offer a meeting as an incentive to get Arafat to take steps to improve security. Zinni said yes. But in the end, Arafat never agreed to the conditions, more evidence to Cheney that the Palestinian was not serious about peace.

In the days after Cheney's visit, violence flared with deadly consequences. Bush was on Air Force One when he heard that a Palestinian suicide bomber had walked into a crowded hotel dining room and detonated an explosion in the middle of a Passover holiday seder dinner, killing 30 and injuring 140. Israelis sent troops into the West Bank and the Gaza Strip.

Bush met with his national security team on April 1, hours after Israeli troops advanced into Bethlehem in Palestinian territory just several hundred yards from the Church of the Nativity, celebrated as the birthplace of Jesus Christ. Bush decided to send Colin Powell on an emergency trip to calm the situation, despite objections by Donald Rumsfeld.

After the meeting, Bush pulled Powell aside and made clear he was counting on the secretary's global standing, aware that it eclipsed his own.

"This is going to be tough," the president said. "You're going to have part of your butt burned off. But you have more butt than any of the rest of us, so you can afford it."

Powell ended up feeling burned back in Washington. He spent ten days in the region without making much headway, and so he finally called for an international peace conference in hopes of demonstrating progress. "It was the only way I could get out of town without being lynched in Jerusalem," Powell later recalled.

Back in Washington, Cheney considered the peace conference the worst kind of freelancing and, after hearing Powell repeat the proposal publicly, called Condoleezza Rice from Air Force Two to suggest she rein him in. Rice called Powell and remembered telling him that the idea "was dead on arrival." He remembered her saying that while she thought a conference was fine, Cheney "was dead set against it and persuaded this was not a good thing." Powell told her, "I am sorry, I have to get out of town with something on my back, and the president needs something."

Cheney later deemed this a critical rupture souring relations with his erstwhile Gulf War partner for the remainder of their time in government together. Powell took the episode "as a personal affront," Cheney wrote in his memoir, and the vice president said he began hearing reports about the secretary whispering disdain for administration policies around Washington. "It was as though a tie had been cut," Cheney said. Powell later disputed that. "That is nonsense," he said. "I don't know why that was a watershed event."

But it is true that Powell was frustrated at the lack of support while he was in the field trying to make peace. When he reported to Bush, he expressed irritation.

"It was a mess, Mr. President," he told Bush. "Don't ever send people off to do missions like that when they are not getting squat."

Worse from Powell's point of view was Bush's comment shortly after the secretary's return. When the two met in the Oval Office on April 18 to discuss the situation, reporters asked the president if he considered Prime Minister Ariel Sharon of Israel a man of peace. "I do believe Ariel Sharon is a man of peace," Bush answered. "I'm confident he wants Israel to be able to exist at peace with its neighbors."

Powell, sitting in the chair to Bush's right, was flabbergasted. Sharon had effectively ignored American pleas to pull back his forces. Powell said nothing with cameras in the room but approached Rice afterward to vent.

"Do you have any idea how this plays on Arab TV?" he asked. "The Israelis are just thumbing their noses at the president. Why is he giving Sharon a pass?"

He was not the only one who wanted to know. Crown Prince Abdullah, the de facto ruler of Saudi Arabia, was livid and flew to America to make his anger known directly to Bush. The president agreed to host him along with Cheney, Powell, and Rice at the Crawford ranch on April 25. Abdullah wanted Bush to pressure Sharon to withdraw from the Palestinian headquarters.

"When will the pig leave Ramallah?" Abdullah asked Bush.

He had tried to persuade him, Bush answered, but Sharon refused.

Abdullah gave Bush a videotape and a book of photographs showing harsh Israeli treatment of Palestinians.

Cheney tried to talk about Iraq, but Abdullah was single-minded and presented an eight-point plan to solve the Palestinian crisis.

"I can't go back empty-handed," the crown prince said.

Abdullah asked to talk privately with his advisers, and Bush and his team stepped out. Suddenly the longtime American translator Gamal Helal rushed in. "Mr. President, I think the Saudis are getting ready to leave," he exclaimed. Evidently, Helal said, Abdullah had expected Bush to force the Israelis out of Ramallah before the visit and wanted him to call Sharon right then. The threatened walkout had been secretly pre-scripted by the Saudis to get Bush's attention.

Bush was annoyed at the showy brinkmanship. He would not be blackmailed.

"Does it matter if they leave?" he asked out loud.

Yes, Rice said. "It would be a disaster."

Powell agreed.

Bush told him to speak with the Saudis. "Go and fix it," Bush said.

Powell found Prince Bandar bin Sultan, the longtime Saudi ambassador to the United States, and tore into him angrily. "What the hell did you do?" Powell demanded. "How did you let it get to this?" The two began shouting loudly enough that Bush came to investigate.

However irritated he was, Bush understood a walkout by America's closest Arab allies would set back his agenda for the region. He went into the living room and asked to see Abdullah alone. Then he tried to interest the crown prince in a discussion of religion, hoping to break the ice as he had with Vladimir Putin a year earlier. But Abdullah sat stone-faced as Bush talked about his faith.

Bush played his last card. "Before you leave, may I show you my ranch?"

He ushered the crown prince outside into his white Ford pickup truck, then zoomed off for a tour of the trees and wildlife around his home. Only when a turkey hen appeared in the road did Abdullah express any interest.

"What's that?" he asked.

Bush told him and mentioned that Benjamin Franklin had wanted to make the turkey the national bird.

"My brother," Abdullah said suddenly, grabbing Bush's arm. "It is a sign from Allah. This is a good omen."

With that, the two returned to the ranch and proceeded with the meeting. After five hours, Abdullah hugged and kissed Bush.

"I love you like a son," Abdullah declared.

Bush never understood why a turkey hen would be taken as such an important sign, but its appearance avoided a foreign policy debacle.

With Israeli tanks still besieging the Church of the Nativity, where Palestinian militants had taken refuge, it took more than a week for negotiators to craft a deal to ease the offensive in exchange for sending certain Palestinians into exile. As the agreement came together, Bush met at the White House on May 8 with another Abdullah, the king of Jordan. Like his counterpart, this Abdullah pressed the president for the withdrawal of Israeli troops. But Bush made clear he had no hope of working with Arafat. "I don't know who else can emerge," the president said. A new generation untainted by terror and corruption had to come forward, he argued.

"I can imagine how Sharon feels when he starts his meeting with me with the news of a suicide bombing," Bush told the king.

Abdullah was struck by how much September 11 had brought the American president closer to Israel, and worried that it meant he did not clearly see the suffering of the Palestinians.

"BUSH KNEW," BLARED the headline on the *New York Post* on the morning of May 16. Senator Hillary Rodham Clinton of New York marched to the Senate floor and held up the newspaper. "The president knew what?" she demanded. "My constituents would like to know the answer to that and many other questions."

Nine months later, word was finally leaking out about the "Bin Ladin Determined" intelligence report presented to Bush at his ranch before the attacks. CBS News first reported that the CIA had briefed him on an al-Qaeda threat, leading to the splashy *New York Post* front page that Clinton was now displaying. The news organizations still did not have the document itself, so Americans had no idea just how sketchy it was, but just like that the politics of September 11 were upended.

Calls for investigation multiplied by the hour. Bush aides were angry at Clinton and other Democrats for insinuating that he had advance warning of the attack. "It didn't rattle him like it rattled a lot of us," Ari Fleischer said. But Bush later admitted, "It bothered me." At a closed lunch with Republican senators that day, Bush declared that had he known, he would have "used the whole force and fury of the United States to stop them." His words quickly leaked, as he knew they would. Then, speaking by phone, Bush agreed to let Cheney push back at a New York fund-raiser that night. "An investigation must not interfere with the ongoing efforts to prevent the next attack," Cheney warned, "because without a doubt, a very real threat of another, perhaps more devastating attack still exists."

Aides to Bush and Cheney knew an investigation would uncover more warnings, the "blinking red lights" George Tenet referred to, and few would spare the president for the vagueness of the information. The next day, May 17, Bush took on critics directly, using a Rose Garden appearance with the U.S. Air Force Academy's championship football team to repeat what he had told the senators.

"Had I known that the enemy was going to use airplanes to kill on that fateful morning, I would have done everything in my power to protect the American people," he said forcefully. "We will use the might of America to protect the American people."

The counterattack succeeded in dousing some of the partisan fire. Clinton backed off, saying she was not "looking to point fingers or place blame on anybody." But demands would only grow by Democrats, families of victims, and some Republicans for a comprehensive investigation into how September 11 happened.

AS SPRING ARRIVED, Bush headed to Moscow to cement improving relations with Russia. The nuclear treaty he had agreed to negotiate with Putin had been finished and encompassed just 475 words, the shortest in the history of Russian-American arms control and less than a third as long as the story about it in the *Washington Post*. It committed each side to shrinking its arsenal to between seventeen hundred and twenty-two hundred warheads by the end of 2012, a dramatic reduction from previous limits. The treaty allowed each side to simply store the weapons rather than destroy them, but it extended mutual inspections that began during the Cold War, and its larger point was symbolic.

Bush went along knowing it was important for Putin to mollify hard-core elements in Moscow—"Putin is at huge risk and he needs to fight off his troglodytes," Bush told advisers at one point—and he hoped it would keep Russia on board as the United States moved toward confrontation with Iraq. He flew to Moscow and entered the gilded St. Andrew's Hall in the Kremlin on May 24, sat down at a table with Putin, and signed the Moscow Treaty, also known as the Strategic Offensive Reductions Treaty. Bush was effusive. "This treaty liquidates the Cold War legacy of nuclear hostility between our countries," he said.

Behind closed doors, though, it did not seem so. Russia had retaliated against Bush's steel tariff by cutting off imports of American chicken drumsticks known as "Bush legs." As they discussed the impasse privately, Putin asserted that the Americans deliberately sent bad poultry to Russia.

"I know you have separate plants for chickens for America and chickens for Russia," Putin told Bush.

Bush was astonished. "Vladimir, you're wrong."

Putin refused to believe him. "My people have told me this is true."

Bush was struck by the old-school Russian paranoia. Putin had surrounded himself with KGB veterans still steeped in the worst suspicions of the Cold War. But if Bush was willing to blame the advisers rather than Putin, it suggested a fundamental misunderstanding of the Russian leader. It was not just his advisers who saw America through the old lens; it was Putin himself.

The meeting was a reminder of how hard it was to shake the past. Bush was trying to redefine national security in an era when Russia was no longer the enemy. The real threats, as he saw them, were stateless extremist groups and the nations that supported them, and he was now putting on paper a fleshed-out version of the doctrine he had begun articulating the night the World Trade Center fell. The United States had always reserved the right to strike first against an enemy gathering to attack, but Bush now wanted to take it a step further. In the post–September 11 world, Bush believed it was not enough to wait until an adversary was on the verge of striking. Instead, the United States would seek out potential threats, what the writer Jacob Weisberg called "Dick Cheney's notion of prophylactic aggression."

Bush unveiled this new strategy during a commencement address at the U.S. Military Academy at West Point. "We cannot defend America and our friends by hoping for the best," he told the first class to graduate since September 11. "We cannot put our faith in the word of tyrants, who solemnly sign non-proliferation treaties, and then systematically break them. If we wait for threats to fully materialize, we will have waited too long."

He added that "our security will require all Americans to be forward-looking and resolute, to be ready for preemptive action when necessary to defend our liberty and to defend our lives."

The approach came to be commonly called preemptive war. Scholars and international legal experts said that confused two concepts. *Preemptive war* refers to striking first when an enemy is about to attack you, much as the Israelis did during the Six-Day War in 1967. What Bush was talking about was *preventive war*, when a country attacks without imminent danger. Some administration officials later argued that Iraq did not qualify as either because it was actually a resumption of a war that started in 1991 and was temporarily halted by a cease-fire whose terms Iraq had been violating. Either way, Bush was not interested in parsing. "He didn't get dragged into the legalistic or theological debate," said Steve Biegun, a senior National Security Council official. "It was ultimately just the clarity of his words, which were we can't stand idly by when we're operating at the intersection of terrorism and weapons of mass destruction. It's unacceptable for us."

THAT WAS OFFENSE. On defense, Bush decided to reorganize the government to better guard against attacks. For the president, this was a reversal. Democrats like Senator Joseph Lieberman had been proposing a new cabinet department focused on homeland security for months, but the White House especially had opposed it, seeing it as a bureaucratic nightmare in the making. As pressure kept building, Bush saw the prospect of Congress approving a new department without him and made a strategic retreat. "Finally, they buckled because it was clear that this was gaining favor," Lieberman said later.

Once Bush had decided to move, his advisers had to figure out how to accomplish the largest bureaucratic restructuring of the American government since the National Security Act at the dawn of the Cold War. Bush believed the more he involved all the agencies, the slower things moved, and the more excuses were found for inaction. Bypassing the endless interagency process would be the only way to accomplish something this complicated. Andy Card quietly tapped five staff members, swore them to secrecy, and sent them to craft a plan in the emergency bunker where Cheney had managed September 11.

The five—Major General Bruce Lawlor, Richard Falkenrath, Joel Kaplan, Brad Berenson, and Mark Everson—were dubbed the Gang of

Five, or G-5, for short, and they met several times a week with a restricted number of senior officials brought in secretly, including Card, Rice, Tom Ridge, Mitch Daniels, and Scooter Libby. On poster board, they scratched out lists of agencies and departments to merge into a single massive Department of Homeland Security, a haphazard process at times. The Federal Aviation Agency, Border Patrol, Customs Service, Drug Enforcement Agency, Coast Guard, Immigration and Naturalization Service, and Secret Service would all be moved. So would the Federal Emergency Management Agency, under Bush's longtime aide Joe Allbaugh. But moving the FBI was an obvious nonstarter politically. Likewise, Card's suggestion to move the National Guard from the Defense Department proved unworkable. Other agencies were thrown in without the young aides grasping what they had done. The Gang of Five assigned the Lawrence Livermore National Laboratory to the new department without realizing it was dedicated to nuclear weapons research.

Word started to leak. When Allbaugh heard FEMA might be folded into the new department, he called Card and declared it a mistake because the agency needed a direct line to the White House.

Card told him it was too late. "This thing has a head of steam on it and I don't think it can be stopped," Card said.

Fuming, Allbaugh resolved to resign as soon as the change happened.

Bush did not tell his cabinet about the radical restructuring until just before it was unveiled, whereupon furious last-minute turf battles ensued. Tommy Thompson, the former Wisconsin governor now serving as health and human services secretary, tried to keep the National Disaster Medical System and the national drug stockpile. Spencer Abraham, the energy secretary, foiled the proposed Livermore transfer once he and his team explained what the lab actually did. Donald Rumsfeld was not told about the creation of the new department until Card called the night before the announcement. "The president will announce it tomorrow, and we are going to take four, five, or six agencies of the Pentagon away and just wanted to give you a heads-up," Rumsfeld remembered Card saying.

Since Libby was working with the Gang of Five, Cheney knew about the plan. He harbored reservations about another big-government response to a problem. But sensing Bush's commitment, Cheney made little protest. The president announced plans for the department on June 6. And then the real turf war began.

CHENEY WAS LESS reticent about Bush's other big initiative as summer arrived. With tanks out of Bethlehem, the president thought it was time for a broader strategy for the Middle East, but the vice president worried he would be undercutting Israel and rewarding Palestinian terrorists.

The thrust behind Bush's new effort was to change the game in a big way. He would call for a Palestinian state side by side with Israel, making an even more explicit commitment to sovereignty for the long-oppressed people than Bill Clinton had made in his peace negotiations. But at the same time, Bush planned to demand that the Palestinians get rid of their longtime leader, Yasser Arafat.

Bush had long since written off Arafat as a liar and unrepentant terrorist. He came into office deeply skeptical, influenced by Clinton's experience. When an intermediary came up during a UN meeting and suggested he shake Arafat's hand, Bush had snapped, "Tell him to shake his own hand." His suspicions only deepened when Israeli commandos stormed aboard a rusty blue cargo ship called the *Karine A* and found fifty tons of rockets, antitank grenades, and other explosives from Iran bound for the Palestinians. "I had to start by saying, I'm not going to deal with Arafat," Bush recalled after his presidency. "He stiffed Bill Clinton. He's a crook. He stole money, and he can't deliver peace, in spite of the fact he got the Nobel Peace Prize."

The idea generated heated debate inside the White House. Cheney agreed they should forswear Arafat but thought they were abandoning Israel by calling for a Palestinian state almost as if it were a reward for terrorism. "He was dead set against that and very disappointed," remembered Dan Bartlett. Colin Powell worried about it from the other end, concerned about alienating moderate Arab leaders who, while aware of Arafat's liabilities, still considered him the most credible voice for Palestinians. But Bush believed a viable Palestinian state with new leadership untainted by the past would allow them to get beyond Arafat, and he sympathized with Palestinians he thought had been betrayed by their own leadership and Arab states. "Whoever gave a damn about the Palestinian people?" he asked in one meeting.

Drafting the speech was torturous; it went through thirty drafts. Even then, Bush entertained doubts. One day he sat with Rice, Karen Hughes, and Michael Gerson.

"Of the three of you in this room," he said, "how many think I should give this speech?"

Rice, Hughes, and Gerson all raised their hands. So did Bush.

The debate went all the way into the weekend before the speech, when Bush finally added the line about Arafat. On a bright afternoon on June 24, Bush marched into the Rose Garden and redefined American policy for the Middle East in seventeen minutes. "I call on the Palestinian people to elect new leaders, leaders not compromised by terror," he said, flanked by Rice, Powell, and Rumsfeld. "I call upon them to build a practicing democracy, based on tolerance and liberty." He added, "And when the Palestinian people have new leaders, new institutions and new security arrangements with their neighbors, the United States of America will support the creation of a Palestinian state whose borders and certain aspects of its sovereignty will be provisional until resolved as part of a final settlement in the Middle East."

Alarm bells immediately went off among the diplomats at the State Department, who started plotting how to undo what they saw as the damage of cutting off Arafat. The speech proved to be controversial within his own family as well.

"How's the first Jewish president doing?" his mother asked when they spoke next. From that tart remark, Bush assumed his mother disapproved and "that meant Dad probably did as well."

The first president Bush had played the Middle East down the middle and, if anything, had closer ties to Arab leaders that he sustained in the years since the White House. But the son was heading in a different direction, nursing a visceral distaste for Arafat and an equally visceral sympathy for the Israelis as victims of terrorism.

The European allies were as upset as the State Department. "Even with our friends, I was Public Enemy Number One," Bush observed years later. " 'What'd you go and do that for?' 'Because,' I said, 'I won't deal with a corrupt thief who doesn't care about his own people and has no commitment to the peace process. Get me a leader who respects human rights and can be a legitimate partner for peace. Until then, I'm out.' "

While many argued that the Israeli-Palestinian conflict was critical to the antipathy fueling anti-American terrorism and therefore critical to solve, Cheney did not see it that way. "You couldn't wait for there to be some kind of solution between the Israelis and Palestinians and then decide you are going to get aggressive on the war on terror," he said later. His attention remained fixed on Iraq. Even as he was losing the debate on the Rose Garden speech, the vice president was pressing Bush to bomb a suspected terrorist camp in northern Iraq.

The CIA had obtained intelligence that a Sunni extremist group known as Ansar al-Islam was operating a chemical weapons laboratory near the Kurdish town of Khurmal in the rugged Zagros Mountains of northeastern Iraq. Analysts believed Abu Musab al-Zarqawi, a Jordanian militant who had run an al-Qaeda training camp in Afghanistan and fled after being wounded during the American-led assault, had taken refuge at Khurmal, joining forces with Ansar al-Islam. The camp was believed to shelter suspected terrorists. Bush was told they were developing ricin and cyanide and had tested their product on animals and even one of their own associates, who died a horrific death as his compatriots watched. One briefing paper given to the White House asserted that "Al-Zarqawi has been directing efforts to smuggle an unspecified chemical material originating in northern Iraq into the United States."

The Joint Chiefs of Staff developed a plan to attack the Khurmal facility and sent it to the White House in late June, unanimously recommending a combined air-ground operation be launched on July 4. An aerial barrage would destroy the camp, followed by a helicopter raid by special operations forces entering through Turkey to kill or capture survivors and scour the site for useful intelligence and evidence of weapons production. The mission would hardly be easy; the high altitude and mountain ridges, not to mention the possibility of a dust storm, would complicate a ground operation. Military planners believed it was "doable, but challenging." The debate at the White House was one of the most contentious to date. Cheney and Rumsfeld argued vigorously for the attack, reasoning this was exactly the definition of Bush's new doctrine. Richard Myers told the president that the Joint Chiefs agreed.

But Powell opposed the operation. There was no conclusive evidence that Saddam Hussein was knowingly harboring Zarqawi in the Kurdish area, which was effectively autonomous from Baghdad. What was presented as a limited strike could easily escalate, effectively opening a war that Bush had not yet decided to wage months before U.S. forces would be prepared. Moreover, Powell maintained an early strike would disrupt efforts to build an international coalition to isolate Hussein. And what if the intelligence was wrong? What would the Turks think of the Americans using their territory? What if there were civilian casualties? Shadowing the moment were memories of Clinton's ill-fated 1998 missile strike against a pharmaceutical plant in Sudan based on questionable intelligence that it was a chemical weapons facility associated with Osama bin Laden.

After one sharp debate over the proposed operation in June, Rice followed Bush back to the Oval Office and told him she agreed with Powell.

Bush told her he shared the concerns and was not ready to start the war. Khurmal would have to wait.

While he would later be accused of a rush to war, Bush at this point wanted to take time for his diplomatic strategy against Hussein to play out. Cheney thought he was making a mistake, undercutting his own Bush Doctrine of going after terrorists wherever they were found.

FOR ALL THE jokes and insinuations about being the secret power behind the throne, Cheney actually got a moment in the big chair on June 29.

With Bush's fifty-sixth birthday approaching, the president agreed to undergo a routine colonoscopy, which would involve an anesthetic that would leave him briefly incapacitated. To be "super cautious" in a time of war, Bush decided to temporarily transfer power to Cheney under the Twenty-Fifth Amendment of the Constitution.

There was little precedent for this. Since the amendment was ratified in 1967, the only other time a president had temporarily passed his powers to a vice president came in 1985 when Bush's father stepped in while Ronald Reagan underwent intestinal surgery. Even then, as Reagan signed letters authorizing the transfer, he wrote that he did not think the Twenty-Fifth Amendment actually applied. The younger Bush had no such constitutional qualms in handing the reins to Cheney. "He's standing by," Bush told reporters, adding mischievously, "He'll realize he's not going to be president that long."

Sitting on a couch in a lounge at the Eucalyptus Cabin at Camp David, Bush signed identical letters to Speaker Dennis Hastert and Senator Robert Byrd, president pro tempore of the Senate, the two next in the line of succession behind Cheney, informing them that he would "transfer temporarily my Constitutional powers and duties to the Vice President during the brief period of the procedure and recovery." Alberto Gonzales, the White House counsel, took the letters by golf cart to the Willow Lodge, where the Camp David communications center faxed them at 7:09 a.m. Colonel Richard J. Tubb of the air force, the White House physician, then performed the procedure, finishing at 7:29 a.m. without finding any polyps. Bush awoke at 7:31 a.m., got up soon thereafter, ate a waffle, and played with his dogs. He signed another pair of letters to Hastert and Byrd "resuming those powers and duties effective immediately" and had them faxed at 9:24 a.m. Cheney spent two hours and fifteen minutes as acting president, mostly at the White House holding national security meetings, but took no publicly recorded actions.

BUSH'S NEW BEST friend increasingly seemed to be Tony Blair. As Bush mapped out a strategy for taking on Iraq, Blair was a full partner. Indeed, if Bush had failed to find his Bob Bullock in Washington, arguably he was finding him in London. "Here you have this liberal Labour leader, Tony Blair, and you have this conservative Republican from Texas, George Bush, and they see exactly eye to eye on the threat in Iraq," noted Karen Hughes.

Blair's team was sensing that summer that Bush's mind was already made up. "There was a perceptible shift in attitude," the British intelligence chief reported to Blair and his team, according to a July 23 memo. "Military action was now seen as inevitable. Bush wanted to remove Saddam, through military action, justified by the conjunction of terrorism and WMD. But the intelligence and facts were being fixed around the policy. The NSC had no patience with the UN route, and no enthusiasm for publishing material on the Iraqi regime's record. There was little discussion in Washington of the aftermath after military action." The same memo summarized the foreign secretary's report: "It seemed clear that Bush had made up his mind to take military action, even if the timing was not yet decided. But the case was thin. Saddam was not threatening his neighbours, and his WMD capability was less than that of Libya, North Korea or Iran."

Bush would later deny that, but indeed every meeting on Iraq through the spring and summer had focused on *how* to attack Iraq—where they would send troops, who would be with them, how long it would take. With Cheney driving the conversation, little if any discussion was devoted to *whether* they should and what the consequences would be. When Richard Haass, the director of policy planning at the State Department, expressed concern to Condoleezza Rice that war with Iraq would dominate the administration's foreign policy, she brushed away his concerns, saying the president had made up his mind, a comment he took to mean that a "political and psychological Rubicon" had been crossed even though it would be months until military action began. "They were really beating the drums," recalled someone in the skeptic camp. Indeed, the British had a point; Bush decided to deal with North Korea through negotiations that included its neighbors in what would become known as the six-party talks. With Iraq, talks were not the goal.

Colin Powell decided to confront the issue one-on-one with the president. "I really have to see the president," he told Rice. "I have to do it alone without all the warlords in the room."

A meeting was set for August 5. Powell, returning from a trip to Asia, scribbled his points on a pad of paper through a long flight over the Pacific.

At 4:30 on the day of the scheduled meeting, Bush, Cheney, Powell, and the rest of the national security team received an update from Tommy Franks on Iraq. Donald Rumsfeld insisted no one take notes and collected the handouts afterward. Franks was planning a light-footprint invasion that would use far fewer troops than during the Gulf War a decade earlier and rely instead on speed and the much more advanced technology wielded by the modern military.

The discussion then turned to postwar planning. Cheney later recalled that Bush looked at George Tenet and asked how the Iraqi people would react to an American invasion. "Most Iraqis will rejoice when Saddam is gone," Tenet said, by Cheney's account. That was almost identical to the prediction Cheney would later make publicly, a forecast that would become a symbol of hubris. Cheney included the conversation in his memoir after leaving office to make clear he had a basis for his forecast, or at least to spread the blame.

After the meeting, Bush brought Powell over to the White House residence for dinner, then invited him to the Treaty Room on the second floor, a private study that had been used in the past for cabinet meetings and the signing of the treaty ending the Spanish-American War. Laura had stocked it with furniture from Ulysses S. Grant's era so Bush could use it as a home office.

Bush listened as Powell ran through the points from his notepad: the consequences of an invasion, the cost to international unity, the possibility of oil price spikes, the potential destabilization of Saudi Arabia and other allies in the region. It would suck all the oxygen out of Bush's term. And most important, it would mean Bush would effectively be responsible for a shattered country, for twenty-five million people and all their hopes and aspirations.

"If you break it, you are going to own it," Powell told Bush. "It isn't getting to Baghdad. It is what happens after you get to Baghdad. And it ain't going to be easy."

Bush asked what he should do.

"We should take the problem to the United Nations," Powell said. "Iraq is in violation of multiple UN resolutions. The UN is the legally aggrieved party."

"Even if the UN doesn't solve it," he added, "making the effort, if you have to go to war, gives you the ability to ask for allies or ask for help."

But Powell also noted Iraq might give in, in which case Bush would have to take yes for an answer, even if it meant Hussein remaining in power.

Bush was struck by Powell's intensity and signaled that he was open to talking about it. "Colin was more passionate than I had seen him at any NSC meeting," Bush recalled.

ON AUGUST 15, ten days after dinner with Powell, Bush was at his ranch scrolling through newspaper clips when he came across an op-ed in the *Wall Street Journal* by Brent Scowcroft, his father's close friend and former national security adviser. "Don't Attack Saddam" read the headline.

The column argued that war in Iraq could distract from the war on terrorism. "The United States could certainly defeat the Iraqi military and destroy Saddam's regime," Bush read. "But it would not be a cakewalk. On the contrary, it undoubtedly would be very expensive—with serious consequences for the U.S. and global economy—and could as well be bloody."

An invasion of Iraq "could well destabilize Arab regimes in the region" and mean "a large-scale, long-term military occupation."

Bush was livid, knowing the piece would be seen as a message from his father or at least repudiation by his father's inner circle. "He was pissed off and let anybody within shouting distance know, including Condi," recalled Dan Bartlett. "He would just rail at her about it—knowing that it wasn't her fault." Rice was a Scowcroft protégée and likewise felt blindsided. She told the president that Scowcroft was just a cautious person on such matters but she would call him. Bush then called his father, who tried to calm him down. "Son, Brent is a friend," he said. Cheney read the piece too and thought Scowcroft was stuck in the past, revealing a "pre-9/11 mind-set, the worldview of a time before we had seen the devastation that terrorists armed with hijacked airplanes could cause."

Rice called Scowcroft and scolded him for taking his views public without talking with her first. "Brent, you know, I wish you had just come and sat down and told me those things," she recalled telling him. Scowcroft responded that he never meant to criticize the president. He just "thought it might be helpful to calm down some of the war talk," as Rice paraphrased him. It was a hard conversation. As Scowcroft later put it, "I got taken to the woodshed." But the reality was that Scowcroft had felt shut out of the new administration and resorted to the pages of a national newspaper because he did not think the White House would listen to him. The headline, written by an editor, may have been blunter than he would have liked, but he did not quarrel with it. He thought the drive for war was a mistake and missed the more fundamental problem in the region, the unsettled dispute between Israelis and Palestinians. Scowcroft felt offended at the notion that the first Bush administration had failed by not taking Hussein out in 1991. "All the neocons were saying, 'Finish the job,'" he said. "In fact, the president said that." While Scowcroft denied writing the piece at the behest of the president's father, there were those who never believed him. "The Scowcroft piece in the *Wall Street Journal* could not have been without HW's approval," said one person close to the Bush family.

The next day, August 16, Powell made his pitch to the National Security Council for the UN route, with Bush participating by video from the ranch and Cheney from his Wyoming home. Cheney understood that Bush had already decided to go along with Powell. But privately he disdained the United Nations as a feckless debating society corrupted by the likes of Hussein and incapable of taking a stand. A lengthy diplomatic campaign would only give Hussein time to expand his arsenal, find a way to hide his weapons, or, worst of all, carry out an attack on the United States or its interests overseas.

Cheney had been meditating on the meaning of September 11 and read a new collection of essays by Victor Davis Hanson called *An Autumn of War*. They made such a powerful impression on him that he invited Hanson for a visit. Cheney was particularly interested in the classically tragic view, from Sophocles to the American Western, that there are not always good and bad choices, but bad and worse choices. For Cheney, leaving Hussein in power was worse than the bad choice of taking him out. He had no doubts that Hussein had weapons. He remembered how wrong intelligence assessments of Iraq had been before the Gulf War. He remembered sitting in his Pentagon office listening to intelligence analysts tell him Iraq was at least five or ten years away from having a nuclear weapon, only to discover after the war that it was in fact much closer, perhaps even just a year away. The lesson he took was clear: if anything, intelligence assessments tended to underestimate the threat, not the other way around.

But Cheney was hearing from friends that Scowcroft's view was on the rise and that the White House had better explain to the public what was so vital about Iraq. On August 18, he heard from Senator Trent Lott, the Republican leader.

"Dick, I think you may have a big problem here with public perceptions of a possible Iraq war," Lott told him. "The case hasn't been made as to why we should do it."

"Don't worry," Cheney said. "We're about to fix all of that. Just hold on."

Before he could fix it, another old friend weighed in. On August 25, Bush and Cheney picked up the *New York Times* and found unsolicited advice from James Baker, the former secretary of state whom Cheney had first plucked out of obscurity in the 1970s and who had overseen the 2000 recount that put the current team into office. Unlike Scowcroft, Baker did not directly oppose war with Iraq, but he urged the president to seek a new UN Security Council resolution requiring Iraq to submit to no-warning inspections and "authorizing all necessary means to enforce it," presumably including force. "Although the United States could certainly succeed, we should try our best not to have to go it alone, and the president should reject the advice of those who counsel doing so," Baker continued. By that, he meant Cheney.

CHENEY TOOK HIS rebuttal public the next day, as he made good on his promise to Lott to fix things. He had commissioned a tough speech to deliver to the Veterans of Foreign Wars. Where Bush would edit speeches line by line, Cheney tended to accept speeches in whole or not, and when he did make changes, they were fully formed paragraphs written out neatly by hand without mistakes. This would be the longest speech of his vice presidency to date, and he wanted it right.

Addressing the aging warriors in the Nashville convention hall, Cheney dispensed with any of the caveats about Iraq. "Simply stated, there is no doubt that Saddam Hussein now has weapons of mass destruction," he said. "There is no doubt he is amassing them to use against our friends, against our allies, and against us." He went beyond simply asserting that Hussein had chemical and biological weapons. "We now know that Saddam has resumed his efforts to acquire nuclear weapons," Cheney said. He added, "Many of us are convinced that Saddam will acquire nuclear weapons fairly soon."

As a result, he went on, there was no point in sending inspectors back in, even though that was exactly what Bush was thinking about doing. "Against that background," Cheney said, "a person would be right to question any suggestion that we should just get inspectors back into Iraq, and then our worries will be over. Saddam has perfected the game of cheat and retreat, and is very skilled in the art of denial and deception. A return of inspectors would provide no assurance whatsoever of his compliance with U.N. resolutions. On the contrary, there is a great danger that it would provide false comfort that Saddam was somehow back in his box."

When Powell heard about the speech, he erupted in anger and called Rice. "Condi, anybody look at this speech?" he demanded, and took her halting answer to mean not really. "He is undercutting the president before the president has tossed the pitch."

Rice agreed Cheney had gone too far. "I will fix it," she told Powell.

The president, vacationing in Crawford, was aggravated too. "Bush was hot about it; he was not pleased," Ari Fleischer said later. "It wasn't him. It wasn't Bush's point of view." But the president chose not to confront Cheney, instead telling Rice to do it.

"Call Dick and tell him I haven't made a decision," he told Rice.

She walked back to the Governor's House, the separate building where she stayed while at the ranch, and got the vice president on the phone. "The president is concerned that your speech is being read as a decision to skip the UN and challenge Saddam unilaterally," Rice recalled telling Cheney. "It's cut off the president's options."

The vice president agreed to soften the language in a follow-up speech to veterans of the Korean War in San Antonio three days later and told her to call Scooter Libby with the exact language she wanted. She did and later claimed he read it verbatim in the next speech.

But the new wording was only slightly less dismissive of the diplomatic route: "Many have suggested that the problem can be dealt with simply by returning inspectors to Iraq. But we must remember that inspections are not an end in themselves. The objective has to be disarmament." Cheney added, "With Saddam's record of thwarting inspections, one has to be concerned that he would continue to plot, using the available time to husband his resources, to invest in his ongoing chemical and biological weapons programs, and to gain the possession of nuclear weapons." Powell did not find the revised version much more to his liking.

At the same time, George Tenet was upset that the speech had never been cleared with his agency and felt the assertions "went well beyond what our analysis could support." But he never challenged Cheney, reluctant to insert himself into policy making—a reluctance he would come to regret. "I should have told the vice president privately that, in my view, his VFW speech had gone too far."

12

"A brutal, ugly, repugnant man"

"What are we talking about Iraq for? Where is this coming from?"

Karen Hughes watched Vice President Cheney's speech from her kitchen table in Austin. President Bush's longtime confidante and muse, she had just recently left her White House job and returned to Texas to spend more time with family. But she remained a key outside adviser to the president and did not like what she was seeing.

As a political specialist, Hughes had not been part of the months of deliberations in the Situation Room or privy to the planning Donald Rumsfeld and Tommy Franks had been conducting at the president's request. To her, the intense focus on Iraq seemed totally out of the blue. The whole idea of going to war with Iraq struck her as a distraction. She did not see the connection to September 11 that Cheney did, and to her it seemed as if Bush were being steered down a path toward a dangerous confrontation.

She called the president in Washington to express her concern. What's going on? she asked. Why is Iraq suddenly so prominent on the agenda?

He told her there were plenty of reasons that he needed to take on Saddam Hussein, not just the connections with terrorists Cheney saw. If she was so troubled by the prospect, he said, then she should get together with Condoleezza Rice, who could walk her through the reasons.

Hughes agreed to do that, and soon she met Rice for dinner. Rice knew how much Hughes cared about Bush and recognized that she needed to reassure the Texas adviser. She laid out for Hughes a series of factors driving the focus on Iraq: It was the only place in the world where American airplanes were being shot at as they enforced the no-fly zone. Hussein had a history of bullying neighbors and using chemical weapons on his own people. The last time America went to war with him, intelligence agencies discovered he was further along in his nuclear program than they had known.

In light of September 11, Rice said, the United States had to reassess threats. Tolerating someone as dangerous as Hussein no longer seemed tenable.

Hughes was impressed by the arguments, but they did not completely convince her. If Bush really was heading toward confrontation with Iraq, then she wanted to make sure he kept as much flexibility as possible so he was not railroaded into a war he did not really want.

She was not the only old friend from Texas who worried as they watched Bush barreling down the road to a clash with Hussein. His lifelong friend Joe O'Neill was among those in the president's longtime circle who agreed that Bush had to attack Afghanistan after September 11 but considered invading Iraq a bad idea. They worried he was being pushed into it. Yet these friends generally kept their doubts to themselves. "I didn't volunteer it," O'Neill recalled. "It's not my job."

The drive to war accelerated after Labor Day as the president and Congress returned to Washington. On September 4, Bush summoned congressional leaders to ask for a resolution of force against Iraq. Some in the room were surprised, having assumed the White House had no intention of seeking congressional input. But now the president was in effect putting them on the hook, forcing them to choose one way or the other—confront Hussein or not?

"Saddam Hussein is a serious threat to the United States, to his neighbors, and to the people who disagree with him inside Iraq," Bush told the leaders. "Doing nothing is not an option and I hope Congress agrees." He added that he planned to press the United Nations to sign on as well. "Saddam Hussein has stiffed the United Nations Security Council," Bush said. "He sidestepped, he crawfished. He has no intention to comply. If the UN wants to be relevant, they need to do something about it. The fact that the world has not dealt with him has created a bigger monster."

After ten minutes, he opened up the floor. The lawmakers asked him what new evidence of banned weapons the United States had and whether military action would be unilateral. Bush said there was plenty of evidence and that he would prefer to have the backing of the United Nations but would go it alone if necessary.

"I will be with you on condition we level with the American people—we have to stay a while," Senator Joseph Biden, the Democratic chairman of the Foreign Relations Committee, told him.

"You're right," Bush responded.

"If you can get it done without staying," Biden added, "we'll give you the Nobel Peace Prize. I'll support you for president."

"I don't know whether that will help me or hurt me," Bush joked.

But other Democrats were upset. Senator Tom Daschle recognized that the timeline would mean Congress would be debating war right before the election. Remembering Karl Rove's comments on taking the war to voters, Daschle suspected political motivations.

Even a Republican leader thought war with Iraq was a fool's errand. "If you invade Iraq, you're going to win the war in two or three weeks and then you're going to own the place and you'll never get out of it," Dick Armey, the House majority leader, told him. "It'll be such a burden on your presidency you'll never be able to complete your domestic agenda."

Bush tried to reassure Armey. "Will you just hold your fire until we have a chance to fully brief you?" he asked.

Armey agreed.

Later that day, Bush sent Rumsfeld to Capitol Hill to brief the Senate. About two-thirds of the members showed up, but the session was "a disaster" that might have "destroyed all of the good will and ground work that the president accomplished during his meeting this morning," a White House aide wrote in a memo that night. "I found myself struggling to keep from laughing out loud at times, especially when Sec. Rumsfeld became a caricature of himself." He refused to share even the most basic intelligence, the aide wrote. "There is a lot of clean up work to do here."

BUSH, CHENEY, AND the rest of the national security team gathered at Camp David on the evening of September 6 in preparation for a meeting the next morning about the president's upcoming speech to the United Nations. It was almost a year to the day since the fateful Camp David meeting that set the administration's course in Afghanistan. Now the team was back in the Maryland mountains to figure out what to do next.

While Powell had won the day by convincing Bush to go to the world body, the unsettled question was whether he would ask for a new resolution. That was a rat hole Cheney wanted to avoid. Tying their hands to the bureaucratic morass to win what he called "yet one more meaningless resolution" was a mistake, one that would only give Hussein more time. When the team sat down in Laurel Lodge, Cheney argued that inspectors would not be Americans and could be fooled by Hussein, muddying the waters. Powell maintained that a resolution was needed to show the world that the United States was willing to do everything possible before turning to force. Then if war did come, Powell said, they would be in a stronger position to build a broad coalition. Bush did not make up his mind at that moment, but issued a dire conclusion. "Either he will come clean about his weapons," he told the group, "or there will be war."

In years to come, some in the war cabinet, including Donald Rumsfeld and George Tenet, would say there was never a single moment when the national security team debated the fundamental question of whether going to war was a good idea, nor any point when Bush asked his advisers directly whether he should attack Iraq. Indeed, the discussion at Camp David that day focused largely on tactics. Yet others saw it as the turning point, the juncture at which Bush resolved to go forward. "It was very much on everybody's minds that you don't give this speech and then not follow through," Dan Bartlett said. Whatever reservations anyone harbored, no one in the room challenged the core judgment that Iraq was worth a war. "In neither this meeting nor any other I attended did any of the president's advisers argue against using military force to remove Saddam from power," Cheney said later. "Nor did anyone argue that leaving Saddam in power, with all the risks and costs associated with that course, was a viable option." Rice, who would clash with Cheney on so many other issues, agreed on that point. "There was no disagreement," she said. "The way ahead could not have been clearer."

For Bush, the decision on how to proceed with the United Nations was sealed that night when he and Cheney had dinner with Tony Blair, who flew from Britain for the sole purpose of convincing the Americans to seek a resolution. Blair told Bush and Cheney that winning a Security Council endorsement would make it easier to forge a true international coalition and expressed fear of the consequences of the United States and Britain going it alone. Cheney looked "very sour throughout," Blair's adviser Alastair Campbell recalled. The British were struck that the vice president attended all the meetings, including the one normally restricted to the leaders, which brought home "as never before Cheney's influence in the Bush administration."

During the session that included aides, Campbell told Bush they needed to understand anti-American sentiment around the world; a lot of it was jealousy, he said, but some was fear of American power. The rhetoric from Washington had not helped.

"You mean we shouldn't talk about democracy?" Cheney snapped.

Not if it came across as a message about Americanization, Campbell retorted.

Bush agreed to seek the resolution from the Security Council. "I think ultimately he bought the idea that this was going to be a whole lot easier if we had a coalition behind us," Blair recalled. That was part of it, but a lot of it was Blair himself. Bush was impressed. "Your man has got *cojones*," he told Campbell. As the prime minister was leaving after just six hours on the ground, Bush joked, "I suppose you can tell the story of how Tony flew in and pulled the crazed unilateralist back from the brink."

Still, Bush and Cheney were ready to take their case to the public. Andy Card had told a *New York Times* reporter in an article that appeared the day Blair visited that they had waited until now because "from a marketing point of view, you don't introduce new products in August." Now it was September, time to launch the product. When reporters from the *Times* called to ask what intelligence agencies knew about Hussein's weapons, officials shared one of the most alarming conclusions found in the reports being sent to Bush and Cheney. On September 8, the *Times* duly reported that Iraq had bought aluminum tubes that could be used for centrifuges to enrich uranium. Officials added that the first sign of a smoking gun might be a mushroom cloud, a clever phrase Michael Gerson had come up with.

That same day, Cheney and Rice went on the Sunday talk shows and cited the story as if it were somehow independent confirmation of their case. "There's a story in the *New York Times* this morning," Cheney said on NBC's *Meet the Press*. "It's now public that, in fact, he has been seeking to acquire, and we have been able to intercept and prevent him from acquiring through this particular channel, the kinds of tubes that are necessary to build a centrifuge." Asked if Hussein already had a nuclear bomb, Cheney said he could not say. "I can say that I know for sure that he's trying to acquire the capability." Rice, on CNN's *Late Edition*, even used the anonymous quotation, saying, "We don't want the smoking gun to be a mushroom cloud."

Cheney rode to the Pentagon on September 11, the first anniversary of the attacks, to join Rumsfeld in briefing three dozen senators about Iraqi weapons. Joined by George Tenet, they were so aggressive that some senators left assuming an invasion was a foregone conclusion. "It was pretty clear that Rumsfeld and Cheney are ready to go to war," Senator Max Cleland wrote afterward in a note to himself. "They have already made the decision to go to war and to them that is the only option."

BUSH FLEW TO New York for the UN General Assembly session the next day. One year after the attacks that had unified the world, he was returning a different figure in a different moment. Anxious about protecting his country, eager to strike out at its enemies, he had lost fifteen pounds and much of whatever innocence he had brought to the office.

The speech was in flux almost until the last minute as Cheney and Powell shadowboxed over how explicitly to ask for a new resolution. Taking the lectern, Bush saw a sea of unsmiling faces, many listening intently to bulky white devices on their ears that would translate his words into dozens of languages. Bush collected himself and launched into his talk, part persuasion, part lecture. He started with the carrot, announcing that the United

States would return to the United Nations Educational, Scientific, and Cultural Organization, or UNESCO, years after withdrawing amid complaints of corruption. The delegates applauded with their approval. It would be the only time they would interrupt to clap.

"Our greatest fear," Bush went on to say, "is that terrorists will find a shortcut to their mad ambitions when an outlaw regime supplies them with the technologies to kill on a massive scale. In one place, in one regime, we find all these dangers, in their most lethal and aggressive forms, exactly the kind of aggressive threat the United Nations was born to confront." He laid out an indictment of Iraq's failure to abide by UN resolutions, daring the body to confront Baghdad. "We know that Saddam Hussein pursued weapons of mass murder even when inspectors were in his country," Bush continued. "Are we to assume that he stopped when they left? The history, the logic, and the facts lead to one conclusion: Saddam Hussein's regime is a grave and gathering danger."

And soon he came to the point: "My nation will work with the U.N. Security Council to meet our common challenge," he said. "If Iraq's regime defies us again, the world must move deliberately, decisively to hold Iraq to account."

Powell and Rice, following along in the audience, realized Bush had left out the critical line about seeking a resolution. After so much back-and-forth, a draft without the updated language had been fed into the teleprompter. All that work, all that fighting, and in the end he would skip the essential point because of a logistical screwup?

As Powell and Rice grew agitated, Bush recognized the omission and ad-libbed it. "We will work with the U.N. Security Council for the necessary resolutions," he said.

His advisers were relieved. But wait a minute. Had he said *resolutions*, plural? Did that extra letter commit them to coming back to the council more than once? That could be a problem.

Just as important, though, were two sentences that followed. "The Security Council resolutions will be enforced—the just demands of peace and security will be met—or action will be unavoidable," Bush went on, picking up the text again. "And a regime that has lost its legitimacy will also lose its power." It was all but a declaration of war dressed up in an ultimatum: *Bow to these demands, or our forces will topple your government.* In the most public of forums, the president of the United States had signaled the coming showdown as clearly as he could.

Twenty-five minutes after he had begun, Bush wrapped up and looked out at the audience knowing he had not won it over. "It's like speaking to the wax museum," he observed afterward. "No one moves."

THE DRIVE FOR war was not helped when Bush saw on September 16 that Lawrence Lindsey, his top economics adviser, had told the *Wall Street Journal* that it could cost $100 billion to $200 billion. In fact, Lindsey was just thinking out loud, not offering a formal projection. He was actually saying that war costs would not have a major economic impact and would be worth it to protect the country from future attack even if it cost between 1 percent and 2 percent of the nation's gross domestic product, which at the time would mean $100 billion to $200 billion. The Gulf War had cost 1 percent of gross domestic product, and Vietnam between 1.5 percent and 2 percent.

But the raw numbers looked enormous compared with predictions by other officials. Lindsey realized his colleagues "were furious" that he was so off message. "At that time, message discipline on Iraq was the functional equivalent of radio silence," he later concluded. Bush himself was edgy the next time he saw him. "So, Lindsey, you're estimating the cost of wars I'm not even planning yet?" Bush asked. Publicly, the White House tried to shoot down his statements. Mitch Daniels, the budget director, was sent out to say that the Lindsey numbers were "likely very, very high."

The issue complicated Bush's campaign to win support in Congress. On September 19, he met behind closed doors with nearly a dozen House members from both parties at the White House, and Representative Howard Berman, a California Democrat, asked if Daniels would be willing to spend the money needed for nation building after Saddam Hussein was toppled.

"Mark my words—yes, we will spend the necessary money," Bush responded.

Several other members urged him to emphasize the threat in his speeches.

"I am well aware," Bush said. "He tried to kill my dad."

With those private words, Bush hinted at the complicated mix of motivations driving him. But he was also thinking bigger than simple retribution. The next day, the White House released a new National Security Strategy, building on the president's West Point speech on preemption. Defeating global terrorism was among the eight goals, as to be expected, but it was the second one listed. Number one was "champion aspirations for human dignity." Many missed the point: Bush was increasingly defining his mission beyond just confronting threats to American security. That evening, he hosted Republican governors for dinner in the State Dining Room. With no reporters present, Bush condemned Saddam Hussein as "a brutal, ugly, repugnant man" but then alluded to the broader agenda. "I'm gonna make a prediction," he told the governors. "Write this down. Afghanistan and Iraq will lead that part of the world to democracy. They are going to be the catalyst to change the Middle East and the world."

At the same time Bush and Cheney were lobbying lawmakers for bipartisan support, they were also waging a fiercely partisan campaign to win the upcoming midterm elections. Just as Karl Rove had forecast, they were taking their national security case to the American public and winning. One of their most cutting arguments concerned the proposed Department of Homeland Security, an idea Bush opposed for nine months after September 11 but now supported, although he was bogged down in a dispute over collective bargaining rights for its employees. Bush wanted to run the department with as little red tape as possible, while Democrats defended the interests of organized labor, a core constituency. To campaign audiences, though, Bush cast it as a sign of Democratic weakness.

"The Senate is more interested in special interests in Washington and not interested in the security of the American people," he declared in a speech in New Jersey on September 23. Democrats were livid. Tom Daschle marched to the Senate floor two days later to denounce Bush's comments as "outrageous, outrageous." But Republican candidates picked up the theme. In Georgia, the Republican challenger, Saxby Chambliss, ran an ad attacking Senator Max Cleland, the incumbent Democrat who had lost three limbs at Khe Sanh in Vietnam. The ad showed pictures of Osama bin Laden and Saddam Hussein, then reported that Cleland voted against Bush's homeland security proposals and therefore lacked "the courage to lead."

THE DAY BEFORE Daschle's speech, Cheney slipped into his official car for the short drive to Capitol Hill. Arriving at his office on the House side, he met with Dick Armey, the skeptical Republican leader.

"Now Dick, when I lay all this out for you and you see all this evidence, I know you're going to agree with me," Cheney said.

Armey could not help noticing that Cheney said he would agree "with me," not "with the president." For a half hour, Cheney laid out the case, showing photographs of aluminum tubes and satellite images of structures he called weapons facilities and walking Armey through the history of the Gulf War and UN inspections. Most ominously, Cheney warned that Hussein might be able to miniaturize weapons and put them in a suitcase. And he emphasized again what he saw as the links between Iraq and al-Qaeda.

Cheney grew grim and laid out the worst-case scenario. "Dick, how would you feel if you voted no on this and the Iraqis brought in a bomb and blew up half the people of San Francisco?"

Armey was suitably scared but still dubious.

"You're going to get mired down there," he predicted.

No, Cheney said. "It'll be like the American troops going through Paris."

In the end, Armey felt he had no choice but to go along. It was a fateful decision. Had the Republican majority leader opposed the authorization of force, it would have freed other nervous Republicans and given cover to Democrats to oppose it as well. Cheney had accomplished his mission. But it would ultimately destroy his relationship with Armey, who came to feel betrayed. "I deserved better than to have been bullshitted by Dick Cheney," he said years later. "I can't definitively say that Cheney purposely lied to me, but if you demonstrated it to me, I wouldn't be surprised."

That same day, the British government released a dossier accusing Iraq of possessing banned weapons and went beyond even what the American intelligence agencies had been saying. Among other things, the dossier asserted that Iraq had sought "significant quantities of uranium from Africa" and claimed that some of Hussein's chemical and biological weapons "are deployable within 45 minutes of an order to use them." That meant mortars and other battlefield tactical weapons, but many assumed from the breathless media coverage that it referred to missiles that could reach London or Washington.

The CIA had warned the British against those claims, but Bush would eventually adopt both of them. "According to the British government, the Iraqi regime could launch a biological or chemical attack in as little as forty-five minutes after the order were given," he said in the Rose Garden on September 26, despite the skepticism of his own CIA.

In a closed meeting with eighteen lawmakers just before heading out to the Rose Garden, Bush had also embraced another unfounded assertion. "Saddam Hussein is a terrible guy who is teaming up with al-Qaeda," he told the lawmakers, ignoring the lack of any hard evidence of such an alliance.

One of the lawmakers asked him what would happen after Hussein was toppled, and Bush seemed to almost dismiss the concern.

"Nothing can be worse than the present situation," he said. The "timeframe," he added, "would be six months."

Later that day, he flew to a fund-raiser in Texas and repeated publicly what he had told lawmakers privately a week earlier about his family's relationship with Hussein. "There's no doubt his hatred is mainly directed at us," Bush said. "There's no doubt he can't stand us. After all, this is the guy that tried to kill my dad at one time."

BUT DID HE have the weapons Bush and Cheney said he did? While they were stretching the case, the reports sent to the president and the vice president suggested Hussein did have at least some weapons. Cheney, a voracious consumer of intelligence since his service on the House Intelligence Committee, even went to the CIA headquarters nearly a dozen times with aides to dive more deeply into the agency's information. At times, George Tenet thought, Cheney and Scooter Libby knew the agency's material better than it did, embarrassing analysts who could not keep up with questions. The visits would become hotly disputed, a sign to many that Cheney pressured the CIA, although subsequent investigations found no evidence that anyone changed an assessment of Iraq's weapons program because of pressure from the vice president.

"There is this mythology that he would come out to the agency frequently for briefings and try to muscle us into stuff," John McLaughlin, the deputy CIA director who sat in on most of the meetings, said later. "We never viewed it that way." Cheney, he said, "wasn't passive at all, but he was not bullying in any sense. He was always very respectful and engaging, and you just have disagreements." Still, less senior analysts might not have seen it so benignly. "They might have had a different feeling than I did," McLaughlin said. "That is always something you have to be on guard for."

Others said that while there was no obvious pressure, at some point analysts knew what the vice president was looking for and were "overly eager to please," as Michael Sulick, then the CIA's associate deputy director of operations, put it. "Analysts feel more politicized and more pushed than many of them can ever remember," an intelligence official told a reporter at the time. Some in the agency even nicknamed the vice president Edgar, as in Bergen, the famous ventriloquist who made his dummy talk. A Cheney aide concluded later that even if the vice president did not intend to influence anyone, "he's a pretty intimidating guy, and he was even more intimidating during that time because people didn't see much of him." Richard Kerr, a former deputy CIA director who led an independent review, concluded the steady requests from the White House created "significant pressure on the Intelligence Community to find evidence that supported a connection" between Iraq and al-Qaeda.

To the extent there was pressure, in McLaughlin's mind it came from a desire to be more definitive in conclusions rather than sticking to typical on-the-one-hand, on-the-other-hand hedging. "In the history of writing National Intelligence Estimates, the pendulum had sort of swung over to the view that in your key judgments, basically you just say what you think," he said. "What do you really think? I don't need the two-armed economists; just tell me what do you think?" That stemmed in part from experience with a 1990s commission on ballistic missile threats headed by Donald Rumsfeld. "They felt our work had been too bound to evidence and there had been too little willingness to go beyond the evidence, to speculate, to infer, to come to the logical conclusion based on what you are seeing or not seeing here," McLaughlin said. And after not connecting the dots prior to September 11, analysts erred on the side of being more aggressive.

So the National Intelligence Estimate, or NIE, sent to Congress on October 1 offered strongly worded key judgments that minimized doubts and dissents. "The nuance was lost," Tenet later admitted. The estimate declared flatly that "Baghdad has chemical and biological weapons," was "reconstituting its nuclear weapons program," and, if it acquired fissile material from abroad, "could make a nuclear weapon within several months to a year." The conclusions were based on poor tradecraft, mistaken assumptions, and overinterpretation. The main evidence of Hussein's attempt to rebuild a nuclear program was the purchase of the aluminum tubes that Cheney had highlighted on television. But the Energy Department believed those tubes were not suited for enriching uranium and instead were for conventional rocket launchers, a conclusion shared by the State Department intelligence unit. Conclusions about biological weapons were based on tenuous sourcing, particularly an Iraqi defector code-named Curveball, who was being held by the German intelligence agency, which had not let the CIA interrogate him. Unmanned aerial vehicles being built, supposedly to deliver biological or chemical weapons, were actually not suited to the task, according to the air force. For what it was worth, the NIE's key judgments did not include the reported uranium deal with Niger that had attracted Cheney's interest, itself based on forged documents provided to the Italian intelligence agency that did not pass basic scrutiny for names, dates, and titles. It was, however, mentioned in the body of the report.

The ninety-two-page NIE included dissents, but mostly in the back of the document. While 71 senators and 161 House members went to the White House for briefings by Bush, Cheney, and their aides, no more than 6 senators and a handful of House members actually went to the secure room on Capitol Hill to read the full NIE past the five pages of key judgments. Even Bush later acknowledged he never read the NIE, in his case figuring he had seen all this intelligence in his daily reports. And those daily reports, Tenet later concluded, were even "more assertive" than the NIE.

The importance of the issue could hardly be overestimated. The day after the NIE was released, Bush sealed a deal with Richard Gephardt, the House Democratic leader, on a resolution authorizing force, and the two appeared in the Rose Garden along with Republican leaders and Senator Joseph Lieberman, increasingly one of the leading hawks among the Democrats. Tom Daschle refused to go along. For Gephardt, the weapons were the issue. "Saddam Hussein is a bad guy, but I didn't think we should go to war in Iraq just because he is a bad guy," Gephardt remembered later. "If that is the test, then we have to go to war in fifty countries." So he told Bush, "If I come to the conclusion that he does not have weapons, I am not going to vote for this."

Largely unnoticed was an exchange during a closed-door meeting on the same day. Senator Carl Levin, the top Democrat on the Armed Services Committee, asked John McLaughlin whether Hussein was likely to attack American interests with biological or chemical weapons. McLaughlin said the chances were low, but if the United States attacked Iraq, then the chances would be "pretty high." In other words, Hussein was a direct threat only if Bush and Cheney acted first. The CIA agreed to declassify that exchange for the public, but it drew little attention. "I always wondered why they never used it more in their debate," McLaughlin said later. "That tells you something about the atmosphere at the time." Because the NIE was classified, the CIA released a white paper summarizing its conclusions for public consumption on October 4. The white paper was even more definitive, generally leaving out the dissents and caveats, such as the State Department doubts about a nuclear program and the air force assessment of the unmanned aerial vehicles.

Fanning the concern about weapons in Hussein's hands was a smooth-talking Iraqi exile named Ahmad Chalabi. A jowly, charming banker with a doctorate from the University of Chicago, Chalabi headed the Iraqi National Congress, a group dedicated to toppling Hussein but deeply distrusted by American intelligence agents. After a CIA-backed coup failed in the 1990s, agency officials blamed Chalabi for exposing the plot and issued a "burn notice" against him, cutting him off from any support. But Chalabi had deftly worked the corridors of Washington, befriending neoconservative figures like Richard Perle, Paul Wolfowitz, Douglas Feith, and John Hannah in the years before they ascended to power with Bush and Cheney. They considered him a hero for his determined opposition to a dictator, an "enormously talented" figure, and a "huge asset for the United States," as Perle put it. The CIA and the State Department, by contrast, considered him a huckster and his cheerleaders inside the administration "like schoolgirls with their first crush," in George Tenet's words. That did not stop information from Chalabi about purported weapons from circulating through government and even onto the front pages of newspapers like the *New York Times*.

All of this fed into what Scott McClellan, then Bush's deputy spokesman and later White House press secretary, called "our campaign to sell the war." After breaking with Bush, McClellan described "a carefully orchestrated campaign to shape and manipulate sources of public approval to our advantage." He said, "We were more focused on creating a sense of gravity and urgency about the threat from Saddam Hussein than governing on the basis of the truth of the situation."

Nor were they focused on what would come next. When a visiting lawmaker noted at a closed meeting on October 1 that the retired general Wesley Clark had predicted the United States would be stuck in Iraq for ten years, Bush brushed it off.

"I don't know how he gets ten years," he said.

WITH THE VOTES in Congress approaching, Bush decided to give a closing argument laying out the case. Advisers had long ago concluded the Oval Office even with its majesty did not suit Bush well as a venue. He needed an audience to play off; just staring into a camera made him look awkward and uncomfortable. So Bush agreed to deliver his prime-time address in front of an audience at a Cincinnati museum, picking a setting metaphorically in the middle of the country.

Much debate went into crafting the speech, both in substance and in style. Adam Levine, a press aide, recognized that it would be delivered almost exactly on the fortieth anniversary of the Cuban missile crisis and suggested harking back to the line John F. Kennedy drew against the threats of his era.

One of the speechwriters protested that Kennedy was a Democrat.

"Yeah, that's right," agreed Karl Rove. "What about that?"

"Yeah," Levine shot back, "the worst you are going to get is Ted Sorensen will write a *New York Times* op-ed that says exactly why everything you have said President Kennedy would have disagreed with."

But if so, Levine went on, it will mean they had struck a chord. Invoking Kennedy would take some of the partisan sheen off the case and summon a memory associated with strength.

A more serious quarrel broke out over the evidence to put in the speech. The drafts written by Michael Gerson and the other speechwriters accused Hussein of building a "massive stockpile" of anthrax and producing "thousands of tons" of mustard gas, sarin nerve gas, and VX nerve gas. It expressed concern that Iraq could use unmanned aerial vehicles to strike the United States. It echoed Cheney's speech from the summer asserting that Hussein was reconstituting his nuclear program, citing the disputed aluminum tubes. The sixth draft of the speech also asserted that Iraq had "been caught attempting to purchase up to 500 metric tons of uranium oxide from sources in Africa—an essential ingredient in the enrichment process." When the text was sent to the CIA for review, analysts objected to the uranium assertion and rushed to see George Tenet on October 5.

Tenet called Stephen Hadley. "Steve, take it out," he said, arguing that Bush should not be a "fact witness" on a disputed issue. Tenet's executive assistant followed up with a memo to Hadley and Gerson, noting that the CIA had already disagreed with the British on the matter. "We told Congress that the Brits have exaggerated this issue," the memo said. The next day, another CIA analyst followed up with a second memo reinforcing the point, noting that "the evidence is weak" and that Iraq would not need the supply since it already had a large stock of uranium oxide. Moreover, the agency had told Congress "that the Africa story is overblown."

The White House complied and deleted the line. Even without it, Bush's speech was plenty provocative. At 8:00 p.m. on October 7, Bush addressed the nation with a compendium of frightening warnings. If Iraq developed nuclear weapons, it would "be in position to dominate the Middle East," "threaten America," and "pass nuclear technology to terrorists." As Levine suggested, he quoted Kennedy declaring that the world could not "tolerate deliberate deception and offensive threat" by any nation or wait until "the actual firing of weapons" to respond to danger. He all but declared war. "Saddam Hussein must disarm himself," he said, "or for the sake of peace, we will lead a coalition to disarm him."

Three days later, on October 10, at 3:05 p.m., the House of Representatives voted 296 to 133 to authorize force in Iraq. With Richard Gephardt's help and Dick Armey's acquiescence, 81 Democrats joined a near-unanimous Republican caucus. Less than ten hours later, voting just past midnight, the Senate followed suit, 77 to 23. Twenty-nine Democrats backed Bush, including Tom Daschle, Joseph Biden, John Kerry, and Hillary Clinton; only one Republican, Lincoln Chafee, balked. After the sun came up, aides sent Bush a memo telling him that he had won bigger majorities than his father had twelve years earlier.

But with lawmakers persuaded about what would go wrong if America did not attack Iraq, Bush and Cheney were confronted with a roster of what could go wrong if it did. Rumsfeld had scrawled out by hand a list of all the possible setbacks, then returned to his office to commit them to a memo. Marked "SECRET" and dated October 15, the three-page document became known as the "Parade of Horribles" and cited twenty-nine possible bad outcomes. Number one was that Bush would fail to win UN approval, meaning that "potential coalition partners may be unwilling to participate." Others included the entry of Israel into the war, a Turkish incursion into Kurdistan, eruption of the Arab street, disruption of oil markets, higher than expected collateral damage, and Iraqi use of weapons of mass destruction against American forces. Number thirteen was "US could fail to find WMD on the ground in Iraq and be unpersuasive to the world." Number nineteen was "Rather than having the post-Saddam effort require 2 to 4 years, it could take 8 to 10 years, thereby absorbing US leadership, military and financial resources." And number twenty-seven was "Iraq could experience ethnic strife among Sunni, Shia and Kurds."

Still, Rumsfeld was not opposing war. He concluded his list by noting that "it is possible of course to prepare a similar illustrative list of all the potential problems that need to be considered if there is no regime change in Iraq."

THROUGH ALL OF this, a separate crisis was brewing with another member of the axis of evil. American intelligence agencies had uncovered evidence that North Korea had a secret uranium enrichment program in addition to the plutonium program it had suspended as part of the Agreed Framework negotiated with Bill Clinton. James Kelly, an assistant secretary of state, was instructed to confront the North Koreans during a trip to Pyongyang. When he did, the North Koreans responded in a way that Kelly took as confirmation.

Suddenly Bush and Cheney had another rogue state developing nuclear weapons. Bush in particular had developed an intense personal animus toward Kim Jong Il, the North Korean dictator. "I loathe Kim Jong Il," he told the journalist Bob Woodward. To Republican senators, Bush had called Kim a "pygmy" and "a spoiled child at a dinner table" who was "starving his own people" and running "a Gulag the size of Houston." But it was not in Bush and Cheney's interest to overemphasize North Korea at the moment, and the announcement on October 16 was largely overlooked amid the public debate on Iraq. "We decided to park this problem in the six-party talks until we dealt with Iraq," Cheney said at one point in the Oval Office.

The skepticism Bush encountered at home was mirrored in the chambers of the Security Council. If they had to seek another resolution, then Cheney wanted it to have teeth and insisted on a draft threatening to use "all necessary means" if Hussein was found in violation. Powell knew that was a nonstarter but sent it up just to make the point; sure enough, every other member of the Security Council, including the British, rejected such explicit language. Powell and the British instead convinced the French to go along with threatening "serious consequences" without explaining what that meant, leaving enough ambiguity for Washington to define it as it chose.

Moreover, Powell set the resolution's terms such that Iraq was almost certain to violate them. "We built a lot of ambushes or traps into 1441 for Saddam Hussein," he said afterward. "The big one was the initial one, where we said, you're in material breach now." Rather than let Iraq off the hook for the past twelve years, the Security Council would start from the premise that it was still in violation of its obligations, putting the burden on Baghdad to establish otherwise. The other "ambush" that Powell helped insert was a requirement that Hussein file a full declaration disclosing all banned weapons programs. Either he would deny having weapons, which would be widely considered a lie, or he would admit having the weapons, which would confirm that he had been lying for years. Then the United States could move straight to "serious consequences."

The drive to war paid off in the midterm elections. As Karl Rove had urged, Bush and Cheney had taken their leadership of the war on terror to the voters. Rove's "72-Hour Project" drove up turnout in the final days of the campaign. On November 5, Bush invited Bill Frist, Dennis Hastert, and other congressional leaders to dinner in the Family Dining Room and then to watch returns. Cheney was not among the guests. Bush was fired up. Republicans defeated Max Cleland and picked up two extra seats in the Senate for a total of fifty-one, recapturing the upper chamber lost when James Jeffords left the party. In the House, Republicans gained eight seats, padding their majority. Bush grabbed Ken Mehlman's cell phone to call winners like Bob Ehrlich, who was elected governor of Maryland. "You won!" Bush exulted.

It was the first time since 1934 that an incumbent president's party picked up seats in both houses in a midterm election. Bush had raised more than $200 million, traveled to forty states, and lent an approval rating that, while down from its post–September 11 high, remained in the mid-sixties. Cheney too dedicated enormous time to the project, making roughly thirty trips in the last couple of months of the campaign and raising more than $40 million. For Bush, it seemed to some advisers that this finally provided him a measure of validation, even legitimacy, after the much-disputed outcome in 2000. If Bush did not win a mandate then, he had won one by proxy in 2002.

Two days after the election, on November 7, Bush was in an expansive mood at a news conference celebrating the victories. He called for a return to the bipartisan spirit that had reigned ever so briefly after September 11.

But with the 2002 election over, the reporters were already turning to 2004. Bill Sammon of the *Washington Times* asked if he would keep Cheney on the ticket.

"Should I decide to run," Bush said flatly, "Vice President Cheney will be my running mate. He's done an excellent job. I appreciate his advice. I appreciate his counsel. I appreciate his friendship. He is a superb vice president, and there's no reason for me to change."

For Cheney, the president's comments were obviously satisfying. But they were not necessarily the final answer.

13

"You could hear the hinge of history turn"

In the fall of 2002, Vice President Cheney allowed himself to muse aloud about the differences between the current White House and previous ones where he had served. "In this White House," he said, "there aren't Cheney people versus Bush people. We're all Bush people." He was talking about the fact that he had no aspirations to run when President Bush was done, a virtually unheard-of situation in modern American politics that meant there was no subtle competition between president and vice president that drove their teams apart, as had happened so often in the past.

Bush thought much the same—at first. He valued Cheney's counsel, and one of the attractions of picking him was that "he didn't want it." While the vice president intimidated others with his quiet, powerful certitude, Cheney was careful to defer to Bush, almost never disagreeing with him in front of others and keeping a low profile to avoid upstaging the president. While outsiders imagined Cheney dominating meetings, in fact Cheney largely kept silent until the president asked for his opinion. When he did talk, he tended to ask questions rather than state his views explicitly, although it was not always hard to tell from his questions which direction he was leaning.

By the time the midterms had passed, though, there were in fact Bush people and Cheney people. In both the national security and the economic teams, fissures had opened that reflected profound differences in policy and personality. Bush and Cheney themselves remained close, and the president still relied heavily on his number two. But the president allowed a fractious struggle to play out beneath him without resolving it firmly one way or the other. Most significantly, Cheney and Donald Rumsfeld were increasingly fighting with Colin Powell, sometimes joined by Condoleezza Rice. At times, Bush grew frustrated enough to demand better behavior, only to retreat when nothing really changed. As the confrontation with Iraq accelerated, there were moments when Cheney worried Bush would not prove decisive enough and those when Bush resented Cheney pushing him.

For all of his Texas swagger, Bush hated conflict within his team and was still a relatively new president with limited experience. He had surrounded himself with some of the nation's most seasoned hands, which at first was reassuring. But friends said it later became something of a straitjacket. "After 9/11, it was, my God, nobody could be luckier having these people there, and he was very fortunate to have them," said Jim Langdon, Bush's longtime friend from Texas. "And with that kind of experience sitting around the table, maybe it did not leave a lot of room for his own judgment in these matters. His team has been there, done it, seen it all, had the context while Bush was governor of Texas."

Bush was often seen as acceding to Cheney's judgment. Yet it was more complicated than that. Even in this period, when Bush and Cheney were closest, the president rejected his advice at key moments. He gave his Middle East speech, he refused to bomb the Khurmal terrorist camp in northern Iraq, and he decided to go to the United Nations, all at odds with Cheney's recommendations. "One of the things people fail to recognize about George W. Bush—he would almost always agree with Cheney and Rumsfeld about what the objectives should be, which was a hawk, but what people miss is that he would agree with Condi Rice and Colin Powell about how to achieve it," reflected Ari Fleischer.

The growing schism between Cheney and Powell was profound and damaging. The two Gulf War partners who rose to prominence side by side in the first Bush administration had become fierce adversaries in the second. Powell had long understood that Cheney was more conservative than he was—a "right-wing nut," as he had once called him semi-jokingly to his face—but now he saw what he considered a fever in Cheney when it came to Iraq and terrorism. The vice president, for his part, increasingly viewed Powell, in the words of his aide Neil Patel, as a "pain in the ass," basically a freelancer more interested in his own press clippings and personal stature than in following orders.

Powell had developed a theory about Cheney and what made things so different this time around. While some believed the vice president had changed, Powell did not think so. In Cheney's past jobs, under Gerald Ford or George H. W. Bush, he was contained. He was too young and inexperienced to impose his will on the Ford White House, and in the first Bush White House he was serving a president who was very sure of himself on foreign policy and national security. As defense secretary, Cheney had often expressed ideas similar to those he would advance as vice president. But back then, he was surrounded by other adults in the room with experience and gravitas—Brent Scowcroft, James Baker, Powell himself, and of course the president. In this White House, Powell believed, Cheney was not effectively contained by anyone. He had a much freer hand with a president whose background gave him little real preparation to be commander in chief. Powell thought Cheney saw himself as Tom Hagen, the mentor-tutor of the *Godfather* movies, the consigliere advising a young mob leader.

Cheney came out on the winning end of these struggles more often than not. Powell recognized that the vice president had the advantage of proximity, seeing Bush multiple times a day, often one-on-one. There was no competing with that. Moreover, Bush did not connect with Powell. "The president was never comfortable with Secretary Powell," said one White House official, "because Powell loomed so large that I always had the sense that the president felt like his all-star quarterback big brother was always around telling him what he should do better."

Bush generally left it to Rice to manage the rivalries, a formidable task even for a more experienced bureaucratic infighter. Rice had never held a government post higher than senior director in the National Security Council, a relatively mid-level position. Now she was charged with riding herd over a vice president who had previously served as secretary of defense and White House chief of staff, a secretary of state who had previously served as four-star general and chairman of the Joint Chiefs of Staff and had held her own position as national security adviser, and a secretary of defense who also had been White House chief of staff and was on his second tour running the Pentagon.

Cheney and Rumsfeld, the two old friends, were a powerful tandem. "He never came over to me and organized against some decision or said we have to marshal support for this or that," Rumsfeld said. But he did not have to. The two were instinctively on the same page. Powerful as Cheney was, it was Rumsfeld with whom Rice tangled most visibly. He was widely regarded as brilliant but prickly and had aggravated his own uniformed officers who thought, as General Hugh Shelton put it, that Rumsfeld ought to put a sign on his desk that said, "Don't Tell Me, I Already Know." Rumsfeld thought the generals had gotten too used to running the show under Clinton and that civilian leadership needed to be reasserted. With everything on his plate, he had little patience for the endless White House meetings Rice called and was dismissive of White House aides who presumed to issue instructions to his people. At times, he called Andy Card and berated him by telling him he was failing at his job. For a while, he resisted sending military officers to staff the NSC or as liaisons to the State Department, as was tradition, asking why he should have to give up his talent for their convenience. And he constantly threw roadblocks at White House efforts to get information, to the point where Rice asked one of her top aides, Frank Miller, to use back-channel Pentagon contacts to ferret out what was happening.

When Rice tried to convene meetings on what to do with captured enemies, Rumsfeld refused to attend. She finally brought it up after a meeting on another subject, only to watch astonished as he got up to walk out.

"Don, where are you going?" she asked.

"I don't do detainees," he said.

The tension came to a head in late 2002 when Rumsfeld sent a testy memo telling Rice to "stop giving tasks and guidance to combatant commanders and the joint staff." He wrote, "You and the NSC staff need to understand that you are not in the chain of command. Since you cannot seem to accept that fact, my only choices are to go to the President and ask him to tell you to stop or to tell anyone in DoD not to respond to you or the NSC staff. I have decided to take the latter course. It [*sic*] it fails, I'll have to go to the President. One way or the other, it will stop, while I am Secretary of Defense."

Rice bristled at the haughtiness but could not figure out how to address it. One day, after another clash during a White House meeting, she found herself walking alone with Rumsfeld through the Colonnade adjacent to the Rose Garden.

"What's wrong between us?" she asked.

"I don't know," he said. "We always got along. You're obviously bright and committed, but it just doesn't work."

Bright? Rice was taken aback. To her, that sounded condescending. She was not a peer in his mind, she concluded, but a subordinate.

Rumsfeld was surprised later to learn she had taken offense, saying, "It certainly was not meant in a derogatory way." His loyalists thought she read too much into a word he used a lot, but agreed it might have been hard for a man who had mentored someone to see her as an equal. That she would presume to oversee his stewardship of the Pentagon, even demanding to clear his travel in advance, just rankled.

Powell, for his part, pressed Rice to ask the president to rein in Rumsfeld. She was reluctant to bring in Bush and wondered why Powell did not take his grievances to him directly. Given his stature, Powell would have more chance of being heard. But he did not, and she concluded that the soldier in Powell resisted a direct confrontation with the commander in chief. Still, one day he asked Rice, "Why doesn't the president just square the circle? One of us needs to go."

As it happened, there was more unanimity on the UN Security Council, which on November 8, just three days after the midterm elections, voted 15 to 0 for Powell's resolution holding Iraq in "material breach" of previous

UN edicts and giving it a "final opportunity to comply" by admitting inspectors and providing a complete accounting of its weapons programs. Failure would result in "serious consequences." In a surprise, even Syria, the only Arab country on the council, voted yes.

IN THE WEEKS after the elections, Bush approved a strategy of "tailored containment" against North Korea, ratcheting up pressure to stop its nuclear program, starting by halting American funding for fuel oil. He also flew to Prague, where he successfully pressed NATO to invite seven Eastern European countries to join, including the former Soviet republics of Latvia, Lithuania, and Estonia. He signed legislation establishing a commission to investigate the September 11 attacks, despite Cheney's concerns. And in the aftermath of the ugly election campaign, he signed legislation creating the Department of Homeland Security, which he would turn over to Tom Ridge.

Most consuming in those days, though, was a raging fight over further tax cuts. Bush wanted to double down on the 2001 plan, hoping it might boost the economy. Cheney had little opportunity to shape the first tax cut plan designed before his arrival on the ticket, but he was determined to play a central role in shaping this one. "I would say all along he was a big driver," recalled Glenn Hubbard, the White House economist. But Cheney found himself at odds with the Treasury secretary he had recruited. Paul O'Neill opposed another package of tax breaks on the grounds that "the economy did not need" it but "we did need the revenue for other important purposes" as the inherited surplus turned into deficit. O'Neill saw the tax cut as purely political. "I think they believed it was a way to assure reelection," he reflected later.

At an economic policy meeting on November 15, O'Neill cautioned that the country was "moving toward a fiscal crisis" with rising deficits.

"Reagan proved deficits don't matter," Cheney countered. "We won the midterms. This is our due."

In saying deficits did not matter, Cheney meant that Ronald Reagan's tax cuts and defense buildup in the 1980s were financed partly through deficit spending but the economy still grew. Cheney's domestic policy adviser, Cesar Conda, had been sending him memos arguing that the size of the deficit did not seem to correlate to interest rates historically, despite conventional wisdom. Either way, the drive for a new tax plan made clear how isolated O'Neill had become from his friend Cheney and the White House staff, who were developing economic policy behind his back. The plan "was designed in the White House and basically handed to us, and it drove him insane," remembered one O'Neill aide.

The debate played out in front of the president in the Roosevelt Room on November 26. Cheney, who participated via secure video, wanted to accelerate the 2001 rate cuts, which had been phased in over time, while reducing the double taxation of dividends and cutting capital gains taxes. Backed by Hubbard and Lawrence Lindsey, Cheney argued that would do the most to assist business expansion and job creation. "The vice president was always interested in just what are the arguments he could make for pro-growth policy, particularly on the tax side," Hubbard recalled. O'Neill made his case for deficit control, joined at times by Mitch Daniels and Joshua Bolten, but Bush seemed less concerned about that than the structure of the tax plan. He favored doing something about double taxation of dividends; companies distributing profits to shareholders had already paid taxes on that money, then the individuals paid taxes on the dividends they received. To Bush, the concept seemed unfair, and he thought they should get rid of it altogether, not just reduce it. But he questioned cutting capital gains taxes because, he said, they were already doing enough for the rich.

"The argument that rang most familiar with the president really wasn't any of those" made by the vice president, Hubbard said. "It was more fairness. He was really concerned about double taxation. The same rhetoric he used to rail against the estate tax—he would call it the death tax—he used on dividend taxes. Frankly, those arguments did very well with the public. All the economist stuff about faster growth and all that, I don't think that's what sold the policy. I think his political instinct was spot-on and people caught on—why should I pay taxes twice?"

ANOTHER MAJOR INITIATIVE was shaping up around the same time. Since taking office, Bush had developed an interest in fighting AIDS in Africa. He had agreed to contribute to an international fund battling the disease and later started a program aimed at providing drugs to HIV-infected pregnant women to reduce the chances of transmitting the virus to their babies. But it had only whetted his appetite to do more. "When we did it, it revealed how unbelievably pathetic the U.S. effort was," Michael Gerson said.

So Bush asked Bolten to come up with something more sweeping. Gerson was already thought of as "the custodian of compassionate conservatism within the White House," as Bolten called him, and he took special interest in AIDS, which had killed his college roommate. Bolten assembled key White House policy aides Gary Edson, Jay Lefkowitz, and Kristen Silverberg in his office. In seeking something transformative, the only outsider they called in was Anthony Fauci, the renowned AIDS researcher and director of the National Institute of Allergy and Infectious Diseases.

"What if money were no object?" Bolten asked. "What would you do?"

Bolten and the others expected him to talk about research for a vaccine because that was what he worked on.

"I'd love to have a few billion more dollars for vaccine research," Fauci said, "but we're putting a lot of money into it, and I could not give you any assurance that another single dollar spent on vaccine research is going to get us to a vaccine any faster than we are now."

Instead, he added, "The thing you can do now is treatment."

The development of low-cost drugs meant for the first time the world could get a grip on the disease and stop it from being a death sentence for millions of people. "They need the money now," Fauci said. "They don't need a vaccine ten years from now."

The aides crafted a plan in secret, keeping it even from Colin Powell and Tommy Thompson, the secretary of health and human services. They were ready for a final presentation to Bush on December 4. Just before heading into the meeting, Bush stopped by the Roosevelt Room to visit with Jewish leaders in town for the annual White House Hanukkah party later that day. The visitors were supportive of Bush's confrontation with Iraq and showered him with praise. One of them, George Klein, founder of the Republican Jewish Coalition, recalled that his father had been among the Jewish leaders who tried to get Franklin Roosevelt to do more to stop the Holocaust. "I speak for everyone in this room when I say that if you had been president in the forties, there could have been millions of Jews saved," the younger Klein said.

Bush choked up at the thought—"You could see his eyes well up," Klein remembered—and went straight from that meeting to the AIDS meeting, the words ringing in his ears. Lefkowitz, who walked with the president from the Roosevelt Room to the Oval Office, was convinced that sense of moral imperative emboldened Bush as he listened to the arguments about what had shaped up as a $15 billion, five-year program. Daniels and other budget-minded aides "were kind of gasping" about spending so much money, especially with all the costs of the struggle against terrorism and the looming invasion of Iraq. But Bush steered the conversation to aides he knew favored the program, and they argued forcefully for it.

"Gerson, what do you think?" Bush asked.

"If we can do this and we don't, it will be a source of shame," Gerson said.

Bush thought so too. So while he mostly wrestled with the coming war, he quietly set in motion one of the most expansive lifesaving programs ever attempted. Somewhere deep inside, the notion of helping the hopeless appealed to a former drinker's sense of redemption, the belief that nobody was beyond saving.

"Look, this is one of those moments when we can actually change the lives of millions of people, a whole continent," he told Lefkowitz after the meeting broke up. "How can we not take this step?"

That was not the end of the fight. In later weeks, Karen Hughes and Mary Matalin tried to prevent Gerson from putting the announcement of the President's Emergency Plan for AIDS Relief, or PEPFAR, in the State of the Union address for fear it would send a message to the American people that Bush cared only about what was happening overseas. But Bush was committed. He would announce it from the biggest platform he had.

BUSH SHARED HIS passion for helping Africa with Paul O'Neill, but that was about all the two shared. Bush "never clicked" with O'Neill and felt his Treasury secretary was too focused on tangential issues, too out of touch with the administration's economic priorities. "He came in and he talked about safety at the mint," Bolten recalled. "Safety at the mint was not a top priority." O'Neill, who had been a corporate chief executive for years, "was not a team player," one aide said.

Bush also worried about repeating his father's mistake by not focusing enough on the economy, so shaking up the economic team might send a useful signal. That would start with O'Neill. Bush also decided to replace Lawrence Lindsey, who had gotten in hot water with his back-of-the-napkin prediction that the Iraq War could cost $200 billion but mainly fell victim to being the coordinator of an economic team that resisted being coordinated. Yet while Bush was willing to make the decision, he left it to Cheney to carry out, avoiding conflict.

Just after lunchtime on December 5, Cheney placed the call to O'Neill at the Treasury Building next door to the White House.

"Paul, the president has decided to make some changes in the economic team," Cheney said. O'Neill would remember a pause before Cheney spoke again. "And you're part of the change."

O'Neill had been meeting with aides on the financial markets when the call came in, and it took him by surprise. He understood he was not always in tune with Bush and Cheney, but he was floored at being unceremoniously shuffled out over the phone.

O'Neill sat down. "The president should have around him the people he wants," he told Cheney. "I'm happy if the president wants to make a change."

With people in his office, O'Neill asked to call back. After reconnecting, Cheney outlined the plan.

"We'd like to have you come over tomorrow or next week and meet with the president, and we'll make an announcement that you've decided to return to the private sector," the vice president said.

O'Neill stiffened. If he was out, then he would announce his resignation the next day. But he would not go along with the cover story.

"I'm too old to begin telling lies, and that's a lie," he said. "I'm not going to do that." He went on, "I'm perfectly okay with people knowing the truth that the president wants to make a change. That's his prerogative."

Again, O'Neill would recall an awkward pause before Cheney replied.

"Okay," the vice president said.

Cheney later tried again to arrange a smooth departure, having Andy Card call O'Neill at home that night to invite the secretary to meet with the president. But O'Neill declined and also rebuffed Card's request to wait to announce his resignation until they were ready to announce Lindsey's departure and the appointment of John Snow, the chief executive of CSX Corporation, to take over Treasury. Instead, O'Neill turned in his resignation letter the following morning.

"It wasn't difficult for me at all," O'Neill recalled, "because I was so disaffected, I was happy to go." He grew even more upset years later when he read Bush's memoir saying that "Paul belittled the tax cuts, which of course got back to me." O'Neill said he was straightforward in his opposition to the tax cuts. "When the president says it got back to him, it's a lie," he said. "I told him three times to his face. I've got to tell you, that's irritating as hell to me that the president would create this impression for the casual reader." O'Neill's departure also disappointed his patron, Alan Greenspan. "The Bush administration turned out to be very different from the reincarnation of the Ford administration that I had imagined," Greenspan said later. "Now, the political operation was far more dominant."

THE POLITICAL OPERATION was quickly absorbed by another drama. Senator Trent Lott, the Republican leader from Mississippi, made remarks at a hundredth-birthday celebration for Senator Strom Thurmond of South Carolina on December 5 that were seen as racially inflammatory. Lott noted that his home state had voted for Thurmond when he ran for president in 1948, adding, "If the rest of the country had followed our lead, we wouldn't have had all these problems over all these years either." What he did not mention was that Thurmond had run on a pro-segregation Dixiecrat ticket. Nick Calio, Bush's top congressional liaison, viewed the comments as just political flattery, a way of buttering up an old man, not a commentary on the issues Thurmond ran on more than a half century earlier. But over the next couple days, in the glare of blogs and cable television, they took on a life of their own, and Lott was forced to issue one apology after another.

By the time Bush flew to Philadelphia a week later for a speech about faith-based initiatives to an audience that included many African Americans, Lott's fellow Republicans were abandoning him. On Marine One heading to his plane on December 12, Bush told aides he felt he had no choice but to admonish Lott in his speech. How else would he have any credibility? If he said nothing, it would be interpreted as condoning a seemingly pro-segregation sentiment.

"People are going to think you are pulling the rug out from under him," Calio warned him.

"We are not doing that," Bush insisted. "We are not pulling the rug out from under him."

"Whether we are or not," Calio replied, "that is what people are going to think."

Calio asked if anyone had told Lott. Bush said no, then turned to Andy Card. "Andy, you are going to need to call him right away," Bush said, once more outsourcing personal conflict.

When Bush arrived in Philadelphia, he took the stage in front of a sign emblazoned "Compassion in Action." About a third of the way into his speech, he raised the Lott contretemps. "Any suggestion that the segregated past was acceptable or positive is offensive and it is wrong," he said to loud applause. "Recent comments by Senator Lott do not reflect the spirit of our country." The applause rose, and Bush raised his voice. "He has apologized and rightly so."

Watching on television, Lott felt sucker punched, especially by Bush's emphasis on the words "and rightly so." He could not quarrel with the conclusion but felt the tone was devastating. Senator Rick Santorum, who had accompanied Bush to Pennsylvania, called Lott from Air Force One. "The president just threw you under the bus," he said.

Lott called Bush to tell him he agreed with his comments, choosing not to express any hurt over the tone.

Bush sounded oddly upbeat. "Hang in there," he said.

He did not. Barely a week later, Lott was out as majority leader, replaced by Senator Bill Frist of Tennessee, a Bush favorite. As Calio predicted, the White House was widely perceived to have cut Lott loose. Lott himself blamed Karl Rove. "I never could prove it was Karl," he said later, "but somebody was doing me in at the White House."

Cheney clearly disagreed with the White House and called Lott to express his concern. "It wasn't a call from the vice president," Lott said. "It was a call from a friend."

THE CONTRETEMPS WAS only a temporary distraction from Iraq. In response to the UN resolution, Saddam Hussein turned in a twelve-thousand-page declaration maintaining he had no banned weapons. Cheney wanted to immediately judge it a lie and declare Iraq in "material breach" of the resolution, but Bush opted to let his government's experts evaluate the document first. In the end, they still wound up at the same place, and on December 19 the United States deemed the declaration inadequate and a "material breach" of Iraq's obligations. But Bush would wait for the newly readmitted UN inspectors to have a chance to work, much to Cheney's frustration.

As Cheney pressed him to move more assertively, Bush received a call one day in December from Karen Hughes, who was back in Texas watching developments with increasing alarm. She worried that he might feel pressured into going through with an invasion even if he did not think it was a good idea simply because he had given the speech at the United Nations. "I suggested that he shouldn't feel that he had to go to war, that there were other ways that we could basically back off of that rhetoric in an effective way," she recalled. Bush assured her he did not feel that way. Once again, Hughes did not tell her friend directly that she opposed going to war, but in her own way she was doing what she could to head it off, offering him an exit ramp.

Whatever doubts Bush harbored were fueled just a few days before Christmas. In the face of Hussein's continued denials, Bush asked the CIA to lay out its best case that Iraq really did have banned weapons. On December 21, with much of Washington out Christmas shopping, Bush and Cheney took their places in the seats in front of the fireplace in the Oval Office. Condoleezza Rice, Andy Card, Scooter Libby, and George Tenet watched from the sofas as John McLaughlin, the deputy CIA director, presented the intelligence.

Where Tenet was a cigar-chewing backslapper, McLaughlin was a professorial agency veteran, as dry in his manner as his boss was exuberant. As he went through the material, he noticed that he did not seem to be persuading anyone. "I was very careful in the presentation," he said later. "I wasn't trying to sell anything. I was basically saying, this is what we think we can confidently say."

Bush was not impressed. "Nice try," he told McLaughlin. "It's not something that Joe Public would understand or would gain a lot of confidence from."

The president turned to Tenet. "I've been told all this intelligence about having WMD, and this is the best we've got?"

"It's a slam dunk," Tenet told Bush, and then repeated the phrase.

Bush took comfort from Tenet's confidence, later calling it "very important" to him. Tenet, however, felt his comment was taken out of context and that he meant that sharpening the public presentation would be a slam dunk, not the intelligence itself, a conclusion McLaughlin shared. It was a subtle distinction, and Tenet had offered strong assurances on other occasions. But in any case, Bush asked some lawyers on his staff to frame the material the way they would in court. The same day, he received a vaccination for smallpox in solidarity with all the troops he had ordered vaccinated.

For a brief moment, Bush confronted uncertainty. After months of barreling toward a seemingly inevitable conflict, he turned to Rice in the Oval Office and directly asked her the question he had not posed to most of his other advisers.

"Do you think we should do this?" he asked abruptly.

Rice felt the weight of the moment.

"Yes," she said. If Hussein did not respond, they would have no choice.

With troops already pouring into the Middle East in preparation for possible action, Bush retreated to Camp David for the holidays. He talked privately with his father. While even the former president's friends believed he opposed the aggressive policy, Bush later wrote that his father backed his approach.

"You've got to try everything you can to avoid war," he quoted his father telling him at Camp David. "But if the man won't comply, you don't have any other choice."

Just as his father wrote him and his siblings a heartfelt letter on the eve of the Gulf War, the younger Bush now sat down to write to his twin daughters.

"I pray that the man in Iraq will disarm in a peaceful way," he wrote. "We are putting pressure on him to do just that and much of the world is with us."

"PEOPLE WILL GREET the troops with sweets and flowers."

Bush and Cheney were meeting in the Oval Office on January 10, 2003, with three Iraqi dissidents, who were reassuring them that American forces would be welcomed if they invaded. Kanan Makiya, author of the book *Republic of Fear,* was painting a picture that resembled the Americans liberating Paris from the Nazis.

How long would American troops have to stay?

Two or three years, the dissidents estimated.

That was longer than the six months Bush had told members of Congress but still a reasonable time frame as far as he was concerned. It was all beginning to feel more real, more inevitable. If diplomacy were ever really an option, by now it felt like a box-checking exercise to get to the war everyone knew was coming.

The day after meeting with the Iraqi dissidents, Cheney summoned Prince Bandar bin Sultan, the longtime Saudi ambassador, to the White House. The vice president asked Donald Rumsfeld and Richard Myers to join them. Just as he had done with Colin Powell before the Gulf War, Cheney gave Bandar a secret heads-up on the war plan.

"The president has made the decision to go after Saddam Hussein," Cheney told Bandar.

Rumsfeld was surprised. That was the first time he had heard it put that definitively.

Bandar was skeptical. "Is Saddam going to survive this time?" he asked.

"Bandar," Cheney said, "once we start this, Saddam is toast."

After Bandar left, Rumsfeld raised Cheney's comment with the vice president. "This is the first time I have heard that," Rumsfeld remembered saying. But Cheney was mum about how he knew that and what the president had told him. Rumsfeld just assumed Bush had clued in his vice president in a way he had not done with the rest of the team yet. "He obviously knew what he was talking about," Rumsfeld later reflected.

While Bush had never directly asked his team the fundamental question of whether they should go to war, he realized as the time approached that he would need to lock down their support. None was more critical than Powell, the one person in government with stature rivaling the president's. Bush asked his secretary of state to stay behind after an Oval Office meeting on January 13.

"I really think I'm going to have to do this," Bush said as they settled into the wing chairs.

"You're sure?" Powell asked.

Yes, he was.

"You understand the consequences," Powell said.

He did. "Are you with me on this?" Bush asked. "I think I have to do this. I want you with me."

Powell had tried to slow the Bush-Cheney war drive and give the president off-ramps to avoid an invasion if possible. He had expressed misgivings about the way the confrontation was being handled. But he had never flatly opposed going to war with Iraq, and he did not in this moment of truth either.

"Yes, sir," he said, "I will support you. I'm with you, Mr. President."

Bush was pleased. "Time to put your war uniform on," he said.

Still, Bush agreed to play out the diplomacy a little longer. He was running into fierce resistance from France and Germany. When the French foreign minister declared that "nothing today justifies" war in Iraq, Powell felt "blindsided" and "was livid." Rumsfeld fired back by dismissing "Old Europe" as opposed to New Europe, meaning the recently liberated countries of Eastern Europe that, fresh from Soviet domination, were more willing to take on another totalitarian regime.

Bush decided to make one more effort to convince the world of Iraq's perfidy, and on January 27 he asked Powell to present evidence to the United Nations. He envisioned a moment like when Adlai Stevenson confronted Soviet envoys with evidence of the deployment of nuclear missiles in Cuba.

"We've really got to make the case and I want you to make it," Bush said. "You have the credibility to do this. Maybe they'll believe you."

Like Bush, Cheney was all too aware that Powell exceeded both of them in international credibility. "You've got high poll ratings," he told Powell after discussing the presentation. "You can afford to lose a few points."

But first, Bush had his own moment on the stage. On the night of January 28, he entered the House chamber glad-handing lawmakers along the aisle as he made his way to the rostrum for his State of the Union address. This would be yet another of those speech-of-a-lifetime moments that he liked to mock, but this speech of a lifetime was a genuine turning point, one leaving little doubt about the looming confrontation with Iraq. Indeed, editors at the *New York Times* initially wanted their story on the speech to say that Bush had, in fact, effectively declared war, until its correspondents in Washington convinced them to tone down the language and stick to what he actually did say.

As he had in Cincinnati three months earlier, Bush laid out his bill of particulars, asserting that the Iraqis at one point had materials sufficient to produce more than twenty-five thousand liters of anthrax, more than thirty-eight thousand liters of botulinum toxin, and as much as five hundred tons of sarin, mustard, and VX nerve agent. He claimed Iraq at one point had several "mobile biological weapons labs," specially equipped trailers designed to produce germ warfare agents. Following Cheney's lead, Bush contended that Hussein was again on the trail of nuclear weapons, citing the much-debated aluminum tubes. And he uttered 16 words that would later overshadow the other 5,400: "The British government has learned that Saddam Hussein recently sought significant quantities of uranium from Africa."

That was the same claim George Tenet had gotten taken out of the Cincinnati speech. But when the State of the Union draft was distributed to top advisers the day before, Tenet handed it off to his staff.

George Walker Bush was raised in Midland, Texas, and tried following in his famous father's footsteps without much success until his young wife, Laura, helped prompt him to quit drinking. "I'm all name and no money," he lamented before buying the Texas Rangers. He translated that success into an underdog election victory for governor of Texas.

Like Bush, Richard Bruce Cheney grew up in the West, playing Little League (top right) and overcoming early troubles with alcohol. With Donald Rumsfeld as his mentor, Cheney became the youngest White House chief of staff in history, under Gerald Ford. He later served as defense secretary under the first George Bush. A friend once asked Cheney what he was after. "To be where the action is," he said.

Cheney initially declined to run on Bush's ticket in 2000. "I'm not going to go for that," he told one friend. But Bush asked him to reconsider and picked him over the objections of his political strategist, Karl Rove, who argued it would look like he was "falling back on his father's administration." Cheney joined the campaign, but eschewed rope lines and baby kissing.

Bush, greeting his father in the Oval Office on Inauguration Day 2001, was determined to avoid the mistakes of the first President Bush. He and Cheney rebuffed pressure to compromise after the disputed election. "Our attitude was hell no," Cheney said.

On September 11, 2001, Andy Card whispered in Bush's ear, "America is under attack." A few minutes later, Bush scribbled out a statement as Dan Bartlett pointed to one of the Twin Towers falling on television. In the White House bunker, Cheney ordered any remaining hijacked planes to be shot down. "If it looks threatening," he said without hesitation, "take it out."

Bush leaned heavily on Cheney and Condoleezza Rice as he tried to figure out war in a new era. "I'm fighting an enemy that I can't see," he said. Cheney flew by helicopter to Camp David to preserve the nation's leadership in case of a decapitating attack on the White House. Bush's impromptu speech with a bullhorn at Ground Zero became an iconic moment, but just as important was what he heard. "Whatever it takes," at least one angry rescue worker told him.

After razzing from New York Yankee Derek Jeter, Bush threw out the first pitch at a World Series game following September 11. Bush agreed to have the "Battle Hymn of the Republic" played at a memorial service at the Washington National Cathedral. "Defiance is good," he said. Just before touring Ground Zero with New York mayor Rudy Giuliani, Cheney learned that he and Bush may have been exposed to the deadly botulinum toxin.

Colin Powell believed Cheney was intent on "keeping me on a much shorter leash" than during the first Bush administration and relations grew so strained that Powell's deputy urged him to resign in protest. Karen Hughes privately expressed doubt about going to war with Iraq. Bush, meeting outside the Oval Office with Cheney and Donald Rumsfeld on the day the war began, was emotional after giving the order. "You could see the weight on his face," an aide said.

BUSH AND CHENEY planned to meet with the generals two days later to go over the war plan. This would be one last chance for the nation's highest-ranking officers to express misgivings.

Bush strode into the Cabinet Room, where he found the Joint Chiefs of Staff and the regional commanders all smartly decked out in uniform. As one person in the room remembered it, the president started out with a full-throated embrace of his defense secretary, who had come to see him right before the meeting. "Don Rumsfeld has my full support," the president said. "I think he's doing a great job."

Then he turned to the topic of the day. "Do any of you have concerns about the war plan?"

At least some in the room got the message. Bush was backing Rumsfeld against any revolt by the uniformed leaders.

Some of the chiefs had been worried about Tommy Franks's light-footprint plan. At one point, they had given him enough of a hard time that he dismissed them to their faces as "Title X motherfuckers," referring to the statute creating the Joint Chiefs. But here in front of Bush and Cheney, they expressed confidence in the plan.

The only one who offered real concerns was General Eric Shinseki, the army chief of staff. He ticked off several issues that worried him, including flow of forces, supply lines, and the lack of a northern approach from Turkey, which so far had not agreed to let American troops use its territory to attack Iraq. Some in the room considered his comments to be relatively minor and not a challenge to the thrust of the war plan. Others saw them as more significant; while delivered in a mild-mannered way, Shinseki's critique undercut the fundamental strategy. "It's the only time in my life where I felt like you could hear the hinge of history turn," said Kori Schake, an NSC official in the room. "The president clearly didn't know what to do." So he thanked Shinseki and moved on.

Bush met the next day, January 31, with Tony Blair, who flew in from London to press the president to seek a second Security Council resolution explicitly declaring Iraq in material breach and authorizing war. The Bush team did not think it was needed, relying on the "serious consequences" language of the November resolution. For once, Cheney and Powell were on the same side. But Blair made a strikingly personal case that his government was at risk of falling. Besides, he argued, it "would give us international cover." Bush agreed, overruling Cheney's objections and promising to "twist arms and even threaten" to get the votes, according to notes taken by the British side paraphrasing him.

During their discussion, Bush made clear he had decided to go to war regardless of what the inspectors found or the Security Council decided. Indeed, he told Blair he had tentatively set the date: March 10. "This was when the bombing would begin," David Manning, a foreign policy adviser to Blair, wrote in a five-page memorandum summarizing the meeting. As a result, Manning wrote, "Our diplomatic strategy had to be arranged around the military planning." Blair indicated that he was "solidly with the President and ready to do whatever it took to disarm Saddam."

Much of the discussion concerned justifying the war, possibly even deceiving the world with a manufactured provocation. "The US was thinking of flying U2 reconnaissance aircraft with fighter cover over Iraq, painted in UN colours," Manning wrote, attributing the idea to Bush. "If Saddam fired on them, he would be in breach." Bush predicted the Iraqi army would "fold very quickly" and the elite Republican Guard would be "decimated by the bombing." Choosing optimism over history, Bush "thought it unlikely that there would be internecine warfare between the different religious and ethnic groups," Manning wrote.

The stakes for Powell's presentation to the United Nations had just gone up. It was not enough to put on a compelling case; it had to be so powerful that it would convince France and other skeptical Security Council members to back a second resolution. Powell was handed a forty-eight-page draft compiled by Cheney's staff, led by Scooter Libby with the help of John Hannah, Neil Patel, and Samantha Ravich, outlining not just alleged weapons but also Hussein's ties to terrorism and human rights abuses. The idea was a two- or three-day presentation. Powell scanned through the report and quickly rejected an extended show. Instead, he would speak for an hour or two, focused largely on weapons. After all, that was the subject of prior resolutions; that was the argument that had sold Richard Gephardt and many Democrats.

Powell handed the Cheney draft to Lawrence Wilkerson, his chief of staff, and asked him to go to the CIA to vet it. Skeptical of Cheney's war fever, Powell wanted everything to be airtight. Wilkerson went to Langley with Hannah and others to go through the draft. But he quickly concluded it was thin. After six hours, he threw the document on the table. "This isn't going to cut it, ladies and gentlemen," he exclaimed. "We're never going to get there." George Tenet suggested they discard the Cheney draft and use the National Intelligence Estimate. By now, Powell had concluded that the Cheney draft was "a disaster" and "incoherent," so he personally went to Langley for three nights, two of them with Rice in tow. The State Department's intelligence unit sent him a memo identifying thirty-eight allegations that were "weak" or "unsubstantiated" and later identified another seven.

Overall, thirty-one of the forty-five weak assertions were taken out. But that meant Powell agreed to make fourteen allegations that his own specialists thought were flimsy, including the claim about aluminum tubes.

Cheney was aggravated that Powell was tossing out most of the terrorism case and pressed him, to no avail, to put some of it back in. Ever since the September 11 attacks, Cheney had been gripped by a report from the Czech intelligence agency that Mohamed Atta, believed to have been the lead hijacker, had been spotted in Prague meeting with an Iraqi intelligence officer on April 9, 2001. But American intelligence had disavowed the report, finding no evidence that Atta had been there other than the single source who told the Czechs, and plenty of evidence that he was not. Among other things, the FBI found indications that Atta was in Virginia Beach on April 4 and Coral Springs, Florida, on April 11, and that his cell phone was used in Florida on several days in between, including April 9. There was no evidence that Atta had left the United States or entered the Czech Republic.

Cheney remained fixed on the supposed Prague meeting long after intelligence analysts had discredited it. He first called it "pretty well confirmed" in a December 2001 interview, then, when more information came in, modified his language in subsequent appearances, saying it was "unconfirmed" but still holding out the possibility that it was true. Indeed, Cheney had been waging a quiet battle with the CIA for a year over suspected ties between Iraq and al-Qaeda. Scooter Libby, Douglas Feith, and others found indications of contacts over the years and argued that showed a relationship even if not an out-and-out alliance. The CIA prepared several reports, including a document on June 21, 2002, titled "Iraq & al-Qa'ida: Interpreting a Murky Relationship." The most recent had been published on January 29, the day after Bush's State of the Union address, but only after Jami Miscik, the deputy director for intelligence, stormed into Tenet's office threatening to resign unless Libby stopped pushing for changes. The paper concluded there had been contacts over the years and moments when Iraq seemed to provide safe haven for terrorists. But it did not connect Iraq with September 11 and found no evidence of "command linkages." Libby and his allies countered that the Taliban did not "command" al-Qaeda either but supported it and that was enough under the Bush Doctrine. Cheney, Libby, Feith, and Paul Wolfowitz thought it was the CIA that was politicizing the intelligence by straining so hard to avoid seeing the ties.

With Powell heading to the United Nations, Rumsfeld revived a favorite idea, suggesting Bush reconsider an immediate strike against the suspected chemical weapons facility run by Ansar al-Islam and Abu Musab al-Zarqawi near Khurmal in northern Iraq. It was not the first time Cheney or Rumsfeld had brought the topic back up since the president rejected it the previous summer. But now Rumsfeld argued that Powell's testimony would make clear the Americans knew about the camp and Zarqawi and his compatriots would evacuate before they could be taken out.

"We should hit Khurmal during the speech," Rumsfeld said, "given that Colin will talk about it."

"That would wipe out my briefing," Powell protested. Besides, he added, "We're going to get Khurmal in a few weeks anyway."

All attention was on the diplomacy and the war plan. With Rumsfeld's Parade of Horribles in mind, Tommy Franks briefed the White House repeatedly on the plans to penetrate a Fortress Baghdad—that is, the urban warfare many feared at the end of the invasion. But there was little focus on what would come next.

When Rice finally managed to arrange a briefing for Bush on "rear-area security," as they called it, the president, knowingly or not, diminished its importance.

"This is something Condi has wanted to talk about," he said, opening the meeting.

Rice immediately detected the generals losing interest, once they realized it was her issue, not the president's.

"If he had done that to me, I would have resigned," Hadley told her afterward.

"Yeah, I know," she said. "But what is that going to solve?"

AFTER DAYS OF scrubbing, Powell flew to New York and took the chair in the Security Council chamber on February 5. He made sure George Tenet sat behind him to show the CIA had endorsed the evidence. Playing recordings of intercepted conversations and holding up a vial to show how little anthrax was needed to inflict mass casualties, Powell went through the case methodically. Bush watched on television in the dining room off the Oval Office, munching crackers and cheese and sipping Diet Coke. Rice joined him toward the end. They felt it went well. "He persuaded me," wrote Mary McGrory, the legendary liberal *Washington Post* columnist, "and I was as tough as France to convince."

Not quite, as it turned out. France remained unconvinced, as did Germany. Bush had been counting on his friend Vladimir Putin to support him, or at least not stand against him. But that reflected a profound misunderstanding of Putin and how Russia saw its place in the world. Putin wanted to be compensated for lost business with Iraq, a demand that went unmet. His shift to overt opposition came during a trip to Berlin and Paris, where he was treated like visiting royalty. Before leaving, Putin had said "we share the position of our American partners" in pushing Iraq to cooperate with inspectors and disarm. But then President Jacques Chirac met him at the Paris airport and escorted him down the Champs-Élysées lined with French and Russian flags for a ceremony at the Arc de Triomphe. On February 10, Putin stood by Chirac's side and declared, "Russia is against the war." The next day he suggested Russia would use its veto at the Security Council to stop "an unreasonable use of force."

In the United States, the bitterness against the French was growing. A Florida bar owner dumped his entire stock of French wines into the street in protest. A North Carolina restaurateur renamed French fries on the menu "freedom fries." Congressional Republicans went one step further, relabeling not only fries at the U.S. Capitol cafeteria but also French toast, which became "freedom toast." More seriously, administration officials proposed blocking France and other countries that opposed them from obtaining postwar oil and reconstruction contracts. "France is clearly trying to destroy NATO in favor of the EU," Rumsfeld told Bush in a memo on February 18, discounting the European view that there were better ways of confronting Hussein than war. "France is trying to define its role in the world by its opposition to almost everything the US proposes." He went on to say that he, Rice, and Powell agreed they should move more NATO decision making away from the North Atlantic Council to the alliance's Defense Policy Committee, an arm that did not include the French. The feelings of animosity were mutual. "We need a lot of Powell and not much of Rumsfeld," Prime Minister José María Aznar of Spain told Bush during a visit to Crawford a few days later.

The diplomatic maneuvering was testing Cheney's patience. He summoned the French ambassador to his residence.

"Is France an ally or a foe?" Cheney asked pointedly.

An ally, the surprised ambassador answered.

"We have many reasons to conclude that you are not really a friend or an ally," Cheney said.

As far as Cheney was concerned, the UN track was a waste of time. Every passing day just increased the threat and gave Hussein more time to prepare. Finally, at one of his weekly lunches with the president in the dining room off the Oval Office, he snapped.

"Are you going to take care of this guy or not?" Cheney demanded impatiently.

It was a particularly impertinent question to ask the president, and Bush was so surprised that it would stick in his mind years later.

He told Cheney that he was not ready to move yet.

"Okay, Mr. President, it's your call," Cheney said. "That's why they pay you the big bucks."

He tempered the sharpness with a smile, but the point was made. Cheney was afraid Bush was going wobbly.

THE STRAIN WAS getting to Bush's father, watching on the sidelines from Texas. When the elder Bush noticed a column supporting his son by the writer Walt Harrington, he picked up a pen and wrote to him: "Walt, he does not want war. He does want Iraq to do what it has pledged to do. Have you ever seen a president face so many tough problems all at once? I haven't."

A few weeks after Bush and Cheney met with the commanders, the quiet tension between Rumsfeld and the uniformed military broke into the open as Eric Shinseki, the army chief of staff, testified before the Senate Armed Services Committee on February 25.

"General Shinseki," asked Senator Carl Levin, the Democratic chairman, "could you give us some idea as to the magnitude of the Army's force requirement for an occupation of Iraq following a successful completion of the war?"

Shinseki ducked. "In specific numbers, I would have to rely on combatant commanders' exact requirements," he said.

Levin pressed. "How about a range?" he asked.

Then Shinseki offered a thought that had been swimming around his head for a while, although he had not offered it during his meeting with the president. "Something on the order of several hundred thousand soldiers are probably, you know, a figure that would be required," he said.

With that, the soft-spoken general stuck a dagger into the heart of the Bush-Cheney team. Whether he meant it or not, his comment became fodder for an enduring indictment of the administration for failing to devote enough resources to the post-Hussein operation. Rumsfeld's vision of a fast-moving, light-footprint military did not include hundreds of thousands of troops hanging around Baghdad and Basra for years. The idea was to get in and get out, turning the country over to a new generation of Iraqis as quickly as possible.

Rumsfeld and his deputy, Paul Wolfowitz, bristled at Shinseki's comment. In testimony before the House Budget Committee two days later, on February 27, Wolfowitz raised the issue without waiting to be asked. "Some of the higher-end predictions that we have been hearing recently, such as the notion that it will take several hundred thousand U.S. troops to provide stability in post-Saddam Iraq, are wildly off the mark," Wolfowitz said. "It's hard to conceive that it would take more forces to provide stability in post-Saddam Iraq than it would take to conduct the war itself and to secure the surrender of Saddam's security forces and his army." The next day, Rumsfeld was asked at a briefing about Shinseki's estimate. "My personal view is that it will prove to be high," he said.

Critics of the administration eventually made Shinseki into something he was not, a martyr who stood up to the president and tried to stop the war train. Despite his off-the-cuff guesstimate, Shinseki never made a proposal for a post-Hussein force of hundreds of thousands of troops. Indeed, in a memo to Rumsfeld upon his retirement in June 2003, Shinseki said his statement had "been misinterpreted" and that he did not "believe there was a 'right' answer on the number of forces" needed to secure Iraq. "I gave an open-ended answer suggesting a non-specific larger, rather than smaller, number to permit you and General Franks maximum flexibility in arriving at a final number."

Rumsfeld glossed over the depth of the tension with Shinseki, dismissing it as a media myth without acknowledging a significant disconnect with his army chief. Neither Rumsfeld nor Wolfowitz ever asked Shinseki about his public estimate and what he meant by it, so it was reasonable for the general to assume his views were not welcomed. Rumsfeld had made his own thoughts so well-known that anyone who dared contradict them risked being marginalized.

Bush felt fortified in his resolve when he stopped by Rice's office one day that week while she was meeting with Elie Wiesel, the famed Holocaust survivor. Bush had just read Michael Beschloss's book *The Conquerors*, about how Franklin Roosevelt and other leaders failed to act to stop the Holocaust. "I'm against silence," Wiesel told him. "I'm against neutrality because it doesn't ever help the victim. It helps the aggressor."

"YOU DON'T UNDERSTAND how big this is."

Bush was excited. On March 1, Khalid Sheikh Mohammed, the mastermind of the September 11 attacks and the killer of Daniel Pearl, a Jewish reporter for the *Wall Street Journal* slain in Pakistan, was captured in Rawalpindi, the military garrison city near the capital of Islamabad. Bush was asleep at Camp David when Rice was notified. She decided not to wake him. But the capture was the biggest since the war on terror began, and by morning Bush was sharing his enthusiasm with Dan Bartlett.

On the same day, though, Bush got bad news from overseas when the Turkish parliament formally rejected an American request to send forces through its territory into Iraq. Cheney and Rumsfeld blamed Powell for not doing more, while he blamed them for making diplomacy impossible. Regardless, without a northern front, the invasion would have to come entirely from Kuwait in the south, leaving Iraqi forces plenty of room to retreat and regroup.

While the British still stood with Bush, his friend Tony Blair was under increasing pressure. The UN inspectors had not found illicit weapons and if Blair went to war without a second UN resolution, Jack Straw, his foreign secretary, warned him privately on March 5, "the only regime change that will be taking place is in this room." It did not help that the case against Saddam Hussein took a hit two days later when the International Atomic Energy Agency concluded the documents reporting the supposed Iraq-Niger uranium deal were forgeries. The basis for the president's claim in the State of the Union had been demolished. The speechwriters had hedged by attributing it to the British, who claimed to have other sources and refused to back off, but it looked dubious.

If the regime was changed in Iraq, the central question was, what would come next? For months, Cheney's allies had been promoting the idea of a new government headed by Ahmad Chalabi, the exile who had been lobbying Washington for years to get rid of Saddam Hussein. But Bush was uncomfortable with that idea, suspicious of the charismatic opposition leader, and wary of looking as if America were simply installing its own favorites.

Bush waited until just a week before the war was to start to sit down with his team to talk about what would come after Hussein was ousted. Leading the briefing on March 10 was Lieutenant General Jay Garner, a retired officer who had managed relief efforts in northern Iraq after the Gulf War and had been tapped to lead the post-Hussein effort. Garner emphasized the importance of paying Iraq's soldiers, police officers, and government workers and using the Iraqi military for reconstruction while bringing in international forces to stabilize the country. A plan presented by Garner envisioned demobilizing soldiers and putting them immediately to work in construction brigades. Bush approved.

In a separate presentation the same day, Frank Miller of the NSC staff briefed the president on Iraq's ruling Baath Party. Miller noted there were 1.5 million official members of the party, but many were simply teachers and public servants who had to join to get jobs. Miller recommended removing between 1 percent and 2 percent of them from their posts, or roughly 25,000 people, the genuine party elite who were part of Hussein's apparatus of fear. Again, Bush approved, though he expressed concern. "It's hard to imagine punishing 25,000 people," he said.

Two days later, on March 12, Bush and Cheney met again with the team to discuss the future of the Iraqi army. At Donald Rumsfeld's request,

Douglas Feith presented Garner's plan to disband Hussein's paramilitary forces and Iraq's premier security units like the Republican Guard and the Special Republican Guard but retain and reconstitute the main army. Three to five divisions would form the nucleus of a new Iraqi army. Feith described the arguments for and against keeping the bulk of the army intact—the utility of having a force to do reconstruction and avoid putting large numbers of armed men out of work versus eliminating a corrupt, abusive, and dysfunctional organization in favor of a completely rebuilt military. No one at the meeting spoke against Garner's recommendation to keep the army, and Bush approved it.

Feith also presented a plan to form a temporary government called the Iraqi Interim Authority. Because of Bush's opposition to simply installing Chalabi, the newly envisioned authority running Iraq would include a mix of "externals" and "internals." The authority would operate under the auspices of the American-led coalition, but at least it would put an Iraqi face on the emerging order and provide a foundation for a future government. Bush agreed to this too.

Bush was still refereeing between Cheney and other members of his team on other fronts. On March 14, Tenet came to him just before the morning intelligence briefing to complain that Cheney was planning to give a speech describing Hussein's ties to terrorism—essentially the material Colin Powell had thrown out of his UN presentation.

"Mr. President, the vice president wants to make a speech about Iraq and al-Qaeda that goes way beyond what the intelligence shows. We cannot support the speech and it should not be given."

Whether Bush intervened, Tenet never learned. But Cheney did not give the speech.

WITH THE SECURITY Council vote approaching, Bush was growing frustrated that even friends like Mexico and Chile were planning to abstain or vote no. His frustration was clear all the way down in Texas, when Karen Hughes called to check in to see if he needed help.

"Would you like me to come up there?" she asked.

"I don't know," he said. "Let's take a vote."

Rice and Laura Bush were with him, among others.

"What's the vote?" Hughes asked.

"Two to two with one abstention," Bush said.

"Who abstained?" she asked.

"I did," Bush answered peevishly. "That's the way everybody is treating me."

Hughes got on a plane.

Bush and Blair decided to meet one last time before the vote, but the question was where. With his government on the line, Blair could not be seen going to Washington, nor was it wise to invite Bush to London, where he would be met by angry protests. Bush's aides suggested Bermuda, but it was too close to the American side of the Atlantic Ocean for Blair's team; instead, they settled on the Azores, the Portuguese islands closer to Europe. Also invited was José María Aznar of Spain, another war supporter, while Prime Minister José Manuel Durão Barroso of Portugal would host.

Before Bush had even landed at Lajes Field, a Portuguese facility long used by the U.S. Air Force, on March 16, Jacques Chirac proposed giving inspectors another thirty days to work and then the Security Council would meet again before any military action. Bush saw it as another delaying tactic benefiting Hussein. Left unsaid was that he had already deployed 240,000 men and women to the region; it was untenable for them to sit in the desert as temperatures rose. The later the invasion started, the greater the chance that troops wearing heavy Kevlar vests and chemical suits would fight in unbearably hot conditions.

Bush huddled with Blair and the other two leaders, telling them that he would issue an ultimatum to Hussein the next day to leave Iraq within forty-eight hours or face war. They had given up hope of success at the Security Council, and to Blair's side the whole exercise felt like just "going through motions." Bush seemed calm but later described himself as "extremely frustrated."

The real question, he believed, was the chance of terrorist groups getting hold of weapons of mass destruction. "I am just not going to be the president on whose watch it happens," he told Blair.

The latest French proposal only exacerbated the aggravation. "If another country tried to introduce a new resolution for the sole purpose of delaying us, we'd have to regard that as a hostile act diplomatically," Blair said.

Bush briefly considered the irony of blocking a French resolution. "I'd be glad to veto something of theirs," he said with delight. "Really glad!"

His irritation with France spilled over into the media appearance that followed as he cast Chirac as little more than Hussein's enabler and insisted that the Security Council vote the next day either way. "It's an old Texas expression—show your cards—when you're playing poker," Bush told reporters. "France showed their cards."

After a quick dinner, Bush prepared to head back to Washington. He asked Blair and his aides about the upcoming parliamentary vote and expressed confidence that the prime minister would survive. In a lighter moment, Alastair Campbell, Blair's senior adviser, who shared Bush's passion for running, asked the president if he would sponsor him for an upcoming marathon.

"If you win the vote in Parliament," Bush replied, "I'll kiss your ass."

Campbell said he would prefer the sponsorship.

As Air Force One headed back out over the ocean, Bush worked on his ultimatum speech with Rice, Michael Gerson, Andy Card, Karen Hughes, and Dan Bartlett. At one point during the five-hour flight, they took a break to watch the movie *Conspiracy Theory*, starring Mel Gibson and Julia Roberts. Bush made fun of the plot.

BACK IN WASHINGTON, Cheney spent part of the day with Tim Russert on the set of *Meet the Press*, making the case for war.

"Do you think the American people are prepared for a long, costly and bloody battle with significant American casualties?" Russert asked.

"Well, I don't think it's likely to unfold that way, Tim," Cheney replied, "because I really do believe that we will be greeted as liberators."

He cited his meetings with Iraqi exiles: "The read we get on the people of Iraq is there is no question but what they want to get rid of Saddam Hussein and they will welcome as liberators the United States when we come to do that."

He added that he was not predicting "a cost-free operation" but said the cost would be far greater if Hussein ever provided al-Qaeda with unconventional weapons. He dismissed Eric Shinseki's warning about force levels. "To suggest that we need several hundred thousand troops there after military operations cease, after the conflict ends, I don't think is accurate. I think that's an overstatement."

Bush met the next day, March 17, with congressional leaders. Some in the room were struck that he turned the discussion over to Rice to explain. She seemed surprised, too, but gamely plowed ahead. Afterward, Senator John Warner of Virginia, the silver-haired patrician Republican chairman of the Armed Services Committee who looked as if he came straight from central casting, pulled Stephen Hadley aside. "You sure better find these stocks of WMD," he said, "or there is going to be hell to pay."

Bush took his place behind the lectern in Cross Hall in the White House that evening to deliver the ultimatum in a nationally televised speech. As he waited for the cameras to go on, the room suddenly went quiet. He noticed Gerson studying the text. "How are you doing, Gerson?" Bush asked. Then he rolled up his own copy of the text and hit his speechwriter playfully on the head with it. Gerson had always been a nervous figure, regularly chewing pens to the point where he once bit through one in the Oval Office, staining a presidential couch with ink. Bush reassured Gerson by telling him the story about how he was so nervous during one of his father's presidential debates that he went to the movies, only to keep sending his brother out to check on the progress. Whether he remembered or not, Bush had told Gerson that story before, but it succeeded in defusing the tension.

At 8:01 p.m., the red light on the camera flashed brightly. "All the decades of deceit and cruelty have now reached an end," Bush declared. "Saddam Hussein and his sons must leave Iraq within forty-eight hours. Their refusal to do so will result in military conflict, commenced at a time of our choosing." There was still hope Hussein might actually leave; Egypt was pushing the idea of giving him $1 billion to leave, and Bush had authorized considerable sums of money, a small price to avoid a bloody war. Still, even then, American forces might have invaded. A team led by Hadley in the weeks leading up to the deadline had run through contingencies and concluded that even if Hussein were deposed or left voluntarily, American troops should still go in temporarily to take control of suspected weapons.

The red light went off. As Bush stood there, he understood he had just passed a point of no return. Barring the unlikely, the country was going to war, and this time, unlike the largely forgotten conflict in Afghanistan, it would be a full-fledged fight, with tens of thousands of ground troops heading into the teeth of what once had been one of the world's largest armies.

PART THREE

14

"Maybe we'll get lucky"

President Bush was unusually formal as he met with his war team one final time on March 19 to give the order setting in motion the start of the war in just two days. He was seated in the Situation Room, surrounded by advisers and facing multiple screens on the wall with the images of his commanders.

"Tommy," he said to General Franks, "I would like to address your team."

Then he turned to the generals one at a time and asked each the same thing. "You have everything you need? Everything you need to accomplish the mission?"

Each answered the same. "Yes, sir."

"Good," he would say, turning to the next one.

Satisfied that he had asked the question, Bush turned to Donald Rumsfeld. He had scripted out what he wanted to say, fully aware of the historic import of the moment.

"Mr. Secretary," he said, "for the peace of the world and the benefit and freedom of the Iraqi people, I hereby give the order to execute Operation Iraqi Freedom. May God bless the troops."

On the video screen, Franks saluted. "Mr. President, may God bless America," he responded.

Bush, still in his seat, saluted back. Everyone sat quietly for a moment, and Colin Powell wordlessly reached out and touched Bush's hand. The president then got up and left. As he strode out of the Situation Room, Eric Draper, the White House photographer standing outside the door, could see Bush's eyes were red and tearing up. Even though he had known this was coming, emotion washed over the president in a way he had not expected. This was it; this was war. He marched upstairs and into the Oval Office without speaking to anyone, headed outside to the South Lawn to collect himself by taking his dog Spot for a walk. Aides could see his feelings were churning and did not follow. When he finally returned to the building, "you could see the weight on his face," recalled Draper.

Bush headed upstairs to the Treaty Room and sat down to write a letter to his father by hand.

> *Dear Dad,*
>
> *At around 9:30 a.m., I gave the order to SecDef to execute the war plan for Operation Iraqi Freedom. In spite of the fact that I had decided a few months ago to use force, if need be, to liberate Iraq and rid the country of WMD, the decision was an emotional one. . . .*
>
> *I know I have taken the right action and do pray few will lose life. Iraq will be free, the world will be safer. The emotion of the moment has passed and now I wait on the covert action that is taking place.*
>
> *I know what you went through.*
>
> *Love,*
>
> *George*

His father replied by fax a few hours later.

> *Dear George,*
>
> *Your handwritten note, just received, touched my heart. You are doing the right thing. Your decision, just made, is the toughest decision you've had to make up until now. But you made it with strength and with compassion. It is right to worry about the loss of innocent life be it Iraqi or American. But you have done that which you had to do. . . .*
>
> *Remember Robin's words "I love you more than tongue can tell." Well, I do.*
>
> *Devotedly,*
>
> *Dad*

Bush later told Dan Bartlett that it just hit him as he gave the formal order launching the war. "All of that comes home to roost at that moment," Bartlett reflected. "But not in the form of doubts. It is almost a release. It is almost, *finally*, exhaled. 'I have made the decision.' You kind of exhale almost."

For a president, the beginning of a war was, in a way, like Election Day. After months of intense work, once he had given the order to go, there was little for Bush himself to actually do but wait and worry. Cheney busied himself with phone calls to the leaders of Egypt, Israel, Hungary, South Korea, and other countries.

But then around 3:40 p.m., Bush received a call from Rumsfeld. "I need your permission to change the plans," he said. "Can I come over?"

Bush summoned Cheney and the rest of his national security team. When Rumsfeld arrived, he had with him George Tenet and Richard Myers. The group retired to the dining room off the Oval Office.

The CIA had heard from its network of Iraqi agents, code-named Rockstar, where Saddam Hussein and his sons, Uday and Qusay, might be that night. Tenet laid out maps on the table showing an estate on the banks of the Tigris River in southern Baghdad owned by Hussein's wife and known as Dora Farms. Aerial reconnaissance of the site showed heavy vehicles, suggesting a large security contingent. While not guaranteed, Tenet felt the information was solid and presented "too good a scenario to pass up." The deadline for Hussein to leave Iraq was not until later that night, and Bush had just approved a carefully laid-out plan to soften up Iraqi defenses with air strikes for two days to start the war. But now it looked as if they had a chance to take out the Iraqi president and, potentially, avert a bloodbath.

Bush was nervous. What if it was a trick? What if they were just plain wrong? The last thing he wanted was a baby-milk-factory situation like his father had faced in the first Gulf War when an errant bomb hit a civilian target. "I was hesitant at first, to be frank with you," he recalled later, "because I was worried that the first pictures coming out of Iraq would be a wounded grandchild of Saddam Hussein." Moreover, they might jeopardize international support with a mistaken strike and potentially even endanger special operations forces that had already snuck into Iraq.

Bush kept pressing Tenet. "How solid are your sources on this?"

Good, Tenet said, but they would never know for sure.

After ninety minutes of deliberation, Bush seemed ready to order a Tomahawk cruise missile strike. "Okay, all right," he said.

But then, as his aides headed for the door, he called them back. "No, wait a minute," he said. He still was not comfortable.

As the discussion moved into the Oval Office itself, officials kept ducking in and out to take or make secure telephone calls seeking more information. Dusk was beginning to settle on the nation's capital, and out the window Myers could see headlights from cars just beginning the evening rush-hour trip home.

The latest report indicated Dora Farms had a bunker, which meant that Tomahawks would not be enough; they would need manned warplanes to drop bunker-busting bombs, which only enhanced the risk since Iraqi air defenses had not yet been neutralized. While Bush absorbed this, the generals ordered a pair of F-117 Nighthawk stealth bombers in Qatar to prepare to take off. Finally, Tenet reported that Hussein had just arrived at the site in a taxicab, a common subterfuge he used.

Bush went around the room, polling his advisers. Everyone agreed he should order the strike. He had to make a decision by 7:15 p.m., or 3:15 a.m. Iraqi time, so the bombers would have enough time to reach the target and get back out by daylight. At 7:00 p.m., the president cleared the room to talk with Cheney alone. For that most fateful decision, he was turning to his trusted vice president.

"Dick, what do you think we ought to do?" Bush asked.

Launch, Cheney said. If the intelligence was right, they had the chance to shorten the war. It was worth the risk.

Bush agreed and called the others back into the office.

"Let's go," he said at 7:12 p.m., beating the deadline by three minutes.

THE STEPPED-UP TIMETABLE disrupted the White House communications plan. Bush was to address the nation at noon on March 21. Cheney briefly argued they should say nothing even after Dora Farms was struck, but Bush concluded that was untenable and decided to go on television that night to announce the start of hostilities. Andy Card, Joe Hagin, the president's assistant Blake Gottesman, and a couple others personally moved the Oval Office couches to make room for cameras rather than summoning the usual workers and potentially letting the secret out.

While the staff prepared, Bush went over to the residence to find Laura, who was with her childhood friend Pamela Hudson Nelson. When he told them he had just ordered the start of war, the two women were as overwhelmed as he had been. They sat down for a quick dinner of chicken potpie as Bush fortified himself for his address. Bush seemed somber, and he expressed hope that the early strike against Dora Farms would prove decisive. "Maybe we'll get lucky," he said. "But it's not going to be easy like the last one." Hussein, he knew, had far more wherewithal than the Taliban. Bush and the two women held hands as the president said a prayer "asking for strength and wisdom."

Bush went to the Treaty Room to go over the speech with Gerson and Hughes. Sitting at his desk, he read through the text one more time. Just after 8:00 p.m., the telephone rang. He picked it up, listened for a moment, and then put it down again. It was Card telling him the deadline for Hussein to leave had passed, with no sign he had complied. Bush said nothing. It was not as if he expected otherwise, but it sank in. It was "the only time I can remember at the White House he looked pale," Gerson said. "I hadn't seen him that way."

At 9:30 p.m. Washington time, just ninety minutes after the deadline passed, two F-117 bombers released four EGBU-27 two-thousand-pound bunker-busting bombs, and thirty-nine Tomahawks smashed into the compound as well. As a makeup artist applied powder to Bush's face for his address, he watched television images of the bombing. Then, at 10:15 p.m., dressed in a dark suit with a red tie and an American flag pin in his lapel, he took his seat behind the *Resolute* desk with pictures of his daughters visible behind him, folded his hands in front of him, and looked at the camera.

"On my orders," he said in an unusually soft, solemn voice, "coalition forces have begun striking selected targets of military importance to undermine Saddam Hussein's ability to wage war. These are the opening stages of what will be a broad and concerted campaign." He made no mention of Dora Farms. But he linked his new war to the attacks of September 11, making the case that by removing Hussein, he was preventing a threat on American soil. "The people of the United States and our friends and allies will not live at the mercy of an outlaw regime that threatens the peace with weapons of mass murder," he said. "We will meet that threat now, with our Army, Air Force, Navy, Coast Guard and Marines, so that we do not have to meet it later with armies of firefighters and police and doctors on the streets of our cities."

Four minutes later, he was done. He headed to the residence to rest. As he and Laura watched the television coverage, they noticed the crawl line at the bottom of the screen reporting that the president and first lady had gone to bed. "Whoops," Laura said, "we'd better go to bed."

Bush woke the next morning, March 20, to disappointing news. Rice called to say that one of the CIA's agents had reported spotting someone resembling Hussein being pulled out of the wreckage at Dora Farms and spirited away in an ambulance. Later reports confirmed it was not him. Whether the attack just missed him or he was never there to begin with was unclear. Either way, the war would proceed.

"We tried everything possible to solve this through peace," Bush told his cabinet that day, justifying his decision to himself as much as anyone. "It was the absolute right decision to commit troops." Recounting some of the abuses of Hussein's regime, Bush added, "Of all things we stand for are human liberty and freedom."

That night, he had dinner in the residence again with Laura and Pamela Nelson. His mind was focused thousands of miles away. Before the food arrived, Bush began talking about the stories of atrocities he had heard about Hussein's Iraq, about the tortures, the rapes, the tongues cut out of mouths. "It was pretty graphic," Nelson recalled later. As they dined, Laura read aloud from the letter Bush's father had sent.

AMERICAN AND BRITISH forces stormed into southern Iraq and pushed quickly toward Baghdad. Many of the worst-case scenarios on Donald Rumsfeld's Parade of Horribles list had not occurred; there was no use of chemical or biological weapons, no massive refugee crisis, no significant attacks bringing Israel into the war, no widespread destruction of the oil fields.

But the troops were meeting resistance. A supply convoy of clerks and cooks was ambushed, leaving several dead and others captured. Irregular Iraqi fighters known as the Fedayeen Saddam played havoc with the Americans in Nasiriyah and elsewhere, disguising themselves as civilians, using children as shields, and pretending to surrender before opening fire. A sandstorm and unanticipated resistance by irregular fighters slowed the advance briefly, and in Washington some of the same concerns about a quagmire that perturbed Bush in the early days of the Afghan war began emerging again.

On the first weekend of the Iraq invasion, Bush headed to Camp David with advisers and friends, hoping to show that he was not obsessing over every incremental development on the battlefield. But in between workouts and walks along the trails, he was glued to television reports from Iraq and talked about little else. "He is just totally immersed," reported Roland Betts, an old college friend who joined him that weekend.

As the invasion accelerated, the military returned to a long-identified target, the Ansar al-Islam camp in Khurmal in northern Iraq, which was bombarded on March 21, the second day of the war, by sixty-four Tomahawk cruise missiles. A week later, on March 28, Special Forces, accompanying Kurdish Peshmerga fighters, arrived at the scene and took on the remaining extremists in a four-day pitched battle. Reports to Bush and Cheney indicated evidence of a chemical weapons facility. Tests detected traces of cyanide salts, ricin, and potassium chloride, and soldiers found chemical hazard suits and Arabic manuals on chemical munitions. But there was no evidence the group was tied to Hussein's regime. Worse, the strike did not succeed in taking out Zarqawi.

On March 27, Bush hosted Tony Blair at Camp David, where the two discussed the war. Bush was looking ahead, hoping the invasion would send a signal to other international outliers. Already there were positive signs. Seif al-Islam el-Qaddafi, the son of Colonel Muammar el-Qaddafi, the longtime dictator of Libya, had just approached the United States through British contacts to open a dialogue about his country's own weapons of mass destruction. The younger Qaddafi indicated that Libya was contemplating a radical rapprochement with the West and that "everything would be on the table," including renunciation of its weapons program. Bush and Blair debated Qaddafi's motivations. Was it a ruse or was he serious?

Libya had been moving to settle accounts for some time, including a settlement admitting culpability in the 1988 terrorist bombing of Pan Am Flight 103 over Lockerbie, Scotland. It was certainly possible that Qaddafi was watching what was happening in Iraq and determined to avoid Hussein's fate. "When Bush has finished with Iraq, we'll quickly have a clear idea of where he's going," Qaddafi had said in a typically fiery interview with the French newspaper *Le Figaro* in which he compared Bush to Adolf Hitler about a week before the invasion. "It won't take long to find out if Iran, Saudi Arabia, or Libya will be targets as well."

Bush and Blair agreed to pursue the outreach to see where it would lead, but keep the discussions secret even from many inside their own governments. Only Bush, Cheney, Rice, Tenet, Stephen Hadley, and a couple of others would know. Powell and Rumsfeld would be told only in very general terms that something was going on, and Bush would leave it to the CIA and his own staff to explore the opportunity. "We had a real concern that if we told the Defense Department, it would leak in ten seconds. If we told the State Department, it would leak in five seconds," Robert Joseph, a National Security Council official tasked with working the issue, said later. "So the goal was to keep it very tightly held."

The tension between State and Defense escalated as the invasion progressed. On March 31, Rumsfeld confronted Powell, accusing his deputy, Richard Armitage, of "badmouthing the Pentagon all over town." Powell countered that Rumsfeld's deputy, Paul Wolfowitz, had clearly been leaking against State, which Rumsfeld denied. The defense secretary was frustrated by the national security team's fractiousness and thought it was moving too slowly in coming up with a replacement for the day Hussein fell. The next day, April 1, he sent a memo to Bush, Cheney, and the rest of the National Security Council urging them to let him set up an interim government. "We have got to get moving on this," he wrote. "We can't afford to have a protracted interagency debate. This is now a matter of operational importance—it is not too much to say that time can cost lives." A new government would convince many Iraqis that the Americans would not stop until Hussein was truly gone, giving them the courage to side with the invaders. Even though Bush had already ruled out a government made up of exiles like Ahmad Chalabi, the fight was not over.

AS AMERICAN FORCES drove toward Baghdad, Bush and his wife boarded Air Force One on April 3 to fly to Camp Lejeune in North Carolina to visit marines. With reports of renewed momentum in the field, Bush was in an upbeat mood as he climbed a makeshift stage set up on a field ringed by tanks and packed with enthusiastic young men and women in uniform. Camp Lejeune had sent 17,500 marines and sailors to Iraq, with more soon to go.

"There's no finer sight, no finer sight, than to see 12,000 United States Marines and corpsmen—unless you happen to be a member of the Iraqi Republican Guard," Bush said to raucous applause. "A vise is closing," he declared, "and the days of a brutal regime are coming to an end."

After ribs and macaroni and cheese with troops in the mess hall, the president and first lady went to a chapel annex to meet families of five marines killed in Iraq, his first such session since the invasion began. So far, thirteen troops from Lejeune had been killed, more than any other military installation, and another six were missing. Each family was seated separately, some wearing pictures of their lost relative on their lapels, and the Bushes offered each words of comfort. "He's in heaven," the president told the relatives of one slain marine. Two of the marines had left behind children they had never met, babies born after their deployment.

Bush met twin six-week-old girls whose father had been lost. How could he not think about his own twin girls, and all they had meant to him, and how these two babies, these two girls who could be so much like Jenna and Barbara, would never know their father? Bush was teary-eyed by the time he left the chapel and boarded Marine One. Usually after such moments, he would bounce back and regain his upbeat demeanor, but not this day. He sat during the twenty-minute helicopter ride in utter silence, staring out the window the whole time. Ari Fleischer had never seen him quite like that, clearly bothered by "that wrenching realization of a family torn apart, broken up, so similar to his."

Aides worried about how Bush was holding up. Stephen Hadley had a moment alone with him after a meeting and asked how he was doing.

"I made the decision," Bush said. "I sleep well at night."

Despite Bush's decision not to install a government of exiles, Ahmad Chalabi's patrons in the Pentagon managed to slip him into Iraq. On the morning of April 5, Powell and Tenet woke to learn that Chalabi and a force of his Free Iraqi Forces had been airlifted to Nasiriyah. Rumsfeld thought the insertion of the Iraqi exiles would be "a useful corrective to the perception that the United States was invading Iraq to occupy the country rather than liberate it." Powell and Tenet thought it was crazy and undercut the argument that America favored Iraqis choosing their own leaders.

ON APRIL 9, one of Bush's assistants called into the Oval Office to tell him he should look at the television. American forces had swarmed into Baghdad, and now in Firdos Square, in the heart of Baghdad, liberated Iraqis were attacking a statue of Saddam Hussein, trying to bring it down. Bush walked to the outer office and glanced at the television as an Iraqi man swung a sledgehammer again and again at the base of the statue. The images were powerful. An American marine unfurled an American flag on the statue, before someone thought better of it and realized it would be politically wiser to put an Iraqi flag there. Finally, a marine tank recovery vehicle arrived to bring down the statue.

"They're hooking it up and they've got the crane out there," one of the assistants called to Bush, who had retreated back into the Oval Office.

"Well, let me know," he said.

"Well, it's about to come down," the assistant replied.

So he hustled back out to watch the fateful fall. Looking back on that moment years later, he described himself feeling "overwhelmed with relief and pride." But others remembered him being more restrained. Eric Draper, his photographer, recalled Bush pausing just for moments to watch the scene. "A second and a half later, he headed back to the Oval," Draper said. "He really wasn't interested. He was so focused on certain things, and what may be dramatic to you and I may not be dramatic to him because he was already past it. He's already thinking ahead."

In reality, it was a small moment in Baghdad involving only a few hundred people. But the symbolic parallels to such iconic scenes as the liberation of Paris and the fall of the Berlin Wall dominated the media. CNN replayed the toppling of the statue that day on average every 7.5 minutes and Fox News every 4.4 minutes. Bush's father sent him an e-mail praising his "conviction and determination." It would be hard for a president not to feel a sense of satisfaction.

Cheney watched in a hotel room in New Orleans, where he had flown to give a speech. By evening, he had returned to Washington and had an unanticipated visit at the White House from Kanan Makiya, the Iraqi exile author who had told him and Bush that Americans would be greeted with "sweets and flowers."

"Thank you for our liberation," Makiya said.

Cheney took Makiya down the hall to the Oval Office so he could thank Bush.

Rice arrived in the Oval Office right around then. "You did this," she congratulated Bush. He did not respond. "He was very much inside his own thoughts," she noticed.

Liberation, however, proved to be messier than anyone had hoped. Cheney and Makiya were right when they said that Americans would be welcomed as liberators by Iraqis. They were, at first. Long-suffering Iraqis were jubilant at Hussein's fall. The stories of torture that spilled out in those days after the statue fell made up a Stalinesque tapestry of cruelty. Where Cheney and Makiya got it wrong was presuming the welcome would last or that the joy over Hussein's overthrow necessarily translated into enduring amity for the overthrowers.

Iraqis had endured a dozen years of international sanctions that Hussein had blamed for widespread malnutrition, disease, and every economic malady. They had been told that a rash of cancers was the result of depleted uranium in American bombs left over from the Gulf War or used to enforce the no-fly zone. Shiites and Kurds were still resentful that after freeing Kuwait, the Americans did nothing to help as Hussein brutally crushed their uprising in 1991. And there was deep-seated suspicion that the Americans had come back not to help them but to take their oil. It did not help that American troops sat by and did little to keep order amid the chaotic scenes following the collapse of the Hussein regime as looters ransacked government buildings. "Stuff happens," Rumsfeld glibly said. But forces were being set loose that would take years to control.

For the moment, that was lost on the White House team. On April 13, Cheney hosted a small dinner to celebrate the fall of Hussein. The few invited included Scooter Libby, Paul Wolfowitz, and Kenneth Adelman, a longtime friend and aide to Cheney and Rumsfeld who had written in the *Washington Post* that the invasion of Iraq would be "a cakewalk." As the vice president welcomed the guests, Adelman surprised him by hugging him, something that generally made Cheney uncomfortable. But emotions were soaring. "We were euphoric," Adelman recalled. "The mood and feeling were just wonderful. I just thought it was a magical moment."

Over dinner, the group toasted Bush and victory in Iraq. Cheney was high on his partner. "It is amazing his courage," the vice president told his guests.

"When do you think this all started?" Adelman asked.

"I am pretty sure it was decided right after 9/11 to go in," Cheney said, "but it took us all too long if you ask me."

The group agreed they had rid America of a terrible enemy, demonstrated the capacity of the U.S. military, and created hope of a genuine ally in the heart of the Middle East. Cheney was not as interested in the democracy experiment that absorbed Bush; he was more focused on American security.

As the evening wound up, Adelman interjected the only sour note. "I wonder why we haven't found WMDs yet," he ventured.

Libby jumped on him. "Oh, we are going to find them," he said. "Don't worry about that."

"They haven't found them, because they have been looking for other stuff," Cheney added.

"Well, if they don't find them pretty soon," Adelman said, "people are going to be pretty pissed off."

WITH HUSSEIN DRIVEN from power and the military engaged in what seemed like mop-up operations, Bush and his team thought the war was all but over. Stephen Hadley even called Richard Armitage to ask how victory parades were organized after the Gulf War.

Tommy Franks was eager for some sort of presidential speech to recognize what his troops had achieved in just a matter of weeks, and Bush wanted to accommodate him.

Joe Hagin came to Bush and told him that the USS *Abraham Lincoln* was returning to port in San Diego after being deployed longer than any vessel since Vietnam; it seemed like the picture-perfect venue. Bush would fly out to the carrier as it approached the coast and deliver a nationally televised speech from the deck. The idea appealed both to the former Air National Guard pilot in Bush and to his inner political showman.

The setting chosen, the question became what to say. When Michael Gerson wrote a lofty speech inspired by Douglas MacArthur's remarks on the deck of the USS *Missouri* ending World War II, it drew plenty of skeptical responses, not least from Rumsfeld. Reading it during his first post-invasion trip to Baghdad, the defense secretary thought the speech "seemed too optimistic" and told the White House to "tone down any triumphalist rhetoric." Rumsfeld wondered where the talk of democracy came from. "Bringing democracy to Iraq had not been among the primary rationales" of the war, he knew. The only one who talked like that in their numerous Situation Room meetings was Rice, "but it was not clear to me whether she was encouraging the president to use rhetoric about democracy or whether it was originating with the president." Rumsfeld was not the only one with concerns; Colin Powell and Karen Hughes weighed in too. But for all the attention to the wording of the speech, what the political advisers did not consider deeply enough was the wording of a banner that the White House had printed up at the request of a proud *Lincoln* crew.

While the White House initially explained that Bush would fly to meet the carrier because it was still too far offshore for a helicopter trip, in fact it had arrived close enough to the West Coast that it had to be repositioned to exclude land from the camera shot. The truth was Bush simply wanted to fly onto the carrier the way a combat pilot did, and his advisers understood the power of the image. To fly to the carrier in an S-3B Viking, Bush and Andy Card had to undergo water-survival training. The president donned an aviator's flight suit and harness and practiced jumping into the White House swimming pool and removing the gear before touching bottom.

On May 1, Bush flew aboard Air Force One to Naval Air Station North Island in San Diego Bay, where he met his pilot. Commander John "Skip" Lussier warned Bush of the inherent dangers of flying a jet onto the deck of a moving ship.

"Ninety-nine point nine percent of the time, everything goes really smoothly," Lussier told him. "But there's always that .1 percent chance that something could happen."

"Luce, you don't need to worry about that," Bush said. "We've got a great vice president."

Bush and Lussier soared into the sky aboard the Viking out toward the Pacific. "Mr. President," Lussier said after a few minutes. "You want the jet?"

Of course he did, excited as a kid to be flying again at four hundred miles per hour, much to the obvious discomfort of the Secret Service agents in the back.

Lussier took the controls back when it came time to land on the *Lincoln*, hitting the deck at 150 miles per hour and catching the fourth and final cable that brought it to an abrupt halt. Bush emerged in his flight suit looking like an older Tom Cruise from *Top Gun*. Any political strategist would have killed for the picture of the manly commander in chief. Except that after he changed back into a suit to give his speech, he now shared the picture with the banner requested by the crew: "Mission Accomplished."

The speech itself was more modulated, after the rewrites Rumsfeld and others insisted on. "My fellow Americans," Bush said, "major combat operations in Iraq have ended. In the battle of Iraq, the United States and our allies have prevailed." The sailors and airmen applauded. "And now our coalition is engaged in securing and reconstructing that country." Bush declared that "we've removed an ally of al-Qaeda," once again advancing a claim that overstated the intelligence. But he made sure to add the important caveat that the fighting was not over. "We have difficult work to do in Iraq. We're bringing order to parts of that country that remain dangerous. We're pursuing and finding leaders of the old regime, who will be held to account for their crimes."

Those sentences became a crutch for Bush aides for years afterward to argue that he was not glossing over what was still to come in Iraq. And certainly, he was correct that "major combat operations" were over in the sense of the big army-on-army battles that ousted a government. That claim hardly seemed controversial; just a week earlier, Tom Brokaw of NBC News had prefaced a question during an interview with Bush with the phrase "Now that the war in Iraq is over." Still, the tone of the speech conveyed triumph, portraying "the battle of Iraq"—which followed "the battle of Afghanistan"—as just another step in a broader campaign as if he were describing the gradual liberation of Europe in World War II.

And the banner, no matter how it got there, no matter what it was intended to mean, became shorthand for the day's message. "Our stagecraft had gone awry," Bush later concluded. "It was a big mistake."

15

"Mr. President, I think we've got a problem"

Five days after the made-for-television landing on the aircraft carrier, President Bush sat down for lunch with the man he wanted to accomplish the next mission in Iraq. Across from him in the dining room off the Oval Office was L. Paul Bremer III, a former ambassador in charge of counterterrorism and former chief of staff to Henry Kissinger. Bremer was Bush's choice to govern Iraq and transition it back to Iraqi hands.

At first glance, Bremer had a background almost designed to draw Bush's skepticism. A product of northeast elite circles, Bremer was the son of the president of Christian Dior Perfumes and an art history lecturer, earned degrees from Andover, Yale, and Harvard, studied at a French political institute, and boasted a résumé of State Department and foreign policy experience a mile long. But at sixty-one, he still had thick, wavy hair and chiseled good looks, worked out vigorously, and, most important, exuded a take-charge energy that appealed to Bush.

From that first meeting on May 6, Bush decided to invest in Bremer. And from the start, Bremer, who went by the name Jerry, laid out a vision in direct conflict with the sketchy plans Bush had made for Iraq. While the president and his team imagined a quick handover of power and a drawdown to thirty thousand troops by September, Bremer saw a longer, much more involved process. And at that lunch just before the announcement of his appointment, he got Bush to buy into his approach.

"We'll stay until the job is done," Bush told him over a salad of pears and greens. "You can count on my support irrespective of the political calendar or what the media might say."

Bush and Cheney had long planned to bring in someone like Bremer to run Iraq, but the plan was accelerated when Jay Garner got off to a rough start as interim administrator. The ease with which Hussein was dispatched had masked the challenge to come and just how unprepared the administration was to deal with it. Even before the fall of the statue at Firdos Square, the struggle for control within Bush's team was escalating to a volatile point. Donald Rumsfeld told Garner to get rid of two people on his team, Thomas Warrick and Meghan O'Sullivan, because a "higher authority" had insisted. The higher authority, Garner later concluded based on sniffing around, was Cheney's office, which regarded the two as insufficiently committed to the mission; Warrick had led a "Future of Iraq" project for the State Department that Cheney's team found suspect, and O'Sullivan had authored a book before the war suggesting alternatives to force for influencing rogue states like Iraq. Eventually, Garner convinced Rumsfeld to let him have O'Sullivan, though not Warrick.

The episode underscored the divisions inside the administration. When Colin Powell sent the Pentagon seven ambassadors with experience in the region, most of them Arabic speakers, Douglas Feith, Rumsfeld's undersecretary and one of the leading neoconservatives in the administration, rejected them. Powell was told the reason was that "we want people who are really committed and believe in what we are doing." Furious, he called Rumsfeld and threatened retaliation. "You know," Powell told him, "you are going to need a lot of help, and I am pulling these guys from embassies and I am pulling anybody who is not in an embassy but can help. But if you are blackballing my seven ambassadors, then I am not sending anybody." Rumsfeld eventually accepted several people from Powell's list.

By that point, Garner had lost support in Washington. He had managed to get crosswise first with Rumsfeld and then with Powell by switching plans for a transition. He did not seem like a decisive enough figure, and he certainly was not seen as part of the team in Cheney's office. Cheney moved quickly to bring in what he hoped would be a stronger figure. Paul Wolfowitz asked to be considered, but he was viewed as more of a thinker than a manager, and his bid went nowhere. Instead, Scooter Libby contacted Bremer and told him he was being considered.

After their lunch, Bush took Bremer into the Oval Office to meet with reporters. With Cheney absent, Bremer sat in the vice president's chair in front of the fireplace as Bush hailed him as "a can-do type person."

Then after the journalists shuffled out, Bush and Bremer sat down privately with Cheney and the rest of the national security team.

"I don't know whether we need this meeting after all," Bush told his advisers. "Jerry and I just had it."

While he was only joshing, Bush had just sent a lasting signal. Bremer took from that that "I was the president's man," not the secretary of defense's. Rumsfeld, ever alert to turf and chain of command, took notice too. "POTUS had lunch with him alone—shouldn't have done so," he jotted down in a note to himself, using the acronym for president of the United States. "POTUS linked him to the White House instead of to DoD or DoS."

What's more, Bush agreed when Bremer insisted he recall Zalmay Khalilzad, a White House aide with deep contacts with Iraqi opposition figures who had been named special envoy. Bremer argued it would be confusing to have two people reporting to the president. Bush styled himself as an MBA president and believed good management was to pick good people and then delegate to them. If Bremer wanted Khalilzad out, Bush would oblige him.

Powell was stunned and called Khalilzad. "Zal, what the hell happened?"

"Colin, you're asking me?" Khalilzad replied. "I'm a poor staffer here."

Colleagues took it as an early indication that Bremer wanted no rivals, but it cost the administration one of its most talented specialists—and one who was determined to facilitate a quick transfer of authority back to the Iraqis. As for Garner, he was asked to stay a while under Bremer, but he got the message and began packing.

Bremer arrived in Baghdad to set up a Coalition Provisional Authority six days later, wearing what would become his trademark outfit, a coat and tie with tan desert boots. On May 16, four days after arriving, he issued Order Number 1, formalizing a ban on Saddam Hussein's Baath Party and removing tens of thousands of its members from government jobs. Garner and the CIA station chief protested to no avail to Bremer, who likened the move to de-Nazification in postwar Germany and based it on a draft given to him by Douglas Feith. A week later, on May 23, Bremer issued Order Number 2, disbanding the army altogether, not just the elite units loyal to Hussein as envisioned by the plan approved by Bush. Bremer reasoned that the army had dissolved itself, its bases effectively stripped and rendered useless. In both cases, he was trying to reassure the Kurds and the Shiites who had long suffered at the hands of Hussein's party and security organs. Restoring the army might have touched off a sectarian backlash. "We would have had a civil war on our hands right away," Bremer said later.

Both orders went against the grain of what Bush originally had in mind, but in neither case did he intervene, continuing the hands-off approach he established during Tora Bora. The two orders put hundreds of thousands of people on the street without jobs, many of them with weapons and military training. Bremer also allowed Ahmad Chalabi to be put in charge of de-Baathification, empowering the controversial figure to decide who kept a job and who was banned. With the passage of time, Bremer would defend his orders, saying "they were the right decisions," and disputing the "encrusted body of mythology around them." But he eventually concluded that his mistake was handing the party-purge process to Chalabi, who used his authority at times indiscriminately.

After just two weeks, Bremer was asserting control and settling in for an extended transition. In his first report to Bush on May 22, Bremer wrote that he had made clear to leaders of Iraq's various tribes and parties that "full sovereignty under an Iraqi government can come after democratic elections, which themselves must be based on a constitution agreed by all the people. This process will take time."

Bush gave his approval the next day, making clear he had switched from a quick-handover strategy to a longer occupation. "You have my full support and confidence," he wrote to Bremer. "You also have the backing of our Administration that knows our work will take time. We will fend off the impatient. . . ."

Among the impatient were those asking where the weapons of mass destruction were. While it had been just weeks, so far none had turned up, and inside the White House there was a growing anxiety about the political dangers if they never did. On the same day that Bush appointed Bremer, White House officials picked up the *New York Times* to find a column crystallizing that hazard in a way no one would immediately recognize.

The column, by Nicholas Kristof, bore the headline "Missing in Action: Truth." Noting that no weapons had been found in Iraq, Kristof suggested the White House had ignored evidence that they were never there. Reprising the sixteen words in the State of the Union about the Niger intelligence, Kristof reported that "the vice president's office asked for an investigation of the uranium deal, so a former U.S. ambassador to Africa was dispatched to Niger." The ambassador reported that "the information was unequivocally wrong and that the documents had been forged."

Kristof was referring to the former ambassador Joseph Wilson, whom he had met days earlier at a Democratic conclave. Wilson, the unnamed source in the column, had exaggerated to Kristof some of the details: he had never seen the documents he supposedly debunked, for example, and congressional investigators later concluded that the results of his trip were not as unequivocal as he averred. Even so, Kristof's reference set in motion a chain of events that would call into question the administration's credibility on the central justification of the war, sow division and mistrust within the White House, and permanently damage the friendship between Bush and Cheney.

BUSH AND CHENEY left Iraq to Bremer while they focused their energies on pushing through the latest tax cut package. After their internal debate, Bush had agreed to seek $726 billion in breaks; Cheney had won on the dividend tax cut and accelerating the 2001 cuts but lost on capital gains so that Bush could give small businesses a bigger break and extend unemployment benefits for the jobless.

As the legislation progressed on Capitol Hill, Cheney's friend Representative Bill Thomas, chairman of the Ways and Means Committee, had slipped the capital gains tax cut back into the bill. But while Republicans controlled both houses again, they were swallowing hard at Bush's bottom line. House Republicans pared it back to $550 billion while Senate Republicans, with just a two-vote majority, deferred to their moderate wing and capped it at $350 billion. The gulf between the houses grew so deep that Thomas and his Senate counterpart, Charles Grassley, were at loggerheads, forcing Bush to intervene.

On May 19, Bush and Cheney hosted Thomas, Grassley, and other Republican leaders on the Truman Balcony of the White House. Cheney had his back to the balcony as Speaker Dennis Hastert launched a direct assault on Grassley. "Mr. President," he said, "I think we've got a problem." Hastert said Grassley had locked himself into a position and should be barred from talks between House and Senate. Hastert noticed Cheney with "his slight little smile" as Grassley's face grew redder.

It fell to Cheney to broker the deal. He spent the next few days shuttling between Thomas and Grassley and other leaders until they finally agreed on a $350 billion package, meeting the Senate's bottom line but adopting some of the ideas of the House plan. Once again, Cheney's tie-breaking vote was required to push it through the Senate on May 23, while the House approved it the same day.

Cheney was deeply involved in another argument with fellow Republicans at the same time, this one inside the administration over environmental regulations. For more than two years, he had been pressing Christine Todd Whitman, the EPA administrator, to approve a new interpretation of clean air rules that would allow utilities more leeway to upgrade their plants without having to install expensive new pollution scrubbers. Whitman had put off revising the so-called New Source Review rules as long as she could but lost a war of attrition when Andy Card finally ordered her to sign it.

Rather than do it, she handed in her resignation on May 21. For public consumption, she said she was eager to spend more time with her family. But the regulations and Card's order, at Cheney's behest, were the final triggers. "It just got to the point where I said I just can't sign this, and that's when Andy called me in and said do it, and they had every right to order me to do it," she recalled. "I didn't exactly stall it for two and a half years, because there really were a lot of questions and a lot of backing and forthing. Andy thought I was stalling, but I wasn't consciously—well, maybe a little bit, but mostly because I didn't want everyone to make a mistake. I thought they were going down the wrong path, and I felt if I just could have a little more time to help him see that there was a way to do this" and provide the certainty industry wanted "but not to let the really bad actors who had been knowingly gaming the system get out."

Cheney was happy to see her go. They had known each other since their days under Donald Rumsfeld in the Nixon administration. But as with Paul O'Neill, they had drifted apart ideologically and personally. "A lot of people I've talked to that have known him, that knew him and worked with him over the years, say there's been a change—whether it was the heart attacks or the working in Halliburton or the combination of the two, but it was a different person who came back in the government than the one they'd known before," Whitman reflected years later. "But I never knew him well enough to make that kind of distinction except that I felt before, he was more approachable."

In the midst of everything else, Bush was busy with reconciliation on another front. After years of estrangement from his alma mater, the president took another step toward peace with Yale University by hosting a reunion for his class of 1968 at the White House. Some of his classmates opted to stay away in protest of the war, an echo of the antiwar passions also roiling campus during Bush's day. But for the president, it was a chance for closure of sorts, to come to terms with the elite side of his multifaceted heritage and put to rest some of the demons that had haunted him since his youth.

It was also a night when the compassionate side of his conservatism was on display. Among those in the receiving line that evening was Petra Leilani Akwai, who had been known in college as Peter Clarence Akwai before undergoing a sex-change operation in 2002. Dressed in an evening gown, Akwai nervously waited her turn.

"Hello, George," she said when presented to the president. "I guess the last time we spoke, I was still living as a man."

Bush did not flinch. "But now you're you," he replied, leaning forward with a warm smile.

BY LATE SPRING, it had been nearly two months since the fall of Saddam Hussein, and Bush was still waiting to find the weapons he had been assured were there.

"What if we don't find them?" he asked one day.

"Oh, we'll find them," Condoleezza Rice reassured him.

Yet no one was taking the lead in the search. Sitting with his war cabinet, he described how he had asked Jerry Bremer and Tommy Franks who was in charge.

"They went—" Bush said, pointing his fingers in opposite directions to indicate the buck-passing he detested.

He turned to George Tenet. "As a result," Bush said, "you are now in charge, George."

Tenet and his slam-dunk certainty had gotten him into this, Bush reasoned, so he should be the one to prove they had been right. Tenet hired David Kay, a former UN weapons inspector who had gone into Iraq after the Gulf War and established himself as one of the premier experts in the field. Like others, he had believed before the war that Iraq had weapons and accepted the challenge.

The pressure to find them only increased. As more media inquiries came in, Cheney was becoming exercised by the story of the unnamed ambassador's mission to Niger supposedly sent at his behest. He had never heard of any such trip or any results from it, and yet he was being accused of ignoring evidence that contradicted his assumptions about Iraq's weapons program.

Finally, Cheney picked up his secure phone and pushed the button that connected him directly to Tenet.

"What the hell is going on, George?" Cheney asked.

In Cheney's memory, Tenet was embarrassed and said he had not known about the trip until the media accounts. In the course of the conversation, Tenet noted that the ambassador's wife "worked in the unit that sent him." He promised to get more information.

Cheney was flabbergasted. He had spent years as a consumer of intelligence and had never heard of an envoy being sent on a trip by his wife, with the director in the dark. "It sounded like amateur hour out at the CIA," Cheney concluded.

Cheney received a call from Scooter Libby, who was preparing to return a call from Walter Pincus of the *Washington Post*. Cheney passed along what he had learned from Tenet and then said in what Libby remembered as "sort of an offhand manner, as a curiosity," that the ambassador's wife worked in the counter-proliferation division of the CIA. Libby, who was taking notes, jotted that down with his blue pen: "CP/his wife works in that divn." Libby also scrawled down the salient talking points: "1) didn't know @ mission, 2) didn't get report back, 3) didn't have any indication of forgery was from IAEA." Libby called Pincus and passed along those points but did not mention the wife. Pincus's story on June 12 recounted the still-unnamed ambassador's trip, questioned the sixteen words from the State of the Union, and reported that the vice president had not known about the trip or received any report about it.

While the vice president's office defended itself, the situation in Iraq developed in troubling ways. Presuming the war was essentially over, short of mop-up operations, Tommy Franks had decided against bringing in the First Cavalry Division as planned and announced his retirement. When Richard Myers asked him to reconsider, Franks lashed out at him. "Not going home?" he said. "Butt-fuck me." His command unit left behind in Iraq then withdrew from the country, and he was replaced by a recently promoted division commander named Ricardo Sanchez. Now the army's most junior lieutenant general, Sanchez found himself in charge with a headquarters designed to run a division, not a country, with just 37 percent of the staff such a post should have had. His ascension went largely overlooked in Washington. Donald Rumsfeld had interviewed Sanchez for his promotion to three stars but later said he had nothing to do with putting him in charge in Iraq, an astonishing disengagement in the most important theater for the American military. (Myers doubted Rumsfeld's account. "I just find that really hard to believe," he said.)

The transition belied the increasing violence on the ground. More than two dozen American soldiers had been killed in combat since Bush declared major operations over under the "Mission Accomplished" banner, and the Pentagon had concluded that it was fighting five distinct groups, even though it refused to call that a guerrilla war or an insurgency. Bush was defiant. Talking with reporters in the Roosevelt Room on July 2, he all but dared the insurgents to escalate their attacks.

"There are some who feel like that the conditions are such that they can attack us there," Bush said. "My answer is: Bring 'em on. We've got the force necessary to deal with the security situation."

The Texas swagger made headlines, but like his "dead or alive" comment in 2001 it drew concern from the first lady and others who deemed it cocky and even insensitive.

"Mr. President, can you imagine how that would sound to a mother who just lost her son in Iraq?" Ari Fleischer asked in a private moment.

Bush said he had not thought of that. "I was just trying to express my confidence in our military."

That offhand bravado became a rallying cry among insurgents in Iraq, who threw it back in Bush's face as the war escalated. And it helped reinforce for Bush what every president ultimately realizes, that words have multiple audiences; what makes sense for one set of ears has a drastically different impact on another. As his presidency wore on, Bush became more aware that he was simultaneously addressing not just the American public but troops in harm's way, the country's allies, the Iraqi people, and the enemy itself. He would eventually consider the "bring 'em on" comment one of his biggest gaffes, although its larger importance lay not in the words themselves but in the flawed analysis they revealed. What he faced in Iraq was not a relatively minor challenge that would be put down expeditiously.

NOR WAS THE Niger question. On July 6, Joseph Wilson unmasked himself, writing an op-ed in the *New York Times*, giving an interview to Walter Pincus and Richard Leiby in the *Washington Post*, and appearing on NBC's *Meet the Press,* all to allege that weapons intelligence "was twisted to exaggerate the Iraqi threat." Cheney read the *Times* op-ed while flying back to Washington on Air Force Two from Wyoming. He clipped it, underlining eleven different parts and scrawling his own reactions above the headline. "Have they done this sort of thing before?" he wrote. "Send an Amb to answer a question? Do we ordinarily send people out pro bono to work for us? Or did his wife send him on a junket?"

The White House was pounded over the sixteen words and decided to retreat. At a briefing on July 7, the day after Wilson's public debut, David Sanger of the *Times* pressed Fleischer on Bush's statement in the State of the Union.

"So it was wrong?" Sanger asked.

"That's what we've acknowledged," Fleischer said.

But that did not end the matter. Cheney was upset and talked it over repeatedly with Libby. The vice president was "very keen to get the truth out," Libby later said. In the days that followed, Libby told Fleischer about Wilson's wife, and the two of them as well as Karl Rove discussed it with reporters. Critics later portrayed that as a systematic campaign to deliberately blow the cover of a covert CIA operative, which would be a crime. All involved denied it, and no one would ever be charged with it. What seems more plausible is that Libby and the others were trying to undercut Wilson's credibility by suggesting he went to Africa at the behest of his wife, not the vice president. Libby was so consumed by the matter that he called Tim Russert, the NBC News bureau chief, to complain about the commentary of the liberal MSNBC talk show host Chris Matthews. What exactly was said during that call would later be in dispute.

Bush was leaving for a weeklong trip to Africa and not eager for the controversy to follow him. The day before he departed, he met with Cheney, Condoleezza Rice, and George Tenet. Rice argued they should "just take the issue off the table" by repudiating the sixteen words and taking responsibility. Cheney opposed that, arguing that the information had been in the National Intelligence Estimate and cited legitimately. Even at that time, it had been reported that an Iraqi delegation had a few years earlier approached Niger about "expanding commercial relations"; Cheney and his allies argued that had to mean uranium, since that was the country's main resource. Besides, Cheney argued, the sixteen words were literally correct because they said the British government had reported this, which it had. But Bush eventually agreed with Rice, who then talked with Tenet about releasing a statement.

The situation worsened as Bush took off on Air Force One. With the president and Rice across the world, Cheney in Washington, and Tenet at a conference in Sun Valley, Idaho, the administration's response over the next few days proved disjointed at best. Before Tenet could finish his statement, Rice felt pressured to put the fire out, so she marched back to the press cabin on Air Force One as it made its way to Entebbe, Uganda, on July 11.

"If the CIA, the director of central intelligence, had said take this out of the speech, it would have been gone, without question," Rice told reporters.

Bush echoed her later that day when asked about it by a reporter at a beachside hotel in Uganda. The speech, he emphasized, "was cleared by the intelligence services."

What Bush and Rice considered factual statements were seen by Tenet as shifting blame, and he wondered if he might be fired or have to resign. In Sun Valley, he grew angrier as he wrote his own statement, going back and forth with the White House. Seventeen drafts later, he took his lumps: "First, CIA approved the President's State of the Union address before it was delivered. Second, I am responsible for the approval process in my Agency. And third, the President had every reason to believe that the text presented to him was sound. These 16 words should never have been included in the text written for the President." But then he offered "a little history," noting that the CIA had disagreed with the British about the validity of the Niger report and had not included it among the key judgments in the National Intelligence Estimate, although it was mentioned in the body of the text. He did not mention that the CIA had gotten the White House to take the same allegation out of Bush's October speech in Cincinnati.

The swirling events opened a permanent rift between Tenet and the White House. Cheney and his allies believed Rice's admission only made matters worse, not better. "You put a bull's-eye on the White House," Robert Joseph, the National Security Council official who had dealt with CIA officials over the speech, told Stephen Hadley that night. Joseph felt the admission fed into the perception that the White House had lied. Rice, Rove, and Dan Bartlett eventually came to the same conclusion, although it was not clear that there was much of a choice.

THE NEXT DAY, July 12, Cheney flew to Norfolk, Virginia, to help commission the USS *Ronald Reagan* aircraft carrier. On the return flight, Libby entered his cabin on Air Force Two to tell him a couple of reporters had called about the Wilson story. Cheney dictated to Libby what he should tell them. Libby later that day talked with four reporters, and Valerie Wilson came up with two or three of them.

On July 14, the conservative columnist Robert Novak published a column identifying Valerie Wilson as a CIA operative. Novak had learned not from the Cheney camp but from one of Cheney's fiercest adversaries, Richard Armitage, Colin Powell's deputy secretary of state, who mentioned it during an interview on other subjects. Armitage, an inveterate gossip, had also mentioned it to Bob Woodward during an interview for a book. Novak got it confirmed to his satisfaction from Karl Rove and then a CIA spokesman. Three days later, Matthew Cooper of *Time*, one of the reporters Libby talked with after the Norfolk trip, posted a story on the magazine's Web site mentioning the ambassador's wife; Cooper, like Novak, had also spoken with Rove. Judith Miller of the *New York Times*, who talked with Libby about Valerie Wilson, never published anything about her.

Libby and Rove at first thought the revelation might help them by making it clear that Joseph Wilson did not go to Africa on Cheney's behalf. But they quickly realized what an enormous miscalculation that was. Although Valerie Wilson was working as an analyst at CIA headquarters, she had previously been overseas undercover, and the Intelligence Identities Protection Act made it a crime to intentionally disclose the identity of a covert agent. Rather than questioning the origin of Wilson's trip, reporters focused on whether the White House had blown the cover of a CIA officer to punish a critic.

Matters got worse over the weekend when Michael Gerson found in his files the memo the CIA had sent him and Hadley warning them to take the Niger uranium story out of the president's Cincinnati speech the previous fall. Gerson brought the memo to Hadley, who was deeply embarrassed. The warning was on page 3 of a three-and-a-half-page memo, and Hadley had forgotten about it, but it was clear the White House had been previously alerted about the veracity problems with the Niger intelligence. It was his responsibility to vet the State of the Union, and he should have remembered the previous episode. Hadley, almost universally considered a soft-spoken, workaholic man of decency and honor, crafted a statement announcing his resignation.

The next morning, July 22, Bush found Hadley coming to see him alone before a meeting.

"Mr. President, I think I need to resign," Hadley said.

"Ugh, Hadley," Bush said, dismissing him.

Hadley raised his voice, something he almost never did. "Mr. President," he said, "you need to hear me out on this."

"All right, Hadley, I will hear you out."

Hadley explained that the president should expect the highest standards and those who work for him were invested with the national trust. It was no disgrace to accept responsibility for a mistake, he said. "In fact, that is exactly how the system should work, and that is what needs to happen here." Hadley mentioned his resignation statement.

"Let me see your statement," Bush said. He read it through. "It is a great statement," he said, "and you can use everything but the last paragraph," meaning the resignation.

"Mr. President, I think this is a mistake," Hadley protested.

"I know you do."

At that point, Cheney and other top advisers arrived for an 8:00 a.m. meeting. Bush decided to needle Hadley a bit. "Hadley wants to resign," he announced to the room.

"What's the matter, Steve?" Cheney asked. "Don't you like it around here?"

Hadley, embarrassed to have this play out in front of the group, made a shorthand version of his case but knew it was for naught. "Give your statement," Bush instructed, "but you are not resigning."

As it happened, Tenet that same morning brought a copy of the memo and a follow-up, intent on making the point that the CIA had warned the White House about the uranium claim in the past. After showing them to Hadley, Tenet went to Andy Card's office. As Tenet recalled, Card shook his head. "I haven't been told the truth," he said.

Hadley that afternoon invited reporters to the Roosevelt Room, where he explained what had happened and took responsibility. He and Bartlett stayed for an hour and twenty-three minutes, letting reporters exhaust every question to prove they were not hiding anything—except, that is, Hadley's attempt to step down. Asked if he had offered to resign, Hadley said, "My conversation with the president I'm not going to talk about."

A week later, the CIA notified the Justice Department that the leak of Valerie Wilson's identity may have constituted a crime.

16

"Welcome to Free Iraq"

Stephen Hadley was not the only one contemplating stepping down that summer. Unbeknownst to almost anyone outside the Oval Office, Vice President Cheney offered three times to drop off the reelection ticket in 2004.

"Mr. President," Cheney said during one of their weekly lunches, "I want you to know that you should feel free to run for reelection with someone else. No hard feelings."

President Bush looked at him with worry. Was he okay? Was there anything wrong with his heart?

No, Cheney said. He just recognized that it might be easier for Bush to win with someone else.

Cheney understood he had become a magnet for attacks, portrayed by critics as the dark force behind the throne. His poll numbers were still relatively strong in those days, far above where they would eventually sink; some 54 percent of the public approved of him, according to Gallup, and 51 percent thought Bush should keep him on the ticket. But the benefit he brought in 2000 as counsel to an inexperienced president no longer applied. Cheney remembered helping to push Nelson Rockefeller off the ticket in 1976 so that Gerald Ford could beat Ronald Reagan for the Republican nomination, and he thought George H. W. Bush should have replaced Dan Quayle in 1992.

"The reason I did it—I believed that it was one of the few things 41 could have done in '92 to change the scenario enough to have a shot," Cheney said years later. "I had been through the thing with Ford and Rockefeller and concluded that we had to get Rockefeller out if we were going to win the nomination." And so, he said, "I always saw the vice president as expendable in a sense. I do today."

Bush, who had urged his father to replace Quayle with Cheney in 1992, brushed off his vice president. But Cheney came back at him during one of their weekly lunches. "The first couple of times I brought it up, I had the impression that he didn't take me seriously," Cheney recalled. "So I brought it up a third time, and he said okay and went away and thought about it." Cheney said it was not an offer made lightly. "I mean, all the president had to say was, 'Dick, I am ready to make a change,' and I was out of there. I would have made it easy."

Bush did think about it and even came up with a potential replacement, Senator Bill Frist, the majority leader from Tennessee. He liked Frist's demeanor, his medical background, the generational change he might represent. Frist had been a key ally on elements of the compassionate conservative agenda, including PEPFAR, and the two were working together on legislation expanding Medicare to cover prescription medicine. But Bush never contacted Frist. He quietly confided in only a few aides, individually and not in a meeting, including Andy Card, Karl Rove, and Dan Bartlett, and it remained a closely held secret. Bush did not mention it to reelection strategists like Ken Mehlman and Matthew Dowd or even to Condoleezza Rice. Cheney kept it secret from most of his staff and even longtime friends like Donald Rumsfeld and Alan Simpson. "I knew nothing about it," Simpson said.

The fact that Bush was tempted, even briefly, suggests that the relationship was beginning to change. As he described it in his memoir, Bush noted that Cheney "helped with important parts of our base" but "had become a lightning rod for criticism from the media and the left. He was seen as dark and heartless—the Darth Vader of the administration." More telling, though, was Bush's mention of the perception that Cheney really ran the White House. "Accepting Dick's offer would be one way to demonstrate that I was in charge," Bush said. All the talk of Cheney as secret puppet master had begun to rankle him, and he wanted to prove he was the boss.

Even though they were unaware of Cheney's offer, the issue was the subject of repeated conversations among the president's campaign advisers. Some like Dowd wanted to replace Cheney—his candidate was Rice—both because of the drag he had become and because they needed to think about the future of the party and who would run for president in 2008. "Many of us came to the conclusion there was a Cheney problem," Dowd said later. Rove, though, would not entertain it, and Bartlett put off the dissidents. "This is being considered," he said. "Stay tuned."

But privately, Bartlett warned Bush against the switch. Even though Bartlett was among the Bush aides who had been most frustrated at times with Cheney, he believed replacing him on the ticket would backfire. "People would say, 'What does it say about Bush?' " he reflected. "The Dems would pile on and would not give any credit. I don't think it would have successfully distanced himself from any of the controversial decisions. For every problem you think you're solving, you're creating two more." While replacing running mates between terms was common early in the country's history, no incumbent president had done it and gone on to win since Franklin Roosevelt. It would call into question the fundamental judgment of the president, suggesting the very first decision he made as a potential national leader had been wrong.

Bush went back to Cheney and turned him down; Cheney thought it was "a few days later," while Bush remembered it being "a few weeks later." Either way, Bush concluded, "I hadn't picked him to be a political asset; I had chosen him to help me do the job. That was exactly what he had done."

For Cheney, the offer was an act of statesmanship, a selfless proposition making it easier for the president to consider what most incumbents entertain in the backs of their minds heading toward reelection year. Yet at the same time, it also had the effect of taking the issue off the table early. Once he made up his mind, Bush rarely revisited a decision, and Cheney had now prompted him to recommit to his vice president.

"It was a clever move by Cheney," said one longtime friend of both men. "Cheney doesn't do things that aren't calculated and thought through." Cheney had given Bush a chance to reassure himself that he really was in charge. "Reminding people that he was the boss was his great weakness, whether it was the shadow of his dad or his own insecurity or Rove or Cheney," said the friend. "It was important to him. Emotionally, he had to remind people he was in charge." Cheney had played to that insecurity. Moreover, in raising the issue, "Cheney reminded Bush of Cheney's place in Bush world, and in the administration, in the White House, and of the centrality of his advice to Bush. 'This is something I value.' It's smart."

BUSH AND CHENEY were both surprised to pick up the *Washington Post* on September 8 and find an op-ed article by Jerry Bremer headlined "Iraq's Path to Sovereignty." In it, Bremer outlined a seven-part plan to turn Iraq back over to Iraqis, one that envisioned writing a constitution, submitting it to a national referendum, and then electing a government before America would pull back.

Bremer had gotten started in July by appointing a twenty-five-member Iraqi Governing Council to advise him on running the country in the interim. The council had thirteen Shiites, five Sunni Arabs, five Kurds, a Turkmen, and a Christian. But recent weeks had seen violence grow. American forces had tracked down Saddam Hussein's sons, Uday and Qusay, notorious for their cruelty, and killed them in a firefight. Hussein vowed revenge by promising to kill Bush's daughters, a threat that George and Laura kept from the twins even as the Secret Service ramped up security.

Then insurgents drove a truck bomb into the Canal Hotel in Baghdad, headquarters for the UN contingent, cratering the building and leaving twenty-three bodies littered amid the rubble. Among them was Sergio Vieira de Mello, the world body's top diplomat in Iraq and a man widely admired by the Bush administration and its critics alike. Bush had met Vieira de Mello when Condoleezza Rice brought him by the Oval Office. Now he was dead, a tragedy that would result in the United Nations pulling most of its foreign workers out of Baghdad.

The Americans increasingly retreated behind the walls of their own fortress, a secured area that became known as the Green Zone. The occupation authority that was building up was a haphazard affair, cobbled together with little understanding of the country it was tasked with running. Muslim workers in the cafeteria were left to serve bacon and pork. Some of the civilians recruited to manage America's new protectorate had been screened by the conservative Heritage Foundation. A twenty-four-year-old who worked at a real estate firm and had never been to the Middle East was assigned to rebuild the stock exchange. An army officer busied himself rewriting Iraq's traffic laws by cutting and pasting from Maryland's code. A twenty-one-year-old who had yet to finish college and whose most significant job until then had been ice-cream truck driver was among those charged with purging the Interior Ministry of militia members.

The American military strategy was still to pull troops out, despite the violence. There was a sense that the armed forces had done their job and the longer they remained, the more it would stimulate resistance. But Robert Blackwill, a longtime diplomat assigned by Rice to study the Iraq situation, sent her a memo urging as many as forty thousand more troops, a recommendation that went unheeded by Rumsfeld and the White House. "You should have flooded the zone in the first place," Powell said. "Rather than flooding the zone, Don wants a moat."

Bremer thought his plan outlined an orderly handover and was in keeping with everything he had been telling Washington for months. But Washington evidently had not gotten the message because his *Post* op-ed set off alarm bells in the White House and the Pentagon. Even Rumsfeld, who had just spent a couple days with Bremer, was surprised to read it in the newspaper. The plan suggested Americans would remain as occupiers for another two years. For Cheney and Rumsfeld, who had been pushing for a quick handover, this was unacceptable. They began thinking about how to accelerate the return of sovereignty.

But as they did so, Cheney's right hand, Scooter Libby, who would normally be the instrument of advancing the vice president's views, was increasingly distracted by the CIA leak scandal. Libby believed Bremer needed to be reversed but felt his own effectiveness was compromised.

On September 16, the CIA gave the Justice Department a memo outlining its internal probe and seeking an FBI investigation into who leaked Valerie Wilson's identity. The same day, Scott McClellan, who had moved up to replace Ari Fleischer as White House press secretary, told reporters that it was "totally ridiculous" to blame Karl Rove but offered no such defense of Libby.

News of the CIA request broke ten days later, when NBC News reported it. At the White House, the report of the investigation request was seen as a deliberate attempt by the CIA to draw attention away from a Senate decision to investigate the agency's flawed intelligence on Iraq. Tenet "was using that as a diversion and it worked," Adam Levine, a White House press aide, said later. Tenet wrote in his memoir that he had nothing to do with making the referral.

The *Washington Post* dealt the next blow, reporting on September 28 that "two top White House officials called at least six Washington journalists" to out Valerie Wilson before Robert Novak's column ran, a sensational claim that roiled Washington with its implication of an orchestrated hit campaign. An unnamed senior official was quoted saying, "Clearly, it was meant purely and simply for revenge." The report was generated partly from a conversation between Mike Allen, a *Post* reporter, and Levine. It was true that Libby, Rove, and Ari Fleischer had talked with several journalists about Valerie Wilson, though not all before the Novak column and not all by making cold calls volunteering the information. And the phrase "before Novak's column ran" had been inserted by an editor who misunderstood the timing. Talking with reporters about Valerie Wilson after her identity was already disclosed by Novak was different from disclosing it in the first place.

The story drove a further wedge into the Bush-Cheney team. McClellan, who had denied that Rove had been involved, now confronted him again. Rove acknowledged that he had spoken with Novak.

"He said he'd heard that Wilson's wife worked at the CIA," Rove explained. "I told him I couldn't confirm it because I didn't know."

McClellan was bothered because Rove had never before volunteered even talking with Novak. "Were you involved in this in any way?" McClellan asked.

"No," Rove said. "Look, I didn't even know about his wife." He did not mention that he had also spoken with Matthew Cooper of *Time* about Wilson's wife.

Bush called to grill Rove too. "Are you the one behind this Novak column?" he remembered asking.

In the president's recollection, Rove told him that he had spoken with Novak but it "had nothing to do with Valerie Plame" and she "had never come up." If Bush's memory was correct, Rove had misled him.

Rove remembered the conversation differently. In his memoir, he wrote that he told Bush that Novak had asked him about Wilson and he replied, "I have heard that too," but that was all. "Bush sounded a little annoyed but took my word," Rove wrote.

The morning after the *Post* story, Bush passed along Rove's assurance to McClellan.

"Karl didn't do it," Bush told McClellan.

"I know—" McClellan began.

"He told me he didn't do it," Bush went on.

Andy Card gestured with his hands to indicate that Bush should not talk about it.

"What?" Bush asked with irritation. "That's what Karl told me."

"I know," Card said. "But you shouldn't be talking about it with anyone, not even me."

McClellan told Bush he planned to say at his briefing that it was a serious issue that should be examined.

"Yeah, I think that's right," Bush said. "I do believe it's a serious matter. And I hope they find who did it."

McClellan returned to let the president know he would say publicly that anyone involved would no longer work in the administration.

Bush agreed. "I would fire anybody involved," he said.

But while Rove and Libby were involved, so was Richard Armitage. Novak wrote a column on October 1 noting that his original source was "no partisan gunslinger," and Armitage realized that meant him. He called Colin Powell to admit his role and then approached prosecutors. While the State Department lawyer told the White House vaguely that the department had information it was sharing with prosecutors, he did not give any details, and the White House lawyers did not want to know. Wary of compromising the investigation, neither Powell nor Armitage told Bush or Cheney. Their caution would permanently sour their relationship with Cheney once he later learned of it.

Cheney was upset Rove had been exonerated from the White House podium while Libby had not. Libby scratched out notes of what he thought McClellan should say on his behalf: "People have made too much of the difference in how I described Karl and Libby. I've talked to Libby. I said it was rediculous [*sic*] about Karl and it is rediculous [*sic*] about Libby.

Libby was not the source of the Novak story. And he did not leak classified information."

Libby showed it to Cheney, who added his own notes to the bottom of the page: "Has to happen today. Call out to key press saying same thing about Scooter as Karl. Not going to protect one staffer and sacrifice the guy that was asked to stick his neck in the meat grinder because of the incompetence of others." Presumably, Cheney meant Libby had been forced to clean up the mess the two of them blamed on the CIA. Cheney took the issue to Bush, who agreed Libby should be cleared from the podium as well.

At 8:30 a.m. on October 4, Card called McClellan at home. "The president and vice president spoke this morning," Card said. "They want you to give the press the same assurance for Scooter that you gave for Karl."

McClellan called Libby to hear his denial directly.

"Were you involved in the leak in any way?" McClellan asked.

"No, absolutely not," Libby said.

McClellan then called four reporters to convey the denial.

THE IRAQ WAR was taking a toll inside the White House, and the situation on the ground was no better. Frustrated by Bremer's performance and Donald Rumsfeld's hands-off management of it, Rice prevailed upon Bush to create the Iraq Stabilization Group under her to improve coordination between Washington and Baghdad. When David Sanger of the *New York Times* heard, Rice confirmed it to him without letting Rumsfeld know the story was coming.

Rumsfeld erupted when he saw the newspaper on October 6. "The story indicates Condi stated that the reorganization was developed by herself, the Vice President, Powell and Rumsfeld," the defense secretary wrote in a memo to Bush and Cheney. "I was not consulted—only advised." If Rice was so eager to run the Iraq political account, Rumsfeld essentially said fine, he would be happy to off-load it. He recommended that "Jerry Bremer's reporting relationship be moved from DoD to the President, Condi Rice or Colin Powell, as you may determine." After all, Rumsfeld wrote with evident pique, Bremer already "has been reporting directly to Colin, Condi and you," and "Condi, in effect has been [*sic*] announced that that is the case."

Bush told Rice to calm Rumsfeld down. "You need to make it right with Don," he said.

He suggested she go to Cheney. She did, and he promised to talk with Rumsfeld.

When she saw Rumsfeld a week later, she pulled him aside and apologized.

Rumsfeld was unforgiving. "You're failing," he told her bluntly. "You could have said something in the NSC meeting in front of the president and the principals."

"Don," Rice replied, "you've made mistakes in your long career."

"Yes," he said, "but I've tried to clean them up."

The schism over Iraq was a decisive turning point in their relationship. For all of their tension in the past, this was the clash from which they never recovered. For the rest of their time in office, Rumsfeld and Rice warily circled each other, ever ready to pounce when possible and nurse grievances when not.

Bush was getting grief on all fronts. The same day, he met with senators in the Roosevelt Room to push an $18.6 billion request for reconstruction, but the senators wanted it to be a loan that Iraq would have to pay back.

"I did not come here to negotiate," Bush said, pounding his fist on the table.

Senator Arlen Specter, a Pennsylvania Republican, said the UN resolution anticipated that Iraq's oil could finance its recovery.

Bush pounded the table again. "Did I make myself clear?" he asked.

Senator Lindsey Graham, a South Carolina Republican, bristled. "Well, I didn't come here to negotiate either," he said. "Let me tell you why I'm gonna vote against you, Mr. President. I'm not worried about pleasing people who think we went to Iraq for oil. They're nuts. I am worried about people back home paying the bill."

The quick, easy victory of May seemed a thousand years ago. Rumsfeld expressed frustration with progress in the war on terror in a memo on October 16. "It is pretty clear that the coalition can win in Afghanistan and Iraq in one way or another," he wrote, "but it will be a long, hard slog."

Bush was sticking by Bremer. As he told a group of current and former officials from the Coalition Provisional Authority one day that October, "I tell members of Congress all the time—if Bremer's happy, I'm happy. If Bremer's worried, I'm worried. If Bremer's frustrated, I'm frustrated."

Bush, Cheney, and the rest of the team met with Bremer in Washington on October 28 to talk about the way forward. Bush then invited the Iraq viceroy to join him for a workout, another signal of confidence in Bremer to the rest of the administration and especially to Rumsfeld. Bush worked the elliptical machine for forty-five minutes while Bremer took the treadmill, and then the two retired to the second floor for sandwiches.

Bush asked about Rumsfeld. "What kind of a person is he to work for? Does he really micromanage?"

Bremer said he liked Rumsfeld and admired him. "But he does micromanage," he said. "Don terrifies his civilian subordinates, so that I can rarely get any decisions out of anyone but him."

Bremer expressed concern that the Pentagon was trying "to set me up as a fall guy" by suggesting they wanted a quick end to the occupation against his resistance, "so any problems from here on out were my fault."

"Don't worry about that," Bush said. "I'll cover you here. And we are *not* going to fail in Iraq."

Bush's commitment to Bremer, though, rankled Rumsfeld further. What were the two of them doing working out together? Did Bremer work for the Pentagon or directly for the president?

"I thought Bremer reported to you?" his friend Kenneth Adelman asked.

"Only on paper," Rumsfeld grumbled.

"That's what paper is for, Don," Adelman said. If Bremer bypassed him, "then just change the paper" so he would formally report to Bush.

BY FALL, WITH weapons nowhere to be found, Bush was looking to advance a more compelling narrative for Iraq. When he learned that the National Endowment for Democracy was celebrating the twentieth anniversary of its founding under Ronald Reagan, he figured that was a perfect setting.

Just as Reagan had emphasized the moral quality of his crusade against the "evil empire," Bush would cast the campaign in Iraq as part of a broader movement toward democracy in the Middle East. While that had not been the driving force behind the decision to invade, these were themes Bush had been thinking about for a while, even including them in his National Security Strategy. Now that America had broken Iraq, it owned it, as Powell had memorably put it, and Bush was looking at how to put it back together again in better shape.

Addressing the democracy group at the U.S. Chamber of Commerce across Lafayette Park from the White House on November 6, Bush dismissed the notion that Muslims were culturally unsuited for democracy, noting that the same was once said about Japan, Germany, and India. "I believe every person has the ability and the right to be free," he declared. To soften the blow against autocratic allies in the Middle East, he was careful to praise Egypt and Saudi Arabia for relatively modest reforms while calling on them to do more. But he made clear he saw democracy as the underpinning of a new doctrine to counter Islamic extremists.

"Iraqi democracy will succeed," Bush said, "and that success will send forth the news, from Damascus to Tehran, that freedom can be the future of every nation. The establishment of a free Iraq at the heart of the Middle

East will be a watershed event in the global democratic revolution. Sixty years of Western nations excusing and accommodating the lack of freedom in the Middle East did nothing to make us safe—because in the long run, stability cannot be purchased at the expense of liberty."

The rhetorical shift excited Michael Gerson and others in the White House, but it was greeted warily by Cheney. The vice president thought democracy was fine as a goal, but he was not a neoconservative crusader; he was much more driven by national security concerns, by the goal of preventing threats from gathering—an "American nationalist," as his aide John Hannah dubbed him. Bush was arguing that those imperatives were no longer at odds, that a freer, more democratic Middle East was in the interest of American national security too. And in that, he had an important ally—Liz Cheney, the vice president's daughter, who as deputy assistant secretary of state for Near Eastern affairs was in charge of the Middle East Partnership Initiative, started in 2002 to promote democratic reform in the region. Liz Cheney increasingly became known as one of the leading voices for democracy promotion.

Yet inside the administration, everyone was growing frustrated with Iraq. While Washington was aggravated by Bremer's plan for an extended occupation, the viceroy in Baghdad was increasingly worried that American forces were not focused on what needed to be done to put down the growing insurgency. "There was a big debate raging," recalled Frederick Jones, the press secretary at the National Security Council. "No one was happy with the direction. There was a lot of tension."

One day, Bremer called Scooter Libby and left a message, only to have Cheney return the call instead. Bremer took the opportunity to lodge his concerns.

"Mr. Vice President, in my view we do not have a military strategy for victory in Iraq," he said. "It seems to me that our policy is driven more by our troop rotation schedule than by a strategy to win."

"I've been asking the same question—what's our strategy to win?" Cheney responded. "My impression is that the Pentagon's mind-set is that the war's over and they're now in the 'mopping up' phase. They fail to see that we're in a major battle against terrorists in Iraq and elsewhere."

Rumsfeld and Powell were advancing separate plans intended to speed up Bremer's timetable for transferring sovereignty. Bremer tried to hold that off by sending a letter to Rumsfeld, Powell, and Rice on November 10, agreeing to pursue an interim constitution, which could accelerate a handover. Rice called him a few hours later and asked him to come to Washington to brief Bush. Bremer raced to catch a military flight and arrived at Andrews Air Force Base at eight o'clock the next morning.

When Bush and Cheney gathered the team to talk with Bremer that day, November 11, they heard a stark warning from the CIA about the growing insurgency. Rumsfeld interrupted.

"Why do you call it an insurgency?" he demanded.

A CIA official outlined the Pentagon's own definition of insurgency, but few wanted to call it that. Acknowledging it was an insurgency would admit the occupation was not going well.

Nor was there much excitement about Bremer's revised transfer plan. Cheney suggested just letting the Iraqi Governing Council choose a transitional government. Bremer thought that was too big a risk, so overnight he reworked his plan with Meghan O'Sullivan and agreed to turn over sovereignty by June 30 of the following year to an interim government chosen through caucuses rather than waiting for elections. When he presented it at the White House the next day, it met with far more approval. "Bremer is doing a fabulous job," Bush told the visiting NATO secretary-general that day. Not everyone on his team agreed. But Bremer had bought himself more time and flew back to Iraq to announce his plan on November 15.

Lieutenant General Ricardo Sanchez, the commander in Iraq, had grown increasingly alienated from Bremer and the White House. He thought Washington had bungled planning for a post-Hussein Iraq and misjudged what was happening on the ground. The decision to transfer sovereignty in his mind was driven by the American political calendar. "The administration knew something had to be done immediately so that the November 2004 presidential election would not be impacted," he concluded. "It was all about winning the presidential election and maintaining power."

If that seemed a cynical interpretation, it was nonetheless hard to separate the political war at home from the military one overseas. As fall headed toward winter, Scooter Libby remained intent on exposing Joseph Wilson as not credible and pressed Kevin Kellems, a newly hired spokesman for the vice president, to attack the ambassador with reporters despite an explicit edict from Bush not to engage in the matter. Kellems was uncomfortable with Libby's requests and went to David Addington for advice. Addington recommended he ignore Libby. "Don't do it," Addington said. "Listen to the president."

CRITICS WERE JUST as cynical about the other big effort Bush was making in those autumn days, this one on the domestic front. Bush had promised during his 2000 campaign to revamp Medicare to cover prescription drugs for older Americans, but as he pressed Congress that fall, many even inside the White House saw it as a calculated move inspired by Karl Rove to win over senior voters in 2004, especially in the retirement havens of Florida, where no one wanted to go through another close call. "This was, I think, a Rove-driven agenda," concluded Senator Judd Gregg, the Republican who helped Bush prepare for the 2000 debates. "They wanted to do something as a statement to senior citizens."

There was certainly a policy argument for the initiative. Since Medicare was enacted in 1965, health care had grown increasingly dependent on prescription medication, and costs for seniors had skyrocketed. The plan Bush was pushing would be the most ambitious expansion of the entitlement program since its inception. But he faced complicated politics in passing it. Democrats generally opposed it, calling it a sop to the pharmaceutical industry and decrying changes Bush and his allies had included in the legislation to make the program more market oriented. Republicans like Gregg and Trent Lott dismissed it as more big government, especially since its $400 billion cost over ten years was not paid for. But Bush did have the critical support of AARP, the retiree group.

Bush was on Air Force One flying back from a visit to London as the House debated deep into the night of November 21. Bush talked with some members from Air Force One.

"I didn't come to Washington to increase the size of government," one balking conservative told him.

"You know what? I didn't either," Bush replied. "I came to make sure the government works. If we're going to have a Medicare program, it ought to be modern, not broken."

By the time Bush landed and returned to the White House, he was still short of a majority. Speaker Dennis Hastert opened voting at three o'clock in the morning and under House rules, members had fifteen minutes to vote. But when time was up, Bush was down by fifteen votes. Hastert held the vote open as party leaders leaned on Republican dissenters to switch. Hastert told David Hobbs, the chief White House lobbyist, that Bush had to talk with more Republicans, but Hobbs could not reach Bush, who had gone to bed. "He was just going crazy because he couldn't get through," Hastert recalled.

Finally, Hobbs woke Bush at 4:45 a.m. and implored him to speak with wavering congressmen. Hobbs wandered around handing his cell phone to Republicans to talk with Bush, putting about twenty on the line, one at a time, so many that he burned out his battery. Then a group of conservatives led by Representative Trent Franks of Arizona said they wanted to speak with the president, so they convened in a room off the House floor and gathered around a phone.

"Congressman, I understand you have a plan for getting the bill passed," Bush told Franks as the others strained to listen.

Franks made clear he and his colleagues actually did not like the bill because they felt it expanded the government role in health care.

"I misunderstood," Bush said. "I thought you had a plan."

"I just needed to tell you that," Franks said, referring to the way conservatives viewed the bill. "The only way they could change their minds on a proposal like that is if they believed they were getting something more important for the country."

"Like what?" Bush asked.

Trying not to sound pushy, Franks switched to the third person. "If we could get the president of the United States to give his word of honor tonight that he would only appoint Supreme Court justices that he knew would overturn *Roe v. Wade*, would uphold personhood of the unborn in the Constitution and be strict constructionists, we could get this done right now," he said.

This went beyond the usual log-rolling for a bill. It was one thing to promise a bridge or a highway project to get a key vote. Bush was being asked to commit to whom he would appoint to the highest court of the land.

"Congressman, I can't do that," Bush said. "If I did that, they'd spoon-feed that to me at the confirmation hearings."

Franks said he did not mean that Bush would have to make it public.

Bush tried to steer the conversation back to the merits of the Medicare bill but Franks persisted. The two went back and forth for several minutes, and Franks made clear they did not mean Bush should directly quiz candidates about *Roe v. Wade* since that would cross a line presidents typically did not cross.

"Okay, give me your criteria one more time," Bush said.

Franks went over it again. Then, even more daring, he added, "Mr. President, that would not include Alberto Gonzales."

Conservatives knew Bush would dearly love to make his White House counsel the nation's first Hispanic justice, but they did not trust Gonzales. There was stunned silence in the room at Franks's brazenness. But Bush let it pass without commenting. What he said next would become a point of dispute.

As at least one of the conservatives in the room remembered it, Bush agreed to the deal. "Congressman," he told Franks in this recollection, "I tell you what, I think I'm going to make that commitment. You know I'm a man of my word."

"I know you're a man of your word," Franks said. "Do I have your word?"

"Yes, congressman, you have my word."

Others did not remember it being that explicit. Hobbs, the White House lobbyist, recalled the president being elliptical. "I don't have a litmus test,"

Bush said in this version. "You know what's in my heart. You know what kind of judicial philosophy I have." Hobbs and Jeff Flake, another congressman in the room, said they did not remember any commitment beyond that. Dennis Hastert too said later that Bush "was very careful not to make hard promises."

Either way, Franks believed he had a commitment from the president to appoint anti-abortion justices; Bush of course was inclined to do so anyway, but the conservatives would try to hold him to it. Franks later sent him a list of ten candidates who fit his criteria. Among them were a couple of appeals court judges named John Roberts and Samuel Alito.

Franks and a few others then switched their no votes, and the bill passed, 220 to 215, at 5:53 a.m. as the sun peeked over the horizon. The two-hour-and-fifty-one-minute vote was twice as long as the longest roll call in history.

The measure headed to the Senate and again stirred drama. Bush allies needed sixty votes to advance the legislation to a final vote on November 24, but they found themselves one short. The only hope for the president, as it turned out, was Trent Lott, who had lost his post as majority leader after Bush took him to task for his controversial comments at Strom Thurmond's birthday party. "I didn't think they were telling the truth about what it was going to cost," Lott recalled. Plus, given the costly growth of the nation's entitlement programs, he thought it was like "putting more chairs on the deck of a sinking ship."

As Lott made his way up the aisle to the clerk's desk to register his vote, he heard Bill Frist, the man who took his post, plead, "Help us out, Trent." Against his better judgment, he did, providing the crucial vote to advance the bill. Bush called minutes later to thank him, but Lott told him it was one of the worst votes of his career. A day later, on November 25, he voted against final passage, but that required only 50 votes, and it passed 54 to 44.

BUSH HEADED TO Crawford for Thanksgiving with another destination in mind. Since mid-October, he had been talking with Andy Card about making a secret trip to Iraq to see firsthand the country that had come to dominate his presidency. The notion seemed almost farcical given the security questions; other presidents had slipped out of the country to visit war zones in secret, but that was before the era of Stinger missiles and twenty-four-hour television.

From the ranch, Bush and Condoleezza Rice convened a videoconference with Cheney and Card on the morning of November 26 to see if everyone still agreed he should go. "We said we thought it was what we should do," Rice recalled. Laura agreed, but their daughters were less sure. Bush told them only thirty minutes before leaving. "I'm scared, Dad," Barbara said. "Be safe. Come home."

Late that afternoon, Bush, wearing jeans, boots, and a work coat, climbed into an unmarked red van with tinted windows along with Rice. Both of them had baseball caps pulled low. "We looked like a normal couple," he said afterward. "We were a casual yuppie couple." To avoid suspicion, the van was driven by a plainclothes Secret Service agent who pulled out of the ranch past guards who did not realize who was in the back of the vehicle. They pulled out onto Interstate 35 toward TSTC Waco Airport, and for once the highway was not shut down for the presidential motorcade. Bush seemed taken aback by the slow pace.

"What is this?" he asked.

"A traffic jam," Rice responded, tweaking him.

They boarded Air Force One with only a handful of aides plus seven journalists who had just been clued in and told to remove batteries from their mobile phones to preserve secrecy. The plane took off at 7:27 p.m. local time and headed to Washington, where the president and his small entourage transferred inside a hangar at Andrews Air Force Base to the second modified Boeing 747 that serves as Air Force One, this one fueled and ready for the trip around the world. Stopping at the top of the ramp, Bush turned to reporters and put his hand with thumb and pinkie apart to his ear as if using a phone and mouthed the words "No calls, got it?" He drew a finger across his neck and repeated, "No calls." Then he slipped into the plane. A few additional aides and reporters joined them, and the president was back in the air at 11:06 p.m. local time.

Bush fell asleep within fifteen minutes of takeoff. As they approached the coast of Great Britain, the distinctive blue-and-white aircraft was spotted by the pilot of a commercial jet who radioed to ground control.

"London, is that Air Force One?" he asked.

"No, that's a Gulfstream V," replied the air traffic controller, reading the cover data that had been fed into the flight system.

The pilot apparently recognized something was up because he just laughed and said, "Okay, London."

Colonel Mark Tillman, the chief Air Force One pilot, alerted Joe Hagin, the deputy chief of staff who had put the trip together. Bush asked whether they should abort. They decided not to but kept watch to make sure the president's absence from Crawford did not show up in any news reports.

As the plane approached Baghdad, Rice, Card, Hagin, and Dan Bartlett grew increasingly tense, and they worried Bush might be too. "Do you think we should go pray with the president?" Rice asked. They went to the president's cabin, everyone held hands, and each of the five then offered a short prayer.

Bush headed to the cockpit to watch the approach to Baghdad. He noticed the minarets in the distance as the sun began to set. "The city seemed so serene from above," he later observed. And yet he understood the dangers and kept his eye on a red light he had been told would flash if a missile were fired at the plane. Just five days before, a cargo plane taking off from the Baghdad airport had been hit by a SAM-7 ground-to-air missile and forced to make an emergency landing. As Air Force One approached, Lieutenant General Ricardo Sanchez, waiting on the tarmac, heard explosions in the distance and worried about a mortar attack.

In the main cabins of Air Force One, the shades were pulled shut and the lights turned off, with only the eerie hue from the digital clocks providing any illumination. Body armor was passed out for the president and passengers, and the pilot took an evasive path to make a sharp, quick landing. Air Force One touched down at 5:32 p.m. local time on Thursday, November 27, in a dusty mist that helped obscure the plane. Bush emerged from the plane in jeans and a blue shirt. At the bottom of the stairs were Sanchez, Jerry Bremer, and a handful of others.

"Welcome to Free Iraq, Mr. President," Bremer declared.

Bush reached out to hug him. Brigadier General Martin Dempsey handed Bush a First Armored Division windbreaker, which he promptly put on.

Bush was then taken to the Bob Hope Dining Facility, which Bremer described as "a sort of overgrown Quonset hut." Bremer had been told about the secret trip while in Washington. Sanchez had learned just three days before the president's arrival. But none of the six hundred troops had a clue.

While the president waited unseen in the wings, Bremer and Sanchez went to the microphone as if they were the main speakers.

"Now, General Sanchez," Bremer started, "it says here I'm supposed to read the president's Thanksgiving proclamation, but I thought the deal was it was the most senior person who reads it. Is that you?"

Sanchez played along. "Sir, I don't know. Maybe we ought to get somebody from the back."

"Let's see if we've got anybody more senior here who can read the president's Thanksgiving speech," Bremer replied. "Is there anybody back there who's more senior than us?"

That was Bush's cue, and he entered to raucous cheers from shocked soldiers. "The building actually shook," one soldier later recorded. The burst of enthusiasm was overwhelming, and as tears ran down Bush's face, aides worried he would be too choked up to speak. "I was swept up by the emotion," Bush recalled.

He tried a weak joke to shake it off. "I was just looking for a warm meal somewhere," he told the soldiers.

He was on the ground just two hours, posing for pictures, and meeting briefly with members of the Iraqi Governing Council. Critics back home later mocked him for holding up a tray of turkey as if serving soldiers when it turned out to be decorative. But for many on the ground, the notion that their commander in chief would fly around the world into danger to spend the holiday with them resonated powerfully. And it would stay with Bush for years after he got back on Air Force One and took off.

Just as important, the secret held until he was out of missile range. Back at the ranch, Laura Bush even grew concerned that she had not seen any television coverage, forgetting that there would be a delay until his departure. She called the Secret Service command post to make sure everything was all right.

"Where's the president?" she asked.

"We show him in the ranch house, ma'am," an agent answered.

She realized they still did not know he was gone. "Oh, I'll go look again," she replied, trying to cover her tracks.

The photogenic trip, with its air of mystery and danger, pumped up Bush, but it did nothing to ameliorate the struggle within his team over what to do about Iraq. Donald Rumsfeld traveled to Iraq shortly after Bush's visit and all but washed his hands of Bremer and his operation. In an airport lounge, Rumsfeld told Bremer it was clear he was reporting to Bush and Rice.

"I'm bowing out of the political process," he told Bremer. "Let Condi and the NSC handle things."

That had become a running theme with Rumsfeld. As far as he was concerned, if others wanted to do his job, fine, let them take responsibility. Leaving a West Wing meeting one day, Rice, a couple of steps behind Rumsfeld in a stairwell, asked him to call Bremer with instructions on something. He refused. "He doesn't work for me," Rumsfeld said. While he maintained he was responding to legitimate chain-of-command issues, colleagues thought he was trying to distance himself from the increasingly messy situation. "Rumsfeld was so disengaged from the political process in Iraq—he had no interest in it at all," said Dan Senor, the Bremer aide. "Rumsfeld kind of tuned out after Baghdad fell," said Richard Perle, who was advising him as a member of the Defense Policy Board. "He was so fed up with the internecine warfare, the interagency warfare, that his basic attitude was, 'Let them do it.'"

BUSH WAS AT Camp David on December 13 when Rumsfeld called.

"Mr. President," he said, "first reports are not always accurate, but—"

Bush interrupted. "This sounds like it's going to be good news."

Rumsfeld said General John Abizaid, the CENTCOM commander, reported that the military might have caught Saddam Hussein.

"Well, that *is* good news," Bush said. "How confident is Abizaid?"

"Very confident."

Acting on information from a captive, Special Forces had raided a remote farm eight miles outside Tikrit, Hussein's hometown, and found a bedraggled, bearded man in a shallow spider hole. The man had a pistol but put up no fight. "I am Saddam Hussein, the president of Iraq, and I am willing to negotiate," he said. A soldier replied, "President Bush sends his regards." The man had a bullet scar on his left leg and distinctive tattoos known to be on the real Iraqi dictator, but the Americans knew he had used body doubles in the past, so they wanted to confirm his identity before making an announcement.

Bush, excited but trying to remain calm, called to inform Rice, who was home in Washington preparing for a Christmas party whose guests were to include Rumsfeld.

"Don just called," Bush said. "The military thinks they've got Saddam." "I'm skeptical," he added. "But we're not breathing a word of this."

"It's probably a double," said Rice.

Bush asked her to let Andy Card and Colin Powell know. He tried to call Cheney, but the vice president was on Air Force Two heading to Newburgh, New York, for a fund-raiser. Cheney got the message when the plane landed and called back. The two connected at 3:43 p.m.

"Dick," Bush began, "it looks like we've captured Saddam Hussein."

Cheney agreed they should proceed cautiously.

Moments after Cheney hung up, Rumsfeld called and said they planned a DNA test to match Hussein with genetic material from one of his slain sons. Assuming it was him, Rumsfeld said, they would announce it the next day. Cheney worked the phone for the next hour and a half as he gathered information, leaving well-heeled Republican donors waiting.

After finally making it to the event, Cheney headed back to Washington and suggested to his daughter Mary, who was traveling with him, that they drop by Rumsfeld's house for his own Christmas party. Lynne Cheney had gone on her own. But Mary thought it was odd since it was already 9:00 p.m. Her father gave her a hint after the plane landed and they had flown by helicopter back to the Naval Observatory grounds. Walking to the limousine that would take them to Rumsfeld's house, Cheney quietly told his daughter there was news out of Iraq but she had to stay mum since it was not confirmed. Once in the car, he handed her a note saying that a "high-value target" had been captured and was being identified by DNA.

Cheney did not say anything more about it for the duration of the party, but he and Rumsfeld were in a festive mood and at the end of the evening sat around a coffee table swapping war stories from the Nixon and Ford administrations. Only after the Cheneys returned to the residence and no one else was around did the vice president finally tell Lynne Cheney that they might have captured Hussein.

Just after three o'clock in the morning of December 14, Bush was jarred out of sleep by a call from Rice.

"I'm sorry to wake you, sir," she said, "but we got him."

"That's fantastic," Bush said. "Are you sure?"

"Yes," she said. She had just heard from Bremer that it really was Hussein.

Among the people Bush told at that point was his father. This was as big a moment for the elder Bush as for the younger. The scourge of their family, the man who had vexed father and son for a dozen years, was now in custody.

"Congratulations," the father told the son. "It's a great day for the country."

The son corrected him gently: "It's a greater day for the Iraqi people."

A few hours later, Bremer appeared before reporters in Baghdad to announce the news. "Ladies and gentlemen, we got him," Bremer said to raucous cheers from Iraqis in the room.

Rumsfeld was annoyed. He had called Ricardo Sanchez and told him to make the announcement; after all, it was the military that had captured Hussein. Rice had a different reaction. It should have been not Bremer or Sanchez but an Iraqi who made the announcement. It was a lost opportunity, she thought, to showcase the fact that Iraqis were taking control of their own fate from the dictator who had brutally repressed them. Still, she did not mention that to Bremer; instead, she called to praise him for a "really first-rate" news conference.

Either way, the capture gave the Bush team hope that Iraqis would see they no longer had anything to fear from Hussein and could therefore embrace the future of their country. Hussein would be put on trial by Iraqi prosecutors in an Iraqi court, albeit with substantial American help, to send a signal: it was time to move on. The picture of a disoriented and disheveled Hussein released by the American military was meant to be a powerful reinforcement of that lesson. "We really believed it was a key to ending the insurgency," Rice remembered.

From the Cabinet Room later that Sunday, Bush made that case directly.

"I have a message for the Iraqi people," he said in remarks televised at 12:15 p.m. Washington time. "You will not have to fear the rule of Saddam Hussein ever again. All Iraqis who take the side of freedom have taken the winning side."

He added, "In the history of Iraq, a dark and painful era is over. A hopeful day has arrived. All Iraqis can now come together and reject violence and build a new Iraq."

THE CAPTURE OF Hussein seemed to help the United States in Libya as well. American and British experts had been secretly visiting Libya and inspecting its weapons program since the outreach from Muammar el-Qaddafi's son back in March. To make sure the rapprochement worked, Bush had kept it secret from even top cabinet officers as he personally oversaw negotiations. "The president was the principal action officer orchestrating the Libya action plan," recalled Robert Joseph, the National Security Council official who led the effort for Bush. By tapping Joseph, one of the administration's most vocal hard-liners, Bush reassured Cheney.

The Libyans had acknowledged a nuclear weapons program and twenty-five tons of mustard chemical weapon agent. They had agreed to submit to international inspections and provided nuclear weapons design materials acquired from A. Q. Khan, the charismatic father of the Pakistani nuclear bomb and mastermind of an illicit proliferation network. But after months of haggling over the details, the Libyans were suddenly ready to finalize the agreement on December 16, just two days after Hussein's capture was announced. Two days later, Tony Blair called Bush. He had reached out to Qaddafi to persuade him to approve the agreement and had promised he and Bush would reciprocate with positive statements.

Bush agreed. At the White House the next day, December 19, he waited for Qaddafi to issue the statement, but hours passed with no word from Tripoli. As morning turned to afternoon and evening, Rice tried "to manage the anxiety" of the president. Only later did they learn Qaddafi was waiting for an important soccer match to finish first. While he was supposed to deliver the statement personally, in the end he put it out in writing. Bush decided that was good enough.

Finally, at 5:30 p.m., the president marched into the briefing room to welcome the agreement. It sent a message, he said, that "leaders who abandon the pursuit of chemical, biological and nuclear weapons, and the means to deliver them, will find an open path to better relations with the United States and other free nations."

The Libyan disarmament was an important victory for Bush and Cheney not only because it took a potentially erratic nuclear player off the board but because it helped finally unravel the nuclear schemes of A. Q. Khan, who turned out to be perhaps the most prolific distributor of dangerous material, technology, and know-how in modern times. As investigators chased his trails, they discovered that he had been a one-man shopping channel not just for Libya but also for North Korea and Iran. Within weeks of the Libya deal, Washington had pressured Pakistan into placing Khan under house arrest and forcing him to issue a public confession.

Just as important, Libya allowed Bush and Cheney to assert that the Iraq War had made it easier to bring other rogue states to the bargaining table. Not every potential threat would require military force if Iraq served as a demonstration project of sorts. "Just simply the fact that Qaddafi gave up his nuclear program because he didn't want to end up like Saddam Hussein is an example of what took place because of what happened," Rumsfeld said years later. But the disappointment for Bush and Cheney was that other states like Iran and North Korea did not follow suit.

WITH THE APPROACH of Christmas, Bush was feeling the effects of time. He was fifty-seven years old and had been running most days since 1972, an activity he pursued with relentless fervor to help clear his head and keep his equilibrium. But now his right knee was hurting, and doctors gave him a magnetic resonance imaging test, or MRI. They concluded he had worn out his knees and needed to give up running and switch to cross-training. It was a significant adjustment, a sign of advancing age, not to mention the stresses of the office.

Bush had little time to get used to the changes in his personal routine. Intelligence agencies had reports of terrorist plots on planes bound for the United States from Europe. It was probably the most serious worry about a specific threat since September 11, and Bush and Cheney were confronted with the question of how to respond: Should they alert the public and cancel planes at the risk of overreacting, disrupting a major holiday, and being accused of stoking fear for political purposes? Or should they let the planes fly, do what they could to hunt down plotters, and pray nothing happened?

"Which one of you, based on this information, would put your family on one of those flights?" Bush asked during a meeting with Tom Ridge and other advisers.

No one said they would. That made the decision easy. The targeted flights would be canceled. The next day, Ridge raised the national threat level to high risk. No attacks materialized, and the holiday passed safely.

For Bush and Cheney, though, the end of the year still brought bad news. John Ashcroft had recused himself from the CIA leak case because Karl Rove used to work for him, so the matter had fallen to his deputy attorney general, James Comey. In turn, Comey had decided to turn it over to a special prosecutor. On December 30, he announced that Patrick Fitzgerald, a boyish-faced U.S. attorney in Chicago and a close friend, would lead the investigation of the White House.

17

"We were almost all wrong"

On January 21, 2004, Vice President Cheney's phone rang. It was his daughter Mary. I need to talk, she said.

There was no mistaking the urgency in her voice, and he told her to come right over. Lynne and Liz Cheney soon heard and rushed over as well. Liz Cheney came so quickly she did not have a chance to change clothes and strode past the Secret Service officers into the West Wing in jeans in violation of the president's dress code.

For the Cheneys, it was a crisis like no other, a clash between personal principle and political loyalty. Mary had agreed to duplicate her 2000 role as her father's campaign operations director heading into 2004, but now she was not sure she could work for a ticket headed by President Bush. In the three years since they took office together, the vice president had never been torn from Bush in such a personal way.

The issue was same-sex marriage. The day before, Bush in his State of the Union address had defended "the sanctity of marriage," which was code for opposing legally sanctioned marriage between gay couples. In an election year, it was an obvious appeal to Bush's conservative base, a way of reminding them that whatever their misgivings about his other policies, this was a president in tune with their social views. But when Mary saw a copy of the speech the day before it was to be delivered, she was shocked. She had planned to sit in the House gallery for the speech but abruptly canceled. "I sure wasn't going to stand up and cheer," she later wrote.

Mary was no liberal; she supported her father on many issues. But this was an existential question. Could she serve a ticket that now officially stood for discriminating against her because of her sexual orientation? Several campaign operatives stopped by to see her at headquarters to express solidarity. It was striking how many people working for the president did not agree with him, a sign of a broader generational shift already under way.

They told Mary that it was not that big a deal since no state actually recognized same-sex marriage, but that was little consolation. She felt she should quit, pack her bags, and head back to her home in Colorado. She had a long, heart-wrenching phone call with her partner, Heather Poe.

On January 21, the four Cheneys closeted themselves in the vice president's office as Mary vented. The vice president had made clear before that he split from conservative orthodoxy when it came to gay rights, declaring in his 2000 debate with Joseph Lieberman that "freedom means freedom for everybody." Now he counseled his daughter that if she felt she had to resign, he would support her. But he said she had played an important role in 2000 and would again if she stayed. The discussion went round and round.

Finally, Cheney noticed the time; he had to leave for New York for a fund-raiser, with Mary slated to join him in her campaign role. Lynne spontaneously decided to go along. While the vice president posed for photographs in a Manhattan apartment, she and Mary found privacy in a bedroom and sat opposite each other on twin beds talking. "If you feel like you have to leave," Lynne said, "then that's the right thing to do."

Ultimately, Mary calmed down and decided to stay. Quitting would call more attention to her. She did not want to be "the vice president's lesbian daughter" or a symbol for a movement; she bristled when activists put her picture on milk cartons because she was "missing" from the fight for gay rights. She loved her father, she supported his political career, and she did not like being used as a wedge against him.

The momentary crisis underscored a rare fault line in the Bush-Cheney partnership. Since the two teamed up on the Republican ticket in the summer of 2000, Bush and Cheney had agreed more than they disagreed. But the signs of change were increasingly there. Bush's brief flirtation with the idea of replacing Cheney "to demonstrate that I was in charge" betrayed his sensitivity. It gnawed at him that they had failed so far to find the weapons Cheney had told Bush were in Iraq, and some close to the president wondered whether he had let himself be led down a dangerous path. By this point, Bush was already talking with Condoleezza Rice about ways to repair the damage with allies and put more emphasis on diplomacy. For his part, Cheney had enjoyed a longer stretch of influence than anyone had expected. When they took office, some on Cheney's team figured the vice president's outsized sway would last six or nine months until Bush grew more comfortable in the job and did not need to lean on his more experienced number two. But Cheney's clout had endured, partly because of the national security issues suddenly thrust to the fore and partly because of his skill at advancing his viewpoint while remaining deferential to Bush.

In the focus on same-sex marriage, Cheney saw the hand of Karl Rove, another powerful force in the White House who had circled carefully around the vice president since arguing against his selection in 2000. Cheney and Rove avoided issues where the other specialized, a tacit arrangement that since September 11 had left the vice president in the dominant position. But now it was 2004 with the next election in sight, putting Rove back at the helm. Rove had been invested in Bush's political success since volunteering in the failed 1978 congressional campaign. A bare-knuckled operative who rattled off poll numbers and election results like others memorized baseball statistics, he orchestrated Bush's two gubernatorial campaigns and the 2000 presidential campaign, then outlasted the other two members of the Iron Triangle, Karen Hughes and Joe Allbaugh, although Hughes still parachuted in at times. Bush called him the "boy genius" when he was happy with him and "turd blossom" when he was not. Critics dubbed him "Bush's brain," underestimating Bush and overestimating Rove.

Heading into 2004, Rove had something to prove. The 2000 campaign that was supposed to be a masterstroke of Rovian politics came unraveled at the end, and now he and Bush both wanted to show they did not need the Supreme Court to win an election. If it took tough tactics, Rove would not shy away; he knew the Democrats would not either. As a result, Cheney figured the line in the State of the Union would probably not be the end of the matter. Armed with Matthew Dowd's analysis of the shrinking political center, Rove was pursuing a strategy focused as much on bolstering Republican turnout as on reaching swing voters.

A squadron of Democrats was vying to challenge Bush, sensing vulnerability born of a war launched on what increasingly looked like false intelligence, including Representative Richard Gephardt, the former House Democratic leader who had supported Bush on Iraq; Senator Joseph Lieberman, the former Democratic vice presidential nominee who had engaged in such a civil debate with Cheney; Senator John Kerry of Massachusetts, a Vietnam War hero who became one of the nation's most prominent antiwar activists; Senator John Edwards of North Carolina, a telegenic trial attorney running on an antipoverty platform; General Wesley Clark, the retired NATO commander who won the Kosovo War; and Governor Howard Dean of Vermont, a physician who pioneered civil unions for gay couples.

Gephardt, Lieberman, Kerry, and Edwards had all voted to authorize war in 2002, complicating their efforts to criticize Bush, while Dean, who had no vote, was making inroads with a vocal antiwar message. Rove conducted an informal survey of the president's political advisers. Four predicted Dean would win the Democratic nomination. Five picked Gephardt, including Bush. No one chose Kerry.

Every weekend, Rove convened "Breakfast Club" meetings at his house, serving scrambled eggs with cheese and cream as well as venison, wild boar, and nilgai sausage while he and other strategists built the architecture of a reelection campaign. The advisers were not the only ones getting geared up. Bush's daughter Jenna dreamed that her father had lost, so she and her sister, Barbara, who had defiantly sat out past campaigns, volunteered to work on this one. If he was going to lose, they reasoned, they wanted to have done what they could. Bush was delighted.

Rove's talent for political forecasting proved no better in Democratic primaries than it had in the 2000 general election. Dean knocked Gephardt out of the race during a brutal campaign in Iowa—with Bush's help. "Dean ran an ad with me in the Rose Garden on that October day with Bush," Gephardt remembered, "and the day the ad appeared, my polls took off. There was nothing to be done." Gephardt, who won Iowa when he ran in 1988, finished fourth on January 19, behind Kerry, Edwards, and Dean. But Dean hurt himself fatally in the process thanks to a whooping scream at the end of his concession speech that got replayed endlessly on cable television.

Rove had been betting colleagues hamburgers that Dean would win the nomination and even now thought he could recover. Bush disagreed.

As he traveled to Ohio and Arizona, Bush offered his verdict. "He's done, it's over," Bush said in his armored car between events.

"Well, your father lost Iowa and went on to win," ventured Matt Schlapp, his political director.

"Yeah, my dad did lose Iowa," Bush said, "but this guy is done."

Dan Bartlett said the concession speech may have played well in the room but was too hot for television. "It's a good reminder," he said.

Bush spent the night of the New Hampshire primary, January 27, with friends and family at the White House. Kerry won with 38 percent, outpacing Dean, who had 26 percent. As the evening progressed, Bush and his guests debated lightly who would be a tougher general election opponent, Kerry or Edwards. Bush thought Edwards was too unseasoned and would be easier to beat, while Kerry would be a formidable opponent. Laura Bush disagreed. She thought Edwards would be the tougher challenger; nobody particularly liked Kerry, she reasoned, while Edwards was young, attractive, southern, and in his own way charming.

WHILE DEAN WAS making Iraq an issue, Bush was coming to terms with the failure to find the weapons. David Kay, the arms inspector hired by the CIA to find the banned arms, decided to step down amid tension with George Tenet, and on January 28, Kay appeared before the Senate Armed Services Committee to give an assessment.

"Let me begin by saying we were almost all wrong," Kay told lawmakers, "and I certainly include myself here."

He noted that even countries that opposed the war, like France and Germany, believed there were weapons. "It turns out that we were all wrong, probably, in my judgment, and that is most disturbing."

Kay rejected the common assertion that intelligence analysts were pressured by political leaders, calling that "a wrong explanation." And he noted that his group had found "hundreds of cases" of prohibited activities involving weapons research by Iraqis, and "not only did they not tell the U.N. about this, they were instructed not to do it and they hid material." But those activities fell short of actually creating or storing weapons, and Kay called it important for Washington to "understand why reality turned out to be different than expectations and estimates."

Bush and Cheney invited Kay to lunch the next day to grill him about his conclusions. Condoleezza Rice and Andy Card joined them. Bush did most of the questioning while Cheney remained silent.

Kay explained that the intelligence was wrong because the Iraqis acted like they had weapons.

"Why would Saddam do something like this?" Bush asked.

Because, encouraged by the French and Russians, he never thought the United States would actually invade, Kay said. Hussein, he added, was more afraid of the Shiites and Kurds he had kept in line with his mythological weapons, not to mention a coup from within his own power structure, and he feared losing stature in the Arab world.

But Kay had criticism for Bush as well. One reason the intelligence community fell down on the job, he told the president, was that he had brought George Tenet across the line between analyst and policy maker. "You're paying a price for having the director of the CIA essentially as a cabinet official and being too close," Kay said. "Every president I know anything about would like to have his own policy and his own facts. The intelligence community should be the holder of the facts. It's very difficult for George if he's sitting at the table."

"Do you think I should meet less with him?" Bush asked.

"Mr. President, this is not something I want to say," Kay said.

The next Monday, February 2, the situation grew worse with an interview that Colin Powell gave the *Washington Post* acknowledging that he might not have supported the invasion had he known there were no weapons. Almost exactly a year to the day after the landmark presentation to the Security Council that had deeply scarred his credibility, Powell admitted they had gone to war on false premises. While he told the newspaper that he still thought the war "was the right thing to do," he hedged when asked whether he would have favored it if he knew then what he knew now. "I don't know," he said, "because it was the stockpile that presented the final little piece that made it more of a real and present danger and threat to the region and to the world." The "absence of a stockpile changes the political calculus," he added, and "changes the answer you get."

Bush and Cheney were furious. Powell tried to backtrack.

"It was something we all agreed to, and would probably agree to again under any other set of circumstances," he told reporters.

George Tenet pushed back three days later with a speech at his alma mater, Georgetown University, where he acknowledged the agency's failures but defended the prewar intelligence. He noted that he had hired another weapons inspector, Charles Duelfer, to replace Kay and that "despite some public statements, we are nowhere near 85 percent finished" looking.

Tenet concluded that the agency was "generally on target" about Hussein's missile program but "may have overestimated the progress Saddam was making" on nuclear weapons. While they had found no chemical or biological weapons, Hussein wanted to make them and had the ability to produce them on short notice. Tenet admitted being influenced by an Iraqi source with "direct access to Saddam" who told the CIA that the Iraqis knew how to fool inspectors. "Could I have ignored or dismissed such reports at the time?" Tenet asked. "Absolutely not."

There was blame enough to go around: A president who arrived in office ready to complete what his father left unfinished. A vice president so convinced of the dangers from Baghdad that he pressed for intelligence to back up his conclusions. A CIA that often overlooked dissenting voices to produce what it thought the nation's leadership wanted. A Democratic opposition cowed by the political winds and too willing to believe the same ultimately flawed evidence. Allied intelligence agencies like the British, Germans, and Italians that passed along thinly supported assertions, fraudulent documents, and wholesale fabrications without fully sharing their sources. An Iraqi dictator who never came clean on the assumption that America would never follow through on its threat. And a news media that got caught up in the post–September 11 moment, trusted official sources too much, and gave prominence to indications of weapons while downplaying doubts.

IF CHENEY HOPED the gay rights issue had blown over in the weeks after the State of the Union, he was soon disappointed. On February 4, the highest court in Massachusetts ruled that same-sex marriage was a right under the state constitution, a decision that turbo-charged the already heated national debate. A week later, the mayor of San Francisco ordered city officials to grant marriage licenses to gay couples contrary to California law.

In the White House, Karl Rove thought the president should go beyond his State of the Union address and explicitly endorse a constitutional amendment defining marriage as the union of a man and a woman. While Bush had always taken a traditional view of marriage, he had never supported rewriting the Constitution to mandate it and indeed had declined to embrace such a proposed amendment when Bill Frist brought it up seven months earlier. But the Massachusetts and San Francisco actions had propelled the issue to new levels, and with the election approaching, it was an issue of great resonance among conservatives. Over the previous year, Tim Goeglein, the White House liaison to evangelical conservative leaders, "heard more about marriage than any other issue."

Bush agreed to consider it. Cheney asked his domestic policy adviser, Neil Patel, to research the issue. Patel assembled a binder with all of the president's past statements on the issue and other material, then gave it to the vice president. Cheney did not volunteer what he would do with it, and it was awkward to ask. Peter Wehner, the speechwriter who had been put in charge of a sort of internal White House think tank called the Office of Strategic Initiatives (sometimes called the Office of Strategery after a mangled Bush term), drafted a briefing laying out both sides of the argument in a dispassionate way, looking at the constitutional ramifications, the institution of marriage, and the state of the law. Bush was turned off by courts seemingly making up rights not explicitly found in law.

As the debate played out, Cheney remained quiet, as he often did. Everyone understood his view. But he chose not to engage, either in larger sessions or even in his one-on-one lunches with Bush. He could have weighed in and possibly tilted the debate but chose discretion. He had never been out front on gay rights, speaking only when asked. And in his calculations about which issues to expend political capital on, same-sex marriage did not make the list. That may have reflected his judgment about where Bush would end up, or it may have reflected a personal discomfort with the topic. In any case, he stayed on the sidelines.

Another person who stayed quiet was Ken Mehlman, the president's campaign manager who was secretly gay but had not yet come to grips with it, much less admitted it to Bush or his colleagues. Some suspected, but others were thrown off by the memory of Mehlman dating a young female campaign worker in 2000. Likewise, Israel Hernandez, Bush's longtime aide going back to the Texas Rangers days, was also secretly gay.

The issue, with all its awkward dynamics, played out against a presidential campaign coming into focus. Bush invited Cheney and top aides to the Yellow Room in the residence at 11:00 a.m. one weekday in February to listen to Rove and other strategists outline their plan for reelection. Rove showed a month-by-month plan of themes, travel, and media for the two principals and their spouses. The strategy was to present Bush as a man of strength and values, a steady leader in a volatile moment. "There is a strong sense that Bush provides security and makes people feel safe," aides wrote about Cleveland focus groups conducted in February. "Subtle images of 9/11 get the message across very effectively." Mark McKinnon, after a technical meltdown with his laptop, played five proposed television ads, including one with images of September 11. If Americans remembered how afraid they were after the attacks, they would side with Bush; if they focused on how astray the Iraq War seemed to be going, he could lose.

Rove, McKinnon, Mehlman, Matthew Dowd, and other political advisers had been preparing for reelection since days after the vote in 2000. Dowd's conclusion during the recount that independent voters were a vanishing force had already driven the White House approach, and now advisers devised a strategy effectively the opposite of the one they advanced four years earlier. Instead of simply devoting resources to a small group of swing voters, they would focus just as intently on identifying and turning out core Republican voters. "That decision influenced everything that we did," Dowd said. "It influenced how we targeted mail, how we targeted phones, how we targeted media, how we traveled, the travel that the president and the vice president did to certain areas, how we did organization, where we had staff."

To research how previous presidents had handled reelection campaigns, Dowd spent the summer of 2002 traveling to presidential libraries, including Ronald Reagan's in California, Gerald Ford's in Michigan, and George H. W. Bush's in Texas. He put together a long memo about the opportunities and traps confronting an incumbent president and presented it to colleagues before the midterm elections. But the strategy Rove, Dowd, and the rest of the team put together was forward-looking, innovative techniques no president had tried before. Adopting the methods of commercial marketing, Rove and his colleagues sliced the electorate using "microtargeting" to tailor messages based on things like what magazines voters subscribed to, what cars they owned, and even what kind of liquor they drank.

For her part, Laura urged her husband not to make same-sex marriage an issue in the campaign. "We have, I reminded him, a number of close friends who are gay or whose children are gay," she remembered. But when Bush and Cheney next had lunch, the president told the vice president he would endorse the constitutional amendment banning same-sex marriage. "He brought up the fact that he knew that I might have a different view because he knew about Mary," Cheney recalled. "He was very gracious about it. I mean, I guess that would be the way I would describe it. I knew going in that this was a place where we differed." Bush was passing along his decision, not soliciting Cheney's advice. He told the vice president to tell Mary that he would understand if she wanted to issue a statement opposing it. The vice president accepted the decision without protest. But he was not happy. "Cheney was pissed off," said a friend, "and I think he blamed Karl for that."

On February 24, Bush made it public. "The union of a man and woman is the most enduring human institution, honored and encouraged in all cultures and by every religious faith," Bush said. At the same time, he said he wanted to make sure states could still pass alternative arrangements, such as civil unions, and he discouraged hateful rhetoric. "We should also conduct this difficult debate in a matter worthy of our country, without bitterness or anger." Bush, who had privately deplored gay bashing and welcomed his transgendered college classmate to the White House, read the statement in a flat tone that suggested his heart was not in it. He was a traditionalist, he did not think courts should be deciding such questions, and he was told it was good politics, but he also knew he was playing to the sorts of antipathies he had resisted in the past.

The vice president called Mary to tell her the president had offered to let her issue her own statement disagreeing with the decision. But the last thing she wanted to do was call more attention to herself. Having wrestled with this issue a month earlier, she had come to terms with remaining on the campaign and keeping her thoughts to herself.

The politics of the decision were clear. A poll taken a week before the announcement showed that 64 percent of Americans opposed same-sex marriage compared with 32 percent who said it should be legal. Among the conservative voters Rove was targeting, the margin was even more lopsided. Eleven states were poised to put the question on the November ballot, drawing out more Bush-Cheney voters. The Bush team would eventually put anti-gay-marriage ads on radio stations oriented to Hispanic and African Americans below the radar screen of the national media; some aides were never sure if Bush even knew about that.

At a private meeting after his announcement, Bush told Republican congressional leaders that he felt his hand had been forced by the courts. But he was also in a feisty mood, focused on the looming campaign. He had "gotten pretty well pummeled" during the Democratic primaries, he told the lawmakers, but was planning to go on offense. "The vice president and I are ready to fight," he said.

IN THE MIDST of a busy February, Bush absorbed a personal blow. His loyal dog Spot had suffered a series of strokes and had to be put to sleep on February 21. The fifteen-year-old English springer was born to Millie, his parents' dog, and had the distinction of being the only canine to live in the White House under two presidents. As with many couples whose children go off to school, Spot along with the Scottish terrier Barney occupied an important part of the president's family life. Where Barney was rambunctious and often had to be corralled, Spot was friendly and obedient, regularly making her way onto Marine One on the South Lawn for trips to Crawford without having to be nudged.

For Bush, the dog's death among all the other tragedy that he had overseen since coming into office, and particularly in the eleven months since invading Iraq, somehow struck home. Before she was to be euthanized, as Laura recalled it, Bush took the ailing dog to the South Lawn, set her down, and then lay on the grass next to her, "encircling her in the chill dusk with the warmth of his body and gently stroking her head for a final farewell."

CHENEY HUSBANDED HIS clout on same-sex marriage, but he used it on North Korea. Sensing weakness, he had been working for months to shore up the American position, insisting that any new round of the six-party talks be based on the goal of a "complete, verifiable and irreversible dismantlement" of Pyongyang's nuclear program. "We don't negotiate with evil," he had declared at a meeting in December. "We defeat it."

By the evening of February 26, talks had opened again, but Cheney heard they were deadlocked over a joint statement. He met with Bush to intercede, fashioning language to force negotiators to take the unyielding line he had been pushing. He spent about an hour on the phone with Michael Green, the president's Asia adviser, wordsmithing the language.

Unaware of the latest intervention were Colin Powell and Richard Armitage, who were attending a black-tie dinner until summoned outside to take a secure phone call in the limousine and work out language with Stephen Hadley. Armitage argued, but Hadley pushed back. "The vice president feels very strongly," he said. Bush went with Cheney's tougher language and Hadley ordered Green to read it over an unsecure telephone to the delegation headed by James Kelly rather than send it through the usual State Department cable. Green said the Chinese would almost certainly be tapping the line and hear. "Yeah," Hadley said. "That's what we want."

Powell only learned later that Cheney's language had been sent when an anxious Chinese foreign minister called to say the American position could blow up the talks. The negotiations wrapped up before the American delegation could execute its new instructions, averting a meltdown. But this was exactly the sort of situation that had been aggravating Powell and Armitage for years. "Diplomacy in the Bush administration is, 'Alright, you fuckers, do what we say,'" Armitage complained at one point.

Powell confronted Bush at the White House the next day, February 27, before a meeting with Germany's visiting chancellor.

"Busy last night, huh?" he asked Bush pointedly.

"Didn't they tell you?" Bush asked.

"No, they didn't," Powell said.

It was lucky the talks adjourned, he scolded the president, because if they had gone ahead with these instructions, the process would have collapsed. "It would have been gone."

To Cheney, such arguments were beside the point. In his mind, Powell had become a captive of the State Department bureaucracy, which cared more about process than results. "The diplomats, whether they knew it or not, in my estimation didn't have license to strike a deal," said Stephen Yates, who was Cheney's Asia adviser. "But they may have thought they did, and so they kept trying to get these joint statements, trying to come up with solutions, which is sort of their job to try. Mysteriously, every time it would come up, they would receive instructions from the White House, from the very highest levels, not to agree to certain things or to remind them of their limited instructions on their interactions. That frustrated the diplomats; it offended people like Powell, Armitage, and Kelly who felt like they were fairly tough-minded people who served in the military, were no pushovers on these kinds of things." They had a point, Yates said, but they were not in charge.

ANOTHER FAULT LINE was opening at the same time. In the two and a half years since Cheney helped usher in the National Security Agency's warrantless surveillance program, it had been reauthorized twenty-two times. Each time, the intelligence agencies produced what had come to be called the "scary memos" outlining the threat to the country justifying renewal of the program. The program remained so secret that Bush personally had to approve telling anyone outside the NSA about it.

But John Yoo was now gone, and a new crop of lawyers had arrived at the Justice Department, only to be shocked at what they found. Jack Goldsmith, a conservative law professor who had taken over as head of the department's Office of Legal Counsel, thought some of the opinions he had inherited were poorly reasoned and unsustainable. As the next reauthorization deadline approached on March 11, he concluded that one element of the program had evolved in a way that went beyond the original presidential authorization and could not be legally supported. Under this part of the program, "metadata" about e-mail and other Internet communications of tens of millions of people was swept up, including names of senders and recipients, and subject lines, but not their content. John Ashcroft was in the hospital with pancreatitis, leaving in charge his deputy, James Comey, the same man who had appointed Patrick Fitzgerald to investigate the CIA leak. Comey agreed with Goldsmith.

Goldsmith went to the White House on March 6 to tell Alberto Gonzales and David Addington the department would not reauthorize the program.

Addington erupted in full volcanic fury. "If you rule that way, the blood of the hundred thousand people who die in the next attack will be on your hands," he thundered.

Goldsmith stood firm. "The president is free to overrule me if he wants."

Addington had been the key architect of the eavesdropping program and a fierce guardian of executive prerogative. He was tall, bearded, intellectually formidable, and profoundly intimidating. He was like a bull confronting a brick wall, Gonzales recalled being told: "Instead of going around it, David will go through that brick wall." Addington kept his office locked at all times and carried a worn copy of the Constitution that he pulled out dramatically to make his arguments. In times of war, he believed that a president's power was largely unfettered. "We're going to push and push and push until some larger force makes us stop," he once said. Since working on the Iran-contra commission with Cheney, Addington had scorned the constraints others tried to apply to a president guarding national security. He particularly disdained the Foreign Intelligence Surveillance Act and the secret court that enforced it. At a meeting just a month earlier, he had said, "We're one bomb away from getting rid of that obnoxious court."

Cheney was alarmed when he heard what the Justice Department was saying. At a meeting at noon on March 9 in Andy Card's office, the vice president consulted with Michael Hayden, the NSA director; John McLaughlin, the deputy CIA director; Robert Mueller, the FBI director; and various White House officials.

Cheney said the legal objections would not stop the program. "The president may have to reauthorize without blessing of DOJ," he said.

"I could have a problem with that," Mueller responded. The FBI would "have to review legality of continued participation in the program."

So now Cheney faced a revolt not just by the lawyers but by the FBI. He summoned Comey, Goldsmith, and other lawyers to the White House later that afternoon.

"How can you possibly be reversing course on something of this importance after all this time?" Cheney demanded. The program was "critically important," he said, and, echoing Addington, asserted that Comey would risk "thousands" of lives if he did not sign off.

Comey said the program's importance did not change the legal issues. "The analysis is flawed, in fact facially flawed," he said. "No lawyer reading that could reasonably rely on it."

"Well, I'm a lawyer and I did," Addington interrupted.

"No *good* lawyer," Comey said.

Thwarted, Cheney invited the congressional Gang of Eight to the White House for an emergency meeting on the afternoon of March 10, the day before the program would expire.

This was an important program, Cheney explained to lawmakers. "We think it is essential," he said. But the lawyers were refusing to sign off.

"You ought to get yourself some new lawyers," said Senator Pat Roberts of Kansas, the Republican chairman of the Senate Intelligence Committee.

After Hayden explained the program for those who had not previously attended such briefings, Cheney asked whether the lawmakers thought it should continue. "None of them says, 'Well, then, you ought to stop the program,' " Hayden recalled. Cheney asked whether they thought the White House should go to Congress to explicitly authorize the program. Again, none did. But several Democrats later said they did not recommend the program proceed either.

That evening, Bush had his staff call Ashcroft at George Washington University Hospital, where he had undergone surgery the day before to remove his gallbladder, but his wife, Janet, had ordered no calls be accepted. So Bush picked up the phone himself and was put through. According to Card, who was listening to Bush's end, the president told Ashcroft he had a reauthorization for the attorney general to sign and the program was about to expire. Ashcroft in this version agreed to sign. "I'll send Alberto and Andy over," Bush said.

Janet Ashcroft quickly told the attorney general's chief of staff, David Ayres, that Card and Gonzales were on their way. Ayres then called Comey, who was in his car on the way home. Sensing an end run, Comey directed his security detail to rush him to the hospital with emergency lights flashing, and he called Mueller and others to urge them to come too.

Arriving at the hospital around 7:10 p.m., Comey did not wait for the elevator and bounded up the stairs, beating the president's emissaries to Ashcroft's room. He called Mueller back and had him instruct the FBI detail that under no circumstances should Comey be removed from Ashcroft's room. Card and Gonzales arrived at 7:35 p.m. with an envelope containing forms to renew the surveillance program. They had brought Addington but Gonzales told him to wait outside so as not "to aggravate the attorney general needlessly."

Gonzales asked Ashcroft how he was feeling.

"Not well," the attorney general said.

"You know, there's a reauthorization that has to be renewed," Gonzales ventured.

Ashcroft, still woozy from the surgery, lifted himself in his bed and outlined the concerns Comey and Goldsmith had expressed, seeming in agreement.

"But that doesn't matter," he added, "because I'm not the attorney general." Pointing to Comey, who was formally acting in his stead, Ashcroft said, "There is the attorney general." Physically spent, he sank back into the bed.

Card and Gonzales later said they did not know that Ashcroft had transferred his power to Comey and were surprised because he seemed so lucid, but they made no further effort. "We said, 'Hope you are doing better,' and left," Card recalled. "We were not trying to get him to sign something that he didn't want to sign."

Janet Ashcroft stuck her tongue out at Card and Gonzales as they walked out. Mueller arrived at 8:00 p.m. and spoke with Ashcroft. "AG in chair; is feeble, barely articulate, clearly stressed," Mueller wrote in his notes.

There are conflicting accounts of key details of the episode. By Card's account, Bush explicitly raised the program on the phone and Ashcroft agreed to sign, only to change his mind after Comey arrived first. In his memoir, though, Bush made no claim that he said anything other than telling Ashcroft he was sending Card and Gonzales over on an urgent matter. Aides to Ashcroft doubt that he agreed on the phone to sign.

The confrontation escalated. After returning to the White House that night, Card called Comey and ordered him to come to his office right away; Comey refused to come without a witness and had Solicitor General Theodore Olson pulled out of a dinner party. Comey met first at the Justice Department with a group of lawyers, and there was broad agreement that they would all resign if the White House overruled their judgment. One of the lawyers quietly e-mailed a friend at the White House, who passed on news of the brewing mass resignation to Card. By the time Comey arrived at the White House at 11:00 p.m., Card realized he faced an insurrection and convinced the acting attorney general to leave Olson outside while they talked. But Comey still refused to budge on the surveillance program.

The next day, March 11, Bush signed the order renewing the surveillance program without Ashcroft or Comey. Addington retyped the order to delete the signature line for the attorney general and substituted the White House counsel instead, so Gonzales could sign it, even though he had no authority. As far as Bush and Cheney were concerned, the importance of the program was brought home all too vividly the same day when terrorists set off ten bombs on four commuter trains in Madrid, killing 191 people and injuring another 1,800 just three days before Spain was to hold elections. It was one of the deadliest such attacks since September 11, and in the heart of Europe, dooming the government of Bush's ally Prime Minister José María Aznar.

Comey and Goldsmith drafted letters of resignation. At 1:30 a.m. on March 12, Mueller scrawled out his own by hand, saying he was "forced to withdraw the FBI from participation in the program." He added, "Further, should the President order the continuation of the FBI's participation in the program, and in the absence of further legal advice from the AG, I would be constrained to resign as Director of the FBI."

Bush did not understand just how far the conflict over the program had gone until later that morning when Card told him Comey and as many as a dozen officials planned to quit because the president had reauthorized it. "I was stunned," Bush said later, asserting that he did not even realize that Ashcroft had transferred his powers to Comey. When Comey showed up for a routine meeting that morning, Bush asked him to stick around afterward.

"I just don't understand why you are raising this at the last minute," Bush said.

Comey was shocked and realized Bush had been kept in the dark. "Mr. President," he said, "your staff has known about this for weeks."

Only then did Bush learn that Mueller also planned to resign. Flashing through his mind were visions of Richard Nixon's "Saturday Night Massacre," when the attorney general and the deputy attorney general both resigned rather than carry out the president's order to fire the Watergate special prosecutor. "I was about to witness the largest mass resignation in modern presidential history, and we were in the middle of a war," Bush concluded. One Justice Department official predicted, with only a bit of hyperbole, that if the top law enforcement officials all walked out, the president would have to resign within seventy-two hours or risk impeachment.

Cheney and others urged Bush not to give in. "I had little patience with what I saw happening," the vice president said. But Bush backed down, modifying the Internet surveillance part of the program that Comey and Mueller objected to. Ultimately, it was restarted several months later under a different legal theory, this time with Comey's assent.

But Cheney struck back at Comey, who had already gotten on the vice president's bad side by appointing the special prosecutor in the CIA leak case; several months later, Cheney blocked a move to make Comey's aide Patrick Philbin deputy solicitor general.

ON THE ELECTORAL front, John Kerry had locked up the Democratic nomination, and the Bush team was feeling on the defensive. Bush tried to settle down his jittery staff during a meeting in the White House residence.

"Listen, I've been involved in a lot of campaigns," he started, implicitly reminding his team that he had already seen five presidential campaigns up close. "The accidental genius of the process in its length is it strips you bare. You're totally revealed to the American people. You can't hide who you are. It's one of the reasons why people made fun of me with my pillow in 2000 and I wanted to get home. But you need your sleep. It's exhausting." The bottom line this year, he added pointedly, was this: "We're going to win because John Kerry is an asshole."

Bush and Cheney wasted little time before going after Kerry. The challenge was to shape his public image before Kerry could do it himself, and the vice president would be the pit bull. "Cheney would be the attack dog who went after Kerry a little more pointedly than the president could," as Scott McClellan, the White House press secretary, later put it. The opening came in mid-March. The campaign team learned that Kerry would be visiting West Virginia, so they decided to try to bait him by airing an ad on local television attacking him for voting against funding for troops in Iraq. When a member of the audience posed the same question at Marshall University in Huntington on March 16, Kerry was already irritated. He explained that he first voted for a Democratic alternative to finance the war by reducing Bush's tax cuts for the wealthy. "I actually did vote for the $87 billion before I voted against it," he said.

There it was, one sentence that neatly summed up the argument that Kerry was an unreliable flip-flopper. Mark McKinnon ran around the Bush-Cheney campaign headquarters wearing a beret and screaming with delight. *Game, set, and match,* he thought. He quickly recut the West Virginia ad to include the Kerry line and sent it out nationally. "When I saw that," Cheney recalled, he thought, "that is a gift." He quickly inserted the line into his stump speech. "I couldn't pass it up and I quoted Kerry saying that and the crowd just roared and I used it in just about every speech."

While exploiting Kerry's gaffe, Bush tried to find a way to minimize his own vulnerability: the missing weapons in Iraq. Humor historically had helped presidents smooth over political problems. So at the black-tie dinner of the Radio and Television Correspondents Association on March 24, Bush presented a slide show of photographs, including a couple of him looking under furniture in the Oval Office.

"Those weapons of mass destruction gotta be somewhere," he joked. When another such picture showed up later in the slide show, he quipped, "Nope, no weapons over there. Maybe under here."

The jokes went over fine in the room at the time, but by morning making light of a colossal intelligence failure that propelled the country to war seemed in poor taste.

In the same performance, Bush needled Cheney, making him a foil, as he did increasingly over the course of his presidency. Bush showed a picture of the two of them in the Oval Office with Andy Card making an odd face as the vice president seemed to be talking to his finger and thumb. "As you can tell from the look on Andy Card's face, we've become a little concerned about the vice president lately," Bush said. "Whenever you ask him a question, he replies, 'Let's see what my little friend says.'"

Other Republicans saw not a punch line but a liability—among them, one of Cheney's most important patrons. A number of Republicans approached Gerald Ford to see if he might help ease Cheney off the ticket. Despite their different political philosophies, Cheney revered Ford, who had entrusted his White House to him at a young age. Ford rebuffed the emissaries who approached him. But Ford told a friendly journalist in March, "Dick has not been the asset I expected on the ticket. As you know, he's a great friend of mine. He did a great job for me. But he has not clicked, if that's the right word."

AS THE CAMPAIGN took shape, Bush was simultaneously juggling the politics of far-off Baghdad, where the fractious Shiite, Sunni, and Kurdish segments of society were overlaid with the personalities and ambitions of exiles who had returned to Iraq. Two separate yet interrelated events inflamed both Shiite and Sunni communities, putting the Americans in between lots of men with guns. On March 28, American troops on Jerry Bremer's orders shut down a newspaper run by Moqtada al-Sadr, a radical Shiite cleric who had been challenging the occupation. In padlocking the gate, they touched off a violent and sustained backlash from Sadr and his supporters in Baghdad, Najaf, and other Shiite areas.

Then, even as American troops were trying to contain Sadr's fighters, four security contractors from the private Blackwater firm were ambushed and killed in Fallujah, the Sunni-dominated city in Anbar Province west of Baghdad where Abu Musab al-Zarqawi and al-Qaeda followers were now based. The charred bodies of the slain contractors were dragged from their sport-utility vehicles into the street and ripped apart by a cheering mob. "Where is Bush? Let him come here and see this!" shouted a boy no older than ten as he ground his heel into a burned head. Two mutilated corpses were hung from a bridge over the Euphrates River. The desire for retaliation among the Americans was overpowering.

The marines resisted suggestions for a full-fledged assault on the city, arguing for a more targeted approach rather than risk further alienating the population. "We ought to probably let the situation settle before we appeared to be attacking out of revenge," Lieutenant General James Conway, commander of the First Marine Expeditionary Force, recalled arguing. His colleagues split; Lieutenant General Ricardo Sanchez agreed, but his superior, General John Abizaid, the CENTCOM commander, thought the marines' indirect approach had failed, and Bremer also favored a strong response. So did Washington. "No, we've got to attack," Sanchez remembered Rumsfeld saying in response to the general's concerns. "We need to make sure that Iraqis in other cities receive our message." In Sanchez's account, the president expressed appreciation for the military's caution, "but then ordered us to attack." After leaving office, Rumsfeld disavowed responsibility for the decision, attributing it to Abizaid. "Military commanders decide that, absolutely," Rumsfeld said.

Now managing simultaneous operations against Sunni and Shiite extremists, Bush, Cheney, and the National Security Council heard from Bremer and Sanchez over a secure videoconference on April 7. Bush was in a feisty mood. He declared that Sadr's Mahdi Army was "a hostile force" and that they could not let a single radical cleric change the course of Iraq. "At the end of this campaign, al-Sadr must be gone," Bush declared. "At a minimum, he will be arrested. It is essential he be wiped out."

Rumsfeld asked whether the effort should be low intensity or high intensity, and the high-intensity president interrupted. As Sanchez remembered it, Bush delivered a sharp tirade. "Kick ass!" Sanchez recalled Bush saying. "If somebody tries to stop the march to democracy, we will seek them out and kill them. We must be tougher than hell." He went on: "Our will is being tested, but we are resolute. We have a better way. Stay strong! Stay the course! Kill them! Be confident! Prevail! We are going to wipe them out. We are not blinking." If it stood out in Sanchez's memory as perhaps more cartoonish than it really was, it reflected the president's state of mind.

Yet the marine assault in Fallujah had already precipitated a crisis in Baghdad that would force Bush to blink. Members of the Iraqi Governing Council threatened to resign if it continued. Tony Blair called Bush asking him to back off, and Bremer agreed they should suspend the operation for fear of losing the government just weeks before the scheduled transfer of sovereignty. Abizaid disagreed, urging that they continue the offensive, even though it would take another two or three weeks. Cheney agreed. "The vice president was pretty adamant about continuing the attack, and he wasn't worried about the government falling," one participant in the discussions recalled. But Bush was. On April 8, Sanchez was ordered to halt the offensive. Once again, the marines were furious. Having launched the operation over their own objections, they now wanted to finish it. Abizaid flew to Fallujah on April 9 to tell the marine commander, Major General James Mattis, whose pants were splattered with blood. Mattis exploded.

"If you are going to take Vienna, take fucking Vienna!" he roared, embellishing Napoleon's famous phrase.

But the order stood. "Let me say again, we're going to stop," Abizaid told him.

Mattis was not the only one unhappy about it. Cheney seemed to have been taken by surprise by the decision. His staff called senior military officers to ask what happened.

The Fallujah episode underscored the uncertain way Bush was managing the war from Washington. One minute he wanted to be tough; the next he was convinced the whole enterprise would unravel. His instinct was to defer to the people on the ground, but when the people on the ground disagreed among themselves, he was reluctant to mediate or insert himself. In his head were images of Lyndon Johnson picking out bombing targets during the Vietnam War, an object lesson, he felt, in what presidents should not do. "You fight the war, and I'll provide you with political cover," he told the generals more than once. But in this instance, his equivocation had a cost. Conway concluded, "We certainly increased the level of animosity that existed." Along with stirring the Sadr hornet's nest without capturing him, the Fallujah debacle led Sanchez to call those days in March and April "a strategic disaster for America's mission in Iraq." Taken together, he said, "our actions had undeniably ignited a civil war in Iraq."

THAT WAR WAS taking a toll on Bush's standing at home, and there was rising pressure on him to admit the invasion had been a misjudgment. At a prime-time news conference in the East Room on April 13, Bush stumbled when John Dickerson of *Time* magazine asked him to name his biggest mistake since September 11. Bush considered it a trap, a way of getting him to backslide on Iraq. But his faltering inability to come up with an answer was perhaps as damaging.

"I wish you would have given me this written question ahead of time so I could plan for it," Bush said, pausing to think. "Uh, John, I'm sure historians will look back and say, gosh, he could have done it better this way, or that way."

Clearly flummoxed, he paused again. Watching from the side of the room, his press secretary, Scott McClellan, thought to himself, *Come on, sir, this one is not difficult!*

"You know," Bush continued, "I just, I'm sure something will pop in my head here in the midst of this press conference, with all the pressure of trying to come up with an answer, but it hadn't yet."

He went on to reaffirm his decision to invade Iraq despite the missing weapons. "You just put me under the spot here," he told Dickerson, "and maybe I'm not as quick on my feet as I should be in coming up with one."

Bush knew he had blown it. Conferring with aides in the darkened State Dining Room afterward, he said, "I kept thinking about what they wanted me to say—that it was a mistake to go into Iraq. And I'm not going to. It was the right decision."

The answer provoked an uproar about a president who could admit no wrong, and it weighed on Bush for weeks. When Adam Levine, a press aide who was leaving the White House, stopped by the Oval Office for a departure photograph, Bush raised the encounter.

"How would you answer the Dickerson question?" Bush asked.

"Mr. President, that isn't fair. I have had three weeks to think about it."

"I know you have, so what would you have said?"

"Well, I would have looked at him and said, 'That's a great question, John. You are right. I make a lot of mistakes. Laura Bush reminds me every night. You probably want to ask her because she keeps better track of them than I do.' "

Bush laughed because of course it was true.

While Bush acknowledged no mistakes, George Tenet became convinced that the president's people were trying to pin them on him instead. When he picked up the *Washington Post* on April 17 to find a story about Bob Woodward's new book, *Plan of Attack*, he read with exasperation that he had told the president the case for weapons in Iraq was a "slam dunk." Tenet felt like "the guy being burned at the stake." He took a few days off work and headed to the New Jersey shore to stew. First, he thought, the White House had hung him out to dry on the sixteen words, and now this.

From his beach getaway, Tenet called Andy Card to vent. "Andy, I'm calling to tell you that I'm really angry," he said. He complained about the leak. "What you guys have gone and done is make me look stupid, and I just want to tell you how furious I am about it. For someone in the administration to now hang this around my neck is about the most despicable thing I have ever seen in my life." Card said little, and Tenet concluded his relationship with the White House was broken beyond repair.

ON THE MORNING of April 29, Bush and Cheney welcomed ten members of a bipartisan commission investigating September 11 into the White House. It was a bright, sunny day, with light beaming through the windows of the Oval Office as the president and the vice president greeted their visitor-inquisitors. Bush was friendly and warm, Cheney quiet and stoic.

The White House, and especially Cheney, had long viewed the inquiry with suspicion, sure that it would turn into an exercise in finger-pointing that could only be damaging in an election year. Richard Clarke had used his appearance before the commission to accuse Bush and his team of not taking the threat of terrorism seriously enough and to dramatically apologize to relatives of the victims of September 11. The White House resisted turning over sensitive intelligence documents or letting aides to the president testify. But eventually the resistance began to look like stonewalling, and the White House agreed to send Condoleezza Rice to testify publicly and to let the commission interview Bush and Cheney—as long as they appeared together and no transcript or recording was made.

The insistence that the two do the interview jointly set tongues wagging about a president who needed to lean on his vice president, feeding into a public perception that it was Cheney who was really in charge, not just in ordering that hijacked planes be shot down on September 11, but in every phase of the war on terror that followed. "My immediate suspicion was that they want to do it together so that we don't get them separately and their stories don't match up, including about the shoot-down episode," recalled Philip Zelikow, the commission's executive director. Timothy J. Roemer, a Democratic member of the commission, said he thought it might be "a way of diluting the time we would have with the president."

But in fact Bush dominated the session. As the commissioners settled into the couches and chairs set up in a semicircle around the president and the vice president, the panel's leaders, Thomas H. Kean, a former Republican governor of New Jersey, and Lee H. Hamilton, a former Democratic congressman from Indiana, opened the questioning for about an hour, taking Bush through the events leading up to September 11 and the day itself. Cheney said nothing unless a question was directed at him or the president asked if he wanted to add something. After Kean and Hamilton were done, the other commissioners were given ten minutes each to pose their own questions.

When one of the Democrats risked straying beyond his time, Kean gently tried to cut in, but Bush waved him off.

"This is the Oval Office," Bush said. "I make the rules."

Then to the commissioner he said, "Go on to your next question."

That defused much of the tension, and Bush gave no appearance of being rushed. Despite the strictures White House lawyers had tried to put on the session, they had actually blocked out the entire morning on the president's schedule so he could give the commission as much time as it wanted. In doing so, he could appear magnanimous and not defensive. "Every time we asked a specific question to the president, he thoroughly answered it or honestly said, 'Here's what I recall,'" Roemer said.

On the shoot-down order, Bush backed Cheney's account that he had obtained permission from the president first. None of the logs or notes taken that day confirmed such a call, but Bush and Cheney were firm in their mutual recollection and attributed the lack of documentation to the confusion of the day. "I just think it was the fog of war and the communications scramble that morning," Cheney said later. "I think there were calls that weren't recorded." Some of the commissioners remained unconvinced, though. While the vice president had no power to issue a military order on his own, few could fault him if he had taken the initiative in the most exigent of circumstances to prevent the destruction of the White House. But some commissioners assumed that the president and the vice president were unwilling to fuel the impression that Cheney was really the dominant member of the tandem, acting on his own.

At one point, Fred Fielding, a Republican commissioner who would later serve as Bush's White House counsel, asked about issues surrounding the Twenty-Fifth Amendment that dealt with the succession of power. Bush replied that his relationship with Cheney was like that of no other president and vice president because there was no political rivalry. "The vice president isn't interested in my job and I'm not interested in his," Bush said.

As they answered questions, though, Bush left little doubt that he was in charge on this day at least. He used no notes and was in full command of the details. "The commissioners go in expecting that Cheney is going to do a lot of talking, except for the few people that know the two men," recalled Zelikow. Instead, "Bush utterly dominates the conversation. The commissioners didn't expect that, a lot of them, especially the Democrats. They had the caricature in their head of Bush, and they didn't understand that the caricature is not quite right." In the end, "Bush probably did 95 percent of the talking. Cheney just stayed silent, which I think he is totally content to do."

So rather than Cheney guarding Bush, it was Cheney who was protected from questioning.

18

"When are we going to fire somebody?"

"This is going to kill us," Alberto Gonzales said quietly as he watched the images on his White House television.

On the night of April 28, the CBS show *60 Minutes II* aired photographs of Iraqi detainees at the Abu Ghraib prison being abused by American soldiers. The photographs were depraved in every way. Several showed Iraqi prisoners stripped naked and blindfolded or hooded, with American soldiers posing next to them smiling or flashing thumbs-ups. One showed naked Iraqi prisoners stacked on top of each other in a pyramid. The most horrific image, one that would be seared into the consciousness of the world as a symbol of American hypocrisy, showed an Iraqi forced to stand on a box of military rations, his head covered with a sandbag and wires attached to his fingers and genitals. He was told if he fell off the box, he would be electrocuted.

President Bush had been told about the Pentagon investigation back in January but had never seen the photographs until now. He felt angry and blindsided. "I had no idea how graphic or grotesque the photos would be," he recalled. Bush understood pictures like this would be interpreted around the world as evidence that the Americans were no better than Saddam Hussein.

Investigators found a broad pattern of abusive behavior at the prison. In a report marked "Secret/No Foreign Dissemination," Major General Antonio M. Taguba concluded that military police had kept detainees naked for days at a time, forced groups of male prisoners to masturbate while being photographed or videotaped, placed a dog chain around a naked detainee's neck so a female guard could pose with him, used unmuzzled military dogs to intimidate detainees and once bite a prisoner, forced male detainees to strip and wear women's underwear, and punched, slapped, and kicked detainees. The abuse did not occur during interrogations, but some guards said they were encouraged by interrogators and believed it helped soften up detainees for later questioning.

At 10:00 a.m. on May 5, Bush met with Rumsfeld, who handed him a handwritten letter. "Read this," the secretary said.

> *Mr. President,*
> *I want you to know that you have my resignation as Secretary of Defense anytime you feel it would be helpful to you.*
> *Don Rumsfeld*

Rumsfeld told the president that there had to be accountability and the furor would just grow until there was a sense that the government had taken it seriously.

Bush agreed. "Don, someone's head has to roll on this one," he said.

Well, Rumsfeld responded, you have my resignation.

The meeting broke up without a decision.

Rumsfeld's letter was not precisely a letter of resignation; it was an offer to resign if the president wanted him to. Generously, it could be read as an honorable act taking responsibility; more cynically, it could be seen as forcing Bush either to support him or cut him loose. Bush saw it as the latter.

"Pretty smooth move by the crusty old guy," Bush told Dan Bartlett. "He called my hand."

Bush thought about accepting but worried about pushing out a defense secretary in the middle of a war and knew Cheney would resist. Moreover, the notion of tossing aside advisers because of a media furor always rankled Bush.

Bush called Rumsfeld at the Pentagon.

"I don't accept your resignation," he said.

"I just don't want to put more rocks in your knapsack," Rumsfeld replied.

Bush asked whether someone else should be fired, like Richard Myers.

"You'd be firing the wrong guy," Rumsfeld responded.

Bush was not willing to let it go. That afternoon, Bartlett popped into the Oval Office. The *Washington Post* had figured out how long Rumsfeld had known about the pictures before Bush found out.

"We have a predicament here," Bartlett told him. "The *Post* has the ticktock on the chronology of the pictures."

Bartlett suggested they leak to the *Post* that the president was "not happy" about the delay and that he had told Rumsfeld so. That would take the heat off Bush and put it where it belonged.

"This is why we have cabinet secretaries," Bartlett told him. "This is why they take the heat."

"I agree," Bush said. "But make sure you let them know what you are going to do."

Bartlett called Larry Di Rita, Rumsfeld's spokesman, to give him a heads-up but never anticipated how the mild phrasing would look. "Bush Privately Chides Rumsfeld," the front-page headline in the *Post* read on May 6. Bartlett got to work that morning at 6:10, certain it was going to be an ugly day. Sure enough, minutes after he arrived, he heard the White House intercom that announced Bush's movements declare: "Trailblazer departs residence." A couple minutes after that, Bartlett's phone rang summoning him to the Oval Office.

This was your work? Bush asked.

It was, Bartlett acknowledged.

"All right," Bush said.

Rumsfeld was angry about the leak—how did airing their dirty laundry help? This was a White House out of control. When he and Bush talked by phone, the defense secretary remonstrated with the president.

"You need to get ahold of your PR team," he complained.

For whatever reason, Bush felt the need to exonerate his political guru. "Don, it was not Karl Rove," he said. He did not volunteer that it was Bartlett, although Di Rita knew.

The next day, May 7, Rumsfeld appeared at a congressional hearing to take responsibility for the scandal. Asked if he might step down, Rumsfeld said, "Certainly since this firestorm has been raging, it's a question that I've given a lot of thought to." He added, "If I felt I could not be effective, I'd resign in a minute." At the White House, it was their turn to be irritated. Rumsfeld had put the president in a box.

Bartlett called Di Rita and pulled him out of the hearing.

"What's he doing?" Bartlett demanded.

"He's telling the truth," Di Rita answered. "He's answering the question."

Others, though, thought it was a mistake to keep Rumsfeld. Matthew Dowd, the reelection strategist, marched into campaign headquarters and pressed for action.

"Rumsfeld has got to be fired," he said. "We can't just blame this on some National Guard general or some shit. This is the guy who ran for office as the accountability president. When are we going to fire somebody?"

Ken Mehlman seemed sympathetic. "I know, I know," he said.

But Rove saw it as giving in to political opponents and the media. "How quickly, Dowd, you throw someone under the bus," he scolded in a phone call.

ON SATURDAY, MAY 8, when few were in the White House to notice, Cheney had an appointment with Patrick Fitzgerald, the special prosecutor investigating the CIA leak. In four months on the case, Fitzgerald had brought Rove, Robert Novak, and Scooter Libby before the grand jury. Joseph Wilson had just published a book on the episode, assailing Bush and Cheney. The situation had put a chill over the White House, where aides worried but were barred from discussing it with one another. Cheney, sour from his fight with James Comey over the surveillance program, viewed Comey's friend Fitzgerald warily. Cheney believed he might be the real target.

But Bush had insisted on cooperation, so Cheney sat down with the prosecutor and gave his account in a matter-of-fact manner while repeatedly saying he did not remember virtually anything of consequence to the investigation. Eventually, he tried to wrap it up by telling his questioners that he had other duties to attend to. Fitzgerald's team had been asking White House officials to sign waivers of any confidentiality agreements with journalists, freeing them to testify about their conversations. When they asked Cheney to sign one, he said he would think about it.

Cheney turned back to the drama involving his friend and mentor. On May 9, Rumsfeld sat down, pulled out stationery emblazoned, "The Secretary of Defense, Washington," and wrote out another letter to the president, this one two pages and more explicit.

> *Dear Mr. President,*
>
> *. . . By this letter I am resigning as Secretary of Defense. During recent days I have given a good deal of thought to the situation, testified before Congress, and considered your views. I have great respect for you, your outstanding leadership in the global war on terror and your hopes for our country. However, I have concluded that the damage from the acts of abuse that happened on my watch, by individuals for whose conduct I am ultimately responsible, can best be responded to by my resignation . . .*
>
> *Respectfully,*
> *Don Rumsfeld*

When Bush and Cheney came to the Pentagon the next morning for a briefing on Iraq and to look at the Abu Ghraib pictures, Rumsfeld handed Bush the new letter.

"Mr. President, the Department of Defense will be better off if I resign," Rumsfeld said.

"That's not true," Bush responded, and pushed the letter back across the table.

Rumsfeld said his mind was made up, but Bush asked for time to think about it. Then they headed to the Pentagon briefing room, where Bush, flanked by Cheney, expressed unstinting confidence in Rumsfeld.

"You are courageously leading our nation in the war against terror," Bush told him before reporters. "You're doing a superb job. You are a strong secretary of defense and our nation owes you a debt of gratitude."

Privately, Bush asked Cheney to talk with his old friend. Cheney went back to the Pentagon the next day, May 11. He sat at a small table while Rumsfeld stood at the standing desk he used near the window.

"Don, thirty-five years ago this week, I went to work for you," Cheney said, "and on this one you're wrong."

Rumsfeld relented and stayed. But he would come to regret it. "It was like a body blow," he said of Abu Ghraib years later. "Unfortunately, the way the chain of command works, there wasn't an obvious person who ought to be fired. I had already replaced some of the senior people of both the administrative and the operational chain of command for different reasons, and so most of the people were brand-new and some of them had just gotten there and were understaffed. And I felt that there really wasn't anyone where you could pin the tail on, and so I stepped up and said if I can't find anyone better than me, it better be me." Looking back, he mused, "Maybe it would have helped the military; maybe it would have helped our cause."

As it was, Bush was left to do damage control. "The pictures made me sick to my stomach," he told the visiting president of Angola. "It hurt us. It gave enemies of freedom the chance to say look at these people." But he said they would also "show the nature of a free society" by having a full investigation and bringing the guilty to justice.

FOR DIFFERENT REASONS, Colin Powell was also contemplating leaving. He had stayed despite his embarrassment over the UN presentation and his battles with Cheney and Rumsfeld. He had stayed even when his deputy and close friend, Richard Armitage, had urged him to resign because he felt Powell had become an enabler for the Bush team, exploited for his political credibility to help every time they got in a jam. But now he was weary of it all and he met privately with Bush to tell the president that he planned to step down after the first term. He then used the opportunity to vent about a dysfunctional war cabinet.

"As I said at the beginning, I only wanted to serve one term, and so after the election I should go," Powell told the president. "But there is another reason, and that is your system is not working well. We are of too many different philosophical views, and we are not reconciling them."

Bush brushed off the criticism. Every administration had tension, particularly between secretaries of state and defense, and he recalled the famous battles between Caspar Weinberger and George Shultz in the Reagan administration.

"Different views are essential," Bush said. "Just like Weinberger and Shultz."

"Mr. President," Powell replied, "I lived through Weinberger and Shultz. I was there. And yes, they had their differences. But they had a system for resolving them. We don't now. We sort of each go our own way and go around."

Bush had heard this from others too. Cheney, Rumsfeld, and Rice all complained about each other. Rumsfeld had told him that Powell's State Department regularly leaked to the media to fight internal battles. Powell bristled at this. Did his team leak? Of course it did. Everyone did. But he could point to particular Rumsfeld advisers who met with reporters to air administration disagreements. And he thought his department's leaking was nothing like that of the White House, including Cheney's office.

Either way, he told Bush, it was time to start fresh. "You need to reconcile this for your second term," Powell told the president, "and I think you should get a whole new team, and it begins with my departure because I am so different from the rest of your team. But I really think you need a new team."

EVEN AS BUSH was trying to manage his fractious team, he was also busy trying to cut off another architect of the Iraq War. For months, he had been stewing about Ahmad Chalabi, the former favorite who had alienated even his admirers in Washington.

Bush was irritated to look up during his State of the Union address and see Chalabi in the first lady's box, and he was angrier when he was told later about an interview where the Iraqi exile bragged about getting the Americans to topple Saddam Hussein even with bad intelligence. "We are heroes in error," Chalabi told the *Telegraph* of London. "As far as we're concerned we've been entirely successful. That tyrant Saddam is gone and the Americans are in Baghdad. What was said before is not important." Bush was "really frosted," Condoleezza Rice told Jerry Bremer. Chalabi tried to repair the damage by sending a message through an intermediary to the White House clarifying he did not mean he manipulated intelligence, but it was too late. "That statement finished him," said Richard Perle, his patron.

By the time May rolled around, evidence emerged that Chalabi had told Iranian intelligence agents that the United States had broken their secret codes.

"What the hell is this?" Bush asked at a meeting.

"This is a compromise of potentially significant ramifications," said Michael Hayden, the NSA director.

Paul Wolfowitz, still sympathetic to Chalabi, warned that they should "make sure this is not something the Iranians are using" to discredit him.

Bush noted media reports that Chalabi's group was still receiving $350,000 a month in American money.

"Who does Chalabi work for?" Bush asked Rumsfeld. "Who pays him?"

"I don't know," Rumsfeld said.

Bush turned to George Tenet. "George, who does he work for?"

"He doesn't work for us," Tenet said, and turned to a deputy. "Isn't that right?"

The deputy said Chalabi was being paid by the Defense Intelligence Agency, part of Rumsfeld's Pentagon.

"If we're paying this guy and he's giving away our secrets," Bush said, "it needs to stop."

Bush was also preparing that spring to replace the two senior Americans on the ground in Iraq. Jerry Bremer and Ricardo Sanchez would both leave with the transfer of sovereignty as part of a transition in leadership. On his way out, Bremer decided to push for more troops. He had watched the situation for a year and concluded that security was slipping away. One day he asked Sanchez what he would do with another two divisions. "I'd control Baghdad," he said. So on May 18, Bremer sent a note to Rumsfeld by courier recommending two more divisions, or thirty thousand to forty thousand troops.

The first time Bush heard about it was two days later, on May 20, when Rumsfeld mentioned it during a meeting. Sanchez was in Washington and in attendance. He remembered Bush and Rumsfeld focusing on why Bremer did not go through the chain of command rather than on the substance of his suggestion.

"What are we going to do about it?" Bush asked.

"Mr. President, you ought to be glad he didn't send it to you, because now you don't have to respond," Condoleezza Rice said. "Bremer is ready to leave. He'll be writing his book. He needs to go."

"Well, this is amazing," Rumsfeld said, shaking his head. "Mr. President, you don't have to do anything. He addressed it to me. I'll take care of responding to him."

After the meeting, Rumsfeld sat down with Sanchez in the Situation Room to tell him the president was not sending his promotion to a fourth star to Congress because of the political debate that would ensue. Instead, he was being replaced in Iraq without the new assignment he expected. Without saying so, Bush had just made Sanchez the highest-ranking officer punished for Abu Ghraib.

And with that, no more was heard by Bush or Cheney about Bremer's proposal for more troops. "I was not pleased that Bremer was recommending more troops for the first time as he was on his way out of Baghdad and not in person to provide his reasoning," Rumsfeld later wrote. Yet Rumsfeld did not contact Bremer to ask his reasoning. Instead, Rumsfeld sent the issue to Richard Myers, who did not respond for two months and then reported that John Abizaid thought he had enough troops. Bush and Rumsfeld had decided that as long as the commanders did not ask for more troops, it was not their business to send more.

What escaped the Bush-Cheney team was that their calculations of how many troops would be needed in Iraq had initially depended on two assumptions that ultimately were not borne out. They had assumed a substantial portion of the Iraqi army would remain intact and that other Arab countries would contribute troops as they did in the Gulf War. After both of those proved false, no one ever thought to compensate for the missing forces. "We never connected it up," Hadley said. "I don't know why. It seems, in retrospect, very clear."

ON JUNE 2, Bush was flying out to Colorado to deliver the commencement address at the Air Force Academy when George Tenet called Andy Card to say he needed to see the president urgently. Tenet did not say why, but Card could guess. Card told Tenet to come by the White House at 8:00 p.m., when the president would be back.

Card ushered Tenet into the residence that evening, and the three men sat down. "It's time for me to go," Tenet said. "I've been doing this a long time. I have a boy who needs me, a family that needs me. I've done all I can do."

Tenet made no mention of the real reason for the decision, his estrangement from the White House. Unlike with Rumsfeld, Bush did not try to change his mind.

"When do you want to announce it?" the president asked.

"Tomorrow morning," Tenet said.

The next day, as Bush headed to Marine One to begin a trip to Europe, he stopped and told reporters Tenet was stepping down. Tenet did not join him. "He's been a strong leader in the war on terror," Bush said, "and I will miss him." Cheney would not. He thought Tenet was cutting and running.

"For him to quit when the going got tough, not to mention in the middle of a presidential campaign, seemed to me unfair to the president, who had put his trust in George Tenet," Cheney observed.

Tenet's departure coincided with a broader turning point for the agency. Less than two weeks after he decided to step down, the Justice Department pulled the plug on the CIA interrogation program Tenet had ushered in. Jack Goldsmith, the head of the Office of Legal Counsel who had objected to the secret NSA surveillance program, was now back announcing that he was withdrawing the August 2002 opinion largely authored by John Yoo and signed by Jay Bybee authorizing waterboarding and other brutal methods of questioning terror suspects. Once again, he was declaring that the president had exceeded his authority.

Goldsmith's decision came just days after the original memo leaked to the media; coming in the aftermath of Abu Ghraib, it painted the picture of a government that had crossed too many lines in the name of national security. Withdrawing an OLC opinion was a rare and extraordinary action, but Goldsmith felt he had no choice, and while some of his colleagues were shocked, he encountered no resistance and heard no one other than David Addington defend the now discredited opinion. At the same time, he knew he could not continue to work in an administration where he was so out of step with important people who doubted his "fortitude for the job." So the day after withdrawing the opinion, Goldsmith handed John Ashcroft his resignation letter.

THAT SPRING, BUSH sought rapprochement on another front. Unlike his father, he had no primary challenger, but he knew he would be better off if he could reach an accommodation with John McCain. As it happened, McCain's camp reached out first. The rivalry between the two men had been fueled by a long-standing feud between their strategists, Karl Rove and John Weaver, two old Texas hands who fell out in 1988 over money. But in early 2004, Weaver called Mark McKinnon, the Bush media adviser, and told him it was time to settle matters with Rove. McKinnon arranged a peace gathering at a Caribou Coffee shop near the White House, where they agreed to put their differences behind them. Within weeks, McCain began campaigning with Bush.

The two traveled together on June 18 to Fort Lewis in Washington State and met privately with families of slain soldiers. Weaver thought "some unspoken bond" formed between Bush and McCain in that moment. All the bitterness was forgotten, at least for a time.

But it was a painful morning for Bush. "You are as big a terrorist as Osama bin Laden," a woman who lost her son in Iraq told him.

Bush did not think there was much to say in response.

During the same session, he met another mother of a slain soldier, Cindy Sheehan, whose twenty-four-year-old son, Casey, had been killed by a rocket-propelled grenade in Sadr City.

Sheehan had grown frustrated with the war and convinced that Bush had "changed his reasons for being over there every time a reason is proven false or an objective reached" but chose not to register her complaints to him directly. Instead, she left the meeting feeling at least somewhat warmly toward the president. "I now know he's sincere about wanting freedom for the Iraqis," she told her local newspaper. "I know he's sorry and feels some pain for our loss."

CHENEY RARELY ROSE to the bait while on the campaign trail, but he lost his famous cool one summer day. Democrats were pounding him for his roots as chief executive of Halliburton, which now had extensive government contracts in Iraq. On June 22, he was in the Senate chamber for a class photograph when Senator Patrick Leahy wandered over and put his arm around him as if they were best friends. Cheney knew Leahy just the day before had kicked off what Democrats were calling "Halliburton Week" with a conference call to reporters calling for an investigation into a Halliburton contract.

Cheney could not stomach what he saw as the rank hypocrisy—impugning his integrity one day and chumming up the next.

"Fuck yourself," he growled at Leahy and stalked away.

The confrontation did not become public for several days, but when it did, even Cheney's family was surprised.

"Did you say that to Pat Leahy?" Liz Cheney asked when she heard.

"Yes, I did," he said matter-of-factly.

White House officials debated whether he should apologize. They need not have bothered. Cheney had no intention of saying he was sorry when he was not.

From Air Force Two, he called Steve Schmidt, his campaign adviser. "You're about the only person who doesn't think I should apologize," Cheney said.

An apology would be contrived and insincere, Schmidt felt, and Leahy had it coming. "Besides, sir, I'm from North Jersey," Schmidt added. "It's a term of affection where I come from."

Cheney laughed. He never did apologize. "It was probably not language

I should have used on the Senate floor," he wrote years later, "but it was completely deserved."

Leahy had never been an administration favorite; after he resisted some provisions of the Patriot Act, White House officials privately nicknamed him Osama bin Leahy. But the Halliburton attacks particularly peeved Cheney. With the wars in Afghanistan and Iraq, the government had dramatically expanded its reliance on private firms to provide everything from food and gasoline to security, and Halliburton had been one of the primary beneficiaries, often through no-bid contracts. Cheney did not help himself by claiming in 2003, "I have no financial interest in Halliburton of any kind and haven't had now for over three years," even though he had received $1.6 million in deferred compensation between the election and the inauguration and had received another $398,548 since taking office.

What Cheney meant was that the deferred compensation was set before he became vice president and not dependent on the company's financial health. Like many corporate executives, Cheney had opted to spread compensation for his work in the 1990s over a number of years. If Halliburton made or lost money, Cheney's checks would be the same, so he did not benefit if the company received contracts. In an abundance of caution, Cheney before taking office had paid $14,903 for an insurance policy to guarantee payments even if Halliburton went out of business, so no one could claim he had any interest in keeping the firm afloat. And before taking office, he gave up $8 million in stock options from Halliburton and other companies, assigning their after-tax profits to charity. In his view, he had done everything he could to avoid conflict, so attacks aggravated him. The Annenberg Public Policy Center agreed that "Cheney doesn't gain financially from the contracts given to the company he once headed," and the journalist Barton Gellman, who wrote a tough-minded book about Cheney, "found no evidence of self-dealing behavior in office, involving Halliburton or anything else."

Others, though, were looking for evidence of wrongdoing in the West Wing, and it was Bush's turn to talk with Patrick Fitzgerald, the prosecutor in the CIA leak case. Unlike Cheney, Bush was friendly and acted perfectly happy to see his visitors. For seventy minutes on June 24, he answered their questions, seemingly in no rush. Without realizing it, he contradicted Karl Rove's version of their conversation, saying Rove had denied he was a source for Robert Novak.

"If Rove said he didn't do it, then he didn't do it," Bush told the prosecutor. "If he was involved, he'd tell me."

When it was over, Fitzgerald pulled out another waiver of confidentiality promises made by reporters.

"Sure, I'll sign that," Bush said instinctively, shrugging off his lawyer as he grabbed the paper, read it over, and pulled out his Sharpie pen.

The next few days brought mixed news for Cheney in his perpetual fight to preserve and expand executive power as the Supreme Court weighed in on two of the biggest controversies of his time in office.

In the first, the justices took the vice president's side in the long-running battle over the secrecy of his 2001 energy task force. In a 7-to-2 decision, the court overturned a lower court's ruling and ordered it to give more weight to Cheney's argument of executive privilege. As a practical matter, that settled the legal battle. Cheney felt vindicated. He had helped reestablish some of the authority that had been chipped away from the executive branch over the past three decades. Others in the White House, though, lamented that the victory on principle had unnecessarily fueled an image of a secretive government in the pocket of corporate titans. And for what? In the end, everyone assumed anyway that the panel's report was shaped by industry, and its recommendations had largely gone nowhere.

Four days later, on June 28, the same court handed Cheney a major defeat, ruling the government could not hold Taliban and al-Qaeda fighters without access to court. Ruling in *Hamdi v. Rumsfeld*, the court affirmed the president's right to declare not just foreigners but even an American citizen caught fighting with the Taliban in Afghanistan like Yaser Esam Hamdi an enemy combatant but required the government to allow such detainees—including those at Guantánamo—to challenge their imprisonment in court. "We have long since made clear that a state of war is not a blank check for the President when it comes to the rights of the Nation's citizens," wrote Sandra Day O'Connor, a stinging rebuke from the justice whose vote had decided *Bush v. Gore* four years earlier.

BUSH WAS IN Istanbul at a NATO summit the same day when Donald Rumsfeld reached over his shoulder and passed him a note from Condoleezza Rice: "Mr. President, Iraq is sovereign. Letter was passed from Bremer at 10:26 a.m., Iraqi time."

Bush picked up a pen and scrawled on it, "Let freedom reign!" Then he turned to his right and shook hands with Tony Blair.

It was an exciting moment for Bush, one he would long cherish. A giant picture of him with the "Let freedom reign!" note was later hung in the West Wing. While others were rotated regularly, that one stayed there for years.

Just like that, the occupation was officially over. But the war was not. As hopeful as Bush was, the very manner in which the transfer took place underscored the decidedly mixed nature of the accomplishment. Bush, worried about terrorist attacks timed to the scheduled transfer of authority on June 30, had suggested through Rice that Bremer secretly move it up a few days. Bremer's aides even confiscated the phones of reporters summoned to hear the announcement so he could leave the country before it was publicly known. Better to live with the troublesome symbolism than to let a bomb go off in the middle of a ceremony.

Bremer's replacement would be an ambassador who would still wield outsized influence in Iraq but no longer as the governing authority. Bush picked John Negroponte, a veteran diplomat who had been serving at the United Nations. Replacing Ricardo Sanchez was General George Casey, a well-respected officer but one who had never served in combat and had no background in the Arab world. Bush invited Casey to the White House for a social dinner with their wives, but otherwise the two men had no substantive meeting before Casey's departure for Baghdad. Bush and Cheney hoped that Iraq might be on a path toward stability, a hope enhanced by the approach of the presidential election.

NEITHER BUSH NOR Cheney was all that impressed with the emerging Democratic ticket. Karl Rove had assumed John Kerry would pick Richard Gephardt as his running mate to lock down labor support, but Matthew Dowd correctly predicted it would be John Edwards.

On July 7, the day after Kerry's announcement, Bush was asked about the choice by a reporter during a stop in Raleigh.

"He's being described today as charming, engaging, a nimble campaigner, a populist, and even sexy," the reporter said. "How does he stack up against Dick Cheney?"

"Dick Cheney can be president," Bush answered sharply, then moved on to another reporter. "Next."

As it happened, the 9/11 Commission had been investigating whether Cheney actually *was* president, at least briefly, on the day of the hijackings. In its draft report, the panel raised questions about whether the vice president gave the order to shoot down threatening planes before getting permission from Bush. Reading over the draft before its release, Cheney grew incensed and called Thomas Kean, the commission chairman.

"Governor, this is not true, just not fair," he told Kean. "The president has told you, I have told you, that the president issued the order. I was following his directions."

Kean said he would ask the staff to review the language in the report again. But the commission ended up releasing the report on July 22 largely unaltered. It came out shortly after another report produced by the Senate Intelligence Committee on the botched prewar intelligence about Iraq's weapons program. The two reports collectively called attention to the lowest moments of Bush and Cheney's tenure, the failure to adequately see the threat of al-Qaeda and move more expeditiously to counter terrorism in the months before September 11 and the fixation on Saddam Hussein that led them to disregard contrary evidence on the preordained path to war. Both reports threw cold water on Cheney's view of the links between al-Qaeda and Hussein's Iraq.

At the same time, the reports also provided balanced portraits that undercut the worst charges lodged against Bush and Cheney by their critics. The Senate report found no evidence that Bush or Cheney had pressured intelligence agencies into skewing reports on Iraq. The 9/11 Commission spread blame around evenly without singling out Bush or Cheney. While the vice president was still irritated, White House officials who had feared the worst in an election year sighed in relief.

A week after the 9/11 Commission report, Democrats officially nominated Kerry and Edwards. Cheney hit the campaign trail with gusto. In Dayton, Ohio, on August 12, he mocked Kerry for being weak. "Senator Kerry has also said that if he were in charge, he would fight a 'more sensitive' war on terror," Cheney said, provoking a wave of laughter. Lincoln and Roosevelt "did not wage sensitive warfare," he added. "Those who threaten us and kill innocents around the world do not need to be treated more sensitively. They need to be destroyed."

Two weeks later, though, Cheney finally got the question he had avoided since January.

"I need to know what do you think about homosexual marriages," a voter asked at a forum in Davenport, Iowa.

Cheney did not duck. "My general view is that freedom means freedom for everyone," he said.

Then he noted that Bush had come out in support of a constitutional amendment banning same-sex marriage. The issue had come up for a vote in the Senate the month before and fell nineteen votes short of passage. Cheney could have ducked, but he acknowledged that he and Bush disagreed.

"My own preference is as I've stated," Cheney said. "But the president makes basic policy for the administration. And he's made it clear that he does, in fact, support a constitutional amendment on this issue."

Aides were surprised that Cheney had just taken on Bush in public. "We were all proud of him because we were all close to Mary," said Neil Patel, his domestic policy adviser. Cheney's traveling press secretary, Anne Womack, e-mailed a heads-up to campaign headquarters and soon received an anxious phone call demanding to know what happened. But then the issue was dropped. Cheney said later that neither Bush nor Karl Rove ever brought it up with him. "They were pretty good about letting me do my thing," he said.

LIFE ON THE ROAD took on a familiar rhythm and drew Bush closer to his aides. After a rally in Taylor, Michigan, on August 30, Bush heard that his deputy chief of staff, Joe Hagin, had lost his mother. Hagin had not told the president or even dropped off the campaign swing.

Bush went to Hagin's hotel room and found him on the phone with his brother. Hagin's back was turned, so Bush just sat down on the bed and waited. Only after five minutes or so had passed did Hagin hang up and realize who was there. Bush spent an hour consoling Hagin, an eternity in the life of a president.

From there, Bush headed to the Republican National Convention, intending to use it to bolster his credentials as America's protector. By holding it in New York, a city not normally friendly to Republicans, he and Cheney reminded everyone of their role in responding to the attacks three years earlier, and they depicted Iraq as a logical extension of the war on terror that followed. What they were not acknowledging was how bad the fighting in Iraq had become. Bush had just gotten a letter from Prime Minister Ayad Allawi making that point. "The situation on the ground in Iraq is grossly unstable," Allawi wrote to Bush. "The threat is now much greater than it was a year ago and it is continuing to escalate."

For public purposes, though, Bush and Cheney depicted Iraq being on the right course and potentially jeopardized by a Democratic victory. In his address the night of September 1, Cheney enthusiastically took on the other ticket. "Senator Kerry's liveliest disagreement is with himself," he said to chants of "flip-flop, flip-flop!" "His back-and-forth reflects a habit of indecision and sends a message of confusion. And it is all part of a pattern. He has, in the last several years, been for the No Child Left Behind Act—and against it. He has spoken in favor of the North American Free Trade Agreement—and against it. He is for the Patriot Act—and against it. Senator Kerry says he sees two Americas. He makes the whole thing mutual—America sees two John Kerrys."

For Bush's speech the next night, aides wanted to strike a more measured tone. Ed Gillespie, the Republican National Committee chairman, was worried about "Bush fatigue"—not the blinding hate felt by many liberals who were never going to vote for him, but a certain weariness among everyday voters. Gillespie suggested the president talk about seeking "a new term" rather than "a second term," to sound fresh rather than more of the same.

As he practiced his speech in a hotel suite, though, Bush kept tripping over a line about holding "the children of the fallen." Invariably, he choked up. However justified he felt the Iraq War was, Bush understood the toll it was taking on families across America. It was the one thing that cracked his Texas bravado.

Maybe it would be safer to just take the line out, someone suggested.

Michael Gerson objected. "Mr. President, we need to do this," Gerson said.

Bush grew snippy. "*We* don't have to do this," he said. "*I* am doing this."

As he stepped onto the stage that night, Bush was greeted by a wave of enthusiasm. He opened with praise for his partner. "I am fortunate to have a superb vice president," he said. "I have counted on Dick Cheney's calm and steady judgment in the difficult days, and I am honored to have him at my side."

As delegates chanted "four more years," Bush outlined what he termed the Ownership Society, ideas like providing tax credits to encourage health savings accounts, allowing workers to invest some of their Social Security payroll taxes in stocks or bonds, and encouraging more home ownership. As a conservative counter to the New Deal and the Great Society, the Ownership Society was intended to give Americans more control to make decisions. Little did he imagine that making it easier for people to buy homes might prove to be a risky venture.

But his main focus was national security, declaring that "freedom is on the march" in places like Iraq and Afghanistan and going directly after Kerry by citing his voted-for-it-before-voting-against-it quote. He mentioned hearing "whatever it takes" at Ground Zero on that wrenching day after the Twin Towers fell. "I will never relent in defending America—whatever it takes," he said. He defended his decision to invade Iraq by recalling that Kerry supported it too, and he linked it to the attack on the city playing host to the convention. "Do I forget the lessons of September the 11th and take the word of a madman?" he asked, referring to Saddam Hussein. "Or do I take action to defend our country? Faced with that choice, I will defend America every time."

He got through the line about the children of the fallen without a problem. After he stepped offstage, Gerson asked how he did it.

"I didn't look at the audience," Bush said. "I just looked up."

Bush had another emotional encounter the next day as he headed out to campaign. At a minor-league baseball stadium in Moosic, Pennsylvania, on September 3, someone in the crowd called out, "Mr. President, we can hear you now!"

The crowd got the reference and cheered, but Bush didn't and apologized for being hoarse. Sitting onstage, Laura Bush looked at the man who had yelled.

"I'm the voice from Ground Zero," he said.

It was Rocco Chierichella, the firefighter who met Bush at the site of the attacks.

Laura whispered in the president's ear, and he turned. "I'll see you later," he told Chierichella.

After the speech, Chierichella and his son were brought into the locker room to meet Bush.

"So you're the guy," Bush said. "I've been using your line for years."

Bush told him he would be in the history books.

Chierichella shrugged. "I couldn't hear you," he said.

Bush shook his hand and grew emotional, wiping tears from his eyes.

"Mr. President, my daughter's going to West Point," the firefighter told him. "Because of you. You changed my life."

Bush shook his head. "No," he said, "*you* changed *my* life."

BUSH AND CHENEY emerged from the convention with the traditional bounce. Karl Rove had left little to chance in building a reelection architecture. From the start, he had set out to fully tap the resources of the federal government within the broad and relatively permissive extent of the law. Other presidential strategists had done much the same over the years, but few as systematically.

Rove oversaw an asset-deployment team that managed high-visibility trips and official grant announcements so as to promote the president's agenda and his Republican allies. Rove's team organized scores of political briefings at federal departments and agencies with election-themed slides. Half of the twenty-two grants released by the Department of Health and Human Services in late September, just weeks before the election, went to targeted states or districts, according to one media analysis; the news release announcing them focused at the top on four recipients, all of which had been highlighted in the political briefings. Secretary of Labor Elaine L. Chao's thirteen official trips in the final weeks before the election all took her to media markets on the political target list, the analysis found. The blending of government and politics triggered investigations by watchdog offices and disgruntled even some of Rove's colleagues. David Kuo, the deputy director of faith-based and community initiatives in the White House, grew alienated when his office volunteered to do roundtables around the country but was then told by a Rove aide to specifically target twenty races during the 2002 midterm elections. In response to the pressure, the office kept a political map with every state shaded according to importance.

Just days after the convention, the campaign faced a tenuous moment. On September 7, the American death toll in Iraq hit one thousand, the vast majority of them taking place after Bush declared major combat operations over in front of the "Mission Accomplished" banner. It was a sobering milestone. But on the campaign trail, Cheney argued that the United States could not afford to give ground.

"It's absolutely essential that eight weeks from today, on November 2nd, we make the right choice," he told supporters in a fiery speech in Des Moines. "Because if we make the wrong choice, then the danger is that we'll get hit again, that we'll be hit in a way that will be devastating."

The line was a sharper articulation of the same argument Bush and Cheney had made for months, that Democrats would return the country to a pre-September 11 mind-set that looked at terrorism as a law enforcement matter rather than a war.

But his stark equation—a vote for Kerry would mean a successful terrorist attack—took it a step further and resulted in gales of protest from the other side. "Dick Cheney's scare tactics crossed the line today, showing once again that he and George Bush will do anything and say anything to save their jobs," John Edwards fired back.

As Cheney flew to his next stop in New Hampshire, cell phones aboard the plane began ringing from campaign headquarters with what-did-he-say questions. Scooter Libby argued that the line was being misread and began quarreling with the stenographer about where a comma should go. Reporters were blamed for blowing it out of proportion, further souring a relationship that had already led Cheney to ban the *New York Times* from Air Force Two and also to try to kick off the Associated Press until he was talked out of it. Anne Womack, his press secretary, was sent into Cheney's cabin to get him to walk back the line. Cheney was irritated. As far as he was concerned, this was just game playing. "That is what I meant," he snapped.

WITH DEBATES APPROACHING, Bush was not as engaged in preparing as four years earlier. A commander in chief in the middle of a war has less time than a challenger. Moreover, Bush was distinctly unenthusiastic about debating and even less so about practicing. The fact that he would go up against Kerry only increased his irritability. Kerry exemplified everything Bush had long despised about the haughty Yale-Eastern-elite culture. "Bush thought Kerry was a pedantic and arrogant flip-flopper and didn't like the Massachusetts senator," as Rove later put it.

Rove worried as he watched Bush glide through debate prep. The president "was rusty," unlike Kerry, who had just emerged from a tough primary battle. Bush misjudged his opponent, telling aides that Kerry would not be overly aggressive because he would want to look presidential. Senator Judd Gregg, who played Al Gore in 2000, put his Democratic mask back on to play Kerry, but he flew to Crawford for prep sessions just three or four times, rather than every week as he had the last time. "You didn't feel the heightened tension or newness or the originality that had to happen with the Gore debates," he recalled. "The president was president. He knew what he wanted to say." Dan Bartlett dubbed this *presidentialitis*—the notion that a president does not need to be prepped, a feeling of "I got this."

Bush arrived in Florida the day before the first debate with a commanding position in the race. The latest Gallup poll showed him with an eight-point lead. The debate could cement that. "If the president does reasonably well, this basically should button down the election," Matthew Dowd concluded. Bush spent part of the day before the evening encounter on September 30 inspecting recent hurricane damage by helicopter and on foot with his brother Jeb. By afternoon, he had returned to his hotel and had a massage to get ready. Only later did advisers come to regret scheduling other activities for the day. Bush was weary.

A couple hours before the debate, the president called Bartlett to his suite. "Now," Bush said, "what do you want me to say about Kerry?"

Bartlett was alarmed. *Houston, we've got a problem*, he thought as he left. He found other members of the campaign team.

"What's wrong?" someone asked.

"I don't think this is going to go well," Bartlett said.

Onstage at the University of Miami that night, Bush found an opponent who quickly got under his skin. Kerry went after the president aggressively, declaring that Bush had made "a colossal error of judgment" in invading Iraq and had "outsourced" the hunt for Osama bin Laden to Afghan warlords. Bush fired back, reminding voters that Kerry had also declared Saddam Hussein a "grave threat" and voted for war.

The exchange flared over the validity of preemptive war. "You have to do it in a way that passes the test," Kerry said, "that passes the global test where your countrymen, your people understand fully why you're doing what you're doing and you can prove to the world that you did it for legitimate reasons."

Bush jumped on that. "I'm not exactly sure what you mean, 'passes the global test,' you take preemptive action if you pass a global test," he said with undisguised scorn. "My attitude is you take preemptive action in order to protect the American people, that you act in order to make this country secure."

The rules required the camera to stay on the candidate who was speaking without reaction shots, but the networks had no intention of obeying a rule they did not negotiate, and the Bush team knew that. Still, his advisers seemed surprised to see a split screen showing the president scowling with disdain as Kerry spoke. After four years in office with a Congress of his own party and a staff that idolized him, Bush had grown unaccustomed to being challenged.

Just as Gore's sighs were off-putting in 2000, so now were Bush's glowers and grimaces. Karen Hughes broke it to him afterward that pundits were offering a harsh judgment.

"They're going to report that you lost the debate," she told him.

"Why?"

"You looked mad."

"I wasn't mad. Tell them that."

"I can't. Because you *did* look mad."

She was not the only one who told him. Rove told him "his dislike for Kerry was making him come across as unlikable." Bartlett, Ken Mehlman, and Mark McKinnon echoed the assessment. Andy Card concluded that "he didn't really want to be at the first debate." Even Laura Bush weighed in. "I don't know what happened," she told him. "You've got to be yourself and you weren't." Even so, it took a review of the pictures to make Bush see. "I don't think I was that irritated," he told a friendly journalist after the election. "My facial expressions must have said that." The polls certainly confirmed the judgment. The eight-point advantage in the Gallup survey disappeared overnight, and suddenly Bush was in a tie. "We came out of that debate and it is a whole new ball game," Dowd concluded. "The performance was a disaster."

CHENEY STARTED DEBATE prep long before Bush did and was determined to help the ticket, but where he was a comforting face in 2000, four years later he had become a forbidding figure to the public. One day after a debate prep session at the vice presidential residence, most of his advisers had drifted off, and Cheney was left with Scooter Libby and Neil Patel. Libby raised the issue that consumed other White House aides but was rarely mentioned around the vice president.

"Sir, have you ever looked at your polls?" Libby asked.

"No, not really," Cheney said, and it seemed possible he really meant it.

"You might want to take a look," Libby said. "They're pretty bad."

"Really? What are they?"

In some polls, his approval rating was below 50 percent.

"You need to remember," Cheney said, "that no one is voting for vice president and that it might help that mine be bad and the president's be a tiny bit better."

"Don't you think during an election that we should work on it a little bit?" Libby asked.

"You've got to remember, no one is voting for the vice president," Cheney repeated. "I really don't care."

Cheney retreated to Jackson Hole for the final debate preparation. He looked up one day to find Dowd, who had flown to Wyoming to see him.

"This is the situation," Dowd told him. "You have to stop the bleeding."

Liz Cheney once again ran debate preparations, and she worried that John Edwards's experience as a trial attorney would make him a formidable opponent. The vice president carved out four or five hours a day to practice. Rob Portman reprised his role as the opposition candidate, and Stuart Stevens was again the moderator. Stevens lightened the mood by asking "insane questions that no one would ever ask," and Cheney gave "the most unbelievable dry answers," recalled Neil Patel. Some in the room thought Cheney did not win the initial practice debates. "In the early ones, Portman did better, and as it went on, Cheney got better and better," said Tevi Troy, another aide. The pressure was on. The night before the debate, Libby told Cheney that it would fall to him to make the case for the Iraq War. Lynne Cheney glared at him with irritation, evidently annoyed that the onus was placed on her husband.

The day before the debate, Cheney went fly-fishing with Portman again, then joined his family for a quiet dinner. He flew on October 5 to Cleveland, where he met Edwards onstage at Case Western Reserve University. He looked down at a note card Liz had given him.

> *Your children and grandchildren will never forget—and will tell their children and grandchildren—everything you have done for this great nation. We love you more than anything. Now go kick some butt.*

If his family was trying to boost him, Democrats were trying to unnerve him. Seated in the audience right in his eyesight was Senator Patrick Leahy, with whom he had skirmished on the Senate floor.

But Cheney held his own, attacking Edwards for inconsistency on the war. Cheney had none of the respect for Edwards that he had had for Joseph Lieberman four years earlier. In Cheney's mind, Edwards was slick and shallow, a presumptuous opportunist, and he did not disguise his contempt.

"Senator, frankly, you have a record in the Senate that's not very distinguished," Cheney said at one point, citing missed meetings and votes. "Now, in my capacity as vice president, I am the president of the Senate, the presiding officer. I'm up in the Senate most Tuesdays when they're in session. The first time I ever met you was when you walked on the stage tonight." Strictly speaking, that was not true. The two had both attended the same National Prayer Breakfast once. But Cheney had made his point: Edwards was not a serious figure.

For Cheney, the most memorable moment of the debate came when the moderator, Gwen Ifill of PBS, asked about his break with Bush over same-sex marriage.

"People ought to be free to choose any arrangement they want," Cheney said. "It's really no one else's business. That's a separate question from the issue of whether or not government should sanction or approve or give some sort of authorization, if you will, to these relationships." That, he said, should be left to the states. But he added that the president set policy for the administration and he supported the president.

When Edwards responded, he mentioned Mary Cheney. "Let me say first that I think the vice president and his wife love their daughter," he began. "I think they love her very much. And you can't have anything but respect for the fact that they're willing to talk about the fact that they have a gay daughter, the fact that they embrace her."

In the audience, Mary Cheney was steaming. *He thinks they love me?* "What gave him the right to use my sexual orientation to try to score political points?" she later asked. She caught Edwards glancing at her, and she mouthed a phrase that had become famous in her family and hoped he could read her lips: "Go fuck yourself." Her mother and sister stuck their tongues out at him.

Edwards went on to say that he and Kerry agreed that marriage is between a man and a woman but they supported partnership benefits for gay couples and criticized Bush for trying to "use the Constitution to divide this country."

When Ifill asked Cheney to respond, he said, "Well, Gwen, let me simply thank the senator for the kind words he said about my family and our daughter. I appreciate that very much."

"That's it?" Ifill asked.

"That's it."

With that, Cheney had fulfilled Dowd's assignment. The slide in the polls was arrested.

THE DAY AFTER the debate, October 6, Charles Duelfer, who had taken over from David Kay as head of the Iraq Survey Group, produced his final report on the hunt for weapons of mass destruction. Just as Kay had, Duelfer concluded Saddam Hussein had no such weapons and was making no concerted effort to develop them. Hussein's illicit weapons capability "was essentially destroyed in 1991" and had not been reestablished. Indeed, Duelfer and his twelve-hundred-member team determined that Iraq, under pressure from the United Nations, had destroyed its last factory capable of producing militarily significant quantities of biological weapons in 1996. And they found no evidence of any attempt to buy uranium from Niger or anywhere else after 1991.

Hussein did harbor a desire to eventually re-create a weapons program after convincing the United Nations to lift sanctions, believing such arms had saved his regime during the war with Iran, deterred the United States from pressing on to Baghdad during the Gulf War, and intimidated Shiite opponents. And he had corrupted the UN oil-for-food program, essentially buying off key French and Russian officials. While Hussein wanted to pursue a nuclear capability, Duelfer reported the Iraqi dictator was focused mainly on ballistic missiles and tactical chemical weapons, and his interest was driven not by conflict with the United States but by fear of Iran, his principal enemy in the region. But this was all notional; there was "no formal written strategy or plan for the revival of WMD after sanctions," Duelfer wrote in the nine-hundred-page report.

Bush and Cheney, naturally, focused on the parts reporting Hussein's ambitions for destructive weapons, but the main message was that the war had been justified on false intelligence. "U.S. Report Finds Iraqis Eliminated Illicit Arms in 90's," read the front-page headline in the *New York Times*. "U.S. 'Almost All Wrong' on Weapons," said the *Washington Post*.

Coming less than a month before the election, the report was politically damaging and exacerbated tensions between the White House and the CIA. Scooter Libby, Stephen Hadley, and other advisers to Bush and Cheney were convinced the CIA was leaking information to the opposition and the media in a deliberate attempt to influence the election. The friction grew so sharp that John McLaughlin, who had stepped in as acting director after Tenet's resignation, personally investigated. "I did some real homework in the agency, and there was no organized campaign there to undermine his election," he said years later. "I am absolutely convinced of that." He told Bush that by phone. "We at CIA are not trying to bring you down," McLaughlin told the president.

Bush met Kerry for their second debate, on October 8, at Washington University in St. Louis. This time it was a town-hall-style format with

Missourians posing the questions, and Bush had worked harder to prepare. Right before going onstage, he asked to be left alone for fifteen minutes to collect himself, a rarity for a president who enjoyed company. It clearly helped. Joining Kerry before the cameras, Bush focused on containing any visible sense of annoyance. Still, as he roamed the stage, he mixed folksy charm with arguments that at times seemed too loud for the medium. Kerry responded by appearing as low-key as possible, although almost to the point of lacking passion.

A focus group convened by the Bush-Cheney campaign in Orlando found that "John Kerry exceeded voters' expectations in the two debates" and was seen as "more likeable, knowledgeable and charismatic than expected." A memo summarizing the focus group said "voters were disappointed by the President in the first debate" but "give him better marks for the second debate and many thought he came across more human than Kerry." For the third debate, Bush's team concluded that "we want to remind voters Kerry's not worth the risk. They know Bush. They don't like the war in Iraq, but they at least know Bush is a decent guy and he stands up for what he believes."

BUSH ARRIVED AT Arizona State University for the final encounter on October 13 accompanied by John McCain. Their events together were awkward. Despite their reconciliation, McCain was reported to have flirted with becoming Kerry's running mate. And the chemistry was still off. McCain kept trying to pump Bush up, sometimes to extremes. In the green room before the Arizona debate, McCain egged Bush on, telling him, "You're going to be great" and "This is how you've got to hit him back." Bush, looking for calm before the televised clash, found McCain's hyper boxing-coach performance off-putting. "Man, is he spun up," Bush marveled to aides afterward.

The Cheneys watched the debate on television at a hotel in Pittsburgh. When the moderator, Bob Schieffer of CBS News, asked if homosexuality was a choice, Kerry, like John Edwards the week before, raised Mary Cheney. "I think if you were to talk to Dick Cheney's daughter, who is a lesbian, she would tell you that she's being who she was, she's being who she was born as," Kerry said.

In her hotel room, Mary looked up from the travel schedule she had been working on and shouted at the television. "You son of a bitch," she said.

Then she went down to her parents' suite to watch the rest of the debate with them. Her mother and sister were equally incensed. "A complete and total sleazeball," fumed Liz. Lynne was so hot she finally retreated to the bedroom to keep from distracting her husband, who was trying to concentrate on the rest of the debate. "Mom was especially furious that John Kerry had just used her child to try to score political points," Liz recalled. "She couldn't quit talking about it, she was so mad."

The Cheneys grew even more incensed afterward when they heard Mary Beth Cahill, the Kerry campaign manager, say on television that Mary was "fair game." The vice president huddled with his family and advisers to decide whether to hit back. The vice president called Steve Schmidt.

"Well, sir, as long as Mary's comfortable with it, I don't see any reason not to," Schmidt said.

Mary overheard. "Make it hurt," she told her father.

Lynne jumped in and said she wanted to address the post-debate rally downstairs, although she had not been scheduled to speak.

Schmidt asked what she would say.

"That this is a man with a dark hole in his soul," she said. "He can have all the fake suntans and manicures he wants, but deep down inside he's rotten."

There was a long pause on the phone, and the campaign staffers on the other end could almost be heard shifting uncomfortably.

Scooter Libby spoke up. Let's just be smart about this, he said.

"She's my daughter and I'm angry and I'm going to say it," Lynne said.

Libby pulled Liz aside and asked her to talk with her mother.

"Look," Lynne said. "I know I'm not going to be stupid. I'm under control. But I'm mad and I'm going to say something about it."

Appearing before the crowd downstairs, the vice president's wife let loose. "I did have a chance to assess John Kerry once more," she said. "And the only thing I could conclude is this is not a good man. This is not a good man. And, of course, I am speaking as a mom and a pretty indignant mom. This is not a good man. What a cheap and tawdry political trick."

Dick Cheney saved his criticism for the next day, October 14, when he addressed a rally of twenty-five hundred supporters at Florida Gulf Coast University in Fort Myers. "You saw a man who will say and do anything in order to get elected," Cheney said. "And I am not speaking just as a father here—though I am a pretty angry father. But I'm also speaking as a citizen."

The Cheneys, both out of genuine anger and with a measure of political calculation, had successfully punished Kerry for bringing Mary into the campaign. Kerry issued a tepid written statement that neither reaffirmed his comment nor apologized for it. "I love my daughters," he said. "They love their daughter. I was trying to say something positive about the way strong families deal with this issue." Elizabeth Edwards, wife of the vice presidential candidate, was less measured, accusing Lynne Cheney of being embarrassed by her daughter. "I think that it indicates a certain degree of shame with respect to her daughter's sexual preferences," she told an interviewer. The public, though, sided with Cheney. He called the bump in the polls the "Mary Cheney bounce."

THE TEAM WAS confident, even cocky, heading into the final stretch. Bush and Cheney had defined Kerry as unreliable. Television ads showed an effete challenger windsurfing one way and then the other. A group of Kerry's war colleagues backed by conservative allies of the president and calling themselves Swift Boat Veterans for Truth challenged his war record with over-the-top attacks that, while factually suspect, took a toll on his national security credentials in a national security election. A counterattack on Bush's own record in the Air National Guard backfired when Dan Rather of CBS News had to retract a story based on forged documents.

By the time Bush landed in Jacksonville, Florida, on October 23, Karl Rove was feeling so sure of victory that he found the White House press pool and started joking around off the record. Rove said he had Osama bin Laden in his basement ready as a last-minute surprise, but the terrorist leader was a real pain, only bathed once a week, ate all the caramel popcorn, and did not even let the dogs out during the day.

No one was laughing a week later when bin Laden appeared in a videotape aired on Al Jazeera. Bin Laden, who had eluded American intelligence since Tora Bora, took on Bush, rebutting his claim that al-Qaeda attacked the United States because it hated freedom—if that were it, he told voters, ask Bush "why we did not attack Sweden." He hinted al-Qaeda would stage another devastating attack if Bush was reelected. "Despite entering the fourth year after September 11, Bush is still deceiving you and hiding the truth from you and therefore the reasons are still there to repeat what happened."

Bush retreated to a private room to discuss the impact. Eventually, he decided it would work in his favor by reminding voters how much bin Laden hated him. But advisers fell into a sharp debate about how to respond. John Ashcroft, with support from Donald Rumsfeld, wanted to raise the nation's threat level. Tom Ridge thought no intelligence justified it. *Is this about security or politics?* he wondered. "A vigorous, some might say dramatic, discussion ensued," he recalled. Ridge had his aide Susan Neely call Air Force One to ask Dan Bartlett to appeal to the president.

Bartlett got the point and raised it with Bush. "I don't have to tell you," Bartlett said, referring to the danger of politicizing national security.

"I know," Bush said. Soon word came down: the threat level would not be raised.

Operating from strength, Cheney engaged in a bit of psychological fake out by making a last-minute foray to Hawaii. While it was a Democratic bastion, polls suggested Republicans were within striking distance, and the campaign brain trust decided that a surprise visit would throw off the opposition. There was a reason no national candidate had campaigned in Hawaii in decades: it's a long flight for little electoral gain. But Lynne Cheney suggested it would be worth it, and the vice president agreed.

On October 31, Cheney started his day in Toledo, Ohio, then flew to Romulus, Michigan; Fort Dodge, Iowa; and Los Lunas, New Mexico, before heading out across the Pacific to hold a late-night rally in Honolulu, where he gamely wore a lei. After just two hours on the ground, he boarded his plane and took off again for Jackson Hole. Over twenty-four hours, he logged nearly eleven thousand miles and eighteen and a half hours in the air.

Still, more than ten thousand people showed up at 11:00 p.m. for the Hawaii rally, possibly his biggest crowd of the campaign. He and his team felt pumped up. Everything, they felt, was in hand.

19

"The election that will never end"

President Bush woke up on Election Day at the ranch and stepped out into the overcast but relatively warm Texas morning. This was the day that would determine whether he would surpass his father by winning a coveted second term or go down in history as a transitional figure who only got into office after a fluky recount. He had rallied the nation after catastrophe, then plunged it into a war on wrong assumptions. Now came the verdict, what he would later call his "accountability moment."

He braced himself for a long day and headed to the Crawford Fire Department to vote. Then he got back into his motorcade for the short ride to the airport.

On the way, he called Matthew Dowd, his chief strategist. "What is going to happen tonight?" he asked.

"You should win," Dowd said. "It will be close, but you should be fine."

His strategists considered Ohio and Florida critical. If he won both, he would be reelected. Just hours earlier, some time after one o'clock in the morning, Karl Rove and Ken Mehlman had tried to figure a last-minute way to get him to both states on Election Day, but Rove checked with Joe Hagin and discovered it was logistically impossible.

"Only one," Rove told Mehlman. "You decide."

"Ohio," Mehlman said.

So Bush flew to Ohio, and his staff set up satellite interviews with Florida television stations. Even then, technical difficulties made it hard to get connected, and Bush grew irritated. "What is Karl making me do on Election Day?" he grumbled.

Bush got back on the plane and headed for Washington, anxious for information. As the plane descended toward Andrews Air Force Base, Rove heard from Sara Taylor, one of his deputies back at campaign headquarters outside Washington. The first exit polls were horrible. Taylor read them over the phone to Rove as matter-of-factly as she could without emotion, but that did not soften the impact. Rove's hand was shaking as he cradled the phone in his ear and tried to scribble down the numbers on a note card on his knee. Dan Bartlett held the paper for him.

The numbers made no sense. They were down in states where they should be up. They were even further down in states where they should at least be competitive. The exit polls had them losing by 18 percentage points in Pennsylvania and by several points in Florida and Ohio; they were fighting just to win stalwart states like South Carolina, Virginia, Mississippi, and Alabama. *How could that be?* If these numbers were right, they were heading for a landslide defeat. As Rove read the numbers aloud, Bush "felt like he had just punched me in the stomach."

Everyone in the cabin was shocked. "That doesn't make any sense—losing Virginia?" said Karen Hughes, who had been traveling with Bush. An upset Condoleezza Rice rushed out and took refuge in the restroom, unable to look Bush in the eye.

Bush was deflated. "Look, if it is what it is, we'll deal with it," he said. "But I don't believe it. We've been here before."

He began working his way around the plane, thanking aides for their hard work. "Whatever happens, I love you guys," he said.

Awash in emotion, he ended up thanking Nicolle Devenish, his communications director, twice. She was crying, as was Mark McKinnon, the media consultant.

Bush phoned Ken Mehlman back at headquarters to learn more. Mehlman ran through the numbers. They were grim. But then Mehlman began pulling them apart.

"Here's why I think it's wrong," he said. Mehlman was a data-driven person, not given to trusting his gut. So he gave his evidence to the president for why the exit polls must be mistaken.

"This is really good," Bush said, momentarily encouraged. "Hold on."

From the plane, the president had the White House switchboard patch in his father, who was waiting back at the mansion.

"Say that again," the president ordered Mehlman, who repeated his analysis.

At the White House and at campaign headquarters, word of the exit polls spread quickly, and a deep depression sank in. Suddenly the spirit and energy of the morning had vanished. Campaign advisers found Dowd in his office despondent, figuratively if not literally in the fetal position, refusing to go downstairs to brief reporters. "He was in a dark place," Taylor recalled.

She went down instead and gamely argued that it was too early to judge. "A lot of people got into an incredible funk," she remembered. "At that moment, it looked real, and people thought, 'Oh my God, we're losing.'"

Despite Mehlman's reassurance, Bush thought so too, and he was gloomy as the plane landed at Andrews, not sure what to think but increasingly worried that he had lost reelection just as his father had. As he prepared to disembark, he told aides, "Whatever happens, we left it all on the field."

Hughes reminded him that everyone was looking to him, so he should keep his game face on. "There are people still voting," she told him. "When you come down the stairs of Air Force One, smile and wave."

Bush complied, smiling and waving for the cameras, but he felt as if he were "in a daze" as he crossed the tarmac to Marine One. The short helicopter flight to the White House seemed to take an hour. He put his happy face on again as he made the short walk across the South Lawn into the mansion. As soon as he crossed the threshold and out of camera range, aides noticed the upward curve of his mouth instantly turn down.

He headed upstairs to the residence, unprepared to face aides who had come with him so far on the journey, only to lose like this. He "moped around the Treaty Room" and tried to gird himself for what could be a crushing night. Just as John Quincy Adams, the only other son of a president to reach the White House, lost reelection, now it looked as if George W. Bush were again following in his footsteps.

ON BOARD Air Force Two, Vice President Cheney maintained more equanimity as Mary got the same bad news from Sara Taylor. His family members, especially Lynne, "were feeling a little sick to our stomachs." But the vice president felt jaded about polls and was willing to believe these were as messed up as the ones in 2000. "I blew it off," he said.

From a last stop in Wisconsin, Cheney flew back to Washington in time to host an election night party at the vice presidential mansion starting at 6:00 p.m. Like Hughes, Lynne kept telling herself to smile, lest her face give away her anxiety. Many of their closest friends came, including Donald Rumsfeld, Alan Simpson, and Nick Brady and their wives, as well as Mary Matalin. Even after four years of partnership, Cheney and Bush were spending the most critical evening of their tenure in their separate spheres. There was the Cheney party, and there was the Bush party. Cheney would join the president for the official declaration of victory, but until then he had his own crowd.

At the White House, Rove set up a war room he called his "bat cave" in the Family Dining Room, complete with two large-screen televisions and a bank of phones and four computers. Rice, oddly bereft of anything to do, helped Rove track key states. Bush fired up a big cigar and from time to time wandered down to check on the latest or called Rove from upstairs in the residence, where he was joined by family and friends for dinner. Later waves of exit polls had narrowed the implausible Kerry leads but still showed Bush losing nearly every battleground state. As the evening drew on, Rove compared county-by-county numbers from 2000 and was certain the exit polls were wrong. Rove, Mehlman, and a recovered Dowd berated network executives about the obvious flaws in the data.

Actual vote counts proved closer to Rove's expectations, and Bush and Cheney began piling up the states they needed. After the early gloom, it looked as if they might pull it off after all. Sometime after 11:00 p.m., Bush went downstairs to Rove's bat cave for an update. "This is the election that will never end," the president moaned. But ten minutes later, ABC News called Florida for Bush and Cheney. The source of so much consternation four years earlier was now in the bag, and more of the president's friends and relatives crowded into the war room. Rove was annoyed since "some of them were a little sloshed and in the way," and he sharply told one Bush pal to stop bothering his staff or "get the hell out."

Andy Card called Mary Beth Cahill, the Kerry campaign manager, to gently sound her out. Should they expect a call from the senator? No, she said.

At 12:41 a.m., Fox News, this time without Bush's cousin, called Ohio for Bush and Cheney, putting them an inch away from an Electoral College victory. Bush, back upstairs chewing on a cigar, got the news from Rove over the phone. With any of several outstanding states, they would go over the top.

The president walked out of his bedroom, found Laura, and hugged and kissed her. "He just looked relieved that it was over," said Eric Draper, the photographer.

But it was not. Around 1:00 a.m., the Cheneys bundled into a motorcade and headed down to the White House, assuming they would soon go to the victory celebration at the Ronald Reagan Building and International Trade Center. But once they arrived, they learned it was not that clear. The networks, burned from 2000, were not calling the race, and Democrats showed no signs of conceding. Card called Cahill again after 1:00 a.m. "We're getting different numbers," she said. Soon after, she announced to the media that Democrats would insist on counting provisional ballots in Ohio. Rove calculated there were not nearly enough such ballots to overcome the Republican lead, but for a while Bush and Cheney feared a repeat of 2000. A plane of operatives and lawyers, including Sara Taylor and Mehlman's brother, was dispatched in the middle of the night to Ohio.

Bush worried about his father. The elder Bush might have been more nervous than anyone, anxious about the prospect of his son facing the same ordeal he had a dozen years earlier. At one point, the eighty-year-old former president distracted himself by launching into a long conversation with Cheney's granddaughter Katie, who was ten years old.

"Katie, you're the youngest person here and I'm the oldest," he told her. "We need to talk."

As the night wore on, the president urged his father to go to sleep. "Go on, nothing's going to happen," he said. "I'm going to win."

With no concession in sight, the Bush and Cheney advisers debated whether to go out and declare victory anyway. Rove, Card, Michael Gerson, and Jim Francis, a close friend of the president's, argued that they should. Why should they be held hostage to the media if the numbers were on their side? The longer they let this drag on, the bigger the risk of Democrats turning it into another Florida. But Nicolle Devenish had been secretly keeping open a back channel with Michael McCurry, a former Clinton White House press secretary who was advising Kerry. She knew McCurry and trusted him. Hold off, he urged. Kerry and Edwards would get there. After what happened in 2000, he said, they just needed time to satisfy themselves there was no real issue in Ohio.

Hughes, Matalin, Dan Bartlett, and Stephen Hadley urged Bush to heed the advice.

"You cannot go out there and put the crown on your own head," Bartlett told Bush. "You just can't do it."

Crucially, Laura agreed. "George, you can't go out there," she said. "Wait until you've been declared the winner." He agreed.

Cheney urged his family to return home and rest, but they refused. The vice president sank into the chair in his office, put his feet up on the desk, and fell asleep. Mary claimed the couch in his office, and her partner, Heather Poe, stretched out between a couple of armchairs. Liz found a sofa in the Roosevelt Room and lay down there. Lynne headed to the White House medical unit, found a pillow and blanket, and slept on an examining table. They did not leave the White House until 6:00 a.m., when they headed home for showers.

THE NEXT MORNING, November 3, dawned with little more clarity. Bush woke around 7:00 a.m. after just two hours of sleep and made it to the Oval Office by 8:00 a.m. His parents had to return to Houston. Advisers discussed how to pressure Democrats without overplaying their hand. Card called James Baker, the man who had secured the 2000 victory, and asked him to see if Vernon Jordan, a prominent Democratic lawyer who had handled debate negotiations for Kerry, could get the challenger to concede. Baker tracked Jordan down at the famed Amen Corner at the Augusta National Golf Club and forwarded the request. Jordan made the call, but suspected Kerry was already getting ready to concede. Bush and Bartlett called Devenish from the Oval Office, telling her to call McCurry and figure out what was going on. She got McCurry on the line. Don't worry, he said. "Kerry is calling now."

While Bush sat in the Oval Office with close advisers waiting for the call, well-wishers began making their way to the White House. Among them was Rumsfeld, who showed up "grinning ear to ear," as Scott McClellan recalled it, to congratulate the reelected president. Rumsfeld knew his future in a second term was uncertain, and Bush saw the visit in that context. "That was a job interview," Bush told aides immediately after Rumsfeld left.

At 11:02 a.m., the president's personal secretary, Ashley Kavanaugh, popped into the Oval Office. "Mr. President, I have Senator Kerry on the line."

Bush picked up the phone. It was a brief conversation but civil. "You were an admirable, worthy opponent," Bush told Kerry. "You waged one tough campaign. I hope you are proud of the effort you put in. You should be."

Just like that, he had won. He had defied the odds, the exit polls, the pundits, and even history. He had achieved what his father could not, entering the elite pantheon of two-term presidents, just the fifteenth incumbent to be elected a second time in a row. It was hardly a landslide; he won with 50.7 percent of the vote to Kerry's 48.3 percent, the smallest margin of any reelected president. But he was the first presidential candidate since his father's election in 1988 to win an absolute majority, and it came without the searing asterisk of 2000. The margin was stronger in the Electoral College, where Bush picked up 286 votes to Kerry's 251. Moreover, he was the first president since 1936 to be reelected to a second term with his party increasing its hold over both houses of Congress. He improved his showing over 2000 among Latinos, Jews, women, voters over sixty, and those without high school degrees. Bush won big among those who named terrorism or moral values as their top issue, and voters in surveys gave him credit for honesty, strong leadership, religious faith, and clear stances on the issues. While Bush lost ground among independents, the base-turnout efforts had succeeded in increasing the conservative share of the voting electorate from 29 percent in 2000 to 34 percent in 2004. Still, buried in the numbers were ominous signs. Just 51 percent of Americans still supported the decision to go to war in Iraq. Kerry won lopsidedly among voters who named Iraq their biggest issue.

The most important result for Bush and Cheney, though, was legitimacy. Now they would have four more years, enough time to finish what they had started in Iraq and bring dramatic change at home as well. Bush already had ideas about how to use the momentum. As he absorbed the news, he exhaled and teared up as he hugged advisers who had come on the journey with him.

"We're going to have fun in the next term," he promised Bartlett. "We're going to have a blast."

He called Laura in the residence to let her know. And then he opened the door and made his way out into the hallway.

"Where's the vice president?" he called out.

Someone told him Cheney was in the Situation Room and went to get him. Bush lingered for a few moments in the corridor waiting and then saw Cheney approach.

"Congratulations, Dick!" Bush said ebulliently.

"Congratulations, Mr. President," Cheney responded more formally.

Bush couldn't help but smile at his famously stiff partner. He stuck his hand out. "I know you're not a big fan of hugs, so we'll just shake hands," the president said.

At 3:00 p.m., the two took the stage at the Ronald Reagan Building for their delayed victory celebration. Cheney lavished praise on Bush. "He's a man of deep conviction, and personal kindness," Cheney told the audience. "His leadership is wise and firm and fearless. Those are the qualities that Americans like in a president—and those are the qualities we will need for the next four years."

Bush had kind words for Cheney as well. "The vice president serves America with wisdom and honor, and I'm proud to serve beside him," Bush said. He spoke for just ten minutes, reiterating his campaign promises and vowing to bring the country together. "A new term is a new opportunity to reach out to the whole nation," he said. "We have one country, one Constitution and one future that binds us. And when we come together and work together, there is no limit to the greatness of America."

IT WAS A heady moment for Bush and Cheney. "Everybody was buoyant," recalled Frederick Jones, who worked at the National Security Council. "People were excited. The president sensed that he could achieve his goals, and there was an optimism."

Bush showed up the next day, November 4, at Bartlett's communications meeting to thank the staff. He singled out Scott McClellan, the press secretary known for his loyalty and tight lips. "I want to especially thank Scotty for saying," Bush said with a waggish pause, "nothing!"

Later that morning, he convened the cabinet and thanked them as well. But he also signaled that some of them would not be sticking around. "I expect there to be lots of rumors and speculation about changes in the cabinet for our second term," he said. "Well, a few changes are very likely, but I haven't had time to think about them yet."

Cheney, who usually remained quiet in meetings like this, took the opportunity to reflect on what had changed in four years. "I remember our conversation coming off the recount of 2000 about whether to trim the sails," he said. "You said it was not an option, and it paid off. This time around, the mandate was clear."

In this case, the mandate included Iraq and Afghanistan. Bush mentioned that he had spoken with Iraqi leaders and they were relieved at the election victory.

"They were toast if you lost," offered Donald Rumsfeld.

"*French* toast," Bush joked.

He did not say so in front of the cabinet, but Bush was already toying with an expansive vision for the second term. He had been talking more about bringing freedom and democracy to the Middle East, an idea that he had raised in speeches even before the invasion of Iraq but that took on greater resonance as the weapons rationale for the war fell apart. Now he was ready to embrace it as the central mission of his presidency, a way of laying down a historical marker that would give definition to his tenure and at the same time provide a fresh ideological underpinning to the war on terror beyond simply killing extremists before they could kill Americans. An optimistic, forward-leaning idealistic call, he felt, would be more inviting for people on both sides of the aisle at home and for skeptical governments abroad.

After the cabinet meeting, he pulled aside Michael Gerson, who was thinking about either leaving or taking on a different role in the second term.

"I hear you're thinking about what you want to do next," Bush said, "but will you help me with my inaugural?"

Of course, Gerson said.

"I want it to be the freedom speech," Bush said. He wanted to "plant a flag" for democracy around the world.

Bush gave a hint of the scale of his new ambition a little while later when he met the White House press corps for his first postelection news conference. "I earned capital in the campaign, political capital," he said exuberantly. "And now I intend to spend it."

20

"Not a speech Dick Cheney would give"

President Bush headed to Camp David to rest after the long campaign and think about his second term. He had gone full tilt for weeks, crisscrossing the country, working endless rope lines, giving the same speech day in and day out, and hitting up a long parade of well-heeled donors. He was ready for a break. He could also use a little time to reflect.

Tellingly, the advisers he invited to join him for part of the weekend were Condoleezza Rice and Andy Card, not the vice president. While Bush had put Cheney in charge of the transition before the first term, he planned to run his own transition to the second. He would consult with Cheney about policy and personnel, but he was not outsourcing them. He had definite ideas, some of which Cheney would agree with, but Bush felt no need to seek concurrence on the ones where he would not.

One thing he needed to do was to overhaul his national security team. The fractiousness of the first term had bothered him for years, and now he had an opportunity to do something about it. Since Colin Powell had told him long ago that he expected to leave after the election, Bush decided he would take advantage of the offer. He admired Powell but understood that he "wasn't fully on board with my philosophy and policies." Cheney supported a change. The vice president considered Powell, his once-trusted sidekick during the first Bush presidency, an increasingly disruptive force who handled policy differences by leaking and undermining the administration while building himself up as some sort of realist hero tilting at the neoconservative hard-liners. From Cheney's point of view, Powell, Richard Armitage, and their team were essentially mounting an "insurgency against the rest of the national security team," as Stephen Yates, a foreign policy adviser to the vice president, put it. "They felt the need to go after the right-wing nut jobs, as they endearingly referred to us," Yates said. "We did not have a similar campaign to go after the left-wing nut jobs, or the State Department folks or the Powell-Armitage folks." In that context, Cheney concluded, Powell's departure "was for the best." The feeling was mutual. To Powell and his team, Cheney and Rumsfeld had formed what Lawrence Wilkerson, the secretary's chief of staff, called a "secretive, little-known cabal" intent on subverting the process to advance a radical agenda. "Powell really thought that Cheney and Rumsfeld were treasonous," said a White House official, "and Cheney and Rumsfeld really thought Powell was treasonous."

Cheney might not have grasped that removing a rival would elevate an even more powerful one. To replace Powell, Bush settled on Rice. Unlike Powell, Rice, as everyone knew, had the president's ear, and she would have the opportunity to transform State into a vehicle for Bush's policies instead of an outpost of resistance. In joining the cabinet, she would finally be freed from the facilitator role she played as national security adviser, making her more of a peer of the vice president than simply a staff person. If he had any qualms, Cheney knew better than to express them. Bush was announcing his decision, not asking him about it. "He had thought about it, and this is the way he wanted to go," Cheney recalled.

Rice had a relationship with Bush like no other adviser. She worked out with him, had dinner with him and Laura in the residence, and spent weekends with them at Camp David. He trusted her implicitly, and she made clear she had no agenda other than his. They were so close that in a strange slip at a dinner party with Washington journalists, some around the table heard the unmarried Rice start to refer to Bush as "my husb—" before catching herself. Rice later denied it and in any case, few if anyone thought their relationship was in any way improper; it seemed more like a big-brother, little-sister connection. "She was treated like the kind of lonely bachelor girl," said one top official who worked with her. Over lunch one day in the first term, Rice told Christine Todd Whitman, "I can count on one hand the days when I have not spoken to the president over the last three years." As Whitman later reflected, "She didn't have a life. Her life was all about that."

The bond between the Texas cowboy and the Stanford Russia scholar confounded many around them. "He was very wary about intellectuals," said David Gordon, a top intelligence official who worked for Rice. "Intellectuals always had to prove something with Bush. And that's why the relationship between Bush and Condi is so interesting because Condi is a serious intellectual. She has all of these other interests obviously. She's a Renaissance woman completely. But she's an intellectual, yet she had developed this really fantastic relationship with the president."

For years, people speculated about her sway over Bush. She told another friend it was the other way around. "People don't understand," she said. "It's not my exercising influence over him. I'm internalizing his world." But if she proved adept at channeling Bush, she was a figure of great frustration to other members of the team who thought she was too eager to erase differences and create false consensus rather than bring difficult choices to the president. She had not been able to manage the sharp rivalries in the war cabinet. Powell thought she should have cracked down on Rumsfeld; Rumsfeld thought she should have cracked down on Powell. And she found herself outmaneuvered by Cheney, who bypassed her on the Kyoto treaty and military commissions.

"I personally favor an NSC and national security process not where you try to bridge everyone's difference and create a blended conclusion but rather taking the different options, different approaches, different views, shoving them up to the president, and having him make a decision," Rumsfeld said later. "That's the healthiest way because people then will salute and go about doing their business. If you have extended delays or you try to compromise different opinions, sometimes you end up with a solution that's worse than either of the options."

Through it all, Rice had somehow escaped blame for the failings of the Iraq War. "I was struck by how deft she is at protecting her reputation," noted Scott McClellan. "No matter what went wrong, she was somehow able to keep her hands clean, even when the problems related to matters under her direct purview," such as the missing weapons, the sixteen words, and inadequate postwar planning. "And in private, she complemented and reinforced Bush's instincts rather than challenging or questioning them."

TO PUT THE changes in place, Bush dropped the news on Rice at Camp David on the afternoon of November 5. "I want you to be secretary of state," he told her.

Rice said she was honored but would need to talk about it first. While hoping he would not take it as criticism, she said they had a lot of "repair work to do with the allies" and would need "to reaffirm the primacy of diplomacy in our foreign policy."

In effect, she was saying, his approach to the outside world had to evolve away from the perception of a unilateral, preemption-minded cowboy who did not care what others thought. She considered that a myth that fundamentally misunderstood Bush, but she also realized that the image was powerful and a major obstacle. Cheney in particular had generated suspicion and hostility unnecessarily. It was time, in her view, to put aside the vice president's posture and return to a more constructive foreign policy like that of the president's father, although she never put it that way publicly. What she did say to Bush was that the new approach would mean, for example, a renewed commitment to resolving the Israeli-Palestinian dispute and establishing a Palestinian state. He was skeptical but agreed.

Rice also insisted on a clear path. "I don't intend to spend my energy sparring with Don," she said of Rumsfeld. "I'm going to lead U.S. foreign policy, and I don't need his input."

Bush seemed taken aback but agreed.

The real question was whether it was time for Rumsfeld to go. Card thought so and urged Bush to think about it. He had a long list of potential successors. Bush was open to the idea. "At times, Don frustrated me with his abruptness toward military leaders and members of my staff," he said later. He was not the only one frustrated. Even Rumsfeld's deputy, Paul Wolfowitz, privately complained to a friend that the secretary was driving him crazy. The way Rumsfeld was handling Iraq, the friend remembered Wolfowitz telling him, "was criminal negligence."

Bush authorized Card to contact Frederick Smith from FedEx, his original choice for defense secretary, but Smith's daughter was ill. Bush also reached out to James Baker, but he had already been secretary of state and Treasury secretary and was not interested in a third cabinet position. Bush mulled Senator Joseph Lieberman, the hawkish Democrat whose own presidential campaign in 2004 fizzled because of his support of the Iraq War. But that did not seem like "the right fit." It was not enough to get rid of Rumsfeld; Bush felt he had to have someone ready to take over. And Cheney strongly opposed replacing his mentor, arguing that changing a defense secretary in the middle of a war was unwise and noting that confirmation hearings would invite a fresh public debate about Iraq.

Bush had other changes to make, some easier than others. John Ashcroft had grown distant from the White House during repeated clashes over the war on terror. He had defied Bush and Cheney on the renewal of the National Security Agency surveillance program and opposed holding detainees indefinitely at Guantánamo without some form of due process. He had fought to guarantee some rights for those tried by military commissions and insisted that Zacarias Moussaoui, an al-Qaeda member arrested before September 11, be prosecuted in civilian courts for conspiring with the hijackers. Sensing he was on the outs, Ashcroft drafted a resignation letter by hand and personally delivered it to Bush on Election Day, deliberately circumventing presidential advisers with whom he had clashed. "He was not going to trust these people to spin his resignation and backstab him any more," said Ashcroft's aide Mark Corallo. The feelings were mutual. Bush's aides saw Ashcroft as "a self-promoter and grandstander."

Bush decided to elevate Alberto Gonzales to attorney general and chose Margaret Spellings, his domestic policy adviser who had followed him from Texas, to replace the departing education secretary, Roderick Paige. In picking Rice, Gonzales, and Spellings, Bush was effectively stocking the cabinet with three of his closest advisers, taking firmer hold over the reins of government for the second term.

ALTHOUGH BUSH HAD already asked Rice to become secretary of state, he had not yet asked Powell to vacate the post. The assumption was that he would, but the president never called to ask if the most prominent member of his cabinet was really ready to step down. Instead, he had Card call Powell on Wednesday, November 10, to ask for his letter of resignation by Friday.

Powell was not surprised, and yet he was a little taken aback by the suddenness. "I thought we were going to talk about it," he told Card, "because frankly I don't know when you want me out but there are some very important conferences coming up. So do you want it right away, or should I stay a couple of months?"

Card explained the plan was to package Powell's resignation with other cabinet changes. "We want the letters right away so they can be announced," Card said.

Powell said fine. Was Rumsfeld going too?

Card said he did not know.

"If I go, Don should go," Powell said.

After they hung up, something got lost in translation because Card took the conversation to mean Powell was hedging on leaving. Bush thought this was coming "out of nowhere" and suspected it was born out of Powell's resentment that he was going but Rumsfeld evidently was not. Powell would later deny any desire to stay beyond a couple of months, which he would end up doing anyway while waiting for Rice to be confirmed by the Senate. But the conflicting signals left a sour taste.

Powell told no one other than his wife and Richard Armitage about Card's call and personally typed his resignation letter at home, using it to reclaim ownership of the decision. "As we have discussed in recent months," he began, "I believe that now that the election is over the time has come for me to step down as Secretary of State and return to private life." The letter was delivered Friday, November 12.

Bush was still torn about what to do about his secretary of defense and cast around for advice. Hours after Powell's letter arrived, the president was talking with his visiting cousin, John Ellis. Bush regaled Ellis with stories from the reelection and then escorted him out to his car on the White House grounds. Just as Ellis was about to head out, Bush stopped him.

"What do you think about Rumsfeld?" he asked.

Ellis didn't hesitate. "I think you should fire him," he said. "I don't know the facts, but I know the building," meaning the Pentagon, "will be very happy if you fire him."

"Well," Bush said, "it's something to think about."

Others were volunteering advice. Michael Gerson ventured that it might be worth making some "personnel changes."

Bush understood the code. "You mean Rumsfeld?" he asked.

He did. Gerson acknowledged he could not speak to the strategic issues, but as a matter of public perception Rumsfeld was too identified with the previous approach. "It's going to be hard to get credit for any improvements in Iraq as long as we have the current leadership," he argued.

Recognizing Bush's strong sense of fidelity to those around him, Gerson said there was no betrayal in remaking the team between terms. "It's not disloyalty when someone's been there four years and there's a natural change," said Gerson, who advocated Lieberman as a replacement.

After another weekend mulling options, Bush announced Powell's resignation on Monday, November 15, in a written statement along with those of the secretaries of energy, education, and agriculture and chairman of the Republican National Committee. Powell was treated as just one more replaceable cabinet member. Bush made no public appearance to discuss Powell's departure, instead dispensing his secretary of state with three paragraphs that praised him as "one of the great public servants of our time." The next day, Bush did appear before cameras in the Roosevelt Room to announce Rice's nomination and the elevation of her deputy, Stephen Hadley, to replace her as national security adviser. Powell was not present. Neither was Cheney.

"WE ARE NOT winning."

Bush and Cheney were meeting with the national security team when they heard Richard Armitage's dour account. Armitage was leaving along with Powell, and he could afford to be blunt in his assessment of the downward spiral in Iraq.

Bush was taken aback. "Are we losing?" he asked.

"Not yet," Armitage said, hardly the answer Bush wanted to hear.

In the days after the election, American forces returned to Fallujah, where they had waged a brief assault on Sunni insurgents in April until being called off. Ever since, the city had become a haven for al-Qaeda, brimming with stockpiles of weapons and laced with an elaborate set of booby traps and improvised bombs awaiting any attackers. Perhaps three thousand Iraqi and foreign insurgents were now estimated to be in the desert city.

About fifteen thousand American and British troops, joined by a contingent of Iraqi forces, launched Operation Phantom Fury on November 8, forcing their way into the hornet's nest while up to 90 percent of the city's 300,000 civilians fled. As in April, the political reaction was explosive. The leading Sunni political party withdrew from the government, and Sunni leaders called for a boycott of national elections scheduled for January. Three relatives of Prime Minister Ayad Allawi were kidnapped in Baghdad and threatened with execution unless the operation was halted. In Fallujah, resistance was fierce, and the house-to-house battle would stretch on for weeks, with 2,175 insurgents reported killed, becoming the bloodiest of the Iraq War.

Amid the violence, Iraq was preparing to put together its first elected government. With Allawi's interim government ready to expire, elections were scheduled for January 30, 2005, to seat a parliament that would govern while a permanent constitution was written. Then elections would be held again in December to pick a full-fledged government that would move Iraq into a new era.

But as fall turned to winter and the vote approached, a debate broke out in Washington and Baghdad about whether to postpone it. With American troops clearing out Sunni militants in Fallujah, leaders of the Sunni minority that had dominated Iraq for decades under Saddam Hussein were calling for a boycott of the elections, fearing they would be marginalized by the newly emergent Shiite majority. Some Bush advisers worried about fueling an insurgency already hijacked by al-Qaeda.

Bush instinctively resisted changing a plan once it was set, and he thought giving in to pressure would be a mistake. Grand Ayatollah Ali Sistani, the foremost Shiite cleric, had rejected any talk of delay, and Allawi, also Shiite, had not asked Bush for one. Postponing the vote might be seen as selling out the Shiite majority. So on December 2, Bush sent a message. Asked about the elections during a photo opportunity in the Oval Office, he said, "The elections should not be postponed. It's time for the Iraqi citizens to go to the polls. And that's why we are very firm on the January 30th date."

The same logic finally brought him to a resolution on Rumsfeld. Just as he did not want to change the elections under pressure, he decided not to change his defense secretary under pressure. Uncertainty at the Pentagon, he reasoned, could not help. Besides, he was reluctant to push out someone he considered completely loyal. If the strategy in Iraq was not working, Bush thought, it was his own responsibility, not Rumsfeld's. And Bush respected the secretary's blunt forcefulness and savvy understanding of how Washington worked. It wasn't at all clear that someone else could do a better job of riding herd over a uniformed military that often viewed political leadership as a transient obstacle. Bush aides spread news of his decision the next day, December 3.

The same day, he disclosed his nomination of Bernard Kerik to take over the Department of Homeland Security from Tom Ridge, who was stepping down. Bush wanted a hard charger who could tame the bureaucratic monster still trying to absorb twenty-two agencies. When Rudy Giuliani, the former New York mayor, called to recommend Kerik, his friend and former police commissioner, Bush jumped at the idea. He had met Kerik in the rubble of the World Trade Center and was instantly impressed. Kerik was the sort of tough, colorful character who appealed to Bush. A high school dropout and son of a prostitute apparently killed by her pimp, Kerik became an undercover narcotics detective wearing a ponytail and diamond earrings before joining Giuliani's 1993 campaign as a driver. He grew close to Giuliani, who made him corrections commissioner and then police commissioner. Bush later sent him to Iraq to train security forces.

Bush had kept his decision to put Kerik in the cabinet secret, instructing Alberto Gonzales to vet him personally. It did not take much to uncover a trove of disturbing details about Kerik—various ethical scrapes, a civil lawsuit, a bankruptcy, a get-rich-quick board appointment to a stun-gun firm seeking business with homeland security agencies, not to mention criticism of his management while in Iraq. Most damning of all, the best man at his wedding worked for a New Jersey construction company with alleged Mafia ties that was seeking a big New York City contract and had provided Kerik with gifts, including $165,000 in apartment renovations. Gonzales, facing his own confirmation process for attorney general, grilled Kerik for hours. But in the end, Bush liked Kerik and brushed aside concerns.

It was a revealing miscalculation. In the week after the announcement, a torrent of media stories highlighted Kerik's checkered past, until finally people at Giuliani's firm scouring Kerik's finances discovered he had not paid Social Security taxes for a nanny who apparently was an illegal immigrant. Kerik later said the White House knew about everything that became public except the nanny. So the nanny became the excuse given for pushing Kerik to withdraw on December 10.

The political damage did not last long, but it should have been an alarm bell inside the White House. With reelection behind them, the danger was the sort of hubris that leads a president to believe that a fundamentally flawed nominee could still be pushed through Senate confirmation. Bush privately blamed Giuliani, angry that an ally would foist on him such a manifestly problematic candidate. But the Kerik case was not a situation where the vetting had failed to turn up negative information; to the contrary, it demonstrated that a president at the peak of his power and influence thought he could dismiss such issues and that the rest of Washington would go along.

Bush was not having an easy time finding someone else to become homeland security secretary. Richard Armitage said no. So did Joseph Lieberman, who also turned down the UN ambassadorship. Eventually, Bush and his team settled on Michael Chertoff, who had been the assistant attorney general at the beginning of the administration and was then appointed to a federal appeals court.

AS HE FINISHED the first term, Bush decided to reward three figures who had played important roles. At a lavish East Room ceremony on December 14, he awarded Presidential Medals of Freedom to George Tenet, Jerry Bremer, and Tommy Franks. "These three men symbolize the nobility of public service, the good character of our country and the good influence of America on the world," Bush declared before draping the medals around their necks. The decision shocked Washington. The three awardees, critics were quick to point out, had been at the heart of the biggest mistakes of the Iraq War—the false intelligence, the heavy-handed occupation, and a postwar plan more intent on pulling troops out than properly securing the country.

In one sense, it demonstrated a president loyal to his people, determined to recognize their patriotism, dedication, and endless hours in service of their country, and unwilling to blame them for errors. In another sense, it was the act of a president fresh off reelection feeling empowered and a little bit defiant. Let the critics wag. He had political capital. And perhaps there was just a bit of calculation as well, keeping three critical players in the fold. Just a week earlier, Tenet had signed a book contract reportedly worth more than $4 million. Given his bitterness, Bush and Cheney had every reason to worry Tenet might come after them in print. Instead, a couple of months after the medal ceremony, Tenet put the book project on hold for a while.

Just three days later, Bush had another task left over from the first term. On December 17, he signed legislation restructuring the nation's spy agencies, a response to two intelligence breakdowns of epic proportions. The legislation passed Congress only after the leaders of the 9/11 Commission, Thomas Kean and Lee Hamilton, went to Cheney asking for him to intervene. He agreed. "You won't hear anything about what I'm doing," he told them, "but that's when I'm most effective." The final bill centralized the sixteen intelligence agencies under a single director of national intelligence, but with billions of dollars and bureaucratic control at stake the measure emerged only after the new position was undercut even before it was filled. Rumsfeld, whose Pentagon controlled most intelligence resources, was unwilling to surrender them. How could a cabinet secretary run his department, he asked, if he did not control the spending of the agencies within it? "The result would be a train wreck," he had written in a memo to Bush during the legislative debate, "or you and your successors will have to spend a great deal of time acting as a referee, with some risk to U.S. intelligence capabilities." Cheney backed him and Bush went along, leaving the new intelligence director without the power to control spending.

The trick now was to find someone to take on the new position without the tools it would really require. Armitage said no thanks. Porter Goss, who had taken over as CIA director from Tenet, was having problems managing the agency, making a promotion implausible. Bush aides approached Robert Gates, a former CIA director under the president's father who was now president of Texas A&M University, but he declined. The search would stretch into the New Year.

The year's end brought one final act of cleanup from the first term. On December 30, the Justice Department adopted a new memo defining the legal contours of the terrorist interrogation program to replace the one first written largely by John Yoo and later abandoned by Jack Goldsmith. The new memo was more restrictive but still granted interrogators a lot of leeway and in one footnote effectively declared that what had been done under the old memo was still legal. This was seen as a quiet victory for Cheney and David Addington. Indeed, Yoo later declared that "the differences in the opinions were for appearances' sake. In the real world of interrogation policy nothing had changed."

AS THE NEW YEAR opened, Bush focused on redefining his presidency. One day Dan Bartlett and Nicolle Devenish found him in the Oval Office standing with his hands in his pockets, staring out the window, and musing about bringing home the troops from Iraq as soon as possible. He knew the public was weary of war. He seemed to be, too.

Bush wanted to use the "freedom speech" he had told Michael Gerson to write for the second inauguration to reorient his administration. His inclination was reinforced when he sat down to leaf through galleys of a book given to him by his friend Tom Bernstein, a former partner in the Texas Rangers. *The Case for Democracy* was a manifesto by Natan Sharansky, the Soviet refusenik, Israeli politician, and neoconservative favorite. Bush found it so riveting he invited Sharansky to visit. In the Oval Office, the president told Sharansky that he had been struck by a metaphor in the book comparing a tyrannical state to a soldier pointing a gun at a prisoner until his arms finally tire, he lowers the gun, and the captive escapes. Sharansky was surprised by how much Bush had internalized the message. "Not only did he read it, he felt it," Sharansky later recalled. "It says what I believe," Bush later told a group of rabbis.

Bush was encouraged in the weeks that followed when hundreds of thousands of people in the former Soviet republic of Ukraine took to the streets of the capital, Kiev, to protest a stolen election and force the end of a calcified regime. The demonstrators, clad in orange scarves, shirts, and hats, were reprising the popular uprising that occurred after a stolen election in Georgia, another former Soviet republic, just a year earlier, an uprising that succeeded in ousting the government in what came to be called the Rose Revolution. The so-called Orange Revolution in Ukraine had a big impact on the White House. It did not go unnoticed either that the revolutionaries in both cases were pro-Westerners standing up to intimidation from Moscow, which thought Washington was behind the uprisings.

The speech-writing process was interrupted when Gerson, at age forty, suffered a mild heart attack in mid-December and had to be rushed to the hospital. Richard Tubb, the White House physician, had the hospital register Gerson under an assumed name, "John Alexandria," to forestall public attention. After doctors inserted two stents into Gerson's chest, Bush called to check in.

"I'm not calling about the second inaugural," he said lightly. "I'm calling to see how the guy who's working on the second inaugural's doing."

Gerson recovered soon and worked closely with his fellow speechwriter John McConnell to come up with the architecture for the speech. They solicited ideas from conservative thinkers. A three-page memo from John Lewis Gaddis, the Yale University scholar, particularly impressed them. "If there is ever to be a moment within the Bush presidency to think big, this is it," Gaddis wrote, matching Bush's own instincts. "The President has a convincing electoral mandate behind him. He's no longer running for anything. He has as much political capital now as he will ever have—and it can only diminish as the second term proceeds." Gaddis argued that the three clearest presidential statements of America's international aspirations in the twentieth century were Woodrow Wilson's address to Congress seeking a declaration of war against Germany to "make the world safe for democracy"; Franklin Roosevelt's "Four Freedoms" address proclaiming the universality of freedom of speech and worship and freedom from want and fear; and Ronald Reagan's London speech declaring that Communism would wind up on the "ash heap of history."

Now, Gaddis argued, was a time for Bush "to think like Wilson, Roosevelt and Reagan." So he proposed that the president set the following goal: "that it will be the objective of the United States, working with the United Nations and all other states who will join in this cause, to ensure that by the year 2030—a quarter century from now—there will be no tyrants left, anywhere in the world."

The Bush team invited Gaddis and others to join them at the White House to talk through possible themes for the second term on January 10, 2005. Joining Gerson were Karl Rove, who was taking on a new title as deputy chief of staff; Dan Bartlett, who was moving up to counselor; and Peter Wehner, the strategic initiatives director. In addition to Gaddis, the outsiders included the conservative scholars and writers Victor Davis Hanson, Charles Krauthammer, Fouad Ajami, and Eliot Cohen. The conversation meandered for a while until there was a pause and Gaddis jumped in.

"Well, I think there ought to be a big idea," said Gaddis, echoing his memo. "I think the president should call for ending tyranny in our time."

No one said anything at first, which Gaddis took as disapproval. Krauthammer thought the idea was "utterly utopian." Cohen considered it "boffo" and wondered why not abolish evil as long as they were at it. But Gerson liked the idea and jotted it down on his notepad.

Bush had talked about freedom and democracy before but never set it out in such striking terms. As Gaddis saw it, to win wider appeal for the notion, the goal should be ending tyranny, not spreading democracy, because spreading democracy smacked of telling people how to live their lives. "Nobody likes tyrants, but not everybody necessarily likes democracy," he said later.

Gerson did not make such a distinction. When he sat down with McConnell, he had a thorough outline with a strong intellectual construct that married Sharansky's notion of promoting democracy with Gaddis's goal of ending tyranny, though without a target date. McConnell thought the outline was really good, and the two writers then managed to script out the entire address in just two or three days. The words "terrorism" and "Iraq" never appeared anywhere in it, nor did Bush want to directly refer to September 11. Instead, the president suggested a metaphor, a "prairie fire." The writers thought that was a little too Texas, so it became "a day of fire." Karen Hughes expressed worry that a fire could become a conflagration, but the rest of the team liked the phrase and it stayed in. When it was done, they were pleased. "John Kennedy could have delivered the same speech," McConnell thought. "Word for word."

SUCH SWEEPING RHETORIC might have generated objections from the professional diplomats at the State Department, whose job was to sweat over how foreign governments react to presidential declarations. "That's why you don't show them the speech," Bartlett said.

The speech was kept secret even from top advisers until the end. Colin Powell saw it only a day or so before the inauguration and thought "it was over the top in terms of the democracy piece of it" but "it was already a done deal and nobody was going to listen to a thing I said anyway." On this, as it happened, he and Rumsfeld actually agreed. Rumsfeld suggested Bush focus on the word "freedom," not "democracy," mindful that America had taken two centuries to get as far as it had in building a democratic system. "I worried that it would be counterproductive to talk about imposing democracy, our kind of democracy, on others," he said.

Condoleezza Rice had her reservations as well. She kept thinking about the operational implications. *How would you implement that? What would that look like?*

"You know," she told Bush gently, "that is kind of a big goal there, end tyranny as we know it."

"Yeah," he said. "But what I really mean, of course, is we have to start toward getting everybody pulling toward this goal of the freedom agenda."

Andy Card was also struck by the idealism of the address. "This is not a speech Dick Cheney would give," he observed.

That much was true. Cheney thought pushing for democracy was fine, but for him it should be in service of the larger goal of securing the United States. Bush thought spreading freedom *was* the larger goal and believed that it would by definition make America more secure. Cheney was not so sure. If the theory was that repression led to extremism and therefore freedom would make America safer, then, he asked, what would explain all the Pakistani youth willing to blow themselves or others up in the United Kingdom, a country with as much freedom as America? Cheney was skeptical that they were properly diagnosing the drivers behind terrorism. Inside his household, Liz Cheney, still working at the State Department, was a passionate believer in the cause, and she was having an impact on her father. He teased her about being his "left-wing daughter," but thanks in part to her influence he was more open to the president's ideas than, for instance, his friend Rumsfeld.

Either way, Cheney played no real role in framing the second inaugural address, arguably the most important speech of the presidency and the foundational document for their remaining four years in office. As central as Cheney had been in setting the agenda for the first term, he was essentially uninvolved in laying out the road map for the second. He had never been much involved in presidential speeches. They were distributed to his office, and he understood they were important, but in the end they were words. He was more focused on the mechanics of governance.

Besides, he knew that Bush cared about them and did not need his help. "Unless there were some reason, I didn't pay a lot of attention to them," Cheney said. "There wasn't a lot I could contribute in that area, so I didn't spend a lot of time on it." But in this case, the words would lay down an important marker for the remainder of the Bush presidency, and in absenting himself from the process, Cheney had essentially sidelined himself.

As the day approached, speech rehearsals in the family theater were unusually free from stress. Bush was feeling good about the coming ceremony. The speech was short, and there were no policy elements to haggle over. Last-minute issues were minor. Dan Bartlett, for instance, wanted to take out the word "subsistence" because he thought Bush might stumble over it.

Bush laughed and needled him. "Dan, subsistence, subsistence, subsistence," he repeated, mantra-like.

He brushed off the concern. "You watch. I will nail it."

ON JANUARY 20, 2005, the day they would take office for the second and final time, Bush and Cheney awoke to a capital covered by a thin layer of snow and swathed in security the likes of which it had never seen. It was the first wartime inauguration in more than three decades. A hundred square blocks of Washington were closed to traffic as black-clad sharpshooters watched from rooftops, fighter jets and helicopters patrolled overhead, bomb-sniffing dogs searched vehicles, and thirteen thousand soldiers and police officers manned the parade route and other key locations. Bush was surrounded by a phalanx of Secret Service agents so tight that he joked he was surprised his Texas friends "were able to penetrate security."

Bush, now fifty-eight years old, and Cheney, just ten days from his sixty-fourth birthday, were a little grayer and a little heavier, weathered by four years of tumult. Cheney was sworn in by his friend Speaker Dennis Hastert. Then, four minutes before the constitutionally prescribed noon hour, Bush again put his hand on the family Bible and took his oath from Chief Justice William Rehnquist, who was leaning on a cane and sounding hoarse in his first public appearance since disclosing that he was battling thyroid cancer.

The twenty-one-minute speech that Michael Gerson and John McConnell had crafted dominated the event, perhaps even more than Bush anticipated. His clarion call for spreading democracy and human rights around the world, while echoing the most memorable words of his predecessors, seemed to go further than any president before in linking principles with policy. No longer was the ideal of democratic aspiration simply the moral cause of the United States. Now it was intrinsically tied to the nation's security.

"We have seen our vulnerability and we have seen its deepest source," Bush declared as Cheney watched. "For as long as whole regions of the world simmer in resentment and tyranny—prone to ideologies that feed hatred and excuse murder—violence will gather and multiply in destructive power and cross the most defended borders and raise a mortal threat. There is only one force of history that can break the reign of hatred and resentment, and expose the pretensions of tyrants, and reward the hopes of the decent and tolerant, and that is the force of human freedom." He went on, "So it is the policy of the United States to seek and support the growth of democratic movements and institutions in every nation and culture, with the ultimate goal of ending tyranny in our world."

It was a bold and sweeping statement, just as Bush had wanted, but the caveats would later be lost alongside the simple declarative nature of his promise. Democratic change, he said, "is not primarily the task of arms," nor did he harbor the illusion that it would happen swiftly; indeed, he said, "the great objective of ending tyranny is the concentrated work of generations." But he vowed to predicate relations with countries around the world on their treatment of their own people. "We will persistently clarify the choice before every ruler and every nation—the moral choice between oppression, which is always wrong, and freedom, which is eternally right. America will not pretend that jailed dissidents prefer their chains, or that women welcome humiliation and servitude, or that any human being aspires to live at the mercy of bullies." To the people of the world he said, "All who live in tyranny and hopelessness can know the United States will not ignore your oppression, or excuse your oppressors. When you stand for your liberty, we will stand with you."

The ceremony was barely over when Gerson, walking back from the Capitol to sit in the White House parade stands, received a call from Stephen Hadley. Already, he told Gerson, there were countries calling to see what this would mean. It was a good question.

Bush didn't care if the foreign policy priesthood was in a dither.

"Don't back down one bit," he told Hadley.

PART FOUR

21

"Who do they think they are? I was reelected too"

Just ten days into his new term, President Bush was already sweating out another election. He worried about turnout, weighed the prospects of different parties, and anticipated policies that might come from a new administration. Most important, he hoped no one would get blown up.

The voters on Bush's mind that January 30 were six thousand miles away in Iraq, which was holding its first national elections since the invasion to install an interim government to transition the country to a constitutional democracy. Bush was anxious. Shortly after waking up, he picked up the phone and asked for the duty officer in the Situation Room to get an update. It was 5:51 a.m. in Washington but eight hours later in Baghdad. Turnout was high, he was told.

The election was a gamble, perhaps the biggest since the invasion itself. The disaffected Sunni minority that dominated Iraq during Saddam Hussein's days had threatened to stay home, and Shiites and Kurds feared violent retaliation if they turned out. For weeks, Bush had been told that holding an election in a war zone without any meaningful reconciliation among the sects could be a disaster. Images of voters being killed at polling places, or the reality of a lopsided Shiite-dominated government, could easily fuel the insurgency. Gloomy CIA warnings had gotten on his nerves so much that at one final briefing Bush clapped his hands sharply, slammed his briefing book shut, and declared defiantly, "We'll see who's right."

Now that the day had arrived, it looked as if it might have been him. Television carried pictures of eager Iraqi voters holding up fingers stained with purple ink indicating they had voted. Lines at polling places stretched out the doors. Eight million people showed up. For the first time since the fall of Saddam Hussein, wrote Anthony Shadid, the Pulitzer Prize–winning correspondent for the *Washington Post*, "the haggard capital and other parts of Iraq took on the veneer of a festival, as crowds danced, chanted and played soccer in streets secured by thousands of Iraqi and American forces." The day was hardly perfect; the military recorded 299 attacks killing about forty-five people, including an American marine. Just as troubling for the long term, Sunnis largely stayed home. But the spirit of the moment, defying months of relentless violence and centuries of ruthless autocracy, was infectious. For one day at least, something extraordinary seemed to be happening, the most audacious experiment in democracy in the history of the Arab world.

Bush was excited as he picked up the phone. Condoleezza Rice was on the line.

"You have to turn on the TV," she said. "You just have to see this."

"Is it good?" he asked. "Is it a good outcome?"

"It's really amazing. It's amazing to see what those Iraqis are doing."

Bush hoped this would turn the naysayers around, both in Washington and in Baghdad. Pressure had been building as the war dragged on. Just days before the election, Senator Ted Kennedy, the president's erstwhile ally on education, had called for withdrawing troops from Iraq. Kennedy had opposed the war from the start, but the last thing Bush or Cheney wanted was for more Democrats to pick up the refrain about pulling out.

In Iraq, the election was to be the first step in undercutting the insurgency by bringing to power a government with popular support. The interim government to be formed out of the elections would oversee Iraq while a commission wrote a new constitution by August 15. Voters would return to the polls on October 15 to ratify the constitution and then again on December 15 to pick a full-fledged government under the terms of the new national charter.

BUSH'S OPTIMISM ON Iraq fed into a strategic calculation about how to frame his second term and spend that political capital he talked about. In those heady winter days shortly after his inauguration, the president felt he was turning a corner in the war and could use his election victory to return to some of the priorities that had animated his run for the White House in the first place. He set four domestic goals for 2005: remaking Social Security, rewriting the tax code, liberalizing immigration laws, and limiting excessive litigation.

He and Karl Rove decided to hold off on immigration and tort reform for now and named a commission headed by the former senators John Breaux, a Democrat, and Connie Mack, a Republican, to craft a tax code overhaul. So they would start with Social Security. Ever since his failed run for Congress in 1978, Bush had talked about restructuring the retirement program so taxpayers could invest some of their payroll taxes in the markets, giving them as he saw it more control over their own futures. Now he and Rove thought it would be the defining domestic legacy of his second term.

The decision was presented without a real debate among his staff, some of whom, like Dan Bartlett, thought it was a mistake. Bush argued he had a mandate on Social Security, but skeptics on his team worried he was misinterpreting the election. He won, they thought, because voters felt safer with him during dangerous times than with John Kerry. Yet Bush had convinced himself that because he mentioned Social Security in, say, minute forty-nine of a fifty-two-minute speech—after spending the previous forty-eight minutes talking about killing terrorists—that meant the public favored changing the storied entitlement program. Others warned Bush and his advisers. Candida Wolff, now his top lobbyist, told Andy Card that the president had never laid out enough of a detailed plan to claim public support. Grover Norquist, president of Americans for Tax Reform and a key conservative ally, told a Bush aide they could never get enough Democrats to overcome a Senate filibuster. And Senator Mitch McConnell, the Republican whip whose wife, Elaine Chao, served in Bush's cabinet as labor secretary, likewise warned Al Hubbard, the president's economics adviser, it might not get done.

Bush dismissed the warnings, confident he could assert his will over Washington. After all, despite similar pessimism, he pushed through tax cuts, education reform, and Medicare prescription drug coverage during his first term. Now he faced what he thought was an opportunity to refashion the liberal New Deal and Great Society into his conservative Ownership Society. "For the first time in six decades," Peter Wehner, his strategic initiatives director, wrote in a memo, "the Social Security battle is one we can win—and in doing so, we can help transform the political and philosophical landscape of the country." A theme was emerging to define the second term, promoting liberty at home and abroad.

Bush and his advisers decided they needed to "create a crisis mentality" about Social Security, as Scott McClellan later put it, to convince the public to go along. Bush would warn of looming fiscal catastrophe as Americans lived longer and stayed on Social Security longer. To be sure, there was an imbalance in the system. While nearly seventeen workers contributed taxes into the system for every retiree benefiting from it in 1950, there were now just three workers per retiree. By 2018, the system would be paying out more in benefits than it was taking in through payroll taxes every year, and by 2042 it would use up the IOUs it had accumulated over time as presidents and Congresses diverted its surpluses to offset deficit spending.

But Medicare actually faced worse financial problems than Social Security; just that year, its hospital insurance expenditures had overtaken revenues, and were projected to exhaust the program's trust funds by 2019, more than two decades sooner than Social Security would. Moreover, the idea of investing some Social Security payroll taxes in stocks and bonds might plausibly produce more retirement benefits for recipients if all worked as planned, but it would do nothing to shore up the overall health of the program. Indeed, in the short term, it would cost at least $700 billion over ten years in transition costs to keep paying current beneficiaries without the money that would be diverted to personal investment accounts for future beneficiaries.

To actually address Social Security's financial issues would require steps like raising the retirement age, increasing payroll taxes, limiting benefits for the wealthy, slowing the growth of benefits for everyone, or some combination. Bush and his advisers debated whether to send Congress a specific plan embracing such ideas. Joshua Bolten favored a detailed proposal, and Keith Hennessey, the president's national economics adviser, agreed, sending Bush a seven-page memo making the case that such an approach "maximizes the chance of getting a good bill," although it "also has a higher chance of producing an unbreachable partisan split that leads to stalemate." Rove opposed sending Congress anything specific, arguing it would just give Democrats something to shoot at and it would be better to stick to broad principles while letting Congress fill in the blanks as it did with No Child Left Behind. Bush sided with Rove.

The president kicked off his Social Security drive in his State of the Union address on the night of February 2. "By the year 2042, the entire system would be exhausted and bankrupt," Bush said, at which point Democrats in the chamber responded with catcalls. "If steps are not taken to avert that outcome, the only solutions would be dramatically higher taxes, massive new borrowing, or sudden and severe cuts in Social Security benefits or other government programs."

The next morning, Bush flew out of Washington for a barnstorming trip, picking five states that he had won in November and were home to seven Democratic senators he hoped to pressure on Social Security. Cheney, on the other hand, remained out of the picture. On the central domestic initiative for the new term, he was neither a force in the internal debate nor a major surrogate in the fight to rally the public and Congress. He would do whatever he was asked, but he was preserving his energy for other fights.

THE UPLIFTING IMAGES of ink-stained voters from Baghdad were soon joined by scenes from Beirut, where tens of thousands were flooding into the streets demanding change in what looked to be a new "color revolution." On February 14, the former prime minister Rafiq Hariri had been assassinated in a brazen act blamed on the Syrians, who had occupied Lebanon for three decades. Now a popular uprising released stored-up frustrations. The Lebanese were calling it the Cedar Revolution.

The succession of developments gave Bush hope that his freedom agenda could result in tangible change. His first real test would come as he met with Russia's Vladimir Putin. Bush prided himself on their friendship despite their break over Iraq. But if he was serious about challenging "every ruler and every nation" over freedom, he could hardly ignore Putin's crackdown on dissent. Since their first soul-gazing meeting in 2001, Putin had taken over television networks, driven business moguls who challenged him out of the country, purged parliament of Western-oriented parties, and eliminated the election of governors. The arrest of the oil tycoon Mikhail Khodorkovsky, the richest man in Russia, had shocked Bush and his team; some, like Condoleezza Rice, knew Khodorkovsky personally. Cheney was following the case and thought it proved Bush should not trust Putin.

When the American and Russian presidents sat down for a long, private discussion in Bratislava, the capital of Slovakia, on February 24, Bush pressed his points about freedom, and Putin grew defensive. As he often did, Putin tried to make equivalences, justifying his actions by comparing them to situations in the United States.

"You talk about Khodorkovsky, and I talk about Enron," Putin told Bush. "You appoint the Electoral College and I appoint governors. What's the difference?"

At another point, Putin defended his control over media in Russia. "Don't lecture me about the free press," he said, "not after you fired that reporter."

Fired a reporter? "Vladimir, are you talking about Dan Rather?" Bush asked.

Yes, that was what he meant.

Rather, the longtime CBS News journalist, was stepping down as anchor and managing editor of the *CBS Evening News* after the previous fall's report accusing Bush of not fulfilling National Guard service based on fraudulent documents. Bush explained he had nothing to do with Rather losing his job. "I strongly suggest you not say that in public," he added. "The American people will think you don't understand our system."

But Putin understood his own system. When the two leaders emerged for a joint news conference, a Russian reporter handpicked by the Kremlin challenged Bush on the same grounds Putin had just been citing in private.

"Why don't you talk a lot about violations of the rights of journalists in the United States?" the reporter asked. "About the fact that some journalists have been fired?"

Bush understood instantly that it was a planted question. Putin had proved Bush's point about the lack of free press in Russia.

"People do get fired in American press," he answered. "They don't get fired by the government, however."

The encounter stuck in Bush's craw, and he was still dwelling on it a week later when he filled in Tony Blair during a videoconference on March 1. "It was fairly unpleasant," Bush told him. "It was not hostile. It was like junior high debating." He recounted the Dan Rather exchange. "Seriously, it was a whole series of these juvenile arguments. There was no breakthrough with this guy." Bush was exasperated at the memory. "I sat there for an hour and forty-five minutes or an hour and forty minutes, and it went on and on. At one point, the interpreter made me so mad that I nearly reached over the table and slapped the hell out of the guy. He had a mocking tone, making accusations about America. He was just sarcastic."

Still, events seemed to validate Bush's optimism. Just four days after Bush's encounter with Putin, fresh protests with tens of thousands in Beirut's Martyrs Square forced the Syrian-backed prime minister, Omar Karami, to resign, emboldening the Lebanese to press Syria to finally pull out. On March 5, President Bashar al-Assad of Syria announced a "gradual and organized withdrawal" of fifteen thousand troops from Lebanon, the beginning of the end of a twenty-nine-year occupation.

The resulting images of democracy on the march made for exhilarating days in the White House and temporarily won over some critics. Walid Jumblatt, a Lebanese Druze leader and socialist who branded American marines "enemy forces" when Ronald Reagan sent peacekeepers to his country, credited Bush for the wave of change sweeping the Middle East. "It's strange for me to say it, but this process of change has started because of the American invasion of Iraq," he said. "I was cynical about Iraq. But when I saw the Iraqi people voting three weeks ago, eight million of them, it was the start of a new Arab world." In the United States, Jon Stewart, the liberal talk show host on Comedy Central who spent most of his time skewering Bush, acknowledged the president might be onto something. "This is the most difficult thing for me because I don't care for the tactics," he said one night, "but I've got to say I've never seen results like this ever in that region." Daniel Schorr, the National Public Radio commentator and frequent Bush critic, said that "he may have had it right." The president's aides were thrilled when *Newsweek* put the Cedar Revolution on the cover with a similar-sounding secondary headline that said "Where Bush Was Right."

Still, there were plenty of signs of trouble ahead. Iraq remained plagued by violence despite its elections. Lebanon was a cauldron of competing sects. Saudi Arabia permitted voting for some seats on municipal councils but continued to bar women from driving cars, much less casting ballots. President Hosni Mubarak of Egypt announced he would allow challengers to run against him, but his government would still control which parties could participate.

Bush made personnel moves intended to advance his democracy agenda. He enlisted Karen Hughes to come back from Texas and serve as undersecretary of state for public diplomacy, asking her to take over the government's moribund campaign to promote American values overseas and wage the battle of ideas with Islamic extremists. And he sent Paul Wolfowitz, the deputy defense secretary, to be president of the World Bank, where he could promote democracy along with development.

The elevation of Rice and the return of Hughes reflected an effort by Bush to cast off some of the unilateralist cowboy image. "The second term is going to be a time of diplomacy," he told aides. Whatever he had to do after September 11 to meet the immediate threat, it was now time to recalibrate. "What I think happened was after 9/11 in terms of the president's personal own philosophy there was probably more of a, maybe a pulling more away from where the president's heart and values really were," Hughes reflected. "And then there was a course correction while Condi was secretary of state. This would have pulled back to where the president really felt in terms of broader engagement and involvement with the world. I think one of the reasons he asked me to do what I did at State was because he wanted somebody close to him to be seen as reaching out to the world on his behalf."

Rice made her new mission clear from the start. She tapped Christopher Hill, a veteran diplomat and protégé of Richard Holbrooke, negotiator of the Dayton Accords ending the Bosnian War, to take over the North Korea portfolio. "Our nation has won two wars," she told him, with a premature declaration of victory, "and now we need diplomats for this term." Rice signaled the shift in her confirmation hearings too, declaring that "the time for diplomacy is now"—a line that generated a fight within the administration, because it either implied there had been no diplomacy in the first term or suggested a retreat from the president's muscular approach. "What it was basically saying is we're sorry for Iraq," said one Rice adviser. As for Rice herself, said another adviser, "that was essentially a declaration that I'm going to now be the leader of this administration."

Cheney was wary. He recognized that the president was heading in a different direction. For Cheney, the second term was already shaping up as a period of waning influence.

During a meeting with the Saudi ambassador, Prince Bandar bin Sultan, his longtime friend dating back to the Gulf War, Cheney complained that others seemed to be trying to elbow him out of even the Iraq portfolio that he cared so much about.

"Who do they think they are?" he asked. "I was reelected too."

WHILE BUSH STUMPED for his Social Security plan, Cheney remained focused on the issues that stimulated him. First among them was terrorism and the defense of the country.

He was a fixture at Terrorism Wednesdays—which later became Terrorism Tuesdays—when the war cabinet gathered in the White House to talk about threats and where they were headed. These meetings, on top of daily intelligence briefings and other sessions, usually included the chief of staff, national security adviser, homeland security secretary, attorney general, director of national intelligence, CIA director, and later the head of the National Counterterrorism Center. Frances Fragos Townsend, who had taken over as the president's homeland security adviser, had tried to recalibrate the White House approach to terrorism by changing the Threat Matrix devised after September 11 into the President's Terrorism Threat Report, shorn of much of the more improbable intelligence so as to present a more realistic picture of actual risks. The idea, she told colleagues, was to "readjust the thermometer."

But Cheney's thermometer ran hot, and he remained as seized by the grim possibilities as he was the day after September 11. While others had moved on to a certain extent, or allowed themselves to begin thinking about a domestic agenda, the vice president stayed locked on target. He was particularly interested in the threat of biological terrorism and what could be done to counter it. While there were medicines for anthrax and other threats, there was a real challenge in distributing them in time. At meeting after meeting, Cheney pushed to hand out medical kits with countermeasures that could be kept at home just in case. But the medicines required prescriptions, and the Food and Drug Administration resisted widespread distribution of drugs without doctor consent.

The vice president was also fighting rearguard actions to protect programs he viewed as critical to the country's security. He was intent on beating back challenges to the warrantless surveillance program and asserting the most expansive position in court fights over detention of terror suspects. He knew challenges were coming from Congress on interrogation methods and understood sentiment was growing within the administration for doing something to close the detention center at Guantánamo. Even Bush had hinted that he wanted to find a way to shutter the prison.

If his mind dwelled on the dark side, as he called it, Cheney did have one domestic assignment from Bush in the early months of 2005. Chief Justice William Rehnquist's health was in obvious decline; he had only just returned to the bench in March after months recovering from thyroid cancer. Since it seemed likely illness would force him to retire before long, the president asked Cheney to launch a clandestine search, in conjunction with Harriet Miers, Bush's former personal attorney from Texas who had taken over for Alberto Gonzales as White House counsel. They wanted a replacement all but ready to go the moment the seat opened up.

While it was unusual to have a nonlawyer head the search, Cheney immediately put together a team. One day in early spring, while flying back to Washington on Air Force Two, Cheney summoned to his cabin Steve Schmidt, his former campaign adviser who was now working as his counselor. On the floor was a large duffel bag filled with binders about possible candidates for the Supreme Court. Cheney pointed to it and told Schmidt to start studying. He wanted strict secrecy. Only a handful of people were to know.

"You're allowed to talk about this with me, with Karl, and with Harriet, and obviously the boss, should he talk to you about it," Cheney instructed. "But figure it out. We haven't done one of these in thirteen years, and there hasn't been one in thirteen years. We think we're going to have an opening. Come up with a plan."

The last time a Republican president filled a Supreme Court vacancy was in 1991, when Bush's father nominated Clarence Thomas. The world had changed dramatically since then. From the start of the administration, Bush and Cheney had anticipated the opportunity to name one or more justices, and the president had tasked the vice president with the project. Cheney and Gonzales had assembled a team of young lawyers to research prospective nominees and write memos about them. In the spring of 2001, Gonzales began meeting with candidates. He went out, for instance, to the Virginia house of J. Michael Luttig, a judge on the Fourth Circuit Court of Appeals who was considered one of the most stellar conservatives on the bench.

In the spring of 2005, Cheney and the team pulled out the old material and began culling through it again. This time, with the odds of a vacancy growing, Cheney wanted to meet top candidates personally. One by one, they were secretly brought to the vice president's residence in April and May for informal interviews with Cheney, who was joined by Gonzales, Miers, Rove, and Andy Card.

On the day of his interview, John G. Roberts, a fifty-year-old judge on the D.C. Circuit Court of Appeals, drove to the vice president's residence forty-five minutes early so as not to be late, then sat in his car until the appointed hour. Ushered into a study, Roberts noticed that most of the books on the shelves were about trout fishing.

"Here, sit in the hot-wired seat," Rove told him with a grin.

Cheney nodded toward Gonzales. "Well, you're the lawyer," he said. "Let's get things started."

Roberts was a leading legal light for Republicans and had first been selected for the appeals court by Bush's father, but his nomination was not acted on by the Senate before the president left office. The younger Bush renominated Roberts, but it took two years to win confirmation, so Roberts had only been on the bench for two years.

With little track record to work from, Gonzales asked Roberts a series of questions to elicit his judicial philosophy. He asked why Roberts had told senators during his 2003 confirmation hearing that he did not label himself a "strict constructionist," the phrase often used by conservatives to signal a judge who does not overinterpret laws or the Constitution. Roberts said the term was not all that meaningful since some liberals considered themselves strict constructionists, an answer that could worry some Republicans but might help him slip through the gauntlet of the confirmation hearings.

Another candidate brought in was Luttig, a protégé of Cheney's friend Justice Antonin Scalia. Probably no other person involved in the process that spring had as much experience with the selection and confirmation of Supreme Court justices as Luttig; as a young government lawyer, he had helped prepare Sandra Day O'Connor, Clarence Thomas, and David Souter for their confirmation hearings, and he had served as a clerk to Scalia and Chief Justice Warren Burger. But this was the first time he was on the receiving end of the questioning.

"Do I have to do this without counsel present?" Luttig joked as he entered the conference room to find a committee waiting for him. "I want my lawyer."

Everyone chuckled. Because he had served as a judge since 1991, Luttig's record as a conservative was clearer, and most of the questions were designed to get a sense of who he was as a person.

But it was not enough to evaluate candidates. The confirmation of Thomas and the failed nomination of Robert H. Bork made clear that Supreme Court selections had become another battleground in the political wars. By filibustering Bush's appointments to lower courts in his first term, Senate Democrats had already demonstrated an appetite for the struggle. Bush was determined to be ready as his father had not been. Rove and Gonzales invited four conservative lawyers to lunch to ask them to coordinate outside interest groups for a confirmation fight: Boyden Gray, the White House counsel to Bush's father; Jay Sekulow, counsel for the American Center for Law and Justice, a group formed by the televangelist Pat Robertson; Edwin Meese III, the attorney general under Ronald Reagan; and Leonard Leo, executive vice president of the conservative Federalist Society. As the White House geared up for battle, they came to be known as the Four Horsemen.

IN EARLY MAY, Bush flew to Moscow for Victory Day ceremonies in Red Square marking the sixtieth anniversary of the end of World War II. Bush understood how important the celebration was for Vladimir Putin, who enjoyed being at the center of world attention. But Bush was not eager to commemorate an event that condemned half of Europe to Soviet domination for four decades, so he stopped first in Riga, capital of the former Soviet republic of Latvia, to express regret over the postwar division of Europe.

Once in Moscow, Bush kept his criticism to himself, hoping to avoid a repeat of the blowup in Bratislava. But Putin had his own way of making a point. During a visit to the Russian president's home outside Moscow, Putin's massive Labrador bounded up.

"Bigger, tougher, stronger, faster, meaner than Barney," Putin said, referring to Bush's Scottish terrier.

Much to Putin's irritation, Bush stopped on the way home in the former Soviet republic of Georgia to celebrate the democratic advances there and signal that he would not accede to Russia's claims to its old sphere of influence. Mikheil Saakashvili, the thirty-seven-year-old revolutionary turned president who had become a favorite of Bush's, went all out and gathered 200,000 people in Tbilisi's Freedom Square to greet the visiting president, an enormous turnout for a country of four million and one of the biggest crowds Bush had seen in his presidency. Bush was invigorated as sunlight bathed the square. "You're making many important contributions to freedom's cause," he told them, "but your most important contribution is your example."

The crowds overwhelmed security checkpoints, and a man in a leather coat who waited hours in the square under the hot sun muttering to himself suddenly hurled a Soviet-made grenade at Bush on the stage. The grenade bounced off a little girl's head and landed sixty-one feet from Bush but did not explode. In the swirl of events, with so many people crowded into the square, neither Bush nor his staff even realized what had happened; it was not until he was on Air Force One flying back to Washington hours later that he learned of the assassination attempt. The attack got relatively little attention because the grenade was initially presumed to be a dud, but authorities later concluded it was live and simply failed to explode because a red plaid cloth wrapped around it prevented the firing pin from deploying fast enough.

RETURNING HOME, BUSH found that his Social Security plan was going nowhere. He had traveled intensively, part of a plan in which he and top administration officials would hold sixty events in sixty days. He had lobbied lawmakers, and even finally embraced measures to slow the growth of benefits except for the poorest Americans in hopes of luring Congress into negotiations. But Democrats had seized on the issue to attack Bush, calculating it was a way of weakening a newly reelected president.

Bush lost Democrats he had collaborated with on tax cuts, like Senator Max Baucus, the ranking Democrat on the Finance Committee, who was offended that the president visited his home state of Montana to pressure him. "Whatever we need to do to beat this thing, I'm in," Baucus told Senator Harry Reid, the Democratic leader. Bush's fellow Republicans were also running for the hills. Dennis Hastert never much cared for the plan and was now willing to let it die. No committee had even produced a written version of legislation, much less voted.

The debate Bush had started was marked by distortion and confusion. The president repeatedly told audiences that Social Security "goes broke" in 2042, which was not exactly the case. In 2042, Social Security would not have enough money to pay out everything recipients had been promised, but it would still have enough to pay out much of it. At the same time, many Democratic opponents misled Americans into thinking the president's plan would force them to put their Social Security money in the stock market. Actually, the plan was entirely voluntary and even then affected only those under fifty-five. Current recipients and near retirees would see no change as a result of the personal investment accounts, and anyone else who thought it was too risky to invest retirement savings in the markets could simply choose not to.

By the time Bush's Social Security tour reached the end of its assigned sixty days, it felt like a past-its-prime Broadway show. Not only was he no closer to success, but he had actually lost ground; support for private accounts had fallen from 58 percent the previous September to 47 percent by May. When he flew to Milwaukee on May 19 for what would amount to the seventy-eighth day of the sixty-day tour, a new poll showed most Americans agreed with his proposed cuts in future benefit increases—until they learned it was Bush's plan. Asked whether they would support trimming the programmed growth of benefits for everyone but the poorest Americans,

53 percent of Americans agreed while 36 percent disagreed. But when the Pew Research Center for the People and the Press changed the question to add the phrase "George W. Bush has proposed," support fell to 45 percent and opposition grew to 43 percent. Bush's own approval rating fell to an anemic 43 percent. For a man who planned to spend political capital after the reelection, the bank account seemed to be draining quickly.

CHENEY CONTINUED TO steer clear of the Social Security campaign, and in May two separate events made it clear that Condoleezza Rice, not the vice president, was the force now driving the administration's international relations.

On the evening of May 13, troops in the central Asian nation of Uzbekistan, a key ally in the war on terror, opened fire on demonstrators protesting poverty and repression in the eastern city of Andijan, killing hundreds of civilians. For Bush, the massacre pitted competing priorities—his vow to hold authoritarian governments accountable for cracking down on dissent versus his need for an airbase to support American troops in Afghanistan. Donald Rumsfeld argued for using American influence to nudge the Uzbeks toward more freedom without escalating into a major conflict. Rice, channeling Bush's freedom agenda, maintained they could not sacrifice the moral high ground.

"The military needs that base," Rumsfeld said. "Our security is at stake."

"Human rights trump security," Rice said.

Rice won when Bush made no effort to rein her in.

The other test in May dealt with the same part of the world. Rice had returned from her first trip to Europe as secretary—the "olive branch tour," as her undersecretary, Nicholas Burns, called it—struck that the one thing her counterparts wanted to talk about was not Iraq but Iran. The Europeans were worried that Bush and Cheney wanted to go after the mullahs of Tehran next. If they wanted to rebuild alliances, Rice told Bush, they should support European efforts to negotiate with Iran over its nuclear program, even if it meant making concessions.

The gestures she proposed were minor. The United States would drop its opposition to World Trade Organization membership talks for Iran and allow the sale of spare parts for American-made civilian airplanes. But they represented a sea change from the policy of confrontation Cheney had advocated in the first term. After all the talk of going it alone if necessary, Bush would now be letting the British, Germans, and French take the lead in pressuring Iran to give up uranium enrichment. Unlike with Andijan, this time Rice moved policy without a major clash. As she sat in the Oval Office one day describing her plan, even Cheney went along without protest. "That makes sense," he said.

The emergence of Rice underscored the evolution of Bush's partnership with Cheney. "There certainly seemed to be a difference in their relationship," Christine Todd Whitman observed from the outside. "At the very beginning the president did lean on him a lot in foreign policy because that was his area of weakness and Cheney's area of strength. And then I think it got to be a little bit of a habit, it just got to be reflexive. And then he suddenly said wait a minute, I'm the president, I'm not going to cede this much, it's getting out of hand now and I'm going to pull it back a bit."

Around the table in the Situation Room, it was evident just how much more of a role Rice was playing. No longer the facilitator, she was now an advocate, pushing for more diplomacy. She viewed this as a natural next step on the continuum from Bush's first term, which after September 11 was necessarily more hard-edged in its approach, and her influence with the president suddenly made the State Department, marginalized under Colin Powell in the first term, a more potent player, all the more so by having Stephen Hadley, her supremely loyal former deputy, now in her old job at the White House. "The interagency dynamic turned 180 degrees," said Kristen Silverberg, a White House aide who became an assistant secretary of state. "If there's an interagency debate and she had a view, that view was 95 percent of the time going to prevail."

Her elevation did not sit well with everyone. And Rice's increasing focus on her own status sometimes rubbed the wrong way. When traveling with the president, she paid attention to which car she was assigned in the motorcade and which helicopter she would fly in. On overseas trips, Rice sometimes insisted on occupying the chair next to the president typically reserved for the ambassador. She was "very, very focused on where she fits into the hierarchy and the appropriate trappings to reinforce to everyone else how important she is," remembered a White House aide. For an African American woman born into the Jim Crow South, life was always about proving herself. She was no longer staff, she was a principal, and she wanted to make sure she was accorded the respect she deserved. After four years in Cheney's shadow, perhaps that was the only way to assert her newfound authority.

CHENEY SEEMED TO disappear further into the shadows amid Rice's rise. "I've never heard him talk in a meeting, not once," said one White House aide. Frederick Jones, who worked at the National Security Council, considered

Cheney as much an idea as a person. "I thought the vice president was a figment of people's imagination," he said, "because I never saw him."

When he did speak publicly, it sometimes came across the wrong way. Talking with CNN's Larry King for an interview aired on Memorial Day, Cheney rejected the conventional Washington gloom and doom about Iraq. "I think they're in the last throes, if you will, of the insurgency," he said. The comment reinforced the sense of a White House out of touch with what was happening on the ground. Even some in the White House were scratching their heads over Cheney's assertion. "Where did that come from?" asked Meghan O'Sullivan, the former Jerry Bremer aide who had become deputy national security adviser overseeing Iraq and Afghanistan. None of the briefings provided to Bush and Cheney offered such a conclusion; in fact, killings were on the rise. In May, 1,330 civilian deaths had been logged in Iraq, twice as many as in the same month a year earlier. In the year to date, killings of civilians were up by a third over 2004. As for coalition soldiers, 366 had been killed so far that year, slightly more than the previous year.

Cheney later explained he meant not that the fighting was ending but that the insurgency was a spent force and on the decline. The violence, he thought or hoped, amounted to "final acts of desperation, last efforts to terrorize and destroy." But looking back, Cheney acknowledged, he "was obviously wrong."

Senator Chuck Hagel, a maverick Republican upset about the "last throes" comment, cornered the president after an event.

"I believe you are getting really bubbled in here in the White House on Iraq," he said. Are you getting other viewpoints?

"Well, I kind of leave that to Hadley," Bush answered.

Hagel later went to see Hadley but remained concerned and told a reporter that "the White House is completely disconnected from reality."

Some Bush friends and advisers worried about the same thing. One person close to the family felt Bush did not have the network of contacts his father did from a lifetime in government and therefore the flow of information was too constricted. "It was analog, not digital," he said. Cheney, by contrast, had such a network but allowed himself to see what he wanted to see.

For months, Bush and his team had largely put Iraq to the side when it came to speeches and public events, a conscious attempt not to let the war consume his presidency while also allowing Iraqis symbolically at least to take the lead in their own country. But the Iraqis were not taking the lead; it had taken months for the Iraqis to settle their own differences and finally pick a prime minister, Ibrahim al-Jaafari, a longtime opponent of Saddam Hussein who had returned from exile in London after the American invasion. The result was a void in leadership both in Washington and in Baghdad, resulting in shrinking public support at home. "No one other than the president was explaining the strategy in Iraq," said Michele Davis, a deputy national security adviser. "Nobody else was echoing him, driving home for the public, here's the path forward."

Finally, prompted by worried advisers, Bush agreed to reengage and give a series of high-profile speeches rallying the country. But aides disagreed on tone. Dan Bartlett, backed by Nicolle Devenish, who had succeeded him as communications director, wanted the president to acknowledge missteps to earn the public's trust; simply claiming that the situation was on the upswing would strain credulity. Karl Rove wanted no retreat, no display of weakness. The opposition would pounce, and Bush would be on the defensive.

On June 28, Bush flew to Fort Bragg in North Carolina to give a prime-time televised speech on the war to an audience of uniformed soldiers. Before going out in front of the cameras, he spent three hours visiting with ninety relatives of slain service members. One of the widows, Crystal Owen, a third-grade teacher, asked the president to wear a metal bracelet memorializing her dead husband, Staff Sergeant Mike Owen. Teary-eyed, Bush agreed.

By the time he went in front of his audience at 8:00 p.m., Bush was emotionally drained. His voice lacked power; his tone was flat and subdued. The soldiers had been told to remain quiet since they were the props for a national address, but the lack of applause that normally greeted Bush in military settings further sapped the energy out of the room as the president tried to thread the needle between Bartlett and Rove.

"Like most Americans," he said, "I see the images of violence and bloodshed. Every picture is horrifying, and the suffering is real. Amid all this violence, I know Americans ask the question: Is the sacrifice worth it? It is worth it, and it is vital to the future security of our country."

It was, thought some aides, a necessary corrective to Cheney's "last throes."

WITH SOCIAL SECURITY going nowhere, Bush wanted to take on another domestic priority, immigration. Since his days as Texas governor, he had favored a more flexible approach to illegal immigration than many in his party, advocating a guest worker program and a route to legal status for some of the ten million undocumented immigrants in the country. It was both his personal conviction and an obvious political calculation. Two days before his first inauguration, Karl Rove had declared that making inroads among Latino voters was "our mission and our goal."

While Bush knew it would be an uphill challenge he figured a newly reelected president was in the best position to make it happen. But when Rove, Frances Townsend, and another White House aide, Brian Hook, went to Capitol Hill to talk with House Republican leaders on June 29, the reception was chilly. The Republicans wanted to talk about securing the border. Anything that smacked of amnesty was a nonstarter. Tom DeLay, the powerful House majority leader, called that "doing something good for someone who has broken the law," according to a White House summary of the conversation. "There was little support among key House Republicans for a comprehensive approach," Hook recalled. "They didn't want to hear what we had to say on anything other than the border. The message was secure the border first and then we'll talk reform."

Which was another way of saying no way.

22

"Whacked upside the head"

President Bush and Vice President Cheney were having their weekly lunch on June 30 when Harriet Miers stuck her head into the private dining room off the Oval Office. She told them that Pamela Talkin, the marshal at the Supreme Court, had called to say she would be delivering a sealed envelope to the White House the next morning. Talkin did not say what would be in the envelope or who was sending it. But the natural assumption was that it was a retirement letter from a justice.

The news surprised Bush and Cheney. The court's term had ended three days earlier without any retirements, which were usually announced on the final day. Evidently, one of the justices had opted to wait until after the cameras had left. The obvious candidate, of course, was Chief Justice William Rehnquist given his health. That afternoon, Bush invited Representative Trent Franks, the conservative who had pressed him to appoint anti-abortion justices in exchange for his vote for the Medicare prescription drug program, to meet in his study in the residence.

Bush had the list of acceptable Supreme Court candidates Franks had sent him and they talked over the possibilities. Franks again spoke against Alberto Gonzales and described Judge Janice Rogers Brown, an African American conservative just confirmed to the D.C. Circuit Court of Appeals, as his favorite. Bush thanked him for his input. That night, the president hosted a dinner party for several lawmakers and ambassadors as he tried out a prospective new White House chef. As they dined on squab, Texas Kobe sirloin steak, salad, and a chocolate mango-tango tart, the conversation turned to the Supreme Court. Senator David Vitter of Louisiana told Bush that if there ever were an opening, he should consider his home-state favorite, Judge Edith Brown Clement. Bush responded with interest but said nothing about what he knew was about to happen.

The next morning, shortly after 9:00, Bush got a phone call from Miers. "It's O'Connor," she said.

Miers had called Talkin to ask her to come a little early, and Talkin revealed the letter was not from Rehnquist but from Justice Sandra Day O'Connor, the first woman to serve on the Supreme Court and as a swing vote its most influential member for a decade.

Bush gathered with Cheney, Miers, Karl Rove, and Dan Bartlett. *O'Connor and not Rehnquist?* Bush and Cheney understood that would change the dynamics. If it were Rehnquist, they could nominate a strong conservative without changing the balance of power. Since it was O'Connor, nominating a true conservative would actually shift the court's makeup—and therefore profoundly raise the stakes of the confirmation battle.

The court's Lincoln Town Car carrying Talkin pulled in to the White House driveway at 10:15 a.m. Miers accepted the plain manila envelope, walked it into the Oval Office, and handed it to Bush. "It has been a great privilege, indeed, to have served as a member of the Court for 24 Terms," O'Connor wrote. "I will leave it with enormous respect for the integrity of the Court and its role under our Constitutional structure."

Some later interpreted that language as an implicit slap at Bush from the justice who wrote in the *Hamdi* case that "a state of war is not a blank check for the President." O'Connor, who had arguably been the critical vote sealing Bush's path to the presidency nearly five years earlier, had grown deeply disenchanted, viewing him as reckless and radical. "What makes this harder," she later told Justice David Souter, "is that it's my party that's destroying the country."

But if Bush harbored any resentment of his own, he kept it to himself. At 10:18 a.m., he picked up the phone to call O'Connor for what ended up being an emotional conversation. She had spent nearly a quarter century on the bench, becoming in the process the most powerful woman in public office in American history. And now it was coming to an end.

"You're one of the great Americans," he told her. Bush could hear her voice breaking with the weight of the moment. "I wish I was there to hug you," he said.

He added a few more words of praise and then concluded in a brotherly tease, "For an old ranching girl, you turned out pretty good."

Bush invited her to the White House to make the announcement together, but she declined, saying she was heading to the airport to escape the inevitable media frenzy.

WITH O'CONNOR'S DECISION, Bush and Cheney finally set in motion a game plan that had been in the works for more than four years. Lawyers working under Cheney had already produced dossiers on eleven candidates, some extending to a hundred pages summarizing information in the public domain, including biographical sketches, journal articles, and past rulings. Bush took the files with him to read on Air Force One during a trip to Europe a few days later.

But even before he had a chance to sort through his choices, he found one of his favorite confidants under attack. Within hours of the O'Connor announcement, conservatives launched preemptive assaults on Alberto Gonzales, concerned that Bush would find the prospect of nominating the nation's first Hispanic justice too appealing. The conservatives viewed Gonzales as a closet moderate, an assessment that overlooked the fact that he approved legal opinions disregarding the Geneva Conventions, ended the long-standing practice of giving the American Bar Association a chance to review judicial nominees in advance, backed Cheney's court fight over the secrecy of his energy task force, and oversaw a judicial selection process that had produced nominees filibustered by Senate Democrats.

Conservative activists focused on a case from his days on the Texas Supreme Court when he voted to allow a seventeen-year-old girl to consult with a judge before having an abortion instead of her parents. Gonzales wrote that while the decision might conflict with his personal beliefs, he had no choice because of state law. But it was enough to convince critics that he was another David Souter, the justice nominated by Bush's father who became a mainstay of the court's liberal bloc. Some joked that "Gonzales is Spanish for Souter." The Four Horsemen went to the White House to warn Andy Card and other Bush aides against Gonzales. "He doesn't quite fit the mold we are looking for," Leonard Leo told the White House officials delicately. "You can and should do better," Boyden Gray said. They recommended, in order, Judges John Roberts of the D.C. Circuit, Samuel Alito of the Third Circuit in Philadelphia, Michael Luttig of the Fourth Circuit in Richmond, and Michael McConnell of the Tenth Circuit in Denver.

The attacks on Gonzales angered Bush, who finally lashed out while in Denmark on July 6, his fifty-ninth birthday. "I don't like it when a friend gets criticized," he told reporters testily. "I'm loyal to my friends. And all of a sudden this fellow, who is a good public servant and a really fine person, is under fire. And so, do I like it? No, I don't like it at all." In other words, *lay off.* But that did little to quell the storm, and for all his irritation Bush turned to other candidates as he returned from Europe, unwilling to push ahead with Gonzales without the support of his base.

He also got some unexpectedly public advice from his wife, who was traveling in South Africa on July 12 when she was asked whether a woman should replace O'Connor. "Sure, I would really like for him to name another woman," she said.

The comment stunned many back in the White House, who knew that was not the direction the search was heading and were unaccustomed to the first lady weighing in publicly. Even the president was surprised. "I didn't realize she'd put this advice in the press," he said when reporters asked about it. "She did? Well, good. I'm definitely considering—we're definitely considering people from all walks of life, and I can't wait to hear her advice in person when she gets back."

By this point, Bush had settled on five finalists, including one woman. All were appellate judges interviewed in the spring by Cheney, and three were on the list of the Four Horsemen: Roberts, Luttig, and Alito plus J. Harvie Wilkinson III of the Fourth Circuit and Edith Brown Clement of the Fifth Circuit in New Orleans, the judge recommended to Bush by Senator David Vitter. Aides wanted to bring the candidates for interviews to Camp David to preserve secrecy, but Card knew he could sneak them into the White House without anyone noticing. He had them brought one at a time through the little-used east entrance and taken up to the residence, where they would not be seen even by other presidential aides.

The first was Wilkinson, who came late in the afternoon on July 14. Luttig and Roberts were brought separately the next afternoon. The next day, Bush had lunch with Clement and then interviewed Alito. As was customary, Bush avoided questions about specific legal issues, for fear of looking as if he were applying a litmus test, and instead focused on life questions, both great and trivial, as he tried to get a sense of the candidates. He also gave each a tour of the residence, showing them the Lincoln Bedroom and the Truman Balcony.

Bush asked Wilkinson about his exercise regime. Wilkinson said he ran three and a half miles a day but had ignored his doctor's advice to do more cross-training. Bush gently scolded the judge, warning that he would blow out his knees. With Luttig, a fellow Texan, the president swapped stories about the Lone Star State and then asked if there was anything that would be particularly controversial if he were nominated. Luttig mentioned that his father had been killed in a botched carjacking in 1994 and that the murderer was executed in Texas in 2002. "Why would that be controversial?" Bush asked. Ever since, Luttig explained, some lawyers had tried to disqualify him from death penalty cases. After Luttig left, Roberts was brought in, having just flown in from London, where he was teaching a summer class. Roberts's timing could not have been better; his appeals court in Washington just hours earlier had issued a ruling in *Hamdan v. Rumsfeld* in which he had voted to put aside the Geneva Conventions and support Bush's plan for military tribunals developed in response to O'Connor's decision in the *Hamdi* case. More important, Bush clicked with Roberts, finding the judge's charm, confidence, and intellect appealing.

After interviews the next day with Clement and Alito, the choice came down to Roberts and Luttig. Wilkinson was courtly and impressive but also sixty years old, and Bush wanted someone young enough to serve for decades. Clement was being pushed not just by David Vitter but also by Bush's longtime friend Donald Ensenat, the State Department chief of protocol. As a woman, she would have Laura's support. But Clement did not have the stature among legal conservatives the others did, and she did not impress Bush during their interview. Alito was Miers's choice; she worried that Roberts did not have the record to prove his conservative bona fides. But Alito was a more reserved figure, without Roberts's easy charm or Luttig's forceful intellect. Cheney supported Luttig, the favorite of conservatives. So did Gonzales. During fourteen years on the bench, Luttig had taken strong stands on hot-button issues like abortion and was seen as the next generation of his mentor, Antonin Scalia. He was the one they had been waiting for. But Roberts had the support of many conservative lawyers who had cycled through the White House counsel's office over the past four years as well as Card and Rove. While he had been on the bench for only two years, he had argued before the Supreme Court thirty-nine times and was considered brilliant. And his decision in *Hamdan* seemed to answer any questions about his judicial viewpoint. Once again, Bush opted against Cheney's choice.

Given that it was O'Connor's seat, it was easier to nominate someone without a record as a full-throated conservative. Roberts might be as conservative as Luttig—indeed, they were close friends, Luttig having served as a groomsman in Roberts's wedding—but Roberts was polished, without Luttig's sharper reputation. At a party in July filled with big-name Washingtonians, someone asked what it meant that O'Connor had retired and not Rehnquist. Boyden Gray and Senator Charles Schumer, a leading Democrat, answered simultaneously, "It probably means Roberts and not Luttig."

Roberts, who had returned to London after his interview, was asked on July 18 to turn around and come back to Washington. That night, Card ran into Clarence Thomas at a state dinner for the prime minister of India. "You're going to love who the president picks," Card reassured him. The next day, Bush excused himself from lunch with the prime minister of Australia to call Roberts at home at 12:35 p.m. and offer the nomination. Bush was exultant, realizing he had made a decision that could shape American jurisprudence for decades. "I just offered the job to a great, smart fifty-year-old lawyer," he told aides.

William Kelley, the deputy White House counsel, picked up Roberts and drove him to the White House. Roberts's family later joined him and the president and first lady for dinner in the residence at 7:00 p.m.

"Does your mother know?" Bush asked.

Roberts's wife, Jane, had called and told his mother to watch the news without saying why.

Bush insisted on calling her.

"Hello, Mrs. Roberts? This is the president," he said. "I just wanted to let you know I'm going to be nominating your son tonight."

At 9:00 p.m., Bush and Roberts strode into the East Room for the announcement. Roberts's four-year-old son, Jack, nearly stole the show, dancing around in short pants and mimicking Spider-Man as Bush spoke. "We're gonna have to grab him," Dan Bartlett whispered to Ed Gillespie, the former Republican National Committee chairman who had been tapped to manage the confirmation battle. "If we grab him, he might scream," Gillespie countered. "Right now, he's not on camera." In fact, the cameras caught the antics, but it proved to be a crowd-pleasing moment.

Bush was pleased too. Two nights later, he appeared at a fund-raiser and saw Boyden Gray, who had helped his father make his own Supreme Court nominations.

"Congratulations on Roberts," Gray told him.

"Yes, I spent a lot of time on that," Bush said. "I hope he is twenty years from now the way he is today."

Just as he had reversed what he saw as his father's mistakes on Iraq and taxes, Bush now believed he was exorcising the ghost of the David Souter nomination.

At the Capitol a few days later, he ran into Representative Trent Franks, the conservative who had pressed him to name anti-abortion justices. "I'm glad you liked my appointment," Bush said. "I told you you would, didn't I?" Franks did like the Roberts choice. "Well," Bush added, "I am just getting started."

THE DAYS LEADING up to Bush's vacation proved busy ones. John McCain was introducing legislation to ban torture in terror interrogations. Cheney, through his counsel, David Addington, quietly slipped a veto threat into an administration statement in response. At the same time, six-party talks on North Korea's nuclear program reopened in Beijing, again under Cheney's watchful eye. As he and Donald Rumsfeld feared, Uzbekistan retaliated for Condoleezza Rice's tough position on the Andijan massacre by kicking out American troops using the airbase in Khanabad. And Bush decided to defy

Senate opposition by using a recess appointment to install John Bolton, a hard-line Cheney ally at the State Department, as ambassador to the United Nations.

Bush had another problem. The CIA leak case had been accelerating that summer. Judith Miller, a reporter for the *New York Times*, had been jailed for refusing to disclose her sources, while Matthew Cooper of *Time* reached a last-minute agreement with Karl Rove's lawyers allowing him to testify about their conversations. News reports revealed that Rove had, in fact, talked with Cooper and Robert Novak about Joseph Wilson's wife. Scott McClellan, who had vouched for Rove from the podium, felt as if he had gotten "whacked upside the head with a two-by-four." Rove had lied to him, he felt. Rove did not agree, arguing that he did not leak Valerie Wilson's identity; he simply told the reporter he had heard the same thing.

Rove tried three times to apologize to McClellan, once by phone, once in a note, and again at the morning senior staff meeting in front of their colleagues. But he was careful to say he was sorry for what McClellan was going through, not for misleading him. McClellan was not satisfied, and their rift cast a pall on the West Wing. Bush avoided intervening, and with Rove now at risk the president refined his previous promise to fire anyone "involved" in the leak. "If someone committed a crime, they will no longer work in my administration," he said at a news conference, a new formula that meant Rove would be pushed out only if charged and convicted.

Happy to escape the tension, Bush boarded Air Force One on August 2 for the flight to Texas. It was his forty-ninth trip to the ranch since taking office, and he planned to stay nearly five weeks, his longest stretch away from the White House. By the time he landed, it would be his 319th day either partially or entirely spent at the ranch, or roughly 20 percent of his presidency. Bush was on track to overtake the most famous presidential vacationer in modern times, Ronald Reagan, who spent 335 days at his ranch in California over eight years; if Bush stayed as long as planned, he would beat Reagan's record with three and a half years remaining in his tenure.

The long getaway touched off the predictable late-night jokes and partisan jibes, reinforcing the impression that Bush took a lackadaisical approach to the world's most important day job. It had not gone unnoticed that Bush spent a month at the ranch before September 11, a period when many believed he should have been more attentive to warning signs. Sensitive to criticism, Bush aides now packed his schedule with plenty of events to foster the image of a "working vacation" at what they styled the "Western White House," right down to a customized "Western White House" seal as a backdrop for press briefings. Bush was slated to leave the ranch at various points to visit seven different states, mostly quick day trips. He would sign energy legislation, host President Álvaro Uribe of Colombia, and then bring down Cheney and the war cabinet for consultations.

It was true, though, that the ranch appealed to Bush in a visceral way. Aides noticed him starting to get visibly excited whenever Air Force One approached Texas airspace. He loved the seclusion, the distance from Washington. He loved the mountain bicycle rides over rough terrain and relished exposing aides and reporters to hundred-degree heat. He loved jumping into his pickup truck and driving himself, something the Secret Service allowed only on the ranch. And he loved clearing brush, of which there seemed to be endless supplies.

Aides would be recruited to join the brush clearing and judged on their prowess and endurance in the sweltering heat. Stephen Hadley, the new national security adviser, was teased for showing up in tasseled loafers. (In fact, they were leather shoes with laces, but the loafers legend stuck.) "There was like a hierarchy that was completely different from any other hierarchy," said Steve Atkiss, the president's trip director who traveled regularly with him. "When you start, your job is basically, after someone cuts down a tree, to drag it out of there and put it wherever it is going to go. Then, if you really did good at that, the next level up was you could be in charge of making a pile of all the things that had been dragged over so that it burned well when you lit it on fire. If you were really good at that, you might be able to, one day, get to use a chain saw."

EVEN SO, IT was hard during those sweaty summer afternoons to avoid the grim news coming out of Iraq. Bush started each morning with a blue sheet overnight intelligence report that among other things listed overnight casualties. On his first morning at the ranch, the blue sheet reported a devastating roadside explosion that killed fourteen marines, ten of them from the same Lima Company of reservists from Columbus, Ohio, that had already suffered extensive losses, including six other marines killed in an ambush two days earlier. Reservists represented the heart of the military, men and women who detached from regular jobs to serve limited tours of duty before returning to civilian life. To have one unit of citizen soldiers hit so hard, so fast was numbing. "That really got him," Hadley remembered.

It got many other Americans as well. As Bush brought Cheney and other advisers to the ranch to talk about Iraq, just 38 percent of Americans approved of the president's handling of the war, and more than half said they believed it was a mistake to invade and favored withdrawing some or all troops.

Bush found a reminder of that closer to home. Just three days after he decamped to the ranch, Cindy Sheehan, the mother of a soldier killed in Iraq, arrived in Crawford aboard a bus painted red, white, and blue and emblazoned with the slogan "Impeachment Tour." She was stopped by police as she tried to approach the ranch, then settled in on the side of the dusty road, vowing to stay until Bush met with her.

Sheehan was one of the mothers Bush had met at Fort Lewis with John McCain a year earlier. While she was a critic even then, she had emerged from that meeting talking about Bush's sincerity and faith. Now as she recounted that meeting, she had a harsher recollection, accusing the president of being disrespectful by referring to her as "Mom" and not knowing her son's name. Suddenly the grieving mother turned peace activist outside the president's ranch became a media sensation, an easy story for White House reporters with little other news on slow summer days.

Sheltered in the ranch, Bush talked with aides about what to do. Should he meet with her? There was some sentiment for that, taking on the issue both to show that he was unafraid and to express the pain he felt for those who had lost loved ones. But he opted not to. He had already met with her once and disliked the idea of giving in to what amounted to a public relations stunt, backed in part by liberal donors and consultants. Instead, he sent Hadley and Joe Hagin to meet with her.

He could not have picked two more sympathetic or patient members of his staff, and for forty-five minutes they talked with Sheehan outside the ranch, listening to her grievances about the war and the president she blamed for her son's death.

"Don't let the president say that he needs to send more troops to get killed in order to honor the sacrifice of my son," she told them.

They promised to convey her message to Bush and made one last attempt to convince her of the president's sincerity.

"I know you feel like he doesn't care," Hagin told her, "but I can tell you, I sit in these meetings, and he cares very, very deeply."

"I don't believe you," Sheehan said.

They reported back to Bush. "We don't think we made a lot of progress," Hagin said.

Bush was bothered she would see him as uncaring.

Within days, other activists made the pilgrimage to Crawford as the protest captured the public imagination. Bush aides found photographs of his 2004 meeting with Sheehan that seemed to refute her depiction of it, about a dozen images of him hugging her, holding her hand, or putting an arm around her shoulder. Some wanted to release them to the media to undercut her account. "We are not going to do that," Bush said.

On August 11, Bush met with Cheney and the national security team at the ranch. Appearing in a short-sleeve shirt before reporters, he used the opportunity to respond to Sheehan.

"You know, listen, I sympathize with Mrs. Sheehan," he said. "She feels strongly about her position. And she has every right in the world to say what she believes. This is America. She has a right to her position. And I've thought long and hard about her position. I've heard her position from others, which is, get out of Iraq now. And it would be a mistake for the security of this country and the ability to lay the foundations for peace in the long run if we were to do so."

Amid the violence in Iraq and discontent at home, Bush clung to the notion that the political process would turn things around. Iraqi negotiators were scrambling to meet an August 15 deadline for producing a new constitution. But in the four-page note he got every night from his Iraq advisers, Meghan O'Sullivan and Brett McGurk, Bush read on the evening of August 12 that there was no way the Iraqis would make the deadline.

Sure enough, a few days later, the deadline passed with no agreement. It would be two more weeks before they finally came up with an accord. Whether the agreement would bring the country together remained to be seen.

23

"This is the end of the presidency"

President Bush pressed his face against the window, staring out at oblivion. As his jet swooped low over New Orleans and the Gulf Coast, the president saw an expansive lake where a city used to be. He saw mile after mile of houses turned into so many matchsticks. He saw highways that disappeared into water, a train plucked off its track, a causeway collapsed into rubble. And he saw the next daunting challenge confronting his presidency.

It was August 31, and Hurricane Katrina had ravaged the shores of Louisiana, Mississippi, and Alabama, laying waste to everything in its path. Hundreds of thousands of people were without shelter, electricity, food, or all three. Just two days earlier, Bush thought the coast had dodged a bullet, only to learn otherwise and belatedly cut short his Texas getaway to fly back to Washington to oversee the crisis response. With rescue efforts still under way, he was told it would be too disruptive to land the plane, but his pilots said they could give him a good look from the air.

Colonel Mark Tillman, the chief Air Force One pilot, pushed the plane down from its cruising altitude of twenty-nine thousand feet and skimmed seventeen hundred feet above the ground for a thirty-five-minute inspection of the arc of devastation. From the air, New Orleans appeared washed out, a city with virtually no visible signs of habitation. Bush noticed the Superdome with part of the roof peeled back and saw a neighborhood of houses where water reached up to and even above the roofs. As Bush watched, a Coast Guard helicopter hovered so low that its rotor blades whipped up the water below, apparently conducting a rescue mission. "It's devastating," Bush told aides. "It's got to be doubly devastating on the ground."

As the jet headed east to the city's outskirts and beyond, Bush saw that some suburban and rural communities were virtually obliterated. Acres of forest were leveled, trees flattened as if stepped on. An amusement park looked like a model in a bathtub, the hills of the roller coaster emerging from the water. Reaching Mississippi, Bush saw the demolished area around the towns of Waveland and Pass Christian, where wooden houses were smashed into scrap lumber. Bush thought it looked like the aftermath of a nuclear bomb. "It's totally wiped out," he murmured. Bush pointed to a church still standing while houses around it were destroyed. In Gulfport and Biloxi, the casinos were partially destroyed. Bush said little as he absorbed the enormity of the disaster.

By the time he got back to the White House, Bush had launched himself into crisis management mode, reviewing the massive relief effort being mobilized—navy ships, medical teams, search-and-rescue squads, electrical generators, a mobile hospital, millions of gallons of water. He agreed to tap the Strategic Petroleum Reserve to replace some of the oil and gasoline that would be temporarily cut off and then he marched out to the Rose Garden to reassure the nation that he was back and in charge. "The challenges that we face on the ground are unprecedented," he said. "But there's no doubt in my mind we're going to succeed."

The I'm-in-charge, we-will-succeed message that worked after the September 11 attacks did not work this time. The image of Bush staring out the window at the damage and the "doubly devastating" quote relayed to the media gave the impression of a leader flying above the fray, dangerously detached from reality on the ground. While he had been briefed repeatedly in the days leading up to the storm, delaying his return to Washington made it look as if he were dithering while New Orleans drowned, touching off a hail of criticism from his adversaries. "He has to get off his mountain bike and back to work," declared Representative Rahm Emanuel, a member of the Democratic leadership.

Now deep in the fifth year of a presidency already marked by one crisis after another, Bush was slow to recognize the scale of the disaster. He and his team were scattered—Bush cutting brush in Texas, Vice President Cheney vacationing in Wyoming, Andy Card celebrating an anniversary in Maine, Condoleezza Rice attending *Spamalot* on Broadway, and others traveling to Greece for the wedding of Nicolle Devenish and another Bush aide, Mark Wallace. By this point, the team had dealt with so many other crises, they had grown "perhaps a little complacent," as Scott McClellan concluded.

To be sure, Bush had received conflicting information. On August 28, before the hurricane hit land, the president walked over to one of the double-wide trailers at the ranch to join a secure videoconference about the storm, studying maps with his reading glasses as experts gave assessments.

"The forecast we have now suggests that there will be minimal flooding in the city of New Orleans itself," Max Mayfield, director of the National

Hurricane Center, told him. But Mayfield emphasized the fluidity of such predictions. "If that track were to deviate just a little bit to the west, it would—it makes all the difference in the world. I do expect there will be some of the levees over top even out here in the western portions here where the airport is."

He added, "I don't think any model can tell you with any confidence right now whether the levees will be topped or not, but that's obviously a very, very grave concern."

Michael Brown, who had succeeded his old college friend Joe Allbaugh as director of the Federal Emergency Management Agency, put it more starkly. "This is, to put it mildly, the Big One I think," he said.

Bush said little on the call other than to thank everyone for their hard work and promise any help the federal government could offer.

In the days and hours leading up to the hurricane's landfall, he received updates from Brown, Mayfield, and Joe Hagin, who was with him at the ranch. Brown called and implored the president to convince leaders in Louisiana to order a mandatory evacuation. "I can't get it through their heads," Brown told him. As the storm bore down on the coast, Bush called Governor Kathleen Babineaux Blanco in Louisiana, reaching her on her mobile phone as she was stepping up to a news conference.

"This is going to be a really, really big storm," he told her.

"Yes, Mr. President," Blanco said.

"I'm calling to ask you to call a mandatory evacuation," Bush said.

"Mr. President, we're on our way out to do that," Blanco said.

But while the city had been encouraging residents to leave for days, the mandatory evacuation order came too late for many to get out. On August 29, Bush left the ranch for a previously scheduled trip to Arizona, where he talked about Social Security and presented John McCain with a birthday cake that melted on the airport tarmac, then headed for California, where he was scheduled to participate the next day in a ceremony marking the end of World War II in the Pacific theater.

At first, he was told the hurricane largely skirted New Orleans, but Blanco called him that evening and asked for help. "We're going to need everything you've got," she said.

Bush told her help was on the way, but it was not clear exactly what she was requesting. Reassured by his aides that the government was on the case, Bush headed to bed.

At 5:00 a.m. Pacific time on August 30, he was woken at his San Diego hotel and told the situation was far worse than initially thought. He joined a videoconference, along with Cheney, Card, Brown, and Michael Chertoff, the homeland security secretary.

"What's the situation?" Bush asked.

"Bad," Brown said. "This was the Big One."

Brown sounded harried as he outlined what he knew. "I can tell you, sir, that 90 percent of the people of New Orleans have been displaced by this event."

Bush was stunned. "Ninety percent?" he asked. "Are you sure?"

The president decided to cut short his vacation. But he went ahead with his day's schedule in California first. While backstage in San Diego, a country music singer gave him a guitar as a gift, and the president gamely strummed it for a moment or two. He did not realize Martha Raddatz of ABC News was backstage at the time, and she caught the all-too-casual moment on film. Exacerbating the lack of urgency, he decided he would stop in Texas for the night before heading back to the White House the next morning.

For the return flight to Washington, Karl Rove suggested flying over New Orleans to demonstrate concern. McClellan and Dan Bartlett opposed the idea. "He's going to be at ten thousand feet, and it's going to make him look out of touch," McClellan complained on a conference call. The idea seemed to go away. But then the next day, the plane began heading toward the Gulf Coast anyway, and McClellan, feeling worn down by the ongoing fight with Rove over the CIA leak, did not protest again. At least don't bring the photographers to the front of the plane, Bartlett urged from Washington. But they were anyway, in keeping with the program Rove had set.

The television coverage that night was brutal, in Bartlett's mind probably the worst of the entire presidency.

"**MR. PRESIDENT,** I definitely need more troops." Blanco was on the phone and desperate for help. She had called the White House that Wednesday looking for Bush, only to be shuffled off to one aide after another. Finally, she and the president connected, and she asked for forty thousand troops. "I just ballparked it; I just did that in my head," she said later.

Without the military, the federal government was ill-equipped to respond to a disaster of this scope. FEMA did not own a single fire truck, boat, or helicopter; it was mainly a check-writing, contracting agency that financed frontline rescue work by states and localities in the days after an initial crisis. But Louisiana and New Orleans leaders were overwhelmed and as far as Bush could tell unable to cope without extraordinary help. On one videoconference, Michael Brown told Bush that Mayor Ray Nagin of New Orleans was behaving like a "crack head" and that Blanco was out of her league.

Bush was fully engaged at this point in leading the government's response. But having pushed every legal boundary in the wake of September 11 to respond to what he saw as the threat to the country, four years later he now went in the other direction, allowing himself to be stymied by legal arguments about the extent of his powers. A nineteenth-century law called the Posse Comitatus Act barred the federal military from exercising police powers on American soil, and Bush was told by advisers that the only way to circumvent that would be to invoke another antiquated statute known as the Insurrection Act or have a state government agree to hand over control of the National Guard.

Donald Rumsfeld resisted sending in the Eighty-Second Airborne Division, arguing that Americans might bristle at seeing soldiers in the streets.

Rice, back from New York, retorted, "They'll welcome the sight of the military."

Some White House officials were angry enough that they thought the president should tell Rumsfeld to issue deployment orders by noon or resign.

Rumsfeld was backed up by Lieutenant General Steven Blum, chief of the National Guard bureau, who argued that federalizing the effort would be "overreach constitutionally" and "a colossal mistake" logistically; instead of helping, he told Bush, such a move would actually hinder the operations of the thousands of guardsmen already streaming into the region from states around the country.

Bush was aggravated but did not take on Rumsfeld. Nor did he call on the carpet Brown, the FEMA director whose background as stewards and judges commissioner of the International Arabian Horse Association did little to prepare him for managing a national catastrophe. Brown at one point on television did not even realize thousands of people had taken refuge at the convention center in New Orleans without food or water. Bush watched with exasperation as rescue efforts faltered. "What the hell is taking so long?" he asked. "Why can't we get these people out of the Superdome?" If the media could get to the convention center, Bush railed, how come rescue workers couldn't? A volatile situation was made worse by false media reports about gunmen, scaring rescue workers away from the Superdome and other locations.

Bush decided to fly to the region on September 2, this time landing to examine the damage up close. As he prepared to leave the White House to board Marine One, Bartlett suggested he express his impatience in front of the cameras waiting on the South Lawn, reasoning that the public wanted to see him as frustrated as they were.

"Tell 'em," Bartlett said.

Bush agreed. "The results are not acceptable," he told reporters sternly, before boarding the helicopter.

Despite oft-repeated denials, Bush did, in fact, read newspapers, although he tended not to watch much television news. To make sure he fully understood just how bad the situation was, Bartlett put together a DVD of newscasts for the president to watch on the flight down to the region to give him a sense of what the rest of the country was seeing—and how much more dire the situation was than it seemed through official channels. Bush was shocked and angry.

At one point, Bush saw a fire burning on the video.

"What's that?" he snapped.

Some isolated fires had broken out along the coast, Michael Chertoff told him.

"Put the fire out now!" Bush said. "I want that fire out."

When he reached Mobile, Alabama, Bush doffed his suit coat, rolled up his sleeves, and met privately with regional leaders. Walking to an airport hangar, Governor Bob Riley of Alabama praised Brown and the federal workers.

"Your guys, Mike Brown, everybody is doing a heck of a job," Riley told Bush.

Evidently, the words stuck in Bush's head, because when he went back out in front of cameras a few minutes later, he repeated them.

"Brownie," he said, "you're doing a heck of a job."

Bush had gone from "not acceptable" to "heck of a job" in just a few hours. Just as he deferred to his generals in Iraq, Bush by inclination was not ready to question how his people on the front lines on the Gulf Coast were performing. But he cemented an impression of disconnect with a gaffe that would harden into one of the worst moments of his presidency.

Bush then flew to New Orleans, where he met with local leaders aboard Air Force One parked on the tarmac at Louis Armstrong New Orleans International Airport. Mayor Nagin, exhausted and sweaty, used the plane's shower. The conversation that ensued was frenzied and unconstructive. Senator Mary Landrieu was distraught, talking through tears and seeming in emotional meltdown.

Bush tired of her. "Would you please be quiet?" he said sharply.

Nagin was frazzled too and "near nervous breakdown," Blanco thought. He lost his temper and slammed his hand down on the conference table, demanding that the president and the governor coordinate. Bush tried to cut through the emotion and figure out the chain of command.

"Who's in charge of the city?" he asked.

Blanco looked over at Nagin but he pointed to her. "The governor's in charge," he said.

Bush was flummoxed.

"Somebody's got to take charge of this," Nagin said.

"I'd like to have a private meeting with the governor," Bush said. Turning to Blanco, he said, "Would you come with me into my office?"

They retreated to his office on the plane, just the two of them and Joe Hagin. Bush asked her what she thought about federalizing the effort. Blanco was put off. The first she had heard about the idea had been a message Senator David Vitter had passed along from Karl Rove. The fact that Rove was mentioned set off her alarm bells. What was a political strategist doing making such a suggestion? To her, it meant the idea had more to do with politics than emergency response. Her advisers had told her federalizing the effort would make things more complicated, not better.

But then as she was leaving his office, she felt a pang of discomfort at stiff-arming the president of the United States, so she said she would consult her National Guard adjutant general. "I'll talk to him again and I'll let you know before twenty-four hours are out," she said. From her point of view, she was just being courteous, not wanting to completely slam the door in the president's face. From Bush's vantage point, though, she sounded more forward leaning than she later remembered it, on the edge of agreeing but dawdling before making a decision at a moment when someone needed to be decisive. If anyone was playing politics, Bush's aides thought it was the governor and her team.

After returning to Washington, Bush and his staff settled on a plan that would put all troops in Louisiana, including the National Guard, under command of the president but, in a face-saving gesture to Blanco, would have Lieutenant General Rossel Honoré, the Pentagon's commander on the scene, report to her as well as to the Defense Department. Card had General Blum, the National Guard Bureau chief, fax a letter outlining the dual-hatted scheme to Blanco at the makeshift governor's mansion in Baton Rouge for her signature at 11:20 p.m.

"I want you to sign it and send it back to me in five minutes," he told her.

Blanco was taken aback. "I'll read your letter but I'm promising you I'm not signing anything until my lawyers look at it," she said.

"It needs to be signed tonight," Blum insisted.

"Why does it need to be signed tonight?"

"The president wants it signed tonight."

Blanco was aggravated. She thought the White House had been trying to pin blame on her through media leaks and now was trying to swoop in to claim credit just when the situation was being brought under control. Complicating the situation was the role of Blum, whom neither side trusted. He had told Blanco's team just what he had told Bush about what a mistake he thought federalizing the guard would be, but now at the direction of the White House, he was repeatedly urging Blanco to sign the document. "I was in a position where I had to read the script," he explained later, "but at that point, she knew the right answer." Finally, Card got on the phone and told Blanco that the president planned to announce the move first thing in the morning.

"I'm not signing anything," she told him angrily. "You guys are now trying to come in and save face. I've got thousands of people here in the trenches while you play your politics."

She added that Bush had the authority to do it without her consent. "You go ahead and declare the Insurrection Act and you take it over that way," she said. "I'm going to go out and say you all care more about politics than about saving lives."

At that point, Bush could have invoked the Insurrection Act, as his father did to restore order during Los Angeles riots in 1992, but in that case he did so at the request of the sitting governor. The last times a president invoked the act against the wishes of a governor were during the civil rights era, when Dwight D. Eisenhower and John F. Kennedy sent troops to enforce desegregation orders in the South. Bush was sensitive to the image of a white male Republican president declaring an African American city with an African American mayor and a female Democratic governor in insurrection. That, he thought, "could unleash holy hell" in the South. "I wanted to overrule them all," he later said. "But at the time, I worried that the consequence could be a constitutional crisis, and possibly a political insurrection as well."

Moreover, he worried about sending eighteen-year-olds armed with assault rifles and trained for Iraq into the Lower Ninth Ward. Bartlett argued that the details were less important than the image of someone taking charge.

"I don't care if we have to put corks in their guns and don't give them bullets," he told Bush. "We should just get them down there."

Bush ultimately finessed the issue by deciding to send seventy-two hundred active-duty troops on a humanitarian mission, rather than in a law enforcement role that would violate the Posse Comitatus Act. But even then he ran into resistance.

Card conveyed the order to Rumsfeld, only to be lectured on protocol. "Look at the chain of command," the defense secretary berated Card. "Where's the chief of staff? I report to the president. I don't report to the chief of staff. If the president really wants me to do this, he'll tell me."

Eventually, Rumsfeld relented and issued the orders. By going house to house looking for survivors, the troops from the Eighty-Second Airborne and the First Cavalry Division freed up National Guard units that were permitted to do law enforcement. But precious days had gone by without visible action, and Bush's public standing would never fully recover. Steve Schmidt, the vice president's counselor, wrote in an e-mail to a colleague, "This is the end of the presidency."

JUST AS HE turned to Cheney after September 11, Bush tried to enlist his vice president to help respond to Katrina. But this time, he was rebuffed. Natural disasters were not a Cheney specialty, nor was public empathy. When Bush told Card to ask Cheney to head a task force overseeing relief efforts, the vice president said he would only if he had real authority and could hire and fire people. He quickly concluded, however, that it was a "primarily symbolic" assignment and made clear he was not interested. "I would be a figurehead without the ability really to do anything about the performance of the federal agencies involved," he recalled. Bush was no longer ceding power to his vice president the way he had in his first term.

Bush was a little edgy about the rejection. At a high-level meeting about the hurricane, he needled the vice president.

"I asked Dick if he'd be interested in spearheading this," Bush announced. "Let's just say I didn't get the most positive response."

He looked over at Cheney. "Will you at least go do a fact-finding trip for us?" Bush asked.

Cheney said yes, but then added, "That'll probably be the extent of it, Mr. President, unless you order otherwise."

The vice president went down to the region on September 8. He quickly concluded that Michael Brown was outmatched and spoke with Michael Chertoff, the homeland security secretary. Chertoff had already come to the same conclusion. Chertoff and Brown had been struggling for control of the crisis for days. Brown felt he needed direct access to the White House, while Chertoff was not about to be bypassed. Chertoff was annoyed that Brown was spending so much time on television instead of overseeing the crisis. He finally ordered the FEMA director not to leave the Baton Rouge operations center. "Get the fuck off television and manage the operation," was how Chertoff remembered his message. Brown disobeyed and left Baton Rouge for a firsthand look at the damage.

Chertoff told Bush he wanted to relieve Brown. "You do whatever you have to do," Bush told him. "It's your show." So Chertoff sent Brown back to Washington, benching him. On September 12, Brown resigned. Brown later acknowledged that he had become "insubordinate" but only because Chertoff "simply did not know how to respond to a disaster and was trying to micromanage our response" from Washington. In the end, the storm and its aftermath cost 1,833 lives, did $108 billion in damage, and left hundreds of thousands without homes. Bush asked his father and Bill Clinton to lead a relief effort.

Amid the dysfunction, Bush felt burned most of all by the accusation that he did not care about the largely African American residents of New Orleans. Whatever Bush's faults, few who knew him included racial insensitivity among them. He told Laura that "it was the worst moment of my presidency."

But he and Michael Gerson thought it might be an opportunity to open a discussion about race and poverty in America, and they crafted a major speech for him to deliver. On September 15, Bush flew to New Orleans, and in a prime-time national address from Jackson Square in the heart of a mostly empty, still flooded city, he promised "one of the largest reconstruction efforts the world has ever seen." He accepted blame for the stutter-start response, saying, "I as president am responsible for the problem, and for the solution."

He tried to open the dialogue he and Gerson wanted. "As all of us saw on television," Bush said, "there is also some deep, persistent poverty in this region as well. That poverty has roots in a history of racial discrimination, which cut off generations from the opportunity of America. We have a duty to confront this poverty with bold action."

But with so much else on his plate, that sort of broader action never took place. Bush and his wife would eventually make dozens of trips to the region, and he ultimately steered $126 billion in federal funds for response and recovery, a historic commitment by some measures equivalent to the Marshall Plan that rebuilt Europe after World War II. But Katrina would remain etched on his record as a failure of leadership, and at times he was bitter. "Can you believe they're blaming me for this?" he once told Kofi Annan in a private conversation.

JUST AS KATRINA took its toll on Bush's reputation, so did it swamp his domestic agenda. By the time the government came up for air, it was clear the president's Social Security plan was struggling. While Bush wanted to blame the Democrats for their lockstep opposition—and to be sure, Democrats made a calculated political decision not to even try to collaborate—it was the Republicans who killed it. Speaker Dennis Hastert delivered the news to Bush at the White House.

"Look, we got another situation where our guys are getting killed on it in an election, and this is a poison pill for us," Hastert told him. "We don't have that big a majority and it is very difficult to carry this load and I don't think we are going to be able to pass it."

Bush was deeply unhappy. "I wish we could be able to do this," he said, "but let's keep working on it and see where we are at."

He would never formally surrender, but just like that, the top item on his second-term domestic agenda was dead.

His second-term foreign agenda was equally shaky. The Cheney camp resisted accommodation with North Korea. Robert Joseph, the hard-liner who negotiated the Libya deal and later moved to the State Department as undersecretary for arms control and international security, was now pushing for a naval blockade to keep Pyongyang from providing fissile material or technology to terrorists. He even handed out a memo outlining how it would work. "If there is a nuclear explosion, this would change the world as we know it," he argued. But few others had much stomach for it with two other wars under way.

With support from Condoleezza Rice, Christopher Hill had labored for months to lure North Korea back into an agreement on its nuclear program, and it looked as if he were about to score a success, despite Cheney's doubts. On September 19, North Korea agreed to scrap its nuclear program in exchange for an American promise not to attack. Bush had already indicated he would rule out hostility if North Korea had no nuclear program. The breakthrough seemed like a major victory for Rice's new approach over Cheney's old one.

But the next day, in quintessential fashion, the mercurial North Korean leadership backed away from its own agreement and upped the ante, demanding the United States provide a civilian nuclear reactor as a tradeoff for giving up its weapons program. That was essentially the same deal that Bill Clinton had made and that Bush had abandoned after taking office. Bush had no interest in reprising Clinton's greatest hits.

Then the standoff took a new twist. The Treasury Department declared Banco Delta Asia, a bank in Macao, a money-laundering operation for sheltering profits from the counterfeiting and money laundering of Kim Jong Il's circle. About $25 million in North Korean accounts at the bank were frozen. The action was not part of Hill's negotiating strategy, but it would come to dominate the talks as the regime found itself cut off from its money.

BUSH WAS IN bed with his wife on September 3 when the phone rang. As he reached for the receiver, he knew it would be bad news. No one called him at that hour with good news.

On the line was Karl Rove. Chief Justice William Rehnquist had died, he reported. The chief justice had been fighting cancer for a year, and it had been clear for months that it was only a matter of time. Bush understood immediately that it gave him an opportunity to further put his stamp on the Supreme Court. John Roberts had made a good impression with a confident demeanor during his courtesy calls on Capitol Hill and practice sessions. Now Bush had a second seat to fill.

The next move was relatively easy. While Cheney briefly floated the notion of promoting his friend, Justice Antonin Scalia, Bush instead decided to nominate Roberts for chief justice, moving him up even before he was confirmed. That had always been a contingency in the minds of the Bush team, but one that was reinforced by the smooth way Roberts handled his confirmation process. And with critics pounding Bush over Katrina, elevating Roberts was the safest choice. The president picked up the phone and called to offer him the job of chief justice, putting him on a path to succeed the man he had once clerked for. Roberts accepted and joined Bush the next morning at the White House to make the announcement.

Roberts was soon cruising to confirmation. He prepared for his hearings with a grueling set of "murder board" practice sessions, with administration lawyers throwing questions at him in a conference room at the Justice Department and measuring the length of his answers with a plastic kitchen timer. With occasional breaks for cookies from Harris Teeter, these sessions stretched on four hours a day, four days a week for four weeks. By the time he arrived on Capitol Hill, Roberts easily deflected Democratic opposition by portraying himself as a nonideological umpire calling balls and strikes.

Under Laura's quiet pressure, Bush was determined to find a woman to fill the other seat replacing O'Connor and told Andy Card to expand the search list. "No white guys," Card told Harriet Miers and her deputy, William Kelley. The list of women on federal appeals courts or in prominent law school positions was finite, and the vetting team quickly went through them. For one reason or another, none of them seemed quite right. Edith Brown Clement, who had made the final cut over the summer, had not impressed Bush in their interview. Edith Jones, a favorite among conservatives, was seen as too provocative. Other candidates included Priscilla Owen, Karen Williams, Alice Batchelder, Diane Sykes, Deanell Reece Tacha, Maura Corrigan, and Maureen Mahoney, but there was always something—either they asked not to be considered, had financial disclosure issues, or were insufficiently conservative. "We looked at every female appellate judge in the country who was plausibly a Republican," Kelley recalled.

Another woman, though, had been on Bush's radar screen even if not deemed a candidate by Cheney or his team: Miers herself. She was no constitutional scholar and had never served as a judge, but she was a pioneer in a way, the first woman to head the State Bar of Texas, a successful corporate attorney, and a former Dallas City Council member. She would bring real-world experience to a chamber filled with Ivy League credentials, just as many justices did before the modern era, when the court became increasingly the province of former appellate judges. Most important of all to Bush was that he knew her and was sure she would be a solid conservative vote. As far back as July, he had talked with Card about whether she might be a good candidate if a second seat opened, and Card had instructed Kelley, her own deputy, to secretly vet her.

Bush's instincts seemed reinforced when he hosted Senate leaders for breakfast on September 21 to talk about O'Connor's seat. Senator Harry Reid, the Democratic minority leader, had been impressed with Miers and declared that she would be someone he could support. "If you nominate Harriet Miers, you'll start with fifty-six votes," he told Bush, meaning the fifty-five Republicans and him. With Katrina, the collapse of his Social Security initiative, and the ongoing spiral of violence in Iraq, an easy confirmation appealed to Bush.

He summoned Miers to the Oval Office later that day and told her to put one more person on her list of candidates—herself.

"What do you mean me?" she asked.

Bush told her she had been vetted secretly, but she demurred, saying she was not the right choice. She still favored Samuel Alito.

"Well, Harriet, look at your résumé," Card told her. "Is that the résumé of someone you would recommend the president consider?"

Yes, she supposed so. If Bush wanted to consider her, she would not say no.

Bush began sounding out others inside the White House. Miers was well liked within the building and respected by many for her prodigious work ethic and unshakable loyalty to the president. But few could envision this graduate of Southern Methodist University's law school as a Supreme Court justice. She was the gatekeeper who made sure paper moved efficiently, who corrected grammar and quizzed aides about their choice of wording in memos, who once rejected the text of a White House Christmas card because she did not think it was well written. She had what the budget director Mitch Daniels called "that schoolmarm voice" that would calm a room, and she was at Bush's side during many of his most critical moments, from Air Force One on September 11 to the USS *Abraham Lincoln* for his speech on Iraq. But around the West Wing, Miers was deemed pedantic, not a deep thinker. She had never expressed a rigorous judicial philosophy. She hardly filled a room as John Roberts did.

Among those affronted by the selection of Miers was Cheney. While his views were tempered somewhat by those of David Addington, who shared a sort of kindred-spirits relationship with Miers as fellow graduates of non-elite law schools, Cheney did not view this as a wise choice. He had spent more than four years searching for the best and the brightest conservative minds to put on the court—at Bush's request. Cheney believed in curbing the liberal tendencies of the bench, if for no other reason than to respect the executive branch's power to wage the war on terror. The Supreme Court's intrusion into a wartime president's defense of the nation in *Hamdi* only reinforced the profound consequences of nominating the right people. And the president's onetime personal lawyer, in his mind, was not among them.

Bush anticipated that Cheney would not be thrilled.

"You probably aren't going to agree with this, Dick," Bush told him, "but I've decided to go with Harriet."

"Well, Mr. President," Cheney said simply, "that's going to be a tough sell."

BUSH TRIED TO figure out just how tough a sell. Even as the Senate Judiciary Committee voted to approve Roberts's nomination on September 23, William Kelley, the deputy White House counsel, called Leonard Leo, one of the Four Horsemen, to take the temperature on Miers. Leo said he thought it would be tough. After hanging up, he thought about it and called back to say they should talk more. Leo and Kelley met the next morning at the Ritz-Carlton in Tysons Corner outside Washington for two and a half hours. "This is going to be a real heavy lift," Leo told Kelley. It could be "a bloodbath" at first, he warned. But if handled properly, she could be confirmed. Still, Leo did not believe Miers was likely to be the candidate, and when he later called other conservatives to ask what they thought of her, they dismissed the question as too implausible to contemplate.

Cheney was not the only one who disagreed with the selection. Alberto Gonzales told Bush that Miers would be viewed as suspiciously as he was in conservative circles. Kelley and Brett Kavanaugh, the staff secretary, urged that Alito be chosen instead. Ed Gillespie, who was running the Roberts confirmation campaign and would presumably do the same for the next nominee, was urging the president to pick someone who would generate a clear-cut ideological fight. "A good, heated debate over striking 'under God' from the pledge, the merits of governments taking property from individual A to give to individual B, the validity of basing court decisions on foreign law and, of course, abortion on demand is not something we should shy away from," Gillespie wrote in a memo.

But Bush was not looking for such a fight. On September 29, Roberts was confirmed 78 to 22 and sworn in as chief justice. Bush invited the new chief justice as well as Gillespie and the former senator Fred Thompson, who had served as Roberts's Sherpa introducing him to the Senate, to the Oval Office, where he solicited advice.

Was it important, he asked, for the next nominee to be a woman?

Thompson said no, it was more important to pick the best-qualified candidate.

Gillespie disagreed. "Mr. President, I think if there's a qualified woman, it would be good," he said. Referring to his wife, he added, "Cathy's a conservative woman, headed up W Stands for Women, as you know, and I know she'll be disappointed if it's not a woman."

"That's pretty telling," Bush said. "My gut's telling me I should find a woman."

Bush headed to Camp David with Andy Card that weekend to think about what to do. He returned to the White House on Sunday, October 2, and summoned Miers to offer her the nomination. She accepted. The two of them joined Laura for a celebratory dinner.

For Bush, the decision fit a long pattern of turning to his own inner circle for appointments and, in a way, resembled the selection of Cheney, who likewise was in charge of finding a candidate, only to turn out to be that candidate. Bush trusted his own judgment of the people around him over the most sterling résumés of people he did not know. To stock his second-term cabinet, he had plucked Condoleezza Rice, Alberto Gonzales, and Margaret Spellings from his White House staff. Sometimes that worked; loyalty forged good working relationships. Other times, it proved to be a disaster.

In this case, Bush thought he was avoiding a fight by picking Miers. But he overestimated the reserve of goodwill he had on the right. Rove that same Sunday tried to reassure the base by calling James Dobson, head of Focus on the Family, a socially conservative advocacy group. Rove told him that Miers was a true-blue conservative who came from a well-known antiabortion church. Dobson agreed to endorse her. But when the White House called Leonard Leo just after 6:00 a.m. on October 3 to let him know that Bush would announce Miers's nomination in less than two hours, he was literally speechless. "Leonard, are you there?" came the voice on the other end.

Bush appeared with Miers in the Oval Office at 8:00 a.m. and called her "exceptionally well suited to sit on the highest court of our nation." At 8:12 a.m., two minutes before Bush even finished speaking, a well-connected conservative lawyer named Manuel Miranda sent out an e-mail message denouncing the choice to his expansive list of activists. "The reaction of many conservatives today will be that the president has made possibly the most unqualified choice since Abe Fortas, who had been the president's lawyer," Miranda wrote, referring to one of Lyndon Johnson's choices for the Supreme Court. Within hours, other conservatives expressed disappointment, including William Kristol, David Frum, Charles Krauthammer, George Will, Robert Bork, and Rush Limbaugh. While conservatives had been uncomfortable with some of Bush's decisions before, like No Child Left Behind, Medicare, and Social Security, this was the first time they revolted in such an overt, unrestrained way.

Cheney jumped in to defend the president's choice, calling Limbaugh to vouch for Miers despite his own doubts. "I'm confident that she has a conservative judicial philosophy that you'd be comfortable with, Rush," Cheney said. "I've worked closely with Harriet for five years." He added, "She believes very deeply in the importance of interpreting the Constitution and the laws as written. She won't legislate from the federal bench, and the president has great confidence in her judicial philosophy, has known her for many years, and I share that confidence based on my own personal experience."

Bush personally responded to the criticism the next day during a Rose Garden news conference, calling Miers "the best person I could find." But when he sent emissaries to meet with conservative groups, they were pummeled. At a luncheon of a hundred activists hosted by Grover Norquist, the antitax leader, on October 5, Ed Gillespie was shocked by the fiery reactions.

"She's the president's nominee," charged David Keene, head of the American Conservative Union. "She's not ours."

Gillespie was offended by what he saw as the notion that Miers was some glorified coffee fetcher for the president. "There is a whiff of sexism and elitism in some of the criticism of Harriet," he told the group.

The room erupted. "Are you saying people in this room are sexist and elitist?" asked Richard Lessner, an editorial writer turned consultant.

Gillespie quickly retreated. "No, I'm not," he said. He only meant some of the criticism of her education, intellect, and even makeup seemed out of place.

The dynamic was repeated at another luncheon with conservatives on the same day hosted by Paul Weyrich, one of the architects of the modern conservative movement. "I've had five 'trust-mes' in my long history here," Weyrich lectured Bush envoys, referring to past Republican court nominees who turned out more liberal than advertised. "I'm sorry, but the president saying he knows her heart is insufficient."

Ken Mehlman, the president's reelection campaign manager who was now chairman of the Republican National Committee, responded that this was not the same. "What's different about this trust-me moment as opposed to the other ones is this president's knowledge of this nominee," he said.

BUSH HAD HAD IT with the conservatives who were beating up Harriet Miers. The more they attacked her, the more he dug in. "I do not care about them at all," he railed to an aide one day. "I don't care what they say. This is my choice. I know who she is. I know what kind of justice she will be. I trust her."

But the situation for Miers was growing worse, not because of the loud activists, but because of the soft-spoken nominee herself. Like John Roberts, Miers would prepare by going through "murder boards," practice sessions where colleagues playing senators would throw questions at her. To get ready, she invited several lawyers to her second-floor office in the West Wing, including William Burck from the White House and Rachel Brand from the Justice Department. They sat down in the paneled office and tried some practice questions, although they were continually interrupted by BlackBerry messages and phone calls as Miers also tended to her White House duties.

Burck quizzed her on criminal law, laying out hypothetical situations. "So, in this particular circumstance," he said at one point, "when you search a car, do you think the law is correct that all you need is reasonable suspicion versus probable cause?"

Miers looked hesitant and confused. "I don't know what either of those two mean," she admitted.

The lawyers were shocked. A corporate lawyer overseeing contracts and financial dealings might not need to know the definition of probable cause, but when it came to the highest court in the land, that was as basic as it got. If she could not handle the most fundamental terminology, how would she survive under the klieg lights of a Senate hearing? They went through more questions and discovered how little she knew. The Fourth Amendment on search and seizure, the Fifth Amendment on self-incrimination, "she literally knew nothing about it at all, nothing," one official recalled.

The formal murder boards were even worse. The prep sessions were so embarrassing that administration officials kept out conservative lawyers who often participated, including Boyden Gray and Leonard Leo of the Four Horsemen. "They wouldn't let us," Gray recalled, "and both of us looked at each other and said that means she isn't going to make it if they can't allow us to see what's going on."

It was not much better on Capitol Hill. When Miers got uncomfortable, she tended to shut down and as she paid courtesy calls on senators, she returned to the White House each day with less support than when she had left, even among the Republicans. "Harriet, you're going to have to say something next time," Senator Jeff Sessions, a conservative from Alabama, told her after one meeting. When Miers asked Senator Tom Coburn of Oklahoma how she did during their session, he responded, "Harriet, you flunked." More critically, Senator Arlen Specter, chairman of the Judiciary Committee, was offended when she contradicted his account of what she had said about privacy rights during their meeting. He was even upset at her written answers to the traditional Senate questionnaire and sent it back to her to do over again, like a teacher forcing a student to redo her homework.

In the end, it was not the attacks by conservatives that would do in Miers. It was her own performance at the murder boards.

"Dan, we can't do this," one of the lawyers told Dan Bartlett.

"We know," he replied. "Give us time."

Andy Card offered a grim report to Bush in the Oval Office on October 25 and suggested Miers withdraw. She would be savaged on national television.

"We cannot put her through that," Bartlett told Bush. "We will forever damage her."

Bush understood and had already begun thinking out loud about who to nominate next. He was mad at his aides, aggravated that they had let this happen. But he realized he was the one who had put his friend in this situation and it was time to find a way out.

Card went to Miers that night and told her it was not going well. He left assuming she understood his meaning, but she did not. The next morning, William Kelley visited and was blunter. "You have to withdraw," her deputy told her. She resisted. But that morning's *Washington Post* had a story reporting that during a speech in 1993 she had suggested that "self-determination" should guide decisions about abortion and warned against "legislating religion or morality," comments that undercut whatever conservative patience remained. Concerned Women for America, a conservative antiabortion group, decided to oppose Miers. Bill Frist, at the White House for a budget meeting, privately told Bush that Miers was in deep trouble.

That much Bush knew. As the sun set, Miers accepted it was over, realizing that Bush, while never telling her himself, had been sending signals through Card and Kelley. Bush was working in his office in the Treaty Room in the residence at 8:30 p.m. when she called to tell him she would drop her nomination. He did not try to talk her out of it. Unaware of the development, White House aides finished revising Miers's rejected Senate questionnaire and delivered it to Capitol Hill at 11:40 p.m., three hours after she gave up. Miers scratched out a formal withdrawal letter and headed into the Oval Office to deliver it the next morning, at 8:30 on October 27, just twenty-four days after her nomination. The White House announced it at 9:00 a.m. Miers went back to the White House counsel's office to begin the search for a new nominee.

The experience would pain Bush for years to come. “If I had it to do over again,” he later wrote, “I would not have thrown Harriet to the wolves of Washington.”

Cheney could only shake his head at the unforced error. “I tried to tell him,” he told an aide.

24

"You could have heard a pin drop"

It was hard to miss the fact that Karl Rove was absent. It was October 28, the morning after Harriet Miers withdrew, and the senior White House staff had gathered for their regular meeting. Everyone knew the moment of truth in the CIA leak case was near and that the president's most prominent adviser could be indicted at any moment.

It had been a surreal environment in the West Wing for months. Aides were fixated on the investigation and what it could mean, yet they could not discuss it with each other, because the lawyers had issued strict instructions not to talk about it. Rove and Scott McClellan were estranged. Legal bills piled up for White House officials forced to testify. Even those not targeted by prosecutors, like Dan Bartlett, had trouble sleeping at times. Moreover, some thought the case had sown distrust between President Bush and Vice President Cheney, that Bush was not happy that Cheney had gotten them into this mess by overreacting to the criticism from Joseph Wilson.

As it turned out that morning, Rove was not the one the staff needed to be worried about. While the aides went over the day's business, someone came in and slipped a note to Scooter Libby. He read it wordlessly, then abruptly got up. He grabbed a pair of crutches he had been using since a recent accident and hobbled out of the room. "You could have heard a pin drop," Scott McClellan recalled. By the time the meeting ended, Libby had turned in his badge and left the White House, never to return.

Bush, who normally disdained television, sat glued to the set in the private dining room off the Oval Office watching as the prosecutor Patrick Fitzgerald announced Libby's indictment on five counts of perjury, obstruction of justice and making false statements. Fitzgerald had not charged Libby with the leak itself, alleging only that he had not told the truth about how he learned about Wilson's wife and whom he told about it. Rove, who had shown up late for work that day, had escaped indictment, at least for now.

For the president and the vice president, the week was already one of the worst of their time in office. The flameout of Miers's candidacy was a shattering blow to Bush and a reminder that Cheney's advice had been disregarded. Now the prospect of a trial of the vice president's chief of staff was devastating. It would go to the heart of the most dangerous political question confronting the administration, namely its veracity in selling the country on war. The Libby case had fueled the suspicion that the White House had deliberately deceived the country; "Bush Lied, People Died" was the favorite bumper sticker of the Left.

While Bush was shaken, Cheney was pained in a far deeper and surprisingly personal way. A politician who had not been reluctant to fire subordinates in the past felt profoundly upset about this adviser, who had become a virtual alter ego. Cheney believed the case was aimed at him and that Libby took his bullet. Some on his staff saw Fitzgerald's zeal as an extension of the fight over the warrantless surveillance program, recalling that he was appointed by his friend James Comey. They suspected the case was prosecuted "essentially to disable the vice president," as one aide put it.

Libby had left a letter of resignation with Andy Card and departed without talking with Bush. Dean McGrath, Libby's deputy, who drove him off the grounds, took him straight to his lawyer's office. In a sign of his sudden turn of fortune, Miers sent out a memo virtually declaring Libby persona non grata, ordering that "all White House staffers should not have any contact with Scooter Libby about any aspect of the investigation." The staff was demoralized; most, though not all, liked Libby. "The lowest point that I can recall was the lead-up to the indictment of Scooter," Peter Wehner said.

Cheney wrote out by hand what he wanted to say in his statement, and Bush aides were struck by how personally he took the case when they compared his draft with the one they had come up with for Bush. "The only hurt I ever saw in him was with Scooter Libby," Alan Simpson said. And just like that, he had lost his most effective lieutenant, his "Cheney's Cheney," as colleagues called him, the alter ego the vice president counted on to keep tabs on what was happening around the West Wing and to make sure his own views were heard.

With Miers shot down and Libby under indictment, Bush retreated to Camp David to talk about what came next. The first task was to find another Supreme Court justice, and at this point Bush wanted no more fuss. To everyone's amazement, Miers resumed her role as counsel, throwing herself into the search for someone to take her place as if nothing had happened. "Her stock went out of the roof internally the week after that, just the way she conducted herself," Bartlett remembered.

Bush went down his list of candidates straight to Samuel Alito, the appeals court judge from New Jersey and Miers's first choice to begin with. Alito, like Michael Luttig, had compiled a strongly conservative record during more than a decade on the bench but was not as prominent and not as easy a target for Democrats. Bush called to offer him the nomination.

THE WHITE HOUSE was pushing through another important appointment at the same time, one not as visible but arguably more important to the rest of their time in office. After eighteen years as the nation's sometimes inscrutable chairman of the Federal Reserve, Alan Greenspan was stepping down. During his long tenure, Greenspan had tamed inflation, coolly managed crises, and presided over a period of significant economic growth with low unemployment. But there were warning signs of trouble ahead.

Riding a wave of easy credit in the form of subprime mortgages, Americans were buying homes as never before, many stretching beyond their means. House prices had jumped nearly 25 percent in two years, creating a bubble that was pushing the economy along. Wall Street was taking those risky mortgages, repackaging them, and selling them as investments. Greenspan had reassured policy makers that this was not actually a bubble, only "froth" in certain local markets that could cool off. Other economists, though, worried that house prices had risen so fast on the backs of unsustainable mortgages that the bubble could collapse and bring on an economic downturn.

To replace Greenspan, Bush again turned to Cheney. Much as he did with the Supreme Court nominees, Cheney winnowed the list, then interviewed finalists in his West Wing office for ninety minutes each. In the end, he settled on Ben Bernanke—a Princeton University economist, former member of the Fed Board of Governors, and current chairman of the president's Council of Economic Advisers—and sent him to the Oval Office to see Bush.

Low-key and professorial, Bernanke was well regarded, one of the nation's foremost experts on the Great Depression. He shared Greenspan's comfort with the housing market, attributing the steep jump in prices to "strong economic fundamentals" like growth in jobs, incomes, and new households. He anticipated the possibility of "a moderate cooling in the housing market" that would not stop economic growth.

Bush announced the selection on October 24, drawing bipartisan support and touching off the biggest stock market rally in six months. Bernanke would go on to be confirmed by the Senate on a voice vote without opposition.

BUSH AND CHENEY increasingly found themselves on the defensive in the area where they had long been strongest, their handling of national security. John McCain, who was tortured in a North Vietnamese prison camp a generation earlier, was leading an uprising against the White House with legislation banning torture and restricting interrogation techniques used with terror suspects.

Cheney was outraged, seeing it as a self-defeating move that would hamstring their efforts to protect the country. He traveled to Capitol Hill to try to stop it, meeting with McCain and his ally Senator Lindsey Graham. He presented intelligence gained through the so-called enhanced interrogation techniques and argued it could not have been obtained any other way. McCain and Graham pushed back. "We are on the defensive all over the world; enemies use this against us," Graham told him. "And there is a better way. You can get good information without abandoning your values."

Their meetings grew heated. At one point, Cheney gave McCain substitute language designed to preserve the interrogators' flexibility, but the senator rejected it. Frustrated, Cheney lashed out and said McCain would have blood on his hands. "Basically, they told me that if our legislation passes, I am going to have planes flying into buildings," McCain told aides afterward. Cheney said later that McCain was not willing even to listen to a briefing on what the interrogations had accomplished. "We had hardly started when he lost his temper and stormed out of the meeting," Cheney said.

McCain responded with a show of force. At the same time the Harriet Miers nomination was foundering, the Senate voted 90 to 9 to approve McCain's Detainee Treatment Act, enough to override a veto. In the White House, some in the Cheney camp wanted to threaten a veto anyway. When John Bellinger, the State Department's top lawyer, saw a draft veto message, he went to Condoleezza Rice and appealed to her to intervene.

He reminded her that she often talked about America being on the right side of history. "I think history is going to judge us badly on our decisions on detention," he said, "but we can change course and you want to be on the right side of history on these issues."

Rice agreed and weighed in at the White House. After a lot of wrangling, the veto threat was quashed. Bush sent Stephen Hadley to negotiate with McCain, benching Cheney. If the vice president was angry, he made no protest that his aides could see.

But even as Bush and Cheney were trying to stave off restrictions on interrogations, one of the most sensitive elements of their war on terror was suddenly exposed when the *Washington Post* reported on November 2 that the CIA had been holding terror suspects in secret "black site" prisons in foreign countries. At the request of the government, the *Post* withheld the names of Eastern European countries hosting secret prisons. Even Bush had not been told which ones they were, according to Michael Hayden, the NSA director who later became CIA director. Subsequent investigations determined that they were Romania, Lithuania, and Poland. Others that had hosted prisons included Thailand and Morocco.

As Thanksgiving approached, Bush and Cheney decided to push back against critics. They were angry at what they saw as the hypocrisy of Democrats jumping all over them for a war many of them had supported too. While Bush headed to Asia for a summit, it fell to Cheney to launch the counteroffensive with a speech at a gala honoring Ronald Reagan sponsored by the Frontiers of Freedom institute in Washington on the evening of November 16. In the hours before the dinner, speechwriters hastily tore up their draft and turned it into a turbocharged assault on the Democrats.

Wearing a tuxedo and his trademark sideways grin, Cheney could hardly have had a friendlier audience as he took the stage at the Mayflower Hotel near the White House.

"Two thousand and eight!" someone in the audience called out.

"Not on your life," Cheney, the noncandidate, quickly retorted.

He wasted no time going after the critics. "I'm sorry we couldn't be joined by Senators Harry Reid, John Kerry, and Jay Rockefeller," Cheney said. "They were unable to attend due to a prior lack of commitment."

To make sure they got the point, he paused amid laughter. "I'll let you think about that one for a minute."

But his point was clear. "The suggestion that's been made by some U.S. senators that the president of the United States or any member of this administration purposely misled the American people on pre-war intelligence is one of the most dishonest and reprehensible charges ever aired in this city," Cheney declared. "Some of the most irresponsible comments have, of course, come from politicians who actually voted in favor of authorizing the use of force against Saddam Hussein. These are elected officials who had access to the intelligence, and were free to draw their own conclusions." Cheney was only getting warmed up as he assailed "a few opportunists" who were "losing their memory or their backbone" and hurling "cynical and pernicious falsehoods" while troops abroad were fighting and dying. "We're not going to sit by and let them rewrite history," Cheney declared. "We're going to continue throwing their own words back at them."

Bush quickly amplified Cheney's attack from the other side of the world. Asked about it a few hours later during a news conference with the South Korean president, Bush said he agreed. "It's patriotic as heck to disagree with the president," he said. "It doesn't bother me. What bothers me is when people are irresponsibly using their positions and playing politics. That's exactly what is taking place in America."

The attacks provoked a furious response. "We need a commander in chief, not a campaigner in chief," Senator Harry Reid, the Democratic minority leader, complained on the Senate floor. "We need leadership from the White House, not more whitewashing of the very serious issues confronting us in Iraq."

But the more potent retort came from Representative Jack Murtha, the hawkish marine veteran of Vietnam and the top Democrat on the subcommittee controlling military spending. Murtha had supported the Iraq War, but on November 17 he declared the war "a flawed policy wrapped in illusion" and called for the "immediate redeployment of U.S. troops consistent with the safety of U.S. forces," which he predicted could take six months. He teared up as he described meeting wounded troops and lashed out at Bush and Cheney. "I like guys who've never been there to criticize us who've been there," he said. "I like that. I like guys who got five deferments and never been there, and send people to war, and then don't like to hear suggestions about what needs to be done."

Murtha's outburst rippled through the president's traveling party in Asia because he was known as one of the most pro-military members of his party. The president's advisers worried that if Murtha could abandon the war, opposition could snowball. Beyond that, it was a personal blow to Cheney. He and Murtha had become good friends in Congress. Murtha had thrown him a dinner upon his appointment as secretary of defense in 1989 and was the Democrat whom Cheney relied on most. "The place where I did my deals that I could count on was Murtha," he once said. Now the man he could count on was calling him a chickenhawk.

In Asia, Bush's advisers argued about how to respond. Some thought Bush should meet with Murtha, but those pushing for a tough slapdown won. The White House issued a statement accusing Murtha of "endorsing the policy positions of Michael Moore and the extreme liberal wing of the Democratic party" and advocating "surrender to the terrorists." That only inflamed the debate. "That was the beginning of keeping our critics at arm's length," Nicolle Devenish, now going by her married name, Wallace, reflected later. "Obviously, it didn't work."

Bush seemed to think better of it too. In between meetings with Chinese leaders in Beijing on November 20, he summoned reporters and raised Murtha without being asked. "Congressman Murtha is a fine man, a good man, who served our country with honor and distinction as a Marine in Vietnam and as a United States congressman," Bush said. "He is a strong supporter of the United States military. And I know the decision to call for an immediate withdrawal of our troops by Congressman Murtha was done in a careful and thoughtful way. I disagree with his position."

Asked by a reporter about Murtha's attack on Cheney, Bush said, "I don't think the vice president's service is relevant in this debate."

WITH AMERICAN MILITARY fatalities in Iraq topping two thousand, the White House worried it was losing the war at home. "We may be running out of time," Stephen Hadley told aides. "I lived through Vietnam. A president cannot continue to fight a protracted war with less than a majority of support from the American people."

The president's advisers decided to revive their plan for the president to wage a concerted public campaign explaining a strategy that Condoleezza Rice had termed "clear, hold and build." This had been the plan for the fall until Hurricane Katrina came along and blew it out of the water. But once again, Karl Rove and Dan Bartlett argued over what tone Bush should take—defiant or humble. Rove wanted an offensive against war opponents, while Bartlett argued that admitting mistakes would do more to restore credibility.

The running debate underscored a broader rift. Ever since Karen Hughes left, Bartlett had become the main counterweight to Rove on the political staff. Lanky and lean with an easy smile, Bartlett had spent his entire adult life working for Bush, joining Rove's consulting firm right out of the University of Texas at Austin just as the first gubernatorial campaign was getting under way. He made a point of showing up early every day and ended up answering the phone when the candidate called in, then bonded with him even more when assigned to research Bush's history to counter negative political attacks. His prematurely graying hair and his confident, mature demeanor made him seem older than his thirty-four years.

But Rove had a hard time seeing Bartlett as a peer, not the kid he had hired right out of college, and the younger man resented what he saw as the patronizing attitude. Eventually, Bartlett stopped returning Rove's calls, infuriating the older man, and the two were barely speaking outside of meetings. A no-better-friend, no-worse-enemy kind of figure, Rove could be funny, charming, and fiercely loyal to his colleagues, but some privately thought the college dropout had an inferiority complex that sometimes manifested itself in condescension. When someone was on his bad side, he did not hide it. His feud with Bartlett spilled over to Wallace, whom he seemed to resent for siding with Bartlett. At one point, he berated her brutally, a "big screaming match," as one colleague termed it, that echoed around the West Wing.

"Karl kicks the shit out of me because he is too scared to kick the shit out of Dan or he's afraid he would push back," Wallace complained to Andy Card over lunch in the White House mess one day.

Card dunked his grilled cheese sandwich in his tomato soup. "I can't do anything about it," he said. "He doesn't listen to me."

Bush was constitutionally loath to admit mistakes, seeing it as a Washington parlor game. But he understood what Bartlett and Wallace were saying. The aides turned to the research of Peter Feaver, a Duke University scholar who had joined the National Security Council staff over the summer. Feaver was an expert on public opinion during wartime and had conducted studies concluding that the key to support even when a war was going badly was whether people believed it could ultimately succeed. Americans turned against Vietnam less because of rising casualties than the sense that leaders no longer believed the United States could win. Most damaging to public opinion, Feaver believed, were public signs of pessimism by a president, whether it was Ronald Reagan after marines were killed in Lebanon or Bill Clinton after the Black Hawk Down battle of Somalia. So while admitting setbacks was okay, it was critical for Bush to convey confidence that victory was achievable.

Bush opened a series of five speeches on the war on November 30 at the U.S. Naval Academy in Annapolis. Feaver helped draft a thirty-five-page "National Strategy for Victory in Iraq" mainly to prove that Bush had one. Feaver originally used the word "success," but the speechwriters insisted on changing it to "victory." "Plan for Victory" signs were hung around the stage, and in his forty-three-minute speech Bush used the word "victory" fifteen times. "We will never back down," he declared. "We will never give in. And we will never accept less than complete victory." Bush did resolve better than regret. He did not use the word "mistakes" but admitted that "we've faced some setbacks" and said "we learned from our earlier experiences."

Bush made more concessions as the series of speeches progressed. By the third outing, on December 12, in a hotel not far from Philadelphia's Independence Hall, he opened the floor to questions. The first person he called on was Didi Goldmark, a sixty-three-year-old former libel lawyer.

"Since the inception of the Iraqi war, I'd like to know the approximate total of Iraqis who have been killed," Goldmark said.

It was a question that the White House and the Pentagon had consistently refused to address. But Bush gave a direct answer.

"I would say 30,000, more or less, have died as a result of the initial incursion and the ongoing violence against Iraqis," he said. "We've lost about 2,140 of our own troops in Iraq."

Bush moved on to the next question without identifying how he arrived at the figure, but he was right on the money, at least according to a group of British researchers and antiwar activists called Iraq Body Count. As of the day he spoke, the group estimated civilian casualties between 27,383 and 30,892. Aides were struck that Bush knew the number without being briefed. It underscored, they thought, just how much he was living and breathing the war.

His plan for turning Iraq around hinged on elections scheduled for three days later, when Iraqis would go to the polls for a third time in 2005 to select a permanent government under the new constitution drafted in August and approved by a referendum in October. This time, the Sunnis, who had boycotted the election in January, were participating. The possibility of reconciliation seemed promising.

IN THE MIDST of his public defense of the Iraq War, Bush spent part of December defending the war on terror on another front. The *New York Times* planned to publish a story disclosing the warrantless surveillance program for the first time.

The *Times* had first learned of the secret program a year earlier, but the White House lobbied editors not to publish on the grounds that it would jeopardize national security. Michael Hayden, the NSA director, had invited Philip Taubman, the newspaper's Washington bureau chief, to visit the agency and hear firsthand from the people doing the eavesdropping—analysts who "were slack-jawed" to be describing one of the nation's deepest secrets to a journalist. The editors were persuaded.

But a year later, more questions were arising over the conduct of the war. James Risen, a reporter working the story along with Eric Lichtblau, was planning to disclose the NSA program in a book. The *Times* editors were revisiting whether it should go in the newspaper too, given what they had learned about the internal debate over the program's legality and the larger pattern of administration policies on interrogation, detention, and rendition.

The White House considered obtaining a court injunction to stop the paper, but instead Bush invited the *Times* leadership to the Oval Office to make a rare personal plea. Hadley and Hayden joined him, but Cheney stayed away, worried that the long-standing tension that led him to kick the newspaper off his plane during the 2004 campaign would be distracting. Taubman brought Bill Keller, the executive editor, and Arthur O. Sulzberger Jr., the chief executive and namesake son of the legendary publisher who resisted government pressure not to publish the Pentagon Papers. As the president welcomed them, he was polite, though not warm. He motioned to Sulzberger to sit in the chair normally occupied by the vice president or visiting foreign leaders.

Sulzberger tried to lighten the mood. "I know what it's like to sit in your father's office," he said lightly.

Bush's face registered no reaction; the *Times* executives thought either the joke went right over his head or he simply did not find it funny.

Bush turned the discussion over to Hayden, who pulled up a chair opposite the president and Sulzberger and laid down briefing materials. Hayden argued the program had prevented terrorist attacks, but one example he shared did not impress the newspaper executives, the case of a would-be terrorist who planned to knock down the Brooklyn Bridge by cutting suspension cables with a tool similar to a blowtorch. Sulzberger and the others found that fanciful at best. *How long would it take to knock down the Brooklyn Bridge with a blowtorch? Hours? Days? And no one would notice?* Sulzberger glanced at Bush and thought he seemed to be snickering at the notion too.

But Bush made the hard pitch, arguing that disclosure could cost lives. There would be another terrorist attack someday, he said sternly, and if administration officials were called to account on Capitol Hill for why they failed to prevent it, the *Times* executives should sit in the dock right next to them. Keller later called that the "blood on our hands" warning. "Whatever you think of Bush," he said later, "hearing the president tell you you're about to do something that will endanger the country is no laughing matter." Yet when they left the White House gates, with a light snow falling, Keller, Sulzberger, and Taubman agreed they had heard nothing to change their minds. It was hard to imagine al-Qaeda militants did not assume their calls might be tapped, warrants or no, so the most compelling issues were the legal questions: Had Bush and Cheney exceeded their powers? Where were lines to be drawn in a democracy during wartime?

They posted the story on the newspaper's Web site on the evening of December 15, shortly after informing the White House. Bush and Cheney felt betrayed by not having much if any real notice, which exacerbated their anger. The story, under the headline "Bush Lets U.S. Spy on Callers Without Courts," caused a sensation. Among those who had been kept in the dark about the program were Michael Chertoff, the secretary of homeland security, and Frances Fragos Townsend, the president's homeland security adviser, not to mention the vast bulk of Congress. Some inside the White House were stunned and wanted nothing to do with it. Frederick Jones, the press secretary for the National Security Council, refused to be part of any defense of the NSA program or, for that matter, the interrogation program many considered torture. "Maybe you should quit," another White House official snapped at him.

Bush ripped up his radio address for Saturday, December 16, to publicly acknowledge the program while defending it. Delivering the address live from the Roosevelt Room, he called the program "a vital tool in our war against the terrorists" and "consistent with U.S. law and the Constitution." Senator Arlen Specter, the Judiciary Committee chairman, vowed to hold hearings. "He's a president, not a king," declared Senator Russell Feingold, a Wisconsin Democrat. The administration, added Senator Patrick Leahy, "seems to believe it is above the law."

The episode prompted a debate inside the White House about openness. Dan Bartlett pushed to be more forthcoming about security initiatives, arguing that Bush was "just carrying too much baggage" from all the secret activities.

"Dan," Cheney replied, "we aren't doing these things for our entertainment. We're doing them because we're at war. These programs—and keeping them secret—are critical for the defense of the nation."

AT THE SAME time, John McCain pressed ahead with the Detainee Treatment Act. After winning the lopsided vote in the Senate, McCain now won an overwhelming nonbinding vote in the House supporting his position as well, 308 to 122, again enough to override a veto. Cheney wanted to keep fighting, but Bush knew he was beaten. On December 15, he endorsed McCain's legislation, taking satisfaction that Stephen Hadley had negotiated protection for interrogators from legal liability for past actions.

Inviting McCain and Senator John Warner to the Oval Office, Bush made the best of the situation, praising his former rival as "a good man who honors the values of America" and declaring himself "happy to work with him to achieve a common objective." McCain responded by thanking Bush no fewer than six times.

Cheney did not show up for the public rapprochement, but he was not done. With the help of allies in Congress, the final bill imposed less restrictive rules on the CIA than on the military, banning its interrogators from using cruel or inhuman treatment but not limiting them to the more conventional techniques outlined in the Army Field Manual. David Addington, who had replaced Scooter Libby as Cheney's chief of staff, made sure the cruel and inhuman standard would be interpreted according to a Supreme Court ruling that defined cruelty as an act that "shocks the conscience." In his view, that provided considerable latitude when measured in the context of a threat of a major terrorist attack. Once again, Addington had worked his will behind the scenes, encouraged by Cheney and tolerated by Bush.

Cheney articulated the more permissive standard during a surprise visit to Iraq. "The rule is whether or not it shocks the conscience," he told ABC

News during a stop on December 18. "Now, you can get into a debate about what shocks the conscience and what is cruel and inhuman. And to some extent, I suppose that's in the eye of the beholder. But I believe, and we think, it's important to remember that we are in a war against a group of individuals, a terrorist organization, that did, in fact, slaughter 3,000 innocent Americans on 9/11, that it's important for us to be able to have effective interrogation of these people when we capture them."

Addington intervened one final time, intercepting a statement the president would release upon signing the Detainee Treatment Act and striking most of the language with a red pen. In its place, he inserted a caveat, asserting that the president would construe the law "in a manner consistent with the constitutional authority of the President to supervise the unitary executive branch and as Commander in Chief" charged with "protecting the American people from further terrorist attacks." John Bellinger, the State Department's top lawyer, was furious and blasted out an e-mail saying they had just unraveled all of Hadley's careful negotiations. McCain was incensed; Bush was saying he would do whatever he chose, law or no.

Bush was operating from a position of weakness. Iraq had sapped his public standing and drained the political capital he believed he had earned a year earlier. Of the four domestic goals he had set for 2005, three were dead. Social Security disappeared without a vote. The Breaux-Mack tax commission produced a plan considered so politically toxic that Bush put it on a shelf never to look at again. And his immigration overhaul had so far gone nowhere amid Republican opposition. Only the fourth goal, a crackdown on court-clogging litigation, had been partially accomplished.

He found himself hamstrung overseas as well. The president who had vowed not to sit by and let another Rwanda genocide occur on his watch was now sitting by and watching what his own government termed genocide in Darfur. While Bush had taken a personal interest in Sudan and managed to broker a deal halting a long-running civil war between the Muslim government and rebels based in the south, authorities had begun arming local Arab militias known as the Janjaweed, which were rampaging through villages, slaughtering hundreds of thousands of people. By late 2005, when he sat down with advisers to ask what could be done, he discovered no options he liked. What about establishing a no-fly zone or sending in combat helicopters to take out militias attacking refugee camps? But Iraq had made that impossible. It would be attacking another Muslim country, he was told, and would inflame much of the Islamic world.

Bush wrapped up his Iraq speeches with a prime-time Oval Office address on December 18, his first since launching the war thirty-three months earlier. This time, more of the concessions favored by Bartlett and Wallace made it into the speech. "This work has been especially difficult in Iraq, more difficult than we expected," he acknowledged to thirty-seven million viewers. "Reconstruction efforts and the training of Iraqi security forces started more slowly than we hoped. We continue to see violence and suffering, caused by an enemy that is determined and brutal, unconstrained by conscience or the rules of war." He offered an olive branch to war opponents. "We will continue to listen to honest criticism and make every change that will help us complete the mission."

The president was pumped up afterward. Instead of heading immediately to bed, as he generally did after a nighttime address, he lingered with aides to chew over themes for his upcoming State of the Union address. The Iraq speeches made him feel he was regaining momentum. He was rewarded with an eight-point bump in his approval rating to 47 percent, suggesting the public was still willing to listen. The lesson he and his staff took was that Iraq had come to consume his presidency and there was little room for much else unless he kept the public behind him on the war. They would have to keep pushing for support on Iraq and take on their critics. Peter Feaver waged an internal campaign to get Cheney to debate Jack Murtha on *Larry King Live*, much as Al Gore had taken on Ross Perot over the North American Free Trade Agreement in the last administration, but the vice president demurred.

Bush was feeling feisty, though, his competitive spirit coming through. On New Year's Eve, he asked Karl Rove about his New Year's resolutions. After an incredibly busy 2005, Rove said he hoped to devote more time to books, a passion that had eluded him lately. His goal for the next year, he said, was to read a book a week.

Three days later, he and Bush were together in the Oval Office when the president turned to him.

"I'm on my second. Where are you?"

With that, a contest was born.

AFTER THE HOLIDAYS, Bush and Cheney focused on confirming Samuel Alito. Senate hearings were turning heated over his memos and other documents from his time working for the Reagan Justice Department. Of particular interest was a 1985 job application when Alito was seeking a promotion after working in the Reagan solicitor general's office. "I am and always have been a conservative," he wrote. He described his "personal satisfaction" in pushing Reagan policies: "I am particularly proud of my contributions in recent cases in which the government has argued in the Supreme Court that racial and ethnic quotas should not be allowed and that the Constitution does not protect a right to an abortion."

Now seeking the role of neutral arbiter, Alito explained that those were the words of an advocate and that his years as a judge had transformed him. But he had little of John Roberts's smooth charm, and Democrats were eager to fight since his replacing Sandra Day O'Connor would move the court to the right. The confrontation peaked on January 11, 2006, when Senator Lindsey Graham, the South Carolina Republican, came to Alito's aid with a series of questions intended to mock the liberal attack on him, particularly his affiliation with a Princeton University alumni group that opposed special efforts to bring more women and minorities to the school.

"Are you really a closet bigot?" Graham asked.

"I'm not any kind of bigot, I'm not," Alito answered.

Graham agreed and said, "I am sorry that your family has had to sit here and listen to this."

Martha-Ann Alito, the nominee's wife, started crying. Rachel Brand, the Justice Department lawyer sitting next to her, leaned over and whispered, "It's okay to step out if you want." And so she left the room. It was a genuine moment of angst, but Cheney's man knew just what to do. Steve Schmidt, the vice president's counselor who was managing the confirmation, immediately sent a note to the dais asking for a recess so the dramatic moment could sink in.

When Martha-Ann had recovered and stood up to return to the hearing room, Schmidt stopped her.

"Sit down," he urged. "Revenge is best served cold. Wait twenty minutes and *then* walk out."

The evening news was approaching, and with any luck her return to the hearing room might be covered live. The episode had made Democrats look mean-spirited. For all intents and purposes, any real suspense over Alito's nomination was now over.

THERE WAS PLENTY of suspense in the Middle East, where Palestinians were preparing for their first parliamentary election in a decade. In the year since Bush vowed to make democracy the touchstone of his presidency, the results had been mixed. The Iraqi elections, Palestinian presidential elections that produced a moderate winner, the Cedar Revolution in Lebanon, the so-called Tulip Revolution in Kyrgyzstan, and various reforms elsewhere gave hope. Yet by the end of the year, there was evidence of retrenchment. Egypt's president, Hosni Mubarak, still receiving billions of American aid dollars, released from prison Ayman Nour, a top opponent, and allowed him to run against him in an election, then after an orchestrated victory reimprisoned him.

The upcoming Palestinian parliamentary elections presented a fresh challenge to Bush. Israel already faced a crisis as Prime Minister Ariel Sharon suffered a massive stroke and his powers were transferred to his deputy, Ehud Olmert. Amid that uncertainty, Israeli officials were nervous that the most violent faction, Hamas, would win the elections. For Bush, it was a fundamental question: Did democracy really mean leaders chosen by popular will even if it resulted in a government run by a party the United States considered a terrorist organization? Some aides, like Elliott Abrams, thought Hamas should not be allowed to run, disqualified by its own history of violence. But he knew where Bush and Rice were coming from and did not fight. Bush made no effort to stop the elections.

On January 25, as Palestinians flocked to the polls, Bush was told in his morning intelligence briefing that Fatah, the more moderate party of President Mahmoud Abbas, would win narrowly. It was not until the next morning as votes were counted that it became clear Hamas had actually won and would claim 76 of 132 seats in the parliament.

Bush talked with Rice by phone that morning. "What do you think we should do now?" he asked.

"The elections were free and fair," she responded.

"So we'll have to accept the result," he said.

But accepting the results did not mean working with Hamas, which had never recognized Israel's right to exist. While Abbas would remain president, the Hamas victory dashed hopes for a peace settlement and prompted the United States and Europe to cut off much of their aid to the Palestinian government. More significantly, perhaps, it struck a debilitating blow to Bush's freedom agenda. Enthusiasm inside the administration for elections faded fast, and the so-called realists who had always been wary of the president's high-flying rhetoric now had something to point to as they argued about the law of unintended consequences; popular will sounds great unless it advances enemies of one of America's closest allies.

WHILE BUSH HOPED to remake the Middle East in a more democratic image, he also aimed to make the United States less dependent on it. Adopting an ambition that had eluded every president since Richard Nixon, he decided as he opened his sixth year in office to focus on reducing America's reliance on foreign oil, seeing it as a way of depriving autocratic regimes in places like Iran and Venezuela of their lifeblood and minimizing American exposure to petro-blackmail. He had long been a fan of alternative energy, lacing speeches with talk of cellulosic ethanol made from corn and switchgrass. Now he wanted to use his upcoming State of the Union address to promote a research revolution.

Cheney was skeptical. He did not share the president's romanticism about alternative fuels. They were fine as far as they went, but the cold truth was that oil and gas were here to stay, at least for decades. Others in the White House shared his doubts. In an interconnected energy market, it was impractical to declare that one barrel of oil came from an undesirable source while another was acceptable, not to mention that allies would still be dependent on the same sources. Energy *independence*, they argued, was something of a misnomer; energy *security* might be better. Besides, while net oil imports had risen from 53 percent of American consumption to 60 percent since the president took office, only 11 percent of the country's oil came from the Persian Gulf, even less than before Bush's arrival. The United States was depending increasingly on Canada and Mexico for oil, much more reliable partners.

None of that dissuaded Bush. His State of the Union would call for a two-decade project to break American energy dependence, echoing promises made by presidents for generations. His goal was to replace more than 75 percent of Middle East oil imports by 2025. After multiple drafts of the speech, he inserted his own catchphrase near the end of the process: "America is addicted to oil." Coming from a former oilman, that would have resonance. And the choice of the word "addicted" for the former drinker was no accident. If Bush believed in redemption for the individual, this was a chance for national salvation. "That was all him," said Jim Connaughton, chairman of the Council on Environmental Quality. "When we put it in, there was a lot of push back." Bush ignored the protests and kept it in.

Just hours before heading to the Capitol to give his address on January 31, Bush finally received one bit of good news. The Senate had confirmed Samuel Alito 58 to 42, overcoming Democratic filibuster threats. Alito was sworn in, just in time to appear in the House chamber in black robes next to the other justices.

"Keeping America competitive requires affordable energy," Bush declared in the fifty-one-minute address. "And here we have a serious problem: America is addicted to oil, which is often imported from unstable parts of the world. The best way to break this addiction is through technology."

The State of the Union was kicking off a new year. Things had to get better. What else could go wrong?

25

"Please do not let anything happen today"

The quail flushed from its covey and flew off into the Texas sky. It was late in the afternoon on February 11, and the sun was dipping below the horizon at the fabled Armstrong Ranch. Vice President Cheney swung around and squeezed the trigger of his 28-gauge Italian-made shotgun. Only after some two hundred lead pellets roared out of the barrel did he notice someone in the line of fire, a fellow hunter dressed in an orange vest but partly obscured as he stood in a gully, only the upper part of his body visible. "The image of him falling is something that I'll never be able to get out of my mind," Cheney said later.

Cheney rushed over to the man. His face, neck, and torso had been shredded by dozens of bird shot and were splattered with blood. The man, a seventy-eight-year-old lawyer named Harry Whittington, was breathing and conscious but badly hurt. Just one eye was open.

"Harry, I had no idea you were there," the vice president said.

Whittington did not answer. He later remembered only the smell of gunpowder before passing out.

A physician's assistant from the vice presidential entourage ran over and administered first aid. Within thirty minutes, they loaded Whittington into the ambulance that followed the vice president wherever he went and transported the wounded man to a local hospital.

Shaken up, Cheney decided to take the night to think about what to do. The Secret Service informed Washington that there had been a hunting accident and that Cheney was unhurt, but when the Situation Room passed word to Andy Card, no one mentioned it was the vice president who had pulled the trigger. Card passed along the incomplete version to Bush. As it happened, Karl Rove was friends with both Whittington and the ranch host, Katharine Armstrong, and spoke with her about the incident at 8:00 p.m., evidently without passing along the information to many people. The Secret

Service called the local sheriff, and he agreed to send a deputy to take statements in the morning.

David Bohrer, the vice president's photographer, called Neil Patel, the highest-ranking Cheney aide traveling with him.

"We have a problem," Bohrer told Patel, who was at a nearby hotel. "The boss shot somebody."

Patel asked what they were planning to do.

Bohrer told him the vice president was planning to wait until morning to make it public. Patel should come to the ranch then.

The news of what really happened made it back to the White House in the most circuitous way, and Bush's advisers were alarmed that the vice president had not publicly disclosed the accident. Even Laura Bush felt compelled to intervene. She was in Italy for the Winter Olympics when her chief of staff, Anita McBride, heard what happened from one of the first lady's Secret Service agents. She quickly called Scott McClellan, the White House press secretary, to find out what was going on, waking him at 6:00 a.m. on Sunday. McClellan had been called by the Situation Room the night before but given the impression that the vice president wasn't involved.

"Has the vice president's office gotten it out yet?" McBride asked.

"Gotten what out yet?" McClellan asked groggily.

"That he shot someone."

"What?" Suddenly McClellan was wide-awake.

She told him she had heard from the Secret Service that Cheney was the one who fired the gun. "Mrs. Bush wants that information out right away," McBride said.

The first lady was agitated that the story was being sat on and told McBride more than once to call Card, first from the ground before taking off and then from her plane as she flew back to Washington. "She felt very strongly that whatever the truth was, immediately it had to be told," McBride recalled later. "There was absolutely no reason in her mind that we did not." While she rarely played a visible role in her husband's political operation, Laura had a clear instinct for the dangers if the story was not disclosed promptly. "She knew herself too that it would fester if they didn't do that," McBride said.

Down in Texas, Gilberto San Miguel Jr., the county's chief deputy sheriff, arrived at the ranch at 8:05 a.m. and was ushered in to meet the vice president. "Mr. Cheney shook my hand and told me he was there to cooperate in any way with the interview," Miguel later reported. The two sat at a table, and Cheney calmly explained what happened. Patel arrived during the interview and saw the vice president get his gun and show it to the deputy.

After the interview was completed, Cheney greeted Patel.

"What are we going to do?" the aide asked.

Cheney was genuinely worried about Whittington. But all around him a furor was growing about disclosing the incident to the public. From Washington, McClellan and Dan Bartlett were calling furiously, but Cheney's staff in Texas refused to take their calls, instead passing them off to Lea Anne McBride, the vice president's spokeswoman (who was not related to Anita McBride). She grew frustrated. "We've got to get back to these guys," she told Patel. "We've got to figure out what we're saying and when we're saying it."

Cheney seemed unusually withdrawn, growing quickly tired and even a little snippy about all the arguing. Liz Cheney called Mary Matalin, her father's former counselor who remained a key adviser from the outside, and asked her to help out. Matalin concluded the fastest and best way to get the information out was to pass it along to a Texas reporter, who would have access to the local sheriff. "Let's get it to the local press," she said.

The vice president got on the phone with Matalin. He did not have enough staff with him to handle something like this.

"It's not going to be a story," she assured him. "Don't worry, I'll get it done."

But she did not understand the agitation building inside the president's team in Washington. Bush's aides were aggravated at being ignored by the vice president. "We couldn't get hold of him for quite a bit of time," Bartlett later recalled. "They were strategizing on their own, which always got me worried."

Finally, when Cheney's team called Bartlett back, they said the vice president planned to tell the *Corpus Christi Caller-Times*. Cheney had no illusions that would keep the story from exploding in the national media, but he saw no need to cater to people in Washington and New York who were eager to skewer him.

The vice president was not surprised that Bush's aides disapproved. Bartlett saw it as a disaster. It would look as if they were trying to hide the situation and would only fuel the fire.

"I have to talk to the vice president directly," Bartlett told the Cheney team.

When the vice president got on the phone, he listened patiently.

"Mr. Vice President, I know you don't have traveling press with you but we need to pull together a pool, get them down there, get you on the phone with them, get this worked out," Bartlett said.

Cheney said nothing. The silence unnerved Bartlett, as Cheney's silences often did.

Finally, Cheney spoke and made clear he had already decided what to do. "This is how we're going to handle it," he said flatly, inviting no further debate.

Not sure what else to do, Bartlett retreated. "Okay, Mr. Vice President," he said.

Cheney likewise "tersely refused" a similar appeal from Rove and headed to the hospital to visit Whittington. While the two traveled in similar circles—Whittington was friends with the elder George Bush and worked on one of his Senate campaigns—they had met only three times before and never hunted together. He was invited only after Robert Gates declined. Cheney did not know what to expect when he walked into the hospital room.

Whittington looked terrible, his face bandaged and red. Bird shot had come close to his heart and carotid artery. While many pellets had been removed, dozens were still lodged in his body and would remain there the rest of his life. But he was incredibly gracious with the man who had shot him.

"How are you doing?" Cheney asked.

"I'm fine, don't worry," Whittington said. "I'm really sorry that this has all happened. How are *you* doing?"

Cheney dismissed the concern. "That's the least of your worries," he said. "Don't worry about it."

CHENEY RETURNED TO Washington later without speaking publicly about the incident. Sure enough, slipping the story to the Texas paper only exacerbated the furor, giving the White House press corps, the cable talk shows, and the bloggers two issues to chew on—the shooting itself and the way it was disclosed. Cheney was disdainful of the frenzy, dismissing it as the arrogance of an elite media that felt entitled to be hand-fed. What difference did it make if it broke in a Texas newspaper? In the Internet age, anyone in the world could read that story. It did not have to be in the *New York Times* first.

But it left McClellan and the White House under siege. At his briefing the next day, February 13, McClellan fended off a barrage of hostile questions. He did not go out of his way to defend the vice president, referring questions to his office, figuring they should have to clean up the mess they had created. Exhausted and beaten down as he left the briefing room, McClellan was handed a notebook and sent to the Oval Office for a meeting. The vice president was already there.

"You did a good job," Cheney told him, evidently having watched the briefing or part of it.

McClellan took no solace from that. *You should be the one out there,* he thought bitterly. But he did not say that out loud.

Cheney showed no interest in meeting the press, and as one news cycle flowed into another dominated by the topic, Bush and his aides grew agitated that the vice president would not simply answer questions and put the issue to rest. Nicolle Wallace suggested Cheney give an interview to Brit Hume on Fox News, someone he would be comfortable with and who would do a professional job but not be innately hostile.

That idea did not go over well in Cheney's camp. Matalin considered the press frenzy crazy and thought all the "mattress mice" in the White House had overreacted to it. She called Wallace on February 14 and ripped into her. "You are a fucking press lover," she snapped.

So Bartlett, Wallace, and McClellan felt they had no choice but to enlist Bush. They were not going to be able to talk about anything else until Cheney did the interview, they told him. Could he ask him? Bush seemed irritated at the distraction and agreed to intervene.

After five years in office together, no one had studied Cheney more intently than Bush, and he understood that a media interview would go against his grain. When Cheney dug in on a question like this, he was hard to move. Cheney hated the phoniness of the public emotional striptease the media demanded of politicians—as if apologizing on television would make a difference one way or the other. "We've got to make him think it's his idea," Bush told his advisers.

How he ultimately did that remains unclear, but Cheney finally backed down and asked Matalin what she thought.

"Is this a big deal?" he asked.

By this point, she had concluded it was time to lance the boil as well. "Yes," she said. "It's spun out of control."

"Is this the best way to fix this?" he asked.

"Yes," she said.

Cheney sat down with Hume on February 15. He was genuinely upset about the shooting, and while he kept his cool, to anyone who had watched him over the years, his distress came across during the interview. "I fired and there's Harry falling, and it was, I'd have to say, one of the worst days of my life," Cheney told Hume. After days of Cheney's defenders essentially blaming Whittington for being where he should not have been, Cheney accepted responsibility. "It's not Harry's fault," he said. "You can't blame anybody else. I'm the guy who pulled the trigger and shot my friend."

The appearance accomplished its purpose. Cheney answered all the obvious questions, ending the firestorm after four days.

Cheney took satisfaction in one last jab at his media tormentors.

"You know why I picked Fox News, don't you?" he asked McClellan.

The press secretary didn't respond.

"Because when all the other media reports this," Cheney said, "I want them to have to cite Fox News."

But the damage went beyond a wounded friend and some political heat. His handling of the shooting was a moment that some inside the White House would call a turning point, an episode that soured the relationship between president and vice president and diminished Cheney's clout within the West Wing. "That had a big effect on the Bush staff and his inner circle," recalled Peter Wehner. Cheney increasingly came to be viewed after the shooting incident less as a sober and intimidating force and more as a political liability. He was even the butt of jokes that would never have been uttered aloud in the corridors of the White House in the first term. "People started rolling their eyes, you know?" said one aide.

Bush had already been pulling away from Cheney, more inclined to see him as one more person in his inner circle with a point of view, rather than the font of wisdom he had been at the start of their tenure. He was still defensive about the mythology that he simply did what Cheney told him to do. One day in that period Bush had lunch with Robert Strauss, the former Democratic power broker who had served as his father's ambassador to Moscow, and Jim Langdon, Bush's friend from Texas and Strauss's law partner.

Without being asked, Bush raised the question of the vice president's influence. "I always value Dick Cheney's advice," Bush told his guests. "There was never a time I didn't value Dick Cheney's advice. But we don't always agree."

THE STRING OF bad news did not let up with the shooting. Just days later, a furious revolt erupted among Republicans on Capitol Hill over a government-approved deal that would turn over management of six ports to a firm from Dubai in the United Arab Emirates. Republicans climbed all over each other to denounce what they called a national security threat. It was a telling indicator of how far Bush and Cheney had fallen that their own party did not hesitate for a moment to abandon them on a matter of security.

On Air Force One flying home from an energy event in Golden, Colorado, on February 21, Bush found Dan Bartlett entering his cabin.

"We've got a problem," Bartlett said, describing the latest moves by lawmakers to overturn the deal.

Bush was aggravated. This whole thing was political pandering, he felt, and an outrageous challenge to his own integrity.

Bring the press pool up here, Bush instructed Bartlett.

The very act of summoning reporters on the plane would send a signal since he almost never did it. By the time they sat down at his conference table, Bush was hot.

"I really don't understand why it's okay for a British company to operate our ports, but not a company from the Middle East when our experts are convinced that port security is not an issue," Bush said sternly.

"What do you say to those in Congress who plan to take legislative action?" a reporter asked.

"They ought to look at the facts and understand the consequences of what they're going to do," Bush said. "But if they pass a law, I'll deal with it, with a veto."

In five years in office, Bush had never vetoed a bill nor even issued quite such an in-your-face threat. A collision course with his own party was looming, and even some advisers were uncomfortable. "I was trying to get him not to," Karl Rove told Ken Mehlman after the plane ride. Republicans on Capitol Hill remained defiant. Shortly after the president's threat, Speaker Dennis Hastert sent him a letter calling for "an immediate moratorium" on the deal and adding that "this proposal may require additional Congressional action in order to ensure that we are fully protecting Americans at home."

The news was about to get worse. By the time Bush and Cheney arrived at work the next morning, on February 22, the war in Iraq had taken a drastic turn. The morning briefing was filled with reports about the bombing of the al-Askari Mosque in the city of Samarra, about sixty miles north of Baghdad. Insurgents dressed as security forces set off two bombs, reducing the gilded dome to a pile of rubble, and with it any remaining shreds of peace. "This is as 9/11 in the United States," declared Adel Abdul Mahdi, one of Iraq's two vice presidents. The shrine, also known as the Golden Mosque, was one of the holiest religious sites in the Shiite world. Moqtada al-Sadr's Mahdi Army was in the streets taking revenge on Sunnis. The attack set off such spasms of anger that Grand Ayatollah Ali Sistani made an unprecedented appearance on national television and issued a written statement ominously warning Iraqi authorities that Shiites might take matters into their own hands.

Bush appealed for calm and hoped to avoid a major rupture. But that quickly proved illusory. Bodies piled up as Shiite and Sunni fighters engaged in open warfare, presumably the goal of the bombing, which was quickly linked to Abu Musab al-Zarqawi, leader of al-Qaeda in Iraq. That evening, Bush read his nightly report on Iraq and found a grim assessment. "For the first time," said the report prepared by Meghan O'Sullivan, Brett McGurk, and the Iraq team, "all of our contacts in Iraq now speak openly of civil war."

The bombing came at a time when the political process Bush and Cheney were counting on had already slowed. It had been two months since the Iraqi parliamentary elections, and there was still no sign of a new government. Ibrahim al-Jaafari, the interim prime minister, was trying to hold on to the post, but he had not impressed the Americans as an effective leader or someone capable of stopping the violence. He was prone to waxing about the founding fathers but referred to them by names like George Jefferson and Jack Washington. Condoleezza Rice considered him "an odd man with the bearing of a humanities professor." O'Sullivan wrote a memo to Bush and Hadley urging them to resist considering Jaafari a fait accompli and arguing that it was in the American interest to push for another outcome. But some in the White House suspected that Zalmay Khalilzad, now the ambassador in Baghdad, was helping Jaafari. He later denied that, attributing such suspicion to his refusal to help a rival candidate, Adel Abdul Mahdi. Either way, Jaafari won the narrow support of his Shiite coalition. "I think this is the day we lost Iraq," McGurk wrote in an e-mail to O'Sullivan.

By the end of the week, Sunni political leaders announced they would drop out of government formation talks, and the Baghdad morgue reported as many as 1,300 corpses. Entire blocks of Sunni families had been wiped out, and reports reaching the Oval Office grew grimmer. On February 25, Bush called seven Iraqi leaders one after the other, imploring them to tamp down the incendiary rhetoric and come to the table. When he reached Abdul Aziz al-Hakim, leader of the Supreme Council for Islamic Revolution in Iraq, a powerful Shiite party, he was met with silence. Then, finally, Hakim said, "Mr. President, please help us. Help us, Mr. President." Shiite, Sunni, and Kurdish leaders appeared in public together later that day to appeal for calm and announce that talks to form a government would go on, but something had changed.

Many would later point to the bombing of the mosque as the tipping point in the war, triggering sectarian conflict that would ultimately claim thousands more lives. The bombing was undoubtedly a grim milestone, but it was also the culmination of tensions ready to burst forth. The elections of 2005, for all their purple-fingered exultation, had papered over fractures tearing apart Iraqi society. The Sunni boycott, the rise of militias, the paralyzing deadlock in forming a government, all set the stage for the tumult that followed the bombing. Zarqawi had merely lit the match. "He actually succeeded and he touched off the sectarian violence and nobody was there in force or in a strategy and was viewed as an honest enough broker to put it down," Stephen Hadley later concluded. "From the bombing of the mosque in Samarra—it had really been building before that—but the real slide begins," recalled his deputy, J. D. Crouch.

Bush turned glum as a bloody winter turned into an even bloodier spring. "I don't think anything disturbed him more than the sectarian violence that occurred in the wake of the Samarra mosque bombing," reflected John Negroponte, the former ambassador to Iraq who was now briefing Bush every morning as the first director of national intelligence. "I think he went through a period for several weeks—I don't know if he went into a state of depression, but I think he was visibly discouraged by the situation in Iraq during this sectarian violence, almost to the point of despondence, because I think it looked to him like the whole game was going down the drain. He was really bothered by that." At some briefings, "it was almost as if he was pleading with us not to give him any more bad news."

Bush's consternation was mirrored by discontent on Capitol Hill, where lawmakers of both parties had concluded that Donald Rumsfeld should bear responsibility for the war. Andy Card tried to use that to convince Bush to finally push out the defense secretary. "Hey, up on the Hill, the drums are beating pretty loudly for change," he told Bush. "I think they're serious and you should think about it."

BUSH TURNED HIS attention briefly to the other war, the largely forgotten conflict in Afghanistan. On March 1, he and Laura made a secret trip to Bagram Air Base north of Kabul, then flew by helicopter to the capital. Bush was struck by the breathtaking scenery, the snowcapped mountains behind brown plains.

With all attention on Iraq, where the bloodshed was unremitting, Afghanistan had gone unnoticed for months, the assumption in Washington being that things were under control. For the moment, they appeared to be, but that misjudgment was fueled by a lack of intelligence, the assets having been moved to the other theater. In reality, Taliban elements were preparing to rally their forces again. "We don't have more troops, and the fighting is getting worse as predicted," Ambassador Ronald Neumann recalled.

Neumann had asked for $600 million for reconstruction projects like roads, power, agricultural development, only to have it cut to $400 million, less than the cost of two days of war in Iraq. So he urged Bush to emphasize American commitment to the Afghans. Over a lunch of *kabuli palau*, Bush assured President Hamid Karzai that America would stay for the long run. Then he went to the embassy to dedicate a new chancery. He didn't much care for the paint job.

"Who picked that baby-shit yellow?" he asked.

"Sir, Secretary Rice owns that building," Neumann replied.

For Laura, the trip was a rare chance to spend concentrated time with her husband on duty. She had watched as he absorbed one blow after another. She knew Bush needed a break from the bad news. "I am certain that all presidents have moments when they simply ask God, 'Please do not let anything happen today,'" she later observed.

Nothing all that bad happened that day. But a week later, the Dubai firm that had won the contract announced it would transfer its port operations to an American company. Bush's opponents had scared it off. His veto threat had failed.

ON THE NIGHT of March 11, Bush and Cheney attended the annual Gridiron Club dinner, a white-tie affair attended by presidents since 1885. If Cheney's mishap had made him the butt of jokes behind his back in the White House, Bush now chose to poke fun to his face.

The president at these dinners was expected to give a humorous talk, so Bush opened with a reference to the shooting incident, alluding to the last time a vice president shot someone, namely Aaron Burr's duel with Alexander Hamilton.

"Mr. Vice President," Bush said, nodding toward Cheney as he greeted the dignitaries onstage. Then, toward Lynne Cheney, he added, "Mrs. Burr."

He went on: "There are all these conspiracy theories that Dick runs the country, or Karl runs the country. Why aren't there any conspiracy theories that I run the country? Really ticks me off."

Bush noted Cheney's middle initial. "B. stands for bull's-eye," he joked. He said the media blew the hunting incident out of proportion. "Good Lord, you'd thought he shot somebody or something."

He kept going: "I really chewed Dick out for the way he handled the whole thing. Dick, I've got an approval rating of 38 percent and you shoot the only trial lawyer in the country who likes me." Bush added, "By the way, when Dick first heard my approval rating was 38 percent, he said, 'What's your secret?'"

Cheney took it with good humor, laughing when he was supposed to. If serving his president meant being the straight man, it was one more service he would provide.

The laughter was a brief interlude in the cascade of bad news. As Bush alluded to, his poll numbers had plummeted to the lowest of any second-term president other than Richard Nixon in the past half century, and Cheney's were worse. Some friends believed Bush needed to shake things up. After all, most of his inner circle had been there since the beginning, more than five years, not counting the campaign. Andy Card got up every day at 4:20 a.m., arrived at the White House an hour later, and did not return home until 9:00 p.m., with phone calls often coming in until 11:00. Then he would get up the next day and do it all over again. No other president's top aide had stayed as long since Sherman Adams under Dwight Eisenhower. Certainly, many of the problems were beyond Card's control, and he enjoyed deep respect inside the White House. But there were some who felt his low-key, self-effacing approach was no longer effective, that he was too weak, that fatigue had led to unforced errors. "We're all burned out," one aide confided at the time. "People are just tired."

Over lunch one day in that period, Bush heard from Clay Johnson, his longtime friend and deputy budget director, that the White House structure was a "clusterfuck," a jumble of crossed lines that he scratched out on a napkin for demonstration purposes. Rather than a commanding figure like other chiefs of staff, Card had been more like the ultimate body man, sticking close to the president through the day and serving as an alter ego; Cheney, in effect, had played the role of chief of staff, dominating the White House operation set up to feed decisions to the president. Card had at times been a punching bag for Rumsfeld, who called to berate him. "You don't know how to be chief of staff," Rumsfeld would tell him, as Card recalled to colleagues. "You're failing the president in your job."

Card at least understood, as Rumsfeld did not, that his time had come; he had been urging Bush to accept his resignation for more than a year, arguing that there were only a handful of people who had enough stature to make a difference in public perceptions by leaving: Cheney, Rice, Rumsfeld, Rove, and himself. Bush had resisted, but now it was time. In March, he summoned Joshua Bolten, now the budget director, and asked if he would be willing to take over.

To break the news, Bush invited Card and his wife, Kathleene, to Camp David on the last weekend of March. When the president stopped by the bowling alley to talk with Card one evening, he did not even have to say the words. "My face must have betrayed my anguish," Bush recalled. He began telling Card how grateful he was for his service, but Card cut him off and said he understood.

Bush announced the decision at 8:30 a.m. on March 28, praising Card for "his calm in crisis, his absolute integrity and his tireless commitment to public service." Bush realized how much he had come to lean on Card. At a later farewell party at Blair House, Bush choked up and could not even get through his remarks.

Bolten had been with Bush even longer than Card and was just as hard a worker, but he arrived at his new assignment determined to "refresh and reenergize" the White House. He was a self-described "policy geek," serious, bright, well liked, "the smartest person in the room," as Nicolle Wallace put it. And yet he was also an avid Harley-Davidson Fat Boy motorcycle rider, a member of a rock band he named Deficit Attention Disorder, and a bachelor once linked to Bo Derek. He brought a dry wit to staff meetings; when someone strayed off course, he would throw a yellow penalty flag onto the conference table like a football referee.

While Cheney respected him, Bolten's selection was another ominous sign for the vice president. For one thing, Bolten intended to be more hands-on than Card, and he planned to make a series of personnel changes. For another, he was not as conservative as Cheney and was more interested in Bush's pet issues like fighting climate change and AIDS in Africa. Most significantly, he had Rumsfeld, Cheney's best friend, in his crosshairs and, unlike Card, would not be deterred for long.

As Bolten looked ahead, Iraq was at the top of the agenda. "Josh viewed his job as getting Bush to understand that Iraq was going to hell in a handbasket and some really big decisions had to be made," observed Michael Gerson. Just days after Bolten's selection, Rumsfeld got into a public spat with Condoleezza Rice that left the impression that he was out of touch with public discontent over Iraq. Rice in London had said that the United States had probably made "thousands" of "tactical errors" in Iraq but had gotten the broader strategy right. Rumsfeld fired back, saying publicly that such a comment betrayed a "lack of understanding" about the war.

Bush still saw the problem as perception as much as reality. He told a visitor that the situation was manageable but exacerbated by a press corps that emphasized failure and gave no credit to success. "The American people are watching—do I have the will to do what I'm doing or will I lose my nerve?" he said. "I will not lose my nerve."

BOLTEN TOOK OVER on April 14, but any ideas of easing out the controversial defense chief were undermined on his first day. Prominent retired army and marine generals had begun speaking out harshly about Rumsfeld and urging that he be fired. Among them were General Anthony C. Zinni, former head of Central Command overseeing operations in the Middle East; Lieutenant General Gregory Newbold, former operations director for the Joint Chiefs of Staff; and Major Generals Paul D. Eaton, who had overseen training of Iraqi troops, and John Batiste, who had commanded a division in Iraq.

But their criticism backfired. Rather than convincing Bush, it got his back up. Although he too had concerns about Rumsfeld, Bush bristled at the idea of military officers, even retired ones, effectively pushing out civilian leadership. Bolten realized any effort to replace Rumsfeld would have to wait.

"We need to step up and give a strong endorsement to Rumsfeld," Bolten told Bush.

Bush agreed and released a statement from Camp David, where he had retreated for Easter: "Secretary Rumsfeld's energetic and steady leadership is exactly what is needed at this critical period. He has my full support and deepest appreciation."

Four days later, addressing reporters in the Rose Garden, Bush went further. "I hear the voices, and I read the front page, and I know the speculation," he said. "But I'm the decider and I decide what is best. And what's best is for Don Rumsfeld to remain as the secretary of defense."

That ended the public discussion for a while, but it did not put an end to it behind closed doors. As the Decider tried to reboot his presidency, Bush invited his closest advisers to the residence one evening in April. Sitting in the Yellow Oval Room, he solicited ideas for how to regain momentum. Ken Mehlman did not hesitate to recommend that Rumsfeld be fired. It was important to show that they understood things were not going well, he said. At the end of the day, it was not about pleasing elites in Washington but about recognizing that the reason a company like Walmart was successful was that every day it adjusted to changing circumstances. Gerson agreed, reprising the argument he made after the 2004 election when he first suggested replacing Rumsfeld.

Bush took that in, then asked for a show of hands. Who thought Rumsfeld should go? Most hands went up, including those of Bolten, Mehlman, Gerson, Rice, Card, Karen Hughes, Ed Gillespie, and Margaret Spellings.

When Joel Kaplan, Bolten's incoming deputy chief of staff, raised his, Bush looked surprised.

"You too?" Bush asked.

"Yes, sir."

But others were skeptical, including Rove, Stephen Hadley, and Dan Bartlett. After the generals' revolt, especially, it just seemed that changing horses at this point would be a mistake. Cheney had been making the same point to Bush in private. Bush agreed.

Bolten might have failed at first to take out Rumsfeld, but he had better luck imposing his will on the West Wing. His first act was to strip Rove of the policy portfolio he had won in the second term, giving it instead to Kaplan. Bolten wanted clearer lines of authority and thought Rove was ill-matched to the role. The new chief also eased out Scott McClellan as the press secretary and public face of the White House. As much as he liked McClellan, Bolten concluded that he was not a natural at the podium and would never be able to change the narrative. Neither move went over well;

Rove simmered over the demotion, while McClellan left bruised and bitter. When Bush heard that McClellan's wife felt it was a betrayal, the president called her, but it did little to salve the hard feelings.

AFTER SOME DISCUSSION, Bush was also coming around to Rice's thinking about Ibrahim al-Jaafari. "The president had not liked Jaafari and found him to be weak and just talking too much but not doing the right thing," recalled one administration official. With Bush's permission, Rice flew to Baghdad to tell Jaafari to drop his bid to remain prime minister. "It is time for you to go," she told him bluntly. "You have no support from any other Iraqi leader besides Sadr, and for that reason you have lost the support of the United States." It was as overt an intervention in the management of a supposedly democratic country as Bush had attempted, but with the war getting worse, there seemed no choice. On April 20, four months after the elections, Jaafari abandoned his candidacy for prime minister.

The same day, much to Cheney's chagrin and against his better judgment, Bush and Rice opened yet another diplomatic front that might have been unthinkable in the first term, a possible grand bargain with North Korea. They decided to broach the idea with China's president, Hu Jintao, during a meeting at the White House. Hu's visit was the first by a Chinese leader in nine years and had been the subject of intense, edgy discussions between the two sides. Beijing wanted a full state visit, including state dinner, seeing it as confirmation of China's international stature. Bush resisted. He was not a fan of state dinners to begin with, and the notion of giving one to the Chinese, who were neither allies nor even reliable partners, would send the wrong message on human rights. Instead, he agreed to most of the trappings of a state visit, including an elaborate welcome ceremony on the South Lawn complete with twenty-one-gun salute and a review of troops, but opted to host Hu at a luncheon rather than a formal dinner. That was good enough for the Chinese. It was too much for Cheney, who swallowed his misgivings while attending the opening ceremony wearing sunglasses.

Bush's carefully laid plans, though, were undercut by two unexpected gaffes. After Hu was welcomed on the South Lawn by a drumroll and trumpet serenade on a sun-splashed morning, the White House announcer told the crowd that the military band would play the national anthem from "the Republic of China"—the formal name for the breakaway republic of Taiwan. Whether Hu noticed was unclear since he did not flinch. Then, moments into Hu's welcome speech, a woman standing on a press riser across the lawn unfurled a yellow protest banner and began screaming.

"President Hu! Your days are numbered," she yelled in English. "President Bush! Stop him from killing!"

The woman had gotten into the White House with a press pass issued to the *Epoch Times*, a newspaper associated with the Falun Gong, a religious sect outlawed in China. Hu froze until Bush encouraged him to continue.

"You're okay," he assured the Chinese leader.

For two and a half minutes, the woman shouted until uniformed Secret Service officers finally made their way through the crowd to take her away.

The flubbed welcome was deeply offensive to the Chinese, who were unaccustomed to the sort of dissent that American leaders experience regularly. Even before the visit, Chinese officials touring the East Room tried to close the curtains so that Hu would not have to see demonstrators outside the White House gates; White House officials had to stop them and explain that was not done. After the heckler, several Chinese officials refused to attend the ceremonial lunch, forcing the White House social secretary, Lea Berman, to scramble to remove empty chairs. Bush was chagrined. When he sat down with Hu in the Oval Office, Bush apologized. "This was unfortunate," he said, "and I'm sorry this happened." He hoped to move past the embarrassment to his North Korea plan, but Hu stuck to his Taiwan-focused talking points.

So when Bush ushered Hu into the East Room for the lunch of butter heirloom corn broth, Alaska halibut, snap peas, and sweet potatoes, he largely ignored the corporate titans from General Motors, Home Depot, Goldman Sachs, and Caterpillar to hurriedly rearrange the seating chart. Michelle Kwan, the Olympic figure skater; Richard Levin, the Yale University president; and Richard Daley, the mayor of Chicago, were shifted around so that Bush sat on one side of Hu and Rice on the other.

"Condi and I have something to talk to President Hu about," Bush apologized.

Speaking softly so no one other than the translator and Hu could hear, Bush and Rice then outlined their idea.

"I want you to know I'm serious about this," Bush said. "I'm going to follow up on it, but if he'll give up his nuclear weapons, I'm ready to end the Korean War basically and to give him a peace treaty, and we need to talk about how to make this happen."

Hu seemed taken aback, so Bush kept repeating himself.

"I understand," Hu replied.

He agreed to deliver the message and ordered a lieutenant to leave Washington immediately for Pyongyang.

26

"I'm not sure how to take good news anymore"

President Bush was already in the Oval Office by the time Joshua Bolten arrived at 6:45 each morning, sitting behind his desk and studying the blue sheet listing overnight casualties, which he had often circled with his Sharpie pen. Iraq was always on Bush's mind. Aides who showed up to talk about other issues often found him distracted and disinterested. Everything kept coming back to Iraq.

Bush was hearing criticism from many different quarters, including friendly ones. On April 23, he paid a courtesy call on Gerald Ford at his home in Rancho Mirage, California, and the ninety-two-year-old former president took the opportunity to lecture him about what was going wrong in Iraq. Ford said he had supported the invasion but felt Bush had done a poor job explaining to the public why it was important and made a mistake by predicating the war on the supposed weapons. "I don't think he admits it," Ford confided to the journalist Tom DeFrank after the meeting, "except that it's a fact."

The news out of Iraq that spring was so grim, so unrelenting. The report Bush got each evening provided increasingly dismal reading—bombings, assassinations, ethnic cleansing, political gridlock, sectarian strife. There were periodic updates on the investigation into the deaths of twenty-four Iraqi civilians, including unarmed women and children, killed in Haditha the previous November by marines upset after a roadside bomb killed one of their own. A trip report prepared by his aide Brett McGurk, who was just back from Baghdad, noted that American civilian officials could leave their fortified Green Zone headquarters only twice a week and with forty-eight hours' notice. Even then, trips were often canceled for security reasons.

In the face of that, it was hard even for the perennially upbeat Bush to keep an optimistic perspective. The jovial demeanor was gone; his face was etched with lines of worry. *What could stop the cycle of violence? What could he do?* He would later call it "the worst period of my presidency" and confessed that "I thought about the war constantly." For the first time, he worried he would not succeed in Iraq, that he had gotten himself and the country enmeshed in another Vietnam—again with devastating consequences for the country.

He was determined not to show it. "He keeps a lot of that very, very locked up inside himself," one longtime friend said. Constitutionally, Bush disdained hand-wringing and what he would mockingly describe as "woe is me" self-pity. Moreover, he was acutely conscious of everyone watching him. From observing his father's presidency, he understood how a White House takes its cues from the man at the top, and it would be even worse if soldiers in the field saw him "wallow in public" and thought he was losing heart. "Can you imagine the signal I would have sent," he asked a visitor after leaving office, "had I said, 'Ah, why me? Why am I thrust in the middle of all this stuff?' "

Bush was a study in contrasts with his fellow Texan LBJ, who agonized over Vietnam. "He never became a Lyndon Johnson figure, oppressed by the office," Michael Gerson believed. "I never saw any of that." Stephen Hadley said that "if he has dark nights of the soul, he doesn't show them to us." Dan Bartlett came to work every morning expecting Bush to finally succumb to the pressure. "He stunned me day after day," Bartlett said. "I am kind of like, this is going to be the day he breaks. This is the day. This has got to be it." Yet it never happened. Laura worried as well and made a point of regularly inviting over the president's brother Marvin, who lived in the Washington suburbs. Despite their ten-year age difference, "Marvelous," as the president called him, was closer to Bush than his other siblings. They sat together on weekends watching sports.

But he was consumed by the war, and friends could tell it was eating away at him even if he refused to admit it. "He did get kind of down," remembered Joe O'Neill, his childhood pal from Texas. "He feels that pain all the time," observed Jim Langdon, another Texas friend who lived in Washington. Bush prayed every day and leaned on religious advisers like Kirbyjon Caldwell, the Texas minister. "Putting parents, children, in harm's way weighed very heavily on him," Caldwell said. The upbeat image Bush conveyed veiled his internal reality. "Anyone who said he didn't care about that, they are just wrong," Caldwell said. "Just flat wrong about it."

Those who saw him for hours a day, like Bolten and Bartlett, noticed the impact in small ways. "It isn't like he's blowing up in rooms and throwing people out or things like that," Bartlett said. "Maybe a little shorter, but I would bet that the typical White House staffer who maybe runs into him every once in a while wouldn't notice it. It was us that were with him all the time and where he is sharing his frustrations" who could tell. "It would always show itself in different ways. It could be 'What the fuck did Rumsfeld say today?'" Or it could be a quiet spell. "Every day would kind of demonstrate and reveal itself in different ways. But he was never sullen. It would be closer to frustration and pissed more than depression and sullen."

How much he blamed himself was unclear. Most of the killings were committed by al-Qaeda affiliates, Shiite or Sunni militias, or other violent elements, not American troops, but he was the one who had failed to foresee the turmoil that would follow the ouster of Saddam Hussein, and he had stood back as it spiraled out of control. His approach was to trust and delegate to his generals and subordinates. "You fight the war, and I'll provide you with political cover," he told them over and over. But it had left him oddly passive as conditions deteriorated. He interposed no objections when Jerry Bremer overruled the plan Bush had approved for how to handle the Iraqi army and Baath Party, nor did he intervene when the six-month time frame he initially imagined extended to a year, then two, then three.

By late spring, whatever blend of optimism, confidence, and wishful thinking had propped up the White House on Iraq had faded. Through the end of 2005, Bush and Cheney had been able to hang on to the timetable of events they had laid out: *Just get to the election for the interim government. Wait till the new constitution is written. Once it's ratified that will make a difference. Look toward the election of a permanent government.*

The series of deadlines became beacons for eventual victory but turned out to be false hope. Instead of looking at the bigger picture, the White House had been fixated on the next date on the calendar. "There's always this kind of optimism, looking toward the next milestone," Frederick Jones of the National Security Council later reflected. "That's why it's always been hard to look back and say cumulatively, this has been a fiasco. It was hard on the inside to look back in a cumulative way." Now there were no more artificial milestones, no more illusions of progress.

McGurk and his boss, Meghan O'Sullivan, were quietly trying to send Bush a message through their nightly reports. An Oxford-trained scholar with little practical Middle East background before the invasion, O'Sullivan by now had as much experience in Iraq as any American official. She served as an aide to Bremer, negotiated the interim constitution, and was once forced to escape a hotel hit by a rocket by climbing out the window onto a tenth-floor ledge. She had deep contacts among Iraqi political figures and was controversial among some Americans on the ground for trying to orchestrate the situation from the White House, an "eight-thousand-mile screwdriver," as some termed micromanagers in Washington. But she had come to the conclusion that the strategy put in place by Generals John Abizaid and George

Casey, and backed by Donald Rumsfeld, was failing. Underlying the strategy was the assumption that control had to be turned over as quickly as possible to Iraqis so that America could reduce its footprint and not be seen as an occupier. It was a reasoned analysis, informed by long study of the region by Abizaid, a Lebanese American who spoke fluent Arabic and was viewed as "our version of Lawrence of Arabia," in the words of John Hannah, who had taken over as Cheney's national security adviser. Perhaps a quick handover at the beginning of the war might have averted the backlash that followed, but there seemed no one capable of leading the country at the time. By the spring of 2006, more than three years after Saddam Hussein was toppled, it was too late to pretend Americans were not occupiers. And the theory that security would follow political reconciliation was proving hollow.

One morning that spring, Bush looked up from a blue sheet casualty report and shook his head.

"This is not working," he said to Stephen Hadley. "We need to take another look at the whole strategy. I need to see some new options."

"Mr. President," Hadley said, "I'm afraid you're right."

WAYLAID IN HIS plan to push out Donald Rumsfeld, Joshua Bolten focused on other changes he thought were needed to shake up the White House. To replace Scott McClellan as press secretary, he came up with a surprising choice—Tony Snow, a high-profile Fox News commentator who had worked as a speechwriter for Bush's father.

Not since the Ford administration had a White House press secretary come directly from the media, but Bolten thought Snow had the right combination of brash charm, nimble debating skills, and disarming humor to pull it off. Moreover, Snow had been tough on the president in his columns and radio show, so he would have credibility. Snow had lambasted Bush as an "impotent" president with a "listless domestic policy" who had "lost control of the federal budget." At one point, Snow said, "George Bush has become something of an embarrassment."

When Bush made the announcement on the morning of April 26, he said slyly, "I asked him about those comments and he said, 'You should have heard what I said about the other guy.'"

Snow's arrival transformed White House press relations. He was the first press secretary for the talk show age, turning daily briefings into cable-style debates with reporters. In a marked shift from the hypercautious McClellan, Snow was not afraid to use bold language and glib repartee that went well beyond the staid talking points. He became an instant rock star, signing autographs, posing for pictures, hitting the lecture circuit, and appearing on television public affairs shows. While his freewheeling style sometimes crossed a line, and his attention to precision was episodic, almost overnight he provided a more popular face for a White House badly in need of it.

Bolten also made two other key changes. Porter Goss, who was constantly at war with the establishment at the CIA, was pushed out as director and replaced by Michael Hayden, the NSA director and architect of the warrantless surveillance program. Engaging, confident, and wise to the ways of Washington, Hayden was a Bush favorite. Now Bolten was ready to reshape the economic team by ousting Secretary of the Treasury John Snow. While Snow got along better with Bush and Cheney than his predecessor did, he was not seen as a powerful public advocate for the administration's economic policies. Besides, Bolten had a nagging sense that the country would be facing a financial crisis before the end of Bush's presidency, just based on the law of averages if nothing else. He figured it would be an international currency crisis of the sort that confronted Bill Clinton, missing early warning signs that it was actually the housing market that was overheating in a dangerous way.

Either way, Snow was not a markets expert, so Bolten set out to find one. Bolten, a former Goldman Sachs executive, pursued Henry Paulson, a onetime junior Nixon White House aide who became chief executive of the storied Wall Street firm, but Paulson said no. Bolten went to other leading Republicans in the financial world, including Charles Schwab, founder of the investment brokerage that used his name; John Thain, chief executive of the New York Stock Exchange; and Kenneth Chenault, chief executive of American Express. But he kept coming back to Paulson, making it a mission to change his mind and devoting hours a day to the project. Paulson was a formidable personality who filled the room. "He's hard to ignore," noted Michele Davis, later one of his chief advisers. "He's tall, but he's even more just gangly with arms flailing and just takes up a lot of space."

With Bush's help, Bolten finally wore him down, much to the chagrin of Paulson's family. His mother cried when Paulson told her he would take the job and expressed hope the Senate would not confirm him. "You started with Nixon and you're going to end with Bush?" she said. "Why would you do such a thing?" Paulson's wife, Wendy, a college classmate of Hillary Clinton's, and their son, Merritt, also opposed his taking the job, although their daughter, Amanda, supported his decision. "You'll be jumping onto a sinking ship," his mother said. But if he was, Paulson at least negotiated terms to his liking. He would run economic policy, not the White House, and not the vice president, who to the outside world seemed to have his hand in every pot.

Actually, Cheney's role was shrinking by the hour. Even as Paulson was boxing him out of economic policy, Rice was elbowing him out of foreign policy. While Iraq was the dominant priority, she was looking for opportunities to make progress on other fronts and saw Iran as a possibility. One night she went home to her apartment in the famed Watergate complex and wrote out a plan for a diplomatic opening in a color-coded chart that proved so complicated only she could read it. But the idea was to propose that the United States come to the negotiating table if Iran suspended its uranium enrichment. At Rice's urging, Bush had been calling other leaders to sound them out. He faced considerable skepticism from some, especially the Russians, who thought the American-led pressure campaign against Tehran risked becoming a repeat of the war in Iraq. "Utter bullshit that I'm going to attack Iran," Bush told Igor Ivanov, the Russian national security adviser, during a visit early in May. "For effectiveness, we can't take the military option off the table. The most important thing is to keep a united front so that there is no way for them to wiggle out of the box."

As Memorial Day approached, Bush finally agreed to make the overture to Iran, if only to keep the Europeans together. Recognizing that the Cheney wing would find it hard to swallow, Rice invited hard-liners to her apartment on the holiday to explain the policy and address objections. She had her collaborator, Nicholas Burns, her undersecretary, lay out the strategy for skeptics like Elliott Abrams, the deputy national security adviser, and John Hannah, Cheney's adviser. Then she invited John Bolton, the hard-line ambassador to the United Nations, to dinner the next night at her favorite restaurant at the Watergate. "I just want to know we are all on the same page," she told him. She announced the new policy the following day, Cheney and his allies quietly going along.

ANOTHER MOMENT OF friction between Bush and Cheney that spring would come over the unlikeliest of issues. On the night of May 20, the FBI raided the Capitol Hill office of Representative William Jefferson, a Louisiana Democrat caught with $90,000 hidden in his freezer. The raid triggered an eruption of anger in Congress that crossed party lines. To lawmakers, it was a violation of separation of powers and the speech-and-debate clause of the Constitution that protects them while performing their duties.

Speaker Dennis Hastert was "livid," as he later recalled, and gave Bush an earful about Attorney General Alberto Gonzales on Air Force One returning to Washington from an event in Illinois.

"This is just unacceptable," he told Bush. "I think you ought to ask for the guy's resignation."

Bush was not about to force Gonzales to resign but grew emotional, with tears in his eyes, during the heated exchange with Hastert. "Let me look into it," he said.

Cheney sided with Hastert and Jefferson. For a vice president fixated on the power of the executive branch, this was one instance where he believed the executive had encroached on the legislative branch.

The White House convened a conference call to review what had happened. David Addington "was just so exercised" and peppered the Justice Department officials with "very tough, aggressive questions" demanding to know the constitutional basis for conducting a search on Capitol Hill, according to Paul McNulty, the deputy attorney general. McNulty argued that separation of powers did not make congressional offices immune from law enforcement, noting that a judge had authorized the search. Bush and Cheney then summoned McNulty to the White House to hear for themselves why the Justice Department thought it had the power to raid Jefferson's office. Bush noted that he had gotten an earful from Hastert, while Cheney pointed out that he was an old House guy and sympathized with their resistance to executive interference.

The dispute put Gonzales in an awkward position, torn between his inherent loyalty to Bush and his responsibility to defend his department. He began shuttling between the White House and the Justice Department looking for a solution, only to return to his office one day having surrendered.

"Well, basically here's the deal," he told aides. "We have to give the evidence back. We have until midnight to give the evidence back, or they are going to order us to give it back."

McNulty, a House Republican lawyer during Bill Clinton's impeachment and the U.S. attorney who prosecuted terrorism cases in Virginia outside Washington, balked. "We can't do that. We can't give the evidence back to the defendant." In fact, he added, "I will resign before I do it, and you can get someone else to do it."

McNulty went to Robert Mueller, the FBI director, and Mueller agreed that he would resign as well if Bush and Cheney forced them to return the evidence.

Just like that, Bush and Cheney found themselves facing another "Saturday Night Massacre"–style situation with the deputy attorney general and the director of the FBI threatening to quit rather than follow what they considered improper orders. A compromise was reached to temporarily put the evidence in a safe, sealed from prosecutors, while a court decided whether the Justice Department had overstepped its bounds. Once again, Bush and Cheney managed to avoid a rupture.

WITH IBRAHIM AL-JAAFARI out, the Iraqis had finally agreed on a little-known Shiite leader named Nouri al-Maliki as the next prime minister. He was sworn in on May 20, a full five months after the elections. American officials knew so little about him that they used the wrong first name for him for a while until Maliki himself corrected them.

Bush and Cheney convened the war cabinet on May 26. Rice, who had been under pressure from Donald Rumsfeld to get more civilians into the effort to remake Iraq, reported that she had forty-eight more on tap to go. General George Casey, on video feed from Baghdad, was not impressed.

"Excuse me, Madame Secretary," he said, "but that's a paltry number."

"You're out of line, General," Rice snapped.

"Well," Bush interjected, "on that happy note, we adjourn."

Rumsfeld was aggravated by what he saw as Rice's breach of the chain of command. It was the first time tensions between his department and State had boiled over so starkly in front of the president. He later told Rice that she should not scold his general; if she had a problem with one of his officers, she should bring it to him.

Despite a growing sense inside the White House that the strategy was not working, there was no consensus on what to do about it. Bush was still reluctant to second-guess commanders, while Cheney was so close to Rumsfeld he seemed unwilling to challenge his friend. Rumsfeld years later said Cheney and he shared the same concerns and recalled no moment when the vice president disagreed with his approach. "Every one of us was worried, wondering about the strategy, what was being done, and asking those questions—should there be more, should there be less, should they be here, should they be there, should their mission be more this than that?" Rumsfeld said. "And those kinds of questions went on continuously from Dick and others."

Hoping to shake up the policy, Stephen Hadley and aides like Meghan O'Sullivan, Brett McGurk, and Peter Feaver proposed a two-day summit on Iraq at Camp David, where the war cabinet could take a deeper look at the situation, a gathering modeled after Dwight Eisenhower's famed sessions in the Solarium when he had analysts present different approaches for dealing with the Soviet Union. Similarly, Bush's advisers hoped to put fundamental issues on the table: Was the current strategy working? How should Shiite militias be tackled? Could further outreach to Sunni insurgents defuse the uprising? Was the Iraqi government helping or making the situation worse? They prepared thick briefing books and invited outside scholars to debate the strategy in front of Bush and Cheney, including some who would advocate sending more troops and switching to a counterinsurgency approach more focused on protecting the population.

Before they could convene, a little good news intervened. On June 7, days before the Camp David session, Bush met in the Roosevelt Room with members of Congress back from Iraq. Representative Ray LaHood, an Illinois Republican, told Bush he should target Abu Musab al-Zarqawi, leader of al-Qaeda in Iraq.

"We really got to get rid of Zarqawi," he said. "It would be like getting Saddam."

Bush quietly chortled at the obvious and elbowed Steny Hoyer, the House Democratic whip, who was sitting next to him.

"Why didn't I think of that?" Hoyer whispered to Bush with a laugh.

Just minutes later, at 3:45 p.m., Hadley was summoned out of the meeting to take a phone call. On the line was Zalmay Khalilzad, the ambassador in Baghdad. They had indications that none other than Zarqawi had just been killed by two five-hundred-pound bombs dropped on a safe house near Baquba. Hadley returned to the meeting. Bush gave him a quizzical look, but Hadley waved him off, reluctant to announce something that had not been confirmed. He got pulled out again a half hour later for another phone call.

Only after the meeting did Hadley go into the Oval Office at 4:35 p.m. to tell Bush, Cheney, Bolten, and Rice the news. They needed to wait to be sure of the identification. Bush offered a restrained response to the possibility that the most potent enemy in Iraq might be gone. "That would be a good thing," he said simply.

It was not until after 9:00 p.m. that Bush received word that fingerprints, tattoos, and scars matched. It was indeed Zarqawi. General Stanley McChrystal, head of special operations forces in Iraq, had personally gone to the bombing site to ensure it was Zarqawi's broken frame pulled out of the wreckage shortly before he died.

Bush announced the news the next morning, June 8, then called Hoyer. "God, I'm so glad that Ray made that suggestion," Bush said.

And he called LaHood to tell him how prescient he was. "Hey, you might go down in history," the president joked.

Zarqawi had been the terrorist Bush declined to bomb in mid-2002 against the advice of Cheney and Rumsfeld for fear of starting a war too soon. He had gone on to become the key figure fomenting sectarian strife in the new Iraq, as lethal a foe as any since the September 11 attacks, responsible for more American deaths in Iraq than any other individual. Finally killing him, however belatedly, was the biggest symbolic victory since Hussein's capture two and a half years earlier. "I was just giddy," Rice recalled. Yet there was no euphoria in the Oval Office. Bush was sober.

"You don't seem happy," O'Sullivan noted.

"I'm not sure how to take good news anymore," he said.

BUSH'S TEAM HEADED to Camp David for their Iraq summit on June 12. Cheney flew by helicopter from his weekend home in St. Michaels, Maryland, landing at Camp David with his mind swirling with questions about the viability of the Iraq venture. O'Sullivan's staff had been up until 3:00 a.m. preparing briefing books, and she hoped the meeting could be a turning point that would force a reappraisal and new strategy.

The war cabinet gathered in Laurel Lodge and sat on one side of a conference table facing screens showing Abizaid, Casey, and Khalilzad in Iraq. Casey reported that the situation had "fundamentally changed" and was no longer just an insurgency against Americans but had become a broader internal struggle for political and economic power. The longer the Americans were there, the longer Iraqis would depend on them to solve their problems, and so he recommended keeping the current strategy to transition responsibility to Iraqi forces. "My view was always we had to draw down," he said later. "For us to be successful, we ultimately had to leave Iraq."

Then four military experts were asked to give presentations: Frederick W. Kagan, a scholar at the American Enterprise Institute; Robert Kaplan, a longtime roving correspondent and writer; Eliot Cohen, a historian at Johns Hopkins University's School of Advanced International Studies; and Michael Vickers, a senior vice president at the Center for Strategic and Budgetary Assessments.

Kagan offered a robust argument for reversing course and adding more troops to implement a counterinsurgency strategy. Iraqi forces were not ready to take over, he said, and until Iraqi civilians felt secure and trusted their government, the strife between Sunni and Shia would continue. The success of the war was too important to wage anything less than a full-fledged effort. This was the message that O'Sullivan, McGurk, and Feaver wanted Bush to hear. Vickers, who had met separately with Bush two weeks earlier, presented the opposite theory. As a young man, he had been an architect of the CIA's successful proxy war against Soviet troops in Afghanistan, a role later popularized in the book and movie *Charlie Wilson's War.* Now he urged a similar approach with Iraqis in the lead. He distributed a four-page paper maintaining that "it is highly unlikely that American forces, even with growing Iraqi security force assistance, will be able to defeat the insurgency within the next 2–3 years." Therefore, the United States should shift to "an indirect approach," withdrawing all but forty thousand troops that would serve as a quick-reaction force supporting Iraqis who would take the lead "no later than summer 2008." Rumsfeld, for one, found Vickers's case "to be persuasive." Worried about just that, Feaver had added Cohen to the list of speakers to bolster Kagan's side.

In the midst of the discussion, Bush got more good news. Karl Rove received word that he would not be indicted. Rove was on a plane around 4:00 p.m. about to take off for New Hampshire when his lawyer called to tell him the prosecutor had informed him no charges would be brought. For Rove, it was a powerful relief. While he had maintained a public stoicism about the investigation, "behind the mask, the whole thing was scaring the hell out of me." Now pumped up, Rove went on to deliver a red-meat speech to a Republican audience that night, accusing Democrats like John Kerry and John Murtha of "cutting and running" in Iraq. "They may be with you at the first shots," he said, "but they are not going to be there for the last tough battles."

At Camp David, Bush excused himself after a long day of discussion. It was late, and everyone assumed he was heading to bed. The next day would be key—a day of closed meetings just with the senior team and a handful of aides as they wrestled with what to do next. But Bush did not go to bed. Instead, he slipped into a car for a short ride to the helipad, where he boarded Marine One and took off for Andrews Air Force Base, flying through the night without lights. With his top advisers at Camp David, it was the perfect cover for another secret trip to Iraq, a "brilliant fake out," as Joshua Bolten saw it. The normally taciturn Cheney was left behind to filibuster since the rest of the team did not know about the trip.

The next morning, June 13, O'Sullivan was at Camp David on the phone with McGurk back in Washington preparing to brief Bush when their colleague Charles Dunne ran into McGurk's office at the White House and announced that the president was on television in Baghdad.

"Meghan, um, where's the president?" McGurk asked.

"He's here," she said. "We're about to get started."

"Charles said he just landed in Baghdad."

"What?" she asked, then quickly hung up.

She headed to the main lodge and found J. D. Crouch. It still had not sunk in until he confirmed what had happened.

"The president's not here," Crouch told her. "The president's in Baghdad."

Bush was at the Green Zone palace with Khalilzad and Nouri al-Maliki. He had flown into the city on an army helicopter that shot off flares to distract heat-seeking missiles. Casey and Khalilzad presented him with a stone from the house where Zarqawi was killed. "He was pumped up about" Zarqawi's death, Casey recalled. Bush took Maliki's measure and was impressed. "I sensed an inner toughness," he concluded.

He also met with Casey, who told him about his plan to launch Operation Together Forward using counterinsurgency techniques that had succeeded in the city of Tal Afar along the Syrian border.

Bush saw a contradiction—true counterinsurgency requires a sizable troop presence—but Casey and Abizaid kept advocating a drawdown.

"I have to do a better job of explaining it to you," Casey said.

"Yes, you do," Bush replied.

But with Zarqawi dead and a new prime minister in place, the stealth trip set back any serious revision of strategy. The bare-it-all Camp David session Bush's advisers anticipated turned out to be just cover for the trip. Cheney, who had grown unsettled about the current strategy, had hoped "to make a big case for how badly things were going," including charts with violence and a discussion of counterinsurgency, according to one adviser. But Bush, sensitive to his commander in the field, returned to Washington willing to give him a chance to turn the corner. "Troop levels will be decided upon by General Casey," Bush told reporters. It was a formulation he had leaned on repeatedly; one study found that he had said troop levels would be decided by ground commanders thirty times in 2006 alone. Joshua Bolten later recalled, "We came away from that trip with a lot of optimism, which was genuine. But it was masking what was going on underneath."

The rump group of insurgents inside the White House pushing for change was disheartened. "What I thought would have started a zero-base review of the strategy miscarries back into debates about implementation on the margins," reflected Feaver. O'Sullivan returned to the White House deeply upset, convinced that their summit had become a "PR session" that "didn't tackle any of the pressing issues of the moment."

27

"Make damn sure we do not fail"

President Bush was in the Oval Office on the morning of June 29 meeting with the visiting prime minister of Japan when Dan Bartlett and Tony Snow interrupted. The Supreme Court, they told him, had just determined that the Geneva Conventions applied to detainees at Guantánamo and threw out the military commission system, ruling that Bush had overstepped his authority. Harriet Miers came downstairs to give the president a "drive-by briefing" before he headed to the East Room for a joint news conference with Prime Minister Junichiro Koizumi. "I will protect the people," Bush told reporters, "and at the same time conform with the findings of the Supreme Court."

Not if Vice President Cheney had his way. He was not ready to conform. The decision in *Hamdan v. Rumsfeld* not only overturned the military commissions that Cheney persuaded Bush to approve that autumn day shortly after the September 11 attacks but also represented a direct blow to the core of the Bush-Cheney war on terror. For nearly five years, Bush and Cheney had waged war largely as they saw fit. If intelligence officers needed to eavesdrop on overseas telephone calls without warrants, Cheney arranged for Bush to authorize it. If the military wanted to hold terrorism suspects without trial, Bush and Cheney agreed to let it.

The two had operated on the principle that it was better to act than ask permission, convinced that protecting the country required the most expansive interpretation of presidential powers. If they were later forced to retreat from controversial decisions, they reasoned, it was worth the price to prevent what in those early hours and days seemed like a certain "second wave" of attacks. Better to "push and push and push until some larger force makes us stop," as David Addington had memorably put it. For years, that had worked. Now the Supreme Court in the latest and broadest of a series of decisions on the war on terror was interposing itself as a larger force.

Cheney and Addington argued for legislation that would overturn the Supreme Court decision. Addington drafted a one-page bill that would strip the court of its jurisdiction over the matter and affirm the president's power to do what he had done. From their point of view, it was outrageous for the Supreme Court to second-guess a wartime commander in chief, especially when it had backed Franklin Roosevelt's military commission scheme to try Nazi saboteurs.

The vice president's move generated a sharp debate. John Bellinger, the State Department's top lawyer, considered resigning if the president sought to reverse the court. "I was just shocked," he said later. "It was just unbelievable to me that anyone would urge the president to overrule the court." His boss, Condoleezza Rice, who had been circumvented by Cheney on the original military commission order, agreed. So did Karen Hughes, now undersecretary of state in charge of repairing America's image in the world. She had concluded that the Guantánamo prison and perceptions of how detainees were treated were overpowering her efforts to win the war of ideas. As far as she was concerned, "we're not going to get anywhere as long as we have this big public relations black eye."

The issue came to a head at a meeting in the Oval Office.

"Mr. President, you cannot overturn the Supreme Court," Rice pleaded.

On Cheney's side were Miers and Alberto Gonzales, who argued that the president should not surrender his powers.

Five years after Bush had readily agreed to sign the military commission order when Cheney brought it to him in 2001, he was no longer willing to go along. "I'm not going to overrule the Supreme Court," he declared.

When someone worried that because of the ruling, international tribunals would try to pick it up and apply the Geneva Conventions to American detainees, Bush brushed it off. "I'm not worried about international tribunals," he said.

Instead, Bush decided to work with Congress to approve a military commission system that would meet the court's guidelines and have buy-in from the elected legislature as well. Some on his staff wondered whether it would have made sense to do that in the first place rather than waste so many years asserting unilateral authority. Either way, this time Bush decided to send Stephen Hadley to Capitol Hill from the start. Cheney was sidelined.

AS SPRING PROGRESSED, Bush found himself increasingly focused on Russia, which was set to host its first Group of Eight, or G-8, summit. To Vladimir Putin, hosting the summit was a validation of his country's reemergence on the world stage, but to critics it reflected badly on the West to give such a prominent stage to a country that did not meet the group's democratic standards. Having promised a freedom agenda favoring dissidents over despots, Bush found himself pressured at home by John McCain and others to boycott the summit. Bush had no intention of snubbing Putin, but he was in an awkward position. "I think we are headed to a firestorm with Putin," Bush confided in Tony Blair.

Among those who thought Bush was on the wrong side of history was Cheney, who had been skeptical of Putin from the beginning. While Bush pondered how to nudge Putin without sacrificing their friendship, the vice president privately launched his own effort to add backbone to American policy. He invited Russia specialists to his office to discuss options for pressuring Moscow, and a Russian opposition leader, Vladimir Ryzhkov, was secretly brought in to meet with the vice president without the Kremlin finding out about it. "He thought the Bush administration had gone too far in embracing Putin," recalled Michael McFaul of Stanford University, one of the scholars Cheney consulted.

With Bush's permission, Cheney flew to Vilnius, the capital of Lithuania, to give a speech on May 4 lacerating Putin's Russia for "unfairly and improperly" restricting the rights of its people and using oil and gas as "tools of intimidation or blackmail" against neighboring countries. "Russia has a choice to make," Cheney said. "And there is no question that a return to democratic reform in Russia will generate further success for its people and greater respect among fellow nations." The speech infuriated Putin. But the message was undermined when Cheney flew next to Kazakhstan, an oil-rich former Soviet republic with no more freedom than Russia, and stood with its autocratic leader, Nursultan Nazarbayev, offering nothing but praise. The Kremlin saw that as the height of cynicism and chose to believe Cheney was just freelancing. But in fact the speech had been vetted at the White House, and Bush was comfortable with Cheney playing the bad cop to his good cop. "The vice president put a stake in the ground with his speech, which helped us," Bush told Blair.

In his more friendly vein, Bush tried to get Putin to put other tangible issues on the table for the summit to keep it from being dominated by the question of Russian democracy. In a phone call on June 5, Bush suggested four subjects—bird flu, Darfur, Iran, and nuclear terrorism. Putin thanked Bush for pushing ahead with Russian membership in the World Trade Organization and said only "a few more moves" and then it "will be finished."

Then, in an odd exchange, Putin mentioned Sergei Lavrov, his chain-smoking, hard-line foreign minister. "Lavrov just returned from London and had problems with his cheeks and lips being swollen," Putin told Bush. "We might need to take a closer look at what Condi did to him."

Bush, awkwardly, played along with what seemed to be a lurid form of sexual innuendo. "Condi is not blind," he joked.

"And she is a very attractive lady," Putin replied.

"She is a wonderful lady," Bush said, then tried to move the conversation along. "Listen, I'd like to get this WTO stuff done in the next couple weeks before we get to St. Petersburg."

The next day, June 9, Bush traveled to Camp David with the visiting Danish prime minister and talked about Putin. "We've had some tough meetings," Bush told his guest. "He's not well informed. It's like arguing with an eighth grader with his facts wrong. I met him in Slovakia. He said, 'You've been saying bad things about me on democracy.' I said, 'Yes. I don't like what our press corps says about me but I don't close them down. You go out and close the media when you don't like what they say.' "

He said Putin had even tried to get to him by offering an oil industry job to Don Evans, the former commerce secretary and one of his closest friends. "Putin asked me, 'Would it help you if I moved Evans to an important position?' What a question! 'Will it help you?' " Bush was exasperated. "What I wanted to say is, 'What would help me is if you make moves on democracy.' It's strange the way he thinks." A few days before leaving for St. Petersburg, Bush confided in the visiting prime minister of Slovenia. "I think Putin is not a democrat anymore," Bush lamented. "He's a tsar. I think we've lost him."

Bush's efforts to divert attention from the democracy dispute by forging a last-minute deal to admit Russia into the World Trade Organization failed. His trade representative, Susan Schwab, negotiated three late nights in a row with the Russians in a frantic effort to reach an accord that Bush and Putin could announce—at one point going twenty-four hours straight and eating pizza for breakfast. They got so close that the Russians publicly declared a deal would be signed by the presidents. But at 2:30 a.m. on July 15, a day after Bush arrived in town, they finally hit a wall.

Disappointed, Bush put a brave face on the visit. After having dinner together, he and Putin appeared in a polite news conference with an undercurrent of tension. Bush's only public mention of Russian democracy was gentle compared with his private frustrations expressed to Blair and others in the months leading up to the summit.

"I talked about my desire to promote institutional change in parts of the world like Iraq, where there's a free press and free religion," Bush told reporters. "And I told him that a lot of people in our country would hope that Russia would do the same thing."

Putin, coiled and ready, seized on the remark. "We certainly would not want to have the same kind of democracy as they have in Iraq, I will tell you quite honestly," he said, provoking laughter from the Russian side.

Bush seemed caught off guard. "Just wait," he replied softly, maintaining a strained smile.

AS IT TURNED out, Bush need not have worried about the summit being dominated by questions of Russian democracy. In the days leading up to the meeting, Israel had invaded Lebanon in response to Hezbollah raids and barrages of rockets, a crisis that had forced its way to the top of the agenda in St. Petersburg.

While Kofi Annan, the UN secretary-general, had been trying to mediate, Bush was fending off pressure from allies to intervene, instead siding with Israel in its outrage over the attacks on its territory. Bush and Annan had what the UN secretary-general called a "charged and pointed debate" in front of the other leaders. "It was clear that Bush saw this as a simple matter of good versus evil," Annan recalled. "A simple battle between good and evil it was not."

Either way, the diplomatic maneuverings underscored just how closely Bush was working with Rice these days. He told her to work out language for a joint statement with the other governments at the summit. In doing so, though, he inadvertently alienated Stephen Hadley, who despite his closeness with Rice felt cut out. Suddenly Bush's tandem with Rice was risking a rupture in his White House team.

"I can't be his national security adviser if he doesn't trust me to do these things for him," Hadley told Rice. "I have to resign."

Rice talked him out of it and then told Bush he could not undercut Hadley like that. Bush meant no insult to Hadley; he was just so comfortable with Rice.

During a private lunch on the summit's final day, Bush shared his frustration over Lebanon with Tony Blair.

"Blair, what are you doing?" he asked. "You leaving?"

"No, no, no, not yet," Blair said.

As Bush ate and Blair stood over him, the two chatted for a couple of minutes about global trade talks and a sweater Blair had given Bush for his birthday.

"I know you picked it out yourself," Bush said sarcastically.

"Oh, absolutely," Blair replied with a laugh.

Then Bush turned the discussion to Annan, telling Blair he was going to send Rice to the region.

Blair offered to make a public statement to prepare the ground. "Obviously, if she goes out, she's got to succeed, as it were, whereas I can just go out and talk," he said, recognizing the different expectations when America got involved.

"What they need to do is get Syria to get Hezbollah to stop doing this shit and it's over," an irritated Bush said with his mouth full as he buttered a piece of bread.

"Who? Syria?" Blair asked.

"Right," Bush said. "What about Kofi? That seems odd. I don't like the sequence of it. His attitude is basically cease-fire and [only then] everything else happens." Instead, he said, Annan should pressure President Bashar al-Assad of Syria to rein in Hezbollah. "I felt like telling Kofi to get on the phone with Assad and make something happen," Bush told Blair.

Bush left St. Petersburg frustrated on multiple fronts. Putin waited until he had cleared Russian airspace to tell a news conference that he would not support Bush in pressuring Iran to give up its nuclear program. "Speaking of sanctions against Iran is premature," Putin said. "We haven't reached that point yet."

Bush and Blair vented their mutual aggravation with Putin during a call two weeks later. "I left St. Petersburg more worried about Russia than ever," Blair told Bush on July 28.

"You should be," Bush agreed. "We talked at dinner. He's okay with centralization, which he thinks leads to stabilization. I told him, 'What happens when the next guy comes and abuses it?' He said, 'I'll stop him.' He thinks he'll be around forever. He asked me why I didn't change the Constitution so I could run again."

WHETHER BUSH WOULD even want to run again was another matter. At home as well as abroad, the challenges were stacking up. After more than five years of working with a Congress mostly under Republican control, Bush was confronted for the first time with a bill he could not live with. Congress sent him legislation lifting his restrictions on federal funding for embryonic stem-cell research. Among those leading the charge was Bill Frist, the senator Bush had privately considered as a replacement for Cheney on the 2004 ticket. Bush decided to veto the measure.

Rather than be defensive, he staged a ceremony on July 19 with "snowflake babies," or children born from discarded embryos adopted by other parents. The pictures on television showed a president surrounded by children, not a rigid conservative preventing lifesaving research. Bush had tempered the fallout from the veto. But the showdown foreshadowed more friction to come between the White House and its Republican allies with elections just months away.

Indeed, as summer progressed and Iraq and other issues soured the public, Republican candidates were going out of their way to avoid Bush and Cheney, and the White House staff was working overtime to find races where the president could help. The last thing they wanted was the perception that Bush was so toxic he was not welcome at the side of Republican candidates. But the ones who did agree to a visit were generally from safe districts. "We were trying to keep his schedule active," recalled Sara Taylor, the White House political director. "We didn't want the president sidelined. Being sidelined would not be a good thing for him. We had people who didn't want him to land at the airport."

The schism between the president and his party was brought home starkly on the same day as the stem-cell veto ceremony when Senator John Thune, one of Karl Rove's pet projects in 2004, distanced himself from Bush. "If I were running in the state this year, you obviously don't embrace the president and his agenda," Thune told reporters at the National Press Club. Rove erupted when he saw the comments. "He thought Thune was ungrateful and whiny," as one White House colleague put it, and told his staff to make sure the Bush donors who had helped Thune in the past knew about his betrayal. His staff balked, deeming it an excessive response, especially since Thune quickly apologized. But Rove persisted. "He would just not let it go," the colleague said. Finally, Joshua Bolten, who had received an apology directly from Thune, stepped in and forced Rove to drop the matter.

Republican lawmakers were not the only ones anxious about Iraq. After the failed reboot at Camp David, Stephen Hadley and the Iraq team tried to find a new way to force a strategy change. Meghan O'Sullivan and Brett McGurk sent Hadley a memo on the same day as Thune's comments pleading for a full-fledged review of the war. The two young advisers reinforced the message directly to Bush the next day in their nightly report. "The deteriorating security situation is outpacing the Iraqi government's ability to respond," Bush read. Turning over the country to Iraqi forces was unrealistic since they were actually part of the problem, engaging in sectarian attacks themselves. "Violence has acquired a momentum of its own *and is now self-sustaining*."

Hadley privately agreed and was trying to nudge the process along subtly while still serving as an arbiter among different factions. If he pushed too hard, too fast, it could generate opposition to change. At Bush's request, Hadley took the questions raised by O'Sullivan and McGurk and presented them to General George Casey during a videoconference on July 22. What was the strategy for Baghdad? Were more troops needed? What was the American mission? Had they let the Iraqis become too dependent on them, or was it the other way around? Casey found the questions demeaning and resented the civilian second-guessing. More forces would not fix the problem. The real solution was political, not military.

A few days later, on July 26, Nouri al-Maliki made his first visit to Washington as Iraq's prime minister. Bush welcomed him to the White House and listened as Maliki let his various ministers present somewhat tedious reports on their areas of responsibility.

Bush tried to lighten the mood. When introduced to the electricity minister, he asked, "Do people call you Sparky?" No one on the Iraqi side seemed to get the joke.

The president's more important message was one of fortitude. "If you take one thing away from this visit, it's that I'm behind you 100 percent," he said. "Don't worry about the politics here. Do the right thing. I'll be with you. Count on it."

CERTAIN ABOUT HIS resolve but uncertain what to do, Bush took off on August 3 for a break at the Crawford ranch, his first summer retreat there since Hurricane Katrina. As soon as he landed, he began pounding the pedals on the bicycle trails he had come to love. Just as exercise helped him purge the toxins of alcohol in his youth, now it helped him flush out the tensions of Washington.

He had just turned sixty that summer, a milestone that had clearly been on his mind. Bush made a point of fighting the advance of age with discipline. He exercised ferociously six days a week with a mountain bike, treadmill, and free-weight resistance training. When in Washington, he went for bike rides as long as two and a half hours at the Secret Service training facility outside the city. With a resting pulse rate of forty-seven beats per minute, a cholesterol count of 178, and a body fat percentage of 15.79, he remained in "superior" shape, according to his doctors.

The devotion to exercise and schedules seemed to stem from the same discipline Bush had summoned to quit drinking at age forty. "He's the first one to admit that he has an addictive personality, and he has to channel this addictiveness to constructive things," Dan Bartlett once observed. "He likes systems; he likes structure. It's interesting—for a personality that's so free-form, he does like structure." He kept a giant wooden jigsaw puzzle set up in the family quarters that he worked on regularly, making order out of the chaos of hundreds of pieces. "It's something you can solve," said Pamela Hudson Nelson, a longtime friend of Laura's. "They have a lot of coping methods." Bush also preferred to look ahead rather than backward. "When you're working for the president," Bartlett said, "you've always got to give him something to look forward to."

He especially looked forward to the long bike rides. He often invited others to join him but asked them not to ride in front of him so he could have the illusion of solitude, a rare sensation of freedom in the eternally scripted, perpetually surrounded life of a president. "Riding helps clear my head, helps me deal with the stresses of the job," Bush, soaked in sweat, said after an eighty-minute ride at the ranch that summer. Mark McKinnon, his consultant and frequent biking partner, said the intensity was directly tied to the burdens of the job. "The more pressure there was at the White House," he said, "the harder he rode."

Biking with the president often seemed to be an exercise in survival as much as serenity, particularly in the sweltering August heat of Texas, where he enrolled those who managed to keep up with him in his Hundred Degree Club. Tony Snow got roped into a ride after making the mistake of telling Bush once that he would enjoy riding with him sometime. "I was just, you know, trying to make nice," he said later. "I was trying to kiss up to the boss."

But now Snow had accompanied Bush to the ranch for the first time.

"Snow, you ready to ride?" Bush asked.

Snow tried to beg off but got nowhere.

The ride was memorable. "You go off-road," he recalled, "and there's a drop of about fifteen or twenty feet. It rises up again and then goes around the curve. The president goes down and goes, 'Woo hoo!' Person behind him goes down and goes, 'Woo hoo!' I'm in the back and I go, 'Waaaah!'"

Right into a tree.

"Snow," Bush called out. "You okay back there?"

"Yes, sir. Just hit a tree."

"Okay, well, come on then."

If anyone had learned the importance of getting up after hitting a tree, it was Bush.

THAT SUMMER IN Crawford, Bush found himself managing a widening divide between his vice president and his secretary of state. The Israeli war in Lebanon had drawn international condemnation, and Europe was pressing for an immediate cease-fire. Bush resisted. He could hardly fault another country for going after terrorists. But he eventually found himself more isolated as the fighting dragged on, especially after Israeli bombs destroyed an apartment complex in the Lebanese village of Qana, killing dozens of civilians, including children.

Condoleezza Rice flew to Texas to confer. She had been working the diplomatic channels and believed it was time to weigh in to halt the violence. Cheney felt otherwise. Israel had every right to protect itself, and stopping the operation before it fully rooted out Hezbollah would leave Lebanon a safe harbor for terrorists. Cheney saw the conflict in the context of America's own struggle. He even thought the Israelis should "crater the runways" at the airport in Damascus on the theory that Iran was using Syria as a conduit for aid to Hezbollah. Even Israel thought that was going too far and urged the Americans to send the opposite message to Syria, that it would be left alone, for fear of a wider war.

On August 5, Bush and Rice strolled over to the double-wide trailer with the communications equipment for a secure videoconference with Cheney and the rest of the national security team. Rice brought everyone up to date on her efforts to win a cease-fire.

Cheney pushed back. "We need to let the Israelis finish off Hezbollah," he argued.

Rice, stunned, scribbled a note to Bush and passed it to him out of sight of the camera. *Where has he been for the last two weeks?* she wrote.

Bush did not say anything but let Cheney make his argument. Rice suspected the vice president had been talking with the Israelis on his own, bypassing her. She grew angrier.

Rice argued that a resolution at the United Nations was close and it was too late to turn back. They owed it to their friends in Lebanon who were trying to stabilize a country fraught with strife after decades of Syrian occupation.

Cheney pushed again to let Israel continue its operation.

Rice turned to the president. "Do that and you are dead in the Middle East," she snapped in a voice loud enough to be picked up by the microphones.

Bush thanked everyone and ended the meeting.

Rice followed him out of the trailer. She was exasperated.

"I've been out there negotiating a resolution and now we don't want one?" she asked.

Bush decided to take the night to think about it. The next morning, when Rice wandered over to the main house for breakfast, he handed her a short memo.

"Here's a copy of something I want you to read," Bush said. "I've already sent it to Dick."

Rice was surprised. Bush had sat down and written out a strategy paper of his own, siding with Rice and agreeing to pursue a UN resolution calling for a cease-fire and sending in international peacekeepers. The paper outlined the reasons why, largely that Iraq was too important and if the Lebanon War continued, it would put that effort at risk, and that it would jeopardize what slim chances there were of getting a Palestinian state. Perhaps as important, he wrote, how could they stand for democracy in Iraq and allow a young democracy in Lebanon to be destroyed?

With Bush's support over Cheney's objections, the cease-fire in Lebanon went into effect August 14, ending the war after thirty-four days. The debate over video link that day in Crawford increasingly represented the pattern of national security meetings as Rice asserted herself more and Cheney found himself on defense. On issue after issue, they would preface their remarks with acknowledgments of their fundamental disconnect. Cheney would open by saying, "It won't surprise you that I disagree with Condi on this one." And Rice would say, "This is about diplomacy, so the vice president won't want to do it." They had become the two poles of the second-term foreign policy. "He is a natural debater and so am I," Rice recalled. "So we would just go at it right there in front of the president. But it was not nasty or personal." Her relationship with Bush gave her an advantage. "It made a difference when you have a secretary of state who's at Camp David every single weekend," noted Michael Gerson. Or, as in the case of the Lebanon War, at the ranch outside Crawford.

For Cheney, the question was less about his own diminishing influence than the gnawing sense that Bush was losing his will. Clearly some of the shift was due to Bush growing more comfortable in the job and more confident in his own judgments, no longer so reliant on the experience his vice president brought to the table. But Cheney thought Bush was letting outside criticism get to him and undermine his faith in the direction the two had taken together in the first term. Bush was listening to Rice, who had become a captive of the pin-striped foreign service set that had never subscribed to administration policies. "It wasn't personal," said Liz Cheney. "He was frustrated that the policy decisions were wrong."

While the vice president maintained a deferential respect for Bush, the people around him engaged in long discussions about when exactly the president changed. Some thought it was as far back as 2003 when it became clear Iraq did not have banned weapons and Bush grew disenchanted with the path Cheney had led him down. Others pointed to the fight over reauthorizing the surveillance program when Bush felt blindsided, or the "last throes" comment when the vice president looked out of touch, or even the shooting accident. And then there were some close to the vice president who pointed to Lebanon, seeing it as a metaphor for Bush's drift from his own record—the president who defied world opinion to take down the dictator of Baghdad was now more intent on currying favor with foreign leaders than doing what was right and standing by Israel against terrorists.

OUTSIDE THE WHITE House, Bush found himself targeted not only by liberals but even by fellow conservatives disenchanted with Iraq and nervous about upcoming midterm elections. On the morning of August 15, Joe Scarborough, a former Republican congressman now hosting a talk show on MSNBC, grilled guests about whether "George Bush's mental weakness is damaging America's credibility at home and abroad," while the bottom of the screen flashed the caption "IS BUSH AN 'IDIOT'?" Other pundits normally sympathetic to the president were jumping ship. Rich Lowry, editor of *National Review*, wrote that "success in Iraq seems more out of reach than it has at any time since the initial invasion," blaming "the administration's on-again-off-again approach." Quin Hillyer, executive editor of the *American Spectator*, added that "we seem not to be winning" and that the administration could not "credibly claim that victory in Iraq is achievable" until it took on militia leaders like Moqtada al-Sadr. George Will, the syndicated columnist, mocked neoconservative aspirations to transform the Middle East.

The White House responded to Will by e-mailing supporters a 2,432-word rebuttal by Peter Wehner—three times as long as the original column—arguing that Will's version of stability meant not confronting oppression and radicalism and "would eventually lead to death and destruction on a scale that is almost unimaginable." But behind the scenes, Wehner was among those in the White House most vocal about the mistakes in Iraq, taking it so personally that he was physically sick and having trouble sleeping at night. To colleagues who blamed media negativity, Wehner argued that "Iraq was not a communications problem, it was a facts-on-the-ground problem." Finally, that August, he took it upon himself to send a memo to Joshua Bolten arguing that Bush should get rid of Rumsfeld. Bolten invited him for a forty-five-minute conversation about the war. Even if the strategy was changed, Wehner told him, no one would perceive it as change as long as Rumsfeld was there. He suggested someone like James Baker, Joseph Lieberman, or Fred Thompson.

Bush returned from Texas more skeptical of his defense chief as well. For inspiration, he had been reading *Lincoln: A Life of Purpose and Power*, by Richard Carwardine, one of fourteen Lincoln biographies he would read during his presidency. Like Bush, Lincoln had issues with generals and struggled to find the right balance between empowering them and imposing his judgment when he thought they were wrong. Under Bush's hands-off approach, Rumsfeld had gotten himself caught in a similarly vicious circle. He had so emphasized the need to transform the military to a lighter, more agile force that when he asked commanders if they needed more troops in Iraq—and he had asked on numerous occasions—the answer came back no, perhaps because the generals had come to internalize his transformation goals or because they assumed they knew the answer he wanted. George Casey said he later found out that junior officers held back making requests. "They weren't pushing things up because they didn't think they'd get approved," he said.

If the generals were not asking for troops, Rumsfeld was not about to overrule them. For all the complaints about his overbearing leadership, on this question he had become all too willing to accept "no, sir." One close aide to the secretary thought that after five years of being called a bully, Rumsfeld had grown gun-shy about pushing too hard in questioning the military's conclusions lest he fuel the still-simmering generals' revolt. Another aide, though, thought the eagerness to transition and withdraw reflected Rumsfeld's own ambivalence. "I'm not sure Rumsfeld believed in the Iraq War," the aide said later. "You can tell by his body language."

The responsibility lay not just with Rumsfeld. Casey and John Abizaid genuinely believed the occupation itself was a spark for the insurgency and so the more the Americans could pull back and put an Iraqi face on the security force, the sooner violence would ebb. For more than two years, Bush had accepted that. But no longer. The president gathered with his national security team on August 17, meeting in the Roosevelt Room because the Situation Room was under renovation. Casey, who, like Abizaid and Ambassador Zalmay Khalilzad, was participating from Iraq via secure video, reported on Operation Together Forward II, the latest effort to secure Baghdad, and said he hoped to turn over security in the capital to the Iraqis by the end of the year.

Bush and Cheney both seemed unconvinced. Over a video link from Wyoming, the vice president asked what could be done to reduce the number of attacks and suggested American forces take on a bigger role, not scale back.

"The situation seems to be deteriorating," Bush said. "I want to be able to say that I have a plan to punch back. Can America succeed? If so, how? How do our commanders answer that?"

Casey maintained that transferring responsibility to the Iraqis faster was key.

Rumsfeld agreed, saying America must "help them help themselves."

Bush found that unsatisfactory. "We must succeed," he said. "If they can't do it, we will. If the bicycle teeters, we're going to put the hand back on. We have to make damn sure we do not fail."

The bicycle analogy was a direct shot at Rumsfeld, who for years had said the United States needed to take its hand off the bicycle seat so the Iraqis could learn to ride on their own. Just like that, Bush made eminently clear that he no longer bought the Rumsfeld-Abizaid-Casey approach. He was so pointed during the conversation that Cheney from Wyoming felt the need to offer praise for Casey and Khalilzad so it would not be taken personally. Bush agreed, saying he supported them "100 percent," but stressed the need to challenge their thinking. "These are difficult times," he said. "We need to ask some difficult questions."

After the meeting, Bush authorized Stephen Hadley to formalize the strategy review already coming together. And if the strategy was to be changed, it followed that there should be changes at the top. It was a telling sign of Bush's anxiety over Iraq that he was finally ready to replace Rumsfeld after years of resisting the advice of even his closest advisers. He respected Rumsfeld and hated tossing overboard a loyal member of his team, particularly one whose ouster would be taken as an acknowledgment of how far off course his presidency had drifted. He hated the satisfaction it would give his critics. But so much was at stake there was little choice.

One solace through much of this period had been the economy. While Bush got little credit for it because of Iraq, 2006 had seen strong growth and falling unemployment and inflation despite fears of recession. But growth was slowing, down from a robust 5.6 percent in the first quarter to half that in the second, and the housing boom that had fueled the economy now appeared at risk. The day after pushing back on Iraq, Bush gathered advisers at Camp David for a long discussion of the economy, led by the newly sworn-in Treasury secretary, Henry Paulson.

Paulson, in his debut, noted economic history and warned that a disruption was due. "We can't predict when the next crisis will come," he told Bush. "But we need to be prepared." As he would later note with chagrin, he correctly foresaw a crisis but not the cause; his presentation made little mention of problems in the overheating housing market.

THE PRESIDENT AND the widow sat on two frayed chairs in a teachers' lounge, just the two of them, so close their knees were almost touching. Bush listened in pain as she held him responsible for her husband's death and begged him to bring home the troops.

"It's time to put our pride behind us and stop the bleeding," she told Bush.

He demurred, unwilling to debate a mourning widow. "We see things differently," he said simply.

As she mentioned two children left fatherless and tears rolled down her face, his eyes welled up too. He hugged her, held her face, kissed her cheek. "I am so sorry for your loss," he kept repeating.

It was August 24. Bush had flown to Kennebunkport, but before heading off for some fishing with his father, he met with relatives of slain soldiers in a local elementary school. One was Hildi Halley, whose husband had died in Afghanistan.

While the public saw Bush's swagger, his private meetings with families that had lost sons and daughters and husbands and wives revealed a different side, one kept out of the media. Typically in such encounters, Bush sat down with each family separately, joined only by a single aide, usually his deputy chief of staff, Joe Hagin. He offered commemorative coins, posed for photographs, or signed autographs, depending on what they wanted. "I do the best I can to cry with them or, you know, laugh with them if they wanna laugh, and hug them," he said. It took a toll. After such meetings, he was drained.

By this point, Bush had served as a wartime president longer than any occupant of the White House since Lyndon Johnson and had presided over more American military casualties than any since Richard Nixon. He avoided military funerals and eschewed public displays that might be seen as weak or doubtful, even when he felt weak and doubtful. Yet he was conscious not to appear indifferent either, giving up golf, except for chipping in the privacy of Camp David, as long as young men and women were dying on his orders. To many of the military relatives who met with him, the private Bush came across as personally tormented by their grief. Laura Bush always knew when her husband had visited the wounded or relatives of the slain because he was uncharacteristically silent, what she called "a deafening kind of quiet." One look at his face told the story. "The grief shone in his eyes," she said.

Meeting with the wounded and the relatives of the dead might have eroded another leader's commitment and convinced him to reverse course. But Bush took the opposite message—in large part because Hildi Halley was the exception. "The number of people that would really say we have to get out, it was a very, very, very small number of people," said Hagin. "By far and away, the most prominent emotion was, they would sort of set their jaw and say, 'Don't let my son have died in vain.'" One mother of a slain soldier told Bush, "He did his job. Now you do yours."

For Bush, withdrawing troops before Iraq was secure would mean admitting their sons and daughters had indeed died in vain, and that was something he just could not let happen.

28

"Don't let this be your legacy"

President Bush was unwilling to give ground on Iraq, but he was more open to strategic retreats elsewhere, much to Vice President Cheney's consternation. One of the most heated debates of the second term took place one August day as the president and the vice president finally confronted the issue of what to do about the secret prisons holding terror suspects overseas. "We had just a huge blood-on-the-floor fight," one official recalled.

The meeting in the Roosevelt Room came almost a year after the *Washington Post* wrote about the so-called black-site prisons and two months after the Supreme Court ruled that the Geneva Conventions applied to al-Qaeda prisoners. It was a time of flux for the interrogation and detention program cobbled together so hastily in the days after the planes hit the World Trade Center and the Pentagon. Bush was faced with taking what was effectively a stopgap system and making it acceptable to courts and Congress.

Michael Hayden, who as NSA director had already pushed the boundaries of counterterrorism with the controversial surveillance program, had spent much of the summer as CIA director getting up to speed on the agency's handling of prisoners and decided he wanted to preserve at least part of the interrogation program that many called torture. "I want to keep some of it even if it is just the ambiguity, you know, that they don't know," he told Stephen Hadley that August. Of thirteen harsh interrogation techniques in the original program, he asked to keep seven. Ultimately, he was allowed to keep six. But he believed it was time to empty the overseas CIA prisons and bring the detainees to Guantánamo, where they would have the same rights as other captives.

Condoleezza Rice also favored closing the secret prisons. They were never as extensive as some thought: fewer than a hundred detainees had been kept in them at various points over the years, fewer than a third of those had been subjected to the so-called enhanced interrogation techniques, and just three had been waterboarded, none since March 2003. But she thought they had taken a disproportionate toll on the nation's image. Everywhere she traveled, she saw an image of America reflected back that was dark and sinister, a place that sounded more like those she had studied years earlier as a Soviet scholar. She did not want to repudiate the decisions made in the early days of the war on terror, when circumstances warranted tough actions. But this was nearly five years later, and like her effort to promote more diplomacy following the Iraq invasion, she felt it was time to recalibrate.

Hadley agreed. The legal, ethical, and security landscapes had changed since the original interrogation and detention policies were put in place. What might have been acceptable at a moment of maximum danger no longer seemed necessary, especially since American intelligence agencies had learned so much more about al-Qaeda by this point and were better positioned to fight the war. Moreover, both Congress and the Supreme Court had weighed in, shifting the ground underneath them. As the president and his team took their seats in the Roosevelt Room that day, Hadley orchestrated the meeting "just like a conductor with a baton," as one person in the room recalled.

Rice gave an impassioned speech. The attacks had happened on our watch, she said, so the perpetrators should be tried on our watch. "Democracies don't disappear people," she said.

Hayden, beaming into the meeting from a secure video connection in Key West, where he was on a brief break, backed Rice. "Mr. President, I think we have to empty the sites," he said. "We are not the nation's jailers."

Cheney strongly disagreed. For some in the room, it was the first time they had ever heard him speak directly on an issue.

"I oppose this, Mr. President," he said. "I think this is a bad idea." Then he gave several reasons why they should keep the selected captives incommunicado. "They might have intelligence value," he argued. Moreover, closing the prisons would embolden critics and betray the countries that hosted them. "We will expose people who helped us."

Some on the other side wondered whether Cheney was so eager to keep the prisons secret because he worried about what might become public about the government's handling of the detainees. *What scandal lurked in the dank cells of Eastern Europe?* Cheney and Rice went back and forth for several minutes as everyone else watched in stunned silence. Rice remembered it as "the most intense confrontation of my time in Washington."

Finally, Rice pulled out the trump card. "Mr. President," she said, "don't let this be your legacy."

When it was over, she could not read Bush, which was rare. Let me think about it, he said.

Only later did he tell Hadley to inform everyone he would empty the prisons and give a speech announcing the decision. But Cheney appealed to him in a one-on-one conversation at least not to close them permanently, keeping options open for the future.

Once he made the decision, Bush seemed oddly pumped up. Finally, after months on the defensive, he could push back against critics and explain what he had been up to. From his perspective, there was a good story to tell. They had captured men who had done grievous damage to the United States and had not simply killed them in revenge. They had not been gentle, to be sure, but their brutal tactics had been enough to extract vital, lifesaving intelligence. "He was very animated" and "extremely excited," recalled William Burck, an aide involved in preparing the speech. "All of this information was stuff he had known and really been the most important information he knew about for three years, and he couldn't tell anybody about it. It was only him and his hard-core, closest national security staff. And now he was able to sort of share it and tell the people, 'Here is what we have been doing, here is what we have been doing to protect you.'"

Just after lunchtime on September 6, Bush strode into the East Room to publicly acknowledge the CIA prisons for the first time and announce that he was sending the fourteen remaining "high-value detainees" to Guantánamo, where they would be made available to the International Committee of the Red Cross and given the same food, clothing, and medical care as other prisoners.

For thirty-seven minutes, Bush defended what he had done, arguing that for a select few captives on the battlefield, the normal rules could not apply. "These are dangerous men with unparalleled knowledge about terrorist networks and their plans for new attacks," Bush said. "The security of our nation and the lives of our citizens depend on our ability to learn what these terrorists know." The detainees in the black-site prisons had been subjected to what he antiseptically referred to as "an alternative set of procedures" that were "tough" but "safe and lawful and necessary." These tactics had "given us information that has saved innocent lives by helping us stop new attacks here in the United States and around the world." He named some detainees who had been held, including Khalid Sheikh Mohammed, Abu Zubaydah, and Ramzi bin al-Shibh, and described how they provided information leading to the other captures and headed off attacks on a marine camp in Djibouti, an American consulate in Pakistan, and civilian targets in London.

What Bush did not describe was exactly what the "alternative set of procedures" were. He did not disclose that Mohammed had been waterboarded 183 times and Zubaydah 83 times. Nor did he describe how Abd al-Rahim al-Nashiri, the Saudi accused of directing the bombing of the USS *Cole* in 2000, was waterboarded twice and threatened with a power drill and a loaded handgun in a mock execution; if Nashiri did not talk, he was told, "we could get your mother in here." Bush did not describe other techniques, including forced nudity, slamming detainees into walls, placing them in a dark, cramped box with insects, dousing them with water as cold as forty-one degrees, and keeping them awake for up to eleven days straight. He rejected the notion that all this constituted torture. "I want to be absolutely clear with our people and the world," Bush said. "The United States does not torture. It's against our laws and it's against our values. I have not authorized it, and I will not authorize it." This reassurance, however, meant only that as long as he and his lawyers determined a tactic was not torture, then he could say he did not authorize torture, even if it was deemed torture by the rest of the world.

Still, as he rhetorically justified his program, Bush was actually moving on. Any future questioning of suspects would be conducted under a new U.S. Army Field Manual issued that same day with more restricted methods of interrogation. And Bush was sending legislation that day to Congress to authorize the creation of new military commissions in response to the Supreme Court ruling, as well as asking lawmakers to pass a law clarifying rules for future interrogations to protect military and intelligence personnel from legal action.

But the tone crushed Rice's camp. What they had hoped would be a speech turning the page on controversial decisions of the past instead became a celebration of them. Marc Thiessen, the chief speechwriter, had crafted an address that gave no ground. "Basically," thought John Bellinger, the top State Department lawyer, "we had clutched defeat from the jaws of victory."

THE WAR WAS driving other fissures among friends. Senator Mitch McConnell, the Republican whip, called Joshua Bolten to ask for a private meeting with the president.

"Of course," Bolten said. "Do you want to tell me what it's about?"

"No," McConnell said.

The senator arrived at the Oval Office at the appointed hour. The midterm campaign was going badly, and he viewed Bush and Iraq as anchors holding the party down.

"Mr. President, your unpopularity is going to cost us control of the Congress," McConnell told Bush.

"Well, Mitch, what do you want me to do about it?" Bush asked.

"Mr. President, bring some troops home from Iraq," McConnell urged.

Bush refused: "I will not withdraw troops unless military conditions warrant."

The desperate plea from the number-two Senate Republican underscored how nervous the party was about the upcoming elections. It also illustrated the disparity between the pro-war statements made for public consumption and the anxious sentiments expressed in private. Just the day before visiting Bush, McConnell had excoriated Democrats for wanting to pull troops out of Iraq. "Cutting and running is not a strategy for protecting the American people here in the United States," he told reporters.

Unbeknownst to the Senate, Bush's advisers were pressing him to do the opposite as part of the strategy review he had requested. After two weeks of intense study, Meghan O'Sullivan and Brett McGurk gave Hadley a thirty-page report pressing for more troops, not fewer, warning of mass killings and a fractured Iraqi army if they did not reinforce the troops. Hadley, still not showing his hand, told them to do it again. When they objected, the typically calm lawyer snapped at them.

"Hey, guys!" he exclaimed. "Do you get it? This is it! You want the president of the United States to send more Americans into Iraq, betting everything on it. Do you get it? You better be damn sure. I'm the one in the Oval with the recommendation. So you better be sure."

They had never heard Hadley use a curse word before.

"We're sure," O'Sullivan said. "We understand and we're sure."

"You better be damn sure," Hadley repeated. "Go back to the table and run the analysis again."

Theirs was not the only review under way. General Peter Pace, chairman of the Joint Chiefs of Staff, had sensed the president's discontent and organized a group of staff officers to examine the war effort, a group that became known as the Council of Colonels. And then there was a rump campaign for change instigated by General Jack Keane, a retired army vice chief of staff serving on the Defense Policy Board, a panel of prominent figures that advised the defense secretary, and a well-respected figure with his own circle of protégés in top positions around the military. Tall, rugged, and barrel-chested, Keane was the picture of an army general, having served in Vietnam, Somalia, Haiti, Bosnia, and Kosovo during thirty-seven years in the military. Although he had been Donald Rumsfeld's choice to become army chief of staff, he retired instead at the end of 2003 to care for his sick wife. But watching from the private sector, he had concluded that the United States was on the verge of defeat in Iraq and could only turn it around with an infusion of troops.

He went to see Rumsfeld on September 19 to urge him to change course and replace John Abizaid and George Casey. It was a radical move for a retired four-star officer to interject himself into policy making and undercut officers in the field. But the stakes were enormous.

"We're edging toward strategic failure," Keane told Rumsfeld. "What's wrong is our strategy. We never adopted a strategy to defeat the insurgency." The Iraqis were not capable of taking over. "We put our money on that horse."

Rumsfeld deflected that to his commanders. "That was Casey and Abizaid's strategy," he said.

Keane replied that Rumsfeld had influence too. In any case, Keane said the only way to win was to protect the population, living with the Iraqi people day and night, not the current strategy of huddling inside isolated bases. "If we don't change it," he said, "we will lose and we will fail."

Keane left thinking Rumsfeld had not really been receptive and set about finding others who would be. Rumsfeld later said he was noncommittal mainly because he had already been talking with the president about moving Abizaid and Casey out. "We were working that problem then before he suggested it, but I didn't feel it was my place to tell him that, because he was an outsider at that stage. He was not an insider; he was not in the government," Rumsfeld said.

Three days later, September 22, Rumsfeld met with another adviser, Kenneth Adelman, who like Keane served on the Defense Policy Board and, more important, had been friends with Rumsfeld for three decades. Adelman had worked for Rumsfeld at three separate stops along their careers. He had stayed in Rumsfeld's houses in Washington, Chicago, Taos, Santo Domingo, and Michigan. They had vacationed together with their families. Adelman had been a vocal proponent of the war, writing the op-ed piece predicting a "cakewalk" and sharing in the celebration at Cheney's house after Saddam Hussein's fall.

But he had grown disenchanted with Rumsfeld's handling of the war, and now was the moment of confrontation. Rumsfeld told Adelman to resign from the Defense Policy Board.

"I wanted to call you in because you have been sounding so negative," Rumsfeld told him.

"Don, you are absolutely right," Adelman replied. "I am sounding negative in the meetings because I feel negative. I feel like you have made terrible decisions."

"Like what?" Rumsfeld asked.

"Well, allowing the looting, Abu Ghraib, the insurgency."

Rumsfeld did not agree, so Adelman ran through his criticisms. It was a travesty, he felt, to brush off the looting in the early days of the war with a dismissive "stuff happens." And Rumsfeld had taken no responsibility, as far as Adelman was concerned, for the abuses at Abu Ghraib that so undermined American credibility. For forty-five minutes, they had it out. Adelman walked out knowing they would never talk again. Cheney's circle was fracturing.

Adelman was not the only one disillusioned. Rumsfeld, perhaps sensing the president's growing impatience, gave him an opening by volunteering at a meeting in September that it might be good to have a "fresh pair of eyes." Bush was not sure whether Rumsfeld was sending a signal, but for the first time he was preparing to act. Rumsfeld told his wife, Joyce, that if Democrats captured one or both houses of Congress in the midterm elections, he should resign because he could foresee two years of hostile hearings. He hinted at his thinking after yet another grim meeting in the Oval Office in early October.

"The good news," Cheney said with his trademark crooked grin, "is that there are only 794 days left until the end of the term."

"Dick," Rumsfeld replied, "there are 794 days left for you. Not for me."

AS BUSH PLOTTED a change, he worried most about Cheney, whose relationship with Rumsfeld remained close after nearly four decades. They had weekend houses next to each other on the Eastern Shore of Maryland, and at events like Mary Cheney's book party at the Palm the previous spring the two men were found huddled alone in a corner, talking animatedly by themselves while everyone else mingled.

It was Rumsfeld who had given Cheney the important breaks leading to a lifetime of success in politics, and it was Rumsfeld who had refused to let his drunk-driving past get in the way. ("He stood by me, and I have never forgotten that.") Cheney had tried to repay him again and again, suggesting Rumsfeld for defense secretary under the first president Bush, then for vice president under the second, and finally for defense secretary again. He had stood by him in all the fights with Colin Powell and Condoleezza Rice, persuaded him to stay after Abu Ghraib, and helped save his job after the 2004 election. "Maybe he didn't have the best bedside manner in the world," Cheney later wrote, "but he is one of the most competent people I've ever met."

For all of that, Cheney had begun drifting away from his friend when it came to Iraq. Rumsfeld worried about nation building run amok; Cheney worried about defeat. "If Rumsfeld saw a Kosovo on steroids, Cheney's image was that last helicopter lifting off the roof of the Saigon embassy," J. D. Crouch said. Cheney's adviser John Hannah had been feeding him excerpts from Lewis Sorley's *Better War*, arguing that in its later years the Vietnam War was being won on the ground and lost in Washington. He had also read a new counterinsurgency manual by Lieutenant General David Petraeus and met privately with critics of the current strategy like Colonel H. R. McMaster, whose success in applying counterinsurgency tactics in the northwestern Iraqi city of Tal Afar had become a model for a different approach. A counterinsurgency strategy would require more troops, and Cheney was amenable but largely kept quiet. "The friendship with Rumsfeld blinded the vice president to some degree to where the responsibility and accountability lay," said one official who worked at different times for both men. "Or maybe it didn't blind him, but it was just too painful to have to deal with it."

Cheney would never blame Rumsfeld. "Even though Cheney knew what the problems were," said a White House official, "he was loyal to the end to Rumsfeld and wasn't going to dime Rumsfeld." In his memoir, Cheney wrote that Casey, Abizaid, and "some in the Pentagon civilian leadership" opposed increasing forces—clearly meaning Rumsfeld without naming him. Like Bush, he made a pointed reference to Rumsfeld's favorite line by saying opponents of a new strategy "continued to argue that the solution was to 'take our hand off the bicycle seat' and put the Iraqis in charge as quickly as we could." Cheney could not bring himself to identify Rumsfeld as one of those opponents. Nor did he confront Rumsfeld directly. "He didn't say it to me," Rumsfeld said after both left office.

If he were to get rid of Rumsfeld, Bush wanted a replacement ready to go. He had long attributed his decisions not to remove Rumsfeld to an inability to come up with a successor. In the past, he had considered Rice, Frederick Smith, James Baker, and Joseph Lieberman, but none of them was available or the right fit. Bush stewed about it and asked advisers and close friends whom they would suggest.

One night he had dinner in the White House with Jack Morrison, a friend from Andover and Yale he had put on the President's Foreign Intelligence Advisory Board. Laura was out of town, so it was just the two of them. The president was clearly wrestling with who should replace Rumsfeld.

"I've got to get someone who's confirmable and acceptable to the military," Bush said.

Morrison had an idea. What about Bob Gates?

That surprised Bush. Gates had been his father's CIA director and was now president of Texas A&M University.

"How do you know Bob Gates?" Bush asked.

"Well, I don't really," Morrison answered, "but I spent a day with him a couple weeks ago, and I came away very impressed."

"That's interesting," Bush said.

BUSH HOSTED ANOTHER dinner at the White House around then that was more delicate. Joining him in the Family Dining Room on the evening of September 27 were Presidents Pervez Musharraf of Pakistan and Hamid Karzai of Afghanistan. In theory, they were allies in the fight against the Taliban and al-Qaeda. But this was a dinner Bush was not looking forward to.

It had been five years almost to the day since the first CIA operatives landed in Afghanistan to insert America into the country's long-running war and topple the Taliban government in retaliation for the attacks on New York and Washington. The quick capture of Kabul and Kandahar and the subsequent invasion of Iraq had drawn attention, resources, and energy away from Afghanistan, on the assumption that the lingering war against insurgents there was relatively in hand. But in fact the Taliban was resurgent again, operating with impunity from Pakistani tribal areas. Insurgent tactics were bleeding over from Iraq as Afghan fighters adopted suicide bombing, and casualties were at a five-year high. Some experts expressed concern about the "Iraqification" of Afghanistan.

By the time he arrived for dinner, Musharraf had just reached an agreement with tribal leaders in the hostile and largely ungoverned border areas near Afghanistan in which he pulled troops back in exchange for cooperation. Joining the visitors and Bush around the table for dinner were Cheney and Rice. Musharraf spent thirty minutes explaining the benefits of the agreement until Karzai began hectoring him for making a deal with terrorists using Pakistan as a safe haven to launch attacks in Afghanistan. Karzai produced a piece of paper that he said proved the Taliban were not to be disturbed under the deal. Musharraf denied that he was harboring the Taliban.

"Tell me where they are," Musharraf demanded.

"You know where they are!" Karzai insisted.

"If I did, I would get them," Musharraf replied.

"Go do it!" Karzai exclaimed.

Bush, wondering whether dinner was a mistake, tried to calm them. Afterward, he walked out shaking his head. "They almost came to blows," he remarked to Rice.

Within weeks, Bush's team concluded that the peace deal in Pakistan was falling apart. As feared, the supposed "live and let live" agreement had merely become license for fighters from al-Qaeda, the Taliban, and the allied

Haqqani group to operate as they pleased. With each passing day, Bush and his advisers grew more aggravated. On October 13, Donald Rumsfeld shot off a memo to Hadley. "I think someone needs to talk to Musharraf—either the President, Abizaid, or I should tell him the deal made in North Waziristan isn't working and is not likely to work," he wrote. "The level of activity has gone up, not down."

"LOOK, I WANT to assure you that this is not the Addington proposal," Hadley told John McCain and other senators.

At Bush's instructions, Hadley headed up to Capitol Hill to negotiate legislation authorizing military commissions. This time, Hadley had a message to deliver. That the president's national security adviser would feel compelled to disavow the vice president's chief of staff spoke volumes about the Bush-Cheney White House in the autumn of its sixth year. Hadley had been through this before and understood that Cheney's intensity and reputation, fairly or not, had colored the talks over the Detainee Treatment Act a year earlier. But it also left McCain's aides wondering if "Cheney was losing steam within the administration a little bit," as one put it.

The Military Commissions Act was a response to the Supreme Court's *Hamdan* ruling, putting the system on a firmer constitutional footing by winning permission from Congress first. Feeling burned by the signing statement Addington had attached to the Detainee Treatment Act the previous year, McCain and Senator Lindsey Graham were determined not to let the White House pull anything over on them. At one point, an aide ran into McCain's office to tell the two senators that Hadley was on the phone at that very moment with the other member of their triumvirate, Senator John Warner of Virginia. McCain and Graham raced down the hall and barged into Warner's office without knocking to ensure he did not give in to White House pressure. "We had to waterboard him," McCain later joked to an aide.

The debate exposed an old rift. From retirement in suburban Virginia, Colin Powell finally reemerged to go public with his years-old fight with Cheney over the Geneva Conventions. "The world is beginning to doubt the moral basis of our fight against terrorism," Powell wrote in a letter made public. "To redefine Common Article 3 would add to those doubts. Furthermore, it would put our own troops at risk."

Eventually, Hadley reached a deal with McCain, Graham, and Warner. The White House would back off the effort to narrow the application of the Geneva Conventions, but the legislation would give the president considerable latitude in determining how to meet the treaty's obligations. Foreigners held as unlawful enemy combatants, even legal residents living in the United States, would have no habeas corpus right to challenge their detention in court. Prosecutors trying terror suspects before military commissions could not introduce secret evidence without letting the defense examine it but could still use evidence obtained from coercive interrogations if a military judge deemed it reliable. The government could detain indefinitely not only American citizens who "engaged in hostilities" against their country but those who "materially supported" the enemy, potentially allowing authorities to imprison without trial people who donated to Middle East charities linked to groups considered terrorist organizations. In the end, Bush was satisfied that the Military Commissions Act "contained everything we asked for." Congress passed it on bipartisan votes at the end of September.

UNMOVED BY BUSH'S latest overture delivered through China's Hu Jintao, North Korea chose the weeks before the congressional election to demand attention again. On the evening of October 8, Bush and his team got frantic messages from China that North Korea was about to test a nuclear bomb. Pyongyang had given Beijing an hour's notice, ignoring the warnings of its most important patron. At 10:36 p.m. Washington time (11:36 a.m. in Korea), a crude nuclear device detonated at the Punggye-ri test site northwest of the capital. Bush spoke with Hu and tried to shame him into taking stronger action. "It's a disgraceful day for China," Bush told him. "You speak out, Mr. President, and Kim Jong Il completely ignored you."

The next morning, October 9, Bush made a short statement in the Diplomatic Reception Room of the White House that laid down a new red line for North Korea. Since Bush could no longer demand that North Korea not test weapons, he insisted that at least it not give them to other rogue nations. "The transfer of nuclear weapons or material by North Korea to states or non-state entities would be considered a grave threat to the United States," he declared, "and we would hold North Korea fully accountable of the consequences of such action."

The explosion proved less than feared. Experts estimated the yield was barely half a kiloton, a fraction of the power of the bomb that destroyed Hiroshima and a pittance compared with modern nuclear weapons. Scientists concluded the bomb probably fizzled, although even a failure can help in understanding what works and what does not. Either way, Bush scorned the North Koreans. "Is this the best they can do?" he asked, shaking his head when advisers briefed him on the findings.

Bush wanted to press the Chinese, who seemed genuinely angry about the test. He decided to send Christopher Hill back to the region. "We cannot solve this by ourselves," Bush said at a session in the Situation Room called to address the issue. The Chinese had to take leadership.

He turned to Hill. "Tell them that they cannot allow this to go on," he said.

"With pleasure," Hill replied.

Within days, Chinese pique cleared the way for the UN Security Council to impose the toughest sanctions on North Korea since the end of the Korean War, banning the sale or transfer of large-scale arms, nuclear technology, or luxury goods and imposing a travel ban and asset freeze on officials connected to the nuclear program.

Cheney was not mollified. While Bush saw the test as a chance to solidify the international coalition against North Korea, Cheney thought the episode showed the utter failure of the policy the administration had been pursuing. On yet another front, the divide between president and vice president had deepened.

WITH THE MIDTERM election drawing near, Bush tried to shift his rhetoric on Iraq. For months, he had been hammering home the need to remain steady. The question he posed after visiting Iraq in June was "whether the United States would have the nerve to stay the course and help them succeed." In Milwaukee in July he declared, "We will win in Iraq so long as we stay the course." In Salt Lake City in August he vowed, "We will stay the course; we will help this young Iraqi democracy succeed."

But support was eroding even among Republicans like Senator John Warner, who returned from Iraq to lament that "the situation is simply drifting sideways." Ed Gillespie called to see if he really meant his comment to be taken as negatively as it was, hoping to perhaps get him to walk it back, but Warner stuck to his view. So Bush was now cutting and running from "stay the course." A phrase meant to connote steely resolve had become a symbol for out-of-touch rigidity and an attack line in Democratic commercials.

In a head-spinning twist, Bush asserted he was never really for "stay the course" at all. "The characterization of 'let's stay the course' is about a quarter right," he told a news conference on October 11. "'Stay the course' means keep doing what you're doing. My attitude is: Don't do what you're doing if it's not working—change. 'Stay the course' also means don't leave before the job is done." Barely a week later, it was no longer even a quarter right. "Listen, we've never been stay the course," he told ABC News. "We have been—we will complete the mission, we will do our job and help achieve the goal, but we're constantly adjusting the tactics. Constantly."

At the time, that seemed more a rhetorical shift than reality. But behind the scenes, momentum for changing course in Iraq was gathering. At a meeting with Bush in the Roosevelt Room, some on the national security team suggested a radical reversal by sending more troops rather than pulling them out. The very idea shocked others, who argued that the military was already overextended. Afterward, Hadley's deputy, J. D. Crouch, grabbed a scrap of paper and sketched out the whole plan in rudimentary form. Then, with Hadley's permission, he assigned William Luti, a navy captain working at the NSC, to quietly study whether it would be possible given the forces available. "If you had a clean sheet of paper," Crouch told him, "what would you do?" Luti came back on October 11 with a set of slides showing the military could muster a "surge" of five brigades. Time was running out. Less than a week later, the military in Baghdad acknowledged that Operation Together Forward II, like its predecessor, had failed to reduce the violence washing over the capital.

Unlike Bush, Cheney saw no need to measure his rhetoric on the campaign trail. It was fine for Bush to reach out to disaffected independents and moderates, but the vice president by both inclination and calculation focused on rallying the conservative base. Some aides later attributed some of the drift between the two men to this different campaign experience: Bush seeing what was necessary to appeal to a broader cross section of Americans and Cheney focused as ever on a narrower audience.

When Scott Hennen, a conservative radio talk show host from Fargo, North Dakota, showed up in the vice president's West Wing office on October 24, Cheney vigorously defended the administration's record.

"I've had people call and say, please let the vice president know that if it takes dunking a terrorist in water, we're all for it, if it saves American lives," Hennen told Cheney. "Again, this debate seems a little silly given the threat we face, would you agree?"

"I do agree," replied Cheney, sitting at his desk without his suit jacket on. "And I think the terrorist threat, for example, with respect to our ability to interrogate high-value detainees like Khalid Sheikh Mohammed, that's been a very important tool that we've had to be able to secure the nation."

"Would you agree a dunk in water is a no-brainer if it can save lives?" the host asked.

"It's a no-brainer for me," Cheney said. "But for a while there, I was criticized as being the Vice President for Torture. We don't torture. That's not what we're involved in. We live up to our obligations in international treaties that we're party to and so forth. But the fact is, you can have a fairly robust interrogation program without torture."

It was perhaps Cheney's most unvarnished public defense to date of waterboarding terror suspects, a "no-brainer" as he measured the trade-offs. When a furor erupted, he told reporters that he "didn't say anything about waterboarding," but that was the obvious reference. In the days to come, Cheney seemed more intent on denying that he disclosed a classified interrogation technique than on distancing himself from waterboarding. But his comments were a genuine reflection of his views: waterboarding did not violate the law on torture, because it did not meet the legal definition crafted by administration lawyers seeking to justify a policy. As for any moral quandaries, the only one Cheney saw was the responsibility to prevent future attacks; everything else took a backseat.

Bush, meanwhile, was determined to maintain a positive outlook in public despite private doubts. He believed that was always his role as commander in chief with troops in the field, and he knew that betraying uncertainty before the election in particular could crater what fragile support his party had left. So when he walked into the East Room for a news conference on October 25, he resolved to remain upbeat.

The first question tested that conviction. Terence Hunt of the Associated Press noted that the Iraq War had now lasted almost as long as the American involvement in World War II.

"Do you think we're winning," Hunt asked, "and why?"

Bush dodged, saying he was "confident we will succeed" and warning that "defeat will only come" if America backs off.

Hunt pressed for an answer. "Are we winning?" he repeated.

This time, Bush offered no equivocation. "Absolutely, we're winning," he said.

In private that same day, though, he offered a much different tone to a group of conservative journalists invited in for an interview. He was certain that, as he put it, "they're coming after us," meaning terrorists, but did not understand why so many others did not see it with the clarity he did. "I am in disbelief that people don't take these problems seriously," he said.

The president's aggravation and isolation were on display. Lawrence Kudlow of CNBC told Bush he had supported the war but was discouraged.

"I need some good news, sir," Kudlow told him.

"Yes, I do, too," Bush replied.

"I really do," Kudlow repeated.

"You're talking to Noah about the flood," Bush said. "I do, too."

The president who kept a chart of al-Qaeda figures in his desk to cross out when one was killed or captured expressed exasperation that he could not find a tangible yardstick to point to victory in Iraq.

"I don't know what Harry Truman was feeling like, or Franklin Roosevelt," he said. "I'm sure there were moments of high frustration for them.

But I do know that at Midway, they were eventually able to say two carriers were sunk and one was damaged. We don't get to say that. A thousand of the enemy killed, or whatever the number was. It's happening; you just don't know it. And there's no scorecard."

THE IDEA OF Robert Gates at the Pentagon gained favor among the small coterie of people Bush had consulted. Condoleezza Rice recommended him enthusiastically, having worked for Gates when they were both at the National Security Council. Gates, a steady figure who had served four presidents and understood the ways of Washington, could be just the ticket. Stephen Hadley and Andy Card had approached him once before about becoming the first director of national intelligence, only to have him decline. Bush instructed Hadley to approach him again about the Pentagon.

Under tight secrecy, Bush instructed Hadley, Joshua Bolten, Karl Rove, Joel Kaplan, and Dan Bartlett to begin planning a change but kept his deliberations secret from Cheney for weeks, obviously concerned about his vice president's reaction. There was probably no more important decision in his presidency that Bush had not shared with his vice president. It was not until October 31 that Bush finally tipped off Cheney, even as he sent Hadley to Baghdad on a fact-finding mission.

"Dick, can I talk to you for a second?" Bush asked after their morning briefings.

The two retreated to the privacy of the small hallway off the Oval Office.

"I've decided to make a change at Defense," Bush said, "and I'm looking at Bob Gates to replace Rumsfeld."

Cheney was struck by the finality of Bush's statement. He was informing Cheney, not soliciting his views. "It wasn't open for discussion by the time he came to me," Cheney recalled.

While Cheney was still processing the surprise, Bush turned around and headed off, not giving his vice president a chance to object as he had so many times before.

Bush was holding back on the public as well as Cheney. Bolten and Bartlett came up with a plan to announce the move the day after the election, reasoning that it would look political to do it before voters headed to the polls. But the day after Bush told Cheney he had decided to remove Rumsfeld, he was asked in the Oval Office by Terence Hunt and two other wire service reporters, Richard Keil of Bloomberg and Steve Holland of Reuters, whether he wanted Rumsfeld and Cheney to stay until the end of his term.

Unwilling to give away his secret, Bush said yes. "Both those men are doing fantastic jobs, and I strongly support them," he said.

Rumsfeld, who had sensed what was coming, was confused when he read about the interview.

ON THE SATURDAY before the elections, nothing much was going right for Bush. He woke up in a hotel in Colorado to find the first fourteen pages of the local newspaper devoted to the drugs-and-gay-sex scandal involving an evangelical pastor who had been among his staunch supporters in the conservative Christian wing of the party. The president's visit to support a Republican congressional candidate did not even make the A section.

Bush stopped in a coffee shop, spoke at an unenthusiastic rally, and called it quits for the day, boarding Air Force One to fly home early to his Texas ranch. His staff told the traveling press corps that the president wanted to celebrate the first lady's birthday over dinner, which was true enough. But he also wanted a chance to meet in private with key advisers to decide what to do next.

Among those at the ranch that afternoon was Ken Mehlman, the rail-thin, hyperkinetic forty-year-old chairman of the Republican National Committee. Mehlman had been a Bush loyalist from the early days—field director during the 2000 election, White House political director through the president's first term, and campaign manager for his reelection in 2004. When it came to his frenetic television appearances, Mehlman never displayed anything but breathless boosterism for the president and the party, making him the most on-message of messengers. Just the night before, Mehlman had been on television confidently forecasting victory. "I predict we will hold both the House and the Senate," he said. But in private, even Mehlman did not believe it.

"Mr. President," he told Bush, "I think we're going to lose twenty-four seats in the House."

Bush seemed stunned. Karl Rove had told him the tide had turned against the Republicans, but he had held out hope that they could keep losses down. Twenty-four seats would be nine more than the Democrats needed to capture control of the House.

Bush told Mehlman he was too pessimistic. He thought they would lose nine or ten seats. Not twenty-four.

As they talked about what would come next, Bush indicated he was ready to make a change at the Pentagon. When should he do it? he asked.

"As soon as possible," Mehlman answered without hesitation. "Tomorrow, even."

Bush was not ready to do that. Pushing out his embattled defense secretary two days before an election would reek of desperation, not to mention politicizing the war. But he used the cover of the ranch to meet secretly with Gates the next day, Sunday, November 5. Bolten and Joe Hagin surreptitiously met Gates in the parking lot of a grocery store in the nearby town of McGregor and, in a bit of CIA-style tradecraft, put him in an unmarked sport-utility vehicle and drove him to the ranch.

Bush and Gates hit it off. Bush said he was considering a troop buildup and strategy change in Iraq. Gates had been serving as a member of the congressionally chartered Iraq Study Group and told Bush he was supporting a recommendation for a temporary surge.

After an hour of discussion, Bush was sold. He leaned forward and asked Gates if he had any more questions. Gates said no.

Bush smiled a bit. "Cheney?" he asked, and then volunteered: "He is a voice, an important voice, but only one voice."

That clarified, the deal was done. Bolten offered to break the news to Rumsfeld, but Bush said he wanted to let Cheney do it. From Air Force One, he called Cheney, who was working in the upstairs family room at home. This time Bush at least let Cheney get in a word of protest.

"I disagree with your decision. I think Don is doing a fine job," Cheney told him. "But it's your call. You're the president."

"Dick, would you like to be the one to tell Don, or should I ask Josh Bolten to make the call?" Bush asked.

"I'll do it, Mr. President," Cheney said. "I owe Don an awful lot and he should hear the news from me."

Cheney's phone call came as Rumsfeld was having dinner with his wife, Joyce, and several friends.

"Don," Cheney said, "the president has decided to make a change."

Rumsfeld was not surprised.

"Fair enough," he said. "I'll prepare a letter of resignation."

Perhaps to soften the blow, or perhaps because he considered Bush's decision political, Cheney attributed it to the election two days away.

"We're going to lose the House of Representatives, and the next two years are going to be rough," Cheney said.

"I agree," Rumsfeld replied. "It's not helpful for the military if I stay. Fresh eyes are a good thing."

He noted that he had been thinking of resigning if Democrats won anyway. "I'm just too much of a target," he said.

HIS DAYS NUMBERED, Rumsfeld focused on a memo laying out options for Iraq. He finished it the next day, November 6, and sent it to the president, the vice president, and others, his last shot at defining the path forward.

He agreed that the war effort was in trouble. "In my view," he wrote, "it is time for a major adjustment. Clearly, what U.S. forces are currently doing in Iraq is not working well enough or fast enough." But in the three pages of options he presented, he continued to argue for those similar to the current strategy.

Among the approaches he listed "above the line," meaning favored ideas, were "an accelerated draw-down of U.S. bases" that would reduce the number of outposts from fifty-five to somewhere between ten and fifteen by April 2007 and just five by July 2007. Other above-the-line ideas were to redefine the mission and "go minimalist"; to "begin modest withdrawals" and "start 'taking our hand off the bicycle seat' "; to withdraw American forces "from vulnerable positions" like cities and turn them into quick-reaction units that could swoop in when Iraqi security forces needed help; and to pull out most combat units, leaving behind enough special operations forces to target al-Qaeda, death squads, and Iranian elements. Among the "below the line" options deemed "less attractive" was a substantial troop increase.

Bush woke up that Monday morning at his Crawford ranch for the last day of the last campaign that would directly affect him. Rove briefed him on critical races. Of twenty recent polls in key districts or states, sixteen had moved in the Republican direction, and three were flat, Rove reported. While conventional wisdom had them losing the House and perhaps the Senate, Rove insisted they had a shot at holding both. He had written off ten or twelve House seats due to corruption scandals but figured Republicans could keep Democrats from capturing the fifteen seats they needed for a majority. Republicans, he added, should hang on to the Senate, albeit by a narrow margin. Bush agreed.

But this last campaign day would bring fresh indignity to the embattled president. He flew to Pensacola, Florida, as a favor to Jeb to boost the Republican candidate running to succeed him as governor, Charlie Crist. The schedule handed out on Air Force One listed Crist introducing the president at a rally. But Crist didn't show; he was too busy, he said, to be with the president of the United States. Instead, he campaigned in Jacksonville with John McCain. Crist was hardly the only Republican eager to keep his distance from a president with a 40 percent approval rating—just the only one impolitic enough to stand him up after inviting him. Bush was irked, and Rove downright angry. Rove "ripped the guy a new one" during a phone call from Air Force One, Joshua Bolten recalled, and Bush aides took to calling the governor "Chickenshit Charlie."

The rest of the president's day underscored his political situation. Rather than parachute into close races where he could make a difference, he made his last two stops in states where the elections were no longer in doubt, first Arkansas, where Asa Hutchinson was heading to a double-digit defeat in his bid for governor, and then Texas, where Governor Rick Perry needed no help cruising to an easy reelection. Bush's aides made sure Laura would be with him, knowing he was less anxious—and less testy—when she was around. At least the day ended with a raucous, pounding-music, shout-to-the-rafters rally that filled Reunion Arena in Dallas with thousands of Texans who welcomed their president with unbridled excitement. Feeling pumped up, Bush launched into a vigorous defense of his presidency and accused Democrats of opposing his national security policies without offering viable alternatives. He led the crowd in a call and repeat, telling them to ask Democrats, "What's your plan?" Bush added, "Harsh criticism is not a plan for victory. Second-guessing is not a strategy. We have a plan. Stick with us and the country will be better off."

But the truth was that Bush was second-guessing his own plan and had no intention of sticking with it. The next morning as the sun was rising just before 7:00 a.m., he left the ranch, his fifteen-vehicle motorcade passing the horses and goats and cows of the Texas countryside to the Crawford fire station, where he voted. Bush then boarded Air Force One bound for Washington and one of the most unpleasant days of his presidency. Arriving at the White House, he met in the Oval Office with Rumsfeld to complete the task he had assigned Cheney to start two days earlier.

"Mr. President, I've prepared this letter for you," Rumsfeld said, handing him his resignation.

Bush, his family instincts kicking in, asked after Rumsfeld's wife. "Is Joyce all right?"

"She's fine. And she's ready. She even typed the letter for me." He added, "Look, Joyce and I are tracking with you on this."

"This is hard for me," Bush said.

Watching election returns that night was no easier. All around the country, Republican incumbents went down. Several prominent members of the class of 1994, swept in by Newt Gingrich's revolution, surrendered seats, including Senators Rick Santorum of Pennsylvania and Mike DeWine of Ohio as well as Representatives Charles Bass of New Hampshire and J. D. Hayworth of Arizona. Bush watched as Republicans lost seats held by scandal-tarred congressmen like Tom DeLay, Mark Foley, and Robert Ney. Worse, with the former navy secretary James Webb clutching a narrow lead in Virginia over Senator George Allen, it looked as if the Senate would fall as well. Bush called some of those who survived and then retreated to another room to smoke cigars with some of the other men.

THE NEXT DAY, Bush arrived in the Oval Office and soon found Joshua Bolten coming in to brief him. Every morning, Bolten made it a habit to begin the day by thanking Bush for the privilege of serving.

"Even today," he added on this morning.

"*Especially* today," Bush retorted lightly.

The president gathered himself and headed to the East Room for a postelection news conference, marching alone down the hall along the red carpet with cameras recording each step. He made a point of being lighthearted. "Why all the glum faces?" he asked. But he acknowledged the defeat and promised to work with Democrats on issues like a minimum wage hike, energy, and immigration. "Look, this was a close election," he said. "If you look at race by race, it was close. The cumulative effect, however, was not too close. It was a thumpin'."

Thumpin' or no, he refused to see it as a repudiation of his leadership, instead blaming congressional scandals, turnout efforts, and even the vagaries of ballot law. "I believe Iraq had a lot to do with the election," he said, "but I believe there were other factors as well."

Still, he tweaked his chief political strategist. Asked to update his reading contest with Rove, Bush said tartly, "I'm losing. I obviously was working harder in the campaign than he was."

Rove, sitting off to the side, forced a smile and looked down at his lap.

The real news of that morning's news conference, of course, was Bush's decision to push out Rumsfeld in favor of Gates. The country was stunned at the bombshell. On Capitol Hill, Republican allies were spitting mad, convinced that waiting until after the election had cost them their majorities. When Bolten called Scott Palmer, the Speaker's chief of staff, to give him a heads up, there was just angry silence on the other end of the phone. Bolten would have to drop off a presidential trip to Asia to stay home, absorb the heat, and calm the caucus. Out in the field, at least some generals and diplomats breathed relief. "We shed no tears in Kabul," noted the ambassador, Ronald Neumann. In the White House complex itself, a day that had begun "in a complete depression" was suddenly transformed, and there was "rejoicing and celebration among White House staff," as one National Security Council official recalled. "It was almost more important" than the election loss. "People were like, thank God, finally it is here, and why didn't he do this earlier? It was seen as liberating at the White House."

In the end, Rumsfeld was a contradiction; demanding yet not decisive, he ran roughshod over subordinates yet deferred to them on a failed strategy for too long. In his memoir years later, he rued not being more interventionist. Bush, though, was careful not to blame Rumsfeld. In his mind, Rumsfeld was only carrying out the direction he himself had set. After resisting pressure to get rid of Rumsfeld for years, Bush was determined to provide as graceful an exit as possible. “Don Rumsfeld has been a superb leader during a time of change,” the president said. “Yet he also appreciates the value of bringing in a fresh perspective during a critical period in this war.”

As Bush talked, he already knew what the audience did not, that he was thinking about sending more troops to Iraq rather than pulling them out as the newly elected Democrats (and even Republicans like Mitch McConnell) wanted him to do. The apostle of staying the course was laying the groundwork for a radical change of strategy. “Somehow it seeped in their conscious,” he said of voters, “that my attitude was just simply ‘stay the course.’ ‘Stay the course’ means, let’s get the job done, but it doesn’t mean staying stuck on a strategy or tactics that may not be working. So perhaps I need to do a better job of explaining that we’re constantly adjusting. And so there’s fresh perspective—so what the American people hear today is we’re constantly looking for fresh perspective.”

Even now, having announced the decision to oust Rumsfeld, Bush misled the public about how long it had been in the works. Reporters reminded him of his interview just a week earlier when the president said Rumsfeld would be around until the end.

“Did you know at that point you would be making a change on Secretary Rumsfeld?” a reporter asked.

“No, I did not,” Bush said. “And the reason I didn’t know is because I hadn’t visited with his replacement—potential replacement.”

“But you knew he would be leaving, just not who would replace him?” the reporter followed up.

“No, I didn’t know that at the time.”

While it was true that Bush had not yet met with Gates at the point he talked with the wire service reporters, he did in fact know he would be moving Rumsfeld out by that point; he had told Cheney just the day before. He did not disclose that to the reporters during either the preelection interview or the postelection news conference. Instead, he tried to parse the question by rationalizing that no decision could be made until he had his final conversation with Rumsfeld and offered the job to Gates.

Richard Keil, the reporter who had gone running with Bush on the morning of September 11, reminded the president that in the same interview he had also said Cheney would be around until the end of the administration.

“Does he still have your complete confidence?” Keil asked.

“Yes, he does,” Bush said. “The campaign is over. Yes, he does.”

“And he’ll be here for the remainder of your term?”

“Yes, he will.”

PART FIVE

29

"The elephants finally threw up on the table"

He had lost Congress, he was at risk of losing the war, and now President Bush was clenching his jaw so hard his teeth were hurting. The uncertainty of the path ahead was gnawing at him, and as he labored to maintain presidential demeanor amid the adversity, he kept grinding his teeth against each other to the point of pain. "I'm just thinking about what I'm going to do in Iraq, and I'm grinding my teeth," he told Dan Bartlett.

Bush knew what many wanted him to do—bring troops home. The newly elected Democratic Congress, the liberal pundits, the generals, some of his father's advisers, and even some Republican allies, all thought it was time to begin withdrawing. In those dark days following the elections, Bush felt as if he were barely holding it all together. "He really felt strongly that it was his sheer force of will that was holding the line between winning and losing the war," recalled Karen Hughes, "that everybody else was ready to abandon it, and that only his force of will was keeping us there and that if he had backed off in any way that it could have ended very differently."

One of the few backing him up was Vice President Cheney, who seemed impervious to outside pressure. But the relationship between president and vice president had grown strained. Bush had cut Cheney out of weeks of deliberations about what to do about Donald Rumsfeld, bringing him in only once the decision had been made. As Bush began reconsidering the transition-and-withdraw strategy implemented by Rumsfeld for three years, he had put Stephen Hadley in charge of reviewing their choices, propelled largely by the young aides Meghan O'Sullivan, Brett McGurk, and Peter Feaver.

With Rumsfeld on the way out, Cheney began to speak up. When Bush invited Cheney, Hadley, and Condoleezza Rice to come upstairs to the residence on November 9, a couple of days after the election, to talk about what to do next, the vice president urged them not to waver. He expressed concern that the election results would convince Iraqis that Americans had lost their will. Bush was on the same wavelength. Even from Baghdad, the change in tone was apparent. On the first videoconference after the election, George Casey, the general advocating a drawdown, was struck by the president's attitude toward him. "He was noticeably colder," Casey recalled.

Hadley gathered advisers in his office two days later to consider how to proceed. From the start, lines were forming. Rice, influenced by two advisers, Philip Zelikow and David Satterfield, argued they could not stop a civil war and should pull back, focusing on a more limited mission of striking al-Qaeda but otherwise letting Iraqi forces deal with sectarian violence and deploying American troops only to stop widespread massacres like the one at Srebrenica during the Bosnian War in 1995.

"It should not take a large force to do that," Rice said. "We find the lower power brokers and deter them, buy them off, cajole. The red line is no mass killings."

Hadley, normally deferential to Rice, pushed back. "So we've gone from clear, hold, build to buy, deter, cajole?" he asked. "That's moving the goal posts."

O'Sullivan argued for an escalation of troops, and for the first time it sounded as if Hadley agreed.

Zelikow pointed out what a major gamble that would be.

"We'd be betting the whole house on it," he said.

"Yeah," Hadley agreed, "the house and the whole farm."

"The house, the whole farm, and the ranch," Rice added pointedly.

Hadley understood the risks, having just returned from a fact-finding mission to Iraq. He was profoundly disturbed about Prime Minister Nouri al-Maliki, who said many of the right things but "is either ignorant of what is going on, misrepresenting his intentions," or "his capabilities are not yet sufficient to turn his good intentions into action," Hadley wrote in a classified memo to Bush. Even if they sent more troops, could they trust their erstwhile partner?

The new order on Capitol Hill would also be an obstacle, and Bush got a vivid taste of it on the evening of November 13. Hosting a reception for new members of Congress, the president sought out James Webb, the Democrat whose victory in Virginia had put his party over the top in the Senate. Bush had read about Webb's emotionally powerful criticism of the Iraq War, born in part out of conversations with a son serving in the marines there. The president wanted to reach out to Webb and praise his son's service. But Webb avoided Bush during the reception in the State Dining Room and refused to go through the receiving line to have his picture taken with the president.

"How's your boy?" Bush asked when he found Webb.

"I'd like to get them out of Iraq, Mr. President," Webb responded brusquely.

"That's not what I asked you," Bush responded. "How's your boy?"

"That's between me and my boy, Mr. President," Webb replied coldly.

IN THE DAYS after the thumpin', Karl Rove pored over the numbers like a forensic scientist, sifting them for evidence that the election was not a repudiation of the president, no matter what everyone else thought. Anyone who wandered into his windowless West Wing office with four Abraham Lincoln portraits would get the riff. "Get me the one-pager!" he would cry out to an aide.

The one-pager, a single sheet of paper filled with a stream of numbers, made the case that Bush was not at fault. Of the twenty-eight House seats Republicans lost, ten were due to individual scandals, Rove concluded. Another six were lost because incumbents did not recognize and react to the threat quickly enough. That left twelve other lost seats, fewer than the fifteen that Democrats needed to capture the House. So without corruption and complacency, Rove argued, Republicans could have kept control despite Bush's troubles and the war. "The Republican philosophy is alive and well and likely to reemerge in the majority in 2008," Rove declared.

Rove had a point. Anyone who thought 2006 represented a lasting shift in American political philosophy was overreading the results, and it was true that corruption scandals had taken a toll. Still, disenchantment with Bush and the war was hardly a minor issue. Exit polls found that 36 percent of those casting ballots said they were voting to oppose Bush, compared with just 22 percent who were voting to support him, a differential that clearly hurt Republican incumbents in close races. Overall, 57 percent of the voting public disapproved of Bush's handling of his job. Those numbers were almost identical with those on Iraq, with 56 percent disapproving of the war and 55 percent favoring withdrawal of some or all troops.

One unlikely source of advice for Bush following the midterm debacle was his predecessor. In the weeks after the election, Bush found himself talking with Bill Clinton about the nature of partisanship in Washington and the opportunities of the presidency. An unlikely friendship was developing. "He would call every now and then," Clinton said later. "We would talk. I just made it a project. I wanted to figure him out and get to know him." In their talks after the midterm elections, Bush complained that no matter how much he wanted to work with the other party, the structural forces of Washington tore them apart—the cable shout-a-thons that encouraged conflict, the congressional leadership organizations that enforced party-line discipline, the rapid-response units that churned out acid e-mails long after campaign season. The mere discussion of bipartisan collaboration, Bush lamented, was seen as a betrayal of principle. Not that Bush was above partisanship. He had just come off a campaign where he had suggested the other party opposed going after terrorists. But now he faced a Congress of another party, much as Clinton had after the midterm elections of 1994.

Bush had no intention of compromising with Democrats on Iraq. With the election over, he ordered Hadley to merge the White House review with those at the Pentagon and State Department. Hadley put his deputy, J. D. Crouch, in charge. Crouch convened hours-long meetings in a conference room named for Cordell Hull in the Eisenhower Executive Office Building next to the White House. The discussion focused at first not on troop levels but on the broader environment. They debated whether Americans were material or immaterial to the fighting going on; in other words, could they really influence the situation, and if so, how? Should they focus on protecting the civilian population, as Lieutenant General David Petraeus described in his new counterinsurgency manual, rather than just killing the enemy and retreating at night to large bases? Everyone agreed that Prime Minister Nouri al-Maliki needed to commit to going after Shia militias, not just Sunni insurgents.

A few days into the review, Hadley dropped by to make clear that whatever they produced, one option had to be a surge of additional troops. Everyone understood this to be where Bush was headed. But other options were debated as well. Zelikow and Satterfield had developed the "ring around the fire" approach that Rice had articulated—pull American troops out of Baghdad while Iraqi forces dealt with the sectarian violence and intervene only to stop mass slaughter. Cheney's national security adviser, John Hannah, presented a paper suggesting the United States had been too eager to woo the disgruntled Sunni minority and perhaps it was better to invest in the Shia and Kurds, a scenario dubbed the "bet on Shiite" approach or the "80 percent solution" after their combined proportion of the population. Hannah had not shown the paper to Cheney but assumed he would agree.

Either way, the military hierarchy, influenced by John Abizaid and George Casey, strongly resisted more troops, viewing it as just worsening the problem. Lieutenant General Douglas Lute, representing the Joint Chiefs of Staff in Crouch's meetings, presented a memo arguing for an accelerated transition and withdrawal, essentially doubling down on the current approach. Crouch, remembering the William Luti study, asked Lute if the military could hypothetically add five brigades. Lute argued no.

During a break, Brett McGurk asked Lute if it was truly impossible.

"You could do it," he replied. "You just won't have an American army left. So you know, it's kind of up to you."

BUSH GATHERED HIS national security team at 5:00 p.m. on November 26, the Sunday after Thanksgiving. He picked the Solarium, a hideaway on the third floor of the White House residence with windows on three sides, olive walls, a magnificent view of the Washington Monument, and a cozier feeling than many rooms in the aging mansion. It had seen its share of history, most famously Dwight Eisenhower's sessions rethinking the Cold War. John F. Kennedy used it as a schoolroom for his daughter, Caroline. Richard Nixon told his family in that room that he would resign the presidency. Ronald Reagan recuperated from his attempted assassination there. Bill Clinton used it to prepare for grand jury testimony in the Monica Lewinsky case. Bush, on the other hand, had rarely used it. Rice, who spent more time in the residence than probably any other adviser, had never seen it before. But Bush hoped to shake things up.

The meeting opened with a briefing by Crouch, who presented a dozen or so slides outlining his team's assessment of where things stood in Iraq. Perhaps the most important was "Key Assumptions," summarizing how the staff had revisited its previous theories to discover that they were no longer true, and some maybe never had been. In the past, the chart read, the White House believed that "political progress will help defuse the insurgency." Now it concluded that "political and economic progress are unlikely absent a basic level of security." In the past, the White House assumed the "majority of Iraqis will support the Coalition and Iraqi efforts to build a democratic state." Now, it read, Iraqis were "increasingly disillusioned with Coalition efforts." The chart indicated the White House wrongly assumed that dialogue with insurgent groups would reduce violence, that other countries in the region had a strategic interest in a stable Iraq, and that Iraqi security forces were gaining strength. Instead, dialogue had not worked, Arab states had not fully supported the Iraqi government, and many Iraqi forces were "not yet ready to handle" the security threat. There on a single page was a revolution in thinking by the Bush team and a remarkable turnaround for a president loath to admit mistakes. Now the question was what to do with the new assumptions.

O'Sullivan had been assigned to prepare the part of the briefing titled "Emerging Consensus" and thought it was "the hardest and worst memo I ever wrote" because, as she told Hadley, "there *is* no emerging consensus." In the Solarium that evening, Crouch took what she had prepared and said that changing the dynamics on the ground in Iraq "may take additional forces." But the lack of consensus quickly became apparent. After all of their clashes over the years, Rice and Donald Rumsfeld, who was a lame duck pending Robert Gates's confirmation hearings, found themselves on the same side opposing a surge, although they advocated different alternatives.

As he had all along, Rumsfeld maintained it would be up to the Iraqis to solve the problem. "The Iraqis need to pull up their socks," he said, a phrase he repeated at least three times by another participant's count. Hedging his bets, Rumsfeld allowed that if more forces were needed temporarily, then the president should do that. But he argued that more forces by themselves were not going to help unless they were doing something concrete. Otherwise, he said, "you are just sending more targets over there."

For her part, Rice again advanced the pullback strategy developed by Zelikow and Satterfield and challenged the notion of American forces providing population security. "So are we now responsible for the security of the Iraqi population or is that the job of their government?" she asked.

The conversation lasted roughly two hours—more informal yet more intense than a Situation Room meeting. Hadley argued something had to be done to stop the violence, while General Peter Pace, the Joint Chiefs chairman, expressed skepticism that the military could pull off what was being asked. Bush let the debate play out, interjecting questions but not tipping his hand. "That meeting is where the elephants finally threw up on the table," Crouch said later. "In other words, they finally expressed their views in front of the president. Everybody knew this was the moment—speak now or forever hold your peace."

Bush made no decision, and Crouch and O'Sullivan left deeply discouraged. "I sort of walked out of that meeting a little bit with my tail between my legs, because it seemed like a morass of contrary views," Crouch said. O'Sullivan thought the meeting "went horrendously" and worried no real change would result. Playing it over in her mind, she decided to stop at a grocery store on the way home. When she made it into the parking lot, her phone rang. It was Dan Bartlett, who wanted to take her temperature.

"How do you think the meeting went?" he asked.

"It is an impending disaster," she said. "Things are being seriously misrepresented to the president."

The two talked for forty-five minutes while the heater in her car ran. She explained they had analyzed a surge and believed it could work. All the alternatives, she said, were much worse, and their current path was catastrophic. When they finally hung up, O'Sullivan discovered her car battery had died.

BUSH KNEW no new strategy would work unless the Iraqis stepped up, and he flew to Amman, Jordan, to meet with Nouri al-Maliki. The meeting was already awkward because Hadley's memo disparaging Maliki had shown up in the *New York Times*, in what many in the White House assumed was a Pentagon leak designed to deflect blame for the deteriorating situation.

Maliki surprised Bush with his own plan for salvaging the war, handing him a PowerPoint document with the seal of the Iraqi government on the cover. Maliki proposed adding four more Iraqi brigades to Baghdad while American troops moved out of the city. He would take charge of reimposing security on the capital. Bush instantly deemed the idea impractical because Iraqi security forces were not up to the task, but he was impressed by the desire to lead.

Bush asked to see Maliki alone, and the two slipped away with their translators.

"The political pressure to abandon Iraq is enormous," Bush told him. "But I am willing to resist that pressure if you are willing to make the hard choices."

For the first time, Bush embraced a surge. "I'm willing to commit tens of thousands of additional American troops to help you retake Baghdad. But you need to give me certain assurances."

Maliki had to promise that Iraqi forces would be evenhanded, challenging Shia as well as Sunni militants, including the powerful Moqtada al-Sadr. Maliki also had to stop interfering with American military operations. Maliki agreed. It was a major turning point. As Bush boarded Air Force One for the flight home, he had all but decided that he would send more troops. Now he had to figure out how to bring along the rest of his government.

On December 6, Bush and Cheney hosted the Iraq Study Group, a bipartisan collection of elder statesmen assigned by Congress to recommend a way forward in the war. It was headed by James Baker, one of the prime architects of the first Bush presidency and the operative who helped ensure the ascension of the second, and Lee Hamilton, the former Democratic congressman and 9/11 commission vice chairman. "The situation in Iraq is grave and deteriorating," read the first line of the group's report. The report outlined a path to what Hamilton would later call "a responsible exit." It recommended opening a new dialogue with Iran and Syria, intensifying Middle East peace efforts, and, most critically, withdrawing all combat forces from Iraq by the first quarter of 2008. In essence, the study group had picked up the Rumsfeld-Abizaid-Casey plan for transferring responsibility to the Iraqis.

"We're not giving you this report to vex you or embarrass you," the former senator Alan Simpson, Cheney's close friend who served on the panel, told the president. These were serious recommendations, and Simpson said he hoped Bush would look at them.

"Oh, I will," Bush said.

Simpson turned to Cheney. "Now you read this, Richard Bruce," Simpson said.

"I will," Cheney said.

Cheney, typically, held his own counsel, although no one in the room thought he agreed with the report. Bush, on the other hand, asked questions and seemed to listen. "While I knew he was not entirely sympathetic with some of the things we were saying," recalled Leon Panetta, a Democratic member who would go on to serve as CIA director and defense secretary after Bush left office, "I felt in the least, especially considering where the war was at that point, that he would think pretty seriously about what we had to say."

For all his politeness, though, Bush had already moved well beyond what the study group was recommending, and Cheney dismissed the report, saying it "was not a strategy for winning the war." Baker tried to help, privately urging Bush aides to read page 50 of the report, where the panel said in passing that it could "support a short-term redeployment or surge of American combat forces to stabilize Baghdad" on the way to the early 2008 withdrawal.

The next morning, December 7, Bush was to see Tony Blair and then jointly address reporters. But when Cheney saw the text of the president's opening remarks, he noticed the word "victory" had been taken out of an earlier draft.

"Mr. President, you can't refuse to talk about winning," he said. "That will be a huge signal that you no longer believe in victory."

Bush agreed and used the word "victory" at the news conference. He tried to finesse the Iraq Study Group report, calling it "worthy of serious study" and insisting he too wanted troops to come home even if he did not accept the study group's timetable. "I've always said we'd like our troops out as fast as possible," he said.

But he bristled when a reporter asked if he was "still in denial about how bad things are in Iraq."

He glared at the reporter. "It's bad in Iraq," he said sharply. "Does that help?"

At 4:00 that afternoon, Cheney and Rice debated Iraq strategy at a national security meeting without Bush. Cheney argued that the outcome mattered too much to simply withdraw and let Iraqis fight among themselves. But Rice remained opposed to a troop buildup. "I was really skeptical of whether a surge was really going to work," she explained later. "If we were going to use the same old strategies, we were just going to get more people killed."

The depth of Bush's political problems became clearer that evening as a Republican senator rose on the floor without warning to deliver an anguished speech breaking with the White House over the war. Senator Gordon Smith of Oregon, a quiet, self-effacing moderate who had "tried to be a good soldier," had grown disaffected. He had read John Keegan's history of World War I and was haunted by its lessons. Next he read *Fiasco*, the history of the first years of the Iraq War by Thomas E. Ricks. That winter morning, he woke up, turned on the news, and saw reports of more American soldiers killed in Iraq.

"I for one am at the end of my rope when it comes to supporting a policy that has our soldiers patrolling the same streets in the same way and being blown up by the same bombs day after day," Smith said on the floor. "That is absurd. It may even be criminal. I cannot support that anymore." A fellow Republican senator called it "a tipping point"—exactly what Bush feared. Republican support for Bush and the war was fraying.

WHEN CHENEY SHOWED UP for an Iraq meeting the next day, December 8, he was disturbed to see that instead of presenting Bush with a crisp choice, the formal agenda papered over the differences he had with Rice. But the real tension during that meeting came between Bush and the woman who was supplanting Cheney as his most influential adviser. Rice made the case that any additional commitment by the United States might be pointless unless Iraqi leaders stepped up.

If they did not want to secure their own population, she argued, why should the United States?

Bush grew testy. "So what's your plan, Condi?" he snapped. "We'll just let them kill each other, and we'll stand by and try to pick up the pieces?"

Rice was offended at the suggestion she was less committed to winning. "No, Mr. President," she shot back. "We just can't win by putting our forces in the middle of their blood feud. If they want to have a civil war we're going to have to let them."

Others in the room were stunned at the confrontation. In Bush's nearly six years in office, they had never seen Bush and Rice bark at each other. The heated exchange revealed just how deeply the war had scarred all of them. Bush seemed desperate for a Hail Mary pass to salvage a deteriorating situation, while Rice seemed to despair that it was too late.

Still angry, Rice followed Bush back to the Oval Office afterward.

"You know that's not what I mean," she told him. "No one has been more committed to winning in Iraq than I have."

Bush had cooled down. "I know, I know," he said softly.

Rice noticed what she thought was profound pain on his face. The war was eating him up inside. She backed off.

Rice was not alone in her skepticism. The same day, Rumsfeld, still a caretaker until Robert Gates was sworn in, sent Bush and Cheney a proposal developed by senior Pentagon generals to "accelerate the transition"—exactly the opposite of where the president was heading. The plan built on the option Rumsfeld had presented in his memo the day before resigning, although the generals' timetable was not as rapid. The number of American bases would be drawn down from fifty-five to thirty-seven by December 2007 and as few as twenty in 2008. Iraqis would assume control of security in all eighteen provinces by November 2007, and the American military mission would "formally conclude" by December 2007. "No increase in the level of U.S. forces can substitute for successful diplomacy in the region and in Iraq in getting the Iraqi Government to act," the memo said.

With the military establishment opposed, Bush turned to a dissident faction that had been urging a more robust troop presence. That weekend, military scholars at the American Enterprise Institute (AEI) led by Frederick W. Kagan, a former West Point professor, conducted a multiday exercise to draft a plan to bolster American forces in Iraq, producing a forty-five-page paper urging that seven more army brigades and marine regiments be sent. General Jack Keane, the retired army vice chairman, then came to the White House on December 11 to make the case.

Keane was one of five military experts to brief Bush and Cheney that afternoon, replaying the Camp David summit, but this time the advocates for change were more determined to get through. Eliot Cohen, who had left Camp David in June kicking himself for not being blunter, did not hold back this time. Reprising arguments from his book *Supreme Command*, which the president had read, Cohen rebutted Bush's Lyndon Johnson analogy, saying the failure in Vietnam was not micromanagement but a failure to force a serious strategic debate. And he argued, it was time to replace his commander.

"One of the biggest problems is leadership," Cohen told Bush. "I have the greatest respect for General Casey but you need different leadership."

Bush was already thinking about that. "So who would you put in?" he asked.

"Petraeus," Cohen said.

Keane agreed, and he was equally direct. "Mr. President, to my mind, this is a major crisis," he said. "Time is running out." The solution, he argued, was a counterinsurgency approach aimed at protecting the population, which required more combat units.

But two other retired generals at the meeting, Barry McCaffrey and Wayne Downing, opposed more troops. "This is a fool's errand," McCaffrey said. Downing advocated a more aggressive use of special operations forces. Stephen Biddle, a scholar at the Council on Foreign Relations, went last and largely sided with Keane.

Biddle was struck by how grim the whole affair was, funereal even. While the experts talked, a phalanx of White House aides lined up behind them like a silent Greek chorus. Bush, he thought, seemed on the verge of clinical depression. "It was clear that Bush thought he was looking at a war he was about to go on the historical record as losing," Biddle recalled later. "He was clearly not happy. Everything suggested weight. His body looked like it felt heavy to him. He didn't smile. The tone was very somber. No joking around. No light-hearted anything."

Afterward, Keane and Kagan gave a private briefing to Cheney, outlining how a surge could work. They had a receptive audience. With his old friend Rumsfeld all but out the door, Cheney was becoming less inhibited about supporting a change in strategy, but he would not be the front man. That would be Keane, who was leading a revolt against the military hierarchy. The retired general had been drumming up support inside the administration and working clandestinely with officers who agreed with him, bypassing George Casey to consult with his deputy, Lieutenant General Ray Odierno, who wanted more forces. Meghan O'Sullivan likewise had been quietly consulting with David Petraeus, everyone's choice to succeed Casey. Keane's maneuvering was driving the military hierarchy crazy. "How is it that Jack Keane's getting in to see the vice president and we're not?" General Peter J. Schoomaker, the army chief of staff, complained to a fellow four-star officer. John Abizaid was equally aggravated. "I guess you have to resign from the military and go work for AEI if you are going to give military advice to the president," he told visiting civilians in Iraq.

Keane's support was critical not because it drove the internal process but because it gave space for Bush to make the strategy change he was already inclined to make. If Bush overrode his commanders and Joint Chiefs, he had to have someone say this reflected good military judgment, not political second-guessing. He could hardly rebuff men with stars on their shoulders for the advice of thirtysomething aides like O'Sullivan with her Oxford doctorate and Brett McGurk with his Columbia law degree, neither of whom had served a day in uniform. "Keane is great as a validator," Hadley said.

But Bush wanted to avoid a confrontation with military leaders if he could help it. He knew that if military leaders testified before Congress opposing the new strategy, what little political support he still had would vanish. "If senior generals had resigned in protest over the surge, that might have been the straw that broke the camel's back in Congress," Karl Rove concluded. "Steve Hadley," recalled William Luti, "kept saying that the surge policy should come from the military." But Casey was "adamantly opposed" to adding more than two additional brigades and told Bush so by videoconference on December 12.

Isolated from his generals and even his closest adviser, Bush found support in an unlikely quarter. John McCain, a staunch supporter of the war and an equally strong critic of the way it was being run, sent Bush a private three-page letter the same day bluntly warning him that he would lose the war without more forces. McCain argued that the administration's approach had it backward: instead of hoping a political settlement would reduce violence, the administration should establish security to create space for political reconciliation. McCain cited Kagan's AEI study. "Without a basic level of security," he wrote, "there will be no political solution, and our mission will fail."

Dan Bartlett noticed how tense Bush was and proposed delaying the announcement of a new strategy.

The president looked relieved. Could they do that?

"We will fade it," Bartlett said, meaning take the heat. "Don't worry."

Even as he was moving toward a troop surge, Bush was entertaining his own doubts. At Henry Kissinger's suggestion, he had been reading *A Savage War of Peace*, Alistair Horne's history of the war in Algeria, and the lesson he took away was that more people actually died after the French withdrew. But when it came to Iraq, perhaps the cause was hopeless. Perhaps Rice was right, and he would be throwing more lives away in a losing cause. On separate occasions, he asked both Hadley and O'Sullivan if the war was lost and hope was gone.

"Hadley, do you think the surge can succeed?" he asked one day.

"Mr. President, I do," Hadley replied.

"Well, that is good," Bush said. "Because if you ever think it can't, you come and tell me. Because as long as we think we can succeed, I am in. But if we ever think we cannot succeed, I can't look the mothers of our men and women in uniform in the eye and keep sending them into battle."

30

"Everybody knew this was the last bullet in the chamber"

As their motorcade crossed the Potomac River, President Bush and Vice President Cheney were on the same page. Increasingly convinced of the need for a surge and strategy change, Bush was determined to bring along the generals, and he needed Cheney to play his wingman.

The two were headed to the Pentagon to meet with the top officers in their supersecret conference center known as the Tank on December 13, going to their turf to show respect. Sitting in the car on the way, Bush and Cheney agreed to a good-cop, bad-cop routine, with the vice president asking tough, pointed questions, while the president held back to avoid chilling the discussion. "The president didn't want to come in with a point of view where the chiefs would say, well, he has already made up his mind," J. D. Crouch remembered. As Dan Bartlett put it, "Cheney was supposed to be the heavy."

General Peter Pace opened the discussion with recommendations from the chiefs to shift to a more advisory and training role, in effect accelerating the current transition strategy.

"The question is when do you shift to advising," the president said. "You don't want to do it too early."

Pace suggested Iraqi troops would be up to the test. "We need to get the Iraqi Security Forces in charge," he said.

As planned, Cheney jumped in, uncharacteristically engaging in debate in front of a group. "We're betting the farm on Iraqi Security Forces," he said. "Wouldn't it be better to make a major push with our forces to get it done?" He offered a grim picture of a destabilizing region if America lost in Iraq. "Suddenly it will be very dangerous to be a friend of the United States. There's an awful lot riding on this."

The case against the surge was made by General Peter Schoomaker, who came of age as part of the daring but failed mission to rescue hostages in Iran in 1980 and then became part of the new special operations forces created in the aftermath, serving in Grenada, Panama, Iraq, and Haiti. He had been lured back from retirement in 2003, in part by Cheney, to take over from Eric Shinseki as army chief of staff and had presided over long, multiple deployments that taxed his troops. As with the other chiefs, his statutory responsibility was the health of the force rather than any operational involvement in Iraq.

Schoomaker argued a surge would not bring down violence, noting that there had been several temporary troop buildups over the years, usually in advance of Iraqi elections in anticipation of possible trouble, without changing the overall arc of violence. In what Bush took to be a reference to the new Democratic Congress, the general seemed to suggest the political system would not tolerate a months-long buildup.

"I don't think that you have the time to surge and generate enough forces for this thing to continue to go," Schoomaker told the president.

"I am the president," Bush shot back. "And I've got the time."

Schoomaker's job was to provide *military* counsel. "Thanks very much for the political advice," Bush said sharply, "but I will take care of the politics. That is my job."

Undeterred, Schoomaker said a surge of five brigades would actually affect fifteen brigades—five in Iraq whose tours would have to be extended, another five whose rotation would have to be accelerated to increase the number of troops in the theater, and another five to move up the queue to backfill. "My concerns were practical ones of force generation and sustainment at that particular point in time," he recalled later.

To Bush, he put it bluntly. "We're concerned we're going to break the army," the general said.

Bush, who was supposed to let Cheney do the debating, could not help himself. He leaned forward. "Let me tell you what's going to break the army," he said. "What's going to break the army is a defeat like we had in Vietnam that broke the army for a generation."

The generals took the point. But they worried that committing everything to Iraq would leave little in case of a flare-up elsewhere in the world.

Again, Bush turned the argument around: better to fight the war America was already in than worry about a war that had not actually happened.

To take the sting out of the encounter, Bush told the generals that he planned to increase the overall size of the armed forces, which should alleviate the pressure, and send more civilians to Iraq, a longtime sore point for the military. But the generals walked out unconvinced. Indeed, Schoomaker took his dissent public the next day, December 14, during testimony before a congressionally chartered commission, warning that "we will break" the military with the current pace of war-zone rotations. Afterward, he told reporters that "we should not surge without a purpose and that purpose should be measurable and get us something."

Two days after the Tank meeting, Bush and Cheney returned to the Pentagon for a full honor review marking Rumsfeld's departure. Bush was gracious, but Cheney heaped praise on his former boss in a way that seemed to hint at loss. Rumsfeld, he said, was "a man of rectitude" and "the very ideal of a public servant," a man who "emanates loyalty, integrity, and above all love for this country and a devotion to its cause." In a comment some took as a subtle rebuke of Bush's decision to oust Rumsfeld, Cheney concluded, "I believe the record speaks for itself: Don Rumsfeld is the finest secretary of defense this nation has ever had."

To win over the Joint Chiefs, Bush decided to publicly signal his willingness to expand the overall size of the military. On December 19, he summoned reporters from the *Washington Post* to the Oval Office to announce that he would support a force increase. "We need to reset our military," he told them. "There's no question the military has been used a lot." The move was a significant reversal after years of denying the need for more men and women in uniform. When John Kerry proposed adding forty thousand to the armed forces during the 2004 campaign, the Bush administration had dismissed him. As late as June 2006, the administration argued that better technology and tactics meant no additional capacity was needed. But now Bush authorized Robert Gates to explore adding seventy thousand soldiers and marines.

As he sat with the reporters in the Oval Office that day, Bush hinted that a surge was on the way, arguing that the midterm election was a mandate not to leave Iraq but to find a way to succeed. Still, he was ready to concede for the first time what everyone else had for a while: the war effort was failing. Just two months after declaring that "absolutely, we're winning" in Iraq, Bush adopted a formulation Peter Pace had used at a congressional hearing. "We're not winning, we're not losing," Bush said. Asked about his previous statement, Bush recast it as a prediction, not an assessment. "Yes, that was an indication of my belief that we're *going* to win," he said.

Robert Gates had just been sworn in as defense secretary, and John Abizaid announced his retirement. George Casey would be on the way out soon too, with David Petraeus on track to be his successor. Within weeks, the president who had boasted of deferring to the military had swept aside the leaders of the war effort. As with Rumsfeld, Bush chose not to blame Abizaid or Casey. He offered Abizaid the position of national intelligence director, only to be turned down. As for Casey, Bush told Gates to take care of him. He would soon be named army chief of staff.

Casey was still fighting the surge, certain that it was a mistake. Recognizing that Bush was determined to add troops, Casey recommended just two brigades be sent, with a third stationed in Kuwait in case it was needed and two others kept on deck in the United States. He convinced Gates when the new defense secretary made his first trip to Iraq since taking office. On the flight back, Gates worked on a recommendation for two brigades. "Our commanders do not want more additional force than these approximately 10,000," he wrote in talking points for a meeting with Bush. "It would be difficult to resource a more aggressive U.S. approach due to the stresses and the strains on the force," and forcing more on a reluctant Iraqi government "would undermine much of what we have accomplished over the past two years."

When Jack Keane heard about the mini-surge plan, he was alarmed and alerted John Hannah, the vice president's national security adviser. Meghan O'Sullivan was equally disturbed and reached out to Petraeus to see if he thought he could do what needed to be done with two brigades; Petraeus made clear he needed as much force as she could deliver. Petraeus, although still not publicly announced to take over in Iraq, called Pace to protest. "Look, Chairman, this is sort of awkward, but I can't go over there if it's two plus three," he said. "Don't bother. You might want to think about a different commander."

Bush headed to Crawford for Christmas, then invited the national security team to come down for a critical meeting on Iraq. Condoleezza Rice arrived the afternoon of December 27, a day early, to visit alone with the president. She found him on the porch of the ranch house and sat down to talk.

She had come to terms with what she knew would be Bush's decision and even convinced herself to support it after calling Ray Odierno in Baghdad and listening to him describe how the extra troops would be married to strategy changes.

"You're going to do it, and it's the right thing to do," she told Bush. "I'm there and I'll do everything I can to support it. But, Mr. President, this is your last card. It had better work."

She got up and walked away.

The next day, the rest of the team arrived. Gates presented the two-brigade mini-surge option advanced by Casey, but Bush shut it down quickly.

"No, I am going to commit five brigades," he said. "If I go to the American people and say I am going to commit two and then more if I need it, what I am really telling them is I don't know what I am doing."

What's more, making the deployment of each additional brigade a separate decision would make each one "another *Washington Post* debate," reopening the fight again and again, as J. D. Crouch put it. If Bush was going to take the heat for an unpopular decision, better to do it all at once. He also decided to send a couple of battalions of marines to Anbar Province, where Sunni leaders alienated by al-Qaeda were beginning to switch sides. Hadley and Crouch had argued for the Anbar deployment as well as reinforcements for Baghdad on the theory that it would be a powerful statement to take back an area deemed lost to the enemy.

So there was a plan. It had taken months, while more blood was spilled. But Bush and Cheney believed they had a chance to turn the situation around. And none too soon. The year ended with two macabre milestones out of Iraq. On December 30, Saddam Hussein was executed in a chaotic scene captured on cell phone video, with Iraqis in the room taunting him in his last moments of life. "Go to hell," one yelled, while others chanted the name of Moqtada al-Sadr before Hussein's neck was snapped by a hangman's noose. A day later, New Year's Eve, the American casualty toll hit three thousand.

BUSH OPENED 2007 preparing for the most explosive move of his presidency. Despite his decision at Crawford, the speech announcing the surge included brackets where the number of new forces would be inserted. Surge advocates were frustrated that the two-brigade option still seemed to be alive. "We've decided to be a bear," Crouch protested to Stephen Hadley. "So let's be a grizzly bear."

But George Casey seemed to have enlisted Nouri al-Maliki and passed word to Washington that the Iraqi leader would only accept two brigades. When Hadley brought the news to Bush on January 4, shortly before a secure videoconference with Maliki, the president snapped.

"Enough! Does the guy want to win or not?" he demanded. Aides were not sure whether he meant Casey or Maliki. "I'm building a plan to win this thing. We're not going to short-change it. Tell him that."

"You might want to tell Maliki that," Hadley offered.

Bush headed out the door toward the Situation Room. "I'm about to," he said. "So let's go."

Mumbling to himself while walking down the corridor, Bush seemed exasperated. "If we're not there to win, why are we there?" he asked out loud.

On the videoconference, Bush asked that both sides clear the room so that he could have a private confrontation with Maliki.

"I'll put my neck out if you put your neck out," Bush told him.

Maliki agreed.

The speechwriters were told to take out the brackets and insert five army brigades for Baghdad plus two marine battalions for Anbar Province. It was the final purge of the old strategy as well as the beginning of a new mentoring relationship between Bush and Maliki. For months to come, Bush would make a point of talking with Maliki every week, nudging him into demonstrating more leadership.

The next morning, Bush made his nomination of Petraeus official. At five feet nine and 150 pounds, Petraeus was surprisingly slight for such a commanding figure. He was legendarily driven, survived a bullet to the chest during a training exercise, and embodied the modern ethos of scholar-soldier. He had led a division in the invasion of Iraq and later returned to train Iraqi troops. He stirred resentment in the Pentagon for his high profile; when *Newsweek* put him on the cover with the headline "Can This Man Save Iraq?" Donald Rumsfeld "went ballistic" on a conference call and snapped, "It is not for David Petraeus to save Iraq." But Petraeus saw from the start what Rumsfeld and others had not. "Tell me how this ends," he remarked to Rick Atkinson, a journalist traveling with him during the original invasion in 2003, a comment that came to define the war: Now it would be up to him to figure that out.

For Bush, there was now the matter of the speech announcing the surge. His advisers debated the best venue. There was talk of the Map Room, but Laura Bush noticed a grandfather clock in the background and thought if it was ticking in the middle of the speech—or frankly, if it was not—it would be a bad metaphor. She suggested the Library instead, deeming it warmer than the Oval Office with its bookshelves and fireplace.

On a morning before the speech, Bush found himself alone in the Oval Office with Meghan O'Sullivan. Bush was about as isolated as a president could be, and his staff felt compelled at times to offer encouragement.

"Mr. President," O'Sullivan ventured, "I know you feel really alone right now, but I want you to know that you are not alone. I am standing there with you."

If Bush was amused or irritated to be getting a pep talk from a young aide, he did not show it. "Thanks, thanks," he said simply, and then walked out the door.

The address was drafted to acknowledge the mistakes made in Iraq while vowing to fix them. More than any speech Dan Bartlett had gotten Bush to give, this would be when the president would most forthrightly admit errors and take responsibility while pivoting to demand that the country not give up yet. It was a hard balance to strike. Too far one way would embolden those ready to pull out; too far the other would only fuel the narrative that Bush was detached from reality.

As Bush practiced, the tension in the room was unlike that before any address he had given. If ever there were a speech with his presidency riding on it, this was it. He had to buy time for Petraeus to build up forces, shift the strategy, and make enough visible progress to keep Congress from cutting off funding. Seventy-three percent of Americans thought the war in Iraq was going badly, 61 percent opposed the idea of sending significantly more troops, and 54 percent wanted to withdraw all American forces immediately or within twelve months.

Bush knew all that as he ran through the text given him by his speechwriters. He fiddled with sections he thought should be clearer, and aides interrupted at times to tell him he was mumbling one passage or another. After one too many suggestions from the staff, Bush told them to stop. He ran through the speech in its final form. Usually, when Bush was done with a practice, he simply bounded away from the lectern and headed off to the next thing on his schedule. This time, though, he just stopped and stared down at the text amid a surreal silence in the room. What exactly was going through his head was anyone's guess, but to aides it seemed as if he were a man on a mountain all by himself, desperately trying to get down.

It only lasted perhaps twenty seconds before Hadley spoke up and said, "Let's go." Bush looked up from his reverie.

"All right," he agreed, "let's go."

WHEN THE RED LIGHT on the camera came on that night, January 10, Bush, as he often did, looked uncomfortable, stiff, and small, "wound tightly," as J. D. Crouch put it, not the robust figure his advisers saw in private. But Bush tried to connect with the frustrations of the country while pleading for more time. "The situation in Iraq is unacceptable to the American people—and it is unacceptable to me," he said. "Our troops in Iraq have fought bravely. They have done everything we have asked them to do. Where mistakes have been made, the responsibility rests with me."

He laid out his plan to send 21,500 more troops—it would later grow to 30,000—to carry out a strategy aimed at protecting the civilian population. The change in strategy was as important as the number of troops, he explained. Bush dismissed calls to leave Iraq, arguing that letting the enemy win would hobble the United States for years. "We carefully considered these proposals," he said of recommendations to withdraw, "and we concluded that to step back now would force a collapse of the Iraqi government, tear the country apart, and result in mass killings on an unimaginable scale. Such a scenario would result in our troops being forced to stay in Iraq even longer, and confront an enemy that is even more lethal. If we increase our support at this crucial moment and help the Iraqis break the current cycle of violence, we can hasten the day our troops begin coming home."

Aides were disappointed. On paper, the speech was coherent and compelling, but Bush's delivery was not. The speech did not have "a lot of persuasive power," Matthew Scully, the speechwriter who had left the White House but came back during this period to help with the next State of the Union address, told colleagues. J. D. Crouch thought the crushing tension and enormous stakes came through in the president's presentation. "Watching his facial expressions, I think you can really see that his heart was in it but his mind was telling him this is going to be bad," Crouch remembered. "Not that he didn't believe. It is like, 'I have to do this, it is the right thing to do, I am going to see it through. But no one is going to stand up and cheer.' You could see it on his face."

To sell the plan, Bush spent the next day surrounded by uniforms. In the morning, he bestowed a Medal of Honor posthumously to a marine who had saved his colleagues by falling on a grenade, tearing up as he presented it to the slain man's family. Then he flew to Fort Benning, Georgia, where he joined camouflage-clad army soldiers in the chow line and made his case again for the surge.

He seemed listless, and so did his audience. At one point, he prepared to meet more families of dead soldiers. As he was about to enter the room, he paused, bowed his head for a moment in seeming prayer, and steeled himself before stepping inside. On Air Force One on the flight back to Washington, he remained cloistered in his cabin, preferring to be alone rather than visit the staff as they had been told he would.

When he returned to the White House, Condoleezza Rice stopped by to check in. She and Robert Gates had been on Capitol Hill testifying on behalf of the surge.

"So how did it go?" Bush asked Rice.

"Not very well," she said, sitting by him in front of the fire. "We have a tough sell."

That barely covered it. The questioning had, in fact, been brutal. Senator Chuck Hagel, the outspoken Republican maverick, accused her of not telling the truth, while condemning the surge as "the most dangerous foreign policy blunder in this country since Vietnam." Senator George V. Voinovich, another Republican, told her he had supported Bush and "bought into his dream" but "at this stage of the game, I don't think it's going to happen." Overall, the reaction to Bush's speech had been almost uniformly negative. Bush aides knew most Democrats would hate it but thought some might be supportive; instead, Democrats universally condemned Bush for ignoring the message of the elections, and Hagel and Voinovich were not the only Republicans jumping ship. House Republicans were collecting signatures on a letter opposing the surge.

Peter Wehner grew so alarmed he sent an e-mail to Joshua Bolten, Karl Rove, and Dan Bartlett on January 12, warning that the presidency was on the line. Wehner envisioned moderate Republican senators like Richard Lugar and John Warner marching to the White House to tell Bush no one would support the war anymore and it was time to get out, not unlike Barry Goldwater and other Republicans finally telling Richard Nixon to resign. "The country was tired of the war, and that was clearly our last chance," Wehner remembered. "Everybody knew this was the last bullet in the chamber."

For the president, it was, as Laura Bush later put it, "the loneliest of George's decisions." Rice saw the isolation as well. "It's such a lonely job," she said. "Nobody, no matter how close you are to the president, he carries that burden in many ways alone." This was never more true than during the run-up to the surge decision. Almost no one, it seemed, supported it, at least at first, not the outgoing commanders in Iraq, not the Joint Chiefs of Staff, not the Iraq Study Group, not the Iraqi prime minister, not Congress, not the public, not even his secretary of state and closest adviser. Against odds, thanks to Hadley's orchestration, Bush had managed the process so that the Joint Chiefs ostensibly had come around with the promise of increases in army and marine corps manpower, Maliki had bought in, and Rice had swallowed her concerns. But papering over differences was not the same thing as forging unity. On this, Bush had Cheney, Hadley, John McCain, Jack Keane, and not many more.

When he felt sorry for himself in those dark days, Laura reminded him that he chose to run for president. "Self-pity is the worst thing that can happen to a presidency," Bush told the writer Robert Draper. "This is a job where you can have a lot of self-pity." He tried to avoid showing it to his staff or the country. "I've got God's shoulder to cry on," he said. "And I cry a lot. I do a lot of crying in this job. I'll bet I've shed more tears than you can count, as president. I'll shed some tomorrow."

A little more than a week after the surge announcement, Bush invited to the Oval Office a dozen aides who helped fashion the new strategy, including Hadley, J. D. Crouch, Meghan O'Sullivan, Brett McGurk, Peter Feaver, and William Luti. He thanked them and posed for photographs. But he lingered afterward and seemed in a rare contemplative mood. He talked about Abraham Lincoln, pointing to the bust in the office and remembering how rough that presidency was.

"Thinking about what Lincoln went through lends some of that perspective to things," he said.

He noted that he had just read a Lincoln biography and during the darkest days only two groups supported the sixteenth president, the evangelicals, although they were not called that at the time, and the army. "You know, I am no Lincoln," aides remembered Bush saying, "but I am in the same boat."

He moved on to Iraq. "I know the decision's unpopular, the decision to surge," he mused. "I made mistakes and said so in my speech. All of the mistakes, they rest right here, with me. But you know what? There's great pressure not to lead—not to act. There's pressure to say, 'Oh, well, this is too damn hard, too risky, let's not do it.'"

He continued, "People say Bush needs to see the world as it is. Well, I've been here six years now and I see the world as it is, maybe better than most." Aides later remembered Bush gesturing with each word. "The world as it is, that world needs America to lead. You know why? Because nothing happens if we don't lead."

For Bush, the Decider, there was no greater sin than giving into *nothing happens*. For three years, yes, he had passively deferred to generals and advisers, seized by his perception of Lyndon Johnson's mistake during Vietnam. But after the war deteriorated drastically, he finally asserted his own judgment over the commanders and made a decision that would determine the remainder of his presidency and the ultimate outcome of his Iraq project.

"The president himself was the guy who was the firmest on the surge," said David Gordon, an intelligence analyst who participated in the White House committee on Iraq. "For a lot of the others of us in the group, I think a lot of people came around to the view that you've got to do the surge before you can move to the next step. So a lot of people ended up, I think, supporting the surge less because they believed in it but more as a step to the Baker-Hamilton approach. But President Bush got it right."

INTRIGUINGLY, IT WAS the first and perhaps only time on a major issue in the second term when Cheney came out on the winning side while Rice was on the losing side. Yet Cheney was not the driving force behind the surge, the way he had been behind the initial invasion in 2003. Only when his friend Donald Rumsfeld was pushed out did Cheney feel liberated enough to exert himself again. By that point, Bush already knew where he was headed. Cheney proved to be a secondary player fortifying the president, not the author of action.

"Bush was very seriously in the driver's seat there," O'Sullivan recalled. "Cheney was part of the process, but this was a Bush-led process." Another official involved thought Cheney "was kind of a nonentity" at that stage in the administration. That is too strong, but it underscored the changing perception of the vice president in the halls of the West Wing. He was becoming more like a regular vice president.

Plenty of other issues were not going Cheney's way. Even as Bush raised the stakes in Iraq, he gave more rope to Christopher Hill to negotiate with North Korea. On January 16, Hill hosted a lavish meal in Berlin for a North Korean delegation, complete with boozy toasts, and the next day came up with the outlines of a deal that Rice called Bush to approve without running it by Cheney. The vice president was angry, wondering how they could toast an outlaw regime just three months after it set off a nuclear test.

Bush also decided to submit the NSA surveillance program to the jurisdiction of the secret foreign intelligence court, the same court David Addington joked about blowing up. And the president embraced an energy plan for his State of the Union calling for a 20 percent reduction in the projected use of gasoline over the next decade through a dramatic expansion of ethanol and tougher fuel economy standards for new cars. Cheney, the old oilman, "thought that was a mistake," deeming ethanol unrealistic given the required subsidy and undesirable side effects like food shortages, Neil Patel recalled. Cheney showed up at one meeting with a digitally altered picture of Al Hubbard, the president's economics adviser, driving a tiny Shriner car to show "what the U.S. auto fleet is going to look like if you approve this policy."

Then there was Scooter Libby, whose trial opened in federal court on January 23, raising tension in the vice president's office, where former colleagues watched with concern for him and for what it might mean for the boss. Among those on the defense team's witness list: Richard Bruce Cheney.

WHILE BUSH AND Cheney were in agreement on the surge, they were taking different approaches rhetorically. In the State of the Union address just hours after the Libby trial started, Bush reached out to opponents, appealing for support for the surge. With just 33 percent of Americans approving of his job performance, only twice before had any president taken the lectern in the House for a State of the Union in weaker condition in the polls—Harry Truman during the Korean War in 1952 and Richard Nixon in the throes of Watergate in 1974. Moreover, opposition to the troop surge had actually grown since Bush announced it, now reaching 65 percent.

Addressing the new Democratic Congress with the newly sworn-in Speaker, Nancy Pelosi, sitting over his left shoulder, Bush pleaded for patience. "I respect you and the arguments you've made," he said. "We went into this largely united in our assumptions and in our convictions. And whatever you voted for, you did not vote for failure. Our country is pursuing a new strategy in Iraq, and I ask you to give it a chance to work."

Sitting over his right shoulder, though, was Cheney, who wanted nothing to do with the contrition strategy. The day after the State of the Union address, he went on CNN and pugnaciously rejected any argument that they were failing in Iraq—as the president himself had concluded.

"With the pressures from some quarters to get out of Iraq, if we were to do that, we would simply validate the terrorists' strategy that says the Americans will not stay to complete the task, that we don't have the stomach for the fight," Cheney told Wolf Blitzer. He dismissed congressional resolutions opposing the surge. "It won't stop us," he vowed. "And it would be, I think, detrimental from the standpoint of the troops." Cheney went on to describe the Iraq War as a success because Saddam Hussein had been ousted.

"If he were still there today," Cheney said, "we'd have a terrible situation."

"But there *is* a terrible situation," Blitzer said.

"No, there is not," Cheney insisted. "There is not. There's problems, ongoing problems, but we have, in fact, accomplished our objectives of getting rid of the old regime and there is a new regime in place that's been there for less than a year, far too soon for you guys to write them off."

He added, "Bottom line is that we've had enormous successes and we will continue to have enormous successes."

He accused Blitzer of siding with cut-and-run Democrats. "What you're recommending, or at least what you seem to believe the right course is, is to bail out," Cheney charged.

"I'm just asking questions," Blitzer protested.

"No, you're not asking questions," Cheney maintained.

Blitzer had been in Cheney's doghouse since the previous October, when he interviewed Lynne Cheney and asked about steamy scenes in a novel she wrote that had been cited by James Webb, the Democratic Senate candidate in Virginia, in defending his own fiction. Lynne had angrily rebuffed Blitzer, and her husband later congratulated her for what he called "the slapdown."

Now Blitzer crossed another line as far as Cheney was concerned by mentioning that Mary Cheney had become pregnant. Did the vice president want to respond to conservatives who had criticized her for having a baby in a lesbian relationship?

"I'm delighted I'm about to have a sixth grandchild, Wolf, and obviously, think the world of both my daughters and all of my grandchildren," Cheney said. "And I think, frankly, you're out of line with that question."

Blitzer tried to defend himself. "I think all of us appreciate—"

Cheney cut him off. "I think you're out of line."

"We like your daughters," Blitzer replied. "Believe me, I'm very, very sympathetic to Liz and to Mary. I like them both. That was just a question that's come up, and it's a responsible, fair question."

"I just fundamentally disagree with you," Cheney retorted.

By this point, Cheney harbored little concern for what the Wolf Blitzers of Washington thought—and not much more for what the White House political operation thought. Speaking with another reporter on January 28, he evinced no worry about the damage to his reputation. "By the time I leave here, it will have been over forty years since I arrived in Washington," he said, "and I've been praised when I didn't deserve it, and probably criticized when I didn't deserve it. And there aren't enough hours in the day for me to spend a lot of time worrying about my image."

Asked about critical comments by onetime friends like the late Gerald Ford, Colin Powell, and Brent Scowcroft, speculation that he had changed or gotten a fever about Saddam Hussein, Cheney just shook his head.

"Well, I'm vice president," he said, "and they're not."

THE TRUTH WAS that neither Bush nor Cheney was a particularly effective front man for the war effort anymore. Their credibility had been so sapped they were mostly talking to each other. So Bush pushed another figure to the fore, his new commander, David Petraeus.

The White House and other Republicans began describing the surge as "the Petraeus plan," exaggerating his authorship to tap his popularity among lawmakers. After the Senate voted 81 to 0 to confirm Petraeus's promotion to a fourth star so he could take over as commander in Iraq, Bush argued that it would make no sense to support the general but not his plan. One day, Senator Lindsey Graham, one of the strongest supporters of the war, planted Petraeus in an office off the Senate floor and one by one fetched fellow Republicans to meet with him.

Petraeus realized he was being lashed to the commander in chief in a way few other commanders had been in modern times. He visited Bush in the Oval Office after his confirmation hearing, and the two reflected on the mission he was about to undertake. The stakes were enormous and the odds of success daunting.

"This is a pretty significant moment," Bush said. "We're going to double down."

Petraeus corrected him. "Mr. President, this is all in."

As part of his confirmation, Petraeus agreed to return to Washington in

September to update Congress on the progress of the surge, a commitment that irritated many in the White House. But it meant that Bush and Cheney needed to buy him time. On February 5, Bush sent Congress a $93 billion spending request to pay for the war. That would be the real test: Would opponents deny funding to an army in the field to force the president to begin winding down the war?

Bush knew the ground had cratered beneath him. The reinforcements he was sending to Iraq would take five months in all to arrive, meaning it could be a while until they achieved results, if any. Bush would have to hold things together until then.

"So now I'm an October–November man," Bush told the writer Robert Draper. "I'm playing for October–November."

31

"I'm going to fire all your asses"

There came a moment, and it was only a moment, when the discussion in the office of the vice president turned to the possibility of a Cheney for President campaign. It was early in 2007, and for the first time since 1928 the country was looking ahead to a presidential election without an incumbent president or vice president in the race. Dick Cheney had made clear he was not interested in running in 2008, but a longtime friend showed up in the West Wing to try to change his mind.

"I've talked to a lot of people around the country," Wayne Berman, one of Washington's most prominent Republican lobbyist-fund-raisers, told Cheney that day, "and I think the money could be raised. I think there's a lot of support for you."

If anyone would know about raising money, it was Berman. A mainstay of Washington power circles, Berman may have been the one who first introduced Cheney to George W. Bush back in 1987 and later became a Pioneer, collecting more than $100,000 for the Bush-Cheney ticket in the 2000 election, and a Ranger, pulling in more than $200,000 in 2004.

His connection to the vice president went beyond political fund-raising. His wife, Lea Berman, had been Cheney's social secretary and later served as Lynne's chief of staff before becoming the White House social secretary responsible for organizing official functions and overseeing the mansion staff. The Cheneys and the Bermans got together occasionally for dinner and gossip about who was up and down in the capital's perennial political games.

Berman's visit in early 2007 came as the Republican field was only beginning to take shape. Senator John McCain was making another run for the White House, but he had considerable vulnerabilities within the party. Others looking at the race included the former mayor Rudy Giuliani of New York; the former governors Mitt Romney of Massachusetts and Mike Huckabee of Arkansas; Senator Sam Brownback of Kansas; the former senator Fred Thompson of Tennessee; and Representative Ron Paul of Texas.

Cheney had steadfastly disavowed interest in running for president and had just begun building a retirement house in Virginia. After exploring the 1996 race, Cheney concluded he did not have the drive for an extended, two-year, all-out national campaign. As recently as the year before, he had told Bob Schieffer of CBS News, "I've taken the Sherman statement—if nominated, I will not run; if elected, I won't serve." Cheney regularly opened speeches by joking that "a warm welcome like that is almost enough to make a guy want to run for office again," then pausing before adding in classic deadpan, "*almost*." Besides, the notion of a Cheney candidacy would strike many as absurd; he had a trunkload of political baggage and an approval rating in the thirties.

Berman knew all that and realized the chances of changing Cheney's mind were slim. But he argued that someone had to carry the Bush-Cheney record into 2008 and defend it against attacks. McCain certainly would not, and, frankly, most of the others probably would not either. For all of Cheney's political problems, he remained popular with the conservative base that dominated the nomination process.

McCain had been recruiting Berman. "I'm going to go work for his campaign and do a whole lot of stuff unless you're going to run," Berman told Cheney. "If you're going to run, I want to work for you, if you want me."

"I'm flattered you came to see me—you've been a great friend of mine for a real long time," said Cheney, who seemed almost emotional to Berman. "For me to do what I want to do around here and finish strong and help the president continue to make sure we protect policies," he had to remain singularly focused on his duties.

Balancing that with frequent trips to Iowa and New Hampshire, punctuated by endless fund-raising calls, would be daunting. "I can't do that, so I'm not going to run."

Cheney added, "McCain's a good man, and he's got a real record. He's an adult, and he's lucky to have you working for him if that's what you decide to do." Cheney then took Berman down to the White House mess for a fat-free hot dog. That wasn't quite what Berman had hoped to get when he arrived at the White House that day.

Cheney's status as a lame duck from the moment he took office made him unique in the annals of the modern vice presidency. For years, he argued it was an asset. He could focus exclusively on advancing Bush's policies without any of the sub-rosa competition that often emerged between presidents and their vice presidents. He had none of the fund-raising and other distractions of those eyeing the big chair. He could take the spears for

Bush for controversial policies, becoming the one blamed for torture and spying and unfounded war.

Still, there was a cost. With no one in the White House with an electoral future, certain incentives were missing. "There were a lot of advantages of having a vice president who was not going to run for president himself," Michael Gerson said. "But one disadvantage was, as things worsened in Iraq, if we had a young vice president that was running for office to replace Bush, they would have been constantly pushing that things have to get better. 'This is going to kill my chances.'" What's more, the White House found itself in a campaign season without anyone to champion its record. "It constitutes a kind of a double lame duck," observed Dean McGrath, the longtime Cheney aide.

WHEN CHENEY TOLD Berman he would forgo a race partly to "protect policies," what he meant was that he was already in a fight inside the White House with those trying to reformulate the legacy of the first term. On interrogation and detention rules, on Middle East policy, and on Iran, Cheney was trying to guard against the wavering and equivocating of those around the president, and perhaps the president himself. On no issue was that battle more pronounced than North Korea.

Much to Cheney's chagrin, the six-party talks reopened in Beijing on February 8, and after a late-night session Christopher Hill emerged on February 13 with a deal. North Korea would shut down its Yongbyon nuclear facility, readmit international inspectors, and pull together a statement accounting for all of its nuclear programs. The United States and its partners would provide fifty thousand tons of heavy fuel as a down payment on a total of one million tons once all nuclear facilities were disabled. Washington would open talks aimed at restoring diplomatic relations with Pyongyang while removing North Korea from the list of state sponsors of terrorism and the list of countries affected by the Trading with the Enemy Act. The deal touched off a backlash among Cheney's allies. Elliott Abrams, the deputy national security adviser, fired off e-mails making clear he thought it was, as he later put it, "a disgraceful policy" and "Clintonism again." The next morning, he found himself in the Oval Office as Bush tried to convince him it was the right approach.

Cheney was no more persuaded and thought they were rewarding North Korea for bad behavior. He believed Rice—as well as Bush—was so eager for an achievement that she was willing to abandon the principles that had undergirded their policies in the first term. "We had a good relationship, so it wasn't personal at all," he reflected later. "I just felt that she was pushing very hard to get something of significance done vis-à-vis the North Koreans, but I thought she was heading in the wrong direction. I didn't agree with the policy." Stephen Yates, the vice president's deputy national security adviser until 2005, put it more bluntly. "North Korea policy was an absolute aberration in terms of the personality of George W. Bush and the instincts that guided the first term," he said. "The first-term president Bush would not have had any part of those shenanigans."

Rice regularly responded to Cheney's skepticism by asking what his plan was. It was true that the North Koreans had proved to be unreliable and manipulative, but what was the alternative to negotiations? "They never had an answer for that," Hill said. "It was sort of, we don't want you to negotiate with them, but, no, we don't have any better idea." While Cheney wanted to stick to a hard line, Hill said, Bush wanted to move beyond his first term. Bush "did not consider himself a warmonger, did not consider it fair that he be regarded in history as someone who always would reach for the gun," Hill said. "He was persuaded by Condi and other people that we should give diplomacy a chance." After all, Rice said, "Even before they exploded a nuclear device, we didn't have a military option." Bush framed it the same way. "I am not going to go to war with North Korea," he told aides. "So what is the alternative?"

Stephen Hadley saw it not as a rejection of Cheney but as an affirmation by Bush of his own judgment. "I don't think he had less influence," Hadley said of Cheney. "But I think what happened is that this president came into his own and he acted more decisively with more confidence." Rice agreed. "I just think he became a lot more confident," she said. By this point in his presidency, Bush was being briefed on North Korea and other issues by aides or CIA analysts who had less experience than he did. No one had to tell him about the North Koreans because he had been dealing with them for six years. "He had a lot of experience under his belt by then and more confidence in his own judgment," Cheney reflected. "And obviously he placed a great store in Condi's experience and her views."

As for Cheney, he was drained, politically and physically, "a spent force," as David Gordon, an adviser to Rice, put it. As a man with a weak heart, Cheney was almost worn-out. Some days he had trouble even climbing the stairs to the second floor of the vice presidential mansion. "He looked tired for the last couple years, for sure," said Neil Patel, his aide. Schedulers tried to ease his load, and Patel told staffers to keep briefings concise. "He would just sort of gloss over half the time, and it's because he's got so much on his plate. You've got to keep it tight and especially in the last couple years."

From time to time, Cheney would even drift off in the Oval Office. "He fell asleep quite often," said one official, who thought Cheney's "energy level by the end was not so high as it had been at the beginning."

One day, after a meeting where Cheney dozed off, Bush and Dan Bartlett chuckled about it as the speechwriter Matt Latimer and others came in for the next meeting.

"Did you see?" Bartlett asked Bush with a big grin.

"Yes," Bush said merrily. "I couldn't look at him."

The two were laughing boisterously. "I saw his head go down and he dropped his papers, and I didn't want to say anything," Bush said.

Latimer thought the two were "like students laughing mischievously at their teacher after class." But it was a sign of the changing relationship that Bush was willing to laugh at Cheney behind his back. Aides in the White House took their cue and were mocking the vice president in a way they never would have in the first term.

On North Korea in particular, Cheney could not stop what he saw as the backsliding, and he was reduced to calling Hadley to gripe without result. He was losing allies. Donald Rumsfeld was gone, and in January, just before the latest agreement, Robert Joseph, the State Department's nonproliferation chief, resigned in protest of Christopher Hill's negotiations. Joseph wrote a memo to Rice on his way out explaining that "as a matter of principle" he could not support the policies that were being pursued, especially dialing back interdiction activities and Hill's efforts to return the $25 million of North Korean funds frozen in Banco Delta Asia in Macao. "This was money traced to North Korea's proliferation activities, counterfeiting American super notes, drug-running profits," Joseph said later. "And we were going to facilitate the return of these illicit funds to the North Koreans?"

Hill had become a deeply controversial figure within the administration. He was a veteran diplomat who had been part of the team led by Richard Holbrooke that negotiated the Dayton Accords ending the Bosnian War in 1995, and he had learned from his mentor the art of creative diplomacy, even if it meant having to outflank bureaucratic adversaries within his own team. Described by Holbrooke as "brilliant, fearless, and argumentative," Hill bridled at the restrictions Cheney and others tried to impose on his negotiations, maneuvered to talk with the North Koreans outside the stiff six-party format, and pushed for more latitude. He held back information from administration rivals and worked around them—doing to Cheney, in effect, what Cheney had done to others in the first term.

Hill made enemies who took his cleverness for dishonesty. "I don't think in my twenty-eight years I have ever met anyone who is as universally distrusted and disliked as Chris Hill," said one of his internal rivals. "He was a junior Holbrooke," said Michael Green, the Asia adviser on the National Security Council. "He saw working for Holbrooke that the bullying and the circumventing the process and all of that could work, and he did it not as effectively but pretty effectively." Rice recognized the dynamic. "I love Chris, and I made him my negotiator because he is creative and he is energetic and he is a go-getter," she said. But "he could be his own worst enemy sometimes."

THE INTERNAL STRUGGLES were overshadowed as 2007 progressed by a momentous showdown with Congress over Iraq. Fresh off their election sweep, Democrats squared off with Bush and Cheney to try to reverse the surge and begin bringing troops home.

On the afternoon of February 16, Speaker Nancy Pelosi pushed through the House 246 to 182 a resolution opposing the surge, with seventeen Republicans breaking ranks to join the majority. But it was a nonbinding resolution. When Senator Harry Reid tried to follow suit by convening the Senate the next day for a rare Saturday session, he failed to break a filibuster. The only way Congress could force a change in the war would be to use its power over purse strings, but Pelosi had already promised to "never cut off funding for our troops when they are in harm's way."

Cheney left the Iraq battle behind that day for a trip to Asia, including stops in Pakistan and Afghanistan to press the governments there to do more to fight al-Qaeda and the Taliban. Along the way, he got a resonant reminder that the Other War, as some called it, remained dangerous and volatile. After landing at Bagram Air Base in Afghanistan on February 26, Cheney was told that heavy snow made it impossible to fly by helicopter to Kabul to meet with President Hamid Karzai. Several aides wanted to go through with the meetings with American military and civilian leaders at the base, apologize to Karzai for missing him, and then leave as scheduled. "No, this is important," Cheney said, deciding he would stay the night in hopes that the weather would clear by morning.

The next day, at around 10:00 a.m., Cheney heard what he described as "a loud boom" and soon found his Secret Service agents rushing into his borrowed quarters at the air base to tell him a suicide bomber had detonated himself at the main gate. Although Cheney was about a mile from the gate and never in danger, the agents moved him to a nearby bomb shelter until they were sure it was not the vanguard of a broader assault.

The Taliban later claimed they were targeting Cheney, but that seemed unlikely given the secrecy surrounding his visit and the change in schedule.

Still, the vice president took it as another sign that Karzai was under siege. "They clearly try to find ways to question the authority of the central government," Cheney, unruffled as ever, told reporters later on Air Force Two after his rescheduled two-hour meeting with Karzai. "Striking at Bagram with a suicide bomber, I suppose, is one way to do that. But it shouldn't affect our behavior at all."

Cheney also briefed reporters about his meetings on background, meaning they could identify him in their reports only as a "senior administration official." Thus shielded, he took issue with media accounts suggesting that he was strong-arming Musharraf and Karzai into more robust action. "I've seen some press reporting says, 'Cheney went in to beat up on them, threaten them,'" Cheney told the reporters. "That's not the way I work. I don't know who writes that, or maybe somebody gets it from some source who doesn't know what I'm doing, or isn't involved in it. But the idea that I'd go in and threaten someone is an invalid misreading of the way I do business."

WHILE TRAVELING AROUND the world, Cheney kept track of Scooter Libby's trial back in Washington. He was prepared to testify, but at the last minute Libby's lawyers decided not to call him or to put Libby on the stand. Instead, they argued that the case boiled down to nothing more than a difference of memories about whether Tim Russert, the NBC bureau chief, first told Libby about Valerie Plame Wilson as Libby claimed and Russert disputed. Even if Russert was right, the lawyers said, Libby could hardly be a criminal for remembering differently. Prosecutors pointed to all the conversations Libby had about Valerie Wilson before talking with Russert, calling it implausible to believe he simply forgot about talking with eight other people over a four-week period.

While Cheney did not testify, the special counsel, Patrick Fitzgerald, put him at the center of the proceedings, declaring in closing arguments that "there is a cloud over the vice president." The jury in a largely Democratic city convicted Libby on March 6. Back from his trip, alone in his office, Cheney watched television reports of the verdict and took calls from Lynne and Liz Cheney. Afterward, he headed to Capitol Hill for the weekly lunch of Senate Republicans, several of whom came up to console him. For Cheney, it was a devastating blow.

Libby was not the only veteran of the Bush-Cheney White House in trouble. Alberto Gonzales was at the center of a full-blown political firestorm over the firing of eight U.S. attorneys over the winter. U.S. attorneys were political appointees serving at the pleasure of the president and could be fired at will; presidents routinely replaced them all with a change of administration. But ousting so many all at once in the middle of a term was unusual and raised suspicions of political interference. The new Democratic Congress smelled scandal, and perhaps opportunity, and immediately launched investigations. E-mails unearthed by investigators showed White House involvement and suggested political motivations. Gonzales's chief of staff, Kyle Sampson, resigned on March 12 after it was revealed that he had not told colleagues about his interactions with the White House regarding the dismissals. The next day, the attorney general acknowledged that "mistakes were made" and took responsibility.

The burgeoning political battle was a jarring wake-up call for the Bush-Cheney White House, which had grown accustomed to working with a Republican Congress for so many years. Now the opposition was in charge, complete with subpoena authority. While a Republican Congress did little oversight of a Republican president, a Democratic Congress would lean the other way, eagerly scrutinizing every possible instance of wrongdoing, especially with an unpopular president. The change was "something of a shock to the system here," Joshua Bolten confided to a writer at the time. "They can dictate what the conversation is about and when it's going to be."

With Bush's public standing at its lowest ebb, he suddenly lost perhaps the most energetic defender he had. At 7:00 a.m. on March 27, the president received a call from Tony Snow, his indefatigable press secretary. Snow told him the cancer he thought he had beaten two years earlier was back. He sounded upbeat, but Bush grasped the seriousness of the threat. Snow, whose mother had died of colon cancer, had long said that he "felt that cancer was stalking me," and now he would have to take leave to fight it again. Bush told him he was praying for him. Snow called his deputy, Dana Perino, at 9:30 a.m. to tell her just before she went into the briefing room for the morning off-camera "gaggle." At the podium, she lost control as she announced the news and began sobbing before finally postponing further questions.

Snow had been a complicated figure in the White House, well liked and admired yet also the subject of quiet dissatisfaction. He had become the face of the White House, a forceful and upbeat defender of an embattled administration and a popular figure in Republican circles, to the point of campaigning during midterm elections, something no predecessor had done. But privately, some in the White House worried he was too glib and not versed enough in the details of policy. Perino and others who worked for him at times resented that he left messes for them to clean up. Yet when his cancer returned, all of that was forgotten, and he suddenly became a popular symbol of defiant heroism in a White House battered in so many ways. His cheery optimism in the face of peril became inspiring. If Snow could confront death, some figured, they could certainly put up with the slings and arrows of political tribulations.

But the arrows kept coming. A few days later, on April 1, Matthew Dowd, the political strategist who helped steer Bush to the White House twice, broke with the president over the war. He wrote an op-ed article titled "Kerry Was Right," arguing that it was time to withdraw from Iraq, and although he could not bring himself to publish it, he gave an interview to Jim Rutenberg of the *New York Times*, making the same point. He expressed disillusionment with the man he had helped elect, over his handling of Hurricane Katrina, Cindy Sheehan, Abu Ghraib, Donald Rumsfeld, and most important Iraq, where his own son was deployed as an army intelligence specialist. "I think he's become more, in my view, secluded and bubbled in," Dowd said of Bush.

Former colleagues whispered that Dowd was bitter at the way Karl Rove had treated him and had descended into a dark place because of a divorce, the death of a premature daughter, and his son's deployment. But while they tried to explain away his defection, word got back to Dowd that it had deeply hurt the president.

It was a raw time for Bush. When Meghan O'Sullivan came to the Oval Office only weeks after the surge to tell him she was stepping down as his deputy national security adviser for Iraq and Afghanistan, she found herself "a little crying heap." She had spent the better part of a year arguing for a major shift in strategy; Bush did not understand why she would leave just as she had succeeded. She reassured him of her loyalty.

"Don't worry," she told him, "I'm not resigning to write a book."

"*You* should be the one to write a book," he told her.

AS BUSH TRIED to get a handle on Iraq, another challenge arose out of public view. In mid-April, Israel asked to show secret material to Bush, and Meir Dagan, the director of the Israeli intelligence agency, Mossad, arrived in Washington. Aides diverted him to sit down instead with Stephen Hadley and Elliott Abrams. Cheney showed up as well. Dagan had startling news: Syria was building a nuclear reactor with help from North Korea. He had aerial images of the facility and pictures of North Koreans helping out—including none other than the North Korean negotiator sent to the six-party talks.

Shortly after the visit, Bush took a call from Israel's prime minister, Ehud Olmert.

"George, I'm asking you to bomb the compound," Olmert told him.

"Give me some time to look at the intelligence and I'll give you an answer," Bush replied.

Cheney had long suspected Syria of nuclear ambitions and now finally had proof. The next time he saw Michael Hayden, the CIA director admitted as much. He walked in, sat down on the couch, and said, "You were right, Mr. Vice President."

Bush wanted more information and options. A special task force was called "the Drafting Committee" on White House schedules so no one else would know its subject. Bush personally approved the list of officials who could be told about the situation. During one early task force meeting in the Situation Room, Bush dropped by unexpectedly and warned its members just how critical it was to keep quiet.

"If this stuff leaks," he told them, "I'm going to fire all your asses."

IN APRIL, CONFLICT with the Democrats over the surge came to a head. Bush had invited Speaker Nancy Pelosi and Senator Harry Reid to meet in the Cabinet Room on April 18, but there was no middle ground. Democrats were prepared to authorize the money Bush had requested for the wars in Iraq and Afghanistan if he followed a timetable for withdrawing troops. Pelosi pressed him to accept the deal.

To Reid, who had made little secret of his antipathy for Bush, the president looked "impatient and spoiled," while Cheney across the table "slumped in his chair, silent."

Reid pointedly told Bush that he was presiding over another Vietnam, where another president kept sending more troops just to avoid being known for losing.

"Mr. President, this war cannot be won militarily," he said. "It is wrong to continue to send soldiers into a war that cannot be won militarily."

Bush bridled at the comparison. "If you think this is about my personal legacy, you're wrong," he told Reid. "I strongly reject that. You don't know what motivates me."

The surge, Bush insisted, could succeed.

The meeting broke up, and no one shook hands on the way out. The next day, Reid told reporters that "this war is lost." Bush was angry at the defeatism. Even some Democrats thought Reid went too far; Senator Carl Levin, chairman of the Armed Services Committee, "chewed my ass" for demoralizing troops, according to Reid.

Bush saw it as crass politics. Just as the Democratic Congress was determined to come after him on the war, so was it intent on going after his friend Alberto Gonzales. Summoned to Capitol Hill to explain the U.S. attorney firings, on the same day as Reid's "lost" remark, Gonzales turned aside help from colleagues like Karen Hughes who wanted to help him prepare. As a result, with the cameras trained on him, Gonzales came across as woefully in over his head or, worse, dishonest. Sixty-four times, he said he could not remember details of the decision. Sixty-four times, his faulty memory was wrapped around his neck.

Still, while some advisers wanted the president to intervene and ease out Gonzales, Bush seemed disengaged from anything other than Iraq. Other issues received his attention in due order but did not animate him as much as they once did. When Bush flew to New York to visit a Harlem school and promote his education program on April 24, he brought along New York congressmen on Air Force One, including Representative Charles Rangel, the Democratic chairman of the House Ways and Means Committee. The White House was in the midst of tough negotiations with Rangel over trade agreements, and it would have been an opportune moment for Bush to weigh in. But Bush made no such effort, chatting with Rangel instead about baseball. "He talked a lot about the Rangers," Rangel said afterward. "I didn't know what the hell he was talking about."

After arriving in New York, Bush was backstage when another local congressman, Peter King, a Republican, introduced him to a soldier who had been injured in one eye. Bush teared up and asked the young man to take off his dark glasses so he could see the wound. "He actually touched the eye a little," King said later. "It was almost as if he felt he had to confront it."

As they headed back to Washington a few hours later with the televisions aboard Air Force One tuned to the New York Mets game, King mused that Bush must be feeling the weight of his office.

"My wife loves you," King said, "but she doesn't know how you don't wake up every morning and say, 'I've had it. I'm out of here.'"

Bush recoiled. "She thinks that?" he said. "Get her on the phone."

King dialed the number and got voice mail.

Bush left a message: "I'm doing okay. Don't worry about me."

A day later, the House passed a spending bill with $95 billion to pay for the wars in Iraq and Afghanistan and mandating a troop withdrawal by March 2008 as urged in the Baker-Hamilton report. The Senate concurred the following day. Bush vetoed the bill on May 1.

Democrats were not the only ones Bush had to worry about. On May 8, a group of moderate House Republicans came to see him. Sitting in the second floor of the White House residence, with Barney lying in the middle of the floor, they lashed out. Representative Tom Davis told Bush that his approval rating was down to 5 percent in part of his suburban Virginia district.

"Why did you replace Rumsfeld the day after the election?" Davis asked Bush. Doing it earlier might have changed enough races to have held the Senate.

"Yeah, I've heard that," Bush said.

"Had you done this thing right, you might have saved some guys," Davis said.

The lawmakers warned Bush that time was running out on Iraq and asked him about the Baker-Hamilton approach.

Bush said he would like to draw down troops but needed the surge to tamp down violence first.

The session was unusually blunt, what Davis later called a "brutal, come-to-Jesus meeting," and it angered Karl Rove, who thought the president deserved more loyalty.

"You guys aren't coming back," he snapped at Representative Mark Kirk, one of the organizers of the session.

WITH MEGHAN O'SULLIVAN leaving, Bush agreed it was time to restructure how he managed the wars. So much was riding on the surge that it was not enough to simply have it be just one of Stephen Hadley's many duties. So Hadley convinced a skeptical Bush and Cheney to appoint a full-time war coordinator with the heft to finally bring more cohesion to the fractured interagency effort. Unlike O'Sullivan, a deputy national security adviser who reported to Hadley, the new "war czar" would report directly to the president. Moreover, the czar would have "tasking authority" to issue instructions to various agencies, so if David Petraeus called to say he needed something and was having trouble getting it, the new official would have the clout to cut through the bureaucracy and get it done.

The idea underscored Hadley's self-effacing personality and genuine commitment to making the Iraq policy succeed; few Washington power brokers willingly give up power. But it also suggested just how dysfunctional the system had become that four years after the Iraq invasion Bush was still trying to figure out how to manage it. The solution itself was unwieldy; the new czar would be equivalent in rank to Hadley but would have the title of deputy national security adviser under Hadley, who himself would still play a role in war policy. Perhaps unsurprisingly, it was hard to find anyone to take the job. Seven retired generals approached by the White House refused to be considered, including Jack Keane, one of the intellectual authors of the surge. Some of them voiced concern about Bush and Cheney. "The very fundamental issue is they don't know where the hell they're going," General John J. "Jack" Sheehan, a retired marine officer, said publicly after turning down the job. "There's the residue of the Cheney view—'we're going to win, al-Qaeda's there'—that justifies anything we did. And then there's the pragmatist view—how the hell do we get out of Dodge and survive? Unfortunately, the people with the former view are still in the positions of most influence."

By that point, the surge troops were only beginning to flow into the theater in force, and casualties had spiked. In April, 104 American troops were killed, and in May the number rose to 126, the highest monthly total since 2004. Rebuffed by Keane and the other retired generals, Bush began looking at active-duty officers, particularly Lieutenant Generals Douglas Lute, who had served in the first Gulf War and in Kosovo and was now chief operations officer of the Joint Chiefs of Staff, and John Sattler, the marine commander during the second battle of Fallujah in 2004 and now chief strategic planner for the Joint Chiefs. In the end, Lute impressed Bush and Hadley the most—which was all the more remarkable because he had been an outspoken opponent of the surge. Bush knew that but did not care as long as Lute would follow the policy that had been set. Bush did not even raise the issue during his interview with Lute, leaving it to the general to mention it just to be sure it was on the table.

"Look, Mr. President, you would know this, but I feel like I need to tell you it's pretty well-known that I didn't support the surge," Lute told him.

"You're right, I did recognize that," Bush replied. It was an awkward moment, but Bush appreciated Lute's candor. "I love you for telling me that," he told Lute.

Lute's appointment was announced on May 15.

CHENEY WAS ANGRY a week later as he picked up the morning newspaper and detected signs of weakness coming out of the White House. He was reading a column on May 22 by David Ignatius in the *Washington Post* headlined "After the Surge," reporting that Bush was discussing a "post-surge" strategy focused on training and advising Iraqi troops, an approach that would "track the recommendations of the Baker-Hamilton report."

Cheney confronted Bush in the Oval Office that morning. "Whoever is leaking information like this to the press is doing a real disservice, Mr. President," he told him, "both to you and to our forces on the ground in Baghdad."

This looked like caving to the Democrats and would undercut Petraeus and the commanders in the field, Cheney complained. "We have to correct this particularly with the generals in the field," he said.

After returning to his office, Cheney looked up to find Hadley coming in and shutting the door. Hadley said he was the one who leaked to Ignatius—and did so on orders from Bush. Hoping to shore up support on Capitol Hill, the president wanted to foreshadow a time when troops would eventually start coming home. Cheney was momentarily nonplussed. The president had not told him he would do so, nor did he admit it even after being asked about it. Once again, they seemed to be on different pages.

The next few days brought moments of good news for Cheney. On May 23, Cheney's daughter Mary had her first child with her partner, Heather Poe, a son named Samuel. And two days after that, Bush signed a spending bill with $95 billion for the wars in Iraq and Afghanistan stripped of the troop withdrawal clause. As weakened as Bush and Cheney were, they had stared down Congress in a test of wills.

But then, on May 26, Cheney was aboard Air Force Two flying to New York to deliver the commencement address at the U.S. Military Academy at West Point when he noticed another leak undercutting the surge. The *New York Times* reported the White House was contemplating cutting combat forces in Iraq by as much as half in 2008.

Cheney was not the only one concerned. David Petraeus raised the issue on May 30 during a videoconference.

"Mr. President, to be quite frank about it, Ray Odierno and I were wondering what's going on?" Petraeus asked.

Bush reassured him. The generals had his 100 percent support.

Cheney was not so sure. The next day, he brought Jack Keane to his weekly lunch with Bush. Keane reinforced Petraeus's concern about the signal to commanders in the field.

Bush brushed it off, saying it was just his advisers working on the political problem in Congress.

Cheney countered that such talk came with a price in terms of confusing troops and risking momentum.

Petraeus understood the president's precarious situation and realized his scheduled testimony after Labor Day had become a deadline for the surge. "My concern was whether we could get it to work sufficiently before September 2007," he recalled. "That was the pistol staring at us out there most importantly."

Petraeus was already fighting a multifront war. While waiting for the last of the surge brigades to arrive, he launched a series of special operations missions targeting insurgent leaders. But he felt constantly undercut by his superior, the new Central Command chief, Admiral William "Fox" Fallon, who was a skeptic of the surge. Fallon, who had pinned his fourth star on before Petraeus pinned on his first, resented his subordinate's independence

Bush's speech under a "Mission Accomplished" banner declaring the end of major combat operations in Iraq became a symbol of premature victory. "Our stagecraft had gone awry," he said later. Bush tapped L. Paul "Jerry" Bremer to run Iraq, abandoning his own plan for a quick transition in favor of a longer occupation. As sovereignty was officially turned over in June 2004, Bush scribbled out a note: "Let freedom reign!"

Mr President,

Iraq is sovereign. Letter was passed from Bremer at 10:26 AM Iraq time —

Condi

Let Freedom reign!

Cheney offered to drop off the ticket in 2004. "I always saw the vice president as expendable in a sense," he said. Bush considered accepting "to demonstrate that I was in charge," but stuck with Cheney. Bush's election-year decision to endorse a constitutional ban on same-sex marriage outraged Cheney's daughter, Mary, who nearly quit the campaign. Bush's second inaugural address outlining a freedom agenda was, according to Andy Card, "not a speech Dick Cheney would give."

Surveying damage from Hurricane Katrina from Air Force One made Bush look removed from the disaster, but privately he was aggravated. "What the hell is taking so long?" he asked. The nomination of Harriet Miers for the Supreme Court collapsed when administration lawyers discovered she could not answer basic questions about constitutional law. After Cheney accidentally shot a fellow hunter, White House aides asked Bush to convince him to go on television to explain.

For two years, Bush resisted aides who urged him to fire Donald Rumsfeld, deferring to Cheney. When Bush finally replaced Rumsfeld after the 2006 midterm elections, he did not consult Cheney. "It wasn't open for discussion," Cheney said later. Appointed secretary of state, Condoleezza Rice supplanted Cheney as the preeminent adviser in the second term and clashed with him over her efforts to moderate policy. Cheney, she concluded, "would have liked to have kept breaking china."

A group of White House aides maneuvered behind the scenes to reverse strategy and send a troop surge to Iraq. TOP ROW, LEFT TO RIGHT: Stephen Hadley, J. D. Crouch; CENTER ROW, LEFT TO RIGHT: Meghan O'Sullivan, Brett McGurk; BOTTOM ROW: Peter Feaver, lower left. Retired General Jack Keane, lower right, was an important "validator" in building support for the course change.

Cheney was not the author of the Iraq surge but became its prime defender as he worried that Bush and his team were going wobbly and undercutting General David Petraeus. Even as Iraq turned around, the domestic economy spiraled into crisis and Bush agreed to the bailout sought by Ben Bernanke and Hank Paulson, who appear here (bottom) with Chris Cox. "Our people are going to hate us for this," Bush confided.

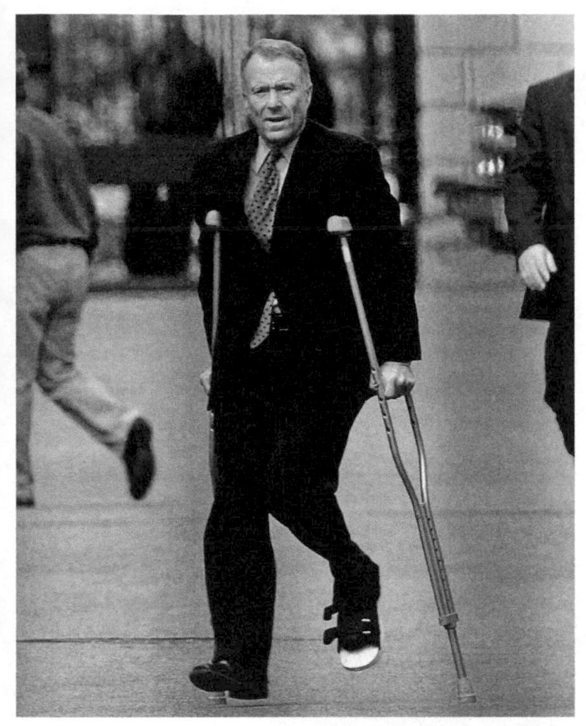

When Scooter Libby was indicted, he got up on crutches and wordlessly left the White House. "You could have heard a pin drop," a colleague recalled. Cheney pressed Bush relentlessly to pardon Libby. Bush refused, concluding that Libby misled investigators because "he was protecting Cheney." Cheney believed it was an injustice and lashed out. "That was wrong, and the president had it within his power to fix it," he said later, "and he chose not to."

Bush left the Oval Office on his last day in power without looking back. Cheney arrived at the White House for the Inauguration Day coffee in a wheelchair after throwing his back out packing. "Cheney looked like hell," said a White House official. Bush said farewell to the new president, Barack Obama, and happily headed to Texas. "He looked relieved, thrilled," an aide said.

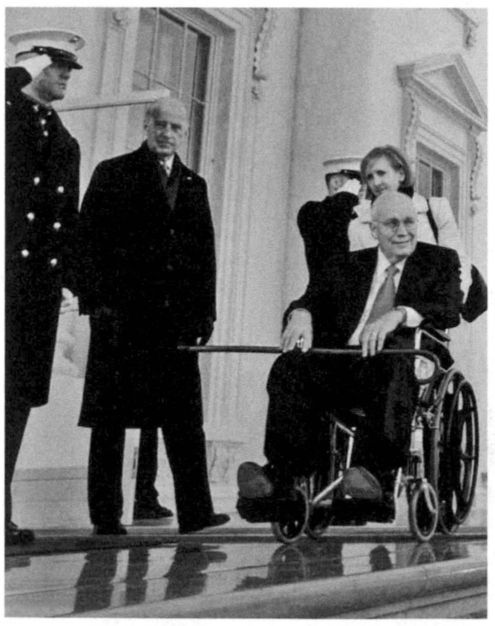

and personal channel to the White House and resolved to reestablish the chain of command. But Petraeus kept asking for more help, only to be frustrated at the negative response or lack of response. "Respectfully, sir, I can take no for an answer," Petraeus wrote to Fallon in one e-mail in May, "but I can't take no answer." Petraeus was flabbergasted. It was the first time in his career his immediate supervisor was not supportive of what he was doing.

The Iraq debate continued to dominate Washington, making it hard for Bush to get traction on anything else. With his Social Security and tax reform ideas dead, Bush was pushing again for a grand bargain on immigration. With the support of John McCain on the right and Ted Kennedy on the left, the president figured it was his best chance for a domestic legacy in his final two years in office. But he found it difficult to rally his own party. No longer afraid of their unpopular president, conservatives roared their opposition to Bush's immigration plan, decrying it more fulsomely than ever as amnesty. Frustrated, Bush unloaded on his erstwhile allies during a speech at a border patrol training facility in Georgia on May 29, saying critics "hadn't read the bill" and were opposing it because "it might make somebody else look good." Addressing thousands of trainees at a sunny outdoor ceremony, Bush turned testy. "If you want to kill the bill, if you don't want to do what's right for America, you can pick one little aspect of it. You can use it to frighten people."

He pressed on a couple of other initiatives at the same time. On May 30, Bush proposed expanding PEPFAR, the anti-AIDS program, which had put lifesaving medicine in the hands of millions of Africans and was rapidly becoming one of the great successes of his administration. He proposed doubling the funding to $30 billion over the next five years, seeing it as a worthy legacy, proving that his presidency was not all about war. The day after that, he reached out to overseas allies alienated by his renunciation of Kyoto with a call for new international talks on climate change.

The crisis atmosphere in the West Wing had taken its toll on Bush's inner circle. His closest aides had been with him longer than White House officials typically stayed and were drained. In late May, Dan Bartlett told the president he was stepping down. After thirteen years at Bush's side, Bartlett knew the president as well as any adviser, literally growing up with the governor turned president. But with a third child on the way, Bartlett believed it was time to move back to Texas.

After letting Bush know, Bartlett announced his decision during an Oval Office meeting of senior staff members. Alluding to his testy encounter with Cheney over disclosure of his shooting incident to a local Texas paper, Bartlett turned to the vice president and joked that he was going to leak his resignation to his neighborhood newsletter. "He didn't laugh," Bartlett recalled.

A few days later, a federal judge sentenced Scooter Libby to two and a half years in prison and a $250,000 fine. Cheney was incensed. Bad enough to convict his former aide on trumped-up charges, but to put him behind bars for longer than many violent criminals seemed like a travesty. Cheney's camp wasted little time lobbying the president. "Pardon Him," read the headline on an editorial posted barely an hour after the sentence was handed down on the Web site of *National Review*, the conservative journal with friends in the vice president's office. William Kristol, editor of the *Weekly Standard*, accused Bush of abandoning Libby. "So much for loyalty, or decency, or courage," the magazine lectured. It added, "Many of us used to respect President Bush. Can one respect him still?" Several Republican presidential candidates debating that night in New Hampshire said they would consider a pardon. Bush, traveling in Europe, found an escape hatch; as his lawyers assured him, there was no need to act as long as Libby had legal avenues to avoid reporting to prison. The judge delayed the sentence until hearing arguments.

ON THE DAY Libby was sentenced, the president arrived in Prague for a democracy conference. Bush was discouraged. He had committed his presidency to working toward "ending tyranny in our world," and yet the march of freedom, as he termed it, seemed stalled. Just as aggravating was the sense that his own government had helped stall it.

For all of Bush's high-flying rhetoric, he had yet to impose his will on the bureaucracy, much of which viewed his inaugural vision as simplistic, naive, and messianic. Badgering foreign governments about how they treated their citizens got in the way of development projects, trade deals, military cooperation, and other priorities. And Iraq haunted the effort, seen, rightly or wrongly, as an extreme example of forcing democracy on other countries.

Even small gestures generated resistance, sometimes from Bush's own friends. The president wanted to invite oppressed Chinese church leaders to the White House, only to run into objections from Clark Randt, a college friend he had made ambassador to Beijing. Randt argued the timing was not right. Bush aides like Michael Gerson and Elliott Abrams, who were leading promoters of the democracy agenda, came to believe the timing would never be right for diplomats who cared more about managing relations than changing the world. As a small concession, Bush agreed to hold the meeting in the residence rather than the Oval Office. When he finally met with the Chinese activists, he ended the session by calling for a prayer. Cheney looked visibly uncomfortable as everyone held hands.

The divisions within the administration grew personal. The advocates gave the professional diplomats derisive nicknames. Christopher Hill was called "Kim Jong Hill," while Richard Boucher, an assistant secretary of state who oversaw central Asia, was dubbed "Boucherbayev," a play off Nursultan Nazarbayev, the autocratic leader of Kazakhstan. John Bolton, whose recess appointment as UN ambassador had expired, referred to the foreign service officers at the State Department's Bureau of East Asian and Pacific Affairs as the "EAPeasers." The professionals were equally scornful of the true believers, viewing them as ideologues. "You can't solve all the problems of the world," Robert Zoellick, deputy secretary of state, lectured Gerson. The conflict persisted in part because Bush himself was conflicted. While he deeply believed in his inaugural aspirations, he repeatedly found himself compromising with allies like Egypt and Saudi Arabia because of other imperatives. The ascension of Hamas in Palestinian elections also cast a shadow, a reminder that popular will in many parts of the world did not favor the United States.

Bush went to Prague at the invitation of Natan Sharansky, the Israeli politician whose book on democracy had inspired him after the 2004 election. Sharansky was disappointed in Bush and hoped to reinvigorate his vision. As Bush met privately with opposition leaders from authoritarian societies, he voiced his own exasperation. "You're not the only dissident," he told Saad Eddin Ibrahim, a leader in the resistance to President Hosni Mubarak of Egypt. "I too am a dissident in Washington. Bureaucracy in the United States does not help change. It seems that Mubarak succeeded in brainwashing them." Bush used the conference to prod his own administration, ordering American ambassadors in unfree nations to meet with dissidents and boasting that he had created a fund to help human rights defenders.

But two months passed without the State Department sending out the cable ordering diplomats to reach out to opposition figures. Frustrated, Elliott Abrams took matters into his own hands and leaked the State Department's failure to follow up to Jackson Diehl of the *Washington Post*. Only after Diehl made inquiries did the State Department suddenly rush to send out the cable ordered by the president.

Returning to Washington, Bush had lunch with Condoleezza Rice, who broached the idea of holding a Middle East peace conference. Since taking office, Bush had avoided the endless shuttle diplomacy between Israelis and Palestinians that had flummoxed other presidents. But with time running short on their administration, Rice believed the moment was ripe to try.

“How do we keep expectations from getting out of control?” Bush asked her. “What if we can’t get an agreement?”

Rice said it was worth the risk.

Bush told her to develop a plan. “And can we call it a meeting?” He was allergic to the word “summit,” with all its grandiose and probably unattainable implications.

“Fine with me,” Rice said. “It’s a meeting.”

32

"Revolt of the radical pragmatists"

"Does anyone here agree with the vice president?"

No hands went up.

The issue of the Syrian nuclear reactor encapsulated all the competing forces of the second term—preemptive war, diplomacy, weapons of mass destruction, and the freedom agenda. And it exposed the widening rift between President Bush and Vice President Cheney in dramatic fashion. The president was reluctant to once more provoke the world with unilateral military action, while the vice president saw it as a test of whether his partner still held to the principles they shared in the days after September 11.

Now more wary of easy intelligence, Bush chose to explore the question only after a methodical review. He gathered his national security team in the Yellow Oval Room in the White House residence at 6:50 p.m. on June 17.

Just how good was the intelligence, anyway? he asked.

"It's about as good as it gets," said Mike McConnell, director of national intelligence.

There was no doubt it was a nuclear reactor. On that, the intelligence agencies had "high confidence." There was convincing, though not indisputable, evidence that the North Koreans were helping the Syrians, so the agencies rated that at "medium confidence." As to whether the reactor was part of a weapons program, the agencies had not found elements that would be definitive, like a plutonium reprocessing operation or a warhead development program, so they had "low confidence" about that. Having said that, Michael Hayden, the CIA director, noted there were no lines connecting the reactor to a power grid. Analysts could not conceive of another explanation for the plant. "Of course it's a weapons program," Hayden said.

Ehud Olmert came to Washington two days later and pressed his case over lunch with Bush and Cheney. The vice president then joined Olmert for dinner that night at Blair House across the street from the White House, and the two kicked staff out for a long private session in which the Israeli leader pleaded for American action. The prospect of a nuclear-armed Syria right on the border was unacceptable, Olmert said. In Cheney, at least, he had a receptive audience.

The national security team reconvened in the Yellow Oval Room to debate the matter. Condoleezza Rice was now bolstered in her struggles with Cheney by a new ally in Robert Gates, who felt the last thing the United States needed was to attack another Arab country and argued that "we don't do Pearl Harbors." The two urged a diplomatic solution—blow the whistle on the Syrians publicly and take them to the UN Security Council to pressure Damascus to give up the plant. If they refused, there would be a better foundation for a military strike. Without that, a surprise attack could trigger a wider regional war and endanger American troops in next-door Iraq, where they would be targets for retaliation. It was also a complicated juncture in the talks with North Korea. Around the same time, Christopher Hill was making a surprise visit to Pyongyang, and a few days after that UN inspectors returned to North Korea for the first time since 2002.

Elliott Abrams, the hawkish deputy national security adviser, felt the diplomatic route advocated by Rice and Gates was ridiculous because the IAEA would never muster the wherewithal to shape events. The moment the Syrians knew their secret was out, it would be much harder to launch a surprise strike. Instead, he advocated letting the Israelis bomb the plant, reasoning that it would help them restore their military reputation following the inconclusive Lebanon War of 2006.

Cheney was the only one to make the case for the United States to bomb the facility itself. To him, it came down to American credibility. After North Korea tested its nuclear bomb in October 2006, Bush had drawn a red line, warning of dire consequences if Pyongyang were caught proliferating nuclear technology. Well, Cheney argued, they had just been caught. Bush's warning had to mean something; otherwise what was the point? If America did not follow through, he said, then the mullahs in Tehran certainly did not have to worry about defying the world on Iran's nuclear program.

Bush listened carefully but seemed disinclined to go along. He even rolled his eyes, according to one report. Several in the room said they did not recall that, but as one participant said, "If not literal rolling of eyes, there was figurative rolling of eyes."

That's when Bush asked for a show of hands and saw none.

It was a far cry from the days when Bush's first instinct was to "call Dick" after the no-fly-zone retaliation against Iraq in 2001 or to clear the room to talk with Cheney alone before launching the strike that opened the Iraq War in 2003. This time, Bush made Cheney offer his case in front of everyone else and then, whether meaning to or not, forced the vice president to confront his own marginalization. On the way out, Abrams apologized to Cheney for leaving him isolated.

As he had repeatedly in the second term, Bush sided with Rice, who thought Cheney's idea of a strike "was, to put it mildly, reckless." Bush would go the diplomatic route. The catastrophic intelligence failure in Iraq still weighed on him. How could he attack a target if the intelligence community was saying it had "low confidence" that it was part of a weapons program? The minute he did that, there would be news stories about him again disregarding evidence to go to war. Instead of rallying the international community against a mutual threat, Washington would have much of the world up in arms.

Bush later called Olmert from the Oval Office to tell him his decision. "I cannot justify an attack on a sovereign nation unless my intelligence agencies stand up and say it's a weapons program," Bush told him.

"That's very disappointing to hear," Olmert told Bush. "We told you at the beginning that at the end of this process that the reactor has to go away, so the reactor is going to go away."

Olmert made clear he would not sit back and wait for diplomacy. For Israel, this was an existential issue. If America would not act, Israel would.

Bush made no real effort to talk him out of it and hung up. "This guy's got balls," the president remarked to aides.

While Gates was furious and thought Israel was holding the United States hostage, Bush told aides to respect the Israeli decision and stay quiet about it. "Look, they view this as a matter of national security, and I'm not going to interfere with their national security, and if this is what he wants to do, everybody shut up," Bush said.

Cheney considered it a lost opportunity. "You can say I am wrong, you can argue with me, but I would have pursued a more robust course in the second term than we did," he said after leaving office. "I would have taken out the Syrian reactor, partly because I thought that had multiple benefits—shut down a major source of proliferation and deliver a real shot across the bow of the Iranians. It would rock the North Koreans back on their haunches in terms of thinking they could peddle their nuclear technology and get away with it. It would mean that our red lines meant something. We threaten action if they proliferate—they proliferate, they get action. But we didn't do it. We passed up the opportunity to really give meaning and substance and consequences to our diplomacy."

CHENEY FOUND HIMSELF embroiled in multiple disputes as summer progressed. In June, House Democrats accused him of acting above the law by refusing to comply with an executive order governing the handling of classified information. Cheney defied the order and the conventions of government on principle. But his explanation held him up for ridicule. The vice president did not need to comply with executive branch rules, David Addington argued, because as the presiding officer of the Senate, he was not strictly an executive branch official.

He had a point. Until recent decades, in fact, the vice president was associated as much with the legislative branch as with the executive branch, working out of the Capitol rather than the White House. But in modern times, that seemed like a mind-boggling argument and triggered an avalanche of criticism from Democrats, mockery by late-night comics, and irritation among the president's team. In their view, just as with the energy task force records, Cheney was stirring trouble unnecessarily. Why not simply comply with an obscure executive order that established a uniform system for safeguarding classified information?

The order, first signed by Bill Clinton in 1995 and later updated and reissued by Bush in 2003, required that any "entity within the executive branch that comes into the possession of classified information" report annually how much it was keeping secret—not even *what* it kept secret, just the quantity. Cheney's office filed reports in 2001 and 2002 but stopped filing in 2003. By 2004, the Information Security Oversight Office at the National Archives and Records Administration responded by ordering an inspection of Cheney's office to see how sensitive material was handled, but his staff blocked the examination. The vice president's team later proposed amending the executive order to abolish the Information Security Oversight Office altogether.

Bush found such disputes baffling. With so much else going on, he was interested in one last chance to achieve a historic domestic initiative, not to poke at a hornet's nest. He was in Rhode Island on June 28 giving a speech on Iraq at the Naval War College when Ted Kennedy called. His on-again, off-again partner asked Bush to press Harry Reid to keep trying on immigration reform. Bush was dumbfounded. If Reid would not listen to Kennedy, he surely would not listen to Bush. Within hours, immigration reform was dead as supporters failed to overcome a filibuster mounted by conservatives who opposed anything they thought smacked of amnesty for foreigners who broke the law to sneak into the country.

Bush looked uncharacteristically dejected as he approached a lectern set up at the war college, fiddling with papers as he talked and avoiding the sort of winking eye contact he often made with reporters. Then he did something he almost never did: he admitted defeat.

"A lot of us worked hard to see if we couldn't find a common ground," he said. "It didn't work."

With that desultory appearance in a college hallway, Bush's second-term domestic legislative agenda died. The Ownership Society he once envisioned had gone nowhere. Social Security, tax reform, and now immigration overhaul had all been thwarted. He had remained supremely confident even in the face of broad opposition; just seventeen days earlier, while in Bulgaria, he had brushed off pessimism about immigration, saying, "I'll see you at the bill signing." Now there would be no bill signing.

This one was especially painful. "The president believed as strongly in that issue as any issue in his time in the White House," Michael Gerson said. White House aides blamed Reid, believing he just wanted to deprive Bush of a bipartisan victory. In any case, Bush and Karl Rove later regretted putting Social Security first in the second term, concluding they should have led off with immigration, where there was at least a possibility of consensus. Now his agenda on Capitol Hill would be defensive, blocking measures he opposed, like stem-cell research, another version of which he just vetoed.

BUSH WAS IN Kennebunkport hosting Vladimir Putin on July 2, when he received word of another thorny challenge. A three-judge appeals court in Washington had ruled that Scooter Libby had to begin his thirty-month sentence immediately. For Bush, there was no more delaying the hard decision. Either he intervened on behalf of a convicted perjurer, or he let one of the early architects of his administration turn in his coat and tie for a prison jumpsuit. He knew Cheney considered it an illegitimate prosecution by an out-of-control prosecutor, Patrick Fitzgerald. "He thought that guy is a zealot," said Alan Simpson, Cheney's friend. But Fred Fielding, the former 9/11 commissioner who had replaced Harriet Miers as White House counsel, did not see it that way and was loath for the president to substitute his judgment for that of a jury that had heard all the evidence.

Bush kept his deliberations exceedingly private, consulting only a handful of advisers like Fielding, Joshua Bolten, and Dan Bartlett. Friends who called the White House to lobby on Libby's behalf were told to stay out of it. Justice Department lawyers who normally reviewed clemency requests were not involved. Nor was Fitzgerald, even though it was typical for the prosecutor to be asked for an opinion. Around the White House, the topic was discussed largely in whispers. As Bush returned to Washington aboard Air Force One, he split the difference: he commuted Libby's prison term without issuing a full pardon voiding the conviction. Two and a half years in prison seemed extreme, but he was not willing to go as far as Cheney wanted him to. "I respect the jury's verdict," Bush said in a written statement crafted with Fielding. "But I have concluded that the prison sentence given to Mr. Libby is excessive." Libby would still have to pay the $250,000 fine and surrender his law license. Bush was careful not to antagonize Fitzgerald; while acknowledging that critics questioned the legitimacy of the prosecution, Bush called Fitzgerald "a highly qualified, professional prosecutor who carried out his responsibilities as charged."

As a political matter, Bush's decision was the worst of both worlds. Democrats excoriated him for protecting a political crony from justice, while Cheney and his allies grew bitter that he did not overturn the conviction altogether. Moreover, Bush only postponed a final reckoning; as long as he remained in office, he would be under pressure from Cheney to go the next step and grant a complete pardon.

AT HOME, THE political ground on Iraq was crumbling. Bush had figured he needed to beat back any congressional efforts to pull out troops until September, when Petraeus would return to report on the results of the surge. But now it looked as if he might not even survive July without a complete collapse in political support. Senator Richard Lugar, one of the leading Republican foreign policy voices, broke with Bush over Iraq. Representative Roy Blunt, the number-two Republican in the House, told Bush, "You have no credibility on communicating about Iraq." And Senator John Warner came to the White House to tell Stephen Hadley he did not think he could hold the line until September—and was unsure even of his own vote if Congress decided to step in. Hadley pleaded for sixty days but got no assurances.

On July 7, Hadley convened a conference call with other White House aides. If Republicans abandoned the war, it was all over. Relating the Warner conversation, Hadley suggested they begin talking about a partial pullout by the end of the year.

"The surge can't last forever—we all know that—so if it would help in the Congress, maybe we can discuss goals for withdrawing some troops," Hadley said.

Karl Rove pushed back hard. "No, no, no," he said. "If we show weakness or let the president talk withdrawal, then we're on a slippery slide. It'll be seen as panicking to the Pelosi-Reid crowd and too enticing to Republicans. No way."

Ed Gillespie, who had replaced Dan Bartlett as presidential counselor, and Candida Wolff, the chief White House legislative liaison, concurred. Hadley backed off.

The next day, Hadley called Cheney aboard Air Force Two as he flew back to Washington from a Wyoming break to tell him about the conversation. It did not escape Cheney's notice that he had not been included in the discussion, and he concluded that even if he had been in town, they might have excluded him since they knew he would disapprove of anything resembling a concession.

Once again, Cheney picked up the newspaper the next day, July 9, to find more evidence of waffling, this one a *New York Times* article reporting that the White House was preparing a narrower mission with a staged pullback if it could not hold political support through September. Cheney noticed at a meeting later that day that no one questioned the validity of the story, only who leaked it. Cheney told them they were panicking and misreading Congress. Afterward, he called Senator Trent Lott, his old friend, and asked him to privately conduct his own vote count.

Concerned that Bush or his people were going soft, Cheney did something the next day that he rarely did. At the weekly Senate Republican lunch, he stood up to press the caucus to stand by the president and the troop buildup. That night, several Republican senators joined him at the vice president's residence for dinner. Lott was there and reported that he thought they had enough votes to make it until September. Mitch McConnell, now the Senate Republican leader, came over as the dinner was breaking up to make the same point. That did not stop the House from voting two days later to pull most troops out by April 2008, but as long as Senate Republicans held firm, they could block a withdrawal.

Hadley and others thought Cheney misunderstood their concerns. "He thought we were going wobbly, which is completely nuts," Hadley said later. "What we were really trying to do was to use the surge to see if we had a chance of getting a bipartisan consensus on the Hill in support of our surge policy." Another official thought Cheney's interpretation of what was happening showed "that he really wasn't in the loop because nobody on that call was thinking of short-circuiting the surge or changing policy. It was really about what's our narrative that could help hold this Congress."

AMID ALL THIS, David Petraeus made a surprising proposal: he wanted to go to Syria to confront President Bashar al-Assad about the foreign militants crossing the border into Iraq to fight Americans. Intelligence agencies believed Syria was the main pipeline for Arab radicals, with as many as 80 percent flying into Damascus and then driving into Iraq. What, if anything, to do about that had been a sore point for months. At one meeting, Elliott Abrams, the deputy national security adviser, literally pounded the table insisting on action such as bombing the Damascus airport and cratering its runways someday at three o'clock in the morning to stop the flow. But others resisted, unwilling to widen the war by bringing in another Muslim country.

Petraeus reported that Assad through intermediaries in the Iraqi government had invited him to visit. He thought it might be an opportunity to tell Assad there would be consequences if he did not shut off the flow of fighters. "I wanted to respectfully confront him on Syria being a transit location for al-Qaeda in Iraq," Petraeus said later. The message would be one of self-interest for Assad: "You're basically allowing poisonous snakes to have a nest in your country with the understanding they only bite the neighbors' kids and sooner or later that backfires and they end up biting your kids and then they do worse." Bush made clear he did not want Petraeus to go, but the general kept raising it. Finally, Admiral Mike Mullen, the Joint Chiefs chairman, privately told him to stop asking. "Forget it," he said. "It's not going to happen in your lifetime in uniform, so there's no reason to bring it up again."

What Petraeus did not know at first was that Israel had already told Bush that it planned to bomb Syria to destroy its fledgling nuclear reactor. Having Petraeus in full military uniform chatting with Assad in the days or weeks before then could send mixed signals. On September 6, Israeli warplanes swooped into Syrian airspace and destroyed the nuclear plant under cover of night. Israel kept quiet about the operation, calculating that Syria would rather absorb the blow in silence than suffer the humiliation of publicly admitting that the Jewish state had successfully raided its territory. The Americans had assumed there would be an uproar in the Arab community. But it turned out the Israelis knew their neighborhood better. Syria kept quiet.

ON JULY 21, Cheney once again took over as acting president while Bush underwent a colonoscopy. Just as he had in 2002, Bush signed letters temporarily transferring power to the vice president under the Twenty-Fifth Amendment. The letters were faxed to Capitol Hill at 7:16 a.m., and Fred Fielding called to inform David Addington, who in turn called Cheney at his weekend home in St. Michaels, Maryland, to let him know he was now in charge. A five-doctor team at Camp David led by Colonel Richard Tubb, the White House physician, removed five polyps from Bush during the procedure. The White House then faxed fresh letters from Bush at 9:21 a.m. reclaiming his powers.

Conservatives playfully imagined all that Cheney could do during his 125-minute presidency—*National Review* collected ideas online, like bomb

Iran and pardon Scooter Libby—but the acting president spent his brief administration writing a letter to his grandchildren as a keepsake.

> *Dear Kate, Elizabeth, Grace, Philip, Richard and Sam,*
>
> *As I write this, our nation is engaged in a war with terrorists of global reach. My principal focus as Vice President has been to help protect the American people and our way of life. The vigilance, diligence and unwavering commitment of those who protect our Nation has kept us safe from terrorist attacks of the kind we faced on September 11, 2001. We owe a special debt of gratitude to the members of our armed forces, intelligence agencies, law enforcement agencies and others who serve and sacrifice to keep us safe and free.*
>
> *As you grow, you will come to understand the sacrifices that each generation makes to preserve freedom and democracy for future generations, and you will assume the important responsibilities of citizens in our society. I ask of you as my grandchildren what I asked of my daughters, that you always strive in your lives to do what is right.*
>
> *May God bless and protect you,*
> *Richard B. Cheney,*
> *Acting President of the United States*
> *(Grandpa Cheney)*

Cheney had his own health issues to address. A week later he underwent surgery to have his defibrillator replaced. Worried that an assassin could hack into the device to kill the vice president by triggering a heart attack, his doctor ordered its wireless capacity turned off.

But it was not just a feared plot giving Cheney fits these days. When Condoleezza Rice and Robert Gates visited Saudi Arabia on July 31, one of Cheney's contacts in the traveling party called him in alarm to tell him the defense secretary had forsworn the use of force against Iran. Gates and Rice had joined King Abdullah in Jeddah, sitting around a modest coffee table with bowls of candy. Abdullah pressed for more aggressive action against Iran. Gates grew angry at what he saw as Saudi willingness to shed American blood and he shut down talk of a military strike. "The American people won't stand for it," he said. Abdullah started to respond when Gates added, "In fact, he will be impeached." Abdullah was furious, and even Rice was flabbergasted. By the time word got back to Cheney, he was both. He sent a message to the Saudis that the defense secretary was freelancing. But as long as Bush resisted any serious discussion of military options against Iran, Cheney's position did not matter much.

Gates was clearly not in sync with the vice president on many of the divisive issues of the latter part of the administration, whether it be Iran, Syria, Guantánamo, or other matters. "In terms of thinking about these kinds of problems, he was a lot closer to Condi than he was me," Cheney said later. The two secretaries "were pretty much on the same page" on most issues, Gates recalled. With their ascendance along with Stephen Hadley and Douglas Lute, it was, in the words of Douglas Ollivant, an NSC official, the "revolt of the radical pragmatists."

In those steamy summer days, the changes in the White House seemed to be coming in rapid succession. In early August, Karl Rove told Bush he would be leaving. The last election was behind him, as was the CIA leak case. He kept in his desk drawer a picture of Scooter Libby clipped from the newspaper the day he was convicted, a reminder of the damage done—and of what Rove himself had avoided. His name was thrown around a lot in the U.S. attorney scandal because he had passed along complaints about some U.S. attorneys who got fired and helped install one of his protégés in one of the prosecutor slots. But that did not concern him much. He saw that as just more partisan noise, and after everything he had been through, he had pretty effective earplugs.

For Rove, it was time to move on. After so much time away, his marriage was in trouble, and he was ready to establish his independence financially and professionally. He wanted to be more than "the Bush guy," as he put it.

Still, he felt guilty. "I feel like I'm deserting you in a time of war," he told Bush.

ALBERTO GONZALES, ON the other hand, refused to leave. Gonzales's tenure as attorney general had become so tumultuous that it was distracting the administration—not just the furor over the U.S. attorneys, but his handling of disputes over the National Security Agency eavesdropping program. Recent congressional testimony by Gonzales on the surveillance program had been so unsteady, so marked by memory lapses and contradictions, that even some inside the White House worried he faced possible perjury prosecution. When White House lawyers asked, David Addington refused to confirm that Gonzales had testified accurately about events surrounding the NSA program.

Like Rove, Bush considered the controversy over the prosecutor firings partisan posturing. Rove kept telling him it was nothing more than a witch hunt, and Bush was not about to cave in to Democrats. Bush's loyalty to Gonzales mystified advisers, many of whom did not think the attorney general was up to the job even in better times. "That was the first time that I ever heard around the watercooler questioning the president's decision on something," one aide recalled, even more than the Harriet Miers nomination.

What bewildered many in Bush's circle was that Gonzales did not realize he should fall on his sword for the president. "I don't understand for the life of me why Al Gonzales is still there," a former top Bush aide groused at the time. Others thought it was time for Bush to recognize reality. "The president," a senior administration official said, "thinks cutting and running on his friends shows weakness. Change shows weakness. Doing what everyone knows has to be done shows weakness."

Only now, after months of painful hearings and headlines, did Bush finally conclude that Gonzales had to go. Questions about the attorney general's credibility on the NSA program struck at the heart of Bush's presidency, namely national security, and risked making it more difficult to win legislation to authorize the eavesdropping. Joshua Bolten raised the issue with him one day.

"We have a big agenda that the attorney general needs to carry for us," he told Bush, "and Alberto can't carry it anymore."

Bush was sad but did not resist. They both thought it was unfair to Gonzales. While he could have handled matters better, Bush thought, the Democrats had intentionally destroyed an honest man's career with no real justification.

Bush left it to Bolten to deliver the news. The chief of staff called Gonzales. He wanted to make clear in a gentle way that he had the president's authority. "Alberto, this makes us all heartsick," he said, "but the best thing you can do for the president right now is resign."

After all these years at Bush's side, it was a hard blow for Gonzales. He insisted on hearing directly from Bush. "I want to talk to the president," he said.

Bolten thought it was a matter of dignity and agreed to set up a meeting. Other officials who heard about it, though, were astonished. When the president sent his top aide to tell a cabinet official to resign, he should simply resign. But Gonzales went to the president's ranch outside Crawford on August 26. Advisers understood how difficult it would be for Bush. For all of his self-description as a decider, Bush hated firing people who had been loyal to him.

In this case, Bush was forced to confront a good friend. As they talked, Gonzales recognized that he had no choice but to accept the decision. If he harbored any illusion that it was not really Bush who wanted him to go, or that he could appeal to his old friend, that vanished. Gonzales flew back to Washington to announce his departure, suggesting the decision was his.

Administration officials quietly put out the cover story that it was Gonzales who offered to resign in a phone call to Bush and that the president was reluctant and suggested he come down for a consolation lunch.

More bad news came on August 31, when Tony Snow announced that he too would resign. His cancer was too advanced to pretend that he would be able to return to the White House podium. Dana Perino stepped in, but a sense of grief pervaded the West Wing, both for the likable press secretary and for a presidency under siege on so many fronts.

BUSH AND CHENEY met that day with the national security team to think about the way forward in Iraq. David Petraeus and his civilian partner, Ambassador Ryan Crocker, were due back in town soon to report to Congress, and while everyone was nervous about getting too far ahead of themselves, it looked as if they might have begun turning the situation around.

After peaking at 126 in May, American military fatalities had fallen by a third, to 84, in August. Iraqi civilian deaths had fallen from 2,796 to 2,384 over that same period. In Baghdad, the center of the violence and the key to creating enough space for political reconciliation, civilian fatalities had fallen by nearly half, from 1,341 to 738. Something was beginning to change on the ground. At least they hoped so.

Staring at the video screen on the wall, Bush and Cheney listened as Petraeus reviewed the situation and anticipated letting a marine expeditionary unit in Anbar go home in December without being replaced and sending the five army surge brigades in Baghdad home by July 2008. It was both an expression of confidence that they had turned a corner and a quiet recognition that the political environment back home required signs that the war was eventually going to end.

Bush pressed Petraeus to ensure it was genuinely his recommendation, not a response to pressure from the Joint Chiefs or his commander, Fox Fallon.

Petraeus assured him it was his own judgment.

"The plan should be this," Bush said. "Keep a boot on the neck and get us in place for the long term." He was in no rush, he said, to bring the troops home if that would endanger the tentative progress on the ground.

At this point, Fallon jumped in. He had been agitating to draw down forces in Iraq for months and offered the president a convoluted analogy about a fighter pilot taking more risk if an enemy had him in his sights. "That's our situation in Iraq," Fallon said. "The bogey on our tail is that the Iraqis still have not made any political progress. We need to force them, take on some more risk by drawing down our forces, force them to step up, take charge."

It was a repeat of the argument of Donald Rumsfeld, John Abizaid, and George Casey a year earlier. The question was whether enough had happened in the interim to justify returning to a transition strategy. Bush did not think so. "I'm not sure we're ready to take on more risk in Iraq," he said.

While Bush was gentle in rebuffing Fallon, Cheney interjected more directly. "Fox, the whole world's betting on our bugging out of Iraq," he said. "You know it. Everyone's watching, asking if we can sustain what's working. Decisions we make now will reverberate for years. And I'm afraid what you present here, to any reasonable person, will be read as surrender."

Fallon was undaunted. "The point is sending a message not to the world but to the Iraqis," he said. "Let them know that they need to step up. It's now or never."

BUSH TOOK ADVANTAGE of the Labor Day holiday to make another secret trip to Iraq, this time leaving from the White House. Rather than be confined to the airport or even to Baghdad, he planned to fly to Anbar Province, once deemed lost to the enemy. It would be a daring display of progress for the audience back home and a chance for the president to see the results of the surge.

First, he had to slip out of the world's most heavily guarded building without detection. Bush found himself in an unmarked vehicle heading to Andrews Air Force Base and stuck in traffic on an often-clogged exit ramp in Washington. For operational security, they posed as a regular vehicle, and no roads were cleared ahead of time.

Suddenly Bush's aides saw a panhandler collecting coins in a McDonald's cup making his way to each of the cars stuck at the traffic light. Bush was in the third one back. Any moment the man would reach them, peer into the window, and notice the president of the United States, blowing the secrecy of the trip.

"Get down," Joe Hagin, the deputy White House chief of staff, told Bush.

"What?" Bush asked.

"Slide down in the seat," Hagin instructed.

Just then, a quick-thinking Secret Service agent in the car following the president's reached into his wallet, pulled out a few dollar bills, and held them out the window. The panhandler skipped right past the president's car to collect the donation.

After a long flight, Bush landed in Iraq on Labor Day, touching down at Al Asad Air Base to meet with Petraeus, Crocker, and Prime Minister Nouri al-Maliki. A furnace wave of 110-degree heat washed over his face as he emerged from Air Force One dressed in a casual dark blue short-sleeve shirt and dark pants. It was an invigorating moment. “They felt the elation of the surprise visit,” Eric Draper, the White House photographer, remembered.

Bush met with sheikhs aligned with the Americans. Many of the sheikhs had been opposed to the new Iraqi government and worked in tandem with al-Qaeda but began switching sides before the surge in what was called the Awakening. The reinforcement of marines in Anbar Province had encouraged and accelerated a shift that was turning the region around. Bush was particularly taken with one young sheikh named Abdul Sattar Abu Risha, a dashing, daring figure. “He’s sent from central casting,” Petraeus remembered. “Very courageous guy, a truly inspirational leader.”

Abu Risha’s spirit was infectious. “My fighters will finish here and go to fight alongside you in Afghanistan,” he told Bush exuberantly.

Bush was pumped up on his way home. *Maybe this was going to work after all.* Now he just had to convince Congress and the American public.

Petraeus and Crocker returned to Washington soon afterward for their report to Congress. Not since Vietnam had there been such an anticipated appearance by a general on Capitol Hill. The liberal activist group MoveOn.org welcomed the general back to America with a full-page ad in the *New York Times* accusing him in advance of cooking the books and dubbing him “General Betray Us.” The inflammatory attack backfired by giving Republicans something to rage about and putting Democrats on the defensive.

Bush watched some of the testimony on September 10 from the West Wing as Petraeus told Congress that American forces “have dealt significant blows” to the enemy in Iraq and outlined his plan to draw down the surge forces by July 2008 while warning of “devastating consequences” of a more rapid withdrawal. Enduring tough questioning from Democrats like Barack Obama and Hillary Clinton, Petraeus and Crocker proved impressive, and it quickly became clear they had bought Bush more time.

When he invited Harry Reid and Nancy Pelosi to the White House the next day, Bush seemed triumphal. “Of course, al-Qaeda needs new recruits,” he said, “because we’re *killin’* ’em.” He smiled. “We’re killin’ ’em all!”

Reid was appalled; Bush, he thought, viewed the war “as if it were some kind of sporting event or action movie.”

That, of course, was not the tone he could take in the national address he planned following Petraeus’s testimony. By putting the general out first, Bush hoped that the timetable for withdrawing the surge brigades would be invested with Petraeus’s credibility; had Bush announced it himself, it would have been seen entirely through the lens of how people viewed Bush. But Cheney read the draft speech and concluded Bush had gone too far the other way, especially by mentioning the Baker-Hamilton report as his ultimate goal.

"Mr. President, you can't refer to Baker-Hamilton," Cheney told him. "Our strategy is Petraeus-Crocker, not Baker-Hamilton."

Bush agreed to strike the reference. While Cheney was not the driving force behind the surge, he had become its most vocal guardian against backtracking.

BUSH WAS PRACTICING the speech in the family theater on September 13 when word arrived that Abdul Sattar Abu Risha, the young Sunni sheikh who had impressed him in Anbar Province just ten days earlier, had been killed by an explosion—the victim, it was said, of his own bodyguard's betrayal. Bush was shaken. At this moment of progress, it was a cruel blow that one of the leaders of the turnaround had been taken down.

Bush worried it was his fault. "Did my visit endanger him?" he asked national security aides. "Did we consider that?"

Douglas Lute, the war coordinator, answered with resignation. "It's just a tough neighborhood," he said.

That night, Bush sat down at his desk in the Oval Office for his address to the nation. He portrayed an Iraq where "ordinary life is beginning to return" at long last. "The principle guiding my decisions on troop levels in Iraq is 'return on success,' " Bush said, adopting a new phrase coined by Ed Gillespie. "The more successful we are, the more American troops can return home." He added, "Some say the gains we are making in Iraq come too late. They are mistaken. It is never too late to deal a blow to al-Qaeda. It is never too late to advance freedom. And it is never too late to support our troops in a fight they can win."

Two days later, September 15, Jack Keane showed up on the porch of Petraeus's house at Fort Myer outside Washington. Petraeus was recovering from a weeklong blitz of congressional committees, White House and Pentagon meetings, and television interviews before heading back to Baghdad.

"I've got a message for you from the president," Keane told him.

"Okay, all right," Petraeus said.

"I was over seeing the vice president," Keane said, "and the president got word I was there and he came over to the office and he said, 'You tell Petraeus, don't let the chain of command filter out any requests. If he needs something, you just tell me. You get the word to me.' "

33

"Don't screw with the president of the United States"

No way, President Bush said. The Boston Red Sox could not hit against John Lackey.

"What are you talking about?" replied a defiant Christopher Hill.

It was early one morning in the fall of 2007, and the president was in the Oval Office trash-talking with Hill, his North Korea negotiator. Bush had invited Vice President Cheney and a handful of other officials to breakfast to hear Hill describe how the talks were progressing. But first he and Hill were engaged in a lighthearted debate about upcoming play-offs between Hill's beloved Red Sox and Lackey's Angels.

Hill noticed Condoleezza Rice out of the corner of his eye staring at him with concern. Maybe "the hired help," as Hill liked to put it, wasn't supposed to argue with the commander in chief, even about baseball. But Bush liked his diplomat's brash fearlessness. The president saw him as someone who cut through the interagency morass.

That did not mean the president overlooked how much Cheney distrusted Hill or how the negotiator was playing his internal adversaries back in Washington to advance his cause, pushing right up against the limits of how far Bush was prepared to go to get a deal. One reason the president wanted to have the breakfast was to lay down his own priorities as they moved forward so that Cheney, Hill, and Rice would know directly what he wanted rather than arguing among themselves.

Bush led his guests into the small dining room adjoining the Oval Office. He sat at the head of the table, with Cheney to his left and Rice to his right. Hill sat next to Rice, and Stephen Hadley next to Cheney, with Joshua Bolten at the opposite end of the table from the president. Robert Gates was traveling, so Eric Edelman, a former Cheney aide now serving as undersecretary of defense, represented him. As the navy steward worked his way around the table taking orders, most of the officials stuck with a simple fruit bowl. Cheney, on the other hand, ordered bacon and eggs. Hill was struck that the vice president would order something so different when everyone else was going light, especially since he had had four heart attacks.

Hill had just brokered a deal in which Pyongyang would disable its nuclear facilities and provide a complete list of all its programs while the United States would remove it from the list of state sponsors of terrorism and the list of countries penalized under the Trading with the Enemy Act, as well as end the banking sanctions that had frozen its $25 million. After years of fitful negotiations and confrontations, resolution seemed possible. If Bush could salvage Iraq and rid North Korea of its nuclear weapons in his final stretch in office, it would go a long way toward shaping a more positive legacy. Cheney was not so optimistic. He saw it as one more ruse by the North Koreans, one made all the more cynical by the secret intelligence showing that Pyongyang had been helping the Syrians build a nuclear capacity, a discovery not acknowledged to the public. How could they make a deal, Cheney wondered, with a country that was double dealing like that?

Bush understood that taking North Korea off the lists would mean little since other sanctions still applied. For years, states had been left on the terrorism and trading with the enemy lists not because they met specific criteria but simply because they were seen as bad actors.

"What we really need," Bush said, "is an assholes list." That would be more accurate.

Edelman served as the most vocal skeptic in the room, pressing Hill about his strategy. "What are you going to do about the stuff they have already weaponized?" he asked.

"You ought to be worried about the loose plutonium," Hill shot back. "That is what could be used by a terrorist to blow us up."

Hill grew so agitated that Bush intervened. "Chris, calm down," he said. The president made clear he wanted to get hold of all of North Korea's weapons and fuel. "They have to give up their nuclear weapons," he said. "That is the whole deal here. It is open kimono. He gets to have his Qaddafi moment now."

Through most of the discussion, Cheney remained silent, as he usually did. Bush finally turned to him. "Dick, would you like to ask something?"

Cheney looked over at Rice and Hill. "Well, I'm not as enthusiastic as some people here," he said, dismissing the whole venture with understatement.

Hill was not sure whether Cheney was looking at him or Rice, but he took it upon himself to push back.

"Mr. Vice President," Hill said, "I want to make something very clear. I'm not enthusiastic about this. I'm simply trying to do my job and get home at night."

Bush interjected. "Oh, Dick didn't mean anything like that," the president said. "He's just concerned about whether the North Koreans will ultimately deliver."

Rice picked up the ball and began explaining the strategy again. No one was overestimating how much they could trust the North Koreans, she said. But they did not have many alternatives.

Cheney remained unconvinced. Had the North Koreans given up their missile program? he asked pointedly. He knew full well they had not and asked the question only to make the point.

Hill started to jump in again, but Rice put her hand across his lap to restrain him and answered herself.

Then Cheney asked, "How do we know they don't have another plutonium reactor?"

The others assured him that a plutonium reactor was much harder to hide than uranium enrichment or other nuclear activities.

No one walked out with their minds changed. "The president is being sold a bill of goods," Edelman complained to Bolten. But Bush had settled the issue for now by blessing Hill's mission. As long as the president was determined to explore diplomacy, Cheney would have to swallow it. But it was not the last time they would debate the matter.

WHILE THE PRESIDENT focused on a possible legacy, the rest of the country was already beginning to move on, tired of the Bush years and fixated by the race to succeed him. For Bush, it was an odd sensation. For the first time in more than thirty years, neither he nor anyone in his family was on the ballot or anticipating being on the next one. And yet it seemed everyone was running against Bush—even the Republicans.

At Republican debates, the candidates were climbing all over each other to distance themselves from him. "I'm not a carbon copy of President Bush," declared Mitt Romney. Mike Huckabee, asked if he agreed with Bush's vision of democracy promotion, replied, "Absolutely not, because I don't think we can force people to accept our way of life, our way of government." On another occasion, John McCain declared that Bush's handling of the Iraq War had been a "train wreck."

Bush recognized that it was a promising cycle for Democrats and expected Hillary Clinton to succeed him. At times, he chortled at the notion. "Wait 'til her fat ass is sitting at this desk," he told aides at one point.

But he respected her strength and leadership skills and hoped that, in a way, her presidency could vindicate his. Clinton, the wife of his predecessor, had staked out a hawkish position since joining the Senate in 2001, even voting for the Iraq War. While harshly critical of Bush's handling of it, she had refused to repudiate that vote despite pummeling from the Left. During an off-the-record chat with television anchors one day, Bush recalled how Dwight Eisenhower criticized Harry Truman's record while running for president in 1952, only to adopt the early Cold War containment strategy he inherited, in effect institutionalizing a bipartisan approach that would endure for decades. The way Bush saw it, Clinton could be the Ike to his Truman. Although she had bashed him on the trail, he felt confident she would continue the broad direction he had set.

Her main opponent for the nomination was a newly elected senator from Illinois, Barack Obama, who even before winning his seat in 2004 had exhilarated Democrats with a stirring keynote address at John Kerry's convention declaring that "there's not a liberal America and a conservative America; there's the United States of America." Bush admired the young senator's skill but seemed offended at his rise from nowhere with pretensions to the presidency. He told visitors that Obama's remark during a Democratic debate that he would be willing to send American forces into Pakistan to chase terrorists even without Islamabad's permission was "stunning" in its "naiveté." On another occasion, after Obama attacked the administration, Bush arrived for a prep session for a speech fuming. "This cat isn't remotely qualified to handle it," Bush told aides. "This guy has no clue, I promise you. You think I wasn't qualified? I was qualified." Still, Bush was pleased that at a debate both Obama and Clinton refused to commit to removing all troops from Iraq in four years; the surge had changed the political dynamics enough to keep his would-be successors from boxing themselves in.

With time ticking down—Joshua Bolten had already given senior White House aides countdown clocks showing exactly how many hours were left to get things done—Bush was thinking about how to leave behind a war on terror that even a President Clinton could largely embrace. With Iraq improving by the month, he hoped to stabilize it enough so the next president would not feel compelled politically to pull out the remaining troops precipitously. He had already emptied the secret CIA prisons, negotiated for congressional authorization of military commissions for suspected terrorists, and pared back the harsh interrogation techniques that critics called torture. He was moving some prisoners out of Guantánamo in hopes of possibly closing it. He was also working with lawmakers to pass legislation explicitly legalizing the National Security Agency's warrantless surveillance program. "He was willing to cut loose some things that weren't going to survive and solidify things that could survive," Rice recalled. "And that was a really important part of the calculation for him."

STILL AT THE top of the list was Iraq. With the surge seemingly helping to turn the security situation around, the president focused on the political situation and pressed to formalize a new relationship between the United States and Iraq.

On the morning of November 26, he arrived at the Situation Room to sign a "declaration of principles" with Prime Minister Nouri al-Maliki that would commit them to negotiating a strategic agreement before Bush left office—an agreement to make an agreement. Just reaching that point had proved problematic enough, foreshadowing difficulties to come. In fact, as Bush took out a pen and signed the document before him, he did not realize that Maliki on the screen from Baghdad was passing his pen over his copies of the papers without actually signing.

At the last minute, Maliki had decided not to sign because he said he had not read the final wording of the document, but no one told Bush that the Iraqi prime minister was faking. Brett McGurk, the president's Iraq adviser, was in the room in Baghdad and waited for the video image to disappear before accosting Maliki's security adviser.

"Don't screw with the president of the United States," he said with barely controlled anger. "Review them now and sign."

Later that afternoon, Maliki's office called and said he had finally reviewed the papers and actually signed them. An embarrassing debacle was avoided.

With Rice's help, Bush was also trying to make progress elsewhere in the Middle East in hopes of leaving behind a better situation for his successor. The next day, November 27, he climbed onto Marine One with Rice for the short flight to Annapolis, where they were convening the Middle East peace talks—not a "summit," but now a "conference" instead of a "meeting," to the irritation of the Israelis who thought it raised the stakes for the event. Elliott Abrams, the deputy national security adviser and a strong Israel supporter, had opposed the session, whatever it was called, fearing that Palestinian sovereignty would simply result in a terrorist state. But he had lost out, convinced that Rice had undergone a "remarkable change" in her approach because of disenchantment with Israel's handling of the Lebanon War.

As Bush settled into the helicopter that would take him to the conference, officials from about forty countries were on hand for the most intense foray into the thicket of Israeli-Palestinian politics of the Bush-Cheney administration.

"Do I have an agreement?" Bush asked Rice.

"No, you don't," she admitted. "I've got them close, but you're going to have to deliver it yourself."

Bush sat back in his seat. "I can do that," he said.

As the helicopter cruised toward the U.S. Naval Academy, Stephen Hadley was busy working out an elaborate orchestration to keep Prime Minister Ehud Olmert and President Mahmoud Abbas in different rooms until Bush could talk with each of them separately. When he arrived, Bush shuttled between the two leaders, making clear they had to agree on a statement or risk failure. Near the end of the seventh year of his presidency, Bush found himself doing almost exactly what Bill Clinton had been doing in his final days in office.

By the time they came upstairs, everyone was ready to deal. Aides were sent to craft the final wording, and soon they had a joint statement pledging to negotiate a full-fledged peace treaty by the end of 2008 that would resolve long-standing disputes, "including all core issues without exception." It was yet another agreement to make an agreement, but one that, if fulfilled, would allow Bush to leave office complementing his legacy of war with a legacy of peace.

As he prepared to announce the agreement, Bush took a look at the final document, but the type was too small. "I can't read this," he said.

"Why?" asked an alarmed Rice, thinking he had a last-minute objection to something in the text.

"No, I really can't read this," he said. "I can't see it."

The next few minutes were a scramble as Hadley ran around trying to find a way to reprint the document in larger type.

Finally, Bush shrugged it off. "Forget it," he said. "They're waiting for us. I'll just use my reading glasses."

As Bush enjoyed the rare moment of accord, Cheney watched with concern. The goal was laudable, he thought, but unrealistic. He was not sure whether it was worth the investment of time and energy to pursue the same dream that had eluded presidents for decades. More significantly, the vice president was aghast that Syria had been invited to the conference. While President Bashar al-Assad had only sent a deputy foreign minister, the very presence of an outlaw state undercut everything they had been working toward. Less than three months after Israeli jets demolished a secret nuclear facility in Syria, the Damascus government was being welcomed to an international gathering with no consequence for its actions.

NOT INVITED AT all was Iran. The day after the summit opened, Bush and Cheney sat down with intelligence officials who briefed them on a new report on Iran's nuclear program that was about to radically alter their campaign against Tehran. After years of assuming that Iran was trying to build a nuclear bomb, the intelligence agencies had made a startling about-face: the new report concluded that while Iran did have a program to develop nuclear weapons in the past, it was shut down in the fall of 2003 just after American troops overthrew Saddam Hussein next door in Iraq.

Bush and Cheney had received updates about this evolving assessment in the months during which the report was being prepared, but it was still shocking. Starting in 2006, Bush had been participating in what aides called "deep dive" sessions with Iran analysts, digging into what was known and not known about the Islamic republic's nuclear quest. By June 2007, the intelligence agencies had assembled a nearly complete draft of a new National Intelligence Estimate about Iran's nuclear program still predicated on the judgment that it was actively seeking weapons.

Then, with Bush pressing for more information, the intelligence agencies came up with something new—a series of intercepted phone calls and e-mails, including some involving Mohsen Fakhrizadeh, Iran's preeminent nuclear scientist, complaining that his funding and work had been frozen by the government. Bush was told about the intercepts by Mike McConnell, the director of national intelligence, during a morning briefing in August. *Could it be?* Bush asked if the intercepts could be an elaborate ruse to throw the Americans off track. But intelligence analysts went back and rescrubbed more than a thousand pieces of evidence while figuring out exactly what would be involved in creating a deception like that, only to conclude that the program really had been shut down. Michael Hayden, the CIA director, and his deputy, Stephen Kappes, even convened a murder board to grill analysts about their data.

Why Iran would have halted weapons design in 2003 became a subject of intense debate within the intelligence community. Some officials credited the Iraq invasion, reasoning that with more than 100,000 American soldiers just across the border, the mullahs in Tehran must have been intimidated. But when Hayden voiced that theory to the analysts, he was shot down. "Sir, that is an interesting theory," he was told, "but there is no evidence." Instead, the analysts said it was likelier that Tehran shut down weapons design after an opposition group exposed to the outside world Iran's undisclosed nuclear facility in Natanz in 2002.

The final study presented to Bush and Cheney on November 28 reported that Iran halted its weaponization program in 2003 "primarily in response to international pressure" and that the intelligence agencies were "moderately confident" that "Tehran had not restarted its nuclear weapons program as of mid-2007." But it added that "we do not know whether it currently intends to develop nuclear weapons." Sophisticated readers understood the report did not mean Iran had given up its aspirations for nuclear weapons. The bomb-making program was the least challenging part of the development of nuclear weapons and the easiest to resume. Iran was still working to master the more difficult science of enriching uranium, the real key to any weapons program; once it succeeded at that, it could restart the bomb-making program that would put the newly enriched uranium to use.

But the report was not written for the general public. Now Bush and Cheney were in a bind. McConnell and Hayden did not want to release the report on the principle that intelligence should remain classified, but if it were ever to leak, it would look as if the administration had covered up evidence undercutting its campaign against Iran. If released as written, on the other hand, it would shatter the international coalition even as they were poised to pass a third round of sanctions at the UN Security Council. Just five years after mistaken intelligence helped lead to war in Iraq, the credibility of American statements would be brought into question. Even after he had been told of the intercepts, Bush in October had publicly warned of the possibility of "World War III" if Iran's nuclear ambitions were not thwarted; this report would make it look as if he were again exaggerating evidence to wage war on a Muslim country.

Cheney suggested simply rejecting the report, but that was quickly dismissed as implausible. Rewriting the report, even just to clarify that the new finding did not mean Iran was not pursuing nuclear weapons through uranium enrichment, would also be unthinkable because, no matter how clean the motives, it would be perceived as manipulating the intelligence.

"This is a disaster," Stephen Hadley told Bush. "I don't think we can make any changes to this NIE."

"You're right," Bush said.

Bush passed along the new report to Prime Minister Olmert while he was in town for the peace conference, and Cheney told Minister of Defense Ehud Barak. But they kept the bombshell news from other participants at the conference, not to mention their European allies, as they tried to figure out what to do. After a weekend of debate, the administration released a declassified version of the report's key judgments on December 3. An uproar ensued. "It was a huge blow, huge blow," Hadley recalled. Chancellor Angela

Merkel had been planning to meet that very week with German industrial leaders to press them to stop doing business with Iran; as soon as she heard about the new American intelligence report, the meeting was canceled.

Bush tried to do damage control, calling other leaders in the coalition to make clear that the report did not change anything and to solicit support for more sanctions. On December 4, he reached Vladimir Putin. It was a measure of how deeply concerned Bush was about losing Russian support against Iran that he buttered up Putin about just-held regional elections that had been widely condemned as unfair.

"The results give us a reason to rejoice," Putin said of the elections.

"You are popular," Bush said. "People like you a lot."

"Other parties did well," Putin said.

"You're being modest," Bush said.

Bush turned to his real purpose in calling, the Iran report. "I'm worried people will see this and want to change policy," he explained. Bush noted a program that once existed could be easily reconstituted. He hoped Russia would send a firm message to Iran that there is a "better way forward."

Putin said he would. "In the waiting room, I have the new Iranian national security adviser," he told Bush. "I will take into account what you told me."

Bush reached Hu Jintao on December 6 and made the same argument. "A country that had one can restart one," he told the Chinese president.

Hu said the report demonstrated that the international community had been successful in pressing Tehran. "We will urge the Iranians to come back to negotiations," he told Bush.

AS WINTER SETTLED IN, Prime Minister Nouri al-Maliki's many foes in Baghdad were plotting to push him out, and some White House officials agreed he should go.

Among them was Cheney, who said the idea "merits our consideration" and favored replacing him with Adel Abdul Mahdi, a Shiite leader who had served as vice president and whose fluent English had helped make him many friends in the administration. Brett McGurk, who had watched Maliki fake signing the agreement with Bush, wrote a memo to Bush declaring Maliki "a significant impediment to our vital objectives in Iraq" because of his governing style and recommending that if his enemies moved against him, "we should not stop it."

But Gates argued against getting involved, foreseeing nothing but problems heading down that road. Bush agreed. "I know there are people in this room who believe Maliki needs to go," he told advisers in the Situation

Room on December 17. "That's not our policy. We're in the middle of the damn surge. It took six damn months to choose Maliki and form a government. Something like that now would be totally destabilizing."

Instead, he sent Rice to Baghdad to tell Maliki to shape up while she blocked the move against him. Sitting down with the prime minister, Rice was as blunt as she had ever been. "You're a terrible prime minister," she told him. "Without progress and without an agreement, you'll be on your own, hanging from a lamppost." Then she met his adversaries and said a change in government would cost them American support.

Amid the international intrigue, Bush continued to fence with the Democratic Congress. He vetoed expansion of a children's health-care program and threatened to veto a bill passed by the House banning the CIA from using harsh interrogation techniques. He refused to send top aides to testify about the U.S. attorney firings, prompting the Senate Judiciary Committee to approve contempt citations against Joshua Bolten and Karl Rove.

But in a rare bipartisan breakthrough, Bush and the Democrats came together on energy legislation that, while not as ambitious as many wanted, represented one of the most significant steps since the oil crises of the 1970s. The measure raised fuel economy standards for cars and light trucks to an average of thirty-five miles per hour by 2020, the first such increase in twenty-two years. It also required a dramatic expansion of ethanol production and began phasing out incandescent lightbulbs. While formulated differently, it tracked the goals Bush had set out in his State of the Union address. A bipartisan commission estimated the law would reduce projected oil consumption by 2.8 million barrels a day by 2020 and reduce projected carbon dioxide emissions by 4 percent. "The legislation I'm about to sign should say to the American people that we can find common ground on critical issues," Bush said at a signing ceremony on December 19, flanked by Nancy Pelosi and Harry Reid. "And there's more we can accomplish together."

Bush headed to the Crawford ranch for the holiday satisfied with the victory and cautiously optimistic about his final year to come. Iraq was looking calmer, with just twenty-three American military fatalities in December, the second-lowest month since the invasion nearly five years earlier. North Korea might not make the end-of-the-year deadline for its declaration, but there was hope for progress. While Bush had gotten little of his agenda through the new Congress, he had used his veto to demonstrate he would not roll over.

But the year would not end without more trouble. Two days after Christmas, Bush woke up to the news that the former prime minister Benazir Bhutto had been assassinated in Pakistan. Bush and Cheney had spent much of the past months managing the volatile political situation with the critical American ally. Bush had been fond of President Pervez Musharraf but found the Pakistani leader an increasingly problematic friend. Musharraf had declared a national emergency, suspended the constitution, and fired the chief justice with whom he had been feuding, precipitating a fresh crisis. Only after months of pressure from Bush did he finally agree to step down as army chief of staff and govern as a civilian. Amid the unrest, Bhutto had returned from years of exile and was campaigning to return to power when a suicide bomber detonated explosives blowing them both up.

Bush put on a suit and rode over to the Crawford Elementary School to address reporters. His face looked drawn and tired. "The United States strongly condemns this cowardly act by murderous extremists who are trying to undermine Pakistan's democracy," he said.

BUSH RETURNED TO Washington after the holiday to begin his final year in office greeted by more bad news, this time domestic. On January 2, 2008, he met with Henry Paulson, who told him that the economy had slowed significantly. For Bush, this chipped away at the one factor that had been a bedrock through international controversy. For fifty-two straight months, the American economy had added jobs, the longest uninterrupted period of job growth on record. But it was relatively weak job creation, and now a bursting housing bubble was beginning to ripple through the system.

Warning signs had been growing for weeks, and Bush authorized Paulson to go to Capitol Hill and take the temperature for a stimulus package that would provide a jolt to the economy. After Paulson's soundings in Congress, Bush on January 18 called for a $145 billion package. Cheney for once showed up to stand behind him during the announcement. With a surprising ease that revealed the degree of bipartisan economic anxiety, Democrats came to an agreement with Paulson and Bush within a week on a $152 billion package that ultimately would give $600 tax breaks to individuals or $1,200 per couple, plus $300 per-child credits and other tax relief for businesses. The package had come together in part because Bush pushed Paulson out in front while largely staying invisible himself.

The economic troubles were already transforming the race to succeed Bush. Where Iraq had dominated the political debate for the past few years, the growing success of the surge had alleviated some of the public anxiety about the war, and the rapidly deteriorating economy had surpassed it on voters' worry list. On the sidelines, Bush watched the vitriolic campaign unfold with a mixture of interest, disaffection, and relief. When Bill Clinton, campaigning for his wife, was called a racist for comments he made the day of the South Carolina primary, Bush sympathized, having been there himself, and called his predecessor to commiserate.

As it turned out, Bush had a little Clinton in him when he took the lectern in the House chamber a couple of days later, on January 28, to deliver the State of the Union address outlining the agenda for his last year. Gone were the grand dreams of remaking Social Security, immigration law, or the tax code. In their place were modest initiatives, like those Clinton used to propose, such as hiring preferences for military spouses. The confrontational foreign policy of old was replaced with talk of Middle East peacemaking and diplomacy with rogue nations.

Bush had taken office with so much derision for his predecessor that critics defined his approach toward governing as ABC, or Anything But Clinton. He would not play "small ball" with incremental policies, he declared, nor would he coddle North Korea or waste time mediating between Israelis and Arabs. But as the end of his tenure neared, Bush appeared to be adopting some of his predecessor's playbook. His ambitions consisted mainly in consolidating what he had achieved, such as pumping $30 billion more into his fight against AIDS in Africa, reauthorizing No Child Left Behind, and codifying policies that steered more federal funds to religious charities.

Hoping to cement his legacy, Bush appealed to lawmakers to set aside the contest already raging for his job. "In this election year, let us show our fellow Americans that we recognize our responsibilities and are determined to meet them," he said. "Let us show them that Republicans and Democrats can compete for votes and cooperate for results at the same time."

34

"What is this, a cruel hoax?"

His advice discarded on Syria, North Korea, the Middle East, secret prisons, and other issues, Vice President Cheney found a new way to express his disenchantment with the direction of the administration that winter. The issue was gun rights.

The dispute concerned a case before the Supreme Court, *District of Columbia v. Heller*, which challenged the constitutionality of a long-standing handgun ban in the city of Washington, D.C. A lower court had ruled that the ban violated the Second Amendment right to bear arms, and for the first time the highest court planned to decide whether the amendment applied to individual Americans or simply to militias as some had long argued.

Rather than weigh in on the side of gun owners, the Justice Department had decided to split the difference with a brief by Solicitor General Paul D. Clement arguing that the court should recognize the individual right but reject the categorical approach of the lower court and send the case back under "a more flexible standard of review" that would not invalidate a host of federal gun laws like the ban on machine guns. Joel Kaplan, the deputy chief of staff, heard of the Justice Department's plan only the night before and was aggravated. He scrambled to see if it could be changed, engaging in a heated discussion with Clement. Finally, he and Joshua Bolten took the issue to Bush.

"What do you want to do?" Bolten asked. "Do you want to let him file? If we try to step in at this point, there's going to be a big dustup."

Bush decided not to intervene, letting the brief be filed.

But Cheney was angry at the Justice Department's equivocation. So when Senator Kay Bailey Hutchison came to him with a friend-of-the-court brief that pro-gun lawmakers were planning to submit and suggested he sign in his capacity as president of the Senate, he was intrigued. He talked with David Addington, who assured him that he would be within his rights. A couple of days later, Cheney called Hutchison and signed on without telling anyone else in the White House.

When Hutchison released the brief on February 8 with the names of 55 senators, 250 House members, and the vice president, the White House was caught off guard. Even though they too had been unhappy with the Justice Department brief, Bolten and Kaplan were were shocked to learn from news reports that Cheney had publicly taken a position at odds with the administration's. Kaplan called Cheney's adviser Neil Patel,

"What the fuck are you guys doing?" he demanded.

Patel had no idea, having just heard about it from a National Rifle Association lobbyist. Patel called Addington, who told him he deliberately left the staff in the dark.

"I want to protect you so you can honestly say you knew nothing about it because the White House is going to be hot," Addington said.

The White House was indeed hot. "They were so angry it's hard to say how angry they were," said Patel.

Bolten went to see Bush and asked for permission to chastise the vice president.

"You can't have more than one administration position," Bolten said, "and the vice president can't have a position different from the rest of the White House."

Bush was more amused than angry and laughed a little. He gave Bolten permission to go see Cheney.

Bolten walked down the hall to the vice president's office and slipped in the door. He explained that the gun brief had crossed a line. But rather than confront Cheney directly, Bolten pinned blame on Addington.

"It's a process foul," he said, "and if I may, I'm going to speak to your chief of staff about it."

"I didn't know you weren't aware," Cheney said. "But I did it in my capacity as president of the Senate." With a half smile, Cheney told Bolten he was free to talk with Addington.

Bolten met with Addington to lay down the law.

Addington, unruffled and clearly confident of Cheney's support, reminded Bolten that he worked for the vice president, not the president's chief of staff, and that his paycheck came from the Senate.

"Understood," Bolten replied, "but if we have another episode like this, I will make sure that all of your belongings and your mail are forwarded to your tiny office in the Senate and you won't be welcome back inside the gates of the White House."

Addington got the point.

The issue went away relatively quickly, and Bush never raised the matter with Cheney, perhaps uncomfortable with a direct confrontation or perhaps regretting his administration's tepid position. Indeed, the same day the brief became public, Bush praised Cheney in a speech to the Conservative Political Action Conference.

"He's the best vice president in history," Bush said, repeating a line he had used in the past, even though it seemed to slight his own father.

Then, with a smile, he added, "Mother may have a different opinion. But don't tell her I said this, but my opinion is the one that counts."

Either way, Cheney's break with Bush on gun rights was seen in some quarters of the White House as a bold act of defiance and frustration by the best vice president in history. "Cheney's view was that all these items—we were not doing these things due to sincerely held policy beliefs but because they were just playing better from a PR perspective," said one White House official. "This was his just a little bit of an F-you to all that."

WITH ALL THE crises at home, Bush found a little respite abroad. On February 15, he boarded Air Force One for a final six-day, five-nation trip to Africa, where he had mounted an unprecedented campaign to fight AIDS, malaria, and poverty in some of the poorest corners of the world. The PEPFAR program he created had invested $15 billion in stemming AIDS on the continent, and Bush was trying to persuade Congress to double it. Another program he started called the Millennium Challenge Corporation had steered billions of dollars to nations that promised concrete progress toward reform. As counterintuitive as it might sound for a conservative Republican, Bush had arguably done more for Africa than any American president before him.

As he made his way across the continent, Bush was showered with appreciation. In Benin, it was proclaimed George W. Bush Day. In Tanzania, tens of thousands thronged the streets to greet his motorcade, and dancing women wore skirts and blouses with his face emblazoned on them. In Ghana, a major road was christened the George Bush Motorway. At his last stop in Liberia, where Bush helped push out President Charles Taylor in 2003 and sent marines and money to help stabilize the country after a fourteen-year civil war, they sang about him on the radio, crooning his name and warbling, "Thank you for the peace process."

Even as Americans back home were considering electing the first black president, the current president had a devoted following in Africa. "Of course, people talk with excitement of Obama," Jakaya Kikwete, the president of Tanzania, said with Bush at his side in the courtyard of his government headquarters in Dar es Salaam. But Kikwete added, "For us, the most important thing is, let him be as good a friend of Africa as President Bush has been." Little wonder. In Tanzania, Bush had spent $817 million to provide medicine and other care to hundreds of thousands of AIDS patients. During his visit, the two leaders signed a $698 million, five-year Millennium Challenge contract to rebuild roads, expand electricity generation, and provide more clean water. Accompanied by Bob Geldof, the rocker-activist, Bush savored the interlude between crises and later called the trip "the best of the presidency." Condoleezza Rice thought that may have been the happiest moment of Bush's tenure. "He loved being in Africa," she observed. "The last trip was very validating."

Bush was not as popular back home, even at the campaign headquarters of the Republican hoping to succeed him. John McCain had sewn up the nomination and was stopping by the White House for the ritual blessing from the incumbent. But that did not mean either man was looking forward to it.

A misunderstanding sent the hates-to-wait president to the North Portico to receive McCain long minutes before the senator actually showed up on March 5. Bush kept his humor with the cameras on, even doing a playful tap dance for reporters, but aides afterward got an earful. When McCain finally arrived, the two went into the Rose Garden.

"I hope that he will campaign for me as much as is keeping with his busy schedule," McCain said.

Bush was more forthright. "If my showing up and endorsing him helps, or if I'm against him and it helps him, either way, I want him to win," Bush said.

While McCain calculated how to distance himself from Bush, the president turned his attention to awkward personnel issues. Tim Goeglein, the White House liaison with the religious conservative community, resigned after he was discovered plagiarizing columns for a hometown newspaper. Bush was pained and summoned Goeglein to the Oval Office. "Tim, I have known mercy and grace in my own life," Bush told him, "and I am offering it to you now. You are forgiven." Bush was somewhat less forgiving of Admiral Fox Fallon, the head of Central Command, who suggested to *Esquire* magazine that he was single-handedly resisting a White House drive to war with Iran. "Do we have a MacArthur problem?" Bush asked Robert Gates, "Is he challenging the commander-in-chief?" But when Bush indicated he might let it pass, Cheney recalled his dismissal of General Michael Dugan during the Gulf War. "I'd fire him in a heartbeat," Cheney told Bush. Admiral Mike Mullen, the chairman of the Joint Chiefs, agreed and with Bush's permission told Fallon to step down.

THE ECONOMIC CRISIS began to worsen dramatically the day after Fallon's resignation. Bush was scheduled to fly to New York to give a speech at the Economic Club on Wall Street amid an accelerating collapse of the housing market and increasing cash flow problems among major investment firms. Bush was going over the text of the speech in the Oval Office on March 12 when Henry Paulson noticed that it ruled out bailouts of any investment banks.

"Don't say that," Paulson cautioned.

"We're not going to do a bailout, are we?" Bush asked.

He was not predicting one, Paulson said, but they did not want to box themselves in either.

"Mr. President, the fact is, the whole system is so fragile we don't know what we might have to do if a financial institution is about to go down."

The next day, Bush got a phone call from Paulson letting him know that they were on the verge of just that scenario. Bear Stearns, one of the venerable investment houses of Wall Street, was about to go under. Bear had been one of the most aggressive players investing in risky home loans and now was paying the price with the meltdown of the subprime mortgage market.

"This is the real thing," Paulson told Bush. "We're in danger of having a firm go down. We're going to have to go into overdrive."

Bush was initially reluctant. A free-market approach had to allow for even large institutions to go out of business if they made bad decisions.

But Paulson argued that Bear's failure would have vast consequences for the whole system.

On Friday morning, March 14, Paulson made clear that the government would have to intervene. "Mr. President," he warned Bush, "you can take out that line in your speech about no bailouts." By the time Air Force One landed in New York, Paulson and Ben Bernanke had orchestrated the takeover of Bear Stearns by JPMorgan Chase, with the help of a $29 billion credit line from the Federal Reserve, effectively ending an eighty-five-year institution but averting a wider calamity.

"It seems like I showed up in an interesting moment," Bush said to laughter as he began his speech to the Economic Club of New York. He praised Paulson and Bernanke but also argued against a broader government action to turn around the housing market. "The temptation of Washington is to say that anything short of a massive government intervention in the housing market amounts to inaction," he said. "I strongly disagree with that sentiment."

He compared government economic policy to driving on a rough patch. "If you ever get stuck in a situation like that, you know full well it's important not to overcorrect—because when you overcorrect, you end up in the ditch."

His critics were not persuaded. Before the end of the day, Democrats like Senator Charles Schumer of New York were already comparing the president to Herbert Hoover.

"We're going to get killed on this, aren't we?" Bush asked Paulson.

BUSH UNDERSTOOD THAT bailing out a Wall Street bank would not be popular, and a part of him was chagrined at that. Not Cheney. As the two of them progressed through their last year in office, their public standing had sunk so low that it had become almost like a badge of honor: what they were doing must be about principle, since it sure was not a political winner.

But there was a fine line between ignoring the fickle winds of popularity and losing the consent of the governed. Cheney skated near that line with defiance. On March 19, the fifth anniversary of the start of the Iraq War, he traveled to the region to highlight the progress of the surge. During a stop in Oman, he gave an interview to Martha Raddatz of ABC News.

"Two-thirds of Americans say it's not worth the fighting," she told him.

"So?" Cheney answered.

Raddatz seemed taken aback.

"So?" she said. "You don't care what the American people think?"

"No," he said, "I think you cannot be blown off course by the fluctuations in the public opinion polls."

The polls actually were not fluctuating; they were heading in one inexorable direction. Even with the evident success of the surge, Bush and Cheney had lost the American public on Iraq. As Cheney saw it, popular opinion should not stop them from doing what was needed to protect the country. "He believed that losing these wars was the worst possible outcome for the United States," said John Hannah, his national security adviser. "He was convinced that we had to win, and you got the sense that he wouldn't be swayed by bad polls or a lack of public support." As Liz Cheney put it, "Everything else was less important, and if it meant your reputation was damaged, that was what you had to live with."

A few days later, the situation in Iraq took a dramatic turn. Shiite militias had fled to the port city of Basra in the southeast near the Iranian border, the hub of the country's oil industry. Prime Minister Nouri al-Maliki had received reports of women being beaten for failing to properly cover up and even mutilated if accused of sexual indiscretions. In a brash move, Maliki ordered the Iraqi army south to take on the militias, only informing David Petraeus after the decision had been made. Petraeus was stunned at the recklessness; without any preparation, there was no way for American forces to support such an operation. "It was very, very precipitous and arguably bordering on impulsive," Petraeus concluded. But Maliki disregarded Petraeus's advice, even traveling to Basra personally to oversee the operation. The American fears were well-founded; Iraqi units were ill-prepared and ran out of ammunition, fuel, and other supplies, and in some cases soldiers refused to fight fellow Shiites. Petraeus ordered Special Forces, Apache helicopters, and Predator drones to follow the prime minister and give him support, but with so little coordination "we couldn't figure out who were the good guys and who were the bad guys."

At the White House, the national security team was in a panic. Condoleezza Rice called Bush to tell him Maliki's government could fall. The CIA offered a grim prognosis. "Everybody here thought this was going to be a disaster," recalled Douglas Lute, the Iraq War coordinator. Lute thought Maliki had gambled everything. "If he doesn't get killed, he's going to cripple himself politically because he's going to be shown as unable to deliver."

But Bush did not see it that way. "Don't tell me this is a bad thing," he said, preempting Stephen Hadley and Brett McGurk when they arrived at the Oval Office to brief him. "Maliki said he would do this and now he's doing it."

For the first time, the Shiite prime minister was taking on Shiite militias as the Americans had asked him to do. Bush believed Maliki, however rashly, was finally showing leadership. While he did not say it out loud, there may have been a part of the old Texan who appreciated the cowboy nature of the move; Maliki was following his gut with bold action, just as Bush believed he did.

When he sat down for a videoconference with Petraeus and Ambassador Ryan Crocker on March 24, Bush stood alone in his assessment.

"This has some potential to be dicey here," Petraeus said with understatement. While the Americans would of course provide support, he told Bush, "you've got to understand there are some serious risks involved here."

Bush said he understood the risks but saw the development as a breakthrough, not a debacle. They had to trust Maliki. "We have wanted him to step up and lead," he said. "Our job here is to support him, not to try to convince him not to do it." They had to make sure Maliki succeeded. "This is going to be a decisive moment."

His team on the ground was not so optimistic. In Baghdad, Crocker, a Bush favorite whose glass-half-empty reports had earned him the presidential nickname Sunshine, turned off the microphone so he could not be heard back in Washington. "I hope it's going to be decisive the way he hopes it will," he told Petraeus.

It very nearly was not. Maliki's headquarters was shelled and his personal bodyguard and childhood friend was killed in the bombardment. Shia militias in Baghdad likewise responded with force, peppering Crocker's palace headquarters in the Green Zone with rockets, nearly a hundred in a forty-eight-hour stretch. But in the end, Petraeus scrambled enough force and Maliki showed enough fortitude that the militias backed off. Maliki reasserted government control over Basra. Suddenly what looked like a breaking point became the moment he finally became a national leader. "He came back from Basra a different Maliki," Lute observed. Senator Lindsey Graham, who talked about it with Maliki afterward, agreed that the Iraqi prime minister was a "changed man" who "went from being docile to being John Wayne."

WITH THE ARRIVAL of spring, Bush was preparing to head to Bucharest, Romania, for his final NATO summit. He had presided over the expansion of NATO in 2004, when seven new countries joined the alliance, including Lithuania, Estonia, and Latvia, the three Baltic states that had once been part of the Soviet Union. Now the alliance was ready to offer membership to two more Eastern European countries: Albania and Croatia.

The real question was what to do about two other former Soviet republics aspiring to membership: Ukraine and Georgia. The issue was extremely sensitive. The so-called color revolutions that toppled calcified regimes and installed democratically elected leaders in Georgia in 2003 and Ukraine in 2004 had deeply alarmed Vladimir Putin, who saw them as American-inspired attempts to establish a ring of pro-Washington allies around Russia. Further integration with the West would only prove the point.

What the two countries were asking for was not NATO membership but a preliminary step called a "membership action plan" that would require them to spend several years upgrading their militaries and solidifying democratic institutions before any decision on actual membership. But even that was enough to become one of the defining foreign policy fights of Bush's final year. Bush found the idea enticing because it seemed to fit the freedom agenda. For once, Cheney was in agreement, though less out of romantic idealism than a hard-eyed geopolitical calculation that it was in the interest of the United States to keep Moscow from reasserting dominance over its neighbors. The louder the Russian opposition grew to Georgia and Ukraine joining NATO, the more convinced Cheney was that it was worth doing.

Germany, joined by France, opposed the idea, seeing it as unnecessarily provocative. Ukraine and Georgia were too volatile. Eastern European countries like Poland and the Baltic states, however, favored reaching out to the two former Soviet republics, mindful of their own years in Moscow's shadow. American intelligence experts briefed Bush, Cheney, and the rest of the national security team, pressing their assessment that European opposition was too great for the United States to succeed. The briefing seemed to rub the vice president the wrong way.

"So you're saying you're against freedom and democracy?" Cheney asked, with a wry look on his face. He was being humorous, and Bush stifled a smirk, but it was barbed humor.

"No, Mr. Vice President," replied Fiona Hill, one of the intelligence analysts. "We didn't say that."

Afterward, Cheney's aide Joe Wood summoned Hill to complain. He thought she was leaning so far forward in her analysis of the obstacles that she was effectively taking sides.

"You're not with the policy," she later remembered him saying.

"We're not supposed to be with the policy, are we?" she retorted. They were there to give their best professional analysis.

The issue came to a head during a National Security Council meeting. Rice and Robert Gates expressed caution, arguing that they did not have to do this now. Gates was hardly soft when it came to Russia; an old cold warrior, he had come back from his first meeting with Putin to tell colleagues that, unlike Bush, "I looked in his eyes and I saw the same KGB killer I've seen my whole life." But Gates thought trying to bring Ukraine and Georgia into NATO "was truly overreaching." Instead, he and Rice recommended a halfway step that would encourage the two former Soviet republics without another blowup with Germany and France.

Hadley, knowing the president was inclined the other way, called on Victoria Nuland, a former Cheney aide who was now ambassador to NATO. Speaking from Brussels on a video connection, Nuland argued that Georgia and Ukraine had done what they had been asked, conducting relatively clean elections, enacting political reforms, fighting corruption, and working to get their economies back on track. "If they want it and they've met the criteria, how can the United States be the ones saying no?" she asked.

Bush agreed. He wanted to push for the two countries. He hoped to make a deal with Chancellor Angela Merkel of Germany, calculating that the French were following Berlin. "This is about me and Angela," Bush told aides.

But during a videoconference, Merkel refused to go along. Bush resigned himself to a fight in Bucharest. As he was about to hang up with Merkel, he told her lightly, "I will see you at the OK Corral."

As if the dynamics were not tricky enough, Putin further complicated them by inviting Bush to visit him in Sochi, a resort town in southern Russia, immediately following the NATO summit. That could be awkward depending on what happened in Bucharest, so Bush was reluctant. He also noticed the harshening of Putin's anti-American rhetoric; at a conference in Munich and a later speech in Moscow, Putin had criticized the United States, once even comparing it to "the Third Reich."

Bush called Putin to see if he could trust that the meeting would not be a setup. "Look, the only way I can come is if you don't pull a Munich on me in Bucharest," Bush told him, as he later described the conversation to aides.

Putin agreed, and Bush accepted the invitation.

Once he got to Bucharest, Bush ran into stiff resistance from Merkel. But leaders of several Eastern European countries defiantly surrounded her, arguing for a stronger statement. No one was more sensitive to Russian intimidation than those who had lived under Soviet domination for decades. In the end, while Georgia and Ukraine were not put on the official membership track, the Eastern Europeans won a formulation in the summit communiqué that actually seemed to offer more certainty: "We agreed today that these countries will become members of NATO." *Will become*, period, no caveats. Bush took that as a victory.

But the decision to split the difference ended up angering both Putin and his Georgian nemesis, President Mikheil Saakashvili, a young firebrand who aligned himself with the United States and went out of his way to provoke Moscow. Putin, invited as a guest to the NATO summit, surprised everyone by showing up in Bucharest early and crashing a dinner of alliance leaders. From Georgia, Saakashvili railed about Western fecklessness. Some back in Washington worried that a hornet's nest had been stirred unnecessarily. "The Russians were furious; the Georgians were furious," remembered Fiona Hill, the intelligence officer who had briefed Cheney. "They weren't listening to all the admonishments to keep a cool head."

After the NATO summit, Bush visited Putin in Sochi. It was their twenty-eighth and final meeting as presidents, with Putin preparing to step down in favor of his handpicked successor, Dmitry Medvedev, while taking up the post of prime minister. Some in Cheney's office later worried that Bush had not been firm enough in warning Putin not to take action against Georgia. Others came away from discussions with the Georgians fearing that Saakashvili had interpreted his talks with Bush to be a "flashing yellow light" subtly supporting him in any military confrontation with Moscow. Bush's staff sent further messages trying to disabuse anyone of such misimpressions, but in the dangerous international game of telephone it was unclear what was being heard.

WITH THE ARRIVAL of spring, the Bush and Cheney camps were wrestling over one last domestic initiative. Bush was itching to do something enduring on climate change, while Cheney viewed it as political pandering with disastrous consequences for the economy.

In the seven years since he renounced the Kyoto climate change treaty and disavowed his campaign promise to impose a cap on power plant emissions, Bush had rarely made the issue a cause. While investing billions of dollars in research and new technologies, he had resisted government mandates that environmentalists insisted were necessary. Bush privately bristled at what he considered sky-is-falling alarmism by the liberal, elitist Hollywood crowd.

But ever so gradually, his views had evolved. He found the science increasingly persuasive and believed more needed to be done. The end of his presidency loomed, and he did not want to be known as the president who stood by while a crisis gathered. Now he bristled not at the Hollywood types but at the notion that he did not care. In the past eighteen months, he had cited the danger of climate change in his State of the Union address for the first time, convened a conference of major world polluters to start working on an international accord to follow Kyoto, and signed legislation cutting gasoline consumption and, by extension, greenhouse gases. He even invited his old rival Al Gore for a forty-minute talk about global warming.

Advisers like Joshua Bolten, Henry Paulson, and Condoleezza Rice were now pushing for more aggressive action, possibly even a version of the so-called cap-and-trade system promoted by his critics, a system in which emissions were limited but polluters could purchase credits to offset them from more efficient energy producers. The White House staff had secretly developed models for a cap-and-trade system for discussion purposes. Jim Connaughton, chairman of the Council on Environmental Quality and Bolten's brother-in-law, and Ed Lazear, chairman of the Council of Economic Advisers, were assigned to produce a policy that addressed the climate concerns without major economic damage. Their review came to be referred to as "Conazear."

Rice, for one, "wanted something more robust on climate change," especially since John McCain supported a cap-and-trade system just as his two Democratic opponents, Barack Obama and Hillary Clinton, did. "We were arguing that the U.S. is going to get into this in a big way in the next administration," said David Gordon, Rice's policy planning director. "They're going to take credit for it. Why don't we set the thing in motion? We won't get it all the way so you won't have to take too much on, Mr. President, but why don't you have part of your legacy being really setting this up?"

Bush concurred. In conversations with aides, he agreed to cap power plant emissions as he had promised in the 2000 campaign, in effect reversing his reversal in the letter Cheney had him sign in the early months of his presidency. But he wanted to structure it in a way that would not drive jobs overseas. Connaughton and Lazear, working with Keith Hennessey, the president's national economics adviser, developed what they called a hybrid model. The government would impose a market-based cap that would reduce emissions as far as possible without making the cost of compliance so expensive that firms felt compelled to relocate. Then, to get the rest of the way to long-term targets, the government would offer financial incentives to encourage industrial polluters to voluntarily curb emissions further. They called it cap and trade with a safety valve.

To Cheney, it seemed that Bush was reversing himself on cap and trade not out of a genuine reevaluation of the policy but out of concerns over legacy and politics. If the president really wanted to do something on climate change, Cheney aides said he should simply impose a tax on carbon emissions. While not enthusiastic about taxes, they argued that it would be the more economically rational way to approach the problem because it would motivate industry to clean up smokestacks without having the government effectively managing a major sector of the economy. And to the extent that a carbon tax would increase energy prices, the government could turn around and give it back to consumers through tax credits. "We had an extremely robust debate over it," remembered Neil Patel, the vice president's domestic policy adviser.

Others in the White House fought the idea too. Ed Gillespie thought that it was way too late in the administration and that the president was far too weak politically to make anything actually happen, but it would alienate the remaining base supporters they still had. He felt strongly enough to bring his concerns to Bush in a one-on-one conversation. But while Cheney and Gillespie could not stop the policy, they did not give up. Bush wanted the speech announcing his new strategy written in a flexible enough way that it would not simply prescribe a solution but outline principles and invite lawmakers to introduce their own ideas. That instruction opened the door to a complex drafting and editing process. Advocates of the new strategy like Connaughton wanted to use the phrase "cap and trade" in the speech, but Cheney and his allies managed to cut it out on the argument that it would close the door to collaboration with Republicans in Congress. "There were a lot of questions whether to say 'cap and trade,' and the reason we didn't is it was so specific as to a particular market-based approach as to not allow room or space for Republicans in particular but also the industrial-state Democrats to get involved in the design of a proper market-based approach," Connaughton recalled. "Maybe we were too intellectual about it, and there's some that clearly wanted to say 'cap and trade' and there's some that clearly did not want to say 'cap and trade,' but the reality is our proposal was based on the combination of a market-based mechanism and incentives."

The final draft of the speech had Bush call for a new national goal of stopping the growth of greenhouse gas emissions by 2025. But rather than outline specifically what needed to be done to achieve such a goal, the president would lay out broad parameters and describe "the right way" and "the wrong way" to proceed. "The wrong way is to raise taxes, duplicate mandates, or demand sudden and drastic emissions cuts that have no chance of being realized and every chance of hurting our economy," Bush said in the Rose Garden on April 16. "The right way is to set realistic goals for reducing emissions consistent with advances in technology, while increasing our energy security and ensuring our economy can continue to prosper and grow."

In the end, Cheney's office had muddied the language enough that no one even realized the president had agreed to a cap-and-trade system. "Most people looked around and had no idea what he just said because it was a big muddle," Patel said. "It was so embarrassing for the Bush folks that they just dropped it." Connaughton was among those who wished the words "cap and trade" had been in the speech. "Looking back, maybe we were too cute by half," he said. "But our intention was to create an opening for the conservatives to engage because that was the only way to get a bill through."

ON THE INTERNATIONAL front, Bush was also rushing to put in place what he could for his successor. He promoted David Petraeus to take over for Fox Fallon as head of Central Command and put Ray Odierno in charge in Iraq. After a furious debate, Bush agreed to go public about what the administration knew about the Syrian nuclear plant. Michael Hayden and other intelligence officials were "going fucking crazy" that they could not even tell Congress what they knew about North Korean involvement in proliferation even as Christopher Hill was closing in on a deal with Pyongyang.

On the Middle East, Bush learned from Rice that the Israelis were willing to make a major breakthrough proposal. While in Jerusalem, Rice had dinner with Prime Minister Ehud Olmert, who outlined a far-reaching plan to finally bridge the differences with the Palestinians. He would give the Palestinians 94 percent of the disputed land as long as they swapped some other territory, and he would agree that Jerusalem would be divided into an Israeli capital in the west and a Palestinian capital in the east. Israel would provide security for the holy sites and would accept the return of some Palestinians, perhaps five thousand. Rice was so excited as she listened she had to force herself to concentrate. Maybe the Annapolis initiative she and Bush had started would yield results.

"It sounds like he's serious—really serious," Bush said when she returned to Washington and briefed him in the Oval Office.

"Yes, he is," she said, "and he knows he's running out of time."

So was Bush. He took a short break from the White House to fly back to Texas for his daughter Jenna's wedding. The twin girls had outgrown their wild college days. Jenna had spent time in Latin America on a UNICEF internship, ultimately writing a book about an HIV-infected single mother she had met. Now she was marrying Henry Hager, a young former assistant to Karl Rove whom she had met during the reelection campaign.

She opted against a fancy White House wedding and for a simpler outdoor ceremony on May 10 at the Crawford ranch, officiated by Kirbyjon Caldwell, the president's minister friend who, as it turned out, was supporting Barack Obama to replace him. Cheney and the rest of the White House team were not invited. Rove, Hager's former boss, was the only boldfaced name outside the family who was present. The president walked his daughter down the aisle to the sound of a mariachi band playing "Trumpet Voluntary" and teared up as the young couple exchanged vows. The early-to-bed president stayed up until 1:00 a.m.

He returned to work shortly afterward and soon found himself on Air Force One to Israel, where he addressed the parliament, reassuring it of his enduring friendship for the Jewish state. He later flew to Sharm el-Sheikh, the Egyptian resort, where he planned to give a strongly worded speech on May 19 reaffirming the vision of his second inaugural address and pressing President Hosni Mubarak to loosen the reins. The speech named Ayman Nour, the opposition leader who had been imprisoned by Mubarak. But on the plane to Egypt, Bush had it rewritten. Mubarak had decided to sit onstage with Bush during the address, presumably assuming the president would be reluctant to challenge him to his face. Stephen Hadley, Elliott Abrams, and Ed Gillespie wanted to keep the reference to Nour, but Rice argued to take it out. It came out, and the speech touched more lightly on the problems with Egyptian autocracy.

If Bush was wary of offending a longtime ally, he found increasingly that longtime allies were no longer wary of offending him. About a week after he returned to Washington, Bush's former press secretary Scott McClellan published a book casting the presidency in a harsh light. He called the decision to go to war in Iraq "a fateful misstep" based on "ambition, certitude, and self-deceit" and a "divinely inspired passion" for a freedom agenda. The war would go down in history as "a serious strategic blunder," and he said Bush's White House had decided "to turn away from candor and honesty when those qualities were most needed."

McClellan was hardly the first to turn on Bush, but it pained him nonetheless. McClellan had been part of the group that came up from Texas, once the most loyal of loyalists. Now he joined a line of disaffected aides and supporters speaking out publicly, including Matthew Dowd, John Bolton, Richard Armitage, Lawrence Wilkerson, John DiIulio, David Kuo, Richard Haass, Kenneth Adelman, and Paul O'Neill.

By this point, so many friends had turned on him that Bush could hardly muster the outrage his aides felt at what they saw as McClellan's betrayal. When Dana Perino, who had been one of McClellan's deputies before succeeding Tony Snow as press secretary, expressed her indignation, Bush sighed and told her to find a way to forgive McClellan or risk being consumed with anger. Karen Hughes was struck by his evolution; the Bush of 1994 might have been mad, but he had grown more forgiving over the years.

Cheney's reaction to the book was one of resignation; he had seen it so many times he was hardly surprised anymore. Sitting at a table waiting for the president to arrive for a meeting shortly after the book came out, Cheney listened as some of the aides expressed their shock.

"The only reason I have the job I have now, or had the job before I have now," he said, "is because I *didn't* write a book about my last job."

IT WAS NO surprise that another prominent Republican also kept his distance. Having wrapped up the Republican presidential nomination, John McCain made clear he wanted nothing to do with Bush, except to tap his fund-raising network.

For what would be their only appearance of the campaign together, McCain invited Bush to a fund-raiser in his home state of Arizona on the day after Memorial Day. What was supposed to be a high-profile convention center event was abruptly switched at the last minute to a private residence closed to journalists.

When advisers told him of the change, Bush snapped, "If he doesn't want me to go, fine. I've got better things to do." When an aide said McCain was having trouble generating a crowd, Bush was exasperated. "He can't get five hundred people to show up for an event in his hometown?" Bush could not believe it. "He couldn't get five hundred people? I could get that many people to turn out in Crawford." He shook his head. "This is a five-spiral crash, boys." After a few minutes, he returned to the topic. "What is this, a cruel hoax?"

In the end, the only public view of the two men together came after the evening news when McCain saw Bush off on the airport tarmac. The presidential limousine pulled up to the foot of Air Force One, and Bush and McCain emerged from opposite sides, circled around to stand side by side, and waved at the assembled cameras for a total of fourteen seconds. Bush then pecked the senator's wife, Cindy, on the cheek, shook McCain's hand, and sprinted up the stairs, disappearing into the plane. It would be the last time the president and the man running to succeed him would see each other for four months.

Obama, on the other hand, seemed to be growing on Bush. The day after the Illinois senator became the first African American to clinch a major-party presidential nomination, Bush raised the subject with aides in the Oval Office.

"What do you guys think about Obama?" he asked.

"He'll be formidable," Ed Gillespie said evenly.

Bush was struck by the history of the day.

"I think it's an amazing moment for America," he said. "Just an amazing moment."

Bush seemed to detect discomfort in Gillespie. "Hey, Ed, don't worry," he said. "Now we'll kick his ass."

ACTUALLY, IT WAS the Supreme Court that kicked Bush's ass. On June 12, the justices once again inserted themselves into the war on terror to rein in the president, rejecting part of the compromise Bush had forged with McCain in the Military Commissions Act. In *Boumediene v. Bush*, the court ruled 5 to 4 that foreign prisoners at Guantánamo Bay had a habeas corpus right to challenge their detention, throwing out the provision stripping federal courts of the jurisdiction to hear such complaints. The Constitution stated that the right of habeas corpus "shall not be suspended, unless when in Cases of Rebellion or Invasion the public Safety may require it." The court ruled it applied even to noncitizens held offshore. "The laws and Constitution are designed to survive, and remain in force, in extraordinary times," wrote Justice Anthony M. Kennedy. Bush's appointees, John Roberts and Samuel Alito, dissented. The White House was so mad it sent out strident talking points for the State Department to use in making a public response; traveling in Paris, Condoleezza Rice agreed with her spokesman, Sean McCormack, that the talking points all but accused the justices of having blood on their hands and she refused to use them or let the department use them.

Bush received happier news when he turned on his television on June 27.

North Korea had finally turned over the declaration of its nuclear programs, nearly six months late. It was a deeply flawed document, full of holes and questionable assertions. It did not disclose exactly how many nuclear bombs the country had, nor did it admit to having a secret uranium enrichment program in addition to its public plutonium fuel-making facility. But in Bush's eyes, it was progress. In exchange, he announced that he would follow through on his promise to take North Korea off the list of state sponsors of terror. "We're just signing a piece of paper," he said repeatedly. Cheney's camp bristled. Eric Edelman, the Cheney aide now serving as undersecretary of defense, passed along a message to Robert Gates requesting not to be asked to testify before Congress on the deal because he would have to criticize it.

On that Friday, North Korean officials demolished the cooling tower at the Yongbyon nuclear weapons plant. Christopher Hill had wanted to go in person, only to be overruled by Rice, who wanted to avoid alienating the Cheney wing by looking as if her side were taking a bow. A cooling tower is not the most important part of a nuclear program and can easily be rebuilt. But on televisions around the world the images of the conical tower disappearing in a puff of smoke served as a stark visual of change.

"Now *that's* verifiable," Bush said with satisfaction as he watched.

35

"Our people are going to hate us for this"

President Bush leaned forward in his chair in the Oval Office, his face alive with irritation. It was his final summer in power, and he found himself besieged by a group of erstwhile supporters accusing him of selling out the principles of his presidency in a vain pursuit of posterity.

He was meeting with conservative scholars and thinkers who had been among his strongest intellectual advocates in the past. Now they were disillusioned and getting in his face about the turnaround they detected, in effect voicing the concerns that Vice President Cheney shared but did not directly confront Bush with, at least not in front of others.

A lot of people think you've changed from your first term to your second term, said Max Boot, a military historian at the Council on Foreign Relations.

"That's ridiculous," Bush interrupted.

Undaunted, Boot continued with the bill of particulars: Iran, North Korea, Egypt, Middle East democracy. Bush, it seemed, was settling for less than he once demanded. Surely, the first-term Bush would not have gone along with the false concessions of a deceptive North Korea the way the second-term Bush had. Surely, the president who envisioned the end of tyranny in his inaugural address would not accept backsliding by Arab autocrats.

Bush snapped back. "That's not true," he said, glaring straight at Boot. Bush seemed most angry at the implication that he was not as committed to his freedom agenda, which in his view had become the philosophical centerpiece of his presidency. "I've been fighting for this from day one," he said. "It's part of everything I do."

Boot remained unimpressed. He cited a column in that morning's *Wall Street Journal* by John Bolton, Bush's former ambassador to the United Nations and a Cheney ally, lacerating the administration for agreeing to lift some sanctions on North Korea in exchange for the incomplete accounting of Pyongyang's nuclear program. "Nothing can erase the ineffable sadness of an American presidency, like this one, in total intellectual collapse," Bolton had written.

Bush grew more agitated at the mention of his own former senior diplomat. "Let me just say from the outset that I don't consider Bolton credible," the president said bitterly. That was quite a statement. Bush, after all, had been the one who sent Bolton to the United Nations in the first place. He had defied the Senate when it refused to confirm Bolton and gave him a recess appointment. Now he was dismissing him as not credible, clearly resenting what he saw as betrayal. "I spent political capital for him," Bush said, and look what he got in return. The president went on to defend his North Korea decision, saying his "action for action" approach held the most hope of getting rid of Pyongyang's nuclear weapons.

Bolton had become something of a public spear-carrier in the private struggle between Bush and Cheney over foreign policy in the final year in office. A colorful figure with a distinctive bushy gray mustache, Bolton had been part of the recount team in Florida and was among the allies Cheney had sprinkled throughout the administration. Cheney urged Colin Powell to appoint Bolton undersecretary of state and later Condoleezza Rice to send him to the United Nations. At the United Nations, Bolton made a point of calling Cheney or his aides anytime he sensed backsliding in Rice's State Department.

Since leaving the administration, Bolton had become increasingly vocal in columns, speeches, and television appearances lambasting the president's second-term shift, although he generally blamed Rice for leading Bush astray. His barrage of criticism, seen by some in the White House as tacitly encouraged by Cheney, aggravated the president and his aides. Christopher Hill, a frequent target of Bolton's barbs, dismissed him as a fringe figure, calling him "Phyllis Schlafly with a mustache."

Bush did not view his policies as changing so much as moving to the next natural step in a continuum. He was acutely aware of the diminishing time left, calculating that it was worth making concessions he might not have made in the past in hopes of leaving his successor a better situation. North Korea was the classic example. "Do you really want to overturn the apple cart and confront the new administration with a crisis in North Korea policy in addition to Iraq, Afghanistan, and the long list of things?" Stephen Hadley recalled. "I was influenced, and I think the president was influenced, by the fact that probably not." Cheney disagreed. Bush's concessions to North Korea "seemed so out of keeping with the clearheaded way I'd seen him make decisions in the past."

CHENEY COULD STILL assert himself on selected issues. More than anyone in the White House, he remained focused on the war on terror, and so while he would engage on other matters like climate change or Middle East peace from time to time, one friend said, "he was only going to fight to the extent that it didn't cost him when he needed to really try to get the president to remain steadfast" on what he considered the central issues.

One area where he called in chits was the warrantless surveillance program he had helped usher into existence after the September 11 attacks. Bush had decided to seek congressional authorization for the program, and lawmakers had already passed a short-term bill making clear it was legal. But as that measure approached expiration, the main sticking point remained immunity for the telecommunications firms that had cooperated with the government from the beginning.

In Cheney's view, it would be an act of treachery to expose companies that had done what their government asked to endless litigation. When some White House political advisers and lawyers at the Justice Department argued for backing off on immunity, Cheney fought even harder. "Cheney won that one, and he did it in a Cheney way," said the friend. "He had different people making different arguments in different places." On July 9, Congress passed the bill permanently authorizing the surveillance program and exempted the telecommunications firms from liability for past actions. Bush and Cheney actually won greater authority from Congress than they had claimed on their own. "On balance," said Michael Hayden, the CIA director, the new law gave the government "far more" latitude, confirming to some in the White House that they would have been better off going to Congress in the first place.

On another important decision in the terror war, Bush and Cheney agreed. For more than a year, officials had been developing a new strategy for the tribal areas of Pakistan where many Islamic militants were hiding. President Pervez Musharraf's deal with tribal leaders had collapsed, and the CIA was detecting signs that al-Qaeda was training a fresh class of terrorists, this time with American passports. To many administration officials, it was clear that relying on the Pakistanis was no longer a tenable strategy, especially with Musharraf embattled at home. The past year had seen little progress. "We have been 0 for '07," complained Hayden, overstating slightly for effect. "We're seeing a dangerous accumulation of breathing space for al-Qaeda," warned Juan Carlos Zarate, the president's deputy national security adviser for combating terrorism.

As the national security team gathered one July day in the Yellow Oval Room on the second floor of the residence, there was a powerful if largely unstated recognition that this might be the last chance to shape terrorism policy before Bush and Cheney left office—and perhaps their last chance to get Osama bin Laden. The plan called for a much more muscular decapitation campaign aimed at killing key al-Qaeda leaders using unmanned drones armed with missiles. Instead of waiting for Pakistani permission, the CIA would strike unilaterally, assuming it had gathered enough indications that there was a high-value target on the ground and that civilian casualties could be kept to a minimum. It would inform Pakistan either as the strike took place or afterward. Special Forces in Afghanistan would also be authorized to conduct raids across the border.

What would make the campaign more effective, Bush was told, was the development of much more intense surveillance of potential targets. Instead of relying simply on fragmentary information from informants or short-lived satellite passes, the CIA was now able to station drones hovering over a target undetected for days or even weeks at a time, gathering a complete picture of a suspected hideout and its occupants. The analysis of what CIA officials called "pattern of life," combined with what Hayden would call "a Home Depot–sized warehouse full of detainee information" gleaned from interrogations, gave agency leaders and commanders a better understanding of the enemy than they had had since September 11. "You need human penetrations, you need signals intelligence, but finally that persistent, godlike stare, unblinking, builds up a level of confidence," Hayden said, referring to drone operations in general.

With so many drones occupied in Iraq, the al-Qaeda hunters until then had been having trouble getting enough to roam the skies over Afghanistan and Pakistan. The strategy was not without risk; hit the wrong house, kill too many civilians, and Pakistan could erupt in an anti-American frenzy. As aggressive as he had been elsewhere, Bush had always taken a measured approach to Pakistan, and had resisted concerted pressure from the military to send troops over the border from Afghanistan for fear of destabilizing the Islamabad government. But with half a year left, Bush was willing to gamble. "We're going to stop playing the game," he told advisers. "These sons of bitches are killing Americans. I've had enough."

IN A NONDESCRIPT suburban office tower across the Potomac River in Virginia where John McCain based his campaign, the putative Republican nominee and his team were trying to figure out how to disinvite the president and the vice president of the United States from their own party's convention.

Bush was arguably the most unpopular president in modern times. His 69 percent disapproval rating in April was the highest of any president since Gallup began polling, surpassing Harry Truman at his worst at 67 percent and Richard Nixon at his worst at 66 percent. By July, as McCain was gearing up for his general election run, just 28 percent supported the president, and 81 percent said the country was on the wrong track. The "Bush Lied, People Died" mantra had been set in concrete for many. For some, normal political opposition had even evolved into deep loathing. By this point, two authors had written fictional books contemplating Bush's assassination, and a filmmaker had made a docudrama about the same scenario. Bush was regularly called a Nazi and depicted on protest signs with a Hitler-like mustache. Beyond the fringe, mainstream pundits debated whether he would go down as the worst president in history.

Democrats asserted that electing John McCain would amount to a "third Bush term," an ironic notion given that the senator had spent much of the previous decade at odds with the president. A *USA Today*/Gallup poll that summer found that 68 percent of Americans were concerned that McCain would pursue policies too similar to those of Bush. "He became an albatross," recalled Senator Joseph Lieberman, the independent Democrat who was supporting McCain.

So McCain and his team brainstormed how to do the unthinkable and keep the sitting president away from the convention in St. Paul, Minnesota. "It wasn't fair," said Charles Black, a McCain strategist, "but the president was unpopular." Eventually, Black was deputized to suggest to the White House that Bush skip the convention in September and leave the country altogether. Perhaps he could go to Africa and beam in a televised message from there highlighting his work against AIDS and malaria, one of the indisputably positive aspects of his legacy.

The idea did not go over well at the White House, where Bush aides grew angry at the affront and thought it was a mistake for McCain to go too far distancing himself from a president who retained the support of a conservative base that distrusted McCain. The McCain staff was already riven between longtime loyalists to the senator and those brought in from the Bush years. "It was so ingrained in the McCain world to hate Bush, and Bush people," said Nicolle Wallace, the former Bush White House communications director who had gone to work for McCain. "I remember being sick at the thought of nickel-and-diming the president of the United States. He was going to be more beloved in the hall than we were. It was awful."

And if Bush was not welcome in McCain's world, Cheney was even less so. The vice president and the senator had clashed most recently over interrogation policy, and feelings were still raw. When McCain kicked off his presidential campaign a year earlier, he had said that Bush "listened too much to the vice president," whom he blamed for the "witch's brew" of a "terribly mishandled war." In hopes of keeping Cheney off the stage at the convention, Black was sent on a separate but parallel mission to ask the vice president whether he would be willing to stay away. "His attitude was, look, I want to help, I'm not sure you're right about this, but I'll think about it because I want to help you win," Black recalled. But in the end, Cheney decided to go to the convention.

While McCain barnstormed the country promising a new start, Bush stewed in the White House, railing about the campaign's undisciplined approach. Through much of 2008, the two men whose relationship had been so fraught for the past decade kept getting crosswise, intentionally or not. Bush was miffed when he hosted the leaders of Mexico and Canada for a summit meeting in New Orleans to show off its recovery from Hurricane Katrina, only to have McCain show up in the Lower Ninth Ward two days later denouncing the administration's response to the storm as "disgraceful." When the two both showed up in Iowa to inspect flood damage, they were just thirty miles apart but effectively undercut each other's effort to show concern. And the McCain camp was aggravated that Bush endorsed lifting restrictions on offshore drilling a day after the candidate did, fueling the "third Bush term" attack line.

Bush understood the treacherous terrain facing McCain and regularly told associates that if he were running as a Republican, he would keep his distance as well. "Republicans will be saying, 'Bush screwed it up,'" he told visitors one day. "If I were running, I guess I would say the same thing. You cannot, I don't care who you are, embrace George W. Bush." But understanding the approach intellectually did not mean he had to like it, and at times Bush thought McCain was taking it too far.

Cheney was just as aggravated at being muzzled. "Personally, I felt that a straightforward defense by the president and me would be better than no rebuttal at all from the White House," he later wrote, "but it was John's campaign and he deserved to run it the way he wanted."

While nursing his frustration, Bush received bad news. On July 12, he learned that Tony Snow had lost his battle with cancer. Five days later, Bush paid tribute to Snow at a Catholic service at Washington's National Shrine of the Immaculate Conception, packed with more than a thousand mourners. "He had the sometimes challenging distinction of working for two presidents named Bush," the president said from the pulpit. "As a speechwriter in my dad's administration, Tony tried to translate the president's policies into English. As a spokesman in my administration, Tony tried to translate my English—into English."

Bush could have used Snow as he tried to cement his achievements and forestall a new crisis. With Iraq calmer, he was trying to negotiate a strategic agreement with Baghdad that would be the framework for American troops remaining after a UN mandate expired at the end of the year. In Baghdad, though, the pact was seen as an occupation agreement.

In a videoconference, Prime Minister Nouri al-Maliki pushed for a withdrawal date. "Mr. President, it is in this garden of success that we can discuss a timetable," Maliki told him. "In the past, to mention a timetable was provocative because it meant enemies could wait and destroy Iraq. But now the enemies cannot defeat the state, so we should not be so sensitive to discussing a timetable."

Bush broke with five years of his own policy. "I agree with you," he said. "And if it's all right with you, I'll put out a statement after this meeting to say I agree with you. Is that all right?"

Maliki said yes. Just like that, Bush was working to seal an agreement that would effectively end the Iraq War. Just a year after it looked as if all were lost, now it seemed possible to negotiate an exit that, if not a clean victory, at least would not look like a retreat under fire.

It had been a long journey. Bush was not one given to reflection, at least not out loud. Yet one day after a meeting, he seemed in a rare introspective mood. Sitting in the Situation Room while waiting for another meeting to begin, the president looked at Robert Gates and Admiral Mike Mullen, who had succeeded Peter Pace as chairman of the Joint Chiefs of Staff, and harked back to the critical days in 2003 before he launched the war that had become so problematic. "You know," he recalled, "when I made the decision on Iraq, I went around the room to everybody at that table, every principal. 'You in? Any doubts?' Nothing from anybody." For Bush, it was an unusual moment of doubt. Was he ruing his own flawed judgment? Bitter that he had been led off track by advisers? Or both? He didn't say.

In the days to come, Bush signed two pieces of important legislation. One expanded his PEPFAR program another five years, allocating $48 billion to fighting AIDS, tuberculosis, and malaria, an extraordinary sum of money to be dedicated to the world's poorest continent. The other made tax dollars available to backstop the two government-chartered housing corporations, Fannie Mae and Freddie Mac. Bush had fought to reform the two entities repeatedly over the years, only to run into a buzz saw of opposition in Congress. "It was literally like William Wallace fighting the British," said Tony Fratto, a deputy press secretary who specialized in economic issues. "It was a slaughter." Now with a housing crisis in full flame, the question was whether it was too late.

A week later, John McCain began airing a new ad with a theme typically used by the party out of power. "We're worse off than we were four years ago," the ad said.

ON AUGUST 8, Bush was standing in a reception line in Beijing about to shake hands with President Hu Jintao marking the opening of the Summer Olympics when his deputy national security adviser, James Jeffrey, sidled up and whispered in his ear. Russian troops were marching into neighboring Georgia after the smaller country shelled a breakaway republic aligned with Moscow. Years of tension had finally exploded into full-fledged war. Caught in the middle was Bush, who had labored so long to keep a constructive relationship with Vladimir Putin but who had also taken great satisfaction out of the democratic revolution that had vaulted Mikheil Saakashvili to power in Georgia.

As he absorbed the news, Bush noticed that just a few places ahead of him in the receiving line was none other than Putin. Although Putin in technical conformance with constitutional term limits had turned the presidency over to his protégé Dmitry Medvedev and assumed the prime ministership, there was little doubt that he was still the country's paramount leader.

Bush chose not to say anything to Putin right then, reasoning that the ceremony presented the wrong venue for a confrontation over war. Besides, protocol demanded that he deal with Medvedev as a fellow head of state. So he waited until he returned to his hotel to call Moscow. He found Medvedev "hot," but "so was I."

"My strong advice is to start deescalating this thing now," Bush lectured him. "The disproportionality of your actions is going to turn the world against you. We're going to be with them."

Medvedev pushed back, comparing Saakashvili to Saddam Hussein and accusing the Georgians of killing fifteen hundred civilians in shelling the pro-Russian separatist republic of South Ossetia. (Later reports indicated only a fraction of that many were actually killed.)

"I hope you're not saying you're going to kill fifteen hundred people in response," Bush said. "You've made your point loud and clear. I hope you consider what I've asked very seriously."

But Bush was dealing with the wrong man. While critics at home casually assumed Cheney was really pulling the strings in the White House, in Russia it was true that the number-two official was the real power. As the opening ceremony for the Olympics commenced, Bush found himself seated in the same row with Putin, so he had Laura and the king of Cambodia shift down a few seats so that the Russian prime minister could sit next to him. Aware of the television cameras focused on them, Bush tried to avoid causing a scene but told Putin that he had made a serious mistake that would leave Russia isolated if it did not get out of Georgia. Putin countered that Saakashvili was a war criminal who had provoked Russia.

"I've been warning you Saakashvili is hot-blooded," Bush told Putin.

"I'm hot-blooded, too," Putin countered.

"No, Vladimir," Bush responded. "You're cold-blooded."

The sudden war in the Caucasus presented a dangerous test for the president. He and his aides worried that Georgia was just the first stone to fall; if Moscow were allowed to roll over a weak neighbor, then it could next try to seize the Crimea region in Ukraine or even make a move in the Baltics, where it ruled until the fall of the Soviet Union. On the other hand, the last thing Bush wanted to do was turn a volatile situation into a Russian-American confrontation and spark a new cold war.

Meetings at the White House were unusually emotional. Saakashvili had cultivated supporters in the administration, particularly in Cheney's camp. When a junior aide suggested that the United States had to step in, Admiral Mike Mullen, the chairman of the Joint Chiefs, interrupted.

"Look, I'm already in a war in Iraq and Afghanistan," he said. He did not want another, especially with Russia.

Mullen was virtually the only American able to reach his counterpart in Moscow. Most Russian officials were ignoring their phones, but Mullen had perhaps seven or eight conversations with General Nikolai Makarov, the Russian chief of staff, over the course of a few days, trying to keep the Russians from marching all the way to the Georgian capital. To avoid framing it as a Russian-American clash, Bush turned to President Nicolas Sarkozy of France, who held the rotating presidency of the European Union, and asked him to take the lead in negotiating a cease-fire. In the meantime, some in the White House kept looking for possible responses, even military ones. Among the options was bombing the Roki Tunnel to block any further Russian advance into Georgia. Cheney had received a call from a frantic Saakashvili requesting military equipment such as Stinger antiaircraft missiles.

The question came up at a meeting after Bush returned from Beijing. Cheney noted the Stinger request from Saakashvili.

"I need to give him an answer," the vice president said.

Condoleezza Rice thought there was "a fair amount of chest beating" and "all kind of loose talk" about a muscular response.

Finally, Stephen Hadley cut to the chase. "Mr. President, I think you need to poll your national security advisers as to whether they recommend to you putting American troops on the ground in Georgia," he said.

Bush looked at Hadley as if he were crazy.

"I think it is important for the historical record to be clear as to whether any of your principals are recommending to you the use of military force," Hadley said.

At that point, Bush got it. Hadley was protecting him, calling the bluff of Cheney and the other hawks. *Were they really ready to go to war with Russia over Georgia?*

Hadley wanted the principals to give their positions explicitly so they could not later write in their memoirs that they had disagreed with the president.

Picking up on that, Bush posed the question. "Does anyone recommend the use of military force?" he asked.

No one did. "It is a very serious matter, but, Mr. President, I think that would be a mistake," Cheney said.

The next day, August 12, Sarkozy reached a cease-fire agreement with both sides, but he had been snookered. The Russians had insisted on a fifteen-kilometer "exclusion zone" for their troops, but the French did not realize that was enough to encompass the Georgian city of Gori. The Russians took advantage and moved in even after the cease-fire. They were on the doorstep of Tbilisi, with regime change as their goal.

"I want to hang Saakashvili by the balls," Putin told Sarkozy.

"Hang him?" Sarkozy asked.

"Why not? The Americans hanged Saddam Hussein."

"But do you want to end up like Bush?"

"Ah," Putin replied, "there you have a point."

Bush decided he could no longer sit on the sidelines. He sent Rice to mediate and authorized humanitarian aid sent on military cargo planes to make a point. With American military planes on the runway at Tbilisi, he calculated, the Russians would be foolish to attack the Georgian capital.

Rice flew to Paris and confronted the French. "Did you look at a map?" she asked.

No, they had not.

Only after consulting their ambassador did they realize she was right and that Gori was within the "exclusion zone."

Rice then flew to Moscow and Tbilisi to broker a new agreement. Walking through the government building in Tbilisi, she and her staff noticed there were no pictures on the walls, just hooks; the Georgians were so panicked about approaching Russian troops they were on the verge of fleeing.

At Rice's instigation, Russia agreed to pull out of Georgia but not from its breakaway republics. The war was over, but the relationship between Bush and Putin that had started with soul gazing seven years earlier was broken. Russia suspended cooperation with NATO and later recognized the independence of South Ossetia and Abkhazia. Bush shelved a civilian nuclear agreement he had spent years negotiating with Putin.

As soon as that crisis was resolved, along came another one. On August 18, Pervez Musharraf resigned as president of Pakistan to avoid impeachment, throwing the American war on terror into uncertainty. For years, Bush had stuck with Musharraf despite his undemocratic reign, tempering his commitment to his freedom agenda in the name of a seemingly loyal ally in the war on terror. But ultimately, Musharraf proved unreliable, never fully able or willing to clean out the tribal areas that remained a safe haven for al-Qaeda and the Taliban. Now Bush would have to find out whether he could work more effectively with Musharraf's untested successor, Asif Ali Zardari, widower of the assassinated Benazir Bhutto.

WITH TIME RUNNING out, Bush grew unusually reflective, and he watched the contest to succeed him with a certain jaundice. One summer day after a meeting, one of Bush's national security aides, William Luti, began chatting with him.

"What's the one thing that surprised you most?" Luti asked.

Bush answered without hesitation. "How little authority I have," he said with a laugh.

Then, turning serious, he added, "The other thing that surprised me—whoever steps into this office, whether it's Obama or McCain, they're going to learn there's a big difference between campaigning and governing."

Bush had no advance warning when John McCain announced his running mate on August 29, and as he happened across a television report, he thought he heard the announcer say "Pawlenty." Only after a moment did he understand that McCain had picked not Tim Pawlenty, the governor of Minnesota, but Sarah Palin, the governor of Alaska.

While Palin initially energized many Republicans, the outgoing president was underwhelmed.

"I'm trying to remember if I've met her before," he told his staff. "I'm sure I must have." He added sarcastically, "What is she, the governor of Guam?"

Ed Gillespie told him that conservatives were enthusiastic.

"Look, I'm a team player. I'm on board," Bush replied.

After a few minutes, he directed the conversation back to Palin. "You know, just wait a few days until the bloom is off that rose," he warned. "This woman is being put into a position she is not even remotely prepared for. She hasn't spent one day on the national level. Neither has her family. Let's wait and see how she looks five days out."

Cheney was no more impressed. McCain, he lamented to associates, had made a "reckless choice" at a time when leadership mattered for the country.

With both Bush and Cheney insisting on attending the convention, the McCain campaign told the White House to keep the president's speech to ten minutes. Go light on the Bush record and praise the nominee, the White House was told. Bush grew irritated. When he read a draft of the speech, he came across a line extolling McCain for seeing the wisdom of a surge in Iraq before Bush's own cabinet, which he took as a slap at Rice.

"You really want me to say that?" Bush asked aides.

Gillespie argued that it was important, but Bush took it out.

The final indignity came when a hurricane named Gustav threatened the Gulf Coast just as Republicans gathered in St. Paul for the convention, prompting McCain to cancel the first night—as it happened, the night when Bush and Cheney were to speak. After Katrina, the last thing any Republican wanted was to be politicking while another killer storm ravaged the American coast. In effect, weather had accomplished what McCain could not. When the hurricane passed with relatively little damage, McCain resumed the convention without Bush or Cheney anywhere to be seen. Bush still wanted to go in person, but the McCain campaign said he could appear via video. "From stem to stern, President Bush resented the fact that we used that as an excuse to knock him off," recalled Wayne Berman, the Bush friend who was working as a McCain fund-raiser. Bush took out one more line from his speech, one praising McCain for "not chasing the public opinion polls." As far as Bush was concerned, that would not be honest.

At 9:54 p.m. on September 2, before the broadcast networks began their one-hour live coverage, Bush's image was projected on a large screen above an empty stage with an empty lectern at the Xcel Energy Center in St. Paul. The delegates greeted him politely as he became the first sitting president to miss his party's convention since Lyndon Johnson stayed away from Chicago in 1968. Speaking by satellite from the White House, Bush offered dutiful praise of the nominee and no celebration of his own eight years in office.

"My fellow citizens, we live in a dangerous world," he told the Republican crowd. "And we need a president who understands the lessons of September the 11th, 2001—that to protect America, we must stay on offense, stop attacks before they happen and not wait to be hit again. The man we need is John McCain."

He made light of McCain's maverick streak, but with a little bit of an edge. "John is an independent man who thinks for himself," Bush said. "Believe me, I know."

Eight minutes later, he was done.

Cheney did not speak at all.

Once Bush's image faded from the screen, none of the marquee speakers for the rest of the convention mentioned his name during the nightly prime-time hour. Indeed, overall, Democrats uttered the word "Bush" twelve times as often at their convention. On September 4, Republican delegates were shown a video about September 11 that included images of Rudy Giuliani and Donald Rumsfeld but none of Bush. In his acceptance speech shortly afterward, McCain thanked "the president," without naming him, for his leadership "in these dark days" and for "keeping us safe from another attack." But he made no further reference to Bush, and when it came to the turnaround in Iraq, McCain credited "the leadership of a brilliant general, David Petraeus."

After the Republicans finished partying without him, Bush took a quiet field trip to tour the battlefield at Gettysburg with some of his old Texas crowd, including Alberto Gonzales, Karen Hughes, Karl Rove, and Margaret Spellings. After taking solace in so many Abraham Lincoln books, Bush on September 5 made the pilgrimage to the site of the defining moment of Honest Abe's presidency.

In front of the Virginia monument, Bush listened as one of the tour guides, Jake Boritt, described how Lincoln saw Lee's strike deep into Union territory as an opportunity.

"Well," Bush asked sardonically, "did the president say, 'Bring it on?'"

"DO THEY KNOW it's coming, Hank?" Bush asked Henry Paulson.

"Mr. President," Paulson said, "we're going to move quickly and take them by surprise. The first sound they'll hear is their heads hitting the floor."

Their heads hit the floor on September 7. With Bush's authorization, Paulson seized control of Fannie Mae and Freddie Mac, the two housing giants that were funding more than two-thirds of the home loans in America, and fired their chief executives and boards of directors.

The stunning move, at that point the most drastic intervention into the private financial markets since the Great Depression, caught much of Washington by surprise and underscored how rapidly the crisis spawned by the housing market was spreading. It also demonstrated how worried Bush was to so easily abandon a lifetime of free-market conservatism.

Fannie Mae and Freddie Mac were government-chartered private corporations with the twin missions of making a profit for shareholders and encouraging home ownership for those who otherwise would find it beyond their reach. Trying to compete in an overheated housing market flooded with subprime mortgages, the two firms were overextended and having trouble raising capital; their shares were off by 90 percent from their highs in the last year. If they had to pare back, it could send mortgage interest rates soaring and push the economy even further to the brink.

The sweeping move by Bush and Paulson was not the end of the crisis, though. Within days, Paulson was back telling Bush that another storied Wall Street brokerage was on the brink of failure, this time Lehman Brothers. Paulson, Ben Bernanke, and the president of the Federal Reserve Bank of New York, Timothy Geithner, plunged into a frenetic, all-hours effort to stop the bleeding and find a buyer, fearing that a Lehman collapse would be the string that pulled apart the whole fabric of the nation's banking system. By the end of the weekend, they were at an impasse. British regulators would not let Barclays buy Lehman, and Bank of America opted to buy Merrill Lynch instead. They had no choice but to let Lehman go down.

"What the hell is going on?" Bush asked Paulson when he reached him on Sunday, September 14. "I thought we were going to get a deal."

"The British aren't prepared to approve," Paulson said.

"Will we be able to explain why Lehman is different from Bear Stearns?" Bush asked.

"Yes, sir. There was just no way to save Lehman. We couldn't find a buyer even with the other private firms' help. We will just have to try to manage this."

Even as they dealt with Lehman's bankruptcy, the government had to make its largest intervention in the private sector to date, pumping a staggering $85 billion into the insurance conglomerate AIG on September 16 in exchange for 80 percent control. AIG was more than an insurance firm. It had ties to every major bank, and if it went down, so would the system.

"How did we get to this point?" Bush asked during a meeting in the Roosevelt Room that afternoon.

"If we don't shore up AIG, we will likely lose several more financial institutions. Morgan Stanley, for one," Paulson said.

Bush was baffled that a single firm had become so important. "Someday you guys are going to have to tell me how we ended up with a system like this and what we need to do to fix it," he said.

Events were moving at a head-snapping pace, each hour bringing more news pointing to a complete meltdown of the nation's financial system. Years of reckless decisions by everyone from unqualified home buyers to profit-hungry investment banks were coming to a head at the eleventh hour of the Bush presidency. "He was pissed off at the banks," Ed Gillespie recalled later. Bush had foreseen problems with Fannie and Freddie and tried to head them off. Still, his own regulators had sat back as Wall Street created ever more exotic and risky investment schemes. How much this was Bush's fault would be debated for years, but there was no question it was unraveling on his watch and he had to stop it.

The crisis came at a time when Bush, Cheney, and their teams were all but wiped out. Nearly eight years of terrorism, war, natural disaster, and scandal had taken their toll. Bush's Texas friend Charlie Younger noticed that Bush had "stopped saying he was glad to be president." Those last months, Younger said, "it got him and he did not enjoy being president." Bush himself later said he felt like "the captain of a sinking ship."

Still, Bush recognized that he was in a better position to confront the catastrophe than his successor would be. He understood by now the levers of government and, moreover, could do what was necessary without worrying about political fallout.

When Karen Hughes called one morning to offer consolation, he was stoic.

"Mr. President, what else can go wrong during your presidency?" she lamented.

"Well, it's a good thing we're here to deal with it," he said.

The economic anxiety had erased any goodwill Bush had earned by turning Iraq around. On September 17, as stock markets were tumbling and banks were failing, Bush welcomed David Petraeus back to the White House. Petraeus was about to take over as commander of the entire Middle East operations from Central Command, based in Tampa, Florida.

In the Oval Office, Bush gave Petraeus presidential cuff links and posed for pictures with his family. The two men started joshing about mountain biking and whether Petraeus could keep up. The president had triggered the general's hypercompetitive spirit.

"Mr. President, do you have a death wish?" Petraeus asked jokingly. "Do you realize who you're talking trash with here? If you weren't the president of the United States, we could provide a workout that you could write off on your income tax as education."

Bush gave as good as he got, boasting about how he had taken out Jim Zorn, the Washington Redskins coach, and left him in the dust. Before it was over, he had challenged Petraeus to a biking contest.

THE LIGHT INTERLUDE was short-lived. The next day, Bush was scheduled to make a fund-raising trip to Alabama and Florida but canceled it to meet in the Roosevelt Room with his economic team. Henry Paulson sat across from the president with Ben Bernanke to his right and Timothy Geithner to his left. Bush was flanked by Joshua Bolten on his left and Ed Gillespie on his right. A moment of truth had arrived. The time for piecemeal fixes was over, the advisers told him. Slapdash rescue efforts for this or that institution were no longer going to hold things together. The Federal Reserve on its own could do no more. Paulson and the others told Bush it was time to go to Congress for extraordinary authority to tackle the underlying problems. They had in mind an eye-popping $500 billion to purchase toxic assets from endangered financial firms.

"What happens if we don't?" Bush asked.

"We're looking at an economy worse than the Great Depression," Paulson said grimly.

Bush was taken aback. "Worse than the Great Depression?" he asked. "Twenty-five percent unemployment?"

He turned to Bernanke. "Ben, do you agree with that?"

"I do, Mr. President."

Bush did not hesitate. After asking some more questions, he signed off immediately.

"I will give you all the backing you need," he told them. "Let's go get it done. This is what the country needs."

What they were talking about went against the grain for a conservative president. "Our people are going to hate us for this," he said in one meeting. "Boy, historians are going to have a fun time with this one," he said at another point. But Bush had grown nervous enough that he did not let old dogma stand in the way. If Paulson said this was what was necessary, then the president was going to support him to the end.

Bush had bonded with Paulson as he never did with his first two Treasury secretaries, seeing a fellow man of action, not a handwringer. In an administration where most cabinet secretaries were invisible, Paulson was a force of nature. He had no time for e-mail, preferring rapid-fire phone calls. He was always moving on to the next thing. If he noticed the person he was talking with understood the point of what he was saying, he often would not bother to finish the thought. For Bush, Paulson would become another Petraeus, a general he would entrust to lead his battle against dark forces. When Bush lost his standing with the public on the war, he knew Petraeus would be a more persuasive front man. If Bush could now no longer command support for his economic policies, then he would let Paulson speak for the government. "In that political environment, we needed Hank to be the voice," said Tony Fratto, the deputy press secretary.

But Bush worried about Paulson. The Treasury secretary had been getting by on barely three hours of sleep a night, running himself into the ground as if single-handedly trying to hold up the world of finance, an Atlas for modern times. As the meeting broke up, Bush pulled aside Michele Davis, a top Paulson adviser.

"Tell Hank to calm down and get some sleep," he advised, "because he's got to be well rested."

Bush walked back to the Oval Office with Ed Gillespie and they stood by a sofa. Joshua Bolten came in behind them and closed the door. Bush stood there for a moment in silence, the words "Great Depression" still echoing in everyone's ears. Then he looked at his aides.

"If we're really looking at another Great Depression," he said, "you can be damn sure I'm going to be Roosevelt, not Hoover."

FOR BUSH, the financial crisis was not the only worry. On September 20, he was told terrorists had bombed the Marriott hotel in the heart of Islamabad, a main gathering area in Pakistan for Americans and other foreigners to meet local contacts, more than fifty of whom were now dead. The day after that, the president watched as Prime Minister Ehud Olmert resigned in Israel amid a corruption investigation, ending any last hopes for a Middle East peace deal during Bush's term despite twenty-five trips by Condoleezza Rice in pursuit of an enduring agreement.

But the firestorm consuming Washington occupied most of Bush's attention. The reaction to the Troubled Asset Relief Program that Paulson and Bernanke had proposed in a scant three-page bill was visceral and unrelenting, from Republicans as much as anyone. Even inside the White House, speechwriters joked that TARP, as it was dubbed, should be called MARX. The notion of bailing out Wall Street after it got the country into the mess in the first place had almost no appeal, especially weeks before an election. Bush needed to calm down the conservatives, and for that there could be no better ambassador than Cheney.

Despite his conservative philosophy, Cheney expressed no hesitation about the bailout program, later calling himself a "strong supporter" of it. In fact, he and his team had little to do with the policy decision. "They were a nonfactor," said Matt Latimer, the speechwriter. But Cheney would help sell it. He climbed into his car at 8:45 a.m. on September 23, joined by Keith Hennessey, the president's economics adviser, and Kevin Warsh, a top Federal Reserve official, and headed to Capitol Hill to meet with the House Republican caucus. Never before had Cheney encountered such hostility from Republican lawmakers. One after another, House members excoriated the bailout. That didn't go so well, Hennessey said in the car on the way back. Cheney was unruffled, calling it a chance for lawmakers to blow off steam. But privately, he thought three-quarters of the caucus would vote against them.

Bush decided to address the nation and prepared a prime-time speech.

But hours before he was to go on the air, he received a call from John McCain asking him to hold a White House meeting on the rescue package. The president was furious. Negotiations were at a delicate stage, and suddenly McCain was going to swoop in to save the day? It was "a stunt," Bush thought. Barry Jackson, his political adviser, was even blunter, calling McCain "a stupid prick." But Bush felt he had no choice and had to convene the meeting McCain had requested. "I could see the headlines: 'Even Bush Thinks McCain's Idea Is a Bad One,'" the president noted later.

He got Barack Obama on the phone to invite him as well. "McCain asked for this meeting and I think I have to give him this meeting and I need you to be here," he told Obama. The Democratic nominee thought the president sounded almost apologetic.

Bush decided to go ahead with the speech anyway. His staff prepared a text sticking to general principles so as not to step on the meeting now scheduled for the next day. But as Bush read it in the family theater, where he was rehearsing, he grew agitated.

"We can't even defend our own proposal?" he asked. "Why did we propose it then?"

He ordered more details put into the speech. "We're buying low and selling high," he said, meaning the toxic assets the government would purchase could still be turned around for a profit eventually.

When he returned to the family theater a few hours later, he read the revised text and was still unhappy.

Why wasn't the buy-low, sell-high concept in there? he demanded.

Because that was not really the concept, someone explained.

Bush was exasperated. "Why did I sign onto this proposal if I don't understand what it does?" he asked.

The president stalked out. He had never seemed more exhausted, his face more drawn, thought Latimer.

The truth was Bush understood it fine. But the proposal was changing faster than anyone could keep up. Paulson was already beginning to rethink the idea of purchasing toxic assets. Ed Lazear, the chairman of the Council of Economic Advisers, had concluded there were $3 trillion in such assets, too many to purchase, and had been urging instead direct infusions of funds to fortify the banks against the financial contagion. Paulson was increasingly worried that the original idea was impractical. The speechwriters were being told to keep light on the details to preserve flexibility, just as the bill itself had been kept vague.

By the time Bush arrived for the 9:00 p.m. speech on the State Floor of the White House residence, he had pulled himself together. He warned Americans that "our entire economy is in danger" and without the massive financial package he was advocating, now $700 billion, the country faced a financial panic, a further collapse in housing prices, spiraling markets, and vanishing credit, all followed by a long and arduous recession. Bush emphasized that "this rescue effort is not aimed at preserving any individual company or industry; it is aimed at preserving America's overall economy."

But he sounded almost as if he were trying to convince himself, almost as if he could not believe that an ardent capitalist would shuck six decades of beliefs for the most intrusive government intervention in the private marketplace of his lifetime. "With the situation becoming more precarious by the day," Bush said, "I faced a choice—to step in with dramatic government action or to stand back and allow the irresponsible actions of some to undermine the financial security of all. I'm a strong believer in free enterprise. So my natural instinct is to oppose government intervention. I believe companies that make bad decisions should be allowed to go out of business. Under normal circumstances, I would have followed this course. But these are not normal circumstances."

THE NEXT DAY, September 25, Bush tried to reassure nervous foreign partners that the bailout would ultimately pass. The issue had global ramifications, with much of the world waiting in suspense for Washington to act.

During a morning telephone call, Angela Merkel of Germany told Bush that banks in her country were watching carefully.

"I don't think Congress has a choice," Bush told her, "so I'm confident it will get done."

But when he hung up, he was still in the dark about McCain's intentions for the White House meeting he had demanded for later that day. Bush worried that the politics of the campaign could make an already difficult situation impossible to manage.

"What's McCain going to say?" Bush asked Ed Gillespie.

"We have no idea," Gillespie responded.

Bush summoned Paulson before the session. It was a damp, chilly afternoon, and the two of them, joined by Joel Kaplan, stood on the terrace outside the president's dining room, Bush chewing on an unlit cigar. Paulson told him that he had had a tense conversation with McCain earlier in the day, all but threatening the senator not to do anything to mess up the financial rescue. Bush seemed astonished by McCain's behavior and said he hoped he knew what he was doing.

"Hank, we are going to get this done," Bush said, summoning his resolve. "There has to be some way Boehner can work this, and maybe I can help with the House Republicans."

Heading back to the Oval Office, they were joined by John Boehner, the House minority leader, and other top Republicans. Boehner said he did not have the votes.

"We need to get there," Bush said.

"I'm trying," Boehner replied. "I don't have the support."

As the congressional leaders filed into the Cabinet Room at 4:00 p.m., Obama worked the room almost as if he already owned the place. McCain stood off to the side. Each took a seat at the polished mahogany table marked by a little white place card. To the president's left were Harry Reid, Mitch McConnell, and then Obama. To his right were Nancy Pelosi, Boehner, and then McCain. Cheney sat opposite Bush.

The president opened the meeting by warning of the consequences. "If money isn't loosened up, this sucker could go down," he said, meaning the entire American economy.

If that were not ominous enough, Bush asked Paulson to give his grim rundown of the situation.

Then, by protocol, Bush turned to Pelosi. "Madam Speaker?"

"Mr. President," she said, "Senator Obama is going to speak for us today."

Bush realized the Democrats had orchestrated their participation and sat back as Obama offered a sober assessment of the situation. "On the way here, we were on the brink of a deal," Obama said. "Now, there are those who think we should start from scratch." It was a trap, Bush realized, putting the blame on McCain for disrupting a deal that in fact was not really there yet. But the president was impressed with Obama's presence and discipline.

Bush turned to McCain. "I think it's fair that I give you the chance to speak next," he said.

"I'll wait my turn," McCain said.

Bush was dumbstruck. *What's going on?* This was McCain's meeting. *He's just going to sit there and let Obama control the conversation?*

The discussion began to devolve. Boehner proposed an alternative plan that his caucus would support, one involving less government intervention. Representative Barney Frank and other Democrats harangued him for failing to produce votes for a deal that House Democrats, Senate Democrats, and Senate Republicans all supported.

"I can't invent votes," Boehner protested. "I have a problem on my own hands."

Finally, about forty minutes into the meeting, Obama interrupted. "Can I hear from Senator McCain?" he asked.

McCain, speaking for the first time, offered generalities, saying the House Republicans had legitimate concerns that needed to be addressed without actually agreeing with them. To many around the table in both parties, it was clear McCain had no clue what he was doing.

Bush was singularly unimpressed and leaned over to Pelosi. "I told you you'd miss me when I'm gone," he whispered.

Within moments, everyone was speaking at once, challenging and baiting each other, talking past one another. Bush gestured with his hands, palms down, trying to calm the room. "It was almost like children sitting at a table throwing food at each other," recalled Eric Draper, the White House photographer. Cheney sat back and could hardly keep from laughing at the spectacle. Obama, he thought, had spoken with authority while McCain had added nothing of substance. It was unclear to Cheney why McCain had returned to Washington and demanded the meeting in the first place. The vice president was overcome with fresh worry for the Republican ticket.

"Well, I've clearly lost control of this meeting," Bush said, standing up to go.

As he left the room, Bush shook his head. That was a joke, a circus, he told aides. What was going on with McCain? "That was the most ridiculous meeting I have ever been a part of," Bush said.

Paulson left the room panicked that the chances of agreement were slipping away. He chased the Democrats into the Roosevelt Room, where they had retreated to confer before going out to the cameras. Somewhat in jest, but trying to make a point about how desperate the circumstances were, Paulson found Pelosi and got down on one knee to beg her to give him time to make it work.

"Gee, Hank, I didn't know you were Catholic," she said with a laugh.

"Don't blow this up," Paulson implored her.

"We're not the ones trying to blow this up," she retorted.

"I know," he said resignedly. "I know."

WHEN THE HOUSE started voting on the bailout program at 1:25 p.m. on September 29, Bush stepped out of the Oval Office to watch on the television in the area where his secretaries sat. The television showed the rolling total as members cast their votes, and the figures looked bad from the start.

Rank-and-file lawmakers were staging a shocking revolt, defying the president, the nominees of both parties, and congressional leaders from both sides of the aisle. In an election year, they were unwilling to vote for hundreds of billions of taxpayer dollars to rescue Wall Street.

"They're not going to get the votes," Bush muttered to no one in particular. "These guys would have voted already."

The markets agreed; without waiting for the voting to finish, investors began selling off, and prices plunged at alarming rates. With each passing moment, billions of dollars of investment value were disappearing. At one point, a Democratic congressman on the floor shouted out the news. "Six hundred points!" he yelled, pointing his thumb downward to indicate the collapsing stock market. The fifteen-minute period for voting expired, but leaders clutching lists of swing members kept the roll call open as they desperately tried to corral a few more votes, all for naught. After another twenty-five minutes, it was over.

As Bush watched from the West Wing, the package went down 228 to 205 with two-thirds of his fellow Republicans voting against it. It was a seismic event. Nearly eight years into his presidency, it was the most decisive congressional repudiation of Bush's leadership—and one with enormous consequences for the country. By the time the day was done, the Dow Jones Industrial Average had plummeted 777 points, the largest single-day point drop in American history. Both sides pointed fingers. As the defeat sank in, a grim Bush called his secretary.

"Let's get Hank back over here," he said. "Get our team together. We got to get back at this and get it done."

Paulson was on edge. He saw the abyss. "Mr. President, this could be worse than 9/11 if we don't do something," he said.

Bush was calm and reassuring. Aides watching him thought he was at his best in a crisis when those below him needed lifting up. His bottomless supply of confidence, no matter how much trouble it had gotten him into in other circumstances, proved reassuring to his staff at those moments.

Bush had let Paulson run with the proposal but believed it was now time to have the White House take over. The Treasury secretary was the expert on finances, but the president's staff was more experienced in working its will on Capitol Hill. "Give us the ball for twenty-four hours," Joshua Bolten told Paulson. "Let us try to figure out how to get this together and get it done."

With lawmakers spooked by the stock market nosedive, Bolten and his team negotiated relatively minor changes in the legislation to give them cover to switch votes. And this time they would vote first in the Senate, where more members were insulated from the pressures of the upcoming election and were traditionally less populist than the House. Cheney implored Republican senators during a meeting in the walnut-paneled Mansfield Room on October 1. "If you don't pass this," he said, "you're going to make George W. Bush into the Herbert Hoover of the twenty-first century."

The Senate passed the slightly revised $700 billion plan 74 to 25 later that day, with both Obama and McCain voting yes. The House followed suit, approving it 263 to 171 two days later, on October 3. Twenty-six Republicans switched to support their president, although a majority of the party still voted no. House officials raced the bill to the White House. Within ninety minutes of the vote, it was on Bush's desk in the Oval Office. He pulled out a pen and signed it without ceremony.

Satisfied, he brought his aide Tony Fratto out to the back patio behind the Oval Office, and the two smoked cigars to mark the hard-won victory.

THAT WEEKEND, BUSH took David Petraeus up on his challenge, bringing the general to Fort Belvoir in suburban Virginia for a vigorous mountain bike ride. Petraeus, decked out in black, brought his son and thought they could keep up with the sixty-two-year-old president. But a bike ride with Bush was not for the faint of heart. As the trail suddenly narrowed, the Secret Service agents riding behind the president would not yield, and Petraeus found himself heading right into a tree. His son also fell off at one point and broke a little finger. "I realized this is not a social occasion," Petraeus said later. That evening, while out with his son for pizza after stopping by Walter Reed Army Medical Center to get the young man's finger treated, Petraeus found his phone ringing. "It's the president checking on our son," he remembered.

With time running out, Condoleezza Rice pressed for one move regarding Iran. For months, she had been urging Bush to open a U.S. interests section in Tehran, an office short of a full-fledged embassy that could issue visas and monitor events. Rice argued that it was not a favor to Iran; if anything, it was a poison pill—an outpost allowing them to encourage Iranians to travel to the United States and to gather firsthand information about what was happening inside the country. Cheney argued against it, deeming it a reward for bad behavior.

In this case, Bush leaned toward Cheney. "How important is this to Condi?" he asked Hadley pointedly. "Does she really think this is the right thing to do? Is this the State Department speaking?"

"This is something Condi really believes in," Hadley told him.

Bush rolled his eyes, but he did not tell Rice no. That was never easy for him.

Hadley eventually realized that it fell to him. After the third time Rice pressed Bush on the proposal, Hadley called her. "You know, Condi, you may be able to get the president to do this because he has great regard for you," Hadley said. "But I have to tell you, he really doesn't want to do it, and he just thinks it is a bad way to end Bush administration policy on Iran."

Rice got the message and a couple of days later told Bush she would drop it.

"Thanks," he said. "I just don't think it is the right thing to do."

"I disagree with that, Mr. President," she said, "but I respect you."

Cheney won one more small victory in the twilight days of the Bush presidency when two dozen Special Forces soldiers in Black Hawk helicopters swooped into Syria six miles across the Iraqi border and killed an al-Qaeda leader named Abu Ghadiya, leader of the network that smuggled foreign fighters into Iraq. Cheney had been pressing for months for someone to go after him, only to be told the intelligence was not definitive enough. For a while, the agencies were not even sure of his name and had no pictures. Then finally a raid on an al-Qaeda hideout captured files proving the connection. For Cheney, it was one small validation in a period of repudiation. He was, said one aide, "quite pleased."

36

"I didn't want to be the president during a depression"

Barack Obama was elected president on Tuesday, November 4, capitalizing on the deep unpopularity of the incumbent in a country tired of war and frightened of financial collapse. Despite his partisan sentiments, President Bush was deeply moved by the historic significance of an African American winning the presidency for the first time.

Even many onetime Bush loyalists got caught up in the moment. Colin Powell voted for Obama, as did Richard Armitage, Scott McClellan, and Matthew Dowd. Jim Wilkinson, who was counselor to Henry Paulson and a self-described rock-ribbed conservative, voted for Obama after watching up close how the two candidates handled the financial crisis. Kenneth Adelman, once a vocal advocate of Bush's war in Iraq, voted for Obama. Neither Paulson nor Condoleezza Rice would say whom they voted for, leading some to assume they too backed Obama.

Bush made clear to his staff that he wanted a seamless transition, and indeed Joshua Bolten had been working for months mapping out a handover of power that would be the most cooperative ever between presidents of different parties. Bush invited Obama to the Oval Office for a long talk while Laura Bush gave Michelle Obama a tour of the residence. The White House produced more than a dozen contingency plans for Obama in case an international crisis erupted in the opening days of his administration, when he would still be short-staffed and not fully prepared. The memos envisioned all sorts of volatile scenarios, like a North Korean nuclear explosion, a cyberattack on American computer systems, a terrorist strike on American facilities overseas, and a fresh outbreak of instability in the Middle East.

The most important thing Bush believed he could bequeath to Obama was a strategic framework agreement with Iraq finally outlining the end of the war. Bush wanted the pact to keep troops there until the end of 2015, while Prime Minister Nouri al-Maliki wanted them out by the end of 2010.

After months of painful haggling, they reached an agreement requiring American troops to withdraw from Iraqi cities by the end of June 2009 and to pull out of the country altogether by the end of 2011. The agreement was controversial inside an administration that had spent years resisting any kind of timetable in Iraq. Ed Gillespie opposed it, calling it an "eviction notice." But Bush signed off on it after David Petraeus and his successor, General Ray Odierno, endorsed it.

Unlike the timetables Democrats wanted to impose in 2007, this withdrawal schedule came after conditions on the ground had improved. Just 14 American troops were killed in October, down from 126 in May 2007. Odierno told Bush that troops could come home with honor. Bush and Maliki finalized the agreement on November 17. Bush hoped it would make it easier for Obama to finish the war in Iraq without feeling pressured to withdraw abruptly. At the same time, he had effectively set Iraq policy for the first three-quarters of his successor's term.

On the same day, Bush found himself making one of the most unexpected telephone calls of his presidency. When he arrived in Washington in 2001, he never imagined he would exchange pleasantries with Colonel Muammar el-Qaddafi, the Libyan dictator once dubbed by Ronald Reagan "the mad dog of the Middle East." But Qaddafi, in keeping with the rapprochement with the West, had provided $1.5 billion to victims of past Libyan terrorism, including the 1988 bombing of Pan Am Flight 103 over Lockerbie, Scotland. The phone call was organized to mark the moment and to try to keep momentum. Just two months earlier, Rice had visited Qaddafi in Libya, where he presented her with a creepy video showing pictures of her with other world leaders set to the tune of a song he had a musician write for her, "Black Flower in the White House." At least Bush would not have to worry about anything like that.

"Colonel Qaddafi?" Bush said on picking up the phone. "George Bush here."

"I'm happy by this telephone call," Qaddafi answered.

"I'm calling to confirm the fact the agreement has been concluded," Bush said, "and now we have a chance to get our relations on a much better basis."

The president called it the "basis of a new beginning" and noted that Qaddafi's son Seif would be welcomed by the administration in Washington the next day. "Good to hear your voice."

Qaddafi said he too was "happy to hear your voice" and called it a "historic moment" between the two countries.

"We still need you in the international affairs of the world," the Libyan added. "Even though you are stepping down, the world needs you." He said he hoped to meet in the future.

Bush responded that he was looking forward to retirement in Texas. "Kind to take my phone call," he added. "Perhaps our paths will cross someday. In the meantime, I ask for God's blessings on you and your people."

WITH THE HOLIDAYS approaching, Bush hosted the annual Kennedy Center honors at the White House on December 7. Among the honorees was the actor Morgan Freeman. Wearing a tuxedo and standing in front of a massive Christmas tree, Bush cited the actor's many credits, including *Deep Impact*, in which Freeman played a president confronted by a civilization-ending comet strike against the earth.

Bush looked up from his notes with a sardonic look on his face. "About the only thing that *hasn't* happened in the last eight years," he ad-libbed, to laughter and applause.

When he took his seat again, Rice leaned over. "Don't tempt fate," she said. "We've still got a few weeks left."

Indeed, while not a killer comet, Bush did face one final crisis in his last weeks as the auto industry teetered on the edge of bankruptcy. The chief executives of General Motors and Chrysler asked Washington for $25 billion in federal loans, then just seventeen days later increased the request to $34 billion.

Bush pushed his staff to negotiate a temporary solution with congressional Democrats, advancing an idea from Joel Kaplan to appoint a financial viability adviser, or car czar, who would have the power to ensure that the auto companies restructured in exchange for federal loans. The White House reached agreement with Nancy Pelosi on a bill that would provide $14 billion from an existing fund dedicated to promoting advanced technology vehicles and give the firms until March to produce plans to turn themselves around. Cheney opposed the plan. Unlike the bank bailout, which he saw as needed to save the economy as a whole, the auto bailout was rewarding private firms that made bad choices.

But having made his case and lost, Cheney agreed to defend the move on Capitol Hill. "If he told me he made a decision, there were very few times where I would say, 'Well, I think that is a really dumb idea, Mr. President,' " he recalled years later. "That is not the way I worked. There was a time to argue and a time to say, 'Yes, sir.' Once he decided it, then he would go to work and away we go." The loyal soldier appeared at the weekly lunch of Republican senators on December 10, only to be slapped down. Senator Bob

Corker, a Tennessee Republican, called the auto plan far too weak. "There is no way in heck that I would support this," he declared. If the automakers wanted their help, he said, they would have to take drastic action like cutting debt, restructuring health care, and trimming wages. Other Republicans said they would oppose any bailout on principle. By the time the Bush-Pelosi bill passed the House that night 237 to 170, it was irrelevant because Corker had taken over the issue in the Senate.

Bush welcomed Paulson into his private dining room off the Oval Office for lunch the next day. Kaplan joined them. As Bush ate small carrots, a chopped apple, and a hot dog, he listened to Paulson make the case that the automakers had not prepared for an orderly bankruptcy. While they had been bleeding slowly for years, the financial crisis had propelled them toward the cliff faster than anyone had anticipated. When Corker's Senate negotiations fell apart that night, the president decided to step in. The next morning, December 12, as he flew back to Texas to give the commencement address at Texas A&M University, Bush issued a statement through his press secretary expressing disappointment that Congress had failed to pass an auto rescue package and vowing to "consider other options if necessary—including the use of the TARP program—to prevent a collapse of troubled automakers."

AFTER THE COMMENCEMENT address, Bush headed to the ranch, providing another opportunity to slip away unnoticed for one last secret trip to Iraq. He landed in Baghdad on December 14 for his fourth visit, having flown around the world to cap his long effort to redeem the ill-fated war he had started. By most measures, it was a different Iraq from the one that had descended into the abyss in 2006. Violence was down, political institutions were developing, and Bush could arrive in the light of day instead of in pitch darkness. Most important, Bush would sign the strategic framework agreement that would lay out the plan for finally ending the war.

The arrival ceremony at the palace, complete with red carpet, marching band, and matching Iraqi and American flags, stirred Bush. Maybe something good would still come out of all this. Bush greeted Nouri al-Maliki like a long-lost brother. The doubts of two years earlier, when Stephen Hadley had written his memo questioning Maliki's fortitude, had disappeared. Bush beamed as Maliki kissed his cheeks.

"I remember what it was like in 2006, and it was bad," Bush recalled. "Now it's better. And you did it."

"We did it together," Maliki said.

Bush alluded to the American doubts about Maliki. "You know, they used to ask me, 'Where's the Iraqi Karzai?' " Bush said. "Karzai's got a pretty face, speaks English. Now they ask me, 'Where's the Afghan Maliki?' Afghanistan needs a Maliki."

It was a bit of flattery, of course, if somewhat awkward, but it also reinforced a defining truth for Bush as he was closing out his term. He had finally turned around Iraq, only to watch Afghanistan unravel in these final months. Sitting on his desk back at the White House was a request for more troops in Afghanistan, a request he would leave to his successor.

But this was not a moment for regrets after years of crises and challenges. Bush finally had something to celebrate.

"Look, I only got a few weeks left," Bush told Maliki. "You'll still be here, but I'll be down in Texas, rockin' on the porch. Never got you to Texas, right?"

"No," Maliki said. "I was quite busy here."

"It's like Iraq," Bush said. "We got desert, oil, tough folks, lots of guns."

"No place is like Iraq," Maliki said. "There's no place like Iraq, believe me."

Maliki held Bush's hand as he led him into a reception room to sign the agreement. A large table with a velvet cloth sat waiting for them with two leather binders holding reciprocal copies of the agreement and a couple of fancy pens. Next to the table were twin wooden lecterns in front of a bank of alternating American and Iraq flags. The room was packed with Iraqi and American journalists.

Suddenly, as they stood at the lecterns, someone was screaming, and something came hurtling at the president. Brett McGurk, the presidential adviser who had negotiated the agreement, thought it was a suicide bomber and assumed they were all about to die. Bush instinctively ducked to his left and the object sailed over him. He realized it was a shoe, thrown by one of the Iraqi journalists in the audience.

"This is the farewell kiss, you dog!" shouted the journalist, who then threw his other shoe. "This is from the widows, the orphans and those who were killed in Iraq!"

This time, Maliki reached out to try to block it, and Bush needed only to turn to the side a bit to dodge the shoe. For Bush, it seemed to happen in slow motion.

The room erupted in chaos as Iraqi security men pounced on the thrower. Don White, the president's lead Secret Service agent, leaped toward him, but Bush waved him off, unwilling to make the incident worse than it already was.

"I'm okay," Bush told the agent.

But his press secretary was not. As White rushed to Bush's side, he knocked into a boom microphone, which struck Dana Perino squarely in the eye. She was escorted out of the room, both hands clutching her head.

For Arabs, showing someone the bottom of a shoe is one of the most profound displays of disrespect, and throwing it at someone much worse. On the day Baghdad was liberated in 2003, Iraqis had slapped the fallen statue of Saddam Hussein with their shoes. Now Bush was the one targeted. Maliki "was white as a sheet," noticed Eric Draper, the White House photographer. But Bush tried to make light of it, smiling and motioning his hands down to calm the other Iraqi journalists, who were apologizing profusely.

"Don't worry about it, don't worry about it," Bush kept saying.

He made a joke. "If you want the facts, it's a size 10 shoe that he threw," Bush said.

The two leaders then signed the documents and proceeded upstairs for a celebratory banquet. Bush aides could hear the shoe thrower screaming as he was pummeled in another room. "Maliki's guards start beating the hell out of this guy," Douglas Lute recalled. "You can hear them laying in the blows." Secret Service agents intervened to spare the man, but to Lute it was a depressing metaphor. "You could capture the whole experience of America and Iraq. You have all the best intentions, so much hard work over the past five years, and it really comes down to the fact that the Iraqis are going to be Iraqis and they'll continue to whale on one another."

Bush tried to avoid letting the episode mar a day of triumph. Maliki was angry and embarrassed, pounding his right fist into his left hand and fuming as Bush and Ryan Crocker, the ambassador, reassured him. "He was almost inconsolable," Lute recalled.

"Hey, please, don't worry about it," Bush told Maliki. "You're making history. That guy's just a momentary thing."

Maliki apologized repeatedly. "Mr. President, you're my guest. This is my home. Please forgive the act of this man. He does not represent Iraq."

Bush brushed it off again and insisted they eat, whereupon Maliki gave a toast that focused on the shoe thrower. "That man, he represents the past," Maliki declared. "He represents everyone who has lost."

By the time Bush got back on Air Force One to head to Afghanistan, he was insisting to everyone that it was no big deal. But aides could tell he was down. The pride and bounce from earlier in the day were gone. After several hours in Kabul, he boarded the plane for the long flight home, wrapping up his final overseas trip as president. As was tradition, he and his staff watched a slide show of pictures taken by Eric Draper on the trip. Draper had captured a series of shots of the shoe whooshing toward the lectern as Bush ducked.

"Good reflexes," Joshua Bolten called out, trying to keep the mood light. Bush did not laugh. "All right," he said flatly. "Next slide."

WHILE AIR FORCE ONE made its way back from Afghanistan, Bush's economic advisers finished a memo outlining four options for the auto industry. The first would provide loans from the TARP fund in exchange for the appointment of a car czar who would require financial viability plans by March. The second would provide loans with the conditions Bob Corker had tried to attach in the Senate requiring the automakers to reduce debt, rewrite work rules, and trim wages. The third would force the companies into immediate bankruptcy and use TARP funds to finance a reorganization. And the fourth would be to do nothing and leave the firms to their fates.

Bush sat down in the Oval Office for nearly an hour and a half to discuss the alternatives. Cheney opposed a bailout and grilled the economic advisers. While the collapse of the auto industry would be damaging, potentially costing 1.1 million jobs, Cheney did not think it would be equivalent to the unraveling of Wall Street and so it did not merit taxpayer intervention. Keith Hennessey, the president's chief economics adviser, agreed. But others, including Ed Lazear, chairman of the Council of Economic Advisers, and Carlos Gutierrez, the commerce secretary, argued they could not let the firms go into Chapter 11 bankruptcy because there was no private financing available to help them restructure. Without federal funds, the result would instead be Chapter 7 liquidation. Henry Paulson and Joel Kaplan favored the second option, giving the companies loans but forcing them to meet the tough Corker conditions. The failure of the automakers, they argued, would cascade through networks of suppliers and dealers at a moment when the economy could ill afford it.

Bush said he would think about it. Paulson urged him to think fast and within a day began pestering Kaplan to find out if the president had made up his mind.

"Look, Hank, you have to give the president time on this decision," Kaplan said. "This is a difficult decision."

"It's not a difficult decision," Paulson replied. "It is an *unpleasant* decision, but it is not difficult." And, he added, "It is not going to get less unpleasant with more time."

"I hear you, Hank," Kaplan said. "But another twenty-four hours for the president to make a decision like this is not unreasonable."

The issue vexed Bush more than TARP for the reasons Cheney had outlined. As a former businessman, Bush believed a company that did not give consumers what they wanted, entered into bad contracts, and made other flawed decisions deserved to fail. That was how the market separated the strong from the weak. Yet with time running out, the argument that resonated most with Bush was not leaving a mess for his successor. Barack Obama had the right to make this call but should not have to make it in the first hours after taking the oath before even figuring out how the phones worked.

Bush, who normally kept his decision making private, wrestled with the issue out loud on the morning of December 18. Appearing before the American Enterprise Institute, he laid out the conflicting pressures on him. "This is a difficult time for a free-market person," he told the institute's president, Chris DeMuth, who interviewed him onstage. "Under ordinary circumstances, failed entities, failing entities, should be allowed to fail. I have concluded these are not ordinary circumstances, for a lot of reasons." He went on to defend his decision on TARP, explaining that the failure of a major financial institution would have "a ripple effect throughout the world" and hurt average people. Recalling Ben Bernanke's warning, Bush said, "I analyzed that and decided I didn't want to be the president during a depression greater than the Great Depression, or the beginning of a depression greater than the Great Depression. So we moved, and moved hard."

As for the auto industry, Bush said the firms "are very fragile" and that he "worried about a disorderly bankruptcy and what it would do to the psychology" of the markets. He did not want to be "putting good money after bad" in untenable enterprises, but he was spending his days imagining what it would be like for Obama taking over the country at such a perilous moment with none of the experience Bush had accumulated the hard way over eight years. "I've thought about what it would be like for me to become president during this period," he mused. "I believe that good policy is not to dump him a major catastrophe in his first day of office."

He made his mind up later that day. Rejecting Cheney's advice, Bush decided he would provide enough money through TARP to get the companies through March. But in a hybrid of the first two options, he insisted they produce plans by then to return to financial viability or risk having the loans called and being forced into bankruptcy. At Keith Hennessey's suggestion, Bush decided against dictating specifically how they fix their problems, recoiling at government getting into the details of how businesses should be run. Instead, he would make the Corker conditions nonbinding as a road map to how the firms should repair themselves; if they wanted to deviate from the Corker ideas, they would have to demonstrate they could achieve the same results. Finally, rather than appoint a car czar, he would have the Treasury secretary oversee the situation. He called Paulson to tell him his decision. It was inelegant, perhaps, and contrary to his own principles. Had it been six months earlier, the decision might have been different.

At 9:00 a.m. the next day, December 19, Bush marched into the Roosevelt Room to announce the decision. The $17.4 billion in loans would become the largest industrial bailout of its kind in American history. "In the midst of a financial crisis and a recession," Bush explained, "allowing the U.S. auto industry to collapse is not a responsible course of action."

By chance, that night Bush hosted the annual holiday dinner for his senior staff. Joshua Bolten stood and led a toast, reviewing the history of gifts the staff had given the president at Christmas over the years.

"And this year, Mr. President," he said, "we chipped in and we bought you Chrysler."

BUSH HOSTED THE world's most exclusive club on January 7, inviting Obama and the three other living presidents to lunch to share their wisdom and experience. The Wall Street bailout had arguably headed off another Great Depression and stabilized the situation, but the country still faced deep problems. Soon Bush would hand them over to Obama, and he was doing what he could to help his successor. Obama was grateful to Bush for how he was handling the transition and expressed no second thoughts about any of the decisions the outgoing president made during the interregnum. "Bush has been extraordinarily gracious toward us," said David Axelrod, Obama's senior adviser.

Joining Bush and Obama that day were Jimmy Carter, Bill Clinton, and the president's father, George H. W. Bush. Clinton, to no one's surprise, did most of the talking. Carter stood off slightly to the side, awkward even with fellow Democrats. The outgoing president was a little antsy. He struck Obama as relieved, clearly ready for the weight of the presidency to be lifted from his shoulders and to escape to Dallas, where he and Laura had bought a retirement house near the site of his future presidential library at her alma mater, Southern Methodist University.

Whatever relief Bush felt, he refused to feel sorry for himself, at least publicly. During his final news conference on January 12, he mocked the phrase "burdens of the office," as if anyone should feel bad for the most powerful man on earth.

"You know, it's kind of like, why me?" he said sarcastically. "Oh, the burdens, you know. Why did the financial collapse have to happen on my watch? It's pathetic, isn't it, self-pity?"

The next day, he invited a group of historians to the Oval Office, including John Lewis Gaddis, Jay Winik, Allen Guelzo, Walter McDougall, and Michael Barone. He was thinking about his memoir, and the historians offered thoughts about how to write it, while Chris Michel, a speechwriter who would help with the book, took notes. Bush's father had never written a traditional memoir, instead publishing a compilation of letters written over a lifetime and a separate foreign policy book with Brent Scowcroft. The younger Bush was mulling a book that, rather than a cradle-to-grave biography, would focus on a series of important decisions and how he confronted them. He had read Clinton's loquacious memoir and wanted something crisper. He mentioned Ulysses Grant's memoir, generally considered the best among presidents, and the historians told him it was a classic because it was spare and unadorned. McDougall also mentioned Harry Truman, who used his book to "remind and explain" after a presidency beset by crisis. Guelzo suggested he focus on four themes: the election and recount; the war on terror; his initiatives in education, faith-based programs and AIDS in Africa; and an articulation of conservatism that understands what government can and cannot do.

It was a long meeting, and Bush was in no hurry. He seemed eager to make sense of his eight years. Some of the visitors were struck by how serene he seemed after everything that had happened. "The presidency did not eat him up or beat him down," Gaddis recalled. "He was still upbeat and optimistic and energetic, as much as when I met him the first time five years earlier." Gaddis had been one of the inspirations for the second inaugural address vow to seek the end of tyranny, only to be disappointed that Bush "never really did anything with the idea." But he respected Bush for his conviction and fortitude.

At one point, one of the historians mentioned Cheney. Bush seized the moment to make a point, saying with a laugh that outsiders imagined his vice president exerted more influence than he really did. He pointed to a telephone on a table beside the sofa and said too many people had the impression that all Cheney had to do was call him up and he would do whatever he was told. He rattled off a series of decisions where he had overruled Cheney, even citing dates. Unknown to the historians, Bush and Cheney at that moment were wrestling over the possible pardon of Scooter Libby, but it was clear the president did not want anyone walking out thinking his vice president had been in charge. "It just came out very quickly," Gaddis said. "He was determined we got that point."

37

"Such a sense of betrayal"

The clemency process had long left a sour taste in President Bush's mouth. His father had been heavily criticized for issuing a series of politically charged pardons in his final weeks in office, most notably to Caspar Weinberger, the former defense secretary under investigation in the Iran-contra affair. Bill Clinton had left office in scandal over his last-minute pardons of a series of sordid characters, including his half brother, Roger; his former business partner Susan McDougal; and, most notoriously, the politically connected financier Marc Rich, who had fled the country to avoid tax fraud and racketeering charges. (Among Rich's lawyers at one point? Scooter Libby.) Bush had not forgotten being kept waiting in his motorcade after church on the morning of his own inauguration eight years earlier because Clinton was not ready to receive him for the traditional White House coffee after spending much of the previous twenty-four hours signing pardons.

Bush was so turned off that he became one of the stingiest presidents in American history when it came to executive clemency. Over the course of eight years, he granted just 189 pardons and 11 commutations, far fewer than any president in at least a century, with the exception of his father. Further coloring the process heading into his final days in office was a little-noticed debacle. Two days before Christmas, the president issued a series of pardons, including one for Isaac Toussie, a Brooklyn developer who had pleaded guilty to mail fraud for falsifying documents for would-be home buyers seeking government-backed mortgages. Toussie's case did not qualify under nonbinding Justice Department guidelines, and the pardon attorney who typically reviewed all applications before they were sent to the president never examined the case. But Toussie had hired Brad Berenson, a former Bush White House lawyer, and the man's father had given $28,500 to the Republican National Committee in April plus another $2,300 to the presidential campaign of John McCain.

When the New York *Daily News* reported the contributions, Joshua Bolten called Bush at Camp David to tell him. The president was already there for Christmas with his family, their final holiday at the presidential retreat. He was irritated. How had they let this happen? This made it look as if he were doling out pardons for political contributors, much as Clinton had seemed to do. Bolten was just as angry.

Bolten found William Burck, the deputy White House counsel.

"Figure out some way to undo this," Bolten told him. "Find out when a pardon is effective. Has the president signed the orders?"

"Yes."

"Have they been notified?"

"Yes."

"Have we announced it?"

"Yes."

Bolten told Burck to research the matter. Burck came back and said a pardon would not be effective until it was delivered to the recipient.

"Where is it?" Bolten asked.

"It's in the pardon attorney's office, and he's gone home for the weekend."

"You call him up," Bolten said. "You meet him as early as he's willing to come in on Saturday morning and you stand outside his office until he shows up and you don't let anybody in or out until you retrieve that pardon grant."

Burck went to the Justice Department to personally retrieve the pardon. "This is a good decision," the Justice Department lawyer who handed him the documents said, "because I don't know if anybody could survive this."

Fred Fielding, Burck's boss, then fell on his sword in a public statement explaining that he had been the one who reviewed the application and recommended it to the president. The only saving grace was that because they did it on Christmas Eve, the reversal drew relatively little attention. For once, the Bush team had caught a break.

But it only reinforced Bush's feelings about the system. "This process is broken," he railed to aides. "It is broken. It doesn't make any sense. Why is it that somebody who knows somebody in the White House gets to have a better shot than somebody who doesn't know somebody in the White House?" It irritated him even more that he was coming under pressure from all directions that season. His lifelong friend Joe O'Neill had written him a letter on behalf of a bank officer who had served time for falsifying documents and was now said to be dying. Another childhood friend from Texas, Charlie Younger, pressed him to pardon a fellow doctor who had served time on child pornography charges. Clay Johnson, his Yale friend and White House aide, was lobbying Bush to commute the sentence of David Safavian, an administration official convicted in the Jack Abramoff lobbying scandal. Supporters importuned Bush on Scooter Libby's behalf in the receiving line at White House Christmas parties. Bush deflected most of them. "Not a chance," he told Younger.

FOR VICE PRESIDENT Cheney, the Libby situation was aggravating. He was bitter that Richard Armitage had admitted to prosecutors that he was the one who originally leaked Valerie Wilson's identity, and yet neither he nor Colin Powell told their colleagues that. "The Powell-Armitage thing was such a sense of betrayal," Liz Cheney said. "They sat there and watched their colleagues in the White House—Scooter and everyone else—go through the ordeal of the investigation, and all that time they both knew Armitage was the leaker." Armitage and Powell maintained they were constrained by lawyers who told them to keep silent. Besides, Armitage said, he was not the one who put others in jeopardy. "I didn't have anything to do with Scooter and Karl," he said.

Aware that his chances were grim, Libby contacted Bolten to ask if he could talk with Bush directly, man-to-man. It seemed like the Texas thing to do.

"I'm sorry, Scooter," said Bolten, who considered Libby a friend. "In fairness to the president, I can't permit that."

Then Cheney went to Bolten.

"Scooter would like to visit with the president."

"I know," Bolten said. "I've already told him no."

"I'm asking you," Cheney said.

Bolten stuck to his guns and said no.

"I'd like you to ask the president directly," Cheney said finally.

"I wish you wouldn't ask me to do that," Bolten said, "but obviously the president would not want me screening him from any request of yours."

In the end, Bush backed up Bolten, refusing to see Libby. Bolten suggested Libby see the White House lawyers instead.

On the final weekend of the administration, as Bush retreated to Camp David for his last getaway, Libby sat down with Fred Fielding and William Burck in a booth at McCormick & Schmick's, a chain seafood restaurant on K Street a few blocks from the White House. It was just after 11:00 a.m. on a weekend, and they hoped no one would recognize them.

For the next ninety minutes, Libby made his case, but the White House lawyers were not swayed. Uncomfortable grilling a former colleague, they nonetheless started going through the evidence. *Isn't it possible? What about this witness?* No, Libby insisted. The point was not what was in the trial record but what was not. The prosecutors had suppressed expert testimony about the unreliability of memory that Libby was sure would have exonerated him. They should look at that, he insisted.

Then Fielding and Burck raised another point: pardons in the modern era were typically issued not to people claiming to be innocent but to convicts who had paid their debts to society and were seeking forgiveness. Under Justice Department guidelines at the time, the pardon attorney who prepared recommendations for the president did not even accept requests until at least five years after applicants had completed their sentences. That did not mean a president could not pardon someone who did not fit that criterion—under the Constitution, the president's pardon power is virtually without limit—but it indicated what was considered an acceptable case for a pardon.

Fielding and Burck asked Libby if he would be willing to admit guilt and ask for forgiveness to obtain a pardon.

No, Libby said. "I am innocent. I did not do this."

FOR A MAN about to win his own freedom, Bush was awfully grumpy. He was at Camp David on that frigid final weekend to mark the end of his presidency and the beginning of a new life back in Texas. With him were his family and a few select friends and advisers, including Bolten, Condoleezza Rice, Henry Paulson, and Stephen Hadley. He had been looking forward to this moment for some time.

If other presidents were reluctant to give up power, Bush was eager to escape Washington and the burdens of an administration that had been consumed by terrorism, war, natural disaster, and now a financial crash rivaling the Great Depression. For this final weekend at the retreat in the Maryland mountains, he planned to celebrate, to focus on the triumphs, not the setbacks, to reflect and remember and soak in his dwindling hours in office. But he was distracted. His mind kept wandering back to his fight with Cheney.

While the rest of his clan was in another room, Bush found a telephone and called Dan Bartlett back in Texas.

"This sucks," Bush said. "Here I am, supposed to be trying to have a great weekend with my family, last weekend, and here I am knowing what a difficult decision it is going to be."

Bartlett reassured him. "You are making the right decision," he said.

Still, Bush's advisers were worried. Bolten felt he had failed the president because he should have protected him from having to confront his own vice president. Rice, who was closer to him than any other adviser, watched Bush as he sulked in the living room of Laurel Lodge and thought he needed to be shaken out of his funk.

"Can I talk to you a minute?" she asked.

They slipped away to the lodge's small presidential office with the sloped ceiling and wooden bookcases.

"Don't let this be a pall over your last days as president," she told him. "You deserve better and you've done so much and you've secured the country and you've done all these things, and this shouldn't be the way that you spend your last hours as president."

Bush nodded. He understood, but he could not help it.

Finally, it fell to his wife, Laura, as it often did, to ground him.

"Just make up your mind," she told him. "You're ruining this for everyone."

He and Laura returned to Washington that Sunday afternoon, January 18, and went to dinner at the spacious home of their friends Jim and Sandy Langdon in the Spring Valley neighborhood of the capital. They had visited any number of times over the past eight years, but this time an official photographer came along to record the evening, a sign of the impending end.

Jim Langdon knew of the president's struggle and interrupted dinner.

"I got this list of people that I need pardons for," he announced jokingly.

Bush laughed.

THE FIGHT OVER the Libby pardon was not the only drama shadowing the final days of the Bush-Cheney administration. By the weekend before the inauguration, intelligence agencies had picked up signs of a plot to attack Barack Obama's swearing-in ceremony. A group of Somali extremists was said to be heading over the border from Canada intent on exploding a bomb on the Mall on Inauguration Day, "the manifestation of one of our worst nightmares," as Juan Carlos Zarate, Bush's counterterrorism chief, put it.

The Bush team briefed their counterparts in the emerging Obama administration, and together they confronted hard choices: An assault on the inaugural ceremony, literally the transfer of power, the most exalted symbol of American democracy, would be devastating, even if it failed to kill the new president. A scene of chaos on the podium could cripple a new commander in chief. What does Obama do if in mid-speech a bomb goes off? asked Hillary Rodham Clinton, the incoming secretary of state, when the two teams met together in the Situation Room. "Is the Secret Service going to whisk him off the podium so the American people see their incoming president disappear in the middle of the inaugural address?" she asked. "I don't think so." No one had a good answer.

The two sides agreed that Robert Gates, who would stay on as Obama's defense secretary, should be kept away from the ceremony to preserve the chain of command in case of disaster. As a sitting cabinet officer with the imprimatur of the new president, Gates was the logical choice to take over the country if everyone above him in the line of succession were to perish. Eventually, the threat turned out to be what intelligence professionals call a "poison pen," when one group of radicals plants a false story to get Americans to take out rivals. But Bush and Cheney could hardly have left their successors a more vivid demonstration of what they had been dealing with for more than seven years or a more fitting lesson in the murky nature of terrorism—distinguishing between what was real and what was not, tracking down where threats began, figuring out the right response, and finding a balance between acknowledging danger and projecting confidence.

On his last full day in office, January 19, Bush put on a suit and arrived at the Oval Office by 7:00 a.m. as usual. He was scheduled to make back-to-back farewell calls to thirteen world leaders, starting with President Mikheil Saakashvili of Georgia at 7:00 a.m., Prime Minister Vladimir Putin at 7:10 a.m., President Lee Myung-bak of South Korea at 7:20 a.m., and so on. The talking points on the presidential memo consisted in their entirety of the following fourteen words:

- "Enjoyed working with you."
- "We have accomplished a lot together."
- "Wish you continued success."

The biggest debate was whether to call both Putin and Dmitry Medvedev. Protocol would usually have the president call only his formal counterpart, which would now be Medvedev. But Bush decided to call both; after all their time together, after all the moments of collaboration and tension, he wanted to say good-bye to "my friend Vladimir." Despite the rupture over the Georgia war, just five months before, Bush wistfully recounted the many visits they had made to each other, at Crawford and the Moscow dacha, in St. Petersburg. He recalled their cooperation on Iran, North Korea, the Middle East, terrorism, arms control, and economics. They had, Bush told Putin, "many fond memories."

Bush had one other final piece of business. At 11:00 a.m., he met in the Oval Office with Fred Fielding and William Burck, who reported to him on their meeting with Scooter Libby over the weekend. They had not changed their minds, they told Bush during a half-hour conversation. Moreover, they pointed out that Libby was not asking for forgiveness because he maintained his innocence. Bush took it all in. He signed clemency orders commuting the sentences of two Border Patrol agents convicted of shooting a Mexican drug dealer, a case that had become a cause célèbre for conservative critics of illegal immigration who thought they were persecuted for doing their jobs. But when Bush put his pen down, that was it. No more clemency meant no pardon for Libby. He would stick to his decision despite Cheney's passionate opposition.

BUSH'S ASTRINGENT ENCOUNTER with Cheney was still fresh when the day came to hand over the Oval Office. On the morning of Inauguration Day, Bush showed up at the Oval Office as usual. His staff had left the office exactly the same as it had been, with all the photographs and paraphernalia still in place. But quietly, the president had given away his cigars, resolving to quit when he moved back to Texas. Bush slipped a handwritten note to the incoming forty-fourth president into a manila envelope marked "The White House" and attached a yellow Post-it note to the outside. He jotted down "44" on it and left it on the *Resolute* desk for Obama.

Bush was to host the Obamas before escorting them down Pennsylvania Avenue to the Capitol for the swearing-in ceremony that would end his presidency after eight turbulent years. But as he waited for the appointed hour, he went wandering around the West Wing with Joshua Bolten. The place was a construction zone as crews rushed to put up more interior walls to make more cubbyholes for the new tenants. "The place was going condo," Bolten recalled. Bush walked past the workmen, who paid no attention to him. He was mellow and reflective.

Eventually, it came time to leave.

"Okay, I'm going over to the residence," he announced to his remaining staff. "Where's my coat?"

He put on his overcoat and cowboy hat in the reception area next to the Oval Office, stepped out the door, walked down the Colonnade in the morning chill toward the East Wing, and never turned back. There was no moment of hesitation to look around the Oval Office one last time.

Just before 10:00 a.m., he and Laura stepped outside the mansion onto the North Portico and greeted Barack and Michelle Obama warmly. They led them inside for the traditional Inauguration Day coffee, a comforting ritual of unity after a campaign season of division. That morning, there were two of everything—two presidents, two vice presidents, two first ladies, two Secret Service details. "It's like Noah's ark," observed Eric Draper, the outgoing Bush photographer.

Cheney showed up in a wheelchair, explaining that he had thrown his back out packing boxes at the vice presidential mansion over the weekend. "Cheney looked like hell," recalled Joel Kaplan, who saw him later in the day. It produced an odd, awkward scene, as if all of Cheney's efforts of the last eight years, all of the fights and the controversy, had finally taken their toll on a nearly sixty-eight-year-old body that had already endured four heart attacks.

"Joe, this is how you're liable to look when your term is up," Cheney joked to his successor, Joseph Biden.

Bush and Cheney separated as they left the White House, each joining his counterpart for the short motorcade to the Capitol. Bush blew a kiss to the White House as he left, then climbed into the armored car with Obama. As the two men settled into the cushioned seats and the tanklike vehicle began its slow, circuitous path past the barricades and out of the White House grounds, Bush took the opportunity to give his successor one last piece of advice.

Whatever you do, Bush said, make sure you set a pardon policy from the start and then stick to it.

In the midst of war and recession, what was on Bush's mind in the final hour of his presidency was his vice president.

When they arrived at the Capitol, Bush took his place on the platform on the West Front. Obama supporters in the crowd chanted, "Nah, nah, nah, nah, hey, hey, hey, good-bye." As Cheney was wheeled to his place, he too heard boos. Democrats buzzed about how the wheelchair-bound vice president had finally made the last transition into Mr. Potter, the cruel tycoon from *It's a Wonderful Life.*

Bush paid no attention. He found Obama's daughters and leaned over to say something to the younger one, Sasha, smiling as he got up close to her face. When he sat down in the big leather chair reserved for him, he and Obama leaned across the aisle separating them and exchanged words that made them both laugh.

Obama began his inaugural address with a note of gratitude for his predecessor. "I thank President Bush for his service to our nation as well as the generosity and cooperation he has shown throughout this transition," he said.

But much of the rest of the speech added up to a repudiation of Bush. Obama criticized "our collective failure to make hard choices and prepare the nation for a new age." He promised to "restore science to its rightful place." He rejected "as false the choice between our safety and our ideals." He assured the rest of the world "that we are ready to lead once more." All in all, it was perhaps the starkest inaugural rejection of a departing president since Franklin Roosevelt took over from Herbert Hoover in 1933.

Bush took it in stride. "That was a hell of a speech," he told Rahm Emanuel, the new president's chief of staff.

Then he headed back through the Rotunda of the Capitol to the marine helicopter waiting on the East Front.

"Come on, Laura," he told his wife, "we're going home."

He gave Obama a hug.

"We will brief you from time to time," Obama told him.

"There is no need for that," Bush said. "I have served my time, and I don't want you to feel like you need to waste a lot of time on me."

Bush was done with Washington. With a last salute, he boarded the helicopter. It was just him, his family, his aide Blake Gottesman, Eric Draper, and some Secret Service agents. Lifting into the air, Bush took Laura's hand and stared out the window at the Capitol and the throngs of people who had come to celebrate his successor's installation—and in effect his own departure. In his other hand, he clutched remarks he planned to give to former aides gathered at Andrews Air Force Base. But something changed in his demeanor on the short flight. Finally, after eight years of living every burden, shouldering every calamity, after all the triumphs and all the misjudgments, he was free. "He looked relieved, thrilled," Draper recalled. "You could see it on his face. His job was over."

At Andrews, Cheney was to introduce Bush during a private ceremony in the hangar. "Frankly, all of us were worried about what he was going to say because we all knew, the people close to the president, how bad and rough the last few days had been," said Joel Kaplan. But Cheney delivered a gracious speech extolling their eight-year partnership. Bush was relieved. After all the tension over the pardon, he had feared their friendship had been broken irretrievably. He took solace from the vice president's words. But it did not close the underlying rift. "George Bush's two terms were almost two different presidencies," David Addington observed. "The second term was rough on both of them, rough on their relationship."

After the two said their farewells, Cheney headed out. Obama had authorized the military to fly the vice president back to Wyoming on the jet he had used as Air Force Two. Once he landed in Casper, his friend Mick McMurry sent his private plane to fly Cheney the rest of the way to Jackson. "Nice plane, Mick," Cheney told him with his wry smile. "I used to have a nice plane."

That evening, Cheney joined friends and family at a welcome-home party. "He was in excruciating pain," his friend Bill Thomson noticed. Cheney refused to take painkillers to avoid a fuzzy head. "He was showing his wear and tear," McMurry said later. "But he seemed to enjoy the evening." Indeed, the taciturn former vice president relaxed. "For Dick, he was pretty talkative that night," McMurry said. "He was out of a job. I guess he could say what he wanted to." While he did not talk much about Bush, McMurry was convinced that "he probably has a firmer relationship with George senior" than with the president he had served the past eight years.

The younger Bush made his way back to Texas aboard one of the special Boeing 747 planes normally designated Air Force One but now just called Special Air Mission 28000. His parents were on board, as were many of the aides who had accompanied him on the journey, most from Texas, like Karl Rove, Karen Hughes, Dan Bartlett, Margaret Spellings, Alberto Gonzales, Mark McKinnon, Joel Kaplan, and Israel Hernandez. They gathered in the conference room to watch a farewell video, including testimonials and tributes from the likes of Tony Blair and Bill Clinton. There was a lot of hugging, a lot of laughing, a lot of relief. "It was a nonstop party the whole way," Draper said. Bush posed for a picture with his mother, resting his chin on her shoulder. "He was very huggy," recalled one aide. "He was hugging everybody. A little weepy, but mostly just hugging people." The tone of Obama's speech produced some grousing among the loyalists, who resented that he had slapped Bush on the way out. But the now-former president did not join in, uttering "not a word" disparaging his successor, as Hughes recalled.

Seventeen hundred miles to the west, Bush landed back in Midland, where he had started his own inaugural journey eight years earlier. He was grayer and worn, now sixty-two years old, and in a sentimental mood. As he got off the plane, he kissed Gonzales on the forehead and said, "Just stay strong." The weather and the crowd were far more forgiving than in Washington. Warmed up by the Gatlin Brothers and Lee Greenwood, more than twenty thousand supporters waving red, white, and blue "W" signs greeted Bush in Centennial Plaza as the sun sank in the west. "There was a moment you got the impression that nobody liked him at all," recalled Hernandez, his longtime aide. "But then he got to Midland and there was a huge crowd. That was very emotional for him."

Bush made a few remarks to the crowd. "Tonight," he told them, "I have the privilege of saying six words that I have been waiting to say for a while—it is good to be home." He offered just a bit of defense of his embattled presidency. "Popularity is as fleeting as the Texas wind," he said. "Character and conscience are as sturdy as our oaks. History will be the judge of my decisions, but when I walked out of the Oval Office this morning, I left with the same values that I took to Washington eight years ago. When I get home tonight and look in the mirror, I am not going to regret what I see—except maybe some gray hair."

EPILOGUE

"There is no middle ground"

One day a couple of years after he left office, Dick Cheney sat down in a small library in the front of his new house in McLean, Virginia, sipped a cup of his favorite Starbucks coffee, and reflected on his time in power.

He was skinnier, his face hollowed out a bit. He was still recovering his strength from a heart attack he suffered after leaving office but had not yet undergone the heart transplant that would come later. He wore a blue Oxford shirt and khaki pants as well as a dark vest that covered the device attached to his chest that kept his weak heart running. He was feeling good, he said. Not running marathons, but going fishing. He spent four months a year in Wyoming, three in the summer, one in winter.

As he talked, Jordan, his black Labrador, lay sleeping nearby, while a yellow Labrador wandered in and out as if checking out the conversation. The off-white house behind a gate in McLean had been built during his last year in office, just down the street from Hickory Hill, the famed estate of Robert F. Kennedy. The Cheneys' retirement home had four bedrooms, six full baths, three half baths, and four fireplaces, large enough for the daughters and their partners and half a dozen grandkids to visit.

On the shelf in the library were the classics expected in a Washington house—Robert Caro, Michael Beschloss, and the like—plus plenty of military histories, including Rick Atkinson's account of the Gulf War, a Cheney favorite. Sitting unread at that point were memoirs by George W. Bush and Condoleezza Rice. But there were also some surprises, including books by critics like Ron Suskind and a volume called *Dick: The Man Who Is President*. On display was a brick from the house of Mullah Muhammed Omar, the Taliban leader, and another from the house where Abu Musab al-Zarqawi was killed. There was, of course, a bust of Winston Churchill. On the wall hung a sword from his great-grandfather, who fought in the Civil War on the Union side.

"It was designed for the two of us. It is a great house," he said. "We can live on one floor. We were thinking about our old age, when we wouldn't be able to get around as easy, so we got a second floor, but we put an elevator in. Made it easy to get to that. We have an apartment over the garage that has been the book office for a lot of what we did this time around, but eventually we'll have someone live in it to look after us. So it has been a lot of fun living here. The only new house we have ever owned, the only one we ever built, and I would never do it again. Everybody always says that, but there are thousands of decisions—doorknobs, by God! It takes a lot of effort to put something like that together. Fortunately, I was an observer and check writer."

Now in retirement, Cheney had taken stock. He took pride in championing what he thought was necessary to protect the country and had no regrets about what others considered the excesses of Iraq, Guantánamo, and waterboarding. "We didn't capture al-Qaeda and say, 'Okay, bring on the water,'" he said. "That is never the way it worked. But as I say, some of our critics would lead us to believe that as soon as we captured these guys, that we started pulling out fingernails and toenails."

Did any part of him feel queasy about what was done in the name of security, even if it was perfectly justified? "No," he said with the calm certitude that marked his tenure in public life. "I firmly believe that it was the right thing to do. It worked. We haven't been hit for seven and a half years, longer than that now."

That was the calculation: means and ends. If the threat was dire enough, then getting rough with a handful of suspects seemed a small price to pay, especially Khalid Sheikh Mohammed, the acknowledged mastermind of September 11. *Whatever it takes.*

"I wasn't concerned just about guarding against another set of airplane hijackings," Cheney went on. "That wasn't the threat. The threat was the ultimate—a possibility of nineteen hijackers armed with a nuke or a biological agent. When you put that out there as the threat that you are trying to guard against, then the question of waterboarding one guy to find out what he knows isn't cause for concern. Thank God we had him and had the ability to get him to talk to us."

As he reflected on eight eventful years, Cheney said he believed he had a "consequential vice presidency," thanks to Bush. "That is the way he wanted it. He is the one who made that possible, not me." He recognized that his influence had faded by the end. He betrayed no anger about that, only acceptance. "Over time, I think I was probably more valuable to the president in the early part than the later part," he said. "Part of that was a learning process for him. By the time we got down toward the later part of the second term, he was much more—well, he had the experience of having been president for all those years, and he relied less, I think, on staff than had been true earlier."

Their parting at Andrews Air Force Base that winter day in 2009 also represented a departure in mission. Bush retreated to Texas, where he quietly went about building a presidential library and developing a public policy institute, while Cheney emerged from his undisclosed location to become a fiery critic of the new president. While Bush resolutely vowed not to pass judgment on his successor, declaring that President Obama "deserves my silence," Cheney had plenty of judgment to pass and thought the country deserved his voice.

What set him off as much as anything was a decision by the new administration to reopen an investigation into CIA interrogations of terror suspects. In Cheney's mind, there could be no more serious betrayal. As he saw it, CIA officers operating under guidelines provided by the Justice Department to break captives and gain information to stop future terrorist attacks were now being treated as criminals. At one point, Cheney gave a speech on the subject on the same day Obama did, offering an unusual split-screen virtual debate between a sitting president and a former vice president. Obama argued for a middle ground between values and security. "The American people are not absolutist," he said in his speech at the National Archives, "and they don't elect us to impose a rigid ideology on our problems." Across town, Cheney argued that absolutism in the defense of liberty was no vice. "In the fight against terrorism," he declared, "there is no middle ground, and half measures keep you half exposed."

Cheney's outspokenness was striking after so many years of staying largely behind the scenes, but it was only a new phase in the same campaign of defending the policies he had helped institute in the first term. "Dick feels an obligation to say what really happened, at least from their perspective," said his friend Bill Thomson. Stephen Hadley thought Cheney was strongly influenced by his experience during Iran-contra, when he believed mid-level officials were sacrificed politically, and saw a parallel with the CIA officers. "Cheney thought that was shameful," Hadley said. "He went out and had an opportunity to throw his body in the way of that freight train." Liz Cheney said her father might have followed Bush's approach and remained quiet had it not been for the investigation. "Threatening to prosecute CIA officials was indefensible," she said. "It was just so far beyond what you could stay silent and watch."

Cheney's public battle with Obama, though, seemed almost like a proxy for his private battle with Bush. Out of deference and his deep respect for protocol, Cheney could say only so much as he watched Bush compromise again and again in their final years in office. But now he could lash out with a Democrat as the target, making the same argument to the nation that he had made in the Situation Room. "He'll never criticize Bush directly," observed David Gordon, an adviser to Condoleezza Rice, "but even the way he criticizes Obama, I think, is implicitly a criticism of the last couple of years" of the Bush administration. In Cheney's mind, the betrayal of the CIA officers became an extension of the betrayal of Scooter Libby. They were all men left behind on the battlefield. "Dick was terribly upset that he didn't pardon him, get him off the hook," recalled his friend Bernie Seebaum. "The man did what he was expected to do, and then he got in trouble for it. Nobody came to his rescue." Cheney felt almost unshackled. "The statute of limitations," he told associates, "has expired." And in the end, Cheney felt he had shifted the public debate; eventually, the Obama administration dropped the investigation.

SITTING IN DALLAS, Bush watched with interest and a little ambivalence. He quizzed visiting friends and former aides on what they thought of the vice president's public campaign but generally did not share his own opinions. He spent his days writing his memoir, building his presidential library, and establishing a public policy institute focused on six main areas: democracy promotion, global health, economic growth, education reform, military service, and women's rights. He gave dozens of speeches and traveled to Africa, expanding his work combating AIDS and malaria to target cervical cancer as well.

He was particularly engaged with veterans. He hosted injured soldiers for hundred-kilometer "wounded warrior" bicycle marathons and visited military hospitals unannounced. He showed up one day at a Texas airport to greet troops coming home from Iraq, a moment that would have gone unnoticed but for the phone cameras that recorded the event and uploaded it to the Internet. Iraq was never far away; he told one former aide who visited him in Dallas that he thought about it every single day. The attention to veterans was his way of grappling with the decision to go to war. "This is not the right word, but that absolves him of guilt," said one friend. "I don't think he feels guilt in any respect or remorse. I think he feels sorrow and sadness for what he's seen have been the consequences of war, but I think the relationship with the military families is a huge part of his life these days."

Bush was determined not to be dragged back into "the swamp," as he put it. No more politics. He told a group of visitors in Dallas that he felt liberated on the day of Obama's inauguration. "When I saw his hand go up, I thought, 'Free at last,'" Bush said. He stayed off the campaign trail during the 2010 midterm elections. When Karl Rove regaled a dinner party at the former president's house in Dallas one night with his analysis of the congressional contests, Bush paid little attention, cracking jokes instead with the wife of a guest sitting next to him. His entire involvement in the 2012 presidential campaign was to offer a four-word endorsement of Obama's Republican opponent when a reporter pursued him after an unrelated event. "I'm for Mitt Romney," Bush said simply as elevator doors shut.

Beyond the largely closed-door speeches and low-profile policy work, Bush enjoyed going to Texas Rangers games, took up painting much as Dwight Eisenhower and Winston Churchill had done, and picked up golf again, years after giving it up out of deference to troops at war. "He's a golf-a-holic now," said his friend Charlie Younger. Bush often played with the first four people who happened to show up at a course, and the Bush family competitive gene kicked in. "I decided I was going to get better at golf, not just *play* golf," he told Walt Harrington, a writer and friend, one day, putting his golf-shoe-clad feet up on his desk and chewing on an unlit cigar. "I have gotten better. The problem is I'm never good enough. That's the problem with the game. It requires discipline, patience, and focus. As you know, I'm long on"—and he paused with a smile—"well, a couple areas where I could use some improvement."

Wayne Berman, who hosted Bush for dinner in Washington after he left office, was struck by his serenity. "I've never seen a happier, more relaxed man than George W. Bush since he left the presidency," he said. While Bill Clinton found departure from the White House a wrenching experience and often talked of how he wished he could have had a third term, Bush seemed to actually mean it when he disclaimed any longing for power. "I'm often asked, do you miss the presidency?" he told one audience. "I really don't." He explained it during a rare visit to the capital to unveil a collection of interviews with dissidents from around the world fighting for freedom in their countries: "I actually found my freedom by leaving Washington."

NEARLY A YEAR to the day after flying home to Texas, Bush returned to the White House. Arriving early, he roamed the halls and greeted the ushers and Secret Service officers by name, joking in a familiar, comfortable way. He had come in response to a request by Obama to team up with Clinton to lead the recovery effort for Haiti after a devastating earthquake. It was Bush's first time back in Washington, and Obama aides were nervous about seeing him, but within a few minutes he had put them at ease. "It was more like meeting an old friend," Valerie Jarrett, Obama's senior adviser, said afterward.

And in a way it was. As much as Obama had run against Bush's legacy in 2008, he ended up embracing much of it in 2009. He kept Bush's defense secretary and many other top national security figures, and he decided to follow Bush's plan for a three-year withdrawal from Iraq. While he jettisoned the term "war on terror" and banned the harsh interrogation techniques that had been so controversial, Obama failed to close the Guantánamo prison, just as Bush had, kept the terrorist surveillance program, authorized the use of military commissions, and decided to hold some terror suspects indefinitely without trial, albeit with more procedural protections built into the process. He more or less adopted Bush's policy toward North Korea, only somewhat modified the approach to Iran, effectively copied the Iraq surge by sending more troops to Afghanistan, and expanded the drone campaign in Pakistan. Arguably, Obama validated some of Bush's most important decisions. By 2013, Ari Fleischer was claiming that Obama was "carrying out Bush's 4th term."

There were more pronounced differences over domestic policy, most notably Obama's expansion of health care and support for marriage and military service for gays and lesbians. But even at home, the new president preserved many of Bush's initiatives. Obama completed the financial and auto industry bailouts that Bush began, largely kept No Child Left Behind and the Medicare drug prescription program, and built on his increases in fuel economy standards and incentives for renewable energy. While Obama ran against Bush's tax cuts, he ended up reauthorizing roughly 85 percent of them, reversing them for just the top 1 percent of American taxpayers. And Obama made one of his highest second-term priorities an overhaul of the immigration system, moving to complete Bush's unfinished mission.

The disparity between Obama's campaign trail rhetoric on national security and his actions upon taking office shocked some of his supporters but should have come as little surprise to anyone who watched the evolution of the previous administration. Obama essentially ran against Bush's first term but inherited his second. By the time Bush left office, he had already shaved off the harsher, more controversial edges of his war on terror, either under pressure from Congress, the courts, and public opinion or out of a conscious effort to put his policies on a firmer foundation with more bipartisan approval. He had emptied the secret CIA prisons, cleared out many of the prisoners at Guantánamo, approved no waterboarding after 2003, and secured the approval of lawmakers for military commissions, expansive surveillance, and other elements of his program.

Bush followed the historical pattern of governments in times of crisis or war, when presidents push the boundaries of the law in the name of protecting the country. Eventually, the system corrects itself and scales back the extremes. John Adams signed the Alien and Sedition Acts that jailed opponents for their political speech. Andrew Jackson forcibly removed Indian tribes that resisted eviction from lands east of the Mississippi. Abraham Lincoln suspended habeas corpus and put American citizens on trial before military commissions even in areas not in rebellion. Woodrow Wilson allowed the imprisonment of a 1912 election opponent for speaking out against World War I. Franklin Roosevelt forced 110,000 Japanese Americans into internment camps during World War II for no other reason than their ethnic background. Bush and Cheney did not go as far as many of these precedents. Although hundreds of Muslims were swept up in the early days after September 11, largely on immigration violations, the wave of arrests paled by comparison to the Japanese roundup in the 1940s, and it subsided quickly. Bush made a point of visiting a mosque, hosting *iftar* dinners at the White House, and repeatedly making clear that he considered Islam a peaceful religion that had been distorted by a relative few radicals. The brutal interrogation techniques used by CIA officers were applied to no more than three dozen prisoners, and just three were waterboarded, although one of them was subjected to it a stunning 183 times. Political opponents were free to lambaste Bush and Cheney as vigorously as they wished without fear of imprisonment. "There's no doubt that whatever President Bush did to curtail civil liberties in the war on terror, a case can be made that a lot of what he did was far less than what other presidents have done in wartime," said Jay Winik, the historian who met with Bush on a few occasions. "In each case our system righted itself. With President Bush, he did respond over time and as conditions allowed."

Still, if history is a defense to an extent, it also is an indictment. Rather than learn from the mistakes of their predecessors, Bush and Cheney repeated them. The most controversial actions of American presidents have proved more durable when they obtained buy-in from other sectors of society, particularly Congress. Bush and Cheney preferred instead to operate on their own, reasoning that disclosure of some techniques would jeopardize security and asserting that the executive had vast, unchecked power when it came to guarding the nation. Congress and the courts would only get in the way. The threat was too serious.

Any number of Bush aides reached the conclusion that it was a mistake, from Jack Goldsmith, the Justice Department lawyer who reversed some of the most sweeping legal interpretations in the terror war, to Donald Rumsfeld, who argued after leaving office that the president would have been better off engaging Congress more. Eventually, Bush came around to the same view. "In retrospect, I probably could have avoided some of the controversy and legal setbacks by seeking legislation on military tribunals, the TSP, and the CIA enhanced interrogation program as soon as they were created," he wrote in his memoir, using the initials for Terrorist Surveillance Program, the administration's name for its warrantless eavesdropping. "If members of Congress had been required to make their decisions at the same time I did—in the immediate aftermath of 9/11—I am confident they would have overwhelmingly approved everything we requested." Or at least forced compromises that might have averted some of the worst abuses.

The unnecessary controversies combined with the devastating misjudgments in Iraq ended up detracting from what otherwise might have been a solid record for the forty-third president. Bush logged major achievements both at home and abroad. He pushed to make education better and saw test scores rise. He helped the elderly afford prescription medicine. He lowered taxes not just for the wealthy but for the middle class and freed millions of lower-income Americans from income taxes altogether. He helped spur a domestic energy boom in both traditional and renewable sectors that dramatically reversed American dependence on foreign oil. He expanded free trade and reduced the nuclear arsenal. He helped arrest the AIDS epidemic in Africa, saving millions of lives. He put two strong conservatives on the Supreme Court. He spoke out for democracy in the Muslim world at a time when others believed it impossible, then took great satisfaction in the Arab Spring that toppled dictators after his presidency. Perhaps most important, while any number of factors were at work, he and his vice president could reasonably claim to have protected the country following September 11.

Whatever the president's virtues, though, they remained unappreciated in his own time. To say that Bush was unpopular only begins to capture the historic depths of his estrangement from the American public in the years before he left office. He was arguably the most disliked president in seven decades. Seventy-one percent of Americans interviewed in a Gallup poll disapproved of his job performance during the worst of the financial crisis in October 2008, the highest negative rate ever recorded for any president since the firm began asking the question in 1938. And while Harry Truman and Richard Nixon at their worst had even fewer supporters—Truman once fell to 22 percent in his job approval rating and Nixon to 24 percent, compared with Bush's low of 25 percent—no president has endured such a prolonged period of public rejection. The last time Bush enjoyed the support of a majority of Americans was March 2005, meaning he went through virtually his entire second term without most of the public behind him. Academic scholars, generally more liberal and never fans of Bush's anti-intellectualism to begin with, ranked him among the five worst presidents in parlor-game polls.

Cheney fared even worse. In Gallup's tracking, which asked about the vice president much less frequently than the president, Cheney slipped into the thirties in 2006 and never recovered. His low of 30 percent found by Gallup in mid-2007 was actually higher than other polls found. At one point in 2006, shortly after the shooting accident, just 18 percent of those surveyed by CBS News approved of the vice president's performance, a number so profoundly low for a political figure of his stature that it became the source of numerous jokes at Cheney's expense, including by the president.

Cheney was unapologetic in the years to come. When he released his own memoir and did the requisite media tour, he gave no ground as he was pressed again and again on issues of torture, war, and surveillance. Asked if the decision to invade Iraq was still the right one given all the costs, he said, "Oh sure. I don't think it damaged our reputation around the world. I just don't believe that." He added, "It was sound policy that dealt with a very serious problem and that eliminated Saddam Hussein."

Bush, never much known for introspection, nonetheless was more willing to identify mistakes, whether it be not sending more troops earlier to Iraq or not acting more decisively to respond to Katrina. But he too stood by the most fundamental decisions, and professed serenity about history's judgment, noting that if George Washington's legacy can still be debated, then his own would not be settled until long after his death. "There's no need to defend myself," he said at one point. "I did what I did and ultimately history will be the judge."

He likewise rejected any suggestion that the myriad crises that confronted him on his watch had weighed him down. "The tendency in life is to feel sorry for yourself—like, 'Oh, man, why me?' You know?" he told an audience at a conference closed to the general public in March 2011. "And particularly when you're president, you know? And then you read about Abraham Lincoln, and you realize that he had a really tough presidency. And so, you know, it helps keep your life in perspective." Bush said he focused on history and tried to avoid the cable chatter. "I didn't watch any TV. 'You didn't watch the news?' I said, 'Hell, no, I didn't watch the news. You know, I *was* the news.' Abraham Lincoln motivated me a lot. He was a great president. Abraham Lincoln understood the president's need to stand on principle no matter how tough the politics might be. So he said all men are created equal under God. In 1863, you know, that wasn't necessarily a given. Lincoln made a great presidential decision in spite of the politics of the moment."

Bush's graceful post-presidency seemed to temper judgments. As he hit the television circuit in 2010 to promote *Decision Points*, his memoir, he found a country a little more open to him, and the book rocketed to the top of the best-seller lists. Most Americans still did not view him favorably, and many still reviled him for invading Iraq, waterboarding terror suspects, and presiding over the worst financial crisis in decades. He was still a punch line, to many a failed president, the source of today's economic and foreign policy troubles. Yet with his successor facing his own difficulties and "Miss Me Yet?" T-shirts with Bush's face on them for sale at Washington's Union Station a short walk from the Capitol, Obama's blame-Bush strategy did not stop voters from returning Republicans to power in the House and handing them more seats in the Senate that fall. By 2013, polls suggested a softening of opinion, with 49 percent of Americans now expressing favorable views, compared with 46 percent who saw him unfavorably, the first time in eight years that he enjoyed a positive balance.

In part, that reflected disenchanted Republicans and conservative independents returning home, especially as they found Obama more unpalatable than Bush. There was also a certain newfound, if limited, appreciation among moderates and some liberals, who contrasted Bush's views on immigration, education, Medicare, and AIDS relief with the harder-edged Republican Party that suceeded him. Senator Charles Schumer, the liberal Democrat who compared Bush to Herbert Hoover in 2008, credited him in 2013 along with Barack Obama and Ben Bernanke with having "saved us from another Great Depression." Many presidents have been viewed more generously in later eras, like Harry Truman, Dwight Eisenhower, Ronald Reagan, and Bill Clinton. Even Lyndon Johnson and Richard Nixon experienced moments of reassessment, their failures in Vietnam and Watergate mitigated to a degree by appreciation for the Great Society or the opening to China. Still, their disappointments seem indelibly marked in the history books, and it may be hard for Bush to shift the narrative as much as he would like. "Decades from now," he wrote, "I hope people will view me as a president who recognized the central challenge of our time and kept my vow to keep the country safe; who pursued my convictions without wavering but changed course when necessary; who trusted individuals to make choices in their lives; and who used America's influence to advance freedom."

ONE DAY IN his new office in Dallas, a visiting former aide asked Bush the question others never would.

"You're leaving as one of the most unpopular presidents ever," the aide noted. "How does that feel?"

Bush pushed back. "I was also the most popular president," he noted.

That true statement underscores a central dynamic of Bush's presidency, the sense of lost opportunity. From the months after September 11, when he reached the stratosphere in popular support, Bush at Cheney's urging pushed forward with a mission that ultimately frittered that away, heroically in the minds of his most fervent admirers, tragically in the minds of others. What might have been had Bush not chosen to invade Iraq?

In the years after he left office, Bush's former inner circle debated the issue, even to the point of questioning whether he would have launched the war at all had he known there were no weapons of mass destruction. Karl Rove and Ari Fleischer, among others, concluded that he would not have. "I just don't think he would have gone to war," said Fleischer. "I think he would have turned up the heat on Saddam, but I don't think he would have gone to war." Richard Armitage agreed. "I'm convinced that President Bush would not have done it absent WMD," he said. Others were not so sure. Rumsfeld, leaning back in a chair in a Washington office after the end of the administration, thought the war was still a worthy one. "I am very respectful of how ugly a war can be and so you say, 'Gee, do you wish it hadn't happened?' The answer of course is yes," he said. "But should it? Did the president make the right decision? Obviously, I thought so and still do. I mean, I think he was faced with a whole set of reasons which seemed to me to be persuasive then, and now."

One thing that is not debatable is that it consumed his presidency. His second-term Ownership Society domestic agenda aimed at overhauling Social Security, immigration policy, and the tax code foundered in large part on the shoals of Iraq. The country and Congress lost interest in anything else from the Bush White House. His hopes of reorienting the Republican Party did not survive his tenure in office, and he privately rued the rise of the populist conservative Tea Party movement after he left. "It breaks my heart that compassionate conservatism has gotten a bad name," Karen Hughes lamented. To the extent that is the case, Bush and Cheney bear responsibility. They rightly note that Democrats like Hillary Clinton and John Kerry also thought Saddam Hussein was a threat and voted for war, but in the end it was their decision. More than twenty-five million Iraqis were freed from Hussein's tyranny, but at the cost of more than four thousand American soldiers and perhaps a hundred thousand or more Iraqis by the time Bush and Cheney departed. The vast majority of the slain civilians died at the hands of insurgents and terrorists, not Americans, but they were forces unleashed by a White House that did not fully understand what it was setting in motion. "The first grave mistake of Bush's presidency was rushing toward military confrontation with Iraq," observed Scott McClellan. "It took his presidency off course and greatly damaged his standing with the public. His second grave mistake was his virtual blindness about the first mistake."

To understand it, it is important to remember the atmosphere in which the decision was made. The anthrax killings, the undisclosed biological scare in the White House, and the discovery of Pakistani nuclear scientists briefing Osama bin Laden created an environment in which the attacks of September 11 looked potentially minor by comparison to what could happen. If Hussein had such weapons, Bush and Cheney concluded, he could no longer be tolerated. "You can say he made a mistake," Senator Joseph Lieberman, the Connecticut Democrat who broke with his party over his support for the war, said of Bush. "We will be debating that part forever. But I think he did it because he really thought it was the right thing to do." The what-ifs, however, haunt some of the war's authors. "If Iraq had gone well," observed Michael Gerson, "the president could have been a colossus in American politics." But it did not, and he was not.

Even to the extent that he salvaged a failing war through the surge after years of letting his generals call the shots, Bush could not ultimately salvage his presidency, thanks to an economic crisis the likes of which no one had faced since Franklin Roosevelt. His final months in office were absorbed by a bruising series of failures on Wall Street due to years of an overheated housing market and exotic, high-risk financial instruments. Bush recognized the syndrome from experience. "Wall Street got drunk," he once explained. "It got drunk and now it's got a hangover." But if Wall Street imbibed too much, Bush was among the bartenders who looked the other way. While it was Bill Clinton who signed the repeal of Glass-Steagall restrictions on banks and Democrats in Congress who helped shield Fannie Mae and Freddie Mac as they binged on unsustainable mortgages, Bush appointed the regulators who remained too hands-off and personally was slow to recognize the severity of the threat. His eventual response in the form of the TARP bailout was almost akin to the Iraq surge, decisively applying the overwhelming force of the federal government to intervene in the markets and prevent the country from falling off a cliff.

To David Frum, the former White House speechwriter, Iraq and the financial crash summed up the Bush presidency. Other than his response to September 11, Bush's two greatest moments in office were arguably his responses to those two crises, ignoring political peril and discarding ideology to do what was necessary to turn things around. Sending more troops to a losing war and spending hundreds of billions of dollars to bail out irresponsible banks had to be two of the boldest and most politically unpopular decisions by any president in modern times. And in both cases, they proved to be critical to the country.

"You have to ask the question, why were they necessary? In both cases there was a long period of antecedent neglect out of which the crisis came, to which the president heroically responded," Frum observed. "Bush made crises through neglect and then resolved crises through courage."

Arguably, Hurricane Katrina fit the same pattern. After stumbling in the early days after the storm, Bush then demonstrated a powerful commitment to rebuilding the region, traveling there seventeen times and devoting vast sums of money over the objections of some in his party. Even Donna Brazile, Al Gore's campaign manager in 2000 and a New Orleans native whose family was displaced by the storm, praised the "intense, personal, dedicated efforts he made to revive and restore people's futures." Bush, in other words, was at his best when he was cleaning up his worst.

ON A BRIGHT, sunny day in the spring of 2013, more than four years after surrendering power, Bush and Cheney reunited for the opening of the George W. Bush Presidential Library and Museum on the campus of Southern Methodist University in Dallas. With thousands of administration veterans and supporters crowded outside the limestone building, Bush and Cheney emerged from the new center along with all the other living presidents and first ladies. But while Bush took a seat onstage along with his peers, Cheney stepped down into the audience to sit with the Bush children. Condoleezza Rice had a speaking role; Cheney did not.

This was only the second time the two men had appeared in public together since leaving office. The first had come when ground was broken on the library in 2010. Cheney was part of the program that day and hailed Bush. "Two years after you left office, judgments are a little more measured than they were," he said that day, speaking of the verdict of history but perhaps also his own judgments of Bush. The former president returned the kind words. "He was a great vice president of the United States and I'm proud to call him friend."

For friends, though, they had had relatively little contact. Most presidents and vice presidents go their separate ways after office, yet no other tandem had worked as closely together in the White House and the new distance spoke volumes about the evolution of their partnership. So did the library that sprouted out of the ground. There were exhibits featuring the first lady and their daughters, videos featuring Rice, Andy Card, and Joshua Bolten, even statues of the presidential dogs and cat. But there was virtually no sign of Cheney. During an interview leading up to the library opening, Bush was asked about their relationship. "You know, it's been cordial," he told C-Span's Steve Scully. "But he lives in Washington and we live in Dallas." Perhaps recognizing the chill that suggested, Bush made sure at the subsequent ceremony to give a shout-out to Cheney. "From the day I asked Dick to run with me, he served with loyalty, principle, and strength," Bush told the audience, and then repeated his words from a few years earlier. "I'm proud to call you friend."

He was blunter later in the year during an off-the-record chat with reporters on Air Force One when he accompanied Obama to South Africa for the funeral of Nelson Mandela. Asked by a reporter how often he talked with Cheney, Bush said tersely, "Never." After all, he said, he had "lots of advisers," and Cheney was just one. They had never really been that close, he added.

As for Cheney, he had been reinvigorated after a near-death experience. Cheney's heart, never strong, had caught up with him once he returned to private life. Around Christmas 2009, he was backing his car out of his garage in Wyoming when "everything went blank." He woke up with Secret Service agents pounding on the windows of the locked car, which was on top of a boulder in an aspen grove in front of the house. His implanted defibrillator had kicked in and saved his life, as it was designed to do.

But within a couple months, he suffered his fifth heart attack and by summer he was heading into end-stage heart failure. He was just hours from death and told his family farewell and instructed them to have his body cremated and the ashes returned to Wyoming. "If this is dying, I remember thinking, it's not all that bad," Cheney recalled later. Doctors rushed him into surgery, where he was on the operating table for nine hours. Cheney spent the next thirty-five days in the hospital, much of it unconscious, dreaming, oddly enough, of a countryside villa north of Rome where he passed the time padding along stone paths to get coffee or newspapers.

Then in 2012, at age seventy-one, Cheney underwent a heart transplant operation. In succeeding months, he regained strength and much of his spirit. By the time he arrived in Dallas for the library opening, he was like a new man. Wearing a cowboy hat, khakis, and a blue blazer, he showed up at a bar the night before the ceremony where more than a thousand administration veterans were partying. More animated than he had been for years, he was mobbed in the parking lot and never even made it into the bar. Instead, he stood outside, happily chatting with Karl Rove about hunting, catching up with colleagues, and posing for pictures with former aides and complete strangers. Asked about a recent documentary about his life, he cheerfully complained that the filmmakers did not include footage of him catching a large fish. He lingered until close to midnight. "Ever since the heart transplant," his daughter Mary observed, "it's been like a miracle."

Never an emotive man, Cheney seemed gripped by the medical heroics that saved his life, talking all the time about the operation and the advances in technology that enabled it and even wrote a book with his cardiologist, Jonathan Reiner, about the experience. At one point after the operation,

Cheney was traveling on the West Coast and dropped by the Los Angeles house of his friend David Hume Kennerly. Sitting at Kennerly's table, the former vice president described his health-care odyssey.

Everyone involved in a heart transplant operation, from the doctors and nurses to the family, viewed it as some sort of spiritual experience, he said.

"Well, if that's true," Kennerly teased, "are you now a Democrat?"

"It wasn't *that* spiritual," Cheney replied.

Kennerly knew better than to expect his old friend to change, new heart or no. Whatever else people said about him, Dick Cheney knew what he believed and felt no need to temper his views to suit others. On some level, his disregard for the vicissitudes of popularity could be seen as admirable in an era of craven politicians. Yet even aides concluded that Cheney took it to such an extreme that his failure to respond to public opinion, or at least try to shape it by explaining and defending his positions, undercut his cause and resulted in his policies ultimately being scaled back.

If Bush thought so, he kept it to himself. While he had clearly moved away from Cheney in the second half of his presidency, he was rarely if ever heard expressing anything but respect for his partner. Some of those around him, though, faulted Cheney for transforming Bush from uniter to divider. "Something happened in Washington," said Sandy Kress, the longtime adviser from Texas who recalled how Bush worked with Democrats in Austin and then initially in Washington on education reform, "and I personally think Dick Cheney was part of the partisanship issue. I don't get it to this day. I don't like it, I didn't like it then, I don't like it now."

And yet to blame or credit Cheney for the president's decisions is to underestimate Bush. "Bush had a little bit of Eisenhower in him," said Wayne Berman, "in that he didn't mind if people thought that he was the sort of guy who was easily manipulated because it also meant that his opponents underestimated him and the people around him thought they were having more influence than they really were. And he used that always to his advantage." While Cheney clearly influenced him in the early years, none of scores of aides, friends, and relatives interviewed after the White House years recalled Bush ever asserting that the vice president talked him into doing something he otherwise would not have done.

Bush, in the end, was the Decider. His successes and his failures through all the days of fire were his own. "He's his own man," said Joe O'Neill, his lifelong friend. "He's got the mistakes to prove it, as we always say. He was his own man."

ACKNOWLEDGMENTS

Every book project is a journey, some longer and more circuitous than others, and I was blessed to have the companionship and support of a phenomenal collection of family, friends, and colleagues along the way. To say this wouldn't have been possible without them may be a cliché, but in this case it is abundantly true.

No one believed in this venture more than Raphael Sagalyn, my agent and friend now for some fifteen years whose talents for hand-holding nervous authors and eliciting their best work are boundless. No one could ask for a better editor than Kris Puopolo at Doubleday, who patiently shepherded this volume through multiple conceptions and drafts, never tiring and never pressuring but always offering insights and counsel that made it stronger at every stage.

Bill Thomas, Doubleday's publisher and editor in chief, saw the value in attempting a neutral history of a White House about which almost no one is neutral, and his faith in that daunting mission despite the obvious challenges proved inspiring. The rest of the team at Doubleday demonstrated why they are collectively the best in the business, including Maria Carella, Todd Doughty, John Fontana, Joe Gallagher, Lorraine Hyland, Dan Meyer, Ingrid Sterner, and Amelia Zalcman.

Jake Schwartz-Forester devoted many months to helping out with research and transcriptions, and I'm especially grateful for all his hard work. He's got a bright future ahead. Cynthia Colonna likewise turned around interview transcripts with speed and precision no matter how many noisy tape backgrounds she had to endure. Clare Sestanovich also helped decipher interviews. Andrew Prokop came along near the end to help save me from myself with a diligent and masterful dissection of flawed chapters. Others who helped with our fact-checking triage have my eternal thanks as well: Margaret Slattery, Julie Tate, Elias Groll, Marya Hannun, and Elizabeth F. Ralph. The crack photographer Doug Mills was kind enough to take the author shot for the book jacket.

The Woodrow Wilson International Center for Scholars gave me a home for several months during the research for this book and I want to thank Lee Hamilton, Jane Harman, Michael Van Dusen, Lucy Jilka, Lindsay Collins, and Blair Ruble for their hospitality. The Hoover Institution at Stanford University has likewise given me several opportunities to come out for short stints that seemed particularly well timed during the process, and I'm grateful to David Brady and Mandy MacCalla.

I have been fortunate to work at the two best newspapers in the world, first at the *Washington Post* for twenty years and then at the *New York Times* for the last five. Both gave me the chance to cover the White House, which for all the tradeoffs is still one of the most challenging and invigorating assignments a reporter could have. Arthur Sulzberger Jr., the chairman and publisher of the *Times*, has done what almost no one else has during the crisis that has transformed our business: he has reinvested in journalism, protecting the franchise at all costs against the winds of financial distress. While others shrank their ambitions, he expanded ours, and he deserves the admiration of anyone who cares about independent reporting. I'm so glad to have worked these last few years for him and for Jill Abramson, Mark Thompson, Dean Baquet, Bill Keller, David Leonhardt, Carl Hulse, Elisabeth Bumiller, Rick Berke, Richard Stevenson, Rebecca Corbett, Bill Hamilton, Gerald Marzorati, Megan Liberman, Chris Suellentrop, Hugo Lindgren, and Joel Lovell. I will always be grateful to Donald Graham, the extraordinary chairman of the Post Company, for his own commitment to quality journalism and for everything he has done for my family over the years. There is no classier person out there.

A number of friends and colleagues played special roles in helping shape this book. Helene Cooper, my partner on the White House beat at the *Times*, came up with the idea of framing the history of the last White House around the unique relationship of President Bush and Vice President Cheney. Michael Abramowitz, who was my partner at the *Post*, spent a lot of time sharing his insights into the Bush-Cheney White House and read the manuscript with a careful eye for how to improve it. Michael Shear, one of my closest friends since we were rookie metro reporters together and now also a partner on the beat, and Bill Hamilton, a first-rate editor at both papers, took time out to read it as well. My other terrific partners, Jackie Calmes and Mark Landler, put up with my absences with patience and support.

Robert Draper, a graceful writer, sharp observer of Texas and Washington politics, and the author of his own excellent book on President Bush, generously shared his research and ministered me through challenging periods with wine and cogent advice. Mark Leibovich, one of the best journalists in this town, was busy birthing his own terrific book over the same period and met with me regularly for breakfast to commiserate and regroup. Rajiv Chandrasekaran and Mark Mazzetti also shared in the joys and travails of the book-writing process.

Matt Bai, Mark Bowden, Steve Coll, Elizabeth Drew, Jane Mayer, Jeff Shesol, Ron Suskind, Leon Wieseltier, and Bob Woodward all offered support and advice. Glenn Frankel and Betsyellen Yeager, and Bill and Ellen Morris graciously opened their homes to me during reporting trips to Texas. Peter Feaver, Meghan O'Sullivan, and William Inboden all brought me to their respective campuses and shared thoughts from their own time in the White House. Peter Wehner went out of his way to open doors. Mark Updegrove, a student of the presidency in general and the Bush family in particular, was a constant source of encouragement and insight.

Thanks too to Mark Knoller of CBS News, an unparalleled archivist of the modern White House and an uncommonly generous colleague, for opening his records. Other colleagues who shared recollections, thoughts, and notes from the Bush-Cheney years included Dan Balz, David Jackson, Richard Keil, Jay Newton-Small, David Sanger, Richard Stevenson, and Philip Taubman. And special appreciation to Gwen Ifill, Chris Guarino, Alla Lora, and the rest of the fine team at *Washington Week*.

It has been humbling to work alongside some of the exceptional reporters at the White House. John Harris first taught me how to cover a president, and after a dozen years of doing it I still aspire to the high standard he set. Other partners over the years at the *Post* and *Times* included Dan Eggen, Michael Fletcher, Jim Rutenberg, Sheryl Gay Stolberg, Jim VandeHei, and Jeff Zeleny. It's daunting to go up against friends-turned-competitors like Mike Allen, Chris Cillizza, Juliet Eilperin, Anne Kornblut, Jonathan Martin, Peter Wallsten, and Scott Wilson, among many, many others. I'm grateful to my neighbors and friends in the bureau who have been so supportive, including John Broder, Adam Liptak, Rachel Swarns, Sabrina Tavernise, and Jonathan Weisman. Alas, the bureau is not the same since the irreplaceable Adam Nagourney decamped for the west.

John Smith has been the best of friends for longer than either of us would care to admit—and has been there for me throughout. I never had a brother but if I did, I would want it to be John. Special thanks to the members of our neighborhood village, Martina Vandenberg and Max, Marshall, and Alan Cooperman, who through years of book work have taken us in once a week for food and friendship. We could not be luckier to share an alley with them. Other friends who have my admiration and appreciation include Gary Bass and Katy Glenn; Marc, Anna, Maria, and Ray

Bonaquist; Natasha and Christian Caryl; Max and Julie Chandrasekaran; Jon Cohen; Karen DeYoung; Mark Franchetti; Somerset, Heather, and Elliott Grant; Michael Grunwald and Cristina Dominguez; Spencer Hsu and Lori Aratani; Indira Lakshmanan and Rohan, Devan, and Dermot Tatlow; Andrew Light; Carlos Lozada and Kathleen McBride; Valerie Mann and Tim Webster; Ellen Nakashima and Alan Sipress; Natalie Nougayrede; Paul Quinn-Judge; Nicole Rabner and Larry Kanarek; Heidi Crebo-Rediker and Charlotte and Doug Rediker; Marilou and Bruce Sanford; Melissa Schwartz and Ben, Emily, and David Muenzer; Sonya Schwartz and Sammy, Harry, and Don Fishman; and Caitlin Shear.

My family deserves singular gratitude because this is the third time they have endured this process and yet for some reason they never give up on me. My love goes to my parents, Ted and Martha Baker, and Linda and Keith Sinrod, for all their support and inspiration over the years, and to my sister, Karin Baker, and her partner, Kait Nolan. Thanks to Steve and Lynn Glasser for welcoming me into their family and for providing a New England escape to get some work done. Thanks too to Laura, Jeffrey, and Jennifer Glasser, Emily Allen, Kasia Nowak, Matthieu Fulchiron, Will and Ben Allen-Glasser. Also to Dan and Sylvia Baker and to Inge Gross and all of their amazing children and grandchildren. We miss Mal Gross terribly. Rosamaria Brizuela has become part of our family and we could not get by without her.

And of course, I could never fully express just how much I owe to Susan and Theo, the loves of my life, who were endlessly understanding through a seemingly endless process. Any author would be lucky to have such a beautiful and brilliant wife but to have one who also happens to be the finest editor of her generation is a gift beyond description. Susan not only provided moral support, she offered crisp and incisive thoughts about how to take a first draft and make it a final draft. Theo, for his part, brightens both of our lives in more ways than we can count. He too read some of the early draft and offered indisputable advice: "Make it compelling." I hope to live up to his expectations.

NOTES

This account emerges from nearly a decade of reporting on President Bush and Vice President Cheney, first for the *Washington Post,* the *New York Times,* and the *New York Times Magazine* and then exclusively for this book. While some of the material appeared in different form in those publications, it is primarily based on nearly 400 original interviews with about 275 sources, including Dick Cheney, Condoleezza Rice, Donald Rumsfeld, Colin Powell, Stephen Hadley, and Joshua Bolten, plus thousands of pages of notes, memos, transcripts, and other internal documents never before released. It involved trips to Dallas, Midland, Austin, Houston, Casper, Cheyenne, New York, Boston, San Francisco, and Durham. Many people sat patiently for hours to describe the events recorded here, some graciously agreeing to be interviewed on multiple occasions. Although some asked to remain unidentified, the vast majority agreed to be cited on the record, making this the most documented history of the Bush-Cheney White House to date.

No book on such a vast subject can be completely original. This one builds on an extraordinary body of work by colleagues at the *Post* and the *Times* and at other news organizations as well as an array of fine books by other authors, especially those of Bob Woodward, Robert Draper, Bill Sammon, Barton Gellman, Stephen Hayes, Karen DeYoung, Bradley Graham, David Sanger, Elisabeth Bumiller, and Jane Mayer. It benefits greatly from the memoirs of participants in these events, particularly those of George W. Bush, Dick Cheney, Condoleezza Rice, and Donald Rumsfeld. Also particularly useful were the repositories of papers at the National Security Archive at George Washington University and oral histories at the Miller Center at the University of Virginia as well as the thousands of documents that Rumsfeld posted online with the publication of his memoir.

In seeking to make this a work of history, I have tried to confirm details and recollections with multiple sources. In general, direct quotations come from transcripts, news accounts, books, contemporaneous notes, or the recollection of at least one person in the room at the time and usually more than one, although of course memories are never as precise as we might wish. No reconstruction of events can be perfect, but I have labored to be as accurate as possible. Although Bush chose not to be interviewed, and his office initially sent an e-mail to former aides explaining that he did not think a *New York Times* reporter could write an objective history of his administration, over time he did not block his many friends and former advisers from talking, and I'm grateful to him for that. His staff in Dallas was always gracious and polite. I also want to thank Cheney and everyone else who did cooperate. Responsibility for this book lies entirely with me, and there will no doubt be elements they do not like, but their cooperation went a long way toward making this the most complete history it can be.

The following people were interviewed in person, by telephone, or via e-mail: John Abizaid, Spencer Abraham, Elliott Abrams, Geoffrey Adams, Ken Adelman, Michael Allen, William Allman, Dick Armey, Richard Armitage, Steve Atkiss, David Axelrod, Michael Barone, Dan Bartlett, John Bellinger, Richard Ben-Veniste, Brad Berenson, Lea Berman, Wayne Berman, Stephen Biddle, Stephen Biegun, Charlie Black, Robert Blackwill, Brad Blakeman, Kathleen Babineaux Blanco, Steven Blum, Joshua Bolten, Stuart Bowen, Nicholas Brady, Rachel Brand, Jerry Bremer, John Bridgeland, Chris Brose, William Burck, Nicholas Burns, Bill Burton, Kirbyjon Caldwell, Nick Calio, Will Cappelletti, George Casey, Dick Cheney, Liz Cheney, Mike Chertoff, Rocco Chierichella, Pratik Chougule, Eliot Cohen, Cesar Conda, Jim Connaughton, Mark Corallo, J. D. Crouch, Robert Dallek, John Danforth, Michele Davis, Tom Davis, Jack Dennis, Larry Di Rita, James Dobbins, Eric Draper, Ken Duberstein, Trent Duffy, Debra Dunn, Charles Dunne, Jennifer Millerwise Dyck, Eric Edelman, John Ellis, Donald Ensenat, Sara Taylor Fagen, Tom Fake, Tony Fauci, Peter Feaver, Howard Fineman, Ari Fleischer, Richard Fontaine, Lea Anne Foster, Tony Fratto, Brad Freeman, David Frum, John Lewis Gaddis, Dick Gephardt, Michael Gerson, Robert Gibbs, Ed Gillespie, James Glassman, Juleanna Glover, Tim Goeglein, David Gordon, Lindsey Graham, Boyden Gray, Michael Green, Stanley Greenberg, Judd Gregg, and Allen Guelzo.

Also: Stephen Hadley, Joe Hagin, John Hannah, Dennis Hastert, Michael Hayden, Israel Hernandez, Christopher Hill, Fiona Hill, David Hobbs, Stuart Holliday, Brian Hook, Al Hubbard, Glenn Hubbard, Karen Hughes, Kay Bailey Hutchison, William Inboden, Valerie Jarrett, Gordon Johndroe, Clay Johnson, Frederick Jones, Vernon Jordan, Robert Joseph, Joel Kaplan, Leon Kass, Ron Kaufman, David Kay, David Keene, Richard Keil, Kevin Kellems, Bill Keller, William Kelley, David Hume Kennerly, Zalmay Khalilzad, George Klein, Anne Womack Kolton, David Kramer, Charles Krauthammer, Sandy Kress, Mark Langdale, Randall Larsen, Matt Latimer, Ed Lazear, Leonard Leo, Richard Lessner, Yuval Levin, Adam Levine, Joseph Lieberman, Trent Lott, Douglas Lute, William Luti, Michael Luttig, Kanan Makiya, Mary Matalin, Anita McBride, Scott McClellan, John McConnell, Mike McConnell, Sean McCormack, Mike McCurry, Walter McDougall, Michael McFaul, Dean McGrath, Brett McGurk, Mark McKinnon, John McLaughlin, Mick McMurry, Paul McNulty, Ken Mehlman, Doug Melton, Joe Meyer, Franklin Miller, Richard Moe, Geoff Morrell, Jack Morrison, Mike Mullen, Richard Myers, John Negroponte, Ben Nelson, Pamela Hudson Nelson, Ronald Neumann, Grover Norquist, Ziad Ojakli, Sean O'Keefe, Marvin Olansky, Douglas Ollivant, Joe O'Neill, Paul O'Neill, Paul Orzulak, Meghan O'Sullivan, Scott Palmer, Leon Panetta, and Neil Patel.

Also: Richard Perle, David Petraeus, Rob Portman, Daniel Price, Blain Rethmeier, Condoleezza Rice, Bob Riley, Timothy Roemer, Ed Rogers, Donald Rumsfeld, Rob Saliterman, David Sanger, Kori Schake, Matt Schlapp, Steve Schmidt, Peter Schoomaker, Brent Scowcroft, Matthew Scully, Bernie Seebaum, Dan Senor, Stephen Sestanovich, Cindy Sheehan, Kristen Silverberg, Alan Simpson, Richard W. Stevenson, Ryan Streeter, Lawrence Summers, Philip Taubman, Bill Thomson, Michael Toner, Frances Fragos Townsend, Tevi Troy, Eric Ueland, John Ullyot, Keith Urbahn, Stewart Verdery, Michael Vickers, Kenneth Wainstein, Nicolle Wallace, John Weaver, Peter Wehner, Christine Todd Whitman, Pete Williams, Damon Wilson, Jay Winik, Candida Wolff, Paul Wolfowitz, Joe Wood, Steve Yates, Charlie Younger, Juan Carlos Zarate, and Philip Zelikow.

PROLOGUE: "BREAKING CHINA"

1 **"Do you think he did it?"**: The account of the pardon deliberations, where not otherwise sourced, is based on author interviews with several administration officials and others who were involved but asked not to be named. See also an early account of the pardon fight, Massimo Calabresi and Michael Weiskopf, "Inside Bush and Cheney's Final Days," *Time*, July 24, 2009. http://www.time.com/time/magazine/article/0,9171,1912414,00.html.

2 **with those of eight other people**: Scooter Libby testified that he learned that Joseph Wilson's wife, Valerie Plame Wilson, worked for the CIA during a telephone conversation with Tim Russert on July 10, 2003, and that he had forgotten that the vice president had previously mentioned it to him, as recorded by notes. Russert testified that he did not know she worked for the CIA and therefore could not have told Libby that. Libby has argued that this was at worst a matter of two people remembering the same conversation differently, hardly a criminal offense. Prosecutors maintained that regardless of whether Libby misremembered one conversation, it was implausible that he actually thought he had learned about Valerie Wilson from Russert because he had talked about her with so many other people before then. Investigators discovered that before his conversation with

Russert, Libby had conversations with at least eight other people in which he either was told that Joseph Wilson's wife worked at the CIA or demonstrated his own knowledge of that: Vice President Cheney; Marc Grossman, undersecretary of state; Robert Grenier, a CIA official; Craig Schmall, Libby's CIA briefer; Cathie Martin, the vice president's spokeswoman; Ari Fleischer, the White House press secretary; Judith Miller, a *New York Times* reporter; and David Addington, the vice president's counsel.

4 **"They weren't personally close":** Ari Fleischer, author interview.

4 **"It was professional":** Dick Cheney, author interview.

4 **"You know, I would, I would":** George W. Bush, interview for Fox News documentary *Dick Cheney: No Retreat*, aired October 2007,

4 **Karl Rove came to call:** Barton Gellman, *The Angler*, p. 160. Gellman reported that Rove denied coining the term but that three White House colleagues confirmed that he did.

4 **"If you spent any time":** Matthew Dowd, author interview.

5 **"He was a black box":** Peter Wehner, author interview.

5 **"Dick here sent over a gift":** Amy Argetsinger and Roxanne Roberts, *The Reliable Source, Washington Post*, January 28, 2008. http://www.washingtonpost.com/wp-dyn/content/article/2008/01/27/AR2008012702668.html.

5 **"Hi, Dick. Have you blown away":** David Hume Kennerly, author interview.

6 **"I'll really miss being president":** Conan O'Brien, *Late Night*, NBC, December 17, 2008.

6 **"doesn't regret any of the decisions":** Jimmy Kimmel, *Jimmy Kimmel Live!*, ABC, May 2009.

6 **"Accepting Dick's offer":** George W. Bush, *Decision Points*, 86–87.

6 **"Am I the evil genius":** Dick Cheney, interview with *USA Today* and *Los Angeles Times*, January 15, 2004. See Maura Reynolds, "Cheney's Lack of Flair Is Just the Ticket for Many in GOP," *Los Angeles Times*, January 19, 2004, http://articles.latimes.com/2004/jan/19/nation/na-cheney19.

6 **Harry Truman as vice president:** Franklin D. Roosevelt Day by Day, Pare Lorentz Center, Franklin D. Roosevelt Presidential Library, http://www.fdrlibrary.marist.edu/daybyday/. A review of FDR's calendars turns up Truman only twice, March 8 and March 19, both for meetings with congressional leaders. Randy Sowell, an archivist at the Harry S. Truman Presidential Library, notes that there may have been other meetings not recorded and also points out that FDR was traveling much of those final months.

6 **"Let me see," he said:** Carl M. Cannon, "The Point Man," *National Journal*, October 21, 2001. http://www3.nationaljournal.com/members/news/2002/10/1011nj1.htm. Cannon retold the story in his book with his father, Lou Cannon, comparing and contrasting Bush with Reagan, *Reagan's Disciple*, 244.

6 **"Are you going to take care":** George W. Bush, *Decision Points*, 251.

6 **"He never did anything in his time":** Alan Simpson, author interview.

7 **"This whole notion that the vice":** Richard Myers, author interview.

7 **"Perhaps my clout was diminished":** Dick Cheney, interview, *Fox News Sunday*, September 5, 2011.

8 **"On top of that, Mr. Vice President":** Ed Gillespie, author interview.

9 **Cheney instructed an aide:** Mann, *Rise of the Vulcans*, 97.

9 **"I didn't change":** Daniel Henninger, *Wall Street Journal*, August 30, 2011, http://online.wsj.com/article/SB10001424053111904199404576536882769562442.html.

9 **"He went from the wise man":** Adam Levine, author interview.

10 **"We had broken a lot of china":** Rice interview.

10 **"Does anyone here agree":** Several participants, author interviews. See also Dick Cheney, *In My Time*, 462–67.

10 **"Whatever you do":** Joshua Bolten and another participant, author interviews. See also Dick Cheney, *In My Time*, 517.

11 **"You are leaving a good man":** Dick Cheney, *In My Time*, 407–10.

11 **"The comment stung":** George W. Bush, *Decision Points*, 104–5.

11 **"Scooter was somebody":** Dick Cheney, author interview.

CHAPTER 1: "ONE OF YOU COULD BE PRESIDENT"

15 **"Roman candle of the family":** Cramer, *What It Takes*, 16–18.

15 **"He's not necessarily what":** Dennis Hastert, author interview.

16 **"not a sport for the impatient":** Lynne Cheney, speech to the Republican National Convention, August 3, 2000, http://partners.nytimes.com/library/politics/camp/080300lynne-txt.html.

16 **"he talks too much":** Kenneth Adelman, author interview.

16 **"asking for grief I didn't need":** Graham, *By His Own Rules*, 169.

16 **"He and Bush hit it off":** Wayne Berman, author interview.

16 **"Bush in those days":** Ibid.

16 **"George is the family clown":** Wead, *All the Presidents' Children*, 4–5.

17 **"Do you have any in yours?":** Koch, *My Father, My President*, 364.

17 **"It is always better to lowball":** Ronald Neumann, author interview.

17 **"His cadence would change":** Kuo, *Tempting Faith*, 117.

17 **Bush's favorite book:** Dana Milbank, "For Bush, War Defines Presidency," *Washington Post*, March 9, 2003.

17 **"His first thought":** Marquis James, *The Raven*, as quoted by Milbank.

17 **"a never-complain, never-explain":** Purdum, *Time of Our Choosing*, 43.

17 **"I suppose it gives him":** Liz Cheney, author interview.

18 **"looked like something a sailor":** Trent Lott, author interview.

18 **"I think years ago, the rooms":** Pete Williams, author interview.

18 **cousin of President Franklin Pierce's:** For a detailed and penetrating analysis of the Bush family tree, and family psychology, see Weisberg, *Bush Tragedy*.

19 **"There is a similarity":** Dean McGrath, author interview.

19 **"little Mayberry type of town":** Joe O'Neill, author interview.

19 **something out of *Happy Days*:** Joe Meyer, author interview.

19 **produced nearly 20 percent:** Diana Davids Hinton, history professor, University of Texas of the Permian Basin, e-mail exchange with author.

19 **Casper had doubled in size:** U.S. Census data compiled by the Wyoming Economic Analysis Division, http://eadiv.state.wy.us/demog_data/cntycity_hist.htm.

19 **Midland had quadrupled:** John Leffler, "Midland, TX," *Handbook of Texas Online*, Texas State Historical Association, http://www.tshaonline.org/handbook/online/articles/hdm03.

19 **215 oil companies had opened:** Ibid.

20 **address him as "Senator":** Schweizer and Schweizer, *Bushes*, xv.

20 **Bush bought for $9,000 in 1951:** The house has been converted into a museum, the George W. Bush Childhood Home. The author toured it in April 2011.

20 **"He lives in his cowboy clothes":** George Bush, *All the Best*, 70.

20 **"Georgie aggravates the hell":** Ibid., 79.

21 **"starkest memory of my childhood":** Wead, *All the Presidents' Children*, 78.

21 **"My mom, dad, and sister are home":** Barbara Bush, *Memoir*, 45.
21 **"She died":** George W. Bush, *Decision Points*, 5–6.
21 **"Why didn't you tell me?":** George Lardner Jr. and Lois Romano, "A Texas Childhood: A Sister Dies, a Family Moves On," *Washington Post*, July 26, 1999, http://www.washingtonpost.com/wp-srv/politics/campaigns/wh2000/stories/bush072699.htm.
21 **"I can't come over to play":** Minutaglio, *First Son*, 45–46.
21 **"That started my cure":** Barbara Bush, *Memoir*, 47.
21 **bought a small $15,000 house:** Lynne Cheney, *Blue Skies, No Fences*, 181–84. The house remained in the family for years, and in fact Cheney stayed there even when he became defense secretary. The author visited the house but did not go inside in July 2011.
21 **"His father had a wry sense":** Williams interview.
21 **"His mom was the real ripsnorter":** Meyer interview.
21 **"We had an A&W on one side":** Bernie Seebaum, author interview.
22 **"too much time wasted foolishly":** Lynne Cheney, *Blue Skies, No Fences*, 181–84.
22 **"We thought we were pretty hot stuff":** Seebaum interview.
22 **"You're kidding!":** Lynne Cheney, *Blue Skies, No Fences*, 259–61.
22 **"like a classic fifties movie":** Dick Cheney, *In My Time*, 23–26.
22 **"We didn't know we were poor":** Mick McMurry, author interview.
22 **"to beat the crap out of each other":** Tom Fake, author interview.
22 **"We went from being the big fish":** Ibid.
22 **"beer was one of the essentials":** Dick Cheney, *In My Time*, 26–28.
22 **"Dick has fallen in with a group":** Ibid.
23 **"She made it clear eventually":** Dick Cheney, oral history, March 17–18, 2000, Miller Center, University of Virginia.
23 **"Andover was cold and distant":** George W. Bush, *Charge to Keep*, 19–21.
23 **He called himself "Tweeds Bush":** Ibid.
23 **"I knew your father":** Schweizer and Schweizer, *Bushes*, 166. After the incident was publicized during the 2000 campaign, Coffin wrote Bush a letter saying he did not remember making the remark but apologizing if he did. Bush accepted the apology. "But his self-righteous attitude was a foretaste of the vitriol that would emanate from many college professors during my presidency," Bush wrote in *Decision Points*, 13–14.
23 **"He was a guy out of water":** O'Neill interview.
24 **"Why don't you try walking":** Lanny Davis, "Farewell to Bush, the President and the Man," *Huffington Post*, January 12, 2009, http://www.huffingtonpost.com/lanny-davis/farewell-to-bush-the-pres_b_157135.html.
24 **"I went to school with him":** Jack Morrison, author interview.
24 **"If you graduate from Yale":** George W. Bush, Yale University commencement address, May 21, 2001, http://georgewbush-whitehouse.archives.gov/news/releases/2001/05/20010521-2.html.
24 **his "nomadic" period:** George Lardner Jr. and Lois Romano, "At Height of Vietnam, Graduate Picks Guard," *Washington Post*, July 28, 1999, http://www.washingtonpost.com/wp-srv/politics/campaigns/wh2000/stories/bush072899.htm.
24 **helped by the Speaker:** Ben Barnes, then the Speaker, said he was contacted by a Bush family friend, Sid Adger, who asked him to help George W. get into the unit. See Barnes interview with Dan Rather of CBS News, http://www.cbsnews.com/2100-500164_162-642060.html.
25 **"I would guess that probably":** Charlie Younger, author interview.

25 **"We went to dinner":** Pete Slover and George Kuempel, "'I Was Young and Irresponsible,'" *Dallas Morning News*, November 15, 1998.
25 **"I hear you're looking for me":** Robert Draper, "Favorite Son," *GQ*, September 1998. See also Laurence I. Barrett, "Junior Is His Own Bush Now," *Time*, July 31, 1989, http://www.time.com/time/magazine/article/0,9171,958244,00.html. And see Wead, *Raising of a President*, 303. Wead cited an interview with Neil Bush. George W. Bush downplayed it in *Decision Points*, saying it had been overblown. He also described Jeb blurting out his admission to Harvard on another night during dinner at a Houston restaurant. See p. 22.
25 **"I had other priorities in the '60s":** George C. Wilson, "Cheney Believes Gorbachev Sincere," *Washington Post*, April 5, 1989.
25 **"It was clear that we hadn't":** Dick Cheney, speech at Hudson Institute luncheon honoring Donald Rumsfeld, May 13, 2003, http://georgewbush-whitehouse.archives.gov/news/releases/2003/05/20030513-9.html. Rumsfeld over the years has taken gentle issue with this account, saying the reason he rejected Cheney was that he wanted a lawyer.
26 **"You're congressional relations":** Ibid.
26 **"But he stood by me":** Dick Cheney, *In My Time*, 51–52.
26 **"Here you are":** George W. Bush, *Charge to Keep*, 60.
26 **Bush had a "rotten time":** Radcliffe, *Simply Barbara Bush*, 139.
26 **"claustrophobic, intellectually and physically":** Minutaglio, *First Son*, 157.
26 **"was a great turning point":** Lardner and Romano, "At Height of Vietnam."
27 **"One of you could be president":** Michael Kranish, "Hallmarks of Bush Style Were Seen at Harvard," *Boston Globe*, December 28, 1999.
27 **Ford considered George H. W.:** The three finalists submitted to the FBI for background checks in August 1974 were Bush, Rumsfeld, and Rockefeller. Dick Cheney, author interview. See also Hartmann, *Palace Politics*, 353.
27 **"All I really had going for me":** Dick Cheney, *In My Time*, 71.
27 **"pragmatic problem solver":** Ford, *Time to Heal*, 324.
27 **"a war that is finished":** Gerald Ford, speech at Tulane University, April 23, 1975, http://www.fordlibrarymuseum.gov/library/speeches/750208.asp.
27 **"Fuck the war":** Nessen, *Making the News, Taking the News*, 9.
27 **"somewhat to the right of Ford":** Hartmann, *Palace Politics*, 283.
27 **"He didn't care much for me":** Cheney interview.
27 **He also thought a vice president:** Cheney said in 1977 that "taking a man or woman who's vice-president of the United States and putting him into that has an impact . . . on the others in the process because they react to the vice-president very differently than they do to the director of the OMB or their colleagues on the staff." Dubose and Bernstein, *Vice*, 39.
27 **urging Ford to stop speaking:** Donald H. Rumsfeld and Dick Cheney to President Ford, memo, October 24, 1975. Accessed at http://www.rumsfeld.com.
28 **referring to them as "the Praetorians":** DeFrank, *Write It When I'm Gone*, 49.
28 **"most distinguishing features":** Hartmann, *Palace Politics*, 283.
28 **"I knew that I could ask Cheney":** Ford, *Time to Heal*, 324.
28 **"intelligent without displaying":** Casserly, *The Ford White House*, 228 and 245.
28 **he dubbed "Errors and No Facts":** Nessen, *It Sure Looks Different from the Inside*, 150.
29 **"We're going to take a dive":** Nessen, *Making the News, Taking the News*, 213.
29 **called Cheney a "son of a bitch":** Hartmann, *Palace Politics*, 406. Rockefeller was also mad that his microphone had been turned down during a speech, which he seemed to blame on Cheney.

29 **"Gentlemen," he proclaimed:** Ibid., 233.
29 **"Mr. President, we lost":** Hayes, *Cheney*, 116–17.
29 **"it would be very hard for me to govern":** Baker, *"Work Hard, Study . . . and Keep out of Politics!,"* 70–71.
29 **"Governor, my voice is gone":** Hayes, *Cheney*, 116–17.
30 **"One of the things he would say":** Donald Rumsfeld, author interview.
30 **"A lot of the things around Watergate":** Dick Cheney, roundtable with reporters, aboard Air Force Two en route to Muscat, Oman, December 20, 2005, http://georgewbush-whitehouse.archives.gov/news/releases/2005/12/20051220-9.html.
30 **"toxic waste dump":** Younger interview.
30 **"So, what's sex like after fifty":** Schweizer and Schweizer, *Bushes*, 305. Bemiss got her revenge later. After Bush passed the half-century mark, she asked him, "So, George, how is it after fifty?" He smiled and said, "Quite good, thank you."
30 **"He always lived on the edge":** Younger interview.

CHAPTER 2: "TO BE WHERE THE ACTION IS"

31 **"Son, you can't win":** George W. Bush, *Charge to Keep*, 37–39.
31 **"I listened to him":** Koch, *My Father, My President*, 145–46.
31 **"Dick, if you run for Senate":** Dick Cheney, commencement address, Natrona County High School, May 29, 2006. In his memoir, Cheney rendered it slightly less G-rated, remembering the quote as "kick your butt."
32 **"He stayed almost past midnight":** Joe O'Neill, author interview.
32 **"Laura stays in her own space":** George W. Bush, *Charge to Keep*, 80–85.
32 **"This guy doesn't give a speech":** Pete Williams, author interview.
32 **"run as Jerry Ford's guy":** Dick Cheney, oral history, Miller Center.
33 **"That was devastating to them":** Joe Meyer, author interview.
33 **"Look, hard work never killed anybody":** Dick Cheney, *In My Time*, 119–24.
33 **viewed it "as a one-off event":** Dick Cheney and Reiner, *Heart*, 45.
33 **Cheney won the primary:** Witzenburger came in second with 31 percent and Gage third with 27 percent. http://www.ourcampaigns.com/RaceDetail.html?RaceID=417083.
33 **A "feisty fighter":** George Bush, *All the Best*, 571.
33 **"I don't think he's ever been":** Minutaglio, *First Son*, 188–91.
33 **Bush was trying "to ride the coattails":** Ibid., 191–93.
33 **"He went to Greenwich Country Day School":** George Lardner Jr. and Lois Romano, "Tragedy Created Bush Mother-Son Bond," *Washington Post*, July 26, 1999, http://www.washingtonpost.com/wp-srv/politics/campaigns/wh2000/stories/bush072699.htm.
33 **"I won't be persuaded by anyone":** Ibid., 188–91.
33 **Hance beat Bush with 53 percent:** U.S. House Clerk's Office, http://clerk.house.gov/member_info/electionInfo/1978election.pdf.
34 **"He allowed Hance to define him":** O'Neill interview.
34 **"We talked on more than":** Dick Cheney, author interview.
34 **from television while dining:** Laura Bush, *Spoken from the Heart*, 103.
34 **it ranked 993rd in oil production:** Minutaglio, *First Son*, 204.
34 **Nearly half of the ninety-five holes:** Mitchell, *W*, 194. By comparison, George H. W. Bush hit oil in all 127 wells he drilled in the 1950s.
34 **with a $75,000-a-year salary:** Ibid., 205.
34 **Cheney supported tax cuts:** Matthew Vita and Dan Morgan, "A Hard-Liner with

a Soft Touch," *Washington Post*, August 5, 2000; and Richard T. Cooper, "Cheney a Man of Big but Limited Ambitions—the Perfect No. 2," *Los Angeles Times*, October 19, 2000, http://articles.latimes.com/2000/oct/19/news/mn-38884.

35 **"never met a weapons system"**: Mann, *Rise of the Vulcans*, 201.

35 **"I had no idea he was that conservative"**: Cooper, "Cheney a Man of Big but Limited Ambitions."

35 **"Nobody ever checked the voting record"**: Cheney interview.

35 **cross out the word "bureaucrat"**: Williams interview.

35 **"The deficit isn't the worst"**: Reeves, *President Reagan*, 92.

35 **"You can't expect them to accept"**: Dubose and Bernstein, *Vice*, 53.

35 **regular participant in a secret program**: Mann, *Rise of the Vulcans*, 138–45.

35 **"the most effective and impressive witness"**: Dubose and Bernstein, *Vice*, 78.

36 **wrote a book, *Kings of the Hill***: Cheney and Cheney, *Kings of the Hill*.

36 **"Dick, what in the hell"**: Meyer interview.

36 **"Go get George"**: Former aide, author interview.

36 **"How do we know we can trust"**: George W. Bush, *Decision Points*, 43–44.

36 **"If someone throws a grenade"**: Ibid.

37 **"planted a seed in my heart"**: Lois Romano and George Lardner Jr., "Bush's Life-Changing Year," *Washington Post*, July 25, 1999, http://www.washingtonpost.com/wp-srv/politics/campaigns/wh2000/stories/bush072599.htm. Some have cast doubt on this story. Jacob Weisberg points out that there is not much of a beach on the rocky shore at Walker's Point and notes that an earlier account did not mention a walk on the beach, only a discussion in the house. See *Bush Tragedy*, 75–78.

37 **"I want to talk to you"**: Arthur Blessitt, "The Day I Prayed With George W. Bush to Receive Jesus!" from his diary, April 3, 1984, http://www.blessitt.com/Inspiration_Witness/PrayingWithGeorgeWBush/Praying_With_Bush_Page1.html.

37 **"I'm all name and no money"**: Robert Reinhold, "In Troubled Oil Business, It Matters Little If Your Name Is Bush, Sons Find," *New York Times*, April 30, 1986.

37 **gave him $600,000 in shares**: Minutaglio, *First Son*, 207.

37 **"You no good fucking sonofabitch"**: Ibid., 208–9. After Minutaglio asked about the incident during research for his book years later, Bush called Hunt to apologize.

37 **"Can you remember the last day"**: George W. Bush, *Decision Points*, 1.

37 **repeated the same toast**: Laura Bush, *Spoken from the Heart*, 118.

37 **"We made a little noise in the dining room"**: O'Neill interview.

37 **"It's either Jim Beam or me"**: Laura Bush, *Spoken from the Heart*, 118.

37 **"He said one day I might be"**: O'Neill interview.

37 **"He was a big, booming personality"**: Debra Dunn, author interview.

37 **driver named Payne was nicknamed**: Steve Atkiss, author interview.

37 **He learned that by showing**: Woodward, *Bush at War*, 235.

38 **"Yeah, I killed them in Atlanta"**: Richard Ben Cramer, author interview.

38 **"You've heard the rumors"**: Un-bylined "Periscope" item in *Newsweek* by Howard Fineman, "Bush and the 'Big A Question,'" June 29, 1987.

38 **"Fighting the 'Wimp Factor'"**: Margaret Warner, *Newsweek*, October 19, 1987.

38 **Bush was "red hot"**: George W. Bush, *Decision Points*, 43–44.

38 **gotten over his "self-pity"**: George W. Bush said this in a 1986 interview with Walt Harrington, a staff writer for the *Washington Post Magazine* who at the time was writing a profile of Bush's father. The quotation did not make the piece, but Harrington later provided it to his *Post* colleagues Lois Romano and George Lardner

Jr. for their enduring 1999 biographical series on the younger Bush. They cited it in "Bush: So-So Student but a Campus Mover," *Washington Post*, July 27, 1999, http://www.washingtonpost.com/wp-srv/politics/campaigns/wh2000/stories/bush072799.htm.

38 **"If there was any sort of"**: Lois Romano and George Lardner Jr., "Bush's Move Up to the Majors," *Washington Post*, July 31, 1999, http://www.washingtonpost.com/wp-srv/politics/campaigns/wh2000/stories/bush073199.htm.

39 **"I got married and gave up"**: Dick Cheney, *In My Time*, 152–58.

39 **"My instinct is to cut him off"**: Woodward, *Commanders*, 44–47.

39 **"General Welch was freelancing"**: Dick Cheney, news conference, Pentagon, March 24, 1989.

39 **Welch "got a bit of a bum rap"**: Cheney, oral history, Miller Center.

39 **"a stroke of genius"**: Ibid.

39 **"a cerebral Wyoming cowboy"**: Powell, *My American Journey*, 412.

39 **"That's because they're all right-wing nuts"**: Ibid., 526.

40 **From the plane, Scowcroft**: Brent Scowcroft, oral history, Miller Center, University of Virginia, November 12–13, 1999. Neither Cheney nor Quayle mentioned this dispute in his memoirs. Powell wrote that Cheney was sick but that he suspected he preferred not to deal with Quayle.

40 **"George, everybody likes you"**: Gerhart, *Perfect Wife*, 83–84.

40 **put in just $606,000 of the $86 million**: Juan B. Elizondo Jr., "Bush Earns $14.9 Million from Team Sale," Associated Press, June 18, 1998.

40 **"How cool is this?"**: Draper, *Dead Certain*, 42–43.

40 **"I can't tell you how many"**: Israel Hernandez, author interview.

40 **went from a losing team**: From 1989 to 1998, the Rangers had seven winning seasons and three losing ones. In the previous decade, the team had three winning seasons and seven losing ones. Total season attendance increased from 1,581,901 before Bush and his partners bought the team to 2,927,409 the year it was sold. (Bush and his partners sold the team in the middle of the 1998 season.) http://mlb.mlb.com/tex/history/year_by_year_results.jsp.

40 **"solved my biggest political problem"**: *Time*, July 31, 1999.

40 **"Did the president have the balls"**: Cheney, oral history, Miller Center.

41 **"It sent a hell of a message"**: Ibid.

41 **Powell later had the study destroyed**: Ibid.

41 **"Lawyers running a war?"**: Powell, *My American Journey*, 483.

41 **"The unanimous view of those of us"**: Cheney, oral history, Miller Center.

41 **just 148 American battle deaths**: Anne Leland and Mari-Jana "M-J" Oboroceanu, "American War and Military Operations Casualties: Lists and Statistics," Congressional Research Service, February 26, 2010, http://www.fas.org/sgp/crs/natsec/RL32492.pdf. The report actually gives two different statistics, 147 and 148, on different pages. The more commonly used figure seems to be 148.

41 **"simple solutionists"**: Powell, *My American Journey*, 511.

41 **"Once we had rounded him up"**: Dick Cheney, speech to Discovery Institute, Seattle, August 14, 1992, Federal News Service transcript.

42 **"I still think we made the right decision"**: Cheney, oral history, Miller Center.

42 **"Smart guy, arrogant, didn't know"**: Ibid.

42 **"You know," he told Sununu**: Duffy and Goodgame, *Marching in Place*, 127–28.

42 **acknowledged that he "blew it"**: Parmet, *George Bush*, 349. According to Parmet, Bush wrote in his diary at the end of the Republican National Convention week in 1988, "It was my decision, and I blew it, but I'm not about to say that I blew it."

42 **"I never completely gave up on my idea":** George W. Bush, *Decision Points*, 49.
42 **"George, you can't win":** Ibid., 52–53.
42 **"I thought she was unbeatable":** Younger interview.
43 **"born with a silver foot":** Ann Richards, keynote address, Democratic National Convention, July 18, 1988, http://gos.sbc.edu/r/richards.html. For video, go to http://www.c-spanvideo.org/program/27252-1.
43 **"I'm not running against her":** Randy Galloway of the *Fort Worth Star-Telegram*, e-mail exchange with author. See also Gail Sheehy, "The Accidental Matter," *Vanity Fair*, October 2000, http://www.vanityfair.com/politics/features/2000/10/bush200010.
43 **"This is going to be rough":** George W. Bush, *Decision Points*, 54.
43 **"He just flat outworked":** O'Neill interview.
43 **"Why do you feel bad":** Schweizer and Schweizer, *Bushes*, xii.
43 **"disappointed, even hurt":** Powell, *My American Journey*, 554. Asked about that during his Miller Center oral history, Cheney said, "I didn't want to go around and throw my arms around people and say, 'Gee, it's been great.'"
43 **"beating the water as hard":** Sean O'Keefe, author interview.
44 **"I just decided I didn't want to do this":** Williams interview.
44 **"You have to first be able to visualize":** Stephen Hadley, author interview.
44 **told a Wyoming newspaper:** Hayes, *Cheney*, 268–69.
44 **"I see you have solved":** Bill Thomson, author interview.
44 **opposing unilateral sanctions:** While at Halliburton, Cheney was an active supporter of a bipartisan group called USA Engage that generally resisted unilateral sanctions. In a speech, Cheney called the sanctions issue "my favorite hobbyhorse" and argued that while he was not opposed to all sanctions, the times they should be used "are relatively rare" and generally when they are multilateral, citing Iraq as an example. Unilateral sanctions, he said, "almost never work" and were "the cheap, easy thing to do" to look like action. "I think it is important for us to recognize as a nation the enormous value of having American businesses engaged around the world." Richard B. Cheney, "Defending Liberty in a Global Economy," Cato Institute, June 23, 1998, http://www.cato.org/speeches/sp-dc062398.html.
44 **bought Dresser for $7.7 billion:** Peter Elkind, "The Truth About Halliburton," *Fortune*, April 18, 2005, http://money.cnn.com/magazines/fortune/fortune_archive/2005/04/18/8257012/index.htm.
45 **would expand to an $11.9 billion giant:** David J. Lesar, chairman, president and chief executive officer, Halliburton, "Letter to Our Shareholders," Halliburton Company 2000 Annual Report. http://media.corporate-ir.net/media_files/IROL/67/67605/reports/company/letter_index_01.html.
45 **"an irascible, crazy old Texas politician":** Sandy Kress, author interview.
45 **"Governor, on this I'm going to":** Dave McNeely, "Missing Bullock's Unvarnished Advice," *Austin American-Statesman*, September 9, 1999. See also McNeely and Henderson, *Bob Bullock*, 262–63; and George W. Bush, *Decision Points*, 57.
45 **"What do you think about us?":** Draper, *Dead Certain*, 50–52. Draper tracked down the teenager, Johnny Demon Baulkmon, in 2006. He had become an adult petty criminal and was serving time in prison. Draper asked him what he thought of Bush. "He doesn't care about anything but himself," Baulkmon said. "He's complete trash, a horrible evil person."
45 **"I didn't have an answer":** Kuo, *Tempting Faith*, 114.
46 **"I just don't know if I can":** Ibid., 111–12.
46 **"I'll never again be able to":** Hughes, *Ten Minutes from Normal*, 4–5.

46 **received a check for $14.9 million:** Elizondo, "Bush Earns $14.9 Million from Team Sale."

46 **"I'm not going to run":** Wead, *All the Presidents' Children*, 4–5.

CHAPTER 3: "THE FIRE HORSE AND THE BELL"

47 **"I feel like a cork":** Dan Balz, e-mail exchange with author. The visiting journalists were Balz and David S. Broder, both of the *Washington Post*. See also Von Drehle, *Deadlock*, 8.

47 **There were not many times:** John Ellis, author interview.

48 **"We have the opportunity":** George W. Bush, *Decision Points*, 60–61.

48 **"He is talking to you":** Ibid. This story changed slightly in the retelling. In his campaign autobiography, *A Charge to Keep*, ghostwritten by Karen Hughes, Bush described his mother saying this after the service and in the past tense: "He was talking to you."

48 **"I feel as if God were talking":** Schweizer and Schweizer, *Bushes*, 438.

48 **"Are you nuts?":** Ibid., 458.

48 **"who makes the Energizer Bunny":** Cannon, Dubose and Reid, *Boy Genius*, 267.

48 **"Huge amounts of charisma":** Ibid., 14.

48 **"I need your help":** Richard Perle, author interview.

49 **"It was very much like":** Marvin Olasky, author interview.

49 **"inherited half of his friends":** George W. Bush, "The First Son," *P.O.V.*, June 1999. This essay honoring his father on his seventy-fifth birthday was republished a decade later by the *Daily Beast*. http://www.thedailybeast.com/articles/2009/06/11/happy-birthday-dad.html.

49 **"Rove let me know that":** Novak, *Prince of Darkness*, 562.

49 **"We had to be the back-of-the-bus":** Ron Kaufman, author interview.

49 **Shultz gave him the blessing:** Draper, *Dead Certain*, 53–54.

49 **"This is your candidate":** David Von Drehle, "In Iowa, Bush Hits Rhetorical Notes, Trail," *Washington Post*, June 13, 1999, http://www.washingtonpost.com/wp-srv/politics/campaigns/wh2000/stories/bush061399.htm.

49 **"the only thing we haven't done":** Milbank, *Smashmouth*, 63.

50 **"Look, I'm really committed":** Hayes, *Cheney*, 276–77.

50 **The dissenters were:** Zakheim, *Vulcan's Tale*, 8–9.

50 **"That mission is to deter wars":** Bush, speech at the Citadel, September 23, 1999. A transcript can be found at http://www3.citadel.edu/pao/addresses/pres_bush.html. But it appears to be the prepared text, as Bush deviated slightly in some parts. A video of the actual speech as delivered can be found at http://www.c-spanvideo.org/program/152320-1.

51 **"grinchy old Republican":** Hughes, *Ten Minutes from Normal*, 109–11.

51 **a term that unbeknownst to her:** Weisberg, *Bush Tragedy*, 92–93. In tracing the origin of the phrase, Weisberg noted that Doug Wead also used it as a chapter title of a book he ghostwrote for James Watt in 1985 and that Karl Rove "was especially concerned" that not become known for fear of association with Ronald Reagan's controversial interior secretary.

51 **"Somewhat different from many":** Glenn Hubbard, author interview.

51 **"sounded less like a philosophy":** Frum, *Right Man*, 6.

52 **"It took a little getting used to":** Michael Gerson, author interview.

52 **"You're going to get asked":** Hughes, *Ten Minutes from Normal*, 124.

52 **"I don't think they ought to":** Terry M. Neal and Juliet Eilperin, "Bush Faults House GOP Spending Plan," *Washington Post*, October 1, 1999, http://www.washingtonpost.com/wp-srv/politics/campaigns/wh2000/stories/congress100199.htm.

52 **"I'm always amazed when I read":** Schweizer and Schweizer, *Bushes*, 334.

52 **his favorite philosopher was Jesus:** John Bachman of WHO-TV asked the candidates which "philosopher or thinker" they identified with the most. Bush answered, "Christ, because he changed my heart." When Bachman said viewers would like to know how, Bush said, "Well, if they don't know, it's going to be hard to explain. When you turn your heart and your life over to Christ, when you accept Christ as the savior, it changes your heart. It changes your life. And that's what happened to me." Republican debate, Des Moines, December 13, 1999, http://www.presidency.ucsb.edu/ws/index.php?pid=76120#axzz1nnD78oFi.

52 **"I don't think your answer":** George W. Bush, *Decision Points*, 71.

52 **Ronald Reagan, who once said:** Lou Cannon, *President Reagan*, 247. Reagan made this comment in an interview with the British television journalist David Frost in 1968 when he was setting his eyes on the White House.

52 **"This is not only no new taxes":** Bush during Republican debate, Durham, N.H., January 6, 2000, http://partners.nytimes.com/library/politics/camp/010700wh-gop-debate-text.html.

52 **"I can see a little chemistry":** Alexandra Pelosi, *Journeys with George*, 2002.

53 **"Please, don't kill me":** Tucker Carlson, "Devil May Care," *Talk*, September 1999.

53 **"I'm not going to kick":** David D. Kirkpatrick, "In Secretly Taped Conversations, Glimpses of the Future President," *New York Times*, February 20, 2005.

53 **"Rarely is the question asked":** Jacob Weisberg of *Slate* magazine made a point of collecting such misstatements and coined a name for them, "Bushisms," that later inspired a book, *The Ultimate George W. Bushisms: Bush at War (with the English Language)*.

53 **"He's going to wear very thin":** Kirkpatrick, "In Secretly Taped Conversations."

53 **McCain thrashed Bush:** John McCain won 48.5 percent of the vote, George W. Bush won 30.4 percent, Steve Forbes won 12.7 percent. Federal Election Commission, February 1, 2000, http://www.fec.gov/pubrec/fe2000/2000presprim.htm#NH.

53 **"Consultants don't concede":** John Weaver, e-mail exchange with author. See also Milbank, *Smashmouth*, 102.

53 **"We said good-bye as friends":** McCain, *Worth the Fighting For*, 378.

53 **"This is my fault, not yours":** Mark McKinnon, author interview.

54 **"He really was like a coach":** Judd Gregg, author interview.

54 **"You got defined":** Draper, *Dead Certain*, 25–26.

54 **"McCain has managed to steal":** Hughes, *Ten Minutes from Normal*, 130–31.

54 **"a combination of the Cowardly Lion":** Yvonne Abraham and Anne E. Kornblut, "McCain to Halt Campaign," *Boston Globe*, March 9, 2000.

54 **"I endorse Governor Bush":** Transcript of Bush-McCain news conference, Pittsburgh, May 9, 2000.

55 **"I cited all the reasons why":** Dick Cheney, author interview.

55 **"Are you on it?":** Alan Simpson, author interview.

56 **"I am so glad to be out":** Pete Williams, author interview.

56 **"If someone says no, do they":** Evan Thomas and Martha Brant, "A Son's Restless Journey," *Newsweek*, August 7, 2000.

56 **"He didn't have any desire":** Liz Cheney, author interview.

56 **"Cheney engineered the whole":** Friend of Cheney's, author interview.

56 **"What do you think about me":** Mary Cheney, *Now It's My Turn*, 1–4.
57 **"You're not going to do this":** Lynne Cheney, unpublished interview with journalist Robert Draper.
57 **"The man I really want":** Hughes, *Ten Minutes from Normal*, 142–46.
57 **"punishingly hot":** Dick Cheney, *In My Time*, 255–59.
57 **harbored "real doubts" about Cheney:** Rove, *Courage and Consequence*, 169–71.
57 **"Tell me why you think":** Ibid.
58 **"falling back on his father's":** Ibid.
58 **"He'd looked at me impassively":** Ibid.
58 **"Dick," Bush said dismissively:** Dick Cheney, *In My Time*, 262–67.
58 **would be funeral director:** George W. Bush, *Decision Points*, 67–69.
58 **"absolutely inaccurate":** Bruni, *Ambling into History*, 151–52.
58 **"the mature person sitting":** Dennis Hastert, author interview.
58 **"He was the most prominent":** Sean O'Keefe, author interview.
58 **"I really wasn't looking":** Bush told this to Christine Todd Whitman, the former governor of New Jersey who would go on to become head of the Environmental Protection Agency in his administration. Roger Simon, "Reporter's Notebook," *U.S. News & World Report* Web site, July 31, 2000, http://www.usnews.com/usnews/news/election/gop/notebook1.htm.
59 **"You'd think it would be about":** John Danforth, author interview.
59 **Cheney told Liz to call back:** Dick Cheney, *In My Time*, 262–67.
59 **David Gribbin called another Cheney:** Joe Meyer, author interview.
59 **Karen Hughes tried to find out:** Dick Cheney, *In My Time*, 262–67.
59 **lied to him:** Rove, *Courage and Consequence*, 173–74.
59 **"You're going to hear something":** David Hume Kennerly, author interview.
60 **"Honey, let's sell the house":** Hayes, *Cheney*, 292.
60 **"I was impressed by the thoughtful":** Bush introduction of Cheney as running mate, July 25, 2000, http://archives.cnn.com/TRANSCRIPTS/0007/25/bn.16.html.
60 **"I was deeply involved":** Ibid.
60 **"the most insignificant office":** John Adams told his wife, Abigail: "My country has in its wisdom contrived for me the most insignificant office that ever the invention of man contrived or his imagination conceived." http://www.whitehouse.gov/about/presidents/johnadams.
60 **"not worth a bucket of warm spit":** The quotation was never reported at the time it was supposedly made, and there remains a debate as to when Garner first said it, and even what word he used. One biographer said he actually said "warm piss," and possibly another four-letter word even more profane. For an interesting essay on the origin of this quotation, see "Not Worth a Bucket of Warm Spit" by Patrick Cox, associate director for American history at the University of Texas at Austin, posted on George Mason University's History News Network, August 20, 2008, http://hnn.us/articles/53402.html.
60 **"I detested every minute of it":** Shesol, *Mutual Contempt*, 75.
60 **"characterized by ambiguity":** Walter F. Mondale to Jimmy Carter, memo, "The Role of the Vice President in the Carter Administration," December 9, 1976, http://www.mnhs.org/collections/upclose/Mondale-CarterMemo-Scanned.pdf. See also Richard Moe, "The Making of the Modern Vice Presidency: A Personal Reflection," *Minnesota History*, fall 2006, http://collections.mnhs.org/MNHistoryMagazine/articles/60/v60i03p088-099.pdf.
60 **"It is a crappy job":** Cheney interview.

61 **"I was impressed and believed":** Ibid.

61 **"The idea of not wearing a tie":** Williams interview.

62 **activists had threatened to out:** Mary Cheney, *Now It's My Turn*, 35. In her book, Mary Cheney wrote that she came out to her parents while a junior in high school. She had just broken up with her first girlfriend and in her sorrow wrecked the family car. She wrote that when she arrived home and told her mother about the crash, she also revealed that she was gay. She added that when she told her father, he said, "You're my daughter and I love you and I just want you to be happy." In his book, though, Dick Cheney wrote that Mary came out to him in the Denver airport during a trip home to Wyoming. *In My Time*, 148.

62 **Howard Fineman of *Newsweek*:** Mary Cheney, *Now It's My Turn*, 12–13.

62 **"Your daughter's sexual orientation":** Howard Fineman, e-mail exchange with author.

62 **"The secretary loves":** Ibid.

62 **"There is one issue we need":** Dan Bartlett, speech to U.S. Chamber of Commerce, September 13, 2007, http://www.leadingauthorities.com/speaker/dan-bartlett.aspx.

63 **It was Lynne who came up with:** John McConnell, author interview.

63 **Cheney ignored them:** Cheney interview.

63 **"I came up and gave them":** Ibid.

63 **"done nothing to help children":** Dick Cheney, acceptance speech, Republican National Convention, Philadelphia, August 2, 2000, http://www.gwu.edu/~action/chen080200.html. For video, go to http://www.c-span.org/Events/Dick-Cheney-2000-Republican-National-Convention-in-Philadelphia-PA/1805/.

63 **"coasted through prosperity":** George W. Bush, acceptance speech, Republican National Convention, Philadelphia, August 3, 2000, http://www.gwu.edu/%7Eaction/bush080300.html. For video, go to http://www.c-span.org/Events/George-W-Bush-2000-Republican-National-Convention-in-Philadelphia-PA/1804/.

64 **"just straining for big themes":** Matthew Scully, author interview.

CHAPTER 4: "WE WRAPPED BILL CLINTON AROUND HIS NECK"

65 **"There were some issues on which":** John McLaughlin, author interview.

66 **"Times Have Never Been Better":** Stevens, *Big Enchilada*, 151.

66 **"pathologically a liar":** Kirkpatrick, "In Secretly Taped Conversations."

66 **"I may have to get a little":** Ibid.

66 **"What we did with Gore":** Dick Cheney, author interview.

66 **"If he decides he can't help":** Halperin and Harris, *Way to Win*, 132.

66 **"The binders came back":** Stuart Holliday, author interview.

66 **"The whole thing was a surprise":** Alan Simpson, author interview.

66 **"He basically sort of laid down":** Holliday interview.

67 **"There's Adam Clymer":** Mike Allen, "Bush Appeals for 'Plain-Spoken Folks' in Office," *Washington Post*, September 5, 2000.

67 **Cheney's staff debated whether:** Former Cheney aide, author interview.

67 **"was careful to break almost every":** Stevens, *Big Enchilada*, 227–28.

67 **"There was no quarter given":** Judd Gregg, author interview.

67 **he was "flat":** Stevens, *Big Enchilada*, 227–28.

67 **"Lambs to the slaughter":** Ibid., 225.

67 **the staff was overwhelmed:** Hughes, *Ten Minutes from Normal*, 163–65.

68 **he called Kirbyjon Caldwell:** Kirbyjon Caldwell, author interview.

68 **"He believes in nation building":** Transcript of Bush-Gore debate, October 3, 2000, http://www.debates.org/index.php?page=october-3-2000-transcript.

68 **"felt like a cross between":** Stevens, *Big Enchilada*, 229–30.

68 **"she would throw him off":** Liz Cheney, author interview.

69 **"He was getting all kinds of advice":** Matthew Dowd, author interview.

69 **"I think that probably includes you":** Democratic talking points provided to author.

69 **"It is a loser, don't attack him":** Joseph Lieberman, author interview.

69 **urged the candidate to go after Cheney:** Stan Greenberg, e-mail exchange with author. In his memoir, Shrum wrote that they advised Lieberman to "go after Bush on the issues, and make sure Cheney didn't break out of his special-interest Halliburton box." Shrum, *No Excuses*, 357–58.

69 **"I'm pleased to see, Dick":** Video clip of Cheney-Lieberman debate, October 5, 2000, http://www.youtube.com/watch?v=xr1O7FaEJ1M&t=7m10s.

69 **overlooked the $763 million:** House Committee on Government Reform Minority Staff, "Dollars Not Sense: Government Contracting Under the Bush Administration," June 2006, http://www.halliburtonwatch.org/reports/waxman0606.pdf.

69 **"The debate was actually":** Lieberman interview.

70 **"He's not going to do that":** Rob Portman, author interview.

70 **"He put the move on me":** Stevens, *Big Enchilada*, 262.

70 **"I'll be the most surprised man":** Von Drehle, *Deadlock*, 16–17. In an e-mail exchange with the author, an aide to Tommy Thompson said he did not recall the conversation.

70 **"'Miss Pessimistic' (me) really":** Barbara Bush, *Reflections*, 365.

70 **"His face didn't change":** Hughes, *Ten Minutes from Normal*, 168–69.

70 **"This thing has gone from probably-win":** Dowd interview. Nationally, Bush's six-point lead in the Gallup/CNN/*USA Today* poll just before the revelation shrank to two points by Election Day. http://www.pollingreport.com/wh2gen1.htm.

70 **four million evangelical voters:** Rove, *Courage and Consequence*, 364.

71 **cost Bush the states:** Stevens, *Big Enchilada*, 275. Gore won New Mexico by just 366 votes, Iowa by 4,144, Oregon by 6,765, and Maine by 33,335, according to the Federal Election Commission. In the case of the first three, that was less than one-half of 1 percent. http://www.fec.gov/pubrec/2000presgeresults.htm.

71 **"The one thing on which":** Michael Toner, author interview. In fact, the lawyers thought if anything out of the ordinary happened, it would be Bush winning the popular vote while losing the electoral vote, and they developed talking points on the virtues of the popular vote—talking points that of course were quickly discarded when the results came in the other way around.

71 **precisely 10:39 p.m. Texas time:** Cannon, Dubose, and Reid, *Boy Genius*, 174.

71 **"It could be a long night":** Von Drehle, *Deadlock*, 31–33.

71 **At 6:48 p.m. in Texas:** Joan Konner, James Risser, and Ben Wattenberg, "Television's Performance on Election Night 2000: A Report for CNN," January 29, 2001, http://archives.cnn.com/2001/ALLPOLITICS/stories/02/02/cnn.report/cnn.pdf.

71 **"I felt like I had let him down":** Koch, *My Father, My President*, 476.

71 **"I'm not going to stay around":** Von Drehle, *Deadlock*, 31–33.

71 **would win with 320 electoral votes:** Cannon, Dubose, and Reid, *Boy Genius*, 171.

71 **"Back from the ashes!":** Koch, *My Father, My President*, 477–78.

72 **At 8:54 p.m. in Texas:** Konner, Risser, and Wattenberg, "Television's Performance on Election Night 2000."

72 **"We're still alive":** Hughes, *Ten Minutes from Normal*, 172–78.
72 **"when she's stressed":** Jenna Bush, interview on *Today*, NBC, November 6, 2012, http://www.today.com/video/today/49708400. "She has a little bit of an OCD issue," Jenna said of her mother.
72 **"suddenly looked old, tired":** Barbara Bush, *Reflections*, 369.
72 **voted Democratic in fourteen:** National Archives and Records Administration, http://www.archives.gov/federal-register/electoral-college/votes/votes_by_state.html.
72 **"What do *you* think?":** Von Drehle, *Deadlock*, 43–44.
72 **at 1:15 a.m. Texas time:** Konner, Risser, and Wattenberg, "Television's Performance on Election Night 2000."
72 **"Congratulations," Gore told him:** Hughes, *Ten Minutes from Normal*, 172–78.
73 **"Dad, you just got elected":** Dick Cheney, *In My Time*, 288.
73 **Mary Cheney remembered her mother:** Mary Cheney, *Now It's My Turn*, 112–16.
73 **"Get up, bastard!":** Alan Simpson, author interview.
73 **"You've just been elected":** Mary Cheney, *Now It's My Turn*, 108–10.
73 **"Circumstances have changed":** This exchange is described in multiple accounts, including Von Drehle, *Deadlock*, 49–50; Toobin, *Too Close to Call*, 24–25; and Simon, *Divided We Stand*, 43. The wording is slightly different in each of the accounts but broadly the same.
73 **"He took it back":** David Hume Kennerly, author interview.
74 **"George, don't do it":** George W. Bush, *Decision Points*, 77–78.
74 **"Bushie," she said teasingly:** Laura Bush, *Spoken from the Heart*, 161–62.
74 **"We spent literally hours":** Andy Card, author interview for unpublished *New York Times* article.
74 **"You are entering a time":** The dinner was at the home of Mary and Tim Herman on the night of November 18. Anne Johnson, the wife of Bush's college friend Clay Johnson, opened the fortune cookie. Clay Johnson, e-mail exchange with author. See also Von Drehle, *Deadlock*, 110.
75 **with instant messages:** Koch, *My Father, My President*, 479.
75 **"We talk all the time":** George Bush, letter to Hugh Sidey, December 16, 2000. See Bush, *All the Best*, 636.
75 **"If they're going to steal":** Fleischer, *Taking Heat*, 11.
75 **"I just can't conceive":** Danforth interview. See also James Baker, *"Work Hard, Study . . . and Keep out of Politics!,"* 380.
75 **under the pseudonym Red Adair:** Dick Cheney and Reiner, *Heart*, 141.
76 **Karen Hughes ordered the doctors:** Dick Cheney, *In My Time*, 292–93.
76 **"I feel good and everything's looking":** *Larry King Live*, CNN, November 22, 2000, http://transcripts.cnn.com/TRANSCRIPTS/0011/22/lkl.00.html.
76 **briefing House Speaker:** Hastert interview.
76 **it ruled 7 to 2:** *George W. Bush et al. v. Albert Gore Jr. et al.*, Supreme Court 00-949, December 12, 2000, http://www.law.cornell.edu/supct/html/00-949.ZPC.html.
76 **"Dick, the Supreme Court":** Kennerly interview.
77 **"Hello, Mr. Vice President–elect":** Dick Cheney, *In My Time*, 296–97. See also Baker, *"Work Hard, Study . . . and Keep out of Politics!,"* 161.
77 **"I'm going to open the good bottle":** Kennerly interview.
77 **"Congratulations, Mr. President":** Toobin, *Too Close to Call*, 267.
77 **"I'm not a lawyer":** Koch, *My Father, My President*, 481.
77 **"I'm not calling back this time":** Hughes, *Ten Minutes from Normal*, 180–81.

78 **Two extensive recounts:** The first study, by *USA Today*, the *Miami Herald*, and Knight Ridder, found that Bush would have actually increased his vote margin under the counting standards advocated by the Gore campaign. If every hanging chad and dimpled ballot had been counted, Bush would have won by 1,665 votes, instead of 537, the study found. The only scenario that would have possibly given Gore a chance was if only ballots with a clean punch were counted, the opposite of what Gore sought. In such a case, the study found Gore with 3 more votes than Bush out of 6 million cast—so razor-thin close that it would be impossible to conclude that Gore would necessarily have won because different counters might have assessed the ballots differently enough to change the margin by 4 votes. http://www.usatoday.com/news/washington/2001-04-03-floridamain.htm. The other study, by a consortium of eight news organizations, including the *New York Times*, the *Washington Post*, and CNN, found that neither the limited statewide recount ordered by the Florida Supreme Court nor the recount sought by Gore in the four Democratic counties would have changed the ultimate outcome. The only scenario for a Gore victory in this study was if Florida had conducted a broader recount in every county, something neither sought by Gore nor ordered by the Florida Supreme Court. Judge Terry Lewis, who was overseeing the recount, said later that he was thinking about ordering a reexamination of ballots rejected by machines because they purportedly recorded more than one vote for president, which theoretically might have resulted in a Gore victory, but neither side had asked that such ballots be counted. It is also fair to assume that the confusion over the butterfly ballot in Palm Beach County cost Gore thousands of votes and, in the end, the election. But his lawyers could not come up with a legal way to address that confusion after the fact, and it was not at issue in the litigation that determined the outcome. In other words, if the U.S. Supreme Court had not issued its controversial ruling in *Bush v. Gore* and the process had gone forward as ordered by the Florida high court, Bush still would have won. http://www.factcheck.org/2008/01/the-florida-recount-of-2000/ or http://www.nytimes.com/images/2001/11/12/politics/recount/preset.html.

78 **"pouring alcohol in an open wound":** Karen Hughes, author interview.

78 **"Here in a place":** George W. Bush, acceptance speech, Austin, Tex., December 13, 2000, http://www3.nationaljournal.com/members/news/2000/12/1213bush_speech.htm.

CHAPTER 5: "I'M GOING TO CALL DICK"

79 **"Our attitude was hell no":** Dick Cheney, unpublished interview with journalist Robert Draper.

79 **"What really unnerved me":** Chafee, *Against the Tide*, 2–10.

80 **"Our votes at this table":** Ibid.

80 **"How will this work?":** Nick Calio, author interview.

81 **"What's CEQ?":** Christine Todd Whitman, author interview. Whitman said she did not know whether Bush was joking or not, so she chose to take it as a joke.

81 **"keeping me on a much shorter":** Colin Powell, author interview.

81 **"To be in a position where":** Dick Cheney, author interview.

81 **Bush attributed the idea:** George W. Bush, *Decision Points*, 83–84.

81 **"awkward issue":** Ibid.

81 **"All I'm going to say to you":** Draper, *Dead Certain*, 282.

82 **"I had no way of knowing":** George W. Bush, *Decision Points*, 83–84.
82 **Rove also argued against:** Rove, *Courage and Consequence*, 220.
82 **"Dick, here's an interesting":** Rumsfeld, *Known and Unknown*, 284–85.
82 **thought it was like the second:** Greenspan, *Age of Turbulence*, 208.
82 **"My God, talk about a replay":** Ottaway, *King's Messenger*, 143.
82 **"We got to be very close":** Daschle, *Like No Other Time*, 51–53. Bush would later tell the author Robert Draper that he doubted he told Daschle not to lie to him that bluntly but may have put it differently, like urging that they both be honest with each other.
83 **"How many more do you":** Dick Cheney, *In My Time*, 302–4.
83 **"I will live and lead":** George W. Bush, inaugural address, January 20, 2001, http://georgewbush-whitehouse.archives.gov/news/inaugural-address.html.
83 **"shockingly good":** Hendrik Hertzberg, "The Word from W.," *New Yorker*, February 5, 2001, http://www.newyorker.com/archive/2001/02/05/010205taco_talk_hertzberg.
83 **"Had you closed your eyes":** Kirbyjon Caldwell, author interview.
84 **"Welcome, Mr. President":** "Bushes: 41 and 43," video made by Mark McKinnon for the Republican National Convention, August 29, 2012, http://www.thedailybeast.com/articles/2012/08/29/backstage-at-the-bush-movie.html.
84 **"I don't think I need a valet":** Laura Bush, *Spoken from the Heart*, 175.
84 **the "Johnny Q Room":** Jay Winik, author interview.
84 **"A Charge to keep I have":** Charles Wesley wrote the hymn in 1762. United Methodist Church, http://gbgm-umc.org/umhistory/wesley/hymns/umh413.stm.
85 **In fact, it was commissioned:** This has been documented in a series of blogs and articles over the years, as well as in Weisberg's *Bush Tragedy*. See in particular http://www.milwaukeeworld.com/html/horne/h-040223.php; http://www.talk2action.org/story/2006/5/12/7393/57216; http://www.salon.com/2007/04/26/torture_policy/.
85 **"a lone, arrogant cowboy":** Cannon and Cannon, *Reagan's Disciple*, 239.
86 **He preferred lunch:** Scheib, *White House Chef*, 232.
86 **His staff had laid out his first:** Brad Blakeman, author interview.
86 **"It was probably the good":** John Bridgeland, author interview.
86 **When Colin Powell showed up late:** Draper, *Dead Certain*, 107. Colin Powell later said he had been "delayed by an important phone call" but added that he did not consider himself dissed because Bush "did it all the time to others," including even "Karl Rove, to my delight." See Powell, *It Worked for Me*, 144.
87 **"No, sir":** Cesar Conda, author interview.
87 **"We said great":** Michael Green, author interview.
87 **"Mr. President, this is what":** Rice, *No Higher Honor*, 17.
87 **"Mr. Vice President, your staff":** Stephen Hadley, author interview.
87 **"seemed very much of one":** Rice, *No Higher Honor*, 17.
88 **Bush's scheduling director:** Blakeman interview.
88 **Juleanna Glover, suggested:** White House official, author interview.
88 **"I think those guys are always":** Neil Patel, author interview.
88 **"We've all done it":** Gellman, *Angler*, 57–58.
89 **"You could lose the 6 or 7":** Matthew Dowd, interview with PBS's *Frontline*, January 4, 2005, http://www.pbs.org/wgbh/pages/frontline/shows/architect/interviews/dowd.html. Dowd confirmed his memo in an e-mail exchange with author. See also Edsall, *Building Red America*, 50.
89 **Bush "was eager and fervent":** Sandy Kress, author interview.

89 **"disaggregation of data":** Peter Baker, "An Unlikely Partnership Left Behind," *Washington Post*, November 5, 2007, http://www.washingtonpost.com/wp-dyn/content/article/2007/11/04/AR2007110401450.html.
89 **"You know, Senator, they are":** Kress interview.
90 **"Who is this guy?":** Pritchard, *Failed Diplomacy*, 52.
90 **"It did not change the president's":** Ibid.
90 **"we *urgently* need":** Richard A. Clarke to Condoleezza Rice, memo, "Subject: Presidential Policy Initiative/Review—the Al-Qaida Network," January 25, 2001, http://www.gwu.edu/~nsarchiv/NSAEBB/NSAEBB147/clarke%20memo.pdf.
90 **"Condi Rice will run these meetings":** Suskind, *Price of Loyalty*, 70–75.
91 **"We're going to correct":** Ibid.
91 **"Almost from the very beginning":** Rice, *No Higher Honor*, 29.
91 **"Why are we even bothering":** DeYoung, *Soldier*, 314–16.
91 **"Factories all over the world":** Paul O'Neill, author interview.
92 **"What's going on?":** Rice, *No Higher Honor*, 27–28.
92 **"a routine mission was conducted":** George W. Bush, news conference, San Cristóbal, Mexico, February 16, 2001, http://georgewbush-whitehouse.archives.gov/news/releases/2001/02/20010216-3.html.
92 **"I'm going to call Dick":** Rice, *No Higher Honor*, 27–28.
92 **"That said something to me":** Condoleezza Rice, author interview.
92 **"relaxed while at the same time":** Campbell, *Blair Years*, 505–6.
92 **"had a certain Soviet woodenness":** Meyer, *DC Confidential*, 176.
93 **"I don't expect that they are":** Ibid., 171.
93 **"He was a curious mix of cocky":** Campbell, *Blair Years*, 505–6.
93 **"self-effacing and self-deprecatory":** Tony Blair, *Journey*, 392.
93 **one American official noticed:** James Dobbins, author interview.
93 **"we both use Colgate toothpaste":** George W. Bush and Tony Blair, joint news conference, February 23, 2001, http://georgewbush-whitehouse.archives.gov/news/releases/2001/02/20010226-1.html.
93 **"Why don't we all watch":** Cherie Blair, *Speaking for Myself*, 261.
93 **"Well, what did they say":** Laura Bush, *Spoken from the Heart*, 179–80.
93 **thirty-seven fishing books:** Labash, *Fly Fishing with Darth Vader*, 57.
93 **Cheney began to feel uncomfortable:** Eric Schmitt, "Cheney Complains of Pains in Chest; Artery Is Cleared," *New York Times*, March 6, 2001.
94 **"Well, I feel great":** *Late Edition*, CNN, March 4, 2001, transcript.
94 **he found a headline:** Steven Mufson, "Bush to Pick Up Clinton Talks on N. Korean Missiles," *Washington Post*, March 7, 2001.
94 **"Have you seen the *Washington Post*?":** Rice, *No Higher Honor*, 35–36.
94 **"the fatal word: 'Clinton'":** DeYoung, *Soldier*, 324–26.
95 **"There was some suggestion":** Colin Powell, remarks to reporters, March 7, 2001, Federal News Service transcript.
95 **"Sometimes you get a little":** Doug Struck, "N. Korean Leader to Continue Sales of Missiles," *Washington Post*, May 5, 2001.
95 **"I oppose the Kyoto Protocol":** George W. Bush to Senators Chuck Hagel, Jesse Helms, Larry Craig, and Pat Roberts, March 13, 2001, http://georgewbush-whitehouse.archives.gov/news/releases/2001/03/20010314.html.
95 **both parties voted 95 to 0:** The nonbinding resolution expressed the "sense of the Senate" that the United States should not sign any agreement at Kyoto that mandated new commitments to limit greenhouse gas emissions unless it included developing countries like China and India. The Senate adopted it July 25, 1997. While it did not hold the force of law, it made pretty clear that ratification was

unlikely to say the least. http://www.senate.gov/legislative/LIS/roll_call_lists/roll_call_vote_cfm.cfm?congress=105&session=1&vote=00205.

96 **"Do you have it?":** Whitman, *It's My Party Too*, 173–79.

96 **"That one was a done deal":** Christine Todd Whitman, author interview.

96 **"Somebody better tell Christie":** Chafee, *Against the Tide*, 105.

96 **"Slow this thing down":** DeYoung, *Soldier*, 327–28. Powell remembered saying he would come, while Rice remembered asking him to come. See Bumiller, *Condoleezza Rice*, 148–49.

96 **"But the letter is already gone":** Rice, *No Higher Honor*, 41–42.

96 **"you're going to see the consequences":** DeYoung, *Soldier*, 327–28.

97 **"The way they did it":** Whitman interview.

97 **"They had built this beautiful":** Gordon Johndroe, author interview.

97 **"While he was right on Kyoto":** Stephen Hadley, author interview.

97 **she was "appalled":** Rice, *No Higher Honor*, 41–42.

97 **"It wasn't that the vice president":** Whitman interview.

97 **"We thought we knew Dick":** Suskind, *Price of Loyalty*, 124–26.

98 **Cheney secretly signed a letter:** Dick Cheney, *In My Time*, 320–22.

98 **"This is not your decision":** Ibid.

CHAPTER 6: "IRON FILINGS MOVING ACROSS A TABLETOP"

99 **"He was not going to be":** Judd Gregg, author interview.

100 **Besides, he said:** Shelton, *Without Hesitation*, 438–41.

100 **"I regret that a Chinese pilot":** George W. Bush statement, April 5, 2001.

100 **"we're sorry" about the death:** Colin Powell, appearance on *Face the Nation*, CBS, April 8, 2001, http://www.cbsnews.com/8301-3460_162-284682.html.

100 **Powell should say "pretty please":** Rice, *No Higher Honor*, 47–48.

100 **The seven-paragraph letter:** Ambassador Joseph W. Prueher to Foreign Minister Tang Jiaxuan of China, April 11, 2001, http://georgewbush-whitehouse.archives.gov/news/releases/2001/04/20010411-1.html.

100 **president's language "was unfortunate":** Rumsfeld, *Known and Unknown*, 314–15.

100 **"they have won":** Robert Kagan and William Kristol, "We Lost," *Washington Post*, April 13, 2001.

100 **"When you're talking to Dick":** Nicholas Lemann, "The Quiet Man," *New Yorker*, May 7, 2001.

101 **"Yes," Lott replied:** Trent Lott, author interview.

101 **"It was good news if the president":** Dennis Hastert, author interview.

101 **Cheney called Tim Pawlenty:** Pawlenty, *Courage to Stand*, p. 112.

101 **"We're asking you for the good":** Edwin Chen and Janet Hook, "Bush Team Plays Role Fit for a Kingmaker," *Los Angeles Times*, April 25, 2001, http://articles.latimes.com/2001/apr/25/news/mn-55164.

101 **"the threat of terrorist attack":** Lemann, "Quiet Man."

101 **he was sharply rebuffed:** Administration official, author interview.

102 **"Stiff 'em," Bush said:** White House official, author interview.

102 **"Now, conservation is an important":** Dick Cheney, speech to the Annual Meeting of the Associated Press, Toronto, April 30, 2001, http://georgewbush-whitehouse.archives.gov/vicepresident/news-speeches/speeches/vp20010430.html.

102 **"battled over the energy policy":** Frum, *Right Man*, 62–64.

102 **"literally defined the next three years"**: Jim Connaughton, author interview.
102 **"It was a way of establishing"**: Brad Berenson, author interview.
102 **"Strom Thurmond Jr., huh?"**: Ibid.
103 **"I won't negotiate with myself"**: Suskind, *Price of Loyalty*, 117.
103 **"I did not foresee how different"**: Greenspan, *Age of Turbulence*, 216–17.
103 **"Nicky," he said, "don't wobble"**: Nick Calio, author interview.
103 **cast his first tie-breaking vote**: David E. Rosenbaum, "Bush Tax Cut Plan Passes First Test in a Split Senate," *New York Times*, April 4, 2001, http://www.nytimes.com/2001/04/04/us/bush-tax-cut-plan-passes-first-test-in-a-split-senate.html. Over the course of his eight years in office, Cheney would break eight ties, the most of any vice president since Richard Nixon during the Eisenhower administration. Senate Historical Office, http://www.senate.gov/artandhistory/history/resources/pdf/VPTies.pdf.
104 **"the Torture Chamber"**: Jeffords, *Independent Man*, 263.
104 **had been jealous**: Rove, *Courage and Consequence*, 230–31.
104 **"relaxed and charming"**: Jeffords, *Independent Man*, 271.
104 **"Here we are in the Oval Office"**: Hughes, *Ten Minutes from Normal*, 211–12.
104 **"a one-term president"**: Jeffords, *Independent Man*, 271.
104 **"You are the swing vote"**: Hughes, *Ten Minutes from Normal*, 211–12.
104 **"It was clear that the deal"**: Calio interview.
104 **"He just said there will be"**: Lott interview.
105 **"It was a big body blow"**: Ari Fleischer, author interview.
105 **scribbling down $1.425 trillion**: Ben Nelson, author interview.
105 **House approved the plan 240 to 154**: U.S. House Clerk's Office, May 26, 2001, http://clerk.house.gov/evs/2001/roll149.xml.
105 **Senate followed barely an hour**: U.S. Senate roll call record, May 26, 2001, http://www.senate.gov/legislative/LIS/roll_call_lists/roll_call_vote_cfm.cfm?congress=107&session=1&vote=00170.
105 **"Don't worry about Susan"**: Chafee, *Against the Tide*, 62–63.
105 **"That's the reason I like"**: Daschle, *Like No Other Time*, 85–88.
106 **"Mr. President, conservatives are"**: Calio interview.
106 **"Mr. President, I got to tell you"**: Ibid.
106 **"one cold dude"**: Bush made the comment to Tony Blair during their first meeting at Camp David in February 2001. Meyer, *DC Confidential*, 178.
106 **"inside our tent"**: Michael McFaul, author interview. McFaul became President Barack Obama's senior adviser on Russia and later ambassador to Moscow.
107 **"I *did* play rugby"**: Hughes, *Ten Minutes from Normal*, 218–19.
107 **"Let me say something"**: Woodward, *Bush at War*, 119–20.
107 **Rice found it hard to believe**: Rice, *No Higher Honor*, 63.
107 **"an honest, straightforward man"**: George W. Bush and Vladimir Putin, news conference, Brdo pri Kranju, Slovenia, June 16, 2001, http://georgewbush-whitehouse.archives.gov/news/releases/2001/06/20010618.html.
107 **"I think KGB, KGB, KGB"**: Baker and Glasser, *Kremlin Rising*, 125.
107 **"A lot of us were kind of rolling"**: Eric Edelman, author interview.
107 **he checked into the hospital**: David E. Sanger and Lawrence K. Altman, "Cheney Gets Heart Device and Declares, 'I Feel Good,'" *New York Times*, July 1, 2001, http://www.nytimes.com/2001/07/01/us/cheney-gets-heart-device-and-declares-i-feel-good.html.
108 **"Well, so what?"**: Jack Dennis, e-mail exchange with author. See also Labash, *Fly Fishing with Darth Vader*, 71.

108 **"literally made my hair stand":** Tenet, *At the Center of the Storm*, 151–54.
108 **she remembered the warning:** Rice, *No Higher Honor*, 64–67.
108 **"I've managed to accommodate":** Cherie Blair, *Speaking for Myself*, 262.
109 **presided over 152 executions:** Execution Database, Death Penalty Information Center.
109 **"Well, that's not the way":** Cherie Blair, *Speaking for Myself*, 263.
109 **"Give the man a break":** Laura Bush, *Spoken from the Heart*, 191–92.
109 **"Within a few years the U.S.":** Donald Rumsfeld to Dick Cheney, Condoleezza Rice, and Colin Powell, memo, July 27, 2001, http://www.gwu.edu/~nsarchiv/NSAEBB/NSAEBB326/doc06.pdf.
109 **"I always felt there wasn't":** Cheney interview.
110 **"Cheney's role was like watching":** David Frum, author interview. Frum used a similar formulation in Jo Becker and Barton Gellman, "A Strong Push from Backstage," *Washington Post*, June 26, 2007, http://blog.washingtonpost.com/cheney/chapters/a_strong_push_from_back_stage/.
110 **"He could care less":** Fleischer interview.
110 **"You don't get it":** Karen Hughes, author interview.
110 **"He was on me all the time":** Whitman interview.
110 **"The vice president didn't have to":** Dean McGrath, author interview.
111 **"We have got to be really cautious":** Jay Lefkowitz, author interview.
111 **"I'm committed to doing everything":** Doug Melton, e-mail exchange with author. See also Jay Lefkowitz, "Stem Cells and the President: An Inside Account," *Commentary*, January 2008.
111 **"I must confess, I am wrestling":** Hughes, *Ten Minutes from Normal*, 227–29.
111 **"We at least owe them the respect":** Leon Kass, e-mail exchange with author. See also Hughes, *Ten Minutes from Normal*, 227–29.
112 **"Are you comfortable with this?":** Hughes, *Ten Minutes from Normal*, 227–29.
112 **"A number of people internally didn't":** Kristen Silverberg, author interview.
112 **"This allows us to explore":** George W. Bush, address to nation, August 9, 2001, http://georgewbush-whitehouse.archives.gov/news/releases/2001/08/20010809-2.html.
112 **"the most unflinchingly pro-life":** Frum, *Right Man*, 109–10.
113 **"Bin Ladin Determined to Strike":** President's Daily Brief, August 6, 2001, http://www.gwu.edu/~nsarchiv/NSAEBB/NSAEBB116/pdb8-6-2001.pdf.
113 **"the system was blinking red":** *9/11 Commission Report*, 259.
113 **"I didn't feel that sense of urgency":** Woodward, *Bush at War*, 39.
114 **called himself a "windshield rancher":** Stevens, *Big Enchilada*, 65.
114 **"I fell in love with it the minute":** George W. Bush, remarks to reporters, Crawford ranch, August 25, 2001, http://georgewbush-whitehouse.archives.gov/news/releases/2001/08/20010825-2.html.
114 **reading Nathaniel Philbrick's:** Notes of conversation with aide, provided to author.
115 **"There wasn't any galvanizing"** Peter Wehner, author interview.
115 **"Decision makers should imagine":** *9/11 Commission Report*, 212.
116 **In none of the morning intelligence:** Ibid., 262.

CHAPTER 7: "SOMEBODY'S GOING TO PAY"

119 **"C'mon, Stretch":** Richard Keil, "With the President: A Reporter's Story of 9/11," *Rochester Review*, University of Rochester, Fall 2004.

120 **"Those were the last carefree":** Sandy Kress, author interview.
120 **The motorcade pulled up:** The times in this chapter are all East Coast time and taken from the report of the 9/11 Commission or the President's Daily Diary.
120 **"This must be a horrible":** Eric Draper, author interview.
120 **"A second plane hit":** *9/11 Commission Report*, 38.
120 **he did not jump up:** For video of the moment in the classroom, see http://www.youtube.com/watch?v=Rg5NvKpJfKE.
121 **"DON'T SAY ANYTHING":** Fleischer, *Taking Heat*, 138–43.
121 **"Whoo, these are great":** Video of school event.
121 **"Nothing much is happening":** Peter Wehner, author interview.
121 **"Turn on the TV right away":** Sean O'Keefe, author interview.
121 **"Boy, it's going to be a bad":** Ibid.
122 **"I need to talk to the president":** Hayes, *Cheney*, 329–32.
122 **Dan Bartlett pointed:** Draper interview.
122 **"Today, we've had a national":** McClellan, *What Happened*, 102.
122 **"We will punish them":** George W. Bush, notes, September 11, 2001, George W. Bush Presidential Library and Museum, http://www.georgewbushlibrary.smu.edu/Photos-and-Videos/Photo-Galleries/Sneak-Peek-Document-Gallery.aspx.
122 **"hunt down and find those folks":** George W. Bush, statement to reporters, September 11, 2001, http://georgewbush-whitehouse.archives.gov/news/releases/2001/09/20010911.html.
123 **"We were flying, faster":** Draper interview.
123 **"Mr. Vice President, we've got to":** Dick Cheney, *In My Time*, 1–5.
123 **"Doors flew open":** O'Keefe interview.
123 **"Get me the president":** Dick Cheney, *In My Time*, 1–5.
124 **"Sounds like we have a minor war":** *9/11 Commission Report*, 39.
124 **"This is what they pay us":** Draper interview.
124 **"I just heard Angel is":** Ibid. The president was told someone calling in a threat had used the code name Angel, which convinced officials that the threat was real. In fact, the caller had not used the word; it was used by a staff person passing along the information.
124 **the bunker was first built:** Bamford, *Pretext for War*, 64.
124 **"shockingly low-tech":** Joshua Bolten, author interview.
124 **"You bet," Bush recalled:** Sammon, *Fighting Back*, 101–2.
124 **But none of about a dozen:** Gellman, *Angler*, 120–21.
125 **"the time it takes a batter":** *9/11 Commission Report*, 41.
125 **"Just confirming, sir":** Several people in the room, author interviews. See also Savage, *Takeover*, 4.
125 **"I don't want it to sound heartless":** Dick Cheney, author interview.
125 **Bolten, who had not heard:** Bolten interview. See also *9/11 Commission Report*, 41.
125 **"I think an act of heroism":** Eric Edelman, author interview.
125 **"You must know whether or not":** Bumiller, *Condoleezza Rice*, xiv.
125 **Cheney's order never got:** The mission commander and the senior weapons director at the Northeast Air Defense Sector said they did not forward the order to pilots "because they were unsure how the pilots would, or should, proceed with this guidance." *9/11 Commission Report*, 43.
126 **One of the pilots:** Steve Hendrix, "F-16 Pilot Was Ready to Down Her Father's Plane," *Washington Post*, September 14, 2011, http://www.washingtonpost.com/lifestyle/style/f-16-pilot-was-ready-to-down-plane-her-father-piloted-on-911/2011/09/13/gIQAHasoSK_story.html.

126 **"Mr. Vice President":** Edelman interview.
126 **"Get that off the screen":** Ibid.
126 **"This is like listening to Alvin":** Ibid.
126 **"Take it out," Cheney ordered:** Dick Cheney, *In My Time*, 1–5.
127 **"There's been at least three":** *9/11 Commission Report*, 43.
127 **"We have canceled our exercises":** Rice, *No Higher Honor*, 74–75.
127 **a "potentially lethal" level of potassium:** Dick Cheney and Reiner, *Heart*, 188.
127 **hitting 630 miles per hour:** "On Board Air Force One," National Geographic Channel, January 25, 2009.
127 **so close he could spot:** Draper, *Dead Certain*, 144.
128 **thought to himself that no American:** George W. Bush, *Decision Points*, 130–31.
128 **"It was surreal":** Ibid.
128 **"Slow down, son":** Ibid.
128 **"The ball will be in your court":** Fleischer, *Taking Heat*, 138–43.
128 **Bush "looked and sounded":** Frum, *Right Man*, 119.
128 **"We need to get back":** Sammon, *Fighting Back*, 119–20.
128 **"Who do you think did this?":** Bowden, *Finish*, 17.
128 **"Who is the asshole":** Clarke, *Against All Enemies*, 18–19.
129 **"Best info fast. Judge whether":** Stephen Cambone, notes, September 11, 2001, available at the National Security Archives at George Washington University, http://www.gwu.edu/~nsarchiv/NSAEBB/NSAEBB326/doc07.pdf.
129 **David Addington asked nonessential:** Hayes, *Cheney*, 342–43.
129 **"We were at war":** Dick Cheney, *In My Time*, 5–10.
129 **"Call the NMCC":** Edelman interview.
130 **"We're at war":** *9/11 Commission Report*, 326.
130 ***"When is this going to end?"*:** George W. Bush, *Decision Points*, 133–34.
130 **"We are at war against terror":** Ibid.
130 **"If I'm in the White House":** Fleischer, *Taking Heat*, 146–50.
130 **"The mightiest building":** Ibid.
131 **"These acts shattered steel":** George W. Bush, address to nation, September 11, 2001, http://georgewbush-whitehouse.archives.gov/news/releases/2001/09/20010911-16.html.
131 **"Awful Office Address":** Frum, *Right Man*, 133.
131 **"unequal to the moment":** Gerson, *Heroic Conservatism*, 69.
131 **"We will make no distinction":** George W. Bush, address, September 11, 2001.
131 **"Not tonight," Cheney said:** Dick Cheney and Reiner, *Heart*, 189. A repeat test the next morning found potassium levels normal. Doctors concluded the high reading on September 11 resulted from a delay in processing the blood sample due to the evacuation of the White House, 193–94.
131 **refused to land:** Parmet, *George Bush*, 271.
131 **"There is no way I'm sleeping":** George W. Bush, *Decision Points*, 138–39.
132 **"Mr. President! Mr. President!":** George W. Bush interview, National Geographic, September 11, 2011, http://video.nationalgeographic.com/video/national-geographic-channel/all-videos/ngc-the-president-looks-back/.
132 **"Don't worry, Mr. President":** Ibid.

CHAPTER 8: "WHATEVER IT TAKES"

133 **piles of strollers on the lawn:** Laura Bush, *Spoken from the Heart*, 206.
133 **Dallek interpreted the call:** Robert Dallek, author interview.

133 **"Don't ever let this happen":** Ashcroft, *Never Again*, 130.
134 **"Whatever it takes":** Woodward, *Bush at War*, 40–41.
134 **"Give me a brief":** Ashcroft, *Never Again*, 132–33.
134 **"Wait a second":** Ibid. Hugh Shelton remembered Ashcroft's outburst being more profane: "Get the damn stuff out on the table, Bob. We've got to catch these guys immediately and make damn sure this doesn't happen tomorrow, so whatever you've got, share it. Right now." See Shelton, *Without Hesitation*, 438–41.
134 **"We simply can't let this":** Ashcroft, *Never Again*, 133.
134 **"This is the beginning of war":** Fleischer, *Taking Heat*, 156–57.
135 **"*War* is a very powerful word":** Ibid. Fleischer, who was taking notes, attributes the comment only to a congressional leader without naming Daschle, but Daschle himself describes the same remarks in *Like No Other Time*, 121–22. So does Karen Hughes in *Ten Minutes from Normal*, 238–70.
135 **"Mr. President, the most important":** Dick Gephardt, author interview.
135 **would "not be cowed":** George W. Bush, remarks, Pentagon, September 12, 2001, http://georgewbush-whitehouse.archives.gov/news/releases/2001/09/20010912-12.html.
135 **"He went down that line":** Joe Hagin, author interview.
135 **"He looked like he wanted":** Clarke, *Against All Enemies*, 32.
135 **"might have spoken":** *9/11 Commission Report*, 334.
135 **"that the President is authorized":** Daschle, *Like No Other Time*, 123–24.
136 **Daschle saw it as a blank check:** Ibid.
136 **"If we think our response":** Gerson, *Heroic Conservatism*, 70.
136 **"Mr. President, by the time":** Cofer Black, interview on "Hank Crumpton: Life as a Spy," *60 Minutes*, CBS, May 13, 2012, http://www.cbsnews.com/8301-18560_162-57433105/hank-crumpton-life-as-a-spy/. See also Woodward, *Bush at War*, 51–53.
136 **"something of a cross between":** Mazzetti, *Way of the Knife*, 11.
136 **"Maybe we should go tomorrow":** Hughes, *Ten Minutes from Normal*, 238–70.
136 **"You've extended me a kind":** George W. Bush, remarks with New York leaders, September 13, 2001, http://georgewbush-whitehouse.archives.gov/news/releases/2001/09/20010913-4.html.
137 **"Could you give us a sense":** Ibid.
137 **"I thought it was an important moment":** Michael Gerson, author interview.
137 **"Sorry about that":** Hughes, *Ten Minutes from Normal*, 238–70.
137 **tapping his wedding ring:** John McConnell, author interview.
137 **"How come you didn't":** Brad Blakeman, author interview.
138 **Bush met Lieutenant Colonel Brian:** White House Staff Secretary's Office to White House Senior Staff, e-mail, September 26, 2001, George W. Bush Presidential Library and Museum, http://www.georgewbushlibrary.smu.edu/Photos-and-Videos/Photo-Galleries/Sneak-Peek-Document-Gallery.aspx. See also Laura Bush, *Spoken from the Heart*, 208.
138 **"We've got another threat":** Woodward, *Bush at War*, 55–57. See also Hughes, *Ten Minutes from Normal*, 238–70.
138 **Over the course of just four hours:** Secret Service log, assembled at request of Vice President Cheney, November 17, 2001, http://www.gwu.edu/~nsarchiv/NSAEBB/NSAEBB358a/doc22.pdf.
139 **"Nous sommes tous Américains":** It headlined an unsigned editorial published on the front page of *Le Monde*, September 13, 2001, http://www.lemonde

.fr/idees/article/2007/05/23/nous-sommes-tous-americains_913706_3232.html. The editorial compared the moment of solidarity to when John F. Kennedy went to divided Berlin and declared, "Ich bin ein Berliner." Having said that, the editorial suggested America to some extent brought the attack on itself because it supported Osama bin Laden and other mujahideen against the Soviets in Afghanistan.

139 **NATO for the first time:** Article 5 further states that when one member is attacked, the others "will assist" with action, "including the use of armed force." http://www.nato.int/terrorism/five.htm.

139 **Condoleezza Rice cried when she:** Meyer, *DC Confidential*, 197.

139 **"We seek your special blessing":** Rumsfeld, *Known and Unknown*, 351–52.

139 **"When I have to give a speech":** George W. Bush, *Decision Points*, 145.

139 **"Defiance is good":** Hughes, *Ten Minutes from Normal*, 238–70.

140 **"May I come with you":** Kirbyjon Caldwell, author interview.

140 **"We are here in the middle hour":** George W. Bush, address at Washington National Cathedral, September 14, 2001, http://georgewbush-whitehouse.archives.gov/news/releases/2001/09/20010914-2.html.

140 **"What is that?":** Caldwell interview.

141 **"You could literally smell":** Ibid.

141 **"like walking into hell":** George W. Bush, interview with National Geographic, September 11, 2011, http://video.nationalgeographic.com/video/national-geographic-channel/all-videos/ngc-the-president-looks-back/.

141 **"look what they've done":** Rocco Chierichella, author interview.

141 **"They want to hear from":** Rove, *Courage and Consequence*, 277.

141 **"Where are you going?":** Bob Beckwith, interview with CNN, September 2005.

142 **"I want you all to know that America":** George W. Bush, remarks to rescue workers in New York, September 14, 2001, http://georgewbush-whitehouse.archives.gov/news/releases/2001/09/20010914-9.html.

142 **"This is my son's badge":** George W. Bush, *Decision Points*, 148–50.

142 **"Put it out":** Fleischer, *Taking Heat*, 167.

142 **"You could tell he was":** Eric Draper, author interview.

143 **"I didn't vote for you":** Keil, "With the President."

143 **renamed the place "Camp Marvin":** George H. W. Bush, *All the Best*, 648.

143 **Rice for once felt:** Rice, *No Higher Honor*, 83.

144 **"the place where great powers":** Ibid., 84.

144 **10 percent to 50 percent chance:** Woodward, *Bush at War*, 75–85.

144 **"No one will understand":** Colin Powell, author interview.

144 **"it is not a coalition worth":** Paul Wolfowitz, author interview. See also Graham, *By His Own Rules*, 290–91.

144 **Shelton outlined three military:** Shelton, *Without Hesitation*, 444–45.

144 **"But we really need to think":** Ibid.

144 **"How many times do I":** Ibid.

145 **"I'm so glad you asked":** Ashcroft, *Never Again*, 141–42.

145 **Bush pulled Card aside:** Rice, *No Higher Honor*, 86–87.

145 **called Lyzbeth Glick:** Dick Cheney, *In My Time*, 332–34.

145 **"Whatever problem Iraq is":** Senior administration official, author interview.

145 **"If we go after Saddam":** Woodward, *Bush at War*, 86–91.

145 **"Well, that is imaginative":** Wolfowitz interview.

145 **"Bay of Goats":** Eric Edelman, author interview.

146 **"We have seen the face of evil":** Rice, *No Higher Honor*, 86–87.

146 **"If you provide sanctuary":** Dick Cheney, *Meet the Press*, NBC, September 16, 2001.
146 **"This crusade, this war":** George W. Bush, remarks to reporters, South Lawn, September 16, 2001, http://georgewbush-whitehouse.archives.gov/news/releases/2001/09/20010916-2.html.
147 **"No, we want to do this":** Debra Dunn, author interview.
147 **"Is that supposed to be there?":** Laura Bush, *Spoken from the Heart*, 209–10.
148 **"Thanks for coming to work":** Matt Schlapp, author interview.
148 **"You were the last person":** Keil, "With the President." Keil in his piece remembered this encounter taking place on Thursday, September 13, but White House schedules show that the event at the Eisenhower Executive Office Building took place on Monday, September 17. In an e-mail exchange with the author, Keil agreed it must have happened on that Monday.
148 **"The purpose of this meeting":** *9/11 Commission Report*, 333.
148 **"quaking in their boots":** Bob Woodward and Dan Balz, "Combating Terrorism: 'It Starts Today,'" *Washington Post*, February 1, 2002, http://www.washingtonpost.com/wp-dyn/content/article/2006/07/18/AR2006071800703.html.
148 **"I believe Iraq was involved":** Ibid.
148 **"I want justice":** George W. Bush, remarks, Pentagon, September 17, 2001, http://georgewbush-whitehouse.archives.gov/news/releases/2001/09/20010917-3.html.
149 **"Bushie, you gonna git 'im?":** Gerhart, *Perfect Wife*, 172.
149 **"The language was a little":** Rice, *No Higher Honor*, 146.
149 **"to get control of Bellinger":** Eichenwald, *500 Days*, 79–80.
149 **if there was even a 10 percent:** *9/11 Commission Report*, 335–36.
149 **no "compelling case" that Iraq:** Ibid., 334.
149 **Unsatisfied, Bush told Tenet:** Suskind, *One Percent Doctrine*, 23.
150 **"I don't want to quote anyone":** Draper, *Dead Certain*, 154–55.
150 **"Is this news enough":** Gerson interview.
150 **exercise called Dark Winter:** Dark Winter exercise overview, http://www.upmc-biosecurity.org/website/events/2001_darkwinter/index.html.
151 **"What does a biological weapon":** Randall Larsen, e-mail exchange with author. See also Larsen, *Our Own Worst Enemy*, 1–3, and Wil S. Hylton, "Warning: There's Not Nearly Enough of This Vaccine to Go Around," *New York Times Magazine*, October 30, 2011, http://www.nytimes.com/2011/10/30/magazine/how-ready-are-we-for-bioterrorism.html?pagewanted=all&_r=0.
151 **"He was unbelievably":** Tony Blair, *Journey*, 354.
151 **"This *is* a time to wobble":** Campbell, *Blair Years*, 573–74.
151 **"God dang, what on earth":** Ibid.
152 **"I said Arafat is not":** Ibid.
152 **"I agree with you, Tony":** Bryan Burrough, Evgenia Peretz, David Rose, and David Wise, "The Path to War," *Vanity Fair*, November 2004, http://www.vanityfair.com/politics/features/2004/05/path-to-war200405.
152 **"He *looked* more like":** Daschle, *Like No Other Time*, 129–31.
152 **"Tonight, the United States":** George W. Bush, speech to Congress, September 20, 2001, http://georgewbush-whitehouse.archives.gov/news/releases/2001/09/20010920-8.html.
153 **"What do you think, Barty?":** Dan Bartlett, author interview.
154 **"I have never felt":** Mike Gerson, author interview. See also Woodward, *Bush at War*, 109.
154 **"Did we get into trouble":** Daschle, *Like No Other Time*, 129–31.

CHAPTER 9: "THE FIRST BATTLE OF THE WAR"

155 **"The whole goal was to keep":** Neil Patel, author interview.
156 **Ron Christie, gave him:** Christie, *Black in the White House*, 164–65.
156 **"one-man Afghani wrecking":** *Saturday Night Live*, NBC, October 13, 2001, http://www.hulu.com/watch/200731/saturday-night-live-drew-barrymore.
156 **"energy-saving mode":** *Saturday Night Live*, NBC, May 12, 2001, http://www.hulu.com/watch/274305/saturday-night-live-dick-cheney-cold-opening.
157 **"We were all under":** Christie, *Black in the White House*, 164.
157 **"You had brothers, sisters":** Joe Hagin, author interview.
157 **White House chef began preparing:** Scheib, *White House Chef*, 268–69.
157 **"cover-your-ass kind of":** Dick Cheney, author interview.
157 **"It had a huge impact":** Condoleezza Rice, author interview.
157 **"anything other than scared":** Tenet, *At the Center of the Storm*, 99.
157 **"He didn't bring it all home":** Laura Bush, *Spoken from the Heart*, 228.
157 **"Bush lacked a big organizing":** Frum, *Right Man*, 274.
157 **"Nine-eleven blew him away":** Joe O'Neill, author interview.
157 **hitting 90 percent:** CNN/*USA Today*/Gallup poll, September 21–22, 2001, http://www.gallup.com/poll/4924/bush-job-approval-highest-gallup-history.aspx. His rating surpassed the previous historic high, held by his father after victory in the Gulf War, by one point.
158 **"I think he has a certain level":** Anne Womack, author interview. Womack later married and now goes by Anne Womack Kolton.
158 **"How are the bad guys":** Kevin Kellems, author interview.
158 **"the country was fundamentally":** Pete Williams, author interview.
158 **"In the period after that":** Patel interview.
158 **"We're okay, Don":** Franks, *American Soldier*, 278–82.
158 **"I'm sharper than a frog hair":** Rumsfeld, *Known and Unknown*, 369.
158 **Bush struck aides:** Shelton, *Without Hesitation*, 227–48.
158 **"You are not going to find":** Rumsfeld, *Known and Unknown*, 370–71.
159 **"had a solid grasp of the tactical":** Shelton, *Without Hesitation*, 447–48.
159 **He wanted a sense of progression:** Myers, *Eyes on the Horizon*, 180–81.
159 **"Mr. President, in about two weeks":** Franks, *American Soldier*, 278–82.
159 **"A large air operation":** Ibid.
159 **"This financial action is the first":** Hughes, *Ten Minutes from Normal*, 261.
159 **"Money is the lifeblood":** George W. Bush, remarks announcing financial actions against al-Qaeda and its supporters, September 24, 2001, http://georgewbush-whitehouse.archives.gov/news/releases/2001/09/20010924-4.html.
159 ***"When justice is done":*** Schweizer and Schweizer, *Bushes*, 517.
159 **"I see things this way":** George W. Bush, speech at FBI headquarters, September 25, 2001, http://georgewbush-whitehouse.archives.gov/news/releases/2001/09/20010925-5.html.
160 **"If this isn't good versus evil":** Fleischer, *Taking Heat*, 34.
160 **"I'm not sure you ought to be":** Hughes, *Ten Minutes from Normal*, 262.
160 **"I want you to develop":** Donald Rumsfeld, notes on his day calendar, September 26, 2001. Accessed at http://www.rumsfeld.com. The notes on the calendar are clear, but they conflict with other accounts. Franks, in *American Soldier*, recalled getting a phone call from Rumsfeld saying the president wanted them to look at Iraq options on November 27, 2001. Richard Myers, the Joint Chiefs chairman, said in an interview that he did not think it happened until November as well since it was unlikely Rumsfeld would have talked with Franks about the

Iraq War plan without mentioning it to him too. "I guess it's possible, but I doubt it," he said.

161 **"No one in the discussions"**: Zalmay Khalilzad, author interview.
161 **"Dick told me about"**: Rumsfeld day calendar. See also George W. Bush, *Decision Points*, 91–94.
162 **"There was a pervasive feeling"**: John McLaughlin, author interview.
162 **"Why do you think nothing"**: Ibid. See also Tenet, *At the Center of the Storm*, 188.
162 **"When Bush got the first"**: Ari Fleischer, author interview.
162 **"I'm here with Ari"**: Hughes, *Ten Minutes from Normal*, 268–69.
162 **"so far this appears to be"**: Department of Health and Human Services statement, October 4, 2001, http://archive.hhs.gov/news/press/2001pres/20011004b.html.
163 **"There was a real, almost fatalistic"**: Dean McGrath, author interview.
163 **Oh, by the way**: Michael Hayden, author interview.
163 **Is there anything else you**: Ibid.
163 **The average wait**: Working draft of NSA inspector general report on surveillance activities, March 24, 2009.
164 **"we can do this, but you know"**: Hayden interview.
164 **"I have some choices here"**: Ibid.
165 **"everybody looked around"**: Dennis Hastert, author interview.
165 **David Addington personally drafted**: Working draft of inspector general report.
165 **Donald Rumsfeld was not informed**: Donald Rumsfeld, author interview.

CHAPTER 10: "WE'RE GOING TO LOSE OUR PREY"

166 **"Are you cleared for any of this?"**: Michael Gerson, author interview.
166 **"You can surmise that"**: Ronald Kessler, *Laura Bush*, 140.
166 **"On my orders, the United States"**: George W. Bush, address to nation, October 7, 2001, http://georgewbush-whitehouse.archives.gov/news/releases/2001/10/20011007-8.html.
167 **"we're just executing"**: John McLaughlin, author interview. See also Woodward, *Bush at War*, 243–44.
168 **"Well, sir, I think it's all FUBAR"**: Richard Armitage, author interview. See also Rice, *No Higher Honor*, 92.
168 **Cheney instructed Libby**: Dick Cheney, *In My Time*, 341–44.
168 **"Good morning, Dick"**: Rice, *No Higher Honor*, 101–2.
169 **"it's nice, for a change"**: Dick Cheney, speech to Alfred E. Smith Memorial Foundation Dinner, October 18, 2001, http://georgewbush-whitehouse.archives.gov/vicepresident/news-speeches/speeches/vp20011018.html.
169 **"Feet down, not up"**: George W. Bush, *Decision Points*, 152–53.
169 **"may have a nuclear device"**: Myers, *Eyes on the Horizon*, 193.
170 **"We have to intensify the hunt"**: Ibid.
170 **Bush was "deeply affected"**: McClellan, *What Happened*, 111.
170 **If it turned left and headed toward**: John Ellis, author interview.
170 **"The threat going forward"**: Dick Cheney, author interview.
170 **"You know, Mr. President"**: Condoleezza Rice, interview with Bob Woodward, August 19, 2002. White House transcript provided to author. See also Woodward, *Bush at War*, 256–58.
171 **"Is there any qualm"**: Woodward, *Bush at War*, 259.
171 **"I just want to make sure"**: George W. Bush, *Decision Points*, 199.
171 **"Anybody have any ideas"**: Woodward, *Bush at War*, 261.

171 **"We're going to stay confident":** George W. Bush, *Decision Points*, 199.

171 **"Hardly able to restrain":** White House weekly legislative report, October 5, 2001. Reviewed by author.

171 **"I should have pushed Congress":** George W. Bush, *Decision Points*, 162.

172 **"Those bastards are going":** Rice interview with Woodward, transcript provided to author. See also Woodward, *Bush at War*, 269–71, and Rice, *No Higher Honor*, 102–3.

172 **"Now, you know the order":** Hayden interview.

172 **Bush signed it November 2:** Shannen W. Coffin (counsel to Dick Cheney) to Patrick Leahy (chairman of the Senate Judiciary Committee), letter, August 20, 2007. The letter disclosed the dates the program was reauthorized up to that point. http://www.scribd.com/fullscreen/599934.

173 **"Mr. President, are you going":** Fleischer, *Taking Heat*, 205.

173 **"The ominous word 'quagmire'":** R. W. Apple Jr., "Afghanistan as Vietnam," *New York Times*, October 31, 2001, http://www.nytimes.com/2001/10/31/international/asia/31ASSE.html.

173 **"They don't get it":** Woodward, *Bush at War*, 279.

173 **"I mean, we were at this":** Sammon, *Fighting Back*, 240.

174 **their "jaws dropped":** Brad Berenson, author interview.

174 **"kind of took control":** Ibid.

174 **attorney general talked over him:** Eichenwald, *500 Days*, 151–52.

174 **"reserve the authority":** George W. Bush's order, "Detention, Treatment, and Trial of Certain Non-citizens in the War Against Terrorism," November 13, 2001, http://georgewbush-whitehouse.archives.gov/news/releases/2001/11/20011113-27.html.

174 **"Don't worry about it":** Stuart Bowen, author interview.

175 **"This is it?":** Ibid.

175 **"more like a scan":** Berenson interview.

175 **signed it, and handed it back:** Bush order, "Detention."

175 **"a real power center":** Berenson interview.

175 **"I think it is a mistake":** Donald Rumsfeld to George W. Bush, memo, November 13, 2001, http://library.rumsfeld.com/doclib/sp/288/2001-11-13%20to%20Bush%20re%20Kabul.pdf#search="kabul."

177 **"Somebody forgot to tell":** Rice, *No Higher Honor*, 174.

177 **"We are seeing a historic":** Hughes, *Ten Minutes from Normal*, 284–85.

178 **"Mr. Vice President, this is the thing":** Suskind, *One Percent Doctrine*, 61–62.

178 **One of the scientists:** Peter Baker, "Pakistani Scientist Who Met Bin Laden Failed Polygraphs, Renewing Suspicions," *Washington Post*, March 3, 2002.

178 **"If there's a one percent":** Suskind, *One Percent Doctrine*, 61–62. See also Tenet, *At the Center of the Storm*, 264–65.

179 **"Where do we stand on":** Rumsfeld, *Known and Unknown*, 427–28.

179 **Fewer than a hundred American:** Senate Foreign Relations Committee Report, "Tora Bora Revisited: How We Failed to Get Bin Laden and Why It Matters Today," November 30, 2009, http://www.foreign.senate.gov/imo/media/doc/Tora_Bora_Report.pdf. See also Susan B. Glasser, "The Battle of Tora Bora: Secrets, Money, Mistrust," *Washington Post*, February 10, 2002.

179 **"We're going to lose our":** Suskind, *One Percent Doctrine*, 59.

180 **commanders estimated that:** Senate Foreign Relations Committee Report, "Tora Bora Revisited."

180 **"He was totally disengaged":** Charlie Younger, author interview.

180 **That "had a big impact on me":** George W. Bush, *Decision Points*, 166.

180 **"Tommy, what's this I hear":** Franks, *American Soldier*, 340–59.

181 **"You've described an Iraqi force":** Ibid.
181 **"We cannot allow weapons":** Ibid.
182 **"flawed but necessary":** Kennedy, *True Compass*, 490.
182 **"There was almost a feeling":** Sandy Kress, author interview.
182 **"I told the folks at the coffee shop":** George W. Bush, remarks, Boston Latin School, January 8, 2002, http://georgewbush-whitehouse.archives.gov/news/releases/2002/01/20020108-5.html.
183 **"The president is in another place":** Kress interview.
183 **the president took umbrage:** Frum, *Right Man*, 205–6. He was referring to an article by Elisabeth Bumiller, "When Lobbying, No. 43 Uses a Lighter Touch," *New York Times*, December 24, 2001.
183 **"most dramatic fiscal deterioration":** Alison Mitchell, "Democrat Assails Bush on Economy," *New York Times*, January 5, 2002.
183 **"Not over my dead body":** George W. Bush, remarks to town hall meeting, Ontario, Calif., January 5, 2002, http://georgewbush-whitehouse.archives.gov/news/releases/2002/01/20020105-3.html.
183 **"This would be a very dangerous":** Shenon, *Commission*, 29–30. Howard Fineman of *Newsweek* was in Daschle's office when the call came in, and the senator allowed him to stay. See "The Battle Back Home," *Newsweek*, February 3, 2002, http://www.thedailybeast.com/newsweek/2002/02/03/the-battle-back-home.html.
183 **"Americans trust the Republicans":** Richard L. Berke, "Bush Adviser Suggests War as Campaign Theme," *New York Times*, January 19, 2002.
184 **A "shameful statement":** Richard Gephardt on CNN, January 19, 2002.
184 **"Nothing short of despicable":** Thomas B. Edsall, "GOP Touts War as Campaign Issue," *Washington Post*, January 19, 2002, http://www.washingtonpost.com/wp-dyn/content/article/2007/08/13/AR2007081300840.html.
184 **"seriously flawed":** William H. Taft IV to John C. Yoo, memo, January 11, 2002, http://www.torturingdemocracy.org/documents/20020111.pdf.
185 **"We have an image to uphold":** Eichenwald, *500 Days*, 229–30.
185 **"You'll notice that everybody":** Myers, *Eyes on the Horizon*, 202–8.
185 **"Would you apply the Geneva":** Ibid.
185 **"We all agree that they'll":** Eichenwald, *500 Days*, 229–30.
185 **"to the extent appropriate":** Order signed by George W. Bush outlining treatment of al-Qaeda and Taliban detainees, February 7, 2002, http://lawofwar.org/bush_torture_memo.htm.
186 **Condoleezza Rice and Stephen Hadley:** Stephen Hadley, author interview.
186 **"No, I want it in":** Ibid.
186 **"States like these and their terrorist":** George W. Bush, State of the Union address, January 29, 2002, http://georgewbush-whitehouse.archives.gov/news/releases/2002/01/20020129-11.html.
186 **"We were more focused on the 'evil'":** Dan Bartlett, author interview.
187 **"quite cowardly for people":** Howard Kurtz, "Straight Man," *Washington Post Magazine*, May 19, 2002.

CHAPTER 11: "AFGHANISTAN WAS TOO EASY"

188 **"Where did Nixon stop?":** Eric Draper, author interview.
188 **a reading contest with Karl Rove:** Karl Rove, "Bush Is a Book Lover," *Wall Street Journal*, December 26, 2008, http://online.wsj.com/article/SB123025595706634689.html.

189 **"political immaturity":** http://news.bbc.co.uk/2/hi/americas/1796034.stm.
189 **"unilateralist overdrive":** Steven Erlanger, "German Joins Europe's Cry That the U.S. Won't Consult," *New York Times*, February 13, 2002.
189 **"Who Is in Axis of Evil?":** William Schneider, "A Reagan Echo," *Los Angeles Times*, February 24, 2002.
189 **"No wonder I think":** Elisabeth Bumiller, "Bush Says the U.S. Plans No Attack on North Korea," *New York Times*, February 20, 2002, http://www.nytimes.com/2002/02/20/world/bush-says-the-us-plans-no-attack-on-north-korea.html?pagewanted=all&src=pm.
189 **A 1992 *New Yorker* article:** Murray S. Waas and Craig Unger, "In the Loop: Bush's Secret Mission," *The New Yorker*, November 2, 1982, http://www.newyorker.com/archive/1992/11/02/1992_11_02_064_TNY_CARDS_000359993.
190 **"No one envisioned him still":** George W. Bush, interview with BBC, November 18, 1999.
190 **"If I found in any way":** George W. Bush, Republican presidential debate, Manchester, N.H., December 2, 1999.
190 **"He cut and run early":** Sammon, *Misunderestimated*, 5.
190 **"Whether he did or not":** Joe O'Neill, author interview.
190 **"Every one of us":** Administration official, author interview.
191 **77 percent of Americans:** CNN/*USA Today*/Gallup poll, taken January 11–14, 2002.
191 **almost an identical number:** Bruce Morton, "Selling an Iraq–al Qaeda Connection," CNN.com, March 11, 2003, http://www.cnn.com/2003/WORLD/meast/03/11/Iraq.Qaeda.link/.
191 **"The only reason we went":** Administration official interview.
191 **"Niamey Signed an Agreement":** Senate Committee on Intelligence, Report on the U.S. Intelligence Community's Prewar Intelligence Assessments on Iraq, July 7, 2004, 38–39, http://web.mit.edu/simsong/www/iraqreport2-textunder.pdf.
192 **enough to make fifty weapons:** A statement cleared by the CIA said that ten tons of uranium ore would be required to enrich enough fuel to make a weapon, so five hundred tons could in theory produce fifty bombs. http://www.globalsecurity.org/wmd/world/iraq/nuke-prewar_intel_2003.htm.
192 **"information on the alleged":** Senate Intelligence Committee report, 38–39.
192 **"If you can't do the right":** Glenn Hubbard, author interview. See also Suskind, *Price of Loyalty*, 216–21.
193 **peppered him with op-ed:** Memos to Dick Cheney. Copies reviewed by author.
193 **"I'm no politician":** Hubbard interview.
193 **"sometimes imports can cause":** George W. Bush, statement announcing steel tariffs, March 5, 2002, http://georgewbush-whitehouse.archives.gov/news/releases/2002/03/20020305-6.html.
193 **Bush by his own account approved all but two:** George W. Bush, *Decision Points*, 168–69. In his own memoir, John Rizzo, the CIA's top lawyer, questions whether Bush actually did, saying he was unaware of Bush ever being briefed on specific interrogation techniques. He wrote that George Tenet told him that he likewise did not remember Bush being briefed on specific techniques. See Rizzo, *Company Man*, 197–99. But Dick Cheney wrote that the program "was approved by the president." See Cheney, *In My Time*, 358. And Condoleezza Rice described several conversations about the interrogation program involving Bush. See Rice, *No Higher Honor*, 117–18. A third official told the author that he too recalled Bush being briefed on the techniques. Bill Harlow, a longtime spokes-

man for Tenet, told the author that the former director did not personally brief Bush on the program but "he has no doubt that either Condi or Steve Hadley did at the time."

194 **waterboarded eighty-three times:** Steven G. Bradbury, principal deputy assistant attorney general, memorandum to John Rizzo, then senior deputy general counsel, Central Intelligence Agency, May 30, 2005, 37, http://media.luxmedia.com/aclu/olc_05302005_bradbury.pdf.

194 **FBI agents said Zubaydah:** Ali Soufan, "My Tortured Decision," *New York Times*, April 22, 2009, http://www.nytimes.com/2009/04/23/opinion/23soufan.html.

194 **Zubaydah was mentally unstable:** Suskind, *One Percent Doctrine*, 95.

194 **George Tenet disputed that:** Tenet, *At the Center of the Storm*, 243.

194 **memo drafted largely by John Yoo:** Memorandum for Alberto R. Gonzales (counsel to the president), "Re: Standards of Conduct for Interrogation Under 18 USC §§ 2340–2340A," August 1, 2002, http://www.justice.gov/olc/docs/memo-gonzales-aug2002.pdf.

194 **who later recanted the statements:** Isikoff and Corn, *Hubris*, 424.

195 **"I stand for 8–10 hours a day":** Handwritten notes on memorandum for Secretary of Defense, from William J. Haynes II (general counsel), "Subject: Counter-Resistance Techniques," November 27, 2002, http://www.defense.gov/news/Jun2004/d20040622doc5.pdf. Rumsfeld indicated his approval of the memo's recommendations, and it was stamped December 2, 2002.

195 **The plane then took off:** Dick Cheney, *In My Time*, 371–80.

195 **Cheney asked if it would be:** Ibid.

196 **"This is going to be tough":** Colin Powell, author interview.

196 **"It was the only way I could":** Ibid.

196 **"was dead on arrival":** Rice, *No Higher Honor*, 139–40.

196 **"was dead set against":** Powell interview.

196 **"I am sorry, I have to get":** Ibid.

196 **"as a personal affront":** Dick Cheney, *In My Time*, 380–82.

196 **"That is nonsense":** Powell interview.

196 **"It was a mess":** Ibid.

197 **"I do believe Ariel Sharon":** George W. Bush, photo opportunity, April 18, 2002, http://georgewbush-whitehouse.archives.gov/news/releases/2002/04/20020418-3.html.

197 **"Do you have any idea":** Rice, *No Higher Honor*, 139–40.

197 **"When will the pig leave":** George W. Bush, *Decision Points*, 401–3.

197 **"I can't go back empty-handed":** DeYoung, *Soldier*, 385–86.

197 **"Mr. President, I think":** George W. Bush, *Decision Points*, 401–3.

197 **"Does it matter":** Rice, *No Higher Honor*, 141.

197 **"What the hell":** DeYoung, *Soldier*, 385–86. See also Ottaway, *King's Messenger*, 237.

198 **"Before you leave":** George W. Bush, *Decision Points*, 401–3.

198 **"My brother":** Ibid.

198 **"I love you like a son":** DeYoung, *Soldier*, 387.

198 **"I don't know who else":** Abdullah II, *Our Last Best Chance*, 208–9.

198 **"I can imagine":** Ibid.

198 **"Bush Knew":** *New York Post*, May 16, 2002.

198 **"The president knew what?":** Dan Balz, "Bush and GOP Defend White House Response," *Washington Post*, May 18, 2002.

199 **CBS News first reported:** David Sanger, "Bush Was Warned bin Laden Wanted

to Hijack Planes," *New York Times*, May 16, 2002, http://www.nytimes.com/2002/05/16/politics/16INQU.html.

199 **"It didn't rattle him like it"**: Ari Fleischer, author interview.

199 **"It bothered me"**: Sammon, *Fighting Back*, 362–63.

199 **"used the whole force"**: Karen Tumulty, James Carney, and Douglas Waller, "Behind All the Finger-Pointing," *Time*, May 27, 2002, http://www.time.com/time/magazine/article/0,9171,1002500,00.html.

199 **"An investigation must not interfere"**: "U.S. Officials Defend Administration's Handling of Terror Warnings," Agence France-Presse, May 17, 2002.

199 **"Had I known that the enemy"**: George W. Bush, remarks upon presenting the Commander-in-Chief's Trophy, May 17, 2002, http://georgewbush-whitehouse.archives.gov/news/releases/2002/05/20020517-1.html.

199 **not "looking to point fingers"**: Tumulty, Carney, and Waller, "Behind All the Finger-Pointing."

200 **"Putin is at huge risk"**: Bolton, *Surrender Is Not An Option*, 77.

200 **"This treaty liquidates"**: George W. Bush, statement at treaty signing, May 24, 2002, http://georgewbush-whitehouse.archives.gov/news/releases/2002/05/20020524-10.html.

200 **"I know you have separate"**: Baker and Glasser, *Kremlin Rising*, 221.

200 **"Dick Cheney's notion of prophylactic aggression"**: Weisberg, *Bush Tragedy*, 197.

200 **"We cannot defend America"**: George W. Bush, commencement address, U.S. Military Academy at West Point, June 1, 2002, http://georgewbush-whitehouse.archives.gov/news/releases/2002/06/20020601-3.html.

201 **"He didn't get dragged"**: Steve Biegun, author interview.

201 **"Finally, they buckled"**: Joseph Lieberman, author interview.

202 **On poster board, they scratched:** Susan B. Glasser and Michael Grunwald, "Department's Mission Was Undermined from Start," *Washington Post*, December 22, 2005, http://www.washingtonpost.com/wp-dyn/content/article/2005/12/21/AR2005122102327.html.

202 **"This thing has a head of steam"**: Cooper and Block, *Disaster*, 76–77.

202 **"The president will announce"**: Donald Rumsfeld, author interview.

203 **"Tell him to shake his"**: Annan, *Interventions*, 273.

203 **"I had to start by saying"**: George W. Bush made this comment during a joint presentation with Bill Clinton at IHS Forum at CERAWeek, Houston, March 11, 2011. The event was closed to reporters, but a transcript was provided to the author.

203 **"He was dead set"**: Dan Bartlett, author interview.

203 **"Whoever gave a damn"**: Michael Gerson, author interview.

203 **went through thirty drafts:** Abrams, *Tested by Zion*, 39–43.

203 **"Of the three of you"**: Hughes, *Ten Minutes from Normal*, 279.

203 **"I call on the Palestinian"**: George W. Bush, address, Rose Garden, June 24, 2002, http://georgewbush-whitehouse.archives.gov/news/releases/2002/06/20020624-3.html.

204 **"How's the first Jewish president"**: George W. Bush, *Decision Points*, 404–5.

204 **"Even with our friends"**: George W. Bush made the comment in an off-the-record session with reporters in the Oval Office on January 4, 2005. The author was not among those reporters but obtained notes taken by a participant.

204 **"You couldn't wait for there"**: Dick Cheney, author interview.

205 **"Al-Zarqawi has been directing"**: Rice, *No Higher Honor*, 178.

205 **"doable, but challenging"**: Micah Zenko, "Foregoing Limited Force: The George W. Bush Administration's Decision Not to Attack Ansar Al-Islam," *Journal of*

Strategic Studies, August 2009, http://www.cfr.org/iraq/foregoing-limited-force-george-w-bush-administrations-decision-not-attack-ansar-al-islam/p20035.

205 **Cheney and Rumsfeld argued:** George W. Bush, *Decision Points*, 236–37. See also Rumsfeld, *Known and Unknown*, 446–47.

205 **After one sharp debate:** Rice, *No Higher Honor*, 178.

206 **"super cautious":** George W. Bush, comments to reporters, South Lawn, June 29, 2002, http://georgewbush-whitehouse.archives.gov/news/releases/2002/06/20020628-8.html.

206 **"He's standing by":** Ibid.

206 **Sitting on a couch:** Mike Allen, "Bush Resumes Power After Test," *Washington Post*, June 30, 2002.

206 **"transfer temporarily":** George W. Bush, letter passing power to Dick Cheney, June 29, 2002, http://georgewbush-whitehouse.archives.gov/news/releases/2002/06/20020629-5.html.

206 **"resuming those powers":** George W. Bush, letter revoking transfer of power, June 29, 2002, http://georgewbush-whitehouse.archives.gov/news/releases/2002/06/20020629-3.html.

206 **"Here you have this liberal":** Karen Hughes, author interview.

206 **"There was a perceptible shift":** The memo was dated July 23, 2002, and written by Matthew Rycroft summarizing a meeting between Tony Blair and top British officials. It was published in the *Sunday Times* of London on May 1, 2005, http://people.virginia.edu/~jrw3k/mediamatters/readings/SundayTimes_SecretDowningStreetMemo.pdf.

207 **she brushed away his concerns:** Haass, *War of Necessity, War of Choice*, 213–16.

207 **"They were really beating":** Senior administration official, author interview.

207 **"I really have to see":** Colin Powell, author interview.

207 **"Most Iraqis will rejoice":** Dick Cheney, *In My Time*, 386.

208 **"If you break it":** Powell interview.

208 **"We should take the problem":** Powell, *It Worked for Me*, 211.

208 **"Even if the UN doesn't solve it":** Powell interview.

208 **"Colin was more passionate":** George W. Bush, *Decision Points*, 237–38.

208 **"The United States could certainly":** Brent Scowcroft, "Don't Attack Saddam," *Wall Street Journal*, August 15, 2002.

209 **"He was pissed off":** Dan Bartlett, author interview.

209 **"Son, Brent is a friend":** George W. Bush, *Decision Points*, 237–38.

209 **"pre-9/11 mind-set":** Dick Cheney, *In My Time*, 388.

209 **"Brent, you know, I wish":** Condoleezza Rice made the recollection during an Aspen Institute panel discussion honoring Scowcroft on August 6, 2011, http://www.aspeninstitute.org/video/summer-celebration-2011.

209 **"thought it might be helpful":** Rice, *No Higher Honor*, 178–79.

209 **"I got taken to the woodshed":** Brent Scowcroft made the remark during the Aspen forum.

209 **"All the neocons were saying":** Jeffrey Goldberg, "Breaking Ranks," *New Yorker*, October 31, 2005.

210 **"Dick, I think you may":** Lott, *Herding Cats*, 235–36.

210 **"authorizing all necessary means":** James Baker, "The Right to Change a Regime," *New York Times*, August 25, 2002, http://www.nytimes.com/2002/08/25/opinion/the-right-way-to-change-a-regime.html?pagewanted=all&src=pm.

211 **"Simply stated, there is no doubt":** Dick Cheney, speech to Veterans of Foreign Wars, August 26, 2002, Nashville, http://georgewbush-whitehouse.archives.gov/news/releases/2002/08/20020826.html.

211 **"Condi, anybody look at":** Senior administration official, author interview.
211 **"Bush was hot about it":** Ari Fleischer, author interview.
211 **"Call Dick and tell him":** Rice, *No Higher Honor*, 180.
211 **"The president is concerned":** Ibid., 180.
211 **"It's cut off the president's":** Hayes, *Cheney*, 381–82.
211 **"Many have suggested":** Dick Cheney, speech to veterans of the Korean War, August 29, 2002, http://georgewbush-whitehouse.archives.gov/news/releases/2002/08/20020829-5.html.
212 **"went well beyond":** Tenet, *At the Center of the Storm*, 315–16.
212 **"I should have told":** Ibid.

CHAPTER 12: "A BRUTAL, UGLY, REPUGNANT MAN"

213 **"What are we talking about Iraq for?":** Karen Hughes, author interview.
213 **Rice knew how much:** Condoleezza Rice, author interview.
214 **"I didn't volunteer it":** Joe O'Neill, author interview.
214 **"Saddam Hussein is a serious threat":** Fleischer, *Taking Heat*, 277–78.
214 **"I will be with you":** Ibid. Fleischer in his book identifies Biden only as a Democratic senator who later voted for the war. But in an e-mail exchange with the author, Fleischer confirmed that the senator in question was Biden.
215 **"If you invade Iraq":** Dick Armey, author interview. See also Isikoff and Corn, *Hubris*, 24–25.
215 **the session was "a disaster":** Christine Ciccone (White House legislative aide) to Nick Calio (director of White House legislative affairs), memo, September 4, 2001. Reviewed by author.
215 **"yet one more meaningless":** Dick Cheney, *In My Time*, 390–91.
215 **"Either he will come clean":** George W. Bush, *Decision Points*, 238–39.
216 **"It was very much on everybody's":** Bartlett interview.
216 **"In neither this meeting":** Dick Cheney, *In My Time*, 390–91.
216 **"There was no disagreement":** Rice, *No Higher Honor*, 181.
216 **"very sour throughout":** Campbell, *Blair Years*, 635.
216 **"as never before Cheney's influence":** Meyer, *DC Confidential*, 251.
216 **"I think ultimately he bought":** Tony Blair, *Journey*, 406.
216 **"Your man has got *cojones*":** George W. Bush, *Decision Points*, 238–39. Alastair Campbell remembered the line as "Your guy's got balls." But Bush was prone to use the word "cojones" and later referred to the session as "the cojones meeting." Christopher Meyer, the British ambassador, likewise remembered it being "cojones," noting that he was probably the only Briton there to understand the reference. See Meyer, *DC Confidential*, 252.
216 **"I suppose you can tell":** Campbell, *Blair Years*, 635.
217 **"from a marketing point of view":** Elisabeth Bumiller, "Bush Aides Set Strategy to Sell Policy on Iraq," *New York Times*, September 7, 2002.
217 **might be a mushroom cloud:** Michael R. Gordon and Judith Miller, "U.S. Says Hussein Intensifies Quest for A-Bomb Parts," *New York Times*, September 8, 2002, http://www.nytimes.com/2002/09/08/world/threats-responses-iraqis-us-says-hussein-intensifies-quest-for-bomb-parts.html?pagewanted=all&src=pm.
217 **"There's a story":** Dick Cheney, *Meet the Press*, NBC, September 8, 2002, http://www.mtholyoke.edu/acad/intrel/bush/meet.htm.
217 **"We don't want the smoking":** Condoleezza Rice, *Late Edition*, CNN, September 8, 2002, http://transcripts.cnn.com/TRANSCRIPTS/0209/08/le.00.html.

217 **"It was pretty clear that"**: Ricks, *Fiasco*, 60.

218 **It would be the only time:** Actually, it would be the only time in eight years of speeches to the General Assembly that Bush would be interrupted by applause.

218 **"Our greatest fear"**: George W. Bush, speech to UN General Assembly, September 12, 2002, http://georgewbush-whitehouse.archives.gov/news/releases/2002/09/20020912-1.html.

218 **"It's like speaking"**: Fleischer, *Taking Heat*, 282. It was a line that clearly stuck with Bush when it came to addressing the General Assembly because he used it again as late as 2008 with an aide just before giving his final speech to that group.

219 **could cost $100 billion to $200 billion:** Bob Davis, "Bush Economic Aide Says the Cost of Iraq War May Top $100 Billion," *Wall Street Journal*, September 16, 2002.

219 **"were furious" that he was so off:** Lindsey, *What a President Should Know*, 36–39.

219 **"So, Lindsey, you're estimating"**: Lawrence Lindsey, unpublished interview with journalist Robert Draper.

219 **"likely very, very high"**: "White House Budget Chief Questions War Cost Estimates," Agence France-Presse, September 18, 2002.

219 **"Mark my words"**: White House notes of meeting, September 19, 2002. Reviewed by author. Howard Berman confirmed asking the question in an e-mail exchange with the author.

219 **"champion aspirations for"**: National Security Strategy, September 20, 2002, http://georgewbush-whitehouse.archives.gov/nsc/nss/2002/.

219 **"I'm gonna make a prediction"**: Notes taken by person in room, September 20, 2002. Reviewed by author. See also McClellan, *What Happened*, 139–40.

220 **"The Senate is more interested"**: George W. Bush, speech to Army National Guard Aviation Support Facility, Trenton, N.J., September 23, 2002, http://georgewbush-whitehouse.archives.gov/news/releases/2002/09/20020923-2.html.

220 **"outrageous, outrageous"**: Tom Daschle, floor speech, September 25, 2002, http://www.washingtonpost.com/wp-srv/politics/transcripts/daschle.html.

220 **The ad showed pictures:** Contrary to enduring misperceptions, the ad did not juxtapose the pictures of Cleland and bin Laden as if to equate the two. It showed the pictures of bin Laden and Hussein to illustrate the threat seen to America and then showed Cleland's picture while criticizing him for his voting record. But Cleland actually co-sponsored legislation creating a department of homeland security in May 2002 while Bush still opposed it; the ad presented Cleland's opposition to Republican proposals to strip collective bargaining rights for employees at the new department as a national security threat. http://www.youtube.com/watch?v KFYpd0q9nE. Cleland was devastated by the campaign and afterward sought psychiatric help and returned to Walter Reed, where he was surrounded by wounded veterans from Iraq and Afghanistan. "I cried uncontrollably for 2½ years," he later said. See Melinda Henneberger, *Politics Daily*, October 6, 2009, http://www.politicsdaily.com/2009/10/06/max-cleland-i-cried-uncontrollably-for-2-1-2-years/.

220 **"Now Dick, when I lay all this out"**: Dick Armey, author interview. See also Isikoff and Corn, *Hubris*, 124–25; and Draper, *Dead Certain*, 178.

221 **"I deserved better than to have been"**: Armey interview.

221 **"significant quantities of uranium"**: Iraq's Weapons of Mass Destruction: The Assessment of the British Government, September 24, 2002, 5, http://www.fas.org/nuke/guide/iraq/iraqdossier.pdf.

221 **"According to the British":** George W. Bush, remarks with congressional leaders, Rose Garden, September 26, 2002, http://georgewbush-whitehouse.archives.gov/news/releases/2002/09/20020926-7.html.
221 **"Saddam Hussein is a terrible guy":** White House notes of meeting, September 26, 2002. Reviewed by author.
221 **"There's no doubt his hatred":** George W. Bush, remarks, reception for Senator John Cornyn, Houston, September 26, 2002, http://georgewbush-whitehouse.archives.gov/news/releases/2002/09/20020926-17.html.
222 **"There is this mythology":** McLaughlin interview.
222 **"overly eager to please":** Isikoff and Corn, *Hubris*, 4–6.
222 **"Analysts feel more":** Greg Miller and Bob Drogin, "CIA Feels Heat on Iraq Data," *Los Angeles Times*, October 11, 2002.
222 **nicknamed the vice president Edgar:** Suskind, *One Percent Doctrine*, 213.
222 **"he's a pretty intimidating guy":** Cheney aide, author interview.
222 **"significant pressure":** Senate Select Committee on Intelligence, Report on the U.S. Intelligence Community's Prewar Intelligence Assessments on Iraq, July 7, 2004, http://web.mit.edu/simsong/www/iraqreport2-textunder.pdf.
222 **"In the history of writing":** McLaughlin interview.
223 **"The nuance was lost":** Tenet, *At the Center of the Storm*, 327.
223 **"Baghdad has chemical and biological":** National Intelligence Estimate, October 1, 2002, http://www.fas.org/irp/cia/product/iraq-wmd-nie.pdf.
223 **Iraqi defector code-named Curveball:** Curveball was the source for more than a hundred reports about Iraqi biological weapons that did not exist, according to Charles Duelfer, who led the search for weapons after the fall of Saddam Hussein. See Duelfer, *Hide and Seek*, 470–71. For a full account of the Curveball saga, see Drogin, *Curveball*.
223 **71 senators and 161 House members:** Woodward, *Plan of Attack*, 203.
223 **no more than 6 senators:** Dana Priest, "Congressional Oversight of Intelligence Criticized," *Washington Post*, April 27, 2004.
223 **even "more assertive":** Tenet, *At the Center of the Storm*, 370.
223 **"Saddam Hussein is a bad guy":** Dick Gephardt, author interview.
224 **chances would be "pretty high":** Isikoff and Corn, *Hubris*, 141.
224 **"I always wondered why":** McLaughlin interview.
224 **issued a "burn notice":** Bonin, *Arrows of the Night*, 115. Chalabi's defenders said he was unfairly blamed and that he tried to warn the CIA that its plan had been compromised. Richard Perle, author interview.
224 **"enormously talented":** Perle interview.
224 **"like schoolgirls with their":** Tenet, *At the Center of the Storm*, 440.
224 **front pages of newspapers:** Judith Miller of the *New York Times* said in an e-mail to a colleague that Chalabi "has provided most of the front page exclusives on WMD to our paper." Howard Kurtz, "Intra-Times Battle over Iraqi Weapons," *Washington Post*, May 26, 2003.
224 **"our campaign to sell":** McClellan, *What Happened*, 120.
224 **"a carefully orchestrated":** Ibid., 125.
224 **"We were more focused":** Ibid., 135.
225 **"I don't know how he gets":** White House notes of meeting, October 1, 2002. Reviewed by author.
225 **"Yeah, that's right":** Adam Levine, author interview.
225 **"been caught attempting":** Tenet, *At the Center of the Storm*, 449–50.
226 **"Steve, take it out":** Ibid.

226 **"be in position to dominate":** George W. Bush, address to nation, Cincinnati, October 7, 2002, http://georgewbush-whitehouse.archives.gov/news/releases/2002/10/20021007-8.html.

226 **voted 296 to 133 to authorize:** U.S. House Clerk's Office. http://clerk.house.gov/evs/2002/roll455.xml.

226 **followed suit, 77 to 23:** U.S. Senate roll call record, http://www.senate.gov/legislative/LIS/roll_call_lists/roll_call_vote_cfm.cfm?congress=107&session=2&vote=00237.

226 **aides sent Bush a memo:** The memo told Bush that his Iraq resolution won forty-six more votes in the House and twenty-five more in the Senate than the Gulf War resolution did in 1991. Memo to Bush from Jack Howard through Nick Calio, October 11, 2002. Reviewed by author.

226 **"Parade of Horribles":** Donald Rumsfeld, memo, October 15, 2002. Accessed at http://www.rumsfeld.com.

227 **"I loathe Kim Jong Il":** Woodward, *Bush at War*, 340.

227 **"pygmy" and "a spoiled child":** Chafee, *Against the Tide*, 95.

227 **"We decided to park this problem":** Michael Green, author interview.

227 **"We built a lot of":** Sammon, *Misunderestimated*, 110–11.

228 **picked up two extra seats:** Republicans emerged from the election with a margin of fifty-one to forty-nine in the Senate. http://uspolitics.about.com/od/elections/l/bl_mid_term_election_results.htm.

228 **gained eight seats:** Ibid.

228 **It was the first time since:** In four other midterm elections after 1934, the president's party gained in one house, though not both: in 1962, John F. Kennedy's Democrats picked up three seats in the Senate while losing four in the House; in 1970, Richard M. Nixon's Republicans picked up two seats in the Senate while losing twelve in the House; in 1982, Ronald Reagan's Republicans picked up one seat in the Senate while losing twenty-six in the House; and in 1998, Bill Clinton's Democrats picked up five seats in the House but made no gain or loss in the Senate. The American Presidency Project, http://www.presidency.ucsb.edu/data/mid-term_elections.php. See also http://uspolitics.about.com/od/elections/l/bl_mid_term_election_results.htm.

228 **raised more than $200 million:** CNN online coverage, http://archives.cnn.com/2002/ALLPOLITICS/11/06/elec02.bush/.

228 **"Should I decide to run":** George W. Bush, news conference, November 7, 2002, http://georgewbush-whitehouse.archives.gov/news/releases/2002/11/20021107-2.html.

CHAPTER 13: "YOU COULD HEAR THE HINGE OF HISTORY TURN"

229 **"In this White House":** Carl M. Cannon, "The Point Man," *National Journal*, October 11, 2002, http://www3.nationaljournal.com/members/news/2002/10/1011nj1.htm.

229 **"he didn't want it":** Draper, *Dead Certain*, 89.

230 **"After 9/11, it was":** Jim Langdon, author interview.

230 **"One of the things":** Ari Fleischer, author interview.

230 **"right-wing nut":** Powell, *My American Journey*, 526.

230 **considered a fever:** Woodward, *Plan of Attack*, 175.

230 **"pain in the ass":** Neil Patel, author interview.

231 **"The president was never":** White House official, author interview.

231 **"He never came over to me"**: Donald Rumsfeld, author interview.
231 **"Don't Tell Me, I Already Know"**: Shelton, *Without Hesitation*, 403.
232 **use back-channel Pentagon**: Frank Miller, author interview.
232 **"Don, where are you going?"**: Rice, *No Higher Honor*, 275. See also Mayer, *Dark Side*, 188.
232 **"stop giving tasks"**: Donald Rumsfeld to Condoleezza Rice, memo, December 1, 2002. Accessed at http://www.rumsfeld.com.
232 **"What's wrong between us?"**: Rice, *No Higher Honor*, 21.
232 **"It certainly was not meant"**: Rumsfeld interview.
232 **"Why doesn't the president"**: Rice, *No Higher Honor*, 22.
232 **holding Iraq in "material breach"**: UN Security Council Resolution 1441, November 8, 2002, http://www.un.org/News/Press/docs/2002/SC7564.doc.htm.
233 **"I would say all along"**: Glenn Hubbard, author interview.
233 **"the economy did not need"**: Paul O'Neill, author interview.
233 **"I think they believed it was"**: Ibid.
233 **"moving toward a fiscal crisis"**: Suskind, *Price of Loyalty*, 291.
233 **"was designed in the White House"**: Aide to Paul O'Neill, author interview.
234 **"The vice president was always"**: Hubbard interview.
234 **"When we did it, it revealed"**: Michael Gerson, author interview.
234 **"the custodian of compassionate"**: Joshua Bolten, author interview.
235 **"What if money were no object?"**: Ibid.
235 **"They need the money now"**: Tony Fauci, author interview.
235 **"I speak for everyone"**: George Klein, author interview.
235 **"were kind of gasping"**: Bolten interview.
235 **"Gerson, what do you think?"**: Gerson, *Heroic Conservatism*, 3. Gerson describes this meeting taking place on November 18, 2002, but other participants said it took place in December, and Bush's office in Dallas confirmed that to the author.
236 **"Look, this is one of those"**: Jay Lefkowitz, author interview.
236 **"never clicked"**: George W. Bush, *Decision Points*, 85.
236 **"He came in and he talked about"**: Bolten interview.
236 **"was not a team player"**: O'Neill aide, author interview.
236 **"Paul, the president has decided"**: O'Neill interview. See also Suskind, *Price of Loyalty*, 309–10.
237 **"It wasn't difficult for me"**: O'Neill interview.
237 **"Paul belittled the tax cuts"**: George W. Bush, *Decision Points*, 85.
237 **"When the president says"**: O'Neill interview.
237 **"The Bush administration turned"**: Greenspan, *Age of Turbulence*, 240–41.
237 **"If the rest of the country"**: Thomas B. Edsall, "Lott Decried for Part of Salute to Thurmond," *Washington Post*, December 7, 2002.
238 **"People are going to think"**: Nick Calio, author interview.
238 **"Any suggestion that"**: George W. Bush, speech, Philadelphia, December 12, 2002, http://georgewbush-whitehouse.archives.gov/news/releases/2002/12/20021212-3.html.
238 **"The president just threw you"**: Trent Lott, author interview.
238 **"I never could prove"**: Ibid.
239 **"I suggested that he shouldn't"**: Karen Hughes, author interview.
239 **"I was very careful"**: John McLaughlin, author interview.
239 **"Nice try," he told McLaughlin**: Ibid. See also Tenet, *At the Center of the Storm*, 360–62; and Woodward, *State of Denial*, 249–50.
240 **Tenet, however, felt his comment**: Tenet, *At the Center of the Storm*, 360–62.
240 **"Do you think we should"**: Bumiller, *Condoleezza Rice*, 197–98.

240 **"You've got to try everything":** George W. Bush, *Decision Points*, 243.
240 **"People will greet the troops":** Kanan Makiya, e-mail exchange with author. See also Fleischer, *Taking Heat*, 298–99.
241 **"The president has made":** Rumsfeld, *Known and Unknown*, 450.
241 **"Is Saddam going to":** Dick Cheney, *In My Time*, 396–97.
241 **"This is the first time":** Rumsfeld interview.
241 **"I really think I'm going":** Woodward, *Plan of Attack*, 269–71. See also DeYoung, *Soldier*, 439.
242 **"nothing today justifies" war:** Julia Preston, "An Attack on Iraq Not Yet Justified, France Warns U.S.," *New York Times*, January 21, 2003, http://www.nytimes.com/2003/01/21/world/threats-responses-diplomacy-attack-iraq-not-yet-justified-france-warns-us.html?pagewanted=all&src=pm.
242 **Powell felt "blindsided":** Powell, *It Worked for Me*, 7.
242 **"Old Europe" as opposed to:** Donald Rumsfeld, news briefing, Foreign Press Center, January 22, 2003, http://www.defense.gov/transcripts/transcript.aspx?transcriptid=1330.
242 **"We've really got to make the case":** DeYoung, *Soldier*, 439.
242 **"You've got high poll ratings":** Ibid., 441.
242 **initially wanted their story:** Richard W. Stevenson and David E. Sanger, author interviews. Instead, Stevenson and Sanger wrote that Bush made "an unflinching threat of military action against Saddam Hussein." See Stevenson and Sanger, "Calling Iraq a Serious Threat, Bush Vows That He'll Disarm It," *New York Times*, January 29, 2003, http://www.nytimes.com/2003/01/29/politics/29BUSH.html.
242 **Bush laid out his bill:** George W. Bush, State of the Union address, January 28, 2003, http://georgewbush-whitehouse.archives.gov/news/releases/2003/01/20030128-19.html.
243 **"Don Rumsfeld has my full support":** Kori Schake, author interview.
243 **"Title X motherfuckers":** Woodward, *Plan of Attack*, 118.
243 **"It's the only time in my life":** Schake interview.
243 **it "would give us international":** David Manning, a foreign policy adviser to Tony Blair, recorded the conversation in a five-page memo, dated the same day, January 31, 2003. The Manning memo was first reported in a book by a British law professor in early 2006. See Sands, *Lawless World*, 273. Don Van Natta Jr. of the *New York Times* later reviewed the memo himself and divulged further details from it. See "Bush Was Set on Path to War, British Memo Says," *New York Times*, March 27, 2006, http://www.nytimes.com/2006/03/27/international/europe/27memo.html?pagewanted=all.
244 **"This isn't going to cut it":** Isikoff and Corn, *Hubris*, 176–78.
244 **"a disaster" and "incoherent":** Powell, *It Worked for Me*, 219.
244 **thirty-eight allegations:** Isikoff and Corn, *Hubris*, 179.
245 **finding no evidence:** *9/11 Commission Report*, 228–29.
245 **"pretty well confirmed":** Dick Cheney, interview, *Meet the Press*, December 9, 2001, http://www.washingtonpost.com/wp-srv/nation/specials/attacked/transcripts/cheneytext_120901.html.
245 **"unconfirmed" but still holding:** On September 8, 2002, for example, Cheney went back on *Meet the Press* and raised the Atta meeting without being asked about it. "Mohamed Atta, who was the lead hijacker, did apparently travel to Prague on a number of occasions. And on at least one occasion, we have reporting that places him in Prague with a senior Iraqi intelligence official a few months before the attack on the World Trade Center." Cheney acknowledged that there was a debate about "was he there or wasn't he there." Asked what the CIA said

about the report, Cheney said, "It's credible [but] unconfirmed at this point." See transcript, http://www.mtholyoke.edu/acad/intrel/bush/meet.htm.

245 **"Iraq & al-Qa'ida: Interpreting a Murky"**: CIA report, June 21, 2002, http://www.levin.senate.gov/imo/media/doc/supporting/2005/CIAreport.062102.pdf.

245 **Jami Miscik, the deputy director**: Suskind, *One Percent Doctrine*, 190–91. See also Tenet, *At the Center of the Storm*, 349–50.

245 **found no evidence of "command"**: CIA report, "Iraqi Support for Terrorism," January 29, 2003, http://www.levin.senate.gov/imo/media/doc/supporting/2005/CIAreport.012903.pdf.

246 **"We should hit Khurmal"**: Rumsfeld, *Known and Unknown*, 446–47.

246 **"This is something Condi has"**: Rice, *No Higher Honor*, 189–90.

246 **"If he had done that to me"**: Stephen Hadley, author interview.

246 **Bush watched on television**: Rice, *No Higher Honor*, 200.

246 **"He persuaded me"**: Mary McGrory, "I'm Persuaded," *Washington Post*, February 6, 2003, http://www.washingtonpost.com/wp-dyn/articles/A32573-2003Feb5.html.

247 **"we share the position"**: Baker and Glasser, *Kremlin Rising*, 225.

247 **"France is clearly trying to"**: Donald Rumsfeld to George W. Bush, memo, February 18, 2003. Accessed at http://www.rumsfeld.com.

247 **"We need a lot of Powell"**: Bryan Burrough, Evgenia Peretz, David Rose, and David Wise, "The Path to War," *Vanity Fair*, November 2004, http://www.vanityfair.com/politics/features/2004/05/path-to-war200405.

247 **"Is France an ally or a foe?"**: Mann, *Rise of the Vulcans*, 355.

247 **"Are you going to take care"**: George W. Bush, *Decision Points*, 251.

248 **"could you give us some idea"**: Senate Armed Services Committee hearing, February 25, 2003.

248 **"Some of the higher-end predictions"**: House Budget Committee hearing, February 27, 2003.

249 **"My personal view is that it will"**: Donald Rumsfeld and General Richard Myers, press briefing, February 28, 2003, http://www.defense.gov/transcripts/transcript.aspx?transcriptid=1976.

249 **had "been misinterpreted"**: Eric Shinseki to Donald Rumsfeld, "End of Tour Memorandum," June 10, 2003, http://media.washingtonpost.com/wp-srv/opinions/documents/shinseki.pdf.

249 **Neither Rumsfeld nor Wolfowitz ever asked**: Graham, *By His Own Rules*, 412.

249 **"I'm against silence"**: Elie Wiesel, e-mail exchange with author through spokesperson. See also Fleischer, *Taking Heat*, 316.

249 **"You don't understand how big"**: Dan Bartlett, author interview.

250 **"the only regime change"**: Campbell, *Blair Years*, 671.

250 **International Atomic Energy Agency concluded**: Mohamed ElBaradei, "The Status of Nuclear Inspections in Iraq: An Update," March 7, 2003, http://www.iaea.org/newscenter/statements/2003/ebsp2003n006.shtml.

250 **refused to back off**: Eventually, Christopher Meyer, the British ambassador, agreed that "the yellow cake claim later turned out to be false." See *DC Confidential*, 259.

250 **removing between 1 percent**: Frank Miller, author interview.

250 **"It's hard to imagine punishing"**: Rumsfeld, *Known and Unknown*, 515–17.

251 **Three to five divisions**: Rice, *No Higher Honor*, 194–95.

251 **No one at the meeting**: Feith, *War and Decision*, 367–68.

251 **"the vice president wants to make"**: Tenet, *At the Center of the Storm*, 341–42.

251 **"Would you like me to come"**: Karen Hughes, author interview.

252 **"going through motions"**: Campbell, *Blair Years*, 679.

252 **"extremely frustrated"**: Sammon, *Misunderestimated*, 178–79.
252 **"I am just not going to be"**: Tony Blair, *Journey*, 341.
252 **"If another country tried to introduce"**: Woodward, *Plan of Attack*, 358.
252 **"It's an old Texas expression"**: George W. Bush, Tony Blair, and other leaders, news conference, March 16, 2003, http://georgewbush-whitehouse.archives.gov/news/releases/2003/03/20030316-3.html.
253 **"If you win the vote in Parliament"**: Campbell, *Blair Years*, 679.
253 **"Do you think the American people"**: Dick Cheney, interview with Tim Russert, *Meet the Press*, NBC, March 16, 2003, http://www.mtholyoke.edu/acad/intrel/bush/cheneymeetthepress.htm.
253 **"You sure better find these"**: Stephen Hadley, author interview.
253 **"How are you doing, Gerson?"**: Michael Gerson, author interview.
254 **"All the decades of deceit"**: George W. Bush, address to nation, March 17, 2003, http://georgewbush-whitehouse.archives.gov/news/releases/2003/03/20030317-7.html.
254 **A team led by Hadley**: Hadley interview.

CHAPTER 14: "MAYBE WE'LL GET LUCKY"

257 **"I would like to address your team"**: Dan Bartlett, author interview. See also George W. Bush, interview with Tom Brokaw of NBC News, April 24, 2003, http://www.presidency.ucsb.edu/ws/index.php?pid=14#axzz1kdCZ5Zoi.
257 **"for the peace of the world"**: George W. Bush, *Decision Points*, 223–25.
257 **Colin Powell wordlessly reached**: Purdum, *Time of Our Choosing*, 106.
258 **"you could see the weight"**: Eric Draper, author interview.
258 **"Dear Dad"**: George W. Bush, *Decision Points*, 223–25.
258 **"All of that comes home to roost"**: Bartlett interview.
259 **"Can I come over?"**: Bush interview with Brokaw.
259 **"too good a scenario to pass up"**: Tenet, *At the Center of the Storm*, 391–95.
259 **"I was hesitant at first"**: Bush interview with Brokaw.
259 **"How solid are your sources"**: Rumsfeld, *Known and Unknown*, 459–60.
259 **"Okay, all right"**: Sammon, *Misunderestimated*, 183–85.
260 **"Dick, what do you think"**: Dick Cheney, *In My Time*, 459–60.
260 **"Let's go," he said**: George W. Bush, *Decision Points*, 254.
260 **moved the Oval Office couches**: Joe Hagin, author interview.
260 **as overwhelmed as he had been**: Pamela Hudson Nelson, author interview.
260 **"Maybe we'll get lucky"**: Ronald Kessler, *Laura Bush*, 160–61.
261 **"the only time I can remember"**: Gerson interview.
261 **thirty-nine Tomahawks**: Gordon and Trainor, *Cobra II*, 172–76. Originally, forty-five Tomahawks were ordered, but an unanticipated problem with the navy's communications system complicated the strike.
261 **"On my orders," he said**: George W. Bush, address to nation, March 19, 2003, http://georgewbush-whitehouse.archives.gov/news/releases/2003/03/20030319-17.html.
261 **"Whoops," Laura said**: Purdum, *Time of Our Choosing*, 111.
261 **"We tried everything possible"**: Fleischer, *Taking Heat*, 339–40.
262 **"It was pretty graphic"**: Nelson interview. See also Ronald Kessler, *Laura Bush*, 160–61.
262 **"He is just totally immersed"**: Purdum, *Time of Our Choosing*, 119.
262 **Reports to Bush and Cheney**: Zenko, "Foregoing Limited Force."

263 **"everything would be on the table":** Joseph, *Countering WMD*, 5–6.

263 **"When Bush has finished with Iraq":** Muammar el-Qaddafi, interview with *Le Figaro*, March 11, 2003, http://worldpress.org/Europe/989.cfm.

263 **"We had a real concern":** Robert Joseph, author interview.

263 **"We have got to get moving":** Donald Rumsfeld to George W. Bush, memo, April 1, 2003, http://library.rumsfeld.com/doclib/sp/321/2003-04-01%20to%20President%20Bush%20re%20Iraqi%20Interim%20Authority.pdf#search="2003-04-01."

264 **Camp Lejeune had sent:** CNN, April 4, 2003, http://articles.cnn.com/2003-04-03/politics/sprj.irq.bush_1_war-criminals-finer-sight-upbeat-progress-report?_s=PM:ALLPOLITICS.

264 **"There's no finer sight":** George W. Bush, address at Camp Lejeune, April 3, 2003, http://georgewbush-whitehouse.archives.gov/news/releases/2003/04/20030403-3.html.

264 **"He's in heaven":** Mike Allen, "Bush Upbeat on War Progress in Visit with Marines," *Washington Post*, April 4, 2003. See also Jennifer Loven, "Bush Seeks to Comfort Families of the Fallen," Associated Press, April 3, 2003.

264 **"that wrenching realization":** Ari Fleischer, author interview.

264 **"I made the decision":** Woodward, *State of Denial*, 155.

264 **"a useful corrective":** Rumsfeld, *Known and Unknown*, 489–94.

265 **"They're hooking it up":** Bush interview with Brokaw.

265 **"overwhelmed with relief and pride":** George W. Bush, *Decision Points*, 256.

265 **"A second and a half later":** Draper interview.

265 **on average every 7.5 minutes:** Peter Maass, ProPublica, December 29, 2010, http://www.youtube.com/user/propublica#p/a/u/0/YDu7bXqx8Ig.

265 **"conviction and determination":** George H. W. Bush, *All the Best*, 661.

265 **"Thank you for our liberation":** Dick Cheney, *In My Time*, 400–401.

265 **"You did this":** Rice, *No Higher Honor*, 208.

266 **"Stuff happens":** Donald Rumsfeld, press briefing with General Richard Myers, April 11, 2003, http://www.defense.gov/transcripts/transcript.aspx?transcriptid=2367.

266 **Iraq would be "a cakewalk":** Kenneth Adelman, "Cakewalk in Iraq," *Washington Post*, February 13, 2002.

266 **"We were euphoric":** Kenneth Adelman, author interview. See also Woodward, *Plan of Attack*, 409–12.

267 **"seemed too optimistic":** Rumsfeld, *Known and Unknown*, 497–99.

267 **"Bringing democracy to Iraq":** Ibid.

268 **"Ninety-nine point nine percent":** Sammon, *Misunderestimated*, 260–66.

268 **"You want the jet?":** Ibid.

268 **"My fellow Americans":** George W. Bush, address to nation, USS *Abraham Lincoln*, May 1, 2003, http://georgewbush-whitehouse.archives.gov/news/releases/2003/05/20030501-15.html.

269 **"Now that the war in Iraq is over":** Bush interview with Brokaw.

269 **"Our stagecraft had gone awry":** George W. Bush, *Decision Points*, 256–57.

CHAPTER 15: "MR. PRESIDENT, I THINK WE'VE GOT A PROBLEM"

270 **"We'll stay until":** Jerry Bremer, author interview. See also Bremer, *My Year in Iraq*, 11–12.

271 **"higher authority":** Ricks, *Fiasco*, 103–4.

271 **"we want people who are":** Colin Powell, author interview.
271 **"you are going to need a lot":** Ibid.
271 **Scooter Libby contacted Bremer:** Bremer, *My Year in Iraq*, 6–7.
271 **"a can-do type person":** George W. Bush, announcement of appointment of L. Paul Bremer III as presidential envoy to Iraq, May 6, 2003, http://georgewbush-whitehouse.archives.gov/news/releases/2003/05/20030506-3.html.
271 **"I don't know whether":** Bremer, *My Year in Iraq*, 12.
271 **"POTUS had lunch with him":** Rumsfeld, *Known and Unknown*, 506.
272 **"Zal, what the hell happened?":** Zalmay Khalilzad, author interview.
272 **he issued Order Number 1:** Coalition Provisional Authority Order Number 1, "De-Ba'athification of Iraqi Society," May 16, 2003, http://www.iraqcoalition.org/regulations/20030516_CPAORD_1_De-Ba_athification_of_Iraqi_Society_.pdf.
272 **Garner and the CIA station chief:** Woodward, *State of Denial*, 193–94.
272 **Bremer issued Order Number 2:** Coalition Provisional Authority Order Number 2, "Dissolution of Entities," May 23, 2003, http://www.iraqcoalition.org/regulations/20030823_CPAORD_2_Dissolution_of_Entities_with_Annex_A.pdf.
272 **"We would have had a civil war":** Bremer interview.
272 **"they were the right decisions":** Ibid.
273 **"full sovereignty under an Iraqi":** L. Paul Bremer III, "Facts for Feith," *National Review Online*, March 19, 2008, http://www.nationalreview.com/node/223954.
273 **"the vice president's office asked":** Nicholas D. Kristof, "Missing In Action: Truth," *New York Times*, May 6, 2003, http://www.nytimes.com/2003/05/06/opinion/missing-in-action-truth.html.
273 **congressional investigators:** Report of the Select Committee on Intelligence on the U.S. Intelligence Community's Prewar Intelligence Assessments on Iraq, July 9, 2004. Wilson said he may have "misspoken" when he told journalists that he debunked the fraudulent documents and must have gotten confused since the documents had since been exposed by others as fraudulent. The Senate report also concluded that to many, though not all, analysts "information in the report lent more credibility" to the allegation, despite Wilson's skepticism. Wilson reported that he talked with Niger's former prime minister Ibrahim Mayaki, who said he knew of no contracts for uranium during his tenure, but he was invited in June 1999 to meet with an Iraqi delegation to discuss "expanding commercial relations" between Niger and Iraq, which he interpreted as meaning uranium, the country's main resource. Nothing ever came of the meeting because of UN sanctions, according to Mayaki. http://www.gpo.gov/fdsys/search/pagedetails.action?browsePath=108/SRPT/%5b300%3b399%5d&granuleId=CRPT-108srpt301&packageId=CRPT-108srpt301.
274 **"I think we've got a problem":** Dennis Hastert, author interview.
274 **push it through the Senate:** U.S. Senate roll call record, Jobs and Growth Tax Relief Reconciliation Act of 2003, 51 to 50, May 23, 2003, http://www.senate.gov/legislative/LIS/roll_call_lists/roll_call_vote_cfm.cfm?congress=108&session=1&vote=00196.
274 **the House approved it:** U.S. House Clerk's Office, 231 to 200, May 23, 2003, http://clerk.house.gov/evs/2003/roll225.xml.
274 **"It just got to the point":** Christine Todd Whitman, author interview.
275 **"A lot of people I've talked to":** Ibid.
275 **"Hello, George," she said:** Elisabeth Bumiller, "On Gay Marriage, Bush May Have Said All He's Going To," *New York Times*, March 1, 2004, http://www.nytimes.com/2004/03/01/us/white-house-letter-on-gay-marriage-bush-may-have-said-all-he-s-going-to.html.

275 **"What if we don't find them?":** Condoleezza Rice, author interview.

276 **"They went—" Bush said:** Tenet, *At the Center of the Storm*, 401.

276 **"What the hell is going on, George?":** Dick Cheney, *In My Time*, 402–6.

276 **"It sounded like amateur hour":** Ibid.

276 **"sort of an offhand manner":** Scooter Libby, grand jury testimony, March 5, 2004, http://www.gwu.edu/~nsarchiv/NSAEBB/NSAEBB215/govt_ex/GX1.pdf.

276 **jotted that down with his blue pen:** Scooter Libby's notes of conversation with Dick Cheney, June 12, 2003, released as part of the investigation and prosecution against Libby, http://www.gwu.edu/~nsarchiv/NSAEBB/NSAEBB215/GX53201.PDF.

276 **Pincus's story on June 12:** Walter Pincus, "CIA Did Not Share Doubt on Iraq Data," *Washington Post*, June 12, 2003.

277 **"Not going home?":** Gordon and Trainor, *Endgame*, 12.

277 **just 37 percent:** Rumsfeld, *Known and Unknown*, 501–2.

277 **Rumsfeld had interviewed:** Rumsfeld spent thirty-five minutes interviewing Sanchez for his promotion to lieutenant general and assignment as commander of V Corps. Sanchez, *Wiser in Battle*, 167–68.

277 **later said he had nothing to do:** Rumsfeld, *Known and Unknown*, 501–2. "I can only speculate that part of the logic behind an otherwise inexplicable selection was that CENTCOM" thought it could begin drawing down, Rumsfeld wrote.

277 **"I just find that really hard":** Richard Myers, author interview. Myers added, "I can't give you chapter and verse on it, but it would be unlike him on every other thing we did."

277 **"There are some who feel":** George W. Bush, comments to reporters, July 2, 2003, http://georgewbush-whitehouse.archives.gov/news/releases/2003/07/20030702-3.html.

277 **"can you imagine how that would":** Draper, *Dead Certain*, 209.

278 **one of his biggest gaffes:** George W. Bush, *Decision Points*, 261. The phrase "left a wrong impression," he wrote, and "I learned from the experience."

278 **Wilson unmasked himself:** Joseph C. Wilson 4th, "What I Didn't Find in Africa," *New York Times*, July 6, 2003, http://www.nytimes.com/2003/07/06/opinion/what-i-didn-t-find-in-africa.html?pagewanted=all&src=pm; Richard Leiby and Walter Pincus, "Retired Envoy: Nuclear Report Ignored," *Washington Post*, July 6, 2003, *Meet the Press*, July 6, 2003, http://justoneminute.typepad.com/footnotes/2004/07/joe_wilson_with.html.

278 **"Have they done this sort":** A copy of Wilson's column with Dick Cheney's notations was released during the subsequent investigation and prosecution of Scooter Libby. http://media.washingtonpost.com/wp-srv/politics/special/plame/GX40201.pdf.

278 **"So it was wrong?":** Ari Fleischer, news briefing, July 7, 2003, http://georgewbush-whitehouse.archives.gov/news/releases/2003/07/20030707-5.html.

278 **"very keen to get the truth out":** Libby testimony.

278 **"just take the issue off":** Rice, *No Higher Honor*, 223.

279 **"expanding commercial relations":** Report of the Select Committee on Intelligence the U.S. Intelligence Community's Prewar Intelligence Assessments on Iraq, July 9, 2004.

279 **"If the CIA, the director":** Condoleezza Rice, press briefing, Air Force One en route to Entebbe, Uganda, July 11, 2003, http://georgewbush-whitehouse.archives.gov/news/releases/2003/07/20030711-7.html.

279 **"was cleared by the intelligence":** George W. Bush, remarks to reporters,

Entebbe, Uganda, July 11, 2003, http://georgewbush-whitehouse.archives.gov/news/releases/2003/07/20030711-6.html.

279 **"CIA approved the President's":** George Tenet, statement, July 11, 2003, https://www.cia.gov/news-information/press-releases-statements/press-release-archive-2003/pr07112003.html.

279 **"You put a bull's-eye":** Administration official, author interview.

280 **Libby later that day:** He spoke with Glenn Kessler of the *Washington Post*, Matthew Cooper of *Time*, Evan Thomas of *Newsweek*, and Judith Miller of the *New York Times*. Libby testified that he talked about Valerie Wilson with Cooper, Miller, and possibly Kessler, but Kessler later said she did not come up in their conversation. See Libby's testimony, http://www.gwu.edu/~nsarchiv/NSAEBB/NSAEBB215/govt_ex/GX1.pdf.

280 **mentioned it during an interview:** Novak, *Prince of Darkness*, 5.

280 **also mentioned it to Bob Woodward:** Woodward interviewed Richard Armitage on June 13, 2003, as part of research for a book. A transcript and recording of the portion where they talked about the uranium story were later made public during the Scooter Libby investigation and trial. See the transcript at http://media.washingtonpost.com/wp-srv/politics/special/plame/woodward_armitage_interview.pdf and listen to the audio clip at http://www.washingtonpost.com/wp-dyn/content/audio/2007/02/13/AU2007021300449.html.

280 **also spoken with Rove:** Cooper's story carried two other bylines, Massimo Calabresi and John F. Dickerson. http://www.time.com/time/nation/article/0,8599,465270,00.html. Cooper recorded his conversation with Rove in an e-mail to his bureau chief. He spoke with Rove briefly about another topic before asking Rove about the Wilson case. Rove warned him not to "get too far out on Wilson" and said it was not Cheney who sent him to Niger. "It was, KR said, [W]ilson's wife, who apparently works at the agency on wmd issues who authorized the trip," Cooper wrote. He said Rove argued that "not only the genesis of the trip is flawed an[d] suspect but so is the report." The e-mail was first reported by Michael Isikoff, "Matt Cooper's Source," *Newsweek*, July 17, 2005, http://www.thedailybeast.com/newsweek/2005/07/17/matt-cooper-s-source.html. Cooper later described his experience in "What I Told the Grand Jury," *Time*, July 17, 2005, http://www.time.com/time/printout/0,8816,1083899,00.html.

280 **talked with Libby:** Libby testimony.

280 **Intelligence Identities Protection Act:** The law protects covert officers but not everyone who works for the CIA, and a debate raged for years about whether Valerie Wilson qualified as a covert officer. http://www.fas.org/irp/offdocs/laws/iipa.html.

280 **page 3 of a three-and-a-half:** Stephen Hadley, press briefing, July 22, 2003, http://www.fas.org/irp/news/2003/07/wh072203b.html.

280 **"I think I need to resign":** Administration official, author interview.

281 **"I haven't been told the truth":** Tenet, *At the Center of the Storm*, 473–74.

281 **"My conversation with the president":** Hadley press briefing.

CHAPTER 16: "WELCOME TO FREE IRAQ"

282 **"I want you to know that you":** George W. Bush, *Decision Points*, 86–87.

282 **54 percent of the public:** Gallup found Dick Cheney at 54 percent in two polls in mid-2003, the first taken June 27–29 and the second taken September 19–21. The question about keeping Cheney on the ticket was asked in a poll taken Octo-

ber 24–26. Forty-two percent said Bush should get someone new. http://www.gallup.com/poll/10696/vice-president-dick-cheney.aspx.

282 **"The reason I did it":** Dick Cheney, author interview.

283 **"The first couple of times":** Ibid.

283 **"I knew nothing about it":** Alan Simpson, author interview.

283 **"helped with important parts":** George W. Bush, *Decision Points*, 86–87.

283 **"Many of us came":** Matthew Dowd, author interview.

283 **"This is being considered":** Ibid. In an interview with the author, Dan Bartlett said he did not remember that specifically but it would not surprise him.

283 **"People would say, 'What does' ":** Dan Bartlett, author interview.

284 **since Franklin D. Roosevelt:** Roosevelt had three vice presidents. In 1944, he dumped his second, Henry Wallace, for a senator he barely knew, Harry Truman.

284 **"a few days later":** Dick Cheney, *In My Time*, 417–18.

284 **"a few weeks later":** George W. Bush, *Decision Points*, 86–87.

284 **"I hadn't picked him to be":** Ibid.

284 **"It was a clever move by Cheney":** Friend of both men, author interview.

284 **op-ed article by Jerry Bremer:** L. Paul Bremer III, "Iraq's Path to Sovereignty," *Washington Post*, September 8, 2003.

285 **George and Laura kept from:** Laura Bush, *Spoken from the Heart*, 285.

285 **A twenty-four-year-old who:** Chandrasekaran, *Imperial Life in the Emerald City*, 95–97, 235–36. See also Chandrasekaran, interview on NPR, March 23, 2010, http://www.npr.org/templates/story/story.php?storyId=125065176.

285 **sent her a memo urging:** Robert Blackwill, e-mail exchange with author. See also Woodward, *State of Denial*, 256.

285 **"You should have flooded":** Colin Powell, author interview.

285 **telling Washington for months:** Jerry Bremer, author interview. By Bremer's count, he had outlined his intentions to Washington thirty-nine times before the article appeared.

285 **surprised to read it in the newspaper:** Rumsfeld, *Known and Unknown*, 522–23.

286 **"totally ridiculous" to blame:** Scott McClellan, press briefing, September 16, 2003, http://georgewbush-whitehouse.archives.gov/news/releases/2003/09/20030916-6.html#27.

286 **"was using that as a diversion":** Adam Levine, author interview.

286 **dealt the next blow:** Mike Allen and Dana Priest, "Bush Administration Is Focus of Inquiry," *Washington Post*, September 28, 2003.

286 **generated partly from a conversation:** Levine interview. Levine acknowledged talking to Allen but declined to discuss what he said in detail, except to say that he was not the only source. "I don't think it was for revenge," he told the author. "I think it was for—if you discredit one thing about the witness, you have to take everything the witness says and throw it out. So they were grasping at straws to discredit."

286 **It was true that Libby, Rove:** Libby had talked with Matthew Cooper and Judith Miller. Rove talked with Robert Novak and Matthew Cooper. Ari Fleischer had mentioned it to David Gregory of NBC News and John Dickerson of *Time*. At this point, Levine did not know that Richard Armitage had also talked with Novak and Bob Woodward.

286 **had been inserted by an editor:** Isikoff and Corn, *Hubris*, 319–20.

286 **"He said he'd heard":** McClellan, *What Happened*, 178–82.

287 **"Are you the one behind this":** Stewart, *Tangled Webs*, 164–65.

287 **"Bush sounded a little annoyed":** Rove, *Courage and Consequence*, 347.

287 **"Karl didn't do it":** McClellan, *What Happened*, 182–84.

287 **"I would fire anybody involved":** Ibid.
287 **"no partisan gunslinger":** Robert Novak, "Columnist Wasn't Pawn for Leak," *Chicago Sun-Times*, October 1, 2003.
287 **"People have made too much":** Handwritten notes, released as part of the investigation and prosecution of Scooter Libby, http://wid.ap.org/documents/libbytrial/jan30/DX802.pdf.
288 **"Has to happen today":** Ibid.
288 **"The president and vice president":** McClellan, *What Happened*, 216–17.
288 **Rice confirmed it to him:** David E. Sanger, "White House to Overhaul Iraq and Afghan Missions," *New York Times*, October 6, 2003.
288 **"The story indicates Condi":** Donald Rumsfeld to George W. Bush, Dick Cheney, and Andy Card, memo, "Iraq Reporting Relationships," October 6, 2003, http://library.rumsfeld.com/doclib/sp/355/2003-10-06%20to%20President%20George%20W%20Bush%20re%20Iraq%20Reporting%20Relationships.pdf#search="2003-10-06."
288 **"You need to make it right":** Rice, *No Higher Honor*, 243–44.
289 **"You're failing," he told her:** Rumsfeld, *Known and Unknown*, 526–27.
289 **"I did not come here to":** Draper, *Dead Certain*, 222.
289 **"It is pretty clear that":** Donald Rumsfeld to Richard Myers, Paul Wolfowitz, Peter Pace, and Douglas Feith, memo, "Global War on Terrorism," October 16, 2003, http://library.rumsfeld.com/doclib/sp/426/2003-10-16%20to%20Myers%20et%20al%20re%20Global%20War%20on%20Terrorism.pdf#search="long%20hard%20slog."
289 **"I tell members of Congress":** Dan Senor, author interview.
289 **"What kind of a person":** Bremer, *My Year in Iraq*, 207–9.
290 **"I thought Bremer reported":** Kenneth Adelman, author interview.
290 **"I believe every person has":** George W. Bush, address marking twentieth anniversary of National Endowment for Democracy, November 6, 2003, http://georgewbush-whitehouse.archives.gov/news/releases/2003/11/20031106-2.html.
291 **an "American nationalist":** John Hannah, author interview.
291 **"There was a big debate":** Frederick Jones, author interview.
291 **"in my view we do not have":** Bremer interview. See also Hayes, *Cheney*, 426–27.
292 **"Why do you call it an insurgency?":** Tenet, *At the Center of the Storm*, 437–38.
292 **"Bremer is doing a fabulous":** Notes of meeting with Lord George Robertson, November 12, 2003. Provided to author.
292 **to announce his plan:** Rajiv Chandrasekaran, "Plan to End Occupation Could Trim U.S. Force," *Washington Post*, November 16, 2003.
292 **"The administration knew something":** Sanchez, *Wiser in Battle*, 283–88.
292 **"Don't do it," Addington said:** Kevin Kellems, author interview.
293 **"This was, I think, a Rove-driven":** Judd Gregg, author interview.
293 **"I didn't come to Washington":** George W. Bush, *Decision Points*, 282–87.
293 **down by fifteen votes:** David S. Broder, "Time Was GOP's Ally on the Vote," *Washington Post*, November 23, 2003.
293 **"He was just going crazy":** Dennis Hastert, author interview.
293 **"Congressman, I understand you have":** Participant in the room, author interview.
294 **"I'm going to make that commitment":** Ibid.
294 **"I don't have a litmus test":** David Hobbs, author interview.
295 **Jeff Flake, another congressman:** Jeff Flake, e-mail exchange with author through a spokeswoman.
295 **"was very careful not to make":** Hastert interview.

295 **Franks later sent him a list:** Trent Franks, letter to George W. Bush, December 6, 2004. Reviewed by author. In addition to Roberts and Alito, the suggested candidates were Michael Luttig, Edith Jones, Janice Rogers Brown, Emilio Garza, Michael McConnell, and Jeffrey Sutton, all appeals court judges, and John Cornyn and Jon Kyl, both Republican senators.

295 **the bill passed:** U.S. House Clerk's Office, Prescription Drug and Medicare Improvement Act of 2003, 220 to 215, November 22, 2003, http://clerk.house.gov/evs/2003/roll669.xml. Sixteen Democrats broke party lines to vote for it, while twenty-five Republicans voted against it.

295 **"I didn't think they were telling":** Trent Lott, author interview.

295 **"Help us out, Trent":** Lott, *Herding Cats*, 292–93. Once Lott and Senator Lindsey Graham, who also opposed the program, switched their votes, Senator Ron Wyden of Oregon switched as well, making the final tally on that crucial procedural vote 61 to 39. Helen Dewar and Amy Goldstein, "Medicare Bill Near Senate Passage," *Washington Post*, November 25, 2003.

295 **it passed 54 to 44:** U.S. Senate roll call record, Drug and Medicare Improvement Act of 2003, 54 to 44, November 25, 2003, http://www.senate.gov/legislative/LIS/roll_call_lists/roll_call_vote_cfm.cfm?congress=108&session=1&vote=00459. Nine Republicans broke ranks and voted against the measure, including Trent Lott and Judd Gregg, while eleven Democrats and the independent James Jeffords voted for it.

295 **other presidents had slipped:** Franklin D. Roosevelt left the United States secretly several times during World War II, including to Casablanca, just two months after Allied troops stormed onto shore there. Dwight D. Eisenhower traveled secretly to Korea during the war there after he was elected president but before he was inaugurated. Both Lyndon B. Johnson, in 1966 and 1967, and Richard M. Nixon, in 1969, traveled to Vietnam.

295 **"We said we thought it was":** Ronald Kessler, *Matter of Character*, 256–57.

296 **"I'm scared, Dad":** George W. Bush, *Decision Points*, 264–66.

296 **"We looked like a normal":** Sammon, *Misunderestimated*, 291–313.

296 **"What is this?":** Rice, *No Higher Honor*, 247.

296 **"No calls, got it?":** Mike Allen, White House press pool report, November 27, 2003, http://www.editorandpublisher.com/Article/Pool-Report-on-Bush-s-Baghdad-Trip.

296 **"London, is that Air Force One?":** Mark Tillman, "My First Time . . . Flying Air Force One into a War Zone," *Washingtonian*, November 2011, as told to Shane Harris, http://www.washingtonian.com/articles/people/21259.html.

296 **"Do you think we should":** Condoleezza Rice, author interview.

297 **"The city seemed so serene":** George W. Bush, *Decision Points*, 264–66.

297 **heard explosions in the distance:** Sanchez, *Wiser in Battle*, 295–97.

297 **"Welcome to Free Iraq":** Bremer, *My Year in Iraq*, 238.

297 **"a sort of overgrown Quonset hut":** Ibid.

297 **"Now, General Sanchez":** Bremer and Sanchez remarks, November 27, 2003, C-Span video, http://www.c-spanvideo.org/program/179325-1.

297 **"The building actually shook":** E-mail from soldier in attendance, posted on *Blackfive*, a military blog, December 4, 2003, http://www.blackfive.net/main/2003/12/email_from_part.html.

298 **"I was swept up by the emotion":** George W. Bush, *Decision Points*, 264–66.

298 **"I was just looking for a warm":** George W. Bush, remarks to troops, Baghdad, November 27, 2003, http://georgewbush-whitehouse.archives.gov/news/releases/2003/11/20031127.html.

298 **"Where's the president?":** Laura Bush, *Spoken from the Heart*, 297.
298 **"I'm bowing out of the political":** Bremer, *My Year in Iraq*, 245. Rumsfeld describes the moment similarly. "As far as I was concerned," he wrote, "any lingering pretense that I oversaw his activities came to an end." See Rumsfeld, *Known and Unknown*, 528.
298 **"He doesn't work for me":** Richard Armitage, author interview.
298 **"Rumsfeld was so disengaged":** Senor interview.
298 **"Rumsfeld kind of tuned out":** Richard Perle, author interview.
299 **"first reports are not always":** Rumsfeld, *Known and Unknown*, 350.
299 **"Well, that *is* good news":** Ronald Kessler, *Matter of Character*, 274–75.
299 **"I am Saddam Hussein":** Phil Zabriskie, "Inside Saddam's Hideout," *Time*, December 15, 2003, http://www.time.com/time/world/article/0,8599,562302,00.html.
299 **"Don just called":** Rice, *No Higher Honor*, 251–52.
299 **"it looks like we've captured":** Dick Cheney, *In My Time*, 411.
300 **"high-value target":** Mary Cheney, *Now It's My Turn*, 146–48.
300 **"I'm sorry to wake you":** Ronald Kessler, *Matter of Character*, 274–75.
300 **"It's a great day for the country":** Sammon, *Misunderestimated*, 317–18.
300 **"Ladies and gentlemen, we got him":** Jerry Bremer, announcement in Baghdad, December 14, 2003, http://www.youtube.com/watch?v=S02BHmWPZNs.
300 **Rumsfeld was annoyed:** Graham, *By His Own Rules*, 447.
300 **Rice had a different reaction:** Rice, *No Higher Honor*, 251–52.
300 **"really first-rate" news:** Bremer, *My Year in Iraq*, 256.
300 **"We really believed it was a key":** Condoleezza Rice, author interview.
301 **"I have a message for the Iraqi":** George W. Bush, address to nation, December 14, 2003, http://georgewbush-whitehouse.archives.gov/news/releases/2003/12/20031214-3.html.
301 **"The president was the principal":** Joseph interview.
301 **"to manage the anxiety":** Rice, *No Higher Honor*, 250.
301 **"leaders who abandon the pursuit":** George W. Bush, remarks, White House briefing room, December 19, 2003, http://georgewbush-whitehouse.archives.gov/news/releases/2003/12/20031219-9.html.
302 **the nuclear schemes of A. Q. Khan:** For more on Khan and his network, see Sanger, *Inheritance*. Khan, who was released from house arrest in 2009, insisted he was not a rogue actor and acted "upon instructions from authorities." See the interview he gave to Simon Henderson, *Foreign Policy*, September 5, 2012, http://www.foreignpolicy.com/articles/2012/09/05/aq_khan_interview.
302 **"Just simply the fact that":** Donald Rumsfeld, author interview.
302 **They concluded he had:** Elisabeth Bumiller and Donald G. McNeil Jr., "Doctors Say Bush Has Typical Runner's Knee," *New York Times*, December 19, 2003, http://www.nytimes.com/2003/12/19/us/doctors-say-bush-has-typical-runner-s-knee.html.
302 **"Which one of you":** Ridge, *Test of Our Times*, 204–5.
303 **announced that Patrick Fitzgerald:** James B. Comey to Patrick Fitzgerald, December 30, 2003, http://www.justice.gov/usao/iln/osc/documents/ag_letter_december_30_2003.pdf.

CHAPTER 17: "WE WERE ALMOST ALL WRONG"

304 **"I sure wasn't going to":** Mary Cheney, *Now It's My Turn*, 173–78.
305 **"If you feel like you have to":** Ibid.

306 **Five picked Gephardt:** Gillespie, *Winning Right*, 51.
307 **Jenna dreamed that her father:** Thomas and the Staff of *Newsweek*, *Election 2004*, xix.
307 **"Dean ran an ad with me":** Dick Gephardt, author interview.
307 **"He's done, it's over":** Matt Schlapp and Dan Bartlett, author interviews.
307 **Kerry won with 38 percent:** New Hampshire Secretary of State's office, http://www.sos.nh.gov/presprim2004/dpressum.htm.
308 **"Let me begin by saying":** David Kay, testimony before the Senate Armed Services Committee, January 28, 2004, http://www.cnn.com/2004/US/01/28/kay.transcript/.
308 **"Why would Saddam do something":** David Kay, author interview.
309 **"was the right thing to do":** Colin Powell, interview with the *Washington Post*, excerpts printed February 3, 2004.
309 **"It was something we all":** Barry Schweid, "Powell Says War Decision Was Correct Even If Weapon Stockpiles Did Not Exist," Associated Press, February 3, 2004.
309 **"despite some public statements":** George Tenet, speech at Georgetown University, February 5, 2004, https://www.cia.gov/news-information/speeches-testimony/2004/tenet_georgetownspeech_02052004.html.
310 **declined to embrace:** Sheryl Stolberg, "White House Avoids Stand on Gay Marriage Measure," *New York Times*, July 2, 2003, http://www.nytimes.com/2003/07/02/us/white-house-avoids-stand-on-gay-marriage-measure.html.
310 **"heard more about marriage":** Goeglein, *Man in the Middle*, 120.
311 **Bush invited Cheney and top aides:** Halperin and Harris, *Way to Win*, 254–55.
311 **"There is a strong sense":** Undated campaign memo, provided to author.
311 **"That decision influenced everything":** Matthew Dowd, interview with PBS's *Frontline*, January 4, 2005, http://www.pbs.org/wgbh/pages/frontline/shows/architect/interviews/dowd.html.
311 **"We have, I reminded him":** Laura Bush, *Spoken from the Heart*, 302–3.
311 **"He brought up the fact":** Dick Cheney, author interview.
312 **"Cheney was pissed off":** Cheney friend, author interview.
312 **"The union of a man and":** George W. Bush, remarks, Roosevelt Room, February 24, 2004, http://georgewbush-whitehouse.archives.gov/news/releases/2004/02/20040224-2.html.
312 **The vice president called Mary:** Mary Cheney, *Now It's My Turn*, 173–78.
312 **64 percent of Americans:** Gallup poll, February 16–17, 2004, http://www.gallup.com/poll/147662/First-Time-Majority-Americans-Favor-Legal-Gay-Marriage.aspx. To get historical numbers, click on the trend data at the bottom of the page.
312 **Eleven states were poised:** All eleven were eventually approved by voters in November, by a collective two-to-one margin. The states were Arkansas, Georgia, Kentucky, Michigan, Mississippi, Montana, North Dakota, Ohio, Oklahoma, Oregon, and Utah. "Voters Pass All 11 Bans on Gay Marriage," Associated Press, November 3, 2004, http://www.msnbc.msn.com/id/6383353/ns/politics/t/voters-pass-all-bans-gay-marriage/#.T2qa-Xgjj-A. Bush won all but two of the states, Michigan and Oregon. http://www.nytimes.com/packages/html/politics/2004_ELECTIONRESULTS_GRAPHIC/.
312 **"gotten pretty well pummeled":** Notes of meeting by participant, provided to author.
313 **suffered a series of strokes:** "Bushes Mourn Death of Their Dog Spot," *New York Times*, February 22, 2004, http://www.nytimes.com/2004/02/22/us/bushes-mourn-death-of-their-dog-spot.html.
313 **"encircling her in the chill dusk":** Laura Bush, *Spoken from the Heart*, 299.

313 **"We don't negotiate with evil":** Glenn Kessler, "Impact from the Shadows: Cheney Wields Power with Few Fingerprints," *Washington Post*, October 4, 2004.
313 **He met with Bush:** Chinoy, *Meltdown*, 203–7.
313 **"The vice president feels very strongly":** Richard Armitage, author interview.
313 **"That's what we want":** Michael Green, author interview.
314 **"Diplomacy in the Bush administration":** Chinoy, *Meltdown*, 136.
314 **"Busy last night, huh?":** DeYoung, *Soldier*, 499–500.
314 **"The diplomats, whether they":** Stephen Yates, author interview.
314 **reauthorized twenty-two times:** Shannen W. Coffin (counsel to Dick Cheney) to Patrick Leahy, August 20, 2007, http://www.scribd.com/fullscreen/5999341. The letter listed all the dates of reauthorization up to that point.
314 **the "scary memos":** Unclassified Report on the President's Surveillance Program, prepared by the inspectors general of the Defense Department, Justice Department, Central Intelligence Agency, National Security Agency, and Office of the Director of National Intelligence, July 10, 2009, 9, http://www.fas.org/irp/eprint/psp.pdf.
315 **Under this part of the program:** Working draft of NSA inspector general report on surveillance activities, March 24, 2009.
315 **"If you rule that way":** Goldsmith, *Terror Presidency*, 71.
315 **"Instead of going around it":** Alberto Gonzales interview with *Frontline*, March 3, 2014.
315 **"We're going to push and push":** Goldsmith, *Terror Presidency*, 126.
315 **"We're one bomb away from":** Ibid., 181.
315 **"The president may have to":** Unclassified Report on the President's Surveillance Program, 22.
316 **"How can you possibly":** Gellman, *Angler*, 295–96.
316 **"critically important":** Unclassified Report on the President's Surveillance Program, 23.
316 **"The analysis is flawed":** Gellman, *Angler*, 295–96.
316 **"We think it is essential":** Michael Hayden, author interview.
316 **"You ought to get yourself":** Ibid.
316 **"None of them says":** Ibid.
316 **According to Card:** Andy Card, unpublished interview with Michael Schmidt of the *New York Times*.
316 **Comey did not wait for:** James Comey, testimony to Senate Judiciary Committee, May 15, 2007, http://gulcfac.typepad.com/georgetown_university_law/files/comey.transcript.pdf.
317 **"to aggravate the attorney general":** Gonzales, *Frontline* interview.
317 **"Not well":** Unclassified Report on the President's Surveillance Program, 25.
317 **"But that doesn't matter":** Comey testimony.
317 **"We said, 'Hope you are doing better' ":** Card, unpublished interview.
317 **stuck her tongue out at Card:** Dan Eggen and Peter Baker, "New Book Details Cheney Lawyer's Efforts to Expand Executive Power," *Washington Post*, September 5, 2007, http://www.washingtonpost.com/wp-dyn/content/article/2007/09/04/AR2007090402292.html. See also Goldsmith, *Terror Presidency*.
317 **"AG in chair; is feeble":** Robert Mueller, notes taken at the time and released three years later to Congress.
317 **One of the lawyers quietly:** Edward Whelan, who was Jack Goldsmith's deputy, sent a message via his BlackBerry to Brett Kavanaugh, a friend working in the White House. Kavanaugh took it to Andy Card. Barton Gellman, *Angler*, 302–7.
317 **Addington retyped the order:** Ibid., 311–13.

318 **terrorists set off ten bombs:** Elaine Sciolino, "Spain Struggles to Absorb Worst Terrorist Attack in Its History," *New York Times*, March 11, 2004, http://www.nytimes.com/2004/03/11/international/europe/11CND-TRAI.html?pagewanted=all. The casualty figures cited in this story were later updated. See "Spain to Mark Eighth Anniversary of Madrid Train Bombings," CNN, March 11, 2012, http://www.cnn.com/2012/03/10/world/europe/madrid-bombing-anniversary/index.html.

318 **"forced to withdraw the FBI":** Unclassified Report on the President's Surveillance Program, 27.

318 **"I was stunned," Bush said:** George W. Bush, *Decision Points*, 173–74.

318 **"I just don't understand":** Ibid.

318 **"I was about to witness":** Ibid.

318 **One Justice Department official:** Justice Department official, author interview.

318 **"I had little patience":** Dick Cheney, *In My Time*, 348–52.

319 **Cheney blocked a move to make:** Comey testimony.

319 **"Listen, I've been involved in":** Campaign adviser, author interview.

319 **"Cheney would be the attack":** McClellan, *What Happened*, 137.

319 **"I actually did vote for":** Richard W. Stevenson and Adam Nagourney, "Bush's Campaign Emphasizes Role of Leader in War," *New York Times*, March 17, 2004. Kerry later compounded the problem with a tortured explanation. "It just was a very inarticulate way of saying something, and I had one of those inarticulate moments late in the evening when I was dead tired in the primaries and I didn't say something very clearly," he told ABC News. See John Kerry, interview with ABC News, transcript, September 29, 2004, http://abcnews.go.com/Politics/Vote2004/story?id=123445&page=1#.UZgaQZV4W0t. He may have been dead tired, but it was not "late in the evening." The speech was at 1:20 in the afternoon. See "Kerry Discusses $87 Billion Comment," CNN, September 30, 2004, http://articles.cnn.com/2004-09-30/politics/kerry.comment_1_kerry-campaign-spokesman-inarticulate-moments-bush-campaign?_s=PM:ALLPOLITICS.

319 ***Game, set, and match*:** Mark McKinnon, author interview.

319 **"When I saw that":** Cheney interview.

320 **"Those weapons of mass":** George W. Bush, address to Radio and Television Correspondents Association dinner, March 24, 2004, http://www.c-spanvideo.org/program/TelevisionCorresp.

320 **"Dick has not been the asset":** DeFrank, *Write It When I'm Gone*, 195–98. DeFrank covered Ford from his days as vice president and had regular conversations in his retirement that, as the title implies, the former president insisted remain off the record until his death.

321 **"Where is Bush? Let him come":** Jeffrey Gettleman, "Enraged Mob in Falluja Kills 4 American Contractors," *New York Times*, March 31, 2004, http://www.nytimes.com/2004/03/31/international/worldspecial/31CND-IRAQ.html?pagewanted=all.

321 **"We ought to probably let":** Rajiv Chandrasekaran, "Key General Criticizes April Attack in Fallujah," *Washington Post*, September 13, 2004.

321 **Bremer also favored a strong:** Jerry Bremer, author interview. See also Bremer, *Year in Iraq*, 317. Bremer wrote that he told Rick Sanchez the morning after the contractors were killed: "We've got to react to this outrage or the enemy will conclude we're irresolute."

321 **"No, we've got to attack":** Sanchez, *Wiser in Battle*, 332–33.

321 **"Military commanders decide":** Donald Rumsfeld, author interview. In his book, Rumsfeld made no mention of opposition by the marines to opening the

assault on Fallujah or to any role by Washington in making the decision. Bush in his memoir made no mention of the April offensive in Fallujah.

321 **"At the end of this campaign":** Sanchez, *Wiser in Battle*, 349–50.

321 **"Kick ass!" Sanchez recalled:** Ibid. Jerry Bremer's description of the scene was more sedate. According to his notes, Bush said, "We need to be tougher than hell now. The American people want to know we're going after the bad guys. We need to get on the offensive and stay on the offensive." Bremer interview. See also Bremer, *My Year in Iraq*, 331–32.

322 **"The vice president was pretty adamant":** Official participant, author interview.

322 **"If you are going to take Vienna":** Cloud and Jaffe, *Fourth Star*, 152–53. Mattis was referring to the famous quotation from Napoleon Bonaparte: "When you set out to take Vienna, take Vienna." A spokeswoman for Mattis confirmed the quotation in an e-mail exchange with the author.

322 **"Let me say again":** John Abizaid, author interview.

322 **"We certainly increased the level":** Chandrasekaran, "Key General Criticizes April Attack in Fallujah."

322 **"a strategic disaster for America's":** Sanchez, *Wiser in Battle*, 369–71.

323 **"I wish you would have given":** George W. Bush, news conference, April 13, 2004, http://georgewbush-whitehouse.archives.gov/news/releases/2004/04/20040413-20.html.

323 ***Come on, sir, this one is:*** McClellan, *What Happened*, 205.

323 **"I kept thinking about what":** Ibid., 207.

323 **"How would you answer":** Adam Levine, author interview.

323 **"the guy being burned":** Tenet, *At the Center of the Storm*, 479–81.

323 **"Andy, I'm calling to tell you":** Ibid., 479–81.

324 **"My immediate suspicion":** Philip Zelikow, author interview.

324 **"a way of diluting":** Timothy Roemer, author interview.

325 **"This is the Oval Office":** There is a conflict about which commissioner was at risk of going over his time. In their book, *Without Precedent*, Tom Kean and Lee Hamilton identify him as Richard Ben-Veniste (pp. 207–10). But in his own book, *The Emperor's New Clothes*, Ben-Veniste says it was Timothy Roemer (p. 299), as does Philip Shenon in his account in *The Commission* (pp. 342–45). In an interview with the author, Roemer said he believed it was him.

325 **"Every time we asked":** Roemer interview.

325 **"I just think it was the fog of war":** Cheney interview.

325 **"The vice president isn't interested":** Ben-Veniste, *Emperor's New Clothes*, 304.

325 **"The commissioners go in":** Zelikow interview.

CHAPTER 18: "WHEN ARE WE GOING TO FIRE SOMEBODY?"

326 **"This is going to kill us":** Goldsmith, *Terror Presidency*, 141.

326 ***60 Minutes II* aired photographs:** "Army Probes POW Abuse," *60 Minutes II*, CBS, April 28, 2004, http://www.cbsnews.com/video/watch/?id=614704n.

326 **"I had no idea how graphic":** George W. Bush, *Decision Points*, 88–89.

326 **Investigators found a broad pattern:** Article 15-6 Investigation of the 800th Military Police Brigade, led by Major General Antonio M. Taguba, http://news.findlaw.com/wsj/docs/iraq/tagubarpt.html.

327 **"Read this," the secretary:** Sammon, *Strategery*, 44–45.

327 **"Mr. President, I want you to know":** Donald Rumsfeld to George W. Bush, handwritten letter, May 5, 2003. Accessed at http://www.rumsfeld.com.

327 **"Don, someone's head has to"**: Rumsfeld, *Known and Unknown*, 545–47.
327 **"Pretty smooth move"**: Dan Bartlett, author interview.
327 **"I don't accept your"**: Rumsfeld, *Known and Unknown*, 545–47.
327 **"I just don't want to put more"**: Latimer, *Speech-Less*, 96.
327 **"You'd be firing the wrong guy"**: Myers, *Eyes on the Horizon*, 262.
327 **"We have a predicament here"**: Bartlett interview.
328 **Bartlett called Larry Di Rita**: Bartlett and Larry Di Rita, author interviews. See also Graham, *By His Own Rules*, 464–67.
328 **"front-page headline"**: Robin Wright and Bradley Graham, "Bush Privately Chides Rumsfeld," *Washington Post*, May 6, 2004.
328 **This was your work?**: Bartlett interview.
328 **"Don, it was not Karl"**: Senior administration official, author interview.
328 **"Certainly since this firestorm"**: Donald Rumsfeld, testimony before Senate Armed Services Committee, May 7, 2003, Federal News Service transcript.
328 **"What's he doing?"**: Di Rita interview.
328 **"Rumsfeld has got to be fired"**: Matthew Dowd, author interview.
329 **had other duties to attend to**: Stewart, *Tangled Webs*, 198–200.
329 **"By this letter I am resigning"**: Donald Rumsfeld to George W. Bush, handwritten letter, May 9, 2003. Accessed at http://www.rumsfeld.com.
329 **"Mr. President, the Department"**: Rumsfeld, *Known and Unknown*, 550–51.
330 **"You are courageously"**: George W. Bush, remarks to reporters, Pentagon, May 10, 2003, http://georgewbush-whitehouse.archives.gov/news/releases/2004/05/20040510-3.html.
330 **"Don, thirty-five years ago"**: Rumsfeld, *Known and Unknown*, 550–51. See also Dick Cheney, *In My Time*, 420–21.
330 **"It was like a body blow"**: Donald Rumsfeld, author interview.
330 **"The pictures made me sick"**: Notes of meeting with President José Eduardo dos Santos of Angola, taken by White House official, May 12, 2004, provided to author.
330 **"As I said at the beginning"**: Colin Powell, author interview.
331 **"We are heroes in error"**: Jack Fairweather and Anton La Guardia, "Chalabi Stands By Faulty Intelligence That Toppled Saddam's Regime," *Telegraph*, February 19, 2004, http://www.telegraph.co.uk/news/worldnews/northamerica/usa/1454831/Chalabi-stands-by-faulty-intelligence-that-toppled-Saddams-regime.html.
331 **Bush was "really frosted"**: Bremer, *My Year in Iraq*, 290–91.
331 **"That statement finished him"**: Richard Perle, author interview.
332 **"What the hell is this?"**: Bonin, *Arrows of the Night*, 236–42. See also Tenet, *At the Center of the Storm*, 445–46.
332 **"I'd control Baghdad"**: Bremer, *My Year in Iraq*, 356–58.
332 **"What are we going to do"**: Sanchez, *Wiser in Battle*, 1–4.
333 **"I was not pleased"**: Rumsfeld, *Known and Unknown*, 661–62.
333 **"We never connected it up"**: Stephen Hadley, author interview.
333 **"It's time for me to go"**: Tenet, *At the Center of the Storm*, 483–84.
333 **"He's been a strong leader"**: George W. Bush, statement to reporters, http://georgewbush-whitehouse.archives.gov/news/releases/2004/06/20040603-2.html.
334 **"For him to quit when"**: Dick Cheney, *In My Time*, 412–16.
334 **"fortitude for the job"**: Goldsmith, *Terror Presidency*, 161.
334 **McKinnon arranged a peace**: Peter Baker, "Alliance and Rivalry Link Bush, McCain," *Washington Post*, April 29, 2007.
334 **"some unspoken bond"**: Ibid.
335 **"You are as big a terrorist"**: George W. Bush, *Decision Points*, 357–58.

335 **"changed his reasons for being":** David Henson, "Bush, Sheehans Share Moments," *Vacaville (Calif.) Reporter*, June 24, 2004.

335 **"Fuck yourself":** Helen Dewar and Dana Milbank, "Cheney Dismisses Critic with Obscenity," *Washington Post*, June 25, 2004.

335 **"Did you say that":** Liz Cheney, author interview.

335 **"You're about the only":** Steve Schmidt, author interview.

335 **"It was probably not language":** Dick Cheney, *In My Time*, 262.

336 **"I have no financial interest":** Dick Cheney, *Meet the Press*, NBC, September 14, 2003, http://www.msnbc.msn.com/id/3080244/ns/meet_the_press/t/transcript-sept/#.T2qjLXgjj-A.

336 **received $1.6 million:** Annenberg Public Policy Center's FactCheck.org, "Kerry Ad Falsely Accuses Cheney on Halliburton," September 30, 2004, http://www.factcheck.org/kerry_ad_falsely_accuses_cheney_on_halliburton.html.

336 **"Cheney doesn't gain financially":** Ibid.

336 **"found no evidence of":** Gellman, *Angler*, 389.

336 **"If Rove said he didn't":** Stewart, *Tangled Webs*, 201–2.

337 **the court overturned a lower:** *Cheney v. United States District Court for the District of Columbia*, June 24, 2004, http://www.law.cornell.edu/supct/search/display.html?terms=cheney&url=/supct/html/03-475.ZS.html.

337 **"We have long since made":** Sandra Day O'Connor, *Hamdi v. Rumsfeld*, June 28, 2004, http://www.law.cornell.edu/supct/html/03-6696.ZO.html.

337 **"Iraq is sovereign":** Condoleezza Rice to George W. Bush, note, June 28, 2004, http://upload.wikimedia.org/wikipedia/commons/2/20/Iraq-sovereign.jpg.

338 **Bush, worried about:** Bremer, *My Year in Iraq*, 384.

338 **had no substantive meeting:** George Casey, author interview.

338 **Karl Rove had assumed:** Thomas and the Staff of *Newsweek*, *Election 2004*, 82.

338 **"He's being described":** George W. Bush, remarks to reporters, July 7, 2004, http://georgewbush-whitehouse.archives.gov/news/releases/2004/07/20040707-3.html.

338 **"Governor, this is not true":** Shenon, *Commission*, 411–12.

339 **The Senate report found:** Report of the Senate Select Committee on Intelligence, http://web.mit.edu/simsong/www/iraqreport2-textunder.pdf.

339 **The 9/11 Commission spread blame:** *9/11 Commission Report*.

339 **"Senator Kerry has also said":** Dick Cheney, speech at Dayton, Ohio, convention center, August 12, 2004, http://georgewbush-whitehouse.archives.gov/news/releases/2004/08/20040812-3.html.

339 **"I need to know what do":** Dick Cheney, town hall meeting, Davenport, Iowa, August 24, 2004, http://georgewbush-whitehouse.archives.gov/news/releases/2004/08/20040824-4.html.

339 **fell nineteen votes short:** Called the Federal Marriage Amendment, the proposed text read, "Marriage in the United States shall consist only of the union of a man and a woman. Neither this Constitution, nor the constitution of any State, shall be construed to require that marriage or the legal incidents thereof be conferred upon any union other than the union of a man and a woman." http://thomas.loc.gov/cgi-bin/query/z?c108:S.J.RES.40:. Sponsored by Senator Wayne Allard, a Colorado Republican, it was defeated 50 to 48 on July 14, 2004, falling nineteen votes short of the two-thirds supermajority required. http://www.senate.gov/legislative/LIS/roll_call_lists/roll_call_vote_cfm.cfm?congress=108&session=2&vote=00155.

339 **"My own preference is as I've":** Cheney, town hall meeting. Oddly, the official White House transcript abruptly cut off Cheney's sentence at "my own pre—,"

omitting the part where he disagreed with Bush. The transcript then continued with more questions. The rest of the quotation cited here is from a transcript prepared by the Federal News Service.

339 **"We were all proud of him"**: Neil Patel, author interview.

340 **"They were pretty good"**: Cheney interview.

340 **Bush went to Hagin's hotel room**: Joe Hagin, author interview.

340 **"The situation on the ground"**: Gordon and Trainor, *Endgame*, 106.

340 **"Senator Kerry's liveliest"**: Dick Cheney, acceptance address at Republican National Convention, September 1, 2004, http://georgewbush-whitehouse.archives.gov/news/releases/2004/09/20040901-7.html.

340 **Gillespie suggested**: Gillespie, *Winning Right*, 29.

341 **"we need to do this"**: Michael Gerson, author interview.

341 **"I am fortunate to have"**: George W. Bush, acceptance address at Republican National Convention, September 2, 2004, http://georgewbush-whitehouse.archives.gov/news/releases/2004/09/20040902-2.html.

341 **"I didn't look at the audience"**: Gerson interview.

342 **"we can hear you now"**: Rocco Chierichella, author interview.

342 **"Mr. President, my daughter's"**: Eric Draper, author interview.

342 **Half of the twenty-two grants**: John Solomon, Alec MacGillis, and Sarah Cohen, "How Rove Directed Federal Assets for GOP Gains," *Washington Post*, August 19, 2007.

343 **grew alienated when his office**: Kuo, *Tempting Faith*, 206–7.

343 **death toll in Iraq hit one thousand**: "U.S. Death Toll in Iraq Tops 1,000," BBC News, September 8, 2004, http://news.bbc.co.uk/2/hi/middle_east/3636340.stm.

343 **"It's absolutely essential that"**: Dick Cheney, town hall meeting, Des Moines, September 7, 2004, http://georgewbush-whitehouse.archives.gov/news/releases/2004/09/20040907-8.html.

343 **"Dick Cheney's scare tactics"**: Amy Lorentzen, "Cheney Says 'Wrong Choice' on Election Day Would Risk Terrorist Attack," Associated Press, September 7, 2004.

343 **to ban the *New York Times***: Rick Lyman of the *Times* wrote an amusing piece about trying to chase Cheney around the country without access to Air Force Two. See Rick Lyman, "Desperately Seeking Dick Cheney," *New York Times*, September 19, 2004, http://www.nytimes.com/2004/09/19/weekinreview/19lyma.html.

343 **"That is what I meant"**: Anne Womack Kolton, author interview.

343 **"Bush thought Kerry"**: Rove, *Courage and Consequence*, 392–93.

344 **"You didn't feel the heightened"**: Judd Gregg, author interview.

344 **dubbed this *presidentialitis***: Bartlett interview.

344 **The latest Gallup poll**: George W. Bush led with 52 percent of likely voters compared with John Kerry's 44 percent in the Gallup poll taken September 24–26, 2004. http://www.gallup.com/poll/18610/trial-heat-bush-vs-kerry-likely-voters.aspx.

344 **"If the president does reasonably"**: Matthew Dowd, author interview.

344 **"what do you want me to say"**: Bartlett interview.

344 **"a colossal error of judgment"**: Bush-Kerry debate transcript, University of Miami, September 30, 2004, http://www.debates.org/index.php?page=september-30-2004-debate-transcript.

345 **"They're going to report"**: Draper, *Dead Certain*, 256–57.

345 **"his dislike for"**: Rove, *Courage and Consequence*, 392–93.

345 **"he didn't really want to be"**: Ronald Kessler, *Laura Bush*, 189.

345 **"I don't know what happened"**: Thomas and the Staff of *Newsweek*, *Election 2004*, 150.

345 **"I don't think I was that"**: Sammon, *Strategery*, 172.
345 **The eight-point advantage**: George W. Bush and John Kerry were tied at 49 percent each in the Gallup poll taken October 1–3, 2004, immediately after the debate. http://www.gallup.com/poll/18610/trial-heat-bush-vs-kerry-likely-voters.aspx.
345 **"We came out of that debate"**: Dowd interview.
345 **"Sir, have you ever looked"**: Patel interview.
346 **"This is the situation"**: Dowd interview.
346 **"insane questions"**: Patel interview.
346 **"In the early ones"**: Tevi Troy, author interview.
346 **The day before the debate**: Hayes, *Cheney*, 457–58.
346 **"Your children and grandchildren"**: Mary Cheney, *Now It's My Turn*, 205–6.
347 **"Senator, frankly, you have"**: Cheney-Edwards debate, Case Western Reserve University, October 5, 2004, http://www.debates.org/index.php?page=october-5-2004-transcript.
347 **"*He thinks they love me*"**: Mary Cheney, *Now It's My Turn*, 205–6.
347 **"use the Constitution"**: Debate transcript.
348 **"was essentially destroyed"**: Report of the Iraq Survey Group, October 6, 2004, https://www.cia.gov/library/reports/general-reports-1/iraq_wmd_2004/Comp_Report_Key_Findings.pdf.
348 **"U.S. Report Finds Iraqis"**: *New York Times*, October 6, 2004, http://www.nytimes.com/2004/10/06/international/middleeast/06CND-INTE.html.
348 **"U.S. 'Almost All Wrong'"**: *Washington Post*, October 6, 2004, http://www.washingtonpost.com/ac2/wp-dyn/A9790-2004Oct5?language=printer.
348 **"I did some real homework"**: John McLaughlin, author interview.
348 **"We at CIA are not trying"**: Suskind, *One Percent Doctrine*, 330.
349 **"John Kerry exceeded voters'"**: Internal campaign summary of Orlando focus group, provided to author.
349 **"You're going to be great"**: Peter Baker, "The Final Days," *New York Times Magazine*, August 31, 2008, http://www.nytimes.com/2008/08/31/magazine/31bush-t.html?pagewanted=all.
349 **"Man, is he spun up"**: Ibid.
349 **"I think if you were to"**: Bush-Kerry debate, Arizona State University, October 13, 2004, http://www.debates.org/index.php?page=october-13-2004-debate-transcript.
349 **"You son of a bitch"**: Mary Cheney, *Now It's My Turn*, 222–27.
349 **"A complete and total sleazeball"**: Ibid.
350 **"Mom was especially furious"**: Liz Cheney, author interview.
350 **Mary was "fair game"**: Chris Wallace of Fox News asked Cahill if it was "over the line" for John Kerry to bring up Mary Cheney's sexual orientation. "There are a lot of questions here about gay marriage," she answered, "and she is someone who's a major figure in the campaign. I think that it's a fair game, and I think she's been treated very respectfully." Fox News Channel, October 13, 2004.
350 **"Well, sir, as long as Mary's"**: Mary Cheney, *Now It's My Turn*, 222–27.
350 **"Make it hurt"**: Ibid.
350 **"That this is a man with a dark"**: Liz Cheney interview.
350 **"She's my daughter"**: Patel interview.
350 **"I did have a chance to assess"**: David Stout, "Cheneys Criticize Kerry's Remarks on Daughter," *New York Times*, October 15, 2004, http://www.nytimes.com/2004/10/14/politics/campaign/14CND-DEBA.html?pagewanted=print&position=.

350 **"You saw a man who will"**: Michael Laris and Mike Allen, "Cheneys Steamed at Kerry Reference to Daughter," *Washington Post*, October 15, 2004, http://www.washingtonpost.com/wp-dyn/articles/A33588-2004Oct14.html.
350 **"I love my daughters"**: John Kerry, statement, October 14, 2004, cited in Tom Vanden Brook, "Kerry Lesbian Remark Angers Cheneys," *USA Today*, October 15, 2004, http://www.usatoday.com/news/politicselections/nation/president/2004-10-14-lynne-cheney_x.htm.
350 **"I think that it indicates a certain"**: Elizabeth Edwards, interview with ABC Radio, October 14, 2004.
351 **"Mary Cheney bounce"**: Dick Cheney interview.
351 **he had Osama bin Laden**: Notes taken by one of the reporters present, provided to author.
351 **"why we did not attack Sweden"**: Osama bin Laden, audiotape, aired October 30, 2004, and translated by Reuters. http://www.nytimes.com/2004/10/29/international/29WIRE-TRANS.html.
351 **"A vigorous, some might say"**: Ridge, *Test of Our Times*, 235–39.
351 **"I don't have to tell you"**: Bartlett interview.
352 **Over twenty-four hours**: David Hume Kennerly, "Dick Cheney's Final Assault Across America," *The Digital Journalist*, November 2004, http://digitaljournalist.org/issue0411/dis_kennerly.html.

CHAPTER 19: "THE ELECTION THAT WILL NEVER END"

353 **call his "accountability moment"**: Jim VandeHei and Michael A. Fletcher, "Bush Says Election Ratified Iraq Policy," *Washington Post*, January 16, 2005, http://www.washingtonpost.com/wp-dyn/articles/A12450-2005Jan15.html.
353 **"What is going to happen"**: Matthew Dowd, author interview.
353 **"Only one"**: Ken Mehlman, author interview.
353 **"What is Karl making me"**: White House official, author interview.
354 **Taylor read them over the phone**: Sara Taylor, author interview. After the White House, Taylor married and changed her name to Sara Taylor Fagen.
354 **"felt like he had just"**: George W. Bush, *Decision Points*, 294–95.
354 **"That doesn't make any"**: Draper, *Dead Certain*, 268–69.
354 **An upset Condoleezza Rice**: Rice, *No Higher Honor*, 287.
354 **"Look, if it is what it is"**: Draper, *Dead Certain*, 268–69.
354 **"Whatever happens, I love you"**: White House official interview.
354 **"Here's why I think it's wrong"**: Mehlman interview.
354 **"He was in a dark place"**: Taylor Fagen interview.
355 **"Whatever happens, we left"**: Nicolle Devenish, author interview. Devenish later married and changed her name to Nicolle Wallace.
355 **"There are people still"**: Sammon, *Strategery*, 185–88.
355 **he were "in a daze"**: George W. Bush, *Decision Points*, 294–95.
355 **"moped around the Treaty Room"**: Ibid.
355 **"were feeling a little sick"**: Lynne Cheney, unpublished interview with journalist Robert Draper.
355 **"I blew it off"**: Sammon, *Strategery*, 185–88.
356 **"This is the election"**: Rove, *Courage and Consequence*, 400.
356 **"some of them were a little"**: Ibid.
356 **At 12:41 a.m., Fox News**: Rachel Smolkin, "Lesson Learned," *American Journalism Review*, December/January 2005, http://www.ajr.org/article.asp?id=3783.

356 **"He just looked relieved"**: Eric Draper, author interview.
356 **"We're getting different"**: Sammon, *Strategery*, 193–98.
357 **"Katie, you're the youngest"**: Lynne Cheney, unpublished Draper interview.
357 **"Go on, nothing's going to"**: Sammon, *Strategery*, 193–98.
357 **Bush and Cheney advisers debated**: Michael Gerson, author interview. Some accounts have Andy Card calling Mary Beth Cahill a third time, but in an e-mail exchange with the author, she said she remembered only two calls.
357 **But Nicolle Devenish had been**: Wallace (Devenish) interview.
357 **Hold off, he urged**: Michael McCurry, author interview.
357 **"You cannot go out there"**: Woodward, *State of Denial*, 348–49.
357 **"George, you can't go out"**: George W. Bush, *Decision Points*, 294–95.
357 **Card called James Baker**: Baker, *"Work Hard, Study . . . and Keep out of Politics!,"* 391–94.
358 **Jordan made the call**: Vernon Jordan, e-mail exchange with author.
358 **"Kerry is calling now"**: Nicolle Wallace (Devenish) interview.
358 **"grinning ear to ear"**: McClellan, *What Happened*, 235.
358 **"That was a job interview"**: Administration official, author interview.
358 **"Mr. President, I have Senator"**: George W. Bush, *Decision Points*, 296.
358 **"You were an admirable"**: Notes of phone call taken by White House official, provided to author.
358 **50.7 percent of the vote**: National Archives and Records Administration, http://www.archives.gov/federal-register/electoral-college/2004/popular_vote.html. History records no popular vote margins for the first four reelected presidents, George Washington, Thomas Jefferson, James Madison, and James Monroe.
358 **to win an absolute majority**: Bill Clinton won 43 percent of the popular vote in 1992 and 49 percent in 1996, with Ross Perot running as an independent in both races. George W. Bush won 48 percent of the popular vote in 2000.
358 **Bush picked up 286 votes**: John Kerry won states totaling 252 electoral votes, but one elector in Minnesota voted for John Edwards instead. National Archives and Records Administration, http://www.archives.gov/federal-register/electoral-college/2004/election_results.html.
358 **party increasing its hold**: Republicans picked up three seats in the House and four in the Senate as George W. Bush won reelection. Dwight D. Eisenhower, Richard M. Nixon, Ronald Reagan, and Bill Clinton all suffered losses in the Senate the years they were reelected, and Eisenhower and Clinton also lost seats in the House. See http://www.presidency.ucsb.edu/data/presidential_elections_seats.php.
358 **He improved his showing**: Exit poll results, 2000 and 2004. Overall, George W. Bush improved his share of the popular vote by three percentage points, but he improved by five points among women, nine points among Latinos, seven points among those sixty and older, ten points among those without a high school degree, and six points among Jews. He won 86 percent of those who named terrorism as the most important issue and 80 percent of those who named moral values, while Kerry won 73 percent of those who named Iraq. Of those voting in 2004, 43 percent said they voted for Bush four years earlier and 37 percent said they voted for Gore, which, given that Gore won the popular vote in 2000, means that Kerry did not get as many Gore voters to the polls as Bush did his own supporters. The 2000 exit polls are available at ABC News at http://abcnews.go.com/sections/politics/2000vote/general/exitpoll_hub.html, while the 2004 exit polls are available at CNN at http://www.cnn.com/ELECTION/2004/pages/results/states/US/P/00/epolls.0.html.

358 **Just 51 percent of Americans:** Exit polls. http://www.cnn.com/ELECTION/2004/pages/results/states/US/P/00/epolls.0.html.
359 **"We're going to have fun":** Draper, *Dead Certain*, 274.
359 **"Where's the vice president?":** White House official, author interview.
359 **"Congratulations, Dick":** Ibid.
359 **"He's a man of deep conviction":** Dick Cheney, victory speech, November 3, 2004, http://georgewbush-whitehouse.archives.gov/news/releases/2004/11/20041103-5.html.
359 **"The vice president serves":** George W. Bush, victory speech, November 3, 2004, http://georgewbush-whitehouse.archives.gov/news/releases/2004/11/20041103-3.html.
359 **"Everybody was buoyant":** Frederick Jones, author interview.
359 **"I want to especially thank Scotty":** Mark Leibovich, "Unanswer Man," *Washington Post*, December 22, 2005, http://www.washingtonpost.com/wp-dyn/content/article/2005/12/21/AR2005122102272.html.
360 **"I expect there to be lots":** Notes of meeting, provided to author.
360 **"I remember our conversation":** Ibid.
360 **"They were toast if you lost":** Ibid.
360 **"I hear you're thinking":** Gerson interview.
360 **"I earned capital":** George W. Bush, news conference, November 4, 2004, http://georgewbush-whitehouse.archives.gov/news/releases/2004/11/20041104-5.html.

CHAPTER 20: "NOT A SPEECH DICK CHENEY WOULD GIVE"

361 **"wasn't fully on board":** George W. Bush, *Decision Points*, 90.
361 **"insurgency against the rest":** Stephen Yates, author interview.
362 **"was for the best":** Dick Cheney, *In My Time*, 425–26.
362 **"secretive, little-known cabal":** Lawrence B. Wilkerson, "The White House Cabal," *Los Angeles Times*, October 25, 2005, http://articles.latimes.com/2005/oct/25/opinion/oe-wilkerson25.
362 **"Powell really thought that":** White House official, author interview.
362 **"He had thought about it":** Dick Cheney, author interview.
362 **refer to Bush as "my husb—":** Condoleezza Rice was at a dinner at the home of Philip Taubman, Washington bureau chief of the *New York Times*, and his wife, Felicity Barringer, a *Times* correspondent, when she was overheard to say, "As I was telling my husb—" before catching herself and saying, "As I was telling President Bush." Deborah Schoeneman, "Condi's Slip," *New York*, April 26, 2004, http://nymag.com/nymetro/news/people/columns/intelligencer/n_10245/. In her book on Rice, Elisabeth Bumiller of the *Times* wrote that two guests heard the remark but she and most others did not. See Bumiller, *Condoleezza Rice*, 228–29, 370.
362 **"She was treated like":** Senior administration official, author interview.
362 **"I can count on one hand":** Christine Todd Whitman, author interview.
362 **"He was very wary":** David Gordon, author interview.
363 **"People don't understand":** Draper, *Dead Certain*, 286.
363 **"I personally favor an NSC":** Donald Rumsfeld, author interview.
363 **"I was struck by how deft":** McClellan, *What Happened*, 243.
363 **"I want you to be secretary":** Condoleezza Rice, author interview.
363 **"repair work to do":** Rice, *No Higher Honor*, 292–93.
364 **"I don't intend to spend":** Ibid., 541.
364 **"At times, Don frustrated":** George W. Bush, *Decision Points*, 91–94.

364 **"was criminal negligence"**: Kenneth Adelman, author interview. Wolfowitz told the author that "I had my differences with Rumsfeld" but "I would not have used those words."

364 **"the right fit"**: George W. Bush, *Decision Points*, 91–94.

364 **"He was not going to trust"**: Peter Baker and Susan Schmidt, "Ashcroft's Complex Tenure at Justice," *Washington Post*, May 20, 2007, http://www.washingtonpost.com/wp-dyn/content/article/2007/05/19/AR2007051901275.html.

364 **"a self-promoter and grandstander"**: Senior administration official, author interview.

365 **"I thought we were going"**: Colin Powell, author interview.

365 **"If I go, Don should go"**: Woodward, *State of Denial*, 362.

365 **"out of nowhere"**: George W. Bush, *Decision Points*, 91–94.

365 **Powell told no one**: DeYoung, *Soldier*, 8–10.

365 **"As we have discussed"**: Colin Powell to George W. Bush, resignation letter, November 12, 2004, http://www.washingtonpost.com/wp-srv/politics/documents/cabinetresignations/powell.pdf.

366 **"You mean Rumsfeld?"**: Michael Gerson, author interview.

366 **"one of the great public"**: George W. Bush, written statement, November 15, 2004, http://georgewbush-whitehouse.archives.gov/news/releases/2004/11/20041115-2.html.

366 **"We are not winning"**: Gordon and Trainor, *Cobra II*, 496.

367 **About fifteen thousand American and British troops**: "US Troops Storm Towards Centre of Fallujah," Agence France-Presse, November 9, 2004.

367 **Three relatives of Prime**: Karl Vick and Naseer Nouri, "3 Allawi Relatives Held Hostage," *Washington Post*, November 11, 2004.

367 **2,175 insurgents reported killed**: Gordon and Trainor, *Endgame*, 120.

367 **"The elections should not be"**: George W. Bush and President Olusegun Obasanjo of Nigeria, remarks to reporters, December 2, 2004, http://georgewbush-whitehouse.archives.gov/news/releases/2004/12/20041202-3.html.

368 **uncover a trove of disturbing**: John Solomon and Peter Baker, "White House Looked Past Alarms on Kerik," *Washington Post*, April 8, 2007, http://www.washingtonpost.com/wp-dyn/content/article/2007/04/07/AR2007040701398.html?hpid opnews.

369 **"These three men symbolize"**: George W. Bush, remarks, Medal of Freedom ceremony, December 14, 2004, http://georgewbush-whitehouse.archives.gov/news/releases/2004/12/20041214-3.html.

369 **Tenet had signed a book contract**: Hillel Italie, "Former CIA Director Tenet Agrees to Book Deal with Crown Publishing," Associated Press, December 7, 2004.

369 **Tenet put the book project**: "Former CIA Director Puts Off Memoir," Associated Press, March 2, 2005.

369 **"You won't hear anything about"**: Kean and Hamilton, *Without Precedent*, 315.

370 **"The result would be a train"**: Donald Rumsfeld to George W. Bush, memo, September 11, 2004, http://library.rumsfeld.com/doclib/sp/390/To%20President%20George%20W.%20Bush%20re%20Intelligence%20'Reform'%2009-11-2004.pdf#search="train%20wreck."

370 **"the differences in the opinions"**: Yoo, *War by Other Means*, 183.

371 **"Not only did he read it"**: Natan Sharansky, author interview.

371 **"It says what I believe"**: Notes of meeting with rabbis and Jewish community leaders, taken by White House official, December 9, 2004, provided to author.

371 **"I'm not calling about":** Gerson interview.
371 **"If there is ever to be a moment":** John Lewis Gaddis to White House, memo, January 2005.
372 **"ought to be a big idea":** John Lewis Gaddis, author interview.
372 **"utterly utopian":** Charles Krauthammer, e-mail exchange with author.
372 **considered it "boffo":** Eliot Cohen, author interview.
372 **"Nobody likes tyrants":** Gaddis interview.
372 **the president suggested a metaphor:** Gerson interview.
372 **"John Kennedy could have":** John McConnell, author interview.
373 **"That's why you don't show":** Bartlett interview.
373 **"it was over the top in terms":** Powell interview.
373 **"I worried that it would be":** Rumsfeld interview.
373 **"that is kind of a big goal":** Condoleezza Rice, author interview.
373 **"This is not a speech Dick":** Woodward, *State of Denial*, 377.
373 **his "left-wing daughter":** Cheney interview.
374 **"Unless there were some reason":** Ibid.
374 **"Dan, subsistence, subsistence":** McConnell interview.
375 **"We have seen our vulnerability":** George W. Bush, inaugural address, January 20, 2005, http://georgewbush-whitehouse.archives.gov/news/releases/2005/01/20050120-1.html.
375 **"Don't back down one bit":** Hadley interview.

CHAPTER 21: "WHO DO THEY THINK THEY ARE? I WAS REELECTED TOO"

379 **asked for the duty officer:** George W. Bush, *Decision Points*, 360.
379 **"We'll see who's right":** Woodward, *State of Denial*, 382.
379 **"the haggard capital":** Anthony Shadid, "Iraqis Defy Threats as Millions Vote," *Washington Post*, January 31, 2005.
380 **the military recorded 299 attacks:** Casey, *Strategic Reflections*, 71.
380 **"You have to turn on":** Woodward, *State of Denial*, 383.
381 **skeptics on his team:** Senior administration officials, author interviews.
381 **told a Bush aide they:** Grover Norquist, author interview.
381 **Senator Mitch McConnell:** Al Hubbard, author interview.
381 **"For the first time in":** Hamburger and Wallsten, *One Party Country*, 201–6.
381 **"create a crisis mentality":** McClellan, *What Happened*, 248.
381 **While nearly seventeen:** In the earliest years of the program, there were actually 42 workers per retiree, but after the program was expanded into closer to what it would become in the modern era, the ratio fell to 16.5 to 1 in 1950 and descended from there. Still, the ratio had largely stabilized in recent years. It had fallen to 3 to 1 by 1975, three decades before Bush would launch his initiative. Social Security Administration, http://www.socialsecurity.gov/OACT/TR/2010/lr4b2.html.
381 **By 2018, the system would:** Status of the Social Security and Medicare Programs, 2004 Annual Reports, http://www.ssa.gov/history/pdf/tr04summary.pdf.
381 **expenditures had overtaken:** Ibid.
382 **at least $700 billion:** Michael A. Fletcher and Peter Baker, "Bush Makes Case for Social Security Plan," *Washington Post*, February 3, 2005.
382 **"maximizes the chance of getting":** Keith Hennessey to Senior Staff, memo, "Subject: Social Security Strategy," January 10, 2005, provided to author.
382 **"By the year 2042":** George W. Bush, State of the Union address, February 2,

2005, http://georgewbush-whitehouse.archives.gov/news/releases/2005/02/2005 0202-11.html.

382 **picking five states that:** George W. Bush traveled to North Dakota, Montana, Nebraska, Arkansas, and Florida. The Democratic senators targeted were Kent Conrad, Byron Dorgan, Max Baucus, Ben Nelson, Mark Pryor, Blanche Lincoln, and Bill Nelson.

383 **Condoleezza Rice, knew Khodorkovsky:** Susan Glasser and Peter Baker, "The Billionaire Dissident," *Foreign Policy*, May/June 2010, http://www.foreignpolicy.com/articles/2010/04/26/the_billionaire_dissident?page=full.

383 **"You talk about Khodorkovsky":** George W. Bush, teleconference with Tony Blair, March 1, 2005. Notes of call, provided to author.

383 **"Don't lecture me about":** George W. Bush, *Decision Points*, 432–33.

383 **"Why don't you talk a lot":** George W. Bush and Vladimir Putin, news conference, Bratislava, Slovakia, July 24, 2005, http://georgewbush-whitehouse.archives.gov/news/releases/2005/02/20050224-9.html.

384 **"It was fairly unpleasant":** Notes of call, provided to author.

384 **"enemy forces":** Reeves, *President Reagan*, 164.

384 **"It's strange for me to say":** David Ignatius, "Beirut's Berlin Wall," *Washington Post*, February 23, 2005.

384 **"This is the most difficult":** Peter Baker, "Mideast Strides Lift Bush, but Challenges Remain," *Washington Post*, March 8, 2005.

384 **"he may have had it right":** Daniel Schorr, "The Iraq Effect? Bush May Have Had It Right," *Christian Science Monitor*, March 4, 2005, http://www.csmonitor.com/2005/0304/p09s03-cods.html.

384 **"Where Bush Was Right":** *Newsweek*, March 14, 2005, http://www.jadaliyya.com/content_images/fck_images/lebanon/2005-03-14_newsweek_cover.jpg. The headline on the cover was slightly different from the one on the story inside by Fareed Zakaria, which was headlined "What Bush Got Right," http://www.thedailybeast.com/newsweek/2005/03/13/what-bush-got-right.html.

385 **"The second term is going":** Stephen Hadley, author interview.

385 **"What I think happened":** Karen Hughes, author interview.

385 **"Our nation has won two wars":** Christopher Hill, author interview.

385 **"the time for diplomacy is now":** Senate Foreign Relations Committee hearing, January 18, 2005, Federal News Service transcript. She actually used the phrase three times during her testimony to emphasize the point.

385 **"What it was basically saying":** Rice adviser, author interview.

385 **"that was essentially a declaration":** Another Rice adviser, author interview.

386 **"Who do they think they":** Woodward, *State of Denial*, 391.

386 **"readjust the thermometer":** Frances Fragos Townsend, author interview.

387 **"You're allowed to talk":** Steve Schmidt, author interview.

388 **"Here, sit in the hot-wired":** Person in the room, author interview.

388 **"Do I have to do this":** Ibid.

389 **"Bigger, tougher, stronger":** Peter Baker and Susan Glasser, *Kremlin Rising* (Dulles, Va.: Potomac Books, 2007), 389.

389 **"You're making many":** George W. Bush, address, Tbilisi, Georgia, May 10, 2005, http://georgewbush-whitehouse.archives.gov/news/releases/2005/05/20050510-2.html.

389 **landed sixty-one feet from Bush:** FBI summary of event and subsequent investigation, January 11, 2006, http://www.fbi.gov/news/stories/2006/january/grenade_attack011106. Georgian authorities working with the FBI later identi-

fied the would-be assassin as Vladimir Arutyunian, an Armenian born in Georgia, and arrested him at his apartment. Arutyunian killed a Georgian police officer during the arrest. His DNA matched a sample found on the red plaid cloth that had been wrapped around the grenade; he was convicted for the attempted assassination and the killing of the police officer and sentenced to life in prison. Arutyunian admitted throwing the grenade, saying he tossed it in a way that he hoped would spread shrapnel over the transparent bulletproof barrier that partially shielded the podium, but his motive remained a mystery.

390 **"Whatever we need to do":** Reid, *Good Fight*, 152. A spokesman for Max Baucus confirmed the account in an e-mail exchange with the author.

390 **had fallen from 58 percent:** Survey released by the Pew Research Center for the People and the Press on May 19, 2005, http://www.people-press.org/2005/05/19/economy-iraq-weighing-down-bush-popularity/.

391 **"The military needs that":** Rice, *No Higher Honor*, 458–59.

391 **"Human rights trump":** Rumsfeld, *Known and Unknown*, 635–36.

391 **the "olive branch tour":** Nicholas Burns, author interview.

392 **"That makes sense":** Condoleezza Rice, author interview.

392 **"There certainly seemed":** Christine Todd Whitman, author interview.

392 **"The interagency dynamic":** Kristen Silverberg, author interview.

392 **"very, very focused":** Administration official, author interview.

392 **"I've never heard him":** White House official, author interview.

393 **"I thought the vice president":** Frederick Jones, author interview.

393 **"they're in the last throes":** Dick Cheney, *Larry King Live*, CNN, May 30, 2005, http://transcripts.cnn.com/TRANSCRIPTS/0505/30/lkl.01.html.

393 **"Where did that come":** Meghan O'Sullivan, author interview.

393 **1,330 civilian deaths:** Iraq Body Count compilation. Iraq Body Count attempted to track civilian casualties in Iraq by assembling all public reports of killings, from media accounts to hospital and morgue records to official and nongovernmental organizations. http://www.iraqbodycount.org/database/.

393 **366 had been killed:** Iraq Coalition Casualty Count, known as icasualties.org, http://icasualties.org/iraq/ByMonth.aspx. Note that this link goes to the page showing all coalition casualties; to get the American casualties requires using the filter at the bottom.

393 **"final acts of desperation":** Dick Cheney, *In My Time*, 433–34.

393 **"was obviously wrong":** Hayes, *Cheney*, 477.

393 **"getting really bubbled":** Woodward, *State of Denial*, 399–400.

393 **"disconnected from reality":** Kevin Whitelaw, "Hit by Friendly Fire," *U.S. News & World Report*, June 19, 2005, http://www.usnews.com/usnews/news/articles/050627/27bush.htm.

393 **"It was analog, not digital":** Person close to George W. Bush, author interview.

394 **"No one other than the president":** Michele Davis, author interview.

394 **wear a metal bracelet:** Peter Baker and Dana Milbank, "Bush Says War Is Worth Sacrifice," *Washington Post*, June 29, 2005.

394 **"Like most Americans":** George W. Bush, address to nation, Fort Bragg, June 28, 2005, http://georgewbush-whitehouse.archives.gov/news/releases/2005/06/20050628-7.html.

394 **"our mission and our goal":** Cannon, Dubose, and Reid, *Boy Genius*, 296.

395 **"doing something good for someone":** White House summary of the meeting, provided to author.

395 **"There was little support among":** Brian Hook, author interview.

CHAPTER 22: "WHACKED UPSIDE THE HEAD"

396 **delivering a sealed envelope:** Notes from senior administration official, provided to author.
396 **Franks again spoke against:** Person familiar with meeting, author interview.
396 **his home-state favorite:** Peter Baker, "Unraveling the Twists and Turns of the Path to a Nominee," *Washington Post*, July 25, 2005.
397 **"It's O'Connor":** George W. Bush, *Decision Points*, 97–99.
397 **"It has been a great privilege":** Sandra Day O'Connor to George W. Bush, July 1, 2005, http://www.supremecourt.gov/publicinfo/press/oconnor070105.pdf.
397 **"What makes this harder":** Toobin, *The Oath*, 209.
397 **"You're one of the great Americans":** Notes of call, provided to author. George W. Bush a few days later wrote O'Connor a heartfelt two-page handwritten note. "Your call reminded me of how lucky we are as a nation to have a decent, honest, and brilliant citizen, you, serve the country," he wrote. "Thanks for a life of public service that will shine the light for others to follow." Letter from Bush, July 4, 2005. George W. Bush Presidential Library and Museum, http://www.georgewbushlibrary.smu.edu/Photos-and-Videos/Photo-Galleries/Sneak-Peek-Document-Gallery.aspx.
398 **"He doesn't quite fit":** Leonard Leo, author interview.
398 **"You can and should do":** Boyden Gray, author interview.
398 **"I don't like it when a friend":** George W. Bush, remarks to reporters, Lyngby, Denmark, July 6, 2005, http://georgewbush-whitehouse.archives.gov/news/releases/2005/07/20050706-3.html.
399 **"Sure, I would really like":** Laura Bush, interview on *Today*, NBC, July 12, 2005.
399 **"I didn't realize she'd put":** George W. Bush, remarks to reporters, Oval Office, July 12, 2005, http://georgewbush-whitehouse.archives.gov/news/releases/2005/07/20050712-1.html.
399 **gave each a tour:** Michael Luttig, author interview.
399 **"Why would that be":** Ibid.
399 **earlier had issued a ruling:** *Hamdan v. Rumsfeld*, U.S. Court of Appeals for the District of Columbia Circuit, July 15, 2005, http://www.mc.mil/Portals/0/Hamdan%20v.%20Rumsfeld,%20415%20F.3d%2033%20(D.C.%20Cir.%202005).pdf.
400 **also by Bush's longtime friend:** Donald Ensenat, e-mail exchange with author.
400 **Cheney supported Luttig:** Administration officials, author interviews. See also George W. Bush, *Decision Points*, 98. In an interview with the author, Cheney did not dispute Luttig was his choice, saying only that Luttig was "one of the top three candidates we had."
400 **thirty-nine times:** John Roberts, official White House biography, http://georgewbush-whitehouse.archives.gov/infocus/judicialnominees/roberts.html.
400 **"It probably means Roberts":** Gray interview.
400 **"You're going to love":** Baker, "Unraveling the Twists and Turns of the Path to a Nominee."
400 **"I just offered the job":** Peter Baker and Jim VandeHei, "Bush Chooses Roberts for Court," *Washington Post*, July 20, 2005, http://www.washingtonpost.com/wp-dyn/content/article/2005/07/19/AR2005071900725.html.
401 **"Does your mother know?":** Crawford Greenburg, *Supreme Conflict*, 209.
401 **"We're gonna have to grab":** Gillespie, *Winning Right*, 195.
401 **"Congratulations on Roberts":** Gray interview.

401 **"I'm glad you liked my appointment":** Person present for conversation, author interview.

401 **slipped a veto threat:** Barton Gellman, *Angler*, 351.

402 **News reports revealed:** *Newsweek* reported on July 10, 2005, that Karl Rove talked with Matthew Cooper about Joseph Wilson's wife, citing the e-mail Cooper sent to editors immediately after their conversation. See Michael Isikoff, "Matt Cooper's Source," *Newsweek*, July 17, 2005, http://www.thedailybeast.com/newsweek/2005/07/17/matt-cooper-s-source.html. On July 15, the *New York Times* reported that Rove had spoken with Robert Novak, who mentioned that Wilson's wife worked at the CIA and had been involved in sending him to Niger. The paper reported that Rove replied, "I heard that too." See David Johnston and Richard W. Stevenson, "Rove Reportedly Held Phone Talk on C.I.A. Officer," *New York Times*, July 15, 2005, http://www.nytimes.com/2005/07/15/politics/15rove.html?pagewanted=all.

402 **"whacked upside the head":** McClellan, *What Happened*, 259.

402 **simply told the reporter:** Rove, *Courage and Consequence*, 329.

402 **"If someone committed a crime":** George W. Bush and Prime Minister Manmohan Singh of India, news conference, July 18, 2008, http://georgewbush-whitehouse.archives.gov/news/releases/2005/07/20050718-1.html.

402 **the 319th day either partially:** Jim VandeHei and Peter Baker, "Vacationing Bush Poised to Set a Record," *Washington Post*, August 3, 2005. By the time he left office after eight years, Bush had spent 490 days at the ranch, according to Mark Knoller, a CBS Radio correspondent and unofficial White House archivist, compared with Reagan's 335 days. Bush also spent part or all of 487 days at Camp David, according to Knoller's count, meaning he spent roughly one out of every three days while in office at one or the other.

403 **they were leather shoes:** Stephen Hadley, author interview.

403 **"There was like a hierarchy":** Steve Atkiss, author interview.

403 **devastating roadside explosion:** John Kifner and James Dao, "Death Visits a Marine Unit, Once Called Lucky," *New York Times*, August 7, 2005.

403 **"That really got him":** Hadley interview.

404 **referring to her as "Mom":** Richard W. Stevenson, "Fallen Soldier's Mother Vows Vigil to See Bush," *New York Times*, August 9, 2005, http://www.nytimes.com/2005/08/08/world/americas/08iht-protester.html.

404 **"Don't let the president":** Joe Hagin, author interview; Cindy Sheehan, e-mail exchange with author.

404 **"We are not going to":** Ibid.

405 **"I sympathize with Mrs. Sheehan":** George W. Bush, remarks to reporters, August 11, 2005, http://georgewbush-whitehouse.archives.gov/news/releases/2005/08/20050811-1.html.

405 **no way the Iraqis would make:** Administration official, author interview.

CHAPTER 23: "THIS IS THE END OF THE PRESIDENCY"

406 **its cruising altitude:** Peter Baker, "Vacation Ends, and Crisis Management Begins," *Washington Post*, September 1, 2005, http://www.washingtonpost.com/wp-dyn/content/article/2005/08/31/AR2005083101283.html.

406 **"It's devastating":** Ibid.

407 **"The challenges that we face":** George W. Bush, remarks to reporters,

August 31, 2005, http://georgewbush-whitehouse.archives.gov/news/releases/2005/08/20050831-3.html.

407 **"He has to get off his"**: Baker, "Vacation Ends."

407 **"perhaps a little complacent"**: McClellan, *What Happened*, 279.

407 **"The forecast we have now"**: Transcript of conference call, August 28, 2005, http://www.popularmechanics.com/science/environment/2413906.

408 **"I can't get it through their heads"**: Joe Hagin, author interview.

408 **"This is going to be a really, really big storm"**: Kathleen Babineaux Blanco, author interview.

408 **"We're going to need everything you've got"**: Ibid. See also Evan Thomas, "How Bush Blew It," *Newsweek*, September 19, 2005, http://www.thedailybeast.com/newsweek/2005/09/18/how-bush-blew-it.html.

409 **"What's the situation?"**: Cooper and Block, *Disaster*, 160–61. See also Michael Brown, interview with Brian Williams, NBC News, March 2, 2006, http://www.nbcnews.com/id/11595834#.UT99fI5RWps.

409 **He did not realize Martha Raddatz**: While White House reporters traveling with Bush were kept in a separate press area, Raddatz was traveling with Donald Rumsfeld and happened to be backstage with Pentagon officials.

409 **"He's going to be at ten thousand"**: Scott McClellan, author interview.

409 **At least don't bring**: Dan Bartlett, author interview.

409 **"Mr. President, I definitely need"**: Brinkley, *The Great Deluge*, 413–14.

409 **"I just ballparked it"**: Blanco interview.

409 **behaving like a "crack head"**: Brown and Schwarz, *Deadly Indifference*, 119–20.

410 **"They'll welcome the sight"**: Rice, *No Higher Honor*, 397.

410 **"overreach constitutionally"**: Steven Blum, author interview.

410 **"What the hell is taking"**: William Burck, author interview.

410 **"Tell 'em," Bartlett said**: Draper, *Dead Certain*, 328–29.

410 **"The results are not acceptable"**: George W. Bush, remarks to reporters, South Lawn, September 2, 2005, http://georgewbush-whitehouse.archives.gov/news/releases/2005/09/20050902.html.

411 **"What's that?" he snapped**: Brinkley, *Great Deluge*, 544–45.

411 **"Your guys, Mike Brown"**: Hagin, Bob Riley and Michael Chertoff, author interviews. In an interview years later, Riley stood by his assessment for his state: "I could not have asked for anyone to be more attentive than Mike was for Alabama."

411 **"Brownie," he said, "you're doing"**: George W. Bush, remarks to reporters, Mobile, Ala., September 2, 2005, http://georgewbush-whitehouse.archives.gov/news/releases/2005/09/20050902-2.html.

411 **"Would you please be quiet?"**: George W. Bush, *Decision Points*, 309.

411 **"near nervous breakdown"**: Brinkley, *Great Deluge*, 570.

411 **"Who's in charge of the city?"**: Blanco interview.

412 **"I'll talk to him again"**: Ibid.

412 **"I want you to sign it"**: Ibid.

413 **"I was in a position"**: Blum interview.

413 **"I'm not signing anything"**: Blanco interview.

413 **"could unleash holy hell"**: George W. Bush, *Decision Points*, 309.

413 **"I don't care if we have to"**: Bartlett interview.

413 **"Look at the chain of command"**: Graham, *By His Own Rules*, 551.

414 **"This is the end of the presidency"**: Steve Schmidt, author interview.

414 **"primarily symbolic"**: Dick Cheney, *In My Time*, 430.

414 **"I asked Dick if he'd be"**: Gellman, *Angler*, 329–30.

414 **"Get the fuck off television":** Chertoff interview.
414 **"You do whatever you":** Ibid.
414 **had become "insubordinate":** Brown and Schwarz, *Deadly Indifference*, 203–4.
414 **cost 1,833 lives, did $108 billion in damage:** Richard D. Knabb, Jamie R. Rhome, and Daniel Brown, *Tropical Cyclone Report: Hurricane Katrina*, National Hurricane Center. First published December 20, 2005; updated September 14, 2011.
415 **"it was the worst moment":** George W. Bush, *Decision Points*, 326.
415 **"one of the largest":** George W. Bush, address to nation, Jackson Square, New Orleans, September 15, 2005, http://georgewbush-whitehouse.archives.gov/news/releases/2005/09/20050915-8.html.
415 **ultimately steered $126 billion:** White House Fact Sheet, http://georgewbush-whitehouse.archives.gov/infocus/katrina/. The United States spent $13 billion on the Marshall Plan from 1948 to 1951. Converted into modern dollars, that would be anywhere between $100 billion and $124 billion. As a share of the economy, however, the Marshall Plan was still significantly larger, roughly 5 percent of the gross domestic product of its time compared with 1 percent for the Katrina aid.
415 **"Can you believe they're":** Person in the room, author interview.
415 **"Look, we got another":** Dennis Hastert, author interview.
416 **"If there is a nuclear explosion":** Christopher Hill, author interview.
416 **Bush was in bed:** George W. Bush, *Decision Points*, 97–99.
417 **While Cheney briefly floated:** Toobin, *The Nine*, 97.
417 **"No white guys":** Crawford Greenburg, *Supreme Conflict*, 245.
417 **"We looked at every female appellate judge":** William Kelley, author interview.
418 **"If you nominate Harriet":** Ibid., 256–57.
418 **"What do you mean me?":** Peter Baker, "Once More, Bush Turns to His Inner Circle," *Washington Post*, October 4, 2005.
418 **"that schoolmarm voice":** Amy Goldstein and Peter Baker, "For Miers, Proximity Meant Power," *Washington Post*, October 13, 2005.
419 **"You probably aren't going":** Dick Cheney, *In My Time*, 324.
419 **"This is going to be a real":** Leonard Leo, author interview.
419 **"A good, heated debate":** Gillespie, *Winning Right*, 217–18.
419 **confirmed 78 to 22:** U.S. Senate roll call record, September 29, 2005, http://www.senate.gov/legislative/LIS/roll_call_lists/roll_call_vote_cfm.cfm?congress=109&session=1&vote=00245.
420 **Thompson said no:** Gillespie, *Winning Right*, 212. Fred Thompson said in an e-mail exchange with the author that he did not recall the exchange but had no reason to question it either.
420 **"if there's a qualified":** Gillespie, *Winning Right*, 212.
420 **"Leonard, are you there?":** Leo interview.
420 **"exceptionally well suited":** George W. Bush, announcement of Harriet Miers nomination, October 3, 2005, http://georgewbush-whitehouse.archives.gov/news/releases/2005/10/20051003.html.
420 **"reaction of many conservatives":** Peter Baker and Amy Goldstein, "Nomination Was Plagued by Missteps from the Start," *Washington Post*, October 28, 2005.
421 **"I'm confident that she":** Dick Cheney, interview with Rush Limbaugh, October 3, 2005, http://www.freerepublic.com/focus/f-news/1495840/posts.
421 **"the best person I could find":** George W. Bush, news conference, October 4, 2005, http://georgewbush-whitehouse.archives.gov/news/releases/2005/10/20051004-1.html.
421 **"She's the president's":** David Keene, e-mail exchange with author.
421 **"There is a whiff of sexism":** Peter Baker and Dan Balz, "Conservatives Con-

front Bush Aides," *Washington Post*, October 6, 2005. See also Gillespie, *Winning Right*, 214–15.

421 **"Are you saying people"**: Richard Lessner, e-mail exchange with author. See also Gillespie, *Winning Right*, 213–14.

421 **"I've had five 'trust-mes'"**: Baker and Balz, "Conservatives Confront Bush Aides."

421 **"What's different about"**: Ibid.

422 **"I do not care about them"**: Burck interview.

422 **"So, in this particular"**: Administration official, author interview.

422 **"she literally knew nothing"**: Ibid.

422 **"They wouldn't let us"**: Boyden Gray, author interview.

422 **"Harriet, you're going to"**: Crawford Greenburg, *Supreme Conflict*, 278–79. A spokesman for Jeff Sessions confirmed the account in an e-mail exchange with the author.

423 **"Harriet, you flunked"**: Ibid. A spokesman for Tom Coburn confirmed the account in an e-mail exchange with the author.

423 **"Dan, we can't do this"**: Bartlett interview.

423 **"We cannot put her through"**: Ibid.

423 **"You have to withdraw"**: Crawford Greenburg, *Supreme Conflict*, 283–84.

423 **"self-determination"**: Jo Becker, "In Speeches from 1990s, Clues About Miers Views," *Washington Post*, October 26, 2005, http://www.washingtonpost.com/wp-dyn/content/article/2005/10/25/AR2005102502038.html.

423 **Bush was working in his office**: Notes taken by White House official, provided to author.

424 **"If I had it to do over again"**: George W. Bush, *Decision Points*, 99–101.

424 **"I tried to tell him"**: Senior administration official, author interview.

CHAPTER 24: "YOU COULD HAVE HEARD A PIN DROP"

425 **had trouble sleeping**: Dan Bartlett, author interview.

425 **"You could have heard a pin"**: Scott McClellan, author interview.

425 **indictment on five counts**: *United States of America v. I. Lewis Libby*, October 28, 2005, http://www.justice.gov/archive/osc/documents/libby_indictment_28102005.pdf.

426 **"essentially to disable the vice president"**: Cheney aide, author interview.

426 **"all White House staffers"**: Peter Baker, "Bush Vows to Keep Focus on His Political Agenda," *Washington Post*, October 29, 2005, http://www.washingtonpost.com/wp-dyn/content/article/2005/10/28/AR2005102802189.html.

426 **"The lowest point that I"**: Peter Wehner, author interview.

426 **"The only hurt I ever saw"**: Alan Simpson, author interview.

426 **"Her stock went out of the roof"**: Bartlett interview.

427 **only "froth" in certain**: Nell Henderson, "Bernanke: There's No Housing Bubble to Go Bust," *Washington Post*, October 27, 2005.

427 **winnowed the list**: The other finalists were Greg Mankiw and Stephen Friedman, both former White House economists under Bush; John Taylor, a former Treasury Department official; and Martin Feldstein, once Ronald Reagan's economics adviser. Wessel, *In Fed We Trust*, 82–84.

427 **"strong economic fundamentals"**: Henderson, "Bernanke."

428 **"We are on the defensive"**: Lindsey Graham, author interview.

428 **"Basically, they told me"**: Aide to John McCain, author interview.

428 **"We had hardly started"**: Dick Cheney, *In My Time*, 358–61.

428 **the Senate voted 90 to 9:** U.S. Senate roll call record, October 5, 2005, http://www.senate.gov/legislative/LIS/roll_call_lists/roll_call_vote_cfm.cfm?congress=109&session=1&vote=00249.

428 **He reminded her that:** John Bellinger, author interview.

428 **the CIA had been holding:** Dana Priest, "CIA Holds Terror Suspects in Secret Prisons," *Washington Post*, November 2, 2005, http://www.washingtonpost.com/wp-dyn/content/article/2005/11/01/AR2005110101644.html. While the story omitted the names of Eastern European "black site" prisons, it reported that the CIA had run covert prisons at various points in eight different countries, including Afghanistan and Thailand.

429 **Even Bush had not been**: Michael Hayden, author interview.

429 **human rights activists:** Human Rights Watch examined flight records to track CIA airplanes making direct flights from Afghanistan to Poland and Romania. Human Rights Watch, Statement on U.S. Secret Detention Facilities in Europe, November 7, 2005, http://www.hrw.org/news/2005/11/06/human-rights-watch-statement-us-secret-detention-facilities-europe. In his book *The Way of the Knife*, Mark Mazzetti reported that Romania and Lithuania definitely hosted the prisons. The fuller list of sites was later reported by Adam Goldman in *The Washington Post* on January 24, 2014. The Poland site was emptied in 2003 and its detainees were scattered to Romania, Morocco and, later, Lithuania. http://www.washingtonpost.com/world/national-security/the-hidden-history-of-the-cias-prison-in-poland/2014/01/23/b77f6ea2-7c6f-11e3-95c6-0a7aa80874bc_story.html.

429 **"Two thousand and eight!":** Dick Cheney, address to Frontiers of Freedom 2005 Ronald Reagan Gala, November 16, 2005, http://georgewbush-whitehouse.archives.gov/news/releases/2005/11/20051116-10.html.

429 **"I'm sorry we couldn't be":** Ibid.

429 **"It's patriotic as heck":** George W. Bush, news conference, Gyeongju, South Korea, November 17, 2005, http://georgewbush-whitehouse.archives.gov/news/releases/2005/11/20051117.html.

430 **"We need a commander in chief":** Harry Reid, transcript of floor remarks released by his office, November 17, 2005.

430 **"a flawed policy wrapped":** John Murtha, news conference, U.S. Capitol, November 17, 2005, Federal News Service transcript.

430 **"The place where I did":** Cheney, oral history, Miller Center.

430 **"endorsing the policy positions":** Scott McClellan, written statement, November 18, 2005, http://georgewbush-whitehouse.archives.gov/news/releases/2005/11/20051118.html.

430 **"That was the beginning of keeping":** Nicolle (Devenish) Wallace, author interview.

430 **"Congressman Murtha is a fine":** George W. Bush, remarks to travel pool, Beijing, November 20, 2005, http://georgewbush-whitehouse.archives.gov/news/releases/2005/11/20051120-9.html.

431 **"We may be running out":** Administration official, author interview.

431 **"big screaming match":** Second administration official, author interview.

432 **"Karl kicks the shit out of me":** Third administration official, author interview.

432 **key to support even when:** Peter Baker and Dan Balz, "Bush Words Reflect Public Opinion Strategy," *Washington Post*, June 30, 2005, http://www.washingtonpost.com/wp-dyn/content/article/2005/06/29/AR2005062902792_pf.html.

432 **"National Strategy for Victory":** White House document, November 30, 2005, http://georgewbush-whitehouse.archives.gov/infocus/iraq/iraq_strategy_nov2005.html#part1.

432 **"We will never back down":** George W. Bush, speech at the U.S. Naval Academy, Annapolis, November 30, 2005, http://georgewbush-whitehouse.archives.gov/news/releases/2005/11/20051130-2.html.

432 **"Since the inception":** George W. Bush, speech and question-and-answer session, Philadelphia, December 12, 2005, http://georgewbush-whitehouse.archives.gov/news/releases/2005/12/20051212-4.html.

433 **casualties between 27,383:** Peter Baker, "Bush Estimates Iraqi Death Toll in War at 30,000," *Washington Post,* December 13, 2005. Iraq Body Count tabulated casualties based on media reports and hospital, morgue, NGO, and official figures. The British journal *Lancet* did an epidemiological study estimating 100,000 deaths in the first eighteen months of the war, based on door-to-door interviews in selected neighborhoods extrapolated nationwide. The *Lancet* methodology was the subject of fierce debate.

433 **analysts who "were slack-jawed":** Philip Taubman, author interview.

433 **planning to disclose the NSA program:** Risen, *State of War.*

433 **The White House considered obtaining:** Alberto Gonzales, interview with *Frontline,* March 3, 2014.

434 **"I know what it's like":** Several participants, author interviews.

434 **the case of a would-be terrorist:** The discussion referred to Iyman Faris, a naturalized American citizen from Kashmir who admitted meeting with al-Qaeda leaders and plotting to destroy the Brooklyn Bridge in 2002. Faris cased the bridge and researched "gas cutters" to sever its suspension cables. But according to the Justice Department, he eventually concluded that the plan "was unlikely to succeed because of the bridge's security and structure" and notified al-Qaeda. After his arrest, he pleaded guilty and was sentenced in 2003 to twenty years in prison for conspiracy and providing material support and resources to al-Qaeda. http://www.justice.gov/opa/pr/2003/October/03_crm_589.htm.

434 **"blood on our hands":** Bill Keller, author interview.

434 **"Whatever you think of Bush":** Ibid.

434 **Bush and Cheney felt betrayed:** White House officials were convinced that the *Times* posted the story before actually notifying them that it would run, despite their agreement. Bill Keller maintains the story did not go up on the Web site until after the call but agrees "we did cut it pretty close." Some of the confusion apparently stems from the time stamp on the Web story; the time listed reflected the time it was put into the *Times*'s internal system rather than the time it actually appeared on the site, so White House officials believed it had been posted earlier than it actually had been. Either way, Philip Taubman regretted the way it was handled. "I felt we hadn't delivered on our promise to give them some warning," he said.

434 **The story, under the headline:** James Risen and Eric Lichtblau, "Bush Lets U.S. Spy on Callers Without Courts," *New York Times,* December 16, 2005, http://www.nytimes.com/2005/12/16/politics/16program.html?pagewanted=all.

434 **"Maybe you should quit":** Frederick Jones, author interview.

435 **"a vital tool in our war":** George W. Bush, radio address, December 16, 2005, http://georgewbush-whitehouse.archives.gov/news/releases/2005/12/20051217.html.

435 **"He's a president, not a king":** Peter Baker, "President Says He Ordered NSA Domestic Spying," *Washington Post,* December 18, 2005.

435 **"seems to believe it is above":** Ibid.

435 **"just carrying too much":** Dick Cheney, *In My Time,* 353.

435 **"we aren't doing these things":** Ibid.

435 **308 to 122, again enough:** U.S. House Clerk's Office. http://clerk.house.gov/evs/2005/roll630.xml.

435 **"a good man who honors":** George W. Bush, remarks to reporters, December 15, 2005, http://georgewbush-whitehouse.archives.gov/news/releases/2005/12/20051215-3.html.

435 **"shocks the conscience":** Gellman, *Angler*, 353.

435 **"The rule is whether":** Dick Cheney, interview with Terry Moran of ABC News, Al Asad Air Base, Iraq, December 18, 2005, http://georgewbush-whitehouse.archives.gov/news/releases/2005/12/20051218-4.html.

436 **"in a manner consistent with":** President's Statement on Signing H.R. 2863, the Department of Defense Emergency Supplemental Appropriations, December 30, 2005, http://georgewbush-whitehouse.archives.gov/news/releases/2005/12/20051230-8.html.

436 **What about establishing:** Michael Abramowitz, "U.S. Promises on Darfur Don't Match Actions," *Washington Post*, October 29, 2007, http://www.washingtonpost.com/wp-dyn/content/story/2007/10/28/ST2007102801732.html.

437 **"This work has been especially":** George W. Bush, address to nation, December 18, 2005, http://georgewbush-whitehouse.archives.gov/news/releases/2005/12/20051218-2.html.

437 **eight-point bump:** George W. Bush's approval rating jumped from 39 percent in November to 47 percent in a survey December 15–18, *Washington Post*–ABC News poll, http://www.washingtonpost.com/wp-dyn/content/article/2005/12/19/AR2005121900924.html.

437 **"I'm on my second":** Rove, "Bush Is a Book Lover."

437 **"I am and always have":** Samuel Alito job application, November 1985.

438 **"Are you really a closet":** Amy Goldstein and Charles Babington, "Alito Leaves Door Open to Reversing 'Roe,'" *Washington Post*, January 12, 2006.

438 **"Sit down," he urged:** Steve Schmidt, author interview.

439 **Elliott Abrams, thought:** Abrams, *Tested by Zion*, 161.

439 **would claim 76 of 132 seats:** Scott Wilson, "Hamas Sweeps Palestinian Elections, Complicating Peace Efforts in Mideast," *Washington Post*, January 27, 2006, http://www.washingtonpost.com/wp-dyn/content/article/2006/01/26/AR2006012600372.html.

439 **"What do you think":** Rice, *No Higher Honor*, 417.

440 **net oil imports had risen:** United States Energy Information Administration, http://www.eia.gov/dnav/pet/pet_move_neti_a_ep00_imn_mbblpd_m.htm.

440 **replace more than 75 percent:** White House Fact Sheet, "Advanced Energy Initiative," January 31, 2006, http://georgewbush-whitehouse.archives.gov/news/releases/2006/01/20060131-6.html.

440 **"That was all him":** Jim Connaughton, author interview.

440 **The Senate had confirmed:** U.S. Senate roll call record, January 31, 2006, http://www.senate.gov/legislative/LIS/roll_call_lists/roll_call_vote_cfm.cfm?congress=109&session=2&vote=00002.

440 **"Keeping America competitive":** George W. Bush, State of the Union address, January 31, 2006, http://georgewbush-whitehouse.archives.gov/news/releases/2006/01/20060131-10.html.

CHAPTER 25: "PLEASE DO NOT LET ANYTHING HAPPEN TODAY"

441 **"The image of him falling":** Dick Cheney, interview with Brit Hume, Fox News, February 16, 2006, http://www.foxnews.com/story/0,2933,185013,00.html.

441 **"Harry, I had no idea you":** Ibid.

442 **"We have a problem"**: Neil Patel, author interview.
442 **"Has the vice president's office"**: Scott McClellan and Anita McBride, author interviews.
442 **"She felt very strongly"**: McBride interview.
442 **"Mr. Cheney shook my hand"**: Gilberto San Miguel Jr., Kenedy County Sheriff's Department, police report, February 15, 2006, http://www.thesmokinggun.com/documents/crime/texas-cops-release-cheney-shooting-report.
443 **"What are we going to do?"**: Patel interview.
443 **"We've got to get back"**: Patel and Lea Anne McBride, author interviews. McBride later married and now goes by Lea Anne Foster.
443 **"Let's get it to the local press"**: Mary Matalin, author interview.
443 **"We couldn't get hold"**: Dan Bartlett, speech to U.S. Chamber of Commerce, September 13, 2007, http://www.leadingauthorities.com/speaker/dan-bartlett.aspx.
444 **"tersely refused"**: Rove, *Courage and Consequence*, 460–61.
444 **"How are you doing?"**: Patel interview.
444 **"You did a good job"**: McClellan interview.
445 **"You are a fucking press"**: Administration official, author interview. In an interview, Matalin said she did not remember saying that but did not deny it either.
445 **"We've got to make him"**: McClellan interview.
445 **"Is this a big deal?"**: Matalin interview.
445 **"I fired and there's Harry"**: Cheney interview with Hume.
445 **"You know why I picked"**: McClellan interview.
446 **"That had a big effect"**: Peter Wehner, author interview.
446 **"People started rolling"**: White House official, author interview.
446 **"I always value Dick"**: Jim Langdon, author interview.
446 **"We've got a problem"**: Draper, *Dead Certain*, 362–63.
447 **"I really don't understand"**: George W. Bush, remarks to reporters, Air Force One, February 21, 2006, http://georgewbush-whitehouse.archives.gov/news/releases/2006/02/20060221-1.html.
447 **"I was trying to get him"**: Draper, *Dead Certain*, 362–63.
447 **"an immediate moratorium"**: Jim VandeHei and Jonathan Weisman, "Bush Threatens Veto Against Bid to Stop Port Deal," *Washington Post*, February 22, 2006.
447 **"This is as 9/11"**: Ellen Knickmeyer and K. I. Ibrahim, "Bombing Shatters Mosque in Iraq," *Washington Post*, February 23, 2006, http://www.washingtonpost.com/wp-dyn/content/article/2006/02/22/AR2006022200454.html.
447 **"For the first time"**: Administration official, author interview. Meghan O'Sullivan, author interview.
448 **"an odd man"**: Condoleezza Rice, *No Higher Honor*, 369.
448 **"I think this is the day"**: Administration official and O'Sullivan interviews.
448 **reported as many as 1,300**: Others disputed that figure. Prime Minister Ibrahim al-Jaafari said the toll was 379, while the Interior Ministry said it was 1,077 and the U.S. military said it had confirmed 220 deaths. A joint Iraqi-American operations center reported receiving accounts of 365 civilian deaths, and officials at the center said the toll could reach 550. Ellen Knickmeyer, "Pressure Seen on Probes at Baghdad Morgue," *Washington Post*, March 1, 2006, http://www.washingtonpost.com/wp-dyn/content/article/2006/02/28/AR2006022801466.html.
448 **"please help us"**: Administration official interview.
448 **"He actually succeeded"**: Stephen Hadley, author interview.
448 **"From the bombing"**: J. D. Crouch, author interview.
449 **"I don't think anything"**: John Negroponte, author interview.

449 **"Hey, up on the Hill":** Graham, *By His Own Rules*, 603–4.
449 **"We don't have more":** Ronald Neumann, author interview.
449 **asked for $600 million:** Neumann, *Other War*, 40–41 and 46–47.
449 **less than the cost of:** The war in Iraq at that time was costing $255 million per day, including both military operations and civilian reconstruction. See John W. Schoen, "How Much Is the War in Iraq Costing Us?," MSNBC, October 22, 2006, http://www.msnbc.msn.com/id/15377059/ns/business-answer_desk/t/how-much-war-iraq-costing-us/#.T3eGo3gjj-B.
449 **"Who picked that baby-shit":** Neumann, *Other War*, 53–57.
450 **"I am certain that all presidents":** Laura Bush, *Spoken from the Heart*, 431.
450 **"Mrs. Burr":** Gridiron Club dinner, March 11, 2006. Author was in attendance.
451 **"We're all burned out":** Peter Baker, "Senior White House Staff May Be Wearing Down," *Washington Post*, March 13, 2006, http://www.washingtonpost.com/wp-dyn/content/article/2006/03/12/AR2006031200821_pf.html.
451 **was a "clusterfuck":** George W. Bush, *Decision Points*, 94–96. In an e-mail exchange with the author, Clay Johnson remembered applying that description specifically to the handling of Hurricane Katrina. Bush in his book remembered it being a more overall assessment of the White House organization.
451 **"You don't know how":** Senior administration official, author interview.
451 **"My face must have betrayed":** George W. Bush, *Decision Points*, 94–96.
451 **"his calm in crisis":** George W. Bush, remarks, Oval Office, March 28, 2006, http://georgewbush-whitehouse.archives.gov/news/releases/2006/03/20060328.html.
451 **Bush choked up:** Hadley interview.
451 **self-described "policy geek":** Peter Baker, "Bringing Evolution, Not Revolution," *Washington Post*, March 29, 2006, http://www.washingtonpost.com/wp-dyn/content/article/2006/03/28/AR2006032801804.html.
451 **"the smartest person":** Nicolle Wallace, author interview.
452 **"Josh viewed his job":** Michael Gerson, author interview.
452 **"thousands" of "tactical":** Condoleezza Rice made the comments in a question session after an address in Blackburn, England. See "Rice Admits Multiple Iraq Errors," BBC News, March 31, 2006, http://news.bbc.co.uk/2/hi/americas/4865344.stm.
452 **"lack of understanding":** Josh White, "Rumsfeld Challenges Rice on 'Tactical Errors' in Iraq," *Washington Post*, April 6, 2006, http://www.washingtonpost.com/wp-dyn/content/article/2006/04/05/AR2006040502269.html.
452 **"The American people are":** Notes of conversation on April 12, 2006, provided to author.
452 **had begun speaking out:** David S. Cloud and Eric Schmitt, "More Retired Generals Call for Rumsfeld's Resignation," *New York Times*, April 14, 2006, http://www.nytimes.com/2006/04/14/washington/14military.html?pagewanted=all.
453 **"We need to step up":** Joshua Bolten, author interview.
453 **"Secretary Rumsfeld's energetic":** George W. Bush, written statement, April 14, 2006, http://georgewbush-whitehouse.archives.gov/news/releases/2006/04/20060414.html.
453 **"I hear the voices":** George W. Bush, remarks to reporters, April 18, 2006, http://georgewbush-whitehouse.archives.gov/news/releases/2006/04/20060418-1.html.
453 **asked for a show:** Several participants, author interviews. Participants remember the timing differently. Some think it took place before the generals' revolt, but Joshua Bolten and Joel Kaplan recall it taking place afterward.
453 **"You too?":** Joel Kaplan, author interview.

454 **"The president had not liked Jaafari":** Administration official, author interview.
454 **"It is time for you to go":** Second administration official, author interview. See also Bumiller, *Condoleezza Rice*, 286.
455 **"President Hu! Your days":** Peter Baker and Glenn Kessler, "Bush, Hu Produce Summit of Symbols," *Washington Post*, April 21, 2006.
455 **"You're okay":** George W. Bush, comment to Hu, audible on CNN video of the event.
455 **refused to attend:** Lea Berman, author interview. See also Harwood and Seib, *Pennsylvania Avenue*, 114–16.
455 **"This was unfortunate":** Baker and Kessler, "Bush, Hu Produce Summit of Symbols."
455 **"Condi and I have something":** Rice, *No Higher Honor*, 526–27.
455 **"I want you to know I'm serious":** Rice interview.

CHAPTER 26: "I'M NOT SURE HOW TO TAKE GOOD NEWS ANYMORE"

456 **done a poor job explaining:** DeFrank, *Write It When I'm Gone*, 221–22.
456 **killed in Haditha:** Tim McGirk, "Collateral Damage or Civilian Massacre in Haditha?," *Time*, March 19, 2006, http://www.time.com/time/world/article/0,8599,1174649,00.html.
457 **"the worst period of my":** George W. Bush, *Decision Points*, 367–68.
457 **"He keeps a lot of that very":** Friend of Bush, author interview.
457 **"Can you imagine the signal":** Walt Harrington, "Dubya and Me," *American Scholar*, Autumn 2011, http://theamericanscholar.org/dubya-and-me/.
457 **"He never became a Lyndon":** Michael Gerson, author interview.
457 **"if he has dark nights of the soul":** Stephen Hadley, author interview.
457 **"He stunned me day after":** Dan Bartlett, author interview.
457 **"He did get kind of down":** Joe O'Neill, author interview.
457 **"He feels that pain":** Jim Langdon, author interview.
457 **"Putting parents, children":** Kirbyjon Caldwell, author interview.
457 **"It isn't like he's blowing up":** Bartlett interview.
458 **"You fight the war, and I'll provide":** John Abizaid, author interview.
458 **"There's always this kind":** Frederick Jones, author interview.
459 **"our version of Lawrence of Arabia":** John Hannah, author interview.
459 **"This is not working":** Hadley interview. See also George W. Bush, *Decision Points*, 363–64.
459 **"impotent" president:** Peter Baker, "Press Secretary Relished Job," *Washington Post*, July 13, 2008.
459 **"I asked him about those":** George W. Bush, remarks announcing Tony Snow's appointment, April 26, 2006, http://georgewbush-whitehouse.archives.gov/news/releases/2006/04/20060426.html.
460 **"He's hard to ignore":** Michele Davis, author interview.
460 **"You started with Nixon":** Paulson, *On the Brink*, 19–20.
461 **"Utter bullshit that I'm":** George W. Bush, meeting with Igor Ivanov, the Russian national security adviser, May 4, 2006. Notes of the conversation provided to author.
461 **"I just want to know we are":** Nicholas Burns, author interview.
461 **speech-and-debate clause:** Article I, Section 6 of the Constitution says members of Congress are "privileged from Arrest during their Attendance at the Session of their respective Houses, and in going to and returning from the same; and for

any Speech or Debate in either House, they shall not be questioned in any other Place." http://www.archives.gov/exhibits/charters/constitution_transcript.html. The point of the clause was to guard the independence of the legislative branch, but how much protection it affords lawmakers has been debated for years. The Congressional Research Service determined that the Jefferson search "appears to be unprecedented in U.S. history and raises serious and significant constitutional questions." See Todd B. Tatelman, "The Speech or Debate Clause: Recent Developments," Congressional Research Service, April 17, 2007, http://www.fas.org/sgp/crs/misc/RL33668.pdf.

461 **Hastert was "livid":** Dennis Hastert, author interview.

462 **"was just so exercised":** Paul McNulty, author interview.

462 **"Well, basically here's the deal":** Ibid.

463 **used the wrong first name:** American officials were calling him Jowad, which was a nom de guerre; Maliki asked them to use Nouri instead.

463 **"Excuse me, Madame Secretary":** George Casey, author interview. See also Graham, *By His Own Rules*, 614.

463 **Rumsfeld was aggravated:** Rumsfeld, *Known and Unknown*, 690–91.

463 **"Every one of us was worried":** Donald Rumsfeld, author interview.

464 **"We really got to get rid":** Ray LaHood, interview with Lynn Sweet, *Chicago Sun-Times*, posted June 8, 2006, http://blogs.suntimes.com/sweet/2006/06/rep_ray_lahood.html.

464 **"Why didn't I think of that?":** Joshua Bolten, author interview.

464 **Hadley was summoned:** Hadley interview.

464 **"That would be a good thing":** Tony Snow, news briefing, June 8, 2006, http://georgewbush-whitehouse.archives.gov/news/releases/2006/06/20060608-7.html.

464 **"God, I'm so glad":** Bolten interview.

464 **"Hey, you might go":** Ray LaHood, interview with Fox News, cited on Web site, June 8, 2006, http://www.foxnews.com/story/0,2933,198657,00.html.

464 **"I was just giddy":** Condoleezza Rice, author interview.

465 **"You don't seem happy":** Meghan O'Sullivan, author interview.

465 **the situation had "fundamentally changed":** George Casey, author interview. See also Casey, *Strategic Reflections*, 105–6.

465 **"My view was always":** Casey interview.

465 **Kagan offered a robust:** O'Sullivan interview.

465 **"it is highly unlikely":** Michael Vickers, e-mail exchange with author. See also Vickers memo, June 12, 2006. Accessed at http://www.rumsfeld.com.

466 **"to be persuasive":** Rumsfeld, *Known and Unknown*, 695–96.

466 **"behind the mask, the whole thing":** Rove, *Courage and Consequence*, 351.

466 **"cutting and running":** Karl Rove, speech on New Hampshire Avenue, played on *Meet the Press*, NBC, June 18, 2006, http://www.msnbc.msn.com/id/13296235/ns/meet_the_press/t/transcript-june/#.T3eEt3gjj-A.

466 **"They may be with you":** David A. Farenthold, "Rove's Speech to N.H. Republicans Keeps to Partisan Line," *Washington Post*, June 13, 2006.

466 **"brilliant fake out":** Bolten interview.

466 **left behind to filibuster:** Sammon, *Strategery*, 109.

466 **"Meghan, um, where's the president?":** Administration official, author interview.

466 **"The president's not here":** O'Sullivan interview. Years later, O'Sullivan did not remember the Brett McGurk phone call but vividly recalled J. D. Crouch telling her the president was in Baghdad. Likewise, in an e-mail exchange with the author, Charles Dunne said he did not recall rushing to McGurk's office.

466 **"He was pumped up":** George Casey, author interview.
467 **"I have to do a better job":** Casey and Hadley interviews.
467 **"to make a big case":** White House official, author interview.
467 **"Troop levels will be decided":** George W. Bush, news conference, June 14, 2006, http://georgewbush-whitehouse.archives.gov/news/releases/2006/06/20060614.html.
467 **one study found that:** Heidi Urben, "'Decider' vs. 'Commander Guy': Presidential Power, Persuasion, and the Surge in Iraq," unpublished manuscript, May 12, 2008. Cited by Peter D. Feaver, "The Right to Be Right: Civil-Military Relations and the Iraq Surge Decision," *International Security*, spring 2011.
467 **"We came away from that":** Sammon, *Evangelical President*, 113.
467 **"What I thought would":** Peter Feaver, author interview.
467 **had become a "PR session":** O'Sullivan interview.

CHAPTER 27: "MAKE DAMN SURE WE DO NOT FAIL"

468 **"drive-by briefing":** Peter Baker and Michael Abramowitz, "A Governing Philosophy Rebuffed," *Washington Post*, June 30, 2006. http://www.washingtonpost.com/wp-dyn/content/article/2006/06/29/AR2006062902300_pf.html.
468 **"I will protect the people":** George W. Bush and Junichiro Koizumi of Japan, news conference, June 29, 2006, http://georgewbush-whitehouse.archives.gov/news/releases/2006/06/20060629-3.html.
469 **"I was just shocked":** John Bellinger, author interview.
469 **"we're not going to get":** Karen Hughes, author interview.
469 **"you cannot overturn":** Condoleezza Rice, author interview.
469 **"I'm not going to overrule":** Senior administration official, author interview.
469 **"I'm not worried about":** Ibid.
470 **"I think we are headed":** George W. Bush, call with Tony Blair, April 2, 2006. Notes of call provided to author.
470 **"He thought the Bush administration":** Michael McFaul, author interview.
470 **"unfairly and improperly":** Dick Cheney, address, Vilnius Conference, May 4, 2006, http://georgewbush-whitehouse.archives.gov/news/releases/2006/05/20060504-1.html.
470 **"The vice president put a stake":** George W. Bush, call with Tony Blair, May 16, 2006. Notes of call provided to author.
470 **"a few more moves":** Vladimir Putin, call with George W. Bush, June 5, 2006. Notes of call provided to author.
471 **"We've had some tough":** George W. Bush, meeting with Prime Minister Anders Fogh Rasmussen of Denmark at Camp David, June 9, 2006. Notes of conversation provided to author.
471 **"I think Putin is not a democrat":** George W. Bush, meeting with Prime Minister Janez Janša of Slovenia, July 10, 2006. Notes of conversation provided to author.
471 **"I talked about my desire":** George W. Bush and Vladimir Putin, remarks to reporters, Strelna, Russia, July 15, 2006, http://georgewbush-whitehouse.archives.gov/news/releases/2006/07/20060715-1.html.
472 **"charged and pointed debate":** Annan, *Interventions*, 4–5.
472 **"I can't be his national security":** Rice, *No Higher Honor*, 478–79.
472 **"Blair, what are you":** Peter Baker, "Bush's Bull Session: Loud and Clear, Chief," *Washington Post*, July 18, 2006. The conversation was mistakenly transmitted via a live microphone to a separate press center where reporters heard it. When he

later heard about the conversation, Kofi Annan wrote that he wished he "could simply 'make something happen' with just a phone call." See Annan, *Interventions*, 4–5.

473 **"Speaking of sanctions against":** Peter Finn and Peter Baker, "Kremlin Sells Russia's Best Self," *Washington Post*, July 18, 2006.

473 **"I left St. Petersburg more":** George W. Bush, call with Tony Blair, July 28, 2006. Notes of call provided to author.

473 **staged a ceremony:** George W. Bush, remarks to audience in East Room, July 19, 2006, http://georgewbush-whitehouse.archives.gov/news/releases/2006/07/20060719-3.html.

474 **"We were trying to keep":** Sara Taylor Fagen, author interview.

474 **"If I were running":** Mary Clare Jalonick, "Thune Says He Would Distance Himself from Bush Agenda," Associated Press, July 19, 2006.

474 **"He thought Thune was ungrateful":** White House official, author interview.

474 **"The deteriorating security":** Administration official, author interview.

475 **"Do people call you Sparky?":** Ibid.

475 **pulse rate of forty-seven:** The White House released a four-page summary after George W. Bush's annual physical exam. http://www.bethesda.med.navy.mil/professional%5Cpublic_affairs%5Cpress_releases%5C2005%5C019_-_pres_annual_physical.htm.

475 **"He's the first one to admit":** Peter Baker, "The Final Days," *New York Times Magazine*, August 29, 2008, http://www.nytimes.com/2008/08/31/magazine/31bush-t.html?pagewanted=all.

475 **"It's something you can solve":** Pamela Hudson Nelson, author interview.

475 **"When you're working for the president":** Baker, "Final Days."

476 **"Riding helps clear my head":** Steve Holland, Reuters, August 5, 2006.

476 **"The more pressure there was":** Mark McKinnon, author interview.

476 **"I was just, you know, trying":** Tony Snow told the story in a commencement address at Catholic University on May 12, 2007. http://publicaffairs.cua.edu/Releases/2007/07CommencementAddress.cfm.

477 **"crater the runways":** John Hannah, author interview.

477 **"We need to let the Israelis":** George W. Bush, *Decision Points*, 414.

477 **"Here's a copy of something":** Condoleezza Rice, author interview.

478 **"He is a natural debater":** Ibid.

478 **"It made a difference when":** Michael Gerson, author interview.

478 **"It wasn't personal":** Liz Cheney, author interview.

479 **"George Bush's mental weakness":** Joe Scarborough, *Scarborough Country*, MSNBC, August 15, 2006, http://www.msnbc.msn.com/id/14375558/#.T3x_Fngjj-A.

479 **"success in Iraq seems more":** "A Fighting Chance in Iraq," *National Review*, August 10, 2006, http://www.nationalreview.com/articles/218448/fighting-chance-iraq/editors.

479 **"we seem not to be winning":** Quin Hillyer, "Lessons from the Black and Silver," *American Spectator*, August 16, 2006, http://spectator.org/archives/2006/08/16/lessons-from-the-black-and-sil.

479 **mocked neoconservative aspirations:** George F. Will, "The Triumph of Unrealism," *Washington Post*, August 15, 2006, http://www.washingtonpost.com/wp-dyn/content/article/2006/08/14/AR2006081401163.html.

479 **"would eventually lead to death":** Peter Wehner, e-mail, August 16, 2006, distributed inside the White House and to a list of outside political figures and journalists. It was posted on the conservative Web site TownHall.com. http://

townhall.com/columnists/peterwehner/2006/08/16/responding_to_george_wills_realism/page/full/.

479 **"Iraq was not a communications"**: Peter Wehner, author interview.

480 **"They weren't pushing things up"**: George Casey, author interview.

480 **One close aide to the secretary**: Pentagon official, author interview.

480 **"I'm not sure Rumsfeld"**: Another Pentagon official, author interview.

480 **"The situation seems to be"**: George W. Bush, *Decision Points*, 371.

481 **But growth was slowing**: Nell Henderson, "Economy Gained Strength in 2006," *Washington Post*, February 1, 2007, http://www.washingtonpost.com/wp-dyn/content/article/2007/01/31/AR2007013100422.html.

481 **"We can't predict when"**: Paulson, *On the Brink*, 47.

481 **"It's time to put our pride"**: Peter Baker, "For Bush, War Anguish Expressed Privately," *Washington Post*, September 25, 2006, http://www.washingtonpost.com/wp-dyn/content/article/2006/09/24/AR2006092400747.html.

482 **"I do the best I can to cry"**: George W. Bush, interview with Katie Couric, CBS News, September 6, 2006, http://www.cbsnews.com/2100-500923_162-1980081.html.

482 **"a deafening kind of quiet"**: Laura Bush, *Spoken from the Heart*, 305.

482 **"The number of people that"**: Joe Hagin, author interview.

482 **"He did his job"**: Stephen Hadley, author interview.

CHAPTER 28: "DON'T LET THIS BE YOUR LEGACY"

483 **"We had just a huge blood"**: Senior administration official, author interview.

483 **"I want to keep some of it"**: Michael Hayden, author interview.

483 **fewer than a hundred detainees**: Michael Hayden and Michael B. Mulkasey, "The President Ties His Own Hands on Terror," *Wall Street Journal*, April 17, 2009, http://online.wsj.com/article/SB123993446103128041.html.

484 **"just like a conductor"**: Senior administration official interview.

484 **"Democracies don't disappear"**: Condoleezza Rice, author interview.

484 **"I think we have to empty"**: Hayden interview.

484 **"I oppose this, Mr. President"**: Senior official interview.

484 **"don't let this be your legacy"**: Rice, *No Higher Honor*, 502.

485 **"He was very animated"**: William Burck, author interview.

485 **"These are dangerous men"**: George W. Bush, speech, September 6, 2006, http://georgewbush-whitehouse.archives.gov/news/releases/2006/09/20060906-3.html.

486 **waterboarded 183 times**: The details of the waterboarding were revealed in April 2009 after President Barack Obama ordered the release of secret legal memos justifying the interrogation program. http://s3.amazonaws.com/nytdocs/docs/151/151.pdf.

486 **threatened with a power drill**: Mark Mazzetti, "Report Provides New Details on C.I.A. Prisoner Abuse," *New York Times*, August 22, 2009, http://www.nytimes.com/2009/08/23/us/politics/23cia.html.

486 **"I want to be absolutely clear"**: George W. Bush, remarks to reporters, September 6, 2006, http://georgewbush-whitehouse.archives.gov/news/releases/2006/09/20060906-3.html.

486 **Bush was sending legislation**: The proposal asked Congress to set up a military commission system built on the traditional military court-martial system but different in important respects. For instance, suspects would not have to

be read *Miranda* warnings about their rights, and classified evidence in some circumstances could be introduced against them without allowing them or their attorneys to review it. http://georgewbush-whitehouse.archives.gov/news/releases/2006/09/20060906-6.html.

486 **"we had clutched defeat":** John Bellinger, author interview.

486 **"Do you want to tell me":** Joshua Bolten, author interview.

487 **"your unpopularity is going":** George W. Bush, *Decision Points*, 355. Mitch McConnell later denied Bush's account of their talk but would not discuss what he recalled saying. "That's not my recollection of the conversation," McConnell told Ryan Alessi, a political talk show host in his home state of Kentucky, in January 2011. "But I'm not going to get into an argument with President Bush and go back and rehash all of that." http://mycn2.com/politics/mcconnell-said-he-had-different-recollection-of-conversation-with-bush. But Cheney in his memoir referenced the same conversation and said he later had a follow-up with McConnell in which the senator admitted he was wrong. *In My Time*, 462. An aide to Bush also recalled the president telling him about the conversation immediately afterward. In an e-mail to the author, a spokesman for McConnell said the senator was only talking about timing, that if the president was going to make a change in Iraq policy, he should do it before the election rather than wait until afterward.

487 **"Cutting and running is not":** Mitch McConnell, remarks to reporters alongside Senator Bill Frist, U.S. Capitol, September 5, 2006, Federal News Service transcript.

487 **"Hey, guys!" he exclaimed:** Administration official and Meghan O'Sullivan, author interviews.

488 **"We're edging toward strategic":** Woodward, *War Within*, 129–38.

488 **"We were working that":** Donald Rumsfeld, author interview.

488 **"I wanted to call you in":** Kenneth Adelman, author interview. See also Jeffrey Goldberg, "The End of the Affair," *New Yorker*, November 20, 2006, http://www.newyorker.com/archive/2006/11/20/061120ta_talk_goldberg.

489 **"fresh pair of eyes":** Rumsfeld, *Known and Unknown*, 2.

489 **"The good news":** Ibid. In actuality, the calculation was wrong, though it is not clear whether Dick Cheney had it wrong or Donald Rumsfeld remembered it wrong. Rumsfeld identified this conversation happening in "early October." But it would not be until November 18 that there would be 794 days left, which was well after Rumsfeld had been forced to resign.

489 **"He stood by me":** Dick Cheney, *In My Time*, 51–52.

489 **"Maybe he didn't have":** Ibid., 442–43.

490 **"If Rumsfeld saw a Kosovo":** J. D. Crouch, author interview.

490 **feeding him excerpts:** John Hannah, author interview.

490 **"The friendship with Rumsfeld":** Senior administration official, author interview.

490 **"Even though Cheney knew":** White House official, author interview.

490 **"some in the Pentagon civilian":** Dick Cheney, *In My Time*, 439.

490 **"He didn't say it to me":** Rumsfeld interview.

490 **"I've got to get someone":** Jack Morrison, author interview.

491 **"Tell me where they are":** George W. Bush, *Decision Points*, 215–16.

491 **"They almost came to blows":** Rice, *No Higher Honor*, 444–45.

492 **"Look, I want to assure you":** Congressional official, author interview.

492 **"Cheney was losing steam":** Ibid.

492 **"We had to waterboard him":** Second congressional official, author interview.

492 **"The world is beginning to":** Colin Powell to John McCain, September 13, 2006. The stationery ignored his service in Bush's cabinet and listed him as "General

Colin L. Powell, USA (Retired)." http://i.a.cnn.net/cnn/2006/images/09/14/powell.article.pdf.

493 **"contained everything we asked":** George W. Bush, *Decision Points*, 179.

493 **"It's a disgraceful day":** Senior White House official, author interview.

493 **"The transfer of nuclear":** George W. Bush, remarks to reporters, October 9, 2006, http://georgewbush-whitehouse.archives.gov/news/releases/2006/10/20061009.html.

493 **"Is this the best they can do?":** Christopher Hill, author interview.

493 **"We cannot solve this":** Ibid.

494 **"whether the United States":** George W. Bush, speech, Washington, D.C., June 19, 2006, http://georgewbush-whitehouse.archives.gov/news/releases/2006/06/20060619-14.html.

494 **"We will win in Iraq so long":** George W. Bush, speech, Milwaukee, July 11, 2006, http://georgewbush-whitehouse.archives.gov/news/releases/2006/07/20060711-11.html.

494 **"We will stay the course":** George W. Bush, speech in Salt Lake City, August 30, 2006, http://georgewbush-whitehouse.archives.gov/news/releases/2006/08/20060830-10.html.

494 **"the situation is simply drifting":** Anne Plummer Flaherty, "Sen. Warner Casts Dismal View of Iraq," Associated Press, October 11, 2006, http://www.washingtonpost.com/wp-dyn/content/article/2006/10/05/AR2006100501364.html.

494 **Ed Gillespie called to see:** Ed Gillespie, author interview.

494 **"The characterization of":** George W. Bush, news conference, October 11, 2006, http://georgewbush-whitehouse.archives.gov/news/releases/2006/10/20061011-5.html.

494 **"Listen, we've never been stay":** George W. Bush, interview on *This Week with George Stephanopoulos*, ABC, aired October 22, 2006, http://abcnews.go.com/ThisWeek/story?id=2594541&page=1&singlePage rue#.TtQfRWAjj-A.

495 **"If you had a clean sheet":** William Luti, author interview.

495 **military in Baghdad acknowledged:** John Ward Anderson, "General Says Mission in Baghdad Falls Short," *Washington Post*, October 20, 2006, http://www.washingtonpost.com/wp-dyn/content/article/2006/10/19/AR2006101900891.html.

495 **"I've had people call":** Dick Cheney, interview with Scott Hennen, WDAY, October 24, 2006, http://georgewbush-whitehouse.archives.gov/news/releases/2006/10/20061024-7.html.

496 **"didn't say anything about":** Dick Cheney, interview with White House reporters, October 27, 2006, http://georgewbush-whitehouse.archives.gov/news/releases/2006/10/20061028-2.html.

496 **"Do you think we're winning":** George W. Bush, news conference, October 25, 2006, http://georgewbush-whitehouse.archives.gov/news/releases/2006/10/20061025.html.

496 **"they're coming after us":** George W. Bush, interview with conservative journalists, October 26, 2006, http://www.nationalreview.com/articles/219056/interview-commander-chief-nro-primary-document.

497 **"Dick, can I talk to you":** Dick Cheney, *In My Time*, 442–43.

497 **"It wasn't open for discussion":** Dick Cheney, author interview.

497 **"Both those men are doing":** Terence Hunt, "Bush Says Rumsfeld, Cheney Should Stay," Associated Press, November 1, 2006, http://www.foxnews.com/wires/2006Nov01/0,4670,Bush,00.html.

498 **"I think we're going to lose":** Ken Mehlman, author interview.

499 **"Cheney?" he asked:** Gates, *Duty*, 6–8
499 **"I disagree with your decision":** George W. Bush, *Decision Points*, 91–94.
499 **"Dick, would you like to be":** Dick Cheney, *In My Time*, 442–43.
499 **"the president has decided":** Rumsfeld, *Known and Unknown*, 705–6.
499 **"I'm just too much of a":** Dick Cheney, *In My Time*, 442–43.
500 **"time for a major adjustment":** Donald Rumsfeld to White House, memo, "Iraq—Illustrative New Courses of Action," November 6, 2006. Accessed at http://www.rumsfeld.com.
500 **Of twenty recent polls:** Peter Baker, "President Who Sees in Absolutes Awaits Voters' Definitive Answer," *Washington Post*, November 7, 2006, http://www.washingtonpost.com/wp-dyn/content/article/2006/11/06/AR2006110601218.html.
500 **"ripped the guy a new one":** Joshua Bolten, author interview.
501 **"What's your plan?":** George W. Bush, rally for Governor Rick Perry of Texas, Dallas, November 6, 2006, http://georgewbush-whitehouse.archives.gov/news/releases/2006/11/20061106-6.html.
501 **"I've prepared this letter":** Rumsfeld, *Known and Unknown*, 707–8.
501 **Republican incumbents went down:** Dan Balz, "Democrats Take House," *Washington Post*, November 8, 2006, http://www.washingtonpost.com/wp-dyn/content/article/2006/11/07/AR2006110701838.html. In the end, thirty seats changed hands in the House, giving Democrats a majority of 233 to 202. Ultimately, Democrats picked up six seats in the Senate, eking out a 51-vote majority with two independents who sided with the party.
502 **"Even today":** Bolten interview.
502 **"Why all the glum faces?":** George W. Bush, news conference, November 8, 2006, http://georgewbush-whitehouse.archives.gov/news/releases/2006/11/20061108-2.html.
502 **there was just angry silence:** Scott Palmer, e-mail exchange with author.
502 **"We shed no tears in Kabul":** Neumann, *Other War*, 144–45.
502 **"in a complete depression":** National Security Council official, author interview.
503 **"Don Rumsfeld has been":** George W. Bush, news conference, November 8, 2006, http://georgewbush-whitehouse.archives.gov/news/releases/2006/11/20061108-2.html.

CHAPTER 29: "THE ELEPHANTS FINALLY THREW UP ON THE TABLE"

507 **"I'm just thinking about":** Dan Bartlett, author interview.
507 **"He really felt strongly that":** Karen Hughes, author interview.
508 **"He was noticeably colder":** George Casey, author interview.
508 **"It should not take a large":** Administration official, author interview.
508 **"We'd be betting the whole house":** Administration official interview.
508 **"is either ignorant of what":** Stephen Hadley to George W. Bush, memo, November 8, 2006, http://www.nytimes.com/2006/11/29/world/middleeast/29mtext.html?_r=1&oref=slogin.
509 **"How's your boy?":** Michael D. Shear, "In Following His Own Script, Webb May Test Senate's Limits," *Washington Post*, November 29, 2006, http://www.washingtonpost.com/wp-dyn/content/article/2006/11/28/AR2006112801582.html.
509 **"Get me the one-pager":** Peter Baker, "Karl Rove Remains Steadfast in the Face of Criticism," *Washington Post*, November 12, 2006, http://www.washingtonpost.com/wp-dyn/content/article/2006/11/11/AR2006111101103.html.

509 **"The Republican philosophy":** Ibid.
509 **Exit polls found that 36 percent:** National Exit Polls, November 8, 2006, http://www.cnn.com/ELECTION/2006/pages/results/states/US/H/00/epolls.0.html.
509 **"He would call every now":** Bill Clinton, author interview. This came from an interview conducted for a piece in the *New York Times Magazine* called "The Mellowing of William Jefferson Clinton," May 31, 2009, http://www.nytimes.com/2009/05/31/magazine/31clinton-t.html?_r=1&pagewanted=print. Some of this was used in the article, and some was not.
511 **"You could do it":** Administration official, author interview.
511 **"political progress will help":** White House briefing slides, later declassified and released when the president made his surge speech to the nation, January 10, 2007.
511 **"the hardest and worst memo":** Meghan O'Sullivan, author interview.
511 **"may take additional forces":** J. D. Crouch, author interview.
512 **"The Iraqis need to pull up":** O'Sullivan interview.
512 **"you are just sending more":** Crouch interview.
512 **"So are we now responsible":** Rice, *No Higher Honor*, 541–42.
512 **"That meeting is where":** Crouch interview.
512 **"went horrendously":** O'Sullivan interview.
512 **"How do you think":** O'Sullivan and Dan Bartlett, author interviews.
513 **shown up in the *New York Times*:** Michael R. Gordon, "Bush Aide's Memo Doubts Iraqi Leader," *New York Times*, November 29, 2006, http://www.nytimes.com/2006/11/29/world/middleeast/29cnd-military.html?pagewanted=all.
513 **"The political pressure":** George W. Bush, *Decision Points*, 374–75.
513 **he had all but decided:** Ibid.
513 **"The situation in Iraq is":** Report of the Iraq Study Group, December 6, 2006, http://media.usip.org/reports/iraq_study_group_report.pdf.
513 **"a responsible exit":** Cullen Murphy and Todd S. Purdum, "Farewell to All That: An Oral History of the Bush White House," *Vanity Fair*, February 2009, http://www.vanityfair.com/politics/features/2009/02/bush-oral-history200902.
513 **"We're not giving you":** Alan Simpson, author interview.
514 **"While I knew he was not":** Leon Panetta, author interview.
514 **"was not a strategy for winning":** Dick Cheney, *In My Time*, 447–49.
514 **"support a short-term":** Iraq Study Group report.
514 **"you can't refuse to talk":** Dick Cheney, *In My Time*, 447–49.
514 **"worthy of serious study":** George W. Bush, news conference, December 7, 2006, http://georgewbush-whitehouse.archives.gov/news/releases/2006/12/20061207-1.html.
514 **"It's bad in Iraq":** Ibid.
514 **"I was really skeptical":** Condoleezza Rice, author interview.
515 **"tried to be a good soldier":** Gordon Smith, speech on the Senate floor, December 7, 2006, http://www.c-spanvideo.org/program/SenateSession3798/start/32510/stop/33526.
515 **"I for one am":** Ibid.
515 **"a tipping point":** Senator Olympia J. Snowe of Maine said, "I think for some, that speech was a tipping point. It was a reality check. We have to admit that something has gone terribly wrong." James Risen, "GOP Senator in Spotlight After a Critical Iraq Speech," *New York Times*, December 28, 2006, http://www.nytimes.com/2006/12/28/washington/28smith.html?pagewanted=all.
515 **"So what's your plan, Condi?":** Rice, *No Higher Honor*, 544.
516 **"accelerate the transition":** Donald Rumsfeld, attachment to memo sent to

George W. Bush and Dick Cheney, December 8, 2006. Accessed at http://www.rumsfeld.com.

516 **producing a forty-five-page paper:** Frederick W. Kagan, "Choosing Victory: A Plan for Success in Iraq," American Enterprise Institute, http://www.aei.org/files/2007/01/05/20070111_ChoosingVictoryupdated.pdf.

516 **"One of the biggest problems":** Eliot Cohen, author interview.

516 **"to my mind, this is a major":** Ricks, *Gamble*, 98–101.

517 **"This is a fool's errand":** Barry McCaffrey, author interview at the time.

517 **"It was clear that Bush thought":** Stephen Biddle, author interview.

517 **"How is it that Jack Keane's getting":** Senior military official, author interview.

517 **"I guess you have to resign":** John Abizaid and Eric Edelman, author interviews.

517 **"Keane is great as a validator":** Stephen Hadley, author interview.

518 **"If senior generals had resigned":** Feaver, "Right to Be Right."

518 **"Steve Hadley," recalled William Luti:** William Luti, author interview.

518 **Casey was "adamantly opposed":** Casey, *Strategic Reflections*, 143–44.

518 **"Without a basic level":** Baker, "Final Days."

518 **"We will fade it":** Bartlett interview.

518 **"Hadley, do you think the surge":** Hadley interview.

CHAPTER 30: "EVERYBODY KNEW THIS WAS THE LAST BULLET IN THE CHAMBER"

519 **"The president didn't want":** J. D. Crouch, author interview.

519 **"Cheney was supposed to":** Dan Bartlett, author interview.

519 **"The question is when do":** Dick Cheney, *In My Time*, 450–52.

519 **"We're betting the farm":** Ibid.

520 **"I don't think that you have":** Several participants, author interviews. See also Woodward, *War Within*, 287–89; and Feaver, "Right to Be Right."

520 **"My concerns were practical":** Peter Schoomaker, e-mail exchange with author.

520 **"We're concerned we're going to break":** Joshua Bolten, author interview.

520 **"we will break" the military:** Ann Scott Tyson, "General Says Army Will Need to Grow," *Washington Post*, December 15, 2006, http://www.washingtonpost.com/wp-dyn/content/article/2006/12/14/AR2006121400803.html.

521 **"a man of rectitude":** Dick Cheney, address, Donald Rumsfeld departure ceremony, December 15, 2006, http://207.245.165.145/news/releases/2006/12/20061215-8.html.

521 **"We need to reset our military":** George W. Bush, interview with Peter Baker, Michael Abramowitz, and Michael Fletcher for the *Washington Post*, December 19, 2006, http://www.washingtonpost.com/wp-dyn/content/article/2006/12/19/AR2006121900880.html.

522 **"Our commanders do not want":** Gordon and Trainor, *Endgame*, 305–6. Robert Gates was so pessimistic about a surge that he recommended developing a "Plan B should the Baghdad effort fail to show much success." Gates confirms this in his memoir, writing that "I had been on the job less than a week, and I was not yet prepared to challenge the commander in the field or other senior general. That would soon change." See Gates, *Duty*, 43–44.

522 **he was alarmed and alerted:** Ricks, *Gamble*, 118; and Woodward, *War Within*, 297–99.

522 **reached out to Petraeus:** O'Sullivan and David Petraeus, author interviews.

522 **"Look, Chairman, this is":** Petraeus interview.

522 **"You're going to do it":** Rice, *No Higher Honor*, 544–45.

522 **"No, I am going to commit":** Crouch interview.
522 **"another *Washington Post* debate":** Ibid.
523 **"Go to hell," one yelled:** Sudarsan Raghavan, "In Hussein's Last Minutes, Jeers and a Cry for Calm," *Washington Post*, December 31, 2006, http://www.washingtonpost.com/wp-dyn/content/article/2006/12/30/AR2006123000392.html.
523 **"We've decided to be a bear":** Administration official, author interview.
523 **"Enough! Does the guy want":** Ibid.
524 **Donald Rumsfeld "went ballistic":** Dan Senor, author interview.
524 **"Tell me how this ends":** Atkinson, *In the Company of Soldiers*, 6.
524 **She suggested the Library:** Draper, *Dead Certain*, 410.
524 **"I know you feel really alone":** O'Sullivan interview.
525 **Seventy-three percent:** *USA Today*/Gallup poll, conducted January 5–7, 2007.
525 **"Let's go":** William Burck, author interview.
525 **"wound tightly":** Crouch interview.
525 **"The situation in Iraq is":** George W. Bush, address to nation, January 10, 2007, http://georgewbush-whitehouse.archives.gov/news/releases/2007/01/20070110-7.html.
526 **"a lot of persuasive power":** Matthew Scully, author interview.
526 **"Watching his facial expressions":** Crouch interview.
526 **"So how did it go?":** Rice, *No Higher Honor*, 547.
526 **"the most dangerous foreign policy":** Senate Foreign Relations Committee hearing, January 11, 2007, Federal News Service transcript.
526 **"bought into his dream":** Ibid.
527 **"The country was tired":** Peter Wehner, author interview.
527 **"the loneliest of George's":** Laura Bush, *Spoken from the Heart*, 421.
527 **"It's such a lonely job":** Rice interview.
527 **"Self-pity is the worst":** Draper, *Dead Certain*, 418.
527 **"Thinking about what Lincoln":** O'Sullivan and administration official interviews.
528 **"You know, I am no Lincoln":** Peter Feaver and O'Sullivan interviews.
528 **"I know the decision's unpopular":** O'Sullivan and administration official interviews.
528 **"The president himself was":** David Gordon, author interview.
528 **"Bush was very seriously":** O'Sullivan interview.
529 **"was kind of a nonentity":** Administration official, author interview.
529 **"thought that was a mistake":** Neil Patel, author interview.
529 **"what the U.S. auto fleet is":** Ibid.
529 **With just 33 percent of Americans:** Peter Baker and Jon Cohen, "Bush to Face Skeptical Congress," *Washington Post*, January 23, 2007, http://www.washingtonpost.com/wp-dyn/content/article/2007/01/22/AR2007012200236.html.
529 **"I respect you and the arguments":** George W. Bush, State of the Union address, January 23, 2007, http://georgewbush-whitehouse.archives.gov/news/releases/2007/01/20070123-2.html.
530 **"With the pressures from some":** Dick Cheney, interview with Wolf Blitzer, *The Situation Room*, CNN, January 24, 2007, http://transcripts.cnn.com/TRANSCRIPTS/0701/24/sitroom.03.html.
531 **"By the time I leave here":** Dick Cheney, interview with Richard Wolffe, *Newsweek*, January 28, 2007, http://georgewbush-whitehouse.archives.gov/news/releases/2007/01/20070128.html.
531 **the Senate voted 81 to 0:** U.S. Senate roll call record, January 26, 2007, http://thomas.loc.gov/cgi-bin/ntquery/z?nomis:110PN0017800:.

531 **planted Petraeus in an office:** Peter Baker, "General Is Front Man for Bush's Iraq Plan," *Washington Post*, February 7, 2007, http://www.washingtonpost.com/wp-dyn/content/article/2007/02/06/AR2007020601918.html.
531 **"This is a pretty significant":** Petraeus interview.
532 **"So now I'm an October":** Draper, *Dead Certain*, 419.

CHAPTER 31: "I'M GOING TO FIRE ALL YOUR ASSES"

533 **first time since 1928:** In 1928, President Calvin Coolidge decided not to run for reelection, and Vice President Charles Dawes did not run. Even then, the incumbent administration had one of its own in the race, in the form of Secretary of Commerce Herbert Hoover. In every election since then, the incumbent president or vice president made a run for the White House, and in every one of those elections but one he won the nomination of his party. The one year that did not happen was 1952, when President Harry Truman gave up his reelection campaign after losing the New Hampshire primary. Vice President Alben Barkley, at age seventy-four, jumped into the race just two weeks before the party convention but lost to Governor Adlai Stevenson of Illinois. Barkley later returned to the Senate.
533 **"I've talked to a lot of":** Wayne Berman, author interview.
533 **a Pioneer, collecting more:** Texans for Public Justice, http://info.tpj.org/docs/pioneers/pioneers_view.jsp?id=156.
534 **"I've taken the Sherman":** Dick Cheney, interview with Bob Schieffer, *Face the Nation*, March 19, 2006. The Sherman statement refers to William Tecumseh Sherman, the Union general from the Civil War who in 1884 gave what became known as the most definitive expression of noninterest that a politician could give: "I will not accept if nominated, and will not serve if elected." In modern politics, anything less definitive often encourages speculation, and often is intended to.
534 **"a warm welcome like that":** For example, see Dick Cheney, speech to the Federalist Society's national convention, November 17, 2006, http://georgewbush-whitehouse.archives.gov/news/releases/2006/11/20061117-11.html.
534 **approval rating in the thirties:** In a survey taken March 11–14, 2007, Gallup found that 34 percent of Americans approved of Dick Cheney's job performance while 56 percent disapproved. http://www.gallup.com/poll/28159/americans-ratings-dick-cheney-reach-new-lows.aspx#2.
534 **"I'm going to go work":** Berman interview.
535 **"There were a lot of":** Michael Gerson, author interview.
535 **"It constitutes a kind of a double":** Dean McGrath, author interview.
535 **"a disgraceful policy":** Elliott Abrams, author interview.
535 **"We had a good relationship":** Dick Cheney, author interview.
536 **"North Korea policy was":** Stephen Yates, author interview.
536 **"They never had an answer":** Christopher Hill, author interview.
536 **"Even before they exploded":** Condoleezza Rice, author interview.
536 **"I am not going to go to war":** Eric Edelman, author interview.
536 **"I don't think he had less":** Stephen Hadley, author interview.
536 **"I just think he became a lot":** Rice interview.
536 **"He had a lot of experience":** Cheney interview.
536 **"a spent force":** David Gordon, author interview.
536 **"He looked tired":** Neil Patel, author interview.
536 **"He fell asleep quite often":** Senior administration official, author interview.
537 **"Did you see?":** Latimer, *Speech-Less*, 168.

537 **"as a matter of principle"**: Robert Joseph, author interview.
537 **"brilliant, fearless, and argumentative"**: Holbrooke, *To End a War*, 80.
537 **"I don't think in my"**: Administration official, author interview.
538 **"He was a junior Holbrooke"**: Michael Green, author interview.
538 **"I love Chris, and I made"**: Rice interview.
538 **pushed through the House**: U.S. House Clerk's Office, http://clerk.house.gov/evs/2007/roll099.xml.
538 **"never cut off funding"**: Nancy Pelosi, interview with ABC News, January 19, 2007, http://abcnews.go.com/GMA/story?id=2805714&page=1#.T4XyOHgjj-A.
538 **"No, this is important"**: Ronald Neumann, author interview.
538 **described as "a loud boom"**: Dick Cheney, remarks to traveling press, Air Force Two, February 27, 2007, http://georgewbush-whitehouse.archives.gov/news/releases/2007/02/20070227.html.
539 **"They clearly try to find"**: Ibid.
539 **"I've seen some press reporting"**: Dick Cheney, briefing for traveling press, Air Force Two, February 27, 2007, http://georgewbush-whitehouse.archives.gov/news/releases/2007/02/20070227-8.html. While the briefing was on "background," meaning Cheney could be identified only as a "senior administration official," his cover was soon blown by the transcript sent out by the White House. The transcript used the "senior administration official" terminology but left the quotations in the first person, as in "That's not the way I work."
539 **"there is a cloud over"**: Byron York, "Scooter Who? In Closing Arguments, Fitzgerald Points the Finger at Dick Cheney," *National Review*, February 21, 2007, http://www.nationalreview.com/articles/220047/scooter-who-closing-arguments-fitzgerald-points-finger-dick-cheney/byron-york.
539 **alone in his office, Cheney**: Hayes, *Cheney*, 519–20.
540 **"mistakes were made"**: Alberto Gonzales, news conference, March 13, 2007, Federal News Service transcript.
540 **"something of a shock"**: Sammon, *Evangelical President*, 189–90.
540 **"felt that cancer was stalking"**: Peter Baker, "White House Spokesman's Colon Cancer Has Returned," *Washington Post*, March 28, 2007, http://www.washingtonpost.com/wp-dyn/content/article/2007/03/27/AR2007032700828.html.
541 **"I think he's become more"**: Jim Rutenberg, "Ex-aide Says He's Lost Faith in Bush," *New York Times*, April 1, 2007, http://www.nytimes.com/2007/04/01/washington/01adviser.html?pagewanted=all.
541 **"a little crying heap"**: Meghan O'Sullivan, author interview.
541 **"George, I'm asking you to"**: George W. Bush, *Decision Points*, 420–22. Elliott Abrams said he did not remember Olmert saying that. See *Tested by Zion*, 246–47.
542 **"You were right"**: Michael Hayden, author interview.
542 **"If this stuff leaks"**: Eric Edelman, author interview.
542 **"impatient and spoiled"**: Reid, *Good Fight*, 4.
542 **"this war cannot be won"**: Ibid., 15.
542 **"If you think this is about"**: Ibid., 18.
542 **"this war is lost"**: The full quotation was "Now, I believe myself that the secretary of state, the secretary of defense and—you have to make your own decision as to what the president knows—that this war is lost and that the surge is not accomplishing anything, as indicated by the extreme violence in Iraq yesterday." Harry Reid, news conference, April 19, 2007, Federal News Service transcript.
542 **"chewed my ass"**: Woodward, *War Within*, 346. While Harry Reid later said he might have chosen his words more carefully, he refused to apologize.

543 **Sixty-four times, he said:** Republican senators were scathing as Alberto Gonzales repeatedly pleaded a bad memory. Tom Coburn of Oklahoma called for his resignation. Arlen Specter of Pennsylvania called his testimony "at variance with the facts." John Cornyn of Texas used the phrase "really deplorable." Dana Milbank, "Maybe Gonzales Won't Recall His Painful Day on the Hill," *Washington Post*, April 20, 2007, http://www.washingtonpost.com/wp-dyn/content/article/2007/04/19/AR2007041902571.html.

543 **"He talked a lot about":** Peter Baker, "A President Besieged and Isolated, yet at Ease," *Washington Post*, July 2, 2007, http://www.washingtonpost.com/wp-dyn/content/article/2007/07/01/AR2007070101356.html.

543 **"He actually touched the eye":** Ibid.

543 **House passed a spending bill:** The bill authorized a total of $124 billion in spending, of which $95 billion would go to the wars. The rest was for Hurricane Katrina recovery, emergency aid to farmers, medical care for veterans, homeland security, and other spending items. The House voted for it 218 to 208, with two Republicans joining the Democratic majority and thirteen Democrats voting no. U.S. House Clerk's Office, April 25, 2007, http://clerk.house.gov/evs/2007/roll265.xml.

544 **"Why did you replace":** Tom Davis, author interview.

544 **"You guys aren't coming":** Ibid.

544 **"The very fundamental issue":** Peter Baker and Thomas E. Ricks, "3 Generals Spurn the Position of War 'Czar,'" *Washington Post*, April 11, 2007, http://www.washingtonpost.com/wp-dyn/content/article/2007/04/10/AR2007041001776.html.

545 **In April, 104 American troops:** Iraq Coalition Casualty Count, known as icasualties.org, http://icasualties.org/iraq/ByMonth.aspx. Note that this link goes to the page showing all coalition casualties; to get the American casualties requires using the filter at the bottom.

545 **"Look, Mr. President":** Douglas Lute, author interview.

545 **He was reading a column:** David Ignatius, "After the Surge," *Washington Post*, May 22, 2007, http://www.washingtonpost.com/wp-dyn/content/article/2007/05/21/AR2007052101439.html.

545 **"Whoever is leaking":** Dick Cheney, *In My Time*, 456–58.

546 **Hadley said he was the one:** Hadley interview.

546 **spending bill with $95 billion:** The overall bill authorized $120 billion in spending, of which about $95 billion was for the wars in Iraq and Afghanistan. As with the previous bill vetoed by George W. Bush, the rest went to a variety of other priorities. It passed the House 221 to 205, with two Republicans joining the Democratic majority and ten Democrats voting no. U.S. House Clerk's Office, May 10, 2007, http://clerk.house.gov/evs/2007/roll333.xml. The Senate passed it 80 to 14, with ten Democrats (including Hillary Clinton and Barack Obama), a Democratic-leaning independent, and three Republicans voting no. U.S. Senate roll call record, May 24, 2007, http://www.senate.gov/legislative/LIS/roll_call_lists/roll_call_vote_cfm.cfm?congress=110&session=1&vote=00181.

546 **another leak undercutting:** David E. Sanger and David S. Cloud, "White House Is Said to Debate '08 Cut in Iraq Combat Forces by 50%," *New York Times*, May 26, 2007, http://www.nytimes.com/2007/05/26/washington/26strategy.html?ex=1180843200&en=4a5b0fcb25dabda6&ei=5065&partner.

546 **"to be quite frank about it":** Woodward, *War Within*, 360.

546 **"My concern was whether":** David Petraeus, author interview.

547 **"Respectfully, sir, I can":** Administration official, author interview.

547 **"hadn't read the bill":** George W. Bush, speech on immigration reform, Federal Law Enforcement Training Center, Glynco, Ga., May 29, 2007, http://georgewbush-whitehouse.archives.gov/news/releases/2007/05/20070529-7.html.

548 **"He didn't laugh":** Dan Bartlett, speech to U.S. Chamber of Commerce, September 13, 2007, http://www.leadingauthorities.com/speaker/dan-bartlett.aspx.

548 **judge sentenced Scooter Libby:** Judge Reggie B. Walton imposed the sentence "with a sense of sadness," he said, because of his respect for those in public service but added that "it is important we expect and demand a lot from people who put themselves in those positions. Mr. Libby failed to meet the bar." Before the sentence was handed down, Scooter Libby asked the judge to "consider, along with the jury verdict, my whole life," but offered no contrition. More than 150 friends and supporters of Libby's sent letters to the judge on his behalf, including Donald Rumsfeld and Douglas Feith. Carol D. Leonnig and Amy Goldstein, "Libby Given 2½-Year Prison Term," *Washington Post*, June 6, 2007, http://www.washingtonpost.com/wp-dyn/content/article/2007/06/05/AR2007060500150.html.

548 **"Pardon Him":** Editorial, "Pardon Him," *National Review*, June 5, 2007, http://www.nationalreview.com/articles/221184/pardon-him/editors.

548 **"So much for loyalty":** William Kristol, "Who, Me?," *Weekly Standard*, June 5, 2007, http://www.weeklystandard.com/Content/Public/Articles/000/000/013/734azcei.asp.

549 **"You can't solve all":** Michael Gerson, author interview.

549 **"You're not the only dissident":** Peter Baker, "As Democracy Push Falters, Bush Feels like a 'Dissident,'" *Washington Post*, August 20, 2007, http://www.washingtonpost.com/wp-dyn/content/article/2007/08/19/AR2007081901720.html.

549 **Diehl made inquiries:** The resulting column ran in the *Washington Post* on August 6, 2007, under the headline "The Rush for a Legacy," without mentioning Abrams. http://www.washingtonpost.com/wp-dyn/content/article/2007/08/05/AR2007080501054.html.

550 **"How do we keep expectations":** Rice, *No Higher Honor*, 600–601.

CHAPTER 32: "REVOLT OF THE RADICAL PRAGMATISTS"

551 **"Does anyone here agree":** Several participants, author interviews. See also Dick Cheney, *In My Time*, 462–67.

551 **"It's about as good as it gets":** Mike McConnell, e-mail exchange with author. See also Dick Cheney, *In My Time*, 462–67.

551 **"Of course it's a weapons":** Michael Hayden, author interview.

552 **"we don't do Pearl Harbors":** Gates, *Duty*, 173.

552 **"If not literal rolling of eyes":** Senior administration official, author interview.

553 **Abrams apologized to Cheney:** Abrams, *Tested by Zion*, 236–39.

553 **"was, to put it mildly, reckless":** Rice, *No Higher Honor*, 713.

553 **"I cannot justify an attack":** George W. Bush, *Decision Points*, 420–22.

553 **"That's very disappointing":** Elliott Abrams, author interview.

553 **"This guy's got balls":** Ibid.

553 **Gates was furious:** Gates, *Duty*, 185.

553 **"Look, they view this as":** Abrams interview.

553 **"You can say I am wrong":** Dick Cheney, author interview.

553 **House Democrats accused:** Peter Baker, "Cheney Defiant on Classified Material," *Washington Post*, June 22, 2007, http://www.washingtonpost.com/wp-dyn/content/article/2007/06/21/AR2007062102309.html.

555 **"A lot of us worked hard":** George W. Bush, remarks to reporters, Naval War College, Newport, R.I., June 28, 2007, http://georgewbush-whitehouse.archives.gov/news/releases/2007/06/20070628-7.html.

555 **"I'll see you at the bill signing":** George W. Bush, remarks to reporters, Sofia, Bulgaria, June 11, 2007, http://georgewbush-whitehouse.archives.gov/news/releases/2007/06/20070611-1.html.

555 **"The president believed as":** Michael Gerson, author interview.

555 **"He thought that guy is a zealot":** Alan Simpson, author interview.

556 **"I respect the jury's":** George W. Bush, written statement on executive clemency for Libby, July 2, 2007, http://georgewbush-whitehouse.archives.gov/news/releases/2007/07/20070702-3.html.

556 **broke with Bush over Iraq:** In a speech on the Senate floor on June 25, 2007, Richard Lugar declared that the surge was unlikely to succeed and called for a change in strategy in Iraq, saying that otherwise "we risk foreign policy failures that could greatly diminish our influence in the region and the world." He said the president would have to downsize troop levels in Iraq and embrace more diplomacy. http://www.c-span.org/Campaign2012/Events/Sen-Richard-Lugar-R-IN-Senate-Floor-Speech-on-the-Iraq-War/7644/.

556 **"You have no credibility":** Woodward, *War Within*, 370.

556 **did not think he could hold:** Administration official, author interview.

556 **"The surge can't last":** Ibid.

557 **reporting that the White House:** David E. Sanger, "In White House, Debate Is Rising on Iraq Pullback," *New York Times*, July 9, 2007, http://www.nytimes.com/2007/07/09/washington/09prexy.html.

557 **Lott was there and reported:** Dick Cheney, *In My Time*, 460–63.

557 **voting two days later:** The bill would require that American force levels in Iraq be reduced to "a limited presence" by April 1, 2008. The House passed it 223 to 201, with four Republicans joining the Democratic majority and ten Democrats voting no. U.S. House Clerk's Office, July 12, 2007, http://clerk.house.gov/evs/2007/roll624.xml.

557 **"He thought we were":** Hadley interview.

557 **"he really wasn't in the loop":** Administration official, author interview.

558 **"I wanted to respectfully":** David Petraeus, author interview.

558 **"It's not going to happen":** Mike Mullen, author interview.

558 ***National Review* collected:** Kathryn Jean Lopez, "A Busy Saturday," *National Review Online*, July 20, 2007, http://www.nationalreview.com/corner/146196/busy-saturday/kathryn-jean-lopez.

559 **"Dear Kate, Elizabeth, Grace":** Dick Cheney, letter to his grandchildren, published in the *Weekly Standard*, August 6, 2007, http://www.weeklystandard.com/Content/Public/Articles/000/000/013/927hkdzx.asp?pg=2.

559 **ordered its wireless capacity turned off:** Dick Cheney and Reiner, *Heart*, 220.

559 **"The American people won't":** Rice interview. See also Gates, *Duty*, 185.

559 **He sent a message to the Saudis:** Dick Cheney, *In My Time*, 478.

560 **"In terms of thinking":** Cheney interview.

560 **"were pretty much on the same page":** Gates, *Duty*, 99.

560 **"revolt of the radical pragmatists":** Douglas Ollivant, author interview.

560 **He kept in his desk drawer:** Peter Baker, "Exit Toward Soul-Searching," *Washington Post*, October 7, 2007, http://www.washingtonpost.com/wp-dyn/content/article/2007/10/06/AR2007100601521.html.

560 **"I feel like I'm deserting you":** Ibid.

560 **"That was the first time":** White House aide, author interview.

561 **"I don't understand":** Baker, "President Besieged and Isolated."
561 **"The president," a senior administration official:** Ibid.
561 **suggesting the decision was:** In his resignation statement on August 27, 2007, Alberto Gonzales said, "Yesterday I met with President Bush and informed him of my decision to conclude my government service." http://www.youtube.com/watch?v=cEm3dTTrLpc.
562 **Tony Snow announced:** Michael Abramowitz, "Tony Snow Resigns as White House Spokesman," *Washington Post*, September 1, 2007, http://www.washingtonpost.com/wp-dyn/content/article/2007/08/31/AR2007083100664.html.
562 **After peaking at 126:** Iraq Coalition Casualty Count, known as icasualties.org, http://icasualties.org/iraq/ByMonth.aspx. Note that this link goes to the page showing all co-alition casualties; to get the American casualties requires using the filter at the bottom.
562 **fallen from 2,796 to 2,384:** Iraq Body Count, http://www.iraqbodycount.org/analysis/numbers/2007/.
562 **from 1,341 to 738:** Ibid.
562 **"The plan should be this":** Administration official interview.
562 **"That's our situation":** Ibid.
563 **"Get down":** Joe Hagin, author interview.
564 **"They felt the elation":** Eric Draper, author interview.
564 **"He's sent from central":** Petraeus interview.
564 **"My fighters will finish here":** Lute interview.
564 **"have dealt significant blows":** David Petraeus, testimony before joint hearing of House Armed Services and Foreign Affairs Committees, September 10, 2007, Federal News Service transcript.
564 **"Of course, al-Qaeda needs":** Reid, *Good Fight*, 10–11.
565 **"you can't refer to Baker":** Dick Cheney, *In My Time*, 460–63.
565 **"Did my visit endanger":** Administration official, author interview.
565 **"ordinary life is beginning":** George W. Bush, address to nation, September 13, 2007, http://georgewbush-whitehouse.archives.gov/news/releases/2007/09/20070913-2.html.
565 **"I've got a message":** Petraeus interview.

CHAPTER 33: "DON'T SCREW WITH THE PRESIDENT OF THE UNITED STATES"

566 **"What are you talking":** Christopher Hill, author interview. John Lackey pitched six innings in the series opener and gave up nine hits and four runs in the loss. The Red Sox swept the series in three games. http://www.baseball-reference.com/postseason/2007_ALDS1.shtml.
567 **"What we really need":** Hill interview.
567 **"What are you going to do":** Eric Edelman, author interview.
567 **"Dick, would you like to ask":** Hill interview.
568 **"The president is being sold":** Edelman interview.
568 **"I'm not a carbon copy":** Mitt Romney, Republican presidential debate sponsored by ABC News, August 5, 2007. See transcript at http://www.nytimes.com/2007/08/05/us/politics/05transcript-debate.html?pagewanted=print.
568 **"Absolutely not, because":** Ibid.
568 **had been a "train wreck":** John McCain, joint appearance with Governor Arnold Schwarzenegger of California, February 21, 2007, http://abcnews.go.com/Politics/story?id=2895526&page=1.

568 **"Wait 'til her fat ass":** Latimer, *Speech-Less*, 269–70.
569 **Clinton could be the Ike:** Peter Baker, "Bush to Hillary Clinton: I'm Truman, You're Ike," The Trail, washingtonpost.com, September 21, 2007, http://voices.washingtonpost.com/44/2007/09/bush-clinton-will-be-democrati.html.
569 **"there's not a liberal America":** Barack Obama, keynote address, Democratic National Convention, July 27, 2004, http://www.washingtonpost.com/wp-dyn/articles/A19751-2004Jul27.html.
569 **"stunning" in its "naiveté":** George W. Bush, off-the-record conversation with journalists on October 9, 2007. The author was not among the journalists invited and therefore not subject to the ground rules. Notes of the meeting were provided to the author by a person in the room.
569 **"This cat isn't remotely":** Latimer, *Speech-Less*, 267–69.
569 **Obama and Clinton refused to commit:** Democratic presidential debate, September 26, 2007.
569 **"He was willing to cut loose":** Condoleezza Rice, author interview.
570 **"Don't screw with the president":** Administration official interview.
570 **undergone a "remarkable change":** Abrams, *Tested by Zion*, 196–97.
571 **"Do I have an agreement?":** Rice interview.
571 **"including all core issues":** Joint Understanding, Annapolis Conference, November 27, 2007, http://georgewbush-whitehouse.archives.gov/news/releases/2007/11/20071127.html.
571 **"I can't read this":** Rice interview.
572 **some involving Mohsen Fakhrizadeh:** Jay Solomon, "Iran's Nuclear-Arms Guru Resurfaces," *Wall Street Journal*, August 30, 2012, http://online.wsj.com/article/SB10000872396390444230504577615971688458892.html.
572 **"Sir, that is an interesting":** Michael Hayden, author interview.
573 **"primarily in response":** Key Judgments, "Iran: Nuclear Intentions and Capabilities," National Intelligence Estimate, November 2007, http://www.dni.gov/press_releases/20071203_release.pdf.
573 **McConnell and Hayden did not want:** Hayden interview and Mike McConnell, e-mail exchange with author.
573 **possibility of "World War III":** George W. Bush, news conference, October 17, 2007, http://georgewbush-whitehouse.archives.gov/news/releases/2008/01/20071017.html.
573 **"This is a disaster":** Stephen Hadley, author interview.
573 **"It was a huge blow":** Ibid.
574 **"The results give us a reason":** George W. Bush, telephone call with Vladimir Putin, December 4, 2007. Notes of call provided to author.
574 **"A country that had one can":** George W. Bush, telephone call with Hu Jintao, December 6, 2007. Notes of call provided to author.
574 **"merits our consideration":** Gordon and Trainor, *Endgame*, 467–68.
574 **"a significant impediment":** Administration official, author interview.
574 **"I know there are people":** Ibid.
575 **"You're a terrible":** Ibid.
575 **A bipartisan commission:** John M. Broder, "House, 314–100, Passes Broad Energy Bill; Bush Plans to Sign It," *New York Times*, December 19, 2007, http://www.nytimes.com/2007/12/19/washington/19energy.html.
575 **"The legislation I'm about to":** George W. Bush, energy bill signing ceremony, December 19, 2007, http://georgewbush-whitehouse.archives.gov/news/releases/2007/12/20071219-6.html.
575 **just twenty-three American:** Iraq Coalition Casualty Count, known as

icasualties.org, http://icasualties.org/iraq/ByMonth.aspx. Note that this link goes to the page showing all coalition casualties; to get the American casualties requires using the filter at the bottom.

576 **"The United States strongly"**: George W. Bush, remarks to reporters, Crawford, December 27, 2007, http://georgewbush-whitehouse.archives.gov/news/releases/2007/12/20071227.html.

576 **told him that the economy**: Paulson, *On the Brink*, 85–86.

576 **Where Iraq had dominated**: A *Washington Post*–ABC News poll released on November 4, 2007, found that 29 percent of those surveyed named Iraq as their top issue, compared with 14 percent who named the economy. In a later poll released January 12, 2008, 29 percent identified the economy as the most important concern compared with 20 percent who said Iraq. http://www.washington post.com/wp-srv/politics/polls/postpoll_011408.html.

577 **called his predecessor to**: Heilemann and Halperin, *Game Change*, 227.

577 **"In this election year"**: George W. Bush, State of the Union address, January 28, 2008, http://georgewbush-whitehouse.archives.gov/news/releases/2008/01/20080128-13.html.

CHAPTER 34: "WHAT IS THIS, A CRUEL HOAX?"

578 **"a more flexible standard"**: Paul D. Clement, Brief for the United States as Amicus Curiae, District of Columbia v. Heller, January 2008. http://www.nraila.org/heller/primaries/07-290_PetitionerAmCuUSA.pdf.

578 **"What do you want to do?"**: Joshua Bolten, author interview.

579 **"What the fuck are you"**: Neil Patel, author interview.

579 **"They were so angry"**: Ibid.

579 **"You can't have more than"**: Bolten interview.

579 **"It's a process foul"**: Ibid. See also Dick Cheney, *In My Time*, 495.

579 **"Understood," Bolten replied**: Bolten interview.

580 **"He's the best vice president"**: George W. Bush, speech to Conservative Political Action Conference, February 8, 2008, http://georgewbush-whitehouse.archives.gov/news/releases/2008/02/20080208.html.

580 **"Cheney's view was that all"**: White House official, author interview.

580 **"Thank you for the peace"**: Peter Baker, "Bush, Feeling Appreciated Abroad," *Washington Post*, February 22, 2008, http://www.washingtonpost.com/wp-dyn/content/article/2008/02/21/AR2008022101585.html.

580 **"Of course, people talk"**: Jakaya Kikwete and George W. Bush, joint news conference, Dar es Salaam, Tanzania, February 17, 2008, http://georgewbush-whitehouse.archives.gov/news/releases/2008/02/20080217.html.

581 **spent $817 million to provide**: Larry E. André Jr., the chargé d'affaires at the U.S. embassy, Dar es Salaam, Tanzania, remarks at relief fund check presentation, May 27, 2009, http://tanzania.usembassy.gov/sp_05272009.html.

581 **"the best of the presidency"**: George W. Bush, *Decision Points*, 352.

581 **"He loved being in Africa"**: Rice interview.

581 **"I hope that he will campaign"**: George W. Bush and John McCain, joint appearance, March 5, 2008, http://georgewbush-whitehouse.archives.gov/news/releases/2008/03/20080305-4.html.

581 **"Tim, I have known mercy"**: Tim Goeglein, author interview.

581 **suggested to *Esquire***: Thomas M. Barnett, "The Man Between War and Peace," *Esquire*, April 2008, http://www.esquire.com/features/fox-fallon.

581 **"Do we have a MacArthur problem?":** Gates, *Duty*, 187–88.
581 **"I'd fire him in a heartbeat":** Senior official, author interview.
582 **"Don't say that":** Sorkin, *Too Big to Fail*, 38–39.
582 **"the fact is, the whole system":** Paulson, *On the Brink*, 92.
582 **"This is the real thing":** Ibid., 96.
582 **"you can take out that":** Ibid., 101–2.
582 **"It seems like I showed up":** George W. Bush, speech to Economic Club of New York, March 14, 2008, http://georgewbush-whitehouse.archives.gov/news/releases/2008/03/20080314-5.html.
583 **comparing the president:** Senator Charles Schumer told a news conference, "The president is looking more and more like Herbert Hoover, sort of whistling a happy tune as the economy heads south." Federal News Service transcript, March 14, 2008.
583 **"We're going to get killed":** Sorkin, *Too Big to Fail*, 38–39.
583 **"Two-thirds of Americans":** Martha Raddatz, interview with Dick Cheney, March 19, 2007. After a furor arose about his answer, Cheney tried to pass it off, saying Raddatz had simply made a statement and he was prompting her for a question. He gave another interview to Raddatz on March 24, 2007, and when she asked about it, he said, "Well, you didn't really ask me a question, Martha, as I recall." But he went on to essentially reaffirm his meaning. "The point I wanted to make and I will make again is the president of the United States under these circumstances dealing with these kinds of issues can't make decisions based on public opinion polls."
583 **"He believed that losing":** John Hannah, author interview.
583 **"Everything else was less important":** Liz Cheney, author interview.
583 **"It was very, very precipitous":** David Petraeus, author interview.
584 **"Everybody here thought this":** Douglas Lute, author interview.
584 **"Don't tell me this is a bad":** George W. Bush, *Decision Points*, 389.
584 **"This has some potential":** Petraeus interview.
584 **"We have wanted him to step up":** Lute interview.
584 **"This is going to be a decisive":** Petraeus interview.
584 **"I hope it's going to be":** Ibid.
585 **"He came back from Basra":** Lute interview.
585 **"went from being docile":** Lindsey Graham, author interview.
586 **"So you're saying you're":** Fiona Hill, author interview.
586 **"You're not with the policy":** Ibid. In an e-mail exchange with the author, Joe Wood said he did not recall saying those words but may have said that "I didn't think she should push any policy view one way or the other."
586 **"I looked in his eyes and I saw":** Administration official, author interview. In his memoir, Gates later wrote that he "had seen a stone-cold killer." Gates, *Duty*, 169.
586 **"was truly overreaching":** Gates, *Duty*, 157–58.
586 **"If they want it and they've":** Second administration official, author interview.
586 **"This is about me and Angela":** Damon Wilson, author interview.
586 **"I will see you at the OK":** Ibid.
587 **Putin had compared the United:** Vladimir Putin, speech, Munich Security Conference, May 9, 2007. He said, "We do not have the right to forget the causes of any war, which must be sought in the mistakes and errors of peacetime. Moreover, in our time, these threats are not diminishing. They are only transforming, changing their appearance. In these new threats, as during the time of the Third Reich, are the same contempt for human life and the same claims of exceptional-

ity and diktat in the world." Andrew E. Kramer, *New York Times*, May 9, 2007, http://www.nytimes.com/2007/05/09/world/europe/10cnd-russia.html.

587 **"Look, the only way I can":** Wilson interview.

587 **"We agreed today that":** Bucharest Summit Declaration, NATO Summit, April 3, 2008, http://www.nato.int/cps/en/natolive/official_texts_8443.htm.

587 **"The Russians were furious":** Hill interview.

587 **"flashing yellow light":** Carl Bildt, the Swedish foreign minister, used the term in describing how Mikheil Saakashvili interpreted messages from Washington. Asmus, *Little War That Shook the World*, 142–44.

588 **"wanted something more robust":** David Gordon, author interview.

588 **"We were arguing that":** Ibid.

589 **"We had an extremely":** Patel interview.

589 **"There were a lot of questions":** Jim Connaughton, author interview.

590 **"The wrong way is":** George W. Bush, speech on climate change, Rose Garden, April 16, 2008, http://georgewbush-whitehouse.archives.gov/news/releases/2008/04/20080416-6.html.

590 **"Most people looked around":** Patel interview.

590 **"Looking back, maybe we":** Connaughton interview.

590 **"going fucking crazy":** Hayden interview.

590 **Palestinians 94 percent:** Rice, *No Higher Honor*, 651–53.

591 **"It sounds like he's serious":** Ibid.

591 **playing "Trumpet Voluntary":** Sandra Sobieraj Westfall and Beth Perry, "Jenna Bush's Texas Style Wedding," *People*, May 26, 2008, http://www.people.com/people/archive/article/0,,20203980,00.html.

591 **Bush had it rewritten:** Ed Gillespie, author interview. See also Matt Latimer, "When Bush Caved to Egypt," *The Daily Beast*, January 30, 2011, http://www.thedailybeast.com/articles/2011/01/30/president-bush-pulled-his-punches-on-egypts-mubarak-too.html.

591 **"a fateful misstep":** McClellan, *What Happened*, xii.

592 **find a way to forgive:** Dana Perino, author interview at the time.

592 **Karen Hughes was struck:** Karen Hughes, author interview.

592 **"The only reason I have":** Brett McGurk, author interview. This was a favorite Cheney line. When Mark Leibovich, then a reporter for the *Washington Post*, asked him in the first term whether he would write a memoir someday, Cheney said, "Sometimes I think I got this job because I didn't write about the last job." See Leibovich, "The Strong, Silent Type," *Washington Post*, January 18, 2004.

592 **"If he doesn't want me to go":** Latimer, *Speech-Less*, 267–69.

592 **"He can't get five hundred":** Ibid.

593 **"What do you guys think about":** Administration official, author interview. In an interview with the author, Ed Gillespie said he did not remember that conversation.

593 **"shall not be suspended":** Article I, Section 9, U.S. Constitution, http://www.archives.gov/exhibits/charters/constitution_transcript.html.

593 **"The laws and Constitution":** Anthony M. Kennedy, majority opinion, *Boumediene v. Bush*, June 12, 2008, http://www.law.cornell.edu/supct/html/06-1195.ZO.html.

593 **she refused to use them:** Sean McCormack, author interview.

594 **"We're just signing a piece of paper":** Matt Latimer, author interview.

594 **"Now *that's* verifiable":** Rice interview.

CHAPTER 35: "OUR PEOPLE ARE GOING TO HATE US FOR THIS"

595 **"That's ridiculous":** Baker, "Final Days."
596 **"Nothing can erase":** John Bolton, "The Tragic End of Bush's North Korea Policy," *Wall Street Journal*, June 30, 2008, http://online.wsj.com/article/SB121478274355214441.html?mod=djemEditorialPage.
596 **"Let me just say from":** Baker, "Final Days."
596 **"Phyllis Schlafly with a mustache":** Christopher Hill, author interview.
596 **"Do you really want to":** Stephen Hadley, author interview.
596 **"seemed so out of keeping":** Dick Cheney, *In My Time*, 486.
597 **"he was only going to fight":** Cheney friend, author interview.
597 **"Cheney won that one":** Ibid.
597 **"On balance":** Michael Hayden, author interview.
597 **"We have been 0 for '07":** Ibid.
597 **"We're seeing a dangerous accumulation":** Juan Carlos Zarate, author interview.
598 **The plan called for a much:** Senior administration officials, author interviews. See also Schmitt and Shanker, *Counterstrike*, 102–3.
598 **"a Home Depot–sized warehouse":** Hayden interview.
598 **"We're going to stop playing the game":** Mazzetti, *Way of the Knife*, 267.
599 **69 percent disapproval:** Gallup Poll, April 18–20, 2008, http://www.gallup.com/poll/106741/bushs-69-job-disapproval-rating-highest-gallup-history.aspx.
599 **just 28 percent supported:** *New York Times*/CBS News poll, March 28–April 2, 2008. http://graphics8.nytimes.com/packages/pdf/politics/20080404_POLL.PDF.
599 **contemplating Bush's assassination:** Nicholson Baker published *Checkpoint* in 2004 about a character who threatens to kill Bush. In 2006, Gabriel Range produced the movie *Death of a President* with computer-generated special effects depicting Bush's assassination. Among those who considered it in poor taste was Hillary Clinton, who called it "despicable" and "absolutely outrageous." Dwight R. Worley, "Sen. Hillary Clinton Blasts Bush Assassination Film," *Journal News*, September 16, 2006, http://web.archive.org/web/20061023003633/http://www.lohud.com/apps/pbcs.dll/article?AID=/20060916/UPDATE/609160394. And in 2007, Krandall Kraus published the novel *The Assassination of George W. Bush: A Love Story*, in which a disillusioned Secret Service agent from Midland, Texas, decides to kill Bush.
599 **68 percent of Americans:** *USA Today*/Gallup poll, June 15–19, 2008, http://www.gallup.com/poll/108490/americans-worry-mccain-would-too-similar-bush.aspx.
599 **"He became an albatross":** Joseph Lieberman, author interview.
599 **"It wasn't fair":** Charles Black, author interview.
599 **Black was deputized:** Ibid. See also Heilemann and Halperin, *Game Change*, 366.
599 **"It was so ingrained in":** Nicolle Wallace, author interview.
600 **"listened too much":** Roger Simon, "McCain Bashes Cheney over Iraq Policy," *Politico*, January 22, 2007, http://www.politico.com/news/stories/0107/2390.html.
600 **"His attitude was, look":** Black interview.
600 **to the storm as "disgraceful":** Elisabeth Bumiller, "McCain Assails Administration for 'Disgraceful' Response to Katrina," *New York Times*, April 25, 2008, http://www.nytimes.com/2008/04/25/world/americas/25iht-mccain.4.12355635.html.

600 **"Republicans will be saying":** Notes taken by participants after private conversations with George W. Bush, provided to author.

600 **"I felt that a straightforward":** Dick Cheney, *In My Time*, 520.

600 **"He had the sometimes":** George W. Bush remarks, Tony Snow memorial service, July 17, 2008, http://georgewbush-whitehouse.archives.gov/news/releases/2008/07/20080717-1.html.

601 **"Mr. President, it is in this":** Administration official, author interview.

601 **"when I made the decision":** Senior official, author interview.

601 **"It was literally like William Wallace":** Tony Fratto, author interview.

602 **"We're worse off than we":** John McCain, campaign ad, "Broken," August 5, 2008, http://www.youtube.com/watch?v=ylJkmMR8Fek.

602 **He found Medvedev "hot":** George W. Bush, *Decision Points*, 434–35.

602 **Later reports indicated:** A European Union investigation, citing a Russian official agency, reported that 162 South Ossetian civilians were killed during the entire course of the war from August 7 to 12. South Ossetia produced a list of 365 residents killed during the entire war, including both civilians and members of the armed services. Independent International Fact-Finding Mission on the Conflict in Georgia, 223–24, http://www.ceiig.ch/pdf/IIFFMCG_Volume_II.pdf.

602 **"I hope you're not":** George W. Bush, *Decision Points*, 434–35.

603 **"I've been warning you":** Ibid.

603 **"Look, I'm already in a war":** Fiona Hill, author interview.

603 **"I need to give him an answer":** Several administration officials, author interviews.

603 **"a fair amount of chest beating":** Rice, *No Higher Honor*, 688–89.

603 **"I think you need to poll":** Stephen Hadley, author interview.

604 **regime change as their goal:** Sergei Lavrov, the Russian foreign minister, told Condoleezza Rice by phone that one condition of a cease-fire was that "Misha Saakashvili has to go." Rice rejected the demand and made it public. See Rice, *No Higher Honor*, 688.

604 **"I want to hang Saakashvili":** French newspaper accounts, cited by Asmus, *Little War That Shook the World*, 199.

604 **"Did you look at a map?":** Condoleezza Rice, author interview.

605 **"What's the one thing":** William Luti, author interview.

605 **the announcer say "Pawlenty":** Heilemann and Halperin, *Game Change*, 382.

605 **"I'm trying to remember":** Latimer, *Speech-Less*, 273. In an interview with the author, Ed Gillespie said that "would capture the sentiment" that the president felt about Palin.

606 **"reckless choice":** Heilemann and Halperin, *Game Change*, 368. In an interview after leaving office, Cheney told Jonathan Karl of ABC News that the Palin pick was a "mistake" because "she'd only been governor for, what, two years" and "I don't think she passed that test" of being prepared to take over the presidency. See Karl, "Dick Cheney: Picking Sarah Palin for VP Was 'a Mistake,'" July 29, 2012, http://abcnews.go.com/blogs/politics/2012/07/dick-cheney-picking-sarah-palin-for-vp-was-a-mistake/.

606 **"You really want me to":** Latimer, *Speech-Less*, 269–70. In an interview with the author, Gillespie said he did not recall that.

606 **"From stem to stern, President Bush":** Wayne Berman, author interview.

606 **"not chasing the public opinion polls":** Latimer, *Speech-Less*, 271.

606 **"My fellow citizens, we live":** George W. Bush, video address to Republican National Convention, September 2, 2008, http://georgewbush-whitehouse.archives.gov/news/releases/2008/09/20080902-11.html.

607 **twelve times as often:** Peter Baker, "The Party in Power, Running as If It Weren't,"

New York Times, September 5, 2008, http://www.nytimes.com/2008/09/05/us/politics/05assess.html.

607 **McCain thanked "the president":** John McCain, acceptance speech, Republican National Convention, September 4, 2008, http://elections.nytimes.com/2008/president/conventions/videos/transcripts/20080904_MCCAIN_SPEECH.html.

607 **"did the president say":** Murphy and Purdum, "Farewell to All That."

607 **"Do they know it's coming, Hank?":** Paulson, *On the Brink*, 1.

608 **"What the hell is going on?":** George W. Bush, *Decision Points*, 456–58.

608 **"Will we be able to explain":** Ibid.

608 **"How did we get to this":** Paulson, *On the Brink*, 235–37.

608 **"If we don't shore up":** Ibid.

608 **"Someday you guys are going":** Ibid.

609 **"stopped saying he was glad":** Charlie Younger, author interview.

609 **"what else can go wrong":** Karen Hughes, author interview.

609 **"do you have a death wish?":** David Petraeus, author interview.

610 **"What happens if we don't?":** Ed Gillespie, author interview. For a slightly different version of the conversation, see Paulson, *On the Brink*, 255–57.

610 **"I will give you all":** Joel Kaplan, author interview.

610 **"Our people are going to hate us":** Tony Fratto, author interview.

610 **"In that political environment":** Ibid.

611 **"Tell Hank to calm down":** Michele Davis, author interview. See also Paulson, *On the Brink*, 255–57.

611 **"If we're really looking at":** George W. Bush, *Decision Points*, 439–40.

611 **despite twenty-five trips by Condoleezza Rice:** Rice visited Israel and the Palestinian territories three times as much as Colin Powell did and twice as much as any other destination during her four years in office. http://history.state.gov/departmenthistory/travels/secretary/rice-condoleezza.

611 **should be called MARX:** Latimer, *Speech-Less*, 265–66.

611 **a "strong supporter" of it:** Dick Cheney, *In My Time*, 506–8.

611 **"They were a nonfactor":** Matt Latimer, author interview.

612 **It was "a stunt":** Latimer, *Speech-Less*, 258–62.

612 **calling McCain a "stupid prick":** Ibid.

612 **"I could see the headlines":** George W. Bush, *Decision Points*, 460–62.

612 **"McCain asked for this":** David Axelrod, author interview.

612 **"We can't even defend":** Latimer, *Speech-Less*, 258–62.

612 **concluded there were $3 trillion:** Ed Lazear, author interview.

612 **"our entire economy":** George W. Bush, address to nation, September 24, 2008, http://georgewbush-whitehouse.archives.gov/news/releases/2008/09/20080924-10.html.

613 **"I don't think Congress has":** George W. Bush, telephone call with Angela Merkel, September 25, 2008. Notes of call provided to author.

613 **"What's McCain going to":** Heilemann and Halperin, *Game Change*, 387–89.

613 **"Hank, we are going to get":** Kaplan interview. See also Paulson, *On the Brink*, 295–300.

614 **"We need to get there":** Kaplan interview. See also Paulson, *On the Brink*, 295–300.

614 **"If money isn't loosened up":** Several participants, author interviews. See also George W. Bush, *Decision Points*, 460–62; Dick Cheney, *In My Time*, 509; Paulson, *On the Brink*, 295–300; Sorkin, *Too Big to Fail*, 492–93; Heilemann and Halperin, *Game Change*, 387–89; and Balz and Johnson, *Battle for America*, 348.

615 **"I told you you'd miss me":** Jonathan Alter, *The Promise: President Obama, Year*

One (New York: Simon & Schuster, 2011), 12. Alter added this to the paperback edition.

615 **"It was almost like children"**: Eric Draper, author interview.
615 **"Well, I've clearly lost control"**: Several participants, author interviews.
615 **"That was the most ridiculous"**: White House official interview.
615 **"Gee, Hank, I didn't know"**: Paulson, *On the Brink*, 295–300.
615 **"They're not going to get"**: Fratto interview.
616 **"Six hundred points!"**: Julie Hirschfeld Davis, "Bailout Bill Slapped Aside; Record Stock Plunge," Associated Press, September 29, 2008.
616 **went down 228 to 205**: U.S. House Clerk's Office. http://clerk.house.gov/evs/2008/roll674.xml.
616 **had plummeted 777 points**: Davis, "Bailout Bill Slapped Aside."
616 **"Let's get Hank back over"**: Fratto interview.
616 **"this could be worse than 9/11"**: Draper interview.
616 **"Give us the ball for twenty-four hours"**: Kaplan interview.
616 **"If you don't pass this"**: Specter, *Life Among the Cannibals*, 141.
616 **74 to 25 later that day**: U.S. Senate roll call record. http://www.senate.gov/legislative/LIS/roll_call_lists/roll_call_vote_cfm.cfm?congress=110&session=2&vote=00212.
617 **263 to 171 two days later**: U.S. House Clerk's Office. http://clerk.house.gov/evs/2008/roll681.xml.
617 **smoked cigars to mark**: Fratto interview.
617 **"I realized this is not"**: Petraeus interview.
617 **"How important is this"**: Stephen Hadley, author interview.
617 **"You know, Condi, you"**: Ibid.
618 **"I just don't think it is"**: Ibid.
618 **"quite pleased"**: Cheney aide, author interview.

CHAPTER 36: "I DIDN'T WANT TO BE THE PRESIDENT DURING A DEPRESSION"

619 **contingency plans for Obama**: Peter Baker, "Bush Prepares Crisis Briefings to Aid Obama," *New York Times*, December 16, 2008, http://www.nytimes.com/2008/12/17/us/politics/17transition.html.
619 **until the end of 2015**: Gordon and Trainor, *Endgame*, 539–41.
620 **an "eviction notice"**: Ed Gillespie, author interview.
620 **Just 14 American troops**: Iraq Coalition Casualty Count, known as icasualties.org, http://icasualties.org/iraq/ByMonth.aspx. Note that this link goes to the page showing all coalition casualties; to get the American casualties requires using the filter at the bottom.
620 **set to the tune of a song**: Rice, *No Higher Honor*, 703.
620 **"Colonel Qaddafi?" Bush said**: George W. Bush, telephone conversation with Muammar el-Qaddafi, November 17, 2008. Notes of call provided to author.
621 **"About the only thing that"**: George W. Bush, remarks, Kennedy Center honors ceremony, White House, December 7, 2008, http://www.youtube.com/watch?v=cXH8ww1XACE.
621 **"We've still got a few weeks"**: Rice, *No Higher Honor*, 722.
621 **asked Washington for**: Bill Vlasic and David M. Herszenhorn, "Pursuing U.S. Aid, G.M. Accepts Need for Drastic Cuts," *New York Times*, December 2, 2008, http://www.nytimes.com/2008/12/03/business/03auto.html?fta=y.
621 **"If he told me he made a decision"**: Dick Cheney, author interview.

622 **"There is no way in heck":** Rattner, *Overhaul*, 34–36.
622 **passed the House that night 237 to 170:** U.S. House Clerk's Office. http://clerk.house.gov/evs/2008/roll690.xml.
622 **"consider other options if":** Dana Perino, statement, December 12, 2008, http://georgewbush-whitehouse.archives.gov/news/releases/2008/12/20081212.html.
622 **"I remember what it was like":** Administration official, author interview.
623 **"This is the farewell kiss":** Steven Lee Myers and Alissa J. Rubin, "Iraqi Journalist Hurls Shoes at Bush and Denounces Him on TV as a 'Dog,'" *New York Times*, December 15, 2008, http://www.nytimes.com/2008/12/15/world/middleeast/15prexy.html?pagewanted=all.
623 **"I'm okay," Bush told:** Video of incident. http://www.youtube.com/watch?v=-xKFh4PYmmc&feature=related.
624 **"was white as a sheet":** Draper interview.
624 **"Don't worry about it":** Video of incident. http://www.youtube.com/watch?v=-xKFh4PYmmc&feature=related.
624 **"Maliki's guards start beating":** Douglas Lute, author interview.
624 **"Hey, please, don't worry":** Administration official interview.
624 **"That man, he represents":** Ibid.
625 **"Good reflexes":** Ibid.
625 **could not let the firms go:** Joel Kaplan and Ed Lazear, author interviews.
625 **"Look, Hank, you have to":** Kaplan interview.
626 **"This is a difficult time":** George W. Bush, speech and question session, American Enterprise Institute, December 18, 2008, http://georgewbush-whitehouse.archives.gov/news/releases/2008/12/20081218-2.html.
627 **"In the midst of a financial":** George W. Bush, remarks announcing auto bailout, December 19, 2008, http://georgewbush-whitehouse.archives.gov/news/releases/2008/12/20081219.html.
627 **"And this year, Mr. President":** Joshua Bolten, author interview. See also Rattner, *Overhaul*, 41–42.
627 **"You know, it's kind of like":** George W. Bush, news conference, January 12, 2009, http://georgewbush-whitehouse.archives.gov/news/releases/2009/01/20090112.html.
628 **"remind and explain":** Walter McDougall, e-mail exchange with author.
628 **Guelzo suggested he focus:** Allen Guelzo, e-mail exchange with author.
628 **"The presidency did not eat":** John Lewis Gaddis, author interview.
628 **"It just came out very quickly":** Ibid.

CHAPTER 37: "SUCH A SENSE OF BETRAYAL"

629 **he granted just 189 pardons:** Office of the Pardon Attorney, U.S. Department of Justice, http://www.justice.gov/pardon/statistics.htm#w-bush. Barack Obama in his first years in office was comparably stingy with pardons.
630 **When the New York *Daily News*:** John Marzulli and James Gordon Meek, "President Bush Pardons Brooklyn Home Scammer," *New York Daily News*, December 23, 2008, http://articles.nydailynews.com/2008-12-23/news/17911607_1_pardon-attorney-ronald-rodgers-isaac-toussie-minority-homebuyers.
630 **"Figure out some way":** The account of the pardon deliberations, where not otherwise sourced, is based on author interviews with several administration officials and others who were involved but asked not to be named.
630 **Clay Johnson, his Yale friend:** Clay Johnson, e-mail exchange with author.

631 **"Not a chance"**: Charlie Younger, author interview.
631 **"The Powell-Armitage thing was"**: Liz Cheney, author interview.
631 **"I didn't have anything to do"**: Richard Armitage, author interview.
631 **"I'm sorry, Scooter"**: Joshua Bolten, author interview.
632 **"I am innocent"**: William Burck, author interview.
632 **"This sucks," Bush said**: Dan Bartlett, author interview.
633 **"Can I talk to you a minute?"**: Condoleezza Rice, author interview.
633 **"Just make up your mind"**: George W. Bush, *Decision Points*, 104–5.
633 **"I got this list of people"**: Jim Langdon, author interview.
633 **"the manifestation of one of our worst"**: Juan Carlos Zarate, author interview.
633 **"Is the Secret Service going"**: Peter Baker, "Obama's War over Terror," *New York Times Magazine*, January 4, 2010, http://www.nytimes.com/2010/01/17/magazine/17Terror-t.html?pagewanted=all.
634 **"Enjoyed working with you"**: White House memo, January 19, 2009, provided to author.
634 **"many fond memories"**: George W. Bush, telephone conversation with Vladimir Putin, January 19, 2009. Notes of call provided to author.
635 **"The place was going condo"**: Bolten interview.
635 **"Okay, I'm going over"**: Draper interview.
635 **"It's like Noah's ark"**: Ibid.
635 **"Cheney looked like hell"**: Joel Kaplan, author interview.
636 **"Joe, this is how you're"**: Dick Cheney, *In My Time*, 517.
636 **"I thank President Bush"**: Barack Obama, inaugural address, January 20, 2009, http://www.whitehouse.gov/the-press-office/president-barack-obamas-inaugural-address.
636 **"That was a hell of a speech"**: Peter Baker, "On Plane to Texas, Critiques of the Speech," *New York Times*, January 22, 2009, http://www.nytimes.com/2009/01/23/us/politics/22web-baker.html.
637 **"Come on, Laura"**: Peter Baker, "Obama Takes Oath, and Nation in Crisis Embraces the Moment," *New York Times*, January 21, 2009, http://www.nytimes.com/2009/01/21/us/politics/21inaug.html?pagewanted=all.
637 **"We will brief you"**: David Axelrod, author interview.
637 **"He looked relieved, thrilled"**: Draper interview.
637 **"Frankly, all of us were worried"**: Kaplan interview.
637 **"George Bush's two terms"**: David Addington, interview with R. J. Cutler for *The World According to Dick Cheney*, a documentary aired on Showtime in spring 2013.
637 **"Nice plane, Mick"**: Mick McMurry, author interview.
637 **"He was in excruciating pain"**: Bill Thomson, author interview.
637 **"For Dick, he was pretty"**: McMurry interview.
638 **"It was a nonstop party"**: Draper interview.
638 **"He was very huggy"**: White House aide, author interview.
638 **"not a word" disparaging**: Baker, "On Plane to Texas."
638 **"Just stay strong"**: Video by Ken Herman, Cox Newspapers, http://www.youtube.com/watch?v=EI0eRJuIrT8.
638 **"I have the privilege"**: George W. Bush, speech to supporters, Midland, Tex., January 20, 2009, http://www.realclearpolitics.com/articles/2009/01/bush_returns_to_texas.html. See also Jim Rutenberg, "Bushes Have a Warm Homecoming in Texas," *New York Times*, January 21, 2009, http://www.nytimes.com/2009/01/21/us/politics/21bush.html. Also see C-Span video, http://www.c-spanvideo.org/program/283465-1.

EPILOGUE: "THERE IS NO MIDDLE GROUND"

640 **"It was designed for the two":** Dick Cheney, author interview.

641 **"deserves my silence":** Ian Austen, "Bush Gives First Speech Since Leaving Office," *New York Times*, March 17, 2009, http://www.nytimes.com/2009/03/18/world/americas/18canada.html?_r=0.

641 **"The American people are not":** Barack Obama, speech, National Archives, May 21, 2009, http://www.whitehouse.gov/the-press-office/remarks-president-national-security-5-21-09.

641 **"In the fight against terrorism":** Dick Cheney, speech, American Enterprise Institute, May 21, 2009, http://www.politico.com/news/stories/0509/22823.html.

641 **"Dick feels an obligation":** Bill Thomson, author interview.

641 **"Cheney thought that was shameful":** Stephen Hadley, author interview.

641 **"Threatening to prosecute CIA":** Liz Cheney, author interview.

642 **"He'll never criticize Bush":** David Gordon, author interview.

642 **"Dick was terribly upset":** Bernie Seebaum, author interview.

642 **"The statute of limitations":** Barton Gellman, "Cheney Uncloaks His Frustration with Bush," *Washington Post*, August 13, 2009, http://articles.washingtonpost.com/2009-08-13/politics/36798654_1_channels-of-american-policy-richard-b-cheney-john-p-hannah.

642 **"This is not the right word":** Bush friend, author interview.

642 **back into "the swamp":** Peter Baker, "Now Appearing: George W. Bush," *New York Times*, November 6, 2010, http://www.nytimes.com/2010/11/07/weekinreview/07baker.html.

642 **"When I saw his hand go":** Dinner party guest, author interview.

643 **"I'm for Mitt Romney":** George W. Bush made the comment on May 15, 2012, when ABC News caught up with him after an event unveiling a collection of interviews with world dissidents. http://abcnews.go.com/blogs/politics/2012/05/george-w-bush-im-for-mitt-romney/.

643 **"He's a golf-a-holic now":** Charlie Younger, author interview.

643 **"I decided I was going to get":** Harrington, "Dubya and Me."

643 **"I've never seen a happier":** Wayne Berman, author interview.

643 **"I'm often asked, do you miss":** George W. Bush, joint presentation with Bill Clinton at IHS Forum at CERAWeek, Houston, March 11, 2011. The event was closed to reporters, but a transcript was provided to the author.

643 **"I actually found my freedom":** Peter Baker, "Bush Dips a Toe Back into Washington," *New York Times*, May 15, 2012, http://www.nytimes.com/2012/05/16/us/politics/george-w-bush-briefly-visits-washington.html.

643 **"It was more like meeting":** Valerie Jarrett, author interview.

644 **"carrying out Bush's 4th term":** Ari Fleischer, Twitter message, June 6, 2013. He wrote: "Drone strikes. Wiretaps. Gitmo. O is carrying out Bush's 4th term. Yet he attacked Bush 4 violating Constitution. # hypocrisy."

645 **"There's no doubt that whatever":** Jay Winik, author interview.

645 **"In retrospect, I probably":** George W. Bush, *Decision Points*, 259.

646 **Seventy-one percent:** Presidential Approval Ratings—George W. Bush, Gallup, http://www.gallup.com/poll/116500/presidential-approval-ratings-george-bush.aspx.

646 **Academic scholars:** Presidential Expert Poll, Siena College Research Institute, July 1, 2010. The survey of 238 presidential scholars ranked Bush at 39th of the 43 presidents, down from 23rd in a 2002 survey. https://www.siena.edu/pages/179.asp?item=2566.

647 **"Oh sure. I don't think":** Dick Cheney, interview with Matt Lauer, *Today*, August 30, 2011, http://video.msnbc.msn.com/msnbc/44328388#44328388.
647 **"There's no need to defend myself":** George W. Bush, interview with *USA Today*, April 21, 2013, http://www.usatoday.com/story/news/nation/2013/04/21/george-w-bush-interview-library/2099093/.
647 **"The tendency in life is to feel":** Bush presentation at CERAWeek.
648 **49 percent of Americans now expressing favorable views:** Gallup poll, June 1–4, 2013, http://www.gallup.com/poll/163022/former-george-bush-image-ratings-improve.aspx.
648 **"saved us from another Great Depression":** John Harwood, "Fed Chairman's Departure Casts a New Light on the Bush Legacy," *New York Times*, July 27, 2013.
648 **"Decades from now":** George W. Bush, *Decision Points*, 476–77.
648 **"You're leaving as one":** Former aide, author interview.
649 **"I just don't think he would":** Ari Fleischer, author interview. In his memoir, Rove wrote: "Would the Iraq War have occurred without WMD? I doubt it." See *Courage and Consequence*, 339.
649 **"I'm convinced that President Bush":** Richard Armitage, author interview.
649 **"I am very respectful of how":** Donald Rumsfeld, author interview.
649 **"It breaks my heart":** Karen Hughes, author interview.
649 **"The first grave mistake":** McClellan, *What Happened*, 210.
650 **"You can say he made":** Joseph Lieberman, author interview.
650 **"If Iraq had gone well":** Michael Gerson, author interview.
650 **"Wall Street got drunk":** George W. Bush, comments during closed fund-raiser caught on amateur video and posted on the Internet. http://www.youtube.com/watch?v=bT29fq0slGc.
650 **"You have to ask the question":** David Frum, author interview.
651 **"intense, personal, dedicated efforts":** Donna Brazile, "Brazile: Bush Came Through on Katrina," CNN.com, April 25, 2013. http://www.cnn.com/2013/04/25/opinion/brazile-katrina-bush.
651 **"Two years after you left":** Peter Baker, "Bush and Cheney, Together Again at Groundbreaking," *New York Times*, November 16, 2010. http://www.nytimes.com/2010/11/17/us/politics/17bush.html?_r=0.
651 **"He was a great vice president":** Ibid.
651 **"You know, it's been cordial":** George W. Bush, interview with C-Span, aired April 24, 2013. http://www.youtube.com/watch?v=R8gMEqiVcr0&feature=youtube.
651 **"From the day I asked Dick":** George W. Bush, speech at opening of George W. Bush Presidential Library and Museum, April 25, 2013. http://foxnewsinsider.com/2013/04/25/transcript-read-fmr-president-george-w-bushs-address-library-dedication.
652 **Bush said tersely, "Never.":** Maureen Dowd, "History: Get Me Rewrite!" *The New York Times,* February 19, 2014. Dowd was not on the plane but later obtained an account of the conversation. Since she was not a participant, she was not bound by the off-the-record ground rules.
652 **"everything went blank":** Dick Cheney, *In My Time*, 524–25.
652 **"If this is dying":** Dick Cheney and Reiner, *Heart*, 1.
652 **"Ever since the heart transplant":** Mary Cheney, conversation with author.
653 **"Well, if that's true":** David Hume Kennerly, author interview.
653 **"Something happened in Washington":** Sandy Kress, author interview.
653 **"Bush had a little bit":** Wayne Berman, author interview.
653 **"He's his own man":** Joe O'Neill, author interview.

BIBLIOGRAPHY

Abdullah II, King. *Our Last Best Chance: The Pursuit of Peace in a Time of Peril*. New York: Viking, 2011.

Abrams, Elliott. *Tested by Zion: The Bush Administration and the Israeli-Palestinian Conflict*. New York: Cambridge University Press, 2013.

Albright, David. *Peddling Peril: How the Secret Nuclear Trade Arms America's Enemies*. New York: Simon & Schuster, 2010.

Annan, Kofi. *Interventions: A Life in War and Peace*. With Nader Mousavizadeh. New York: Penguin Press, 2012.

Ashcroft, John. *Never Again: Securing America and Restoring Justice*. New York: Center Street, 2006.

Asmus, Ronald D. *A Little War That Shook the World: Georgia, Russia, and the Future of the West*. New York: Palgrave Macmillan, 2010.

Atkinson, Rick. *In the Company of Soldiers: A Chronicle of Combat in Iraq*. New York: Henry Holt, 2004.

Baker, James A., III. *The Politics of Diplomacy: Revolution, War, and Peace, 1989–1992*. With Thomas M. DeFrank. New York: Putnam, 1995.

———. *"Work Hard, Study . . . and Keep out of Politics!": Adventures and Lessons from an Unexpected Public Life*. With Steve Fiffer. New York: G. P. Putnam's Sons, 2006.

Baker, Peter, and Susan Glasser. *Kremlin Rising: Vladimir Putin and the End of Revolution*. New York: Scribner, 2005.

Balz, Dan, and Haynes Johnson. *The Battle for America, 2008: The Story of an Extraordinary Election*. New York: Viking, 2009.

Bamford, James. *Pretext for War: 9/11, Iraq, and the Abuse of America's Intelligence Agencies*. New York: Doubleday, 2004.

Ben-Veniste, Richard. *The Emperor's New Clothes: Exposing the Truth from Watergate to 9/11*. New York: Thomas Dunne Books, 2009.

Bergen, Peter. *The Longest War: Inside the Enduring Conflict Between America and al-Qaeda*. New York: Free Press, 2011.

———. *Manhunt: The Ten-Year Search for bin Laden—from 9/11 to Abbottabad*. New York: Crown, 2012.

Blair, Cherie. *Speaking for Myself: My Life from Liverpool to Downing Street*. New York: Little, Brown, 2008.

Blair, Tony. *A Journey: My Political Life*. New York: Knopf, 2010.

Bolton, John. *Surrender Is Not an Option: Defending America at the United Nations.* New York: Threshold, 2007.

Bonin, Richard. *Arrows of the Night: Ahmad Chalabi's Long Journey to Triumph in Iraq.* New York: Doubleday, 2011.

Bowden, Mark. *The Finish: The Killing of Osama bin Laden.* New York: Atlantic Monthly Press, 2012.

Brady, John. *Bad Boy: The Life and Politics of Lee Atwater.* New York: Addison-Wesley, 1996.

Bremer, L. Paul, III. *My Year in Iraq: The Struggle to Build a Future of Hope.* With Malcolm McConnell. New York: Simon & Schuster, 2006.

Bridgeland, John M. *Heart of the Nation: Volunteering and America's Civic Spirit.* Lanham, Md.: Rowman & Littlefield, 2012.

Brinkley, Douglas. *The Great Deluge: Hurricane Katrina, New Orleans, and the Mississippi Gulf Coast.* New York: Morrow, 2006.

Broadwell, Paula. *All In: The Education of General David Petraeus.* With Vernon Loeb. New York: Penguin Press, 2012.

Brown, Michael, and Ted Schwarz. *Deadly Indifference: The Perfect (Political) Storm: Hurricane Katrina, the Bush White House, and Beyond.* Lanham, Md.: Taylor Trade Publishing, 2011.

Bruni, Frank. *Ambling into History: The Unlikely Odyssey of George W. Bush.* New York: HarperCollins, 2002.

Bumiller, Elisabeth. *Condoleezza Rice: An American Life: A Biography.* New York: Random House, 2007.

Bush, Barbara. *Barbara Bush: A Memoir.* New York: Charles Scribner's Sons, 1994.

———. *Reflections: Life After the White House.* New York: Scribner, 2003.

Bush, George H. W. *All the Best, George Bush: My Life in Letters and Other Writings.* New York: Scribner, 1999. Rereleased in 2013 with additional letters from during his son's presidency.

Bush, George, and Brent Scowcroft. *A World Transformed.* New York: Knopf, 1998.

Bush, George W. *A Charge to Keep.* New York: William Morrow, 1999.

———. *Decision Points.* New York: Crown, 2010.

Bush, Laura. *Spoken from the Heart.* New York: Scribner, 2010.

Campbell, Alastair. *The Blair Years: The Alastair Campbell Diaries.* New York: Knopf, 2007.

Cannon, Carl, Lou Dubose, and Jan Reid. *Boy Genius: Karl Rove, the Architect of George W. Bush's Remarkable Political Triumphs.* New York: PublicAffairs, 2005.

Cannon, Lou. *President Reagan: The Role of a Lifetime.* New York: Simon & Schuster, 1991.

Cannon, Lou, and Carl Cannon. *Reagan's Disciple: George W. Bush's Troubled Quest for a Presidential Legacy.* New York: PublicAffairs, 2008.

Casey, George W., Jr. *Strategic Reflections: Operation Iraqi Freedom, July 2004–February 2007.* Washington: National Defense University Press, 2012.

Casserly, John J. *The Ford White House: The Diary of a Speechwriter* Boulder: Colorado Associated University Press, 1977.

Chafee, Lincoln. *Against the Tide: How a Compliant Congress Empowered a Reckless President.* New York: Thomas Dunne Books, 2008.

Chandrasekaran, Rajiv. *Imperial Life in the Emerald City: Inside Iraq's Green Zone.* New York: Knopf, 2006.

Cheney, Dick. *In My Time: A Personal and Political Memoir.* New York: Threshold, 2011.

Cheney, Dick and Jonathan Reiner. *Heart: An American Medical Odyssey.* New York: Scribner, 2013. With Liz Cheney.

Cheney, Lynne. *Blue Skies, No Fences: A Memoir of Childhood and Family*. New York: Pocket Books, 2007.

Cheney, Mary. *Now It's My Turn: A Daughter's Chronicle of Political Life*. New York: Threshold, 2006.

Cheney, Richard B., and Lynne V. Cheney. *Kings of the Hill: How Nine Powerful Men Changed the Course of American History*. New York: Touchstone, 1996.

Chertoff, Michael. *Homeland Security: Assessing the First Five Years*. Philadelphia: University of Pennsylvania Press, 2009.

Chinoy, Mike. *Meltdown: The Inside Story of the North Korean Nuclear Crisis*. New York: St. Martin's Press, 2008.

Chirac, Jacques. *My Life in Politics*. Translated by Catherine Spencer. New York: Palgrave Macmillan, 2012.

Christie, Ron. *Black in the White House: Life Inside George W. Bush's West Wing*. Nashville: Thomas Nelson, 2006.

Clarke, Richard A. *Against All Enemies: Inside America's War on Terror*. New York: Free Press, 2004.

Clinton, Bill. *My Life*. New York: Knopf, 2004.

Cloud, David, and Greg Jaffe. *The Fourth Star: Four Generals and the Epic Struggle for the Future of the United States Army*. New York: Crown, 2009.

Coll, Steve. *Private Empire: ExxonMobil and American Power*. New York: Penguin Press, 2012.

Cooper, Christopher, and Robert Block. *Disaster: Hurricane Katrina and the Failure of Homeland Security*. New York: Times Books, 2006.

Cramer, Richard Ben. *What It Takes: The Way to the White House*. New York: Random House, 1992.

Crawford Greenburg, Jan. *Supreme Conflict: The Inside Story of the Struggle for Control of the United States Supreme Court*. New York: Penguin Press, 2007.

Danforth, John. *Faith and Politics: How the "Moral Values" Debate Divides America and How to Move Forward Together*. New York: Viking, 2006.

Daschle, Tom. *Like No Other Time: The 107th Congress and the Two Years That Changed America Forever*. New York: Crown, 2003.

DeFrank, Thomas M. *Write It When I'm Gone: Remarkable Off-the-Record Conversations with Gerald R. Ford*. New York: G. P. Putnam's Sons, 2007.

DeLay, Tom. *No Retreat, No Surrender: One American's Fight*. With Stephen Mansfield. New York: Sentinel, 2007.

DeYoung, Karen. *Soldier: The Life of Colin Powell*. New York: Knopf, 2006.

Dobbins, James F. *After the Taliban: Nation-Building in Afghanistan*. Dulles, Va.: Potomac Books, 2008.

Dobbins, James F., Seth G. Jones, Benjamin Runkle, and Siddharth Mohandas. *Occupying Iraq: A History of the Coalition Provisional Authority*. Arlington, Va.: Rand, 2009.

Draper, Robert. *Dead Certain: The Presidency of George W. Bush*. New York: Free Press, 2007.

Drew, Elizabeth. *Citizen McCain*. New York: Simon & Schuster, 2002.

Drogin, Bob. *Curveball: Spies, Lies, and the Con Man Who Caused a War*. New York: Random House, 2007.

Dubose, Lou, and Jake Bernstein. *Vice: Dick Cheney and the Hijacking of the American Presidency*. New York: Random House, 2006.

Duelfer, Charles. *Hide and Seek: The Search for Truth in Iraq*. New York: PublicAffairs, 2009.

Duffy, Michael, and Dan Goodgame. *Marching in Place: The Status Quo Presidency of George Bush*. New York: Simon & Schuster, 1992.

Edsall, Thomas Byrne. *Building Red America: The New Conservative Coalition and the Drive for Permanent Power.* New York: Basic Books, 2006.

Eichenwald, Kurt. *500 Days: Secrets and Lies in the Terror Wars.* New York: Touchstone, 2012.

Eisner, Peter, and Knut Royce. *The Italian Letter: How the Bush Administration Used a Fake Letter to Build the Case for War in Iraq.* New York: Rodale, 2007.

Feith, Douglas J. *War and Decision: Inside the Pentagon at the Dawn of the War on Terrorism.* New York: Harper, 2008.

Fleischer, Ari. *Taking Heat: The President, the Press, and My Years in the White House.* New York: William Morrow, 2005.

Ford, Gerald R. *A Time to Heal: The Autobiography of Gerald R. Ford.* New York: Harper & Row, 1979.

Franks, Tommy. *American Soldier.* With Malcolm McConnell. New York: HarperCollins, 2004.

Freeh, Louis J. *My FBI: Bringing Down the Mafia, Investigating Bill Clinton, and Fighting the War on Terror.* New York: St. Martin's Press, 2005.

Frist, William H. *A Heart to Serve: The Passion to Bring Health, Hope, and Healing.* New York: Center Street, 2009.

Frum, David. *The Right Man: An Inside Account of the Bush White House.* New York: Random House, 2003.

Gates, Robert M., *Duty: Memoirs of a Secretary at War.* New York: Knopf, 2014.

Gellman, Barton. *Angler: The Cheney Vice Presidency.* New York: Penguin Press, 2008.

Gergen, David. *Eyewitness to Power: The Essence of Leadership: Nixon to Clinton.* New York: Simon & Schuster, 2001.

Gerhart, Ann. *The Perfect Wife: The Life and Choices of Laura Bush.* New York: Simon & Schuster, 2004.

Gerson, Michael J. *Heroic Conservatism: Why Republicans Need to Embrace America's Ideals (and Why They Deserve to Fail if They Don't).* San Francisco: HarperOne, 2007.

Gillespie, Ed. *Winning Right: Campaign Politics and Conservative Policies.* New York: Threshold, 2006.

Goeglein, Tim. *The Man in the Middle: An Inside Account of Faith and Politics in the George W. Bush Era.* Nashville: B&H, 2011.

Goldsmith, Jack L. *The Terror Presidency: Law and Judgment Inside the Bush Administration.* New York: W. W. Norton, 2007.

Gordon, Michael, and Bernard E. Trainor. *Cobra II: The Inside Story of the Invasion and Occupation of Iraq.* New York: Pantheon, 2006.

———. *The Endgame: The Hidden History of America's Struggle to Build Democracy in Iraq.* New York: Pantheon, 2012.

Graham, Bradley. *By His Own Rules: The Ambitions, Successes, and Ultimate Failures of Donald Rumsfeld.* New York: PublicAffairs, 2009.

Greenspan, Alan. *Age of Turbulence: Adventures in a New World.* New York: Penguin, 2008.

Haass, Richard N. *War of Necessity, War of Choice: A Memoir of Two Iraq Wars.* New York: Simon & Schuster, 2009.

Halperin, Mark, and John F. Harris. *The Way to Win: Taking the White House in 2008.* New York: Random House, 2006.

Hamburger, Tom, and Peter Wallsten. *One Party Country: The Republican Plan for Dominance in the 21st Century.* New York: Wiley, 2006.

Hanson, Victor Davis. *An Autumn of War: What America Learned from September 11 and the War on Terrorism.* New York: Anchor, 2002.

Harris, Katherine. *Center of the Storm: Practicing Principled Leadership in Times of Crisis*. Nashville: Thomas Nelson, 2002.

Hartmann, Robert. *Palace Politics: An Inside Account of the Ford Years*. New York: McGraw-Hill, 1980.

Harwood, John, and Gerald F. Seib. *Pennsylvania Avenue: Profiles in Backroom Power.* New York: Random House, 2008.

Hastert, Denny. *Speaker: Lessons from Forty Years in Coaching and Politics*. Washington, D.C.: Regnery, 2004.

Hayes, Stephen F. *Cheney: The Untold Story of America's Most Powerful and Controversial Vice President*. New York: HarperCollins, 2007.

Heilemann, John, and Mark Halperin. *Game Change: Obama and the Clintons, McCain and Palin, and the Race of a Lifetime*. New York: Harper, 2010.

Helgerson, John L. *Getting to Know the President: Intelligence Briefings of Presidential Candidates, 1952–2004*. Langley, Va.: Center for the Study of Intelligence, 2012.

Holbrooke, Richard. *To End a War.* New York: Random House, 1998.

Hughes, Karen. *Ten Minutes from Normal*. New York: Viking, 2004.

Iraq Study Group. *The Iraq Study Group Report: The Way Forward—a New Approach*. New York: Vintage, 2006.

Isikoff, Michael, and David Corn. *Hubris: The Inside Story of Spin, Scandal, and the Selling of the Iraq War.* New York: Crown, 2006.

Jeffords, James M. *An Independent Man: Adventures of a Public Servant*. New York: Simon & Schuster, 2003.

Joseph, Robert G. *Countering WMD: The Libya Experience*. Fairfax, Va.: National Institute Press, 2009.

Kean, Thomas H., and Lee H. Hamilton. *Without Precedent: The Inside Story of the 9/11 Commission*. With Benjamin Rhodes. New York: Knopf, 2006.

Kennedy, Edward M. *True Compass: A Memoir.* New York: Twelve, 2009.

Kessler, Glenn. *The Confidante: Condoleezza Rice and the Creation of the Bush Legacy*. New York: St. Martin's Press, 2007.

Kessler, Ronald. *Laura Bush: An Intimate Portrait of the First Lady*. New York: Broadway, 2007.

———. *A Matter of Character: Inside the White House of George W. Bush*. New York: Sentinel, 2004.

Kitfield, James. *War and Destiny: How the Bush Revolution in Foreign and Military Affairs Redefined American Power.* Dulles, Va.: Potomac Books, 2005.

Koch, Dorothy Bush. *My Father, My President: A Personal Account of the Life of George H. W. Bush*. New York: Warner Books, 2006.

Kuo, David. *Tempting Faith: An Inside Story of Political Seduction*. New York: Free Press, 2006.

Labash, Matt. *Fly Fishing with Darth Vader: And Other Adventures with Evangelical Wrestlers, Political Hitmen, and Jewish Cowboys*. New York: Simon & Schuster, 2010.

Larsen, Randall J. *Our Own Worst Enemy: Asking the Right Questions About Security to Protect You, Your Family and America*. New York: Grand Central Publishing, 2007.

Latimer, Matt. *Speech-Less: Tales of a White House Survivor.* New York: Crown, 2009.

Lichtblau, Eric. *Bush's Law: The Remaking of American Justice*. New York: Pantheon, 2008.

Lindsey, Lawrence. *What a President Should Know . . . but Most Learn Too Late: An Insider's View on How to Succeed in the Oval Office*. With Marc Sumerlin. Lanham, Md.: Rowman & Littlefield, 2008.

Lott, Trent. *Herding Cats: A Life in Politics*. New York: Regan Books, 2005.
Mabry, Marcus. *Twice as Good: Condoleezza Rice and Her Path to Power*. New York: Modern Times, 2007.
Mann, James. *Rise of the Vulcans: The History of Bush's War Cabinet*. New York: Viking, 2004.
Mansfield, Stephen. *The Faith of George W. Bush*. New York: Tarcher/Penguin, 2003.
Mayer, Jane. *The Dark Side: Inside the Story of How the War on Terror Turned into a War on American Ideals*. New York: Doubleday, 2008.
Mazzetti, Mark. *The Way of the Knife: The CIA, a Secret Army, and a War at the Ends of the Earth*. New York: Penguin Press, 2013.
McCain, John. *Worth the Fighting For: A Memoir*. With Mark Salter. New York: Random House, 2002.
McChrystal, Stanley. *My Share of the Task: A Memoir*. New York: Portfolio/Penguin, 2013.
McClellan, Scott. *What Happened: Inside the Bush White House and Washington's Culture of Deception*. New York: PublicAffairs, 2008.
McNeely, Dave, and Jim Henderson. *Bob Bullock: God Bless Texas*. Austin: University of Texas Press, 2008.
Meyer, Christopher. *DC Confidential: The Controversial Memoirs of Britain's Ambassador to the U.S. at the Time of 9/11 and the Run-Up to the Iraq War*. London: Orion, 2006.
Milbank, Dana. *Smashmouth: Two Years in the Gutter with Al Gore and George W. Bush*. New York: Basic Books, 2001.
Minutaglio, Bill. *First Son: George W. Bush and the Bush Family Dynasty*. New York: Crown, 1999.
———. *The President's Counselor: The Rise to Power of Alberto Gonzales*. New York: Rayo, 2006.
Mitchell, Elizabeth. *W: The Revenge of the Bush Dynasty*. New York: Hyperion, 2000.
Musharraf, Pervez. *In the Line of Fire: A Memoir*. New York: Free Press, 2006.
Myers, Richard B. *Eyes on the Horizon: Serving on the Front Lines of National Security*. With Malcolm McConnell. New York: Threshold, 2010.
Nessen, Ronald. *It Sure Looks Different from the Inside*. New York: Simon & Schuster, 1978.
———. *Making the News, Taking the News: From NBC to the Ford White House*. Middletown, Conn.: Wesleyan University Press, 2011.
Neumann, Ronald E. *The Other War: Winning and Losing in Afghanistan*. Dulles, Va.: Potomac Books, 2009.
9/11 Commission. *The 9/11 Commission Report: Final Report of the National Commission on Terrorist Attacks upon the United States*. New York: W. W. Norton, 2004.
Novak, Robert D. *Prince of Darkness: Fifty Years of Reporting in Washington*. New York: Crown, 2007.
Obama, Barack. *The Audacity of Hope*. New York: Crown, 2006.
Ottaway, David B. *The King's Messenger: Prince Bandar bin Sultan and America's Tangled Relationship with Saudi Arabia*. New York: Walker, 2008.
Paige, Rod. *The War Against Hope: How Teachers' Unions Hurt Children, Hinder Teachers, and Endanger Public Education*. Nashville: Thomas Nelson, 2007.
Parmet, Herbert S. *George Bush: The Life of a Lone Star Yankee*. New York: Scribner, 1997.
Paulson, Henry M., Jr. *On the Brink: Inside the Race to Stop the Collapse of the Global Financial System*. New York: Business Plus, 2010.

Pawlenty, Tim. *Courage to Stand: An American Story.* Carol Stream, Ill.: Tyndale House Publishers, 2011.

Phillips, Kevin. *American Dynasty: Aristocracy, Fortune, and the Politics of Deceit in the House of Bush.* New York: Viking, 2004.

Plouffe, David. *The Audacity to Win: The Inside Story and Lessons of Barack Obama's Historic Victory.* New York: Viking Penguin, 2009.

Powell, Colin L. *It Worked for Me: In Life and Leadership.* With Tony Koltz. New York: Harper, 2012.

———. *My American Journey: An Autobiography.* With Joseph E. Persico. New York: Random House, 1995.

Pritchard, Charles L. *Failed Diplomacy: The Tragic Story of How North Korea Got the Bomb.* Washington, D.C.: Brookings Institution, 2007.

Purdum, Todd S. *A Time of Our Choosing: America's War in Iraq.* With the Staff of the *New York Times.* New York: Times Books, 2003.

Quayle, Dan. *Standing Firm.* New York: HarperCollins, 1994.

Radcliffe, Donnie. *Simply Barbara Bush: A Portrait of America's Candid First Lady.* New York: Grand Central, 1989.

Rattner, Steven. *Overhaul: An Insider's Account of the Obama Administration's Emergency Rescue of the Auto Industry.* New York: Houghton Mifflin Harcourt, 2010.

Reeves, Richard. *President Reagan: The Triumph of Imagination.* New York: Simon & Schuster, 2005.

Reid, Harry. *The Good Fight: Hard Lessons from Searchlight to Washington.* With Mark Warren. New York: G. P. Putnam's Sons, 2008.

Rice, Condoleezza. *Extraordinary, Ordinary People: A Memoir of Family.* New York: Crown, 2010.

———. *No Higher Honor: A Memoir of My Years in Washington.* New York: Crown, 2011.

Ricks, Thomas E. *Fiasco: The American Military Adventure in Iraq.* New York: Penguin Press, 2006.

———. *The Gamble: General David Petraeus and the American Military Adventure in Iraq, 2006–2008.* New York: Penguin Press, 2009.

Ridge, Tom. *The Test of Our Times: America Under Siege . . . and How We Can Be Safe Again.* With Lary Bloom. New York: Thomas Dunne Books, 2009.

Risen, James. *State of War: The Secret History of the CIA and the Bush Administration.* New York: Free Press, 2006.

Rizzo, John. *Company Man: Thirty Years of Controversy and Crisis in the CIA.* New York: Scribner, 2014.

Robinson, Linda. *Tell Me How This Ends: General David Petraeus and the Search for a Way out of Iraq.* New York: PublicAffairs, 2009.

Rodman, Peter W. *Presidential Command: Power, Leadership, and Foreign Policy from Richard Nixon to George W. Bush.* New York: Knopf, 2009.

Rothkopf, David. *Running the World: The Inside Story of the National Security Council and the Architects of American Power.* New York: PublicAffairs, 2005.

Rove, Karl. *Courage and Consequence: My Life as a Conservative in the Fight.* New York: Threshold, 2010.

Rumsfeld, Donald. *Known and Unknown: A Memoir.* New York: Sentinel, 2011.

———. *Rumsfeld's Rules: Leadership Lessons in Business, Politics, War, and Life.* New York: Broadside, 2013.

Sammon, Bill. *The Evangelical President: George Bush's Struggle to Spread a Moral Democracy Throughout the World.* Washington, D.C.: Regnery, 2007.

———. *Fighting Back: The War on Terrorism from Inside the Bush White House.* Washington, D.C.: Regnery, 2002.

———. *Misunderestimated: The President Battles Terrorism, John Kerry, and the Bush Haters.* New York: William Morrow, 2004.

———. *Strategery: How George W. Bush Is Defeating Terrorists, Outwitting Democrats, and Confounding the Mainstream Media.* Washington, D.C.: Regnery, 2006.

Sanchez, Ricardo S. *Wiser in Battle: A Soldier's Story.* With Donald T. Phillips. New York: Harper, 2008.

Sands, Philippe. *Lawless World: Making and Breaking Global Rules.* London: Penguin, 2006.

Sanger, David E. *The Inheritance: The World Obama Confronts and the Challenges to American Power.* New York: Crown, 2009.

Savage, Charlie. *Takeover: The Return of the Imperial Presidency and the Subversion of American Democracy.* New York: Little, Brown, 2007.

Scheib, Walter. *White House Chef: Eleven Years, Two Presidents, One Kitchen.* Hoboken, N.J.: John Wiley & Sons, 2007.

Schmitt, Eric, and Thom Shanker. *Counterstrike: The Untold Story of America's Secret Campaign Against Al Qaeda.* New York: Times Books, 2011.

Schwarzkopf, H. Norman. *It Doesn't Take a Hero: The Autobiography.* New York: Bantam, 1992.

Schweizer, Peter, and Rochelle Schweizer. *The Bushes: Portrait of a Dynasty.* New York: Doubleday, 2004.

Shelton, Hugh. *Without Hesitation: The Odyssey of an American Warrior.* With Ronald Levinson and Malcolm McConnell. New York: St. Martin's Press, 2010.

Shenon, Philip. *The Commission: The Uncensored History of the 9/11 Investigation.* New York: Twelve, 2008.

Shesol, Jeff. *Mutual Contempt: Lyndon Johnson, Robert Kennedy, and the Feud That Defined a Decade.* New York: W. W. Norton, 1997.

Shirley, Craig. *Reagan's Revolution. The Untold Story of the Campaign That Started It All.* Nashville: Thomas Nelson, 2005.

Shrum, Robert. *No Excuses: Concessions of a Serial Campaigner.* New York: Simon & Schuster, 2007.

Sietzen, Frank, Jr., and Keith L. Cowing. *New Moon Rising: The Making of America's New Space Vision and the Remaking of NASA.* Burlington, Ont.: Apogee Books, 2004.

Simon, Roger. *Divided We Stand: How Al Gore Beat George Bush and Lost the Presidency.* New York: Crown, 2001.

Sorkin, Andrew Ross. *Too Big to Fail: The Inside Story of How Wall Street and Washington Fought to Save the Financial System—and Themselves.* New York: Viking Penguin, 2009.

Specter, Arlen. *Life Among the Cannibals: A Political Career, a Tea Party Uprising, and the End of Governing as We Know It.* With Charles Robbins. New York: Thomas Dunne Books, 2012.

Stevens, Stuart. *The Big Enchilada: Campaign Adventures with the Cockeyed Optimists from Texas Who Won the Biggest Prize in Politics.* New York: Free Press, 2001.

Stewart, James B. *Tangled Webs: How False Statements Are Undermining America: From Martha Stewart to Bernie Madoff.* New York: Penguin Press, 2011.

Stothard, Peter. *Thirty Days: Tony Blair and the Test of History.* London: HarperCollins, 2003.

Suskind, Ron. *The One Percent Doctrine: Deep Inside America's Pursuit of Its Enemies Since 9/11.* New York: Simon & Schuster, 2006.

———. *The Price of Loyalty: George W. Bush, the White House, and the Education of Paul O'Neill*. New York: Simon & Schuster, 2004.

———. *The Way of the World: A Story of Truth and Hope in an Age of Extremism*. New York: Harper, 2008.

Tenet, George. *At the Center of the Storm: My Years at the CIA*. New York: HarperCollins, 2007.

Thiessen, Marc A. *Courting Disaster: How the CIA Kept America Safe and How Barack Obama Is Inviting the Next Attack*. Washington, D.C.: Regnery, 2010.

———, ed. *A Charge Kept: The Record of the Bush Presidency, 2001–2009*. New York: Morgan James, 2009.

Thomas, Evan, and the Staff of *Newsweek*. *Election 2004: How Bush Won and What You Can Expect in the Future*. New York: PublicAffairs, 2004.

Toobin, Jeffrey. *The Nine: Inside the Secret World of the Supreme Court*. New York: Doubleday, 2007.

———. *The Oath: The Obama White House and the Supreme Court*. New York: Doubleday, 2012.

———. *Too Close to Call: The Thirty-Six-Day Battle to Decide the 2000 Election*. New York: Random House, 2001.

Tyler, Patrick. *A World of Trouble: The White House and the Middle East—from the Cold War to the War on Terror*. New York: Farrar, Straus and Giroux, 2009.

Von Drehle, David, and the Staff of the *Washington Post*. *Deadlock: The Inside Story of America's Closest Election*. New York: PublicAffairs, 2001.

Warshaw, Shirley Anne. *The Co-presidency of Bush and Cheney*. Stanford, Calif.: Stanford Politics and Policy, 2009.

Wead, Doug. *All the Presidents' Children: Triumph and Tragedy in the Lives of America's First Families*. New York: Atria, 2004.

———. *The Raising of a President: The Mothers and Fathers of Our Nation's Leaders*. New York: Atria, 2007.

Weisberg, Jacob. *The Bush Tragedy*. New York: Random House, 2008.

Werth, Barry. *31 Days: Gerald Ford, the Nixon Pardon, and a Government in Crisis*. New York: Anchor, 2006.

Wessel, David. *In Fed We Trust: Ben Bernanke's War on the Great Panic*. New York: Crown, 2009.

West, Bing. *The Strongest Tribe: War, Politics, and the Endgame in Iraq*. New York: Random House, 2008.

Whitman, Christine Todd. *It's My Party, Too: The Battle for the Heart of the GOP and the Future of America*. New York: Penguin Press, 2005.

Wilson, Joseph. *The Politics of Truth: Inside the Lies That Led to War and Betrayed My Wife's CIA Identity: A Diplomat's Memoir*. New York: Carroll & Graf, 2004.

Wilson, Valerie Plame. *Fair Game: My Life as a Spy, My Betrayal by the White House*. New York: Simon & Schuster, 2007.

Witcover, Jules. *Marathon: The Pursuit of the Presidency, 1972–1976*. New York: Viking Penguin, 1977.

Woodward, Bob. *Bush at War*. New York: Simon & Schuster, 2002.

———. *The Commanders*. New York: Simon & Schuster, 1991.

———. *Plan of Attack*. New York: Simon & Schuster, 2004.

———. *State of Denial: Bush at War, Part III*. New York: Simon & Schuster, 2006.

———. *The War Within: A Secret White House History, 2006–2008*. New York: Simon & Schuster, 2008.

Yoo, John. *Crisis and Command: A History of Executive Power from George Washington to George W. Bush*. New York: Kaplan, 2009.

———. *The Powers of War and Peace: The Constitution and Foreign Affairs After 9/11.* Chicago: University of Chicago Press, 2005.

———. *War by Other Means: An Insider's Account of the War on Terror.* New York: Atlantic Monthly Press, 2006.

Zakheim, Dov S. *A Vulcan's Tale: How the Bush Administration Mismanaged the Reconstruction of Afghanistan.* Washington, D.C.: Brookings Institution Press, 2011.

Zelnick, Bob. *Winning Florida: How the Bush Team Fought the Battle.* Palo Alto, Calif.: Hoover Institution, 2001.

INDEX

ILLUSTRATION CREDITS

Bush and Cheney in limousine: Eric Draper, George W. Bush Presidential Library and Museum; Bush as toddler on father's shoulders: George Bush Presidential Library and Museum; Bush as governor: Mark Graham, *New York Times*; Bush with Laura, twins: George Bush Presidential Library and Museum; Cheney as child: AP Photo; Cheney with Ford and Rumsfeld: Gerald R. Ford Presidential Library; Cheney with Bush 41: George Bush Presidential Library and Museum; Bush and Cheney on train: AP Photo/Eric Draper; Karl Rove: George W. Bush Presidential Library and Museum; Bush and father in Oval Office: Eric Draper, George W. Bush Presidential Library and Museum; Bush and Cheney checking watches: Eric Draper, George W. Bush Presidential Library and Museum; Andy Card whispering in Bush's ear: REUTERS/Win McNamee/Landov; Dan Bartlett pointing to TV: George W. Bush Presidential Library and Museum; Cheney in bunker: Presidential Materials Division, National Archives and Records Administration; Bush, Cheney and Rice: George W. Bush Presidential Library and Museum; Cheney on helicopter: Presidential Materials Division, National Archives and Records Administration; Bush at Ground Zero: George W. Bush Presidential Library and Museum; Bush throws out first pitch: George W. Bush Presidential Library and Museum; Bush and father at National Cathedral: George W. Bush Presidential Library and Museum; Cheney with Giuliani at Ground Zero: Presidential Materials Division, National Archives and Records Administration; Cheney with Powell, Rumsfeld and Rice: Presidential Materials Division, National Archives and Records Administration; Karen Hughes: George W. Bush Presidential Library and Museum; Bush, Cheney and Rumsfeld on lawn: Eric Draper, George W. Bush Presidential Library and Museum; Bush with "Mission Accomplished" banner: AP Photo/J. Scott Applewhite; Bush with Bremer: George W. Bush Presidential Library and Museum; "Let Freedom Reign" note: George W. Bush Presidential Library and Museum; Bush and Cheney at 2004 convention: Doug Mills, *New York Times*; Mary Cheney: George W. Bush Presidential Library and Museum; Bush and Cheney at 2005 inauguration: George W. Bush Presidential Library and Museum; Bush surveying Katrina damage: George W. Bush Presidential Library and Museum; Harriet Miers: George W. Bush Presidential Library and Museum; Cheney interview on shooting: David Bohrer/Presidential Materials Division, National Archives and Records Administration; Bush with Rumsfeld after resignation: George W. Bush Presidential Library and Museum; Cheney and Rice in Red Room: Presidential Materials Division, National Archives and Records Administration; Stephen Hadley: George W. Bush Presidential Library and Museum; Meghan O'Sullivan: Stephen Crowley, *New York Times*; J. D. Crouch: Paul Hosefros, *New York Times*; Peter Feaver: C-SPAN; Jack Keane: C-SPAN; Brett McGurk: C-SPAN; Cheney with Petraeus: Presidential Materials Division, National Archives and Records Administration; Bush with Paulson and Bernanke: George W. Bush Presidential Library and Museum; Scooter Libby on crutches: Doug Mills, *New York Times*; Bush and Cheney on Colonnade: Presidential Materials Division, National Archives and Records Administration; Bush leaving Oval Office: Eric Draper, George W. Bush Presidential Library and Museum; Cheney in wheelchair: Andrew Councill, *New York Times*; Bush with Obama: Ruth Fremson, *New York Times*